FIFTEENTH EDITION
GLOBAL EDITION

Strategic Management *and* Business Policy

GLOBALIZATION, INNOVATION, AND SUSTAINABILITY

Thomas L. Wheelen
Formerly with University of Virginia, Trinity College, Dublin, Ireland

J. David Hunger
Formerly with Iowa State University, St. John's University

Alan N. Hoffman
Bentley University

Charles E. Bamford
University of Notre Dame

Pearson

Harlow, England • London • New York • Boston • San Francisco • Toronto • Sydney • Dubai • Singapore • Hong Kong
Tokyo • Seoul • Taipei • New Delhi • Cape Town • Sao Paulo • Mexico City • Madrid • Amsterdam • Munich • Paris • Milan

Vice President, Business Publishing: Donna Battista
Director of Portfolio Management: Stephanie Wall
Director, Courseware Portfolio Management:
Ashley Dodge
Senior Sponsoring Editor: Neeraj Bhalla
Associate Acquisitions Editor, Global Edition:
Ishita Sinha
Associate Project Editor, Global Edition: Paromita
Banerjee
Editorial Assistant: Linda Siebert Albelli
Vice President, Product Marketing: Roxanne
McCarley
Director of Strategic Marketing: Brad Parkins
Strategic Marketing Manager: Deborah Strickland
Product Marketer: Becky Brown
Field Marketing Manager: Lenny Ann Kucenski
Field Marketing Assistant: Kristen Compton
Product Marketing Assistant: Jessica Quazza
**Vice President, Production and Digital Studio, Arts
and Business:** Etain O'Dea

Director of Production, Business: Jeff Holcomb
Senior Manufacturing Controller, Global Edition:
Kay Holman
Content Producer, Global Edition: Pooja Aggarwal
Managing Producer, Business: Ashley Santora
Operations Specialist: Carol Melville
Creative Director: Blair Brown
Manager, Learning Tools: Brian Surette
Content Developer, Learning Tools: Lindsey Sloan
**Managing Producer, Digital Studio, Arts and
Business:** Diane Lombardo
Digital Studio Producer: Darren Cormier
Digital Studio Producer: Alana Coles
Media Production Manager, Global Edition:
Vikram Kumar
Full-Service Project Management and Composition: SPi Global
Interior Design: SPi Global
Cover Art: kaband/Shutterstock

Acknowledgments of third-party content appear on the appropriate page within the text.

Pearson Education Limited
KAO Two
KAO Park
Harlow
CM17 9NA
United Kingdom

and Associated Companies throughout the world

Visit us on the World Wide Web at: www.pearsonglobaleditions.com

© Pearson Education Limited 2018

The rights of Thomas L. Wheelen, J. David Hunger, Alan N. Hoffman, and Charles E. Bamford to be identified as the authors of this work have been asserted by them in accordance with the Copyright, Designs and Patents Act 1988.

Authorized adaptation from the United States edition, entitled Strategic Management and Business Policy: Globalization, Innovation, and Sustainability, 15th Edition, ISBN 978-0-13-452205-0 by Thomas L. Wheelen, J. David Hunger, Alan N. Hoffman, and Charles E. Bamford, published by Pearson Education © 2018.

ISBN 10:   1-292-21548-8
ISBN 13: 978-1-292-21548-8

British Library Cataloguing-in-Publication Data
A catalogue record for this book is available from the British Library

10 9 8 7 6 5 4 3 2 1

Typeset in Times Ten Lt Std by SPi Global
Printed and bound by Vivar in Malaysia

Dedicated to

TOM WHEELEN AND DAVID HUNGER

Tom originated this book in the late 1970s and with his friend David Hunger brought the first edition to fruition in 1982. What a ride it was! We lost both of these extraordinary men in rapid succession. After battling bone cancer, Tom died in Saint Petersburg, Florida, on December 24, 2011. David died in St. Joseph, Minnesota on April 10, 2014 after fighting cancer himself. It was Tom's idea from the very beginning to include the latest research and useful material written in such a way that the typical student could read and understand the book without outside assistance. That has been a key reason for the success of the book through its many editions. Tom and David worked in adjoining offices at the McIntire School of Commerce at the University of Virginia where their lifelong collaboration blossomed. Tom's last months were spent working with the two new co-authors to map out the direction for the 14th edition and we were fortunate to work with David through the early part of the 14th edition update until his fight against his cancer took priority. We thank you both and bid you a fond farewell! This 15th edition is for you!

Alan N. Hoffman
Charles E. Bamford

SPECIAL DEDICATION TO DAVID HUNGER

A special dedication in honor of David Hunger to his colleagues, friends, and students—

It is our hope and prayer that you found, and continue to find, some joy in your study of Strategic Management and Business Policy and, perhaps, experience a sense of the passion behind the subject matter presented in this textbook. It was originated by two men who were the best of friends and colleagues, Dr. Tom Wheelen (May 30, 1935 – December 24, 2011) and our Dad, Dr. J. David Hunger (May 17, 1941 – April 10, 2014). This will be the first edition we will see without a handwritten note in the front and a dedication to us all. Dad came alive discussing strategy, case management, theory, entrepreneurship, and the daily happenings in the field of management. Even relaxing at the end of the day, he could be found thumbing through a Business Week or journal. Colleagues always knew when he was in their presentations because he was fully engaged, offering questions and happy to share in an animated dialogue. Students speak fondly of being in his class. His dedication to the field never ended. Even up to a month before he died (still undergoing chemotherapy) he insisted on travelling by train from Minnesota to Chicago for a Case Research Conference to run a panel. We are so proud and thankful that Drs. Alan Hoffman and Chuck Bamford knew Tom and Dad and are carrying the torch forward. As his 4 daughters and 6 grandchildren, we miss him daily. We lost him far too soon. Finally, our mom, Betty Hunger, who lived with the authorship of this textbook for three quarters of their 45 years together and joked that it was their 5th child, wishes to express just how much she misses Dad and looks forward to seeing him again.

Betty, Kari and Jeff, Madison and Megan, Suzi and Nick, Summer and Kacey, Lori and Derek, Merry and Dylan, and Edan and Greyson.

We love you David/Dad/GrandDad.

To Will Hoffman, the greatest son in the world…. and to our saint Wendy Appel. …. and to Jodi L. Silton, thank you for your kindness and understanding.

Alan Hoffman

To Yvonne, for your support, advice, encouragement, love, and confidence. To my children Ada, Rob, and Sean and my grandchildren Silas, Isaac, and Clara.

Chuck Bamford

Brief Contents

Contents

Preface

Welcome to the 15th edition of *Strategic Management and Business Policy*! All of the chapters have been updated and we have added one new chapter on Global Strategy. In addition, we have added 13 brand-new cases (**Target, American Red Cross, Sonic Restaurants, Harley Davidson, Staples, Chipotle, Uber, Pandora Internet Radio, Snap-on Tools, Google, Pepsi, Town Sports International, and JC Penney**). Many of the cases are exclusive to this edition! Although we still make a distinction between full-length and mini cases, we have interwoven them throughout the book to better identify them with their industries.

The theme that runs throughout all 13 chapters of this edition continues our view from the 14th edition that there are three strategic issues that comprise the cornerstone all organizations must build upon to push their businesses forward. Those are *globalization, innovation, and sustainability*. Each chapter incorporates specific vignettes about these three themes. We strive to be the most comprehensive and practical strategy book on the market, with chapters ranging from corporate governance and social responsibility to competitive strategy, functional strategy, and strategic alliances.

FEATURES NEW TO THIS 15TH EDITION

This edition of the text has:

- A completely new Chapter (9) on Global Strategy. While we discuss globalization in every chapter of the book, including a Global Issues section in each chapter, we have called out a stand-alone chapter to address the key issues of entry, international coordination, stages of international development, international employment, and measurement of performance.

- New and updated vignettes on sustainability (which is widely defined as business sustainability), globalization (which we view as an expectation of business), and innovation (which is the single most important element in achieving competitive advantage) appear in every chapter of the text.

- Every example, chapter opening, and story has been updated. This includes chapter opening vignettes examining companies such as: Tesla, Pizza Hut, UNIQLO, Kärcher, Purbani Group, and United Airlines among many others.

- Resource-based analysis and more specifically the VRIO framework (Chapter 5) has been added to the toolbox of students' understanding of core competencies and competitive advantage with a significant addition of material and a practical example.

- Extensive additions have been made to the text from both strategy research and practical experience.
- Thirteen new comprehensive cases have been added to support the 14 popular full-length cases and 6 mini-cases carried forward from past editions. Of the 33 cases appearing in this book, 19 are exclusive and do not appear in other books.
- One of the new cases deals with privacy (**Google and the Right to Be Forgotten**).
- One of the new cases deals with governance (**American Red Cross**).
- One of the new cases deals with conscious capitalism (**Chipotle**).
- Two of the new cases deal with international issues (**Uber**, **Harley Davidson**).
- One of the new cases involves Internet companies (**Pandora Internet Radio**).
- One of the new cases deals with Sports and Leisure (**Town Sports Int'l**).
- One of the new cases deals with Apparel (**J.C. Penney**).
- Three of the new cases deal with Food and Beverages (**Pepsi, Sonic Restaurants**).
- Two of the new cases deal with Retailing (**Target, Staples**).
- One of the new cases deals with Manufacturing (**Snap-on Tools**).

HOW THIS BOOK IS DIFFERENT FROM OTHER STRATEGY TEXTBOOKS

This book contains a **Strategic Management Model** that runs through the first 12 chapters and is made operational through the **Strategic Audit**, a complete case analysis methodology. The Strategic Audit provides a professional framework for case analysis in terms of external and internal factors and takes the student through the generation of strategic alternatives and implementation programs.

To help the student synthesize the many factors in a complex strategy case, we developed three useful techniques:

- **The External Factor Analysis (EFAS) Table in Chapter 4**
- This reduces the external opportunities and threats to the 8 to 10 most important external factors facing management.
- **The Internal Factor Analysis (IFAS) Table in Chapter 5**
- This reduces the internal strengths and weaknesses to the 8 to 10 most important internal factors facing management.
- **The Strategic Factor Analysis Summary (SFAS) Matrix in Chapter 6**
  This condenses the 16 to 20 factors generated in the EFAS and IFAS tables into the 8 to 10 most important (strategic) factors facing the company. These strategic factors become the basis for generating alternatives and act as a recommendation for the company's future direction.

Suggestions for case analysis are provided in **Appendix 13.B (end of Chapter 13)** and contain step-by-step procedures on how to use a strategic audit in analyzing a case. This appendix includes an example of a student-written strategic audit. Thousands of students around the world have applied this methodology to case analysis with great success. *The Case Instructor's Manual* contains examples of student-written strategic audits for each of the full-length comprehensive strategy cases.

FEATURES

This edition contains many of the same features and content that helped make previous editions successful. Some of the features include the following:

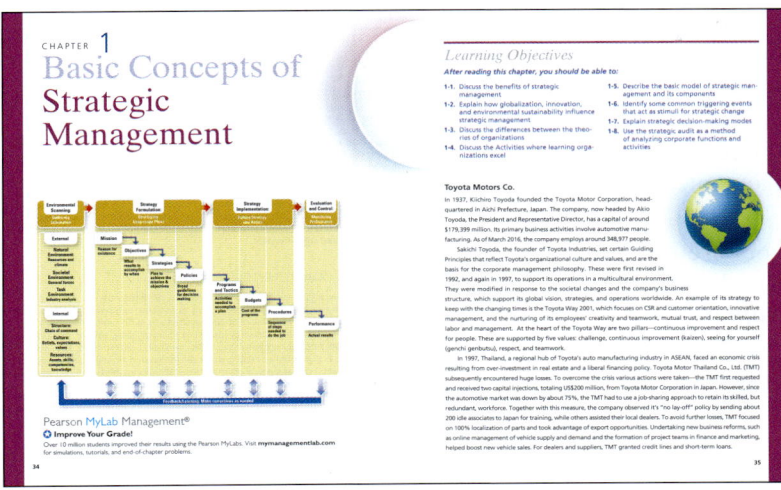

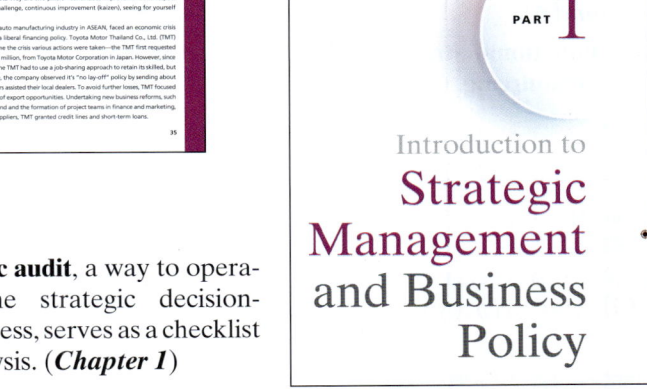

- A **strategic management model** runs throughout the first 12 chapters as a unifying concept. (Explained in *Chapter 1*)

Introduction to

Strategic Management and Business Policy

- The **strategic audit**, a way to operationalize the strategic decision-making process, serves as a checklist in case analysis. (*Chapter 1*)

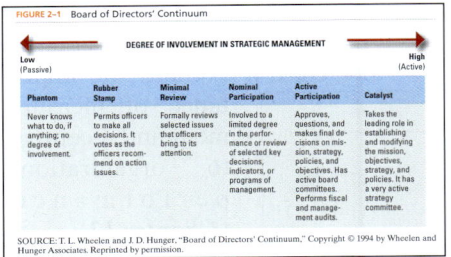

- **Corporate governance** is examined in terms of the roles, responsibilities, and interactions of top management and the board of directors. (*Chapter 2*)

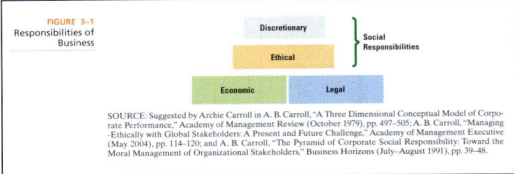

- **Social responsibility and managerial ethics** are examined in detail in terms of how they affect strategic decision making. They include the process of stakeholder analysis and the concept of social capital. (*Chapter 3*)

■ Equal emphasis is placed on **environmental scanning** of the societal environment as well as on the task environment. Topics include forecasting and Miles and Snow's typology in addition to competitive intelligence techniques and Porter's industry analysis. (***Chapter 4***)

■ **Core and distinctive competencies** are examined within the framework of the resource-based view of the firm and utilizing the VRIO framework. (***Chapter 5***)

■ **Organizational analysis** includes material on business models, supply chain management, and corporate reputation. (***Chapter 5***)

■ Internal and external strategic factors are emphasized through the use of specially designed **EFAS**, **IFAS**, and **SFAS** tables. (***Chapters 4, 5, and 6***)

■ **Functional strategies** are examined in light of **outsourcing**. (***Chapter 8***)

Pierre Beaudoin stepped down in 2015 as the company continued to spiral downward. The C-Series has yet to make any real penetration in the market with orders of less than 250 planes (and none in the past 1½ years) as of 12/31/15 compared to 3,072 orders for Boeing's 737 and 4,471 for Airbus's 320. As the investment of billions in the program was underway, the company decided to launch two new business jets further stretching resources.

The company has invested over $5 billion in the C-Series alone and has had a net negative cash burn for the past five years. The stock is now worth one-tenth of what it was in 2011 and the company is asking for a bailout from the Canadian government as they lay off nearly 10% of their workforce.

SOURCES: S. Deveau & F. Tomesco, "Why Bombardier Is Struggling to Build Bigger Planes," *Bloomberg Business*, February 18, 2016; A. Petroff, "Bombardier cutting 7,000 jobs," *CNN Money*, February 17, 2016 (money.cnn.com/2016/02/17/news/companies/bombardier-job-cuts-canada-europe/index.html); http://www.bombardier.com/en/about-us/history.html; F. Tomesco, "Quebec eyes fresh Bombardier aid absent federal investment," *The Globe and Mail*, February 10, 2016, http://www.theglobeandmail.com/report-on-business/quebec-eyes-fresh-bombardier-aid-absent-federal-investment/article28701038/

A Resource-Based Approach to Organizational analysis—Vrio

5-1. Apply the resource-based view of the firm and the VRIO framework to determine core and distinctive competencies

Scanning and analyzing the external environment for opportunities and threats is necessary for the firm to be able to understand its competitive environment and its place in that environment. It is the absolute starting place for strategic analysis. However, in order for the organization to thrive, the senior leadership team must look within the corporation itself to identify *internal strategic factors*—critical *strengths and weaknesses* that are likely to determine whether a firm will be able to take advantage of opportunities while avoiding threats. This internal scanning, often referred to as **organizational analysis**, is concerned with identifying, developing, and taking advantage of an organization's resources and competencies.

CORE AND DISTINCTIVE COMPETENCIES

Resources are an organization's assets and are thus the basic building blocks of the organization. They include *tangible assets* (such as its plant, equipment, finances, and location), *human assets* (the number of employees, their skills, and motivation), and *intangible assets* (such as its technology [patents and copyrights], culture, and reputation).[1] **Capabilities** refer to a corporation's ability to exploit its resources. They consist of business processes and routines that manage the interaction among resources to turn inputs into outputs. For example, a company's marketing capability can be based on the interaction among its marketing specialists, distribution channels, and salespeople. A capability is functionally based and is resident in a particular function. Thus, there are marketing capabilities, manufacturing capabilities, and human resource management capabilities. When these capabilities are constantly being changed and reconfigured to make them more adaptive to an uncertain environment, they are called *dynamic capabilities*.[2] A **competency** is a cross-functional integration and coordination

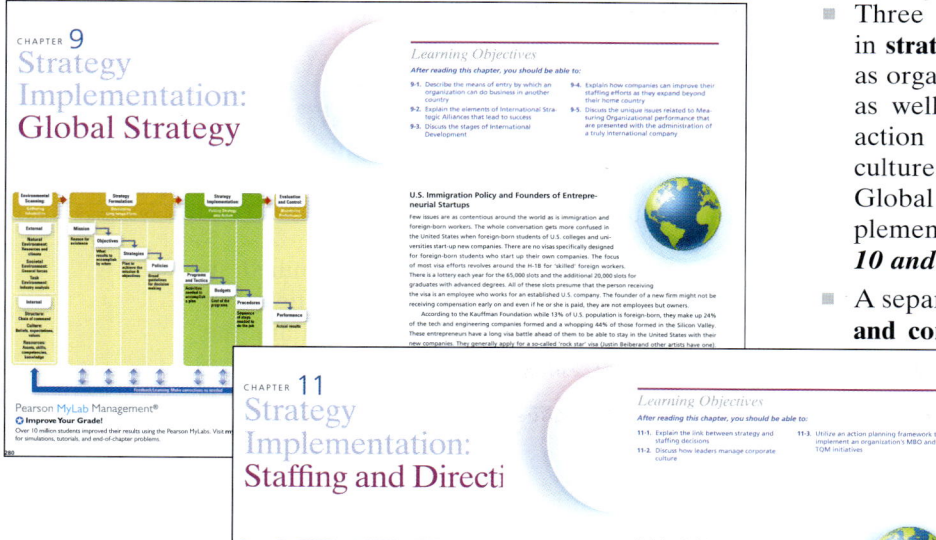

■ Three chapters deal with issues in **strategy implementation**, such as organizational and job design, as well as strategy-manager fit, action planning, and corporate culture. In addition we address Global Strategy as a unique implementation issue. (***Chapters 9, 10 and 11***)

■ A separate chapter on **evaluation and control** explains the importance of measurement and incentives to organizational performance. (***Chapter 12***)

■ **Suggestions for in-depth case analysis** provide a complete listing of financial ratios, recommendations for oral and written analysis, and ideas for further research. (***Chapter 13***)

■ The **strategic audit worksheet** is based on the time-tested strategic audit and is designed to help students organize and structure daily case preparation in a brief period of time. The worksheet works exceedingly well for checking the level of daily student case preparation—especially for open class discussions of cases. (*Chapter 13*)

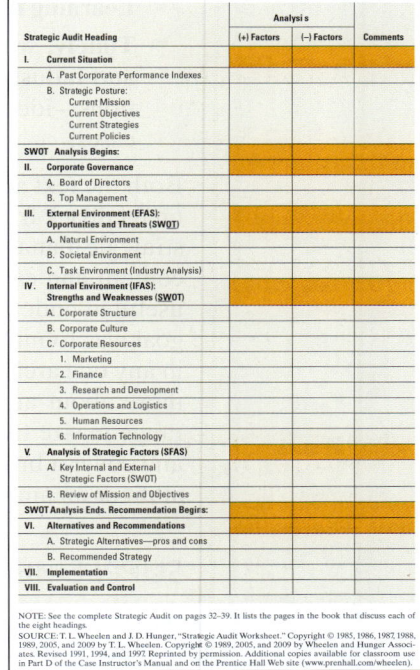

Strategic Audit Heading	Analysis		
	(+) Factors	(−) Factors	Comments
I. Current Situation			
A. Past Corporate Performance Indexes			
B. Strategic Posture: Current Mission, Current Objectives, Current Strategies, Current Policies			
SWOT Analysis Begins:			
II. Corporate Governance			
A. Board of Directors			
B. Top Management			
III. External Environment (EFAS): Opportunities and Threats (SWOT)			
A. Natural Environment			
B. Societal Environment			
C. Task Environment (Industry Analysis)			
IV. Internal Environment (IFAS): Strengths and Weaknesses (SWOT)			
A. Corporate Structure			
B. Corporate Culture			
C. Corporate Resources			
1. Marketing			
2. Finance			
3. Research and Development			
4. Operations and Logistics			
5. Human Resources			
6. Information Technology			
V. Analysis of Strategic Factors (SFAS)			
A. Key Internal and External Strategic Factors (SWOT)			
B. Review of Mission and Objectives			
SWOT Analysis Ends. Recommendation Begins:			
VI. Alternatives and Recommendations			
A. Strategic Alternatives—pros and cons			
B. Recommended Strategy			
VII. Implementation			
VIII. Evaluation and Control			

NOTE: See the complete Strategic Audit on pages 32–39. It lists the pages in the book that discuss each of the eight headings.
SOURCE: T. L. Wheelen and J. D. Hunger, "Strategic Audit Worksheet." Copyright © 1985, 1986, 1987, 1988, 1989, 2005, and 2009 by T. L. Wheelen. Copyright © 1989, 2005, and 2009 by Wheelen and Hunger Associates. Revised 1991, 1994, and 1997. Reprinted by permission. Additional copies available for classroom use in Part D of the Case Instructor's Manual and on the Prentice Hall Web site (www.prenhall.com/wheelen).

End of Chapter SUMMARY

Every day, about 17 truckloads of used diesel engines and other parts are dumped at a receiving facility at Caterpillar's remanufacturing plant in Corinth, Mississippi. The filthy iron engines are then broken down by two workers, who manually hammer and drill for half a day until they have taken every bolt off the engine and put each component into its own bin. The engines are then cleaned and remade at half of the cost of a new engine and sold for a tidy profit. This system works at Caterpillar because, as a general rule, 70% of the cost to build something new is in the materials and 30% is in the labor. Remanufacturing simply starts the manufacturing process over again with materials that are essentially free and which already contain most of the energy costs needed to make them. The would-be discards become fodder for the next product, eliminating waste, and cutting costs. Caterpillar's management was so impressed by the remanufacturing operation that they made the business a separate division in 2005. The unit earned more than US$1 billion in sales in 2005 and by 2012 employed more than 8500 workers in 16 countries.

Caterpillar's remanufacturing unit was successful not only because of its ability to wring productivity out of materials and labor, but also because it designed its products for reuse. Before they are built new, remanufactured products must be designed for disassembly. In order to achieve this, Caterpillar asks its designers to check a "Reman" box on Caterpillar's product development checklist. The company also needs to know where its products are being used in order to take them back—known as the art of *reverse logistics*. This is achieved by Caterpillar's excellent relationship with its dealers throughout the world, as well as through financial incentives. For example, when a customer orders a crankshaft, that customer is offered a remanufactured one for half the cost of a new one—assuming the customer turns in the old

■ An **experiential exercise** focusing on the material covered in each chapter helps the reader apply strategic concepts to an actual situation.

■ A list of **key terms** and the pages on which they are discussed let the reader keep track of important concepts as they are introduced in each chapter.

End of Chapter SUMMARY

Strategy implementation is where "the rubber hits the road." Environmental scanning and strategy formulation are crucial to strategic management but are only the beginning of the process. The failure to carry a strategic plan into the day-to-day operations of the workplace is a major reason why strategic planning often fails to achieve its objectives. It is discouraging to note that in one study nearly 70% of the strategic plans were never successfully implemented.[76]

For a strategy to be successfully implemented, it must be made action-oriented. This is done through a series of programs that are funded through specific budgets and contain new detailed procedures. This is what Sergio Marchionne did when he implemented a turnaround strategy as the new Fiat Group CEO in 2004. He attacked the lethargic, bureaucratic system by flattening Fiat's structure and giving younger managers a larger amount of authority and responsibility. He ordered managers worked to reduce the number of auto platforms from 19 to 6 by 2012. The time from the completion of the design process to new car production was cut from 26 to 18 months. By 2008, the Fiat auto unit was again profitable. Marchionne reintroduced Fiat to the U.S. market in 2012 after a 27-year absence.[77] Unfortunately, Fiat struggled to gain any traction in the U.S. market. Despite a strong marketing campaign and a number of cars designed specifically for the market, by 2016 sales had stalled at 44,000 cars a year. The company has remained strongly profitable and even acquired 100% of Chrysler in 2014.[78]

This chapter explains how jobs and organizational units can be designed to support a change in strategy. We will continue with staffing and directing issues in strategy implementation in the next chapter.

Pearson MyLab Management®
Go to **mymanagementlab.com** to complete the problems marked with this icon.

KEY TERMS

budget (p. 301)
cellular/modular organization (p. 314)
first mover (p. 299)
geographic-area structure (p. 317)
job design (p. 316)
late movers (p. 299)
market location tactic (p. 299)

matrix structures (p. 310)
network structure (p. 312)
organizational life cycle (p. 309)
procedures (p. 301)
product-group structure (p. 317)
program (p. 298)
reengineering (p. 314)

Six Sigma (p. 315)
stages of corporate development (p. 304)
strategy implementation (p. 296)
structure follows strategy (p. 303)
synergy (p. 302)
timing tactic (p. 299)
virtual organization (p. 312)

- **Learning objectives** begin each chapter.
- **Timely, well-researched, and class-tested cases** deal with interesting companies and industries. Many of the cases are about well-known, publicly held corporations—ideal subjects for further research by students wishing to "update" the cases.

Both the text and the cases have been class-tested in strategy courses and revised based on feedback from students and instructors. The first 12 chapters are organized around a strategic management model that begins each chapter and provides a structure for both content and case analysis. We emphasize those concepts that have proven to be most useful in understanding strategic decision making and in conducting case analysis. Our goal was to make the text as comprehensive as possible without getting bogged down in any one area. Extensive endnote references are provided for those who wish to learn more about any particular topic. All cases are about actual organizations. The firms range in size from large, established multinationals to small, entrepreneurial ventures, and cover a broad variety of issues. As an aid to case analysis, we propose the strategic audit as an analytical technique.

SUPPLEMENTS

At www.pearsonglobaleditions.com/Wheelen instructors can access teaching resources available with this text in a downloadable, digital format. Registration is simple and gives you immediate access to new titles and editions. Please contact your Pearson sales representative for your access code. As a registered faculty member, you can download resource files and receive immediate access and instructions for installing course management content on your campus server. In case you ever need assistance, our dedicated technical support team is ready to assist instructors with questions about the media supplements that accompany this text. Visit for answers to frequently asked questions. This title has the following electronic resources.

Instructor's Manuals

Two comprehensive Instructor's Manuals have been carefully constructed to accompany this book. The first one accompanies the concepts chapters; the second one accompanies the cases.

Concepts Instructor's Manual

To aid in discussing the 13 strategy chapters, the *Concepts Instructor's Manual* includes:

- **Suggestions for Teaching Strategic Management:** These include various teaching methods and suggested course syllabi.
- **Chapter Notes:** These include summaries of each chapter, suggested answers to discussion questions, and suggestions for using end-of-chapter cases/exercises and part-ending cases, plus additional discussion questions (with answers) and lecture modules.

Case Instructor's Manual

To aid in case method teaching, the *Case Instructor's Manual* includes detailed suggestions for its use, teaching objectives, and examples of student analyses for each of the full-length comprehensive cases. This is the most comprehensive instructor's manual available in strategic management. A standardized format is provided for each case:

1. Case Abstract
2. Case Issues and Subjects
3. Steps Covered in the Strategic Decision-Making Process
4. Case Objectives
5. Suggested Classroom Approaches
6. Discussion Questions
7. Case Author's Teaching Note (if available)
8. Student-Written Strategic Audit (if appropriate)
9. EFAS, IFAS, and SFAS Exhibits
10. Financial Analysis—ratios and common-size income statements (if appropriate)

PowerPoint Slides

PowerPoint slides, provided in a comprehensive package of text outlines and figures corresponding to the text, are designed to aid the educator and supplement in-class lectures.

Test Item File

The Test Item File contains over 1200 questions, including multiple-choice, true/false, and essay questions. Each question is followed by the correct answer, AACSB category, and difficulty rating.

TestGen

TestGen software is preloaded with all of the *Test Item File* questions. It allows instructors to manually or randomly view test questions, and to add, delete, or modify testbank questions as needed to create multiple tests.

VIDEO LIBRARY

Videos illustrating the most important subject topics are available in the following format:

- MyLab—available for instructors and students, provides round the clock instant access to videos and corresponding assessment for Pearson textbooks.
  Contact your local Pearson representative to request access to either format.

Acknowledgments

We would like to thank the many people at Pearson who helped make this edition possible. We are especially grateful to our senior sponsoring editor, Neeraj Bhalla, who managed to keep everything on an even keel. We also would like to thank Greetal Carolyn Jayanandan, Nicole Suddeth, Dan Tylman, Claudia Fernandes and everyone at Pearson who guided the book through the production and marketing processes. Special thanks to Kaitlyn Dell'Aquila at Pearson for her hard work in the trenches.

We are very thankful to Paul D. Maxwell, *St. Thomas University, Miami, FL*; Terry J. Schindler, *University of Indianapolis*; Anne Walsh, *La Salle University*; Angelo Camillo, *Woodbury University*; Jeannine L. Scherenberg, *Rockford College*; William Reisel, *St. John's University*; Ronaldo Parente, *Florida International University*; Roxana Wright, *Plymouth State University*; J. Barry Dickinson, *Holy Family University*; Theodore E. Davis, *Jr., PhD, SUNY College at Buffalo*; Manzoor Chowdhury, *Lincoln University*; David Olson, *California State University at Bakersfield*; and Janis Dietz, *University of La Verne* for their constructive criticism of the 14th edition.

We are especially thankful to the many students who tried out the cases we chose to include in this book. Their comments helped us find any flaws in the cases before the book went to the printer.

We also offer a big thanks to the many case authors who have provided us with excellent cases for the 15th edition of this book. We consider many of these case authors to be our friends. A special thanks to you!! The adage is true: The path to greatness is through others.

Alan Hoffman would like to thank the following colleagues for their valuable insight, support, and feedback during the writing process: Anne Nelson, Trena Depel, Kathy Connolly, John Nicholson, Robert Frisch, Barbara Gottfried, Bonnie Kornman, Gail Goldman, Raj Sisodia, Ken Kornman, Donna Gallo, Jeff Shuman, Anna Forte, Deb Kennedy, Paula Josephs, Lisa Dinsmore, Alyssa Goldman, Susan Fleming, Jill Brown, Lucia Gumbs, Jadwiga Supryn, Cynthia Clark, Natalia Gold, Aileen Cordette, Andrea Harding, Martha Bailey, Lew Sudarsky, Ed Ottensmeyer, Tim Stearns, Christopher Forte, Roberta Francis, Abbey Nicholson, Sam Vitali, Michael Page, Chip Wiggins, Jon Horlink, Vicki Lafarge, Dorothy Feldmann, Susan Adams, Josh Senn, Gary Cordette, Merle Gordon, Thom McGillvray, Bob Cronin, Arthur Hughes, Jayne Pollack, Susan McGrath, Joe Goldman, Ed Harding, Lynne Young, Rick Vitali, Catherine Usoff, and Beverley Earle. Special thanks to Joyce Vincelette, Kathryn Wheelen, Patricia Ryan, Jim Schwartz, and Pamela Goldberg Schwartz.

Lastly, to the many strategy instructors and students who have relayed to us their thoughts about teaching the strategy course: We have tried to respond to your problems and concerns as best we could by providing a comprehensive yet usable text coupled with recent and complex cases. To you, the people who work hard in the strategy trenches, we acknowledge our debt. This book is yours.

A. N. H.
Needham Heights, Massachusetts

C. E. B.
Durham, North Carolina

Global Edition Acknowledgments

Pearson would like to thank Georg Hauer, *Stuttgart Technology University of Applied Sciences,* Humphry Hung, *Tung Wah College,* Krish Saha, *Birmingham City University,* and Sununta Siengthai, *Asian Institute of Technology (A.I.T.),* for their contributions to the Global Edition.

We would also like to thank David Ahlstrom, *Chinese University of Hong Kong,* Nazih El-Jor, *Universite du Saint Esprit Kaslik,* Goh See Kwong, *Taylor's University Malaysia,* and Tan Wei Lian, *Taylor's University.*

About the Authors

THOMAS L. WHEELEN, May 30, 1935 – December 24, 2011. DBA, MBA, BS Cum Laude (George Washington University, Babson College, and Boston College, respectively), College, MBA (1961); Boston College, BS cum laude (1957). Teaching Experience: Visiting Professor— Trinity College—University of Dublin (Fall 1999); University of South Florida—Professor of Strategic Management (1983–2008); University of Virginia - McIntire School of Commerce; Ralph A. Beeton Professor of Free Enterprise (1981–1985); Professor (1974–1981); Associate Professor (1971–1974); and Assistant Professor (1968–1971); Visiting Professor—University of Arizona (1979–1980 and Northeastern University (Summer 1975, 1977, and 1979). **Academic, Industry, and Military Experience:** University of Virginia College of Continuing Education: (1) Coordinator for Business Education (1978–1983, 1971–1976)—approved all undergraduate courses offered at seven Regional Centers and approved faculty; (2) Liaison Faculty and Consultant to the National Academy of the FBI Academy (1972–1983) and; (3) developed, sold, and conducted over 200 seminars for local, state, and national governments, and companies for the McIntire School of Commerce and Continuing Education. General Electric Company—various management positions (1961–1965); U.S. Navy Supply Corps (SC)—Lt. (SC) USNR—assistant supply officer aboard nuclear support tender (1957–1960). **Publications:** (1) *Monograph, An Assessment of Undergraduate Business Education in the United States* (with J. D. Hunger), 1980; (2) Books: **60 books published; 14 books translated into eight languages** (Arabic, Bahasa-Indonesian, Chinese, Chinese Simplified, Greek, Italian, Japanese, Portuguese, and Thai); (3) Books—co-author with J. D. Hunger—five active books: *Strategic Management and Business Policy*, 10th edition (2006); *Cases in Strategic Management and Business Policy*, 10th edition (2006); *Concepts in Strategic Management and Business Policy*, 10th edition (2006); *Strategic Management and Business Policy*, 10th edition; *International Edition* (2006); and *Essentials of Strategic Management*, 3rd edition (2003); (4) Co-editor: *Developments in Information Systems* (1974) and *Collective Bargaining in the Public Sector* (1977); and (5) Co-developer of software—STrategic Financial ANalyzer (ST. FAN) (1993, 1990, 1989—different versions); (6) Articles—authored over 40 articles that have appeared in such journals as the *Journal of Management, Business Quarterly, Personnel Journal, SAM Advanced Management Journal, Journal of Retailing, International Journal of Management,* and the *Handbook of Business Strategy*; (6) Cases—have about 280 cases appearing in over 83 text and case books, as well as the *Business Case Journal, Journal of Management Case Studies, International Journal of Case Studies and Research,* and the *Case Research Journal.* **Awards:** (1) Fellow elected by the Society for Advancement of Management in 2002; (2) Fellow elected by the North American Case Research Association in 2000; (3) Fellow elected by the Text and Academic Authors Association in 2000; (4) the 1999 Phil Carroll Advancement of Management Award in Strategic Management from the Society for Advancement of Management; (5) 1999 McGuffey Award for Excellence and Longevity for Strategic Management and Business Policy, 6th edition, from the Text and Academic Authors Association; (6) 1996/97 Teaching Incentive Program Award for teaching undergraduate strategic management; (7) Fulbright, 1996–1997, to Ireland but had to turn it down; (8) Endowed Chair, Ralph A.

Beeton Professor, at University of Virginia (1981–1985); (9) a Sesquicentennial Associateship research grant from the Center for Advanced Studies at the University of Virginia, 1979–1980; (10) Small Business Administration (Small Business Institute), supervised undergraduate team that won District, Regional III, and Honorable Mention Awards; and (11) awards for two articles. **Associations:** Dr. Wheelen served on the Board of Directors of the Adhia Mutual Fund, the Society for Advancement of Management, and on the Editorial Board and as Associate Editor of *SAM Advanced Management Journal*. He served on the Board of Directors of Lazer Surgical Software Inc. and the Southern Management Association, and on the Editorial Boards of the *Journal of Management* and *Journal of Management Case Studies*, the *Journal of Retail Banking*, the *Case Research Journal*, and *the Business Case Journal*. He was Vice President of Strategic Management for the Society for the Advancement of Management, and President of the North American Case Research Association. Dr. Wheelen was a member of the Academy of Management, Beta Gamma Sigma, the Southern Management Association, the North American Case Research Association, the Society for Advancement of Management, the Society for Case Research, the Strategic Management Association, and the World Association for Case Method Research and Application. He has been listed in *Who's Who in Finance and Industry*, *Who's Who in the South and Southwest*, and *Who's Who in American Education*.

J. DAVID HUNGER, Ph.D. (Ohio State University), is currently Strategic Management Scholar in Residence at Saint John's University in Minnesota. He is also Professor Emeritus at Iowa State University where he taught for 23 years. He previously taught at George Mason University, the University of Virginia, and Baldwin-Wallace College. He worked in brand management at Procter & Gamble Company, as a selling supervisor at Lazarus Department Store, and served as a Captain in U.S. Army Military Intelligence. He has been active as a consultant and trainer to business corporations, as well as to state and federal government agencies. He has written numerous articles and cases that have appeared in the *Academy of Management Journal, International Journal of Management, Human Resource Management, Journal of Business Strategies, Case Research Journal, Business Case Journal, Handbook of Business Strategy, Journal of Management Case Studies, Annual Advances in Business Cases, Journal of Retail Banking, SAM Advanced Management Journal,* and *Journal of Management,* among others. Dr. Hunger is a member of the Academy of Management, the North American Case Research Association, the Society for Case Research, the North American Management Society, the Textbook and Academic Authors Association, and the Strategic Management Society. He is past-President of the North American Case Research Association, the Society for Case Research, and the Iowa State University Press Board of Directors. He also served as a Vice President of the U.S. Association for Small Business and Entrepreneurship. He was Academic Director of the Pappajohn Center for Entrepreneurship at Iowa State University. He has served on the editorial review boards of *SAM Advanced Management Journal,* the *Journal of Business Strategies,* and the *Journal of Business Research*. He has served on the board of directors of the North American Case Research Association, the Society for Case Research, the Iowa State University Press, and the North American Management Society. He is co-author with Thomas L. Wheelen of *Strategic Management and Business Policy* and *Essentials of Strategic Management* plus *Concepts in Strategic Management and Business Policy* and *Cases in Strategic Management and Business Policy,* as well as *Strategic Management Cases* (PIC: Preferred Individualized Cases), and a monograph assessing undergraduate business education in the United States. The 8th edition of *Strategic Management and Business Policy* received the McGuffey

Award for Excellence and Longevity in 1999 from the Text and Academic Authors Association. Dr. Hunger received the Best Case Award given by the McGraw-Hill Publishing Company and the Society for Case Research in 1991 for outstanding case development. He is listed in various versions of *Who's Who*, including *Who's Who in the United States* and *Who's Who in the World*. He was also recognized in 1999 by the Iowa State University College of Business with its Innovation in Teaching Award and was elected a Fellow of the Teaching and Academic Authors Association and of the North American Case Research Association.

ALAN N. HOFFMAN, MBA, DBA (Indiana University), is Professor of Strategic Management at Bentley University in Waltham, Massachusetts. He is the former Director of the MBA Program at Bentley University. He served as the course coordinator and Visiting Professor of Strategic Management for the Global Strategy course in the OneMBA Program at the Rotterdam School of Management at Erasmus University, Rotterdam, The Netherlands. He is also the owner of *Dr. Alan N. Hoffman Investment Management*, founded in 1995. His major areas of interest include strategic management, global competition, investment strategy, design thinking, and technology. Professor Hoffman is coauthor of *The Strategic Management Casebook and Skill Builder* textbook (with Hugh O'Neill). His academic publications have appeared in the *Academy of Management Journal, Human Relations*, the *Journal of Business Ethics*, the *Journal of Business Research*, and *Business Horizons*. He has authored more than 40 strategic management cases, including The Boston YWCA, Ryka Inc., Liz Claiborne, Ben & Jerry's, Cisco Systems, Sun Microsystems, Palm Inc., Handspring, eBay, AOL/Time Warner, McAfee, Apple Computer, TiVo Inc., Wynn Resorts, TomTom, Blue Nile, GE, Amazon, Netflix, Delta Airlines, A123, Tesla Motors, Chipotle, Staples, Target, Sonic Restaurants, Harley Davidson, and Whole Foods Market. He is the recipient of the 2004 Bentley University Teaching Innovation Award for his course: "The Organizational Life Cycle—The Boston Beer Company Brewers of Samuel Adams Lager Beer." He teaches strategic management in many executive programs and also teaches business to artists at The Massachusetts College of Art and Design.

CHARLES E. BAMFORD, Ph.D. (University of Tennessee), MBA (Virginia Tech), and BS (University of Virginia). He is an adjunct professor at the University of Notre Dame, where he has been awarded the EMBA Professor of the Year Award four times. Chuck worked in industry for 12 years prior to pursuing his Ph.D. His last position was as the Manager of Business Analysis (Mergers & Acquisitions, Dispositions, and Business Consulting) for Dominion Bankshares Corporation (now Wells Fargo). Three years ago Chuck founded Bamford Associates, LLC and relocated to Durham, NC. He has worked with thousands of managers in the development of implementable strategic plans and an entrepreneurial orientation to growth.

His research has been published in the *Strategic Management Journal, Journal of Business Venturing, Entrepreneurship Theory & Practice, Journal of Business Research, Journal of Business Strategies, Journal of Technology Transfer*, and *Journal of Small Business Management*, among others. Chuck has co-authored four other textbooks and is the author of the fiction novel *Some Things Are Never Forgiven* (Penguin Press).

He has taught courses in strategy and entrepreneurship at the undergraduate, graduate, and executive levels. His teaching experience includes courses taught at universities in Scotland, Hungary, and the Czech Republic. He was a Professor and the Dennis Thompson Chair of Entrepreneurship at Queens University of Charlotte. He also held positions as an Associate Professor at Texas Christian University and at the University of Richmond. He has taught Executive MBA courses at The University of Notre Dame, Texas Christian University, Tulane University, and at Queens University of Charlotte.

Chuck has won 19 individual teaching excellence awards during his career, including 10 Executive MBA Professor of the Year Awards. He is also a Noble Foundation Fellow in Teaching Excellence.

PART 1

Introduction to Strategic Management and Business Policy

CHAPTER 1

Basic Concepts of Strategic Management

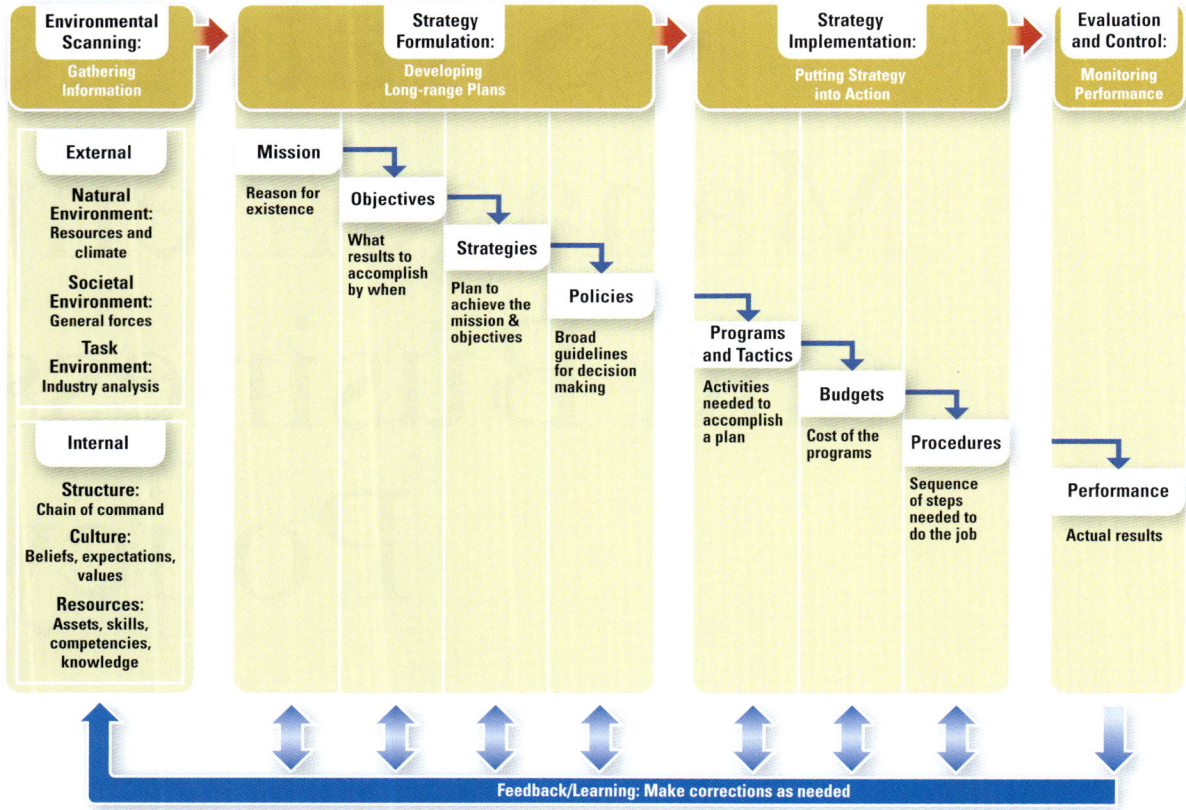

Pearson MyLab Management®

⭐ Improve Your Grade!

Over 10 million students improved their results using the Pearson MyLabs. Visit **mymanagementlab.com** for simulations, tutorials, and end-of-chapter problems.

Learning Objectives

After reading this chapter, you should be able to:

1-1. Discuss the benefits of strategic management

1-2. Explain how globalization, innovation, and environmental sustainability influence strategic management

1-3. Discuss the differences between the theories of organizations

1-4. Discuss the Activities where learning organizations excel

1-5. Describe the basic model of strategic management and its components

1-6. Identify some common triggering events that act as stimuli for strategic change

1-7. Explain strategic decision-making modes

1-8. Use the strategic audit as a method of analyzing corporate functions and activities

Toyota Motors Co.

In 1937, Kiichiro Toyoda founded the Toyota Motor Corporation, headquartered in Aichi Prefecture, Japan. The company, now headed by Akio Toyoda, the President and Representative Director, has a capital of around $179,399 million. Its primary business activities involve automotive manufacturing. As of March 2016, the company employs around 348,977 people.

Sakichi Toyoda, the founder of Toyota Industries, set certain Guiding Principles that reflect Toyota's organizational culture and values, and are the basis for the corporate management philosophy. These were first revised in 1992, and again in 1997, to support its operations in a multicultural environment. They were modified in response to the societal changes and the company's business structure, which support its global vision, strategies, and operations worldwide. An example of its strategy to keep with the changing times is the Toyota Way 2001, which focuses on CSR and customer orientation, innovative management, and the nurturing of its employees' creativity and teamwork, mutual trust, and respect between labor and management. At the heart of the Toyota Way are two pillars—continuous improvement and respect for people. These are supported by five values: challenge, continuous improvement (kaizen), seeing for yourself (genchi genbutsu), respect, and teamwork.

In 1997, Thailand, a regional hub of Toyota's auto manufacturing industry in ASEAN, faced an economic crisis resulting from over-investment in real estate and a liberal financing policy. Toyota Motor Thailand Co., Ltd. (TMT) subsequently encountered huge losses. To overcome the crisis various actions were taken—the TMT first requested and received two capital injections, totaling US$200 million, from Toyota Motor Corporation in Japan. However, since the automotive market was down by about 75%, the TMT had to use a job-sharing approach to retain its skilled, but redundant, workforce. Together with this measure, the company observed it's "no lay-off" policy by sending about 200 idle associates to Japan for training, while others assisted their local dealers. To avoid further losses, TMT focused on 100% localization of parts and took advantage of export opportunities. Undertaking new business reforms, such as online management of vehicle supply and demand and the formation of project teams in finance and marketing, helped boost new vehicle sales. For dealers and suppliers, TMT granted credit lines and short-term loans.

At the time, the former king of Thailand, Bhumibol Adulyadej, showed concern for the issues of possible unemployment and granted a purchase order to TMT to produce a Toyota Soluna (Vios) and prolong the working period of Thai workers. Instead of selling the vehicle, TMT presented it to the king as a gift; the King, in turn, granted $17,518 (600,000 baht) to TMT to help establish the Rachamongkol Rice Mill, a project spearheaded by Ninnart Chaithi-rapinyo, the Vice Chairman of TMT. As an ongoing TMT-CSR activity, the mill still helps rice farmers maintain their crop prices and benefits TMT associates and the overall community. In brief, TMT overcame the crisis of 1997 by using Kaizen to strengthen its competitiveness and improving communication among top management and all of its associates.

In its developmental path towards sustainability, Toyota Motors set a Global Vision. The medium- to long-term management plan is prepared and implemented with the controlling measures as a feedback in its management system. In the implementation process, the Toyota Way 2001 and the Toyota Code of Conduct serves as an important global guideline for daily business operations for all employees.

Toyota's divisional organization structure is based on varied business operations, but is linked to the traditional Japanese organizational structures. In 2013, as a response to the safety issues and corresponding product recalls crisis of 2009, the centralized hierarchical structure underwent significant changes to become more decentralized. After the re-organization, Toyota's new organizational structure has the following main characteristics: global hierarchy, geographic divisions, and product-based divisions. The company is now more capable of responding to regional market conditions and is empowered to speedily respond to issues and to provide higher quality products. However, the increased decision-making power of regional heads has reduced headquarters' control over the global organization. Still, this organizational structure facilitates business resilience and continued growth.

A study by Wells and Orsato (2005) suggests that there is currently a shift away from the current all-steel, internal combustion engine car, which requires automakers to fundamentally reform their systems of production. The business challenges and the governmental regulations to preserve the environment means cars of the future have to be eco-friendly. This created a big challenge for auto firms that have sunk investments in the existing traditional car manufacturing technology.

In 2009, as a result of its worldwide recall-crisis and with over 8 million vehicles addressing issues related to 'unintended acceleration,' Toyota had a great lesson in keeping up with its production and leveraging of quality, durability, safety, and reliability issues. The company continued to develop innovative models to overcome environmental regulation challenges and to add a 'humanistic' dimension to consumers' image of auto companies. Its strategic direction is to go beyond zero environmental impact and achieve a net positive impact and sustainability.

SOURCES: Orsato, R. J. and P.Wells (2007a) "The Automobile Industry & Sustainability", *Journal of Cleaner Production* 15 (2007) 989-993; Orsato, R.J. and P. Wells (2007b) "U-Turn: The Rise And Demise Of The Automobile Industry," *Journal of Cleaner Production*, 15 (2007) 994-1006; Wells P, Orsato R. Redesigning the industrial ecology of the automobile; *Journal of Industrial Ecology* 2005;9(3):15e30; Prahalad C, Hamel G. "The core competence of the corporation," *Harvard Business Review*, Vol. 79-91, May and June, 1990; "Top 100 Most Innovative Companies Shift Focus from Quantity To Quality," Clarivate Analytics, http://www.prnewswire.com, accessed January 2017; "The Most Innovative Companies 2016: Getting Past "Not Invented Here"," The Boston Consulting Group, https://media-publications.bcg.com, accessed January, 2017; Guiding Principles at Toyota, http://www.toyota-global.com/company/vision_philosophy/guiding_principles.html; Jon Miller, "Challenging 'Challenge' Within the Toyota Way," *Quality Digest*, November 19, 2012, https://www.qualitydigest.com; Lawrence Gregory, "Toyota's Organizational Structure: An Analysis," *Panmore Institute*, February 1, 2017, http://panmore.com/toyota-organizational-structure-analysis; and http://www.toyota-global.com/sustainability/environment/challenge2050/

The Study of Strategic Management

1-1. Discuss the benefits of strategic management

Strategic management is a set of managerial decisions and actions that help determine the long-term performance of an organization. It includes environmental scanning (both external and internal), strategy formulation (strategic or long-range planning), strategy implementation, and evaluation and control. Originally called *business policy,* strategic management has advanced substantially with the concentrated efforts of researchers and practitioners. Today, we recognize both a science and an art to the application of strategic management techniques.

PHASES OF STRATEGIC MANAGEMENT

Many of the concepts and techniques that deal with strategic management have been developed and used successfully by the largest business organizations in the world as well as the newest startups. Over time, business practitioners and academic researchers have expanded and refined these concepts. One of the most critical drivers of business success is a leader's ability to design and implement a strategy for the company. Increasing risks of error, costly mistakes, and even economic ruin are causing today's professional managers in all organizations to take strategic management seriously in order to keep their companies competitive in an increasingly volatile environment.

As managers attempt to better deal with their changing world, a firm generally evolves through the following four **phases of strategic management**:[1]

Phase 1—Basic financial planning: Managers initiate serious planning when they are requested to propose the following year's budget. Projects are proposed on the basis of very little analysis, with most information coming from within the firm. The sales force usually provides the small amount of environmental information used in this effort. Such simplistic operational planning only pretends to be strategic management, yet it is quite time consuming. Normal company activities are often suspended for weeks while managers try to cram ideas into the proposed budget. The time horizon is usually one year.

Phase 2—Forecast-based planning: As annual budgets become less useful at stimulating long-term planning, managers attempt to propose five-year plans. At this point, they consider projects that may take more than one year. In addition to internal information, managers gather any available environmental data—usually on an ad hoc basis—and extrapolate current trends. This phase is also time consuming, often involving a full month or more of managerial activity to make sure all the proposed budgets fit together. The process gets very political as managers compete for larger shares of limited funds. Seemingly endless meetings take place to evaluate proposals and justify assumptions. The time horizon is usually three to five years.

Phase 3—Externally oriented (strategic) planning: Frustrated with highly political yet ineffectual five-year plans, top management takes control of the planning process by initiating a formal strategic planning system. The company seeks to increase its responsiveness to changing markets and competition by thinking and acting strategically. Planning is taken out of the hands of lower-level managers and concentrated in a planning staff whose task is to develop strategic plans for the corporation. Consultants often provide the sophisticated and innovative techniques that the planning staff uses to gather information and forecast future trends. Organizations start competitive intelligence units. Upper-level managers meet once a year at a resort "retreat" led by key members of the planning staff to evaluate and update the current strategic plan. Such top-down planning emphasizes formal strategy formulation and leaves the implementation issues to lower-management levels. Top management typically develops long-term plans with help from consultants but minimal input from lower levels.

Phase 4—Strategic management: Realizing that even the best strategic plans are worthless without the input and commitment of lower-level managers, top management forms planning groups of managers and key employees at many levels, from various departments and workgroups. They develop and integrate a series of plans focused on emphasizing the company's true competitive advantages. Strategic plans at this point detail the implementation, evaluation, and control issues. Rather than attempting to perfectly forecast the future, the plans emphasize probable scenarios and contingency strategies. The sophisticated annual five-year strategic plan is replaced with strategic thinking at all levels of the organization throughout the year. Strategic information, previously available only centrally to top management, is used by people throughout the organization. Instead of a large centralized planning staff, internal and external planning consultants are available to help guide group strategy discussions. Although top management may still initiate the strategic planning process, the resulting strategies may come from anywhere in the organization. Planning is typically interactive across levels and is no longer strictly top down. People at all levels are now involved.

General Electric, one of the pioneers of strategic planning, led the transition from strategic planning to strategic management during the 1980s.[2] By the 1990s, most other corporations around the world had also begun the conversion to strategic management.

BENEFITS OF STRATEGIC MANAGEMENT

Strategic management emphasizes long-term performance. Many companies can manage short-term bursts of high performance, but only a few can sustain it over a longer period of time. Since the release of the original *Fortune 500* companies listing in 1955, more than 1,800 companies have made the list. In 2015, 18 new companies joined the list for the first time meaning that 18 others fell from the list.[3] To be successful in the long-run, companies must not only be able to *execute* current activities to satisfy an existing market, but they must also *adapt* those activities to satisfy new and changing markets.[4]

Research reveals that organizations that engage in strategic management generally outperform those that do not.[5] The attainment of an appropriate match, or "fit," between an organization's environment and its strategy, structure, and processes has positive effects on the organization's performance.[6] Strategic planning becomes increasingly important as the environment becomes more unstable.[7] For example, studies of the impact of deregulation on the U.S. railroad and trucking industries found that companies that changed their strategies and structures as their environment changed outperformed companies that did not change.[8]

A survey of nearly 50 corporations in a variety of countries and industries found the three most highly rated benefits of strategic management to be:

- A clearer sense of strategic vision for the firm.
- A sharper focus on what is strategically important.
- An improved understanding of a rapidly changing environment.[9]

A survey by McKinsey & Company of 800 executives found that formal strategic planning processes improved overall satisfaction with strategy development.[10] To be effective, however, strategic management need not always be a formal process. It can begin with a few simple questions:

- Where is the organization now? (Not where do we hope it is!)
- If no significant changes are made, where will the organization be in one year? Two years? Five years? Ten years? Are the answers acceptable?
- If the answers are not acceptable, what specific actions should management undertake? What are the risks and payoffs involved?

The Bain & Company's *2015 Management Tools and Trends* survey of 1,067 global executives revealed that strategic planning was the number two tool used by decision makers just behind customer relationship management. Other highly ranked strategic management tools were mission and vision statements, change management programs, and balanced scorecards.[11] A study by Joyce, Nohria, and Roberson of 200 firms in 50 subindustries found that devising and maintaining an engaged, focused strategy was the first of four essential management practices that best differentiated between successful and unsuccessful companies.[12] Based on these and other studies, it can be concluded that strategic management is crucial for long-term organizational success.

Research into the planning practices of companies in the oil industry concludes that the real value of modern strategic planning is more in the *strategic thinking* and *organizational learning* that is part of a future-oriented planning process than in any resulting written strategic plan.[13] Small companies, in particular, may plan informally and irregularly. Nevertheless, studies of small- and medium-sized businesses reveal that the greater the level of planning intensity, as measured by the presence of a formal strategic plan, the greater the level of financial performance, especially when measured in terms of sales increases.[14]

Planning the strategy of large, multidivisional corporations can be complex and time consuming. It often takes slightly more than a year for a large company to move from situation assessment to a final decision agreement. For example, strategic plans in the global oil industry tend to cover four to five years. The planning horizon for oil exploration is even longer—up to 15 years.[15] Because of the relatively large number of people affected by a strategic decision in a large firm, a formalized, more sophisticated system is needed to ensure that strategic planning leads to successful performance. Otherwise, top management becomes isolated from developments in the business units, and lower-level managers lose sight of the corporate mission and objectives.

Globalization, Innovation, and Sustainability: Challenges to Strategic Management

1-2. Explain how globalization, innovation, and environmental sustainability influence strategic management

Not too long ago, a business corporation could be successful by focusing only on making and selling goods and services within its national boundaries. International considerations were minimal. Profits earned from exporting products to foreign lands were considered frosting on the cake, but not really essential to corporate success. During the 1960s, most U.S. companies organized themselves around a number of product divisions that made and sold goods only in the United States. All manufacturing and sales outside the United States were typically managed through one international division. An international assignment was usually considered a message that the person was no longer promotable and should be looking for another job.

Similarly, for a very long time, many established companies viewed innovation as the domain of the new entrant. The efficiencies that came with size were considered to be the core competitive advantage of the large organization. That view has proven to be a recipe for failure. The ability to create unique value and grow an organization organically requires innovation skills. A strategic management approach suggests that if an organization stands still, it will be run over by the competition. What was extraordinary last year is the standard expectation of customers this year. We have watched many large corporations succumb to the lack of innovation in their organization. Sears was the dominant retailer in the United States for more than 70 years. Today, it is struggling to find an approach that will give it a competitive advantage. IBM was a company that dominated mainframe computing and was fortunate enough to find a visionary CEO when the mainframe market was crushed by the advent of the PC. That CEO (Louis V. Gerstner, Jr.) transformed the organization with innovation that was cultural, structural, and painful for the company employees. Innovation is rarely easy and it is almost never painless. Nonetheless, it is a core element of successful strategic management.

Lastly, until the later part of the 20th century, a business firm could be very successful without considering sustainable business practices. Companies dumped their waste products in nearby streams or lakes and freely polluted the air with smoke containing noxious gases. Responding to complaints, governments eventually passed laws restricting the freedom to pollute the environment. Lawsuits forced companies to stop old practices. Nevertheless, until the dawn of the 21st century, most executives considered pollution abatement measures to be a cost of business that should be either minimized or avoided. Rather than clean up a polluting manufacturing site, they often closed the plant and moved manufacturing offshore to a developing nation with fewer environmental restrictions. The issues of recycling and refurbishing, as well as a company's responsibility to both the local inhabitants and the environment where it operated, were not considered mainstream business approaches, because it was felt these concerns did not help maximize shareholder value. In those days, the word *sustainability* was used to describe competitive advantage, not the environment.

Today, the term used to describe a business's sustainability is the **triple bottom line**. This phrase was first used by John Elkington in 1994 to suggest that companies prepare three different bottom lines in their annual report.[16]

- Traditional Profit/Loss
- People Account—The social responsibility of the organization
- Planet Account—The environmental responsibility of the organization

This triple bottom line has become increasingly important to business today. Companies seek Leadership in Energy and Environmental Design (LEED) certification for their buildings and mold a reputation for being a business that is friendly to the world. LEED certification is available for all structures and includes a number of levels depending upon the efforts made to have a building be self-sustaining or to have as little impact (the smallest footprint) on the environment as possible.[17]

IMPACT OF GLOBALIZATION

Today, everything has changed. **Globalization**, the integrated internationalization of markets and corporations, has changed the way modern corporations do business. As Thomas Friedman points out in *The World Is Flat*, jobs, knowledge, and capital are now able to move across borders with far greater speed and far less friction than was possible only a few years ago.[18]

For example, the interconnected nature of the global financial community meant that the mortgage lending problems of U.S. banks led to a global financial crisis that started in 2008 and impacted economies for years. The worldwide availability of the Internet and supply-chain logistical improvements, such as containerized shipping, mean that companies can now locate anywhere and work with multiple partners to serve any market. For companies seeking a low-cost approach, the internationalization of business has been a new avenue for competitive advantage. Nike and Reebok manufacture their athletic shoes in various countries throughout Asia for sale on every continent. Many other companies in North America and Western Europe are outsourcing their manufacturing, software development, or customer service to companies in China, Eastern Europe, or India. English language proficiency, lower wages in India, and large pools of talented software programmers now enable IBM to employ an estimated 100,000 people in its global delivery centers in Bangalore, Delhi, or Kolkata to serve the needs of clients in Atlanta, Munich, or Melbourne.[19] Instead of using one international division to manage everything outside the home country, large corporations are now using matrix structures in which product units are interwoven with country or regional units. Today, international assignments are considered key for anyone interested in reaching top management.

As more industries become global, strategic management is becoming an increasingly important way to keep track of international developments and position a company for long-term competitive advantage. For example, General Electric moved a major research and development lab for its medical systems division from Japan to China in order to learn more about developing new products for developing economies. Microsoft's largest research center outside Redmond, Washington, is in Beijing.

The formation of regional trade associations and agreements, such as the European Union, NAFTA, Mercosur, Andean Community, CAFTA, and ASEAN, is changing how international business is being conducted. See the **Global Issue** feature to learn how regional trade associations are pushing corporations to establish a manufacturing presence wherever they wish to market goods. These associations have led to the increasing harmonization of standards so that products can more easily be sold and moved across national boundaries. International considerations have led to the strategic alliance between British Airways and American Airlines and to the acquisition of the Anheuser-Busch Companies by the Belgium company InBev, creating AB InBev, among others.

IMPACT OF INNOVATION

Innovation, as the term is used in business, is meant to describe new products, services, methods, and organizational approaches that allow the business to achieve extraordinary returns. Boston Consulting Group (BCG) found that innovation is a top 3 priority for three-quarters of the companies in the 2014 BCG global innovation survey.[20] They also found that:

- 61% were spending more money on innovation in 2014 than in 2013
- 75% of respondents reported that innovation investment was primarily aimed at long-term advantage and current competitive advantage
- The top five most innovative companies were Apple, Google, Samsung, Microsoft, and IBM
- 70% of executives felt their own companies' innovation capabilities were only average and 13% felt they were weak.

GLOBAL issue

ASEAN: REGIONAL TRADE ASSOCIATIONS

The Association of Southeast Asian Nations (ASEAN) was formed in 1967 with 5 founding members: Indonesia, Malaysia, the Philippines, Singapore, and Thailand in an effort to reduce regional hostilities and to fight the potential threat of communist-led insurgencies at the height of the U.S. war in Vietnam. They signed the Treaty of Amity and Cooperation emphasizing ASEAN's promotion of peace, prosperity and stability. Later in 1990s, Brunei (1984), Vietnam (1995), Laos and Myanmar (1997), and Cambodia (1999) joined the ASEAN. Along with the regional security objectives, ASEAN have established its regional economic integration, ASEAN economic community (AEC). The AEC's four pillars include: the creation of a single market with the free flow of goods, services, investment, and skilled labor; fair economic competition; sustainable and equitable economic development; and integrating ASEAN into the global economy. ASEAN have liberalized intra-ASEAN trade over the last 20 years by establishing the ASEAN Free Trade Area (AFTA).

The region accounts for over 600 million people and a combined GDP of about $2.6 trillion in 2014. Historically, ASEAN has been one of the most liberal and attractive investment regimes among developing countries. It has liberalized intra-ASEAN trade over the last 20 years by establishing the ASEAN Free Trade Area (AFTA). During 2001-2013, it was the second fastest growing economy in Asia, i.e., China (575%) and ASEAN (313%), while those in the U.S. and E.U. have slowed down significantly. It is expected to rank as the world's fourth-largest economy by 2050. With the drop in FDI from developed countries, the emergence of FDI from ASEAN, which is rising, could complement the drop. Furthermore, ASEAN countries such as Singapore, Malaysia, and Thailand are also gradually extending their contribution to world FDI.

....

SOURCES: Lee, C. and y. Fukunaga,"ASEAN Regional Cooperation on Competition Policy", *Journal of Asian Economics,* (2014), 77–91; and Eleanor Albert, "ASEAN: The Association of Southeast Asian Nations," Council on Foreign Relations, (September 1, 2016), www.cfr.org.

Innovation is the machine that generates business opportunities in the market; however, it is the implementation of potential innovations that truly drives businesses to be remarkable. Although there is a value in being a first mover, there is also a tremendous value in being a second or third mover with the right implementation. PC tablets had been developed and sold for more than two decades before the iPad stormed the market. Many people forget that Apple released the Newton tablet back in 1992.[21] Not only was the timing not right, but the product was not promoted in a way that consumers felt a compelling need to buy one. Many elements have to come together for an innovation to bring long-term success to a company.

IMPACT OF SUSTAINABILITY

Sustainability refers to the use of business practices to manage the triple bottom line as was discussed earlier. That triple bottom line involves (1) the management of traditional profit/loss; (2) the management of the company's social responsibility; and (3) the management of its environmental responsibility.

The company has a relatively obvious long-term responsibility to the shareholders of the organization. That means that the company has to be able to thrive despite changes in the industry, society, and the physical environment. This is the focus of much of this textbook and the focus of strategy in business.

The company that pursues a sustainable approach to business has a responsibility to its employees, its customers, and the community in which it operates. Companies

that have embraced sustainable practices have seen dramatic increases in risk mitigation and innovation, and an overall feeling of corporate social responsibility.
The 2014 Sustainability & Employee Engagement survey managed by GreenBiz
in association with the National Environmental Education Foundation found that
employees at companies who focused on business sustainability reported 57%
applied more effort in their jobs and 87% were less likely to leave the company. In
addition, more than 50% of companies place at least some or a great deal of value
on a job candidate's sustainability knowledge.[22] In fact, a Gallop research study
found that these engaged organizations had 3.9 times the earnings per share (EPS)
growth rates when compared to organizations with lower engagement in the same
industry.[23]

The company also has a responsibility to treat the environment well. This is usually
defined as trying to achieve (or approach) zero impact on the environment. Recycling,
increased use of renewable resources, reduction of waste, and refitting buildings to
reduce their impact on the environment, among many other techniques, are included
in this element of the triple bottom line. The most recognized worldwide standard for
environmental efficiency is the ISO 14001 designation. It is not a set of standards, but a
framework of activities aimed at effective environmental management.[24]

South American countries are also working to harmonize their trading relationships
with each other and to form trade associations. The establishment of the **Mercosur
(Mercosul** in Portuguese) free-trade area among Argentina, Brazil, Paraguay, Uruguay,
and Venezuela brings together a group that includes 295 million people and $3.5 tril-
lion in combined GDP. As of late 2015 Bolivia was in the final stages of accession. The
Andean Community (Comunidad Andina de Naciones) is a free-trade alliance composed of Columbia, Ecuador, Peru, and Bolivia (until its acceptance into Mercosur).
On May 23, 2008, the **Union of South American Nations** was formed to unite the two
existing free-trade areas with a secretariat in Ecuador and a parliament in Bolivia. It
consists of 12 South American countries.

In 2004, the five Central American countries of El Salvador, Guatemala, Honduras,
Nicaragua, and Costa Rica, plus the United States, signed the **Central American Free
Trade Agreement (CAFTA)**. The Dominican Republic joined soon thereafter. Previously, Central American textile manufacturers had to pay import duties of 18%–28%
to sell their clothes in the United States unless they bought their raw material from
U.S. companies. Under CAFTA, members can buy raw material from anywhere, and
their exports are duty free. In addition, CAFTA eliminated import duties on 80% of
U.S. goods exported to the region, with the remaining tariffs being phased out over
10 years.

The **Association of Southeast Asian Nations (ASEAN)**—composed of Brunei
Darussalam, Cambodia, Indonesia, Laos, Malaysia, Myanmar, Philippines, Singapore,
Thailand, and Vietnam—is in the process of linking its members into a border-
less economic zone by 2020. Increasingly referred to as ASEAN+3, ASEAN now
includes China, Japan, and South Korea in its annual summit meetings. The ASEAN
nations negotiated linkage of the ASEAN Free Trade Area (AFTA) with the existing free-trade area of Australia and New Zealand. With the EU extending eastward
and NAFTA extending southward to someday connect with CAFTA and the Union
of South American Nations, pressure is building on the independent Asian nations to
join ASEAN.

Porter and Reinhardt warn that "in addition to understanding its emissions costs,
every firm needs to evaluate its vulnerability to climate-related effects such as regional
shifts in the availability of energy and water, the reliability of infrastructures and supply chains, and the prevalence of infectious diseases."[25] The National Centers for

Environmental Information has calculated that there were 178 weather and climate disasters where damages exceeded $1 billion between 1980 and 2014. The total cost of these 178 events exceeded $1 trillion.[26]

Theories of Organizational Adaptation

1-3. Discuss the differences between the theories of organizations

Globalization, innovation, and sustainability present real challenges to the strategic management of businesses. How can any one company keep track of all the changing technological, economic, political–legal, and sociocultural trends around the world in order to make the necessary adjustments? This is not an easy task. Various theories have been proposed to account for how organizations obtain fit with their environment and how these approaches have been used to varying degrees by researchers trying to understand firm performance. The theory of **population ecology** suggests that once an organization is successfully established in a particular environmental niche, it is unable to adapt to changing conditions. Inertia prevents the organization from changing in any significant manner. The company is thus replaced (is bought out or goes bankrupt) by other organizations more suited to the new environment. Although it is a popular theory in sociology, research fails to support the arguments of population ecology.[27] **Institution theory**, in contrast, proposes that organizations can and do adapt to changing conditions by imitating other successful organizations. Many examples can be found of companies that have adapted to changing circumstances by imitating an admired firm's strategies and management techniques.[28] The theory does not, however, explain how or by whom successful new strategies are developed in the first place. The **strategic choice perspective** goes a significant step further by proposing that not only do organizations adapt to a changing environment, but they also have the opportunity and power to reshape their environment. This perspective is supported by research indicating that the decisions of a firm's management have at least as great an impact on firm performance as overall industry factors.[29] Because of its emphasis on managers making rational strategic decisions, the strategic choice perspective is the dominant one taken in strategic management. Its argument that adaptation is a dynamic process fits with the view of **organizational learning theory**, which says that an organization adjusts defensively to a changing environment and uses knowledge offensively to improve the fit between itself and its environment. This perspective expands the strategic choice perspective to include people at all levels becoming involved in providing input into strategic decisions.[30]

In agreement with the concepts of organizational learning theory, an increasing number of companies are realizing that they must shift from a vertically organized, top-down type of organization to a more horizontally managed, interactive organization. They are attempting to adapt more quickly to changing conditions by becoming "learning organizations."

Creating a Learning Organization

1-4. Discuss the Activities where learning organizations excel

Strategic management has now evolved to the point that its primary value is in helping an organization operate successfully in a dynamic, complex environment. To be competitive in dynamic environments, corporations are becoming less bureaucratic and more flexible. In stable environments such as those that existed in years past, a competitive strategy simply involved defining a competitive position and then defending it.

As it takes less and less time for one product, service, or technology to replace another, companies are finding that there is no such thing as a permanent competitive advantage. Many agree with Richard D'Aveni, who says in his book *Hypercompetition* that any sustainable competitive advantage lies not in doggedly following a centrally managed five-year plan but in stringing together a series of strategic short-term thrusts (as Apple does by cutting into the sales of its own offerings with periodic introductions of new products).[31] This means that corporations must develop *strategic flexibility*—the ability to shift from one dominant strategy to another.[32]

Strategic flexibility demands a long-term commitment to the development and nurturing of critical resources and capabilities. It also demands that the company become a **learning organization**—an organization skilled at creating, acquiring, and transferring knowledge and at modifying its behavior to reflect new knowledge and insights. Organizational learning is a critical component of competitiveness in a dynamic environment. It is particularly important to innovation and new product development.[33] Siemens, a major electronics company, created a global knowledge-sharing network, called ShareNet, in order to quickly spread information technology throughout the firm. Based on its experience with ShareNet, Siemens established PeopleShareNet, a system that serves as a virtual expert marketplace for facilitating the creation of cross-cultural teams composed of members with specific knowledge and competencies.[34]

Learning organizations are skilled at four main activities:

- Solving problems systematically
- Experimenting with new approaches
- Learning from their own experiences and past history as well as from the experiences of others
- Transferring knowledge quickly and efficiently throughout the organization.[35]

Business historian Alfred Chandler proposes that high-technology industries are defined by "paths of learning" in which organizational strengths derive from learned capabilities.[36] According to Chandler, companies spring from an individual entrepreneur's knowledge, which then evolves into organizational knowledge. This organizational knowledge is composed of three basic strengths: technical skills; functional knowledge, such as production and marketing; and managerial expertise. This knowledge leads to new areas in which the company can succeed and creates an entry barrier to new competitors. Chandler believes that once a corporation has built its learning base to the point where it has become a core company in its industry, entrepreneurial startups are rarely able to successfully enter. Thus, organizational knowledge becomes a competitive advantage that is difficult to understand and imitate.

Strategic management is essential for learning organizations to avoid stagnation through continuous self-examination and experimentation. People at all levels, not just top management, participate in strategic management—helping to scan the environment for critical information, suggesting changes to strategies and programs to take advantage of environmental shifts, and working with others to continuously improve work methods, procedures, and evaluation techniques. The Toyota production system is famous for empowering employees to improve. If an employee spots a problem on the line, he/she pulls the cord, which immediately starts a speedy diagnosis. The line continues if the problem can be solved within one minute. If not, the production line is shut down until the problem is solved. At Toyota, they learn from their mistakes as much as they learn from their successes. Improvements are sent to all factories worldwide.[37]

Organizations that are willing to experiment and are able to learn from their experiences are more successful than those that are not.[38] This was seen in a study of U.S. manufacturers of diagnostic imaging equipment, the most successful firms were those that improved products sold in the United States by incorporating some of what they had learned from their manufacturing and sales experiences in other countries. The less successful firms used their foreign operations primarily as sales outlets, not as important sources of technical knowledge.[39] Research also reveals that multidivisional corporations that establish ways to transfer knowledge across divisions are more innovative than other diversified corporations that do not.[40]

Basic Model of Strategic Management

Strategic management consists of four basic elements:

1-5. Describe the basic model of strategic management and its components

- Environmental scanning
- Strategy formulation
- Strategy implementation
- Evaluation and control.

Figure 1–1 illustrates how these four elements interact; **Figure 1–2** expands each of these elements and serves as the model for this book. This model is both rational and prescriptive. It is a planning model that presents what a corporation *should* do in terms of the strategic management process, not what any particular firm may actually do. The rational planning model predicts that as environmental uncertainty increases, corporations that work diligently to analyze and predict more accurately the changing situation in which they operate will outperform those that do not. Empirical research studies support this model.[41] The terms used in **Figure 1–2** are explained in the following pages.

ENVIRONMENTAL SCANNING

Environmental scanning is the monitoring, evaluating, and disseminating of information from the external and internal environments to key people within the corporation. Its purpose is to identify **strategic factors**—those external and internal elements that will assist in the analysis of the strategic decisions of the corporation. The simplest way to represent the outcomes of environmental scanning is through a **SWOT approach**. SWOT is an acronym used to describe the particular **S**trengths, **W**eaknesses, **O**pportunities, and **T**hreats that appear to be strategic factors for a specific company. The **external environment** consists of variables (opportunities and threats) that are outside the organization and not typically within the short-run control of top management. These variables form the context within which the corporation exists.

FIGURE 1–1
Basic Elements of the Strategic Management Process

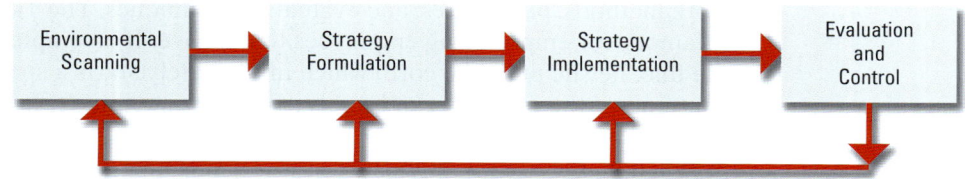

FIGURE 1–2 Strategic Management Model

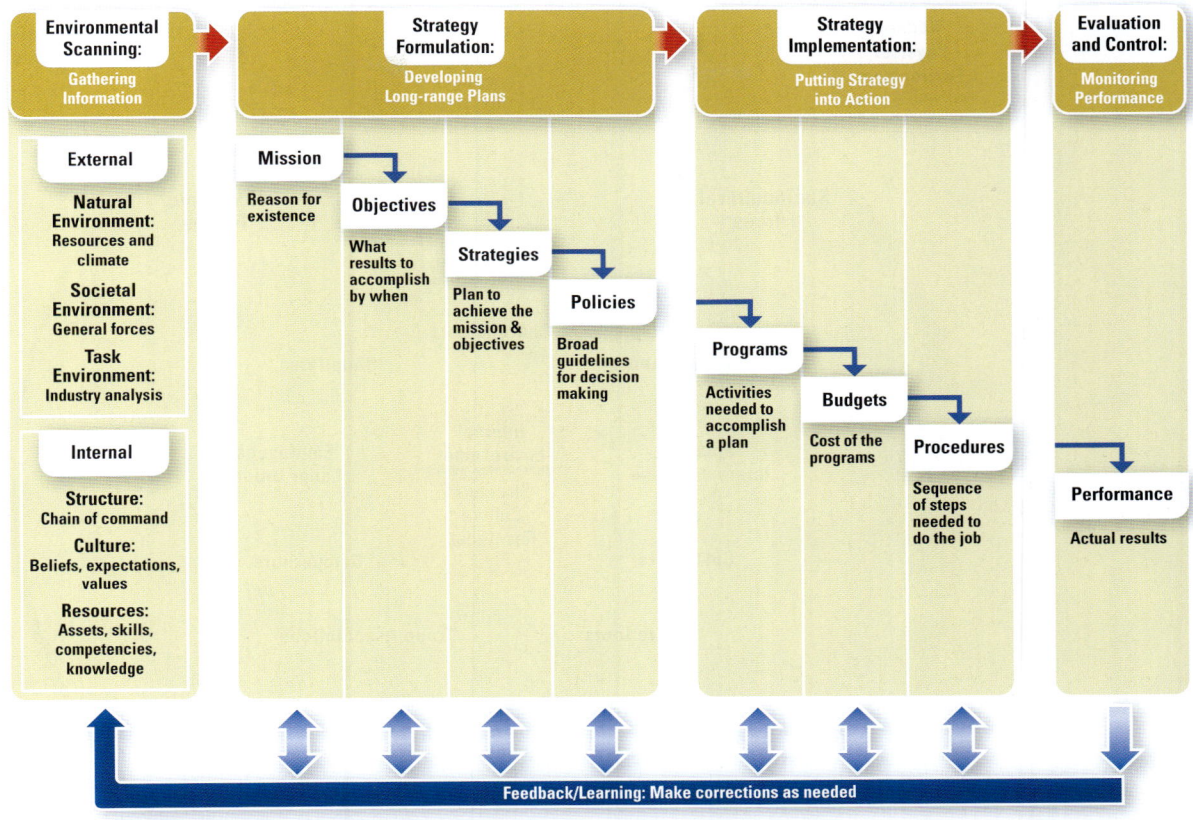

SOURCE: T. L. Wheelen, "Strategic Management Model," adapted from "Concepts of Management," presented to Society for Advancement of Management (SAM), International Meeting, Richmond, VA, 1981. Kathryn E. Wheelen solely owns all of (Dr.) Thomas L. Wheelen's copyright materials. Kathryn E. Wheelen requires written reprint permission for each book that this material is to be printed in. Copyright © 1981 by T. L. Wheelen and SAM. Copyright © 1982, 1985, 1988, and 2005 by T. L. Wheelen and J. D. Hunger. Revised 1989, 1995, 1998, 2000, 2005, 2009, and 2013. Reprinted by permission of the copyright holders.

Figure 1–3 depicts key environmental variables. They may be general forces and trends within the natural or societal environments or specific factors that operate within an organization's specific task environment—often called its *industry*. The analysis techniques available for the examination of these environmental variables are the focus of **Chapter 4**.

The **internal environment** of a corporation consists of variables (strengths and weaknesses) that are within the organization itself and are within the short-run control of top management. These variables form the context in which work is done. They include the corporation's structure, culture, capabilities, and resources. Key strengths form a set of core competencies that the corporation can use to gain competitive advantage. Although strategic management is fundamentally concerned with what constitutes an organization's strengths, weaknesses, opportunities, and threats, the methods to analyze each has developed substantially in the past two decades. No longer do we simply list the SWOT variables and have employees try to populate the quadrants. Each of the four is rich with processes and techniques that will allow for a robust and sophisticated understanding of the company. This will be examined in detail beginning with **Chapter 5** of the text.

FIGURE 1–3 Environmental Variables

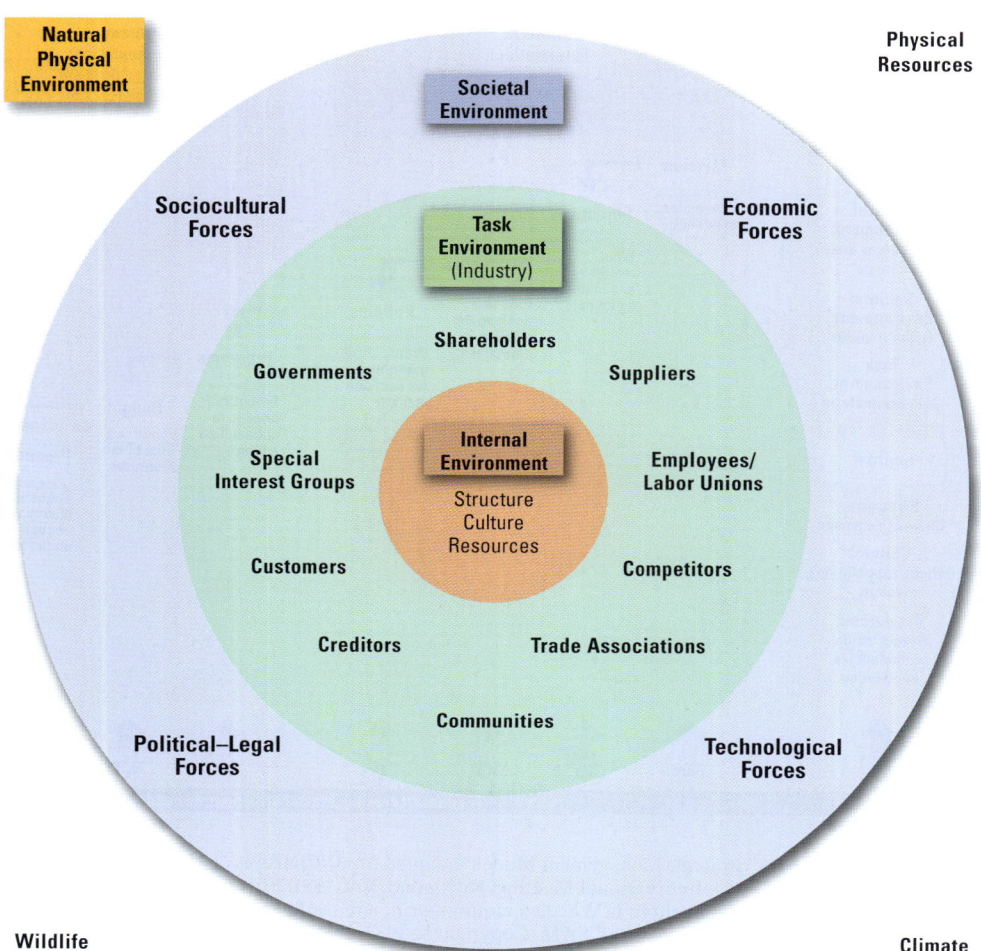

STRATEGY FORMULATION

Strategy formulation is the process of investigation, analysis, and decision making that provides the company with the criteria for attaining a competitive advantage. It includes defining the competitive advantages of the business, identifying weaknesses that are impacting the company's ability to grow, crafting the corporate mission, specifying achievable objectives, and setting policy guidelines.

Mission: Stating Purpose

An organization's **mission** is the purpose or reason for the organization's existence. It announces what the company is providing to society—either a service such as consulting, a set of products such as automobile tires, or a combination of the two such as tablets and their associated Apps. A well-conceived mission statement defines the fundamental, unique purpose that sets a company apart from other firms of its type. Research reveals that firms with mission statements containing explicit descriptions of their competitive advantages have significantly higher growth than firms without such statements.[42] A mission statement may also include the firm's values and philosophy about how it does business and treats its employees; however, that is usually better kept as a separate document. A well-crafted mission statement describes what the company is now and what it wants to become—management's strategic vision of the firm's future. The mission statement promotes a sense of shared expectations in employees and communicates a public image to important stakeholder groups in the company's task environment. Some people like to consider vision and mission as two different concepts: Mission describes what the organization is now; **vision** describes what the organization would like to become. We prefer to combine these ideas into a single mission statement.[43]

A classic example is that etched in bronze at Newport News Shipbuilding, unchanged since its founding in 1886:

> *We shall build good ships here—at a profit if we can—at a loss if we must—but always good ships.*[44]

A mission may be defined narrowly or broadly in scope. An example of a *broad* mission statement is that used by many corporations: "Serve the best interests of shar-eowners, customers, and employees." A broadly defined mission statement such as this keeps the company from restricting itself to one field or product line, but it fails to clearly identify either what it makes or which products/markets it plans to emphasize. Broad statements are relatively useless while narrow statements provide direction and value to the organization.

Objectives: Listing Expected Results

Objectives are the end results of planned activity. They should be stated as *action verbs* and tell employees what is to be accomplished and when, with appropriate metrics. The achievement of corporate objectives should result in the fulfillment of a corporation's mission. In effect, this is what society gives back to the corporation when the corporation does a good job of fulfilling its mission. Coca-Cola has set the standard of a focused, international company. In their Vision 2020 plan, they have laid out specific objectives including reducing the overall carbon footprint of their business operations by 15% by 2020, as compared to the 2007 baseline, and reducing the impact of their packaging by maximizing their use of renewable, reusable, and recyclable resources to recover the equivalent of 100% of their packaging. This type of focus has made Coca-Cola a perennial member of the Fortune 500, one of the Fortune 50 Most Admired Companies, one of Barron's Most Respected Companies in the World, and a Diversity, Inc. Top 50 company. Over the past 10 years, they have raised their dividend an average of 9.8% per year and the company's earnings per share have jumped 11.3% per year over the past five years.[45]

The term *goal* is often used interchangeably with the term objective. In this book, we prefer to differentiate the two terms. In contrast to an objective, we consider a *goal* as an open-ended statement of what one wants to accomplish, with no quantification of what is to be achieved and no time criteria for completion. For example, a simple statement of "increased profitability" is thus a goal, not an objective, because it does not state how much profit the firm wants to make the next year. A good objective should be action-oriented and begin with the word *to*. An example of an objective is "to increase the firm's profitability in 2017 by 10% over 2016."

Some of the areas in which a corporation might establish its goals and objectives are:

- Profitability (net profits)
- Efficiency (low costs, etc.)
- Growth (increase in total assets, sales, etc.)
- Shareholder wealth (dividends plus stock price appreciation)
- Utilization of resources (Return on Equity (ROE) or Return on Investment (ROI))

- Reputation (being considered a "top" firm)
- Contributions to employees (employment security, wages, diversity)
- Contributions to society (taxes paid, participation in charities, providing a needed product or service)
- Market leadership (market share)
- Technological leadership (innovations, creativity)
- Survival (avoiding bankruptcy)
- Personal needs of top management (using the firm for personal purposes, such as providing jobs for relatives)

Strategy: Defining the Competitive Advantages

An organization must examine the external environment in order to determine who constitutes the perfect customer for the business as it exists today, who the most direct competitors are for that customer, what the company does that is necessary to compete, and what the company does that truly sets it apart from its competitors. These elements can be rephrased into the strengths of the business, the understanding of its weaknesses relative to its competitors, what opportunities would be most prudent, and what threats might affect the business's primary competitive advantages.

A **strategy** of a business forms a comprehensive master approach that states how the business will achieve its mission and objectives. It maximizes competitive advantage and minimizes competitive disadvantage. Pfizer, the giant drug company has embraced the need for this type of approach. Faced with the rapid fall-off of its biggest blockbuster drugs (patents expiring), Pfizer was faced with the question of how to generate the R&D to create new drugs. Historically, the company had relied upon its cadre of scientists, but this changed in the past few years. Pfizer moved aggressively to acquire drug makers in the emerging biosimiliar market (small molecule biologics made from living cells). Pfizer's late-stage biosimiliar drugs have a very good chance of allowing the company to capture a significant part of what is expected to be a US$20 billion market by 2020. This is the crucial new ground from which they hope to replace such blockbusters as Lipitor, which saw its sales drop from US$12 billion in 2012 to just over US$2 billion in 2015 after the patent expired.[46]

The typical larger business addresses three types of strategy: corporate, business, and functional.

- **Corporate strategy** describes a company's overall direction in terms of growth and the management of its various businesses. Corporate strategies generally fit within the three main categories of stability, growth, and retrenchment.

- **Business strategy** usually occurs at the business unit or product level, and it emphasizes improvement of the competitive position of a corporation's products or services in the specific industry or market segment served by that business unit. Business strategies may fit within the two overall categories: *competitive* and *cooperative* strategies. For example, Staples, the U.S. office supply store chain, has used a competitive strategy to differentiate its retail stores from its competitors by adding services to its stores, such as copying, UPS shipping, and hiring mobile technicians who can fix computers and install networks. British Airways has followed a cooperative strategy by forming an alliance with American Airlines in order to provide global service. Cooperative strategy may be used to provide a competitive advantage in situations where the cooperating entities are not in direct competition for customers. Intel, a manufacturer of computer microprocessors, uses its alliance (cooperative strategy) with Microsoft to differentiate itself (competitive strategy) from AMD, its primary competitor.

- **Functional strategy** is the approach taken by a functional area to achieve corporate and business unit objectives and strategies by maximizing resource productivity. It is concerned with developing and nurturing a distinctive competence to provide a company or business unit with a competitive advantage. Examples of research and development (R&D) functional strategies are technological followership (imitation of the products of other companies) and technological leadership (pioneering an innovation). For years, Magic Chef had been a successful appliance maker by spending little on R&D but by quickly imitating the innovations of other competitors. This helped the company keep its costs lower than those of its competitors and consequently to compete with lower prices. In terms of marketing functional strategies, Procter & Gamble (P&G) is a master of marketing "pull"—the process of spending huge amounts on advertising in order to create customer demand. This supports P&G's competitive strategy of differentiating its products from those of its competitors.

Business firms use all three types of strategy simultaneously. A **hierarchy of strategy** is a grouping of strategy types by level in the organization. Hierarchy of strategy is a nesting of one strategy within another so that they complement and support one another. (See **Figure 1–4**.) Functional strategies support business strategies, which, in turn, support the corporate strategy(ies).

Policies: Setting Guidelines

A **policy** is a broad guideline for decision making that links the formulation of a strategy with its implementation. Companies use policies to make sure that employees throughout the firm make decisions and take actions that support the corporation's mission, objectives, and strategies. For example, when Cisco decided on a strategy of growth through acquisitions, it established a policy to consider only companies with no more than 75 employees, 75% of whom were engineers.[47] Consider the following company policies:

- **3M:** 3M says researchers should spend 15% of their time working on something other than their primary project. (This supports 3M's strong product development strategy.)

FIGURE 1–4
Hierarchy of
Strategy

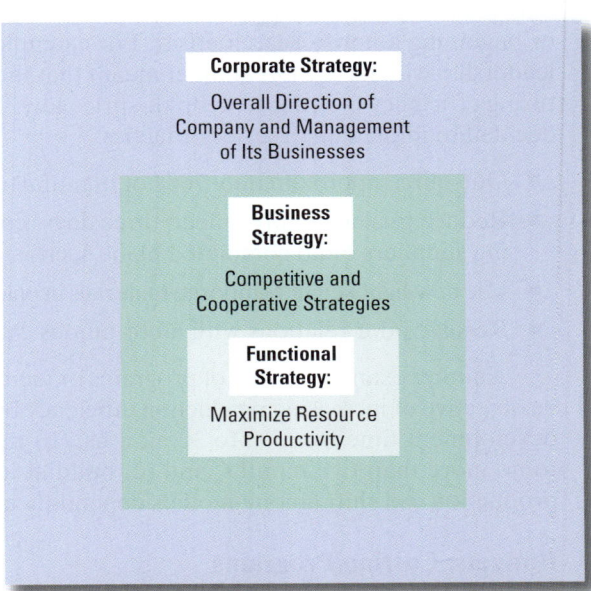

- **Google:** Google's health care plan includes their onsite medical staff. Any employee who feels ill at work can make an appointment with the doctor at the Googleplex. This supports the Google HRM functional strategy to support its employees.
- **General Electric:** GE must be number one or two wherever it competes. (This supports GE's objective to be number one in market capitalization.)
- **Starbucks:** All Starbucks employees are offered a Total Pay Package that includes a 401(k) savings plan, stock options, and an employee stock purchase plan. This goes a long way toward their goal of having every employee feel like a partner in the business.
- **Ryanair:** Ryanair charges for everything a passenger might want or need on a flight. The only thing you get with your ticket is the right to a seat on the plane (and that seat depends upon how fast you can run across the tarmac to the plane).

Policies such as these provide clear guidance to managers throughout the organization. (Strategy formulation is discussed in greater detail in **Chapter 6, 7,** and **8**.)

STRATEGY IMPLEMENTATION

Strategy implementation is a process by which strategies and policies are put into action through the development of programs, budgets, and procedures. This process might involve changes within the overall culture, structure, and/or management system of the entire organization. Except when such drastic corporatewide changes are needed, however, the implementation of strategy is typically conducted by middle- and lower-level managers, with review by top management. Sometimes referred to as *operational planning*, strategy implementation often involves day-to-day decisions in resource allocation.

Programs and Tactics: Defining Actions

A **program** or a **tactic** is a statement of the activities or steps needed to support a strategy. The terms are interchangeable. In practice, a program is a collection of tactics where a tactic is the individual action taken by the organization as an element of the effort to accomplish a plan. A program or tactic makes a strategy action-oriented. It may involve restructuring the corporation, changing the company's internal culture, or beginning a new research effort. For example, Boeing's strategy to regain industry leadership with its 787 Dreamliner meant that the company had to increase its manufacturing efficiency in order to keep the price low. To significantly cut costs, management decided to implement a series of tactics:

- Outsource approximately 70% of manufacturing.
- Reduce final assembly time to three days (compared to 20 for its 737 plane) by having suppliers build completed plane sections.
- Use new, lightweight composite materials in place of aluminum to reduce inspection time.
- Resolve poor relations with labor unions caused by downsizing and outsourcing.

Another example is a set of programs or tactics used by automaker BMW to achieve its objective of increasing production efficiency by 5% each year: (a) shorten new model development time from 60 to 30 months, (b) reduce preproduction time from a year to no more than five months, and (c) build at least two vehicles in each plant so that production can shift among models depending upon demand.

Budgets: Costing Programs

A **budget** is a statement of a corporation's programs in terms of dollars. Used in planning and control, a budget lists the detailed cost of each program. Many corporations demand a certain percentage return on investment, often called a "hurdle rate," before management will approve a new program. This is done so that the new program has the potential to significantly add to the corporation's profit performance and thus build shareholder value. The budget not only serves as a detailed plan of the new strategy in action, it also specifies through proforma financial statements the expected impact on the firm's financial future.

A company that has really invested in the future is Nordstrom. The company plans to spend upwards of US$4.3 billion over the next few years to dramatically grow their online and store presence. The company has a goal of reaching US$20 billion in sales by 2020 (up from roughly US$13 billion in 2015). The CEO is aiming to integrate their ecommerce platform and store operations, both in their luxury stores as well as their rack outlets.[48]

Procedures: Detailing Activities

Procedures, sometimes termed Standard Operating Procedures (SOP), are a system of sequential steps or techniques that describe in detail how a particular task or job is to be done. They typically detail the various activities that must be carried out in order to complete the corporation's program. For example, when the home improvement retailer Home Depot noted that sales were lagging because its stores were full of clogged aisles and had long checkout times and too few salespeople, management changed its procedures for restocking shelves and pricing the products. Instead of requiring its employees to do these activities at the same time they were working with customers, management moved these activities to when the stores were closed at night. Employees were then able to focus on increasing customer sales during the day. Both UPS and FedEx put such an emphasis on consistent, quality service that both companies have strict rules for employee behavior, ranging from how a driver dresses to how keys are held when approaching a customer's door. (Strategy implementation is discussed in more detail in **Chapter 9** and **10**.)

EVALUATION AND CONTROL

Evaluation and control is a process in which corporate activities and performance results are monitored so that actual performance can be compared with desired performance. Managers at all levels use the resulting information to take corrective action and resolve problems. Although evaluation and control is the final major element of strategic management, it can also pinpoint weaknesses in previously implemented strategic plans and thus stimulates the entire process to begin again.

Performance is the end result of activities.[49] It includes the actual outcomes of the strategic management process. The practice of strategic management is justified in terms of its ability to improve an organization's performance, typically measured in terms of profits and return on investment. For evaluation and control to be effective, managers must obtain clear, prompt, and unbiased information from the people below them in the corporation's hierarchy. Using this information, managers compare what is actually happening with what was originally planned in the formulation stage.

Starbucks had created a mystique around the enjoyment of coffee. Carefully designed stores and an experience that encouraged people to stay and chat had built Starbucks into a powerhouse. Howard Schultz (founder and CEO) stepped down from active management of the business and Jim Donald took over as CEO and drove the company toward efficiency, pricing growth, and diversification. The company went from an American success story to one with a 97% drop in net income and same store sales in negative territory. Despite a well-known e-mail from Schultz to Donald in 2007 encouraging him to return to core elements of the business, things did not improve, and in January 2008 Schultz replaced Donald as CEO. In February 2008, all 7,100+ Starbucks in North America shut their doors for a three-hour video conference with Schultz so they could reset the Starbucks experience. He shut down almost 1,000 outlets and instituted a series of moves aimed at returning the company to its preeminent position. The turnaround at Starbucks has been a remarkable story of regaining the cache they almost lost.[50]

The evaluation and control of performance completes the strategic management model. Based on performance results, management may need to make adjustments in its strategy formulation, in implementation, or in both. (Evaluation and control is discussed in more detail in **Chapter 12**.)

FEEDBACK/LEARNING PROCESS

Note that the strategic management model depicted in **Figure 1–2** includes a feedback/learning process. Arrows are drawn coming out of each part of the model and taking information to each of the previous parts of the model. As a firm or business unit develops strategies, programs, and the like, it often must go back to revise or correct decisions made earlier in the process. For example, poor performance (as measured in evaluation and control) usually indicates that something has gone wrong with either strategy formulation or implementation. It could also mean that a key variable, such as a new competitor, a change in the environment, or a significant regulatory change has occurred. Just after Shultz took back the reigns at Starbucks, the recession hit and the mantra in the country became, "save money, don't buy Starbucks." The business was built on an image as the comfortable place away from home, but had trended toward a fast-food operation. Schultz eliminated hot sandwiches which were filling the place with the smell of burnt cheese instead of coffee, refocused on the services provided by the baristas, started grinding coffee on-site to add the smells so loved at a Starbucks, and put in new coffee machines that allowed baristas to talk with customers. Starbucks reassessed the environment and found a better way to profitably apply its core competencies.

Initiation of Strategy: Triggering Events

1-6. Identify some common triggering events that act as stimuli for strategic change

After much research, Henry Mintzberg concluded that strategy formulation is not a regular, continuous process: "It is most often an irregular, discontinuous process, proceeding in fits and starts. There are periods of stability in strategy development, but also there are periods of flux, of groping, of piecemeal change, and of global change."[51] This view of strategy formulation as an irregular process can be explained by the very human tendency to continue on a particular course of action until something goes wrong or a person is forced to question his or her actions. This period of strategic drift may result from inertia on the part of the organization, or it may reflect management's belief that the current strategy is still appropriate and needs only some fine-tuning.

Most large organizations tend to follow a particular strategic orientation for a period of years before making a significant change in direction.[52] This phenomenon, called *punctuated equilibrium*, describes corporations as evolving through relatively long periods of stability (equilibrium periods) punctuated by relatively short bursts of fundamental change (revolutionary periods).[53] After this rather long period of fine-tuning an existing strategy, some sort of shock to the system is needed to motivate management to seriously reassess the corporation's situation.

A **triggering event** is something that acts as a stimulus for a change in strategy. Some possible triggering events are:[54]

- **New CEO:** By asking a series of embarrassing questions, a new CEO cuts through the veil of complacency and forces people to question the very reason for the corporation's existence.

- **External intervention:** A firm's bank suddenly refuses to approve a new loan or suddenly demands payment in full on an old one. A key customer complains about a serious product defect.

- **Threat of a change in ownership:** Another firm may initiate a takeover by buying a company's common stock.

- **Performance gap:** A *performance gap* exists when performance does not meet expectations. Sales and profits either are no longer increasing or may even be falling.

- **Strategic inflection point:** Coined by Andy Grove, past-CEO of Intel Corporation, a *strategic inflection point* is what happens to a business when a major change takes place due to the introduction of new technologies, a different regulatory environment, a change in customers' values, or a change in what customers prefer.[55]

Strategic Decision Making

1-7. Explain strategic decision-making modes

A distinguishing characteristic of strategic management is its emphasis on strategic decision making. As organizations grow larger and more complex, with more uncertain environments, decisions become increasingly complicated and difficult to make. In agreement with the strategic choice perspective mentioned earlier, this book proposes a strategic decision-making framework that can help people make these decisions regardless of their level and function in the corporation.

WHAT MAKES A DECISION STRATEGIC?

Unlike many other decisions, **strategic decisions** deal with the long-term future of an entire organization and have three characteristics:

- **Rare:** Strategic decisions are unusual and typically have no precedent to follow.

- **Consequential:** Strategic decisions commit substantial resources and demand a great deal of commitment from people at all levels.

- **Directive:** Strategic decisions set precedents for lesser decisions and future actions throughout an organization.[56]

One example of a strategic decision with all of these characteristics was that made by Genentech, a biotechnology company that had been founded in 1976 to produce protein-based drugs from cloned genes. After building sales to US$9 billion and profits to US$2 billion in 2006, the company's sales growth slowed and its stock price dropped in 2007. The company's products were reaching maturity with few new ones in the pipeline. To regain revenue growth, management decided to target autoimmune diseases, such as multiple sclerosis, rheumatoid arthritis, lupus, and 80 other ailments for which there was no known lasting treatment. This was an enormous opportunity, but also a very large risk for the company. Existing drugs in this area either were not effective for many patients or caused side effects that were worse than the disease. Competition from companies like Amgen and Novartis were already vying for leadership in this area. A number of Genentech's first attempts in the area had failed to do well against the competition.

The strategic decision to commit resources to this new area was based on a report from a British physician that Genentech's cancer drug Rituxan eased the agony of rheumatoid arthritis in five of his patients. CEO Arthur Levinson was so impressed with this report that he immediately informed Genentech's board of directors. He urged them to support a full research program for Rituxan in autoimmune disease. With the board's blessing, Levinson launched a program to study the drug as a treatment for rheumatoid arthritis, MS, and lupus. The company deployed a third of its 1,000 researchers to pursue new drugs to fight autoimmune diseases. In 2006, Rituxan was approved to treat rheumatoid arthritis and captured 10% of the market. By 2014, Rituxan had sales of more than US$7 billion. The research mandate was to consider ideas others might overlook. This has led to a series of FDA-approved drugs for breast cancer and vision loss. "There's this tremendous herd instinct out there," said Levinson. "That's a great opportunity, because often the crowd is wrong."[57]

MINTZBERG'S MODES OF STRATEGIC DECISION MAKING

Some strategic decisions are made in a flash by one person (often an entrepreneur or a powerful chief executive officer) who has a brilliant insight and is quickly able to convince others to adopt his or her idea. Other strategic decisions seem to develop out of a series of small incremental choices that over time push an organization more in one direction than another. According to Henry Mintzberg, the three most typical approaches, or modes, of strategic decision making are entrepreneurial, adaptive, and planning (a fourth mode, logical incrementalism, was added later by Quinn):[58]

- **Entrepreneurial mode:** Strategy is made by one powerful individual. The focus is on opportunities; problems are secondary. Strategy is guided by the founder's own vision of direction and is exemplified by large, bold decisions. The dominant goal is growth of the corporation. Amazon.com, founded by Jeff Bezos, is an example of this mode of strategic decision making. The company reflects Bezos' vision of using the Internet to market everything that can be bought.

- **Adaptive mode:** Sometimes referred to as "muddling through," this decision-making mode is characterized by reactive solutions to existing problems, rather than a proactive search for new opportunities. Much bargaining goes on concerning the priority of objectives. Strategy is fragmented and is developed to move a corporation forward incrementally. This mode is typical of most universities, many large hospitals, a large number of governmental agencies, and a surprising number of large corporations. Encyclopedia Britannica Inc. operated successfully for many years in this mode, but it continued to rely on the door-to-door selling of its prestigious books long after dual-career couples made that marketing approach obsolete. Only after it was acquired in 1996 did the company change its door-to-door sales to television advertising and Internet marketing. The company now charges libraries and individual subscribers for complete access via its Web site and has apps for the iPad and iPhone that cost users US$50. In May 2012, the company stopped producing the bound set of encyclopedias that had been in print for over 244 years.[59]

- **Planning mode:** This decision-making mode involves the systematic gathering of appropriate information for situation analysis, the generation of feasible alternative strategies, and the rational selection of the most appropriate strategy. It includes both the proactive search for new opportunities and the reactive solution of existing problems. IBM under CEO Louis Gerstner is a great example of the planning mode. When Gerstner accepted the position of CEO in 1993, he realized that IBM was in serious difficulty. Mainframe computers, the company's primary product line, were suffering a rapid decline both in sales and market share. One of Gerstner's first actions was to convene a two-day meeting on corporate strategy with senior executives. An in-depth analysis of IBM's product lines revealed that the only part of the company that was growing was services, but it was a relatively small segment and not very profitable. Rather than focusing on making and selling its own computer hardware, IBM made the strategic decision to invest in services that integrated information technology. IBM thus decided to provide a complete set of services from building systems to defining architecture to actually running and managing the computers for the customer—regardless of who made the products. Because it was no longer important that the company be completely vertically integrated, it sold off its DRAM, disk-drive, and laptop computer businesses and exited software application development. Since making this strategic decision in 1993, 80% of IBM's revenue growth has come from services. Most of this is chronicled in an outstanding business practices book written by Gerstner himself entitled *Who Says Elephants Can't Dance?* It should be one of the top reads for anyone really interested in this topic.[60]

■ **Logical incrementalism:** A fourth decision-making mode can be viewed as a synthesis of the planning, adaptive, and, to a lesser extent, the entrepreneurial modes. In this mode, top management has a reasonably clear idea of the corporation's mission and objectives, but, in its development of strategies, it chooses to use "an interactive process in which the organization probes the future, experiments, and learns from a series of partial (incremental) commitments rather than through global formulations of total strategies."[61] Thus, although the mission and objectives are set, the strategy is allowed to emerge out of debate, discussion, and experimentation. This approach appears to be useful when the environment is changing rapidly and when it is important to build consensus and develop needed resources before committing an entire corporation to a specific strategy. In his analysis of the petroleum industry, Grant described strategic planning in this industry as "planned emergence." Corporate headquarters established the mission and objectives but allowed the business units to propose strategies to achieve them.[62]

STRATEGIC DECISION-MAKING PROCESS: AID TO BETTER DECISIONS

Good arguments can be made for using the entrepreneurial, adaptive modes, or logical incrementalism approaches in certain specific situations.[63] This book proposes, however, that in most situations the planning mode, which includes the basic elements of the strategic management process, is a more rational, better tested, and more complete method for making strategic decisions. Research indicates that the planning mode is not only more analytical and less political than are the other modes, but it is also more appropriate for dealing with complex, changing environments.[64] We therefore propose the following eight-step **strategic decision-making process** to improve the making of strategic decisions (see **Figure 1–5**):

■ **Evaluate current performance results** in terms of (a) return on investment, profitability, and so forth, and (b) the current mission, objectives, strategies, and policies.

■ **Review corporate governance**—that is, the performance of the firm's board of directors and top management.

■ **Scan and assess the external environment** to determine the strategic factors that pose opportunities and threats.

■ **Scan and assess the internal corporate environment** to determine the strategic factors that are strengths (especially core competencies) and weaknesses.

■ **Analyze strategic factors** to (a) pinpoint problem areas and (b) review and revise the corporate mission and objectives, as necessary.

■ **Generate, evaluate, and select the best alternative strategies** in light of the analysis conducted in the previous step.

■ **Implement selected strategies** via programs, budgets, and procedures.

■ **Evaluate implemented strategies** via feedback systems, and the control of activities to ensure their minimum deviation from plans.

FIGURE 1–5
Strategic Decision-
Making Process

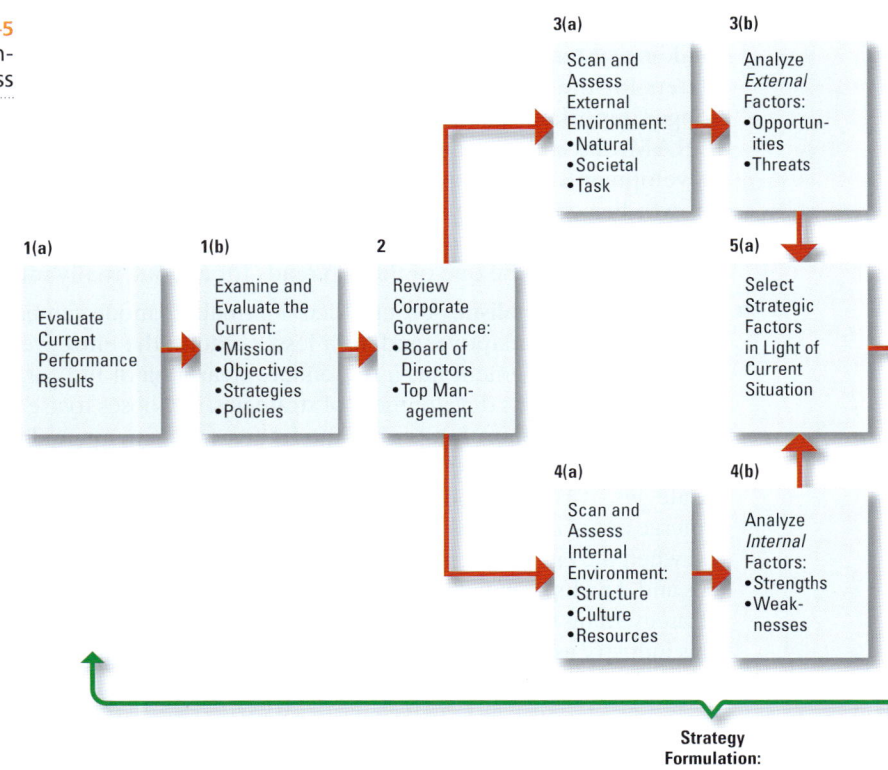

SOURCE: T. L. Wheelen and J. D. Hunger, "Strategic Decision-Making Process." Copyright © 1994 and 1977 by Wheelen and Hunger Associates. Reprinted by permission.

The Strategic Audit: Aid to Strategic Decision Making

1-8. Use the strategic audit as a method of analyzing corporate functions and activities

One effective means of putting the strategic decision-making process into action is through a technique known as the strategic audit. A **strategic audit** provides a checklist of questions, by area or issue, that enables a systematic analysis to be made of various corporate functions and activities. (See **Appendix 1.A** at the end of this chapter.) Note that the numbered primary headings in the audit are the same as the numbered blocks in the strategic decision-making process in **Figure 1–5**. Beginning with an evaluation of current performance, the audit continues with environmental scanning, strategy formulation, and strategy implementation, and it concludes with evaluation and control. A strategic audit is a type of management audit and is extremely useful as a diagnostic tool for pinpointing corporatewide problem areas and to highlight organizational strengths and weaknesses.[65] A strategic audit can help determine why a certain area is creating problems for a corporation and help generate solutions to the problem.

A strategic audit is not all-inclusive, but it asks many of the critical questions needed for a detailed strategic analysis of any business. Some questions, or even some areas, might be inappropriate for a particular company; in other cases, the questions may be insufficient for a complete analysis. However, each question in a particular area of a strategic audit can be broken down into an additional series of sub questions. An analyst can develop responses to these sub questions when they are needed for a complete strategic analysis of a company.

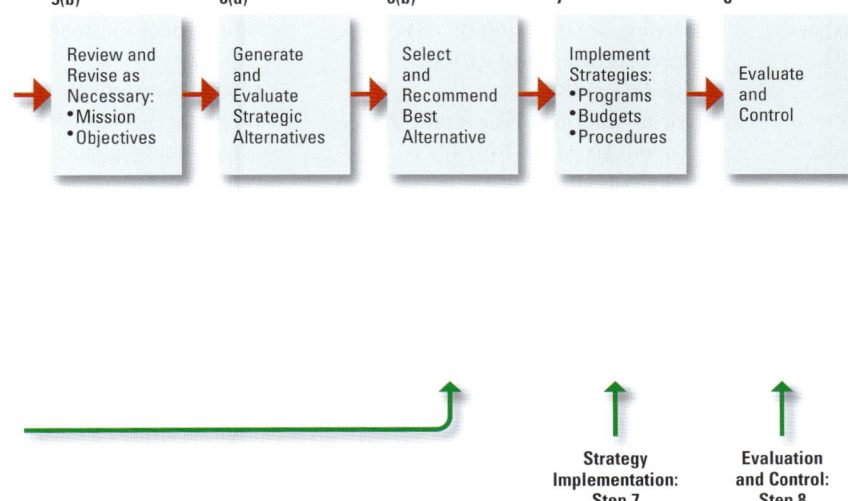

End of Chapter SUMMARY

Strategy scholars Donald Hambrick and James Fredrickson propose that a good strategy has five elements, providing answers to five questions:

- Arenas: Where will we be active?
- Vehicles: How will we get there?
- Differentiators: How will we win in the marketplace?
- Staging: What will be our speed and sequence of moves?
- Economic logic: How will we obtain our returns?[66]

This chapter introduces you to a well-accepted model of strategic management (**Figure 1–2**) in which environmental scanning leads to strategy formulation, strategy implementation, and evaluation and control. It further shows how that model can be put into action through the strategic decision-making process (**Figure 1–5**) and a strategic audit (**Appendix 1.A**). As pointed out by Hambrick and Fredrickson, "strategy consists of an integrated set of choices."[67] The questions "Where will we be active?" and "How will we get there?" are dealt with by a company's mission, objectives, and corporate strategy. The question "How will we win in the marketplace?" is the concern of business strategy. The question "What will be our speed and sequence of moves?" is answered not only by business strategy and tactics but also by functional strategy and by implemented programs, budgets, and procedures. The question "How will we obtain our returns?" is the primary emphasis of the evaluation and control element of the strategic management model. Each of these questions and topics will be dealt with in greater detail in the chapters to come. Welcome to the study of strategic management!

Pearson MyLab Management®

Go to **mymanagementlab.com** to complete the problems marked with this icon .

KEY TERMS

Andean Community (p. 43)
Association of Southeast Asian
    Nations (ASEAN) (p. 43)
budget (p. 52)
business strategy (p. 50)
Central American Free Trade
    Agreement (CAFTA) (p. 43)
corporate strategy (p. 50)
environmental scanning (p. 46)
European Union (EU) (p. 42)
evaluation and control (p. 53)
external environment (p. 46)
functional strategy (p. 51)
globalization (p. 40)
hierarchy of strategy (p. 51)
innovation (p. 41)
institution theory (p. 44)

internal environment (p. 47)
learning organization (p. 45)
Mercosur/Mercosul (p. 43)
mission (p. 48)
North American Free Trade Agree-
    ment (NAFTA) (p. 42)
objectives (p. 49)
organizational learning theory
    (p. 44)
performance (p. 53)
phases of strategic management
    (p. 37)
policy (p. 51)
population ecology (p. 44)
procedures (p. 53)
program (p. 52)
strategic audit (p. 58)

strategic choice perspective (p. 44)
strategic decision-making process
    (p. 57)
strategic decisions (p. 55)
strategic factors (p. 46)
strategic management (p. 37)
strategy (p. 50)
strategy formulation (p. 48)
strategy implementation (p. 52)
sustainability (p. 42)
SWOT approach (p. 46)
tactic (p. 52)
triggering event (p. 54)
triple bottom line (p. 40)
Union of South American Nations
    (p. 43)
vision (p. 49)

Pearson MyLab Management®

Go to **mymanagmentlab.com** for the following assisted-graded writing questions:

⭐ **1-1.** How do the three elements of globalization, innovation, and sustainability impact your understanding of strategy?

⭐ **1-2.** Organizational strategy can be divided roughly into two categories: (a) formulation and (b) implementation. Although there is legitimate crossover between the two, how would you characterize the issues involved in each effort?

DISCUSSION QUESTIONS

⭐ **1-3.** Why is strategic management considered important for global market competition?

1-4. What is the impact of sustainability on business practice?

⭐ **1-5.** Define strategic flexibility and explain its implications. Why is organizational learning important to the long-term development of strategic flexibility

of organizations that intend to enter overseas markets?

1-6. What is a triggering event? List a few triggering events that stimulate strategic changes.

⭐ **1-7.** What is the most preferred planning mode of strategic decision-making for organizations competing internationally?

STRATEGIC PRACTICE EXERCISES

Advanced economies are emerging from the worst financial recessions in modern times. Many developed nations have implemented austerity measures to adjust the deficit caused by massive spending during the years of cheap and available credit facilities. New industrial policies are also implemented at national and regional levels to police banks and financial institutions as measures of avoiding further economic problems in the future. The austerity measures and policy changes have forced industries and business practices to change. How do you think these act as strategic change stimuli?

1-8. What changes do you think this might cause in the immediate task environment for a business operating within the financial service industry? Look at the *Financial Times* online for information.

1-9. How do these changes impact on corporate, business, and functional level strategies of financial service businesses? Are these changes going to affect you as customers?

1-10. How do you think a learning organization would act in this dynamic environment? What survival chances do the stagnant organizations have?

NOTES

1. F. W. Gluck, S. P. Kaufman, and A. S. Walleck, "The Four Phases of Strategic Management," *Journal of Business Strategy* (Winter 1982), pp. 9–21.
2. M. R. Vaghefi and A. B. Huellmantel, "Strategic Leadership at General Electric," *Long Range Planning* (April 1998), pp. 280–294. For a detailed description of the evolution of strategic management at GE, see W. Ocasio and J. Joseph, "Rise and Fall—or Transformation?" *Long Range Planning* (June 2008), pp. 248–272.
3. B. Geier, "26 companies join this year's Fortune 500," *Fortune* http://www.fortune.com/2015/06/04/fortune-500-newcomers/. June 4, 2015.
4. E. D. Beinhocker, "The Adaptable Corporation," *McKinsey Quarterly* (2006, Number 2), pp. 77–87.
5. B. W. Wirtz, A. Mathieu, and O. Schilke, "Strategy in High-Velocity Environments," *Long Range Planning* (June 2007), pp. 295–313; L. F. Teagarden, Y. Sarason, J. S. Childers, and D. E. Hatfield, "The Engagement of Employees in the Strategy Process and Firm Performance: The Role of Strategic Goals and Environment," *Journal of Business Strategies* (Spring 2005), pp. 75–99; T. J. Andersen, "Strategic Planning, Autonomous Actions and Corporate Performance," *Long Range Planning* (April 2000), pp. 184–200; C. C. Miller and L. B. Cardinal, "Strategic Planning and Firm Performance: A Synthesis of More than Two Decades of Research," *Academy of Management Journal* (December 1994), pp. 1649–1665; P. Pekar Jr. and S. Abraham, "Is Strategic Management Living Up to Its Promise?" *Long Range Planning* (October 1995), pp. 32–44; W. E. Hopkins and S. A. Hopkins, "Strategic Planning—Financial Performance Relationship in Banks: A Causal Examination," *Strategic Management Journal* (September 1997), pp. 635–652.
6. E. J. Zajac, M. S. Kraatz, and R. F. Bresser, "Modeling the Dynamics of Strategic Fit: A Normative Approach to Strategic Change," *Strategic Management Journal* (April 2000), pp. 429–453; M. Peteraf and R. Reed, "Managerial Discretion and Internal Alignment Under Regulatory Constraints and Change," *Strategic Management Journal* (November 2007), pp. 1089–1112; C. S. Katsikeas, S. Samiee, and M. Theodosiou, "Strategy Fit and Performance Consequences of International Marketing Standardization," *Strategic Management Journal* (September 2006), pp. 867–890.
7. P. Brews and D. Purohit, "Strategic Planning in Unstable Environments," *Long Range Planning* (February 2007), pp. 64–83.
8. K. G. Smith and C. M. Grimm, "Environmental Variation, Strategic Change and Firm Performance: A Study of Railroad Deregulation," *Strategic Management Journal* (July–August 1987), pp. 363–376; J. A. Nickerson and B. S. Silverman, "Why Firms Want to Organize Efficiently and What Keeps Them from Doing So: Inappropriate Governance, Performance, and Adaptation in a Deregulated Industry," *Administrative Science Quarterly* (September 2003), pp. 433–465.
9. I. Wilson, "Strategic Planning Isn't Dead—It Changed," *Long Range Planning* (August 1994), p. 20.
10. R. Dye and O. Sibony, "How to Improve Strategic Planning," *McKinsey Quarterly* (2007, Number 3), pp. 40–48.
11. D. Rigby and B. Bilodeau, *Management Tools and Trends 2007* (Bain & Company, 2007); D. Rigby and B. Bilodeau, *Management Tools and Trends 2015* (Bain & Company, 2015).
12. W. Joyce, "What Really Works: Building the 4+2 Organization," *Organizational Dynamics* (Vol. 34, Issue 2, 2005), pp. 118–129. See also W. Joyce, N. Nohria, and B. Roberson, *What Really Works: The 4+2 Formula for Sustained Business Success* (HarperBusiness, 2003).
13. R. M. Grant, "Strategic Planning in a Turbulent Environment: Evidence from the Oil Majors," *Strategic Management Journal* (June 2003), pp. 491–517.
14. M. J. Peel and J. Bridge, "How Planning and Capital Budgeting Improve SME Performance," *Long Range Planning* (December 1998), pp. 848–856; L. W. Rue and N. A. Ibrahim, "The Relationship Between Planning Sophistication and Performance in Small Businesses," *Journal of Small Business Management* (October 1998), pp. 24–32; J. C. Carland and J. W. Carland, "A Model of Entrepreneurial Planning and Its Effect on Performance," paper presented to Association for Small Business and Entrepreneurship (Houston, TX, 2003).
15. R. M. Grant, "Strategic Planning in a Turbulent Environment: Evidence from the Oil Majors," *Strategic Management Journal* (June 2003), pp. 491–517.
16. "Triple Bottom Line," *The Economist* (November 17, 2009), (www.economist.com/node/14301663).
17. www.usgbc.org/.

18. T. L. Friedman, *The World Is Flat* (NY: Farrar, Strauss & Giroux, 2005).

19. R. Cohen, "America Abroad," *The New York Times*, January 9, 2012, (www.nytimes.com/2012/01/10/opinion /america-abroad.html); A. K. Gupta, V. Govindarajan, and H. Wang, *The Quest for Global Dominance*, 2nd ed. (San Francisco: Jossey-Bass, 2008).

20. K. Wagner, A. Taylor, H. Zablit, and E. Foo. "Innovation in 2014," *BCG Perspectives*, October 28, 2014, https://www.bcgperspectives.com/content/articles /innovation_growth_digital_economy_Innovation_in_2014.

21. http://www.ign.com/articles/2010/01/26/apples-first-tablet.

22. J. Davies, "Sustainability & Employee Engagement," September 2014. GreenBiz.com.

23. R. Sylvan and K. Rainey, "2012 Workplace Trends Report: Workplaces that Promote Sustainability," (www.sodexousa .com/usen/roles/facilmgmt/workplaces_that_promote_ sustainability.asp).

24. www.iso.org/iso/iso14000.

25. M. E. Porter and F. L. Reinhardt, "A Strategic Approach to Climate," *Harvard Business Review* (October 2007), p. 22.

26. "Billion-Dollar Weather and Climate Disasters: Overview," *Department of Commerce, 2015.* (www.ncdc.noaa .gov/billions/).

27. J. A. C. Baum, "Organizational Ecology," in *Handbook of Organization Studies*, edited by S. R. Clegg, C. Handy, and W. Nord (London: Sage, 1996), pp. 77–114.

28. B. M. Staw and L. D. Epstein, "What Bandwagons Bring: Effects of Popular Management Techniques on Corporate Performance, Reputation, and CEO Pay," *Administrative Science Quarterly* (September 2000), pp. 523–556; M. B. Lieberman and S. Asaba, "Why Do Firms Imitate Each Other?" *Academy of Management Review* (April 2006), pp. 366–385.

29. T. W. Ruefli and R. R. Wiggins, "Industry, Corporate, and Segment Effects and Business Performance: A Non-Parametric Approach," *Strategic Management Journal* (September 2003), pp. 861–879; Y. E. Spanos, G. Zaralis, and S. Lioukas, "Strategy and Industry Effects on Profitability: Evidence from Greece," *Strategic Management Journal* (February 2004), pp. 139–165; E. H. Bowman and C. E. Helfat, "Does Corporate Strategy Matter?" *Strategic Management Journal* (January 2001), pp. 1–23; T. H. Brush, P. Bromiley, and M. Hendrickx, "The Relative Influence of Industry and Corporation on Business Segment Performance: An Alternative Estimate," *Strategic Management Journal* (June 1999), pp. 519–547; K. M. Gilley, B. A. Walters, and B. J. Olson, "Top Management Team Risk Taking Propensities and Firm Performance: Direct and Moderating Effects," *Journal of Business Strategies* (Fall 2002), pp. 95–114.

30. For more information on these theories, see A. Y. Lewin and H. W. Voloberda, "Prolegomena on Coevolution: A Framework for Research on Strategy and New Organizational Forms," *Organization Science* (October 1999), pp. 519–534, and H. Aldrich, *Organizations Evolving* (London: Sage, 1999), pp. 43–74.

31. R. A. D'Aveni, *Hypercompetition* (New York: The Free Press, 1994). Hypercompetition is discussed in more detail in Chapter 4.

32. R. S. M. Lau, "Strategic Flexibility: A New Reality for World-Class Manufacturing," *SAM Advanced Management Journal* (Spring 1996), pp. 11–15.

33. M. A. Hitt, B. W. Keats, and S. M. DeMarie, "Navigating in the New Competitive Landscape: Building Strategic Flexibility and Competitive Advantage in the 21st Century," *Academy of Management Executive* (November 1998), pp. 22–42.

34. S. C. Voelpel, M. Dous, and T. H. Davenport, "Five Steps to Creating a Global Knowledge-Sharing System: Siemens' ShareNet," *Academy of Management Executive* (May 2005), pp. 9–23.

35. D. A. Garvin, "Building a Learning Organization," *Harvard Business Review* (July/August 1993), p. 80. See also P. M. Senge, *The Fifth Discipline: The Art and Practice of the Learning Organization* (New York: Doubleday, 1990).

36. A. D. Chandler, *Inventing the Electronic Century* (New York: The Free Press, 2001).

37. N. Collier, F. Fishwick, and S. W. Floyd, "Managerial Involvement and Perceptions of Strategy Process," *Long Range Planning* (February 2004), pp. 67–83; J. A. Parnell, S. Carraher, and K. Holt, "Participative Management's Influence on Effective Strategic Planning," *Journal of Business Strategies* (Fall 2002), pp. 161–179; M. Ketokivi and X. Castaner, "Strategic Planning as an Integrative Device," *Administrative Science Quarterly* (September 2004), pp. 337–365; Edmondson, A. "Strategies for Learning from Failure," *Harvard Business Review* (April 2011).

38. E. W. K. Tsang, "Internationalization as a Learning Process: Singapore MNCs in China," *Academy of Management Executive* (February 1999), pp. 91–101; J. M. Shaver, W. Mitchell, and B. Yeung, "The Effect of Own-Firm and Other Firm Experience on Foreign Direct Investment Survival in the U.S., 1987–92," *Strategic Management Journal* (November 1997), pp. 811–824; P. Kale and H. Singh, "Building Firm Capabilities through Learning: The Role of the Alliance Learning Process in Alliance Capability and Firm-Level Alliance Success," *Strategic Management Journal* (October 2007), pp. 981–1000; H. Barkema and M. Schijven, "How Do Firms Learn to Make Acquisitions? A Review of Past Research and an Agenda for the Future," *Journal of Management* (June 2008), pp. 594–634; D. D. Bergh and E. N-K Lim, "Learning How to Restructure: Absorptive Capacity and Improvisational Views of Restructuring Actions and Performance," *Strategic Management Journal* (June 2008), pp. 593–616.

39. W. Mitchell, J. M. Shaver, and B. Yeung, "Getting There in a Global Industry: Impacts on Performance of Changing International Presence," *Strategic Management Journal* (September 1992), pp. 419–432.

40. D. J. Miller, M. J. Fern, and L. B. Cardinal, "The Use of Knowledge for Technological Innovation Within Diversified Firms," *Academy of Management Journal* (April 2007), pp. 308–326.

41. R. Wiltbank, N. Dew, S. Read, and S. D. Sarasvathy, "What to Do Next? The Case for Non-Predictive Strategy," *Strategic Management Journal* (October 2006), pp. 981–998; J. A. Smith, "Strategies for Start-Ups," *Long Range Planning* (December 1998), pp. 857–872.

42. J. S. Sidhu, "Business-Domain Definition and Performance: An Empirical Study," *SAM Advanced Management Journal* (Autumn 2004), pp. 40–45.

43. See A. Campbell and S. Yeung, "Brief Case: Mission, Vision, and Strategic Intent," *Long Range Planning* (August 1991), pp. 145–147; S. Cummings and J. Davies, "Mission, Vision, Fusion," *Long Range Planning* (December 1994), pp. 147–150.

44. *J. Cosco, "Down to the Sea in Ships," Journal of Business Strategy (November/December 1995), p. 48.*

45. "Is PepsiCo a Better Dividend Stock than Coca-Cola?" *Seeking Alpha* (August 7, 2012), (www.seekingalpha.com /article/786211-is-pepsi-a-better-dividend-stock-than-coca-cola); www.thecoca-colacompany.com.

46. T. Campbell, "Pfizer boosts its guidance, suggesting better times may be coming," The Motley Fool (9/30/2015) (www.fool.com/investing/general/2015/09/30/pfizer-boosts-its-guidance-suggesting-better-times.aspx).

47. K. M. Eisenhardt and D. N. Sull, "Strategy as Simple Rules," *Harvard Business Review* (January 2001), p. 110.

48. P. Wahba, "Nordstrom's multi-billion dollar plan for e-commerce domination," *Fortune*, February 20, 2015. (fortune.com/2015/02/20/Nordstrom-ecomerce/).

49. H. A. Simon, *Administrative Behavior*, 2nd edition (New York: The Free Press, 1957), p. 231.

50. "Starbucks to Close All U.S. Stores for Training," MSNBC (February 26, 2008), (www.msnbc.com/id/23351151/ns /business-us_business/t/starbucks-close-all-us-stores-trainign/#.uco_I2t5mk0); "Howard Schultz on How Starbucks Got Its Groove Back," careerbuilder.com (June 3, 2011), (http://www.thehiringsite.careerbuilder.com/2011/06/03 /howard-schultz-on-how-starbucks-got-its-groove-back/); A. Clark. "Starbucks revival is a credit to founder Schultz," *The Guardian* (December 11, 2010), (www.theguardian. com/business/2010/dec/12/starbucks-revival-comment-andrew-clark), B. Stone. "Starbucks Profits Down Sharply on Restructuring Costs," *The New York Times* (November 10, 2008), (http://www.nytimes.com/2008/11/11/business/11sbux .html).

51. H. Mintzberg, "Planning on the Left Side and Managing on the Right," *Harvard Business Review* (July–August 1976), p. 56.

52. R. A. Burgelman and A. S. Grove, "Let Chaos Reign, Then Reign in Chaos—Repeatedly: Managing Strategic Dynamics for Corporate Longevity," *Strategic Management Journal* (October 2007), pp. 965–979.

53. E. Romanelli and M. L. Tushman, "Organizational Transformation as Punctuated Equilibrium: An Empirical Test," *Academy of Management Journal* (October 1994), pp. 1141–1166.

54. S. S. Gordon, W. H. Stewart Jr., R. Sweo, and W. A. Luker, "Convergence versus Strategic Reorientation: The Antecedents of Fast-Paced Organizational Change," *Journal of Management* (Vol. 26, No. 5, 2000), pp. 911–945.

55. Speech to the 1998 Academy of Management, reported by S. M. Puffer, "Global Executive: Intel's Andrew Grove on Competitiveness," *Academy of Management Executive* (February 1999), pp. 15–24.

56. D. J. Hickson, R. J. Butler, D. Cray, G. R. Mallory, and D. C. Wilson, *Top Decisions: Strategic Decision Making in Organizations* (San Francisco: Jossey-Bass, 1986), pp. 26–42.

57. Top Pharma List 2015, PMLive. (www.pmlive.com/top_ pharma_list/top_50_pharmaceutical_products_by_global_ sales (accessed January, 2016); A. Weintraub, "Genentech's Gamble," *BusinessWeek* (December 17, 2007), pp. 44–48; http:// www.fiercepharma.com/special-reports/top-10-best-selling-cancer-drugs/rituxan-3-billion; http://diabetes.webmd.com /news/20120814/new-drug-for-diabetes-related-vision-loss.

58. H. Mintzberg, "Strategy-Making in Three Modes," *California Management Review* (Winter 1973), pp. 44–53.

59. Stern, J. 2012, "Encyclopedia Britannica Kills Its Print Edition," *ABC News* (March 13, 2012), (http://abcnews.go.com/blogs/technology/2012/03 /encyclopaedia-britannica-kills-its-print-edition/).

60. L. V. Gerstner, *Who Says Elephants Can't Dance?* (New York: HarperCollins, 2002).

61. J. B. Quinn, *Strategies for Change: Logical Incrementalism* (Homewood, IL.: Irwin, 1980), p. 58.

62. R. M. Grant, "Strategic Planning in a Turbulent Environment: Evidence from the Oil Majors," *Strategic Management Journal* (June 2003), pp. 491–517.

63. G. Gavetti and J. W. Rivkin, "Seek Strategy the Right Way at the Right Time," *Harvard Business Review* (January 2008), pp. 22–23.

64. P. J. Brews and M. R. Hunt, "Learning to Plan and Planning to Learn: Resolving the Planning School/Learning School Debate," *Strategic Management Journal* (October 1999), pp. 889–913; I. Gold and A. M. A. Rasheed, "Rational Decision-Making and Firm Performance: The Moderating Role of the Environment," *Strategic Management Journal* (August 1997), pp. 583–591; R. L. Priem, A. M. A. Rasheed, and A. G. Kotulic, "Rationality in Strategic Decision Processes, Environmental Dynamism and Firm Performance," *Journal of Management*, Vol. 21, No. 5 (1995), pp. 913–929; J. W. Dean Jr., and M. P. Sharfman, "Does Decision Process Matter? A Study of Strategic Decision-Making Effectiveness," *Academy of Management Journal* (April 1996), pp. 368–396.

65. T. L. Wheelen and J. D. Hunger, "Using the Strategic Audit," *SAM Advanced Management Journal* (Winter 1987), pp. 4–12; G. Donaldson. "A New Tool for Boards: The Strategic Audit," *Harvard Business Review* (July–August 1995), pp. 99–107.

66. D. C. Hambrick and J. W. Fredrickson, "Are You Sure You Have a Strategy?" *Academy of Management Executive* (November, 2001), pp. 48–59.

67. Hambrick and Fredrickson, p. 49.

1.A
Strategic Audit of a Corporation

I. Current Situation

A. Current Performance

How did the corporation perform in the past year overall in terms of return on investment, market share, and profitability?

B. Strategic Posture

What are the corporation's current mission, objectives, strategies, and policies?

1. Are they clearly stated, or are they merely implied from performance?
2. **Mission:** What business(es) is the corporation in? Why?
3. **Objectives:** What are the corporate, business, and functional objectives? Are they consistent with each other, with the mission, and with the internal and external environments?
4. **Strategies:** What strategy or mix of strategies is the corporation following? Are they consistent with each other, with the mission and objectives, and with the internal and external environments?
5. **Policies:** What are the corporation's policies? Are they consistent with each other, with the mission, objectives, and strategies, and with the internal and external environments?
6. Do the current mission, objectives, strategies, and policies reflect the corporation's international operations, whether global or multidomestic?

II. Corporate Governance

A. Board of Directors

1. Who is on the board? How many are internal (employees) or external members?
2. Which board members own significant shares of stock? What percentage?
3. Is the stock privately held or publicly traded? Are there different classes of stock with different voting rights?

SOURCE: T. L. Wheelen and J. D. Hunger, *Strategic Audit of a Corporation*, Copyright © 1982 and 2005 by Wheelen and Hunger Associates. Thomas L. Wheelen, "A Strategic Audit," paper presented to Society for Advancement of Management (SAM). Presented by J. D. Hunger and T. L. Wheelen in "The Strategic Audit: An Integrative Approach to Teaching Business Policy," *Academy of Management* (August 1983). Published in "Using the Strategic Audit," by T. L. Wheelen and J. D. Hunger in *SAM Advanced Management Journal* (Winter 1987), pp. 4–12. Reprinted by permission of the copyright holders. Revised 1988, 1994, 1997, 2000, 2002, 2004, 2005, 2009, and 2013.

4. What do the board members contribute to the corporation in terms of knowledge, skills, background, and connections? If the corporation has international operations, do any board members have international experience? Are board members concerned with environmental sustainability?

5. How long have the board members served on the board?

6. What is their level of involvement in strategic management? Do they merely rubber-stamp top management's proposals or do they actively participate and suggest future directions? Do they evaluate management's proposals in terms of environmental sustainability?

B. Top Management

1. What person or group constitutes top management?

2. What are top management's chief characteristics in terms of knowledge, skills, background, and style? If the corporation has international operations, does top management have international experience? Are executives from acquired companies considered part of the top management team?

3. Has top management been responsible for the corporation's performance over the past few years? How many managers have been in their current position for less than three years? Were they promoted internally or externally hired?

4. Has top management established a systematic approach to strategic management?

5. What is top management's level of involvement in the strategic management process?

6. How well does top management interact with lower-level managers and with the board of directors?

7. Are strategic decisions made ethically in a socially responsible manner?

8. Are strategic decisions made in an environmentally sustainable manner?

9. Do top executives own significant amounts of stock in the corporation?

10. Do you believe that top management is sufficiently skilled to cope with likely future challenges?

III. External Environment: Opportunities and Threats (SW**OT**)

A. Natural Physical Environment: Sustainability Issues

1. What forces from the natural physical environment are currently affecting the corporation and the industries in which it competes? How would you categorize current or future threats? Opportunities?
   a. Climate, including global temperature, sea level, and fresh water availability
   b. Weather-related events, such as severe storms, floods, and droughts
   c. Solar phenomena, such as sunspots and solar wind

2. Do these forces have different effects in other regions of the world?

B. Societal Environment

1. What general environmental forces are currently affecting both the corporation and the industries in which it competes? Which present current or future threats? Opportunities?
   a. Economic
   b. Technological

    c. Political–legal

    d. Sociocultural

2. Are these forces different in other regions of the world?

C. Task Environment

1. What forces drive industry competition? Are these forces the same globally or do they vary from country to country? Rate each force as **high**, **medium**, or **low**.

    a. Threat of new entrants

    b. Bargaining power of buyers

    c. Threat of substitute products or services

    d. Bargaining power of suppliers

    e. Rivalry among competing firms

    f. Relative power of unions, governments, special interest groups, etc.

2. What key factors in the immediate environment (that is, customers, competitors, suppliers, creditors, labor unions, governments, trade associations, interest groups, local communities, and shareholders) are currently affecting the corporation? Which are current or future threats? Opportunities?

D. Summary of External Factors
(List in the EFAS Table 4–5, p. 153)

Which of these forces and factors are the most important to the corporation and to the industries in which it competes at the present time? Which will be important in the future?

IV. Internal Environment: Strengths and Weaknesses (<u>SW</u>OT)

A. Corporate Structure

1. How is the corporation structured at present?

    a. Is the decision-making authority centralized around one group or decentralized to many units?

    b. Is the corporation organized on the basis of functions, projects, geography, or some combination of these?

2. Is the structure clearly understood by everyone in the corporation?

3. Is the present structure consistent with current corporate objectives, strategies, policies, and programs, as well as with the firm's international operations?

4. In what ways does this structure compare with those of similar corporations?

B. Corporate Culture

1. Is there a well-defined or emerging culture composed of shared beliefs, expectations, and values?

2. Is the culture consistent with the current objectives, strategies, policies, and programs?

3. What is the culture's position on environmental sustainability?

4. What is the culture's position on other important issues facing the corporation (that is, on productivity, quality of performance, adaptability to changing conditions, and internationalization)?

5. Is the culture compatible with the employees' diversity of backgrounds?

6. Does the company take into consideration the values of the culture of each nation in which the firm operates?

C. Corporate Resources

1. **Marketing**
   a. What are the corporation's current marketing objectives, strategies, policies, and programs?
      i. Are they clearly stated or merely implied from performance and/or budgets?
      ii. Are they consistent with the corporation's mission, objectives, strategies, and policies, and with internal and external environments?
   b. How well is the corporation performing in terms of analysis of market position and marketing mix (that is, product, price, place, and promotion) in both domestic and international markets? How dependent is the corporation on a few customers? How big is its market? Where is it gaining or losing market share? What percentage of sales comes from developed versus developing regions? Where are current products in the product life cycle?
      i. What trends emerge from this analysis?
      ii. What impact have these trends had on past performance and how might these trends affect future performance?
      iii. Does this analysis support the corporation's past and pending strategic decisions?
      iv. Does marketing provide the company with a competitive advantage?
   c. How well does the corporation's marketing performance compare with that of similar corporations?
   d. Are marketing managers using accepted marketing concepts and techniques to evaluate and improve product performance? (Consider product life cycle, market segmentation, market research, and product portfolios.)
   e. Does marketing adjust to the conditions in each country in which it operates?
   f. Does marketing consider environmental sustainability when making decisions?
   g. What is the role of the marketing manager in the strategic management process?

2. **Finance**
   a. What are the corporation's current financial objectives, strategies, policies, and programs?
      i. Are they clearly stated or merely implied from performance and/or budgets?
      ii. Are they consistent with the corporation's mission, objectives, strategies, and policies, and with internal and external environments?
   b. How well is the corporation performing in terms of financial analysis? (Consider ratio analysis, common size statements, and capitalization structure.) How balanced, in terms of cash flow, is the company's portfolio of products and businesses? What are investor expectations in terms of share price?
      i. What trends emerge from this analysis?
      ii. Are there any significant differences when statements are calculated in constant versus reported dollars?
      iii. What impact have these trends had on past performance and how might these trends affect future performance?
      iv. Does this analysis support the corporation's past and pending strategic decisions?
      v. Does finance provide the company with a competitive advantage?
   c. How well does the corporation's financial performance compare with that of similar corporations?
   d. Are financial managers using accepted financial concepts and techniques to evaluate and improve current corporate and divisional performance? (Consider financial leverage, capital budgeting, ratio analysis, and managing foreign currencies.)
   e. How does finance adjust to the conditions in each country in which the company operates?
   f. How does finance cope with global financial issues?
   g. What is the role of the financial manager in the strategic management process?

3. **Research and Development (R&D)**
   a. What are the corporation's current R&D objectives, strategies, policies, and programs?
      i. Are they clearly stated or merely implied from performance or budgets?
      ii. Are they consistent with the corporation's mission, objectives, strategies, and policies, and with internal and external environments?
      iii. What is the role of technology in corporate performance?
      iv. Is the mix of basic, applied, and engineering research appropriate given the corporate mission and strategies?
      v. Does R&D provide the company with a competitive advantage?
   b. What return is the corporation receiving from its investment in R&D?
   c. Is the corporation competent in technology transfer? Does it use concurrent engineering and cross-functional work teams in product and process design?
   d. What role does technological discontinuity play in the company's products?
   e. How well does the corporation's investment in R&D compare with the investments of similar corporations? How much R&D is being outsourced? Is the corporation using value-chain alliances appropriately for innovation and competitive advantage?
   f. Does R&D adjust to the conditions in each country in which the company operates?
   g. Does R&D consider environmental sustainability in product development and packaging?
   h. What is the role of the R&D manager in the strategic management process?

4. **Operations and Logistics**
   a. What are the corporation's current manufacturing/service objectives, strategies, policies, and programs?
      i. Are they clearly stated or merely implied from performance or budgets?
      ii. Are they consistent with the corporation's mission, objectives, strategies, and policies, and with internal and external environments?
   b. What are the type and extent of operations capabilities of the corporation? How much is done domestically versus internationally? Is the amount of outsourcing appropriate to be competitive? Is purchasing being handled appropriately? Are suppliers and distributors operating in an environmentally sustainable manner? Which products have the highest and lowest profit margins?
      i. If the corporation is product-oriented, consider plant facilities, type of manufacturing system (continuous mass production, intermittent job shop, or flexible manufacturing), age and type of equipment, degree and role of automation and/or robots, plant capacities and utilization, productivity ratings, and availability and type of transportation.
      ii. If the corporation is service-oriented, consider service facilities (hospital, theater, or school buildings), type of operations systems (continuous service over time to the same clientele or intermittent service over time to varied clientele), age and type of supporting equipment, degree and role of automation and use of mass communication devices (diagnostic machinery, video machines), facility capacities and utilization rates, efficiency ratings of professional and service personnel, and availability and type of transportation to bring service staff and clientele together.
   c. Are manufacturing or service facilities vulnerable to natural disasters, local or national strikes, reduction or limitation of resources from suppliers, substantial cost increases of materials, or nationalization by governments?
   d. Is there an appropriate mix of people and machines (in manufacturing firms) or of support staff to professionals (in service firms)?
   e. How well does the corporation perform relative to the competition? Is it balancing inventory costs (warehousing) with logistical costs (just-in-time)? Consider costs per unit of labor, material, and overhead; downtime; inventory

control management and scheduling of service staff; production ratings; facility utilization percentages; and number of clients successfully treated by category (if service firm) or percentage of orders shipped on time (if product firm).

    i. What trends emerge from this analysis?

    ii. What impact have these trends had on past performance and how might these trends affect future performance?

    iii. Does this analysis support the corporation's past and pending strategic decisions?

    iv. Do operations provide the company with a competitive advantage?

  f. Are operations managers using appropriate concepts and techniques to evaluate and improve current performance? Consider cost systems, quality control and reliability systems, inventory control management, personnel scheduling, Total Quality Management (TQM), learning curves, safety programs, and engineering programs that can improve efficiency of manufacturing or of service.

  g. Do operations adjust to the conditions in each country in which it has facilities?

  h. Do operations consider environmental sustainability when making decisions?

  i. What is the role of the operations manager in the strategic management process?

5. **Human Resources Management (HRM)**

  a. What are the corporation's current HRM objectives, strategies, policies, and programs?

    i. Are they clearly stated or merely implied from performance and/or budgets?

    ii. Are they consistent with the corporation's mission, objectives, strategies, and policies and with internal and external environments?

  b. How well is the corporation's HRM performing in terms of improving the fit between the individual employee and the job? Consider turnover, grievances, strikes, layoffs, employee training, and quality of work life.

    i. What trends emerge from this analysis?

    ii. What impact have these trends had on past performance and how might these trends affect future performance?

    iii. Does this analysis support the corporation's past and pending strategic decisions?

    iv. Does HRM provide the company with a competitive advantage?

  c. How does this corporation's HRM performance compare with that of similar corporations?

  d. Are HRM managers using appropriate concepts and techniques to evaluate and improve corporate performance? Consider the job analysis program, performance appraisal system, up-to-date job descriptions, training and development programs, attitude surveys, job design programs, quality of relationships with unions, and use of autonomous work teams.

  e. How well is the company managing the diversity of its workforce? What is the company's record on human rights? Does the company monitor the human rights record of key suppliers and distributors?

  f. Does HRM adjust to the conditions in each country in which the company operates? Does the company have a code of conduct for HRM for itself and key suppliers in developing nations? Are employees receiving international assignments to prepare them for managerial positions?

  g. What is the role of outsourcing in HRM planning?

  h. What is the role of the HRM manager in the strategic management process?

6. **Information Technology (IT)**

  a. What are the corporation's current IT objectives, strategies, policies, and programs?

    i. Are they clearly stated or merely implied from performance and/or budgets?

    ii. Are they consistent with the corporation's mission, objectives, strategies, and policies, and with internal and external environments?

b. How well is the corporation's IT performing in terms of providing a useful database, automating routine clerical operations, assisting managers in making routine decisions, and providing information necessary for strategic decisions?

   i. What trends emerge from this analysis?

   ii. What impact have these trends had on past performance and how might these trends affect future performance?

   iii. Does this analysis support the corporation's past and pending strategic decisions?

   iv. Does IT provide the company with a competitive advantage?

c. How does this corporation's IT performance and stage of development compare with that of similar corporations? Is it appropriately using the Internet, intranet, and extranets?

d. Are IT managers using appropriate concepts and techniques to evaluate and improve corporate performance? Do they know how to build and manage a complex database, establish Web sites with firewalls and virus protection, conduct system analyses, and implement interactive decision-support systems?

e. Does the company have a global IT and Internet presence? Does it have difficulty with getting data across national boundaries?

f. What is the role of the IT manager in the strategic management process?

D. Summary of Internal Factors
(List in the IFAS Table 5–2, p. 186)

Which of these factors are core competencies? Which, if any, are distinctive competencies? Which of these factors are the most important to the corporation and to the industries in which it competes at the present time? Which might be important in the future? Which functions or activities are candidates for outsourcing?

V. Analysis of Strategic Factors (SWOT)

A. Situational Analysis
(List in SFAS Matrix, Figure 6–1, pp. 198–199)

Of the external (EFAS) and internal (IFAS) factors listed in III.D and IV.D, which are the strategic (most important) factors that strongly affect the corporation's present and future performance?

B. Review of Mission and Objectives

1. Are the current mission and objectives appropriate in light of the key strategic factors and problems?

2. Should the mission and objectives be changed? If so, how?

3. If they are changed, what will be the effects on the firm?

VI. Strategic Alternatives and Recommended Strategy

A. Strategic Alternatives

1. Can the current or revised objectives be met through more careful implementation of those strategies presently in use (for example, fine-tuning the strategies)?

2. What are the major feasible alternative strategies available to the corporation? What are the pros and cons of each? Can corporate scenarios be developed and agreed on? (Alternatives must fit the natural physical environment, societal environment, industry, and corporation for the next three to five years.)
   a. Consider *stability*, *growth*, and *retrenchment* as corporate strategies.
   b. Consider *cost leadership* and *differentiation* as business strategies.
   c. Consider any functional strategic alternatives that might be needed for reinforcement of an important corporate or business strategic alternative.

B. Recommended Strategy

1. Specify which of the strategic alternatives you are recommending for the corporate, business, and functional levels of the corporation. Do you recommend different business or functional strategies for different units of the corporation?
2. Justify your recommendation in terms of its ability to resolve both long- and short-term problems and effectively deal with the strategic factors.
3. What policies should be developed or revised to guide effective implementation?
4. What is the impact of your recommended strategy on the company's core and distinctive competencies?

VII. Implementation

A. What Kinds of Programs or Tactics Should Be Developed to Implement the Recommended Strategy?

1. Who should develop these programs/tactics?
2. Who should be in charge of these programs/tactics?

B. Are the Programs/Tactics Financially Feasible? Can Pro Forma Budgets Be Developed and Agreed On? Are Priorities and Timetables Appropriate to Individual Programs/Tactics?

C. Will New Standard Operating Procedures Need to Be Developed?

VIII. Evaluation and Control

A. Is the Current Information System Capable of Providing Sufficient Feedback on Implementation Activities and Performance? Can It Measure Strategic Factors?

1. Can performance results be pinpointed by area, unit, project, or function?
2. Is the information timely?
3. Is the corporation using benchmarking to evaluate its functions and activities?

B. Are Adequate Control Measures in Place to Ensure Conformance with the Recommended Strategic Plan?

1. Are appropriate standards and measures being used?
2. Are reward systems capable of recognizing and rewarding good performance?

CHAPTER 2
Corporate Governance

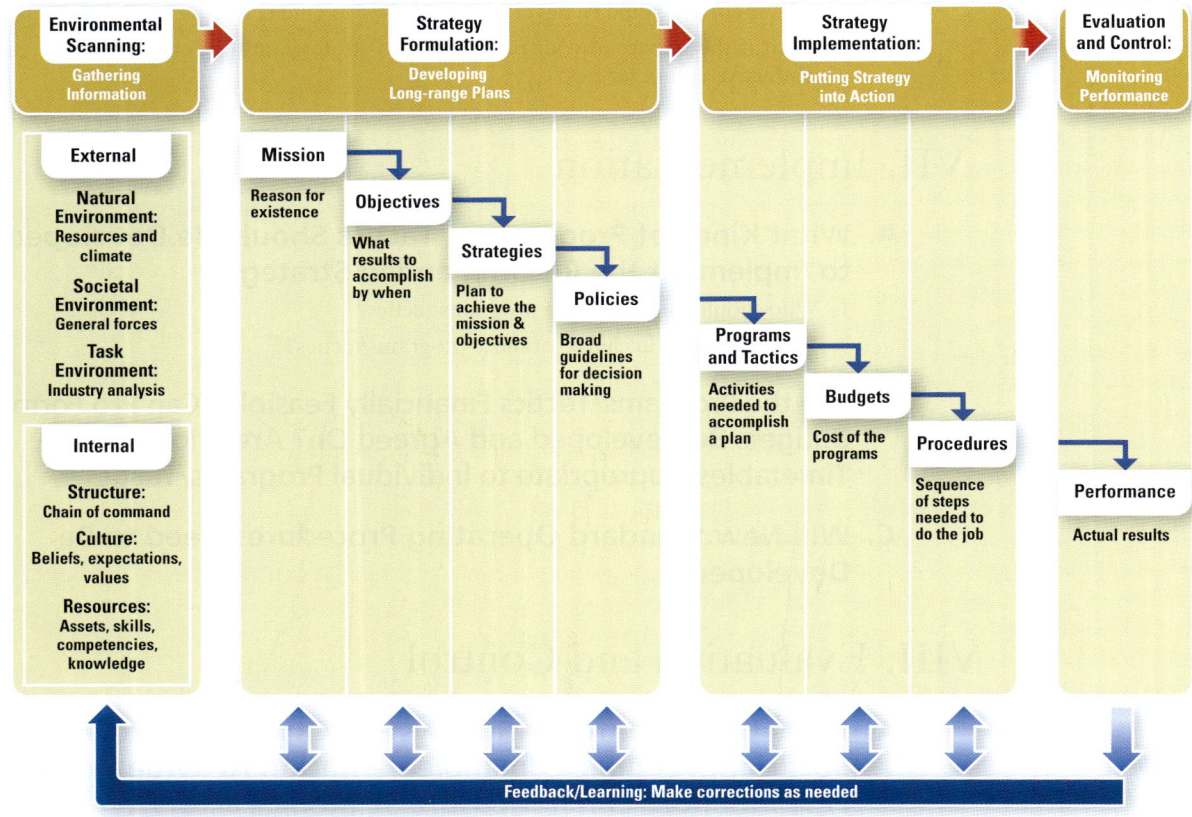

Environmental Scanning: Gathering Information → Strategy Formulation: Developing Long-range Plans → Strategy Implementation: Putting Strategy into Action → Evaluation and Control: Monitoring Performance

External

Natural Environment: Resources and climate

Societal Environment: General forces

Task Environment: Industry analysis

Internal

Structure: Chain of command

Culture: Beliefs, expectations, values

Resources: Assets, skills, competencies, knowledge

Mission — Reason for existence

Objectives — What results to accomplish by when

Strategies — Plan to achieve the mission & objectives

Policies — Broad guidelines for decision making

Programs and Tactics — Activities needed to accomplish a plan

Budgets — Cost of the programs

Procedures — Sequence of steps needed to do the job

Performance — Actual results

Feedback/Learning: Make corrections as needed

Pearson MyLab Management®

⭐ **Improve Your Grade!**

Over 10 million students improved their results using the Pearson MyLabs. Visit **mymanagementlab.com** for simulations, tutorials, and end-of-chapter problems.

Learning Objectives

After reading this chapter, you should be able to:

2-1. Describe the role and responsibilities of the board of directors in corporate governance

2-2. Explain how the composition of a board can affect its operation

2-3. Describe the impact of the Sarbanes–Oxley Act on corporate governance in the United States

2-4. Discuss trends in corporate governance

2-5. Explain how executive leadership is an important part of strategic management

Disarray with the HP Board of Directors

Sometimes an activist or even catalyst board does more harm than good. This has certainly been the case at Hewlett-Packard Company, the Palo Alto pioneer in technology.

Lewis Platt was only the fourth CEO in the history of the company, and like his predecessor (John A. Young); he was a long-time engineering employee of the company. Under his leadership, the company prospered as it had through most of its 50-year history up to that point. With the support of the board, he spun off the Medical Instruments division and made tentative moves toward the new information age, but was slow to recognize the importance of the Internet.

In 1999, along with the board of directors, he decided to look outside the company for the first time and try to hire a visible, passionate leader for the staid engineering-oriented firm. On July 19, 1999, HP announced that Carly Fiorina would be the new CEO, making her the first woman to head a DOW 30 company. Fiorina made her name at Lucent Technologies where she was President of a company that made a remarkable turnaround in the face of the huge changes in technology of the day.

Some of the same board members that hired her then turned against her in one of the most public proxy battles of our times when she announced a US$25 billion merger with Compaq Computer Company in September 2001. Walter Hewlett and Lewis Platt openly opposed the merger. The plan to move HP into an innovation machine in the Internet age was now being sidelined to put most of its resources in a low-margin, shrinking PC manufacturing business. Wall Street hated the idea. HP stock lost 18% of its value on the day the merger was announced and many analysts in the industry thought this was a bad move. Fiorina forced the merger forward with the support of the majority of the board of directors.

On February 22, 2002, the HP Board of Directors sent a very public and stinging letter of criticism against Walter Hewlett to all of its shareholders. Hewlett responded by taking out ads in major newspapers opposing the acquisition. In the end, the merger was approved, but by only a scant 3% majority.

The history of acquisitions is not a good one. Very few bring real value to the companies that are the acquirer. The bigger the acquisition, the more likely this is the case. Such was the fate of HP. By the end of 2004, the board was fed up with Carly Fiorina's inability to move the new, huge HP forward. The board began meeting in private without their high-profile CEO. On February 6, 2005, the board met with Fiorina at Chicago's O'Hare Hyatt Hotel and expressed their frustration with her leadership and her unwillingness to work with the board of directors on the future of the company. The next day they asked her to resign.

Believing that it was a failure of execution, the board moved to hire someone with strict operating credentials. The result was Mark Hurd, the 25-year veteran CEO at NCR Corporation. Hurd roared into the company, eliminating 15,000+ jobs, cutting R&D, and attempting to automate consulting services. A leak of information discussed at a board of director's strategy meeting in late 2005 led then–Board Chairman Patricia Dunn and CEO Mark Hurd to initiate an investigation of fellow board members. Using detectives who posed as reporters, they obtained phone records of those people on the board that they suspected, and the spying scandal exploded into the open.

Dunn was fired from her board seat in 2006 and *Newsweek* magazine put her on the cover with the title "The Boss Who Spied on Her Board." Mark Hurd escaped any serious repercussions from the scandal and announced a new, very strict code of conduct for the corporation.

By all accounts, Mark Hurd was successful at turning the company around and was listed as one of the best CEOs in 2009. However, another scandal broke, Hurd was accused of sexual harassment with an HP marketing consultant. While the board found that he did not actually violate the company's sexual-harassment policies, they did find that he submitted inaccurate expense reports intended to conceal the relationship. He was forced to resign in August 2010 by a powerful but small group of directors.

In the wake of the Hurd resignation, there was a major board shakeup. Four directors involved in forcing the Hurd resignation resigned their board seats and five new board members were named. In November, 2010, the board named Leo Apotheker as the new CEO. He was the former head of Global Field Operations at SAP, and would remain the company's CEO for little more than 10 months.

Apotheker's move to push forward the HP TouchPad tablet was a commercial failure at the same time that HP phones were taking a beating in the market. In a stunning announcement in September 2011, he stated that HP would exit the PC business entirely. HP was the leader in PC sales both within the United States and globally. The outrage was immediate and overwhelming. The company reversed position two weeks later, but the board was appalled at his lack of leadership. After firing Apotheker, the board named one of its own members, former eBay CEO Meg Whitman to run the company.

The board turmoil did not end. After a contentious annual meeting in 2013, the Chairman of the Board stepped down and two other board members resigned. In 2014

Meg Whitman was named Chairman of the Board and two new members were added at the same time that the company was in the process of the most significant layoffs in its history. From 2011 when Whitman took over as CEO to 2015, the company laid off more than 55,000 employees. Effective November 1, 2015 the company split into two publically traded companies in an effort to separate the slow growing PC and printer business from the potentially fast growing cloud technology and cyber security businesses.

One of the most important responsibilities that a board of directors has is to effectively recruit and work with management to lead the business. The CEO revolving door at HP has cost the company more than US$83 million in severance pay for CEOs that the board no longer wants to run the company. *CNN Money* reported in 2012 that "Before Apotheker ever came to HP, the company was known for its fractious board. Individual directors would cycle in and out, yet somehow the group seemed constantly divided by personal rivalries, bickering, and leaks to the press."

SOURCES: "HP's Meg Whitman: More Job Cuts Ahead," CNN Money, June 4, 2015. (money. cnn.com/2015/06/04/news/economy/hp-job-cuts-meg-whitman.index.html accessed January, 2016.), "HP Announces Changes to Board of Directors," Yahoo Finance, April 4, 2013. (finance. yahoo.com/news/hp-announces-changes-board-directors-203303763.html), "HP Announces Changes to Its Board of Directors," MarketWatch, July 17, 2014. (www.marketwatch.com/sotry /hp-announces-changes-to-its-board-of-directors-2014-01-17), Bandler, J. and Burke, D. "How Hewlett-Packard Lost Its Way," Accessed 5/30/13, www.tech.fortune.cnn.com/2012/05/08 /500-hp-apotheker/ (accessed January, 2016); Lohr, S. "Lewis E. Platt, 64, Chief of Hewlett-Packard in 1990's Dies," nytimes.com, Accessed 5/30/13, www.nytimes.com/2005/09/10 /technology/10platt.html; Stanford Graduate School of Business Case SM-130. "HP and Compaq Combined: In Search of Scale and Scope," Accessed 5/30/13, www.cendix.com/downloads/education/HP%20 Compaq.pdf; Elgin, B. "The Inside Story of Carly's Ouster," Accessed 5/30/13, www.businessweek.com/ stories/2005-02-20/the-inside-story-of-carlys-ouster; Oracle.com, "Mark Hurd – President," Accessed, 5/30/13, www.oracle.com/us/corporate/press/executives/mark-hurd-170533.html (accessed January, 2016); Gregory, S. "Corporate Scandals: Why HP had to Oust Mark Hurd," Accessed 5/30/13, www. time.com/time/business/article/0,8599,2009617,00.html; Arnold, L. and Turner, N. "Patricia Dunn, HP Chairman Fired in Spying Scandal, Dies at 58," Accessed 5/30/13, www.businessweek.com/news/2011-12-05/patricia-dunn-hp-chairman-fired-in-spying-scandal-dies-at-58.html (accessed January, 2016).

Role of the Board of Directors

2-1. Describe the role and responsibilities of the board of directors in corporate governance

A *corporation* is a mechanism established to allow different parties to contribute capital, expertise, and labor for their mutual benefit. The investor/shareholder participates in the profits (in the form of dividends and stock price increases) of the enterprise without taking responsibility for the operations. Management runs the company without being responsible for personally providing the funds. To make this possible, laws have been passed that give shareholders limited liability and, correspondingly, limited involvement in a corporation's activities. That involvement does include, however, the right to elect directors who have a legal duty to represent the shareholders and protect their interests. As representatives of the shareholders, directors have both the authority and the responsibility to establish basic corporate policies and to ensure that they are followed.[1]

The board of directors, therefore, has an obligation to approve all decisions that might affect the long-term performance of the corporation. This means that the corporation is fundamentally governed by the *board of directors* overseeing *top management*, with the concurrence of the *shareholder*. The term **corporate governance** refers to the relationship among these three groups in determining the direction and performance of the corporation.[2]

Increasingly, shareholders, activist investors, and various interest groups have seriously questioned the role of the board of directors in corporations. They are concerned that inside board members may use their position to feather their own nests and that outside board members often lack sufficient knowledge, involvement, and enthusiasm to do an adequate job of monitoring and providing guidance to top management. Instances of widespread corruption and questionable accounting practices at Enron, Global Crossing, WorldCom, Tyco, Bernard L. Madoff Investment Securities, and Qwest, among others, seem to justify their concerns. The board at HP appeared to be incapable of deciding upon the direction of the business, moving CEOs in and out as its ideas changed.

The general public has not only become more aware and more critical of many boards' apparent lack of responsibility for corporate activities, it has begun to push government to demand accountability. As a result, the board as a rubber stamp of the CEO or as a bastion of the "old-boy" selection system is slowly being replaced by more active, more professional boards.

RESPONSIBILITIES OF THE BOARD

Laws and standards defining the responsibilities of boards of directors vary from country to country. For example, board members in Ontario, Canada, face more than 100 provincial and federal laws governing director liability. The United States, however, has no clear national standards or federal laws. Specific requirements of directors vary, depending on the state in which the corporate charter is issued. There is, nevertheless, a developing worldwide consensus concerning the major responsibilities of a board. An article by Spencer Stuart written by an international team of contributors suggested the following five **board of director responsibilities**:

1. Effective board leadership including the processes, makeup, and output of the board
2. Strategy of the organization
3. Risk vs. initiative and the overall risk profile of the organization
4. Succession planning for the board and top management team
5. Sustainability[3]

These suggested responsibilities are in agreement with a survey by the National Association of Corporate Directors, in which U.S. CEOs reported that the four most important issues boards should address are corporate performance, CEO succession, strategic planning, and corporate governance.[4] Directors in the United States must make certain, in addition to the duties just listed, that the corporation is managed in accordance with the laws of the state in which it is incorporated. Because more than half of all publicly traded companies in the United States are incorporated in the state of Delaware, this state's laws and rulings have more impact than do those of any other state.[5] Directors must also ensure management's adherence to laws and regulations, such as those dealing with the issuance of securities, insider trading, and other conflict-of-interest situations. They must also be aware of the needs and demands of constituent groups so that they can achieve a judicious balance among the interests of these diverse groups while ensuring the continued functioning of the corporation.

In a legal sense, the board is required to direct the affairs of the corporation but not to manage them. It is charged by law to act with **due care**. If a director or the board as a whole fails to act with due care and, as a result, the corporation is in some way harmed, the careless director or directors can be held personally liable for the harm done. This is no small concern given that one survey of outside directors revealed that more than 40% had been named as part of lawsuits against corporations.[6] In 2015 the courts ruled that shareholders could pursue claims against Zynga (Farmville and Words with Friends among many others). Based upon the testimony of at least a half-dozen confidential witnesses, it appears that Zynga management intended to hide information detrimental to the price of the stock. Shareholders claim that insiders (Members of the Senior Management Team and Board of Directors) were allowed to sell $593 million in stock before a post-IPO lockup was to expire. The stock dropped 75% over the next four months as declining user activity information was released.[7] Most corporations have found that they need directors' and officers' liability insurance in order to attract people to become members of boards of directors.

McKinsey & Company began surveying the board of directors about their understanding of company issues in 2011. Their latest survey results revealed the following statistics about board members who felt they had a complete or a good understanding of the following: [8]

- Financial Position – 91%
- Current Strategy – 87%
- Value Creation – 74%
- Industry Dynamics – 77%
- Risks the company faces – 69%

In addition, 73% now report that they believe they have a high or very high impact on company financial success.

Role of the Board in Strategic Management

How does a board of directors fulfill their many responsibilities? The *role of the board of directors in strategic management* is to carry out three basic tasks:

- **Monitor:** By acting through its committees, a board can keep abreast of developments inside and outside the corporation, bringing to management's attention developments it might have overlooked. A board should, at the minimum, carry out this task.
- **Evaluate and influence:** A board can examine management's proposals, decisions, and actions; agree or disagree with them; give advice and offer suggestions; and outline alternatives. More active boards perform this task in addition to monitoring.
- **Initiate and determine:** A board can delineate a corporation's mission and specify strategic options to its management. Only the most active boards take on this task in addition to the two previous ones.

Board of Directors' Continuum

A board of directors is involved in strategic management to the extent that it carries out the three tasks of monitoring, evaluating and influencing, and initiating and determining. The **board of directors' continuum** shown in **Figure 2–1** shows the possible degree of involvement (from low to high) in the strategic management process. Boards can range from phantom boards with no real involvement to catalyst boards with a very high degree of involvement.[9] Research suggests that active board involvement in strategic management is positively related to a corporation's financial performance and its credit rating.[10]

FIGURE 2–1   Board of Directors' Continuum

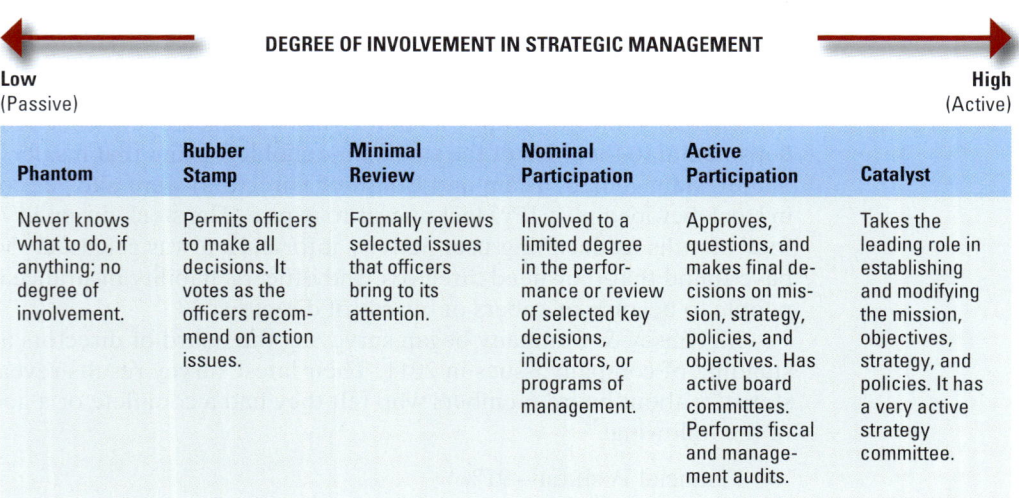

DEGREE OF INVOLVEMENT IN STRATEGIC MANAGEMENT

Low (Passive) ←———→ High (Active)

Phantom	Rubber Stamp	Minimal Review	Nominal Participation	Active Participation	Catalyst
Never knows what to do, if anything; no degree of involvement.	Permits officers to make all decisions. It votes as the officers recommend on action issues.	Formally reviews selected issues that officers bring to its attention.	Involved to a limited degree in the performance or review of selected key decisions, indicators, or programs of management.	Approves, questions, and makes final decisions on mission, strategy, policies, and objectives. Has active board committees. Performs fiscal and management audits.	Takes the leading role in establishing and modifying the mission, objectives, strategy, and policies. It has a very active strategy committee.

SOURCE: T. L. Wheelen and J. D. Hunger, "Board of Directors' Continuum," Copyright © 1994 by Wheelen and Hunger Associates. Reprinted by permission.

Highly involved boards tend to be very active. They take their tasks of monitoring, evaluating and influencing, and initiating and determining very seriously; they provide advice when necessary and keep management alert. As depicted in **Figure 2–1**, their heavy involvement in the strategic management process places them in the active participation or even catalyst positions. Although 74% of public corporations have periodic board meetings devoted primarily to the review of overall company strategy, the boards may not have had much influence in generating the plan itself.[11] The same global survey of directors by McKinsey & Company found that directors devote more time to strategy than any other area. Those boards reporting high influence typically shared a common plan for creating value and had healthy debate about what actions the company should take to create value. Together with top management, these high-influence boards considered global trends and future scenarios and developed plans. In contrast, those boards with low influence tended not to do any of these things.[12] Nevertheless, studies indicate that boards are becoming increasingly active.

These and other studies suggest that most large publicly owned corporations have boards that operate at some point between nominal and active participation. As a board becomes less involved in the affairs of the corporation, it moves farther to the left on the continuum (see **Figure 2–1**). On the far left are passive phantom or rubber-stamp boards that typically never initiate or determine strategy unless a crisis occurs. In these situations, the CEO who also usually serves as Chairman of the Board (although we see the same situation in active boards), personally nominates all directors and works to keep board members under his or her control by giving them the "mushroom treatment"—throw manure on them and keep them in the dark!

Generally, the smaller the corporation, the less active is its board of directors in strategic management.[13] In an entrepreneurial venture, for example, the privately held corporation may be 100% owned by the founders—who also manage the company. In this case, there is no need for an active board to protect the interests of the owner-manager shareholders—the interests of the owners and the managers are identical.

In this instance, a board is really unnecessary and only meets to satisfy legal requirements. If stock is sold to outsiders to finance growth, however, the board becomes more active. Key investors want seats on the board so they can oversee their investment. To the extent that they still control most of the stock, however, the founders dominate the board. Friends, family members, and key shareholders usually become members, but the board acts primarily as a rubber stamp for any proposals put forward by the owner-managers. In this type of company, the founder tends to be both CEO and Chairman of the Board and the board includes few people who are not affiliated with the firm or family.[14] This cozy relationship between the board and management should change, however, when the corporation goes public and stock is more widely dispersed. The founders, who are still acting as management, may sometimes make decisions that conflict with the needs of the other shareholders (especially if the founders own less than 50% of the common stock). In this instance, problems could occur if the board fails to become more active in terms of its roles and responsibilities. This situation can occur in large organizations as well. Even after the high-profile IPO, Facebook was still more than 50% controlled by founder Mark Zuckerberg and he used his position to make significant strategic decisions without input from the board of directors. In 2012, just ahead of the IPO of Facebook, he bought Instagram for roughly US$1 billion and only then informed the board of his move.[15]

Board of Directors Composition

2-2. Explain how the composition of a board can affect its operation

The boards of most publicly owned corporations are composed of both inside and outside directors. **Inside directors** (sometimes called management directors) are typically officers or executives employed by the corporation. **Outside directors** (sometimes called non-management directors) may be executives of other firms but are not employees of the board's corporation. Although there is yet no clear evidence indicating that a high proportion of outsiders on a board results in improved financial performance,[16] there is a trend in the United States to increase the number of outsiders on boards and to reduce the total size of the board.[17] The board of directors of a typical large U.S. corporation has an average of 10 directors, 2 of whom are insiders.[18] In 1998 there were no non-executives (outside directors) that served as Chairman of the Board for the S&P 500 companies. By 2012 these outsiders comprised 23% of the Chair positions. Not surprisingly, in 1998 84% of the S&P 500 companies had their CEO in a dual role as Chairman. By 2012 that number had dropped to 56%.[19]

Outsiders thus account for 80% of the board members in large U.S. corporations (approximately the same as in Canada). Boards in the United Kingdom typically have 5 inside and 5 outside directors, whereas in France boards usually consist of 3 insiders and 8 outsiders. Japanese boards, in contrast, contain 2 outsiders and 12 insiders.[20] The board of directors in a typical small U.S. corporation has 4 to 5 members, of whom only 1 or 2 are outsiders.[21] Research from large and small corporations reveals a negative relationship between board size and firm profitability.[22]

People who favor a high proportion of outsiders state that outside directors are less biased and more likely to evaluate management's performance objectively than are inside directors. This is the main reason why the U.S. Securities and Exchange Commission (SEC) in 2003 required that a majority of directors on the board be independent outsiders. The SEC also required that all listed companies staff their audit, compensation, and nominating/corporate governance committees entirely with independent, outside members. This view is in agreement with **agency theory**, which states

INNOVATION issue

JCPENNEY AND INNOVATION

Ron Johnson joined erstwhile retailer JCPenney in November 2011 with a mandate from the board of directors to shake up the organization. The board members were not interested in another decade of classic retailer wisdom, they wanted someone who would create a new JCPenney. They got exactly what they were looking for. The question was whether that bold move would allow the company to thrive, limp along, or go out of business.

Johnson was the architect behind the "cheap chic" approach at Target before he moved to Apple with the mandate to create "THE" store experience. He designed an Apple retail approach that is the envy of the retailer world and in the process created the world's most profitable stores. Johnson was personally recruited to take over JCPenney by Bill Ackman. His company (Pershing Square Capital Management) owned 18% of JCPenney.

Johnson's vision was to create a company that was not dependent upon sales coupons or continuous promotions for its survival. He joined a 110-year-old company that was running 590 different promotions a year that cost the company (in promotion costs alone) more than US$1 billion. Ninety-nine percent of those promotions were ignored by their primary customer group. The real sales price for virtually every product in the store was substantially less than the list price on the shelf.

The fundamental strategic approach was conceptually sound. He was separating the company from its competitors and doing so with an approach that was rare in the retailing world, durable as long as the competitors didn't believe that approach would work, and might have been valuable for the company both from a cost containment approach as well as its potential to draw in new customers. Unfortunately for JCPenny the story was over almost before it began. Sales plummeted, profits evaporated, and after 18 months on the job, Johnson was fired only to be replaced by the former CEO of the company. Perhaps Johnson's biggest failure was rollout. Rather than experimenting with the new concept to refine the effort, he demanded that it be put in place systemwide. He had the support of the board until his unwillingness to compromise or reevaluate his strategy drove the board to act.

....

SOURCES: Berfield, S. and Maheshwari, S. 2012. "J.C. Penney vs. The Bargain Hunters," *Bloomberg BusinessWeek*, May 28–June 3, 2012, pp. 21–22. Rooney, J. "JCPenney's New Strategy a Tough Sell on the Sales Floor," Forbes.com, Accessed 5/30/13, www.forbes.com/sites/jenniferrooney/2012/03/14/jc-penneys-new-strategy-a-tough-sell-on-the-sales-floor/

that problems arise in corporations because the agents (top management) are not willing to bear responsibility for their decisions unless they own a substantial amount of stock in the corporation. The theory suggests that a majority of a board needs to be from outside the firm so that top management is prevented from acting selfishly to the detriment of the shareholders. For example, proponents of agency theory argue that managers in management-controlled firms (contrasted with owner-controlled firms in which the founder or family still own a significant amount of stock) select less risky strategies with quick payoffs in order to keep their jobs.[23] This view is supported by research revealing that manager-controlled firms (with weak boards) are more likely to go into debt to diversify into unrelated markets (thus quickly boosting sales and assets to justify higher salaries for themselves). These actions result in poorer long-term performance than would be seen with owner-controlled firms.[24] Boards with a larger proportion of outside directors tend to favor growth through international expansion and innovative venturing activities than do boards with a smaller proportion of outsiders.[25] Outsiders tend to be more objective and critical of corporate activities. For example, research reveals that the likelihood of a firm engaging in illegal behavior or being sued declines with the addition of outsiders on the board.[26] Research on family businesses has found that boards with a larger number of outsiders on the board tended to have better corporate governance and better performance than did boards with fewer outsiders.[27]

In contrast, those who prefer inside over outside directors contend that outside directors are less effective than are insiders because the outsiders are less likely to have the necessary interest, availability, or competency. **Stewardship theory** proposes that, because of their long tenure with the corporation, insiders (senior executives) tend to identify with the corporation and its success. Rather than use the firm for their own ends, these executives are thus most interested in guaranteeing the continued life and success of the corporation. (See the **Strategy Highlight** feature for a discussion of agency theory contrasted with stewardship theory.) Excluding all insiders but the CEO reduces the opportunity for outside directors to see potential successors in action or to obtain alternate points of view of management decisions. Outside directors may sometimes serve on so many boards that they spread their time and interest too thin

STRATEGY highlight

AGENCY THEORY VERSUS STEWARDSHIP THEORY IN CORPORATE GOVERNANCE

Managers of large, modern, publicly held corporations are typically not the owners. In fact, most of today's top managers own only nominal amounts of stock in the corporation they manage. The real owners (shareholders) elect boards of directors who hire managers as their agents to run the firm's day-to-day activities. Once hired, how trustworthy are these executives? Do they put themselves or the firm first? There are two significant schools of thought on this.

Agency Theory. As suggested in the classic study by Berle and Means, top managers are, in effect, "hired hands" who are very likely more interested in their personal welfare than that of the shareholders. For example, management might emphasize strategies, such as acquisitions, that increase the size of the firm (to become more powerful and to demand increased pay and benefits) or that diversify the firm into unrelated businesses (to reduce short-term risk and to allow them to put less effort into a core product line that may be facing difficulty) but that result in a reduction of dividends and/or stock price.

Agency theory is concerned with analyzing and resolving two problems that occur in relationships between principals (owners/shareholders) and their agents (top management):

1. *Conflict of interest* arises when the desires or objectives of the owners and the agents conflict. For example, attitudes toward risk may be quite different. Agents may shy away from riskier strategies in order to protect their jobs.

2. *Moral hazard* refers to the situation where it is difficult or expensive for the owners to verify what the agents are actually doing.

According to agency theory, the likelihood that these problems will occur increases when stock is widely held (that is, when no one shareholder owns more than a small percentage of the total common stock), when the board of directors is composed of people who know little of the company or who are personal friends of top management, and when a high percentage of board members are inside (management) directors.

To better align the interests of the agents with those of the owners and to increase the corporation's overall performance, agency theory suggests that top management have a significant degree of ownership in the firm and/or have a strong financial stake in its long-term performance. In support of this argument, research indicates a positive relationship between corporate performance and the amount of stock owned by directors.

Stewardship Theory. In contrast, stewardship theory suggests that executives tend to be more motivated to act in the best interests of the corporation than in their own self-interests. Whereas agency theory focuses on extrinsic rewards that serve lower-level needs, such as pay and security, stewardship theory focuses on the higher-order needs, such as achievement and self-actualization. Stewardship theory argues that senior executives over time tend to view the corporation as an extension of themselves. Rather than use the firm for their own ends, these executives are most interested in guaranteeing the continued life and success of the corporation. The relationship between the board and top management is thus one of principal and steward, not principal and agent ("hired hand"). Stewardship theory notes that in a widely held corporation, the shareholder is free to sell his or her stock at any time. In fact, the average share of stock is held less than 10 months. A diversified investor or speculator may care little about risk at the company level—preferring management to assume extraordinary risk so long as the return is adequate. Because executives in a firm cannot easily leave their jobs when in difficulty, they are more interested in a merely satisfactory return and put heavy emphasis on the firm's continued survival. Thus, stewardship theory argues that in many instances top management may care more about

a company's long-term success than do more short-term–oriented shareholders.

....

SOURCES: For more information about agency and stewardship theory, see A. A. Berle and G. C. Means, *The Modern Corporation and Private Property* (NY: Macmillan, 1936). Also see J. H. Davis, F. D. Schoorman, and L. Donaldson, "Toward a Stewardship Theory of Management," *Academy of Management Review* (January 1997), pp. 20–47; P. J. Lane, A. A. Cannella Jr., and M. H. Lubatkin, "Agency Problems as Antecedents to Unrelated Mergers and Diversification: Amihud and Lev Reconsidered," *Strategic Management Journal* (June 1998), pp. 555–578; M. L. Hayward and D. C. Hambrick, "Explaining the Premiums Paid for Large Acquisitions: Evidence of CEO Hubris," *Administrative Science Quarterly* (March 1997), pp. 103–127; and C. M. Christensen and S. D. Anthony, "Put Investors in Their Place," *BusinessWeek* (May 28, 2007), p. 108.

to actively fulfill their responsibilities. The average board member of a U.S. Fortune 500 firm serves on three boards. Research indicates that firm performance decreases as the number of directorships held by the average board member increases.[28] Although only 40% of surveyed U.S. boards currently limit the number of directorships a board member may hold in other corporations, 60% limit the number of boards on which their CEO may be a member.[29]

Those who question the value of having more outside board members point out that the term *outsider* is too simplistic because some outsiders are not truly objective and should be considered more as insiders than as outsiders. For example, there can be:

1. **Affiliated directors**, who, though not really employed by the corporation, handle the legal or insurance work for the company or are important suppliers (and thus dependent on the current management for a key part of their business). These outsiders face a conflict of interest and are not likely to be objective. As a result of recent actions by the U.S. Congress, the Securities and Exchange Commission, the New York Stock Exchange, and NASDAQ, affiliated directors are being banned from U.S. corporate boardrooms. U.S. boards can no longer include representatives of major suppliers or customers or even professional organizations that might do business with the firm, even though these people could provide valuable knowledge and expertise.[30] The New York Stock Exchange decided in 2004 that anyone paid by the company during the previous three years could not be classified as an independent outside director.[31]

2. **Retired executive directors**, who used to work for the company, such as the past CEO who is partly responsible for much of the corporation's current strategy and who probably groomed the current CEO as his or her replacement. In the recent past, many boards of large firms kept the firm's recently retired CEO on the board for a year or two after retirement as a courtesy, especially if he or she had performed well as the CEO. It is almost certain, however, that this person will not be able to objectively evaluate the corporation's performance. Because of the likelihood of a conflict of interest, only 30% of boards in the Americas and 28% in Europe now include the former CEO on their boards.[32]

3. **Family directors,** who are descendants of the founder and own significant blocks of stock (with personal agendas based on a family relationship with the current CEO). The Schlitz Brewing Company, for example, was unable to complete its turnaround strategy with a non-family CEO because family members serving on the board wanted their money out of the company, forcing it to be sold.[33]

The majority of outside directors are active or retired CEOs and COOs of other corporations. Others are major investors/shareholders, academicians, attorneys, consultants, former government officials, and bankers. Given that 66% of the outstanding stock in the largest U.S. and UK corporations is now owned by institutional investors, such as mutual funds and pension plans, these investors are taking an increasingly active role in board membership and activities.[34] For example, TIAA-CREF's Corporate Governance team monitors governance practices of the 4000 companies in which it invests its pension funds through its Corporate Assessment Program. If its analysis of a company reveals problems, TIAA-CREF first sends letters stating its concerns, followed up by visits, and it finally sponsors a shareholder resolution in opposition to management's actions.[35] Institutional investors are also powerful in many other countries. In Germany, bankers are represented on almost every board—primarily because they own large blocks of stock in German corporations. In Denmark, Sweden, Belgium, and Italy, however, investment companies assume this role. For example, the investment company Investor casts 42.5% of the Electrolux shareholder votes, thus guaranteeing itself positions on the Electrolux Board.

Boards of directors have been working to increase the number of women and minorities serving on boards and well they should. A 2012 study of 2360 companies found that shares of companies with female board members outperformed comparable businesses with all-male boards by 26% worldwide over a six-year time period.[36] Korn/Ferry International reported that amongst the 100 largest companies listed in 2011 96% of boards of directors had at least one female director, while at the same time women made up only 16% of all directors.

This number was quite different when we look at the situation in some other countries. A 2011 study by Korn/Ferry examined the 100 largest companies in seven countries across the Pacific Rim. They found female board representation to be:

- Australia—11.2%
- China—8.1%
- Hong Kong—8.6%
- India—4.7%
- Malaysia—7.8%
- Singapore—6.4%
- New Zealand—7.5%[37]

Korn/Ferry's survey also revealed that 78% of the U.S. boards had at least one ethnic minority in 2007 (African-American, 47%; Latino, 19%; Asian, 11%) as director compared to only 47% in 1995, comprising around 14% of total directors.[38] Among the top 200 S&P companies in the United States, however, 84% have at least one African-American director.[39] The globalization of business is having an impact on board membership. According to the Spencer Stuart executive recruiting firm, 33% of U.S. boards had an international director.[40] Europe was the most "globalized" region of the world, with most companies reporting one or more non-national directors.[41] Although Asian and Latin American boards are still predominantly staffed by nationals, they are working to add more international directors.[42]

A 2015 study of the top 100 public firms in the United States found that 4% of the companies paid their directors more than US$150K as a cash retainer (not counting money paid for meeting attendance or other obligations). The same study found that the median cash retainer was between US$75K and US$100K (38%).[43] Directors serving on the boards of small companies usually received much less compensation (around US$10,000).

One study found directors of a sample of large U.S. firms to hold, on average, 3% of their corporations' outstanding stock.[44]

The vast majority of inside directors are the chief executive officer and either the chief operating officer (if not also the CEO) or the chief financial officer. Presidents or vice presidents of key operating divisions or functional units sometimes serve on the board. Few, if any, inside directors receive any extra compensation for assuming this extra duty. Very rarely does a U.S. board include any lower-level operating employees.

Codetermination: Should Employees Serve on Boards?

Codetermination, the inclusion of a corporation's workers on its board, began only recently in the United States. Corporations such as Chrysler, Northwest Airlines, United Airlines (UAL), and Wheeling-Pittsburgh Steel added representatives from employee associations to their boards as part of union agreements or Employee Stock Ownership Plans (ESOPs). For example, United Airlines workers traded 15% in pay cuts for 55% of the company (through an ESOP) and 3 of the firm's 12 board seats. In this instance, workers represent themselves on the board not so much as employees but primarily as owners. At Chrysler, however, the United Auto Workers union obtained a temporary seat on the board as part of a union contract agreement in exchange for changes in work rules and reductions in benefits. This was at a time when Chrysler was facing bankruptcy in the late 1970s. In situations like this, when a director represents an internal stakeholder, critics raise the issue of conflict of interest. Can a member of the board, who is privy to confidential managerial information, function, for example, as a union leader whose primary duty is to fight for the best benefits for his or her members? Although the movement to place employees on the boards of directors of U.S. companies shows little likelihood of increasing (except through employee stock ownership), the European experience reveals an increasing acceptance of worker participation (without ownership) on corporate boards.

Germany pioneered codetermination during the 1950s with a two-tiered system: (1) a supervisory board elected by shareholders and employees to approve or decide corporate strategy and policy and (2) a management board (composed primarily of top management) appointed by the supervisory board to manage the company's activities. Most other Western European countries have either passed similar codetermination legislation (as in Sweden, Denmark, Norway, and Austria) or use worker councils to work closely with management (as in Belgium, Luxembourg, France, Italy, Ireland, and the Netherlands).

CEOs often nominate chief executives (as well as board members) from other firms to membership on their own boards in order to create an interlocking directorate. A *direct* **interlocking directorate** occurs when two firms share a director or when an executive of one firm sits on the board of a second firm. An *indirect* interlock occurs when two corporations have directors who also serve on the board of a third firm, such as a bank.

Although the Clayton Act and the Banking Act of 1933 prohibit interlocking directorates by U.S. companies competing in the same industry, interlocking continues to occur in almost all corporations, especially large ones. Interlocking occurs because large firms have a large impact on other corporations and these other corporations, in turn, have some control over the firm's inputs and marketplace. For example, most large corporations in the United States, Japan, and Germany are interlocked either directly or indirectly with financial institutions.[45] Eleven of the 15 largest U.S. corporations have at least two board members who sit together on another board. Twenty percent of the 1000 largest U.S. firms share at least one board member.[46]

Interlocking directorates are useful for gaining both inside information about an uncertain environment and objective expertise about potential strategies and tactics.[47] For example, Kleiner Perkins, a high-tech venture capital firm, not only has seats on the boards of the companies in which it invests, but it also has executives (which Kleiner Perkins hired) from one entrepreneurial venture who serve as directors on others. Kleiner Perkins refers to its network of interlocked firms as its *keiretsu*, a Japanese term for a set of companies with interlocking business relationships and share-holdings.[48] Family-owned corporations, however, are less likely to have interlocking directorates than are corporations with highly dispersed stock ownership, probably because family-owned corporations do not like to dilute their corporate control by adding outsiders to boardroom discussions.

There is some concern, however, when the chairs of separate corporations serve on each other's boards. Twenty-two such pairs of corporate chairs (who typically also served as their firm's CEO) existed in 2003. In one instance, the three chairmen of Anheuser-Busch, SBC Communications, and Emerson Electric served on all three of the boards. Typically, a CEO sits on only one board in addition to his or her own—down from two additional boards in previous years. Although such interlocks may provide valuable information, they are increasingly frowned upon because of the possibility of collusion.[49] Nevertheless, evidence indicates that well-interlocked corporations are better able to survive in a highly competitive environment.[50]

NOMINATION AND ELECTION OF BOARD MEMBERS

Traditionally, the CEO of a corporation decided whom to invite to board membership and merely asked the shareholders for approval in the annual proxy statement. All nominees were usually elected. There are some dangers, however, in allowing the CEO free rein in nominating directors. The CEO might select only board members who, in the CEO's opinion, will not disturb the company's policies and functioning. Given that the average length of service of a U.S. board member is three 3-year terms (but can range up to 20 years for some boards), CEO-friendly, passive boards are likely to result. This is especially likely given that only 7% of surveyed directors indicated that their company had term limits for board members. Nevertheless, 60% of U.S. boards and 58% of European boards have a mandatory retirement age—typically around 70.[51] Research reveals that boards rated as least effective by the Corporate Library, a corporate governance research firm, tend to have members serving longer (an average of 9.7 years) than boards rated as most effective (7.5 years).[52] Directors selected by the CEO often feel that they should go along with any proposal the CEO makes. Thus board members find themselves accountable to the very management they are charged to oversee. Because this is likely to happen, more boards are using a nominating committee to nominate new outside board members for the shareholders to elect. Ninety-seven percent of large U.S. corporations now use nominating committees to identify potential directors. This practice is less common in Europe where 60% of boards use nominating committees.[53]

Many corporations whose directors serve terms of more than one year divide the board into classes and stagger elections so that only a portion of the board stands for election each year. This is called a *staggered board*. Sixty-three percent of U.S. boards currently have staggered boards.[54] Arguments in favor of this practice are that it provides continuity by reducing the chance of an abrupt turnover in its membership and that it reduces the likelihood of electing people unfriendly to management (who might be interested in a hostile takeover) through cumulative voting. An argument against staggered boards is that they make it more difficult for concerned shareholders to curb a

CEO's power—especially when that CEO is also Chairman of the board. An increasing number of shareholder resolutions to replace staggered boards with annual elections of all board members are currently being passed at annual meetings.

When nominating people for election to a board of directors, it is important that nominees have previous experience dealing with corporate issues. For example, research reveals that a firm makes better acquisition decisions when the firm's outside directors have had experience with such decisions.[55]

A survey of directors of U.S. corporations revealed the following as the main reasons for which individuals serve on a board:

- Interested in the Business—79%
- Make a Difference—65%
- Stay Active in Business Community—50%
- Recruited by Friend on the Board—25%
- Compensation—14%
- Networking Opportunities—11%
- Notoriety/Prestige—9%
- Recruited by Friend Not on the Board—4%[56]

ORGANIZATION OF THE BOARD

The size of a board in the United States is determined by the corporation's charter and its bylaws, in compliance with state laws. Although some states require a minimum number of board members, most corporations have quite a bit of discretion in determining board size. The average large, publicly held U.S. firm has 10 directors on its board. The average small, privately held company has 4 to 5 members. The average size of boards elsewhere is Japan, 14; Non-Japan Asia, 9; Germany, 16; UK, 10; and France, 11.[57]

Approximately 47% of the S&P 500 boards have split the role of Chairman and CEO. In addition, 28% of boards now have a truly independent chair.[58] The combined Chair/CEO position is being increasingly criticized because of the potential for conflict of interest. The CEO is supposed to concentrate on strategy, planning, external relations, and responsibility to the board. The Chairman's responsibility is to ensure that the board and its committees perform their functions as stated in the board's charter. Further, the Chairman schedules board meetings and presides over the annual shareholders' meeting. Critics of having one person in the two offices ask how the board can properly oversee top management if the Chairman is also a part of top management. For this reason, the Chairman and CEO roles are separated by law in Germany, the Netherlands, South Africa, and Finland. A similar law has been considered in the United Kingdom and Australia. Although research is mixed regarding the impact of the combined Chair/CEO position on overall corporate financial performance, firm stock price and credit ratings both respond negatively to announcements of CEOs also assuming the Chairman position.[59] Research also shows that corporations with a combined Chair/CEO have a greater likelihood of fraudulent financial reporting when CEO stock options are not present.[60]

Many of those who prefer that the Chairman and CEO positions be combined agree that the outside directors should elect a **lead director**. This person is consulted by the Chair/CEO regarding board affairs and coordinates the annual evaluation of the CEO.[61] The lead director position is very popular in the United Kingdom, where it originated. Of those U.S. companies combining the Chairman and CEO positions, 96% had a lead director.[62] Korn/Ferry found that in 2003 72% of respondents thought having a lead director was the right thing to do, while 85% thought so in 2007. A lead director creates a balance in power when the CEO is also the Chair of the Board. The same survey showed that board members are spending 16 hours a month on board business and that 86% were either very satisfied or extremely satisfied with their role in the business. The lead director becomes increasingly important because 94% of U.S. boards in 2007 (compared to only 41% in 2002) held regular executive sessions without the CEO being present.[63] Nevertheless, there are many ways in which an unscrupulous Chair/CEO can guarantee a director's loyalty. Research indicates that an increase in board independence often results in higher levels of CEO ingratiation behavior aimed at persuading directors to support CEO proposals. Long-tenured directors who support the CEO may use social pressure to persuade a new board member to conform to the group. Directors are more likely to be recommended for membership on other boards if they "don't rock the boat" and engage in low levels of monitoring and control behavior.[64] Even in those situations when the board has a nominating committee composed only of outsiders, the committee often obtains the CEO's approval for each new board candidate.[65]

The most effective boards accomplish much of their work through committees. Although they do not usually have legal duties, most committees are granted full power to act with the authority of the board between board meetings. Typical standing committees (in order of prevalence) are the audit (100%), compensation (99%), nominating (97%), corporate governance (94%), stock options (84%), director compensation (52%), and executive (43%) committees.[66] The executive committee is usually composed of two inside and two outside directors located nearby who can meet between board meetings to attend to matters that must be settled quickly. This committee acts as an extension of the board and, consequently, may have almost unrestricted authority in certain areas.[67] Except for the executive, finance, and investment committees, board committees are now typically staffed only by outside directors. Although each board committee typically meets four to five times annually, the average audit committee meets nine times.[68]

Impact of Sarbanes–Oxley on U.S. Corporate Governance

2-3. Describe the impact of the Sarbanes–Oxley Act on corporate governance in the United States

In response to the many corporate scandals uncovered since 2000, the U.S. Congress passed the **Sarbanes–Oxley Act** in June 2002. This act was designed to protect shareholders from the excesses and failed oversight that characterized criminal activities at Enron, Tyco, WorldCom, Adelphia Communications, Qwest, and Global Crossing, among other prominent firms. Several key elements of Sarbanes–Oxley were designed to formalize greater board independence and oversight. For example, the act requires that all directors serving on the audit committee be independent of the firm and receive no fees other than for services of the director. In addition, boards may no longer grant loans to corporate officers. The act has also established formal procedures for individuals (known as "whistleblowers") to report incidents of questionable accounting or auditing. Firms are prohibited from retaliating against anyone reporting wrongdoing. Both the CEO and CFO must certify the corporation's financial information. The act bans auditors from providing both external and internal audit services to the same company. It also requires that a firm identify whether it has a "financial expert" serving on the audit committee who is independent from management.

Although the cost to a large corporation of implementing the provisions of the law was US$8.5 million in 2004, the first year of compliance, the costs to a large firm fell to US$1–$5 million annually during the following years as accounting and information processes were refined and made more efficient.[69] Pitney Bowes, for example, saved more than US$500,000 in 2005 simply by consolidating four accounts receivable offices into one. Similar savings were realized at Cisco and Genentech.[70] An additional benefit of the increased disclosure requirements is more reliable corporate financial statements. Companies are now reporting numbers with fewer adjustments for unusual charges and write-offs, which in the past have been used to boost reported earnings.[71] The new rules have also made it more difficult for firms to post-date executive stock options. "This is an unintended consequence of disclosure," remarked Gregory Taxin, CEO of Glass, Lewis & Company, a stock research firm.[72] See the **Global Issue** feature to learn how board activism affects the managing of a global company.

GLOBAL issue

GLOBAL BUSINESS BOARD ACTIVISM AT YAHOO!

In the digital age in general and with Internet-based companies in particular, the impact of board activism now cuts across geographic boundaries like nothing has in the past. Yahoo! grew to become the largest Internet search engine company in the world used by individuals in their own language.

Yahoo! was founded in a Stanford University campus trailer in early 1994 by Ph.D. candidates David Filo and Jerry Yang as a means for people to keep track of their favorite interests on the Internet. Yahoo! is an acronym for "Yet Another Hierarchical Officious Oracle." Young companies often see dramatic moves by the board of directors who are unaccustomed to the growth phases in a business. An activist board will hold management responsible for their actions and may take on the role of a catalyst board in some circumstances.

Yahoo! grew quickly before the Internet bubble nearly bankrupted the company. Terry Semel, a legendary Hollywood dealmaker who didn't even use e-mail, was hired to turn the company into a media giant. In the summer of 2002, Semel tried to buy Google for roughly US$3 billion (this was two years before Google went public). At the time, Google's revenue stood at a paltry US$240 million, while Yahoo!'s was in excess of US$800 million. Despite failures to purchase Google, Facebook, and YouTube, Yahoo! became an Internet search giant serving more than 345 million individuals a month. By 2005, Yahoo! was the number one global Internet brand. Forbes listed Semel's total compensation as US$230.6 million. His reign saw both the rise and fall of the company. The board grew increasingly dissatisfied. By 2007, the company was losing market share and repeated acquisitions had failed to produce any real bump in the stock price. The board moved to act in June 2007. Semel assumed the role of non-executive chairman and Jerry Yang became the CEO once again.

Things did not improve. There were regular calls for Yang's resignation as the company continued to flounder.

At a time when tech companies were growing dramatically, Yahoo! continued its long, slow slide. Frustrated by his inability to strike deals with rivals Microsoft and Google, Yang and the board agreed that it was best for him to resign as CEO. His tenure lasted a scant 18 months.

Carol Bartz was hired in January 2009 to turn the company around and help it regain its stature. She was the former CEO of Autodesk and was viewed as a no-nonsense industry veteran. She instituted layoffs, reshuffled management, and turned over search operations to Microsoft in a deal that brought US$900 million to Yahoo!. However, shares remained effectively flat during her tenure and market share continued to drop. The board became increasingly dissatisfied with her performance and acted suddenly in September 2011. Without a replacement in hand, she was notified via a phone call from the Chairman of the Board that she was fired.

After a lengthy search, Scott Thompson was hired as the CEO in January 2012. He had previously been the CEO of eBay's PayPal unit and had done what most experts believed was a very good job. Unfortunately, he listed a computer science degree from Stonehill College that he had not earned. He did graduate, but with an accounting degree. Activist shareholder group Third Point (who has a chair on the board and owns 5.8% of the company) released details about his resumé padding. The information was part of a proxy fight that led to a board shakeup in February of 2012. That shakeup saw most of the previous board members removed and a new group of members (approved of by Third Point) elected.

Thompson resigned and Ross Levinsohm, the former head of global media for the company, was named the interim CEO while the company did yet another search. That search ended in July 2012 when the company named Marissa Mayer as the new CEO. Mayer was a longtime Google executive who ran their search group. While Mayer has struggled to turn the fortunes of the company around, at least there has been some consistency in the leadership. In her first two years, Mayer acquired 37 companies in an effort to build out some much needed capability at the company.

The continuous changes at Yahoo! have served to damage the company's ability to perform. It is difficult to gain any momentum in an industry when the top management changes so often and with such dramatic flair. The board of directors has a responsibility to the shareholders. The question is: At what point have they failed to do their job?

....

SOURCES: S. Loeb, "Analysis of Yahoo's acquisitions under Marissa Mayer," Vatornews (February 13, 2014), vator.tv/news/2014-02-03-analysis-of-yahoos-acquisitions-under-marissa-mayer (accessed January, 2016), B. Stone, "Marissa Mayer Is Yahoo's New CEO," *Bloomberg BusinessWeek* (July 16, 2012), (www.businessweek.com/articles/2012-07-16/marissa-mayer-isthe-new-yahoo-ceo accessed January, 2016); Yahoo! Website - http://pressroom.yahoo.net/pr/ycorp/overview.aspx; N. Damouni, "Yahoo CEO Search down to Leninsohn, Hulu CEO's Jason Kilar," Accessed 5/30/13, www.huffingtonpost.com/2012/07/05/yahoo-ceo-search-down-to-levinsohn-kilar_n_1652674.html; D. Temin, "Little Lies; Big Lies - Yahoo! CEO Scott Thompson's Revisionist History", Accessed 5/30/13; www.forbes.com/sites/daviatemin/2012/05/07/little-lies-big-lies-yahoo-ceo-scott-thompson-revisionist-history.html; J. Pepitone, "Yahoo confirms CEO is out after resume scandal," Accessed 5/30/13. www.money.cnn.com/2012/05/13/technology/yahoo-ceo-out/index.html (accessed January, 2016); V. Kopytoff and C. Miller, "Yahoo Board Fires Chief Executive," Accessed 5/30/13 www.nytimes.com/2011/09/07/technology/carol-bartz-yahoos-chief-executive-is-fired.html; T. Carmody, "Co-Founder, Ex-CEO Jerry Yang Resigns From Yahoo's Board," Accessed 5/30/13, www.wired.com/business/2012/01/jerry-yang-resigns-yahoo/; Compensation - Terry S Semel, Accessed 5/30/13, www.forbes.com/static/pvp2005/LIRXC25.html; F. Vogelstein, "How Yahoo! Blew It," Accessed 5/30/13, www.wired.com/wired/-archive/15.02/yahoo.html (accessed January, 2016).

IMPROVING GOVERNANCE

In implementing the Sarbanes–Oxley Act, the U.S. Securities and Exchange Commission (SEC) required in 2003 that a company disclose whether it has adopted a code of ethics that applies to the CEO and to the company's principal financial officer. Among other things, the SEC requires that the audit, nominating, and compensation committees be staffed entirely by outside directors. The New York Stock Exchange reinforced the mandates of Sarbanes–Oxley by requiring that companies have a nominating/governance committee composed entirely of independent outside directors. Similarly, NASDAQ rules require that nominations for new directors be made by either a nominating committee of independent outsiders or by a majority of independent outside directors.[73]

Partially in response to Sarbanes–Oxley, a survey of directors of Fortune 1000 U.S. companies by Mercer Delta Consulting and the University of Southern California revealed that 60% of directors were spending more time on board matters than before Sarbanes–Oxley, with 85% spending more time on their company's accounts, 83% more on governance practices, and 52% on monitoring financial performance.[74] Newly elected outside directors with financial management experience increased to 10% of all outside directors in 2003 from only 1% of outsiders in 1998.[75] Seventy-eight percent of Fortune 1000 U.S. boards in 2006 required that directors own stock in the corporation, compared to just 36% in Europe, and 26% in Asia.[76]

EVALUATING GOVERNANCE

To help investors evaluate a firm's corporate governance, a number of independent rating services, such as Standard & Poor's (S&P), Moody's, Morningstar, The Corporate Library, Institutional Shareholder Services (ISS), and Governance Metrics International (GMI), have established criteria for good governance. *Bloomberg BusinessWeek* annually publishes a list of the best and worst boards of U.S. corporations. Whereas rating service firms like S&P, Moody's, and The Corporate Library use a wide mix of research data and criteria to evaluate companies, ISS and GMI have been criticized because they primarily use public records to score firms, using simple checklists.[77] In contrast, the S&P Corporate Governance Scoring System researches four major issues:

- Ownership Structure and Influence
- Financial Stakeholder Rights and Relations

- Financial Transparency and Information Disclosure
- Board Structure and Processes

Although the S&P scoring system is proprietary and confidential, independent research using generally accepted measures of S&P's four issues revealed that moving from the poorest to the best-governed categories nearly doubled a firm's likelihood of receiving an investment-grade credit rating.[78]

AVOIDING GOVERNANCE IMPROVEMENTS

A number of corporations are concerned that various requirements to improve corporate governance will constrain top management's ability to effectively manage the company. For example, more U.S. public corporations have gone private in the years since the passage of Sarbanes–Oxley than before its passage. Other companies use multiple classes of stock to keep outsiders from having sufficient voting power to change the company. Insiders, usually the company's founders, get stock with extra votes, while others get second-class stock with fewer votes. For example, in 2012 Mark Zuckerberg, the CEO of Facebook, owned approximately 28% of the outstanding shares, but because of a two-class stock system, he controlled 57% of the voting shares.[79] A comprehensive analysis of firms completed in 2006 reported that approximately 6% of the companies had multiple classes of stock.[80]

Another approach to sidestepping new governance requirements is being used by corporations such as Google, Infrasource Services, Orbitz, and W&T Offshore. If a corporation in which an individual group or another company controls more than 50% of the voting shares decides to become a "controlled company," the firm is then exempt from requirements by the New York Stock Exchange and NASDAQ that a majority of the board and all members of key board committees be independent outsiders. It is easy to see that the minority shareholders have virtually no power in these situations.

Trends in Corporate Governance

The role of the board of directors in the strategic management of a corporation is likely to be more active in the future. Although neither the composition of boards nor the board leadership structure has been consistently linked to firm financial performance, better governance does lead to higher credit ratings and stock prices. A McKinsey survey reveals that investors are willing to pay 16% more for a corporation's stock if it is known to have good corporate governance. The investors explained that they would pay more because, in their opinion (1) good governance leads to better performance over time, (2) good governance reduces the risk of the company getting into trouble, and (3) governance is a major strategic issue.[81]

2-4. Discuss trends in corporate governance

Some of today's trends in governance (particularly prevalent in the United States and the United Kingdom) that are likely to continue include the following:

- Boards are getting more involved not only in reviewing and evaluating company strategy but also in shaping it.
- Institutional investors, such as pension funds, mutual funds, and insurance companies, are becoming active on boards and are putting increasing pressure on top management to improve corporate performance. This trend is supported by a U.S. SEC requirement that a mutual fund must publicly disclose the proxy votes cast at

company board meetings in its portfolio. This reduces the tendency for mutual funds to rubber-stamp management proposals.[82]

- Shareholders are demanding that directors and top managers own more than token amounts of stock in the corporation. Research indicates that boards with equity ownership use quantifiable, verifiable criteria (instead of vague, qualitative criteria) to evaluate the CEO.[83] When compensation committee members are significant shareholders, they tend to offer the CEO less salary but with a higher incentive component than do compensation committee members who own little to no stock.[84]

- Non-affiliated outside (non-management) directors are increasing their numbers and power in publicly held corporations as CEOs loosen their grip on boards. Outside members are taking charge of annual CEO evaluations.

- Women and minorities are being increasingly represented on boards.

- Boards are establishing mandatory retirement ages for board members—typically around age 70.

- Boards are evaluating not only their own overall performance, but also that of individual directors.

- Boards are getting smaller—partially because of the reduction in the number of insiders but also because boards desire new directors to have specialized knowledge and expertise instead of general experience.

- Boards continue to take more control of board functions by either splitting the combined Chair/CEO into two separate positions or establishing a lead outside director position.

- Boards are eliminating 1970s anti-takeover defenses that served to entrench current management. In just one year, for example, 66 boards repealed their staggered boards and 25 eliminated **poison pills**. (A poison pill is a term that refers to a dramatic event that empowers the current owners which will take place upon receiving an unwanted attempt at acquisition.)[85]

- As corporations become more global, they are increasingly looking for board members with international experience.

- Instead of merely being able to vote for or against directors nominated by the board's nominating committee, shareholders may eventually be allowed to nominate board members. This was originally proposed by the U.S. Securities and Exchange Commission in 2004, but was not implemented. Supported by the AFL-CIO, a more open nominating process would enable shareholders to vote out directors who ignore shareholder interests.[86]

- Society, in the form of special interest groups, increasingly expects boards of directors to balance the economic goal of profitability with the social needs of society. Issues dealing with workforce diversity and environmental sustainability are now reaching the board level.

The Role of Top Management

2-5. Explain how executive leadership is an important part of strategic management

The top management function is usually conducted by the CEO of the corporation in coordination with the COO (Chief Operating Officer) or president, executive vice president, and vice presidents of divisions and functional areas.[87] Even though strategic management involves everyone in the organization, the board of directors holds top management primarily responsible for the strategy and implementation of that strategy at the firm.[88]

RESPONSIBILITIES OF TOP MANAGEMENT

Top management responsibilities, especially those of the CEO, involve getting things accomplished through and with others in order to meet the corporate objectives. Top management's job is thus multidimensional and is oriented toward the welfare of the total organization. Specific top management tasks vary from firm to firm and are developed from an analysis of the mission, objectives, strategies, and key activities of the corporation. Tasks are typically divided among the members of the top management team. A diversity of skills can thus be very important. Research indicates that top management teams with a diversity of functional backgrounds, experiences, and length of time with the company tend to be significantly related to improvements in corporate market share and profitability.[89] In addition, highly diverse teams with some international experience tend to emphasize international growth strategies and strategic innovation, especially in uncertain environments, as a means to boost financial performance.[90] The CEO, with the support of the rest of the top management team, has two primary responsibilities when it comes to strategic management. The first is to provide executive leadership and a vision for the firm. The second is to manage a strategic planning process. (See the **Sustainability Issue** feature for an example of how CEO pay is affecting the economic viability of corporations.)

SUSTAINABILITY issue

CEO PAY AND CORPORATE PERFORMANCE

What leads a CEO to perform in the best interests of the shareholders? This has been a question for some time (see STRATEGY highlight). Egregious pay for CEOs who don't perform has been a contention for many years. Leo Apotheker was paid over US$30 million dollars during his 11-month tenure at HP despite making strategic choices that cost the company hundreds of millions in sales and a share price that dropped almost in half. Financial research firm Obermatt did a study on CEO pay and company performance between 2008 and 2010. They calculated a "deserved pay" based upon earnings growth and shareholder return. They found that there is no correlation in the S&P 100 between CEO pay and company performance.

The 2015 median pay for the nation's 200 top-paid CEOs was US$11.5 million and the CEO pay as multiple of the typical worker pay was over 295 times, according to a study conducted for *The New York Times*.

In 2010, the Dodd–Frank financial reform law was enacted, which requires companies to submit executive compensation packages for a nonbinding shareholder vote at least once every three years even though most public companies now do so annually. The changes in the boardroom to the means and methods of executive compensation have been affected because of the potential for public embarrassment. These votes have done little to curb CEO pay. Since the legislation went into effect, CEO pay has risen 12% annually. There have been some notable exceptions, in 2011, shareholders rejected CEO Vikram Pandit's (Citigroup) US$14.8 million pay package after the stock dropped over 40%, and in 2012 shareholders rejected Chiquita Brands CEO pay package by a 4-to-1 margin.

BusinessWeek reported that companies who suffered shareholder rejections of executive pay packages, as well as those that received yes votes, changed their compensation systems to align them with the interest of shareholders. By 2012, a *Wall Street Journal* analysis of the top 300 U.S. companies found that pay now generally tracked performance. Balancing the interests of the owners of a corporation with those who run the corporation is one of the most important issues in sustainable business practices.

SOURCES: A. Ahmed, "Research Finds No Correlation of CEO Pay and Performance/Market Capitalisation," Obermatt, February 9, 2012, G. Morgenson, "Despite Federal Regulation, C.E.O.-Worker Pay Gap Data Remains Hidden," *New York Times*, April 10. 2015. (www.nytimes.com/2015/04/12/business/despite-federal-regulation-ceo-worker-pay-gap-remains-hidden.html?_r=0 accessed January, 2016); G. Morgenson, "Shareholders' Votes Have Done Little to Curb Lavish Executive Pay," *New York Times*, May 16, 2015. (www.nytimes.com/2015/05/17/business/ shareholders-votes-have-done-little-to-curb-lavish-executive-pay .html); "Executive Pay and Performance," Accessed 5/30/13, www .economist.com/blogs/graphicdetail/2012/02/focus-O; Brady, D. "Say on Pay: Boards Listen When Shareholders Speak," Accessed 5/30/13, www.businessweek.com/articles/2012-06-07/say-on-pay-boards-listen-when-shareholders-speak.html (accessed January, 2016); Popper, N. "C.E.O. Pay Is Rising Despite the Din," Accessed 5/30/13, www.nytimes.com/2012/06/17 /business/executive-pay-still-climbing-despite-a-shareholder-din.html.

Executive Leadership and Strategic Vision

Executive leadership is the directing of activities toward the accomplishment of corporate objectives. Executive leadership is important because it sets the tone for the entire corporation. A **strategic vision** is a description of what the company is capable of becoming. It is often communicated in the company's vision statement (as described in **Chapter 1**). People in an organization want to have a sense of direction, but only top management is in the position to specify and communicate their unique strategic vision to the general workforce. Top management's enthusiasm (or lack of it) about the corporation tends to be contagious. The importance of executive leadership is wonderfully illustrated by the quote in the United States Infantry Journal from 1948: "No man is a leader until his appointment is ratified in the minds and hearts of his men."[91]

Successful CEOs are noted for having a clear strategic vision, a strong passion for their company, and an ability to communicate with others. They are often perceived to be dynamic and charismatic leaders—which is especially important for high firm performance and investor confidence in uncertain environments.[92] They have many of the characteristics of **transformational leaders**—that is, leaders who provide change and movement in an organization by providing a vision for that change.[93] The positive attitude characterizing many well-known current and former leaders—such as Bill Gates at Microsoft, Anita Roddick at the Body Shop, Richard Branson at Virgin, Steve Jobs at Apple Computer, Meg Whitman at eBay and now HP, Howard Schultz at Starbucks, and Herb Kelleher at Southwest Airlines—energized their respective corporations at important times. These transformational leaders have been able to command respect and execute effective strategy formulation and implementation because they have exhibited three key characteristics:[94]

1. **The CEO articulates a strategic vision for the corporation:** The CEO envisions the company not as it currently is but as it can become. The new perspective that the CEO's vision brings gives renewed meaning to everyone's work and enables employees to see beyond the details of their own jobs to the functioning of the total corporation.[95] Louis Gerstner proposed a new vision for IBM when he proposed that the company change its business model from computer hardware to services. In a survey of 1,500 senior executives from 20 different countries, when asked the most important behavioral trait a CEO must have, 98% responded that the CEO must convey "a strong sense of vision."[96]

2. **The CEO presents a role for others to identify with and to follow:** The leader empathizes with followers and sets an example in terms of behavior, dress, and actions. The CEO's attitudes and values concerning the corporation's purpose and activities are clear-cut and constantly communicated in words and deeds. For example, when design engineers at General Motors had problems with monitor resolution

using the Windows operating system, Steve Ballmer, then CEO of Microsoft personally crawled under conference room tables to plug in PC monitors and diagnose the problem.[97] People need to know what to expect and have trust in their CEO. Research indicates that businesses in which the general manager has the trust of the employees have higher sales and profits with lower turnover than do businesses in which there is a lesser amount of trust.[98]

3. **The CEO communicates high-performance standards and also shows confidence in the followers' abilities to meet these standards:** The leader empowers followers by raising their beliefs in their own capabilities. No leader ever improved performance by setting easily attainable goals that provided no challenge. Communicating high expectations to others can often lead to high performance.[99] The CEO must be willing to follow through by coaching people. As a result, employees view their work as very important and thus motivating.[100] Ivan Seidenberg, chief executive of Verizon Communications, was closely involved in deciding Verizon's strategic direction, and he showed his faith in his people by letting his key managers handle important projects and represent the company in public forums. Grateful for his faith in them, his managers were fiercely loyal both to him and the company.[101]

The negative side of confident executive leaders is that their very confidence may lead to *hubris*, in which their confidence blinds them to information that is contrary to a decided course of action. For example, overconfident CEOs tend to charge ahead with mergers and acquisitions even though they are aware that most acquisitions destroy shareholder value. Research by Tate and Malmendier found that overconfident CEOs were most likely to make acquisitions when they could avoid selling new stock to finance them, and they were more likely to do deals that diversified their firm's lines of businesses.[102] Carly Fiorina used the power of her office and her considerable influence with a relatively weak board of directors to push through the Compaq Computer acquisition over the objections of the founders family and many significant shareholders.

Managing the Strategic Planning Process

As business corporations adopt more of the characteristics of a learning organization, strategic planning initiatives can come from any part of an organization. A survey of 156 large corporations throughout the world revealed that, in two-thirds of the firms, strategies were first proposed in the business units and sent to headquarters for approval.[103] However, unless top management encourages and supports the planning process, it is unlikely to result in a strategy. In most corporations, top management must initiate and manage the strategic planning process. It may do so by first asking business units and functional areas to propose strategic plans for themselves, or it may begin by drafting an overall corporate plan within which the units can then build their own plans. Research suggests that bottom-up strategic planning may be most appropriate in multidivisional corporations operating in relatively stable environments but that top-down strategic planning may be most appropriate for firms operating in turbulent environments.[104] Other organizations engage in concurrent strategic planning in which all the organization's units draft plans for themselves after they have been provided with the organization's overall mission and objectives.

Regardless of the approach taken, the typical board of directors expects top management to manage the overall strategic planning process so that the plans of all the units and functional areas fit together into an overall corporate plan. Top management's job, therefore, includes the tasks of evaluating unit plans and providing feedback. To do this, it may require each unit to justify its proposed objectives, strategies, and programs in terms of how well they satisfy the organization's overall objectives in light of available resources. If a company is not organized into business units, top managers may work together as a team to do strategic planning. CEO Jeff Bezos tells how this is done at Amazon.com:

> We have a group called the S Team—S meaning "senior" [management]—that stays abreast of what the company is working on and delves into strategy issues. It meets for about four hours every Tuesday. Once or twice a year the S Team also gets together in a two-day meeting where different ideas are explored. Homework is assigned ahead of time. . . . Eventually we have to choose just a couple of things, if they're big, and make bets.[105]

In contrast to the seemingly continuous strategic planning being done at Amazon.com, most large corporations conduct the strategic planning process just once a year—often at offsite strategy workshops attended by senior executives.[106]

Many large organizations have a *strategic planning staff* charged with supporting both top management and the business units in the strategic planning process. This staff may prepare the background materials used in senior management's offsite strategy workshop. This planning staff typically consists of fewer than 10 people, headed by a senior executive with the title of Director of Corporate Development or Chief Strategy Officer. The staff's major responsibilities are to:

1. Identify and analyze companywide strategic issues, and suggest corporate strategic alternatives to top management.
2. Work as facilitators with business units to guide them through the strategic planning process.[107]

End of Chapter SUMMARY

Who determines a corporation's performance? According to the popular press, it is the Chief Executive Officer who seems to be personally responsible for a company's success or failure. When a company is in trouble, one of the first alternatives usually presented is to fire the CEO. That was certainly the case at the Walt Disney Company under Michael Eisner, as well as Hewlett-Packard under Carly Fiorina. Both CEOs were first viewed as transformational leaders who made needed strategic changes to their companies. Later both were perceived to be the primary reason for their company's poor performance and were fired by their boards. The truth is rarely this simple.

According to research by Margarethe Wiersema, firing the CEO rarely solves a corporation's problems. In a study of CEO turnover caused by dismissals and retirements in the 500 largest public U.S. companies, 71% of the departures were involuntary. In those firms in which the CEO was fired or asked to resign and replaced by another, Wiersema found *no* significant improvement in the company's operating earnings or stock price. She couldn't find a single measure suggesting that CEO dismissal had a positive effect on corporate performance! Wiersema placed the blame for the poor results squarely on the shoulders of the boards of directors. Boards typically lack an in-depth understanding of the business and consequently rely too heavily on executive search firms that know even less about the business. According to Wiersema, boards that successfully managed the executive succession process had three things in common:

- The board set the criteria for candidate selection based on the strategic needs of the company.
- The board set realistic performance expectations rather than demanding a quick fix to please the investment community.

■ The board developed a deep understanding of the business and provided strong strategic oversight of top management, including thoughtful annual reviews of CEO performance.[108]

As noted at the beginning of this chapter, corporate governance involves not just the CEO or the board of directors. It involves the combined active participation of the board, top management, and shareholders. One positive result of the many corporate scandals occurring over the past decade is the increased interest in governance. Institutional investors are no longer content to be passive shareholders. Thanks to new regulations, boards of directors are taking their responsibilities more seriously and including more independent outsiders on key oversight committees. Top managers are beginning to understand the value of working with boards as partners, not just as adversaries or as people to be manipulated. Although there will always be passive shareholders, rubber-stamp boards, and dominating CEOs, the simple truth is that good corporate governance means better strategic management.

Pearson MyLab Management®

Go to **mymanagementlab.com** to complete the problems marked with this icon .

KEY TERMS

affiliated directors (p. 82)
agency theory (p. 79)
board of directors' continuum (p. 77)
board of director responsibilities (p. 76)
codetermination (p. 84)
corporate governance (p. 75)

due care (p. 76)
executive leadership (p. 93)
inside directors (p. 79)
interlocking directorate (p. 84)
lead director (p. 86)
outside directors (p. 79)
poison pills (p. 91)

retired executive directors (p. 82)
Sarbanes–Oxley Act (p. 87)
stewardship theory (p. 81)
strategic vision (p. 93)
top management responsibilities (p. 92)
transformational leaders (p. 93)

Pearson MyLab Management®

Go to **mymanagementlab.com** for the following assisted-graded writing questions:

✪ **2-1.** What are the roles and responsibilities of an effective and active Board of Directors?
✪ **2-2.** What are the issues that suggest the need for oversight of a particular company's management team?

DISCUSSION QUESTIONS

✪ **2-3.** Explain the role of executive leadership in building the strategic vision in corporations.

2-4. Is there a close relationship between the composition of a board of directors and the organizational performance?

✪ **2-5.** Why is the combined Chair/CEO (or Managing Director) positions being increasingly criticized by most management scholars?

2-6. What is the role of codetermination? In your opinion, is the incorporation of lower-level employees on the board appropriate?

✪ **2-7.** How should a board of directors be involved in the executive leadership of an organization?

STRATEGIC PRACTICE EXERCISE

A. Think of the **best manager** for whom you have ever worked. What was it about this person that made him or her such a good manager in your eyes? Consider the following statements as they pertain to that person. Fill in the blank *in front of each statement* with one of the following values:

STRONGLY AGREE = 5; AGREE = 4; NEUTRAL = 3;
DISAGREE = 2; STRONGLY DISAGREE = 1

1. ____ I respect him/her personally, and want to act in a way that merits his/her respect and admiration.

2. ____ I respect her/his competence about things she/he is more experienced about than I.

3. ____ He/she can give special help to those who co-operate with him/her.

4. ____ He/she can apply pressure on those who don't cooperate with him/her.

5. ____ He/she has a legitimate right, considering his/her position, to expect that his/her suggestions will be carried out.

6. ____ I defer to his/her judgment in areas with which he/she is more familiar than I.

7. ____ He/she can make things difficult for me if I fail to follow his/her advice.

8. ____ Because of his/her job title and rank, I am obligated to follow his/her suggestions.

9. ____ I can personally benefit by cooperating with him/her.

10. ____ Following his/her advice results in better decisions.

11. ____ I cooperate with him/her because I have a high regard for him/her as an individual.

12. ____ He/she can penalize those who do not follow his/her suggestions.

13. ____ I feel I have to cooperate with him/her.

14. ____ I cooperate with him/her because I wish to be identified with him/her.

15. ____ Cooperating with him/her can positively affect my performance.

SOURCE: Questionnaire developed by J. D. Hunger from the article "Influence and Information: An Exploratory Investigation of the Boundary Role Person's Bases of Power" by Robert Spekman, *Academy of Management Journal*, March 1979. Copyright © 2004 by J. David Hunger.

B. Now think of the **worst manager** for whom you have ever worked. What was it about this person that made him or her such a poor manager? Please consider the statements earlier as they pertain to that person. Please place a number *after each statement* with one of the values, from 5 = strongly agree to 1 = strongly disagree.

C. Add the values you marked for the best manager within each of the five categories of power below. Then, do the same for the values you marked for the worst manager.

BEST MANAGER

Reward	Coercive	Legitimate	Referent	Expert
3.	4.	5.	1.	2.
9.	7.	8.	11.	6.
15.	12.	13.	14.	10.
Total	Total	Total	Total	Total

WORST MANAGER

Reward	Coercive	Legitimate	Referent	Expert
3.	4.	5.	1.	2.
9.	7.	8.	11.	6.
15.	12.	13.	14.	10.
Total	Total	Total	Total	Total

D. Consider the differences between how you rated your best and your worst manager. How different are the two profiles? In many cases, the best manager's profile tends to be similar to that of transformational leaders in that the best manager tends to score highest on referent, followed by expert and reward, power—especially when compared to the worst manager's profile. The worst manager often scores highest on coercive and legitimate power, followed by reward power. The results of this survey may help you answer discussion question 2-7 for this chapter.

NOTES

1. A. G. Monks and N. Minow, *Corporate Governance* (Cambridge, MA: Blackwell Business, 1995), pp. 8–32.
2. Ibid., p. 1.
3. C. Corsi, G. Dale, J. H. Daum, J. W. Mumm, and W. Schoppen, "5 Things Boards of Directors Should Be Thinking About," *Point of View*: A special issue focusing on today's board and CEO agenda (2010), Spencer Stuart. © 2010 Spencer Stuart. All rights reserved. For information about copying, distributing, and displaying this work, contact permissions@spencerstuart.com.
4. Reported by E. L. Biggs in "CEO Succession Planning: An Emerging Challenge for Boards of Directors," *Academy of Management Executive* (February 2004), pp. 105–107.
5. A. Borrus, "Less Laissez-Faire in Delaware?" *BusinessWeek* (March 22, 2004), pp. 80–82.
6. L. Light, "Why Outside Directors Have Nightmares," *BusinessWeek* (October 23, 1996), p. 6.
7. J. Stempel, "Zynga must face U.S. lawsuit alleging fraud tied to IPO," Reuters, March 26, 2015. (www.reuters.com/article/2015/03/26/us-zynga-lawsuit-IdUSKBN0MM1XP20150326 accessed January, 2016), www.zynga.com.
8. C. Bhagat, M. Hirt, & C. Kehoe, "Improving board governance: McKinsey Global Survey results," *McKinsey & Company Insigts & Publications*, August 2013. (www.mckinsey.com/insights/strategy/improving_board_governance_mckinsey_global_survey_results).
9. Nadler proposes a similar five-step continuum for board involvement ranging from the least involved "passive board" to the most involved "operating board," plus a form for measuring board involvement in D. A. Nadler, "Building Better Boards," *Harvard Business Review* (May 2004), pp. 102–111.
10. H. Ashbaugh, D. W. Collins, and R. LaFond, "The Effects of Corporate Governance on Firms' Credit Ratings," unpublished paper (March, 2004); W. Q. Judge Jr., and C. P. Zeithaml, "Institutional and Strategic Choice Perspectives on Board Involvement in the Strategic Choice Process," *Academy of Management Journal* (October 1992), pp. 766–794; J. A. Pearce II, and S. A. Zahra, "Effective Power-Sharing Between the Board of Directors and the CEO," *Handbook of Business Strategy*, 1992/93 Yearbook (Boston: Warren, Gorham, and Lamont, 1992), pp. 1.1–1.16.
11. *Current Board Practices*, American Society of Corporate Secretaries, 2002 as reported by B. Atkins in "Directors Don't Deserve such a Punitive Policy," *Directors & Boards* (Summer 2002), p. 23.
12. A. Chen, J. Osofsky, and E. Stephenson, "Making the Board More Strategic: A McKinsey Global Survey," *McKinsey Quarterly* (March 2008), pp. 1–10.

13. M. K. Fiegener, "Determinants of Board Participation in the Strategic Decisions of Small Corporations," *Entrepreneurship Theory and Practice* (September 2005), pp. 627–650.
14. A. L. Ranft and H. M. O'Neill, "Board Composition and High-Flying Founders: Hints of Trouble to Come?" *Academy of Management Executive* (February 2001), pp. 126–138.
15. B. Stone, D. MacMilan, A. Vance, A. Satariano, and D. Bass, "How Zuck Hacked the Valley," *BusinessWeek* (May 21, 2012).
16. D. R. Dalton, M. A. Hitt, S. Trevis Certo, and C. M. Dalton, "The Fundamental Agency Problem and Its Mitigation," Chapter Chapter One in *Academy of Management Annals*, edited by J. F. Westfall and A. F. Brief (London: Rutledge, 2007); Y. Deutsch, "The Impact of Board Composition on Firms' Critical Decisions: A Meta-Analytic Review," *Journal of Management* (June 2005), pp. 424–444; D. F. Larcher, S. A. Richardson, and I. Tuna, "Does Corporate Governance Really Matter?" *Knowledge @ Wharton* (September 8–21, 2004); J. Merritt and L. Lavelle, "A Different Kind of Governance Guru," *BusinessWeek* (August 9, 2004), pp. 46–47; A. Dehaene, V. DeVuyst, and H. Ooghe, "Corporate Performance and Board Structure in Belgian Companies," *Long Range Planning* (June 2001), pp. 383–398; M. W. Peng, "Outside Directors and Firm Performance During Institutional Transitions," *Strategic Management Journal* (May 2004), pp. 453–471.
17. D. R. Dalton, M. A. Hitt, S. Trevis Certo, and C. M. Dalton, "The Fundamental Agency Problem and Its Mitigation," Chapter One in *Academy of Management Annals*, edited by J. F. Westfall and A. F. Brief (London: Rutledge, 2007).
18. *33rd Annual Board of Directors Study* (New York: Korn/Ferry International, 2007), p. 11.
19. R. Hallagan, D. Carey, K. Daly, and P. Gleason, "Annual Survey of Board Leadership 2014," Korn Ferry Institute. (www.kornferry.com/institute/816-korn-ferry-nacd-annual-survey-of-board-leadership-2014 accessed January, 2016).
20. *30th Annual Board of Directors Study* (New York: Korn/Ferry International, 2003).
21. M. K. Fiegerer, "Determinants of Board Participation in the Strategic Decisions of Small Corporations," *Entrepreneurship Theory and Practice* (September 2005), pp. 627–650; S. K. Lee and G. Filbeck, "Board Size and Firm Performance: Case of Small Firms," *Proceedings of the Academy of Accounting and Financial Studies* (2006), pp. 43–46; W. S. Schulze, M. H. Lubatkin, R. N. Dino, and

A. K. Buchholtz, "Agency Relationships in Family Firms: Theory and Evidence," *Organization Science* (March–April, 2001), pp. 99–116.

22. S. K. Lee and G. Filbeck, "Board Size and Firm Performance: The Case of Small Firms," *Proceedings of the Academy of Accounting and Financial Studies* (2006), pp. 43–46.

23. J. J. Reur and R. Ragozzino, "Agency Hazards and Alliance Portfolios," *Strategic Management Journal* (January 2006), pp. 27–43.

24. M. Goranova, T. M. Alessandri, P. Brades, and R. Dharwadkar, "Managerial Ownership and Corporate Diversification: A Longitudinal View," *Strategic Management Journal* (March 2007), pp. 211–225; B. K. Boyd, S. Gove, and M. A. Hitt, "Consequences of Measurement Problems in Strategic Management Research: The Case of Amihud and Lev," *Strategic Management Journal* (April 2005), pp. 367–375; J. P. Katz and B. P. Niehoff, "How Owners Influence Strategy—A Comparison of Owner-Controlled and Manager-Controlled Firms," *Long Range Planning* (October 1998), pp. 755–761; M. Kroll, P. Wright, L. Toombs, and H. Leavell, "Form of Control: A Critical Determinant of Acquisition Performance and CEO Rewards," *Strategic Management Journal* (February 1997), pp. 85–96.

25. L. Tihanyi, R. A. Johnson, R. E. Hoskisson, and M. A. Hitt, "Institutional Ownership Differences and International Diversification: The Effects of Boards of Directors and Technological Opportunity," *Academy of Management Journal* (April 2003), pp. 195–211; A. E. Ellstrand, L. Tihanyi, and J. L. Johnson, "Board Structure and International Political Risk," *Academy of Management Journal* (August 2002), pp. 769–777; S. A. Zahra, D. O. Neubaum, and M. Huse, "Entrepreneurship in Medium-Size Companies: Exploring the Effects of Ownership and Governance Systems," *Journal of Management* (Vol. 26, No. 5, 2000), pp. 947–976.

26. G. Kassinis and N. Vafeas, "Corporate Boards and Outside Stakeholders as Determinants of Environmental Litigation," *Strategic Management Journal* (May 2002), pp. 399–415; P. Dunn, "The Impact of Insider Power on Fraudulent Financial Reporting," *Journal of Management* (Vol. 30, No. 3, 2004), pp. 397–412.

27. R. C. Anderson and D. M. Reeb, "Board Composition: Balancing Family Influence in S&P 500 Firms," *Administrative Science Quarterly* (June 2004), pp. 209–237; W. S. Schulze, M. H. Lubatkin, R. N. Dino, and A. K. Buchholtz, "Agency Relationships in Family Firms: Theory and Evidence," *Organization Science* (March–April, 2001), pp. 99–116.

28. M. N. Young, A. K. Buchholtz, and D. Ahlstrom, "How Can Board Members Be Empowered If They Are Spread Too Thin?" *SAM Advanced Management Journal* (Autumn 2003), pp. 4–11.

29. *33rd Annual Board of Directors Study* (New York: Korn/Ferry International, 2007), p. 21.

30. C. M. Daily and D. R. Dalton, "The Endangered Director," *Journal of Business Strategy*, (Vol. 25, No. 3, 2004), pp. 8–9.

31. I. Sager, "The Boardroom: New Rules, New Loopholes," *BusinessWeek* (November 29, 2004), p. 13.

32. *34th Annual Board of Directors Study* (New York: Korn/Ferry International, 2008), pp. 25–32.

33. See S. Finkelstein and D. C. Hambrick, *Strategic Leadership: Top Executives and Their Impact on Organizations* (St. Paul, MN: West, 1996), p. 213.

34. D. R. Dalton, M. A. Hitt, S. Trevis Certo, and C. M. Dalton, "The Fundamental Agency Problem and Its Mitigation," Chapter One in *Academy of Management Annals*, edited by J. F. Westfall and A. F. Brief (London: Rutledge, 2007).

35. "TIAA-CREF's Role in Corporate Governance," *Investment Forum* (June 2003), p. 13.

36. Credit Suisse Research Institutes (July 31, 2012), (www.credit-suisse.com/news/en/media_release.jsp).

37. M. Teen, "The Diversity Scorecard," (Korn/Ferry Institute, 2011).

38. *33rd Annual Board of Directors Study* (New York: Korn/Ferry International, 2007), p. 11 T. Neff and J. H. Daum, "The Empty Boardroom," *Strategy + Business* (Summer 2007), pp. 57–61.

39. R. O. Crockett, "The Rising Stock of Black Directors," *BusinessWeek* (February 27, 2006), p. 34.

40. J. Daum, "Portrait of Boards on the Cusp of Historic Change," *Directors & Boards* (Winter 2003), p. 56 J. Daum, "SSBI: Audit Committees Are Leading the Change," *Directors & Boards* (Winter 2004), p. 59.

41. *30th Annual Board of Directors Study* (New York: Korn/Ferry International, 2003) p. 38.

42. *Globalizing the Board of Directors: Trends and Strategies* (New York: The Conference Board, 1999).

43. "The Korn/Ferry Market Cap 100 – 2015," p. 20.

44. R. W. Pouder and R. S. Cantrell, "Corporate Governance Reform: Influence on Shareholder Wealth," *Journal of Business Strategies* (Spring 1999), pp. 48–66.

45. M. L. Gerlach, "The Japanese Corporate Network: A Block-Model Analysis," *Administrative Science Quarterly* (March 1992), pp. 105–139.

46. W. E. Stead and J. G. Stead, *Sustainable Strategic Management* (Armonk, NY: M. E. Sharp, 2004), p. 47.

47. J. D. Westphal, M. L. Seidel, and K. J. Stewart, "Second-Order Imitation: Uncovering Latent Effects of Board Network Ties," *Administrative Science Quarterly* (December 2001), pp. 717–747; M. A. Geletkanycz, B. K. Boyd, and S. Finkelstein, "The Strategic Value of CEO External Directorate Networks: Implications for CEO Compensation," *Strategic Management Journal* (September 2001), pp. 889–898; M. A. Carpenter and J. D. Westphal, "The Strategic Context of External Network Ties: Examining the Impact of Director Appointments on Board Involvement in Strategic Decision Making," *Academy of Management Journal* (August 2001), pp. 639–660.

48. M. Warner, "Inside the Silicon Valley Money Machine," *Fortune* (October 26, 1998), pp. 128–140.

49. D. Jones and B. Hansen, "Chairmen Still Doing Do-Si-Do," *USA Today* (November 5, 2003), p. 3B; J. H. Daum and T. J. Neff, "SSBI: Audit Committees Are Leading the Charge," *Directors & Boards* (Winter 2003), p. 59.

50. J. A. C. Baum and C. Oliver, "Institutional Linkages and Organizational Mortality," *Administrative Science Quarterly* (June 1991) pp. 187–218; J. P. Sheppard, "Strategy and Bankruptcy: An Exploration into Organizational Death," *Journal of Management* (Winter 1994), pp. 795–833.

51. *33rd Annual Board of Directors Study* (New York: Korn/Ferry International, 2007), p. 44, and *Directors' Compensation and Board Practices in 2003*, Research Report R-1339-03-RR (New York: Conference Board, 2003) Table 49, p. 38.

52. J. Canavan, B. Jones, and M. J. Potter, "Board Tenure: How Long Is Too Long?" *Boards & Directors* (Winter 2004), pp. 39–42.

53. *34th Annual Board of Directors Study* (New York: Korn/Ferry International, 2008), p. 18, and *30th Annual Board of Directors Study Supplement: Governance Trends of the Fortune 1000* (New York: Korn/Ferry International, 2004), p. 5.

54. D. F. Larcker and S. A. Richardson, "Does Governance Really Matter?" *Knowledge @ Wharton* (September 8–21, 2004).

55. M. L. McDonald, J. D. Westphal, and M. E. Graebner, "What Do they Know? The Effects of Outside Director Acquisition Experience on Firm Acquisition Experience," *Strategic Management Journal* (November 2008), pp. 1155–1177.

56. *33rd Annual Board of Directors Study* (New York: Korn/Ferry International, 2008), p. 22.

57. *30th Annual Board of Directors Study* (New York: Korn/Ferry International, 2003), pp. 8, 31, 44.

58. "2014 Spencer Stuart Board Index," (www.spencer-stuart.com/~/media/pdf%20files/research%20and%20insight%20pdfs/ssbi2014web14nov2014.pdf).

59. A. Desai, M. Kroll, and P. Wright, "CEO Duality, Board Monitoring, and Acquisition Performance," *Journal of Business Strategies* (Fall 2003), pp. 147–156; D. Harris and C. E. Helfat, "CEO Duality, Succession, Capabilities and Agency Theory: Commentary and Research Agenda," *Strategic Management Journal* (September 1998), pp. 901–904; C. M. Daily and D. R. Dalton, "CEO and Board Chair Roles Held Jointly or Separately: Much Ado About Nothing," *Academy of Management Executive* (August 1997), pp. 11–20; D. L. Worrell, C. Nemec, and W. N. Davidson III, "One Hat Too Many: Key Executive Plurality and Shareholder Wealth," *Strategic Management Journal* (June 1997), pp. 499–507; J. W. Coles and W. S. Hesterly, "Independence of the Chairman and Board Composition: Firm Choices and Shareholder Value," *Journal of Management*, Vol. 26, No. 2 (2000), pp. 195–214; H. Ashbaugh, D. W. Collins, and R. LaFond, "The Effects of Corporate Governance on Firms' Credit Ratings," unpublished paper, March 2004.

60. J. P. O'Connor, R. I. Priem, J. E. Coombs, and K. M. Gilley, "Do CEO Stock Options Prevent or Promote Fraudulent Financial Reporting?" *Academy of Management Journal* (June 2006), pp. 483–500.

61. N. R. Augustine, "How Leading a Role for the Lead Director?" *Directors & Boards* (Winter 2004), pp. 20–23.

62. D. R. Dalton, M. A. Hitt, S. Trevis Certo, and C. M. Dalton, "The Fundamental Agency Problem and Its Mitigation," Chapter One in *Academy of Management Annals*, edited by J. F. Westfall and A. F. Brief (London: Rutledge, 2007).

63. *33rd Annual Board of Directors Study* (New York: Korn/Ferry International, 2008), p. 19.

64. J. D. Westphal and I. Stern, "Flattery Will Get You Everywhere (Especially If You Are a Male Caucasian): How Ingratiation, Boardroom Behavior, and Demographic Minority Status Affect Additional Board Appointments at U.S. Companies," *Academy of Management Journal* (April 2007), pp. 267–288; J. D. Westphal, "Board Games: How CEOs Adapt to Increases in Structural Board Independence from Management," *Administrative Science Quarterly* (September 1998), pp. 511–537; J. D. Westphal and P. Khanna, "Keeping Directors in Line: Social Distancing as a Control Mechanism in the Corporate Elite," *Administrative Science Quarterly* (September 2003), pp. 361–398.

65. H. L. Tosi, W. Shen, and R. J. Gentry, "Why Outsiders on Boards Can't Solve the Corporate Governance Problem," *Organizational Dynamics* (Vol. 32, No. 2, 2003), pp. 180–192.

66. *33rd Annual Board of Directors Study* (New York: Korn/Ferry International, 2007), p. 12. Other committees are succession planning (39%), finance (30%), corporate responsibility (17%), and investment (15%).

67. Perhaps because of their potential to usurp the power of the board, executive committees are being used less often.

68. *34th Annual Board of Directors Study* (New York: Korn/Ferry International, 2008), p. 19.

69. "The Trial of Sarbanes–Oxley," *The Economist* (April 22, 2006), pp. 59–60; *33rd Annual Board of Directors Study* (New York: Korn/Ferry International, 2007), p. 14; S. Wagner and L. Dittmar, "The Unexpected Benefits of Sarbanes–Oxley," *Harvard Business Review* (April 2006), pp. 133–140.

70. A. Borrus, "Learning to Love Sarbanes–Oxley," *BusinessWeek* (November 21, 2005), pp. 126–128.

71. D. Henry, "Not Everyone Hates SarbOx," *BusinessWeek* (January 29, 2007), p. 37.

72. D. Henry, "A SarbOx Surprise," *BusinessWeek* (January 12, 2006), p. 38.

73. *30th Annual Board of Directors Study Supplement: Governance Trends of the Fortune 1000* (New York: Korn/Ferry International, 2004), p. 5.

74. "Where's All the Fun Gone?" *The Economist* (March 20, 2004), pp. 75–77.

75. Daum and Neff (2004), p. 58.

76. *33rd Annual Board of Directors Study* (New York: Korn/Ferry International, 2007), p. 7.

77. J. Sonnenfeld, "Good Governance and the Misleading Myths of Bad Metrics." *Academy of Management Executive* (February 2004), pp. 108–113.

78. H. Ashbaugh, D. W. Collins, and R. LaFond, "The Effects of Corporate Governance on Firms' Credit Ratings," unpublished paper (March 2002).

79. M. Hiltzik, "Facebook Shareholders Are Wedded to the Whims of Mark Zuckerberg," *The Los Angeles Times* (May 20, 2012), (www.articles.latimes.com/2012/may/20/business/la-fi-hiltzik-20120517 accessed January, 2016).

80. P. A. Gompers, J. Ishii, and A. Metrick, "*Extreme Governance: An Analysis of Dual-Class Firms in the United States*," (2006), (www.hbs.edu/units/am/pdf/dual.pdf), pp. 1–48.

81. D. R. Dalton, C. M. Daily, A. E. Ellstrand, and J. L. Johnson, "Meta-Analytic Reviews of Board Composition, Leadership Structure, and Financial Performance," *Strategic Management Journal* (March 1998), pp. 269–290; G. Beaver, "Competitive Advantage and Corporate Governance—Shop Soiled and Needing Attention!" *Strategic Change* (September–October 1999), p. 330.

82. A. Borrus and L. Young, "Nothing Like a Little Exposure," *BusinessWeek* (September 13, 2004), p. 92.

83. P. Silva, "Do Motivation and Equity Ownership Matter in Board of Directors' Evaluation of CEO Performance?" *Journal of Management Issues* (Fall 2005), pp. 346–362.

84. L. He and M. J. Conyon, "The Role of Compensation Committees in CEO and Committee Compensation Decisions," paper presented to *Academy of Management* (Seattle, WA, 2003).

85. P. Coy, E. Thornton, M. Arndt, B. Grow, and A. Park, "Shake, Rattle, and Merge," *BusinessWeek* (January 10, 2005), pp. 32–35.

86. L. Lavelle, "A Fighting Chance for Boardroom Democracy," *BusinessWeek* (June 9, 2003), p. 50 L. Lavelle, "So That's Why Boards Are Waking Up," *BusinessWeek* (January 19, 2004), pp. 72–73.

87. For a detailed description of the COO's role, see N. Bennett and S. A. Miles, "Second in Command," *Harvard Business Review* (May 2006), pp. 71–78.

88. S. Finkelstein and D. C. Hambrick, *Strategic Leadership: Top Executives and Their Impact on Organizations* (St. Louis: West, 1996).

89. H. G. Barkema and O. Shvyrkov, "Does Top Management Team Diversity Promote or Hamper Foreign Expansion?" *Strategic Management Journal* (July 2007), pp. 663–680; D. C. Hambrick, T. S. Cho, and M-J Chen, "The Influence of Top Management Team Heterogeneity on Firms' Competitive Moves," *Administrative Science Quarterly* (December 1996), pp. 659–684.

90. P. Pitcher and A. D. Smith, "Top Management Heterogeneity: Personality, Power, and Proxies," *Organization Science* (January–February 2001), pp. 1–18; M. A. Carpenter and J. W. Fredrickson, "Top Management Teams, Global Strategic Posture, and the Moderating Role of Uncertainty," *Academy of Management Journal* (June 2001), pp. 533–545; M. A. Carpenter, "The Implications of Strategy and Social Context for the Relationship Between Top Management Team Heterogeneity and Firm Performance," *Strategic Management Journal* (March 2002), pp. 275–284; L. Tihanyi, A. E. Ellstrand, C. M. Daily, and D. R. Dalton, "Composition of the Top Management Team and Firm International Expansion," *Journal of Management* (Vol. 26, No. 6, 2000), pp. 1157–1177.

91. "One on One with Steve Reinemund," *BusinessWeek* (December 17, 2001), special advertising insert on leadership by Heidrick & Struggles, executive search firm.

92. D. A. Waldman, G. G. Ramirez, R. J. House, and P. Puranam, "Does Leadership Matter? CEO Leadership Attributes and Profitability Under Conditions of Perceived Environmental Uncertainty," *Academy of Management Journal* (February 2001), pp. 134–143; F. J. Flynn and B. M. Staw, "Lend Me Your Wallets: The Effect of Charismatic Leadership on External Support for an Organization," *Strategic Management Journal* (April 2004), pp. 309–330.

93. J. Burns, *Leadership* (New York: HarperCollins, 1978); B. Bass, "From Transactional to Transformational Leadership: Learning to Share the Vision," *Organizational Dynamics* (Vol. 18, 1990), pp. 19–31; W. Bennis and B. Nanus, *Leaders: Strategies for Taking Charge* (New York: HarperCollins, 1997).

94. Based on R. J. House, "A 1976 Theory of Charismatic Leadership," in J. G. Hunt and L. L. Larson (Eds.), *Leadership: The Cutting Edge* (Carbondale, IL: Southern Illinois University Press, 1976), pp. 189–207. Also see J. Choi, "A Motivational Theory of Charismatic Leadership: Envisioning, Empathy, and Empowerment," *Journal of Leadership and Organizational Studies* (Vol. 13, No. 1, 2006), pp. 24–43.

95. I. D. Colville and A. J. Murphy, "Leadership as the Enabler of Strategizing and Organizing," *Long Range Planning* (December 2006), pp. 663–677.

96. M. Lipton, "Demystifying the Development of an Organizational Vision," *Sloan Management Review* (Summer 1996), p. 84.

97. S. Hahn, "Why High Tech Has to Stay Humble," *BusinessWeek* (January 19, 2004), pp. 76–77.

98. J. H. David, F. D. Schoorman, R. Mayer, and H. H. Tan, "The Trusted General Manager and Business Unit Performance: Empirical Evidence of a Competitive Advantage," *Strategic Management Journal* (May 2000), pp. 563–576.

99. D. B. McNatt and T. A. Judge, "Boundary Conditions of the Galatea Effect: A Field Experiment and Constructive Replication," *Academy of Management Journal* (August 2004), pp. 550–565.

100. R. F. Piccolo and J. A. Colquitt, "Transformational Leadership and Job Behaviors: The Mediating Role of Core Job Characteristics," *Academy of Management Journal* (April 2006), pp. 327–340; J. E. Bono and T. A. Judge, "Self-Concordance at Work: Toward Understanding the Motivational Effects of Transformational Leaders," *Academy of Management Journal* (October 2003), pp. 554–571.

101. T. Lowry, R. O. Crockett, and I. M. Kunii, "Verizon's Gutsy Bet," *BusinessWeek* (August 4, 2003), pp. 52–62.

102. G. Tate and U. Malmendier, "Who Makes Acquisitions? CEO Overconfidence and the Market's Reaction," summarized by *Knowledge @ Wharton* (February 25, 2004).

103. M. C. Mankins and R. Steele, "Stop Making Plans, Start Making Decisions," *Harvard Business Review* (January 2006), pp. 76–84.

104. T. R. Eisenmann and J. L. Bower, "The Entrepreneurial M Form: Strategic Integration in Global Media Firms," *Organization Science* (May–June 2000), pp. 348–355.

105. J. Kirby and T. A. Stewart, "The Institutional Yes," *Harvard Business Review* (October 2007), p. 76.

106. M. C. Mankins and R. Steele, "Stop Making Plans, Start Making Decisions," *Harvard Business Review* (January 2006), pp. 76–84; G. P. Hodgkinson, R. Whittington, G. Johnson, and M. Schwarz, "The Role of Strategy Workshops in Strategy Development Processes: Formality, Communication, Co-ordination and Inclusion," *Long Range Planning* (October 2006), pp. 479–496; B. Frisch and L. Chandler, "Off-Sites that Work," *Harvard Business Review* (June 2006), pp. 117–126.

107. For a description of the Chief Strategy Officer, see R. T. S. Breene, P. F. Nunes, and W. E. Shill, "The Chief Strategy Officer," *Harvard Business Review* (October 2007), pp. 84–93; R. Dye, "How Chief Strategy Officers Think about Their Role: A Roundtable," *McKinsey Quarterly* (May 2008), pp. 1–8.

108. M. Wiersema, "Holes at the Top: Why CEO Firings Backfire," *Harvard Business Review* (December 2002), pp. 70–77.

CHAPTER **3**

Social Responsibility and Ethics in Strategic Management

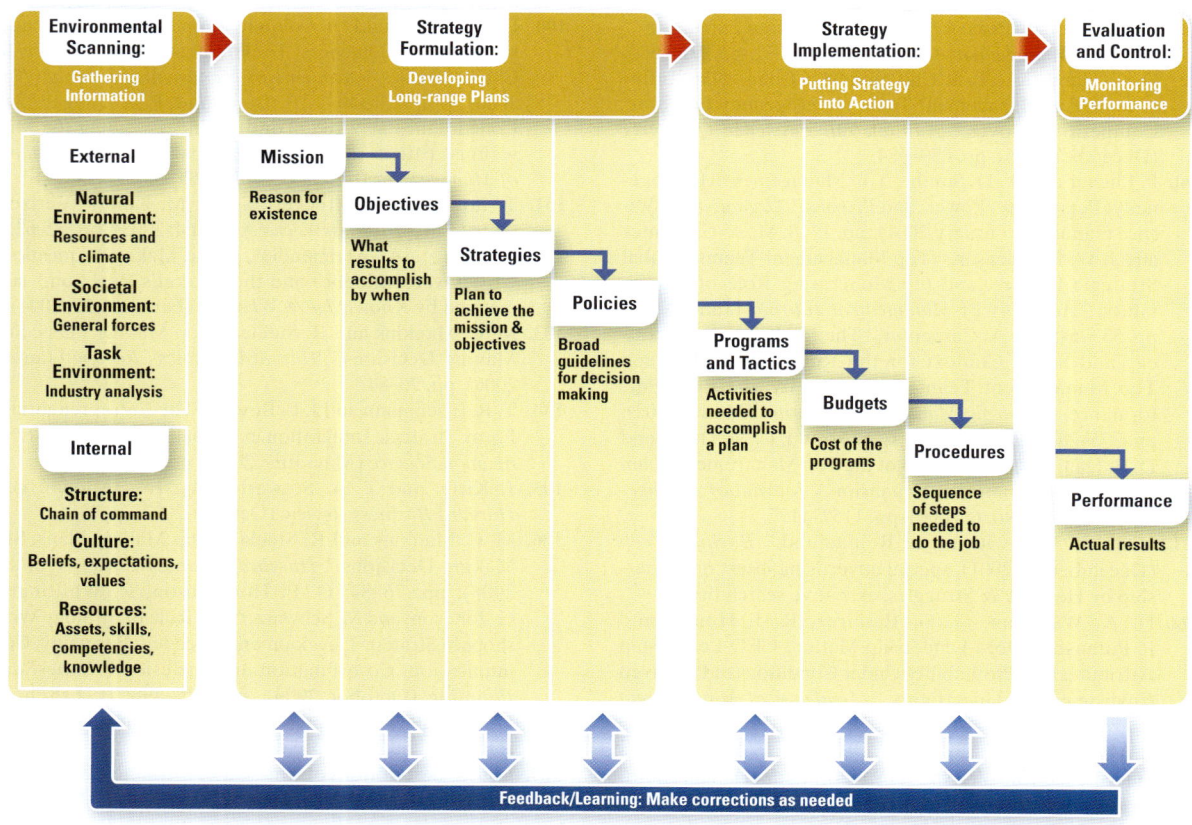

| Environmental Scanning: Gathering Information | | Strategy Formulation: Developing Long-range Plans | | | | Strategy Implementation: Putting Strategy into Action | | | Evaluation and Control: Monitoring Performance |

Pearson MyLab Management®

⭐ **Improve Your Grade!**

Over 10 million students improved their results using the Pearson MyLabs. Visit **mymanagementlab.com** for simulations, tutorials, and end-of-chapter problems.

Learning Objectives

After reading this chapter, you should be able to:

3-1. Discuss the relationship between social responsibility and corporate performance

3-2. Explain the concept of sustainability

3-3. Conduct a stakeholder analysis

3-4. Explain why people may act unethically

3-5. Describe different views of ethics according to the utilitarian, individual rights, and justice approaches

Purbani Group—The CSR Pioneer in Bangladesh

Purbani Group is one of the largest suppliers of garments to the world's leading fashion brands and retailers such as H&M, K-Mart, and Hanes. In the 1970s, it started as small textile yarn trader in Dhaka, Bangladesh, and is now a vertically integrated apparel production facility. It's annual turnover is around $150 million and it employs 7000 people.

The group has several vertically integrated spinning, knitting, apparel, dying, and yarn trading companies. The business model is a self-sufficient one, as it produces yarn from imported cotton, used to produce fabrics in its textile mills and feed the 100% export-oriented apparel manufacturing facilities.

Committed to social responsibility, Purbani's recent collaboration with The Deutsche Gesellschaft für Internationale Zusammenarbeit GmbH (GIZ) is underway to implement an energy services company model, or ESCO model, to transform energy usage. The group's implementation of the ESCO model helps combine various energy sources to maximize cleaner energy use and reduce energy waste by improving building facilities, lighting, and air-cooling system.

It's also a pioneer in women empowerment through employment. More than 60% of its workforce is young women. Given the demography, many of the female employees are young mothers. Purbani has created nursery and schooling facilities within its factory premises, allowing parents to bring their children to work and be taken care of by the nursery staff until the end of shifts. Also, frequent breaks allows mothers to check on and feed their babies, reducing the number of skilled–female workers quitting after childbirth, and enhancing job satisfaction. Purbani understands that their initiatives in environmental and social welfare have created a virtuous cycle of sustainability, CSR, productivity, and brand image.

SOURCES: Purbani Group Web site, HYPERLINK "http://www.purbanigroup.com/web/"http://www.purbanigroup.com/ ; H&M, "Our Supplier Factory List," H&M Group Web site, http://sustainability.hm.com/en/sustainability/downloads-resources/resources/supplier-list.html (February, 2017); Kmart Factory List, http://www.kmart.com.au/ethical-factories, (accessed February, 2017); and GIZ Web site, https://www.giz.de/en/html/our_services.html (accessed February, 2017).

Social Responsibilities of Strategic Decision Makers

3-1. Discuss the relationship between social responsibility and corporate performance

Should strategic decision makers be responsible only to shareholders, or do they have broader responsibilities? The concept of **social responsibility** proposes that a private corporation has responsibilities to society that extend beyond making a profit. Strategic decisions often affect more than just the corporation. A decision to retrench by closing some plants and discontinuing product lines, for example, affects not only the firm's workforce but also the communities where the plants are located and the customers with no other source for the discontinued product. Such situations raise questions about the appropriateness of certain missions, objectives, and strategies of business corporations. Managers must be able to deal with these conflicting interests in an ethical manner to formulate a viable strategic plan.

RESPONSIBILITIES OF A BUSINESS FIRM

What are the responsibilities of a business firm and how many of them must be fulfilled? Milton Friedman and Archie Carroll offer two contrasting views of the responsibilities of business firms to society.

Friedman's Traditional View of Business Responsibility

Urging a return to a laissez-faire worldwide economy with minimal government regulation, Milton Friedman argued against the concept of social responsibility as a function of business. A business person who acts "responsibly" by cutting the price of the firm's product to aid the poor, or by making expenditures to reduce pollution, or by hiring the hard-core unemployed, according to Friedman, is spending the shareholder's money for a general social interest. Even if the businessperson has shareholder permission or even encouragement to do so, he or she is still acting from motives other than economic and may, in the long run, harm the very society the firm is trying to help. By taking on the burden of these social costs, the business becomes less efficient—either prices go up to pay for the increased costs or investment in new activities and research is postponed. These results negatively affect—perhaps fatally—the long-term efficiency of a business. Friedman thus referred to the social responsibility of business as a "fundamentally subversive doctrine" and stated that:

> There is one and only one social responsibility of business—to use its resources and engage in activities designed to increase its profits so long as it stays within the rules of the game, which is to say, engages in open and free competition without deception or fraud.[1]

Following Friedman's reasoning, the management of Caterpillar may be guilty of misusing corporate assets and negatively affecting shareholder wealth. The millions spent on recycling could have been invested in new product development or given back as dividends to the shareholders. Instead of Caterpillar's management acting on its own, shareholders could have decided which charities to support.

Carroll's Four Responsibilities of Business

Friedman's contention that the primary goal of business is profit maximization is only one side of an ongoing debate regarding corporate social responsibility (CSR). According to William J. Byron, Distinguished Professor of Ethics at Georgetown University and past President of Catholic University of America, profits are merely a means to an end, not an end in itself. Just as a person needs food to survive and grow, so does a business corporation need profits to survive and grow. "Maximizing profits is like maximizing food." Thus, contends Byron, maximization of profits cannot be the primary obligation of business.[2]

As shown in **Figure 3–1**, Archie Carroll proposed that the managers of business organizations have four responsibilities: economic, legal, ethical, and discretionary.[3]

1. **Economic** responsibilities of a business organization's management are to produce goods and services of value to society so that the firm may repay its creditors and increase the wealth of its shareholders.

2. **Legal** responsibilities are defined by governments in laws that management is expected to obey. For example, U.S. business firms are required to hire and promote people based on their credentials rather than to discriminate on non-job-related characteristics such as race, gender, or religion.

3. **Ethical** responsibilities of an organization's management are to follow the generally held beliefs about behavior in a society. For example, society generally expects firms to work with the employees and the community in planning for layoffs, even though no law may require this. The affected people can get very upset if an organization's management fails to act according to generally prevailing ethical values.

4. **Discretionary** responsibilities are the purely voluntary obligations a corporation assumes. Examples are philanthropic contributions, training the hard-core unemployed, and providing day-care centers. The difference between ethical and discretionary responsibilities is that few people expect an organization to fulfill discretionary responsibilities, whereas many expect an organization to fulfill ethical ones.[4]

Carroll lists these four responsibilities *in order of priority*. A business firm must first make a profit to satisfy its economic responsibilities. To continue in existence, the firm must follow the laws, thus fulfilling its legal responsibilities. There is evidence that companies found guilty of violating laws have lower profits and sales growth after conviction.[5] On this point, Carroll and Friedman are in agreement. Carroll, however, goes further by arguing that business managers have responsibilities beyond economic and legal ones.

Having satisfied the two basic responsibilities, according to Carroll, a firm should look to fulfilling its social responsibilities. Social responsibility, therefore, includes both ethical and discretionary, but not economic and legal, responsibilities. A firm can fulfill its ethical responsibilities by taking actions that society tends to value but has not yet put into law. When ethical responsibilities are satisfied, a firm can focus on discretionary responsibilities—purely voluntary actions that society has not yet decided to expect

FIGURE 3–1
Responsibilities of
Business

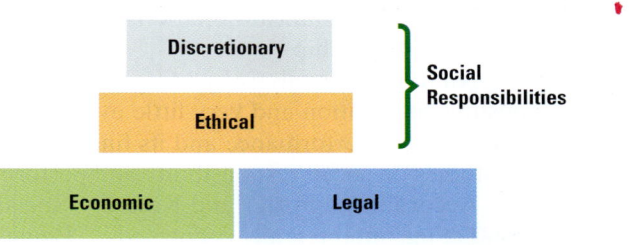

SOURCE: Suggested by Archie Carroll in A. B. Carroll, "A Three Dimensional Conceptual Model of Corporate Performance," Academy of Management Review (October 1979), pp. 497–505; A. B. Carroll, "Managing-Ethically with Global Stakeholders: A Present and Future Challenge," Academy of Management Executive (May 2004), pp. 114–120; and A. B. Carroll, "The Pyramid of Corporate Social Responsibility: Toward the Moral Management of Organizational Stakeholders," Business Horizons (July–August 1991), pp. 39–48.

from every company. For example, when Cisco Systems decided to dismiss 6000 full-time employees, it provided a novel severance package. Those employees who agreed to work for a local nonprofit organization for a year would receive one-third of their salaries plus benefits and stock options and be the first to be rehired. Nonprofits were delighted to hire such highly qualified people and Cisco was able to maintain its talent pool for when it could hire once again.[6]

As societal values evolve, the discretionary responsibilities of today may become the ethical responsibilities of tomorrow. For example, in 1990, 86% of people in the United States believed that obesity was caused by the individuals themselves, with only 14% blaming either corporate marketing or government guidelines. By 2003, however, only 54% blamed obesity on individuals and 46% put responsibility on corporate marketing and government guidelines. Thus, the offering of healthy, low-calorie food by food processors and restaurants is moving rapidly from being a discretionary to an ethical responsibility.[7] In recent years, school cafeterias across the United States have added fresh vegetables, removed soda machines, and in 2012, many school systems also moved to eliminate the much maligned *pink slime* from their beef product lines.

Carroll suggests that to the extent that business corporations fail to acknowledge discretionary or ethical responsibilities, society, through government, will act, making them legal responsibilities. Government may do this, moreover, without regard to an organization's economic responsibilities. As a result, the organization may have greater difficulty in earning a profit than it would have if it had voluntarily assumed some ethical and discretionary responsibilities.

Both Friedman and Carroll argue their positions based on the impact of socially responsible actions on a firm's profits. Friedman says that socially responsible actions hurt a firm's efficiency. Carroll proposes that a lack of social responsibility results in increased government regulations, which reduce a firm's efficiency because it must not only comply with the law, but must prove its compliance with regulators.

Friedman's position on social responsibility appears to be losing traction with business executives. For example, a 2006 survey of business executives across the world by McKinsey & Company revealed that only 16% felt that business should focus solely on providing the highest possible returns to investors while obeying all laws and regulations, contrasted with 84% who stated that business should generate high returns to investors but balance it with contributions to the broader public good.[8] The United National Global Compact was started in 2001 as an initiative for a company to voluntarily commit to aligning their operations with 10 principles covering human rights, the environment, labor, and corruption among others. By 2012, over 6800 companies in 140 countries had signed the compact. Those CEOs have agreed to report on their activities annually.[9]

Empirical research now indicates that socially responsible actions may have a positive effect on a firm's financial performance. Although a number of studies in the past have found no significant relationship,[10] an increasing number are finding a small, but positive relationship.[11]

An in-depth analysis by Margolis and Walsh of 127 studies found that "there is a positive association and very little evidence of a negative association between a company's social performance and its financial performance."[12] Another meta-analysis of 52 studies on social responsibility and performance reached this same conclusion.[13]

According to Porter and Kramer, "social and economic goals are not inherently conflicting, but integrally connected."[14] Being known as a socially responsible firm may provide a company with *social capital*, the goodwill of key stakeholders, that can be used for competitive advantage.[15] Target, for example, tries to attract socially concerned younger consumers by offering brands from companies that can boast ethical track records and community involvement.[16] A 2008 study conducted by Grant Thornton found that privately held businesses were forgoing the big publicity campaigns run by multinational companies and focusing their attention on CSR as a means for recruitment and retention of the best employees. In the same report, they found that 58% of these private companies had formally adopted transparent CSR policies as a means of influencing larger companies that may use their services/products.[17]

Being socially responsible does provide a firm with a more positive overall reputation.[18] A survey of more than 700 global companies by The Conference Board reported that 60% of the managers state that citizenship activities had led to (1) goodwill that opened doors in local communities and (2) an enhanced reputation with consumers.[19] Another survey of 140 U.S. firms revealed that being more socially responsible regarding environmental sustainability resulted not only in competitive advantages but also in cost savings.[20] For example, companies that take the lead in being environmentally friendly, such as by using recycled materials preempt attacks from environmental groups and enhance their corporate image. Programs to reduce pollution, for example, can actually reduce waste and maximize resource productivity. One study that examined 70 ecological initiatives taken by 43 companies found the average payback period to be 18 months.[21] Other examples of benefits received from being socially responsible are:[22]

- Their environmental concerns may enable them to charge premium prices and gain brand loyalty (for example, Stoneyfield Yogurt, Whole Foods, and Ben & Jerry's Ice Cream).
- Their trustworthiness may help them generate enduring relationships with suppliers and distributors without requiring them to spend a lot of time and money policing contracts.
- They can attract outstanding employees who prefer working for a responsible firm (for example, Procter & Gamble and Starbucks).
- They are more likely to be welcomed into a foreign country (for example, Levi Strauss).
- They can utilize the goodwill of public officials for support in difficult times.
- They are more likely to attract capital infusions from investors who view reputable companies as desirable long-term investments. For example, mutual funds investing only in socially responsible companies more than doubled in size from 1995 to 2007 and outperformed the S&P 500 list of stocks.[23]

Sustainability

3-2. Explain the concept of sustainability

As we pointed out in **Chapter 1**, sustainability includes much more than just ecological concerns and the natural environment. Crane and Matten point out that the concept of sustainability should be broadened to include economic and social as well as environmental concerns. They argue that it is sometimes impossible to address the sustainability of the natural environment without considering the social and economic aspects of relevant communities and their activities. For example, even though environmentalists may oppose road building programs because of their effect on wildlife and conservation efforts, others point to the benefits to local communities of less traffic congestion and more jobs.[24] Dow Jones & Company, a leading provider of global business news and information, developed a sustainability index that considers not only environmental, but also economic and social factors. See the **Sustainability Issue** feature to learn how a global company is using environmental sustainability efforts to improve its bottom line.

SUSTAINABILITY issue

MARKS & SPENCER LEADS THE WAY

There have been many moves over the past few years to increase the sustainability of business practices. The idea that waste is not a given in the operation of businesses has led to new ways of doing business that not only make a business a good citizen, but save a company a substantial amount of money. None has been more focused than Marks and Spencer Group (M&S), the enormous retailer of goods from clothing to food that is based in the United Kingdom M&S announced in June 2012 that it had achieved its goal of going "carbon neutral."

A huge financial incentive exists in the United Kingdom to do so. There is a landfill tax of 64 pounds (roughly US$100) per ton, and that number is slated to increase by 8 pounds a year indefinitely because the country is rapidly running out of landfill space. M&S now recycles 90% of its food waste and 100% of store, office, and warehouse waste. The company is currently 100% carbon neutral.

The effort was started in 2007 with what the company called Plan A. Plan A was designed to transform the company into the carbon neutral firm it is today. The company's efforts in this area extend to everything in their operation. As of 2016, they have worked with suppliers and cut food packaging by 60%, made hanger recycling the norm, and have seen overall energy efficiency improve by more than 36% since inception of the program.

Management takes the whole business very seriously. Progress on Plan A is reviewed by a "how we do business" committee and reported annually. Furthermore, progress on Plan A constitutes 20% of the bonuses for the CEO and the directors of the company.

M&S is not done, however. In 2010, they started a new five-year plan (also called Plan A) aimed at making M&S the most sustainable major retailer in the world. Their efforts have been good for their business and good for society at large.

....

SOURCES: http://planareport.marksandspencer.com/M&S_PlanAReport2015_Performance.pdf; "Finally, a Use for Sandwich Crusts," *BusinessWeek* (June 18, 2012); L. Thorpe, "Marks & Spencer—An Ambitious Commitment to Tackling Waste," *The Guardian* (2011), (http://www.guardian.co.uk/sustainable-business/marks-spencer-waste-recycling).

The broader concept of sustainability has much in common with Carroll's list of business responsibilities presented earlier. In order for a business corporation to be sustainable—that is, to be successful over a long period of time—it must satisfy all of its economic, legal, ethical, and discretionary responsibilities. Sustainability thus involves many issues, concerns, and tradeoffs—leading us to an examination of corporate stakeholders.

CORPORATE STAKEHOLDERS

The concept that business must be socially responsible sounds appealing until we ask, "Responsible to whom?" A corporation's task environment includes a large number of groups with interest in a business organization's activities. These groups are referred to as **stakeholders** because they affect or are affected by the achievement of the firm's objectives.[25] Should a corporation be responsible only to some of these groups, or does business have an equal responsibility to all of them?

A survey of the U.S. general public by Penn Schoen Berland of Corporate Social Responsibility found that companies utilize a number of activities to appease their stakeholders and provide something back to a wide range of stakeholders. This included 33% that practiced recycling and energy savings approaches and 24% that donated to charities.[26] As scandal after scandal breaks in the press, support for corporate leaders plunges. A 2012 survey of 169 Chief Financial Officers at publicly traded companies in the United States found that 20% intentionally misrepresented their economic performance primarily to influence stock price.[27]

In any one strategic decision, the interests of one stakeholder group can conflict with those of another. For example, a business firm's decision to use only recycled materials in its manufacturing process may have a positive effect on environmental groups, but a negative effect on shareholder dividends. In another example, arguably the worst environmental disaster in the past decade occurred in the Gulf of Mexico when the Deepwater Horizon platform exploded, killing 11 workers and unleashing the worst oil spill in the nation's history. Much of the investigation since that explosion centered on a series of cost-saving approaches used by Trans Ocean (under contract to BP). On the one hand, shareholders were being rewarded with lower costs and higher profits. Had the rig not exploded, the focus would have remained on extracting the oil at the least possible cost. On the other hand, officials and the population along the gulf coast were decimated by the economic and environmental impact of a spill that was entirely preventable.[28] Which group's interests should have priority?

In order to answer this question, the corporation may need to craft an *enterprise strategy* —an overarching strategy that explicitly articulates the firm's ethical relationship with its stakeholders. This requires not only that management clearly state the firm's key ethical values, but also that it understands the firm's societal context, and undertakes stakeholder analysis to identify the concerns and abilities of each stakeholder.[29]

Stakeholder Analysis

Stakeholder analysis is the identification and evaluation of corporate stakeholders. This can be done in a three-step process.

3-3. Conduct a stakeholder analysis

The *first step* in stakeholder analysis is to identify primary stakeholders, those who have a *direct connection* with the corporation and who have sufficient bargaining power to *directly* affect corporate activities. Primary stakeholders include customers, employees, suppliers, shareholders, and creditors.

Unfortunately, determining exactly who constitutes the firm's customers and exactly what they want is difficult. This is particularly difficult when companies sell items for other companies (many retail organizations are simply flow-through operations for the products on their shelf, e.g., Wal-Mart, Target, etc.) or they sell items for which they have only limited influence. Coca-Cola Bottling Company Consolidated (CCBCC) is the largest independent bottler for Coca-Cola. Although they are in direct contact with the retailers who display their products, most of those products are controlled by Coca-Cola in Atlanta, Georgia. Furthermore, these retailers although customers of CCBCC, are really just conduits for the consumer of the beverage. Marketing outwardly focuses on the end consumer of the beverage, but that same consumer probably has no idea that CCBCC has done all the work to ensure that the shelves are stocked. Coca-Cola in Atlanta may create a new flavor or drink brand (think Coconut Water) and pressure CCBCC to find a way to get those products accepted by the retailer who really only wants the product if it will outsell what was on the shelf before it arrived.

Although difficult at times, it is nonetheless important for businesses to determine who their stakeholders are and what they want. The corporation systematically monitors these stakeholders because they are important to a firm meeting its economic and legal responsibilities. Employees want a fair pay and fringe benefits. Customers want safe products and a value for the price they pay. Shareholders want dividends and stock price appreciation. Suppliers want predictable orders and bills paid. Creditors want commitments to be met on time. In the normal course of affairs, the relationship between a firm and many of its primary stakeholders is regulated by written or verbal agreements and laws. Once a problem is identified, negotiation takes place based on costs and benefits to each party. (Government is not usually considered a primary stakeholder because laws apply to everyone in a particular category and usually cannot be negotiated.)

The *second step* in stakeholder analysis is to identify the *secondary stakeholders* — those who have only an *indirect* stake in the corporation but who are also affected by corporate activities. These usually include nongovernmental organizations (NGOs, such as Greenpeace), activists, local communities, trade associations, competitors, and governments. Because the corporation's relationship with each of these stakeholders is usually not covered by any written or verbal agreement, there is room for misunderstanding. As in the case of NGOs and activists, there actually may be no relationship until a problem develops—usually brought up by the stakeholder. In the normal course of events, these stakeholders do not affect the corporation's ability to meet its economic or legal responsibilities. Aside from competitors, these secondary stakeholders are not usually monitored by the corporation in any systematic fashion. As a result, relationships are usually based on a set of questionable assumptions about each other's needs and wants. Although these stakeholders may not directly affect a firm's short-term profitability, their actions could impact a corporation's reputation and thus its long-term performance.

The *third step* in stakeholder analysis is to estimate the effect on each stakeholder group from any particular strategic decision. Because the primary decision criteria used by management is generally economic, this is the point where secondary stakeholders may be ignored or discounted as unimportant. For a firm to fulfill its ethical or discretionary responsibilities, it must seriously consider the needs and wants of its secondary stakeholders in any strategic decision. For example, how much will specific stakeholder groups lose or gain? What other alternatives do they have to replace what may be lost?

Stakeholder Input

Once stakeholder impacts have been identified, managers should decide whether stakeholder input should be invited into the discussion of the strategic alternatives. A group is more likely to accept or even help implement a decision if it has some input into which alternative is chosen and how it is to be implemented. In the case of the huge BP oil spill, the company originally committed more than US$20 billion to the restoration of the gulf coast and the reimbursement of lost earnings to businesses affected by the spill. Although there are still outstanding lawsuits and many claim not to have been made whole, BP has paid out more than $28 billion as of 2015 without any legal requirement.[30]

Given the wide range of interests and concerns present in any organization's task environment, one or more groups, at any one time, will probably be dissatisfied with an organization's activities—even if management is trying to be socially responsible. A company may have some stakeholders of which it is only marginally aware and in some cases does not seem interested in appeasing. For example, when Chick-fil-A announced their support for a ban on gay marriage, a firestorm of protests erupted. The mayors of Chicago and Boston opposed moves by Chick-fil-A to add stores in their area, The Jim Henson Company pulled their Muppet toys from the kids meals and gay-rights groups called for a boycott. On the other hand, the company found a quick and vocal group of supporters. Radio talk show host and former Presidential candidate, Mike Huckabee called for a "Chick-fil-A Appreciation Day."[31]

Therefore, before making a strategic decision, strategic managers should consider how each alternative will affect various stakeholder groups. What seems at first to be the best decision because it appears to be the most profitable may actually result in the worst set of consequences to the corporation. One example of a company that does its best to consider its responsibilities to its primary and secondary stakeholders when making strategic decisions is Johnson & Johnson. See the Strategy Highlight feature for the J & J Credo.

STRATEGY highlight

JOHNSON & JOHNSON CREDO

We believe our first responsibility is to the doctors, nurses, and patients, to mothers and fathers and all others who use our products and services. In meeting their needs everything we do must be of high quality. We must constantly strive to reduce our costs in order to maintain reasonable prices. Customers' orders must be serviced promptly and accurately. Our suppliers and distributors must have an opportunity to make a fair profit.

We are responsible to our employees, the men and women who work with us throughout the world. Everyone must be considered as an individual. We must respect their dignity and recognize their merit. They must have a sense of security in their jobs. Compensation must be fair and adequate, and working conditions clean, orderly, and safe. We must be mindful of ways to help our employees fulfill their family responsibilities. Employees must feel free to make suggestions and complaints. There must be equal opportunity for employment, development, and advancement for those qualified. We must provide competent management, and their actions must be just and ethical.

We are responsible to the communities where we live and work and to the world community as well. We must be good citizens—support good works and charities and bear our fair share of taxes. We must encourage civic improvements and better health and education. We must maintain in good order the property we are privileged to use, protecting the environment and natural resources.

Our final responsibility is to our stockholders. Business must make a sound profit. We must experiment with new ideas. Research must be carried on, innovative programs developed, and mistakes paid for. New equipment must be purchased, new facilities provided, and new products launched. Reserves must be created for adverse times. When we operate according to these principles, the stockholders should realize a fair return.

. . . .

Ethical Decision Making

3-4. Explain why people may act unethically

Some people joke that there is no such thing as "business ethics." They call it an oxymoron—a concept that combines opposite or contradictory ideas. Unfortunately, there is some truth to this sarcastic comment. The Ethics Resource Center has been measuring the state of ethics in organizations since 2007. The 2013 (released in 2014) survey found that 41% of employees surveyed said that they had witnessed misconduct at work, but only 63% reported it. The latest study saw some significant positive trends; the percentage of organizations providing ethics training rose to an all-time high of 81% and 74% of companies now provide communication internally about disciplinary actions when wrongdoing occurs.[32] In a survey from 1996 to 2005 of top managers at 2270 firms, researchers found that 29.2% of the firms analyzed had backdated or otherwise manipulated stock option grants to take advantage of favorable share-price movements.[33]

The Financial Crimes Enforcement Network found that mortgage fraud cases jumped by over 88% from 2010 to 2011 to just over 29,500. The most common types of mortgage fraud are debt-elimination scams, falsifying information on loan applications, and identity theft.[34] In one instance, Allison Bice, office manager at Leonard Fazio's RE/MAX A-1 Best Realtors in Urbandale, Iowa, admitted that she submitted fake invoices and copies of checks drawn on a closed account as part of a scheme to obtain more money from Homecoming Financial, a mortgage company that had hired Fazio's agency to resell foreclosed homes.

A study of more than 5000 graduate students at 32 colleges and universities in the United States and Canada revealed that 56% of business students and 47% of non-business students admitted to cheating at least once during the past year. Cheating was more likely when a student's peers also cheated.[35] In another example, 6000 people paid US$30 to enter a VIP section on ScoreTop.com's Web site to obtain access to actual test questions posted by those who had recently taken the Graduate Management Admission Test (GMAT). In response, the Graduate Management Admission Council promised to cancel the scores of anyone who posted "live" questions to the site or knowingly read them.[36] Given this lack of ethical behavior among students, it is easy to understand why some could run into trouble if they obtained a job at a corporation having an unethical culture, such as Enron, WorldCom, or Tyco.

SOME REASONS FOR UNETHICAL BEHAVIOR

Why are many business people perceived to be acting unethically? It may be that the involved people are not even aware that they are doing something questionable. There is no worldwide standard of conduct for business people. This is especially important given the global nature of business activities. Cultural norms and values vary between countries and even between different geographic regions and ethnic groups within a country. For example, what is considered in one country to be a bribe to expedite service is sometimes considered in another country to be normal business practice. Some of these differences may derive from whether a country's governance system is *rule-based* or *relationship-based*. Relationship-based countries tend to be less transparent and have a higher degree of corruption than do rule-based countries.[37] See the **Global Issue** feature for an explanation of country governance systems and how they may affect business practices.

Another possible reason for what is often perceived to be unethical behavior lies in differences in values between business people and key stakeholders. Some business people may believe profit maximization is the key goal of their firm, whereas concerned interest groups may have other priorities, such as the hiring of minorities and women or the safety of their neighborhoods. Of the six values measured by the Allport-Vernon-Lindzey Study of Values test (aesthetic, economic, political, religious, social, and theoretical), both U.S. and UK executives consistently score highest on economic and political values and lowest on social and religious ones. This is similar to the value profile of managers from Japan, Korea, India, and Australia, as well as those of U.S. business school students. U.S. Protestant ministers, in contrast, score highest on religious and social values and very low on economic values.[38]

This difference in values can make it difficult for one group of people to understand another's actions. For example, Michael Bloomberg, (former mayor of New York City) pushed through regulations that changed the type of oil that fast-food companies could use in their fryers, mandated calorie listings for all eating establishments, and in 2012 presented a plan that would prohibit food-service establishments from selling sodas and similarly sweet drinks in sizes larger than 16 oz. That plan was invalidated by the courts before it could ever be implemented. "*Let the buyer beware*" is a traditional saying by free-market proponents who argue that customers in a free market democracy have the right to choose how they spend their money and live their lives. Social progressives contend that business people working in tobacco, alcoholic beverages, gambling, and maybe now the soft drink industries are acting unethically by making and advertising products with potentially dangerous and expensive side effects, such as cancer, alcoholism, obesity, and addiction. People working in these industries could respond by asking whether it is ethical for people who don't smoke, drink, or gamble to reject another person's right to do so.

GLOBAL issue

HOW RULE-BASED AND RELATIONSHIP-BASED GOVERNANCE SYSTEMS AFFECT ETHICAL BEHAVIOR

The developed nations of the world operate under governance systems quite different from those used by developing nations. Developed nations and the business firms within them follow well-recognized rules in their dealings and financial reporting. To the extent that a country's rules force business corporations to publicly disclose in-depth information about the company to potential shareholders and others, that country's financial and legal system is said to be *transparent*. Transparency helps simplify transactions and reduces the temptation to behave illegally or unethically. Finland, the United Kingdom, Hong Kong, the United States, and Australia have very transparent business climates. The Kurtzman Group, a consulting firm, developed an *opacity index* that measures the risks associated with unclear legal systems, regulations, economic policies, corporate governance standards, and corruption in 48 countries. The countries with the most opaque/least transparent ratings are Indonesia, Venezuela, China, Nigeria, India, Egypt, and Russia.

Developing nations tend to have *relationship-based governance*. Transactions are based on personal and implicit agreements, not on formal contracts enforceable by a court. Information about a business is largely local and private—thus, it cannot be easily verified by a third party. In contrast, *rule-based governance* relies on publicly verifiable information—the type of information that is typically not available in a developing country. The rule-based system has an infrastructure, based on accounting, auditing, ratings systems, legal cases, and codes, to provide and monitor this information. If present in a developing nation, the infrastructure is not very sophisticated. This is why investing in a developing country is very risky. The relationship-based system in a developing nation is inherently nontransparent due to the local and non-verifiable nature of its information. A business person needs to develop and nurture a wide network of personal relationships. *What* you know is less important than *who* you know.

The investment in time and money needed to build the necessary relationships to conduct business in a developing nation creates a high entry barrier for any newcomers to an industry. Thus, key industries in developing nations tend to be controlled by a small number of companies, usually privately owned, family-controlled conglomerates. Because public information is unreliable and insufficient for decisions, strategic decisions may depend more on a CEO playing golf with the prime minister than with questionable market share data. In a relationship-based system, the culture of the country (and the founder's family) strongly affects corporate culture and business ethics. What is "fair" depends on whether one is a family member, a close friend, a neighbor, or a stranger. Because behavior tends to be less controlled by laws and agreed-upon standards than by tradition, business people from a rule-based developed nation perceive the relationship-based system in a developing nation to be less ethical and more corrupt. According to Larry Smeltzer, ethics professor at Arizona State University, "The lack of openness and predictable business standards drives companies away. Why would you want to do business in, say Libya, where you don't know the rules?"

....

SOURCES: S. Li, S. H. Park, and S. Li, "The Great Leap Forward: The Transition from Relation-Based Governance to Rule-Based Governance," *Organizational Dynamics* (Vol. 33, No. 1, 2003), pp. 63–78; M. Davids, "Global Standards, Local Problems," *Journal of Business Strategy* (January/February 1999), pp. 38–43; "The Opacity Index," *The Economist* (September 18, 2004), p. 106.

Seventy percent of executives representing 111 diverse national and multinational corporations reported that they bend the rules to attain their objectives.[39] The three most common reasons given were:

- Organizational performance required it—74%
- Rules were ambiguous or out of date—70%
- Pressure from others and everyone does it—47%

The financial community's emphasis on short-term earnings performance is a significant pressure for executives to "manage" quarterly earnings. For example, a company achieving its forecasted quarterly earnings figure signals the investment community that its strategy and operations are proceeding as planned. Failing to meet its targeted objective signals that the company is in trouble—thus causing the stock price to fall and shareholders to become worried. Research by Degeorge and Patel involving more than 100,000 quarterly earnings reports revealed that a preponderance (82%) of reported earnings *exactly* matched analysts' expectations or exceeded them by 1%. The disparity between the number of earnings reports that missed estimates by a penny and the number that exceeded them by a penny suggests that executives who risked falling short of forecasts "borrowed" earnings from future quarters.[40]

In explaining why executives and accountants at Enron engaged in unethical and illegal actions, former Enron Vice-President Sherron Watkins used the *"frogs in boiling water"* analogy. If, for example, one were to toss a frog into a pan of boiling water, according to the folk tale, the frog would quickly jump out. It might be burned, but the frog would survive. However, if one put a frog in a pan of cold water and turned up the heat very slowly, the frog would not sense the increasing heat until it was too lethargic to jump out and would be boiled.

Moral Relativism

Some people justify their seemingly unethical positions by arguing that there is no one absolute code of ethics and that morality is relative. Simply put, **moral relativism** claims that morality is relative to some personal, social, or cultural standard and that there is no method for deciding whether one decision is better than another.

At one time or another, most managers have probably used one of the four types of moral relativism—naïve, role, social group, or cultural—to justify questionable behavior.[41]

Naïve relativism: Based on the belief that all moral decisions are deeply personal and that individuals have the right to run their own lives, adherents of moral relativism argue that each person should be allowed to interpret situations and act according to his or her own moral values. This is not so much a belief as it is an excuse for not having a belief or is a common excuse for not taking action when observing others lying or cheating.

Role relativism: Based on the belief that social roles carry with them certain obligations to that role, adherents of role relativism argue that a manager in charge of a work unit must put aside his or her personal beliefs and do instead what the role requires—that is, act in the best interests of the unit. Blindly following orders was a common excuse provided by Nazi war criminals after World War II.

Social group relativism: Based on a belief that morality is simply a matter of following the norms of an individual's peer group, social group relativism argues that a decision is considered legitimate if it is common practice, regardless of other considerations ("everyone's doing it"). A real danger in embracing this view is that the person may incorrectly believe that a certain action is commonly accepted practice in an industry when it is not.

Cultural relativism: Based on the belief that morality is relative to a particular culture, society, or community, adherents of cultural relativism argue that people should understand the practices of other societies, but not judge them. This view not only suggests that one should not criticize another culture's norms and customs, but also that it is acceptable to personally follow these norms and customs. ("When in Rome, do as the Romans do.")

Although each of these arguments has some element that may be understandable, moral relativism could enable a person to justify almost any sort of decision or action, so long as it is not declared illegal.

Kohlberg's Levels of Moral Development

Another reason why some business people might be seen as unethical is that they may have no well-developed personal sense of ethics. A person's ethical behavior is affected by his or her level of moral development, certain personality variables, and such situational factors as the job itself, the supervisor, and the organizational culture.[42] Kohlberg proposes that a person progresses through three **levels of moral development**.[43] Similar in some ways to Maslow's hierarchy of needs, in Kohlberg's system, the individual moves from total self-centeredness to a concern for universal values. Kohlberg's three levels are as follows:

1. **The preconventional level:** This level is characterized by a concern for self. Small children and others who have not progressed beyond this stage evaluate behaviors on the basis of personal interest—avoiding punishment or quid pro quo.

2. **The conventional level:** This level is characterized by considerations of society's laws and norms. Actions are justified by an external code of conduct.

3. **The principled level:** This level is characterized by a person's adherence to an internal moral code. An individual at this level looks beyond norms or laws to find

INNOVATION issue

TURNING A NEED INTO A BUSINESS TO SOLVE THE NEED

Tying an innovative idea to a social problem and turning it into a viable business is no small feat. Putting those three concepts together was exactly what David Auerbach accomplished. After returning from a two-year fellowship in China's Hunan province, he and several of his MIT classmates put their heads together to solve a horrifying problem that he encountered. He found that vast rural stretches of the Chinese provinces had no adequate sanitation. Pit latrines that spread disease and made life miserable were more the norm than he realized.

Today, 2.6 billion people on the earth have no access to adequate sanitation. The resulting disease and pollution cause more than 1.7 million deaths and the loss of some US$84 billion in worker time each year. A particularly poor area of the world is Kenya, where some 8 million people lack any access to adequate sanitation.

The key was to turn this issue into something more than a charity. Charities come and go with the interest level of donors. If Auerbach and his team could figure out how to make it into a business, then the potential for vastly improving the lives of millions might be possible. With that, he and his classmates put together a business plan and won the 2009 business plan competition at MIT. Armed with their prize money and US$20,000 from the Eleos Foundation (a nonprofit that makes venture capital investments in social businesses), they set off to start a company in Kenya.

Today that company is Sanergy (http://saner.gy). They build prefab concrete toilets and sell them to local entrepreneurs for US$500. Those entrepreneurs charge "customers" roughly 5 cents per use. The units are well stocked with toilet paper, soap, and water. The waste is collected by the company at the end of each day and is processed and sold as fertilizer. By 2016, they had created more than 779 jobs and installed 772 toilets serving more than 31,000 residents. The team is looking at pitching the toilets to landlords as a means for them to charge a bit more in rent but provide better sanitation to their tenants. The company has extended their reach into transforming the waste into usable fertilizer.

There are no easy answers in addressing some of these almost intractable problems, but a consistent theme of success is turning a "good" into a business that thrives for local residents.

....

SOURCES: http://saner.gy; "Getting to Sanitation for All: Always Be Closing," (July 9, 2012), (http://saner.gy/2012/07/09/getting-to-sanitation-for-all-always-be-closing); P. Clark, "Innovator Cleaning Up," *BusinessWeek* (October 17, 2011).

universal values or principles. See the Innovation Issue to see how someone turned a pressing world need into a viable business.

Kohlberg places most people in the conventional level, with fewer than 20% of U.S. adults in the principled level of development.[44] Research appears to support Kohlberg's concept. For example, one study found that individuals higher in cognitive moral development, lower in Machiavellianism, with a more internal locus of control, a less-relativistic moral philosophy, and higher job satisfaction are less likely to plan and enact unethical choices.[45]

ENCOURAGING ETHICAL BEHAVIOR

Following Carroll's work, if business people do not act ethically, government will be forced to pass laws regulating their actions—and usually increasing their costs. For self-interest, if for no other reason, managers should be more ethical in their decision making. One way to do that is by developing codes of ethics. Another is by providing guidelines for ethical behavior.

Codes of Ethics

A **code of ethics** specifies how an organization expects its employees to behave while on the job. Developing a code of ethics can be a useful way to promote ethical behavior, especially for people who are operating at Kohlberg's conventional level of moral development. Such codes are currently being used by more than half of U.S. business corporations. A code of ethics (1) clarifies company expectations of employee conduct in various situations and (2) makes clear that the company expects its people to recognize the ethical dimensions in decisions and actions.[46]

Various studies indicate that an increasing number of companies are developing codes of ethics and implementing ethics training workshops and seminars. However, research also indicates that when faced with a question of ethics, managers tend to ignore codes of ethics and try to solve dilemmas on their own.[47] To combat this tendency, the management of a company that wants to improve its employees' ethical behavior should not only develop a comprehensive code of ethics but also communicate the code in its training programs; in its performance appraisal system, policies, and procedures; and through its own actions.[48] It may even include key values in its values and mission statements. According to a 2011 survey conducted by the National Business Ethics Survey (NBES), the strength of ethics cultures declined dramatically in 2011 with 42% of respondents finding that their corporate ethics culture was either weak or weak leaning. This was an increase from the 2009 survey that found only 35% in the same situation. Specific findings of interest were:

- 90% of employees who observed corporate misconduct rated their cultures as weak.
- 34% of employees felt that their supervisor did not display ethical behavior.
- 34% said their management watches them more closely.[49]

In addition, U.S. corporations have attempted to support **whistle-blowers**, those employees who report illegal or unethical behavior on the part of others. The U.S. False Claims Act gives whistle-blowers 15% to 30% of any damages recovered in cases where the government is defrauded. Even though the Sarbanes–Oxley Act forbids firms from retaliating against anyone reporting wrongdoing, 22% of employees who reported misconduct in one study said they experienced retaliation, which was up from 15% in 2009 and 12% in 2007.[50]

Corporations appear to benefit from well-conceived and implemented ethics programs. For example, companies with strong ethical cultures and enforced codes of conduct have fewer unethical choices available to employees—thus fewer temptations.[51] A study by the Open Compliance and Ethics Group found that no company with an ethics program in place for 10 years or more experienced "reputational damage" in the last five years.[52] Some of the companies identified in surveys as having strong moral cultures are Canon, Hewlett-Packard, Johnson & Johnson, Levi Strauss, Medtronic, Motorola, Newman's Own, Patagonia, S. C. Johnson, Shorebank, Smucker, and Sony.[53]

A corporation's management should consider establishing and enforcing a code of ethical behavior not only for itself, but also for those companies with which it does business—especially if it outsources its manufacturing to a company in another country. Apple is one of the most profitable and powerful companies in the world. Much of their product manufacturing is outsourced to Chinese factories that have a reputation for harsh working conditions. Apple has a supplier code of conduct and a relatively vigorous auditing effort. Despite those efforts, *The New York Times* reported in 2012 that some of the suppliers audited by Apple had violated at least one aspect of the code every year since 2007. Critics have pointed out that for a variety of reasons Apple is relatively lax in its enforcement of the code. *The New York Times* reported that Apple conducted 312 audits over a three-year time period finding more than half the companies in violation and 70 core violations. Yet, despite all the evidence, Apple has terminated only 15 contracts over the past five years.[54]

Recent surveys of over one hundred companies in the Global 2000 uncovered that 64% have some code of conduct that regulates supplier conduct, but only 40% require suppliers to actually take any action with respect to the code, such as disseminating it to employees, offering training, certifying compliance, or even reading or acknowledging receipt of the code.[55]

It is important to note that having a code of ethics for suppliers does not prevent harm to a corporation's reputation if one of its offshore suppliers is able to conceal abuses. Numerous Chinese factories, for example, keep double sets of books to fool auditors and distribute scripts for employees to recite if they are questioned. Consultants have found new business helping Chinese companies evade audits.[56]

Views on Ethical Behavior

3-5. Describe different views of ethics according to the utilitarian, individual rights, and justice approaches

Ethics is defined as the consensually accepted standards of behavior for an occupation, a trade, or a profession. **Morality**, in contrast, constitutes one's rules of personal behavior based on religious or philosophical grounds. **Law** refers to formal codes that permit or forbid certain behaviors and may or may not enforce ethics or morality.[57] Given these definitions, how do we arrive at a comprehensive statement of ethics to use in making decisions in a specific occupation, trade, or profession? A starting point for such a code of ethics is to consider the three basic approaches to ethical behavior:[58]

1. **Utilitarian approach:** The **utilitarian approach** proposes that actions and plans should be judged by their consequences. People should, therefore, behave in a way that will produce the greatest benefit to society and produce the least harm or the lowest cost. A problem with this approach is the difficulty in recognizing all the benefits and costs of any particular decision. Research

reveals that only the stakeholders who have the most *power* (ability to affect the company), *legitimacy* (legal or moral claim on company resources), and *urgency* (demand for immediate attention) are given priority by CEOs.[59] It is, therefore, likely that only the most obvious stakeholders will be considered, while others are ignored.

2. **Individual rights approach:** The **individual rights approach** proposes that human beings have certain fundamental rights that should be respected in all decisions. A particular decision or behavior should be avoided if it interferes with the rights of others. A problem with this approach is in defining "fundamental rights." The U.S. Constitution includes a Bill of Rights that may or may not be accepted throughout the world. The approach can also encourage selfish behavior when a person defines a personal need or want as a "right."

3. **Justice approach:** The **justice approach** proposes that decision makers be equitable, fair, and impartial in the distribution of costs and benefits to individuals and groups. It follows the principles of *distributive justice* (people who are similar on relevant dimensions such as job seniority should be treated in the same way) and *fairness* (liberty should be equal for all persons). The justice approach can also include the concepts of *retributive justice* (punishment should be proportional to the offense) and *compensatory justice* (wrongs should be compensated in proportion to the offense). Affirmative action issues such as reverse discrimination are examples of conflicts between distributive and compensatory justice.

Cavanagh proposes that we solve ethical problems by asking the following three questions regarding an act or a decision:

1. **Utility:** Does it optimize the satisfactions of all stakeholders?
2. **Rights:** Does it respect the rights of the individuals involved?
3. **Justice:** Is it consistent with the canons of justice?[60]

For example, what if a company allows one vice-president to fly first class to Europe, but not others? Using the utility criterion, this action increases the company's costs and thus does not optimize benefits for shareholders or customers. Using the rights approach, the VP allowed to fly first class might argue that he or she is owed this type of reward for the extra strain that an international trip puts on personal relationships or work performance. Using the justice criterion, unless everyone at the VP level is allowed to fly first class, the privilege is not justifiable.

Another approach to resolving ethical dilemmas is by applying the logic of the philosopher Immanuel Kant. Kant presents two principles (called **categorical imperatives**) to guide our actions:

1. A person's action is ethical only if that person is willing for that same action to be taken by everyone who is in a similar situation. This is the same as the Golden Rule: Treat others as you would like them to treat you. For example, staying at upscale hotels while on the trip to Europe is only ethical if the same opportunity is available to others in the company at the same level.

2. A person should never treat another human being simply as a means but always as an end. This means that an action is morally wrong for a person if that person uses others merely as a means for advancing his or her own interests. To be moral, the act should not restrict other people's actions so they are disadvantaged in some way.[61]

End of Chapter SUMMARY

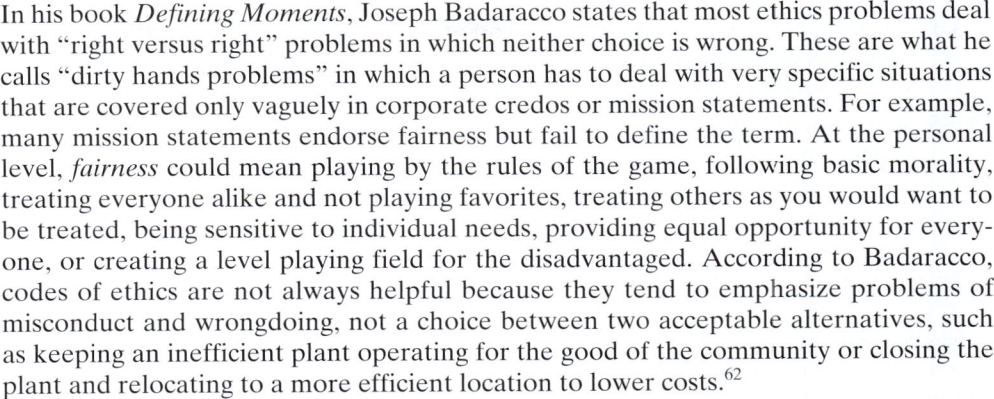

In his book *Defining Moments*, Joseph Badaracco states that most ethics problems deal with "right versus right" problems in which neither choice is wrong. These are what he calls "dirty hands problems" in which a person has to deal with very specific situations that are covered only vaguely in corporate credos or mission statements. For example, many mission statements endorse fairness but fail to define the term. At the personal level, *fairness* could mean playing by the rules of the game, following basic morality, treating everyone alike and not playing favorites, treating others as you would want to be treated, being sensitive to individual needs, providing equal opportunity for everyone, or creating a level playing field for the disadvantaged. According to Badaracco, codes of ethics are not always helpful because they tend to emphasize problems of misconduct and wrongdoing, not a choice between two acceptable alternatives, such as keeping an inefficient plant operating for the good of the community or closing the plant and relocating to a more efficient location to lower costs.[62]

This chapter provides a framework for evaluating the social responsibilities of a business. Following Carroll, it proposes that a manager should consider not only the economic and legal responsibilities of the business but also its ethical and discretionary responsibilities. It also provides a method for making ethical choices, whether they are right versus right or some combination of right and wrong. It is important to consider Cavanaugh's questions about using the utilitarian, individual rights, and justice approaches, plus Kant's categorical imperatives, when making a strategic decision. In general, a corporation should try to move from Kohlberg's conventional development to a principled level of ethical development. If nothing else, the frameworks should contribute to well-reasoned strategic decisions that a person can defend when interviewed by hostile media or questioned in a court room.

Pearson MyLab Management®

Go to **mymanagementlab.com** to complete the problems marked with this icon .

KEY TERMS

categorical imperatives (p. 118)
code of ethics (p. 116)
cultural relativism (p. 114)
ethics (p. 117)
individual rights approach (p. 118)
justice approach (p. 118)

law (p. 117)
levels of moral development (p. 115)
morality (p. 117)
moral relativism (p. 114)
naïve relativism (p. 114)
role relativism (p. 114)

social group relativism (p. 114)
social responsibility (p. 104)
stakeholder analysis (p. 109)
stakeholders (p. 108)
utilitarian approach (p. 117)
whistle-blowers (p. 116)

Pearson MyLab Management®

Go to **mymanagmentlab.com** for the following assisted-graded writing questions:

⭐ **3-1.** How has moral relativism led to criminal activities by some employees in companies?
⭐ **3-2.** How does a company ensure that its code of ethics is integrated into the daily decision-making process of the company and is not just a symbolic trophy or plaque hanging on the wall?

DISCUSSION QUESTIONS

⭐**3-3.** What is hypercompetition? Is the outcome positive for corporations in the IT industry?

3-4. What is your opinion of Apple having a code of conduct for its suppliers? What would Milton Friedman say? Contrast his view with Archie Carroll's view.

⭐**3-5.** Why should a profit-making organization be socially responsible to its various stakeholders?

3-6. What is stakeholder analysis? Explain the steps taken to achieve the identification and evaluation.

⭐**3-7.** Why do some employees of an organization behave unethically? Why is it necessary for an organization to develop employees' ethics?

STRATEGIC PRACTICE EXERCISE

It was certainly not the first time it had happened to the new social gaming company, but it was more of a worry this time. It was taking a lot longer to release the first version of the game being designed than had ever been anticipated. The firm had raised money four times already, but this round was more of an issue. The company probably needed an additional US$25 million, and more and more it was looking like the sales projections were far too optimistic.

The original idea for the game had morphed quite a bit and now was slated to use Facebook as its platform. The problem had occurred during the almost three years it had taken to bring the product to market. Two other games had been released that had taken the wind out of the new offering.

Knowing this, the company had quietly begun work on a new gaming platform. The problem was that it would take another 18 months before it had any marketability, and investors were unlikely to provide the type of valuations the company needed to keep afloat. The key to raising the funds needed was to keep talking about the existing game and getting it released into the market.

Private company valuations and market potential is difficult under the best circumstances. They are not required to provide audited financials, the risk of failure is quite high, and sales projections are at best a guess. They do not exist in the marketplace, so there is no history from which to judge their performance. In addition, competitor reactions to their entry into the market is unknown.

All of this is hard enough for investors, let alone the issue of management trying to hide known issues. The management of the business is convinced that they can be a big player in the market with their newer product; however, to get there they need the finances that may only be available if they act as if the product closer to release will be THE ONE. What should the manager do? Why do you believe so? What are the ethical implications of your decision?

NOTES

1. M. Friedman, "The Social Responsibility of Business Is to Increase Its Profits," *The New York Times Magazine* (September 13, 1970), pp. 30, 126–127; M. Friedman, *Capitalism and Freedom* (Chicago: University of Chicago Press, 1963), p. 133.

2. W. J. Byron, *Old Ethical Principles for the New Corporate Culture*, presentation to the College of Business, Iowa State University, Ames, Iowa (March 31, 2003).

3. A. B. Carroll, "A Three-Dimensional Conceptual Model of Corporate Performance," *Academy of Management Review* (October 1979), pp. 497–505. This model of business responsibilities was reaffirmed in A. B. Carroll, "Managing Ethically with Global Stakeholders: A Present and Future Challenge," *Academy of Management Executive* (May 2004), pp. 114–120.

4. Carroll refers to discretionary responsibilities as philanthropic responsibilities in A. B. Carroll, "The Pyramid of

Corporate Social Responsibility: Toward the Moral Management of Organizational Stakeholders," *Business Horizons* (July–August 1991), pp. 39–48.

5. M. S. Baucus and D. A. Baucus, "Paying the Piper: An Empirical Examination of Longer-Term Financial Consequences of Illegal Corporate Behavior," *Academy of Management Journal* (February 1997), pp. 129–151.

6. J. Oleck, "Pink Slips with a Silver Lining," *BusinessWeek* (June 4, 2001), p. 14.

7. S. M. J. Bonini, L. T. Mendonca, and J. M. Oppenheim, "When Social Issues Become Strategic," *McKinsey Quarterly* (2006, Number 2), pp. 20–31.

8. "The McKinsey Global Survey of Business Executives: Business and Society," *McKinsey Quarterly*, Web edition (March 31, 2006).

9. "Corporate Social Responsibility Now a Staple at Davos," *CNBC* (January 22, 2012), (www.cnbc.com/id/45856248/

corporate_social_responsibility_now_a_staple_at_Davos accessed January, 2016).

10. A. McWilliams and D. Siegel, "Corporate Social Responsibility and Financial Performance: Correlation or Misspecification?" *Strategic Management Journal* (May 2000), pp. 603–609; P. Rechner and K. Roth, "Social Responsibility and Financial Performance: A Structural Equation Methodology," *International Journal of Management* (December 1990), pp. 382–391; K. E. Aupperle, A. B. Carroll, and J. D. Hatfield, "An Empirical Examination of the Relationship Between Corporate Social Responsibility and Profitability," *Academy of Management Journal* (June 1985), p. 459.

11. M. M. Arthur, "Share Price Reactions to Work-Family Initiatives: An Institutional Perspective," *Academy of Management Journal* (April 2003), pp. 497–505; S. A. Waddock and S. B. Graves, "The Corporate Social Performance—Financial Performance Link," *Strategic Management Journal* (April 1997), pp. 303–319; M. V. Russo and P. A. Fouts, "Resource Based Perspective on Corporate Environmental Performance and Profitability" *Academy of Management Journal* (July 1997), pp. 534–559; H. Meyer, "The Greening of Corporate America," *Journal of Business Strategy* (January/February 2000), pp. 38–43.

12. J. D. Margolis and J. P. Walsh, "Misery Loves Companies: Re-thinking Social Initiatives by Business," *Administrative Science Quarterly* (June 2003), pp. 268–305.

13. M. F. L. Orlitzky, F. L. Schmidt, and S. L. Rynes, "Corporate Social and Financial Performance: A Meta Analysis," *Organization Studies* (Vol. 24, 2003), pp. 403–441.

14. M. Porter and M. R. Kramer, "The Competitive Advantage of Corporate Philanthropy," *Harvard Business Review* (December 2002), p. 59.

15. P. S. Adler and S. W. Kwon, "Social Capital: Prospects for a New Concept," *Academy of Management Journal* (January 2002), pp. 17–40. Also called "moral capital" in P. C. Godfrey, "The Relationship Between Corporate Philanthropy and Shareholder Wealth: A Risk Management Perspective," *Academy of Management Review* (October 2005), pp. 777–799.

16. L. Gard, "We're Good Guys, Buy from Us," *BusinessWeek* (November 22, 2004), pp. 72–74.

17. G. Thornton, "Corporate Social Responsibility – A Necessity Not a Choice for Privately Held Businesses," (2008), (www.internationalbusinessreport.com/2008/corporate-social-responsibility.asp).

18. C. J. Fombrun, "Corporate Reputation as an Economic Asset," in M. A. Hitt, E. R. Freeman, and J. S. Harrison (Eds.), *The Blackwell Handbook of Strategic Management* (Oxford: Blackwell Publishers, 2001), pp. 289–310.

19. S. A. Muirhead, C. J. Bennett, R. E. Berenbeim, A. Kao, and D. J. Vidal, *Corporate Citizenship in the New Century* (New York: The Conference Board, 2002), p. 6.

20. *2002 Sustainability Survey Report*, PriceWaterhouseCoopers, reported in "Corporate America's Social Conscience," Special Advertising Section, *Fortune* (May 26, 2003), pp. 149–157.

21. C. L. Harman and E. R. Stafford, "Green Alliances: Building New Business with Environmental Groups" *Long Range Planning* (April 1997), pp. 184–196.

22. D. B. Turner and D. W. Greening, "Corporate Social Performance and Organizational Attractiveness to Prospective Employees," *Academy of Management Journal* (July 1997), pp. 658–672; S. Preece, C. Fleisher, and J. Toccacelli, "Building a Reputation Along the Value Chain at Levi Strauss," *Long Range Planning* (December 1995), pp. 88–98; J. B. Barney and M. H. Hansen, "Trustworthiness as a Source of Competitive Advantage," *Strategic Management Journal* (Special Winter Issue, 1994), pp. 175–190; R. V. Aguilera, D. E. Rupp, C. A. Williams, and J. Ganapathi, "Putting the S Back in Corporate Social Responsibility: A Multilevel Theory of Social Change in Organizations," *Academy of Management Review* (July 2007), pp. 836–863; S. Bonini and S. Chenevert, "The State of Corporate Philanthropy: A McKinsey Global Survey," *McKinsey Quarterly*, Web edition (March 1, 2008); P. Kotler and N. Lee (Eds.), *Corporate Social Responsibility: Doing the Most Good for Your Company and Your Cause* (Hoboken, NJ: Wiley, 2005).

23. "Numbers: Do-Good Investments Are Holding Up Better," *BusinessWeek* (July 14 and 21, 2008), p. 15.

24. A. Crane and D. Matten, *Business Ethics: A European Perspective* (Oxford: Oxford University Press, 2004), p. 22.

25. R. E. Freeman and D. R. Gilbert, *Corporate Strategy and the Search for Ethics* (Upper Saddle River, NJ: Prentice Hall, 1988), p. 6.

26. "CSR Branding Survey 2010," (www.slideshare.net/bmglobalnews/csr-branding-survey-2010-final).

27. M. Boesler, "Study: 20% of Companies Lie on Earnings Reports, Top Reason Is to Boost Stock Price," *Business Insider* (July 25, 2012), (www.businessinsider.com/study-20-of-companies-lie-earnings-stock-prices-2012-7).

28. "BP expert defends controversial cost saving decision before blast," ProjectNola.com (July 22, 2010), (http://projectnola.com/the-news/news/42-fox-8/98578-bp-expert-defends-controversial-cost-saving-decision-before-blast accessed January, 2016).

29. W. E. Stead and J. G. Stead, *Sustainable Strategic Management* (Armonk, NY: M. E. Sharpe, 2004), p. 41.

30. D. Elliott, "5 Years After BP Oil Spill, Effects Linger And Recovery Is Slow," *NPR* (April 20, 2015), http://www.npr.org/2015/04/20/400374744/5-years-after-bp-oil-spill-effects-linger-and-recovery-is-slow.

31. B. Barrow, "Chick-fil-A Sandwiches at Center of Latest Political Storm," *The Charlotte Observer* (July 27, 2012), pg. A1.

32. The National Business Ethics Survey 2013 (http://www.ethics.org/research/eci-research/nbes/nbes-reports/nbes-2013).

33. "Dates from Hell," *The Economist* (July 22, 2006), pp. 59–60.

34. B. O'Connell, "Mortgage Fraud Cases Climbing," NuWire Investor (2011), www.nuwireinvestor.com/articles/mortgage-fraud-cases-climbing-57871.aspx.

35. D. L. McCabe, K. D. Butterfield, and L. K. Trevino, "Academic Dishonesty in Graduate Business Programs: Prevalence, Causes, and Proposed Action," *Academy of Management Learning & Education* (September 2006), pp. 294–305.

36. L. Lavelle, "The GMAT Cheat Sheet," *BusinessWeek* (July 14 and 21, 2008), p. 34.

37. S. Li, S. H. Park, and S. Li, "The Great Leap Forward: The Transition from Relation-Based Governance to Rule-Based Governance," *Organizational Dynamics* (Vol. 33, No. 1, 2004), pp. 63–78; M. Davids, "Global Standards, Local Problems," *Journal of Business Strategy* (January/

February 1999), pp. 38–43; "The Opacity Index," *The Economist* (September 18, 2004), p. 106.

38. K. Kumar, "Ethical Orientation of Future American Executives: What the Value Profiles of Business School Students Portend," *SAM Advanced Management Journal* (Autumn 1995), pp. 32–36, 47; M. Gable and P. Arlow, "A Comparative Examination of the Value Orientations of British and American Executives," *International Journal of Management* (September 1986), pp. 97–106; W. D. Guth and R. Tagiuri, "Personal Values and Corporate Strategy," *Harvard Business Review* (September–October 1965), pp. 126–127; G. W. England, "Managers and Their Value Systems: A Five Country Comparative Study," *Columbia Journal of World Business* (Summer 1978), p. 35.

39. J. F. Veiga, T. D. Golden, and K. Dechant, "Why Managers Bend Company Rules," *Academy of Management Executive* (May 2004), pp. 84–91.

40. H. Collingwood, "The Earnings Game," *Harvard Business Review* (June 2001), pp. 65–74; J. Fox, "Can We Trust Them Now?" *Fortune* (March 3, 2003), pp. 97–99.

41. R. E. Freeman and D. R. Gilbert Jr., *Corporate Strategy and the Search for Ethics* (Englewood Cliffs, NJ: Prentice Hall, 1988), pp. 24–41.

42. L. K. Trevino, "Ethical Decision Making in Organizations: A Person-Situation Interactionist Model," *Academy of Management Review* (July 1986), pp. 601–617.

43. L. Kohlberg, "Moral Stage and Moralization: The Cognitive-Development Approach," in T. Lickona (Ed.), *Moral Development and Behavior* (New York: Holt, Rinehart & Winston, 1976).

44. L. K. Trevino, "Ethical Decision Making in Organizations: A Person-Situation Interactionist Model," *Academy of Management Review* (July 1986), p. 606 L. K. Trevino, G. R. Weaver, and S. J. Reynolds, "Behavioral Ethics in Organizations: A Review," *Journal of Management* (December 2006), pp. 951–990.

45. J. K. Gephart, D. A. Harrison, and L. K. Trevino, "The Who, When, and Where of Unethical Choices: Meta-Analytic Answers to Fundamental Ethics Questions." Paper presented to the *Academy of Management* annual meeting, Philadelphia, PA (2007).

46. J. Keogh (Ed.), *Corporate Ethics: A Prime Business Asset* (New York: The Business Roundtable, 1988), p. 5.

47. G. F. Kohut and S. E. Corriher, "The Relationship of Age, Gender, Experience and Awareness of Written Ethics Policies to Business Decision Making," *SAM Advanced Management Journal* (Winter 1994), pp. 32–39; J. C. Lere and B. R. Gaumitz, "The Impact of Codes of Ethics on Decision Making: Some Insights from Information

Economics," *Journal of Business Ethics* (Vol. 48, 2003), pp. 365–379.

48. W. I. Sauser, "Business Ethics: Back to Basics," *Management in Practice* (2005, No. 2), pp. 2–3; J. M. Stevens, H. K. Steensma, D. A. Harrison, and P. L. Cochran, "Symbolic or Substantive Document? The Influence of Ethics Codes on Financial Executives' Decisions," *Strategic Management Journal* (February 2005), pp. 181–195.

49. M. Oxley and P. Harned, "2011 National Business Ethics Survey," (2012), pp. 1–62.

50. Ibid.

51. J. K. Gephart, D. A. Harrison, and L. K. Trevino, "The Who, When, and Where of Unethical Choices: Meta-Analytic Answers to Fundamental Ethics Questions." Paper presented to the *Academy of Management* annual meeting, Philadelphia, PA (2007).

52. "A 'How Am I Doing?' Guide for Ethics Czars," *Business Ethics* (Fall 2005), p. 11.

53. S. P. Feldman, "Moral Business Cultures: The Keys to Creating and Maintaining Them," *Organizational Dynamics* (Vol. 36, No. 2, 2007), pp. 156–170. Also see the "World's Most Ethical Companies," published annually by Ethisphere at http://ethisphere.com.

54. "In China, Human Costs Are Built into an iPad," *The New York Times* (January 25, 2012), (www.nytimes.com/2012/01/26/business/ieconomy-apples-ipad-and-the-human-costs-for-workers-in-china.html accessed January, 2016).

55. M. Levin, "Building an Ethical Supply Chain," *Sarbanes–Oxley Compliance Journal* (April 3, 2008).

56. A. Bernstein, S. Holmes, and X. Ji, "Secrets, Lies, and Sweat-shops," *BusinessWeek* (November 27, 2006), pp. 50–58.

57. T. J. Von der Embse, and R. A. Wagley, "Managerial Ethics: Hard Decisions on Soft Criteria," *SAM Advanced Management Journal* (Winter 1988), p. 6.

58. G. F. Cavanagh, *American Business Values*, 3rd ed. (Upper Saddle River, NJ: Prentice Hall, 1990), pp. 186–199.

59. B. R. Agle, R. K. Mitchell, and J. A. Sonnenfeld, "Who Matters Most to CEOs? An Investigation of Stakeholder Attributes and Salience, Corporate Performance, and CEO Values," *Academy of Management Journal* (October 1999), pp. 507–525.

60. G. F. Cavanagh, *American Business Values*, 3rd ed. (Upper Saddle River, NJ: Prentice Hall, 1990), pp. 195–196.

61. I. Kant, "The Foundations of the Metaphysic of Morals," in *Ethical Theory: Classical and Contemporary Readings*, 2nd ed., by L. P. Pojman (Belmont, CA: Wadsworth Publishing, 1995), pp. 255–279.

62. J. L. Badaracco Jr., *Defining Moments* (Boston: Harvard Business School Press, 1997).

PART 2

Scanning the
Environment

CHAPTER 4

Environmental Scanning and Industry Analysis

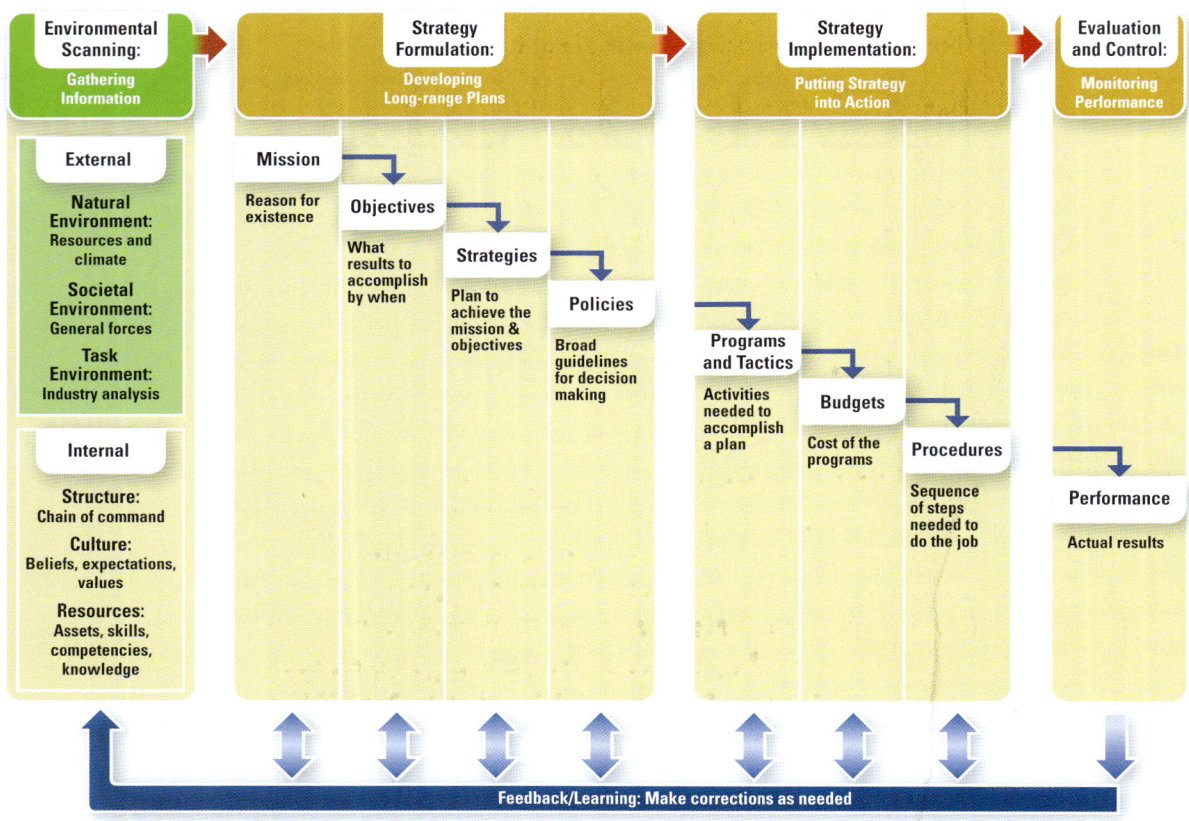

Pearson MyLab Management®

⭐ Improve Your Grade!

Over 10 million students improved their results using the Pearson MyLabs. Visit **mymanagementlab.com** for simulations, tutorials, and end-of-chapter problems.

Learning Objectives

After reading this chapter, you should be able to:

4-1. List the aspects of an organization's environment that can influence its long-term decisions

4-2. Identify the aspects of an organization's environment that are most strategically important

4-3. Conduct an industry analysis to explain the competitive forces that influence the intensity of rivalry within an industry

4-4. Discuss how industry maturity affects industry competitive forces

4-5. Categorize international industries based on their pressures for coordination and local responsiveness

4-6. Identify key success factors and develop an industry matrix

4-7. Construct strategic group maps to assess the competitive positions of firms in an industry

4-8. Develop an industry scenario as a forecasting technique

4-9. Use publicly available information to conduct competitive intelligence

4-10. Construct an EFAS table that summarizes external environmental factors

Kodak—What Happened to a Great Company?

Yes, Kodak is still a company, having emerged from a 2013 bankruptcy that was preceded by a decade of selling off intellectual property; failed investments in cameras, printers, and medical devices; and sharp reductions in their workforce. Of the more than 200 buildings that once stood on the 1,300-acre campus in Rochester, NY, more than 80 have been demolished and 59 others have been sold off to other companies.

Eastman Kodak was founded officially in 1881 as the Eastman Dry Plate Company. In 1888 the name "Kodak" was born and the KODAK camera appeared on the market, with the slogan, "You press the button—we do the rest." The company grew rapidly on the back of research and patents that set the standards for decades. By 1990 it had sales of $19 billion and employed more than 145,000 employees worldwide.

Kodak actually created digital photography and put the technology into professional cameras in the early 1990s. While they were the founders of what would eventually mean the demise of the company, they did little with it, only dabbling in cameras for consumers. It wasn't that the company didn't see the decline in film coming; it was just so profitable to keep producing film that everyone assumed the company had time to change.

The end began to become very clear. Starting in 2001 film sales began plummeting by 20%–30% a year. The company poured a fortune into a very unsuccessful attempt to enter the digital printing market. Like so many companies that are unable to adapt to new market conditions, the company suffered through many rounds of layoffs, restructurings, and asset sales as management teams floundered.

In 2013 the company sold off a majority of its remaining valuable patents to a group of companies including Apple, Samsung, and Facebook for just over $500 million. Today the company is owned by a group of Private Equity investors and the CEO lives in San Francisco and is trying to manage the remaining intellectual property and employees to find some areas of growth. The company excels at high-speed printing and digital imaging. Some Hollywood directors still use film (Quentin Tarantino & J.J. Abrams) which Kodak continues to produce, but the future of the company is murky at best. Kodak, once a brand name that rivaled the greatest in the world may go the way of other legacy companies that failed to change with the environment.

SOURCE: Quentin Hardy, "At Kodak, Clinging to a Future Beyond Film," *The New York Times,* March 20, 2015. (http://www.nytimes.com/2015/03/22/business/at-kodak-clinging-to-a-future-beyond-film .html?ref=topics&_r=0); http://www.kodak.com/ek/us/en/corp/aboutus/heritage/milestones/default.htm

A changing environment can help as well as hurt a company. Many pioneering companies have gone out of business because of their failure to adapt to competitive and environmental change or, even worse, because of their failure to create change. For example, Baldwin Locomotive, the major manufacturer of steam locomotives, was very slow in making the switch to diesel locomotives. General Electric and General Motors soon dominated the diesel locomotive business and Baldwin went out of business. The dominant manufacturers of vacuum tubes failed to make the change to transistors and consequently lost this market. Eastman Kodak, the pioneer and market leader of chemical-based film photography, has been in a long decline as it struggles to find its place in the post-film world. Failure to adapt is, however, only one side of the coin. A changing environment usually creates new opportunities at the same time it destroys old ones. The lesson is simple: To be successful over time, an organization needs to be in tune with its external environment. There must be a strategic fit between what the environment wants and what the corporation has to offer, as well as between what the corporation needs and what the environment can provide.

Current predictions are that the environment for all organizations will become even more uncertain with every passing year. What is **environmental uncertainty**? It is the *degree of complexity* plus the *degree of change* that exists in an organization's external environment. As more and more markets become global, the number of factors a company must consider in any decision increases in size and difficulty. With new technologies being discovered every year, markets change and products must change with them.

On the one hand, environmental uncertainty is a threat to strategic managers because it hampers their ability to develop long-range plans and to make strategic decisions to keep the corporation in equilibrium with its external environment. On the other hand, environmental uncertainty is an opportunity because it creates a new playing field in which creativity and innovation can play a major part in strategic decisions.

Aspects of Environmental Scanning

4-1. List the aspects of an organization's environment that can influence its long-term decisions

Before managers can begin strategy formulation, they must understand the context of the environment in which their organization competes. It is virtually impossible for a company to design a strategy without a deep understanding of the external environment. Once management has framed the aspects of the environment that impact the business, they are in a position to determine the firm's competitive advantages. **Environmental scanning** is an overarching term encompassing the monitoring, evaluation, and dissemination of information relevant to the organizational development of strategy. A corporation uses this tool to avoid strategic surprise and to ensure its long-term health. Research has found a positive relationship between environmental scanning and profits.[1] A 2011 study by McKinsey & Company found that executives ranked macrolevel trends as the most important input to be considered when developing corporate strategy.[2]

IDENTIFYING EXTERNAL ENVIRONMENTAL VARIABLES

In undertaking environmental scanning, strategic managers must first be aware of the many variables within a corporation's natural, societal, and task environments (see **Figure 1–3**). The **natural environment** includes physical resources, wildlife, and climate that are an inherent part of existence on Earth. These factors form an ecological system of interrelated life. The **societal environment** is mankind's social system that includes general forces that do not directly touch on the short-run activities of the organization, but that can influence its long-term decisions. These factors affect multiple industries and are as follows:

- **Economic forces** that regulate the exchange of materials, money, energy, and information.
- **Technological forces** that generate problem-solving inventions.
- **Political–legal forces** that allocate power and provide constraining and protecting laws and regulations.
- **Sociocultural forces** that regulate the values, mores, and customs of society.

The **task environment** includes those elements or groups that directly affect a corporation and, in turn, are affected by it. These are governments, local communities, suppliers, competitors, customers, creditors, employees/labor unions, special-interest groups, and trade associations. A corporation's task environment is typically focused on the industry within which the firm operates. **Industry analysis** refers to an in-depth examination of key factors within a corporation's task environment. The natural, societal, and task environments must be monitored to examine the strategic factors that have a strong impact on corporate success or failure. Significant changes in the natural environment tend to impact the societal environment of the business (resource availability and costs), and finally the task environment because it impacts the growth or decline of whole industries.

Scanning the Natural Environment

The natural environment includes physical resources, wildlife, and climate that are an inherent part of existence on Earth. Until the 20th century, the natural environment was generally perceived by business people to be a given—something to exploit, not conserve. It was viewed as a free resource, something to be taken or fought over, like arable land, diamond mines, deep water harbors, or fresh water. Once they were controlled by a person or entity, these resources were considered assets and thus valued as part of the general economic system—a resource to be bought, sold, or sometimes shared. Side effects, such as pollution, were considered to be *externalities*, costs not included in a business firm's accounting system, but felt by others. Eventually these externalities were identified by governments, which passed regulations to force business corporations to deal with the side effects of their activities.

The concept of sustainability argues that a firm's ability to continuously renew itself for long-term success and survival is dependent not only upon the greater economic and social system of which it is a part, but also upon the natural ecosystem in which the firm is embedded.[3] For more information on innovative approaches to this issue, see the **Sustainability Issue** feature.

A business must scan the natural environment for factors that might previously have been taken for granted, such as the availability of fresh water and clean air. Global warming means that aspects of the natural environment, such as sea level, weather, and climate, are becoming increasingly uncertain and difficult to predict. Management must scan not only the natural environment for possible strategic factors, but also include in its strategic decision-making processes the impact of its activities upon the natural environment. In a world concerned with climate change, a company could measure and reduce its *carbon footprint*—the amount of greenhouse gases it is emitting into the air. Research reveals that scanning the market for environmental issues is positively related to firm performance because it helps management identify opportunities to fulfill future market demand based upon environmentally friendly products or processes.[4] See the **Sustainability Issue** feature to learn how the high-end car companies saw an opportunity in green cars.

SUSTAINABILITY issue

GREEN SUPERCARS

The move to greener cars has finally reached ultra-high-end car companies, including Porsche, Ferrari, and Bentley. The push to get car manufacturing companies to increase gas mileage and reduce emissions has come from a combination of regulations, purchasing patterns, and pressure from environmental groups. Although some form of hybrid vehicle technology has been around since the beginning of the automobile, the Toyota Prius, introduced to the Japanese market in 1997, quickly became the standard of economy in the industry.

Higher-end car makers have been making hybrid vehicles for some time, even though the price of these vehicles has kept their sales relatively modest. BMW offers the 750i, four-door sedan for US$101,000, while the equivalent Mercedes sedan (S400) goes for roughly US$92,000. Despite this, ultra-luxury car makers waited until the 2013 model year to release their hybrid models.

Ferrari announced the F70, which has two electric motors along with a 12-cylinder gasoline engine that cuts fuel consumption by more than 40%. The price tag is something to see, however. The vehicle will most likely be priced above US$850,000. Porsche already has hybrid versions of its Cayenne SUV and Panamera four-door cars, clocking in at US$70,000 and US$96,000, respectively. In 2015 Porsche released the new 918 Spyder sports coupe hybrid with a base price between US$850,000 to US$930,000. Even venerable Bentley is planning a plug-in hybrid version of its SUV that will come with a price tag above US$300,000.

All of these vehicles require battery packs that weigh in excess of 1000 pounds and must be disposed of when the vehicle is no longer useful. The increase in sustainability from an environmental approach on one end triggers an environmental issue at the other end of the product's useful life. So what is the right answer for these companies? And what about the environment?

SOURCES: http://www.hybridcars.com/history/history-of-hybrid-vehicles.html (accessed January, 2016); T. Ebhardt, "Supercar Makers Seek a Different Shade of Green," *BusinessWeek* (May 28, 2012), (www.businessweek.com).

Strategic Importance of the External Environment

SCANNING THE SOCIETAL ENVIRONMENT: STEEP ANALYSIS

4-2. Identify the aspects of an organization's environment that are most strategically important

The number of possible strategic factors in the societal environment is very high. The number becomes enormous when we realize that, generally speaking, each country in the world can be represented by its own unique set of societal forces—some of which are very similar to those of neighboring countries and some of which are very different.

For example, even though Korea and China share Asia's Pacific Rim area with Thailand, Taiwan, and Hong Kong (sharing many similar cultural values), they have very different views about the role of business in society. It is generally believed in Korea and China (and to a lesser extent in Japan) that the role of business is primarily to contribute to national development. However, in Hong Kong, Taiwan, and Thailand (and to a lesser extent in the Philippines, Indonesia, Singapore, and Malaysia), the role of business is primarily to make profits for the shareholders.[5] Such differences may translate into different trade regulations and varying difficulty in the *repatriation of profits* (the transfer of profits from a foreign subsidiary to a corporation's headquarters) from one group of Pacific Rim countries to another.

STEEP Analysis: Monitoring Trends in the Societal and Natural Environments

As shown in **Table 4–1**, large corporations categorize the natural and societal environments in any one geographic region into five areas and focus their scanning in each area on trends that have corporatewide relevance. For ease of remembering the approach,

TABLE 4–1 Some Important Variables in the Societal Environment

Sociocultural	Technological	Economic	Ecological	Political–Legal
Lifestyle changes	Total government spending for R&D	GDP trends	Environmental protection laws	Antitrust regulations
Career expectations		Interest rates	Global warming impacts	Environmental protection laws
Consumer activism	Total industry spending for R&D	Money supply	Non-governmental organizations	Global warming legislation
Rate of family formation	Focus of technological efforts	Inflation rates		Immigration laws
Growth rate of population	Patent protection	Unemployment levels	Pollution impacts	Tax laws
Age distribution of population	New products	Wage/price controls	Reuse	Special incentives
Regional shifts in population	New developments in technology transfer from lab to marketplace	Devaluation/revaluation	Triple bottom line	Foreign trade regulations
Life expectancies	Productivity improvements through automation	Energy alternatives	Recycling	Attitudes toward foreign companies
Birthrates	Internet availability	Energy availability and cost		Laws on hiring and promotion
Pension plans	Telecommunication infrastructure	Disposable and discretionary income		Stability of government
Health care	Computer hacking activity	Currency markets		Outsourcing regulation
Level of education		Global financial system		Foreign "sweatshops"
Living wage				
Unionization				

this scanning can be called **STEEP Analysis**, the scanning of Sociocultural, Technological, Economic, Ecological, and Political–legal environmental forces.[6] (It may also be called *PESTEL Analysis* for Political, Economic, Sociocultural, Technological, Ecological, and Legal forces.) Obviously, trends in any one area may be very important to firms in one industry but of lesser importance to firms in other industries.

Demographic trends are part of the *sociocultural* aspect of the societal environment. Although the world's population has grown from 3.71 billion people in 1970 to 7.3 billion in 2015 and is expected to increase to between 8.3 and 10.9 billion by 2050, not all regions will grow equally.[7] Most of the growth will be in the developing nations. It is predicted that the population of the developed nations will fall from 14% of the total world population in 2000 to only 10% in 2050.[8] Around 75% of the world will live in a city by 2050, compared to little more than half in 2008.[9] Developing nations will continue to have more young than old people, but it will be the reverse in the industrialized nations. For example, the demographic bulge in the U.S. population caused by the baby boom after WWII continues to affect market demand in many industries. This group of 77 million people now in their 50s and 60s is the largest age group in all developed countries, especially in Europe. (See **Table 4–2**.) Although the median age in the United States will rise from 35 in 2000 to 40 by 2050, it will increase from 40 to 47 during the same time period in Germany, and it will increase to up to 50 in Italy as soon as 2025.[10] By 2050, one in three Italians will be over 65, nearly double the number in 2005.[11] With its low birthrate, Japan's population is expected to fall from 127.6 million in 2004 to around 100 million by 2050.[12] China's stringent birth control policy (which was recently relaxed to allow couples to have two children) is predicted to cause the ratio of workers to retirees to fall from 20 to 1 during the early 1980s to 2.5 to one by 2020.[13] Companies with an eye on the future can find many opportunities to offer products and services to the growing number of "woofies" (well-off old folks)—defined as people over 50 with money to spend.[14] These people are very likely to purchase recreational vehicles (RVs), take ocean cruises, and enjoy leisure sports, in addition to needing complex financial services and health care. Anticipating the needs of seniors for prescription drugs is one reason Walgreens has grown so fast. It opened its 7000th store in 2009 and by mid-year 2015 had over 8100 stores![15]

To attract older customers, retailers will need to place seats in their larger stores so aging shoppers can rest. Washrooms will need to be more handicap-accessible. Signs will need to be larger. Restaurants will need to raise the level of lighting so people can read their menus. Home appliances will require simpler and larger controls. Automobiles will need larger door openings and more comfortable seats. Zimmer Holdings, an innovative

TABLE 4–2		Generation	Born	Age in 2015	% of Total Adult Population
Current U.S. Generations	Current U.S. Generations	Greatest	Before 1928	88–100	2%
		WWII / Silent Generation	1928–1945	70–87	11%
		Baby Boomers	1946–1964	51–69	30%
		Generation X	1965–1980	35–50	27%
		Millennials	1980–1996	18–34	30%

SOURCES: Developed from Pew Research Center analysis of census bureau population projections (September 3, 2015), (http://www.people-press.org/2015/09/03/the-whys-and-hows-of-generations-research/generations_2/).

manufacturer of artificial joints, is looking forward to its market growing rapidly over the next 20 years. According to J. Raymond Elliot, Chair and CEO of Zimmer, "It's simple math. Our best years are still in front of us."[16]

Eight current sociocultural trends are transforming North America and the rest of the world:

1. **Increasing environmental awareness:** Recycling and conservation are becoming more than slogans. Busch Gardens, for example, has eliminated the use of disposable Styrofoam trays in favor of washing and reusing plastic trays.

2. **Growing health consciousness:** Concerns about personal health fuel the trend toward physical fitness and healthier living. There has been a general move across the planet to attack obesity. The U.S. Centers for Disease Control and Prevention cites that more than two-thirds of American adults and one-third of American youth are now obese or overweight. A number of states have enacted provisions to encourage grocery stores to open in so-called "food deserts" where the population has virtually no access to fresh foods.[17] In 2012, Chile decided to ban toys that are included in various fast-food meals aimed at children in order to increase the fight against childhood obesity.[18]

3. **Expanding seniors market:** As their numbers increase, people over age 55 will become an even more important market. Already some companies are segmenting the senior population into Young Matures, Older Matures, and the Elderly—each having a different set of attitudes and interests. Both mature segments, for example, are good markets for the health care and tourism industries; whereas, the elderly are the key market for long-term care facilities. The desire for companionship by people whose children are grown is causing the pet care industry to grow by more than 5% annually in the United States. In 2014, for example, 73 million households in the United States spent US$58 billion on their pets. That was up from just above US$41 billion 2007.[19]

4. **Impact of millennials:** Born between 1980 and 1996 to the baby boomers and Generation Xers, this cohort is almost as large as the baby boomer generation. In 1957, the peak year of the postwar boom, 4.3 million babies were born. In 1990, there were 4.2 million births; the Millennials' peak year. By 2000, they were overcrowding elementary and high schools and entering college in numbers not seen since the baby boomers. Now in its 20s and 30s, this cohort is expected to have a strong impact on future products and services.

5. **Declining mass market:** Niche markets are defining the marketers' environment. People want products and services that are adapted more to their personal needs. For example, Estée Lauder's "All Skin" and Maybelline's "Shades of You" lines of cosmetic products are specifically made for African-American women. "Mass customization"—the making and marketing of products tailored to a person's requirements is replacing the mass production and marketing of the same product in some markets. The past 10 years have seen a real fracturing of the chocolate market with the advent of craft chocolate making and flavored chocolates. These products command significantly higher margins and have become a force in the retailing environment. By 2010, 43% of chocolate sales occurred in nontraditional channels.[20]

6. **Changing pace and location of life:** Instant communication via e-mail, cell phones, and overnight mail enhances efficiency, but it also puts more pressure on people. Merging the personal or tablet computer with the communication and entertainment industries through telephone lines, satellite dishes, and Internet connections increases consumers' choices and allows workers to telecommute from anywhere.

7. **Changing household composition:** Single-person households, especially those consisting of single women with children, could soon become the most common household type in the United States. According to the U.S. Census, married-couple households slipped from nearly 80% in the 1950s to 48% of all households by 2010.[21] By 2007, for the first time in U.S. history, more than half the adult female population was single.[22] Those women are also having more children. As of 2012, 41% of all births in the United States were to unmarried women.[23] A typical family household is no longer the same as it was once portrayed in *Happy Days* in the 1970s.

8. **Increasing diversity of workforce and markets:** Between now and 2050, minorities will account for nearly 90% of population growth in the United States. Over time, group percentages of the total U.S. population are expected to change as follows: Non- Hispanic Whites—from 90% in 1950 to 74% in 1995 to 53% by 2050; Hispanic Whites—from 9% in 1995 to 22% in 2050; Blacks—from 13% in 1995 to 15% in 2050; Asians—from 4% in 1995 to 9% in 2050; American Indians—1%, with slight increase.[24]

Heavy immigration from developing to developed nations is increasing the number of minorities in all developed countries and forcing an acceptance of the value of diversity in races, religions, and lifestyles. For example, 24% of the Swiss population was born elsewhere.[25] Traditional minority groups are increasing their numbers in the workforce and are being identified as desirable target markets. Coca-Cola, Nestlé, and Pepsi have targeted African-American and Latino communities for the sale of bottled water after a study by the department of pediatrics at the Medical College of Wisconsin in 2011 found that African-American and Latino families were three times more likely to give their children bottled water as compared to white families.[26]

Changes in the *technological* part of the societal environment can also have a great impact on multiple industries. Improvements in computer microprocessors have not only led to the widespread use of personal computers but also to better automobile engine performance in terms of power and fuel economy through the use of microprocessors to monitor fuel injection. Digital technology allows movies and music to be available instantly over the Internet or through cable service, but it has also meant falling fortunes for movie rental shops such as Blockbuster and CD stores like Tower Records. Advances in nanotechnology are enabling companies to manufacture extremely small devices that are very energy efficient. Developing biotechnology, including gene manipulation techniques, is already providing new approaches to dealing with disease and agriculture. Researchers at George Washington University have identified a number of technological breakthroughs that are already having a significant impact on many industries:

■ **Portable information devices and electronic networking:** Combining the computing power of the personal computer, the networking of the Internet, the images of television, and the convenience of the telephone, tablets and Smartphones will soon be used by a majority of the population of industrialized nations to make phone calls, stay connected in business and personal relationships, and transmit documents and other data. Homes, autos, and offices are rapidly being connected (via wires and wirelessly) into intelligent networks that interact with one another. This trend is being accelerated by the development of *cloud computing*, in which a person can access their data anywhere through a Web connection.[27] This is being dramatically improved by companies like Microsoft who are releasing *cloud* versions of their Office package available for rent.[28] The traditional stand-alone desktop computer will someday join the manual typewriter as a historical curiosity.

- **Alternative energy sources:** The use of wind, geothermal, hydroelectric, solar, biomass, and other alternative energy sources should increase considerably. Over the past two decades, the cost of manufacturing and installing a photovoltaic solar-power system has decreased by 20% with every doubling of installed capacity.[29]

- **Precision farming:** The computerized management of crops to suit variations in land characteristics will make farming more efficient and sustainable. Farm equipment dealers such as Case and John Deere now add this equipment to tractors for an additional fee. It enables farmers to reduce costs, increase yields, and decrease environmental impact. The old system of small, low-tech farming is becoming less viable as large corporate farms increase crop yields on limited farmland for a growing population.

- **Virtual personal assistants:** Very smart computer programs that monitor e-mail, faxes, and phone calls will be able to take over routine tasks, such as writing a letter, retrieving a file, making a phone call, or screening requests. Acting like a secretary, a person's virtual assistant could substitute for a person at meetings or in dealing with routine actions.

- **Genetically altered organisms:** A convergence of biotechnology and agriculture is creating a new field of life sciences. Plant seeds can be genetically modified to produce more needed vitamins or to be less attractive to pests and more able to survive. Animals (including people) could be similarly modified for desirable characteristics and to eliminate genetic disabilities and diseases.

- **Smart, mobile robots:** Robot development has been limited by a lack of sensory devices and sophisticated artificial intelligence systems. Improvements in these areas mean that robots will be created to perform more sophisticated factory work, run errands, do household chores, and assist the disabled.[30]

Trends in the *economic* part of the societal environment can have an obvious impact on business activity. For example, an increase in interest rates means fewer sales of major home appliances. Why? A rising interest rate tends to be reflected in higher mortgage rates. Because higher mortgage rates increase the cost of buying a house, the demand for new and used houses tends to fall. Because most major home appliances are sold when people change houses, a reduction in house sales soon translates into a decline in sales of refrigerators, stoves, and dishwashers and reduced profits for everyone in the appliance industry. Changes in the price of oil have a similar impact upon multiple industries, from packaging and automobiles to hospitality and shipping.

The rapid economic development of Brazil, Russia, India, and China (often called the *BRIC* countries) is having a major impact on the rest of the world. By 2007, China had become the world's second-largest economy according to the World Bank. With India graduating more English-speaking scientists, engineers, and technicians than all other nations combined, it has become the primary location for the outsourcing of services, computer software, and telecommunications.[31] Eastern Europe has become a major manufacturing supplier to the European Union countries. According to the International Monetary Fund, emerging markets make up less than one-third of total world gross domestic product (GDP), but account for more than half of GDP growth.[32]

Trends in the *ecological* part of the environment have been accelerating at a pace that is difficult to stay up with. This element is focused upon the natural environment and its consideration/impacts upon the operation of a business. The effects of climate change on companies can be grouped into six categories of risks: regulatory, supply chain, product and technology, litigation, reputational, and physical.[33]

1. **Regulatory Risk:** Companies in much of the world were already subject to the first commitment period of the *Kyoto Protocol*, which required 37 industrialized countries and the European Community to reduce Greenhouse Gases (GHG) emissions to an average of 5% against 1990 levels. During the second commitment period, parties committed to reduce GHG emissions by at least 18% below 1990 levels in the eight-year period from 2013 to 2020. The European Union has an emissions trading program that allows companies that emit greenhouse gases beyond a certain point to buy additional allowances from other companies whose emissions are lower than that allowed. Companies can also earn credits toward their emissions by investing in emissions abatement projects outside their own firms. Although the United States withdrew from the Kyoto Protocol, various regional, state, and local government policies affect company activities in the United States. For example, seven Northeastern states, six Western states, and four Canadian provinces have adopted proposals to cap carbon emissions and establish carbon-trading programs.

2. **Supply Chain Risk:** Suppliers will be increasingly vulnerable to government regulations—leading to higher component and energy costs as they pass along increasing carbon-related costs to their customers. Global supply chains will be at risk from an increasing intensity of major storms and flooding. Higher sea levels resulting from the melting of polar ice will create problems for seaports. China, where much of the world's manufacturing is currently being outsourced, is becoming concerned with environmental degradation. Twelve Chinese ministries produced a report on global warming foreseeing a 5%–10% reduction in agricultural output by 2030; more droughts, floods, typhoons, and sandstorms; and a 40% increase in population threatened by plague.[34]

   The increasing scarcity of fossil-based fuel is already boosting transportation costs significantly. For example, Tesla Motors, the maker of an electric-powered sports car, transferred assembly of battery packs from Thailand to California because Thailand's low wages were more than offset by the costs of shipping thousand-pound battery packs across the Pacific Ocean.[35]

3. **Product and Technology Risk:** Environmental sustainability can be a prerequisite to profitable growth. Sixty percent of U.S. respondents to an Environics study stated that knowing a company is mindful of its impact on the environment and society makes them more likely to buy their products and services.[36] Carbon-friendly products using new technologies are becoming increasingly popular with consumers. Those automobile companies, for example, that were quick to introduce hybrid or alternative energy cars gained a competitive advantage.

4. **Litigation Risk:** Companies that generate significant carbon emissions face the threat of lawsuits similar to those in the tobacco, pharmaceutical, and building supplies (e.g., asbestos) industries. For example, oil and gas companies were sued for greenhouse gas emissions in the federal district court of Mississippi, based on the assertion that these companies contributed to the severity of Hurricane Katrina.

5. **Reputational Risk:** A company's impact on the environment can affect its overall reputation. The Carbon Trust, a consulting group, found that in some sectors the value of a company's brand could be at risk because of negative perceptions related to climate change. In contrast, a company with a good record of environmental sustainability may create a competitive advantage in terms of attracting and keeping loyal consumers, employees, and investors. For example, Wal-Mart's

pursuit of environmental sustainability as a core business strategy has helped soften its negative reputation as a low-wage, low-benefit employer. By setting objectives for its retail stores of reducing greenhouse gases by 20%, reducing solid waste by 25%, increasing truck fleet efficiency by 25%, and using 100% renewable energy, it is also forcing its suppliers to become more environmentally sustainable.[37] Tools have recently been developed to measure sustainability on a variety of factors. For example, the SAM (Sustainable Asset Management) Group of Zurich, Switzerland, has been assessing and documenting the sustainability performance of over 1000 corporations annually since 1999. SAM lists the top 15% of firms in its *Sustainability Yearbook* and classifies them into gold, silver, and bronze categories.[38]

BusinessWeek published its first list of the world's 100 most sustainable corporations January 29, 2007. The *Dow Jones Sustainability Indexes* and the *KLD Broad Market Social Index*, which evaluate companies on a range of environmental, social, and governance criteria are used for investment decisions.[39] Financial services firms, such as Goldman Sachs, Bank of America, JPMorgan Chase, and Citigroup have adopted guidelines for lending and asset management aimed at promoting clean-energy alternatives.[40]

6. **Physical Risk:** The direct risk posed by climate change includes the physical effects of droughts, floods, storms, and rising sea levels. Average Arctic temperatures have risen four to five degrees Fahrenheit (two to three degrees Celsius) in the past 50 years, leading to melting glaciers and sea levels rising one inch per decade.[41] Industries most likely to be affected are insurance, agriculture, fishing, forestry, real estate, and tourism. Physical risk can also affect other industries, such as oil and gas, through higher insurance premiums paid on facilities in vulnerable areas. Coca-Cola, for example, studies the linkages between climate change and water availability to decide the location of new bottling plants. The warming of the Tibetan plateau has led to a thawing of the permafrost—thereby threatening the newly-completed railway line between China and Tibet.[42]

Trends in the *political–legal* part of the societal environment have a significant impact not only on the level of competition within an industry but also on which strategies might be successful.[43] For example, periods of strict enforcement of U.S. antitrust laws directly affect corporate growth strategy. As large companies find it more difficult to acquire another firm in the same or a related industry, they are typically driven to diversify into unrelated industries.[44] High levels of taxation and constraining labor laws in Western European countries stimulate companies to alter their competitive strategies or find better locations elsewhere. It is because Germany has some of the highest labor and tax costs in Europe that German companies have been forced to compete at the top end of the market with high-quality products or else move their manufacturing to lower-cost countries.[45] Government bureaucracy can create regulations that make it almost impossible for a business firm to operate profitably in some countries. The World Bank report on red tape around the world found amazing examples of government bureaucracy, including: (1) A company in the Congo with a profit margin of 20% or more faces a tax bill of 340% of profits; (2) obtaining a construction permit in Russia requires 51 steps; (3) enforcing a contract through the courts takes 150 days in Singapore and 1,420 in India; (4) while winding up an insolvent firm, creditors in Japan can recover 92.7 cents on the dollar, those in Chad get nothing.[46]

The US$66 trillion global economy operates through a set of rules established by the World Trade Organization (WTO). Composed of 155 member nations and 29 observer nations, the WTO is a forum for governments to negotiate trade agreements and settle trade disputes. Originally founded in 1947 as the General

Agreement on Tariffs and Trade (GATT), the WTO was created in 1995 to extend the ground rules for international commerce. The system's purpose is to encourage free trade among nations with the least undesirable side effects. Among its principles is trade without discrimination. This is exemplified by its *most-favored nation* clause, which states that a country cannot grant a trading partner lower customs duties without granting them to all other WTO member nations. Another principle is that of lowering trade barriers gradually though negotiation. It implements this principle through a series of rounds of trade negotiations. As a result of these negotiations, industrial countries' tariff rates on industrial goods had fallen steadily to less than 4% by the mid-1990s. The WTO is currently negotiating its latest round of negotiations, called the Doha Round. The WTO is also in favor of fair competition, predictability of member markets, and the encouragement of economic development and reform. As a result of many negotiations, developed nations have started to allow duty-free and quota-free imports from almost all products from the least-developed countries.[47]

International Societal Considerations. Each country or group of countries in which a company operates presents a unique societal environment with a different set of sociocultural, technological, economic, ecological, and political–legal variables for the company to face. International societal environments vary so widely that a corporation's internal environment and strategic management process must be very flexible. Cultural trends in Germany, for example, have resulted in the inclusion of worker representatives in corporate strategic planning. Because Islamic law (*sharia*) forbids interest (*riba*), loans of capital in Islamic countries must be arranged on the basis of profit-sharing instead of interest rates.[48]

Differences in societal environments strongly affect the ways in which a **multinational corporation (MNC)**, a company with significant assets and activities in multiple countries, conducts its marketing, financial, manufacturing, and other functional activities. For example, Europe's lower labor productivity, due to a shorter work week and restrictions on the ability to lay off unproductive workers, forces European-based MNCs to expand operations in countries where labor is cheaper and productivity is higher.[49] Moving manufacturing to a lower-cost location, such as China, was a successful strategy during the 1990s, but a country's labor costs rise as it develops economically. For example, China required all firms in January 2008 to consult employees on material work-related issues, enabling the country to achieve its stated objective of having trade unions in all of China's non-state-owned enterprises. By September 2008, the All-China Federation of Trade Unions had signed with 80% of the largest foreign companies.[50] See the Global Issues feature to see how demand for SUVs has exploded in China.

To account for the many differences among societal environments from one country to another, consider **Table 4–3**. It includes a list of economic, technological, political–legal, and sociocultural variables for any particular country or region. For example, an important economic variable for any firm investing in a foreign country is currency convertibility. Without convertibility, a company cannot convert its money into currencies of other countries. Almost all nations allow for some method of currency conversion. As of 2016, only the Cuban national peso and the North Korean won are nonconvertible. In terms of sociocultural variables, many Asian cultures (especially China) are less concerned with a Western version of human rights than are European and North American cultures. Some Asians actually contend that U.S. companies are trying to impose Western human rights requirements on them in an attempt to make Asian products less competitive by raising their costs.[51]

GLOBAL issue

SUVS POWER ON IN CHINA

U.S. and European automakers are looking to China for most of their growth potential in the next two decades. The Chinese middle class is expected to grow to 600 million by 2020. That is a market that is equivalent to the ENTIRE population of the Unites States AND every country in the European Union combined.

This growing middle class in China (it stood at less than 300 million in 2012) has spurred a huge demand for sport utility vehicles (SUVs). Ford, BMW, Mercedes-Benz, and Porsche are all selling SUVs at a significant clip. The success of these brands spurred Chinese auto makers to dramatically grow their SUV offerings. Chinese automakers now sell 8 of the 10 bestselling sport utility vehicles.

The total SUV market in China is predicted to reach more than 7.04 million units in 2018, up from 4.32 million in 2014, according to researcher IHS Automotive.

Growing consumer prosperity is leading to the push for SUVs. *BusinessWeek* reported seeing the same trend in China that has been seen in the United States, with women in particular being drawn to the flexibility of the SUV. A Ford spokesperson said that "For Tiger Moms—and other moms—SUVs offer great appeal as the whole family can be transported safely and in style." The sharp increase in demand has drawn in the ultra-high-end car companies as well. Maserati and Lamborghini have both announced new SUVs for the Chinese market.

BMW has approached the market with products that they sell around the world, including the BMW X5. This is an example of a global organization. On the other hand, Mercedes-Benz is producing a Chinese-built GLK SUV that is tailored to the market. This is an example of a multidomestic organization. Figuring out how to address global markets is a key strategic area for any management team.

....

SOURCES: "How China Brands Took Over the World's Hottest SUV Market," *Bloomberg BusinessWeek* (April 16, 2015), (http://www.bloomberg.com/news/articles/2015-04-16/how-china-brands-took-over-the-world-s-hottest-suv-market); "China's Soccer Moms Want SUVs, Too," *Bloomberg BusinessWeek* (May 7, 2012), (www.businessweek.com/articles/2012-05-03/chinas-soccer-moms-want-suvs-too); Eurostat news release, "EU27 population 502.5 million at 1 January 2011." Accessed 5/30/13, http://epp.eurostat.ec.europa.eu/cache/ITY_PUBLIC/3-28072011-AP/EN/3-28072011-AP-EN.PDF).

TABLE 4–3	Some Important Variables in *International* Societal Environments			
Sociocultural	**Technological**	**Economic**	**Ecological**	**Political–Legal**
Customs, norms, values	Regulations on technology transfer	Economic development	Non-governmental groups	Form of government
Language	Energy availability/cost	Per capita income	Passion for environmental causes	Political ideology
Demographics	Natural resource availability	Climate	Infrastructure to handle recycling	Tax laws
Life expectancies	Transportation network	GDP trends		Stability of government
Social institutions	Skill level of workforce	Monetary and fiscal policies		Government attitude toward foreign companies
Status symbols	Patent-trademark protection	Unemployment levels		Regulations on foreign ownership of assets
Lifestyle	Internet availability	Currency convertibility		Strength of opposition groups
Religious beliefs	Telecommunication infrastructure	Wage levels		Trade regulations
Attitudes toward foreigners	Computer hacking technology	Nature of competition		Protectionist sentiment
Literacy level	New energy sources	Membership in regional economic associations—e.g., EU, NAFTA, ASEAN		Foreign policies
Human rights		Membership in World Trade Organization (WTO)		Terrorist activity
Environmentalism		Outsourcing capability		Legal system
"Sweatshops"		Global financial system		Global warming laws
Pension plans				Immigration laws
Health care				
Slavery				

Before planning its strategy for a particular international location, a company must scan that country's environment(s) for its similarities and differences when compared with the company's home country. Focusing only on developed nations may cause a corporation to miss important market opportunities. Although those nations may not have developed to the point that they have significant demand for a broad spectrum of products, they may very likely be on the threshold of rapid growth in the demand for specific products. Using the concept of entering where the competition is not, this may be an opportunity for a company to enter this market—before competition is established. The key is to be able to identify the *trigger point* when demand for a particular product or service is ready to boom.

Creating a Scanning System.   Although the Internet has opened up a tremendous volume of information, scanning and making sense of that data is one of the important skills of an effective manager. It is a daunting task for even a large corporation with many resources. To deal with this problem, in 2002 IBM created a tool called *WebFountain* to help the company analyze the vast amounts of environmental data available on the Internet. WebFountain is an advanced information discovery system designed to help extract trends, detect patterns, and find relationships within vast amounts of raw data. For example, IBM sought to learn whether there was a trend toward more positive discussions about e-business. Within a week, the company had data that experts within the company used to replace their hunches with analysis.

Scanning the Task Environment

As shown in **Figure 4–1**, a corporation's scanning of the environment includes analyses of all the relevant elements in the task environment. These analyses take the form of individual reports written by various people in different parts of the firm. At Procter & Gamble (P&G), for example, people from each of the brand management

FIGURE 4–1
Scanning External
Environment

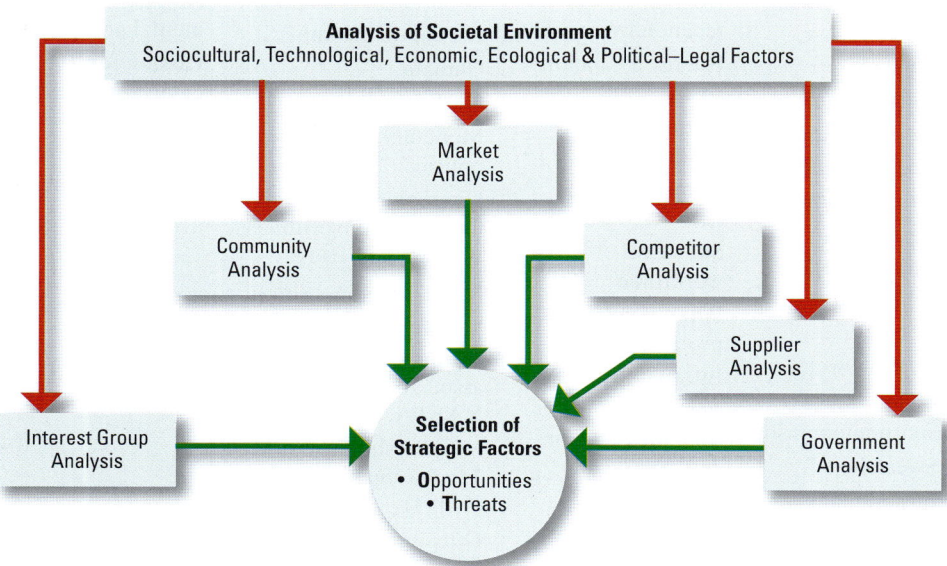

teams work with key people from the sales and market research departments to research and write a "competitive activity report" each quarter on each of the product categories in which P&G competes. People in purchasing also write similar reports concerning new developments in the industries that supply P&G. These and other reports are then summarized and transmitted up the corporate hierarchy for top management to use in strategic decision making. If a new development is reported regarding a particular product category, top management may then send memos asking people throughout the organization to watch for and report on developments in related product areas. The many reports resulting from these scanning efforts, when boiled down to their essentials, act as a detailed list of external strategic factors.

IDENTIFYING EXTERNAL STRATEGIC FACTORS

The origin of competitive advantage lies in the ability to identify and respond to environmental change well in advance of competition.[52] Although this seems obvious, why are some companies better able to adapt than others? One reason is because of differences in the ability of managers to recognize and understand external strategic issues and factors. Booz & Company found that companies that are most successful at avoiding surprises had a well-defined system that integrated planning, budgeting, and business reviews.[53]

No firm can successfully monitor all external factors. Choices must be made regarding which factors are important and which are not. Even though managers agree that strategic importance determines what variables are consistently tracked, they sometimes miss or choose to ignore crucial new developments.[54] Personal values and functional experiences of a corporation's managers, as well as the success of current strategies, are likely to bias both their perception of what is important to monitor in the external environment and their interpretations of what they perceive.[55]

This willingness to reject unfamiliar as well as negative information is called *strategic myopia*.[56] If a firm needs to change its strategy, it might not be gathering the appropriate external information to change strategies successfully. For example, when Daniel Hesse became CEO of Sprint Nextel in December 2007, he assumed that improving customer service would be one of his biggest challenges. He quickly discovered that none of the current Sprint Nextel executives were even thinking about the topic. "We weren't talking about the customer when I first joined," said Hesse. "Now this is the No. 1 priority of the company."[57]

Hesse insists that "great customer service costs less—when we were last in the industry, we were spending twice as much." By 2012, Sprint had closed down 29 call centers and was answering calls faster than ever. The second quarter of 2012 saw Sprint receiving the fewest calls ever from customers.[58]

Industry Analysis: Analyzing the Task Environment

4-3. Conduct an industry analysis to explain the competitive forces that influence the intensity of rivalry within an industry

An **industry** is a group of firms that produces a similar product or service, such as soft drinks or financial services. An examination of the important stakeholder groups, like suppliers and customers, in a particular corporation's task environment is a part of industry analysis.

PORTER'S APPROACH TO INDUSTRY ANALYSIS

Michael Porter, an authority on competitive strategy, contends that a corporation is most concerned with the intensity of competition within its industry. The level of this intensity is determined by basic competitive forces, as depicted in **Figure 4–2**. "The collective strength of these forces," he contends, "determines the ultimate profit potential in the industry, where profit potential is measured in terms of long-run return on invested capital."[59] In carefully scanning its industry, a corporation must assess the importance to its success of each of six forces: threat of new entrants, rivalry among existing firms, threat of substitute products or services, bargaining power of buyers, bargaining power of suppliers, and relative power of other stakeholders.[60] The stronger each of these forces is, the more limited companies are in their ability to raise prices and earn greater profits. Although Porter mentions only five forces, a sixth—other stakeholders—is added here to reflect the power that governments, local communities, and other groups from the task environment wield over industry activities.

Using the model in **Figure 4–2**, a high force can be regarded as a threat because it is likely to reduce profits. A low force, in contrast, can be viewed as an opportunity because it may allow the company to earn greater profits. In the short run, these forces act as constraints on a company's activities. In the long run, however, it may be possible for a company, through its choice of strategy, to change the strength of one or more of the forces to the company's advantage. For example, Dell's early use of the Internet to market its computers was an effective way to negate the bargaining power of distributors in the PC industry.

A strategist can analyze any industry by rating each competitive force as high, medium, or low in strength. For example, the global athletic shoe industry could be rated as follows: rivalry is high (Nike, Reebok, New Balance, Converse, and Adidas are strong competitors worldwide), threat of potential entrants is high (the industry has seen clothing firms such as UnderArmour and Fila as well as specialty shoe brands like the wildly popular Vibram Five Fingers shoes), threat of substitutes is low (other shoes

FIGURE 4–2
Forces Driving
Industry
Competition

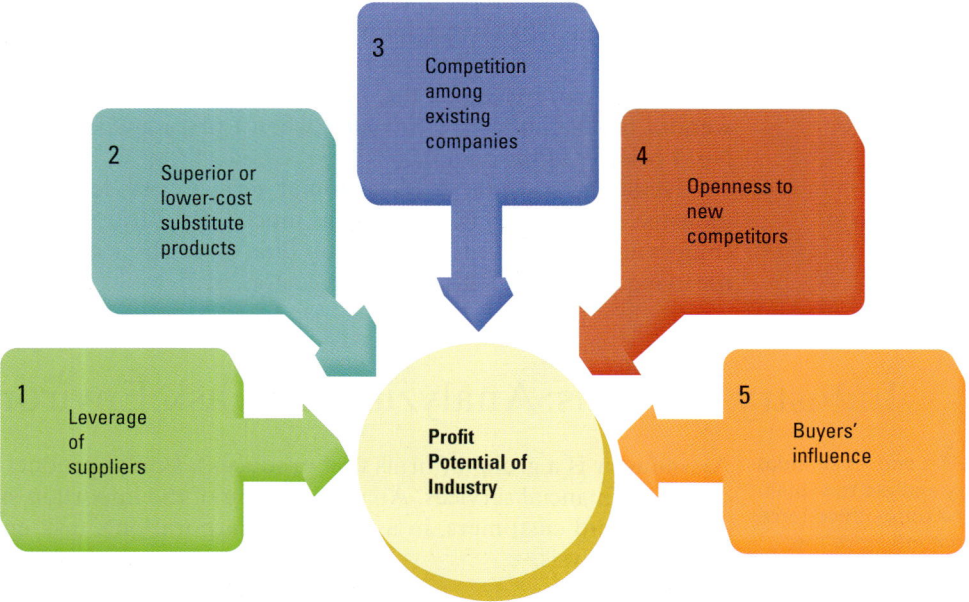

don't provide support for sports activities), bargaining power of suppliers is medium but rising (suppliers in Asian countries are increasing in size and ability), bargaining power of buyers is medium but increasing (prices are falling as the low-priced shoe market has grown to be half of the U.S.-branded athletic shoe market), and threat of other stakeholders is medium to high (government regulations and human rights concerns are growing). Based on current trends in each of these competitive forces, the industry's level of competitive intensity will continue to be high—meaning that sales increases and profit margins should continue to be modest for the industry as a whole.[61]

Threat of New Entrants

New entrants to an industry typically bring to it new capacity, a desire to gain market share, and potentially substantial resources. They are, therefore, threats to an established corporation. The threat of entry depends on the presence of entry barriers and the reaction that can be expected from existing competitors. An **entry barrier** is an obstruction that makes it difficult for a company to enter an industry. For example, no new, full-line domestic automobile companies have been successfully established in the United States since the 1930s (although Tesla is now growing its line of vehicles) because of the high capital requirements to build production facilities and to develop a dealer distribution network. Some of the possible barriers to entry are:

- **Economies of scale:** Scale economies in the production and sale of microprocessors, for example, gave Intel a significant cost advantage over any new rival.

- **Product differentiation:** Corporations such as Procter & Gamble and General Mills, which manufacture products such as Tide and Cheerios, create high entry barriers through their high levels of advertising and promotion.

- **Capital requirements:** The need to invest huge financial resources in manufacturing facilities in order to produce large commercial airplanes creates a significant barrier to entry to any competitor for Boeing and Airbus.

- **Switching costs:** Once a software program such as Excel or Word becomes established in an office, office managers are very reluctant to switch to a new program because of the high training costs.

- **Access to distribution channels:** Smaller new firms often have difficulty obtaining supermarket shelf space for their goods because large retailers charge for space on their shelves and give priority to the established firms who can pay for the advertising needed to generate high customer demand.

- **Cost disadvantages independent of size:** Once a new product earns sufficient market share to be accepted as the *standard* for that type of product, the maker has a key advantage. Microsoft's development of the first widely adopted operating system (MS-DOS) for the IBM-type personal computer gave it a significant competitive advantage over potential competitors. Its introduction of Windows helped to cement that advantage so that the Microsoft operating system is now on more than 90% of personal computers worldwide.

- **Government policy:** Governments can limit entry into an industry through licensing requirements by restricting access to raw materials, such as oil-drilling sites in protected areas.

Rivalry among Existing Firms

In most industries, corporations are mutually dependent. A competitive move by one firm can be expected to have a noticeable effect on its competitors and thus may cause retaliation. For example, the successful entry by companies such as Samsung and Amazon and unsuccessful entries by HP and RIM into a tablet industry previously dominated by Apple changed the level of competitive activity to such an extent that each new product change was quickly followed by similar moves from other tablet makers. The same is true of prices in the United States airline industry. According to Porter, intense rivalry is related to the presence of several factors, including:

- **Number of competitors:** When competitors are few and roughly equal in size, such as in the auto and major home appliance industries, they watch each other carefully to make sure they match any move by another firm with an equal countermove.

- **Rate of industry growth:** Any slowing in passenger traffic tends to set off price wars in the airline industry because the only path to growth is to take sales away from a competitor.

- **Product or service characteristics:** A product can be very unique, with many qualities differentiating it from others of its kind, or it may be a *commodity*, a product whose characteristics are the same, regardless of who sells it. For example, most people choose a gas station based on location and pricing because they view gasoline as a commodity.

- **Amount of fixed costs:** Because airlines must fly their planes on a schedule, regardless of the number of paying passengers for any one flight, some offer cheap standby fares whenever a plane has empty seats.

- **Capacity:** If the only way a manufacturer can increase capacity is in a large increment by building a new plant (as in the paper industry), it will run that new plant at full capacity to keep its unit costs as low as possible—thus producing so much that the selling price falls throughout the industry.

- **Height of exit barriers: Exit barriers** keep a company from leaving an industry. The brewing industry, for example, has a low percentage of companies that voluntarily leave the industry because breweries are specialized assets with few uses except for making beer.

- **Diversity of rivals:** Rivals that have very different ideas of how to compete are likely to cross paths often and unknowingly challenge each other's position. This happens frequently in the retail clothing industry when a number of retailers open outlets in the same location—thus taking sales away from each other. This is also likely to happen in some countries or regions when multinational corporations compete in an increasingly global economy.

Threat of Substitute Products or Services

A **substitute product** is a product that appears to be different but can satisfy the same need as another product. For example, texting is a substitute for e-mail, Stevia is a substitute for sugar, the Internet is a substitute for video stores, and bottled water is a substitute for a cola. Effective substitutes are a limiting factor for companies. To the extent that switching costs are low, substitutes may have a strong effect on an industry. Tea can be considered a substitute for coffee. If the price of coffee goes up high enough, coffee drinkers will slowly begin switching to tea. The price of tea thus puts a price ceiling on the price of coffee. Sometimes a difficult task, the identification of possible substitute products or services means searching for products or services that can perform the same function, even though they have a different appearance and may not appear to be easily substitutable.

The Bargaining Power of Buyers

Buyers affect an industry through their ability to force down prices, bargain for higher quality or more services, and play competitors against each other. A buyer or a group of buyers is powerful if some of the following factors hold true:

- A buyer purchases a large proportion of the seller's product or service (for example, oil filters purchased by a major automaker).

- A buyer has the potential to integrate backward by producing the product itself (for example, a newspaper chain could make its own paper).

- Alternative suppliers are plentiful because the product is standard or undifferentiated (for example, motorists can choose among many gas stations).

- Changing suppliers costs very little (for example, office supplies are easy to find).

- The purchased product represents a high percentage of a buyer's costs, thus providing an incentive to shop around for a lower price (for example, gasoline purchased for resale by convenience stores makes up half their total costs).

- A buyer earns low profits and is thus very sensitive to costs and service differences (for example, grocery stores have very small margins).

- The purchased product is unimportant to the final quality or price of a buyer's products or services and thus can be easily substituted without affecting the final product adversely (for example, electric wire bought for use in lamps).

The Bargaining Power of Suppliers

Suppliers can affect an industry through their ability to raise prices or reduce the quality of purchased goods and services. A supplier or supplier group is powerful if some of the following factors apply:

- The supplier industry is dominated by a few companies, but it sells to many (for example, the petroleum industry).

- Its product or service is unique and/or it has built up switching costs (for example, word processing software).

- Substitutes are not readily available (for example, electricity).

- Suppliers are able to integrate forward and compete directly with their present customers for example, a microprocessor producer such as Intel can make PCs).

- A purchasing industry buys only a small portion of the supplier group's goods and services and is thus unimportant to the supplier (for example, sales of lawn mower tires are less important to the tire industry than are sales of auto tires).

The Relative Power of Other Stakeholders

A sixth force should be added to Porter's list to include a variety of stakeholder groups from the task environment. Some of these groups are governments (if not explicitly included elsewhere), local communities, creditors (if not included with suppliers), trade associations, special-interest groups, unions (if not included with suppliers), shareholders, and complementors. According to Andy Grove, Chairman and past CEO of Intel, a **complementor** is a company (e.g., Microsoft) or an industry whose product works well with a firm's (e.g., Intel's) product and without which the product would lose much of its value.[62]

The importance of these stakeholders varies by industry. For example, environmental groups in Maine, Michigan, Oregon, and Iowa successfully fought to pass bills outlawing disposable bottles and cans, and thus deposits for most drink containers are now required. This effectively raised costs across the board, with the most impact on the marginal producers who could not internally absorb all these costs. The traditionally strong power of national unions in the United States' auto and railroad industries has effectively raised costs throughout these industries but is of little importance in computer software.

Industry Evolution

4-4. Discuss how industry maturity affects industry competitive forces

Over time, most industries evolve through a series of stages from growth through maturity to eventual decline. The strength of each of the six forces mentioned earlier varies according to the stage of industry evolution. The industry life cycle is useful for explaining and evaluating trends among the six forces that drive industry competition. For example, when an industry is new, people might buy the product, regardless of price, because it uniquely fulfills an existing need. This usually occurs in a **fragmented industry**—where no firm has a large market share, and each firm serves only a small piece of the total market in competition with others (for example, cleaning services).[63] As new competitors enter the industry, prices drop as a result of competition. Companies use the experience curve(discussed in **Chapter 5**) and economies of scale to reduce costs faster than the competition. Companies integrate to reduce costs even further sometimes by acquiring their suppliers and distributors. Competitors try to differentiate their products from one another's in order to avoid the fierce price competition common to a maturing industry.

By the time an industry enters maturity, products tend to become more like commodities. This is now a **consolidated industry**—dominated by a few large firms, each of which struggles to differentiate its products from those of the competition. As buyers become more sophisticated over time, purchasing decisions are based on better information. Price becomes a dominant concern, given a minimum level of quality and features, and profit margins decline. The automobile, petroleum, and major home appliance industries are examples of mature, consolidated industries, each controlled by a few large competitors. In the case of the United States' major home appliance industry, the industry changed from being a fragmented industry (pure competition) composed of hundreds of appliance manufacturers in the industry's early years to a consolidated industry (mature oligopoly) composed of three companies controlling over 90% of U.S. appliance sales. A similar consolidation is occurring now in European major home appliances.

As an industry moves through maturity toward possible decline, its products' growth rate of sales slows and may even begin to decrease. To the extent that exit barriers are low, firms begin converting their facilities to alternate uses or sell them to other firms. The industry tends to consolidate around fewer but larger competitors. The tobacco industry is an example of an industry currently that appeared to be in decline just a few years ago but has been re-born with the advent of e-cigarettes.

Categorizing International Industries

4-5. Categorize international industries based on their pressures for coordination and local responsiveness

According to Porter, worldwide industries vary on a continuum from multidomestic to global (see **Figure 4–3**).[64] **Multidomestic industries** are specific to each country or group of countries. This type of international industry is a collection of essentially domestic industries, such as retailing and insurance. The activities in a subsidiary of a multinational corporation (MNC) in this type of industry are essentially

INNOVATION issue

TAKING STOCK OF AN OBSESSION

It is worth periodically taking stock of innovations to understand their profound impact upon consumers, competitors, and perhaps in the following case, every business operation in the world. The Apple iPhone was released to great fanfare on June 29, 2007 and by mid-2012 more than 217 million had been sold. As of late 2014, the world had 7.2 billion mobile devices, and they're multiplying five times faster than the world population. In his book *iDisorder: Understanding Our Obsession with Technology and Overcoming Its Hold on Us*, psychologist Larry Rosen observes that "the iPhone has changed everything about how we relate to technology, for both good and bad."

The iPhone led the way to using a touchscreen for every aspect of the phone's use. The Apple focus on simplicity in design and functionality changed the way that phones would look and be used. The laptop computer was the state-of-the-art mobile business platform when the iPhone was released. More and more people not only realized that they could use their phone to keep up with e-mails, make calls, and check Web pages, but more importantly, they were exposed to the App for the first time.

The app (a staple of the iPhone's capability and increasingly for all devices) provides people with a means to achieve a result with a minimum of additional effort. Besides playing games, the business application apps have become a time-saver and confidence builder for people throughout the world. By July 2015, there were more than 1.8 million apps in the iTunes App Store up from half a million apps just three years earlier. Apps run the gamut from games that probably waste productive time, to translators that quickly help international travelers, to digital books that allow one to take any book with them wherever they go, to programs that allow one to access all their files wherever they may be.

Mobile access is accelerating with the introduction of the iPad tablet, along with the many look-alike tablets and Smartphones. Where will this all go? What will business communication look like in 10 years? No one predicted that a phone would become our computer.

....

SOURCES: P. Burrows, "The First Five Years of Mass Obsession," *Bloomberg BusinessWeek* (June 25, 2012), www.apple.com/iphone/built-in-apps/app-store.html; http://www.statista.com/statistics/268251/number-of-apps-in-the-itunes-app-store-since-2008/.

FIGURE 4–3
Continuum of International Industries

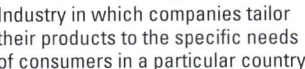

Multidomestic ⟷ **Global**

Industry in which companies tailor their products to the specific needs of consumers in a particular country.
- Retailing
- Insurance
- Banking

Industry in which companies manufacture and sell the same products, with only minor adjustments made for individual countries around the world.
- Automobiles
- Tires
- Television sets

---

independent of the activities of the MNC's subsidiaries in other countries. Within each country, it has a manufacturing facility to produce goods for sale within that country. The MNC is thus able to tailor its products or services to the very specific needs of consumers in a particular country or group of countries having similar societal environments.

Global industries, in contrast, operate worldwide, with MNCs making only small adjustments for country-specific circumstances. In a global industry an MNC's activities in one country are not significantly affected by its activities in other countries. MNCs in global industries produce products or services in various locations throughout the world and sell them, making only minor adjustments for specific country requirements. Examples of global industries are commercial aircraft, retail electronics, semiconductors, copiers, automobiles, watches, and tires. The largest industrial corporations in the world in terms of sales revenue are, for the most part, MNCs operating in global industries.

The factors that tend to determine whether an industry will be primarily multidomestic or primarily global are:

1. **Pressure for coordination** within the MNCs operating in that industry
2. **Pressure for local responsiveness** on the part of individual country markets

To the extent that the pressure for coordination is strong and the pressure for local responsiveness is weak for MNCs within a particular industry, that industry will tend to become global. In contrast, when the pressure for local responsiveness is strong and the pressure for coordination is weak for multinational corporations in an industry, that industry will tend to be multidomestic. Between these two extremes lie a number of industries with varying characteristics of both multidomestic and global industries. These are **regional industries**, in which MNCs primarily coordinate their activities within regions, such as the Americas or Asia.[65] The major home appliance industry is a current example of a regional industry becoming a global industry. Japanese appliance makers, for example, are major competitors in Asia, but only minor players in Europe or America. The dynamic tension between the pressure for coordination and the pressure for local responsiveness is contained in the phrase, "Think globally but act locally."

INTERNATIONAL RISK ASSESSMENT

Some firms develop elaborate information networks and computerized systems to evaluate and rank investment risks. Small companies may hire outside consultants to provide political-risk assessments. Among the many systems that exist to assess political and economic risks are the Business Environment Risk Index, the Economist Intelligence Unit, and Frost and Sullivan's World Political Risk Forecasts. The Economist Intelligence Unit, for example, provides a constant flow of analysis and forecasts on more than 200 countries and eight key industries. Regardless of the source of data, a firm must develop its own method of assessing risk. It must decide on its most important risk factors and then assign weights to each.

STRATEGIC GROUPS

A **strategic group** is a set of business units or firms that "pursue similar strategies with similar resources."[66] Categorizing firms in any one industry into a set of strategic groups is very useful as a way of better understanding the competitive environment.[67] Research shows that some strategic groups in the same industry are more profitable than others.[68] Because a corporation's structure and culture tend to reflect the kinds of strategies it follows, companies or business units belonging to a particular strategic group within the same industry tend to be strong rivals and tend to be more similar to each other than to competitors in other strategic groups within the same industry.[69]

For example, although McDonald's and Olive Garden are a part of the same industry, the restaurant industry, they have different missions, objectives, and strategies, and thus they belong to different strategic groups. They generally have very little in common and pay little attention to each other when planning competitive actions. Burger King and Wendy's, however, have a great deal in common with McDonald's in terms of their similar strategy of producing a high volume of low-priced meals targeted for sale to the average family. Consequently, they are strong rivals and are organized to operate similarly.

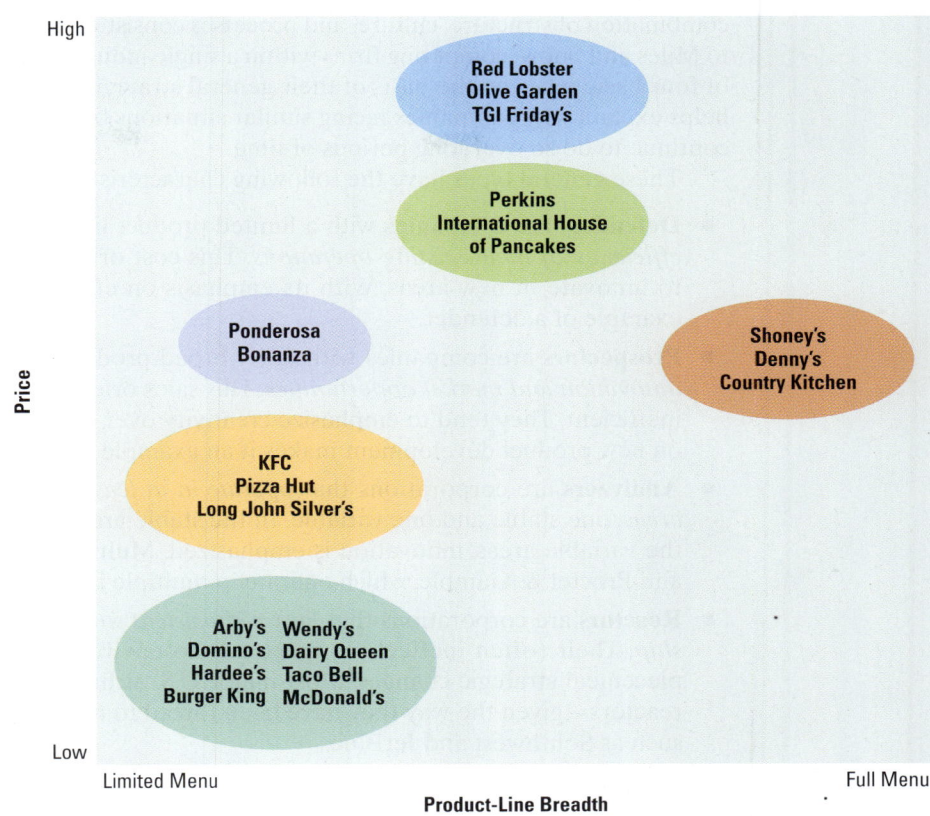

FIGURE 4–4
Mapping Strategic Groups in the U.S. Restaurant Chain Industry

Strategic groups in a particular industry can be mapped by plotting the market positions of industry competitors on a two-dimensional graph, using two strategic variables as the vertical and horizontal axes (**Figure 4–4**):

1. Select two broad characteristics, such as price and menu that differentiate the companies in an industry from one another.

2. Plot the firms, using these two characteristics as the dimensions.

3. Draw a circle around those companies that are closest to one another as one strategic group, varying the size of the circle in proportion to the group's share of total industry sales. (You could also name each strategic group in the restaurant industry with an identifying title, such as quick fast food or buffet-style service.)

Other dimensions, such as quality, service, location, or degree of vertical integration, could also be used in additional graphs of the restaurant industry to gain a better understanding of how the various firms in the industry compete. Keep in mind, however, that the two dimensions should not be highly correlated; otherwise, the circles on the map will simply lie along the diagonal, providing very little new information other than the obvious.

STRATEGIC TYPES

In analyzing the level of competitive intensity within a particular industry or strategic group, it is useful to characterize the various competitors for predictive purposes. A **strategic type** is a category of firms based on a common strategic orientation and a combination of structure, culture, and processes consistent with that strategy. According to Miles and Snow, competing firms within a single industry can be categorized into one of four basic types on the basis of their general strategic orientation.[70] This distinction helps explain why companies facing similar situations behave differently and why they continue to do so over long periods of time.[71]

These general types have the following characteristics:

- **Defenders** are companies with a limited product line that *focus on improving the efficiency of their existing operations*. This cost orientation makes them unlikely to innovate in new areas. With its emphasis on efficiency, Lincoln Electric is an example of a defender.

- **Prospectors** are companies with fairly broad product lines that *focus on product innovation and market opportunities*. This sales orientation makes them somewhat inefficient. They tend to emphasize creativity over efficiency. Frito Lay's emphasis on new product development makes it an example of a prospector.

- **Analyzers** are corporations that *operate in at least two different product-market areas*, one stable and one variable. In the stable areas, efficiency is emphasized. In the variable areas, innovation is emphasized. Multidivisional firms, such as BASF and Procter & Gamble, which operate in multiple industries, tend to be analyzers.

- **Reactors** are corporations that *lack a consistent strategy-structure-culture relationship*. Their (often ineffective) responses to environmental pressures tend to be piecemeal strategic changes. Most major U.S. airlines have recently tended to be reactors—given the way they have been forced to respond to more nimble airlines such as Southwest and JetBlue.

Dividing the competition into these four categories enables the strategic manager not only to monitor the effectiveness of certain strategic orientations, but also to develop scenarios of future industry developments (discussed later in this chapter).

HYPERCOMPETITION

Most industries today are facing an ever-increasing level of environmental uncertainty. They are becoming more complex and more dynamic. Industries that used to be multidomestic are becoming global. New flexible, aggressive, innovative competitors are moving into established markets to rapidly erode the advantages of large previously dominant firms. Distribution channels vary from country to country and are being altered daily through the use of sophisticated information systems. Closer relationships with suppliers are being forged to reduce costs, increase quality, and gain access to new technology. Companies learn to quickly imitate the successful strategies of market leaders, and it becomes harder to sustain any competitive advantage for very long. Consequently, the level of competitive intensity is increasing in most industries.

Richard D'Aveni contends that as this type of environmental turbulence reaches more industries, competition becomes **hypercompetition**. According to D'Aveni:

> *In hypercompetition the frequency, boldness, and aggressiveness of dynamic movement by the players accelerates to create a condition of constant disequilibrium and change. Market stability is threatened by short product life cycles, short product design cycles, new technologies, frequent entry by unexpected outsiders, repositioning by incumbents, and tactical redefinitions of market boundaries as diverse industries merge. In other words, environments escalate toward higher and higher levels of uncertainty, dynamism, heterogeneity of the players and hostility.[72]*

In hypercompetitive industries such as information technology, competitive advantage comes from an up-to-date knowledge of environmental trends and competitive activity, coupled with a willingness to risk a current advantage for a possible new advantage. Companies must be willing to *cannibalize* their own products (that is, replace popular products before competitors do so) in order to sustain their competitive advantage. (Hypercompetition is discussed in more detail in **Chapter 6**.)

Using Key Success Factors to Create an Industry Matrix

4-6. Identify key success factors and develop an industry matrix

Within any industry, there are usually certain variables—key success factors—that a company's management must understand in order to be successful. **Key success factors** (sometimes referred to as Key Performance Indicators) (KSF or KPI) are variables that can significantly affect the overall competitive positions of companies within any particular industry. They typically vary from industry to industry and are crucial to determining a company's ability to succeed within that industry. They are usually determined by the economic and technological characteristics of the industry and by the competitive weapons on which the firms in the industry have built their strategies.[73] For example, in the major home appliance industry, a firm must achieve low costs, typically by building large manufacturing facilities dedicated to making multiple versions of one type of appliance, such as washing machines. Because 60% of major home appliances in the United States are sold through "power retailers" such as Sears and Best Buy, a firm must have a strong presence in the mass merchandiser distribution channel. It must offer a full line of appliances and provide a just-in-time delivery system to keep store inventory and ordering costs to a minimum. Because the consumer expects reliability and durability in an appliance, a firm must have excellent process R&D. Any appliance manufacturer that is unable to deal successfully with these key success factors will not survive long in the U.S. market.

An **industry matrix** summarizes the key success factors within a particular industry. As shown in **Table 4–4**, the matrix gives a weight for each factor based on how important that factor is for success within the industry. The matrix also specifies how well various competitors in the industry are responding to each factor. To generate an industry matrix using two industry competitors (called A and B), complete the following steps for the industry being analyzed:

1. In Column 1 (Key Success Factors), list the 8 to 10 factors that appear to determine success in the industry.

TABLE 4–4	Industry Matrix					
Key Success Factors		**Weight**	**Company A Rating**	**Company A Weighted Score**	**Company B Rating**	**Company B Weighted Score**
	1	2	3	4	5	6
Total		1.00		=		=

SOURCE: T. L. Wheelen and J. D. Hunger, *Industry Matrix*. Copyright © 1997, 2001, and 2005 by Wheelen & Hunger Associates. Reprinted with permission.

2. In Column 2 (Weight), assign a weight to each factor, from 1.0 (Most Important) to 0.0 (Not Important) based on that factor's probable impact on the overall industry's current and future success. (All weights must sum to 1.0 regardless of the number of strategic factors.)

3. In Column 3 (Company A Rating), examine a particular company within the industry—for example, Company A. Assign a rating to each factor from 5 (Outstanding) to 1 (*Poor*) based on Company A's current response to that particular factor. Each rating is a judgment regarding how well that company is specifically dealing with each key success factor.

4. In Column 4 (Company A Weighted Score) multiply the weight in Column 2 for each factor by its rating in Column 3 to obtain that factor's weighted score for Company A.

5. In Column 5 (Company B Rating) examine a second company within the industry—in this case, Company B. Assign a rating to each key success factor from 5.0 (Outstanding) to 1.0 (Poor), based on Company B's current response to each particular factor.

6. In Column 6 (Company B Weighted Score) multiply the weight in Column 2 for each factor times its rating in Column 5 to obtain that factor's weighted score for Company B.

7. Finally, add the weighted scores for all the factors in Columns 4 and 6 to determine the total weighted scores for companies A and B. **The total weighted score indicates how well each company is responding to current and expected key success factors in the industry's environment.** Check to ensure that the total weighted score truly reflects the company's current performance in terms of profitability and market share. (An average company should have a total weighted score of 3.)

The industry matrix can be expanded to include all the major competitors within an industry through the addition of two additional columns for each additional competitor.

Competitive Intelligence

4-7. Construct strategic group maps to assess the competitive positions of firms in an industry

Most external environmental scanning is done on an informal and individual basis. Information is obtained from a variety of sources—suppliers, customers, industry publications, employees, industry experts, industry conferences, and the Internet.[74] For example, scientists and engineers working in a firm's R&D lab can learn about new products and competitors' ideas at professional meetings; someone from the purchasing department, speaking with supplier representatives' personnel, may also uncover valuable bits of information about a competitor. A study of product innovation found that 77% of all product innovations in scientific instruments and 67% in semiconductors and printed circuit boards were initiated by the customer in the form of inquiries and complaints.[75] In these industries, the sales force and service departments must be especially vigilant.

A recent survey of global executives by McKinsey & Company found that the single factor contributing most to the increasing competitive intensity in their industries was the improved capabilities of competitors.[76] Yet, without competitive intelligence, companies run the risk of flying blind in the marketplace. According to work by Ryall, firms can have competitive advantages simply because their rivals have erroneous beliefs about them.[77] This is why competitive intelligence has become an important part of environmental scanning in most companies.

Competitive intelligence (CI) is a formal program of gathering information on a company's competitors. Often called *business intelligence*, it is one of the fastest growing fields within strategic management. Research indicates that there is a strong association between corporate performance and competitive intelligence activities.[78] The 2015 Global Market Intelligence Survey found that more than 50% reported a high return on investment (ROI) on CI operations while 80% of competitive intelligence professionals gather information from social media. According to a 2011 survey of competitive intelligence by the Global Intelligence Alliance, nearly 70% of North American companies plan to increase their budgets for competitive intelligence. Ninety-four percent felt that they had benefited from their competitive intelligence efforts, while 42% of those companies without a competitive intelligence program intend to start one within the year.[79]

In about a third of the firms, the competitive/business intelligence function is housed in its own unit, with the remainder being housed within marketing, strategic planning, information services, business development (merger and acquisitions), product development, or other units.[80] Competitive Intelligence software maker Good-Data estimated that the total spent on competitive intelligence activities was more than US$25 billion in 2012.[81] At General Mills, for example, all employees have been trained to recognize and tap sources of competitive information. Janitors no longer simply place orders with suppliers of cleaning materials; they also ask about relevant practices at competing firms!

SOURCES OF COMPETITIVE INTELLIGENCE

Most corporations use outside organizations to provide them with environmental data. Firms such as A. C. Nielsen Co. provide subscribers with bimonthly data on brand share, retail prices, percentages of stores stocking an item, and percentages of stock-out stores. Strategists can use this data to spot regional and national trends as well as to assess market share. Information on market conditions, government regulations, industry competitors, and new products can be bought from "information brokers" such as Market Research.com (Findex), LexisNexis (company and country analyses), and Finsbury Data Services. Company and industry profiles are generally available from the Hoover's Web site at www.hoovers.com. Many business corporations have established their own in-house libraries and computerized information systems to deal with the growing mass of available information.

The Internet has changed the way strategists engage in environmental scanning. It provides the quickest means to obtain data on almost any subject. Although the scope and quality of Internet information is increasing rapidly, it is also littered with "noise," misinformation, and utter nonsense. Unlike the library, the Internet lacks the tight bibliographic control standards that exist in the print world. There is no ISBN or Dewey Decimal System to identify, search, and retrieve a document. Many Web documents lack the name of the author and the date of publication. A Web page providing useful information may be accessible on the Web one day and gone the next. Unhappy ex-employees, far-out extremists, and prank-prone hackers create "blog" Web sites to attack and discredit an otherwise reputable corporation. Rumors with no basis in fact are spread via chat rooms and personal Web sites. This creates a serious problem for researchers. How can one evaluate the information found on the Internet? For a way to evaluate intelligence information, see the Strategy Highlight on evaluating competitive intelligence.

STRATEGY highlight

EVALUATING COMPETITIVE INTELLIGENCE

A basic rule in intelligence gathering is that before a piece of information can be in any report or briefing, it must first be evaluated in two ways. *First*, the source of the information should be judged in terms of its truthfulness and reliability. How trustworthy is the source? How well can a researcher rely upon it for truthful and correct information? One approach is to rank the reliability of the source on a scale from A (extremely reliable), B (reliable), C (unknown reliability), D (probably unreliable), to E (very questionable reliability). The reliability of a source can be judged on the basis of the author's credentials, the organization sponsoring the information, and past performance, among other factors. *Second*, the information or data should be judged in terms of its likelihood of being correct. The correctness of the data may be ranked on a scale from 1 (correct), 2 (probably correct), 3 (unknown), 4 (doubtful), to 5 (extremely doubtful). The correctness of a piece of data or information can be judged on the basis of its agreement with other bits of separately obtained information or with a general trend supported by previous data. For every piece of information found on the Internet, for example, list not only the URL of the Web page, but also the evaluation of the information from A1 (trusted) to E5 (highly questionable). Information found through library research in sources such as Moody's Industrials, Standard & Poor's, or Value Line can generally be evaluated as having a reliability of A. The correctness of the data can still range anywhere from 1 to 5, but in most instances is likely to be either 1 or 2, but probably no worse than 3 or 4. Web sites are quite different.

Web sites, such as those sponsored by the U.S. Securities and Exchange Commission (www.sec.gov), *The Economist* (www.economist.com), or Hoovers Online (www.hoovers.com) are extremely reliable. Company-sponsored Web sites are generally reliable, but are not the place to go for trade secrets, strategic plans, or proprietary information. For one thing, many firms think of their Web sites primarily in terms of marketing and provide little data aside from product descriptions and distributors. Other companies provide their latest financial statements and links to other useful Web sites. Nevertheless, some companies in very competitive industries may install software on their Web site to ascertain a visitor's Web address. Visitors from a competitor's domain name are thus screened before they are allowed to access certain Web sites. They may not be allowed beyond the product information page or they may be sent to a bogus Web site containing misinformation. Cisco Systems, for example, uses its Web site to send visitors coming in from other high-tech firm Web sites to a special Web page asking if they would like to apply for a job at Cisco!

Some companies choose to use industrial espionage or other intelligence-gathering techniques to get their information straight from their competitors. According to a survey by the American Society for Industrial Security, PricewaterhouseCoopers, and the United States Chamber of Commerce, Fortune 1000 companies lost an estimated US$59 billion in one year alone due to the theft of trade secrets.[82] By using current or former competitors' employees and private contractors, some firms attempt to obtain trade secrets, technology, business plans, and pricing strategies. In a well-documented case, Avon Products hired private investigators to retrieve from a public dumpster documents (some of them shredded) that Mary Kay Corporation had thrown away. Oracle Corporation hired detectives to obtain the trash of a think tank that had defended the pricing practices of its rival Microsoft. Studies reveal that 32% of the trash typically found next to copy machines contains confidential company data, in addition to personal data (29%) and gossip (39%).[83] Even P&G, which defends itself like a fortress from information leaks, is vulnerable. A competitor was able to learn the precise launch date of a concentrated laundry detergent in Europe when one of its people visited the factory where machinery was being made. Simply asking a few questions about what a certain machine did, whom it was for, and when it would be delivered was all that was necessary.

Some of the firms providing investigatory services are Altegrity Inc. with 11,000 employees in 30 countries, Fairfax, Security Outsourcing Solutions, Trident Group, and Diligence Inc.[84]

Trident, for example, specializes in helping American companies enter the Russian market and is a U.S.-based corporate intelligence firm founded and managed by former veterans of Russian intelligence services, like the KGB.[85]

To combat the increasing theft of company secrets, the U.S. government passed the Economic Espionage Act in 1996. The law makes it illegal (with fines up to US$5 million and 10 years in jail) to steal any material that a business has taken "reasonable efforts" to keep secret and that derives its value from not being known.[86] The Society of Competitive Intelligence Professionals (www.scip.org) urges strategists to stay within the law and to act ethically when searching for information. The society states that illegal activities are foolish because the vast majority of worthwhile competitive intelligence is available publicly via annual reports, Web sites, and libraries. Unfortunately, a number of firms hire "kites," consultants with questionable reputations, who do what is necessary to get information when the selected methods do not meet SPIC ethical standards or are illegal. This allows the company that initiated the action to deny that it did anything wrong.[87]

MONITORING COMPETITORS FOR STRATEGIC PLANNING

The primary activity of a competitive intelligence unit is to monitor **competitors**—organizations that offer the same, similar, or substitutable products or services in the business area in which a particular company operates. To understand a competitor, it is important to answer the following 10 questions:

1. Why do your competitors exist? Do they exist to make profits or just to support another unit?

2. Where do they add customer value—higher quality, lower price, excellent credit terms, or better service?

3. Which of your customers are the competitors most interested in? Are they cherry-picking your best customers, picking the ones you don't want, or going after all of them?

4. What is their cost base and liquidity? How much cash do they have? How do they get their supplies?

5. Are they less exposed with their suppliers than your firm? Are their suppliers better than yours?

6. What do they intend to do in the future? Do they have a strategic plan to target your market segments? How committed are they to growth? Are there any succession issues?

7. How will their activity affect your strategies? Should you adjust your plans and operations?

8. How much better than your competitor do you need to be in order to win customers? Do either of you have a competitive advantage in the marketplace?

9. Will new competitors or new ways of doing things appear over the next few years? Who is a potential new entrant?

10. If you were a customer, would you choose your product over those offered by your competitors? What irritates your current customers? What competitors solve these particular customer complaints?[88]

To answer these and other questions, competitive intelligence professionals utilize a number of analytical techniques. In addition to the previously discussed industry forces analysis, and strategic group analysis, some of these techniques can be found in Porter's four-corner exercise, Treacy and Wiersema's value disciplines, Gilad's blind spot analysis, and war gaming.[89] Done right, competitive intelligence is a key input to strategic planning.

Forecasting

4-8. Develop an industry scenario as a forecasting technique

Environmental scanning provides reasonably hard data on the present situation and current trends, but intuition and luck are needed to accurately predict whether these trends will continue. The resulting forecasts are, however, usually based on a set of assumptions that may or may not be valid.

DANGER OF ASSUMPTIONS

Faulty underlying assumptions are the most frequent cause of forecasting errors. Nevertheless, many managers who formulate and implement strategic plans rarely consider that their success is based on a series of basic assumptions. Many strategic plans are simply based on projections of the current situation. For example, few people in 2007 expected the price of oil (light, sweet crude, also called West Texas intermediate) to rise above US$80 per barrel and were extremely surprised to see the price approach US$150 by July 2008, especially as the price had been around US$20 per barrel in 2002. U.S. auto companies in particular had continued to design and manufacture large cars, pick-up trucks, and SUVs under the assumption of gasoline being available for around US$2.00 a gallon. Market demand for these types of cars collapsed when the price of gasoline passed US$3.00 to reach US$4.00 a gallon in July 2008. The volatile oil market saw the price of a gallon of gas drop below US$2.00 again in 2015. Car makers shifted again to larger SUVs and trucks while trying to increase efficiency in all vehicles. In another example, many banks made a number of questionable mortgages based on the assumption that housing prices would continue to rise as they had in the past. When housing prices began to fall in late 2006, these "sub-prime" mortgages were almost worthless—causing the banking crisis that gripped the nation for the next three plus years. The lesson here: Assumptions can be dangerous to your business's health!

USEFUL FORECASTING TECHNIQUES

Various techniques are used to forecast future situations. They do not tell the future; they merely state what can be, not what will be. As such, they can be used to form a set of reasonable assumptions about the future. Each technique has its proponents and its critics. A study of nearly 500 of the world's largest corporations revealed trend extrapolation to be the most widely practiced form of forecasting—over 70% use this technique either occasionally or frequently.[90] Simply stated, *extrapolation* is the extension of present trends into the future. It rests on the assumption that the world is reasonably consistent and changes slowly in the short run. Time-series methods are approaches of this type. They attempt to carry a series of historical events forward into the future. The basic problem with extrapolation is that a historical trend is based on a series of patterns or relationships among so many different variables that a change in any one can drastically alter the future direction of the trend. As a rule of thumb, the further back into the past you can find relevant data supporting the trend, the more confidence you can have in the prediction.

Brainstorming, expert opinion, and statistical modeling are also very popular forecasting techniques. *Brainstorming* is a non-quantitative approach that simply requires the presence of people with some knowledge of the situation in order to concept out the future. The basic ground rule is to propose ideas without first mentally screening them. No criticism is allowed. "Wild" ideas are encouraged. Ideas should build on previous ideas until a consensus is reached.[91] This is a good technique to use with operating managers who have more faith in "gut feel" than in more quantitative number-crunching techniques. *Expert opinion* is a non-quantitative technique in which experts in a particular area attempt to forecast likely developments. This type of forecast is based on the ability of a knowledgeable person(s) to construct probable future developments based on the interaction of key variables. One application, developed by the RAND Corporation, is the *Delphi Technique*, in which separate experts independently assess the likelihoods of specified events. These assessments are combined and sent back to each expert for fine-tuning until agreement is reached. These assessments are most useful if they are shaped into several possible scenarios that allow decision makers to more fully understand their implication.[92] *Statistical modeling* is a quantitative technique that attempts to discover causal or at least explanatory factors that link two or more time series together. Examples of statistical modeling are regression analysis and other econometric methods. Although very useful in the grasping of historic trends, statistical modeling, such as trend extrapolation, is based on historical data. As the patterns of relationships change, the accuracy of the forecast deteriorates.

Prediction markets is a recent forecasting technique enabled by easy access to the Internet. As emphasized by James Surowiecki in *The Wisdom of Crowds*, the conclusions of large groups can often be better than those of experts because such groups can aggregate a large amount of dispersed wisdom.[93] Prediction markets are small-scale electronic markets, frequently open to any employee, that tie payoffs to measurable future events, such as sales data for a computer workstation, the number of bugs in an application, or product usage patterns. These markets yield prices on prediction contracts—prices that can be interpreted as market-aggregated forecasts.[94] Companies including Microsoft, Google, and Eli Lilly have asked their employees to participate in prediction markets by betting on whether products will sell, when new offices will open, and whether profits will be high in the next quarter. Early predictions have been exceedingly accurate.[95] Intrade.com offers a free Web site in which people can buy or sell various predictions in a manner similar to buying or selling common stock. On August 17, 2012, for example, Intrade.com listed the bidding price for democratic presidential candidate Barack Obama as US$5.62 compared to US$4.26 for Mitt Romney. Thus far, prediction markets have not been documented for long-term forecasting, so its value in strategic planning has not yet been established. Other forecasting techniques, such as *cross-impact analysis (CIA)* and *trend-impact analysis (TIA)*, have not established themselves successfully as regularly employed tools.[96]

Scenario writing is the most widely used forecasting technique after trend extrapolation. Originated by Royal Dutch Shell, scenarios are focused descriptions of different likely futures presented in a narrative fashion. A scenario thus may be merely a written description of some future state, in terms of key variables and issues, or it may be generated in combination with other forecasting techniques. Often called scenario planning, this technique has been successfully used by 3M, Levi Strauss, General Electric, United Distillers, Electrolux, British Airways, and Pacific Gas and Electricity, among others.[97] According to Mike Eskew, Chairman and CEO of United Parcel Service, UPS uses scenario writing to envision what its customers might need 5 to 10 years in the future.[98]

An **industry scenario** is a forecasted description of a particular industry's likely future. Such a scenario is developed by analyzing the probable impact of future societal forces on key groups in a particular industry. The process may operate as follows:[99]

1. Examine possible shifts in the natural environment and in societal variables globally.
2. Identify uncertainties in each of the six forces of the task environment (i.e., potential entrants, competitors, likely substitutes, buyers, suppliers, and other key stakeholders).
3. Make a range of plausible assumptions about future trends.
4. Combine assumptions about individual trends into internally consistent scenarios.
5. Analyze the industry situation that would prevail under each scenario.
6. Determine the sources of competitive advantage under each scenario.
7. Predict competitors' behavior under each scenario.
8. Select the scenarios that are either most likely to occur or most likely to have a strong impact on the future of the company. Use these scenarios as assumptions in strategy formulation.

The Strategic Audit: A Checklist for Environmental Scanning

4-9. Use publicly available information to conduct competitive intelligence

One way of scanning the environment to identify opportunities and threats is by using the Strategic Audit found in **Appendix 1.A** at the end of **Chapter 1**. The audit provides a checklist of questions by area of concern. For example, Part III of the audit examines the natural, societal, and task environments. It looks at the societal environment in terms of economic, technological, political–legal, and sociocultural forces. It also considers the task environment (industry) in terms of the threat of new entrants, the bargaining power of buyers and suppliers, the threat of substitute products, rivalry among existing firms, and the relative power of other stakeholders.

Synthesis of External Factors

4-10. Construct an EFAS table that summarizes external environmental factors

After strategic managers have scanned the natural, societal, and task environments and identified a number of likely external factors for their particular corporation, they may want to refine their analysis of these factors by using a form such as that given in **Table 4–5**. Using an **EFAS table** (External Factors Analysis Summary) is one way to organize the external factors into the generally accepted categories of opportunities

TABLE 4–5	External Factor Analysis Summary (EFAS Table): Maytag as Example				
External Factors	**Weight**	**Rating**	**Weighted Score**	**Comments**	
	1	2	3	4	5
Opportunities					
▪ Economic integration of European Community	.20	4.1	.82	Acquisition of Hoover	
▪ Demographics favor quality appliances	.10	5.0	.50	Maytag quality	
▪ Economic development of Asia	.05	1.0	.05	Low Maytag presence	
▪ Opening of Eastern Europe	.05	2.0	.10	Will take time	
▪ Trend to "Super Stores"	.10	1.8	.18	Maytag weak in this channel	
Threats					
▪ Increasing government regulations	.10	4.3	.43	Well positioned	
▪ Strong U.S. competition	.10	4.0	.40	Well positioned	
▪ Whirlpool and Electrolux strong globally	.15	3.0	.45	Hoover weak globally	
▪ New product advances	.05	1.2	.06	Questionable	
▪ Japanese appliance companies	.10	1.6	.16	Only Asian presence in Australia	
Total Scores	1.00		3.15		

NOTES:

1. List opportunities and threats (8–10) in Column 1.
2. Weight each factor from 1.0 (Most Important) to 0.0 (Not Important) in Column 2 based on that factor's probable impact on the company's strategic position. **The total weights must sum to 1.00.**
3. Rate each factor from 5.0 (Outstanding) to 1.0 (Poor) in Column 3 based on the company's response to that factor.
4. Multiply each factor's weight times its rating to obtain each factor's weighted score in Column 4.
5. Use Column 5 (comments) for the rationale used for each factor.
6. Add the individual weighted scores to obtain the total weighted score for the company in Column 4. This tells how well the company is responding to the factors in its external environment.

SOURCE: Thomas L. Wheelen. Copyright © 1982, 1985, 1987, 1988, 1989, 1990, 1991, 1998, and every year after that. Kathryn E. Wheelen solely owns all of (Dr.) Thomas L. Wheelen's copyrighted materials. Kathryn E. Wheelen requires written reprint permission for each book that this material is to be printed in. Thomas L. Wheelen and J. David Hunger, copyright © 1991–first year "External Factor Analysis Summary" (EFAS) appeared in this text (4th ed). Reprinted by permission of the copyright holders.

and threats, as well as to analyze how well a particular company's management (rating) is responding to these specific factors in light of the perceived importance (weight) of these factors to the company. To generate an EFAS Table for the company being analyzed, complete the following steps:

1. In Column 1 (External Factors), list the 8 to 10 most important opportunities and threats facing the company.
2. In Column 2 (Weight), assign a weight to each factor from 1.0 (Most Important) to 0.0 (Not Important) based on that factor's probable impact on a particular company's current strategic position. The higher the weight, the more important is this factor to the current and future success of the company. (All weights must sum to 1.0 regardless of the number of factors.)

3. In Column 3 (Rating), assign a rating to each factor from 5.0 (Outstanding) to 1.0 (Poor) based on that particular company's specific response to that particular factor. Each rating is a judgment regarding how well the company is currently dealing with each specific external factor.

4. In Column 4 (Weighted Score), multiply the weight in Column 2 for each factor times its rating in Column 3 to obtain that factor's weighted score.

5. In Column 5 (Comments), note why a particular factor was selected and how its weight and rating were estimated.

6. Finally, add the weighted scores for all the external factors in Column 4 to determine the total weighted score for that particular company. The **total weighted** score indicates how well a particular company is responding to current and expected factors in its external environment. The score can be used to compare that firm to other firms in the industry. Check to ensure that the total weighted score truly reflects the company's current performance in terms of profitability and market share.? **The total weighted score for an average firm in an industry is always 3.0.**

As an example of this procedure, **Table 4–5** includes a number of external factors for Maytag Corporation with corresponding weights, ratings, and weighted scores provided. This table is appropriate for 1995, long before Maytag was acquired by Whirlpool. Note that Maytag's total weight was 3.15, meaning that the corporation was slightly above average in the major home appliance industry at that time.

End of Chapter SUMMARY

Wayne Gretzky was one of the most famous people ever to play professional ice hockey. He wasn't very fast. His shot was fairly weak. He was usually last in his team in strength training. He tended to operate in the back of his opponent's goal, anticipating where his team members would be long before they got there and fed them passes so unsuspected that he would often surprise his own team members. In an interview with *Time* magazine, Gretzky stated that the key to winning is skating not to where the puck is but to where it is going to be. "People talk about skating, puck handling and shooting, but the whole sport is angles and caroms, forgetting the straight direction the puck is going, calculating where it will be diverted, factoring in all the interruptions," explained Gretzky.[100]

Environmental scanning involves monitoring, collecting, and evaluating information in order to understand the current trends in the natural, societal, and task environments. The information is then used to forecast whether these trends will continue or whether others will take their place. How will developments in the natural environment affect the world? What kind of developments can we expect in the societal environment to affect our industry? What will an industry look like in 10 to 20 years? Who will be the key competitors? Who is likely to fall by the wayside? We use this information to make certain assumptions about the future—assumptions that are then used in strategic planning. In many ways, success in the business world is like ice hockey: The key to winning is not to assume that your industry will continue as it is now but to assume that the industry will change and to make sure your company will be in position to take advantage of those changes.

Pearson MyLab Management®

Go to **mymanagementlab.com** to complete the problems marked with this icon .

KEY TERMS

analyzers (p. 148)
competitive intelligence (p. 151)
competitors (p. 153)
complementor (p. 143)
consolidated industry (p. 144)
defenders (p. 148)
EFAS table (p. 156)
entry barriers (p. 141)
environmental scanning (p. 126)
environmental uncertainty (p. 126)
exit barrier (p. 142)

fragmented industry (p. 144)
global industries (p. 145)
hypercompetition (p. 148)
industry (p. 139)
industry analysis (p. 127)
industry matrix (p. 149)
industry scenario (p. 156)
key success factor (p. 149)
multidomestic industries (p. 144)
multinational corporation (MNC)
   (p. 136)

natural environment (p. 127)
new entrants (p. 141)
prospectors (p. 148)
reactors (p. 148)
regional industries (p. 146)
societal environment (p. 127)
STEEP analysis (p. 130)
strategic group (p. 146)
strategic type (p. 147)
substitute product (p. 142)
task environment (p. 127)

Pearson MyLab Management®

Go to **mymanagementlab.com** for the following assisted-graded writing questions:

4-1. How does STEEP analysis aid in the development of the strategy of a company?

4-2. The effects of climate change on companies can be grouped into six categories of risks. Use any two of these to explain the impact upon the resort hotel industry?

DISCUSSION QUESTIONS

4-3. Explain why environmental analysis is considered to be an important activity for the strategy formulation process of an organization.

4-4. How do corporations analyze the societal environment? Is STEEP Analysis an appropriate tool?

4-5. Differentiate between fragmented and consolidated industry.

4-6. What are the most significant implications of a strategic group analysis of an organization?

4-7. How is Porter's five force framework related to the identification of key success factors?

STRATEGIC PRACTICE EXERCISE

How far should people in a business firm go in gathering competitive intelligence? Where do you draw the line?

4-1. Take a look at each of the following approaches that a person might use to gather information about competitors. Which do you believe are techniques that you might use? Why?

- Using a "clipping agency" to scour the popular press for information on competitors
- Being a customer of competitors

- Creating a phony company to act as a potential customer
- Reverse engineering competitors' products
- Hiring consultants who have worked for competitors
- Asking suppliers about your competitors
- Hiring companies to collect and examine competitors' garbage

- Changing the interview process for a new position when a candidate is from a direct competitor
- Taking public tours of competitors' facilities
- Using social media to cause competitors harm
- Using trade shows and conferences to learn more about competitors

- Hiring key employees from competitors
- What other approaches came to your mind as you considered the above? Add those ideas and evaluate the approach.

4-2. Go to the Web site of the Society for Competitive Intelligence Professionals (www.scip.org). What does SCIP say about these approaches?

NOTES

1. J. B. Thomas, S. M. Clark, and D. A. Gioia, "Strategic Sense-making and Organizational Performance: Linkages Among Scanning, Interpretation, Action, Outcomes," *Academy of Management Journal* (April 1993), pp. 239–270; J. A. Smith, "Strategies for Start-Ups," *Long Range Planning* (December 1998), pp. 857–872.
2. M. Birshan, R. Dye, and S. Hall, "Creating More Value with Corporate Strategy: McKinsey Global Survey Results," (2011), (www.mckinseyquarterly.com/surveys/creating_more_value_with_corporate_strategy_McKinsey_Global_Survey_results_2733).
3. W. E. Stead and J. G. Stead, *Sustainable Strategic Management* (Armonk, NY: M. E. Sharpe, 2004), p. 6.
4. F. Montabon, R. Sroufe, and R. Narasimhan, "An Examination of Corporate Reporting, Environmental Management Practices and Firm Performance," *Journal of Operations Management* (August 2007), pp. 998–1014.
5. P. Lasserre and J. Probert, "Competing on the Pacific Rim: High Risks and High Returns," *Long Range Planning* (April 1994), pp. 12–35.
6. J. J. McGonagle, "Mapping and Anticipating the Competitive Landscape," *Competitive Intelligence Magazine* (March–April 2007), p. 49.
7. www.census.gov/popclock/.
8. M. J. Cetron and O. Davies, "Trends Now Shaping the Future," *The Futurist* (March–April 2005), pp. 28–29; M. Cetron and O. Davies, "Trends Shaping Tomorrow's World," *The Futurist* (March–April 2008), pp. 35–52.
9. "Trend: Urbane Urban Portraits," *BusinessWeek* (April 28, 2008), p. 57.
10. "Old Europe," *The Economist* (October 2, 2004), pp. 49–50.
11. M. J. Cetron and O. Davies, "Trends Now Shaping the Future," *The Futurist* (March–April 2005), p. 30.
12. "The Incredible Shrinking Country," *The Economist* (November 13, 2004), pp. 45–46.
13. D. Levin, "Tradition Under Stress," *AARP Bulletin* (July–August 2008), pp. 16–18.
14. J. Wyatt, "Playing the Woofie Card," *Fortune* (February 6, 1995), pp. 130–132.
15. www.news.walgreens.com/article_display.cfm?article_id=831 (accessed January, 2016); http://news.walgreens.com/fact-sheets/store-count-by-state.htm; http://www.walgreens.com/topic/about/press/facts.jsp (accessed January, 2016).
16. M. Arndt, "Zimmer: Growing Older Gracefully," *BusinessWeek* (June 9, 2003), pp. 82–84.
17. "Healthy Eating" Public Health Law Center—William Mitchell College of Law (2012), (www.publichealthlawcenter.org/topics/healthy-eating).
18. "Chile Bans Toys in Fast Food to Attack Child Obesity," *Fox News Latino* (August 2, 2012), (www.latino.foxnews.com/latino/lifestyle/2012/08/02/chile-bans-toys-in-fast-food-to-attack-child-obesity accessed January, 2016).
19. H. Yen, "Empty Nesters Push Growth of Pet Health Care Businesses," *The* (Ames, IA) *Tribune* (September 27, 2003), p. C8; "Industry Statistics and Trends—2012," American Pet Products Association, (www.americanpetproducts.org/press_industrytrends.asp); "Pampering Your Pet," *St. Cloud (MN) Times* (September 8, 2007), p. 3A.
20. "Chocolate Candy Market in the U.S.: Trends and Opportunities in Premium, Gourmet and Mass Market Products," *Packaged Facts* (www.packagedfacts.com/chocolate-2505082).
21. S. Tavernise, "Married Couples Are No Longer a Majority, Census Finds," *The New York Times*, May 26, 2011, (www.nytimes.com/2011/05/26/us/26marry.html).
22. "The Power of One," *Entrepreneur* (June 2007), p. 28.
23. "Unmarried Childbearing," Centers for Disease Control and Prevention, 2012, (www.cdc.gov/nchs/fastats/unmarry.html accessed January, 2016).
24. N. Irvin II, "The Arrival of the Thrivals," *The Futurist* (March–April 2004), pp. 16–23.
25. "The Trouble with Migrants," *The Economist* (November 24, 2007), pp. 56–57.
26. G. Cheeseman, "Bottled Water Marketing Campaigns Target Minorities," (November 29, 2011), (www.triplepundit.com/2011/11/bottled-water-brands-target-minorities/).
27. E. Knorr and G. Gruman, "What Cloud Computing Really Means," *InfoWorld* (2012), (www.infoworld.com/d/cloud-computing/what-cloud-computing-really-means-031).
28. K. Boehret, "Is Hotmail Hotter Now than It's Outlook.com?" *The Wall Street Journal* (August 1, 2012), (http://online.wsj.com/article/SB10000872396390444226904577561131545052576.html?KEYWORDS=microsoft+and+cloud).
29. P. Lorenz, D. Pinner, and T. Seitz, "The Economics of Solar Power," *McKinsey Quarterly* (June 2008), p. 2.

30. W. E. Halal, "The Top 10 Emerging Technologies," *Special Report* (World Future Society, 2000).

31. M. J. Cetron, "Economics: Prospects for the 'Dragon' and the 'Tiger,'" *Futurist* (July–August 2004), pp. 10–11; "A Less Fiery Dragon," *The Economist* (December 1, 2007), p. 92.

32. "Investing Without Borders: A Different Approach to Global Investing," *T. Rowe Price Report* (Fall 2007), p. 1.

33. J. Lash and F. Wellington, "Competitive Advantage on a Warming Planet," *Harvard Business Review* (March 2007), pp. 95–102.

34. "Melting Asia," *The Economist* (June 7, 2008), pp. 29–32.

35. P. Engardia, "Can the U.S. Bring Jobs Back from China?" *BusinessWeek* (June 30, 2008), pp. 39–43.

36. D. Rigby, "Growth through Sustainability," Presentation to the 2008 Annual Meeting of the Consumer Industries Governors, World Economic Forum (January 24, 2008).

37. J. Carey and L. Woellert, "Global Warming: Here Comes the Lawyers," *BusinessWeek* (October 30, 2006), pp. 34–36.

38. C. Laszlo, *Sustainable Value: How the World's Leading Companies Are Doing Well by Doing Good* (Stanford: Stanford University Press, 2008), pp. 89–99.

39. R. Ringger and S. A. DiPizza, *Sustainability Yearbook 2008* (PricewaterhouseCoopers, 2008).

40. L. T. Mendonca and J. Oppenheim, "Investing in Sustainability: An Interview with Al Gore and David Blood," *McKinsey Quarterly* (May 2007).

41. A. J. Hoffman, *Getting Ahead of the Curve: Corporate Strategies that Address Climate Change* (Ann Arbor: University of Michigan, 2006), p. 2.

42. J. K. Bourne Jr., "Signs of Change," *National Geographic* (Special Report on Changing Climate, 2008), pp. 7–21.

43. F. Dobbin and T. J. Dowd, "How Policy Shapes Competition: Early Railroad Foundings in Massachusetts," *Administrative Science Quarterly* (September 1997), pp. 501–529.

44. A. Shleifer and R. W. Viskny, "Takeovers in the 1960s and the 1980s: Evidence and Implications," in R. P. Rumelt, D. E. Schendel, and D. J. Teece (Eds.), *Fundamental Issues in Strategy: A Research Agenda* (Boston: Harvard Business School Press, 1994), pp. 403–418.

45. "The Problem with Solid Engineering," *The Economist* (May 20, 2006), pp. 71–73.

46. "Doing Business," *The Economist* (October 22, 2011), (www.economist.com/node/21533395).

47. Web site, *World Trade Organization*, www.wto.org (accessed August 3, 2012).

48. "Islamic Finance: West Meets East," *The Economist* (October 25, 2003), p. 69.

49. "Giants Forced to Dance," *The Economist* (May 26, 2007), pp. 67–68.

50. "Membership Required," *The Economist* (August 2, 2008), p. 66.

51. J. Naisbitt, *Megatrends Asia* (New York: Simon & Schuster, 1996), p. 79.

52. I. M. Cockburn, R. M. Henderson, and S. Stern, "Untangling the Origins of Competitive Advantage," *Strategic Management Journal* (October–November, 2000), Special Issue, pp. 1123–1145.

53. J. Kerins and C. McNeese, "No Surprises: Creating an Effective "Early Warning" System," (October 2008), (www.booz.com/media/uploads/no_surprises.pdf).

54. H. Wissema, "Driving through Red Lights," *Long Range Planning* (October 2002), pp. 521–539; B. K. Boyd and J. Fulk, "Executive Scanning and Perceived Uncertainty: A Multidimensional Model," *Journal of Management* (Vol. 22, No. 1, 1996), pp. 1–21.

55. P. G. Audia, E. A. Locke, and K. G. Smith, "The Paradox of Success: An Archival and a Laboratory Study of Strategic Persistence Following Radical Environmental Change," *Academy of Management Journal* (October 2000), pp. 837–853; M. L. McDonald and J. D. Westphal, "Getting By with the Advice of Their Friends: CEOs Advice Networks and Firms' Strategic Responses to Poor Performance," *Administrative Science Quarterly* (March 2003), pp. 1–32; R. A. Bettis and C. K. Prahalad, "The Dominant Logic: Retrospective and Extension," *Strategic Management Journal* (January 1995), pp. 5–14; J. M. Stofford and C. W. F. Baden-Fuller, "Creating Corporate Entrepreneurship," *Strategic Management Journal* (September 1994), pp. 521–536; J. M. Beyer, P. Chattopadhyay, E. George, W. H. Glick, and D. Pugliese, "The Selective Perception of Managers Revisited," *Academy of Management Journal* (June 1997), pp. 716–737.

56. H. I. Ansoff, "Strategic Management in a Historical Perspective," in *International Review of Strategic Management* (Vol. 2, No. 1, 1991), D. E. Hussey (Ed.), (Chichester, England: Wiley, 1991), p. 61.

57. S. E. Ante, "Sprint's Wake-Up Call," *BusinessWeek* (March 3, 2008), p. 54.

58. I. Fried, "Sprint CEO Hesse: Good Customer Service Costs Less," *All Things D* (August 7, 2012), (www.allthingsd.com/20120807/sprint-ceo-hesse-good-customer-service-costs-less accessed January, 2016).

59. M. E. Porter, *Competitive Strategy* (New York: The Free Press, 1980), p. 3.

60. This summary of the forces driving competitive strategy is taken from Porter, *Competitive Strategy*, pp. 7–29.

61. M. McCarthy, "Rivals Scramble to Topple Nike's Sneaker Supremacy," *USA Today* (April 3, 2003), pp. B1–B2; S. Holmes, "Changing the Game on Nike," *BusinessWeek* (January 22, 2007), p. 80.

62. A. S. Grove, "Surviving a 10x Force," *Strategy & Leadership* (January/February 1997), pp. 35–37.

63. A fragmented industry is defined as one whose market share for the leading four firms is equal to or less than 40% of total industry sales. See M. J. Dollinger, "The Evolution of Collective Strategies in Fragmented Industries," *Academy of Management Review* (April 1990), pp. 266–285.

64. M. E. Porter, "Changing Patterns of International Competition," *California Management Review* (Winter 1986), pp. 9–40.

65. A. M. Rugman, *The Regional Multinationals: MNEs and Global Strategic Management* (Cambridge: Cambridge University Press, 2005).

66. K. J. Hatten and M. L. Hatten, "Strategic Groups, Asymmetrical Mobility Barriers, and Contestability," *Strategic Management Journal* (July–August 1987), p. 329.

67. J. C. Short, D. J. Ketchen Jr., T. B. Palmer, and G. T. M. Hult, "Firm, Strategic Group, and Industry Influences on Performance," *Strategic Management Journal* (February 2007), pp. 147–167; J. D. Osborne, C. I. Stubbart, and A. Ramaprasad, "Strategic Groups and Competitive Enactment: A Study of Dynamic Relationships Between Mental Models and Performance," *Strategic Management Journal* (May 2001), pp. 435–454; A. Fiegenbaum and H. Thomas, "Strategic Groups as Reference Groups: Theory, Modeling and Empirical Examination of Industry and Competitive Strategy," *Strategic Management Journal* (September 1995), pp. 461–476; H. R. Greve, "Managerial Cognition and the Mimetic Adoption of Market Positions: What You See Is What You Do," *Strategic Management Journal* (October 1998), pp. 967–988.

68. G. Leask and D. Parker, "Strategic Groups, Competitive Groups and Performance Within the U.K. Pharmaceutical Industry: Improving Our Understanding of the Competitive Process," *Strategic Management Journal* (July 2007), pp. 723–745.

69. C. C. Pegels, Y. I. Song, and B. Yang, "Management Heterogeneity, Competitive Interaction Groups, and Firm Performance," *Strategic Management Journal* (September 2000), pp. 911–923; W. S. Desarbo and R. Grewal, "Hybrid Strategic Groups," *Strategic Management Journal* (March 2008), pp. 293–317.

70. R. E. Miles and C. C. Snow, *Organizational Strategy, Structure, and Process* (New York: McGraw-Hill, 1978). See also D. J. Ketchen Jr., "An Interview with Raymond E. Miles and Charles C. Snow," *Academy of Management Executive* (November 2003), pp. 97–104.

71. B. Kabanoff and S. Brown, "Knowledge Structures of Prospectors, Analyzers, and Defenders: Content, Structure, Stability, and Performance," *Strategic Management Journal* (February 2008), pp. 149–171.

72. R. A. D'Aveni, *Hypercompetition* (New York: The Free Press, 1994), pp. xiii–xiv.

73. C. W. Hofer and D. Schendel, *Strategy Formulation: Analytical Concepts* (St. Paul, MN: West Publishing Co., 1978), p. 77.

74. "Information Overload," *Journal of Business Strategy* (January–February 1998), p. 4.

75. E. Von Hipple, *Sources of Innovation* (New York: Oxford -University Press, 1988), p. 4.

76. "An Executive Takes on the Top Business Trends: A McKinsey Global Survey," *McKinsey Quarterly* (April 2006).

77. M. D. Ryall, "Subjective Rationality, Self-Confirming Equilibrium, and Corporate Strategy," *Management Science* (Vol. 49, 2003), pp. 936–949.

78. C. H. Wee and M. L. Leow, "Competitive Business Intelligence in Singapore," *Journal of Strategic Marketing* (Vol. 2, 1994), pp. 112–139.

79. Global Market Intelligence Survey 2015 (https:// dfsm9194vna0o.cloudfront.net/1605036-0-MBrainMISurvey2015.pdf); Miller, G. 2011. "Online Retailers will spend more $$$ on competitive intelligence in 2012," Upstream Commerce (November 19, 2011), (www.upstreamcommerce. com/blog/2011/11/19/north-american-companies-spend-bit-on-competitive-intelligence-2012 accessed January, 2016).

80. D. Fehringer, B. Hohhof, and T. Johnson, "State of the Art: Competitive Intelligence," Research Report of the *Competitive Intelligence Foundation* (2006), p. 6.

81. A. Andreescu, "GoodData Delivers Record-Breaking Second Quarter 2012," (August 6, 2012), (www.gooddata .com/blog/gooddata-delivers-record-breaking-second-quarter-2012).

82. E. Iwata, "More U.S. Trade Secrets Walk Out Door with Foreign Spies," *USA Today* (February 13, 2003), pp. B1, B2.

83. "Twenty-nine Percent Spy on Co-Workers," *USA Today* (August 19, 2003), p. B1.

84. M. Orey, "Corporate Snoops," *BusinessWeek* (October 9, 2006), pp. 46–49; E. Javers, "Spies, Lies, & KPMG," *BusinessWeek* (February 26, 2007), pp. 86–88; "Altegrity to Acquire Kroll, the World's Leading Risk Consulting Firm," from Marsh & McLennan, *Business Wire* (www.businesswire.com/news/home/20100607005989/en /altegrity-acquire-kroll-world-leading-risk-consulting).

85. E. Javers, "I Spy—For Capitalism," *BusinessWeek* (August 13, 2007), pp. 54–56.

86. B. Flora, "Ethical Business Intelligence in NOT Mission Impossible," *Strategy & Leadership* (January/February 1998), pp. 40–41.

87. A. L. Penenberg and M. Berry, *Spooked: Espionage in Corporate America* (Cambridge, MA: Perseus Publishing, 2000).

88. T. Kendrick and J. Blackmore, "Ten Things You Really Need to Know About Competitors," *Competitive Intelligence Magazine* (September–October 2001), pp. 12–15.

89. For the percentage of CI professionals using each analytical technique, see A. Badr, E. Madden, and S. Wright, "The Contributions of CI to the Strategic Decision Making Process: Empirical Study of the European Pharmaceutical Industry," *Journal of Competitive Intelligence and Management* (Vol. 3, No. 4, 2006), pp. 15–35; and D. Fehringer, B. Hohhof, and T. Johnson, "State of the Art: Competitive Intelligence," Research Report of the *Competitive Intelligence Foundation* (2006).

90. H. E. Klein and R. E. Linneman, "Environmental Assessment: An International Study of Corporate Practices," *Journal of Business Strategy* (Summer 1984), p. 72.

91. A. F. Osborn, *Applied Imagination* (NY: Scribner, 1957); R. C. Litchfield, "Brainstorming Reconsidered: A Goal-Based View," *Academy of Management Review* (July 2008), pp. 649–668; R. I. Sutton, "The Truth About Brainstorming," *Inside Innovation*, insert to *BusinessWeek* (September 26, 2006), pp. 17–21.

92. R. S. Duboff, "The Wisdom of Expert Crowds," *Harvard Business Review* (September 2007), p. 28.

93. J. Surowiecki, *The Wisdom of Crowds* (NY: Doubleday, 2004).

94. R. Dye, "The Promise of Prediction Markets: A Roundtable," *McKinsey Quarterly* (April 2008), pp. 83–93.

95. C. R. Sunstein, "When Crowds Aren't Wise," *Harvard Business Review* (September 2006), pp. 20–21.

96. See L. E. Schlange and U. Juttner, "Helping Managers to Identify the Key Strategic Issues," *Long Range Planning* (October 1997), pp. 777–786, for an explanation and application of the cross-impact matrix.

97. G. Ringland, *Scenario Planning: Managing for the Future* (Chichester, England: Wiley, 1998); N. C. Georgantzas and W. Acar, *Scenario-Driven Planning: Learning to Manage Strategic Uncertainty* (Westport, CN: Quorum Books, 1995); L. Fahey and R. M. Randall (Eds.), *Learning from the Future: Competitive Foresight Scenarios* (New York: John Wiley & Sons, 1998).

98. M. Eskew, "Stick with Your Vision," *Harvard Business Review* (July–August 2007), pp. 56–57. This process of scenario development is adapted from M. E. Porter, *Competitive Advantage* (New York: The Free Press, 1985), pp. 448–470.

99. This process of scenario development is adapted from M. E. Porter, *Competitive Advantage* (New York: The Free Press, 1985), pp. 448–470.

100. H. C. Sashittal and A. R. Jassawalla, "Learning from Wayne Gretzky," *Organizational Dynamics* (Spring 2002), pp. 341–355.

CHAPTER **5**

Organizational Analysis and Competitive Advantage

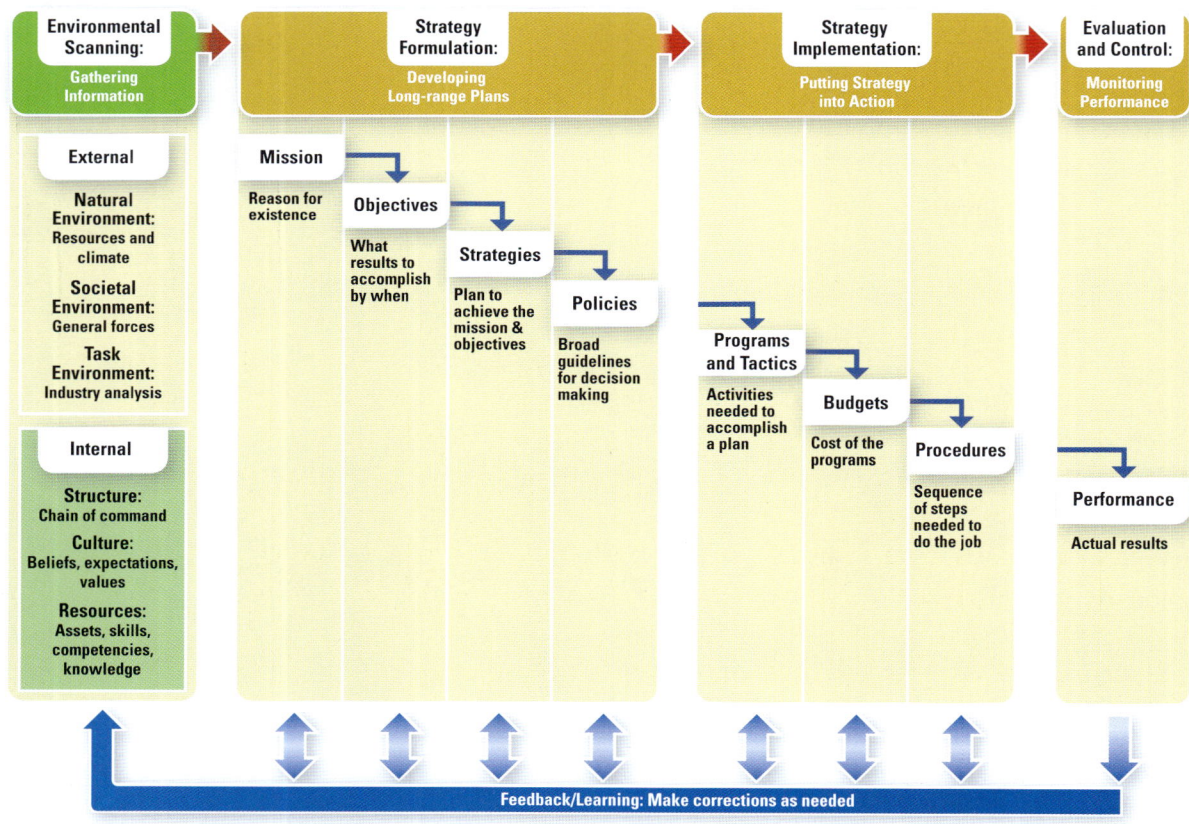

| Environmental Scanning: Gathering Information | | Strategy Formulation: Developing Long-range Plans | | | | Strategy Implementation: Putting Strategy into Action | | | Evaluation and Control: Monitoring Performance |

External

Natural Environment: Resources and climate

Societal Environment: General forces

Task Environment: Industry analysis

Internal

Structure: Chain of command

Culture: Beliefs, expectations, values

Resources: Assets, skills, competencies, knowledge

Mission — Reason for existence

Objectives — What results to accomplish by when

Strategies — Plan to achieve the mission & objectives

Policies — Broad guidelines for decision making

Programs and Tactics — Activities needed to accomplish a plan

Budgets — Cost of the programs

Procedures — Sequence of steps needed to do the job

Performance — Actual results

Feedback/Learning: Make corrections as needed

Pearson MyLab Management®

⭐ **Improve Your Grade!**

Over 10 million students improved their results using the Pearson MyLabs. Visit **mymanagementlab.com** for simulations, tutorials, and end-of-chapter problems.

Learning Objectives

After reading this chapter, you should be able to:

5-1. Apply the resource-based view of the firm and the VRIO framework to determine core and distinctive competencies

5-2. Explain company business models and how they can be imitated

5-3. Use value chain to assess the activities of an industry and of an organization

5-4. Explain why different organizational structures are utilized in business

5-5. Assess a company's corporate culture and how it might affect a proposed strategy

5-6. Construct an IFAS Table that summarizes internal factors

Understanding Capabilities—Bombardier and the C-Series Aircraft

Bombardier started in 1942 as a commercial snowmobile company in Quebec, Ontario to take advantage of the breakthrough multipassenger snowmobile that Joseph-Armand Bombardier created back in 1937. Over the years, the company adapted and diversified, first into a multipassenger truck manufacturer for hard to reach locations and then, in his quest to develop the perfect personal snowmobile, he created the Ski-Doo in 1959. Riding the back of the phenomenally successful Ski-Doo, the company acquired rail/ transportation companies and became a leader in the industry during the 1960s and 1970s.

It was in 1986 that the company acquired Canadair and moved aggressively into the aerospace industry. The company scrapped Canadair's wide-body jet and, in 1989, released the first CRJ regional aircraft for which the company has been so well known. It is hard to travel to smaller airports in the modern era without spending some time in a CRJ.

Over the next few years the company acquired storied names in the industry including Learjet and de Havilland and, in 1995, it was one of the very first companies to introduce fractional aircraft ownership with Flexjet! All of these strategic moves worked well for Bombardier as they were a dominant player in a market where the competition was generally absent. The two behemoths in the aircraft manufacturing industry are Boeing and Airbus. Both concentrate on larger aircraft that have longer range capabilities.

The Bombardier Company was profitable, growing, and financially sound in 2008 when they announced plans to take on Boeing and Airbus by entering the single-aisle wide-body jet market. This move instantly put them into a field of competition that managed by different rules and demanded new skills from both the sales and engineering sides. Bombardier grossly underestimated the depth of those capabilities.

So sure was the Pierre Beaudoin (CEO in 2008 and third generation member of the founding family) that Bombardier's new C-Series would be successful that he refused to offer bulk discounts to the major carriers as was common in the wide-body aircraft industry. The C-Series was hit by numerous missteps and delays as the company tried to move into larger jet production.

Pierre Beaudoin stepped down in 2015 as the company continued to spiral downward. The C-Series has yet to make any real penetration in the market with orders of less than 250 planes (and none in the past 1½ years) as of 12/31/15 compared to 3,072 orders for Boeing's 737 and 4,471 for Airbus's 320. As the investment of billions in the program was underway, the company decided to launch two new business jets further stretching resources.

The company has invested over $5 billion in the C-Series alone and has had a net negative cash burn for the past five years. The stock is now worth one-tenth of what it was in 2011 and the company is asking for a bailout from the Canadian government as they lay off nearly 10% of their workforce.

SOURCES: S. Deveau & F. Tomesco, "Why Bombardier Is Struggling to Build Bigger Planes," *Bloomberg Business*, February 4, 2016; A. Petroff, "Bombardier cutting 7,000 jobs," *CNN Money*; February 17, 2016 (money.cnn.com/2016/02/17/news/companies/bombardier-job-cuts-canada-europe/index.html); http://www.bombardier.com/en/about-us/history.html; F. Tomesco, "Quebec eyes fresh Bombardier aid absent federal investment," *The Globe and Mail*, February 10, 2016, http://www.theglobeandmail.com /report-on-business/quebec-eyes-fresh-bombardier-aid-absent-federal-investment/article28701038/

A Resource-Based Approach to Organizational analysis—Vrio

5-1. Apply the resource-based view of the firm and the VRIO framework to determine core and distinctive competencies

Scanning and analyzing the external environment for opportunities and threats is necessary for the firm to be able to understand its competitive environment and its place in that environment. It is the absolute starting place for strategic analysis. However, in order for the organization to thrive, the senior leadership team must look within the corporation itself to identify *internal strategic factors*—critical *strengths and weaknesses* that are likely to determine whether a firm will be able to take advantage of opportunities while avoiding threats. This internal scanning, often referred to as **organizational analysis**, is concerned with identifying, developing, and taking advantage of an organization's resources and competencies.

CORE AND DISTINCTIVE COMPETENCIES

Resources are an organization's assets and are thus the basic building blocks of the organization. They include *tangible assets* (such as its plant, equipment, finances, and location), *human assets* (the number of employees, their skills, and motivation), and *intangible assets* (such as its technology [patents and copyrights], culture, and reputation).[1] **Capabilities** refer to a corporation's ability to exploit its resources. They consist of business processes and routines that manage the interaction among resources to turn inputs into outputs. For example, a company's marketing capability can be based on the interaction among its marketing specialists, distribution channels, and salespeople. A capability is functionally based and is resident in a particular function. Thus, there are marketing capabilities, manufacturing capabilities, and human resource management capabilities. When these capabilities are constantly being changed and reconfigured to make them more adaptive to an uncertain environment, they are called *dynamic capabilities*.[2] A **competency** is a cross-functional integration and coordination of capabilities. For example, a competency in new product development in one division of a corporation may be the consequence of integrating information systems capabilities, marketing capabilities, R&D capabilities, and production capabilities within the division. **A core competency** is a collection of competencies that crosses divisional boundaries, is widespread within the corporation, and is something that the corporation can do exceedingly well. Thus, new product development is a core competency if it goes beyond one division.[3] For example, a core competency of Avon Products is its expertise in door-to-door selling. FedEx has a core competency in its application of information technology to all its operations. A company must continually reinvest in a core competency or risk its becoming a *core rigidity* or *deficiency*—that is, a strength that over time matures and becomes a weakness.[4] Although it is typically not an asset in the accounting sense, a core competency is a very valuable capability—it does not "wear out" with use. In general, the more core competencies are used, the more refined they get, and the more valuable they become. When unique resources and/or core competencies are superior to those of the competition, they are called **distinctive competencies**. For example, General Electric is well known for its distinctive competency in management development. Its executives are sought out by other companies hiring top managers.[5]

Resources and capabilities are only of value if they provide the organization an ability to make extraordinary returns. The resource-based approach is a well-researched, very effective means of analyzing resources and capabilities in order to determine which might provide the organization with real competitive advantages.

The approach used today has its roots in works by Wernerfelt in 1984 followed by an effective operationalization by Jay Barney who first proposed a VRIN framework that he later developed into the **VRIO framework** of analysis, proposing four questions to evaluate a firm's competencies:

1. **Valuable:** Does it provide customer value and competitive advantage?
2. **Rareness:** Does only one other competitor or preferably do no competitors possess it at relatively the same level?
3. **Imitability: Do the competitors have the financial ability** (viewed in the widest sense) to imitate?
4. **Organization:** Is the firm organized to exploit the resource?

If the answer to each of these questions is *yes* for a particular competency, it is considered to be a strength and thus a distinctive competence.[6] This should provide the company with a possible competitive advantage and lead to higher performance.[7]

Let's look at each of the elements and how you can use them to evaluate resources and capabilities. Each resource or capability (R/C) of the firm should be examined separately. Only if they pass all of the four elements are they true competitive advantages.

In order for a resource/capability to be, valuable it must allow the organization to either charge more for its offerings than competitors do for theirs or have a lower cost structure than those of the competitors. This is generally accomplished by providing a value proposition for the customer that exceeds that of the competitors. The customers are drawn to the organization by the improved value proposition. Tesla has been able to consistently charge a premium price for a battery powered car because of a set of distinctive competencies. If it fails at Valuable, then this R/C generally falls into one of two categories – either it is part of the table stakes of the industry and simply expected or it is something that the organization can consider for elimination.

If it passes the Valuable test, then the approach moves to examine the rareness of the R/C. In order for it to be useful as a competitive advantage it must not be possessed by the competitors of the organization. The rule of thumb is that if one competitor has the same resource/capability at even the equivalent level then it is still relatively rare; however, if more than one competitor has the same R/C then it fails at Rareness and would be eliminated as a potential competitive advantage. Buc-ee's focuses on the size and cleanliness of their bathrooms as a competitive advantage. They have one massive service station in Texas that has 60 gas pumps and 83 restroom stalls that are cleaned 24/7 by a team of five employees. The bathroom at that Buc-ee's in New Braunfels, TX was voted the best in the country.[8]

Any R/C that passes both Valuable and Rareness should be examined for competitor's ability to imitate. If an organization has a true competitive advantage, it is likely that competitors will look to find a way to match what is being offered in the market either by imitating it or attempting to substitute for it. The longer an organization can retain a competitive advantage, the better off it will be.

Imitability is the rate at which a firm's underlying resources, capabilities, or core competencies can be duplicated by others. To the extent that a firm's distinctive competency gives it competitive advantage in the marketplace, competitors will do what they can to learn and imitate that set of skills and capabilities. Competitors' efforts may range from *reverse engineering* (which involves taking apart a competitor's product in order to find out how it works), to hiring employees from the competitor, to outright patent infringement. A core competency can be easily imitated to the extent that it is transparent, transferable, and replicable.

- **Transparency** is the speed with which other firms can understand the relationship of resources and capabilities supporting a successful firm's strategy. Gillette has always supported its dominance in the marketing of razors with excellent R&D. A competitor could never understand how the Fusion razor was produced simply by taking one apart. Gillette's razor designs are very difficult to copy, partly because the manufacturing equipment needed to produce it is so expensive and complicated.

- **Transferability** is the ability of competitors to gather the resources and capabilities necessary to support a competitive challenge. For example, it may be very difficult for a winemaker to duplicate a French winery's key resources of land and climate, especially if the imitator is located in Iowa.

- **Replicability** is the ability of competitors to use duplicated resources and capabilities to imitate the other firm's success. For example, even though many companies have tried to imitate Procter & Gamble's success with brand management by hiring brand managers away from P&G, they have often failed to duplicate P&G's success. The competitors failed to identify less visible P&G coordination mechanisms or to realize that P&G's brand management style conflicted with the competitor's own corporate culture.

It is relatively easy to learn and imitate another company's core competency or capability if it comes from **explicit knowledge**—that is, knowledge that can be easily articulated and communicated. This is the type of knowledge that competitive intelligence activities can quickly identify and communicate. **Tacit knowledge**, in contrast, is knowledge that is *not* easily communicated because it is deeply rooted in employee experience or in a corporation's culture.[9] Tacit knowledge is more valuable and more likely to lead to a sustainable competitive advantage than is explicit knowledge because it is much harder for competitors to imitate.[10] The knowledge may be complex and combined with other types of knowledge in an unclear fashion in such a way that even management cannot clearly explain the competency.[11] Tacit knowledge is thus subject to a paradox. For a corporation to be successful and grow, its tacit knowledge must be clearly identified and codified if the knowledge is to be spread throughout the firm. Once tacit knowledge is identified and written down, however, it is easily imitable by competitors.[12] This forces companies to establish complex security systems to safeguard their key knowledge.

An organization's resources and capabilities can be placed on a continuum to the extent they are durable and can't be imitated (that is, aren't transparent, transferable, or replicable) by another firm. At one extreme are resources which are sustainable because they are shielded by patents, geography, strong brand names, or tacit knowledge. These resources and capabilities are distinctive competencies because they provide a sustainable competitive advantage. Gillette's razor technology is a good example of a product built around slow-cycle resources. The other extreme includes resources which face the highest imitation pressures because they are based on a concept or technology that can be easily duplicated, such as streaming movies. To the extent that a company has fast-cycle resources, the primary way it can compete successfully is through increased speed from lab to marketplace. Otherwise, it has no real sustainable competitive advantage.

The estimation of what it will take for a competitor to match the R/C determines its imitability. If the organization believes that it will take significant resources and time to match the R/C, then we move on with the analysis. If it can be matched relatively easily, then we would eliminate this R/C as a potential true competitive advantage. This is a qualitative estimation based on a deep understanding of the competitors.

Finally, all R/Cs that have survived the three previous tests are evaluated for the ability of the organization to take advantage of it. Organizational capability is rooted in the policies, procedures, culture, and norms of the organization. The organizational elements of implementation are discussed in detail in later chapters of this textbook. The key to remember is that the organization must be structured and aligned around the true competitive advantages of the business.

It is important to evaluate the importance of a company's resources, capabilities, and competencies to ascertain whether they are internal strategic factors—that is, particular strengths (true competitive advantages) or weaknesses (areas that must be addressed) that will help determine the future of the company. This can be done by comparing measures of these factors with measures of (1) the company's past performance, (2) the company's key competitors, and (3) the industry as a whole.

Even though a distinctive competency is certainly considered to be a corporation's key strength, a key strength may not always be a distinctive competency. As competitors attempt to imitate another company's competency (especially during hypercompetition), what was once a distinctive competency becomes a minimum requirement to compete in the industry.[13] Even though the competency may still be a core competency and thus a strength, it is no longer unique. Apple is well known for their functional design ability. The iPod, iPad, and iPhone are examples of their distinctive competency. As other phone manufacturers imitated Apple's designs and released ever more stylish phones, we would say that this continued to be a key strength (that is, a core competency) of Apple, but it was less and less a distinctive competency.

USING RESOURCES/CAPABILITIES TO GAIN COMPETITIVE ADVANTAGE

Where do these resources/competencies come from? A corporation can gain access to a distinctive competency in four ways:

- It may be an asset endowment, such as a key patent, coming from the founding of the company. Such was the case with Xerox, which grew on the basis of its original copying patent.
- It may be acquired from someone else. Disney bought Pixar in order to reestablish itself in the animated movie market.

- It may be shared with another business unit or alliance partner. LG has taken its electronics and production expertise into appliances with astonishing success in the market.

- It may be carefully built and accumulated over time within the company. For example, Honda carefully extended its expertise in small motor manufacturing from motorcycles to autos, boat engines, generators, and lawnmowers.[14]

There is some evidence that the best corporations prefer organic internal growth over acquisitions. One study of large global companies identified firms that outperformed their peers on both revenue growth and profitability over a decade. These excellent performers generated value from knowledge-intensive intangibles, such as copyrights, trade secrets, or strong brands, not from acquisitions.[15]

The desire to build or upgrade a set of resources and core competencies is one reason entrepreneurial and other fast-growing firms tend to locate close to their competitors. They form *clusters*—geographic concentrations of interconnected companies and industries. Examples in the United States are computer technology in Silicon Valley in northern California; biotechnology in the Research Triangle area of North Carolina; financial services in New York City; clean energy in Colorado; and aviation in the Miami/Ft. Lauderdale area.[16] According to Michael Porter, clusters provide access to employees, suppliers, specialized information, and complementary products.[17] Being close to one's competitors makes it easier to measure and compare performance against rivals. Resources are more easily acquired and capabilities may be formed externally through a firm's network resources. An example is the presence of many venture capitalists located in Silicon Valley who provide financial support and assistance to high-tech startup firms in the region. Employees from competitive firms in these clusters often socialize. As a result, companies learn from each other while competing with each other. Interestingly, research reveals that companies with strong core competencies have little to gain from locating in a cluster with other firms and therefore do not do so. In contrast, firms with the weakest technologies, human resources, training programs, suppliers, and distributors are strongly motivated to cluster. They have little to lose and a lot to gain from locating close to their competitors.[18]

Business Models

5-2. Explain company business models and how they can be imitated

When analyzing a company, it is helpful to learn what sort of business model it is following. A **business model** is a company's method for making money in the current business environment. It includes the key structural and operational characteristics of a firm—how it earns revenue and makes a profit. A business model is usually composed of five elements:

- Who it serves
- What it provides
- How it makes money
- How it differentiates and sustains competitive advantage
- How it provides its product/service.[19]

The simplest business model is to provide a good or service that can be sold such that revenues exceed costs and all expenses. Other models can be much more complicated. Some of the many possible business models are:

- **Customer solutions model:** IBM uses this model to make money not by selling IBM products, but by selling its expertise to improve its customers' operations. This is a consulting model.

- **Profit pyramid model:** General Motors offers a full line of automobiles in order to close out any niches where a competitor might find a position. The key is to get customers to buy in at the low-priced, low-margin entry point (Chevrolet Spark—manufacturer's suggested retail price US $13,485)[20] and move them up to high-priced, high-margin products (Cadillac and Buick) where the company makes its money.

- **Multicomponent system/installed base model:** Gillette invented this classic model to sell razors at break-even pricing in order to make money on higher-margin razor blades. HP does the same with printers and printer cartridges. The product is thus a system, not just one product, with one component providing most of the profits.

- **Advertising model:** Similar to the multicomponent system/installed base model, this model offers its basic product free in order to make money on advertising. Originating in the newspaper industry, this model is used heavily in commercial radio and television. Many web-based firms offer freemium versions to users in order to expose them to the basics and then hope to sell premium features to a smaller set of customers.

- **Switchboard model:** In this model, a firm acts as an intermediary to connect multiple sellers to multiple buyers. Financial planners juggle a wide range of products for sale to multiple customers with different needs. This model has been successfully used by eBay and Amazon.com.

- **Time model:** Product R&D and speed are the keys to success in the time model. Being the first to market with a new innovation allows a pioneer such as Google to earn extraordinary returns. By the time the rest of the industry catches up, Google has moved on to a newer, more innovative approach to keep people coming back.

- **Efficiency model:** In this model, a company waits until a product becomes standardized and then enters the market with a low-priced, low-margin approach that appeals to the mass market. This model is used by Spirit Airlines, KIA Motors, and Vanguard.

- **Blockbuster model:** In some industries, such as pharmaceuticals and motion picture studios, profitability is driven by a few key products. The focus is on high investment in a few products with high potential payoffs—especially if they can be protected by patents.

- **Profit multiplier model:** The idea of this model is to develop a concept that may or may not make money on its own but, through synergy, can spin off many profitable products. Walt Disney invented this concept by using cartoon characters to develop high-margin theme parks, merchandise, and licensing opportunities.

- **Entrepreneurial model:** In this model, a company offers specialized products/services to market niches that are too small to be worthwhile to large competitors but have the potential to grow quickly. Small, local brew pubs have been very successful in a mature industry dominated by AB InBev and MillerCoors. This model has often been used by small high-tech firms that develop innovative prototypes in order to sell off the companies (without ever selling a product) to bigger players.

- **De facto industry standard model:** In this model, a company offers products free or at a very low price in order to saturate the market and become the industry standard. Once users are locked in, the company offers higher-margin products using this standard. LinkedIn has used this approach very successfully while TurboTax makes its most basic program free.

In order to understand how some of these business models work, it is important to learn where on the value chain the company makes its money. Although a company might offer a large number of products and services, one element of the business might contribute most of the profits. Back when Hewlett-Packard was a single company, the printer and imaging division represented more than 20% of the company's revenues, with operating margins that exceeded 15% compared to the PC division's 6% margins.[21]

Value-Chain Analysis

5-3. Use value chain to assess the activities of an industry and of an organization

A **value chain** is a linked set of value-creating activities that begin with basic raw materials coming from suppliers, moving on to a series of value-added activities involved in producing and marketing a product or service, and ending with distributors getting the final goods into the hands of the ultimate consumer. Value-chain analysis works for every type of business regardless of whether they provide a service or manufacture a product. See **Figure 5–1** for an example of a typical value chain for a manufactured product. The focus of value-chain analysis is to examine the corporation in the context of the overall chain of value-creating activities, of which the firm may be only a small part.

Very few corporations have a product's entire value chain in-house. Out of sheer necessity, Ford Motor Company did when it was managed by its founder, Henry Ford. During the 1920s and 1930s, the company owned its own iron mines, ore-carrying ships, and a small rail line to bring ore to its mile-long River Rouge plant in Detroit. Visitors to the plant would walk along an elevated walkway, where they could watch iron ore being dumped from the rail cars into huge furnaces. The resulting steel was poured and rolled out onto a moving belt to be fabricated into auto frames and parts while the visitors watched in awe. As visitors moved along the walkway, they observed an automobile being built piece by piece. Reaching the end of the moving line, the finished automobile was driven out of the plant into a vast adjoining parking lot. Ford trucks would then load the cars for delivery to dealers. Interestingly, Ford dealers had almost no power in the value chain of the company. Dealerships were awarded by the company and taken away if a dealer was at all disloyal. Dealers received new vehicles not necessarily because they needed those particular models, but because Ford Motor chose those vehicles for sale at that dealership. Ford Motor Company at that time was completely vertically integrated—that is, it controlled (usually by ownership) every stage of the value chain, from the iron mines to the retailers.

INDUSTRY VALUE-CHAIN ANALYSIS

The value chains of most industries can be split into two segments, *upstream* and *downstream*. In the petroleum industry, for example, *upstream* refers to oil exploration, drilling, and moving the crude oil to the refinery, and *downstream* refers to refining the oil plus transporting and marketing gasoline and refined oil to distributors and gas station retailers. Even though most large oil companies are completely integrated, they often vary in the amount of expertise they have at each part of the value chain. Amoco, for

FIGURE 5–1
Typical Value Chain for a Manufactured Product

example, had strong expertise downstream in marketing and retailing. British Petroleum, in contrast, was more dominant in upstream activities like exploration. That's one reason the two companies merged to form BP Amoco in 1998. The company has since changed its name to simply BP.[22]

An industry can be analyzed in terms of the profit margin available at any point along the value chain. For example, the U.S. auto industry's revenues and profits are divided among many value-chain activities, including manufacturing, new and used car sales, gasoline retailing, insurance, after-sales service and parts, and lease financing. From a revenue standpoint, auto manufacturers dominate the industry, accounting for almost 60% of total industry revenues. Profits, however, are a different matter. The various North American automakers have gone from earning most of their profit from leasing, insurance, and financing operations just a few years ago, to a resurgence of the manufacturing part of the value chain as the driver of profits. After undergoing a painful few years from 2008–2010, the automakers have emerged again as manufacturing-driven organizations. In 2016, the once bankrupt General Motors reported income for the year of $9.7 billion, up from $2.8 billion in 2014 and Ford Motor Company which took no bailout from the government, reported profits of $7.4 billion.[23]

In analyzing the complete value chain of a product, note that even if a firm operates up and down the entire industry chain, it usually has an area of expertise where its primary activities lie. A company's *center of gravity* is the part of the chain where the company's greatest expertise and capabilities lie—its core competencies. According to Galbraith, a company's center of gravity is usually the point at which the company started. After a firm successfully establishes itself at this point by obtaining a competitive advantage, one of its first strategic moves is to move forward or backward along the value chain in order to reduce costs, guarantee access to key raw materials, or to guarantee distribution.[24] This process, called *vertical integration*, is discussed in more detail in **Chapter 7**.

In the paper industry, for example, Weyerhauser's center of gravity is in the raw materials and primary manufacturing parts of the value chain shown in **Figure 5–2**. Weyerhauser's expertise is in lumbering and pulp mills, which is where the company

FIGURE 5–2
A Corporation's
Value Chain

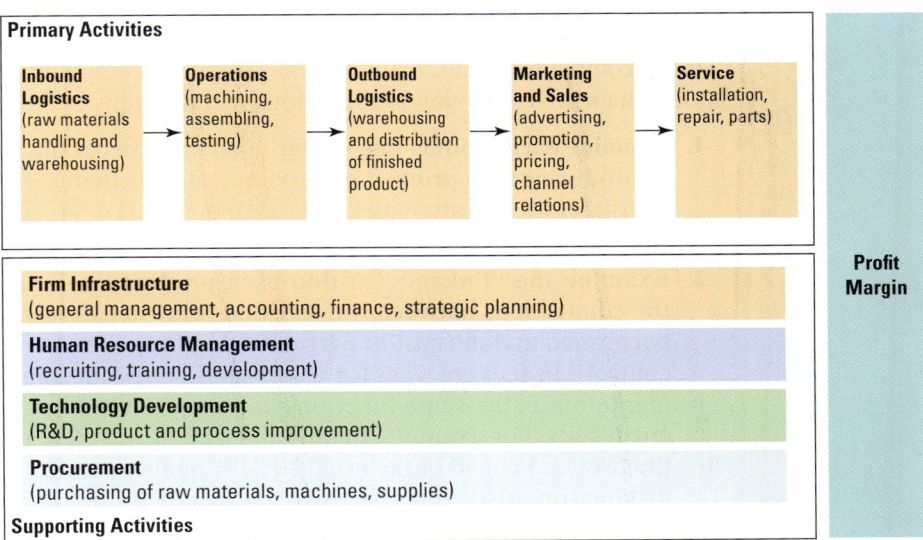

SOURCE: Based on The Free Press, a division of Simon & Schuster, from Competitive Advantage: *Creating and Sustaining Superior Performance* by Michael E. Porter. © Thomas L. Wheelen.

started. It integrated forward by using its wood pulp to make paper and boxes, but its greatest capability still lies in getting the greatest return from its lumbering activities. In contrast, P&G is primarily a consumer products company that also owned timberland and operated pulp mills. Its expertise is in the fabrication and distribution parts of the **Figure 5–2** value chain. P&G purchased these assets to guarantee access to the large quantities of wood pulp it needed to expand its disposable diaper, toilet tissue, and napkin products. P&G's strongest capabilities have always been in the downstream activities of product development, marketing, and brand management. It has never been as efficient in upstream paper activities as Weyerhauser. It had no real distinctive competency on that part of the value chain. When paper supplies became more plentiful (and competition got rougher), P&G gladly sold its land and mills to focus more on the part of the value chain where it could provide the greatest value at the lowest cost—creating and marketing innovative consumer products. As was the case with P&G's experience in the paper industry, it may make sense for a company to outsource any weak areas it may control internally on the industry value chain.

CORPORATE VALUE-CHAIN ANALYSIS

Each corporation has its own internal value chain of activities. See **Figure 5–2** for an example of a corporate value chain. Porter proposes that a manufacturing firm's *primary activities* usually begin with inbound logistics (raw materials handling and warehousing), go through an operations process in which a product is manufactured, and continue on to outbound logistics (warehousing and distribution), to marketing and sales, and finally to service (installation, repair, and sale of parts). Several *support activities*, such as procurement (purchasing), technology development (R&D), human resource management, and firm infrastructure (accounting, finance, strategic planning), ensure that the primary value-chain activities operate effectively and efficiently. Each of a company's product lines has its own distinctive value chain. Because most corporations make several different products or services, an internal analysis of the firm involves analyzing a series of different value chains.

The systematic examination of individual value activities can lead to a better understanding of a corporation's strengths and weaknesses. According to Porter, "Differences among competitor value chains are a key source of competitive advantage."[25] Corporate value-chain analysis involves the following three steps:

1. **Examine each product line's value chain in terms of the various activities involved in producing that product or service:** Which activities passed the VRIO test and are therefore true strengths (core competencies) or areas where the organization is substantially behind and therefore weaknesses (core deficiencies)?

2. **Examine the "linkages" within each product line's value chain:** *Linkages* are the connections between the way one value activity (for example, marketing) is performed and the cost of performance of another activity (for example, quality control). In seeking ways for a corporation to gain competitive advantage in the marketplace, the same function can be performed in different ways with different results. For example, quality inspection of 100% of output by the workers themselves instead of the usual 10% by quality control inspectors might increase production costs, but that increase could be offset by the savings obtained from reducing the number of repair people needed to fix defective products and increasing the amount of salespeople's time devoted to selling instead of

exchanging already-sold but defective products. It could also be used by the overall company as a differentiator when compared to competitors and allow the company to charge more.

3. **Examine the potential synergies among the value chains of different product lines or business units:** Each value element, such as advertising or manufacturing, has an inherent economy of scale in which activities are conducted at their lowest possible cost per unit of output. If a particular product is not being produced at a high enough level to reach economies of scale in distribution, another product could be used to share the same distribution channel. This is an example of **economies of scope**, which result when the value chains of two separate products or services share activities, such as the same marketing channels or manufacturing facilities. The cost of joint production of multiple products can be lower than the cost of separate production.

SCANNING FUNCTIONAL RESOURCES AND CAPABILITIES

The simplest way to begin an analysis of a corporation's value chain is by carefully examining its traditional functional areas for potential strengths and weaknesses. Functional resources and capabilities include not only the financial, physical, and human assets in each area but also the ability of the people in each area to formulate and implement the necessary functional objectives, strategies, and policies. These resources and capabilities include the knowledge of analytical concepts and procedural techniques common to each area, as well as the ability of the people in each area to use them effectively. If used properly, these resources and capabilities serve as strengths to carry out value-added activities and support strategic decisions. In addition to the usual business functions of marketing, finance, R&D, operations, human resources, and information systems/technology, we also discuss structure and culture as key parts of a business corporation's value chain.

Basic Organizational Structures

5-4. Explain why different organizational structures are utilized in business

Although there is an almost infinite variety of structural forms, certain basic types predominate in modern complex organizations. **Figure 5–3** illustrates three basic **organizational structures**. The conglomerate structure is a variant of the divisional structure and is thus not depicted as a fourth structure. If one of the basic structures does not easily support a strategy under consideration, top management must decide whether the proposed strategy is feasible or whether the structure should be changed to a more complicated structure such as a matrix or network. (Other structural designs including the matrix and network are discussed in **Chapter 9**.) Generally speaking, each structure tends to support some corporate strategies better than others:

■ **Simple structure** has no functional or product categories and is appropriate for a small, entrepreneur-dominated company with one or two product lines that operates in a reasonably small, easily identifiable market niche. Employees tend to be generalists and jacks-of-all-trades. In terms of stages of development (to be discussed in **Chapter 9**), this is a Stage I company.

FIGURE 5–3
Basic Organiza-
tional Structures

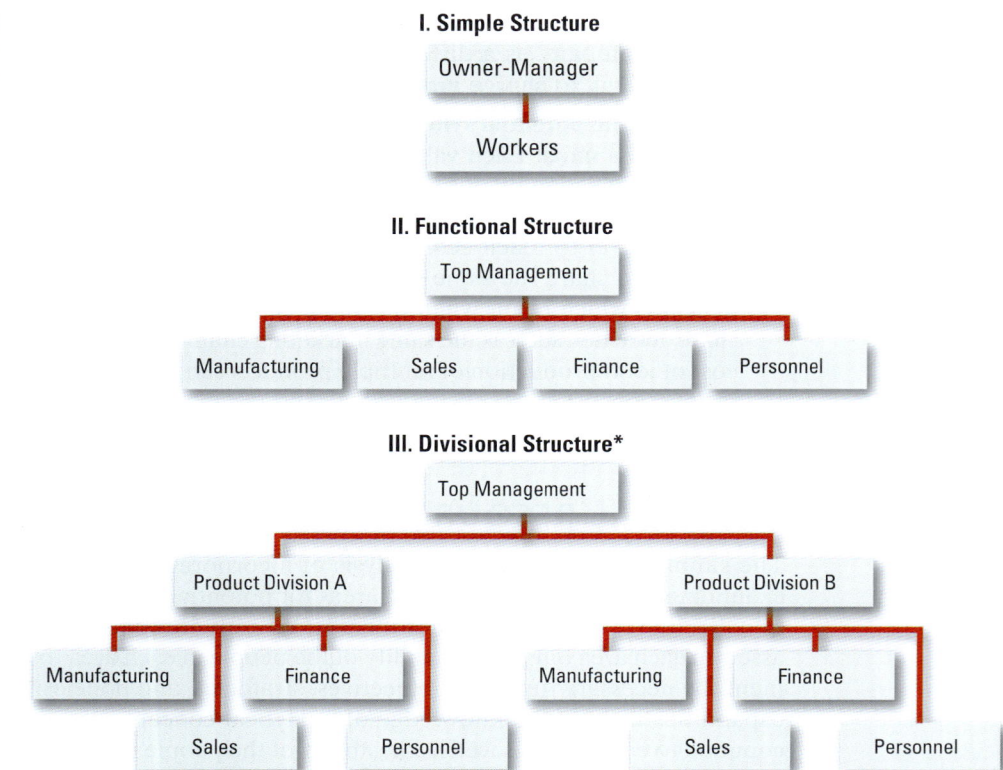

I. Simple Structure

Owner-Manager

Workers

II. Functional Structure

Top Management

Manufacturing | Sales | Finance | Personnel

III. Divisional Structure*

Top Management

Product Division A

Manufacturing | Finance

Sales | Personnel

Product Division B

Manufacturing | Finance

Sales | Personnel

*Strategic Business Units and the conglomerate structure are variants of the divisional structure.

- **Functional structure** is appropriate for a medium-sized firm with several product lines in one industry. Employees tend to be specialists in the business functions that are important to that industry, such as manufacturing, marketing, finance, and human resources. In terms of stages of development (discussed in **Chapter 9**), this is a Stage II company.

- **Divisional structure** is appropriate for a large corporation with many product lines in several related industries. Employees tend to be functional specialists organized according to product/market distinctions. The Clorox Company is made up of five big divisions: (1) Cleaning (e.g., Clorox, 409, and Tilex); (2) Household (e.g., Glad, Kingsford, and Fresh Step); (3) Lifestyle (e.g., Brita and Burt's Bees); (4) Professional (Commercial Solutions); and (5) International (e.g., Chux and Poett).[26] Management attempts to find some synergy among divisional activities through the use of committees and horizontal linkages. In terms of stages of development (to be discussed in **Chapter 9**), this is a Stage III company.

- **Strategic business units (SBUs)** are a modification of the divisional structure. Strategic business units are divisions or groups of divisions composed of independent product-market segments that are given primary responsibility and authority for the management of their own functional areas. *An SBU may be of any size or level,* *but it must have (1) a unique mission, (2) identifiable competitors, (3) an external market focus, and (4) control of its business functions.*[27] The idea is to decentralize on the basis of strategic elements rather than on the basis of size, product characteristics, or span of control and to create horizontal linkages among units previously kept separate. For example, rather than organize products on the basis of packaging technology like frozen foods, canned foods, and bagged foods, General Foods organized its products into SBUs on the basis of consumer-oriented menu segments: breakfast food, beverage, main meal, dessert, and pet foods. In terms of stages of development (to be discussed in **Chapter 9**), this is also a Stage III company.

- **Conglomerate structure** is appropriate for a large corporation with many product lines in several unrelated industries. A variant of the divisional structure, the conglomerate structure (sometimes called a holding company) is typically an assemblage of legally independent firms (subsidiaries) operating under one corporate umbrella but controlled through the subsidiaries' boards of directors. The unrelated nature of the subsidiaries prevents any attempt at gaining synergy among them. In terms of stages of development (discussed in **Chapter 9**), this is also a Stage III company.

Culture

5-5. Assess a company's corporate culture and how it might affect a proposed strategy

There is an oft-told story of a person new to a company asking an experienced co-worker what an employee should do when a customer calls. The old-timer responded: "There are three ways to do any job—the right way, the wrong way, and the company way. Around here, we always do things the company way." In most organizations, the "company way" is derived from the corporation's culture. **Corporate culture** is the collection of beliefs, expectations, and values learned and shared by a corporation's members and transmitted from one generation of employees to another. The corporate culture generally reflects the values of the founder(s) and the mission of the firm.[28] It gives a company a sense of identity: "This is who we are. This is what we do. This is what we stand for." The culture includes the dominant orientation of the company, such as R&D at 3M, shared responsibility at Nucor, customer service at Nordstrom, innovation at Google, or product quality at BMW. It often includes a number of informal work rules (forming the "company way") that employees follow without question. These work practices over time become part of a company's unquestioned tradition. The culture, therefore, reflects the company's values.

Corporate culture has two distinct attributes, intensity and integration.[29] *Cultural intensity* is the degree to which members of a unit accept the norms, values, or other cultural content associated with the unit. This shows the culture's depth. Organizations with strong norms promoting a particular value, such as quality at BMW, have intensive cultures, whereas new firms (or those in transition) have weaker, less intensive cultures. Employees in an intensive culture tend to exhibit consistent behavior—that is, they tend to act similarly over time. *Cultural integration* is the extent to which units throughout an organization share a common culture. This is the culture's breadth. Organizations with a pervasive dominant culture may be hierarchically controlled and power-oriented, such as a military unit, and have highly integrated cultures. All employees tend to hold the same cultural values and norms. In contrast, a company that is structured into diverse units by functions or divisions usually exhibits some strong subcultures (for example, R&D versus manufacturing) and a less integrated corporate culture.

Corporate culture fulfills several important functions in an organization:

1. Conveys a sense of identity for employees

2. Helps generate employee commitment to something greater than themselves

3. Adds to the stability of the organization as a social system

4. Serves as a frame of reference for employees to use to make sense of organizational activities and to use as a guide for appropriate behavior.[30]

Corporate culture shapes the behavior of people in a corporation, thus affecting corporate performance. For example, corporate cultures that emphasize the socialization of new employees have less employee turnover, leading to lower costs.[31] Because corporate cultures have a powerful influence on the behavior of people at all levels, they can strongly affect a corporation's ability to shift its strategic direction. A strong culture should not only promote survival, but it should also create the basis for a superior competitive position by increasing motivation and facilitating coordination and control.[32] For example, a culture emphasizing constant renewal may help a company adapt to a changing, hypercompetitive environment.[33] To the extent that a corporation's distinctive competence is embedded in an organization's culture, it will be a form of tacit knowledge and very difficult for a competitor to imitate. The **Global Issue** feature shows the differences between ABB ASEA Brown Boveri AG and Panasonic Corporation in terms of how they manage their corporate cultures in a global industry.

A change in mission, objectives, strategies, or policies is not likely to be successful if it is in opposition to the accepted culture of a firm. Foot-dragging and even sabotage may result, as employees fight to resist a radical change in corporate philosophy. As with structure, if an organization's culture is compatible with a new strategy, it is an internal strength. On the other hand, if the corporate culture is not compatible with the proposed strategy, it is a serious weakness. Circuit City ceased operations in January 2009 after a disastrous set of moves by then CEO Philip Schoonover. The history of Circuit City and its competitive advantage for years had been built around a level of expertise simply not available at other big box stores like Best Buy. However, in a move to save money, Schoonover fired 3400 of Circuit City's most experienced employees and replaced them with low-wage, low-level clerks. Analysts blasted the move for the devastating loss of morale and associated decline in customer service. The misalignment with the organization's culture spelled doom for the organization.[34]

Corporate culture is also important when considering an acquisition. The merging of two dissimilar cultures, if not handled wisely, can create some serious internal conflicts. Procter & Gamble's management knew, for example, that their 2005 acquisition of Gillette might create some cultural problems. Even though both companies were strong consumer goods marketers, they each had a fundamental difference that led to many, subtle differences between the cultures: Gillette sold its razors, toothbrushes, and batteries to men; whereas, P&G sold its health and beauty aids to women. Art Lafley, P&G's CEO, admitted a year after the merger that it would take an additional year to 15 months to align the two companies.[35]

GLOBAL issue

MANAGING CORPORATE CULTURE FOR GLOBAL COMPETITIVE ADVANTAGE: ABB VS. PANASONIC

Zurich-based ABB ASEA Brown Boveri AG (ABB) is a world-builder of power plants and electrical equipment with industrial factories in 140 countries. By establishing one set of multicultural values throughout its global operations, ABB's management believes that the company will gain an advantage over its rivals Siemens AG of Germany, France's Alcatel-Alsthom NV, and the U.S.'s General Electric Company. ABB is a company with no geographic base. Instead, it has many "home" markets so it can draw on expertise from around the globe. ABB created a set of 500 global managers who could adapt to local cultures while executing ABB's global strategies. These people are multilingual and move around each of ABB's 5000 profit centers in 140 countries. Their assignment is to cut costs, improve efficiency, and integrate local businesses with the ABB worldview.

Few multinational corporations are as successful as ABB in getting global strategies to work with local operations. In agreement with the resource-based view of the firm, the past Chairman of ABB, Percy Barnevik stated, "Our strength comes from pulling together . . . . If you can make this work real well, then you get a competitive edge out of the organization which is very, very difficult to copy."

Contrast ABB's globally oriented corporate culture with the more parochial culture of Panasonic Corporation of Japan. Panasonic is the third-largest electrical company in the world. Konosuke Matsushita founded the company in 1918. His management philosophy led to the company's success but became institutionalized in the corporate culture—a culture that was more focused on Japanese values than on cross-cultural globalization. As a result, Panasonic corporate culture does not adapt well to local conditions. Not only is Panasonic's top management *exclusively* Japanese, its subsidiary managers are *overwhelmingly* Japanese. The company's distrust of non-Japanese managers in the United States and some European countries results in a "rice-paper ceiling" that prevents non-Japanese people from being promoted into Panasonic subsidiaries' top management. Foreign employees are often confused by the corporate philosophy that has not been adapted to suit local realities. Panasonic's corporate culture perpetuates a cross-cultural divide that separates the Japanese from the non-Japanese managers, leaving the non-Japanese managers feeling frustrated and undervalued. This divide prevents the flow of knowledge and experience from regional operations to the headquarters and may hinder Panasonic's ability to compete globally.

....

SOURCES: Summarized from J. Guyon, "ABB Fuses Units with One Set of Values," *The Wall Street Journal* (October 2, 1996), p. A15, and N. Holden, "Why Globalizing with a Conservative Corporate Culture Inhibits Localization of Management: The Telling Case of Matsushita Electric," *International Journal of Cross Cultural Management* (Vol. 1, No. 1, 2001), pp. 53–72.

STRATEGIC MARKETING ISSUES

The marketing manager is a company's primary link to the customer and the competition. The manager, therefore, must be especially concerned with the market position and marketing mix of the firm as well as with the overall reputation of the company and its brands.

Market Position and Segmentation

Market position deals with the question, "Who are our customers?" It refers to the selection of specific areas for marketing concentration and can be expressed in terms of market, product, and geographic locations. Through market research, corporations are able to practice *market segmentation* with various products or services so that managers can discover what niches to seek, which new types of products to develop, and how to ensure that a company's many products do not directly compete with one another.

Marketing Mix

Marketing mix refers to the particular combination of key variables under a corporation's control that can be used to affect demand and to gain competitive advantage.

TABLE 5–1	Product	Place	Promotion	Price
Marketing Mix Variables	Quality	Channels	Advertising	List price
	Features	Coverage	Personal selling	Discounts
	Options	Locations	Sales promotion	Allowances
	Style	Inventory	Publicity	Payment periods
	Brand name	Transport		Credit items
	Packaging			
	Sizes			
	Services			
	Warranties			
	Returns			

SOURCE: Philip Kotler, *Marketing Management,* 11th edition © 2003, p. 16. Reprinted by Pearson Education Inc., Upper Saddle River, NJ.

These variables are product, place, promotion, and price. Within each of these four variables are several sub-variables, listed in **Table 5–1**, that should be analyzed in terms of their effects on divisional and corporate performance.

Product Life Cycle

As depicted in **Figure 5–4**, the **product life cycle** is a graph showing time plotted against the sales of a product as it moves from introduction through growth and maturity to decline. This concept is used by marketing managers to discuss the marketing mix of a particular product or group of products in terms of where it might exist in the life cycle. From a strategic management perspective, this concept is of little value because the real position of any product and the actual curve of that product can only be ascertained in hindsight. Strategy is about making decisions in real-time for the future of the business. The Innovation Issue feature shows how a company can use the conventional wisdom of the product life cycle to its advantage against leading-edge competitors.

FIGURE 5–4
Product Life Cycle

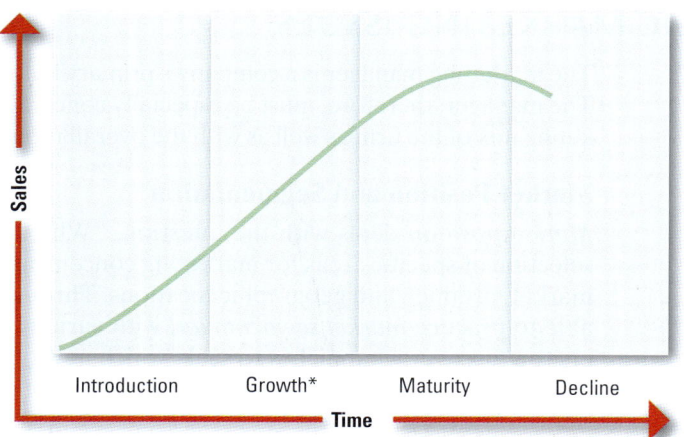

* The right end of the Growth stage is often called Competitive Turbulence because of price and distribution competition that shakes out the weaker competitors. For further information, see C. R. Wasson, *Dynamic Competitive Strategy and Product Life Cycles.* 3rd ed. (Austin, TX: Austin Press, 1978).

INNOVATION issue

DOCOMO MOVES AGAINST THE GRAIN

Years ago, DoCoMo (Japan's largest cell phone service provider in Japan) chose not to be a part of the iPhone phenomenon. The expense of the iPhone to the company was key in this decision. Sometimes innovation is needed because of strategic decisions. In this case, the iPhone has come to symbolize what constitutes "hip," so the company went on a search for opportunities in the market where they had core strengths that were not being addressed.

The fastest-growing demographic in Japan is the elderly. People age 65 and older make up 23% of the population and their needs are substantially different than those of the younger set. This is especially true in the cell phone market, where the latest iPhone helped push the percentage of adults age 20–29 with a Smartphone in Japan to over 51%. That compares to less than 6% of people age 65 or older who own a Smartphone.

The small screen and apps designed for the latest desires of the younger set simply don't appeal to an audience with weaker eyesight and a focus on more practical applications. DoCoMo seized on this apparent opportunity and went to work to create a must-have Smartphone experience for those over 60.

Today, the company is offering phones with larger keys, apps that are easier to understand and use, a new voice-recognition software that allows its customers to send e-mails, and is holding training sessions around the country to teach older customers how to use a Smartphone. In each of these areas, they are separating themselves from the competition, which is far more interested in being seen as the most cutting-edge in the industry. While other competitors battle it out for the younger set, DoCoMo has captured the imagination of the older set. People over the age of 60 now account for more than 24% of the company's business, and DoCoMo's goal is to stay in the lead with the elderly market by anticipating their desires and providing innovative solutions that in some cases are more retro than cutting-edge.

....

SOURCES: R. Martin, "DoCoMo Shuns iPhone, Pushes Android Options," *The Japan Times* (May 23, 2012), (http://www.japantimes.co.jp/text/nc20120523ga.html); M. Yasu and S. Ozasa, "DoCoMo Savors an Older Vintage," *Bloomberg Businessweek* (July 2, 2012), (http://www.businessweek.com/articles/2012-06-28/docomo-looks-for-growth-among-japans-elderly).

Brand and Corporate Reputation

A **brand** is a name given to a company's product which embodies all of the characteristics of that item in the mind of the consumer. Over time and with effective advertising and execution, a brand connotes various characteristics in the consumers' minds. For example, Disney stands for family entertainment. Carnival has the "fun ships." BMW means high-performance autos. A brand can thus be an important corporate resource. If done well, a brand name is connected to the product to such an extent that a brand may stand for an entire product category, such as Kleenex for facial tissue. The objective is for the customer to ask for the brand name (Coke or Pepsi) instead of the product category (cola). The world's 10 most valuable brands in 2015 were Apple, Microsoft, Google, Coca-Cola, IBM, McDonald's, Samsung, Toyota, General Electric, and Facebook, in that order. According to *Forbes*, the value of the Apple brand is US$145.3 billion.[36]

A *corporate brand* is a type of brand in which the company's name serves as the brand. Of the top 10 world brands listed previously, all are company names. The value of a corporate brand is that it typically stands for consumers' impressions of a company and can thus be extended onto products not currently offered—regardless of the company's actual expertise. For example, Caterpillar, a manufacturer of heavy earth-moving equipment, used consumer associations with the Caterpillar brand (*rugged*, *masculine*, *construction-related*) to market work boots. While this type of move may not be strategically advisable, consumer impressions of a brand can at least suggest new product categories to enter even though a company may have no competencies in making or marketing that type of product or service.[37]

A **corporate reputation** is a widely held perception of a company by the general public. It consists of two attributes: (1) stakeholders' perceptions of a corporation's ability to produce quality goods and (2) a corporation's prominence in the minds of stakeholders.[38] A good corporate reputation can be a strategic resource. It can serve in marketing as both a signal and an entry barrier. It contributes to its goods having a price premium.[39] Reputation is especially important when the quality of a company's product or service is not directly observable and can be learned only through experience. For example, retail stores are willing to stock a new product from P&G or Coca-Cola because they know that both companies market only good-quality products that are highly advertised. Like tacit knowledge, reputation tends to be long-lasting and hard for others to duplicate. It can deteriorate over time without constant vigilance, but has the potential to provide a sustainable competitive advantage.[40] It might also have a significant impact on a firm's stock price.[41] Research reveals a positive relationship between corporate reputation and financial performance.[42]

STRATEGIC FINANCIAL ISSUES

A financial manager must ascertain the best sources of funds, uses of funds, and the control of funds. All strategic issues have financial implications. Cash must be raised from internal or external (local and global) sources and allocated for different uses. The flow of funds in the operations of an organization must be monitored. To the extent that a corporation is involved in international activities, currency fluctuations must be dealt with to ensure that profits aren't wiped out by the rise or fall of the dollar versus the yen, euro, or other currencies. Benefits in the form of returns, repayments, or products and services must be given to the sources of outside financing. All these tasks must be handled in a way that complements and supports overall corporate strategy. A firm's capital structure (amounts of debt and equity) can influence its strategic choices. Corporations with increased debt tend to be more risk-averse and less willing to invest in R&D.[43]

Financial Leverage

The mix of externally generated short-term and long-term funds in relation to the amount and timing of internally generated funds should be appropriate to the corporate objectives, strategies, and policies. The concept of **financial leverage** (the ratio of total debt to total assets) is helpful in describing how debt is used to increase the earnings available to common shareholders. When the company finances its activities by sales of bonds or notes instead of through stock, the earnings per share are boosted: the interest paid on the debt reduces taxable income, but fewer shareholders share the profits than if the company had sold more stock to finance its activities. The debt, however, does raise the firm's break-even point above what it would have been if the firm had financed from internally generated funds only. High leverage may, therefore, be perceived as a corporate strength in times of prosperity and increasing sales, or as a weakness in times of a recession and falling sales. This is because leverage acts to magnify the effect on earnings per share of an increase or decrease in actual sales. Research indicates that greater leverage has a positive impact on performance for firms in stable environments, but a negative impact for firms in dynamic environments.[44]

Capital Budgeting

Capital budgeting is the analyzing and ranking of possible investments in fixed assets such as land, buildings, and equipment in terms of the additional outlays and additional receipts that will result from each investment. A good finance department will be able to prepare such capital budgets and to rank them on the basis of some accepted criteria or *hurdle rate* (for example, years to pay back investment, desired rate of return, or time to break-even point) for the purpose of strategic decision making. Most firms have more than one hurdle rate and vary it as a function of the type of project being considered. Projects with high strategic significance, such as entering new markets or defending market share, will often have lower hurdle rates.[45]

STRATEGIC RESEARCH AND DEVELOPMENT (R&D) ISSUES

The R&D manager is responsible for suggesting and implementing a company's technological strategy in light of its corporate objectives and policies. The manager's job, therefore, involves (1) choosing among alternative new technologies to use within the corporation, (2) developing methods of embodying the new technology in new products and processes, and (3) deploying resources so that the new technology can be successfully implemented.

R&D Intensity, Technological Competence, and Technology Transfer

The company must make available the resources necessary for effective research and development. A company's **R&D intensity** (its spending on R&D as a percentage of sales revenue) is a principal means of gaining market share in global competition. The amount spent on R&D varies dramatically. In 2014, *Fortune* reported on the top 10 companies in R&D money spent. The top company was Volkswagen ($13.5 billion) (5.2% of revenue) followed by Samsung ($13.4 billion) (6.4% of revenue) and Intel ($10.6 billion) (20.1%) of revenue.[46] A good rule of thumb for R&D spending is that a corporation should spend at a "normal" rate for that particular industry unless its strategic plan calls for unusual expenditures.

Simply spending money on R&D or new projects does not mean, however, that the money will produce useful results. Apple is one of the most profitable and admired companies in the world and yet there are seven firms that spend more in terms of R&D than Apple's $4.7 billion. The top five on the list of companies that invest in R&D were Microsoft (US$10.9b), Intel (US$10.6b), J&J (US$8.1b), Google (US$7.9b), and Amazon (US$6.5b).[47]

A company's R&D unit should be evaluated for **technological competence** in both the development and use of innovative technology. Not only should the corporation make a consistent research effort (as measured by reasonably constant corporate expenditures that result in usable innovations), it should also be proficient in managing research personnel and integrating their innovations into its day-to-day operations. A company should also be proficient in **technology transfer**, the process of taking a new technology from the laboratory to the marketplace. Aerospace parts maker Rockwell Collins, for example, is a master of developing new technology, such as the "heads-up display" (transparent screens in an airplane cockpit that tell pilots speed, altitude, and direction), for the military and then using it in products built for the civilian market.[48]

R&D Mix

Basic R&D is conducted by scientists in well-equipped laboratories where the focus is on theoretical problem areas. The best indicators of a company's capability in this area are its patents and research publications. *Product R&D* concentrates on marketing and is concerned with product or product-packaging improvements. The best measurements of ability in this area are the number of successful new products introduced and the percentage of total sales and profits coming from products introduced within the past five years. *Engineering (or process) R&D* is concerned with engineering, concentrating on quality control, and the development of design specifications and improved production equipment. A company's capability in this area can be measured by consistent reductions in unit manufacturing costs and by the number of product defects.

Most corporations will have a mix of basic, product, and process R&D, which varies by industry, company, and product line. The balance of these types of research is known as the **R&D mix** and should be appropriate to the strategy being considered and to each product's life cycle. For example, it is generally accepted that product R&D normally dominates the early stages of a product's life cycle (when the product's optimal form and features are still being debated), whereas process R&D becomes especially important in the later stages (when the product's design is solidified and the emphasis is on reducing costs and improving quality).

Impact of Technological Discontinuity on Strategy

The R&D manager must determine when to abandon present technology and when to develop or adopt new technology. Richard Foster of McKinsey and Company states that the displacement of one technology by another (**technological discontinuity**) is a frequent and strategically important phenomenon. Such a discontinuity occurs when a new technology cannot simply be used to enhance the current technology, but actually substitutes for that technology to yield better performance. According to Foster, for each technology within a given field or industry, the plotting of product performance against research effort/expenditures on a graph results in an S-shaped curve.

Information technology is still on the steep upward slope of its S-curve in which relatively small increments in R&D effort result in significant improvement in performance. This is an example of *Moore's Law* (which is really a rule of thumb and not a scientific law), which states that the number of transistors that can fit on a computer chip (microprocessors) will double (in other words, computing power will double) every 18 months.[49] The presence of a technological discontinuity in the world's steel industry during the 1960s explains why the large capital expenditures by U.S. steel companies failed to keep them competitive with the Japanese firms that adopted the new technologies. As Foster points out, "History has shown that as one technology nears the end of its S-curve, competitive leadership in a market generally changes hands."[50]

Christensen explains in *The Innovator's Dilemma* why this transition occurs when a "disruptive technology" enters an industry. In a study of computer disk drive manufacturers, he explains that established market leaders are typically reluctant to move in a timely manner to a new technology. This reluctance to switch technologies (even when the firm is aware of the new technology and may have even invented it!) is because the resource allocation process in most companies gives priority to those projects (typically based on the old technology) with the greatest likelihood of generating a good return on investment—those projects appealing to the firm's current customers (whose products are also based on the characteristics of the old technology). For example, in the 1980s a disk drive manufacturer's customers (PC manufacturers) wanted a better (faster) 5¼″ drive with greater capacity. These PC makers were not interested in the new 3½″ drives based on the new technology because (at that time) the smaller drives were slower and had less capacity. Smaller size was irrelevant because these companies primarily made desktop personal computers, which were designed to hold large drives.

The new technology is generally riskier and of little appeal to the current customers of established firms. Products derived from the new technology are more expensive and do not meet the customers' requirements—requirements based on the old technology. New entrepreneurial firms are typically more interested in the new technology because it is one way to appeal to a developing market niche in a market currently dominated by established companies. Even though the new technology may be more expensive to develop, it offers performance improvements in areas that are attractive to this small niche, but of no consequence to the customers of the established competitors.

This was the case with the entrepreneurial manufacturers of 3½″ disk drives. These smaller drives appealed to the PC makers who were trying to increase their small PC market share by offering laptop computers. Size and weight were more important to these customers than were capacity and speed. By the time the new technology was developed to the point that the 3½″ drive matched and even surpassed the 5¼″ drive in terms of speed and capacity (in addition to size and weight), it was too late for the established 5¼″ disk drive firms to switch to the new technology. Once their customers begin demanding smaller products using the new technology, the established firms were unable to respond quickly and lost their leadership position in the industry. They were able to remain in the industry (with a much reduced market share) only if they were able to utilize the new technology to be competitive in the new product line.[51]

The same phenomenon can be seen in many product categories ranging from flat-panel display screens to railroad locomotives to digital photography to musical recordings. For example, George Heilmeier created the first practical liquid-crystal display (LCD) in 1964 at RCA Labs. RCA unveiled the new display in 1968 with much fanfare about LCDs being the future of TV sets, but then refused to fund further development of the new technology. In contrast, Japanese television and computer manufacturers invested in long-term development of LCDs. Today, Japanese, Korean, and Taiwanese companies dominate a market that is estimated will be US$155 billion by 2020. RCA no longer makes televisions. Interestingly, Heilmeier received the Kyoto Prize in 2005 for his LCD invention.[52]

STRATEGIC OPERATIONS ISSUES

The primary task of the operations (manufacturing or service) manager is to develop and operate a system that will produce the required number of products or services, with a certain quality, at a given cost, within an allotted time. Many of the key concepts and techniques popularly used in manufacturing can be applied to service businesses.

In very general terms, manufacturing can be intermittent or continuous. In *intermittent systems* (job shops), the item is normally processed sequentially, but the work and sequence of the process vary. An example is an auto body repair shop. At each location, the tasks determine the details of processing and the time required for them. These job shops can be very labor-intensive. For example, a job shop usually has little automated machinery and thus a small amount of fixed costs. It has a fairly low break-even point, but its variable cost line (composed of wages and the costs of special parts) has a relatively steep slope. Because most of the costs associated with the product are variable (many employees earn piece-rate wages), a job shop's variable costs are higher than those of automated firms. Its advantage over other firms is that it can operate at low levels and still be profitable. After a job shop's sales reach break-even, however, the huge variable costs as a percentage of total costs keep the profit per unit at a relatively low level. In terms of strategy, this firm should look for a niche in the marketplace for which it can produce and sell a reasonably small quantity of custom-made goods.

In contrast, *continuous systems* are those laid out as lines on which products can be continuously assembled or processed. An example is an automobile assembly line. A firm using continuous systems invests heavily in fixed investments such as automated processes and highly sophisticated machinery. Its labor force, relatively small but highly skilled, earns salaries rather than piece-rate wages. Consequently, this firm has a high amount of fixed costs. It also has a relatively high break-even point, but its variable cost line rises slowly. This is an example of **operating leverage**, the impact of a specific change in sales volume on net operating income. The advantage of high operating leverage is that once the firm reaches break-even, its profits rise faster than do those of less automated firms having lower operating leverage. Continuous systems reap benefits from economies of scale. In terms of strategy, this firm needs to find a high-demand niche in the marketplace for which it can produce and sell a large quantity of goods. However, a firm with high operating leverage is likely to suffer huge losses during a recession. During an economic downturn, the firm with less automation and thus less leverage is more likely to survive comfortably because a drop in sales primarily affects variable costs. It is often easier to lay off labor than to sell off specialized plants and machines.

Experience Curve

A conceptual framework that many large corporations have used successfully is the experience curve (originally called the learning curve). The **experience curve** suggests that unit production costs decline by some fixed percentage (commonly 20%–30%) each time the total accumulated volume of production in units doubles. The actual percentage varies by industry and is based on many variables: the amount of time it takes a person to learn a new task, scale economies, product and process improvements, and lower raw materials costs, among others. For example, in an industry with an 85% experience curve, a corporation might expect a 15% reduction in unit costs for every doubling of volume. The total costs per unit can be expected to drop from US$100 when the total production is 10 units, to US$85 (US$100 × 85%) when production increases to 20 units, and to US$72.25 (US$85 × 85%) when it reaches 40 units. Achieving these results often means investing in R&D and fixed assets; higher fixed costs and less flexibility thus result. Nevertheless, the manufacturing strategy is one of building capacity ahead of demand in order to achieve the lower unit costs that develop from the experience curve. On the basis of some future point on the experience curve, the corporation should price the product or service very low to preempt competition and increase market demand. The resulting high number of units sold and high market share should result in high profits, based on the low unit costs.

Management commonly uses the experience curve in estimating the production costs of (1) a product never before made with the present techniques and processes or (2) current products produced by newly introduced techniques or processes. The concept was first applied in the airframe industry and can be applied in the service industry as well. For example, a cleaning company can reduce its costs per employee by having its workers use the same equipment and techniques to clean many adjacent offices in one office building rather than just cleaning a few offices in multiple buildings. Although many firms have used experience curves extensively, an unquestioning acceptance of the industry norm (such as 80% for the airframe industry or 70% for integrated circuits) is very risky. The experience curve of the industry as a whole might not hold true for a particular company for a variety of reasons.[53]

Flexible Manufacturing for Mass Customization

The use of large, continuous, mass-production facilities to take advantage of experience-curve economies has recently been criticized. The use of **C**omputer-**A**ssisted **D**esign and **C**omputer-**A**ssisted **M**anufacturing (CAD/CAM) and robot technology means that learning times are shorter and products can be economically manufactured in small, customized batches in a process called *mass customization*—the low-cost production of individually customized goods and services.[54] Economies of scope (in which common parts of the manufacturing activities of various products are combined to gain economies even though small numbers of each product are made) replace **economies of scale** (in which unit costs are reduced by making large numbers of the same product) in flexible manufacturing. *Flexible manufacturing* permits the low-volume output of custom-tailored products at relatively low unit costs through economies of scope. It is thus possible to have the cost advantages of continuous systems with the customer-oriented advantages of intermittent systems. The automaker Hyundai/Kia is designing all of its manufacturing facilities so that any assembly line can build any car in the fleet with minimal change. They are automating plants so that robots are able to handle parts regardless of the model being produced. Previously, robots were capable of handling parts for only one model line at a time.[55]

STRATEGIC HUMAN RESOURCE MANAGEMENT (HRM) ISSUES

The primary task of the manager of human resources is to improve the match between individuals and jobs. Research indicates that companies with good HRM practices have higher profits and a better survival rate than do firms without these practices.[56] A good HRM department should know how to use attitude surveys and other feedback devices to assess employees' satisfaction with their jobs and with the corporation as a whole. HRM managers should also use job analysis to obtain job description information about what each job needs to accomplish in terms of quality and quantity. Up-to-date job descriptions are essential not only for proper employee selection, appraisal, training, and development for wage and salary administration, and for labor negotiations, but also for summarizing the corporate-wide human resources in terms of employee-skill categories. Just as a company must know the number, type, and quality of its manufacturing facilities, it must also know the kinds of people it employs and the skills they possess. The best strategies are meaningless if employees do not have the skills to carry them out or if jobs cannot be designed to accommodate the available workers. IBM, Procter & Gamble, and Hewlett-Packard, for example, use employee profiles to ensure that they have the best mix of talents to implement their planned strategies. Because project managers at IBM are now able to scan the company's databases to identify employee capabilities and availability, the average time needed to assemble a team has declined 20% for a savings of US$500 million overall.[57]

Increasing Use of Teams

Management practice has moved to more flexible utilization of employees in order for human resources to be classified as a strength. Human resource managers, therefore, need to be knowledgeable about work options such as part-time work, job sharing, flex-time, extended leaves, and contract work, and especially about the proper use of teams. Over two-thirds of large U.S. companies are successfully using *autonomous (self-managing) work teams* in which a group of people work together without a supervisor to plan, coordinate, and evaluate their own work.[58] Connecticut Spring & Stamping is using self-directed work teams to achieve the dual goals of 100% on-time delivery and 100% quality. Since installing the work teams, the company has gone from what it referred to as a "very low on-time delivery performance" to an on-time delivery rate of 96%.[59]

As a way to move a product more quickly through its development stage, companies like Harley-Davidson, KPMG, Wendy's, LinkedIn, and Pfizer are using *cross-functional work teams*. Instead of developing products/services in a series of steps, companies are tearing down the traditional walls separating the departments so that people from each discipline can get involved in projects early on. In a process called *concurrent engineering*, the once-isolated specialists now work side-by-side and compare notes constantly in an effort to design cost-effective products with features customers want. Taking this approach enabled Chrysler Corporation to reduce its product development cycle from 60 to 36 months.[60] For such cross-functional work teams to be successful, the groups must receive training and coaching. Otherwise, poorly implemented teams may worsen morale, create divisiveness, and raise the level of cynicism among workers.[61]

Virtual teams are groups of geographically and/or organizationally dispersed co-workers that are assembled using a combination of telecommunications and information technologies to accomplish an organizational task.[62] A study conducted in 2012 found that 46% of organizations polled used virtual teams and that multinational companies were twice as likely (66%) to use virtual teams as compared to those having U.S.-based operations (28%).[63] According to the Gartner Group, more than 60% of professional employees now work in virtual teams.[64] Internet, intranet, and extranet systems are combining with other new technologies, such as desktop videoconferencing and collaborative software, to create a new workplace in which teams of workers are no longer restrained by geography, time, or organizational boundaries. This technology allows about 12% of the U.S. workforce, who have no permanent office at their companies, to do team projects over the Internet and report to a manager thousands of miles away. A 2015 poll by the Gallup organization found that 37% of U.S. workers have telecommuted and the average worker telecommutes two days a month. That percentage is up substantially from 1995 when the number was only 9%.[65]

As more companies outsource some of the activities previously conducted internally, the traditional organizational structure is being replaced by a series of virtual teams, which rarely, if ever, meet face to face. Such teams may be established as temporary groups to accomplish a specific task or may be more permanent to address continuing issues such as strategic planning. Membership on these teams is often fluid, depending upon the task to be accomplished. They may include not only employees from different functions within a company, but also members of various stakeholder groups, such as suppliers, customers, and law or consulting firms. The use of virtual teams to replace traditional face-to-face work groups is being driven by five trends:

1. Flatter organizational structures with increasing cross-functional coordination needs
2. Turbulent environments requiring more interorganizational cooperation
3. Increasing employee autonomy and participation in decision making
4. Higher knowledge requirements derived from a greater emphasis on service
5. Increasing globalization of trade and corporate activity.[66]

Union Relations and Temporary/Part-Time Workers

If part of the organization is unionized, a good human resource manager should be able to work closely with the union. Even though union membership had dropped to only 11.1% of the U.S. workforce by 2015 compared to 20.1% in 1983, it still included 14.8 million people. Nevertheless, only 6.7% of private sector employees belonged to a union (compared to 35.2% of public sector employees).[67] To save jobs, U.S. unions are increasingly willing to support new strategic initiatives and employee involvement programs. For example, United Steel Workers hired Ron Bloom, an investment banker, to propose a strategic plan to make Goodyear Tire & Rubber globally competitive in a way that would preserve as many jobs as possible. In their landmark 2003 contract, the union gave up US$1.15 billion in wage and benefit concessions over three years in return for a promise by Goodyear's top management to invest in 12 of its 14 U.S. factories, to limit imports from its factories in Brazil and Asia, and to maintain 85% of its 19,000-person workforce. The company also agreed to aggressively restructure the firm's US$5 billion debt. According to Bloom, "We told Goodyear, 'We'll make you profitable, but you're going to adopt this strategy.'. . . We think the company should be a patient, long-term builder of value for the employees and shareholders." In their most recent contract, the U.S. tire maker expects to save some US$500+ million over four years and invest US$600 million in unionized plants.[68]

Outside the United States, the average proportion of unionized workers among major industrialized nations is around 50%. European unions tend to be militant, politically oriented, and much less interested in working with management to increase efficiency. Nationwide strikes can occur quickly. In contrast, Japanese unions are typically tied to individual companies and are usually supportive of management. These differences among countries have significant implications for the management of multinational corporations.

To increase flexibility, avoid layoffs, and reduce labor costs, corporations are using more temporary (also known as contingent) workers. Over 90% of U.S. and European firms use temporary workers in some capacity; 43% use them in professional and technical functions.[69] As of 2016, approximately 18.2% of the U.S. workforce consisted of part-time workers.[70] The percentage is even higher in Japan, where 26% of workers are part-time, and in the Netherlands, where 36% of all employees work part-time.[71] Labor unions are concerned that companies use temps to avoid hiring costlier unionized workers.

Quality of Work Life and Human Diversity

Human resource departments have found that to reduce employee dissatisfaction and unionization efforts (or, conversely, to improve employee satisfaction and existing union relations), they must consider the *quality of work life* in the design of jobs. Partially a reaction to the traditionally heavy emphasis on technical and economic factors in job design, quality of work life emphasizes improving the human dimension of work. The knowledgeable human resource manager, therefore, should be able to improve the corporation's quality of work life by (1) introducing participative problem solving, (2) restructuring work, (3) introducing innovative reward systems, and (4) improving the work environment. It is hoped that these improvements will lead to a more participative corporate culture and thus higher productivity and quality products. Ford Motor Company, for example, rebuilt and modernized its famous River Rouge plant using flexible equipment and new processes. Employees work in teams and use Internet-connected PCs on the shop floor to share their concerns instantly with suppliers or product engineers. Workstations were redesigned to make them more ergonomic and reduce repetitive-strain injuries. "If you feel good while you're working, I think quality and productivity will increase, and Ford thinks that too, otherwise they wouldn't do this," observed Jerry Sullivan, president of United Auto Workers Local 600.[72]

Companies are also discovering that by redesigning their plants and offices for improved energy efficiency, they can receive a side effect of improving their employees' quality of work life—that is, raising labor productivity. See the **Sustainability Issue** feature to learn how improved environmental sustainability programs have changed the Olympic Games.

Human diversity refers to the mix in the workplace of people from different races, cultures, and backgrounds. Realizing that the demographics are changing toward an increasing percentage of minorities and women in the U.S. workforce, companies are now concerned with hiring and promoting people without regard to ethnic background. Research does indicate that an increase in racial diversity leads to an increase in firm performance.[73] In a survey of 131 leading European companies, 67.2% stated that a diverse workforce can provide competitive advantage.[74] A manager from Nestlé stated: "To deliver products that meet the needs of individual consumers, we need people who respect other cultures, embrace diversity, and never discriminate on any basis."[75] Good human resource managers should be working to ensure that people are treated fairly on the job and not harassed by prejudiced co-workers or managers. Otherwise, they may find themselves subject to lawsuits. Coca-Cola Company, for example, agreed to pay US$192.5 million because of discrimination against African-American salaried employees in pay, promotions, and evaluations from 1995 and 2000. According to then Chairman and CEO Douglas Daft, "Sometimes things happen in an unintentional manner. And I've made it clear that can't happen anymore."[76]

An organization's human resources may be a key to achieving a sustainable competitive advantage. Advances in technology are copied almost immediately by competitors around the world. People, however, are not as willing to move to other companies in other countries. This means that the only long-term resource advantage remaining to corporations operating in the industrialized nations may lie in the area of skilled human resources.[77] Research does reveal that competitive strategies are more successfully executed in those companies with a high level of commitment to their employees than in those firms with less commitment.[78]

STRATEGIC INFORMATION SYSTEMS/TECHNOLOGY ISSUES

The primary task of the manager of information systems/technology is to design and manage the flow of information in an organization in ways that improve productivity and decision making. Information must be collected, stored, and synthesized in such a manner that it will answer important operating and strategic questions. A corporation's

SUSTAINABILITY issue

THE OLYMPIC GAMES—LONDON 2012/SOCHI 2014/RIO 2016 & TOKYO 2020

Prior to the 2012 Olympic Games in London, there had never been a plan in place for any sustainability standards for the event sector. The 2012 London Olympic Committee decided not only to make sustainability a cornerstone of that Olympics, but also to establish standards for future Olympics and other major events.

Rather than dictating a set of specific targets or checklists, the committee established a method for organizers to work with the local community, suppliers, and participants to identify the key impact areas of the event and a means to mitigate the negative impacts, measure progress, make improvements, and report those results. The committee worked with representatives from over 30 countries including the hosts for the 2014 and 2016 games. There were five areas of focus for the group: (1) Climate Change, (2) Waste, (3) Bio-diversity, (4) Inclusion, and (5) Healthy Living.

The results were stunning. Not only did the committee succeed in codifying the new standards (now referred to as ISO 20121), they also used the standards to design and run the games. Here are two of many examples of their success:

1. An industrial dump had existed in East London for over 100 years. The site was famous with the locals as an eyesore and a dangerous place. The committee took this on as one of their sustainability projects by cleaning the entire area up, putting many of the new sports venues on the site and creating what is now one of Europe's largest urban parks. The area has been transformed and eventually will see thousands of new homes in the heart of London.

2. The "Food Vision" program aimed to mitigate the impact of having to serve more than 14 million meals across 40 different venues during the 17 days of the Olympics. It required suppliers to use local sources as much as possible, and certify that food met a number of food-related standards including Fairtrade, Marine Stewardship Council Certified Fish, and Farm Assured Red Tractor. Sponsor companies such as McDonald's, Coca-Cola, and Cadbury voluntarily applied the standards to all of their meals.

There was a significant setback with the Sochi Winter Olympics in 2014. Despite significant promises by the organizers and substantial financial resources, it appears that very few of the sustainability promises were kept. Unlicensed landfills, damage to pristine environments and the reported harassing of environmental activists set the Olympic sustainability efforts back.

The Rio 2016 games moved aggressively to implement the sustainability standards and on January 27, 2016 they received a plaque confirming ISO 20121 certification. The Tokyo 2020 committee developed and published a High-level Sustainability Plan and has pledged a minimal impact and sustainable games.

Although there is no way to have a zero-impact event with something the size of the Olympic games, the work done for the 2012 Olympics seems to be changing the way that all organizations plan for large events.

················

SOURCES: Olympics.org/news/Tokyo-2020-reveals-plans-for-sustainable-and-minimal-impact-games/247577; Olympic.org/new/rio-2016-organizers-receive-sustainability-certification/247862; A. Aston, "Winter Olympics 2014: a missed opportunity to advance sustainability," *The Guardian* (February 4, 2014) (theguardian.com /sustainable-business/2014/feb/04/sochi-winter-olympics-missed-opportunity-sustainability); "London 2012 – Helping Set Sustainability Standards," *The Guardian* (August 10, 2012), (http://www. guardian.co.uk/sustainable-business/blog/london-2012-helping-set-sustainability-standards); http://www.london2012.com /about-us/publications/publication=london-2012-sustainability-plan-summary/; http://ukinjapan.fco.gov.uk/en/visiting-the-uk /london-2012-olympics/sustainability/.

information system can be a strength or a weakness in multiple areas of strategic management. Not only can it aid in environmental scanning and in controlling a company's many activities, it can also be used as a strategic weapon in gaining competitive advantage.

Impact on Performance

Information systems/technology offers four main contributions to corporate performance. *First*, (beginning in the 1970s with mainframe computers) it is used to automate existing back-office processes, such as payroll, human resource records, accounts payable and receivable, and to establish huge databases. *Second*, (beginning in the 1980s) it is used to automate individual tasks, such as keeping track of clients and expenses, through the use of personal computers with word processing and spreadsheet software. Corporate databases are accessed to provide sufficient data to analyze and to create what-if scenarios. These first two contributions tend to focus on reducing costs. *Third*, (beginning in the 1990s) it is used to enhance key business functions, such as marketing and operations. This third contribution focuses on productivity improvements. The system provides customer support and help in distribution and logistics. For example, in an early effort on the Internet, FedEx found that by allowing customers to directly access its package-tracking database via the Web instead of having to ask a human operator, the company saved up to US$2 million annually.[79] Business processes are analyzed to increase efficiency and productivity via reengineering. Enterprise resource planning (ERP) application software, such as SAP, PeopleSoft, Oracle, Baan, and J.D. Edwards (discussed further in **Chapter 10**), is used to integrate worldwide business activities so that employees need to enter information only once and that information is available to all corporate systems (including accounting) around the world. *Fourth*, (beginning in 2000) it is used to develop competitive advantage. For example, American Hospital Supply (AHS), a leading manufacturer and distributor of a broad line of products for doctors, laboratories, and hospitals, developed an order entry distribution system that directly linked the majority of its customers to AHS computers. The system was successful because it simplified ordering processes for customers, reduced costs for both AHS and the customer, and allowed AHS to provide pricing incentives to the customer. As a result, customer loyalty was high and AHS's share of the market became large.

A current trend in corporate information systems/technology is the increasing use of the Internet for marketing, intranets for internal communication, and extranets for logistics and distribution. An *intranet* is an information network within an organization that also has access to the external worldwide Internet. Intranets typically begin as ways to provide employees with company information such as lists of product prices, fringe benefits, and company policies. They are then converted into extranets for supply chain management. An *extranet* is an information network within an organization that is available to key suppliers and customers. The key issue in building an extranet is the creation of "fire walls" to block extranet users from accessing the firm's or other users' confidential data. Once this is accomplished, companies can allow employees, customers, and suppliers to access information and conduct business on the Internet in a completely automated manner. By connecting these groups, companies hope to obtain a competitive advantage by reducing the time needed to design and bring new products to market, slashing inventories, customizing manufacturing, and entering new markets.[80]

There has been an explosion of wikis, blogs, RSS (Really Simple Syndication), social networks (e.g., LinkedIn and Facebook), podcasts, online video conferencing, video sharing, and mash-ups through company Web sites to forge tighter links with customers and suppliers and to engage employees more successfully. For example, LEGO invited customers to suggest new models interactively and then financially rewarded the people whose ideas proved marketable.[81]

Supply Chain Management

The expansion of the marketing-oriented Internet into intranets and extranets is making significant contributions to organizational performance through supply chain management. **Supply chain management** is the forming of networks for sourcing raw materials, manufacturing products or creating services, storing and distributing the goods, and delivering them to customers and consumers.[82] Research indicates that supplier network resources have a significant impact on firm performance.[83] A survey of global executives revealed that their interest in supply chains was first to reduce costs, and then to improve customer service and get new products to market faster.[84] More than 85% of senior executives stated that improving their firm's supply-chain performance was a top priority. Companies like Wal-Mart, Dell, and Toyota, who are known to be exemplars in supply-chain management, spend only 4% of their revenues on supply-chain costs compared to 10% by the average firm.[85]

Industry leaders are integrating modern information systems into their corporate value chains to harmonize companywide efforts and to achieve competitive advantage. For example, Heineken beer distributors input actual depletion figures and replenishment orders to the Netherlands brewer through their linked Web pages. This interactive planning system generates time-phased orders based on actual usage rather than on projected demand. Distributors are then able to modify plans based on local conditions or changes in marketing. Heineken uses these modifications to adjust brewing and supply schedules. As a result of this system, lead times have been reduced from the traditional 10–12 weeks to 4–6 weeks. This time savings is especially useful in an industry competing on product freshness. In another example, Procter & Gamble participates in an information network to move the company's line of consumer products through Wal-Mart's many stores. *Radio-frequency identification (RFID)* tags containing product information are used to track goods through inventory and distribution channels. As part of the network with Wal-Mart, P&G knows by cash register and by store what products have passed through the system every hour of each day. The network is linked by satellite communications on a real-time basis. With actual point-of-sale information, products are replenished to meet current demand and minimize stockouts while maintaining exceptionally low inventories.[86]

The Strategic Audit: A Checklist for Organizational Analysis

5-6. Construct an IFAS Table that summarizes internal factors

One way of conducting an organizational analysis to examine a company's strengths and weaknesses is by using the Strategic Audit found in **Appendix 1.A** at the end of **Chapter 1**. The audit provides a checklist of questions by area of concern. For example, Part IV of the audit examines corporate structure, culture, and resources. It looks at organizational resources and capabilities in terms of the functional areas of marketing, finance, R&D, operations, human resources, and information systems, among others.

SYNTHESIS OF INTERNAL FACTORS (IFAS)

After strategists have scanned the internal organizational environment and identified factors for their particular corporation, they may want to summarize their analysis of these factors using a form such as that given in **Table 5–2**. This **IFAS (Internal Factor Analysis Summary) Table** is one way to organize the internal factors into the generally accepted categories of strengths and weaknesses as well as to examine how well a particular company's management is responding to these specific factors in light of the perceived importance of these factors to the company. Use the VRIO framework (**V**alue, **R**areness, **I**mitability, and **O**rganization) to assess the importance of each of the factors that might be considered strengths. Except for its internal orientation, this IFAS Table is built the same way as the EFAS Table described in **Chapter 4** (in **Table 4–5**). To use the IFAS Table, complete the following steps:

1. In Column 1 (Internal Factors), list the 8 to 10 most important strengths and weaknesses facing the company.

2. In Column 2 (Weight), assign a weight to each factor from 1.0 (Most Important) to 0.0 (Not Important) based on that factor's probable impact on a particular company's current strategic position. The higher the weight, the more important is this factor to the current and future success of the company. **All weights must sum to 1.0 regardless of the number of factors.**

3. In Column 3 (Rating), assign a rating to each factor from 5.0 (Outstanding) to 1.0 (Poor) based on management's specific response to that particular factor. Each rating is a judgment regarding how well the company's management is currently dealing with each specific internal factor.

TABLE 5–2 Internal Factor Analysis Summary (IFAS Table): Maytag as Example

Internal Factors	Weight	Rating	Weighted Score	Comments
1	2	3	4	5
Strengths				
▪ Quality Maytag culture	.15	5.0	.75	Quality key to success
▪ Experienced top management	.05	4.2	.21	Know appliances
▪ Vertical integration	.10	3.9	.39	Dedicated factories
▪ Employer relations	.05	3.0	.15	Good, but deteriorating
▪ Hoover's international orientation	.15	2.8	.42	Hoover name in cleaners
Weaknesses				
▪ Process-oriented R&D	.05	2.2	.11	Slow on new products
▪ Distribution channels	.05	2.0	.10	Superstores replacing small dealers
▪ Financial position	.15	2.0	.30	High debt load
▪ Global positioning	.20	2.1	.42	Hoover weak outside the United Kingdom and Australia
▪ Manufacturing facilities	.05	4.0	.20	Investing now
Total Scores	1.00		3.05	

NOTES:

1. List strengths and weaknesses (8–10) in Column 1.
2. Weight each factor from 1.0 (Most Important) to 0.0 (Not Important) in Column 2 based on that factor's probable impact on the company's strategic position. **The total weights must sum to 1.00.**
3. Rate each factor from 5.0 (Outstanding) to 1.0 (Poor) in Column 3 based on the company's response to that factor.
4. Multiply each factor's weight times its rating to obtain each factor's weighted score in Column 4.
5. Use Column 5 (comments) for the rationale used for each factor.
6. Add the individual weighted scores to obtain the total weighted score for the company in Column 4. This tells how well the company is responding to the factors in its internal environment.

SOURCE: Thomas L. Wheelen, copyright © 1982, 1985, 1987, 1988, 1989, 1990, 1991, 1995, and every year after that. Kathryn E. Wheelen solely owns all of (Dr.) Thomas L. Wheelen's copyrighted materials. Kathryn E. Wheelen requires written reprint permission for each book that this material is to be printed in. Thomas L. Wheelen and J. David Hunger, copyright © 1991—first year "Internal Factor Analysis Summary (IFAS) appeared in this text (4th ed.) Reprinted by permission of the copyright holders".

4. In Column 4 (Weighted Score), multiply the weight in Column 2 for each factor times its rating in Column 3 to obtain that factor's weighted score.

5. In Column 5 (Comments), note why a particular factor was selected and/or how its weight and rating were estimated.

6. Finally, add the weighted scores for all the internal factors in Column 4 to determine the total weighted score for that particular company. The **total weighted score** indicates how well a particular company is responding to current and expected factors in its internal environment. The score can be used to compare that firm to other firms in its industry. Check to ensure that the total weighted score truly reflects the company's current performance in terms of profitability and market share. **The total weighted score for an average firm in an industry is always 3.0**.

As an example of this procedure, **Table 5–2** includes a number of internal factors for Maytag Corporation in 1995 (before Maytag was acquired by Whirlpool) with corresponding weights, ratings, and weighted scores provided. Note that Maytag's total weighted score is 3.05, meaning that the corporation is about average compared to the strengths and weaknesses of others in the major home appliance industry.

End of Chapter SUMMARY

Every day, about 17 truckloads of used diesel engines and other parts are dumped at a receiving facility at Caterpillar's remanufacturing plant in Corinth, Mississippi. The filthy iron engines are then broken down by two workers, who manually hammer and drill for half a day until they have taken every bolt off the engine and put each component into its own bin. The engines are then cleaned and remade at half of the cost of a new engine and sold for a tidy profit. This system works at Caterpillar because, as a general rule, 70% of the cost to build something new is in the materials and 30% is in the labor. Remanufacturing simply starts the manufacturing process over again with materials that are essentially free and which already contain most of the energy costs needed to make them. The would-be discards become fodder for the next product, eliminating waste, and cutting costs. Caterpillar's management was so impressed by the remanufacturing operation that they made the business a separate division in 2005. The unit earned more than US$1 billion in sales in 2005 and by 2012 employed more than 8500 workers in 16 countries.

Caterpillar's remanufacturing unit was successful not only because of its ability to wring productivity out of materials and labor, but also because it designed its products for reuse. Before they are built new, remanufactured products must be designed for disassembly. In order to achieve this, Caterpillar asks its designers to check a "Reman" box on Caterpillar's product development checklist. The company also needs to know where its products are being used in order to take them back—known as the art of *reverse logistics*. This is achieved by Caterpillar's excellent relationship with its dealers throughout the world, as well as through financial incentives. For example, when a customer orders a crankshaft, that customer is offered a remanufactured one for half the cost of a new one—assuming the customer turns in the old crankshaft to Caterpillar. The products also should be built for performance with little regard for changing fashion. Because diesel engines change little from year to year, a remanufactured engine is very similar to a new engine and might perform even better.

Monitoring the external environment is only one part of environmental scanning. Strategists also need to scan a corporation's internal environment to identify its resources, capabilities, and competencies. What are its strengths and weaknesses? At Caterpillar, management clearly noted that the environment was changing in a way to make its remanufactured product more desirable. It took advantage of its strengths in manufacturing and distribution to offer a recycling service for its current customers and a low-cost alternative product for those who could not afford a new Caterpillar engine. It also happened to be an environmentally friendly, sustainable business model. Caterpillar's management felt that remanufacturing thus provided them with a strategic advantage over competitors who don't remanufacture. This is an example of a company using its capabilities in key functional areas to expand its business by moving into a new profitable position on its value chain.[87]

Pearson MyLab Management®

Go to **mymanagementlab.com** to complete the problems marked with this icon 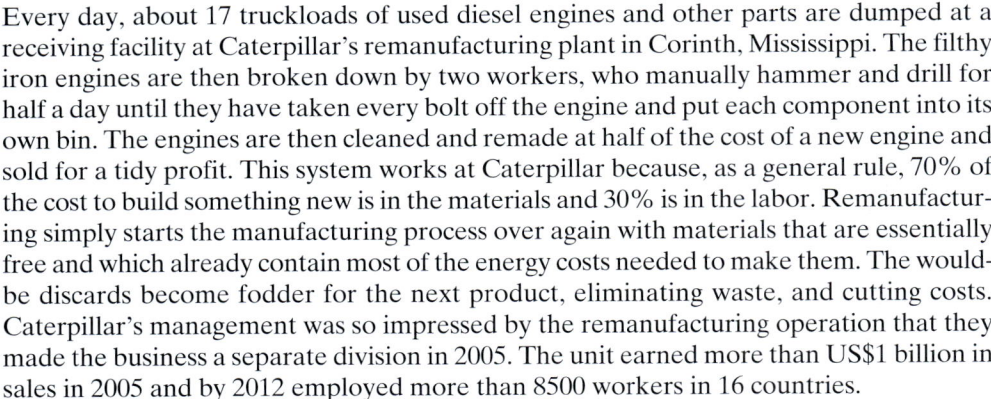.

KEY TERMS

brand (p. 181)
business model (p. 170)
capabilities (p. 166)
capital budgeting (p. 182)

competency (p. 166)
conglomerate structure (p. 177)
a core competency (p. 167)
corporate culture (p. 177)

corporate reputation (p. 182)
distinctive competencies (p. 167)
divisional structure (p. 176)
economies of scale (p. 186)

Pearson MyLab Management®

Go to **mymanagmentlab.com** for the following assisted-graded writing questions:

5-1. How does the resource-based view of the firm provide a superior means of evaluating a company's competitive advantage?

5-2. Explain how using an IFAS table impacts the understanding of a company's internal resources and capabilities?

DISCUSSION QUESTIONS

5-3. How does the resource-based view of firms help in determining the sustainability of a competitive advantage?

5-4. How does VRIO framework analysis help in evaluating a company's competencies?

5-5. Why is organizational culture important for a business to effectively formulate its strategy?

5-6. How are organizational resources linked to the competitive advantages and corporate performance of an organization?

5-7. How is the possession of valuable and scarce resources of an organization related to the planning and formulation of its corporate-level strategy for enhancing its competitive advantages in the market?

STRATEGIC PRACTICE EXERCISES

Today, the primary means of information collection is through the Internet. Try the following exercise.

5-1. Form into teams of around three to five people. Select a well-known publicly-owned company to research. Inform the instructor of your choice.

5-2. Assign each person a separate task. One task might be to find the latest financial statements. Another would be to learn as much as possible about its top management and board of directors. Yet another might be to identify its business model, or its key competitors. Conduct research on the company *using the Internet only*.

  a. Apply the resource-based view of the firm to determine core and distinctive competencies of your selected company.

  b. Use the VRIO framework and the value chain to assess the company's competitive advantage, and how it can be sustained.

  c. Understand the company's business model, and how it could be imitated.

  d. Assess the company's corporate culture, and how it might affect a proposed strategy.

  e. Scan functional resources to determine their fit with the company strategy.

  f. What is your prediction about the future of this firm if it continues on its current path?

5-3. Would you buy a stock in this company? Assume that your team has U.S. $25,000 to invest. Allocate the money among the four or five primary competitors in this industry. List the companies, the number of shares purchased of each, the cost of each share as of a given date, and the total cost for each purchase assuming a typical commission used by an Internet broker, such as E-Trade or Scottrade.

5-4. Meet with your team members to discuss what you have found. What are the company's opportunities, threats, strengths, and weaknesses? Go back to the Internet for more information if needed.

NOTES

1. R. M. Grant, *Contemporary Strategy Analysis*, 6th edition (Malden, MA: Blackwell Publishing, 2008), pp. 130–131.

2. G. Schreyogg and M. Kliesch-Eberl, "How Dynamic Can Organizational Capabilities Be? Towards a Dual-Process Model of Capability Dynamization," *Strategic Management Journal* (September 2007), pp. 913–933.

3. M. Javidan, "Core Competence: What Does It Mean in Practice?" *Long Range Planning* (February 1998), pp. 60–71.

4. M. A. Hitt, B. W. Keats, and S. M. DeMarie, "Navigating in the New Competitive Landscape: Building Strategic Flexibility and Competitive Advantage in the 21st Century," *Academy of Management Executive* (November 1998), pp. 22–42; C. E. Helfat and M. A. Peteraf, "The Dynamic Resources-Based View: Capability Life Cycles," *Strategic Management Journal* (October 2003), pp. 997–1010.

5. D. Brady and K. Capell, "GE Breaks the Mold to Spur Innovation," *BusinessWeek* (April 26, 2004), pp. 88–89.

6. J. B. Barney, *Gaining and Sustaining Competitive Advantage*, 2nd ed. (Upper Saddle River, NJ: Prentice Hall, 2002), pp. 159–172. Barney's VRIO questions are very similar to those proposed by G. Hamel and S. K. Prahalad in their book, *Competing for the Future* (Boston: Harvard Business School Press, 1994) on pages 202–207 in which they state that to be distinctive, a competency must (a) provide customer value, (b) be competitor unique, and (c) be extendable to develop new products and/or markets.

7. S. L. Newbert, "Value, Rareness, Competitive Advantage, and Performance: A Conceptual-Level Empirical Investigation of the Resource-Based View of the Firm," *Strategic Management Journal* (July 2008), pp. 745–768.

8. http://www.kens5.com/story/news/local/2014/06/25/10319134/

9. M. Polanyi, *The Tacit Dimension* (London: Routledge & Kegan Paul, 1966).

10. S. K. McEvily and B. Chakravarthy, "The Persistence of Knowledge-Based Advantage: An Empirical Test for Product Performance and Technological Knowledge," *Strategic Management Journal* (April 2002), pp. 285–305.

11. P. E. Bierly III, "Development of a Generic Knowledge Strategy Typology," *Journal of Business Strategies* (Spring 1999), p. 3.

12. R. W. Coff, D. C. Coff, and R. Eastvold, "The Knowledge Leveraging Paradox: How to Achieve Scale Without Making Knowledge Imitable," *Academy of Management Review* (April 2006), pp. 452–465.

13. Barney, p. 161.

14. P. J. Verdin and P. J. Williamson, "Core Competencies, Competitive Advantage and Market Analysis: Forging the Links," in G. Hamel and A. Heene (Eds.), *Competence-Based Competition* (New York: John Wiley and Sons, 1994), pp. 83–84; S. K. Ethiraj, P. Kale, M. S. Krishnan, and J. V. Singh, "Where Do Capabilities Come From and How Do They Matter? A Study in the Software Services Industry," *Strategic Management Journal* (January 2005), pp. 701–719.

15. J. Devan, M. B. Klusas, and T. W. Ruefli, "The Elusive Goal of Corporate Outperformance," *McKinsey Quarterly Online* (April 2007).

16. "Aviation Industry Clusters in U.S. Metros," June 2015, *Garner Economics*, http://www.garnereconomics.com/pdf/Garner%20Economics%20Aviation%20Cluster%202015%20final.pdf; P. Davidson, "To Get Jobs, Areas Develop Industry Hubs in Emerging Fields," *USA Today* (June 7, 2011).

17. M. E. Porter, "Clusters and the New Economics of Competition," *Harvard Business Review* (November–December 1998), pp. 77–90.

18. J. M. Shaver and F. Flyer, "Agglomeration Economies, Firm Heterogeneity, and Foreign Direct Investment in the United States," *Strategic Management Journal* (December 2000), pp. 1175–1193; W. Chung and A. Kalnins, "Agglomeration Effects and Performance: A Test of the Texas Lodging Industry," *Strategic Management Journal* (October 2001), pp. 969–988.

19. S. Abraham, "Experiencing Strategic Conversations about the Central Forces of Our Time," *Strategy & Leadership* (Vol. 31, No. 2, 2003), pp. 61–62.

20. http://autocontentexp.com/least-expensive-cars-of-2016/

21. K. Kelleher, "HP's Printer Problem," *CNNMoney* (March 29, 2012), (www.tech.fortune.cnn.com/2012/03/29/hps-printer-problem/); P. Burrows, "Ever Wonder Why Ink Costs So Much?" *BusinessWeek* (November 14, 2005), pp. 42–44.

22. http://www.bp.com/sectiongenericarticle.do?categoryId=9014445&contentId=7027526.

23. https://media.ford.com/content/dam/fordmedia/North%20America/US/2016/01/28/4qfinancials.pdf; O. Lowenberg, "GM made record profits in 2015 thanks to North American sales," *The Christian Science Monitor*, February 3, 2016 (http://www.csmonitor.com/Business/In-Gear/2016/0203/GM-made-record-profits-in-2015-thanks-to-North-American-sales-video).

24. J. R. Galbraith, "Strategy and Organization Planning," in H. Mintzberg and J. B. Quinn (Eds.), *The Strategy Process: Concepts, Contexts, and Cases*, 2nd ed. (Englewood Cliffs, N.J.: Prentice Hall, 1991), pp. 315–324.

25. M. Porter, *Competitive Advantage: Creating and Sustaining Superior Performance* (New York: The Free Press, 1985), p. 36.

26. www.thecloroxcompany.com/products/our-brands/.

27. M. Leontiades, "A Diagnostic Framework for Planning," *Strategic Management Journal* (January–March 1983), p. 14.

28. E. H. Schein, *The Corporate Culture Survival Guide* (San Francisco: Jossey-Bass, 1999), p. 12; L. C. Harris and E. Ogbonna, "The Strategic Legacy of Company Founders," *Long Range Planning* (June 1999), pp. 333–343.

29. D. M. Rousseau, "Assessing Organizational Culture: The Case for Multiple Methods," in B. Schneider (Ed.), *Organizational Climate and Culture* (San Francisco: Jossey-Bass, 1990), pp. 153–192.

30. L. Smircich, "Concepts of Culture and Organizational Analysis," *Administrative Science Quarterly* (September 1983), pp. 345–346; D. Ravasi and M. Schultz, "Responding to Organizational Identity Threats: Exploring the Role of Organizational Culture," *Academy of Management Journal* (June 2006), pp. 433–458.

31. D. G. Allen, "Do Organizational Socialization Tactics Influence Newcomer Embeddedness and Turnover?" *Journal of Management* (April 2006), pp. 237–256.

32. J. B. Sorensen, "The Strength of Corporate Culture and the Reliability of Firm Performance," *Administrative Science Quarterly* (March 2002), pp. 70–91; R. E. Smerek and D. R. Denison, "Social Capital in Organizations: Understanding the Link to Firm Performance," presentation to the *Academy of Management* (Philadelphia, 2007).

33. K. E. Aupperle, "Spontaneous Organizational Reconfiguration: A Historical Example Based on Xenophon's Anabasis," *Organization Science* (July–August 1996), pp. 445–460.

34. P. Gogoi, "Circuit City: Due for a Change?" *Bloomberg Businessweek* (February 29, 2008), (www.businessweek.com/stories/2008-02-29/circuit-city-due-for-a-change-businessweek-business-news-stock-market-and-financial-advice; E. Gruenwedel, "Circuit City Ceases Operations," *HomeMedia Magazine* (January 16, 2009), (http://www.homemediamagazine.com/news/circuit-city-ceases-operations-14346).

35. "Face Value: A Post-Modern Proctoid," *The Economist* (April 15, 2006), p. 68.

36. http://www.forbes.com/powerful-brands/list/#tab:rank; K. Badenhausen, "Apple And Microsoft Head The World's Most Valuable Brands 2015," *Forbes* (May 13, 2015), (http://www.forbes.com/sites/kurtbadenhausen/2015/05/13/apple-and-microsoft-head-the-worlds-most-valuable-brands-2015/#2232cef72875).

37. R. T. Wilcox, "The Hidden Potential of Powerful Brands," *Batten Briefings* (Summer 2003), pp. 1, 4–5.

38. V. P. Rindova, I. O. Williamson, A. P. Petkova, and J. M. Sever, "Being Good or Being Known: An Empirical Examination of the Dimensions, Antecedents, and Consequences of Organizational Reputation," *Academy of Management Journal* (December 2005), pp. 1033–1049.

39. Ibid.

40. C. Fombrun and C. Van Riel, "The Reputational Landscape," *Corporate Reputation Review* (Vol. 1, Nos. 1 & 2, 1997), pp. 5–13.

41. P. Engardio and M. Arndt, "What Price Reputation?" *BusinessWeek* (July 9 and 16, 2007), pp. 70–79.

42. P. W. Roberts and G. R. Dowling, "Corporate Reputation and Sustained Financial Performance," *Strategic Management Journal* (December 2002), pp. 1077–1093; J. Shamsie, "The Context of Dominance: An Industry-Driven Framework for Exploiting Reputation," *Strategic Management Journal* (March 2003), pp. 199–215; M. D. Michalisin, D. M. Kline, and R. D. Smith, "Intangible Strategic Assets and Firm Performance: A Multi-Industry Study of the Resource-Based View," *Journal of Business Strategies* (Fall 2000), pp. 91–117; S. S. Standifird, "Reputation and E-Commerce: eBay Auctions and the Asymmetrical Impact of Positive and Negative Ratings," *Journal of Management* (Vol. 27, No. 3, 2001), pp. 279–295.

43. R. L. Simerly and M. Li, "Environmental Dynamism, Capital Structure and Performance: A Theoretical Integration and an Empirical Test," *Strategic Management Journal* (January 2000), pp. 31–49.

44. R. L. Simerly and M. Li, "Environmental Dynamism, Capital Structure and Performance: A Theoretical Integration and an Empirical Test," *Strategic Management Journal* (January 2000), pp. 31–49; A. Heisz and S. LaRochelle-Cote, "Corporate Financial Leverage in Canadian Manufacturing: Consequences for Employment and Inventories," *Canadian Journal of Administrative Science* (June 2004), pp. 111–128.

45. J. M. Poterba and L. H. Summers, "A CEO Survey of U.S. Companies' Time Horizons and Hurdle Rates," *Sloan Management Review* (Fall 1995), pp. 43–53.

46. M. Casey & R. Hackett, "The 10 biggest R&D spenders worldwide," *Fortune*, (November 17, 2014) (http://fortune.com/2014/11/17/top-10-research-development/).

47. M. Krantz, "7 companies outspend Apple on innovation," *USA Today* (September 9, 2014), (http://americasmarkets.usatoday.com/2014/09/09/7-companies-outspent-apple-on-innovation/)

48. C. Palmeri, "Swords to Plowshares—And Back Again," *BusinessWeek* (February 11, 2008), p. 66.

49. G. E. Moore, "Cramming More Components onto Integrated Circuits," *Electronics* (38:8), April 19, 1965); D. J. Yang, "Leaving Moore's Law in the Dust," *U.S. News & World Report* (July 10, 2000), pp. 37–38; R. Fishburne and M. Malone, "Laying Down the Laws: Gordon Moore and Bob Metcalfe in Conversation," *Forbes ASAP* (February 21, 2000), pp. 97–100.

50. P. Pascarella, "Are You Investing in the Wrong Technology?" *Industry Week* (July 25, 1983), p. 38.

51. C. M. Christensen, *The Innovator's Dilemma* (Boston: Harvard Business School Press, 1997).

52. Markets & Markets, 2015 (http://www.marketsandmarkets.com/Market-Reports/display-market-925.html); O. Port, "Flat-Panel Pioneer," *BusinessWeek* (December 12, 2005), p. 22. This phenomenon has also been discussed in terms of paradigm shifts in which a new development makes the old game obsolete—See Joel A. Barker, *Future Edge* (New York: William Morrow and Company, 1992).

53. For examples of experience curves for various products, see M. Gottfredson, S. Schaubert, and H. Saenz, "The New Leader's Guide to Diagnosing the Business," *Harvard Business Review* (February 2008), pp. 63–73.

54. B. J. Pine, *Mass Customization: The New Frontier in Business Competition* (Boston: Harvard Business School Press, 1993).

55. J. Buckley, "Korea's Flexible Carmakers," *AMS* (May/June 2009), pp. 18–29.

56. S. L Rynes, K. G. Brown, and A. E. Colbert, "Seven Common Misconceptions about Human Resource Practices: Research Findings Versus Practitioner Belief," *Academy of Management Executive* (August 2002), pp. 92–103; R. S. Schuler and S. E. Jackson, "A Quarter-Century Review of Human Resource Management in the U.S.: The Growth in Importance of the International Perspective," in R. S. Schuler and S. E. Jackson (Eds.), *Strategic Human Resource Management*, 2nd ed. (Malden, MA: Blackwell Publishing, 2007), pp. 214–240; M. Guthridge and A. B. Komm, "Why Multinationals Struggle to Manage Talent," *McKinsey Quarterly* (May 2008), pp. 1–5.

57. J. McGregor and S. Hamm, "Managing the Global Work-force," *BusinessWeek* (January 28, 2008), pp. 34–48; D. A. Ready and J. A. Conger, "Make Your Company a Talent Factory," *Harvard Business Review* (June 2007), pp. 68–77.

58. E. E. Lawler, S. A. Mohrman, and G. E. Ledford, Jr., *Creating High Performance Organizations* (San Francisco: Jossey-Bass, 1995), p. 29.

59. "Building Perfection: Self-Directed Work Teams Deliver on Quality," *QualityDigest* (February 1, 2012), (www.qualtydigest.com/inside/quality-insider-article/connecticut-company-uses-self-directed-work-teams-improve-time.html).

60. R. Sanchez, "Strategic Flexibility in Product Competition," *Strategic Management Journal* (Summer 1995), p. 147.

61. A. R. Jassawalla and H. C. Sashittal, "Building Collaborative Cross-Functional New Product Teams," *Academy of Management Executive* (August 1999), pp. 50–63.

62. A. M. Townsend, S. M. DeMarie, and A. R. Hendrickson, "Virtual Teams' Technology and the Workplace of the Future," *Academy of Management Executive* (August 1998), pp. 17–29.

63. S. A. Furst, M. Reeves, B. Rosen, and R. S. Blackburn, "Managing the Life Cycle of Virtual Teams," *Academy of Management Executive* (May 2004), pp. 6–20; L. L. Martins, L. L. Gilson, and M. T. Maynard, "Virtual Teams: What Do We Know and Where Do We Go From Here?" *Journal of Management* (Vol. 30, No. 6, 2004), pp. 805–835; T. Minton-Eversole, "Virtual Teams Used Most by Global Organizations, Survey Says," *SHRM* (July 19, 2012), (www.shrm.org/hrdisciplines/orgempdev/articles/pages/virtualteamsusedmostbyglobalorganizations,surveysays.aspx).

64. C. B. Gibson and J. L. Gibbs, "Unpacking the Concept of Virtuality: The Effects of Geographic Dispersion, Electronic Dependence, Dynamic Structure, and National Diversity on Team Innovation," *Administrative Science Quarterly* (September 2006), pp. 451–495.

65. J. Jones, "In U.S., Telecommuting for Work Climbs to 37%," *Gallup* (August 19, 2015) (www.gallup.com/poll/184649/telecommuting-work-climbs.aspx).

66. Townsend, DeMarie, and Hendrickson, p. 18.

67. "Economic News Release," *Bureau of Labor Statistics*, U.S. Department of Labor (January 28, 2016) (www.bls.gov/news.release/union2.nr0.htm).

68. D. Welsh, "What Goodyear Got from Its Union," *BusinessWeek* (October 20, 2003), pp. 148–149; "Update 1 – Goodyear Union Contract Saves $215 Mln over 4-Yrs," *Reuters* (September 29, 2009), (www.reuters.com/articles/2009/09/29/goodyear-idUSN2915419220090929).

69. S. F. Matusik and C. W. L. Hill, "The Utilization of Contingent Work, Knowledge Creation, and Competitive Advantage," *Academy of Management Executive* (October 1998), pp. 680–697; W. Mayrhofer and C. Brewster, "European Human Resource Management: Researching Developments Over Time," in *Strategic Human Resource Management*, 2nd ed. (Malden, MA: Blackwell Publishing, 2007), pp. 241–269.

70. Economic News Release, Bureau of Labor Statistics, U.S. Department of Labor (February 5, 2016) (www.bls.gov/news.release/empsit.nr0.htm).

71. "Part-Time Work," *The Economist* (June 24, 2006), p. 112, (www.statistica.com/statistics/192342/unadjusted-monthly-number-of-part-time-employees-in-the-us/).

72. J. Muller, "A Ford Redesign," *BusinessWeek* (November 13, 2000), Special Report.

73. O. C. Richard, B. P. S. Murthi, and K. Ismail, "The Impact of Racial Diversity on Intermediate and Long-Term Performance: The Moderating Role of Environmental Context," *Strategic Management Journal* (December 2007), pp. 1213–1233; G. Colvin, "The 50 Best Companies for Asians, Blacks, and Hispanics," *Fortune* (July 19, 1999), pp. 53–58.

74. V. Singh and S. Point, "Strategic Responses by European Companies to the Diversity Challenge: An Online Comparison," *Long Range Planning* (August 2004), pp. 295–318.

75. Singh and Point, p. 310.

76. J. Bachman, "Coke to Pay $192.5 Million to Settle Lawsuit," *The* (Ames, IA) *Tribune* (November 20, 2000), p. D4.

77. O. Gottschalg and M. Zollo, "Interest Alignment and Competitive Advantage," *Academy of Management Review* (April 2007), pp. 418–437.

78. J. Lee and D. Miller, "People Matter: Commitment to Employees, Strategy, and Performance in Korean Firms," *Strategic Management Journal* (June 1999), pp. 579–593.

79. A. Cortese, "Here Comes the Intranet," *BusinessWeek* (February 26, 1996), p. 76.

80. D. Bartholomew, "Blue-Collar Computing," *Information Week* (June 19, 1995), pp. 34–43.

81. "Business and Web 2.0: An Interactive Feature," McKinsey & Company, (November 2013) (www.mckinsey.com/business-functions/business-technology/our-insights/business-and-web-20-an-interactive-feature); J. Bughin, J. Manyika, A. Miller, and M. Chui, "Building the Web 2.0 Enterprise," *McKinsey Quarterly Online* (December 2010); J. Bughin and M. Chui, "The Rise of the Networked Enterprise: Web 2.0 Finds Its Payday," *McKinsey Quarterly Online* (December 2010), pp. 1–4.

82. C. C. Poirier, *Advanced Supply Chain Management* (San Francisco: Berrett-Koehler Publishers, 1999), p. 2.

83. J. H. Dyer and N. W. Hatch, "Relation-Specific Capabilities and Barriers to Knowledge Transfers: Creating Advantage through Network Relationships," *Strategic Management Journal* (August 2006), pp. 701–719.

84. D. Paulonis and S. Norton, "Managing Global Supply Chains," *McKinsey Quarterly Online* (August 2008).

85. M. Cook and R. Hagey, "Why Companies Flunk Supply-Chain 101: Only 33 Percent Correctly Measure Supply-Chain Performance; Few Use the Right Incentives," *Journal of Business Strategy* (Vol. 24, No. 4, 2003), pp. 35–42.

86. C. C. Poirer, pp. 3–5. For further information on RFID technology, see F. Taghaboni-Dutta and B. Velthouse, "RFID Technology is Revolutionary: Who Should Be Involved in This Game of Tag?" *Academy of Management Perspectives* (November 2006), pp. 65–78.

87. M. Arndt, "Everything Old Is New Again," *BusinessWeek* (September 25, 2006), pp. 64–70, (www.cat.com/).

PART 3

Strategy
Formulation

CHAPTER 6

Strategy Formulation: Business Strategy

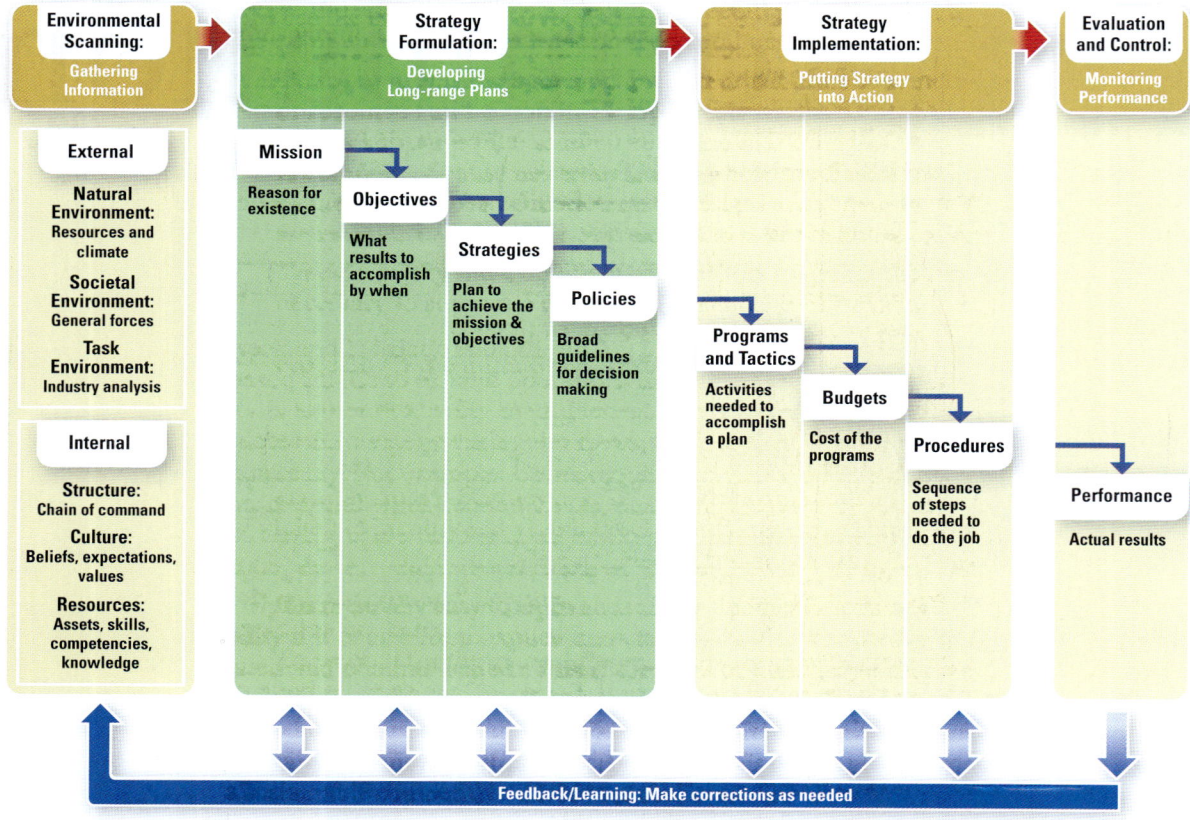

| Environmental Scanning: Gathering Information | Strategy Formulation: Developing Long-range Plans | Strategy Implementation: Putting Strategy into Action | Evaluation and Control: Monitoring Performance |

Feedback/Learning: Make corrections as needed

Pearson MyLab Management®

⭐ **Improve Your Grade!**

Over 10 million students improved their results using the Pearson MyLabs. Visit **mymanagementlab.com** for simulations, tutorials, and end-of-chapter problems.

Learning Objectives

After reading this chapter, you should be able to:

6-1. Utilize the SFAS matrix and a SWOT diagram to examine business strategy.

6-2. Develop a mission statement that addresses the five elements of good design

6-3. Explain the competitive and cooperative strategies available to corporations

6-4. Identify the types of strategic alliances

Kärcher – Evolutionary Diversification Strategy

Based in Winnenden, Germany, Alfred Kärcher GmbH & Co KG is a family-owned company and a market leader for cleaning equipment and services. In 1935, it began as a small engineering office that developed and marketed product ideas in the field of heating technology and grew with its niche product—high pressure cleaners. In 2013, Kärcher surpassed its €2 billion turnover mark (compared to €1.3 billion in 2009) with 12.5 million machines sold. It now has more than 10.600 employees worldwide serving its customers on a global scale. In 2015, it showed a new record with sales totaling €2.22 billion.

The company went through a period of stagnation after Alfred's death. In1974, to turn this slump around, Kärcher shifted its strategy by focusing all its resources on its core competencies: developing and selling high-pressure cleaning equipment. Former CEO, Roland Kamm, was inspired by the example of the Galápagos finches, which were similar in size, but had different sized and shaped beaks. According to English naturalist and geologist, Charles Darwin, this was a result of geographical isolation with different species developing from "ancestral finches." Based on this example, Kamm approached Kärcher's high-pressure steam cleaners as the ancestral finch. In a then-unsegmented market, Kärcher's growth had stagnated after its core product had gained a large share. However, like the birds that had evolved and adapted with modified beaks, a differentiation strategy would solve Kärcher's cleaning problems. The company's new vision statement and motto was " Kärcher: cleaning is our business," and it was now a solution provider that meets the cleaning challenges of target customer groups.

In the 1980s, Kärcher chose to enter the consumer business with a new product—a portable pressure washer. It created a new market and became the leading manufacturer of cleaning equipments for homes and cars. It also led global cleaning projects. For example, in 2005, Kärcher was chosen to clean Mount Rushmore National Memorial. Kärcher's products successfully removed organic dirt that would have damaged the monument in the long term as a result of biocorrosion. By 2006, it addressed the cleaning needs of target customer groups and sold about 2,500 products, most being sold to private households.

SOURCES: https://www.kaercher.com/int/inside-kaercher/company/about-kaercher.html; and B. Venohr and K. E. Meyer, "The German Miracle Keeps Running: How Germany's Hidden Champions Stay Ahead in the Global Economy," *Berlin School of Economics*, May, 2007 (http://hwr-berlin.com/fileadmin/downloads_internet/Forschung/Veroeffentlichungen/Working_paper/working_paper_30.pdf).

A Framework for Examining Business Strategy

6-1. Utilize the SFAS matrix and a SWOT diagram to examine business strategy

Strategy Formulation, often referred to as strategic planning or long-range planning, is concerned with developing a corporation's mission, objectives, strategies, and policies. It begins with situation analysis: the process of finding a strategic fit between external opportunities and internal strengths while working around external threats and internal weaknesses. As shown in the Strategic Decision-Making Process in **Figure 1–5**, step 5(a) is analyzing strategic factors in light of the current situation. As was discussed in **Chapter 5**, the VRIO framework is extraordinarily effective in not only analyzing potential competitive advantages to determine which are true competitive advantages, but also in examining whether the company is organized to take advantage of those strengths.

Many executives prefer to present their analysis using a SWOT chart. **SWOT** is an acronym used to describe the four quadrants of **S**trengths, **W**eaknesses, **O**pportunities, and **T**hreats for a specific company.

It can be said that the essence of strategy is opportunity divided by capacity.[1] An opportunity by itself has no real value unless a company has the capacity (i.e., resources) to take advantage of that opportunity. By itself, a distinctive competency in a key resource or capability is no guarantee of competitive advantage. Weaknesses in other resource areas can prevent a strategy from being successful. SWOT, as a conceptual tool can be used to take a broader view of strategy through the formula SA = O/(S–W)—that is, (Strategic Alternative equals Opportunity divided by Strengths minus Weaknesses). This reflects an important issue strategic managers face: Should we invest more in our strengths to make them even stronger (a distinctive competence) or should we invest in our weaknesses to at least make them competitive?

Populating a SWOT chart, by itself, is just the start of a strategic analysis. Some of the primary criticisms of SWOT are:

- It is simply the opinions of those filling out the boxes
- Virtually everything that is a strength is also a weakness
- Virtually everything that is an opportunity is also a threat
- Adding layers of effort does not improve the validity of the list
- It uses a single point in time approach
- There is no tie to the view from the customer
- There is no validated evaluation approach.

Originally developed in the 1970s, SWOT was one of the original approaches as the field moved from business policy (looking at examples and inferring long-range plans) to strategy. In the intervening years, many techniques have developed that provide strategists with keener insights into the elements of SWOT. However, as strategists, we need to understand our strengths, calculate the impact of weaknesses (whether they are real or perceived), take advantage of opportunities that match our strengths and minimize the impact of outside threats to the success of the organization. Thus, SWOT as a means of conceptualizing the organization is quite effective.

GENERATING A STRATEGIC FACTORS ANALYSIS SUMMARY (SFAS) MATRIX

The EFAS and IFAS Tables plus the SFAS Matrix were developed to deal with some of the criticisms of SWOT analysis and have been very effective. The **SFAS (Strategic Factors Analysis Summary) Matrix** summarizes an organization's strategic factors by combining the external factors from the EFAS Table with the internal factors from the IFAS Table. The EFAS and IFAS examples given of Maytag Corporation (as it was in 1995) in **Table 4–5** and **Table 5–2** list a total of 20 internal and external factors. These are too many factors for most people to use in strategy formulation. The SFAS Matrix requires a strategic decision maker to condense these strengths, weaknesses, opportunities, and threats into fewer than 10 strategic factors. This is done with a management team review and then by revising the weight given each factor. The revised weights reflect the priority of each factor as a determinant of the company's future success. The highest-weighted EFAS and IFAS factors should appear in the SFAS Matrix.

As shown in **Figure 6–1**, you can create an SFAS Matrix by following these steps:

1. In Column 1 (Strategic Factors), list the most important EFAS and IFAS items. After each factor, indicate whether it is a Strength **(S)**, Weakness **(W)**, an Opportunity **(O)**, or a Threat **(T)**.

2. In Column 2 (Weight), assign weights for all of the internal and external strategic factors. As with the EFAS and IFAS Tables presented earlier, the **weight column must total 1.00**. This means that the weights calculated earlier for EFAS and IFAS will probably have to be adjusted.

3. In Column 3 (Rating) assign a rating of how the company's management is responding to each of the strategic factors. These ratings will probably (but not always) be the same as those listed in the EFAS and IFAS Tables.

4. In Column 4 (Weighted Score) multiply the weight in Column 2 for each factor by its rating in Column 3 to obtain the factor's rated score.

5. In Column 5 (Duration), depicted in **Figure 6–1**, indicate short-term (less than one year), intermediate-term (one to three years), or long-term (three years and beyond).

6. In Column 6 (Comments), repeat or revise your comments for each strategic factor from the previous EFAS and IFAS Tables. **The total weighted score for the average firm in an industry is always 3.0.**

The resulting SFAS Matrix is a listing of the firm's external and internal strategic factors in one table. The example given in **Figure 6–1** is for Maytag Corporation in 1995, before the firm sold its European and Australian operations and it was acquired by Whirlpool. The SFAS Matrix includes only the most important factors gathered from environmental scanning, and thus provides information that is essential for strategy formulation. The use of EFAS and IFAS Tables together with the SFAS Matrix deals

FIGURE 6–1 Strategic Factor Analysis Summary (SFAS) Matrix

Internal Strategic Factors	Weight	Rating	Weighted Score	Comments
	1	2	3	4	5
Strengths				
S1 Quality Maytag culture	.15	5.0	.75	Quality key to success
S2 Experienced top management	.05	4.2	.21	Know appliances
S3 Vertical integration	.10	3.9	.39	Dedicated factories
S4 Employee relations	.05	3.0	.15	Good, but deteriorating
S5 Hoover's international orientation	.15	2.8	.42	Hoover name in cleaners
Weaknesses				
W1 Process-oriented R&D	.05	2.2	.11	Slow on new products
W2 Distribution channels	.05	2.0	.10	Superstores replacing small dealers
W3 Financial position	.15	2.0	.30	High debt load
W4 Global positioning	.20	2.1	.42	Hoover weak outside the United Kingdom and Australia
W5 Manufacturing facilities	.05	4.0	.20	Investing now
Total Scores	1.00		3.05	

External Strategic Factors	Weight	Rating	Weighted Score	Comments
	1	2	3	4	5
Opportunities				
O1 Economic integration of European Community	.20	4.1	.82	Acquisition of Hoover
O2 Demographics favor quality appliances	.10	5.0	.50	Maytag quality
O3 Economic development of Asia	.05	1.0	.05	Low Maytag presence
O4 Opening of Eastern Europe	.05	2.0	.10	Will take time
O5 Trend to "Super Stores"	.10	1.8	.18	Maytag weak in this channel
Threats				
T1 Increasing government regulations	.10	4.3	.43	Well positioned
T2 Strong U.S. competition	.10	4.0	.40	Well positioned
T3 Whirlpool and Electrolux strong globally	.15	3.0	.45	Hoover weak globally
T4 New product advances	.05	1.2	.06	Questionable
T5 Japanese appliance companies	.10	1.6	.16	Only Asian presence is Australia
Total Scores	1.00		3.15	

*The most important external and internal factors are identified in the EFAS and IFAS Tables as shown here by shading these factors.

Strategic Factors (Select the most important opportunities/threats from EFAS, Table 4–5 and the most important strengths and weaknesses from IFAS, Table 5–2)	Weight (1)	Rating (2)	Weighted Score (3)	Duration (4) SHORT	INTERMEDIATE	LONG (5)	Comments (6)
S1 Quality Maytag culture (S)	.10	5.0	.50			X	Quality key to success
S5 Hoover's international orientation (S)	.10	2.8	.28	X	X		Name recognition
W3 Financial position (W)	.10	2.0	.20	X	X		High debt
W4 Global positioning (W)	.15	2.2	.33		X	X	Only in N.A., U.K., and Australia
O1 Economic integration of European Community (O)	.10	4.1	.41			X	Acquisition of Hoover
O2 Demographics favor quality (O)	.10	5.0	.50		X		Maytag quality
O5 Trend to super stores (O + T)	.10	1.8	.18	X			Weak in this channel
T3 Whirlpool and Electrolux (T)	.15	3.0	.45	X			Dominate industry
T5 Japanese appliance companies (T)	.10	1.6	.16			X	Asian presence
Total Scores	1.00		3.01				

NOTES:
1. List each of the most important factors developed in your IFAS and EFAS Tables in Column 1.
2. Weight each factor from 1.0 (Most Important) to 0.0 (Not Important) in Column 2 based on that factor's probable impact on the company's strategic position. The total weights must sum to 1.00.
3. Rate each factor from 5.0 (Outstanding) to 1.0 (Poor) in Column 3 based on the company's response to that factor.
4. Multiply each factor's weight times its rating to obtain each factor's weighted score in Column 4.
5. For the duration in Column 5, check the appropriate column (short term—less than 1 year; intermediate—1 to 3 years; long term—over 3 years).
6. Use Column 6 (comments) for rationale used for each factor.

with some of the criticisms of SWOT analysis. For example, the use of the SFAS Matrix reduces the list of factors to a manageable number, puts weights on each factor, and allows one factor to be listed as both a strength and a weakness (or as an opportunity and a threat).

FINDING MARKET NICHES

One desired outcome of analyzing strategic factors is identifying niches where an organization can use its core competencies to take advantage of a particular market opportunity. A niche is a need in the marketplace that is currently unsatisfied. This is the premise of the book *Blue Ocean Strategy* and many other popular press books on strategy. The goal is to find a **propitious niche**—an extremely favorable niche—that is so well suited to the firm's competitive advantages that other organizations are not likely to challenge or dislodge it.[2] A niche is propitious to the extent that it currently is just large enough for one firm to satisfy its demand. After a firm has found and filled that niche, it is not worth a potential competitor's time or money to also go after the same niche.

Finding such a niche or sweet spot is not easy. A firm's management must continually look for a *strategic window*—that is, a unique market opportunity that is available only for a particular time. The first firm through a strategic window can occupy the market and discourage competition (if the firm has the required internal strengths). One company that successfully found a propitious niche was Frank J. Zamboni & Company, the manufacturer of the machines that smooth the ice at ice skating rinks. Frank Zamboni invented the unique tractor-like machine in 1949 and no one yet has found a way to dislodge this company from the market. Before the machine was invented, people had to clean and scrape the ice by hand to prepare the surface for skating. Now hockey fans look forward to intermissions just to watch "the Zamboni" slowly drive up and down the ice rink, turning rough, scraped ice into a smooth mirror surface—almost like magic. So long as Zamboni's company is able to produce the machines in the quantity and quality desired, at a reasonable price, it was not worth another company's effort.

As a niche grows, so can a company within that niche—by increasing its operations' capacity or through alliances with larger firms. The key is to identify a market opportunity in which the first firm to reach that market segment can obtain and keep dominant market share. Church & Dwight was the first company in the United States to successfully market sodium bicarbonate for use in cooking. Its Arm & Hammer brand baking soda is still found in 95% of all U.S. households. This niche concept is crucial to the software industry. Small initial demand in emerging markets allows new entrepreneurial ventures to go after niches too small to be noticed by established companies. When Microsoft developed its first disk operating system (DOS) in 1980 for IBM's personal computers, for example, the demand for such open systems software was very small—a small niche for a then very small Microsoft. The company was able to fill that niche and to successfully grow with it.

Niches can also change—sometimes faster than a firm can adapt to that change. A company's management may discover in their situation analysis that they need to invest heavily in the firm's capabilities to keep them competitively strong in a changing niche. South African Breweries (SAB), for example, took this approach when management realized that the only way to keep competitors out of its market was to continuously invest in increased productivity and infrastructure in order to keep its prices very low.

Mission and Objectives

6-2. Develop a mission statement that addresses the five elements of good design

One of the first steps in good strategy design should be crafting the mission statement for the organization. A mission statement has a unique ability to focus the efforts of every employee in the company if and only if it is designed well and is implemented with a singular focus. Once a company has crafted the elements that constitute their competitive advantages, the implementation of that strategy (the competitive advantages) logically begins with a useful, focused mission grounded in those advantages that every individual in the company can use to make decisions. Well-trained, motivated employees absent an effective, unifying mission will head in the direction that they believe is the best for the company. This may or may not align with the focus of the top management team. An effective mission statement not only needs to be specific to that organization; it must enable a **common thread** to highlight and focus the energy of everyone in the organization in the direction that the top management team believes is best for the business. A well-crafted mission statement has five common elements:

1. It must be short so that every employee can remember the statement.
2. The design must be simple so that everyone in the company can understand what the senior leadership team desires.
3. It has to provide direction to the activities of company employees.
4. The statement should enable employees knowing exactly what the company does and what it does not do.
5. The statement should be measurable so that the company can visibly see progress.[3]

A company's objectives are also critical to the effort to implement a strategy. They can either focus too much on short-term operational goals or be so general that they provide little real guidance. There may be a gap between planned and achieved objectives. When such a gap occurs, either the strategies have to be changed to improve performance or the objectives need to be adjusted downward to be more realistic. Consequently, objectives should be constantly reviewed to ensure their usefulness. This is what happened at Boeing when management decided to change its primary objective from being the largest in the industry to being the most profitable. This had a significant effect on its strategies and policies. Following its new objective, the company canceled its policy of competing with Airbus on price and abandoned its commitment to maintaining a manufacturing capacity that could produce more than half a peak year's demand for airplanes.[4]

Business Strategies

6-3. Explain the competitive and cooperative strategies available to corporations

Business strategy focuses on improving the competitive position of a company's or business unit's products or services within the specific industry or market segment that the company or business unit serves. Business strategy is extremely important because research shows that business unit effects have double the impact on overall company performance than do either corporate or industry effects.[5] Business strategy can be competitive (battling against all competitors for advantage) and/or cooperative (working with one or more companies to gain advantage against other competitors). Just as corporate strategy asks what industry(ies) the company should be in, business strategy asks how the company or its units should compete or cooperate in each industry.

PORTER'S COMPETITIVE STRATEGIES

Competitive strategy raises the following questions:

- Should we compete on the basis of lower cost, or should we differentiate our products or services on some basis other than cost, such as quality or service?
- Should we compete head to head with our major competitors for the biggest but most sought-after share of the market, or should we focus on a niche in which we can satisfy a less sought-after but also profitable segment of the market?

Michael Porter proposed three "generic" competitive strategies for outperforming other organizations in a particular industry: overall cost leadership, differentiation, and focus.[6] These strategies are called generic because they can be pursued by any type or size of business firm, even by not-for-profit organizations:

- **Cost leadership** is the ability of a company or a business unit to design, produce, and market a comparable product or service more efficiently than its competitors.

- **Differentiation** is the ability of a company to provide unique and superior value to the buyer. This may include areas such as product quality, special features, or after-sale service.

- **Focus** is the ability of a company to provide unique and superior value to a particular buyer group, segment of the market line, or geographic market.

Porter proposed that a firm's competitive advantage in an industry is determined by its **competitive scope**—that is, the breadth of the company's or business unit's target market. Simply put, a company or business unit can choose a broad target (aim at the middle of the mass market) or a narrow target (aim at a market niche). Combining these two types of target markets with the three competitive strategies results in four variations of generic strategies. When the lower-cost and differentiation strategies have a broad mass-market target, they are simply called *cost leadership* and *differentiation*. When they are focused on a market niche (narrow target), however, they are called *cost focus* and *differentiation focus*. Research does indicate that established firms pursuing broad-scope strategies outperform firms following narrow-scope strategies in terms of Return on Assets (ROA). Even though research has found that new entrepreneurial firms increase their chance of survival if they follow a narrow-scope strategy, it has unfortunately also found that new firms that take the risk and pursue a broad-scope strategy will significantly outperform those that follow a narrow-scope strategy regardless of the size and breadth of their initial resources.[7]

Cost leadership is a lower-cost competitive strategy that aims at the broad mass market and requires "aggressive construction of efficient-scale facilities, vigorous pursuit of cost reductions from experience, tight cost and overhead control, avoidance of marginal customer accounts, and cost minimization in areas like R&D, service, sales force, advertising, and so on."[8] Because of its lower costs, the cost leader is able to charge a lower price for its products than its competitors and still make a satisfactory profit. Although it may not necessarily have the lowest costs in the industry, it has lower costs than its competitors. Some companies successfully following this strategy are Wal-Mart (discount retailing), Taco Bell (fast-food restaurants), HP (computers), Enterprise (rental cars), Aldi (grocery stores), Southwest Airlines, and Timex (watches). Having a lower-cost position also gives a company or business unit a defense against rivals. Its lower costs allow it to continue to earn profits during times of heavy competition. Its high market share means that it will have high bargaining power relative to its suppliers (because it buys in large quantities). Its low price will also serve as a barrier to entry because few new entrants will be able to match the leader's cost advantage. As a result, cost leaders are likely to earn above-average returns on investment.

Differentiation is aimed at the broad mass market and involves the creation of a product or service that is perceived throughout its industry as having passed through the elements of VRIO. The company or business unit may then (if they choose to) charge a premium. Differentiation is a viable strategy for earning above-average returns in a specific business because the resulting increased value to the customer lowers price sensitivity. Increased costs can usually be passed on to the buyers. Buyer loyalty also serves as an entry barrier; new firms must develop their own distinctive competence to differentiate their products or services in some way in order to compete successfully. Examples of companies that successfully use a **differentiation strategy** are Walt Disney Company (entertainment), BMW (automobiles), Apple (computers, tablets, watches, and cell phones), and Five Guys (fast food). Research does suggest that a differentiation strategy is more likely to generate higher profits than does a **lower-cost strategy** because differentiation creates a better entry barrier. A low-cost strategy is more likely, however, to generate increases in market share.[9] For an example of how companies approach generic strategies, see the **Global Issue** feature on Emirates and globalization.

Cost focus is a low-cost competitive strategy that focuses on a particular buyer group or geographic market and attempts to serve only this niche, to the exclusion of others. In using cost focus, the company or business unit seeks a cost advantage in its target segment. A good example of this strategy is Potlach Corporation, a manufacturer of toilet tissue. Rather than compete directly against Procter & Gamble's Charmin, Potlach makes the house brands for Albertson's, Safeway, Jewel, and many other grocery store chains. It matches the quality of the well-known brands, but keeps costs low by

GLOBAL issue

HAS EMIRATES REACHED THE LIMIT OF GLOBALIZATION?

The Dubai-based Emirates group is the holding company of the Emirates Airline and Dnata Travel, and is wholly owned by the Dubai Government. Emirates operates the largest fleet of the most advanced Airbus A380 and Boeing 777, and Dnata is one of the largest combined air service providers in the world. The group's financial performance reported AED 96.4 billion operating income and AED 6.8 billion operating profit for the 2014–15 financial year. The group's success is attributed to its operational focus, global ambition, proximity to power and geographical location. To refuel its global ambition the government is investing $32 billion to build a five-runway mega-hub called the Dubai World Centre, with a handling capacity of 220 million passengers a year. Upon completion, the Dubai World Centre will have a capacity four times higher than the JFK International Airport.

However, a closer look at its financial data will bring out the bleak profit margins of recent years. Is it indicative of the end of continuous expansion for Emirates? There are several challenges looming at Emirates' horizon. It is facing decreasing demand from emerging markets, and its business and first class bookings are ebbing due to sluggish economic growth in western

countries. On top of this, international rivals are intensifying lobbying against Emirates' perceived government backings and asking for a more level playing field. Certain airlines from other Persian Gulf countries are also following a similar locational advantage-based strategy that supported Emirates' astounding success. Airlines like Qatar, Etihad, and Turkish are competing more or less for the same customer groups and routes usually served by Emirates. Emirates is also running overcapacity in most of its profitable routes. The question civil aviation experts are asking is how Emirates will fill the seats of the planes yet to join the fleet in the near future. Dnata will also struggle in a future where Emirates carries fewer passengers and flies to fewer destinations. It seems Emirates may need to scale down its global expansion to be sustainable.

For an example of how companies approach generic strategies, see the Global Issue feature on Emirates and globalization.

SOURCES: The Emirates Group Annual Report 2014-15 (http://content.emirates.com/downloads/ek/pdfs/report/annual_report_2015.pdf accessed February, 2017); and The Emirates Group Environmental report 2011-12 (https://www.emirates.com/english/images/2011_12%20Emirates%20Environment%20Report%20secured_tcm233-888462.pdf accessed February, 2017).

eliminating advertising and promotion expenses. As a result, Spokane-based Potlach makes 92% of the private-label bathroom tissue and one-third of all bathroom tissue sold in Western U.S. grocery stores. The phenomenal growth of store brand purchases is a testament to the power of a cost focus as a means to sell at lower prices. A study by Accenture found that annual sales of store brands had increased 40% over the past decade. A total of 64% of U.S. shoppers said that store brands comprised 50% of their groceries. The same study asked why people purchased store brands. They found that 66% of shoppers bought store brands because they were cheaper, and 87% said they would buy brand-name products but only if they were the same price as the store brand.[10]

Differentiation focus, like cost focus, concentrates on a particular buyer group, product line segment, or geographic market. This is the strategy successfully followed by Midamar Corporation (distributor of halal foods), Morgan Motor Car Company (a manufacturer of classic British sports cars), Nickelodeon (a cable channel for children), OrphageniX (pharmaceuticals), and local ethnic grocery stores. In using differentiation focus, a company or business unit seeks differentiation in a targeted market segment. This strategy is valued by those who believe that a company or a unit that focuses its efforts is better able to serve the special needs of a narrow strategic target more effectively than can its competition. For example, OrphageniX is a small biotech pharmaceutical company that avoids head-to-head competition with big companies like AstraZenica and Merck by developing drug therapies for "orphan" diseases. That is, diseases that are rare and often life threatening but do not have effective treatment options—for instance, diseases such as sickle cell anemia and spinal muscular atrophy; diseases that big drug makers are overlooking.[11]

Risks in Competitive Strategies

No one competitive strategy is guaranteed to achieve success, and some companies that have successfully implemented one of Porter's competitive strategies have found that they could not sustain the strategy. Each of the generic strategies has risks. For example, a company following a differentiation strategy must ensure that the higher price it charges for its higher quality is not too far above the price of the competition, otherwise customers will not see the extra quality as worth the extra cost. For years, Deere & Company was the leader in farm machinery until low-cost competitors from India and other developing countries began making low-priced products. Deere responded by building high-tech flexible manufacturing plants using mass-customization to cut its manufacturing costs and using innovation to create differentiated products which, although higher-priced, reduced customers' labor and fuel expenses.[12]

Issues in Competitive Strategies

Porter argues that to be successful, a company or business unit must achieve one of the previously mentioned generic competitive strategies. Otherwise, the company or business unit is *stuck in the middle* of the competitive marketplace with no competitive advantage and is doomed to below-average performance. A classic example of a company that found itself stuck in the middle was K-Mart. The company spent a lot of money trying to imitate both Wal-Mart's low-cost strategy and Target's quality differentiation strategy. The result was a bankruptcy filing and its continuation today as a floundering company with poor performance and no clear strategy. Although some studies do support Porter's argument that companies tend to sort themselves into either lower cost or differentiation strategies and that successful companies emphasize only one strategy,[13] other research suggests that some combination of the two competitive strategies may also be successful.[14]

The Toyota and Honda auto companies are often presented as examples of successful firms able to achieve both of these generic competitive strategies. Thanks to advances in technology, a company may be able to design quality into a product or service in such a way that it can achieve both high quality and lower costs thus achieving a higher market share.[15] Although Porter agrees that it is possible for a company or a business unit to achieve low cost and differentiation simultaneously, he suggests that this state is often temporary.[16] Porter does admit, however, that many different kinds of potentially profitable competitive strategies exist. Although there is generally room for only one company to successfully pursue the mass market cost leadership strategy (because it is so often tied to maintaining a dominant market share), there is room for an almost unlimited number of differentiation and focus strategies (depending on the range of possible desirable features and the number of identifiable market niches).

Most entrepreneurial ventures follow focus strategies. The successful ones differentiate their product or service from those of others by focusing on customer wants in a segment of the market, thereby achieving a dominant share of that part of the market. Adopting guerrilla warfare tactics, these companies often go after opportunities in market niches too small to justify retaliation from the market leaders.

Industry Structure and Competitive Strategy

Although each of Porter's generic competitive strategies may be used in any industry, certain strategies are more likely to succeed depending upon the type of industry. In a **fragmented industry**, for example, where many small- and medium-sized local companies compete for relatively small shares of the total market, focus strategies will likely predominate. Fragmented industries are typical for products in the early stages of their life cycles. If few economies are to be gained through size, no large firms will emerge and entry barriers will be low—allowing a stream of new entrants into the industry. Sandwich shops, veterinary care, used-car lots, dry cleaners, and nail salons are examples. Even though P.F. Chang's and the Panda Restaurant Group have firmly established themselves as chains in the United States, local family-owned restaurants still comprise 86% of Asian casual dining restaurants.[17,18]

If a company is able to overcome the limitations of a fragmented market, however, it can reap the benefits of a broadly targeted cost-leadership or differentiation strategy. Until Pizza Hut was able to use advertising to differentiate itself from local competitors, the pizza fast-food business was a fragmented industry composed primarily of locally owned pizza parlors, each with its own distinctive product and service offering. Subsequently, Domino's used the cost-leadership strategy to achieve the number two U.S. national market share.

As an industry matures, fragmentation is overcome, and the industry tends to become a **consolidated industry** dominated by a few large companies. Although many industries start out being fragmented, battles for market share and creative attempts to overcome local or niche market boundaries often increase the market share of a few companies. After product standards become established for minimum quality and features, competition shifts to a greater emphasis on cost and service. Slower growth, overcapacity, and knowledgeable buyers combine to put a premium on a firm's ability to achieve cost leadership or differentiation along the dimensions most desired by the market. R&D shifts from product to process improvements. Overall product quality improves, and costs are reduced significantly.

The *strategic rollup* was developed in the mid-1990s as an efficient way to quickly consolidate a fragmented industry. With the aid of money from venture capitalists and private equity firms, a single company acquires hundreds of owner-operated small businesses. The resulting large firm creates economies of scale by building regional or national brands, applies best practices across all aspects of marketing and operations, and hires more sophisticated managers than the small businesses could previously afford. Rollups differ from conventional mergers and acquisitions in three ways: (1) they involve large numbers of firms, (2) the acquired firms are typically owner operated, and (3) the objective is not to gain incremental advantage, but to reinvent an entire industry.[19] Examples of rollups are in the anti-freeze (waste glycol) recycling industry led by GlyEco Inc. and legendary rollup artist John Lorenz, and in the shredding and record storage industry led by Business Records Management and Cornerstone Records Management.[20]

Once consolidated, an industry will become one in which cost leadership and differentiation tend to be combined to various degrees, even though one competitive strategy may be primarily emphasized. A firm can no longer gain and keep high market share simply through low price. The buyers are more sophisticated and demand a certain minimum level of quality for price paid. Colgate Palmolive Company, a leader in soap, toothpaste, and toothbrushes used the U.S. obsession for whiter teeth to create Colgate Optic White toothpaste (at a premium price) helping increase the company's overall market share in toothpaste to more than 41%.[21] The same is true for firms emphasizing high quality. Either the quality must be high enough and valued by the customer enough to justify the higher price, or the price must be dropped (through lowering costs) to compete effectively with the lower-priced products. Apple has consistently chosen to increase the capabilities of their products instead of dropping the price. Even though tablets are now available in a wide variety of sizes, capabilities, and price points, Apple has chosen to maintain their premium price and add features. They allow no discounting and no sales of their products. Consolidation is taking place worldwide in the banking, airline, cell phone, and home appliance industries. For an example of how a company can challenge what is still a fragmented industry and change the way the whole industry operates, see the **Innovation Issue** feature on CHEGG.

INNOVATION issue

CHEGG AND COLLEGE TEXTBOOKS

Innovation in strategy sometimes means being able to gain advantage in an industry that refuses to acknowledge a change in customer behavior. One market that has remained mired in the past has been that of college textbooks. The business model dates back a long time and most colleges and universities used (or still use) the on-campus bookstore as a cash generator. Textbooks are chosen by professors, not students, to fit the mindset the professor wants for that particular class. Once chosen, the professors post the required material to their syllabus and let the bookstore know what they have chosen.

For many decades, students lined up to buy their books and pay whatever the bookstore charged (usually an amount that was staggering). The advent of the Internet and some very creative companies have changed the entire industry, upending both the bookstores and the publishers' means for generating income. Beyond the obvious avenue of used textbook sales, there were innovative companies taking advantage of the stagnation in the industry.

In 2007, CHEGG launched its online rental site for textbooks. Rather than paying hundreds of dollars for an "Introduction to Biology" textbook, you could rent it from CHEGG for as much as 80% off the cover price. CHEGG quickly became known as the Netflix of textbooks and their bright orange boxes became a staple at campuses throughout the United States. The company had sales of over US$300 million by 2016. However, not all was well at the company. Book rentals started to level off long before

CHEGG hit any type of market saturation and the company has not had positive net income in the past five years.

The winds had started changing again with the move to digital books, digital rentals, and a number of companies who were reimagining an industry where the textbook was not the center of the learning environment. CHEGG chose to move as well, but it moved in a different direction. The company saw the college experience as the new center for their business model and moved with it, spending US$50 million and buying up six companies in an effort to become the hub of the college student experience, offering discounts on dorm room decorations, homework help, professor recommendations, digital books, and connecting the whole operation to Facebook. CHEGG's rental book market acts as the core of its business, while CHUBB.com is used as a focused networking site for college students.

....

SOURCES: quotes.wsj.com/CHGG; http://www.chegg.com/; A. Levy, "A College Hub. Togas Not Included," *Bloomberg Businessweek* (June 4, 2012), (http://www.businessweek.com /articles/2012-05-31/chegg-acollege-hub-dot-togas-not-included).

Hypercompetition and Competitive Advantage Sustainability

Some firms are able to sustain their competitive advantage for many years,[22] but most find that competitive advantage erodes over time. In his book *Hypercompetition*, D'Aveni proposes that it is becoming increasingly difficult to sustain a competitive advantage for very long. "Market stability is threatened by short product life cycles, short product design cycles, new technologies, frequent entry by unexpected outsiders, repositioning by incumbents, and tactical redefinitions of market boundaries as diverse industries merge."[23] Consequently, a company or business unit must constantly work to improve its competitive advantage. It is not enough to be just the lowest-cost competitor. Through continuous improvement programs, competitors are usually working to lower their costs as well. Firms must find new ways not only to reduce costs further but also to add value to the product or service being provided.

The same is true of a firm or unit that is following a differentiation strategy. Maytag Corporation, for example, was successful for many years by offering the most reliable brand in North American major home appliances. It was able to charge the highest prices for Maytag brand washing machines. When other competitors improved the quality of their products, however, it became increasingly difficult for customers to justify Maytag's significantly higher price. Consequently, Maytag Corporation was forced not only to add new features to its products but also to reduce costs through improved manufacturing processes so that its prices were no longer out of line with those of the competition. D'Aveni's theory of hypercompetition is supported by developing research on the importance of building *dynamic capabilities* to better cope with uncertain environments (discussed previously in **Chapter 5** in the resource-based view of the firm).

D'Aveni contends that when industries become hypercompetitive, they tend to go through escalating stages of competition. Firms initially compete on cost and quality, until an abundance of high-quality, low-priced goods result. This occurred in the U.S. major home appliance industry up through 1980. In a second stage of competition, the competitors move into untapped markets. Others usually imitate these moves until their actions become too risky or expensive. This epitomized the major home appliance industry during the 1980s and 1990s, as strong U.S. and European firms like Whirlpool, Electrolux, and Bosch-Siemens established a presence in both Europe and the Americas and then moved into Asia. Strong Asian firms like LG and Haier likewise entered Europe and the Americas in the late 1990s.

According to D'Aveni, firms then raise entry barriers to limit competitors. Economies of scale, distribution agreements, and strategic alliances made it all but impossible for a new firm to enter the major home appliance industry by the end of the 20th century. After the established players have entered and consolidated all new markets, the next stage is for the remaining firms to attack and destroy the strongholds of other firms. Maytag's inability to hold onto its North American stronghold led to its acquisition by Whirlpool in 2006. Eventually, according to D'Aveni, the remaining large global competitors can work their way to a situation of perfect competition in which no one has any advantage and profits are minimal.

Before hypercompetition, strategic initiatives provided competitive advantage for many years, perhaps for decades. Except for a few stable industries, this is no longer the case. According to D'Aveni, as industries become hypercompetitive, there is no such thing as a sustainable competitive advantage. Successful strategic initiatives in this type of industry typically last only months to a few years. According to D'Aveni, the only way a firm in this kind of dynamic industry can sustain any competitive advantage is through a continuous series of multiple short-term initiatives aimed at replacing a firm's current successful products with the next generation of products before the competitors can do so. Consumer product companies like Procter & Gamble, Kraft, and Kimberly Clark are taking this approach in the hypercompetitive household products industry.

Hypercompetition views competition, in effect, as a distinct series of ocean waves on what used to be a fairly calm stretch of water. As industry competition becomes more intense, the waves grow higher and require more dexterity to handle. Although a strategy is still needed to sail from point A to point B, more turbulent water means that a craft must continually adjust course to suit each new large wave. One danger of D'Aveni's concept of hypercompetition, however, is that it may lead to an overemphasis on short-term **tactics** (discussed in the next section) over long-term strategy. Too much of an orientation on the individual waves of hypercompetition could cause a company to focus too much on short-term temporary advantage and not enough on achieving its long-term objectives through building sustainable competitive advantage. Nevertheless, research supports D'Aveni's argument that sustained competitive advantage is increasingly a matter not of a single advantage maintained over time, but more a matter of sequencing advantages over time.[24]

For an example of a how a company can achieve sustainable competitive advantages in a hypercompetitive market, see the **Sustainability Issue** feature about ESPN.

SUSTAINABILITY issue

STRATEGIC SUSTAINABILITY—ESPN

A sustainable strategy has many components. This is especially true in the hyper-competitive sports entertainment industry. Around the world, there is an almost maniacal love of sports, sports teams, sports superstars, and sports trivia. While this phenomenon is nothing new, technology advances have raised this "want" to an instant gratification level.

This was not always the way it was. Way back in the 1970s, we watched sports when the three networks deemed that we were to watch sports. We watched only the teams that they chose and it was rare to see any sports that were not considered to be mainstream. When you think about the staggering number of sporting events that occur every day around the world, it was amazing how few were shown on television.

All that changed with the founding of ESPN (Entertainment and Sports Programming Network) in 1979 in Bristol, Connecticut. Aired with little content, a show called *Sports Center*, and a lot of Australian Rules Football, the company sought out an approach in a field that had been dominated by the major league sports teams. The new

ESPN moved to 24-hour broadcasting on September 1, 1980. ESPN quickly realized that a sustainable competitive advantage required contracts. All the analysis in the world would not make up for the fact that fans were watching other channels. The top management at ESPN also realized that it would not just be about keeping viewers tied to a single television channel as the industry standard was at the time.

The company opened up new television channels, created a radio station broadcast for stations across the country, moved aggressively into the Internet, and is the leader in mobile broadcasting of sports. Today, despite the issue of viewers unplugging from cable subscriptions, ESPN is still the undisputed king of sports broadcasting with over 95 million cable subscribers. Now a part of Disney, its 2015 revenue was just over US$9.5 billion. ESPN charges cable companies US$6.55 per month/per subscriber in an industry where the average is US$0.20/month/subscriber. The company has bet its sustainability in this market on its contracts with the NFL (through 2021), MLB (2021), NBA (2025), College Football Playoffs (2025), US Open (2026), and Wimbledon (2023), as well as a series of exclusive or partially shared contracts with major colleges and conferences. It caters to the sports enthusiast by providing that customer with the access and information they desire in the manner they desire it. The company then takes each successful platform to advertisers and monetizes the platform. ESPN is unconcerned about cannibalizing platforms because they seek to continually reinvent the company.

....

SOURCES: R Nakashima, "Sports Costs at ESPN weigh down Disney's Force-ful quarter," *TheLedger.com*, February 9, 2016 (www.theledger.com/article/20160209/news/160209388&tc=yahoo?p=3&tc=pg); F. Bi, "ESPN Leads All Cable Networks in Affiliate Fees," *Forbes*, January 8, 2015 (www.forbes.com/sites/frankbi/2015/08/espn-leads-all-cable-networks-in-affiliate-fees/#104711cce60c); espn.go.com; K. T. Greenfeld, "ESPN Is Running Up the Score," *Bloomberg Businessweek* (September 3, 2012), pp. 58–64; http://frontrow.espn.go.com/category/espn-history/; http://a.espncdn.com/espninc/pressreleases/chronology.html; Hawkins, S. "Big 12 reaches $2.6B deal with ESPN, Fox Sports," Accessed 6/1/13, http://www.boston.comsports/colleges/2012/09/07/big-reaches-deal-with-espn-fox-sports/MbkpeOW4xEyX78F3FfHPcl/story.html.

COOPERATIVE STRATEGIES

A company uses competitive strategies to gain competitive advantage within an industry by battling against other firms. These are not, however, the only business strategy options available to a company or business unit for competing successfully within an industry. A company can also use **cooperative strategies** to gain competitive advantage within an industry by working with other firms. The two general types of cooperative strategies are collusion and strategic alliances.

Collusion

Collusion is the active cooperation of firms within an industry to reduce output and raise prices in order to get around the normal economic law of supply and demand. Collusion may be explicit, in which case firms cooperate through direct communication and negotiation, or tacit, in which case firms cooperate indirectly through an informal system of signals. Explicit collusion is illegal in most countries and in a number of regional trade associations, such as the European Union. For example, Archer Daniels Midland (ADM), the large U.S. agricultural products firm, conspired with its competitors to limit the sales volume and raise the price of the food additive lysine. Executives from three Japanese and South Korean lysine manufacturers admitted meeting in hotels in major cities throughout the world to form a "lysine trade association." The three companies were fined more than US$20 million by the U.S. federal government.[25] Professional sports is big business and a fascinating collusion lawsuit was filed in May 2012 (*Reggie White, et al. v. NFL*) against the National Football League. The players contended they lost US$1 billion because of a secret salary cap for the 2010 season. As stipulated by collectively bargained language, such damages, if proved, would be automatically trebled to US$3 billion.[26]

Collusion can also be tacit, in which case there is no direct communication among competing firms. According to Barney, tacit collusion in an industry is most likely to be successful if (1) there are a small number of identifiable competitors, (2) costs are similar among firms, (3) one firm tends to act as the price leader, (4) there is a common industry culture that accepts cooperation, (5) sales are characterized by a high frequency of small orders, (6) large inventories and order backlogs are normal ways of dealing with fluctuations in demand, and (7) there are high entry barriers to keep out new competitors.[27]

Even tacit collusion can, however, be illegal. For example, when General Electric wanted to ease price competition in the steam turbine industry, it widely advertised its prices and publicly committed not to sell below those prices. Customers were even told that if GE reduced turbine prices in the future, it would give customers a refund equal to the price reduction. GE's message was not lost on Westinghouse, the major competitor in steam turbines. Both prices and profit margins remained stable for the next 10 years in this industry. The U.S. Department of Justice then sued both firms for engaging in "conscious parallelism" (following each other's lead to reduce the level of competition) in order to reduce competition.

Strategic Alliances

6-4. Identify the types of strategic alliances

A **strategic alliance** is a long-term cooperative arrangement between two or more independent firms or business units that engage in business activities for mutual economic gain.[28] Alliances between companies or business units have become a fact of life in modern business. Each of the top 500 global business firms now averages 60 major alliances.[29] Some alliances are very short term, only lasting long enough for one partner to establish a beachhead in a new market. Over time, conflicts over objectives and control often develop among the partners. For these and other reasons, around half of all alliances (including international alliances) perform unsatisfactorily.[30] Others are more long-lasting and may even be preludes to full mergers between companies.

Many alliances do increase profitability of the members and have a positive effect on firm value.[31] A study by Cooper & Lybrand found that firms involved in strategic alliances had 11% higher revenue and a 20% higher growth rate than did companies not involved in alliances.[32] Forming and managing strategic alliances is a capability that is learned over time. Research reveals that the more experience a firm has with strategic alliances, the more likely that its alliances will be successful.[33] (There is some evidence, however, that too much partnering experience with the same partners generates diminishing returns over time and leads to reduced performance.)[34] Consequently, leading firms are making investments in building and developing their partnering capabilities.[35]

Companies or business units may form a strategic alliance for a number of reasons, including:

1. **To obtain or learn new capabilities:** In 2015, General Motors formed an alliance with the car sharing service Lyft by purchasing a 9% equity ownership interest in the firm. They plan to put multiple car-sharing programs under a single brand called Maven. Lyft has proven its expertise in the area and General Motors is looking for appropriate outlets for a fleet of new electric vehicles and a market leadership position.[36] Alliances are especially useful if the desired knowledge or capability is based on tacit knowledge or on new poorly understood technology.[37] A study found that firms with strategic alliances had more modern manufacturing technologies than did firms without alliances.[38]

2. **To obtain access to specific markets:** Rather than buy a foreign company or build breweries of its own in other countries, AB InBev chose to license the right to brew and market Budweiser to other brewers, such as Labatt in Canada, Modelo in Mexico, and Kirin in Japan. As another example, U.S. defense contractors and aircraft manufacturers selling to foreign governments are typically required by these governments to spend a percentage of the contract/purchase value, either by purchasing parts or obtaining sub-contractors, in that country. This is often achieved by forming value-chain alliances with foreign companies either as parts suppliers or as sub-contractors.[39] In a survey by the *Economist Intelligence Unit*, 59% of executives stated that their primary reason for engaging in alliances was the need for fast and low-cost expansion into new markets.[40]

3. **To reduce financial risk:** Alliances take less financial resources than do acquisitions or going it alone and are easier to exit if necessary.[41] For example, because the costs of developing new large jet airplanes were becoming too high for any one manufacturer, Aerospatiale of France, British Aerospace, Construcciones Aeronáuticas of Spain, and Daimler-Benz Aerospace of Germany formed a joint consortium called Airbus Industrie to design and build such planes. Using alliances with suppliers is a popular means of outsourcing an expensive activity.

4. **To reduce political risk:** Forming alliances with local partners is a good way to overcome deficiencies in resources and capabilities when expanding into international markets.[42] To gain access to China while ensuring a positive relationship with the often restrictive Chinese government, Maytag Corporation formed a joint venture with the Chinese appliance maker, RSD.

Cooperative arrangements between companies and business units fall along a continuum from weak and distant to strong and close. (See **Figure 6–2**.) The types of alliances range from mutual service consortia to joint ventures and licensing arrangements to value-chain partnerships.[43]

Mutual Service Consortia. A **mutual service consortium** is a partnership of similar companies in similar industries that pool their resources to gain a benefit that is too expensive to develop alone, such as access to advanced technology. For example, IBM established a research alliance with Sony Electronics and Toshiba to build its next generation of computer chips. The result was the "cell" chip, a microprocessor running at 256 gigaflops—around 10 times the performance of the fastest chips currently used in desktop computers. Referred to as a "supercomputer on a chip," cell chips are used by Sony in its PlayStation 3, by Toshiba in its high-definition televisions, and by IBM in its super computers.[44] The mutual service consortia is a fairly weak and distant alliance—appropriate for partners that wish to work together but

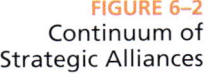

FIGURE 6–2
Continuum of
Strategic Alliances

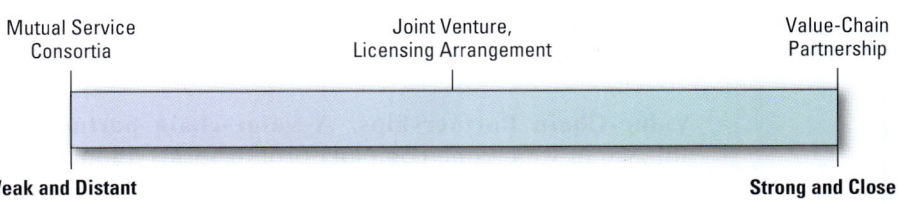

SOURCE: Based on Collaborative Advantage: The Art of Alliances by R. M. Kanter (July–August 1994). *Harvard Business Review*. © Thomas L. Wheelen.

not share their core competencies. There is very little interaction or communication among the partners.

Joint Venture. A **joint venture** is a "cooperative business activity, formed by two or more separate organizations for strategic purposes, that creates an independent business entity and allocates ownership, operational responsibilities, and financial risks and rewards to each member, while preserving their separate identity/autonomy."[45] Along with licensing arrangements, joint ventures lie at the midpoint of the continuum and are formed to pursue an opportunity that needs a capability from two or more companies or business units, such as the technology of one and the distribution channels of another.

Joint ventures are the most popular form of strategic alliance. They often occur because the companies involved do not want to or cannot legally merge permanently. Joint ventures provide a way to temporarily combine the different strengths of partners to achieve an outcome of value to all. For example, Proctor & Gamble formed a joint venture with Clorox to produce food-storage wraps. P&G brought its cling-film technology and 20 full-time employees to the venture, while Clorox contributed its bags, containers, and wraps business.[46]

Extremely popular in international undertakings because of financial and political–legal constraints, forming joint ventures is a convenient way for corporations to work together without losing their independence. Between 30% and 55% of international joint ventures include three or more partners.[47] The disadvantages of joint ventures include loss of control, lower profits, probability of conflicts with partners, and the likely transfer of technological advantage to the partner. Joint ventures are often meant to be temporary, especially by some companies that may view them as a way to rectify a competitive weakness until they can achieve long-term dominance in the partnership. Partially for this reason, joint ventures have a high failure rate. Research indicates, however, that joint ventures tend to be more successful when both partners have equal ownership in the venture and are mutually dependent on each other for results.[48]

Licensing Arrangements. A **licensing arrangement** is an agreement in which the licensing firm grants rights to another firm in another country or market to produce and/or sell a product. The licensee pays compensation to the licensing firm in return for technical expertise. Licensing is an especially useful strategy if the trademark or brand name is well known but the MNC does not have sufficient funds to finance its entering the country directly. For example, Yum! Brands successfully used franchising and licensing to establish its KFC, Pizza Hut, Taco Bell, Long John Silver's, and A&W restaurants throughout the world. By 2016, Yum! Brands had used that strategy to open more than 7,100 restaurants in China and had plans to open 600 more by year's end.[49] This strategy also becomes important if the country makes entry via investment either difficult or impossible. The danger always exists, however, that the licensee might develop its competence to the point that it becomes a competitor to the licensing firm. Therefore, a company should never license its distinctive competence, even for some short-run advantage.

Value-Chain Partnerships. A **value-chain partnership** is a strong and close alliance in which one company or unit forms a long-term arrangement with a key supplier or distributor for mutual advantage. In 2015 Facebook partnered with nine news organizations to allow the news organizations (including powerhouses like the

New York Times and *NBC News*) to post stories on the Facebook site. The partnership allows the news organizations to keep the advertising revenue from those posts while Facebook increases the amount of time that a particular customer is on their site.[50]

To improve the quality of parts it purchases, companies in the U.S. auto industry, for example, have decided to work more closely with fewer suppliers and to involve them more in product design decisions. Activities that had previously been done internally by an automaker are being outsourced to suppliers specializing in those activities. The benefits of such relationships do not just accrue to the purchasing firm. Research suggests that suppliers that engage in long-term relationships are more profitable than suppliers with multiple short-term contracts.[51]

All forms of strategic alliances involve uncertainty. Many issues need to be dealt with when an alliance is initially formed, and others emerge later. Many problems revolve around the fact that a firm's alliance partners may also be its competitors, either immediately or in the future. According to Professor Peter Lorange, one thorny issue in any strategic alliance is how to cooperate without giving away the company or business unit's core competence: "Particularly when advanced technology is involved, it can be difficult for partners in an alliance to cooperate and openly share strategic know-how, but it is mandatory if the joint venture is to succeed."[52] It is, therefore, important that a company or business unit that is interested in joining or forming a strategic alliance consider the strategic alliance success factors listed in **Table 6–1.**

TABLE 6–1 Strategic Alliance Success Factors	<ul><li>Have a clear strategic purpose. Integrate the alliance with each partner's strategy. Ensure that mutual value is created for all partners.</li><li>Find a fitting partner with compatible goals and complementary capabilities.</li><li>Identify likely partnering risks and deal with them when the alliance is formed.</li><li>Allocate tasks and responsibilities so that each partner can specialize in what it does best.</li><li>Create incentives for cooperation to minimize differences in corporate culture or organization fit.</li><li>Minimize conflicts among the partners by clarifying objectives and avoiding direct competition in the marketplace.</li><li>In an international alliance, ensure that those managing it have comprehensive cross-cultural knowledge.</li><li>Exchange human resources to maintain communication and trust. Don't allow individual egos to dominate.</li><li>Operate with long-term time horizons. The expectation of future gains can minimize short-term conflicts.</li><li>Develop multiple joint projects so that any failures are counterbalanced by successes.</li><li>Agree on a monitoring process. Share information to build trust and keep projects on target. Monitor customer responses and service complaints.</li><li>Be flexible in terms of willingness to renegotiate the relationship in terms of environmental changes and new opportunities.</li><li>Agree on an exit strategy for when the partners' objectives are achieved or the alliance is judged a failure.</li></ul>

SOURCES: Compiled from B. Gomes-Casseres, "Do You Really Have an Alliance Strategy?" *Strategy & Leadership* (September/October 1998), pp. 6–11; L. Segil, "Strategic Alliances for the 21st Century," *Strategy & Leadership* (September/October 1998), pp. 12–16; and A. C. Inkpen and K-Q. Li, "Joint Venture Formation: Planning and Knowledge Gathering for Success," *Organizational Dynamics* (Spring 1999), pp. 33–47. Inkpen and Li provide a checklist of 17 questions on p. 46.

End of Chapter SUMMARY

Once environmental scanning is completed, situational analysis calls for the integration of this information. Utilizing the elements of a SWOT chart is one of the more popular methods for classifying external and internal information. We recommend using the SFAS Matrix as one way to identify a corporation's strategic factors.

Business strategy is composed of both competitive and cooperative strategy. As the external environment becomes more uncertain, an increasing number of corporations are choosing to simultaneously compete *and* cooperate with their competitors. These firms may cooperate to obtain efficiency in some areas, while each firm simultaneously tries to differentiate itself for competitive purposes. Raymond Noorda, Novell's founder and former CEO, coined the term *co-opetition* to describe such simultaneous competition and cooperation among firms.[53] One example is the collaboration between competitors DHL and UPS in the express delivery market. DHL's American delivery business was losing money and UPS' costly airfreight network had excess capacity. Under the terms of a 10-year agreement signed back in 2008, UPS carries DHL packages in its American airfreight network for a fee. The agreement covers only air freight, leaving both firms free to compete in the rest of the express parcel business.[54] A careful balancing act, co-opetition involves the careful management of alliance partners so that each partner obtains sufficient benefits to keep the alliance together. A long-term view is crucial. An unintended transfer of knowledge could be enough to provide one partner a significant competitive advantage over the others.[55] Unless that company forebears from using that knowledge against its partners, the alliance will be doomed.

Pearson MyLab Management®

Go to **mymanagementlab.com** to complete the problems marked with this icon ✪.

KEY TERMS

business strategy (p. 207)
collusion (p. 215)
common thread (p. 207)
competitive scope (p. 208)
competitive strategy (p. 207)
consolidated industry (p. 211)
cooperative strategy (p. 215)
cost focus (p. 209)
cost leadership (p. 208)

differentiation (p. 208)
differentiation focus (p. 210)
differentiation strategy (p. 209)
fragmented industry (p. 211)
joint venture (p. 218)
licensing arrangement (p. 218)
lower-cost strategy (p. 209)
mutual service consortium (p. 217)
propitious niche (p. 206)

SFAS (Strategic Factors Analysis Summary) Matrix (p. 203)
strategic alliance (p. 216)
strategy formulation (p. 202)
SWOT (p. 202)
tactics (p. 214)
value-chain partnership (p. 218)

Pearson MyLab Management®

Go to **mymanagementlab.com** for the following assisted-graded writing questions:

6-1. How does a hypercompetitive environment change the strategic approach for a company?

6-2. Explain how our understanding of the three generic strategic approaches available to companies can be used to direct the efforts of all employees at those companies.

DISCUSSION QUESTIONS

6-3. Discuss how industry structure impacts competitive strategy choices.

⭐ **6-4.** What are the major sources of competitive advantages of an organization that can be effectively developed to support a cost leadership strategy for competing in the market?

⭐ **6-5.** How can an organization develop a competitive advantage internally without the help of outsiders?

⭐ **6-6.** Explain the importance of strategic alliances.

STRATEGIC PRACTICE EXERCISE

Select two publicly-owned companies within a particular industry, and perform a comparative SWOT analysis for the selected companies.

INDUSTRY:_____

Companies:_____

Strengths:_____

Weaknesses:_____

Opportunities:_____

Threats:_____

NOTES

1. T. Brown, "The Essence of Strategy," *Management Review* (April 1997), pp. 8–13.
2. W. H. Newman, "Shaping the Master Strategy of Your Firm," *California Management Review* (Vol. 9, No. 3, 1967), pp. 77–88.
3. C. Bamford, 2015. *The Strategy Mindset*, CreateSpace Publishing, North Charleston, SC.
4. D. J. Collis and M. G. Rukstad, "Can You Say What Your Strategy Is?" *Harvard Business Review* (April 2008), p. 86.
5. V. F. Misangyi, H. Elms, T. Greckhamer, and J. A Lepine, "A New Perspective on a Fundamental Debate: A Multilevel Approach to Industry, Corporate, and Business Unit Effects," *Strategic Management Journal* (June 2006), pp. 571–590.
6. M. E. Porter, *Competitive Strategy* (New York: The Free Press, 1980), pp. 34–41 as revised in M. E. Porter, *The Competitive Advantage of Nations* (New York: The Free Press, 1990), pp. 37–40.
7. J. O. DeCastro and J. J. Chrisman, "Narrow-Scope Strategies and Firm Performance: An Empirical Investigation," *Journal of Business Strategies* (Spring 1998), pp. 1–16; T. M. Stearns, N. M. Carter, P. D. Reynolds, and M. L. Williams, "New Firm Survival: Industry, Strategy, and Location," *Journal of Business Venturing* (January 1995), pp. 23–42; C. E. Bamford, T. J. Dean, and P. P. McDougall, "Reconsidering the Niche Prescription for New Ventures: A Study of Initial Strategy and Growth," *Advances in Entrepreneurship: Firm Emergence and Growth* (Vol. 11, 2009). pp. 9–39.
8. Porter, *Competitive Strategy*, p. 35.
9. R. E. Caves, and P. Ghemawat, "Identifying Mobility Barriers," *Strategic Management Journal* (January 1992), pp. 1–12.
10. "Private Label Brands Winning the Retail Sales Game," *Food Product Design* (July 27, 2012), (http://www.food productdesign.com/news/2012/07/private-label-brands -winning-theretail-sales-gam.aspx).
11. "Company Targets 'Orphan Drugs,'" *St. Cloud (MN) Times* (May 9, 2007), p. 2A, http://www.orphagenix.com/Home /research-technology-1.
12. M. Arndt, "Deere's Revolution on Wheels," *BusinessWeek* (July 2, 2007), pp. 78–79.
13. S. Thornhill and R. E. White, "Strategic Purity: A Multi-Industry Evaluation of Pure vs. Hybrid Business Strategies," *Strategic Management Journal* (May 2007), pp. 553–561; M. Delmas, M. V. Russo, and M. J. Montes-Sancho, "Deregulation and Environmental Differentiation in the Electric Utility Industry," *Strategic Management Journal* (February 2007), pp. 189–209.
14. C. Campbell-Hunt, "What Have We Learned About Generic Competitive Strategy? A Meta Analysis," *Strategic Management Journal* (February 2000), pp. 127–154.
15. M. Kroll, P. Wright, and R. A. Heiens, "The Contribution of Product Quality to Competitive Advantage: Impacts on Systematic Variance and Unexplained Variance in Returns," *Strategic Management Journal* (April 1999), pp. 375–384.
16. R. M. Hodgetts, "A Conversation with Michael E. Porter: A 'Significant Extension' Toward Operational Improvement and Positioning," *Organizational Dynamics* (Summer 1999), pp. 24–33.
17. M. Morrison, "Table Set for Fast Casual Asian Invasion," *Advertising Age* (May 16, 2011), (http://adage.com/article /news/table-set-fast-casual-asian-invasion/227577/); D. Banerjee and L. Patton, "P.F. Chang's to Be Bought by

Centerbridge for $1 Billion," *Bloomberg Businessweek* (May 1, 2012), (http://www.businessweek.com/news/2012-05-01/p-dot-f-dot-chang-s-is-bought-by-centerbridge-for-1-dot-1-billion).

18. Pizza Industry Report 2011, (http://www.franchisedirect.com/foodfranchises/pizzafranchises/pizzaindustryreport2011productdiversitymarketleadersbusinessmodels2/80/294).

19. P. F. Kocourek, S. Y. Chung, and M. G. McKenna, "Strategic Rollups: Overhauling the Multi-Merger Machine," *Strategy + Business* (2nd Quarter 2000), pp. 45–53.

20. J. A. Tannenbaum, "Acquisitive Companies Set Out to 'Roll Up' Fragmented Industries," *The Wall Street Journal* (March 3, 1997), pp. A1, A6; 2007 Form 10-K and Quarterly Report (July 2008); VCA Antech Inc. "A Best Idea", "Legendary Roll-Up Virtuoso John Lorenz Inks Acquisition #7 in just over Four Months," *SmallCap Network* (June 14, 2012), (http://www.smallcapnetwork.com/A-Best-Idea-Legendary-roll-up-virtuoso-John-Lorenz-inks-acquisition-7-in-just-over-four-months/s/via/8996/article/view/p/mid/1/id/43/); "BRM Acquires Paper Exchange," *Shred Nations* (August 31, 2012), (http://www.shrednations.com/news/category/acquisition/).

21. "Colgate Announces Fourth Quarter and Full Year 2015 Results," (January 29, 2016), (investor.colgate.com/releaseddetailpop.cfm?ReleaseID=952369).

22. J. C. Bou and A. Satorra, "The Persistence of Abnormal Returns at Industry and Firm Levels: Evidence from Spain," *Strategic Management Journal* (July 2007), pp. 707–722.

23. R. A. D'Aveni, *Hypercompetition* (New York: The Free Press, 1994), pp. xiii–xiv.

24. R. R. Wiggins and T. W. Ruefli, "Schumpeter's Ghost: Is Hypercompetition Making the Best of Times Shorter?" *Strategic Management Journal* (October 2005), pp. 887–911.

25. T. M. Burton, "Archer-Daniels Faces a Potential Blow as Three Firms Admit Price-Fixing Plot," *The Wall Street Journal* (August 28, 1996), pp. A3, A6; R. Henkoff, "The ADM Tale Gets Even Stranger," *Fortune* (May 13, 1996), pp. 113–120.

26. M. McCann, "Proving that NFL Teams Agreed to a Secret Salary Cap Will Not Be Easy," *Sports Illustrated* (May 24, 2012), (http://sportsillustrated.cnn.com/2012/writers/michael_mccann/05/23/nfl/index.html).

27. Much of the content on cooperative strategies was summarized from J. B. Barney, *Gaining and Sustaining Competitive Advantage* (Reading, MA: Addison-Wesley, 1997), pp. 255–278.

28. A. C. Inkpen and E. W. K. Tsang, "Learning and Strategic Alliances," *Academy of Management Annals* (Vol. 1, December 2007), J. F. Walsh and A. F. Brief (Eds.), pp. 479–511.

29. R. D. Ireland, M. A. Hitt, and D. Vaidyanath, "Alliance Management as a Source of Competitive Advantage," *Journal of Management* (Vol. 28, No. 3, 2002), pp. 413–446.

30. S. H. Park and G. R. Ungson, "Interfirm Rivalry and Managerial Complexity: A Conceptual Framework of Alliance Failure," *Organization Science* (January–February 2001), pp. 37–53; D. C. Hambrick, J. Li, K. Xin, and A. S. Tsui, "Compositional Gaps and Downward Spirals in International Joint Venture Management Groups," *Strategic Management Journal* (November 2001), pp. 1033–1053;

T. K. Das and B. S. Teng, "Instabilities of Strategic Alliances: An Internal Tensions Perspective," *Organization Science* (January–February 2000), pp. 77–101; J. F. Hennart, D. J. Kim, and M. Zeng, "The Impact of Joint Venture Status on the Longevity of Japanese Stakes in U.S. Manufacturing Affiliates," *Organization Science* (May–June 1998), pp. 382–395.

31. N. K. Park, J. M. Mezias, and J. Song, "A Resource-Based View of Strategic Alliances and Firm Value in the Electronic Marketplace," *Journal of Management* (Vol. 30, No. 1, 2004), pp. 7–27; T. Khanna and J. W. Rivkin, "Estimating the Performance Effects of Business Groups in Emerging Markets," *Strategic Management Journal* (January 2001), pp. 45–74; G. Garai, "Leveraging the Rewards of Strategic Alliances," *Journal of Business Strategy* (March–April 1999), pp. 40–43.

32. L. Segil, "Strategic Alliances for the 21st Century," *Strategy & Leadership* (September/October 1998), pp. 12–16.

33. R. C. Sampson, "Experience Effects and Collaborative Returns in R&D Alliances," *Strategic Management Journal* (November 2005), pp. 1009–1031; J. Draulans, AP deMan, and H. W. Volberda, "Building Alliance Capability: Management Techniques for Superior Alliance Performance," *Long Range Planning* (April 2003), pp. 151–166; P. Kale, J. H. Dyer, and H. Singh, "Alliance Capability, Stock Market Response, and Long-Term Alliance Success: The Role of the Alliance Function," *Strategic Management Journal* (August 2002), pp. 747–767.

34. H. Hoang and F. T. Rothaermel, "The Effect of General and Partner-Specific Alliance Experience on Joint R&D Project Performance," *Academy of Management Journal* (April 2005), pp. 332–345; A. Goerzen, "Alliance Networks and Firm Performance: The Impact of Repeated Partnerships," *Strategic Management Journal* (May 2007), pp. 487–509.

35. A. MacCormack and T. Forbath, "Learning the Fine Art of Global Collaboration," *Harvard Business Review* (January 2008), pp. 24–26.

36. J. Parker, "What to Expect from GM's Strategic Alliance with Lyft in 2016," Market Realist, February 10, 2016 (marketrealist.com/2016/02/expect-gms-strategic-alliance-lyft-2016/).

37. H. Bapuji and M. Crossan, "Knowledge Types and Knowledge Management Strategies," in M. Gibbert and T. Durand (Eds.) *Strategic Networks: Learning to Compete* (Malden, MA: Blackwell Publishing, 2007), pp. 8–25; F. T. Rothaermel and W. Boeker, "Old Technology Meets New Technology: Complementarities, Similarities, and Alliance Formation," *Strategic Management Journal* (January 2008), pp. 47–77.

38. M. M. Bear, "How Japanese Partners Help U.S. Manufacturers to Raise Productivity," *Long Range Planning* (December 1998), pp. 919–926.

39. According to M. J. Thome of Rockwell Collins in a June 26, 2008, e-mail, these are called "international offsets."

40. P. Anslinger and J. Jenk, "Creating Successful Alliances," *Journal of Business Strategy* (Vol. 25, No. 2, 2004), p. 18.

41. X. Yin and M. Shanley, "Industry Determinants of the 'Merger Versus Alliance' Decision," *Academy of Management Review* (April 2008), pp. 473–491.

42. J. W. Lu and P. W. Beamish, "The Internationalization and Performance of SMEs," *Strategic Management Journal* (June–July 2001), pp. 565–586.

43. R. M. Kanter, "Collaborative Advantage: The Art of Alliances," *Harvard Business Review* (July–August 1994), pp. 96–108.

44. "The Cell of the New Machine," *The Economist* (February 12, 2005), pp. 77–78.

45. R. P. Lynch, *The Practical Guide to Joint Ventures and Corporate Alliances* (New York: John Wiley and Sons, 1989), p. 7.

46. "Will She, Won't She?" *The Economist* (August 11, 2007), pp. 61–63.

47. Y. Gong, O. Shenkar, Y. Luo, and M-K. Nyaw, "Do Multiple Parents Help or Hinder International Joint Venture Performance? The Mediating Roles of Contract Completeness and Partner Cooperation," *Strategic Management Journal* (October 2007), pp. 1021–1034.

48. L. L. Blodgett, "Factors in the Instability of International Joint Ventures: An Event History Analysis," *Strategic Management Journal* (September 1992), pp. 475–481; J. Bleeke and D. Ernst, "The Way to Win in Cross-Border Alliances," *Harvard Business Review* (November–December 1991), pp. 127–135; J. M. Geringer, "Partner Selection Criteria for Developed Country Joint Ventures," in H. W. Lane and J. J. DiStephano (Eds.), *International Management Behavior*, 2nd ed. (Boston: PWS-Kent, 1992), pp. 206–216.

49. www.yum.com/brands/china.asp; Schreiner, B. 2012, "YUM Brands Posts Rare Profit Setback in China," *USA Today* (July 18, 2012), (http://www.usatoday.com/money/companies/earnings/story/2012-07-18/yum-brands-earnings/56321222/1).

50. B. Stelter, "Why Facebook is starting a new partnership with 9 news publishers," *CNN Money*, May 13, 2015 (money.cnn.com/2015/05/13/media/facebook-instant-articles-news-industry/index.html).

51. K. Z. Andrews, "Manufacturer/Supplier Relationships: The Supplier Payoff," *Harvard Business Review* (September–October 1995), pp. 14–15.

52. P. Lorange, "Black-Box Protection of Your Core Competencies in Strategic Alliances," in P. W. Beamish and J. P. Killing (Eds.), *Cooperative Strategies: European Perspectives* (San Francisco: The New Lexington Press, 1997), pp. 59–99.

53. E. P. Gee, "Co-opetition: The New Market Milieu," *Journal of Healthcare Management* (Vol. 45, 2000), pp. 359–363.

54. "Make Love—and War," *The Economist* (August 9, 2008), pp. 57–58.

55. D. J. Ketchen Jr., C. C. Snow, and V. L. Hoover, "Research on Competitive Dynamics: Recent Accomplishments and Future Challenges," *Journal of Management* (Vol. 30, No. 6, 2004), pp. 779–804.

CHAPTER **7**

Strategy Formulation:
Corporate Strategy

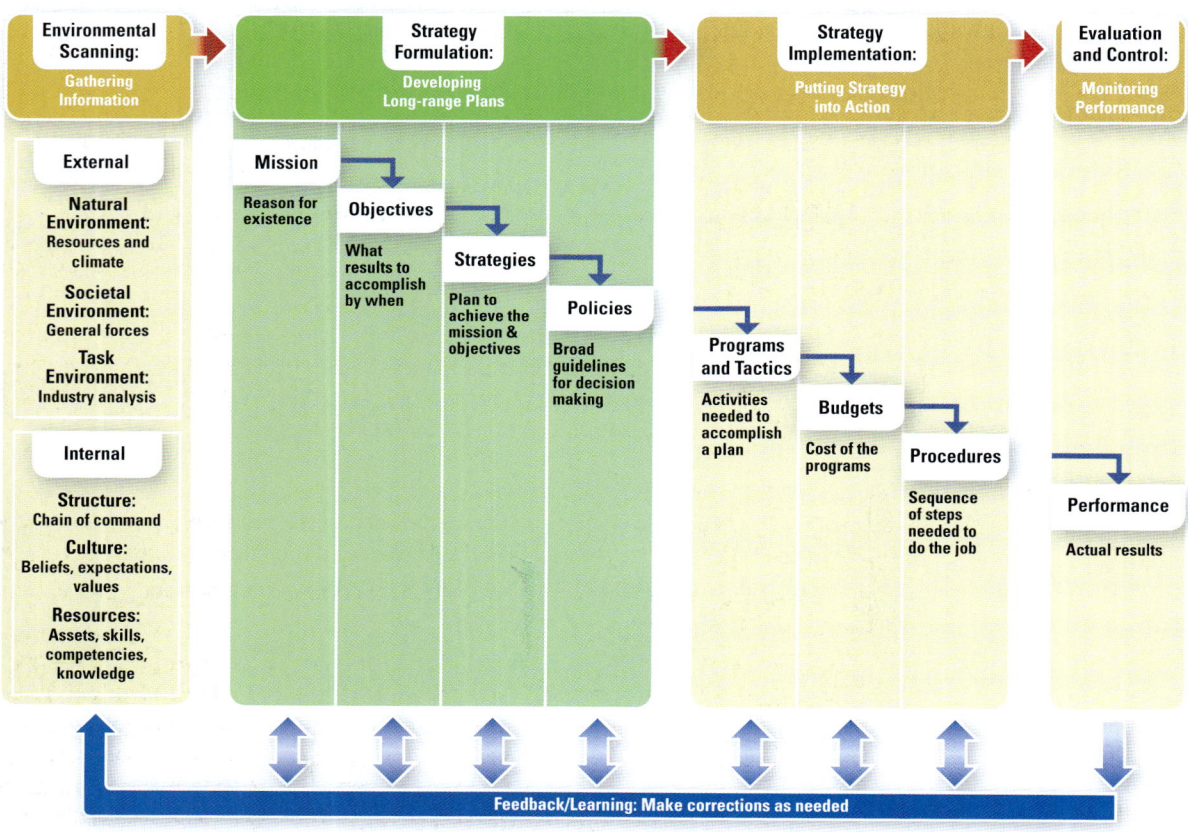

| Environmental Scanning: Gathering Information | Strategy Formulation: Developing Long-range Plans | Strategy Implementation: Putting Strategy into Action | Evaluation and Control: Monitoring Performance |

External

Natural Environment: Resources and climate

Societal Environment: General forces

Task Environment: Industry analysis

Internal

Structure: Chain of command

Culture: Beliefs, expectations, values

Resources: Assets, skills, competencies, knowledge

Mission

Reason for existence

Objectives

What results to accomplish by when

Strategies

Plan to achieve the mission & objectives

Policies

Broad guidelines for decision making

Programs and Tactics

Activities needed to accomplish a plan

Budgets

Cost of the programs

Procedures

Sequence of steps needed to do the job

Performance

Actual results

Feedback/Learning: Make corrections as needed

Pearson MyLab Management®

⭐ **Improve Your Grade!**

Over 10 million students improved their results using the Pearson MyLabs. Visit **mymanagementlab.com** for simulations, tutorials, and end-of-chapter problems.

Learning Objectives

After reading this chapter, you should be able to:

7-1. Explain the three key issues that corporate strategy addresses

7-2. Apply the directional strategies of growth, stability, and retrenchment to the organizational environment in which they work best

7-3. Apply portfolio analysis to guide decisions in companies with multiple products and businesses

7-4. Develop a parenting strategy for a multiple-business corporation

How Does a Company Grow if Its Primary Business Is Maturing?

Pfizer Remakes the Company

Pfizer, Inc. was founded in 1849 by Charles Pfizer and Charles Erhart. The company was the breakthrough leader in the development of the means for producing penicillin on a large scale. In fact, most of the penicillin carried by troops on D-Day in 1944 was made by Pfizer. The company became a major research lab for the development of drugs. In 1972, Pfizer increased funding of research and development from 5% of sales (an astounding figure in any industry) to 20% of sales. The company viewed its mission as discovering and developing innovative pharmaceuticals. In 2011, the company had sales of US$67.4 billion but had also absorbed several very large acquisitions from 1999–2009, including Wyeth, Warner-Lambert, and Pharmacia. A number of blockbuster drugs had come or were coming off patent protection and new ones were becoming increasingly difficult to find. Most of the diseases that still lacked effective treatment, such as Alzheimer's, were more complicated.

The company poured US$2.8 billion into an inhalable insulin (Exubera) and a cholesterol-reducing replacement for Lipitor (Torcetrapib), but both failed to take hold in the market. History has shown that only 16% of drugs under development ever get regulatory approval.

In a bold move, Pfizer's CEO, Ian Read, made the decision in 2012 to consolidate around five areas: cardiovascular diseases, cancer, neuroscience, vaccines, and inflammation/immunology. Over the next four years they added a rare disease area to the group. Redirecting resources in the company, Pfizer closed the famed Sandwich, England, research campus (the birthplace of Viagra) laying off more than 2000 employees because its focus was on areas not included in the new direction of the company. It then divested its animal health and infant nutrition businesses. It also cut more than 3000 research jobs at its flagship New London, Connecticut, campus.

All of the cuts were plowed into one of the focus areas. The company continued to acquire other companies and in a very controversial move purchased Allergan (based in Ireland) and announced that it was moving its corporate headquarters to Ireland. The move is now expected to provide a tax windfall to the company of as much as US$35 billion.

This type of corporate repositioning is an example of portfolio management.

SOURCES: R. Merle, "Giving up its US citizenship could save Pfizer $35 billion in taxes," *The Washington Post*, February 25, 2016 (https://www.washingtonpost.com/news/business/wp/2016/02/25/giving-up-its-u-s-citizenship-could-save-pfizer-35-billion-in-taxes/); "Pfizer Embarks on an Overdue Crash Diet," *Bloomberg Businessweek* (March 12, 2012), pp. 24–25; http://www.pfizer.com/about/history/history.jsp; http://www.pfizer.com/about/history/1951_1999.jsp.

Corporate Strategy

7-1. Explain the three key issues that corporate strategy addresses

The vignette about Pfizer illustrates the importance of corporate strategy to a firm's survival and success. Corporate strategy addresses three key issues facing the corporation as a whole:

1. The firm's overall orientation toward growth, stability, or retrenchment (**directional strategy**)
2. The industries or markets in which the firm competes through its products and business units (**portfolio analysis**)
3. The manner in which management coordinates activities, transfers resources, and cultivates capabilities among product lines and business units (**parenting strategy**).

Corporate strategy is primarily about the choice of direction for a firm as a whole and the management of its business or product portfolio.[1] This is true whether the firm is a small company or a large multinational corporation (MNC). In a large multiple-business company, in particular, corporate strategy is concerned with managing various product lines and business units for maximum value. In this instance, corporate headquarters must play the role of the organizational "parent," in that it must deal with various product and business unit "children." Even though each product line or business unit has its own competitive or cooperative strategy that it uses to obtain its own competitive advantage in the marketplace, the corporation must coordinate these different business strategies so that the corporation as a whole succeeds as a "family."[2]

Corporate strategy, therefore, includes decisions regarding the flow of financial and other resources to and from a company's product lines and business units. Through a series of coordinating devices, a company transfers skills and capabilities developed in one unit to other units that need such resources. In this way, it attempts to obtain synergy among numerous product lines and business units so that the corporate whole is greater than the sum of its individual business unit parts.[3] All corporations, from the smallest company offering one product in only one industry to the largest conglomerate operating in many industries with many products, must at one time or another consider one or more of these issues.

To deal with each of the key issues, this chapter is organized into three parts that examine corporate strategy in terms of *directional strategy* (orientation toward growth), *portfolio analysis* (coordination of cash flow among units), and *corporate parenting* (the building of corporate synergies through resource sharing and development).[4]

Directional Strategy

Just as every product or business unit must follow a business strategy to improve its competitive position, every corporation must decide its orientation toward growth by asking the following three questions:

7-2. Apply the directional strategies of growth, stability, and retrenchment to the organizational environment in which they work best

1. Should we expand, cut back, or continue our operations unchanged?

2. Should we concentrate our activities within our current industry, or should we diversify into other industries?

3. If we want to grow and expand nationally and/or globally, should we do so through internal development or through external acquisitions, mergers, or strategic alliances?

A corporation's directional strategy is composed of three general orientations (sometimes called *grand strategies*):

- **Growth strategies** expand the company's activities.
- **Stability strategies** make no change to the company's current activities.
- **Retrenchment strategies** reduce the company's level of activities.

Having chosen the general orientation (such as growth), a company's managers can select from several more specific corporate strategies such as concentration within one product line/industry or diversification into other products/industries. (See **Figure 7–1**.) These strategies are useful both to corporations operating in only one industry with one product line and to those operating in many industries with many product lines.

GROWTH STRATEGIES

By far, the most widely pursued corporate directional strategies are those designed to achieve growth in sales, assets, profits, or some combination of these. Companies that do business in expanding industries must grow to survive. Continuing growth means increasing sales and a chance to take advantage of the experience curve to reduce the per-unit cost of products sold, thereby increasing profits. This cost reduction becomes extremely important if a corporation's industry is growing quickly or consolidating and if competitors are engaging in price wars in attempts to increase their shares of the market. Firms that have not reached "critical mass" (that is, gained the necessary economy of production) face large losses unless they can find and fill a small, but profitable, niche where higher prices can be offset by special product or service features. That is why Oracle has been on the acquisition trail. In the past four years the company has added 31 new companies to the organization focused on four major areas (Applications, Middleware, Industry Solutions, and Servers/Storage/Networking). Although still growing, the software industry is dominated by a handful of large firms. According to CEO Larry Ellison, Oracle needs to grow by buying smaller and weaker rivals if it wants to compete with SAP and Microsoft.[5] Growth is a popular strategy because larger businesses tend to survive longer than smaller companies due to the greater availability of financial resources, organizational routines, and external ties.[6]

FIGURE 7–1   Corporate Directional Strategies

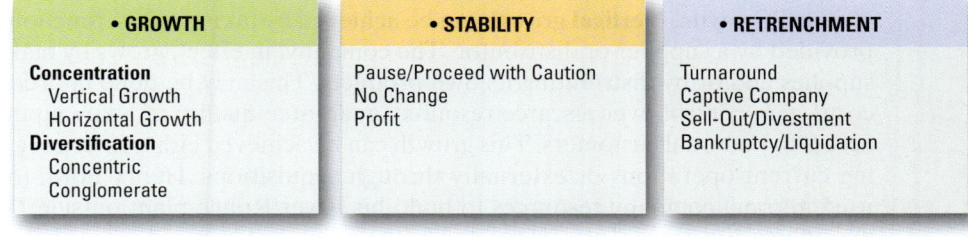

• GROWTH	• STABILITY	• RETRENCHMENT
Concentration Vertical Growth Horizontal Growth **Diversification** Concentric Conglomerate	Pause/Proceed with Caution No Change Profit	Turnaround Captive Company Sell-Out/Divestment Bankruptcy/Liquidation

A corporation can grow internally by expanding its operations both globally and domestically, or it can grow externally through mergers, acquisitions, and strategic alliances. In practice, the line between mergers and acquisitions has been blurred to the point where it is difficult to tell the difference. In general, we regard a **merger** as a transaction involving two or more corporations in which both companies exchange stock in order to create one new corporation. Mergers that occur between firms of somewhat similar size are referred to as a "merger of equals." Most mergers are "friendly"—that is, both parties believe it is in their best interests to combine their companies. The resulting firm is likely to have a name derived from its composite firms. One of the largest such mergers was between Heinz and Kraft Foods in 2015 that formed the new company Kraft Heinz Company. That merger created a company with annual revenues of over US$28 billion.[7] An **acquisition** is a purchase of another company. In some cases, the company continues to operate as an independent entity and in others it is completely absorbed as an operating subsidiary or division of the acquiring corporation. In July 2015, Duke Energy acquired Piedmont Natural Gas, making the latter a wholly owned unit of Duke Energy. With the acquisition, Duke Energy tripled the number of natural gas customers it served and took more control of a key resource for electricity production.[8] Acquisitions usually occur between firms of different sizes and can be either friendly or hostile. Hostile acquisitions are often called *takeovers*.

From management's perspective (but perhaps not a stockholder's), growth is very attractive for two key reasons:

- Growth based on increasing market demand may mask flaws in a company—flaws that would be immediately evident in a stable or declining market. A growing flow of revenue into a highly leveraged corporation can create a large amount of *organization slack* (unused resources) that can be used to quickly resolve problems and conflicts between departments and divisions. Growth also provides a big cushion for turnaround in case a strategic error is made. Larger firms also have more bargaining power than do small firms and are more likely to obtain support from key stakeholders in case of difficulty.

- A growing firm offers more opportunities for advancement, promotion, and interesting jobs. Growth itself is exciting and ego-enhancing for everyone. The marketplace and potential investors tend to view a growing corporation as a "winner" or "on the move." Executive compensation tends to get bigger as an organization increases in size. Large firms are also more difficult to acquire than smaller ones—thus, an executive's job in a large firm is more secure.

The two basic growth strategies are **concentration** on the current or innovative product line(s) in one industry and **diversification** into other product lines or other industries.

Concentration

If a company's current product lines have real growth potential, the concentration of resources on those product lines makes sense as a strategy for growth. The two basic concentration strategies are vertical growth and horizontal growth. Growing firms in a growing industry tend to choose these strategies before they try diversification.

Vertical Growth. **Vertical growth** can be achieved by taking over a function previously provided by a supplier or distributor. The company, in effect, grows by making its own supplies and/or by distributing its own products. This may be done in order to reduce costs, gain control over a scarce resource, guarantee quality of a key input, or obtain access to potential customers. This growth can be achieved either internally by expanding current operations or externally through acquisitions. Henry Ford, for example, used internal company resources to build his River Rouge plant outside Detroit. The manufacturing process was integrated to the point that iron ore entered one end of the long plant, and finished automobiles rolled out the other end into a huge parking lot. In contrast, Cisco Systems, a maker of Internet hardware, chose the external route to vertical growth by purchasing Scientific-Atlanta Inc., a maker of set-top boxes for television programs and movies-on-demand. This acquisition gave Cisco access to technology for distributing television to living rooms through the Internet.[9]

Vertical growth results in **vertical integration**—the degree to which a firm operates vertically in multiple locations on an industry's value chain from extracting raw materials to manufacturing to retailing. More specifically, assuming a function previously provided by a supplier is called **backward integration** (going backward on an industry's value chain). The purchase of Carroll's Foods for its hog-growing facilities by Smithfield Foods, the world's largest pork processor, is an example of backward integration.[10] Assuming a function previously provided by a distributor is labeled **forward integration** (going forward on an industry's value chain). FedEx, for example, used forward integration when it purchased Kinko's in order to provide store-front package drop-off and delivery services for the small-business market.[11]

Vertical growth is a logical strategy for a corporation or business unit with a strong competitive position in a highly attractive industry—especially when technology is predictable and markets are growing.[12] To keep and even improve its competitive position, a company may use backward integration to minimize resource acquisition costs and inefficient operations, as well as forward integration to gain more control over product distribution. The firm, in effect, builds on its distinctive competence by expanding along the industry's value chain to gain greater competitive advantage.

Although backward integration is often more profitable than forward integration (because of typical low margins in retailing), it can reduce a corporation's strategic flexibility. The resulting encumbrance of expensive assets that might be hard to sell could create an exit barrier, preventing the corporation from leaving that particular industry. Examples of single-use assets are blast furnaces and refineries. When demand drops in either of these industries (steel or oil and gas), these assets have no alternative use, but continue to cost money in terms of debt payments, property taxes, and security expenses.

Transaction cost economics proposes that vertical integration is more efficient than contracting for goods and services in the marketplace when the transaction costs of buying goods on the open market become too great. When highly vertically integrated firms become excessively large and bureaucratic, however, the costs of managing the internal transactions may become greater than simply purchasing the needed goods externally—thus justifying outsourcing over vertical integration. This is why vertical integration and outsourcing are situation specific. Neither approach is best for all companies in all situations.[13] See the **Strategy Highlight** feature on how transaction cost economics helps explain why firms vertically integrate or outsource important activities. Research thus far provides mixed support for the predictions of transaction cost economics.[14]

Of course a company's degree of vertical integration can range from total ownership of the value chain needed to make and sell a product to no ownership at all.[15] Under **full integration**, a firm internally makes 100% of its key supplies and completely controls its distributors. Large oil companies, such as British Petroleum and Royal Dutch Shell, are fully integrated. They own the oil rigs that pump the oil out of the ground, the ships and pipelines that transport the oil, the refineries that convert the oil to gasoline, and the trucks that deliver the gasoline to company-owned and franchised gas stations. Sherwin-Williams Company, which not only manufactures paint, but also sells it in its own chain of 3000 retail stores, is another example of a fully integrated firm.[16] If a corporation does not want the disadvantages of full vertical integration, it may choose either taper or quasi-integration strategies.

With **taper integration** (also called concurrent sourcing), a firm internally produces less than half of its own requirements and buys the rest from outside suppliers (backward taper integration).[17] In the case of Smithfield Foods, its purchase of Carroll's

STRATEGY highlight

TRANSACTION COST ECONOMICS ANALYZES VERTICAL GROWTH STRATEGY

Why do corporations use vertical growth to permanently own suppliers or distributors when they could simply purchase individual items when needed on the open market? Transaction cost economics is a branch of institutional economics that attempts to answer this question. Transaction cost economics proposes that owning resources through vertical growth is more efficient than contracting for goods and services in the marketplace when the transaction costs of buying goods on the open market become too great. Transaction costs include the basic costs of drafting, negotiating, and safeguarding a market agreement (a contract) as well as the later managerial costs when the agreement is creating problems (goods aren't being delivered on time or quality is lower than needed), renegotiation costs (e.g., costs of meetings and phone calls), and the costs of settling disputes (e.g., lawyers' fees and court costs).

According to Williamson, three conditions must be met before a corporation will prefer internalizing a vertical transaction through ownership over contracting for the transaction in the marketplace: (1) a high level of uncertainty must surround the transaction, (2) assets involved in the transaction must be highly specialized to the transaction, and (3) the transaction must occur frequently. If there is a high level of uncertainty, it will be impossible to write a contract covering all contingencies, and it is likely that the contractor will act opportunistically to exploit any gaps in the written agreement—thus creating problems and increasing costs. If the assets being

contracted for are highly specialized (e.g., goods or services with few alternate uses), there are likely to be few alternative suppliers—thus allowing the contractor to take advantage of the situation and increase costs. The more frequent the transactions, the more opportunity for the contractor to demand special treatment and thus increase costs further.

Vertical integration is not always more efficient than the marketplace, however. When highly vertically integrated firms become excessively large and bureaucratic, the costs of managing the internal transactions may become greater than simply purchasing the needed goods externally—thus justifying outsourcing over ownership. The usually hidden management costs (e.g., excessive layers of management, endless committee meetings needed for interdepartmental coordination, and delayed decision making due to excessively detailed rules and policies) add to the internal transaction costs—thus reducing the effectiveness and efficiency of vertical integration. The decision to own or to outsource is, therefore, based on the particular situation surrounding the transaction and the ability of the corporation to manage the transaction internally both effectively and efficiently.

....

SOURCES: O. E. Williamson and S. G. Winter (Eds.), *The Nature of the Firm: Origins, Evolution, and Development* (New York: Oxford University Press, 1991); E. Mosakowski, "Organizational Boundaries and Economic Performance: An Empirical Study of Entrepreneurial Computer Firms," *Strategic Management Journal* (February 1991), pp. 115–133; P. S. Ring and A. H. Van de Ven, "Structuring Cooperative Relationships Between Organizations," *Strategic Management Journal* (October 1992), pp. 483–498.

allowed it to produce 27% of the hogs it needed to process into pork. In terms of forward taper integration, a firm sells part of its goods through company-owned stores and the rest through general wholesalers. Although Apple had 246 of its own retail stores in 2012, much of the company's sales continued to be through national chains such as Best Buy and through independent local and regional dealers.

With **quasi-integration**, a company does not make any of its key supplies but purchases most of its requirements from outside suppliers that are under its partial control (backward quasi-integration). A company may not want to purchase outright a supplier or distributor, but it still may want to guarantee access to needed supplies, new products, technologies, or distribution channels. For example, the pharmaceutical company Bristol-Myers Squibb purchased 17% of the common stock of ImClone in order to gain access to new drug products being developed through biotechnology. An example of forward quasi-integration would be a paper company acquiring part interest in an office products chain in order to guarantee that its products had access to the distribution channel.

Purchasing part interest in another company usually provides a company with a seat on the other firm's board of directors, thus guaranteeing the acquiring firm both information and control. As in the case of Bristol-Myers Squibb and ImClone, a quasi-integrated firm may later decide to buy the rest of a key supplier that it did not already own.[18]

Long-term contracts are agreements between two firms to provide agreed-upon goods and services to each other for a specified period of time. This cannot really be considered to be vertical integration unless it is an *exclusive* contract that specifies that the supplier or distributor cannot have a similar relationship with a competitive firm. In that case, the supplier or distributor is really a *captive company* that, although officially independent, does most of its business with the contracted firm and is formally tied to the other company through a long-term contract.

Some companies have moved away from vertical growth strategies (and thus vertical integration) toward cooperative contractual relationships with suppliers and even with competitors.[19] These relationships range from *outsourcing*, in which resources are purchased from outsiders through long-term contracts instead of being done in-house (Coca-Cola Enterprises eliminated jobs in three U.S. centers by contracting with Capgemini for accounting and financial services), to strategic alliances, in which partnerships, technology licensing agreements, and joint ventures supplement a firm's capabilities (Toshiba has used strategic alliances with GE, Siemens, and Ericsson to become one of the world's leading electronic companies).[20]

Horizontal Growth. A firm can achieve **horizontal growth** by expanding its operations into other geographic locations and/or by increasing the range of products and services offered to current markets. Research indicates that firms that grow horizontally by broadening their product lines have high survival rates.[21] Horizontal growth results in **horizontal integration**—the degree to which a firm operates in multiple geographic locations at the same point on an industry's value chain. The Walt Disney Company is one of the world's most powerful brands. The company consists of a deep portfolio of entertainment and information in locations around the world. Not only does the company continually add to its existing product, service, and entertainment lines to reduce possible niches that competitors may enter, but also introduces successful ideas from one part of the world to another.[22]

Horizontal growth can be achieved through internal development or externally through acquisitions and strategic alliances with other firms in the same industry. In late 2013, U.S. Airways acquired American Airlines (American Airlines was then trying to emerge from bankruptcy) and took the American name for the organization. The primary goals were to obtain routes that they could not access and establish the organization as the leader in the industry. Of the 900+ routes that the two airlines flew at the time, only 12 overlapped.[23] In contrast, many small commuter airlines engage in long-term contracts with major airlines in order to offer a complete arrangement for travelers. For example, the regional carrier Mesa Airlines arranged long-term contractual agreements with United Airlines (2028) and American Airlines (2025) to be listed on their computer reservations, respectively, as United Express and American Eagle.[24]

Horizontal growth is increasingly being achieved through international expansion. America's Wal-Mart, France's Carrefour, and Britain's Tesco are examples of national supermarket discount chains expanding horizontally throughout the world. This type of growth can be achieved internationally through many different strategies.

Diversification Strategies

According to strategist Richard Rumelt, companies begin thinking about diversification when their growth has plateaued and opportunities for growth in the original business have been depleted.[25] This often occurs when an industry consolidates, becomes mature, and most of the surviving firms have reached the limits of growth using vertical and

GLOBAL issue

GLOBAL EXPANSION IS NOT ALWAYS A PATH TO GROWTH

The mantra in U.S. business growth for the past few decades has been to look to international markets for growth, and especially to China. Company after company poured into China with their successful U.S. business models and touted their global growth plans. Entering a new market, and especially a new market that is in a new country, often requires an adjustment to the nuances of that market.

McDonald's learned that lesson long ago when it modified its menu for the Indian market by eliminating pork and beef products and offering such unique offerings as the McAloo Tikkiburger with a mashed potato patty and the McPuff, which is a vegetable and cheese pastry. In China-based McDonald's outlets, a favorite drink is "bubble tea," which is tea with tapioca balls in the bottom. Unfortunately, many large U.S. companies are pulling out of China completely or they are having to completely rewrite their business models in order to succeed.

Home Depot Inc. closed all seven of its remaining Chinese big-box stores in 2012 (they started with 12 stores through an acquisition in 2006). Unlike the U.S. market, the Chinese consumer is far more interested in finished goods and paying someone to complete a project than they are in doing it themselves. IKEA struggled for years in the Chinese market until they began offering assembly and delivery services. The DIY (do-it-yourself) market does not appear to translate well into some cultures.

Best Buy closed all of its nine stores in 2011 after discovering that Chinese consumers were far more interested in appliances than its predominantly entertainment-based product line. Best Buy experimented with a small-sized appliance store, but eventually decided to pull out of China completely and focus on their North American markets.

This is not to say that some businesses don't translate easily. Yum Brands Inc. had over 7100 restaurants in over 1100 cities in China in 2016 following its business model (much like McDonald's) but modifying the approach (which is selling fast food) to its market. KFC sells egg tarts and soy milk in China while not offering those menu items outside the Chinese market.

Global success is a function of many different elements. Some businesses that are wildly successful in their home country will not find an easy path to growth in international expansion.

....

SOURCES: "Best Buy considers sale of China business: WSJ," Reuters, January 24, 2014 (www.reuters.com/articles/us-best-buy-china-idUSKBN0EZ2YE20140642); www.yum.com/brands/china.asp; "McDonald's Going Vegetarian," *Bloomberg Businessweek* (September 10, 2012), p. 30; L. Burkitt, "Home Depot: Chinese Prefer Do-It-for-Me," *The Wall Street Journal* (September 15, 2012), p. B1.

---

horizontal growth strategies. Unless the competitors are able to expand internationally into less mature markets, they may have no choice but to diversify into different industries if they want to continue growing. The two basic diversification strategies are concentric and conglomerate and both require very sophisticated management techniques in order to keep the elements of the company moving in relatively the same direction.

Concentric (Related) Diversification. Growth through **concentric diversification** into a related industry may be a very appropriate corporate strategy when a firm has a strong competitive position but industry attractiveness is low.

Research indicates that the probability of succeeding by moving into a related business is a function of a company's position in its core business. For companies in leadership positions, the chances for success are nearly three times higher than those for followers.[26] By focusing on the characteristics that have given the company its distinctive competence, the company uses those very strengths as its means of diversification. The firm attempts to secure strategic fit in a new industry where the firm's product knowledge, its manufacturing capabilities, and/or the marketing skills it used so effectively in the original industry can be put to good use.[27] The corporation's products or processes are related in some way: They possess some common thread.

A firm may choose to diversify concentrically through either internal or external means. Electrolux, for example, has diversified externally globally through acquisitions.

Toro, in contrast, grew internally in North America by using its current manufacturing processes and distributors to make and market snow blowers in addition to lawn mowers.[28]

Conglomerate (Unrelated) Diversification. When management realizes that the current industry is unattractive and that the firm lacks outstanding abilities or skills that it could easily transfer to related products or services in other industries, the most likely strategy is **conglomerate diversification**—diversifying into an industry unrelated to its current one. Rather than maintaining a common thread throughout their organization, strategic managers who adopt this strategy are primarily concerned with financial considerations of cash flow or risk reduction. This is also a good strategy for a firm when its core capability is its own excellent management systems. Berkshire Hathaway is one of the best examples of a company that has used conglomerate diversification to grow successfully. Founded by Warren Buffet, the company has more than 60 companies in its portfolio including Benjamin Moore, BNSF Railway, Fruit of the Loom, GEICO, and See's Candies.[29]

The emphasis in conglomerate diversification is on sound investment and value-oriented management rather than on the product-market synergy common to concentric diversification. A cash-rich company with few opportunities for growth in its industry might, for example, move into another industry where opportunities are great but cash is hard to find. Another instance of conglomerate diversification might be when a company with a seasonal and, therefore, uneven cash flow purchases a firm in an unrelated industry with complementing seasonal sales that will level out the cash flow. CSX management considered the purchase of a natural gas transmission business (Texas Gas Resources) by CSX Corporation (a railroad-dominated transportation company) to be a good fit because most of the gas transmission revenue was realized in the winter months—the lean period in the railroad business.

CONTROVERSIES IN DIRECTIONAL GROWTH STRATEGIES

Is vertical growth better than horizontal growth? Is concentration better than diversification? Is concentric diversification better than conglomerate diversification? Research reveals that companies following a related diversification strategy appear to be higher performers and survive longer than do companies with narrower scope following a pure concentration strategy.[30] Although the research is not in complete agreement, growth into areas related to a company's current product lines is generally more successful than is growth into completely unrelated areas.[31] While there has only been limited research in the area, one study of various growth projects examined how many were considered successful—that is, still in existence after 22 years. The results were vertical growth, 80%; horizontal growth, 50%; concentric diversification, 35%; and conglomerate diversification, 28%.[32] This supports the conclusion from a later study of 40 successful European companies that companies should first exploit their existing assets and capabilities before exploring for new ones, but that they should also diversify their portfolio of products.[33]

In terms of diversification strategies, research suggests that the relationship between relatedness and performance follows an inverted U-shaped curve. If a new business is very similar to that of the acquiring firm, it adds little new to the corporation and only marginally improves performance. If the new business is completely different from the acquiring company's businesses, there may be very little potential for any synergy. If, however, the new business provides new resources and capabilities in a different but similar business, the likelihood of a significant performance improvement is high.[34]

Is internal growth better than external growth? Corporations can follow the growth strategies of either concentration or diversification through the internal development of new products and services, or through external acquisitions, mergers, and strategic alliances. The value of global acquisitions and mergers was US$5.03 trillion in 2015, a rise of more than 37% from 2014.[35] According to a McKinsey & Company survey, managers are primarily motivated to purchase other companies in order to add capabilities, expand geographically, and buy growth.[36] Research generally concludes, however, that firms growing through acquisitions do not perform financially as well as firms that grow through internal means.[37] For example, on September 3, 2001, the day *before* HP announced that it was purchasing Compaq, HP's stock was selling at US$23.11. After the announcement, the stock price fell to US$18.87. Three years later, on September 21, 2004, the shares sold at US$18.70.[38] One reason for this poor performance may be the typically high price of the acquisition itself. Studies reveal that over half to two-thirds of acquisitions are failures primarily because the premiums paid were too high for them to earn their cost of capital.[39] Another reason for the poor stock performance is that the customers of the current firms see a lot of negatives in mergers. A coalition of consumer groups opposed the proposed merger between Time-Warner Cable and Charter citing the power of the new entity to stifle innovation, reduce competition and raise rates to consumers.[40] It is likely that neither strategy is best by itself and that some combination of internal and external growth strategies is better than using one or the other.[41]

What can improve acquisition performance? For one thing, the acquisition should be linked to strategic objectives and support corporate strategy. Some consultants have suggested that a corporation must be prepared to identify roughly 100 candidates and conduct due diligence investigation on around 40 companies in order to ultimately purchase 10 companies. This kind of effort requires the capacity to sift through many candidates while simultaneously integrating previous acquisitions.[42] A study by Bain & Company of more than 11,000 acquisitions by companies throughout the world concluded that successful acquirers make small, low-risk acquisitions before moving on to larger ones.[43] Previous experience between an acquirer and a target firm in terms of R&D, manufacturing, or marketing alliances improves the likelihood of a successful acquisition.[44]

STABILITY STRATEGIES

A corporation may choose stability over growth by continuing its current activities without any significant change in direction. Although sometimes viewed as a lack of strategy, the stability family of corporate strategies can be appropriate for a successful corporation operating in a reasonably predictable environment.[45] They are very popular with small business owners who have found a niche and are happy with their success and the manageable size of their firms. Stability strategies can be very useful in the short run, but they can be dangerous if followed for too long. Some of the more popular of these strategies are the pause/proceed-with-caution, no-change, and profit strategies.

Pause/Proceed-with-Caution Strategy

A **pause/proceed-with-caution strategy** is, in effect, a timeout—an opportunity to rest before continuing a growth or retrenchment strategy. It is a very deliberate attempt to make only incremental improvements until a particular environmental situation changes. It is typically conceived as a temporary strategy to be used until the environment becomes more hospitable or to enable a company to consolidate its resources after prolonged rapid growth. A great example of this was during the heyday of personal computer growth in the early 1990s. This was the strategy Dell followed after its growth strategy had resulted in more growth than it could handle. Explained CEO Michael Dell at the time, "We grew 285% in two years, and we're having some growing pains." Selling personal computers by mail enabled Dell to underprice competitors, but it could not keep up with the needs of a US$2 billion, 5600-employee company selling PCs in 95 countries. Dell did not give up on its growth strategy, though. It merely put it temporarily in limbo until the company was able to hire new managers, improve the structure, and build new facilities.[46]

No-Change Strategy

A **no-change strategy** is a decision to do nothing new—a choice to continue current operations and policies for the foreseeable future. Rarely articulated as a definite strategy, a no-change strategy's success depends on a lack of significant change in a corporation's situation. The relative stability created by the firm's modest competitive position in an industry facing little or no growth encourages the company to continue on its current course, making only small adjustments for inflation in its sales and profit objectives. There are no obvious opportunities or threats and the status quo is a viable alternative. Few aggressive new competitors are likely to enter such an industry. The corporation has probably found a reasonably profitable and stable niche for its products. Unless the industry is undergoing consolidation, the relative comfort a company in this situation experiences is likely to encourage the company to follow a no-change strategy in which the future is expected to continue as an extension of the present. Many small-town businesses followed this strategy before Wal-Mart moved into their areas and forced them to rethink their strategy or drove them out of business before they could react.

Profit Strategy

A **profit strategy** is a decision to do nothing new in a worsening situation but instead to act as though the company's problems are only temporary. The profit strategy is an attempt to artificially support profits when a company's sales are declining by reducing investment and short-term discretionary expenditures. Rather than announce the company's poor position to shareholders and the investment community at large, top management may be tempted to follow this very seductive approach. Blaming the company's problems on a hostile environment (such as antibusiness government policies, unethical competitors, finicky customers, and/or greedy lenders), management defers investments and/or cuts core business expenses (such as R&D, maintenance, and advertising) to stabilize profits during this period. It may even sell one of its product lines for the cash-flow benefits.

   The profit strategy is useful only to help a company get through a temporary difficulty. It may also be a way to boost the value of a company in preparation to be acquired or for going public via an initial public offering (IPO). Unfortunately, the strategy is seductive and if continued long enough it will lead to a serious deterioration in a corporation's competitive position. The profit strategy is typically top management's passive, short-term, and often self-serving response to a difficult situation. In such situations, it is often better to face the problem directly by choosing a retrenchment strategy.

RETRENCHMENT STRATEGIES

A company may pursue retrenchment strategies when it has a weak competitive position in some or all of its product lines resulting in poor performance—sales are down and profits are becoming losses. These strategies impose a great deal of pressure to improve performance. In an attempt to eliminate the weaknesses that are dragging the company down, management may follow one of several retrenchment strategies, ranging from turnaround or becoming a captive company to selling out, bankruptcy, or liquidation.

Turnaround Strategy

Turnaround strategy (sometimes referred to as transformation)emphasizes the improvement of operational efficiency and is probably most appropriate when a corporation's problems are pervasive but not yet critical. Research shows that poorly performing firms in mature industries have been able to improve their performance by cutting costs and expenses and by selling off assets.[47] For these efforts to be something more than a profit protection, the company has to deal with three phases of the effort—Contraction, Consolidation, and Rebirth.

Contraction is the initial effort to quickly "stop the bleeding" with a general, across-the-board cutback in size and costs. NetApp faced a revenue decline of 19% and a third straight year of layoffs to mitigate the profit impact. In mid-2016 they announced plans to cut more than 12% of its employees as part of a huge, US$400 million cost-cutting move.[48] The second phase, *consolidation*, implements a program to stabilize the now-leaner corporation. To streamline the company, plans are developed to reduce unnecessary overhead and to make functional activities cost-justified. This is a crucial time for the organization. If the consolidation phase is not conducted in a positive manner, many of the best people leave the organization. An overemphasis on downsizing and cutting costs coupled with a heavy hand by top management is usually counterproductive and can actually hurt performance.[49] If, however, all employees are encouraged to get involved in productivity improvements, the firm is likely to emerge from this retrenchment period a much stronger and better-organized company. NetApp aimed to reset the organization around cloud-based storage solutions that would not require the same level of employees to develop and support. The last phase, *re-birth*, happens if the company is successful with its efforts and starts growing profitably again.

Captive Company Strategy

A **captive company strategy** involves giving up independence in exchange for security. A company with a weak competitive position may not be able to successfully implement a full-blown turnaround strategy for a variety of reasons. The industry may not be sufficiently attractive to justify such an effort from either the current management or investors. Nevertheless, a company in this situation faces poor sales and potentially increasing losses unless it takes some action. Management searches for an "angel" by offering to be a captive company to one of its larger customers or another player in the industry in order to guarantee the company's continued existence. In this way, the corporation may be able to reduce the scope of some of its functional activities thus significantly reducing costs. In the case of selling to a customer, the weaker company gains certainty of sales and production in return for becoming heavily dependent on another firm for most of its sales. In the case of selling to a competitor, the company is generally able to protect many of the jobs and in many cases operate as an independent entity. After years of cost cutting moves, acquisitions, and selling off assets, Yahoo! finally gave in to the captive strategy by hiring investment bankers to sell the company.[50]

Sell-Out/Divestment Strategy

If a corporation with a weak competitive position in an industry is unable either to pull itself up by its bootstraps or to find a customer or competitor to which it can become a captive company, it may have no choice but to sell out. The **sell-out strategy** makes sense if management can still obtain a good price for its shareholders and the employees can keep their jobs by selling the entire company to another firm. The hope is that another company will have the necessary resources and determination to return the company to profitability. Marginal performance in a troubled industry was one reason American Airlines was willing to be sold to U.S. Airways.

If the corporation has multiple business lines and it chooses to sell off a division with low growth potential, this is called **divestment**. This was the strategy P&G used when it sold more than half of its brands and consolidated others in order to focus on just 65 brands.[51]

Divestment is often used after a corporation acquires a multiunit corporation in order to shed the units that do not fit with the corporation's new strategy. This is why Whirlpool sold Maytag's Hoover vacuum cleaner unit after Whirlpool purchased Maytag. Divestment was also a key part of Lego's turnaround strategy when management decided to divest its theme parks to concentrate more on its core business of making toys.[52]

Bankruptcy/Liquidation Strategy

When a company finds itself in the worst possible situation with a poor competitive position in an industry with few prospects, management has only a few alternatives—all of them distasteful. Because no one is interested in buying a weak company in an unattractive industry, the firm must pursue a bankruptcy or liquidation strategy. **Bankruptcy** involves giving up management of the firm to the courts in return for some settlement of the corporation's obligations. Top management hopes that once the court decides the claims on the company, the company will be stronger and better able to compete in a more attractive industry. A controversial approach was used by Delphi Corporation when it filed for **Chapter 11** bankruptcy only for its U.S. operations, which employed 32,000 high-wage union workers, but not for its foreign factories in low-wage countries.[53]

In contrast to bankruptcy, which seeks to perpetuate a corporation, **liquidation** is the termination of the firm. When the industry is unattractive and the company too weak to be sold as a going concern, management may choose to convert as many saleable assets as possible to cash, which is then distributed to the shareholders after all obligations are paid. Liquidation is a prudent strategy for distressed firms with a small number of choices, all of which are problematic.[54] This was Circuit City's situation when it liquidated its retail stores. The benefit of liquidation over bankruptcy is that the board of directors, as representatives of the shareholders, together with top management, make the decisions instead of turning them over to the bankruptcy court, which may choose to ignore shareholders completely.

At times, top management must be willing to select one of these less desirable strategies. Unfortunately, many top managers are unwilling to admit that their company has serious weaknesses for fear that they may be personally blamed. Even worse, top management may not even perceive that crises are developing. When these top managers eventually notice trouble, they are prone to attribute the problems to temporary environmental disturbances and tend to follow profit strategies. Even when things are going terribly wrong, top management is greatly tempted to avoid liquidation in the hope of a miracle. Top management then enters a *cycle of decline*, in which it goes through a process of secrecy and denial, followed by blame and scorn, avoidance and turf protection, ending with passivity and helplessness.[55] Thus, a corporation needs a strong board of directors who, to safeguard shareholders' interests, can tell top management when to quit.

Portfolio Analysis

7-3. Apply portfolio analysis to guide decisions in companies with multiple products and businesses

Chapter 6 dealt with how individual product lines and business units can gain competitive advantage in the marketplace by using competitive and cooperative strategies. Companies with multiple product lines or business units must also ask themselves how these various products and business units should be managed to boost overall corporate performance:

- How much of our time and money should we spend on our best products and business units to ensure that they continue to be successful?

- How much of our time and money should we spend developing new costly products, most of which will never be successful?

One of the most popular aids to developing corporate strategy in a multiple-business corporation is portfolio analysis. Although its popularity has dropped since the 1970s and 1980s, when more than half of the largest business corporations used portfolio analysis, it is still used in corporate strategy formulation.[56] Portfolio analysis puts corporate headquarters into the role of an internal banker. In portfolio analysis, top management views its product lines and business units as a series of investments from which it expects a profitable return. The product lines/business units form a portfolio of investments that top management must constantly juggle to ensure the best return on the corporation's invested money. Although not conclusive, a McKinsey & Company study of the performance of the most active companies acquiring and divesting in their portfolio found that they are perceived to be more successful.[57] Given the increasing number of strategic alliances in today's corporations, portfolio analysis is also being used to evaluate the contribution of alliances to corporate and business unit objectives.

One of the most popular portfolio techniques is the BCG Growth-Share Matrix.

BCG GROWTH-SHARE MATRIX

Using the **BCG (Boston Consulting Group) Growth-Share Matrix** depicted in **Figure 7–2** is the simplest way to portray a corporation's portfolio of investments. Each of the corporation's product lines or business units is plotted on the matrix according to both the growth rate of the industry in which it competes and its relative market share. A unit's relative competitive position is defined as its market share in the industry divided by that of the largest other competitor. By this calculation, a relative market share above 1.0 belongs to the market leader. The business growth rate is the percentage of market growth—that is, the percentage by which sales of a particular business unit classification of products have increased. The matrix assumes that, other things being equal, a growing market is attractive.

The line separating areas of high and low relative competitive position is set at 1.5 times. A product line or business unit must have relative strengths of this magnitude to ensure that it will have the dominant position needed to be a "star" or "cash cow." On the other hand, a product line or unit having a relative competitive position less than 1.0 has "dog" status.[58] Each product or unit is represented in **Figure 7–3** by a circle. The

FIGURE 7–2 Vertical Integration Continuum

SOURCE: *Suggested by K. R. Harrigan, Strategies for Vertical Integration* (Lexington, MA: Lexington Books, D.C. Heath, 1983), pp. 16–21.

FIGURE 7–3 BCG Growth-Share Matrix

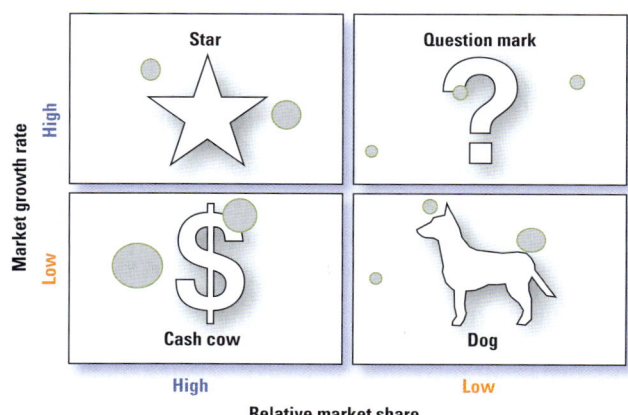

SOURCE: Based on *Long Range Planning,* Vol. 10, No. 2, 1977, Hedley, "Strategy and the Business Portfolio." p. 12. Copyright © 1977.

area of the circle represents the relative significance of each business unit or product line to the corporation in terms of assets used or sales generated.

The BCG Growth-Share Matrix has some common attributes and, therefore, common problems with the product life cycle. As a product moves through its perceived life cycle, it is generally categorized into one of four types for the purpose of funding decisions:

- **Question marks** (sometimes called "problem children" or "wildcats") are new products with the potential for success, but needing a lot of cash for development. If such a product is to gain enough market share to become a market leader and thus a star, money must be taken from more mature products and spent on the question mark. This is a "fish or cut bait" decision in which management must decide if the business is worth the investment needed. For example, after years of fruitlessly experimenting with an electric car, General Motors finally decided in 2006 to take a chance on developing the Chevrolet Volt.[59] To learn more of GM's decision to build the electric car, see the **Sustainability Issue** feature.

- **Stars** are market leaders that are typically at or nearing the peak of their perceived product life cycle and are able to generate enough cash to maintain their high share of the market and usually contribute to the company's profits. The Fitbit bracelet has been a star performer for the company with the product still commanding more than 30% of the market share in 2016.[60,61]

- **Cash cows** typically bring in far more money than is needed to maintain their market share. In this maturing or even declining stage of their life cycle, these products are "milked" for cash that will be invested in new question marks. Expenses such as advertising and R&D are reduced. Apple's iPhone (once a true star) represented more than 60% of Apple revenues even as sales started falling in 2016. This flagship product of the company provides vast resources that have been poured into the Apple Watch among others.[62] Question marks unable to obtain dominant market share (and thus become stars) by the time the industry growth rate inevitably slows become dogs.

- **Dogs** have low market share and do not have the potential (usually because they are in an unattractive industry without a significant market position) to bring in much cash. According to the BCG Growth-Share Matrix, dogs should be either sold off or managed carefully for the small amount of cash they can generate. IBM sold its PC business to China's Lenovo Group in order to focus on its growing services business.

Underlying the BCG Growth-Share Matrix is the concept of the experience curve (discussed in **Chapter 5**). The key to success with this model is assumed to be market leadership. Firms with higher market share tend to have a cost leadership position based on economies of scale, among many other things. If a company is able to use the experience curve to its advantage, it should be able to manufacture and sell new products at a price low enough to garner early market share leadership (assuming no successful imitation by competitors).

Having plotted the current positions of its product lines or business units on a matrix, a company can project its future positions; however, this assumes no change in strategy by either the company with the portfolio or its competitors—a very unrealistic assumption. That said, present and projected matrixes can be used to help identify major strategic issues facing the organization. The goal of any company using a portfolio approach is to maintain a balanced portfolio so it can be self-sufficient in cash and always working to harvest mature products in declining or stagnant industries in order to support new ones in growing industries.

The BCG Growth-Share Matrix is a very well-known portfolio concept with some clear advantages. It is quantifiable and easy to use. *Cash cow*, *dog*, *question mark*, and *star* are easy-to-remember terms for referring to a corporation's business units

SUSTAINABILITY issue

GENERAL MOTORS AND THE ELECTRIC CAR

In 2003, top management at General Motors (GM) decided to discontinue further work on its EV1 electric automobile. Working versions of the car had been leased to a limited number of people, but never sold. GM required every EV1 to be returned to the company. Environmentalists protested that GM stopped making the car just to send a message to government policy makers that an electric car was bad business. Management responded by stating that the car would never have made a profit.

In an April 2005 meeting of GM's top management team, Vice Chairman Robert Lutz suggested that it might be time to build another electric car. He noted that Toyota's Prius hybrid had made Toyota look environmentally sensitive, whereas GM was viewed as making gas "hogs." The response was negative. Lutz recalled one executive saying, "We lost $1 billion on the last one. Do you want to lose $1 billion on the next one?"

Even though worldwide car ownership was growing 5% annually, rising fuel prices in 2005 reduced sales of GM's profitable SUVs, resulting in a loss of US$11 billion. Board members began signaling that it was time for management to take some riskier bets to get the company out of financial trouble. In February 2006, management reluctantly approved developmental work on another electric car. At the time, no one in GM knew if batteries could be made small enough to power a car, but they knew that choices were limited. According to Larry Burns, Vice President of R&D and Strategic Planning, "This industry is 98% dependent on petroleum. GM has concluded that that's not sustainable." In the meantime, Tesla Motors had been founded and was planning an all-battery powered model to be released in 2008.

Chairman and CEO Richard Wagoner Jr. surprised the world at the January 2007 Detroit Auto Show with a vow to start developing an electric car called the Chevrolet Volt. It would plug into a regular electric outlet, leapfrog the established competition, and be on sale in 2010.

Management created a new team dedicated to getting hybrid and electric cars to market. The R&D budget was increased from US$6.6 billion in 2006 to US$8.1 billion in 2007. Several new models were canceled to free up resources. The battery lab was under pressure to design batteries that could propel the Volt 40 miles before a small gasoline engine would recharge the battery and extend the range to 600 miles. Douglas Drauch, battery lab manager, said. "Fifty years from now, people will remember the Volt—like they remember a '53 Corvette."

The Volt was released with much fanfare in October, 2010, and by 2012 GM was selling 2500 a month at just over US$40,000 per car. The company was still struggling to match manufacturing with sales and still make a profit. In the meantime, Nissan, Ford, and Toyota were making significant moves in the battery-powered car business. Nissan released the Leaf, Ford released the electric Focus, and Toyota offered the Plug-in Prius and the all-electric RAV4, which claimed to get 103 MPG. Overarching all of the established car company efforts was Tesla. In 2012 they launched the Model S that was 100% electric and could travel 265 miles per charge. By 2016, Tesla had 50,000 vehicles on the road and was seen as the leader in electric car technology.

The Volt remained a hybrid vehicle and sales limped along. By mid-2015 the Volt was selling less than 9,000 units a year and the Leaf was only a bit better selling roughly 15,000 units a year. So, in late 2016, Chevy planned to release the Chevy Bolt. The Bolt is an all-electric vehicle with a range of 200 miles and a price tag in the $38,000 range. It has yet to be seen if the electric car can gain a significant foothold on the U.S. market.

. . . .

SOURCES: www.chevrolet.com/bolt-ev-electric-vehicle.html; www.teslamotors.com/about; S. Blanco, "Nissan Leaf, Chevy Volt have best sales month of 2015," *Autoblog*, (www.autoblog.com/2015/06/02/nissan-leaf-chevy-volt-best-sales-month-2015/); J. Bennett, "GM Expects Volt Sales to Set Monthly Record," *The Wall Street Journal* (August 30, 2012), (http://blogs.wsj.com/drivers-seat/2012/08/30/gm-expects-volt-sales-to-set-monthly-record/?KEYWORDS=volt); "12 Electric Cars for 2012," *CNN Money*, (http://money.cnn.com/galleries/2012/autos/1201/gallery.electric-hybrid-cars.fortune/9.html); D. Welch, "GM: Live Green or Die," *BusinessWeek* (May 26, 2008), pp. 36–41; "The Drive for Low Emissions," *The Economist's Special Report on Business and Climate Change* (June 2, 2007), pp. 26–28.

or products. Unfortunately, the BCG Growth-Share Matrix also has some serious limitations:

- The use of highs and lows to form four categories is too simplistic.
- The link between market share and profitability is questionable.[63] Low-share businesses can also be profitable.[64] The long-play record virtually disappeared in the

1990s and early 2000s as CDs, downloads, and then streaming music took hold of the masses. Today, there are still companies pressing in-house vinyl records and doing so very profitably. At the same time there has been a resurgence in demand for cassette tapes![65]

- Growth rate is only one aspect of industry attractiveness.
- Product lines or business units are considered only in relation to one competitor: the market leader. Small competitors with fast-growing market shares are ignored.
- Market share is only one aspect of overall competitive position.

ADVANTAGES AND LIMITATIONS OF PORTFOLIO ANALYSIS

Portfolio analysis is commonly used in strategy formulation because it offers certain *advantages:*

- It encourages top management to evaluate each of the corporation's businesses individually and to set objectives and allocate resources for each.
- It stimulates the use of externally oriented data to supplement management's judgment.
- It raises the issue of cash-flow availability for use in expansion and growth.
- Its graphic depiction facilitates communication.

Portfolio analysis does, however, have some very real *limitations* that have caused some companies to reduce their use of this approach:

- Defining product/market segments is difficult.
- It suggests the use of standard strategies that can miss opportunities or be impractical.
- It provides an illusion of scientific rigor, when in reality positions are based on subjective judgments.
- Its value-laden terms such as cash cow and dog can lead to self-fulfilling prophecies.
- It is not always clear what makes an industry attractive or where a product is in its life cycle.
- Naively following the prescriptions of a portfolio model may actually reduce corporate profits if they are used inappropriately. For example, General Mills' immensely successful Bisquick brand of baking mix would have been written off years ago based on portfolio analysis.

MANAGING A STRATEGIC ALLIANCE PORTFOLIO

Just as product lines/business units form a portfolio of investments that top management must constantly juggle to ensure the best return on the corporation's invested money, strategic alliances can also be viewed as a portfolio of investments—investments of money, time, and energy. The way a company manages these intertwined relationships can significantly influence corporate competitiveness. Alliances are thus recognized as an important potential source of competitive advantage and superior performance.[66]

Managing groups of strategic alliances is primarily the job of the business unit. Its decisions may escalate, however, to the corporate level.

There appear to be four tasks of multi-alliance management that are necessary for successful alliance portfolio management:

1. **Developing and implementing a portfolio strategy for each business unit and a corporate policy for managing all the alliances of the entire company:** Alliances are primarily determined by business units. The corporate level develops general rules concerning when, how, and with whom to cooperate. The task of alliance policy is to strategically align all of the corporation's alliance activities with corporate strategy and corporate values. Every new alliance is thus checked against corporate policy before it is approved.

2. **Monitoring the alliance portfolio in terms of implementing business unit strategies and corporate strategy and policies:** Each alliance is measured in terms of achievement of objectives (e.g., market share), financial measures (e.g., profits and cash flow), contributed resource quality and quantity, and the overall relationship. The more a firm is diversified, the less the need for monitoring at the corporate level.

3. **Coordinating the portfolio to obtain synergies and avoid conflicts among alliances:** Because the interdependencies among alliances within a business unit are usually greater than among different businesses, the need for coordination is greater at the business level than at the corporate level. The need for coordination increases as the number of alliances in one business unit and the company as a whole increases, the average number of partners per alliance increases, and/or the overlap of the alliances increases.

4. **Establishing an alliance management system to support other tasks of multi-alliance management:** This infrastructure consists of formalized processes, standardized tools, and specialized organizational units. Many companies establish centers of competence for alliance management. The centers are often part of a department for corporate development or a department of alliance management at the corporate level. In other corporations, specialized positions for alliance management are created at both the corporate and business unit levels or only at the business unit level. Most corporations prefer a system in which the corporate level provides the methods and tools to support alliances centrally, but decentralizes day-to-day alliance management to the business units.[67]

Corporate Parenting

7-4. Develop a parenting strategy for a multiple-business corporation

It has been suggested that portfolio-based corporate strategists address two crucial questions:

- What businesses should this company own and why?
- What organizational structure, management processes, and philosophy will foster superior performance from the company's business units?[68]

Portfolio analysis typically attempts to answer these questions by examining the attractiveness of various industries and by managing business units for cash flow—that is, by using cash generated from mature units to build new product lines. Unfortunately, portfolio analysis fails to deal with the question of what industries a corporation should enter or how a corporation can attain synergy among its product lines and business units. As suggested by its name, portfolio analysis tends to primarily view matters financially, regarding business units and product lines as separate and independent investments. Calculating the impact and fit of entering a new industry or a new business acquisition within the current industry can be quite difficult as shown in the **Innovation Issue** feature.

INNOVATION issue

TO RED HAT OR NOT?

Many large, established organizations including IBM, Hewlett-Packard, Oracle, and Intel were looking closely at acquiring a business that had grown to a US$1 billion business in a niche area of the industry. Red Hat was a business founded on supporting what amounts to a free software system called Linux.

The precursor to the Internet was born in 1968, and in 1969 a researcher at Bell Labs created UNIX as an open-source operating system. Being open sourced meant that anyone who wanted to volunteer their time could add to the capability of the software. Fast forward to 1995 and a new company called Red Hat was born as an accessory, books, and magazine company focused on what had then become known as Linux—the latest version of Unix.

Red Hat, based in the Raleigh-Durham area of North Carolina, released its own version of Linux in 1995 and promised to support companies who used that version. It was still freeware, but now it had a company of engineers to support it at that particular point in time. This became the core of the business. The company would freeze Linux periodically and then support that "version" for a 10-year period of time. This gave corporate managers the confidence to use Linux as their operating system.

The company experienced phenomenal growth by focusing on Data Centers and supporting each version with more than 150 engineers. Red Hat charged a substantial premium to its customers who pay a subscription fee for Red Hat support.

With the winds of a potential acquisition behind it, the company's share price surged 66% between 2010 and 2012. Red Hat was the only company that had found a business model that made substantial profits on open-sourced software. Whether this fit with the needs of such major companies as IBM or not was the open question.

In the end Red Hat remained an independent company that had a 2016 market capitalization of over US$12 billion and is moving aggressively into cloud computing.

....

SOURCES: http://www.redhat.com/about/company/history.html; "Red Hat Sees Lots of Green," *Bloomberg Businessweek* (April 2, 2012), pp. 41–43.

Corporate parenting, or parenting strategy, in contrast, views a corporation in terms of resources and capabilities that can be used to build business unit value as well as generate synergies across business units. A widely accepted definition is that:

Multibusiness companies create value by influencing—or parenting—the businesses they own. The best parent companies create more value than any of their rivals would if they owned the same businesses. Those companies have what we call parenting advantage.[69]

Corporate parenting generates corporate strategy by focusing on the core competencies of the parent corporation and on the value created from the relationship between the parent and its businesses. In the form of corporate headquarters, the parent has a great deal of power in this relationship. If there is a good fit between the parent's skills and resources and the needs and opportunities of the business units, the corporation is likely to create value. If, however, there is not a good fit, the corporation is likely to destroy value.[70] Research indicates that companies that have a good fit between their strategy and their parenting roles are better performers than those companies that do not have a good fit.[71] This approach to corporate strategy is useful not only in deciding what new businesses to acquire but also in choosing how each existing business unit should be best managed. This appears to have been one of the key elements to the success of General Electric under CEO Jack Welch.

The primary job of corporate headquarters is, therefore, to obtain synergy among the business units by providing needed resources to units, transferring skills and capabilities among the units, and coordinating the activities of shared unit functions to attain economies of scope (as in centralized purchasing).[72] This is in agreement with the concept of the learning organization discussed in **Chapter 1** in which the role of a large firm is to facilitate and transfer the knowledge assets and services throughout the corporation.[73] This is especially important given that 75% or more of a modern company's market value stems from its intangible assets—the organization's knowledge and capabilities.[74] At Proctor & Gamble, for example, the various business units are expected to work together to develop innovative products. Crest Whitestrips, which controlled 67% of the at-home tooth-whitening market by 2014, was based on the P&G laundry division's knowledge of whitening agents.[75]

DEVELOPING A CORPORATE PARENTING STRATEGY

The search for appropriate corporate strategy involves three analytical steps:

1. **Examine each business unit (or target firm in the case of acquisition) in terms of its strategic factors:** People in the business units probably identified the strategic factors when they were generating business strategies for their units. One popular approach is to establish centers of excellence throughout the corporation. A **center of excellence** is "an organizational unit that embodies a set of capabilities that has been explicitly recognized by the firm as an important source of value creation, with the intention that these capabilities be leveraged by and/or disseminated to other parts of the firm."[76]

2. **Examine each business unit (or target firm) in terms of areas in which performance can be improved:** These are considered to be parenting opportunities. For example, two business units might be able to gain economies of scope by combining their sales forces. In another instance, a unit may have good, but not great, manufacturing and logistics skills. A parent company having world-class expertise in these areas could improve that unit's performance. The corporate parent could also transfer some people from one business unit who have the desired skills to another unit that is in need of those skills. People at corporate headquarters may, because of their experience in many industries, spot areas where improvements are possible that even people in the business unit may not have noticed. Unless specific areas are significantly weaker than the competition, people in the business units may not even be aware that these areas could be improved, especially if each business unit monitors only its own particular industry.

3. **Analyze how well the parent corporation fits with the business unit (or target firm):** Corporate headquarters must be aware of its own strengths and weaknesses in terms of resources, skills, and capabilities. To do this, the corporate parent must ask whether it has the characteristics that fit the parenting opportunities in each business unit. It must also ask whether there is a misfit between the parent's characteristics and the critical success factors of each business unit.

HORIZONTAL STRATEGY AND MULTIPOINT COMPETITION

A **horizontal strategy** is a corporate strategy that cuts across business unit boundaries to build synergy between business units and to improve the competitive position of one or more business units.[77] When used to build synergy, it acts like a parenting strategy. When used to improve the competitive position of one or more business units, it can be thought of as a corporate competitive strategy. In **multipoint competition**, large multibusiness corporations compete against other large multibusiness firms in a number of markets. These multipoint competitors are firms that compete with each other not only in one business unit, but also in a number of business units. At one time or another, a cash-rich competitor may choose to build its own market share in a particular market to the disadvantage of another corporation's business unit. Although each business unit has primary responsibility for its own business strategy, it may sometimes need some help from its corporate parent, especially if the competitor business unit is getting heavy financial support from its corporate parent. In this instance, corporate headquarters develops a horizontal strategy to coordinate the various goals and strategies of related business units.

P&G, Kimberly-Clark, Scott Paper, and Johnson & Johnson (J&J) compete with one another in varying combinations of consumer paper products, from disposable diapers to facial tissue. If (purely hypothetically) J&J had just developed a toilet tissue with which it chose to challenge Procter & Gamble's high-share Charmin brand in a particular district, it might charge a low price for its new brand to build sales quickly. P&G might not choose to respond to this attack on its share by cutting prices on Charmin. Because of Charmin's high market share, P&G would lose significantly more sales dollars in a price war than J&J would with its initially low-share brand. To retaliate, P&G might challenge J&J's high-share baby shampoo with P&G's own low-share brand of baby shampoo in a different district. Once J&J had perceived P&G's response, it might choose to stop challenging Charmin so that P&G would stop challenging J&J's baby shampoo.

Multipoint competition and the resulting use of horizontal strategy may actually slow the development of hypercompetition in an industry. The realization that an attack on a market leader's position could result in a response in another market leads to mutual forbearance in which managers behave more conservatively toward multimarket rivals and competitive rivalry is reduced.[78] There are examples of multipoint competition that have resulted in firms being less likely to exit a market. "Live and let live" replaced strong competitive rivalry.[79]

Multipoint competition is likely to become even more prevalent in the future, as corporations become global competitors and expand into more markets through strategic alliances.[80]

End of Chapter SUMMARY

Corporate strategy is primarily about the choice of direction for the firm as a whole. It deals with three key issues that a corporation faces: (1) the firm's overall orientation toward growth, stability, or retrenchment; (2) the industries or markets in which the firm competes through its products and business units; and (3) the manner in which management coordinates activities and transfers resources and cultivates capabilities among product lines and business units. These issues are dealt with through directional strategy, portfolio analysis, and corporate parenting.

Managers must constantly examine their corporation's entire portfolio of products, businesses, and opportunities as if they were planning to reinvest all of its capital.[81]

Pearson MyLab Management®

Go to **mymanagementlab.com** to complete the problems marked with this icon ⭐.

KEY TERMS

acquisition (p. 228)
backward integration (p. 229)
bankruptcy (p. 237)
BCG (Boston Consulting Group)
    Growth-Share Matrix (p. 238)

captive company strategy (p. 236)
cash cows (p. 239)
center of excellence (p. 244)
concentration (p. 228)
concentric diversification (p. 232)

conglomerate diversification (p. 233)
corporate parenting (p. 243)
corporate strategy (p. 226)
directional strategy (p. 226)
diversification (p. 228)

divestment (p. 236)
dogs (p. 239)
forward integration (p. 229)
full integration (p. 229)
growth strategies (p. 227)
horizontal growth (p. 231)
horizontal integration (p. 231)
horizontal strategy (p. 244)
liquidation (p. 237)
long-term contracts (p. 231)
merger (p. 228)

multipoint competition (p. 244)
no-change strategy (p. 235)
parenting strategy (p. 226)
pause/proceed-with-caution
    strategy (p. 234)
portfolio analysis (p. 226)
profit strategy (p. 235)
quasi-integration (p. 230)
question marks (p. 239)

retrenchment strategies (p. 227)
sell-out strategy (p. 236)
stability strategies (p. 227)
stars (p. 239)
taper integration (p. 229)
transaction cost economics (p. 229)
turnaround strategy (p. 235)
vertical growth (p. 228)
vertical integration (p. 229)

Pearson MyLab Management®

Go to **mymanagementlab.com** for the following assisted-graded writing questions:

7-1. List the means available to a company for horizontal growth and explain why a company might pursue one over another?

7-2. Evaluate the types of retrenchment strategies that might be used by companies in stagnant industries.

DISCUSSION QUESTIONS

✪ **7-3.** How is a diversification strategy related to the sustainable growth and development of an organization?

✪ **7-4.** What are the major factors that an organization needs to analyze before it can consider entering a foreign market?

7-5. Explain the vertical integration continuum.

✪ **7-6.** How is corporate parenting different from portfolio analysis? How is it alike? Is it a useful concept in a global industry?

STRATEGIC PRACTICE EXERCISE

7-1. Form into small groups in the class to discuss the future of electronic publishing.

7-2. Consider the following questions as discussion guides:

- What are the pros and cons of electronic publishing?
- What is the impact of electronic publishing on the environment?
- Should newspaper and book publishers completely convert to electronic publishing over

paper? (*The New York Times* and *The Wall Street Journal* publish in both paper and electronic formats. Why have they been successful when so many others have not been able to make money with this approach?)

- Would you prefer this textbook and others in an electronic format? What prevents this move?
- What business model should publishers use to make money publishing electronically?

7-3. Present your group's conclusions to the class.

NOTES

1. R. P. Rumelt, D. E. Schendel, and D. J. Teece, "Fundamental Issues in Strategy," in R. P. Rumelt, D. E. Schendel, and D. J. Teece (Eds.), *Fundamental Issues in Strategy: A Research Agenda* (Boston: HBS Press, 1994), p. 42.

2. This analogy of corporate parent and business unit children was initially proposed by A. Campbell, M. Goold, and M. Alexander. See "Corporate Strategy: The Quest for Parenting Advantage," *Harvard Business Review* (March–April, 1995), pp. 120–132.

3. M. E. Porter, "From Competitive Strategy to Corporate Strategy," in D. E. Husey (Ed.), *International Review of Strategic Management, Vol. 1* (Chichester, England: John Wiley & Sons, 1990), p. 29.

4. This is in agreement with Toyohiro Kono when he proposes that corporate headquarters has three main functions: formulate corporate strategy, identify and develop the company's core competencies, and provide central resources. See T. Kono, "A Strong Head Office Makes a Strong Company," *Long Range Planning* (April 1999), pp. 225–236.

5. www.oracle.com/corporate/acquisitions/index.html (February 22, 2016); "Larry Ups the Ante," *The Economist* (February 7, 2004), pp. 59–60, (http://www.oracle.com/us/corporate/acquisitions/index.html).

6. J. Bercovitz and W. Mitchell, "When Is More Better? The Impact of Business Scale and Scope on Long-Term Business Survival, While Controlling for Profitability," *Strategic Management Journal* (January 2007), pp. 61–79.

7. G. Smith, "Heinz, Kraft agree to merge, forming a new food giant," *Fortune*, (March 25, 2015) (fortune.com/2015/03/25/heinz-kraft-to-merge-to-form-new-food-giant/).

8. www.duke-energy.com/PNG/

9. "Cisco Inc. Buys Top Technology Innovator," *St. Cloud (MN) Times* (November 19, 2005), p. 6A.

10. J. Perkins, "It's a Hog Predicament," *Des Moines Register* (April 11, 1999), pp. J1–J2.

11. C. Woodyard, "FedEx Ponies Up $2.4B for Kinko's," *USA Today* (December 31, 2003), p. B1.

12. J. W. Slocum Jr., M. McGill, and D. T. Lei, "The New Learning Strategy: Anytime, Anything, Anywhere," *Organizational Dynamics* (Autumn 1994), p. 36.

13. M. J. Leiblein, J. J. Reuer, and F. Dalsace, "Do Make or Buy Decisions Matter? The Influence of Organizational Governance on Technological Performance," *Strategic Management Journal* (September 2002), pp. 817–833.

14. I. Geyskens, J-B. E. M. Steenkamp, and N. Kumar, "Make, Buy, or Ally: A Transaction Cost Theory Meta-Analysis," *Academy of Management Journal* (June 2006), pp. 519–543; R. Carter and G. M. Hodgson, "The Impact of Empirical Tests of Transaction Cost Economics on the Debate on the Nature of the Firm," *Strategic Management Journal* (May 2006), pp. 461–476; T. A. Shervani, G. Frazier, and G. Challagalla, "The Moderating Influence of Firm Market Power on the Transaction Cost Economics Model: An Empirical Test in a Forward Channel Integration Context," *Strategic Management Journal* (June 2007), pp. 635–652; K. J. Mayer and R. M. Solomon, "Capabilities, Contractual Hazards, and Governance: Integrating Resource-Based and Transaction Cost Perspectives," *Academy of Management Journal* (October 2006), pp. 942–959.

15. K. R. Harrigan, *Strategies for Vertical Integration* (Lexington, MA.: Lexington Books, 1983), pp. 16–21.

16. M. Arndt, "Who's Afraid of a Housing Slump?" *BusinessWeek* (April 30, 2007), p. 76.

17. A. Parmigiani, "Why Do Firms Both Make and Buy? An Investigation of Concurrent Sourcing," *Strategic Management Journal* (March 2007), pp. 285–311; F. T. Rothaermel, M. A. Hitt, and L. A. Jobe, "Balancing Vertical Integration and Strategic Outsourcing: Effects on Product Portfolio, Product Success, and Firm Performance," *Strategic Management Journal* (November 2006), pp. 1033–1056.

18. "Converge or Conflict?" *The Economist* (August 30, 2008), pp. 61–62.

19. M. G. Jacobides, "Industry Change Through Vertical Disintegration: How and Why Markets Emerged in Mortgage Banking," *Academy of Management Journal* (June 2005), pp. 465–498.

20. For a discussion of the pros and cons of contracting versus vertical integration, see J. T. Mahoney, "The Choice of Organizational Form: Vertical Financial Ownership Versus Other Methods of Vertical Integration," *Strategic Management Journal* (November 1992), pp. 559–584; J. Helyar, "Outsourcing: A Passage Out of India," *Bloomberg Businessweek* (March 15, 2012), (www.businessweek.com/articles/2012-03-15/outsourcing-a-passage-out-of-india).

21. G. Dowell, "Product Line Strategies of New Entrants in an Established Industry: Evidence from the U.S. Bicycle Industry," *Strategic Management Journal* (October 2006), pp. 959–979; C. Sorenson, S. McEvily, C. R. Ren, and R. Roy, "Niche Width Revisited: Organizational Scope, Behavior and Performance," *Strategic Management Journal* (October 2006), pp. 915–936.

22. https://thewaltdisneycompany.com/investor-relations/

23. CBS News, " American Airlines CEO: Nothing about this merger should affect prices," December 10, 2013 (www.cbsnews.com/news/american-airlines-ceo-nothingabout-this-merger-should-affect-prices/).

24. www.mesa-air.com/content.aspx?pageID=16425

25. D. P. Lovallo and L. T. Mendonca, "Strategy's Strategist: An Interview with Richard Rumelt," *McKinsey Quarterly Online* (2007, No. 4).

26. C. Zook, "Increasing the Odds of Successful Growth: The Critical Prelude to Moving 'Beyond the Core.'" *Strategy & Leadership* (Vol. 32, No. 4, 2004), pp. 17–23.

27. A. Y. Ilinich and C. P. Zeithaml, "Operationalizing and Testing Galbraith's Center of Gravity Theory," *Strategic Management Journal* (June 1995), pp. 401–410; H. Tanriverdi and N. Venkatraman, "Knowledge Relatedness and the Performance of Multibusiness Firms," *Strategic Management Journal* (February 2005), pp. 97–119.

28. "Electrolux turns to emerging markets after GE bid collapse," RTE News, February 24, 2016 (www.rte.ie/news/business/2016/0224/770407-electrolux/).

29. www.berkshirehathaway.com/subs/sublinks.html

30. J. Bercovitz and W. Mitchell, "When Is More Better? The Impact of Business Scale and Scope on Long-Term Business Survival, While Controlling for Profitability," *Strategic Management Journal* (January 2007), pp. 61–79; D. J. Miller, "Technological Diversity, Related Diversification, and Firm Performance," *Strategic Management Journal* (July 2006), pp. 601–619; C. Stadler, "The Four Principles of Enduring Success," *Harvard Business Review* (July–August 2007), pp. 62–72.

31. K. Carow, R. Heron, and T. Saxton, "Do Early Birds Get the Returns? An Empirical Investigation of Early-Mover Advantages in Acquisitions," *Strategic Management Journal* (June 2004), pp. 563–585; K. Ramaswamy, "The Performance Impact of Strategic Similarity in Horizontal Mergers: Evidence from the U.S. Banking Industry," *Academy of Management Journal* (July 1997), pp. 697–715; D. J. Flanagan, "Announcements of Purely Related

and Purely Unrelated Mergers and Shareholder Returns: Reconciling the Relatedness Paradox," *Journal of Management* (Vol. 22, No. 6, 1996), pp. 823–835; D. D. Bergh, "Predicting Diversification of Unrelated Acquisitions: An Integrated Model of Ex Ante Conditions," *Strategic Management Journal* (October 1997), pp. 715–731.

32. J. M. Pennings, H. Barkema, and S. Douma, "Organizational Learning and Diversification," *Academy of Management Journal* (June 1994), pp. 608–640.

33. C. Stadler, "The Four Principles of Enduring Success," *Harvard Business Review* (July–August 2007), pp. 62–72.

34. L. E. Palich, L. B. Cardinal, and C. C. Miller, "Curvilinearity in the Diversification-Performance Linkage: An Examination of over Three Decades of Research," *Strategic Management Journal* (February 2000), pp. 155–174; M. S. Gary, "Implementation Strategy and Performance Outcomes in Related Diversification," *Strategic Management Journal* (July 2005), pp. 643–664; G. Yip and G. Johnson, "Transforming Strategy," *Business Strategy Review* (Spring 2007), pp. 11–15.

35. "Global mergers and acquisitions volume hits record in 2015," *Yahoo!News*, December 29, 2015 (news.yahoo.com/global-mergers-acquisitions-volume-hits-record-2015-163303085.html).

36. R. N. Palter and D. Srinivasan, "Habits of Busiest Acquirers," *McKinsey on Finance* (Summer 2006), pp. 8–13.

37. D. R. King, D. R. Dalton, C. M. Daily, and J. G. Covin, "Meta-Analyses of Post-Acquisition Performance: Indications of Unidentified Moderators," *Strategic Management Journal* (February 2004), pp. 187–200; W. B. Carper, "Corporate Acquisitions and Shareholder Wealth: A Review and Exploratory Analysis" *Journal of Management* (December 1990), pp. 807–823; P. G. Simmonds, "Using Diversification as a Tool for Effective Performance," in H. E. Glass and M. A. Hovde (Eds.), *Handbook of Business Strategy, 1992/93 Yearbook* (Boston: Warren, Gorham & Lamont, 1992), pp. 3.1–3.7; B. T. Lamont and C. A. Anderson, "Mode of Corporate Diversification and Economic Performance," *Academy of Management Journal* (December 1985), pp. 926–936.

38. "The HP–Compaq Merger Two Years Out: Still Waiting for the Upside," *Knowledge@Wharton* (October 6–19, 2004).

39. A. Hinterhuber, "When Two Companies Become One," in S. Crainer and D. Dearlove (Eds.), *Financial Times Handbook of Management*, 3rd ed. (Harlow, UK: Pearson Education, 2004), pp. 824–833; D. L. Laurie, Y. L. Doz, and C. P. Sheer, "Creating New Growth Platforms," *Harvard Business Review* (May 2006), pp. 80–90; R. Langford and C. Brown III, "Making M&A Pay: Lessons from the World's Most Successful Acquirers," *Strategy & Leadership* (Vol. 32, No. 1, 2004), pp. 5–14; J. G. Lynch and B. Lind, "Escaping Merger and Acquisition Madness," *Strategy & Leadership* (Vol. 30, No. 2, 2002), pp. 5–12; M. L. Sirower, *The Synergy Trap* (New York: Free Press, 1997); B. Jensen, "Make It Simple! How Simplicity Could Become Your Ultimate Strategy," *Strategy & Leadership* (March/April 1997), p. 35.

40. "Why consumer groups are fighting the Charter-Time Warner cable merger," Fox News, January 27, 2016 (www.foxnews.com/tech/2016/01/27/why-consumer-groups-are-fighting-charter-time-warner-cable-merger.html).

41. S. Karim and W. Mitchell, "Innovating through Acquisition and Internal Development: A Quarter-Century of Boundary Evolution at Johnson & Johnson," *Long Range Planning* (December 2004), pp. 525–547; L. Selden and G. Colvin, "M&A Needn't Be a Loser's Game," *Harvard Business Review* (June 2003), pp. 70–79; E. C. Busija, H. M. O'Neill, and C. P. Zeithaml, "Diversification Strategy, Entry Mode, and Performance: Evidence of Choice and Constraints," *Strategic Management Journal* (April 1997), pp. 321–327; A. Sharma, "Mode of Entry and Ex-Post Performance," *Strategic Management Journal* (September 1998), pp. 879–900.

42. R. T. Uhlaner and A. S. West, "Running a Winning M&A Shop," *McKinsey Quarterly* (March 2008), pp. 1–7.

43. S. Rovitt, D. Harding, and C. Lemire, "A Simple M&A Model for All Seasons," *Strategy & Leadership* (Vol. 32, No. 5, 2004), pp. 18–24.

44. P. Porrini, "Can a Previous Alliance Between an Acquirer and a Target Affect Acquisition Performance?" *Journal of Management* (Vol. 30, No. 4, 2004), pp. 545–562; L. Wang and E. J. Zajac, "Alliance or Acquisition? A Dyadic Perspective on Interfirm Resource Combinations," *Strategic Management Journal* (December 2007), pp. 1291–1317.

45. A. Inkpen and N. Choudhury, "The Seeking of Strategy Where It Is Not: Towards a Theory of Strategy Absence," *Strategic Management Journal* (May 1995), pp. 313–323.

46. P. Burrows and S. Anderson, "Dell Computer Goes into the Shop," *BusinessWeek* (July 12, 1993), pp. 138–140.

47. M. Brauer, "What Have We Acquired and What Should We Acquire in Divestiture Research? A Review and Research Agenda," *Journal of Management* (December 2006), pp. 751–785; J. L. Morrow Jr., R. A. Johnson, and L. W. Busenitz, "The Effects of Cost and Asset Retrenchment on Firm Performance: The Overlooked Role of a Firm's Competitive Environment," *Journal of Management* (Vol. 30, No. 2, 2004), pp. 189–208.

48. "NetApp launches cost-cutting plan, reports drop in earnings," *Nasdaq*, February 17, 2016 (www.nasdaq.com/article/netapp-launches-costcutting-plan-reports-drop-in-earnings-20160217-01260).

49. F. Gandolfi, "Reflecting on Downsizing: What Have We Learned?" *SAM Advanced Management Journal* (Spring 2008), pp. 46–55; C. Chadwick, L. W. Hunter, and S. L. Walston, "Effects of Downsizing Practices on the Performance of Hospitals," *Strategic Management Journal* (May 2004), pp. 405–427; J. R. Morris, W. F. Cascio, and C. E. Young, "Downsizing After All These Years," *Organizational Dynamics* (Winter 1999), pp. 78–87; P. H. Mirvis, "Human Resource Management: Leaders, Laggards, and Followers," *Academy of Management Executive* (May 1997), pp. 43–56; J. K. DeDee and D. W. Vorhies, "Retrenchment Activities of Small Firms During Economic Downturn: An Empirical Investigation," *Journal of Small Business Management* (July 1998), pp. 46–61.

50. Solomon, "Yahoo's Decision to explore a sale exposes a weak board," *The New York Times*, February 22, 2016 (www.nytimes.com/2016/02/26/businesss/dealbook/yahoos-decision-to-explore-a-sale-exposes-a-weak-board.html?_r=0).

51. Trefis Team, "With brand divestments almost over, here's how P&G plans to cut costs next year," *Forbes*, May 7, 2015 (www.forbes.com/sites/greatspeculations/2015/05/07

/with-brand-divestments-almost-over-heres-pg-plans-to
-cut-costs-next/#20b1e81164bb).

52. For more on divestment, see C. Dexter and T. Mellewight, "Thirty Years After Michael E. Porter: What Do We Know about Business Exit?" *Academy of Management Perspectives* (May 2007), pp. 41–55.

53. D. Welch, "Go Bankrupt, Then Go Overseas," *BusinessWeek* (April 24, 2006), pp. 52–55.

54. D. D. Dawley, J. J. Hoffman, and B. T. Lamont, "Choice Situation, Refocusing, and Post-Bankruptcy Performance," *Journal of Management* (Vol. 28, No. 5, 2002), pp. 695–717.

55. R. M. Kanter, "Leadership and the Psychology of Turnarounds," *Harvard Business Review* (June 2003), pp. 58–67.

56. B. C. Reimann and A. Reichert, "Portfolio Planning Methods for Strategic Capital Allocation: A Survey of Fortune 500 Firms," *International Journal of Management* (March 1996), pp. 84–93.

57. "How M&A practitioners enable their success," McKinsey & Co., October 2015 (http://www.mckinsey.com/business -functions/strategy-and-corporate-finance/our-insights /how-m-and-a-practitioners-enable-their-success).

58. B. Hedley, "Strategy and the Business Portfolio," *Long Range Planning* (February 1977), p. 9.

59. D. Welch, "GM: Live Green or Die," *BusinessWeek* (May 26, 2008), pp. 36–41.

60. "Fitbit shares fall on fears for the long run," *Yahoo! News*, February 23, 2016 (news.yahoo.com/fitbit-shares-fall-fears-long-run-234734838.html).

61. "Android vs iPhone Market Share, 52 against 33 percent," *Phones Review* (September 5, 2012), (http://www.phones review.co.uk/2012/09/05/android-vs-iphone-market-share -52-against-33-percent/).

62. A. Rogers, "Will Apple Witness Its first year-over -year iPhone sales fall?" *Yahoo! Finance*, February 23, 2016 (finance.yahoo.com/news/apple-witness-first-over -iphone-060703317.html).

63. C. Anterasian, J. L. Graham, and R. B. Money, "Are U.S. Managers Superstitious About Market Share?" *Sloan Management Review* (Summer 1996), pp. 67–77.

64. D. Rosenblum, D. Tomlinson, and L. Scott, "Bottom-Feeding for Blockbuster Businesses," *Harvard Business Review* (March 2003), pp. 52–59.

65. S. Poulter, "Cassettes roll back into fashion: Format follows vinyl with huge boost in sales after acts start releasing albums on tape," *Daily Mail*, February 21, 2016 (www.dailymail.co.uk/news/article-3457561/Cassettes -role-fashion-format-follows-vinyl-huge-boost-sales-acts -start-releasing-albums-tape.html).

66. W. H. Hoffmann, "Strategies for Managing a Portfolio of Alliances," *Strategic Management Journal* (August 2007), pp. 827–856; D. Lavie, "Alliance Portfolios and Firm Performance: A Study of Value Creation and Appropriation in the U.S. Software Industry," *Strategic Management Journal* (December 2007), pp. 1187–1212.

67. W. H. Hoffmann, "How to Manage a Portfolio of Alliances," *Long Range Planning* (April 2005), pp. 121–143.

68. A. Campbell, M. Goold, and M. Alexander, *Corporate-Level Strategy: Creating Value in the Multibusiness Company* (New York: John Wiley & Sons, 1994). See also M. Goold, A. Campbell, and M. Alexander, "Corporate Strategy and Parenting Theory," *Long Range Planning* (April 1998), pp. 308–318, and M. Goold and A. Campbell, "Parenting in Complex Structures," *Long Range Planning* (June 2002), pp. 219–243.

69. A. Campbell, M. Goold, and M. Alexander, "Corporate Strategy: The Quest for Parenting Advantage," *Harvard Business Review* (March–April 1995), p. 121.

70. Ibid., p. 122.

71. A. van Oijen and S. Douma, "Diversification Strategy and the Roles of the Centre," *Long Range Planning* (August 2000), pp. 560–578.

72. D. J. Collis, "Corporate Strategy in Multibusiness Firms," *Long Range Planning* (June 1996), pp. 416–418; D. Lei, M. A. Hitt, and R. Bettis, "Dynamic Core Competencies Through Meta-Learning and Strategic Context," *Journal of Management* (Vol. 22, No. 4, 1996), pp. 549–569.

73. D. J. Teece, "Strategies for Managing Knowledge Assets: The Role of Firm Structure and Industrial Context," *Long Range Planning* (February 2000), pp. 35–54.

74. R. S. Kaplan and D. P. Norton, "The Strategy Map: Guide to Aligning Intangible Assets," *Strategy & Leadership* (Vol. 32, No. 5, 2004), pp. 10–17; L. Edvinsson, "The New Knowledge Economics," *Business Strategy Review* (September 2002), pp. 72–76; C. Havens and E. Knapp, "Easing into Knowledge Management," *Strategy & Leadership* (March/April 1999), pp. 4–9.

75. S. Decker, "Diaper-War Veteran Wages New Patent War Over White Teeth," *BloombergBusiness*, May 5, 2014 (http://www.bloomberg.com/news/articles/2014-05-05 /diaper-war-veteran-wages-new-patent-war-over-white -teeth); J. Scanlon, "Cross-Pollinators," *BusinessWeek's Inside Innovation* (September 2007), pp. 8–11.

76. T. S. Frost, J. M. Birkinshaw, and P. C. Ensign, "Centers of Excellence in Multinational Corporations," *Strategic Management Journal* (November 2002), pp. 997–1018.

77. M. E. Porter, *Competitive Advantage* (New York: The Free Press, 1985), pp. 317–382.

78. H. R. Greve, "Multimarket Contact and Sales Growth: Evidence from Insurance," *Strategic Management Journal* (March 2008), pp. 229–249; L. Fuentelsaz and J. Gomez, "Multipoint Competition, Strategic Similarity and Entry Into Geographic Markets," *Strategic Management Journal* (May 2006), pp. 477–499; J. Gimeno, "Reciprocal Threats in Multi-market Rivalry: Staking Out 'Spheres of Influence' in the U.S. Airline Industry," *Strategic Management Journal* (February 1999), pp. 101–128; J. Baum and H. J. Korn, "Dynamics of Dyadic Competitive Interaction," *Strategic Management Journal* (March 1999), pp. 251–278; J. Gimeno and C. Y. Woo, "Hypercompetition in a Multimarket Environment: The Role of Strategic Similarity and Multimarket Contact in Competitive De-escalation," *Organization Science* (May/June 1996), pp. 322–341.

79. W. Boeker, J. Goodstein, J. Stephan, and J. P. Murmann, "Competition in a Multimarket Environment: The Case of Market Exit," *Organization Science* (March/April 1997), pp. 126–142.

80. J. Gimeno and C. Y. Woo, "Multimarket Contact, Economies of Scope, and Firm Performance," *Academy of Management Journal* (June 1999), pp. 239–259.

81. L. Carlesi, B. Verster, and F. Wenger, "The New Dynamics of Managing the Corporate Portfolio," *McKinsey Quarterly Online* (April 2007).

CHAPTER **8**

Strategy Formulation:
Functional Strategy
and Strategic Choice

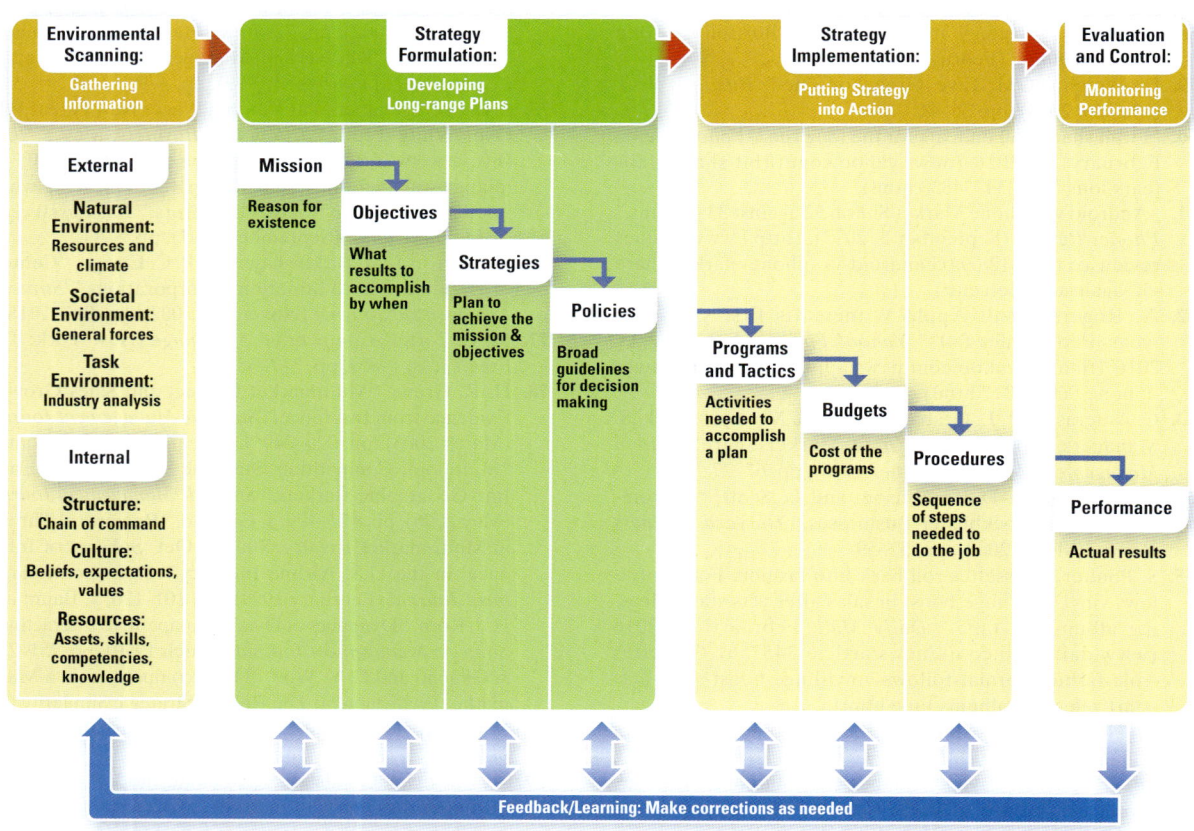

| Environmental Scanning: Gathering Information | Strategy Formulation: Developing Long-range Plans | Strategy Implementation: Putting Strategy into Action | Evaluation and Control: Monitoring Performance |

External

Natural Environment: Resources and climate

Societal Environment: General forces

Task Environment: Industry analysis

Internal

Structure: Chain of command

Culture: Beliefs, expectations, values

Resources: Assets, skills, competencies, knowledge

Mission — Reason for existence

Objectives — What results to accomplish by when

Strategies — Plan to achieve the mission & objectives

Policies — Broad guidelines for decision making

Programs and Tactics — Activities needed to accomplish a plan

Budgets — Cost of the programs

Procedures — Sequence of steps needed to do the job

Performance — Actual results

Feedback/Learning: Make corrections as needed

Pearson MyLab Management®

⭐ **Improve Your Grade!**

Over 10 million students improved their results using the Pearson MyLabs. Visit **mymanagementlab.com** for simulations, tutorials, and end-of-chapter problems.

Learning Objectives

After reading this chapter, you should be able to:

8-1. Discuss the impact that the various types of functional strategies have on the achievement of organizational goals and objectives

8-2. Explain which activities and functions are appropriate to outsource/offshore in order to gain or strengthen competitive advantage

8-3. List and explain the strategies to avoid

8-4. Construct corporate scenarios to evaluate strategic options

Can Research in Motion (BlackBerry) Be Saved?

Research in Motion (RIM) was founded in 1984 by Jim Balsillie and Mike Lazaridis as a business focused on providing the backbone for the two-way pager market. In 1999, they released the first BlackBerry device with an embedded full QWERTY keyboard. The "BlackBerry" set the bar for the connected business person. The term "crack berry" was even coined for those business people who could not put down their BlackBerry. The company focused almost exclusively on the integrity of the network on which their phones operated. They provided security measures that made RIM the choice of data managers.

When developing a strategy, companies have to bring together all the elements in a manner that provides them with a unique position relative to their competitors. At the time of its release, most competitors provided cell phones that could make calls and little more. BlackBerry changed the nature and use of a portable device at the same time it provided a secure platform for IT managers wary of allowing remote devices to access their systems. BlackBerry sales peaked in 2008 about the same time that Apple released the iPhone.

Despite that, the company still has tens of millions of users worldwide, a cash hoard in excess of US$2.7 billion and a reputation for being a best-in-class device for the business community. The company has made a number of missteps along the way, including a touchscreen BlackBerry that didn't catch on, a tablet that lacked e-mail connectivity, and an approach to the market that made it clear that the company believed the backbone was of more value than the device used.

The two founders stepped down in 2012 and the company continued to fumble with its strategy. New CEO Thorsten Heins asserted in January 2012 that RIM needed to focus on consumers rather than the enterprise. Then, in March 2012, he told analysts that RIM will focus on the enterprise instead of consumers. Heins was replaced less than a year later by John Chen. By late 2015, the company had seen a 46% drop in revenues from a year earlier and had sold less than 800,000 handsets in the previous quarter. A year earlier in the same quarter RIM had sold 2.4 million units. How can RIM align the elements of its strategy? Can RIM be saved?

SOURCES: "Blackberry: Sales continue to deteriorate, competition rife," Zaks Equity Research, Yahoo! Finance, September 29, 2015 (finance.yahoo.com/news/blackberry-sales-continue-deteriorate-competition-162004893.html); us.blackberry.com/company/investors/documents .html; S. Jakab, "RIM Seeks to Avoid Its Own Waterloo," *The Wall Street Journal* (September 27, 2012), (http://online.wsj.com/article/SB10000872396390444549204578020473252582296 .html?KEYWORDS=RIM+waterloo); D. Meyer, "How RIM Found Itself on the Wrong Side of History," *ZDNet* (July 1, 2012), (http://www.zdnet.com/how-rim-found-itself-on-the-wrong-side-of -history-3040155462/); http://www.rim.com/company/index.shtml; "Research in Motion Co-founders Step Down," (New York) *Daily News* (January 23, 2012), (http://articles.nydailynews.com/2012-01-23 /news/30653912_1_balsillie-and-mike-lazaridis-rim-founders).

Functional Strategy

8-1. Discuss the impact that the various types of functional strategies have on the achievement of organizational goals and objectives

Functional strategy is the approach a functional area takes to achieve corporate and business unit objectives and strategies by maximizing resource productivity. It is concerned with developing and nurturing a distinctive competence to provide a company or business unit with a competitive advantage. Just as a multidivisional corporation has several business units, each with its own business strategy, each business unit has its own set of departments, each with its own functional strategy.

The orientation of a functional strategy is dictated by its parent business unit's strategy.[1] For example, a business unit following a competitive strategy of differentiation through high quality might require a manufacturing functional strategy that emphasizes expensive quality assurance processes over cheaper, high-volume production; a human resource functional strategy that emphasizes the hiring and training of a highly skilled, but costly, workforce; and a marketing functional strategy that emphasizes distribution channel "pull," using advertising to increase consumer demand, over "push," using promotional allowances to retailers. If a business unit were to follow a low-cost competitive strategy, however, a different set of functional strategies would be needed to support the business strategy.

Just as competitive strategies may need to vary from one region of the world to another, functional strategies may need to vary from region to region. When Mr. Donut expanded into Japan, for example, it had to market donuts not as breakfast, but as snack food. Because the Japanese had no breakfast coffee-and-donut custom, they preferred to eat the donuts in the afternoon or evening. Mr. Donut restaurants were thus located near railroad stations and supermarkets. All signs were in English to appeal to the Western interests of the Japanese.

MARKETING STRATEGY

Marketing strategy deals with pricing, selling, and distributing a product. Using a **market development** strategy, a company or business unit can (1) capture a larger share of an existing market for current products through market saturation and market penetration or (2) develop new uses and/or markets for current products. Consumer product giants such as P&G, Colgate-Palmolive, and Unilever are experts at using advertising and promotion to implement a market saturation/penetration strategy to gain the dominant market share in a product category. As seeming masters of the product life cycle, these companies are able to extend product life almost indefinitely through "new and improved" variations of product and packaging that appeal to most market niches.

A company, such as Church & Dwight, follows the second market development strategy by finding new uses for its successful current product: Arm & Hammer brand baking soda.

Using the **product development** strategy, a company or unit can (1) develop new products for *existing markets* or (2) develop new products for *new markets*. Church & Dwight has had great success by following the first product development strategy developing new products to sell to its current customers in its existing markets. Acknowledging the widespread appeal of its Arm & Hammer brand baking soda, the company has generated new uses for its sodium bicarbonate by reformulating it as toothpaste, deodorant, and detergent. In another example, Ocean Spray developed Craisins, mock berries, more than 50 variations of juice, sauces, flavored snacks, and juice boxes in order to market its cranberries to current customers.[2] Using a successful brand name to market other products is called *brand extension*, and it is a good way to appeal to a company's current customers. Smith & Wesson, famous for its handguns, has taken this approach by using licensing to put its name on men's cologne and other products like the Smith & Wesson 357 Magnum Wood Pellet Smoker (for smoking meats).[3] Church & Dwight has also successfully followed the second product development strategy (new products for new markets) by developing new pollution-reduction products (using sodium bicarbonate compounds) for sale to coal-fired electric utility plants—a very different market from grocery stores.

There are numerous other marketing strategies. For advertising and promotion, for example, a company or business unit can choose between "push" and "pull" marketing strategies. Many large food and consumer products companies in the United States and Canada follow a *push strategy* by spending a large amount of money on trade promotion in order to gain or hold shelf space in retail outlets. Trade promotion includes discounts, in-store special offers, and advertising allowances designed to "push" products through the distribution system. The Kellogg Company decided a few years ago to change its emphasis from a push to a *pull strategy*, in which advertising "pulls" the products through the distribution channels. The company now spends more money on consumer advertising designed to build brand awareness so that shoppers will ask for the products. Research has found that a high level of advertising (a key part of a pull strategy) is beneficial to leading brands in a market.[4] Strong brands provide a competitive advantage to a firm because they act as entry barriers and usually generate higher market share.[5]

Other marketing strategies deal with distribution and pricing. Should a company use distributors and dealers to sell its products, should it sell directly to mass merchandisers, or should it use the direct marketing model by selling straight to the consumers via the Internet? Using multiple channels simultaneously can lead to problems. In order to increase the sales of its lawn tractors and mowers, for example, John Deere decided to sell the products not only through its current dealer network but also through mass merchandisers such as Home Depot. Deere's dealers, however, were furious. They considered Home Depot to be a key competitor. The dealers were concerned that Home Depot's ability to underprice them would eventually lead to their becoming little more than repair facilities for their competition and be left with insufficient sales to stay in business. However, the bulk (US$23 billion) of John Deere's US$32 billion in revenue comes from equipment sold to farmers. Home Depot sells the average lawn mower/tractor that was never a big part of the dealer's business.[6]

When pricing a new product, a company or business unit can follow one of two strategies. For new-product pioneers, *skim pricing* offers the opportunity to "skim the cream" from the top of the demand curve with a high price while the product is novel and competitors are few. *Penetration pricing*, in contrast, attempts to hasten market development and offers the pioneer the opportunity to use the experience curve to gain market share with a low price and then dominate the industry. Depending on corporate and business unit objectives and strategies, either of these choices may be desirable to a particular company or unit. Penetration pricing is, however, more likely than skim pricing to raise a unit's operating profit in the long term.[7] The use of the Internet to market goods directly to consumers allows a company to use *dynamic pricing*, a practice in which prices vary frequently based upon demand, market segment, and product availability.[8]

FINANCIAL STRATEGY

Financial strategy examines the financial implications of corporate and business-level strategic options and identifies the best financial course of action. It can also provide competitive advantage through a lower cost of funds and a flexible ability to raise capital to support a business strategy. Financial strategy usually attempts to maximize the financial value of a firm.

The trade-off between achieving the desired debt-to-equity ratio and relying on internal long-term financing via cash flow is a key issue in financial strategy. Many small-and medium-sized family-owned companies try to avoid all external sources of funds in order to avoid outside entanglements and to keep control of the company within the family. Most large publicly held firms have long-term debt and keep a large amount of money in cash and short-term investments. One of these is Apple Inc., which had more than a US$215 billion cash hoard by early 2016.[9] Many financial analysts believe, however, that only by financing through long-term debt can a corporation use financial leverage to boost earnings per share—thus raising stock price and the overall value of the company. Research indicates that higher debt levels not only deter takeover by other firms (by making the company less attractive) but also lead to improved productivity and improved cash flows by forcing management to focus on core businesses.[10] High debt can be a problem, however, when the economy or the company falters and a company's cash flow drops.

Research reveals that a firm's financial strategy is influenced by its corporate diversification strategy. Equity financing, for example, is preferred for related diversification, whereas debt financing is preferred for unrelated diversification.[11]

A very popular financial strategy that ebbs and flows with the economy is the leveraged buyout (LBO). Goldman Sachs Group is one of the largest financers of LBOs in the world. They raised over US$26 billion in the past 10 years and completed the largest single raise of funds in history with over US$8 billion in 2016.[12] In a **leveraged buyout**, a company is acquired in a transaction financed largely by debt, usually obtained from a third party, such as an insurance company or an investment banker. Ultimately, the debt is paid with money generated from the acquired company's operations or by sales of its assets. The acquired company, in effect, pays for its own acquisition. Management of the LBO is then under tremendous pressure to keep the highly leveraged company profitable. Unfortunately, the huge amount of debt on the acquired company's books may actually cause its eventual decline by focusing management's attention on short-term matters. For example, one year after the buyout, the cash flow of eight of the largest LBOs made during 2006–2007 was barely enough to cover interest payments.[13] One study of LBOs (also called MBOs—Management Buy Outs if they are led by a company's current management) revealed that the financial performance of the typical LBO usually falls below the industry average in the fourth year after the buyout. The firm declines because of inflated expectations, utilization of all slack, management burnout, and a lack of strategic management.[14] Often, the only solutions are to sell the company or to again go public by selling stock to finance growth.[15]

The management of dividends and stock price is an important part of a corporation's financial strategy. Corporations in fast-growing industries such as computers and computer software often do not declare dividends. They use the money they might have spent on dividends to finance rapid growth. If the company is successful, its growth in sales and profits is reflected in a higher stock price, eventually resulting in a hefty capital gain when shareholders sell their common stock. Other corporations, such as Diebold Inc., that do not face rapid growth, must support the value of their stock by offering consistent dividends. Instead of raising dividends when profits are high, a popular financial strategy is to use excess cash (or even use debt) to buy back a company's own shares of stock. In 2015, U.S.-based publicly traded companies spent more than US$568 billion buying back stock. Because stock buybacks increase earnings per share, they typically increase a firm's stock price and make unwanted takeover attempts more difficult. Such buybacks do send a signal to investors that management may not have been able to find any profitable investment opportunities for the company or that it is anticipating reduced future earnings.[16]

A number of firms have been supporting the price of their stock by using *reverse stock splits*. Contrasted with a typical forward 2-for-1 stock split in which an investor receives an additional share for every share owned (with each share being worth only half as much), in a reverse 1-for-2 stock split, the number of shares an investor owns is reduced by half for the same total amount of money (with each share now being worth twice as much). Thus, 100 shares of stock worth US$10 each are exchanged for 50 shares worth US$20 each. A reverse stock split may successfully raise a company's stock price, but it does not solve underlying problems. A study by Credit Suisse First Boston revealed that almost all 800 companies that had reverse stock splits in a five-year period performed worse than their peers over the long term.[17]

A rather novel financial strategy is the selling of a company's patents. Companies such as AT&T, Bellsouth, American Express, Kimberly Clark, and 3Com have been selling patents for products that they no longer wish to commercialize or are not a part of their core business. Kodak has been selling off virtually its entire portfolio of patents in a desperate attempt to raise enough money to survive while management tries to figure out what the company should do if it can emerge from bankruptcy. Companies like Apple, Microsoft, and Google have bought patents in order to protect their competitive positions. Patents are also bought by patent accumulators who seek to sell groups of patents to other companies. A more sinister version of these are known as Patent Trolls who collect patents in order to sue other companies, but not use the patents themselves.[18]

RESEARCH AND DEVELOPMENT (R&D) STRATEGY

R&D strategy deals with product and process innovation and improvement. It also deals with the appropriate mix of different types of R&D (basic, product, or process) and with the question of how new technology should be accessed—through internal development, external acquisition, or strategic alliances. RIM has floundered by going back and forth among these approaches rather than choosing an approach and investing their resources.

One of the R&D choices is to be either a **technological leader**, pioneering an innovation, or a **technological follower**, imitating the products of competitors.

Nike, Inc. has utilized a *leader* R&D functional strategy to achieve a differentiation competitive advantage. Nike spends more than most in the industry on R&D to differentiate the performance of its athletic shoes from that of its competitors. As a result, its products have become the favorite of serious athletes. This happened despite the fact that Nike simultaneously pursues a low-cost manufacturing approach. An example of the use of the *follower* R&D functional strategy to achieve a low-cost competitive advantage is Dean Foods Company, maker of such brands as Dairy Pure, Land O'Lakes, and TruMoo.

An increasing number of companies are working with their suppliers to help them keep up with changing technology. They are beginning to realize that a firm cannot be competitive technologically only through internal development. For example, Chrysler Corporation's skillful use of parts suppliers to design everything from car seats to drive shafts has enabled it to spend consistently less money than its competitors to develop new car models. Using strategic technology alliances is one way to combine the R&D capabilities of two companies. One UK study found that 93% of UK auto assemblers and component manufacturers use their suppliers as technology suppliers.[19]

A newer approach to R&D is *open innovation*, in which a firm uses alliances and connections with corporate, government, academic labs, and consumers to develop new products and processes. Open innovation (OI) has been widely accepted and applied to a wide variety of companies in every industry including some state governments and the National Football League.[20] Intel opened four small-scale research facilities adjacent to universities to promote the cross-pollination of ideas. Thirteen U.S. university labs engaging in nanotechnology research have formed the National Nanotechnology Infrastructure Network in order to offer their resources to businesses for a fee.[21] Mattel, Wal-Mart, and other toy manufacturers and retailers use idea brokers to scout for new toy ideas. IBM adopted the open operating system Linux for some of its computer products and systems, drawing on a core code base that is continually improved and enhanced by a massive global community of software developers, of whom only a fraction work for IBM.[22] To open its own labs to ideas being generated elsewhere, P&G's CEO Art Lafley decreed that half of the company's ideas must come from outside, up from 10% in 2000. P&G instituted the use of *technology scouts* to search beyond the company for promising innovations. By 2007, the objective was achieved: 50% of the company's innovations originated outside P&G. Unfortunately, the unintended consequence was a sharp reduction in breakthrough products overall. Most of the innovations were relatively minor changes to existing products or products with very limited markets.[23]

A slightly different approach to technology development is for a large firm such as IBM or Microsoft to purchase minority stakes in relatively new high-tech entrepreneurial ventures that need capital to continue operation. Investing corporate venture capital is one way to gain access to promising innovations at a lower cost than by developing them internally.[24]

OPERATIONS STRATEGY

Operations strategy determines how and where a product or service is to be manufactured, the level of vertical integration in the production process, the deployment of physical resources, and relationships with suppliers. It should also deal with the optimum level of technology the firm should use in its operations processes. See the **Global Issue** feature to see how operational differences in national conditions can impact the global efforts of a worldwide brand.

Advanced manufacturing technology (AMT) is revolutionizing operations worldwide and should continue to have a major impact as corporations strive to integrate diverse business activities by using computer-assisted design and manufacturing (CAD/CAM) principles. The use of CAD/CAM, flexible manufacturing systems, computer

GLOBAL issue

WHY IS STARBUCKS AFRAID OF ITALY?

The concept of the Starbucks café (as it exists today) started in Milan, Italy, when Howard Schultz, then the Marketing Director for a coffee roasting business called Starbucks, saw how people talked to the folks making their coffee at the many coffee houses there. He came back to the United States and unable to convince his bosses about the idea, started up his own café in Seattle. Within three years, he had grown his company to such a size that he bought out the original Starbucks roasting business.

By early 2016 Starbucks had more than 21,000 cafés in 65 countries worldwide. Interestingly, it does not have one outlet in Italy even though rumors are swirling that they may open one in Milan in late 2016.

Why are there no Starbucks in Italy? Italy is the home of coffee culture and their approach to coffee is quite different. Italians primarily drink espresso and do so in one quick gulp. Cappuccino is strictly a breakfast drink, and while coffee stands are a gathering point, people rarely hang out after they have received their coffee.

That said, McDonald's has had significant success with its McCafé offering of traditional American style coffee, as well as Italian espresso. It encourages customers to linger much like the Starbucks model. McDonald's has more than 400 locations in Italy that serve coffee, including more than 100 that have a traditional Italian coffee bar.

So, should Starbucks make the move into Italy?

....
SOURCES: http://www.starbucks.com/business/international-stores; http://www.lifeinitaly.com/lifestyle/starbucks-in-italy; http://www.aboutmcdonalds.com/content/mcd/investors/news-events/financial-news.html; S. Faris, "Grounds Zero," *Bloomberg Businessweek* (February 13, 2012), (http://www.businessweek.com/magazine/grounds-zero-a-starbucksfree-italy-02092012.html); http://www.starbucks.com/about-us/our-heritage; "Starbucks Outlines Strategy for Accelerating Profitable Global Growth" (http://news.starbucks.com/article_display.cfm?article_id=342).

---

numerically controlled systems, automatically guided vehicles, robotics, manufacturing resource planning (MRP II), optimized production technology, and just-in-time techniques contribute to increased flexibility, quick response time, and higher productivity. Such investments also act to increase the company's fixed costs and could cause significant problems if the company is unable to achieve economies of scale or scope.

A firm's manufacturing strategy is often affected by a product's popularity. As the sales of a product increase, there will be an increase in production volume ranging from lot sizes as low as one in a *job shop* (one-of-a-kind production using skilled labor) through *connected line batch flow* (components are standardized; each machine functions like a job shop but is positioned in the same order as the parts are processed), to lot sizes as high as 100,000 or more per year for *flexible manufacturing systems* (parts are grouped into manufacturing families to produce a wide variety of mass-produced items), and *dedicated transfer lines* (highly automated assembly lines making one mass-produced product using little human labor). According to this concept, the product becomes standardized into a commodity over time in conjunction with increasing demand. Flexibility thus gives way to efficiency.[25]

Increasing competitive intensity in many industries has forced companies to switch from traditional mass production using dedicated transfer lines to a continuous improvement production strategy. A *mass-production* system was an excellent method to produce a large number of low-cost, standard goods and services. Employees worked on narrowly defined, repetitive tasks under close supervision in a bureaucratic and hierarchical structure. Quality, however, often tended to be fairly low. Learning how to do something better was the prerogative of management; workers were expected only to learn what was assigned to them. This system tended to dominate manufacturing until the 1970s. Under the *continuous improvement* system developed by W. Edwards Deming and perfected by Japanese firms, companies empowered cross-functional teams to constantly strive to improve production processes. Managers are more like coaches than bosses. The result is a large quantity of low-cost, standard goods and services, but with high quality. The key to continuous improvement is the acknowledgment that workers' experience and knowledge can help managers solve production problems and contribute to tightening variances and reducing errors. Because continuous improvement enables firms to use the same low-cost competitive strategy as do mass-production firms but at a significantly higher level of quality, it is rapidly replacing mass production as an operations strategy.

The automobile industry is aggressively moving forward with a strategy approach referred to as *modular manufacturing* in which preassembled subassemblies are delivered as they are needed (i.e., just-in-time) to a company's assembly-line workers, who quickly piece the modules together into a finished product. General Motors is on a path to reduce their current approach of 22 different platforms down to just 4 by 2025. The move to modular tool kits attached to standard platforms is an approach that General Motors has no choice but to apply. Ford, Toyota, and VW are also working on this approach. The savings in the cost of development and the dramatic improvement in the speed of delivering new models is core to the investment.[26]

The concept of a product's life cycle eventually leading to one-size-fits-all mass production has been successfully challenged by the concept of mass customization. Appropriate for an ever-changing environment, *mass customization* requires that people, processes, units, and technology reconfigure themselves to give customers exactly what they want, when they want it. The advent of high-speed 3D printers, the success of small business websites like etsy.com and the increasing ability to have items delivered quickly and directly to your door has changed the nature of the business model. In contrast to continuous improvement, mass customization requires flexibility and quick responsiveness. Managers coordinate independent, capable individuals. An efficient linkage system is crucial. The result is low-cost, high-quality, customized goods and services appropriate for a large number of market niches.

PURCHASING STRATEGY

Purchasing strategy deals with obtaining the raw materials, parts, and supplies needed to perform the operations function. A contentious issue for manufacturing companies throughout the world is the availability of resources needed to operate a modern factory. The dramatic swings in the fundamental elements of business (oil, electricity, and rare earth materials among many others) has drastically boosted costs, only some of which can be passed on to the customers in a competitive environment. The likelihood that fresh water will become an equally scarce resource is causing many companies to rethink water-intensive manufacturing processes. To learn how companies are beginning to deal with global warming and increasing fresh water scarcity, see the **Sustainability Issue** feature.

The basic purchasing choices are multiple, sole, and parallel sourcing. Under *multiple sourcing*, the purchasing company orders a particular part from several vendors. Multiple sourcing has traditionally been considered superior to other purchasing approaches because (1) it forces suppliers to compete for the business of an important buyer, thus reducing purchasing costs, and (2) if one supplier cannot deliver, another usually can, thus guaranteeing that parts and supplies are always on hand when needed. Multiple sourcing has been one way for a purchasing firm to control the relationship with its suppliers. So long as suppliers can provide evidence that they can meet the product specifications, they are kept on the purchaser's list of acceptable vendors for

SUSTAINABILITY issue

HOW HOT IS HOT?

July 2015 was the hottest month in the recorded history of the Earth and 2015 was the hottest year on record. Eight of the world's 10 deadliest heat waves have occurred since 1997.

The impact on fresh water availability is more than significant not only to individuals, but also the operations of companies. The United Nations reported that by the mid-1990s, some 40% of the world's population was suffering water shortages. Thirty-seven countries in the world already face "extremely high" levels of water stress with the 5 most stressed locations being Western Sahara, UAE, Trinidad and Tobago, Singapore, and San Marino.

Nestlé, Unilever, Coca-Cola, AB Inbev, and Danone consume almost 575 billion liters of water a year, enough to satisfy the daily water needs of every person on the planet. It takes about 13 cubic meters of fresh water to produce a single 200-mm semiconductor wafer. As a result, chip making is believed to account for 25% of the water consumption in Silicon Valley. According to José Lopez, Nestlé's COO, it takes four liters of water to make one liter of product in Nestlé's factories, but 3000 liters of water are needed to grow the agricultural produce that supplies them. Each year, around 40% of the fresh water withdrawn from lakes and aquifers in America is used to cool power plants. Separating one liter of oil from Canada's tar sands requires up to five liters of water!

"Water is the oil of the 21st century," contends Andrew Liveris, CEO of the chemical company Dow. Like oil, supplies of clean, easily accessible fresh water are under a growing strain because of the growing population and widespread improvements in living standards. Industrialization in developing nations is contaminating rivers and aquifers. Climate change is altering the patterns of fresh water availability so that droughts are more likely in many parts of the world. According to a survey by the Marsh Center for Risk Insights, 40% of Fortune 1000 companies stated that the impact of a water shortage on their business would be "severe" or "catastrophic," but only 17% said that they were prepared for such a crisis. Of Nestlé's 481 factories worldwide, 49 are located in water-scarce regions. Environmental activists have attacked PepsiCo and Coca-Cola for allegedly depleting groundwater in India to make bottled drinks.

There are a number of companies that are taking action to protect their future supply of fresh water. Starbucks has reduced the water consumption in their stores by 23% in the past seven years and Abbot Laboratories which has operations in over 130 countries has reduced fresh water consumption by 18% in the past four years.

SOURCES: J. Gillis, "2015 Was Hottest Year in Historical Record, Scientists Say," *The New York Times*, January 20, 2016 (http://www.nytimes.com/2016/01/21/science/earth/2015-hottest-year-global-warming.html?_r=0); M. Ferner, "These Are The Most Water-Stressed Countries In The World," *The Huffington Post*, December 13, 2013 (http://www.huffingtonpost.com/2013/12/13/water-stressed-countries_n_4434115.html); http://www.starbucks.com/responsibility/environment/water-and-energy; http://www.edie.net/news/4/Water-reduction-efforts-keep-Abbott-on-track-to-meet-2020-targets/27429/; "The Impact of Global Change on Water Resources," UNESCO Report, (http://unesdoc.unesco.org/images/0019/001922/192216e.pdf); K. Kube, "Into the Wild Brown Yonder," *Trains* (November 2008), pp. 68–73; "Running Dry," *The Economist* (August 23, 2008), pp. 53–54.

specific parts and supplies. Unfortunately, the common practice of accepting the lowest bid often compromises quality.

W. Edwards Deming, a well-known management consultant, strongly recommended *sole sourcing* as the only manageable way to obtain high supplier quality. Sole sourcing relies on only one supplier for a particular part. Given his concern with designing quality into a product in its early stages of development, Deming argued that the buyer should work closely with the supplier at all stages. This reduces both cost and time spent on product design thus improving quality. It can also simplify the purchasing company's production process by using the *just-in-time* (JIT) concept of having the purchased parts arrive at the plant just when they are needed rather than keeping inventories. The concept of sole sourcing is taken one step further in JIT II, in which vendor sales representatives actually have desks next to the purchasing company's factory floor, attend production status meetings, visit the R&D lab, and analyze the purchasing company's sales forecasts. These in-house suppliers then write sales orders for which the purchasing company is billed. Developed by Lance Dixon at Bose Corporation, JIT II is used as a technique that provides a competitive advantage.

Sole sourcing reduces transaction costs and builds quality by having the purchaser and supplier work together as partners rather than as adversaries. With sole sourcing, more companies will have longer relationships with fewer suppliers. Research has found that buyer- supplier collaboration and joint problem solving with both parties dependent upon the other results in the development of competitive capabilities, higher quality, lower costs, and better scheduling.[27] Sole sourcing does, however, have limitations. If a supplier is unable to deliver a part, the purchaser has no alternative but to delay production. Multiple suppliers can provide the purchaser with better information about new technology and performance capabilities. The limitations of sole sourcing have led to the development of parallel sourcing. In *parallel sourcing*, two suppliers are the sole suppliers of two different parts, but they are also backup suppliers for each other's parts. If one vendor cannot supply all of its parts on time, the other vendor is asked to make up the difference.[28]

The Internet has changed the ability of procurement managers to compare and source supplies for their organization. Research indicates that companies using Internet-based technologies are able to lower administrative costs and purchase prices.[29] Sometimes innovations tied to the use of the Internet for one strategy are adopted by other areas. See the **Innovation Issue** regarding the use and misuse of QR codes.

INNOVATION issue

WHEN AN INNOVATION FAILS TO LIVE UP TO EXPECTATIONS

Sometimes a promising innovation has to find the right application for it to have an impact on strategy formulation. Such has been the fate of QR codes. QR codes, or quick response codes, are those dense, square, grids of black and white that seem to be everywhere. Invented in 1994 by Denso Wave (a subsidiary of Toyota Group), the original intent of the little block was to improve the inventory tracking of auto parts. While the QR code is patented, the company published complete specifications online and allowed anyone to use the codes for free.

The codes were adopted by advertisers as a means to improve the connection between a company and its customers. In December 2011, more than 8% of magazine ads contained the codes, up from just over 3% at the beginning of the year. Unfortunately, most companies seem to have little idea how to use the codes to engage the consumer. Most direct the consumer's cell phone to the corporate Web site, and therein lies much of the issue with using this as a part of a company's strategy. The QR code requires the consumer to download an app that reads the codes onto their cell phone and then hold the phone very steady as they take a picture of the code that they want to follow. The codes have found a real value in the movie theater and airline ticket businesses as more people buy their tickets online. The codes are downloaded to a consumer's Smartphone and scanned as a ticket upon entering the theater or the TSA line. They could also be used to help prevent counterfeit goods, but some companies have put the codes on billboards (virtually impossible to scan), the inside of liquor bottles, and on subway posters (low light prevents the app from working). As of 2015 only 15% of Smart device users knew how to correctly scan a QR code. In fact, there is no standard QR scanner app included on smart devices.

Not all innovations that businesses can adopt should be adopted. Finding the value and aligning the innovation with the competitive advantages of the business are crucial. Where do you believe QR codes could be put to their best use?

....

SOURCES: I. Nass, "Why did QR code die despite the smartphone revolution" Dazeinfo, March 20, 2015 (dazeinfo.com/2015/03/20/why-did-qr-code-die-despite-exploding-adoption-of-smartphone); "QR Code Fatigue," *Bloomberg Businessweek* (July 2, 2012), pp. 28–29; https://www.denso-wave.com/en/; http://www.qrcode.com/en/index.html

LOGISTICS STRATEGY

Logistics strategy deals with the flow of products into and out of the manufacturing process. Three trends related to this strategy are evident: centralization, outsourcing, and the use of the Internet. To gain logistical synergies across business units, corporations began centralizing logistics in the headquarters group. This centralized logistics group usually contains specialists with expertise in different transportation modes such as rail or trucking. They work to aggregate shipping volumes across the entire corporation to gain better contracts with shippers. Companies such as Georgia-Pacific, Marriott, and Union Carbide view the logistics function as an important way to differentiate themselves from the competition, to add value, and to reduce costs.

In the past few years, a diverse set of firms from around the world have moved quickly on the logistics front pushed by Amazon's ability to provide same-day service—a logistical feat in business. Most providers cannot match Amazon's efficiency (a result of a massive investment in logistics) and have still had to create complex systems to match rising customer expectations. Amazon changed the whole game by introducing one-hour delivery in major American cities and even a series of Wi-Fi-connected buttons that allow consumers to simply push to re-order select products.[30]

HUMAN RESOURCE MANAGEMENT (HRM) STRATEGY

HRM strategy, among many other things, addresses issues that range from whether a company or business unit should hire a large number of low-skilled employees who receive low pay, perform repetitive jobs, and will most likely quit after a short time (the fast-food restaurant strategy) to whether they should hire skilled employees who receive relatively high pay and are cross-trained to participate in *self-managing work teams*. As work increases in complexity, it becomes more suited for teams, especially in the case of innovative product development efforts. These self-managed work teams are the hallmark of the Silicon Valley startup and have been successfully used in a wide range of industries.[31] Research on large, multinational established companies indicates that the use of work teams leads to increased quality and productivity as well as to higher employee satisfaction and commitment.[32]

Companies following a competitive strategy of differentiation through high quality use input from subordinates and peers in performance appraisals to a greater extent than do firms following other business strategies.[33] A complete *360-degree appraisal*, in which performance input is gathered from multiple sources, is considered to be a standard expectation of good HR management practices.[34]

Companies are finding that having a *diverse workforce* is a competitive advantage. Research reveals that firms with a high degree of diversity following a growth strategy have higher productivity than do firms with less racial diversity.[35] Avon Company, for example, was able to turn around its unprofitable inner-city markets by putting African-American and Hispanic managers in charge of marketing to these markets.[36] Diversity in terms of age and national origin also offers benefits. DuPont's use of multinational teams has helped the company develop and market products internationally. McDonald's found that older workers performed as well as, if not better than, younger employees.[37]

INFORMATION TECHNOLOGY STRATEGY

Corporations have always used an **information technology strategy** to provide their business units with competitive advantage. When FedEx first provided its customers with PowerShip computer software to store addresses, print shipping labels, and track package location, its sales jumped significantly. UPS soon followed with its own Maxi-Ships software. Viewing its information system as a distinctive competency, FedEx continued to push for further advantage over UPS by using its Web site to enable customers to track their packages. FedEx used this competency in its advertisements by showing how customers could track the progress of their shipments. Soon thereafter, UPS provided the same service. Although it can be argued that information technology has now become so pervasive that it no longer offers companies a competitive advantage, Gartner Worldwide reported that in 2015 corporations worldwide spent over US$3.5 trillion annually on information technology with that number forecasted to approach US$4 trillion by 2019.[38]

Multinational corporations use sophisticated intranets to allow employees to practice *follow-the-sun management*, in which project team members living in one country can pass their work to team members in another country in which the work day is just beginning. Thus, night shifts are no longer needed.[39] The development of instant translation software is also enabling workers to have online communication with co-workers in other countries who use a different language.[40]

The Sourcing Decision: Location of Functions

For a functional strategy to have the best chance of success, it should be built on a distinctive competency residing within that functional area. If a corporation does not have a distinctive competency in a particular functional area, that functional area could be a candidate for outsourcing.

8-2. Explain which activities and functions are appropriate to outsource/offshore in order to gain or strengthen competitive advantage

Outsourcing is purchasing a product or service externally that had been previously provided internally. Thus, it is the reverse of vertical integration. Outsourcing is becoming an increasingly important part of the strategic decision-making discussion. There are many pros and cons to outsourcing with managers increasingly focusing on non-strategically critical parts of the business as categories for outsourcing. However, there are specific examples in which companies have outsourced as a means of increasing efficiency and in some cases quality. Boeing used outsourcing as a way to reduce the cost of designing and manufacturing its new 787 Dreamliner. Up to 70% of the plane was outsourced. In a break from past practice, suppliers make large parts of the fuselage, including plumbing, electrical, and computer systems, and ship them to Seattle for assembly by Boeing.[41]

According to the latest bi-annual survey by Deloitte Consulting, 53% of the companies surveyed outsourced some elements of their IT function. Interestingly, 16% outsource their HR function with 22% of those who do not currently outsource HR planning to do so in the near future. The top factors in a successful outsourcing relationship seemed to be a spirit of partnership, a well-designed agreement, joint governance, and consistent communication.[42] **Offshoring** is the outsourcing of an activity or a function to a wholly owned company or an independent provider in another country. Offshoring is a simple reality of business operations that has been supported by advances in information and communication technologies, the development of stable, secure, and high-speed data transmission systems, and logistical advances like containerized shipping. In 2016, 53% of U.S. manufacturing companies outsource with offshore operations. The leading countries are India, Indonesia, China, Bulgaria, and the Philippines.[43] These countries have low-cost qualified labor and an educated workforce. The pay gap can be so dramatic that it overwhelms almost all other considerations. Consider that a Mexican assembly line worker earns an average of US$4.00 to US$5.00 an hour plus benefits compared to US$28 an hour plus benefits for the top paid Detroit worker and still substantially less than the lowest paid U.S. auto plant worker who earns US$15 to US$20 an hour plus benefits.[44]

Software programming and customer service, in particular, are being outsourced to India. For example, General Electric's back-office services unit, GE Capital International Services which was spun off into a new company called Genpact, is one of the oldest and biggest of India's outsourcing companies. From only US$26 million in 1999, its annual revenues grew to over US$2.5 billion by 2016.[45] As part of this trend, IBM acquired Daksh eServices Ltd., one of India's biggest suppliers of remote business services.[46]

Outsourcing, including offshoring, has significant disadvantages as well. For example, mounting complaints forced Dell Computer to stop routing corporate customers to a technical support call center in Bangalore, India.[47] GE's introduction of a new washing machine was delayed three weeks because of production problems at a supplier's company to which it had contracted out key work. Some companies have found themselves locked into long-term contracts with outside suppliers that are no longer competitive.[48] Some authorities propose that the cumulative effects of continued outsourcing steadily reduces a firm's ability to learn new skills and to develop new core competencies.[49] One survey of 129 outsourcing firms revealed that half the outsourcing projects undertaken in one year failed to deliver anticipated savings. This is in agreement with a survey by Bain & Company in which 51% of large North American, European, and Asian firms stated that outsourcing (including offshoring) did not meet their expectations.[50] Another survey of software projects, by MIT, found that the median Indian project had 10% more software bugs than did comparable U.S. projects.[51] A study of 91 outsourcing efforts conducted by European and North American firms found seven major errors that should be avoided:

1. **Outsourcing activities that should not be outsourced:** Companies failed to keep core activities in-house.

2. **Selecting the wrong vendor:** Vendors were not trustworthy or lacked state-of-the-art processes.

3. **Writing a poor contract:** Companies failed to establish a balance of power in the relationship.

4. **Overlooking personnel issues:** Employees lost commitment to the firm.

5. **Losing control over the outsourced activity:** Qualified managers failed to manage the outsourced activity.[52]

6. **Overlooking the hidden costs of outsourcing:** Transaction costs overwhelmed other savings.

7. **Failing to plan an exit strategy:** Companies failed to build reversibility clauses into the contract.[53]

The key to outsourcing is to purchase from outside only those activities that are not key to the company's distinctive competencies. Otherwise, the company may give up the very capabilities that made it successful in the first place—thus putting itself on the road to eventual decline. This is supported by research reporting that companies that have more experience with a particular manufacturing technology tend to keep manufacturing in-house.[54] J. P. Morgan Chase & Company terminated a seven-year technology outsourcing agreement with IBM because the bank's management realized that information technology (IT) was too important strategically to be outsourced.[55]

In determining functional strategy, the strategist must:

- Identify the company's or business unit's core competencies.
- Ensure that the competencies are continually being strengthened.
- Manage the competencies in such a way that best preserves the competitive advantage they create.

An outsourcing decision depends on the fraction of total value added that the activity under consideration represents and on the amount of potential competitive advantage in that activity for the company or business unit. See the outsourcing matrix in **FIGURE 8–1**. A firm should consider outsourcing any activity or function that has low potential for competitive advantage. If that activity constitutes only a small part of the total value of the firm's products or services, it could be purchased on the open market (assuming that quality providers of the activity are plentiful). If, however, the activity contributes highly to the company's products or services, the firm should purchase it through long-term contracts with trusted suppliers or distributors. A firm should always produce at least some of the activity or function (i.e., taper vertical integration) if that activity has the potential for providing the company some competitive advantage. However, full vertical integration should be considered only when that activity or function adds significant value to the company's products or services in addition to providing competitive advantage.[56]

FIGURE 8–1
Proposed Outsourcing Matrix

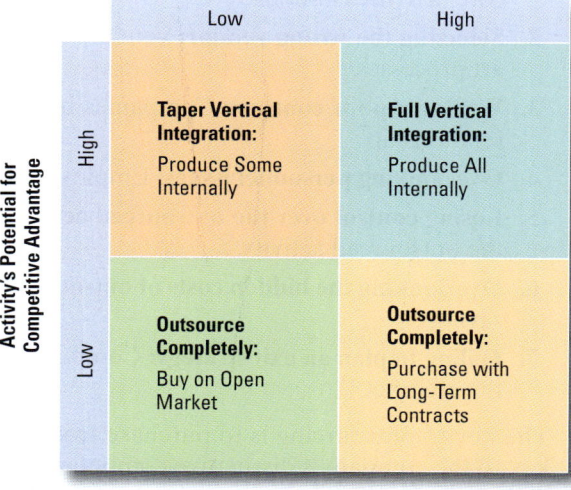

SOURCE: J. D. Hunger and T. L. Wheelen, "Proposed Outsourcing Matrix." Copyright © 1996 and 2005 by Wheelen and Hunger Associates. Reprinted by permission.

Strategies To Avoid

8-3. List and explain the strategies to avoid

Several strategies that could be considered corporate, business, or functional are very dangerous. Managers who have made poor analyses or lack creativity may be trapped into considering some of the following strategies that should be avoided:

- **Follow the leader:** Imitating a leading competitor's strategy might seem to be a good idea, but it ignores a firm's particular competitive advantages and the possibility that the leader may be wrong. Fujitsu Ltd., the world's second-largest computer maker, had been driven since the 1960s by the sole ambition of catching up to IBM. Like IBM at the time, Fujitsu competed primarily as a mainframe computer maker. So devoted was it to catching IBM, however, that it failed to notice that the mainframe business had reached maturity by 1990 and was no longer growing.

- **Hit another home run:** If a company is successful because it pioneered an extremely successful product, it tends to search for another super product that will ensure growth and prosperity. As in betting on long shots in horse races, the probability of finding a second winner is slight. Polaroid spent a lot of money developing an "instant" movie camera, but the public ignored it in favor of the camcorder.

- **Arms race:** Entering into a spirited battle with another firm for increased market share might increase sales revenue, but that increase will probably be more than offset by increases in advertising, promotion, R&D, and manufacturing costs. Since the U.S. deregulation of airlines, price wars and rate specials have contributed to the bankruptcies of many major airlines, such as Eastern, Pan American, TWA, and the consolidation of virtually every major airline into just four major players.

- **Do everything:** When faced with several interesting opportunities, management might tend to leap at all of them. At first, a corporation might have enough resources to develop each idea into a project, but money, time, and energy are soon exhausted as the many projects demand large infusions of resources. Yahoo! went on an acquisition spree for years under CEO Marissa Mayer spending more than US$1 billion for one acquisition alone. Searching for something that would provide growth for the company, the company invested in a wide swath of companies involved in mobile, search, and content. All failed to provide the company with any real growth.[57]

- **Losing hand:** A corporation might have invested so much in a particular strategy that top management is unwilling to accept its failure. Believing that it has too much invested to quit, management may continue to "throw good money after bad." RIM's BlackBerry phone was the undisputed leader in Smartphone technology and acceptance. They were so focused on their approach to how users needed to access information that they missed seeing how the new entrants in the industry had changed the industry. By the time they accepted that a change had really occurred, they were so far behind that catching up was virtually impossible.

Strategic Choice: Constructing Scenarios

8-4. Construct corporate scenarios to evaluate strategic options

After the pros and cons of the potential strategic alternatives have been identified and evaluated, one must be selected for implementation. By now, it is likely that many feasible alternatives will have emerged. How is the best strategy determined?

An important consideration in the selection of a strategy is the ability of each alternative to satisfy agreed-upon objectives with the least resources and the fewest negative side effects. The competitive advantages developed earlier using the VRIO framework is an excellent place to start. It is, therefore, important to develop a tentative implementation plan in order to address the difficulties that management is likely to face. This should be done in light of societal trends, the industry, and the company's situation based on the construction of scenarios.

CONSTRUCTING CORPORATE SCENARIOS

Corporate scenarios are *pro forma* (estimated future) balance sheets and income statements that forecast the effect each alternative strategy and its various programs will likely have on division and corporate return on investment. (Pro forma financial statements are discussed in **Chapter 12**.)

The recommended scenarios are simply extensions of the industry scenarios discussed in **Chapter 4**. If, for example, industry scenarios suggest the probable emergence of a strong market demand in a specific country for certain products, a series of alternative strategy scenarios can be developed. The alternative of acquiring another firm having these products in that country can be compared with the alternative of a green-field development (e.g., building new operations in that country). Using three sets of estimated sales figures (optimistic, pessimistic, and most likely) for the new products over the next five years, the two alternatives can be evaluated in terms of their effect on future company performance as reflected in the company's probable future financial statements. Pro forma balance sheets and income statements can be generated with spreadsheet software, such as Excel, on a personal computer. Pro forma statements are based on financial and economic scenarios.

To construct a corporate scenario, follow these steps:

1. Use industry scenarios (as discussed in **Chapter 4**) to develop a set of assumptions about the task environment (in the specific country under consideration). For example, 3M requires the general manager of each business unit to describe annually what his or her industry will look like in 15 years. List *optimistic, pessimistic*, and *most likely* assumptions for key economic factors such as the GDP (Gross Domestic Product), CPI (consumer price index), and prime interest rate and for other key external strategic factors such as governmental regulation and industry trends. This should be done for every country/region in which the corporation has significant operations that will be affected by each strategic alternative. These same underlying assumptions should be listed for each of the alternative scenarios to be developed.

2. Develop common-size financial statements (as discussed in **Chapter 12**) for the company's or business unit's previous years to serve as the basis for the trend analysis projections of pro forma financial statements. Use the *Scenario Box* form shown in **TABLE 8–1**:
   a. Use the historical common-size percentages to estimate the level of revenues, expenses, and other categories in estimated pro forma statements for future years.
   b. Develop for each strategic alternative a set of *optimistic (O), pessimistic (P),* and *most likely (ML)* assumptions about the impact of key variables on the company's future financial statements.
   c. Forecast three sets of sales and cost of goods sold figures for at least five years into the future.
   d. Analyze historical data and make adjustments based on the environmental assumptions listed earlier. Do the same for other figures that can vary significantly.
   e. Assume for other figures that they will continue in their historical relationship to sales or some other key determining factor. Plug in expected inventory levels,

TABLE 8–1	Scenario Box for Use in Generating Financial Pro Forma Statements												
				Projections[1]									
				200–			200–			200–			
Factor	Last Year	Historical Average	Trend Analysis	O	P	ML	O	P	ML	O	P	ML	Comments
GDP													
CPI													
Other													
Sales units													
Dollars													
COGS													
Advertising and marketing													
Interest expense													
Plant expansion													
Dividends													
Net profits													
EPS													
ROI													
ROE													
Other													

NOTE 1: O = Optimistic; P = Pessimistic; ML = Most Likely.

SOURCE: T. L. Wheelen and J. D. Hunger. Copyright © 1987, 1988, 1989, 1990, 1992, 2005, and 2009 by T. L. Wheelen. Copyright © 1993 and 2005 by Wheelen and Hunger Associates. Reprinted with permission.

accounts receivable, accounts payable, R&D expenses, advertising and promotion expenses, capital expenditures, and debt payments (assuming that debt is used to finance the strategy), among others.

f. Consider not only historical trends but also programs that might be needed to implement each alternative strategy (such as building a new manufacturing facility or expanding the sales force).

3. Construct detailed pro forma financial statements for each strategic alternative:

a. List the actual figures from this year's financial statements in the left column of the spreadsheet.

b. List to the right of this column the optimistic figures for years 1 through 5.

c. Go through this same process with the same strategic alternative, but now list the pessimistic figures for the next five years.

d. Do the same with the most likely figures.

e. Develop a similar set of optimistic (O), pessimistic (P), and most likely (ML) pro forma statements for the second strategic alternative. This process generates six different pro forma scenarios reflecting three different situations (O, P, and ML) for two strategic alternatives.

f. Calculate financial ratios and common-size income statements and create balance sheets to accompany the pro forma statements.

g. Compare the assumptions underlying the scenarios with the financial statements and ratios to determine the feasibility of the scenarios. For example, if cost of goods sold drops from 70% to 50% of total sales revenue in the pro forma income statements, this drop should result from a change in the production process or a shift to cheaper raw materials or labor costs rather than from a failure to keep the cost of goods sold in its usual percentage relationship to sales revenue when the predicted statement was developed.

The result of this detailed scenario construction should be anticipated net profits, cash flow, and net working capital for each of three versions of the two alternatives for five years into the future. A strategist might want to go further into the future if the strategy is expected to have a major impact on the company's financial statements beyond five years. The result of this work should provide sufficient information on which forecasts of the likely feasibility and probable profitability of each of the strategic alternatives could be based.

Obviously, these scenarios can quickly become very complicated, especially if three sets of acquisition prices and development costs are calculated. Nevertheless, this sort of detailed what-if analysis is needed to realistically compare the projected outcome of each reasonable alternative strategy and its attendant programs, budgets, and procedures. Regardless of the quantifiable pros and cons of each alternative, the actual decision will probably be influenced by several subjective factors such as those described in the following sections.

Management's Attitude Toward Risk

The attractiveness of a particular strategic alternative is partially a function of the amount of risk it entails. **Risk** is composed not only of the *probability* that the strategy will be effective but also of the *amount of assets* the corporation must allocate to that strategy and the *length of time* the assets will be unavailable for other uses. Because of variation among countries in terms of customs, regulations, and resources, companies operating in global industries must deal with a greater amount of risk than firms operating only in one country.[58] The greater the assets involved and the longer they are committed, the more likely top management is to demand a high probability of success. Managers with no ownership position in a company are unlikely to have much interest in putting their jobs in danger with risky decisions. Research indicates that managers who own a significant amount of stock in their firms are more likely to engage in risk-taking actions than are managers with no stock.[59]

A high level of risk was why Intel's board of directors found it difficult to vote for a proposal in the early 1990s to commit US$5 billion to making the Pentium microprocessor chip—five times the amount of money needed for its previous chip. In looking back on that board meeting, then-CEO Andy Grove remarked, "I remember people's eyes looking at that chart and getting big. I wasn't even sure I believed those numbers at the time." The proposal committed the company to building new factories—something Intel had been reluctant to do. A wrong decision would mean that the company would end up with a killing amount of overcapacity. Based on Grove's presentation, the board decided to take the gamble. Intel's resulting manufacturing expansion eventually cost US$10 billion but resulted in Intel's obtaining 75% of the microprocessor business and huge cash profits.[60]

Risk might be one reason that significant innovations occur more often in small firms than in large, established corporations. A small firm managed by an entrepreneur is often willing to accept greater risk than is a large firm of diversified ownership run by professional managers.[61] It is one thing to take a chance if you are the primary shareholder and are not concerned with periodic changes in the value of the company's common stock. It is something else if the corporation's stock is widely held and acquisition-hungry competitors or takeover artists surround the company like sharks every time the company's stock price falls below some external assessment of the firm's value.

Another approach to evaluating alternatives under conditions of high environmental uncertainty is to use the real-options theory. According to the **real-options** approach, when the future is highly uncertain, it pays to have a broad range of options open. This is in contrast to using *net present value (NPV)* to calculate the value of a project by predicting its payouts, adjusting them for risk, and subtracting the amount invested. By boiling everything down to one scenario, NPV doesn't provide any flexibility in case circumstances change. NPV is also difficult to apply to projects in which the potential payoffs are currently unknown. The real-options approach, however, deals with these issues by breaking the investment into stages. Management allocates a small amount of funding to initiate multiple projects, monitors their development, and then cancels the projects that aren't successful and funds those that are doing well.[62] This approach is very similar to the way venture capitalists fund an entrepreneurial venture in stages of funding based on the venture's performance.

Research indicates that the use of the real-options approach does improve organizational performance.[63] Some of the corporations using the real-options approach are Chevron for bidding on petroleum reserves, Airbus for calculating the costs of airlines changing their orders at the last minute, and the Tennessee Valley Authority for outsourcing electricity generation instead of building its own plant. There is an international conference on Real Options, but because of its complexity, the real-options approach is probably not worthwhile for minor decisions or for projects requiring a full commitment at the beginning.[64]

Pressures from Stakeholders

The attractiveness of a strategic alternative is affected by its perceived compatibility with the key stakeholders in a corporation's task environment. Creditors want to be paid on time. Unions exert pressure for comparable wage and employment security. Governments and interest groups demand social responsibility. Shareholders want dividends. All these pressures must be given some consideration in the selection of the best alternative.

Stakeholders can be categorized in terms of their (1) interest in the corporation's activities and (2) relative power to influence the corporation's activities. As shown in **Figure 8–2**, each stakeholder group can be shown graphically based on its *level of interest* (from low to high) in a corporation's activities and on its *relative power* (from low to high) to influence a corporation's activities.

Strategic managers should ask four questions to assess the importance of stakeholder concerns in a particular decision:

1. How will this decision affect each stakeholder, especially those given high and medium priority?
2. How much of what each stakeholder wants is he or she likely to get under this alternative?
3. What are the stakeholders likely to do if they don't get what they want?
4. What is the probability that they will do it?

Strategy makers should choose strategic alternatives that minimize external pressures and maximize the probability of gaining stakeholder support. Managers may, however, ignore or take some stakeholders for granted—leading to serious problems later. The Tata Group, for example, failed to consider the unwillingness of farmers in Singur, India, to accept the West Bengal government's compensation for expropriating their land so that Tata could build its Nano auto plant. Farmers formed rallies against the plant, blocked roads, and even assaulted an employee of a Tata supplier.[65]

FIGURE 8–2
Stakeholder
Priority Matrix

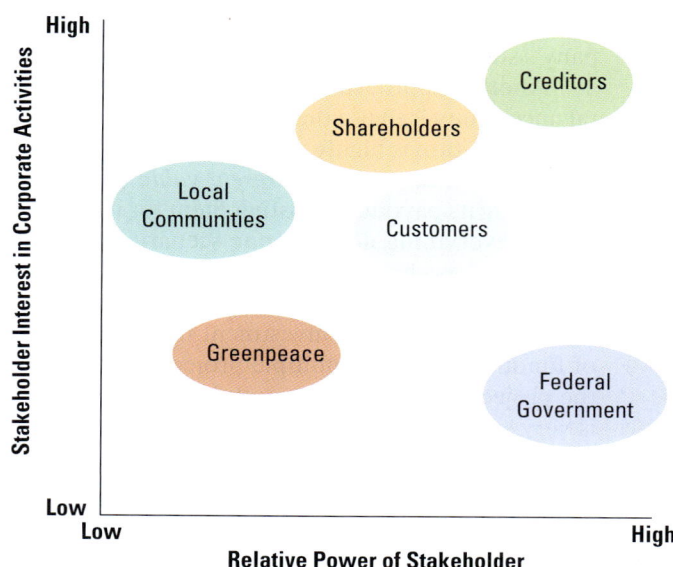

SOURCE: Suggested by C. Anderson in "Values-Based Management," Academy of Management Executive (November 1997), pp. 25–46.

Top management can also propose a political strategy to influence its key stakeholders. A **political strategy** is a plan to bring stakeholders into agreement with a corporation's actions. Some of the most commonly used political strategies are constituency building, political action committee contributions, advocacy advertising, lobbying, and coalition building. Research reveals that large firms, those operating in concentrated industries, and firms that are highly dependent upon government regulation are more politically active.[66] Political support can be critical in entering a new international market, especially in transition economies where free market competition did not previously exist.[67]

Pressures from the Corporate Culture

If a strategy is incompatible with a company's corporate culture, the likelihood of its success is very low. Foot-dragging and even sabotage will result as employees fight to resist a radical change in corporate philosophy. Precedents from the past tend to restrict the kinds of objectives and strategies that are seriously considered.[68] The "aura" of the founders of a corporation can linger long past their lifetimes because their values are imprinted on a corporation's members.

In evaluating a strategic alternative, strategy makers must consider pressures from the corporate culture and assess a strategy's compatibility with that culture. If there is little fit, management must decide if it should:

- Take a chance on ignoring the culture.
- Manage around the culture and change the implementation plan.
- Try to change the culture to fit the strategy.
- Change the strategy to fit the culture.

Further, a decision to proceed with a particular strategy without a commitment to change the culture or manage around the culture (both very tricky and time consuming) is dangerous. Nevertheless, restricting a corporation to only those strategies that are completely compatible with its culture might eliminate from consideration the most profitable alternatives. (See **Chapter 10** for more information on managing corporate culture.)

Needs and Desires of Key Managers

Even the most attractive alternative might not be selected if it is contrary to the needs and desires of important top managers. Personal characteristics and experience affect a person's assessment of an alternative's attractiveness.[69] For example, one study found that narcissistic (self-absorbed and arrogant) CEOs favor bold actions that attract attention, like many large acquisitions—resulting in either big wins or big losses.[70] A person's ego may be tied to a particular proposal to the extent that all other alternatives are strongly lobbied against. As a result, the person may have unfavorable forecasts altered so that they are more in agreement with the desired alternative.[71] In a study by McKinsey & Company of over 2500 executives from around the world, 36% responded that managers hide, restrict, or misrepresent information at least "somewhat" frequently when submitting capital-investment proposals. In addition, an executive might influence other people in top management to favor a particular alternative so that objections to it are overruled. In the same McKinsey study of global executives, more than 60% of the managers reported that business unit and divisional heads form alliances with peers or lobby someone more senior in the organization at least "somewhat" frequently when resource allocation decisions are being made.[72]

Industry and cultural backgrounds affect strategic choice. For example, executives with strong ties within an industry tend to choose strategies commonly used in that industry. Other executives who have come to the firm from another industry and have strong ties outside the industry tend to choose different strategies from what is being currently used in their industry.[73] Country of origin often affects preferences. For example, Japanese managers prefer a cost-leadership strategy more than do United States managers.[74] Research reveals that executives from Korea, the United States, Japan, and Germany tend to make different strategic choices in similar situations because they use different decision criteria and weights. For example, Korean executives emphasize industry attractiveness, sales, and market share in their decisions, whereas U.S. executives emphasize projected demand, discounted cash flow, and ROI.[75]

There is a tendency to maintain the status quo, which means that decision makers continue with existing goals and plans beyond the point when an objective observer would recommend a change in course.[76] Some executives show a self-serving tendency to attribute the firm's problems not to their own poor decisions but to environmental events out of their control, such as government policies or a poor economic climate.[77] For example, a CEO is more likely to divest a poorly performing unit when its poor performance does not incriminate that same CEO who had acquired it.[78] Negative information about a particular course of action to which a person is committed may be ignored because of a desire to appear competent or because of strongly held values regarding consistency. It may take a crisis or an unlikely event to cause strategic decision makers to seriously consider an alternative they had previously ignored or discounted.[79] It wasn't until the CEO of ConAgra, a multinational food products company, had a heart attack that ConAgra started producing the Healthy Choice line of low-fat, low-cholesterol, low-sodium frozen-food entrees.

THE PROCESS OF STRATEGIC CHOICE

Strategic choice is the evaluation of alternative strategies and selection of the best alternative. According to Paul Nutt, an authority in decision making, half of the decisions made by managers are failures.[80] After analyzing 400 decisions, Nutt found that failure almost always stems from the actions of the decision maker, not from bad luck or situational limitations. In these instances, managers commit one or more key blunders: (1) their desire for speedy actions leads to a rush to judgment, (2) they apply failure-prone decision-making practices such as adopting the claim of an influential stakeholder, and (3) they make poor use of resources by investigating only one or two options. These three blunders cause executives to limit their search for feasible alternatives and look for a quick consensus. Only 4% of the 400 managers set an objective and considered several alternatives. The search for innovative options was attempted in only 24% of the decisions studied.[81] Another study of 68 divestiture decisions found a strong tendency for managers to rely heavily on past experience when developing strategic alternatives.[82]

There is mounting evidence that when an organization is facing a dynamic environment, the best strategic decisions are not arrived at through **consensus** when everyone agrees on one alternative. They actually involve a certain amount of heated disagreement, and even conflict.[83] Many diverse opinions are presented, participants trust in one another's abilities and competencies, and conflict is task-oriented, not personal.[84] This is certainly the case for firms operating in global industries. Because unmanaged conflict often carries a high emotional cost, authorities in decision making propose that strategic managers use "programmed conflict" to raise different opinions, regardless of the personal feelings of the people involved.[85] Two techniques help strategic managers avoid the consensus trap that Alfred Sloan found:

1. **Devil's advocate:** The idea of the **devil's advocate** originated in the medieval Roman Catholic Church as a way of ensuring that impostors were not canonized as saints. One trusted person was selected to find and present all the reasons why a person should not be canonized. When this process is applied to strategic decision making, a devil's advocate (who may be an individual or a group) is assigned to identify potential pitfalls and problems with a proposed alternative strategy in a formal presentation.

2. **Dialectical inquiry:** The dialectical philosophy, which can be traced back to Plato and Aristotle and more recently to Hegel, involves combining two conflicting views—the thesis and the antithesis—into a synthesis. When applied to strategic decision making, **dialectical inquiry** requires that two proposals using different assumptions be generated for each alternative strategy under consideration. After advocates of each position present and debate the merits of their arguments before key decision makers, either one of the alternatives or a new compromise alternative is selected as the strategy to be implemented.

Research generally supports the conclusion that the devil's advocate and dialectical inquiry methods are equally superior to consensus in decision making, especially when the firm's environment is dynamic. The debate itself, rather than its particular format, appears to improve the quality of decisions by formalizing and legitimizing constructive conflict and by encouraging critical evaluation. Both lead to better assumptions and recommendations and to a higher level of critical thinking among the people involved.[86]

Regardless of the process used to generate strategic alternatives, each resulting alternative must be rigorously evaluated in terms of its ability to meet four criteria:

1. **Mutual exclusivity:** Doing any one alternative would preclude doing any other.

2. **Success:** It must be feasible and have a good probability of success.

3. **Completeness:** It must take into account all the key strategic issues.

4. **Internal consistency:** It must make sense on its own as a strategic decision for the entire firm and not contradict key goals, policies, and strategies currently being pursued by the firm or its units.[87]

USING POLICIES TO GUIDE STRATEGIC CHOICES

The selection of the best strategic alternative is not the end of strategy formulation. The organization must then engage in developing policies. Policies define the broad guidelines for implementation. Flowing from the selected strategy, policies provide guidance for decision making and actions throughout the organization. They are the principles under which the corporation operates on a day-to-day basis. At General Electric, for example, Chairman Jack Welch initiated the policy that any GE business unit must be number one or number two in whatever market it competes. This policy gave clear guidance to managers throughout the organization.

When crafted correctly, an effective policy accomplishes three things:

- It forces trade-offs between competing resource demands.
- It tests the strategic soundness of a particular action.
- It sets clear boundaries within which employees must operate, while granting them the freedom to experiment within those constraints.[88]

Policies tend to be rather long lived and can even outlast the particular strategy that created them. These general policies—such as "The customer is always right" (Nordstrom) or "Always Low Prices" (Wal-Mart)—can become, in time, part of a corporation's culture. Such policies can make the implementation of specific strategies easier. They can also restrict top management's strategic options in the future. Thus, a change in strategy should be followed quickly by a change in policies. Managing policy is one way to manage the corporate culture.

End of Chapter SUMMARY

This chapter completes the part of this book on strategy formulation and sets the stage for strategy implementation. Functional strategies must be formulated to support business and corporate strategies; otherwise, the company will move in multiple directions and eventually pull itself apart. For a functional strategy to have the best chance of success, it should be built on a distinctive competency residing within that functional area. If a corporation does not have a distinctive competency in a particular functional area, that functional area could be a candidate for outsourcing.

When evaluating a strategic alternative, the most important criterion is the ability of the proposed strategy to deal with the competitive advantages of the organization. If the alternative doesn't take advantage of environmental opportunities and corporate advantages, it will probably fail. Developing corporate scenarios and pro forma projections for each alternative are rational aids for strategic decision making. This logical approach fits Mintzberg's planning mode of strategic decision making, as discussed earlier in **Chapter 1**. Nevertheless, some strategic decisions are inherently risky and are often resolved on the basis of one person's "gut feel." This is an aspect of the entrepreneurial mode and is seen in large established corporations as well as in new venture startups. Various management studies have found that executives routinely rely on their intuition to solve complex problems. The effective use of intuition has been found to differentiate successful top executives and board members from lower-level managers and dysfunctional boards.[89] According to Ralph Larsen, former Chair and CEO of Johnson & Johnson, "Often there is absolutely no way that you could have the time to thoroughly analyze every one of the options or alternatives available to you.

So you have to rely on your business judgment."[90] For managerial intuition to be effective, however, it requires years of experience in problem solving and is founded upon a complete understanding of the details of the business.[91]

When Bob Lutz, then President of Chrysler Corporation, was enjoying a fast drive in his Cobra roadster one weekend in 1988, he wondered why Chrysler's cars were so dull. "I felt guilty: there I was, the president of Chrysler, driving this great car that had such a strong Ford association," said Lutz, referring to the original Cobra's Ford V-8 engine. That Monday, Lutz enlisted allies at Chrysler to develop a muscular, outrageous sports car that would turn heads and stop traffic. Others in management argued that the US$80 million investment would be better spent elsewhere. The sales force warned that no U.S. auto maker had ever succeeded in selling a US$50,000 car. With only his gut instincts to support him, he pushed the project forward with unwavering commitment. The result was the Dodge Viper—a car that single-handedly changed the public's perception of Chrysler. Years later, Lutz had trouble describing exactly how he had made this critical decision. "It was this subconscious, visceral feeling. And it just felt right," explained Lutz.[92]

Pearson MyLab Management®

Go to **mymanagementlab.com** to complete the problems marked with this icon .

KEY TERMS

consensus (p. 272)
corporate scenarios (p. 266)
devil's advocate (p. 272)
dialectical inquiry (p. 272)
financial strategy (p. 254)
functional strategy (p. 252)
HRM strategy (p. 261)
information technology strategy (p. 262)

leveraged buyout (p. 254)
logistics strategy (p. 261)
market development (p. 252)
marketing strategy (p. 252)
offshoring (p. 262)
operations strategy (p. 256)
outsourcing (p. 262)
political strategy (p. 270)

product development (p. 253)
purchasing strategy (p. 258)
R&D strategy (p. 255)
real options (p. 269)
risk (p. 268)
strategic choice (p. 271)
technological follower (p. 255)
technological leader (p. 255)

Pearson MyLab Management®

Go to **mymanagmentlab.com** for the following Assisted-graded writing questions:

8-1. How can an operations strategy be used to understand and exploit a particular product offering?

8-2. How are corporate scenarios used in the development of an effective strategy?

DISCUSSION QUESTIONS

8-3. Explain how functional strategies can support an organization's corporate strategy.

8-4. What are the reasons for strategic planners to pay more attention to the importance of planning and implementing an effective pricing strategy in a competitive market?

8-5. Explain the new real-options approach used in conditions of high environmental uncertainty.

8-6. Identify the common signs that indicate an outsourcing strategy is not executed effectively.

8-7. How does a business evaluate its strategic choices?

STRATEGIC PRACTICE EXERCISE

The political situation in Lebanon always seems to be changing. At times, like the saying goes, political calm only precedes chaos. At others, this political calm truly stabilizes the economy and growth follows. Encouraging news about the potential formation of a new government, at one point, pushed the Beirut Stock Exchange (BSE) higher with Solidere A and B shares having gained 7.87 percent and 6.18 percent, respectively. Investors, whether local or foreign, seemed optimistic. The beneficial impact of this rise led to more sales: the trade of Solidere A was 86,111 while Solidere B was 24,060. The total number of shares traded that day was 307,667 with a trading value of $4.47 million, meaning that the stock capitalization of the listed companies increased by 1.30 percent to reach $10.848 billion rather than the $10.707 billion for the previous session. Despite the increase in trades on the BSE

following the news, the volume remained relatively low compared to historic levels. Trade was local; it was not foreign. Foreign investors who normally do not buy less than 50,000 shares are rarely found on the Beirut Stock Exchange. It is their capital that is acutely needed in Lebanon today!

1. What is the problem Solidere faces?

2. Should Solidere adopt a marketing strategy? Why? Why not?

3. 3. If you were part of the decision-making team in Solidere, which functional level strategy would you adopt to improve the position of Solidere?

SOURCE: Dana Halawi, "Hope for cabinet lift Solidere Shares," *The Daily Star (January 15, 2014)*, p. 5.

NOTES

1. S. F. Slater and E. M. Olson, "Market's Contribution to the Implementation of Business Strategy: An Empirical Analysis," *Strategic Management Journal* (November 2001), pp. 1055–1067; B. C. Skaggs and T. R. Huffman, "A Customer Interaction Approach to Strategy and Production Complexity Alignment in Service Firms," *Academy of Management Journal* (December 2003), pp. 775–786.

2. A. Pressman, "Ocean Spray's Creative Juices," *BusinessWeek* (May 15, 2006), pp. 88–89; http://www.oceanspray.com/Products.aspx

3. A. Pressman, "Smith & Wesson: A Gunmaker Loaded with Offshoots," *BusinessWeek* (June 4, 2007), p. 66. A *line extension,* in contrast to brand extension, is the introduction of additional items in the same category under the same brand name, such as new flavors, added ingredients, or package sizes.

4. S. M. Oster, *Modern Competitive Analysis*, 2nd ed. (New York: Oxford University Press, 1994), p. 93.

5. J. M. de Figueiredo and M. K. Kyle, "Surviving the Gales of Creative Destruction: The Determinants of Product Turnover," *Strategic Management Journal* (March 2006), pp. 241–264.

6. J. Gruley and S. D. Singh, "Deere's Big Green Profit Machine," *Bloomberg Businessweek* (July 5, 2012), (http://www.businessweek.com/articles/2012-07-05/

deeres-big-green-profit-machine); M. Springer, "Plowed Under," *Forbes* (February 21, 2000), p. 56.

7. W. Redmond, "The Strategic Pricing of Innovative Products," *Handbook of Business Strategy, 1992/1993 Yearbook*, edited by H. E. Glass and M. A. Hovde (Boston: Warren, Gorham & Lamont, 1992), pp. 16.1–16.13; A. Hinterhuber, "Towards Value-Based Pricing—An Integrative Framework for Decision Making," *Industrial Marketing Management* (Vol. 33, 2004), pp. 765–778.

8. A. Kambil, H. J. Wilson III, and V. Agrawal, "Are You Leaving Money on the Table?" *Journal of Business Strategy* (January/February 2002), pp. 40–43.

9. J.C. Owens, "Apple isn't really sitting on $216 billion in cash," *MarketWatch*, January 27, 2016 (http://www.marketwatch.com/story/apple-isnt-really-sitting-on-216-billion-in-cash-2016-01-26).

10. A. Safieddine and S. Titman in April 1999 *Journal of Finance,* as summarized by D. Champion, "The Joy of Leverage," *Harvard Business Review* (July–August 1999), pp. 19–22.

11. R. Kochhar and M. A. Hitt, "Linking Corporate Strategy to Capital Structure: Diversification Strategy, Type and Source of Financing," *Strategic Management Journal* (June 1998), pp. 601–610.

12. O. Oran, G. Roumeliotis, and K. Haunss, "Goldman fills vacuum in leveraged buyout market with $8 billion

fund), *Reuters*, January 8, 2016 (http://www.reuters.com/article/us-goldmansachs-mezzaninefund-idUSKBN0UM0G320160108).

13. "Private Investigations," *The Economist* (July 5, 2008), pp. 84–85.

14. D. Angwin and I. Contardo, "Unleashing Cerberus: Don't Let Your MBOs Turn on Themselves," *Long Range Planning* (October 1999), pp. 494–504.

15. For information on different types of LBOs, see M. Wright, R. E. Hoskisson, and L. W. Busenitz, "Firm Rebirth: Buyouts as Facilitators of Strategic Growth and Entrepreneurship," *Academy of Management Executive* (February 2001), pp. 111–125.

16. B. Nichols, "Why Stock Buybacks Will Be Stronger Than Ever in 2016 (SPY, AAPL, NKE)," *InvestorPlace*, January 6, 2016 (http://investorplace.com/2016/01/stock-buybacks-will-stronger-ever-2016-spy-aapl-nke/#.VtDIJ4-cGP8); D. N. Hurtt, J. G. Kreuze, and S. A. Langsam, "Stock Buybacks and Their Association with Stock Options Exercised in the IT Industry," *American Journal of Business* (Spring 2008), pp. 13–21.

17. B. Deener, "Back Up and Look at Reasons for Reverse Stock Split," *The (St. Petersburg, FL) Times* (December 29, 2002), p. 3H.

18. H. Wee, "Patent trolls target US businesses, consumers ultimately foot the bill," *CNBC*, March 31, 2014 (http://www.cnbc.com/2014/03/31/); T. Francis, "Can You Get a Patent on Being a Patent Troll?" NPR, August 2, 2012. (http://www.npr.org/blogs/money/2012/08/01/157743897/can-you-get-a-patent-on-being-a-patent-troll); M. Orey, "A Sotheby's for Investors," *BusinessWeek* (February 13, 2006), p. 39.

19. L-E. Gadde and H. Hakansson, "Teaching in Supplier Networks," in M. Gibbert and T. Durand (Eds.), *Strategic Networks: Learning to Compete* (Malden, MA: Blackwell Publishing, 2007), pp. 40–57.

20. D. Resnick, "Transparency is Key to Open Innovation," *R&D Magazine*, February 26, 2016 (http://www.rdmag.com/articles/2016/02/transparency-key-open-innovation).

21. "Schools Rent Out Labs to Businesses," *St. Cloud (MN) Times* (December 11, 2007), p. 3A.

22. J. Bughin, M. Chui, and B. Johnson, "The Next Step in Open Innovation," *McKinsey Quarterly* (June 2008), pp. 1–8.

23. L. Coleman-Lochner and C. Hymowitz, "At P&G, the Innovation Well Runs Dry," *Bloomberg Businessweek* (September 10, 2012), pp. 24–26; J. Greene, J. Carey, M. Arndt, and O. Port, "Reinventing Corporate R&D," *BusinessWeek* (September 22, 2003), pp. 74–76; J. Birkinshaw, S. Crainer, and M. Mol, "From R&D to Connect + Develop at P&G," *Business Strategy Review* (Spring 2007), pp. 66–69; L. Huston and N. Sakkab, "Connect and Develop: Inside Proctor & Gamble's New Model for Innovation," *Harvard Business Review* (March 2006), pp. 58–66.

24. G. Dushnitsky and M. J. Lenox, "When Do Firms Undertake R&D by Investing in New Ventures?" Paper presented to the annual meeting of the *Academy of Management*, Seattle, WA (August 2003).

25. J. R. Williams and R. S. Novak, "Aligning CIM Strategies to Different Markets," *Long Range Planning* (February 1990), pp. 126–135.

26. B. Levisohn, "Morgan Stanley: General Motors Didn't Warn So We'll Do It For Them," *Barrons*, October 7, 2014 (http://blogs.barrons.com/stockstowatchtoday/2014/10/07/morgan-stanley-general-motors-didnt-warn-so-well-do-it-for-them/).

27. M. Hoegl and S. M. Wagner, "Buyer-Supplier Collaboration in Product Development Projects," *Journal of Management* (August 2005), pp. 530–548; B. McEvily and A. Marcus, "Embedded Ties and the Acquisition of Competitive Capabilities," *Strategic Management Journal* (November 2005), pp. 1033–1055; R. Gulati and M. Sytch, "Dependence Asymmetry and Joint Dependence in Interorganizational Relationships: Effects of Embeddedness on a Manufacturer's Performance in Procurement Relationships," *Administrative Science Quarterly* (March 2007), pp. 32–69.

28. J. Richardson, "Parallel Sourcing and Supplier Performance in the Japanese Automobile Industry," *Strategic Management Journal* (July 1993), pp. 339–350.

29. D. H. Pearcy, D. B. Parker, and L. C. Giunipero, "Using Electronic Procurement to Facilitate Supply Chain Integration: An Exploratory Study of U.S.-Based Firms," *American Journal of Business* (Spring 2008), pp. 23–35.

30. M. Lierow, "Amazon Is Using Logistics To Lead A Retail Revolution," *Forbes*, February 18, 2016 (http://www.forbes.com/sites/oliverwyman/2016/02/18/amazon-is-using-logistics-to-lead-a-retail-revolution/#2e2624a51309).

31. B. L. Kirkman and Debra L. Shapiro, "The Impact of Cultural Values on Employee Resistance to Teams: Toward a Model of Globalized Self-Managing Work Team Effectiveness," *Academy of Management Review* (July 1997), pp. 730–757.

32. R. D. Banker, J. M. Field, R. G. Schroeder, and K. K. Sinha, "Impact of Work Teams on Manufacturing Performance: A Longitudinal Field Study," *Academy of Management Journal* (August 1996), pp. 867–890; B. L. Kirkman and B. Rosen, "Beyond Self-Management: Antecedents and Consequences of Team Empowerment," *Academy of Management Journal* (February 1999), pp. 58–74.

33. V. Y. Haines III, S. St. Onge, and A. Marcoux, "Performance Management Design and Effectiveness in Quality-Driven Organizations," *Canadian Journal of Administrative Sciences* (June 2004), pp. 146–160.

34. "Talent Acquisition, biggest challenge and business aligned HR, top HR game changer in 2016," *The Economic Times*, February 25, 2016 (http://economictimes.indiatimes.com/jobs/talent-acquisition-biggest-challenge-and-business-aligned-hr-top-hr-game-changer-in-2016-survey/articleshow/51137601.cms).

35. O. C. Richard, "Racial Diversity, Business Strategy, and Firm Performance: A Resource-Based View," *Academy of Management Journal* (April 2000), pp. 164–177.

36. G. Robinson and K. Dechant, "Building a Business Case for Diversity," *Academy of Management Executive* (August 1997), pp. 21–31.

37. K. Labich, "Making Diversity Pay," *Fortune* (September 9, 1996), pp. 177–180.

38. "Gartner Worldwide IT Spending Forecast," (gartner.com/technology/research/it-spending-forecast); N. G. Carr, "IT Doesn't Matter," *Harvard Business Review* (May 2003), pp. 41–50.

39. J. Greco, "Good Day Sunshine," *Journal of Business Strategy* (July/August 1998), pp. 4–5.

40. W. Howard, "Translate Now," *PC Magazine* (September 19, 2000), p. 81.

41. S. Holmes and M. Arndt, "A Plane that Could Change the Game," *BusinessWeek* (August 9, 2004), p. 33.

42. "2014 Global Outsourcing and Insourcing Survey," (February 2014), (www2.deloitte.com/us/en/pages/strategy /articles/2014-global-outsourcing-and-insourcing-survey .html).

43. http://www.statisticbrain.com/outsourcing-statistics-by -country/

44. "Mexico's auto boom is about wages," *Automotive News*, February 1, 2012 (autonews.com/article/20120201/blog06 /120209989/mexico%E2%80%99s-auto-boom-is-about -wages).

45. "Genpact reports results for the first quarter of 2015," *PRNewswire*, April 30, 2015 *(prnnewswire.com/news-releases/genpact-reports-results-for-the-first-quarter-of-2015-300075473.html).*

46. "IBM's Plan to Buy India Firm Points to Demand for Outsourcing," *Des Moines Register* (April 11, 2004), p. 2D.

47. A. Castro, "Complaints Push Dell to Use U.S. Call Centers," *Des Moines Register* (November 25, 2003), p. 1D.

48. J. A. Byrne, "Has Outsourcing Gone Too Far?" *Business-Week* (April 1, 1996), pp. 26–28.

49. R. C. Insinga and M. J. Werle, "Linking Outsourcing to Business Strategy," *Academy of Management Executive* (November 2000), pp. 58–70; D. Lei and M. A. Hitt, "Strategic Restructuring and Outsourcing: The Effect of Mergers and Acquisitions and LBOs on Building Firm Skills and Capabilities," *Journal of Management* (Vol. 21, No. 5, 1995), pp. 835–859.

50. "Outsourcing: Time to Bring It Back Home?" *The Economist* (May 5, 2005), p. 63.

51. S. E. Ante, "Shifting Work Offshore? Outsourcer Beware," *BusinessWeek* (January 12, 2004), pp. 36–37.

52. A. Takeishi, "Bridging Inter- and Intra-Firm Boundaries: Management of Supplier Involvement in Automobile Product Development," *Strategic Management Journal* May 2001), pp. 40-43.

53. J. Barthelemy, "The Seven Deadly Sins of Outsourcing," *Academy of Management Executive* (May 2003), pp. 87–98.

54. M. J. Leiblein and D. J. Miller, "An Empirical Examination of Transaction and Firm-Level Influences on the Vertical Boundaries of the Firm," *Strategic Management Journal* (September 2003), pp. 839–859.

55. S. Hamm, "Is Outsourcing on the Outs?" *BusinessWeek* (October 4, 2004), p. 42.

56. For further information on effective offshoring, see R. Aron and J. V. Singh, "Getting Offshoring Right," *Harvard Business Review* (December 2005), pp. 135–143.

57. S. Nielson, "Why Yahoo! acquisitions have not accelerated revenue growth," MarketRealist, October 14, 2014 (finance.yahoo.com/news/why-yahoo-acquisitions-not-accelerated-170017478.html).

58. N. Checa, J. Maguire, and J. Berry, "The New World Disorder," *Harvard Business Review* (August 2003), pp. 70–79.

59. T. B. Palmer and R. M. Wiseman, "Decoupling Risk Taking from Income Stream Uncertainty: A Holistic Model of Risk," *Strategic Management Journal* (November 1999),

pp. 1037–1062; W. G. Sanders and D. C. Hambrick, "Swinging for the Fences: The Effects of CEO Stock Options on Company Risk Taking and Performance," *Academy of Management Journal* (October 2007), pp. 1055–1078.

60. D. Clark, "All the Chips: A Big Bet Made Intel What It Is Today; Now It Wagers Again," *The Wall Street Journal* (June 6, 1995), pp. A1, A5.

61. L. W. Busenitz and J. B. Barney, "Differences Between Entrepreneurs and Managers in Large Organizations: Biases and Heuristics in Strategic Decision-Making," *Journal of Business Venturing* (January 1997), pp. 9–30.

62. J. J. Janney and G. G. Dess, "Can Real-Options Analysis Improve Decision-Making? Promises and Pitfalls," *Academy of Management Executive* (November 2004), pp. 60–75; S. Maklan, S. Knox, and L. Ryals, "Using Real Options to Help Build the Business Case for CRM Investment," *Long Range Planning* (August 2005), pp. 393–410.

63. J. Rosenberger and K. Eisenhardt, "What Are Real Options: A Review of Empirical Research," Paper presented to annual meeting of the *Academy of Management*, Seattle, WA (August 2003).

64. P. Coy, "Exploiting Uncertainty," *BusinessWeek* (June 7, 1999), pp. 118–124. For further information on real options, see M. Amram and N. Kulatilaka, *Real Options* (Boston, Harvard University Press, 1999). For a simpler summary, see R. M. Grant, *Contemporary Strategy Analysis*, 5th ed. (Malden, MA: Blackwell Publishing, 2005), pp. 48–50.

65. "Nano Wars," *The Economist* (August 30, 2008), p. 63.

66. J-P. Bonardi, A. J. Hillman, and G. D. Keim, "The Attractiveness of Political Markets: Implications for Firm Strategy," *Academy of Management Review* (April 2005), pp. 397–413.

67. J. G. Frynas, K. Mellahi, and G. A. Pigman, "First Mover Advantages in International Business and Firm-Specific Political Resources," *Strategic Management Journal* (April 2006), pp. 321–345. For additional information about political strategies, see C. Oliver and I. Holzinger, "The Effectiveness of Strategic Political Management: A Dynamic Capabilities Framework," *Academy of Management Review* (April 2008), pp. 496–520.

68. H. M. O'Neill, R. W. Pouder, and A. K. Buchholtz, "Patterns in the Diffusion of Strategies Across Organizations: Insights from the Innovation Diffusion Literature," *Academy of Management Executive* (January 1998), pp. 98–114; C. G. Gilbert, "Unbundling the Structure of Inertia: Resource Versus Routine Rigidity," *Academy of Management Journal* (October 2005), pp. 741–763.

69. B. B. Tyler and H. K. Steensma. "Evaluating Technological Collaborative Opportunities: A Cognitive Modeling Perspective," *Strategic Management Journal* (Summer 1995), pp. 43–70; D. Duchan, D. P. Ashman, and M. Nathan, "Mavericks, Visionaries, Protestors, and Sages: Toward a Typology of Cognitive Structures for Decision Making in Organizations," *Journal of Business Strategies* (Fall 1997), pp. 106–125; P. Chattopadhyay, W. H. Glick, C. C. Miller, and G. P. Huber, "Determinants of Executive Beliefs: Comparing Functional Conditioning and Social Influence," *Strategic Management Journal* (August 1999), pp. 763–789; B. Katey and G. G. Meredith, "Relationship Among Owner/Manager Personal Values, Business Strategies, and Enterprise Performance," *Journal of Small Business Management* (April 1997), pp. 37–64.

70. A. Chatterjee and D. C. Hambrick, "It's All About Me: Narcissistic Executive Officers and Their Effects on Company Strategy and Performance," *Administrative Science Quarterly* (September 2007), pp. 351–386.

71. C. S. Galbraith and G. B. Merrill, "The Politics of Forecasting: Managing the Truth*," California Management Review* (Winter 1996), pp. 29–43.

72. M. Garbuio, D. Lovallo, and P. Viguerie, "How Companies Spend Their Money: A McKinsey Global Survey," *McKinsey Quarterly Online* (June 2007).

73. M. A. Geletkanycz and D. C. Hambrick, "The External Ties of Top Executives: Implications for Strategic Choice and Performance," *Administrative Science Quarterly* (December 1997), pp. 654–681.

74. M. Song, R. J. Calantone, and C. A. Di Benedetto, "Competitive Forces and Strategic Choice Decisions: An Experimental Investigation in the United States and Japan," *Strategic Management Journal* (October 2002), pp. 969–978.

75. M. A. Hitt, M. T. Dacin, B. B. Tyler, and D. Park, "Understanding the Differences in Korean and U.S. Executives' Strategic Orientation," *Strategic Management Journal* (February 1997), pp. 159–167; L. G. Thomas III and G. Waring, "Competing Capitalisms: Capital Investment in American, German, and Japanese Firms," *Strategic Management Journal* (August 1999), pp. 729–748.

76. M. H. Bazerman and D. Chugh, "Decisions Without Blinders," *Harvard Business Review* (January 2006), pp. 88–97.

77. J. A. Wagner III and R. Z. Gooding, "Equivocal Information and Attribution: An Investigation of Patterns of Managerial Sensemaking," *Strategic Management Journal* (April 1997), pp. 275–286; K. Shimizu and M. A. Hitt, "Strategic Flexibility: Organizational Preparedness to Reverse Ineffective Strategic Decisions," *Academy of Management Executive* (November 2004), pp. 44–59.

78. M. L. A. Hayward and K. Shimizu, "De-Commitment to Losing Strategic Action: Evidence from the Divestiture of Poorly Performing Acquisitions," *Strategic Management Journal* (June 2006), pp. 541–557.

79. J. Ross and B. M. Staw, "Organizational Escalation and Exit: Lessons from the Shoreham Nuclear Power Plant," *Academy of Management Journal* (August 1993), pp. 701–732; P. W. Mulvey, J. F. Veiga, and P. M. Elsass, "When Teammates Raise a White Flag," *Academy of Management Executive* (February 1996), pp. 40–49.

80. P. C. Nutt, *Why Decisions Fail* (San Francisco: Berrett-Koehler, 2002).

81. P. C. Nutt, "Expanding the Search for Alternatives During Strategic Decision-Making," *Academy of Management Executive* (November 2004), pp. 13–28.

82. K. Shimizu, "Prospect Theory, Behavioral Theory, and the Threat-Rigidity Thesis: Combinative Effects on Organizational Decisions to Divest Formerly Acquired Units," *Academy of Management Journal* (December 2007), pp. 1495–1514.

83. G. P. West III and G. D. Meyer, "To Agree or Not to Agree? Consensus and Performance in New Ventures," *Journal of Business Venturing* (September 1998), pp. 395–422; L. Markoczy, "Consensus Formation During Strategic Change," *Strategic Management Journal* (November 2001), pp. 1013–1031.

84. B. J. Olson, S. Parayitam, and Y. Bao, "Strategic Decision Making: The Effects of Cognitive Diversity, Conflict, and Trust on Decision Outcomes," *Journal of Management* (April 2007), pp. 196–222.

85. A. C. Amason, "Distinguishing the Effects of Functional and Dysfunctional Conflict on Strategic Decision Making: Resolving a Paradox for Top Management Teams," *Academy of Management Journal* (February 1996), pp. 123–148; A. C. Amason and H. J. Sapienza, "The Effects of Top Management Team Size and Interaction Norms on Cognitive and Affective Conflict," *Journal of Management* (Vol. 23, No. 4, 1997), pp. 495–516.

86. D. M. Schweiger, W. R. Sandberg, and P. L. Rechner, "Experiential Effects of Dialectical Inquiry, Devil's Advocacy, and Consensus Approaches to Strategic Decision Making," *Academy of Management Journal* (December 1989), pp. 745–772; G. Whyte, "Decision Failures: Why They Occur and How to Prevent Them," *Academy of Management Executive* (August 1991), pp. 23–31; R. L. Priem, D. A. Harrison, and N. K. Muir, "Structured Conflict and Consensus Outcomes in Group Decision Making," *Journal of Management* (Vol. 21, No. 4, 1995), pp. 691–710.

87. S. C. Abraham, "Using Bundles to Find the Best Strategy," *Strategy & Leadership* (July/August/September 1999), pp. 53–55.

88. O. Gadiesh and J. L Gilbert, "Transforming Corner-Office Strategy into Frontline Action," *Harvard Business Review* (May 2001), pp. 73–79.

89. E. Dane and M. G. Pratt, "Exploring Intuition and Its Role in Managerial Decision Making," *Academy of Management Review* (January 2007), pp. 33–54.

90. A. M. Hayashi, "When to Trust Your Gut," *Harvard Business Review* (February 2001), pp. 59–65.

91. E. Dane and M. G. Pratt, "Exploring Intuition and Its Role in Managerial Decision Making," *Academy of Management Review* (January 2007), pp. 33–54.

92. A. M. Hayashi, pp. 59–60.

93. C. Holahan, "Going, Going . . . Everywhere," *BusinessWeek* (June 18, 2007), pp. 62–64.

94. S. Mitra, "eBay floundering again," SeekingAlpha, February 23, 2016 (seekingalpha.com/article/3921686-ebay-floundering); investors.ebayinc.com/releasedetail.cfm.

PART 4

Strategy
Implementation
and Control

CHAPTER **9**

Strategy Implementation: Global Strategy

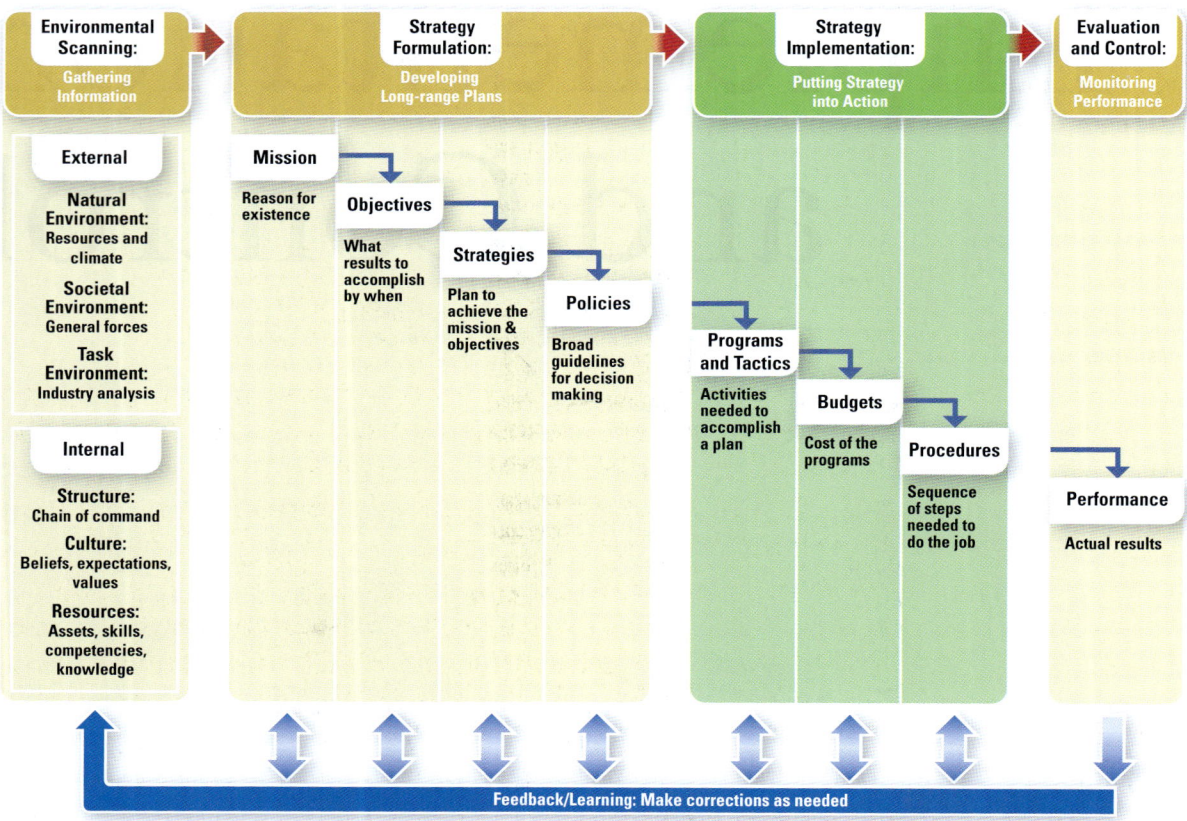

Environmental Scanning:	Strategy Formulation:	Strategy Implementation:	Evaluation and Control:
Gathering Information	Developing Long-range Plans	Putting Strategy into Action	Monitoring Performance

External

Natural Environment: Resources and climate

Societal Environment: General forces

Task Environment: Industry analysis

Internal

Structure: Chain of command

Culture: Beliefs, expectations, values

Resources: Assets, skills, competencies, knowledge

Mission — Reason for existence

Objectives — What results to accomplish by when

Strategies — Plan to achieve the mission & objectives

Policies — Broad guidelines for decision making

Programs and Tactics — Activities needed to accomplish a plan

Budgets — Cost of the programs

Procedures — Sequence of steps needed to do the job

Performance — Actual results

Feedback/Learning: Make corrections as needed

Pearson MyLab Management®

⭐ **Improve Your Grade!**

Over 10 million students improved their results using the Pearson MyLabs. Visit **mymanagementlab.com** for simulations, tutorials, and end-of-chapter problems.

Learning Objectives

After reading this chapter, you should be able to:

9-1. Describe the means of entry by which an organization can do business in another country

9-2. Explain the elements of International Strategic Alliances that lead to success

9-3. Discuss the stages of International Development

9-4. Explain how companies can improve their staffing efforts as they expand beyond their home country

9-5. Discuss the unique issues related to Measuring Organizational performance that are presented with the administration of a truly international company

UNIQLO – From Japan to Asia to the World

Founded in 1949, UNIQLO, a Japanese fashion retailer from the Fast Retailing group, opened a unisex casual wear store in Fukuro-machi, Naka-ku, Hiroshima, under the name "Unique Clothing Warehouse," and later converted to its current brand name. As of November 2016, UNIQLO Japan had 841 stores. By 2016, UNIQLO has over 1,700 stores worldwide and around 40,000 global employees.

Fast Retailing adopted a set of strategies from the American retailer GAP Inc. known as "SPA" (specialty-store/retailer of private-label apparel), under which they produce their own clothing and sell it exclusively. By having a SPA business model, UNIQLO could deliver high-quality, affordable, and innovative apparel to consumers. The concept of this brand is "Made for All." It means UNIQLO offers a basic casual outfit that everyone can wear daily.

There has been major growth in Asia, with 497 stores in Greater China (Mainland China, Hong Kong, and Taiwan), 178 in South Korea, and 248 in Southeast Asia and Oceania. However, the Fast Retailing group currently ranks as the forth place as global fashion retailer, just behind Inditex (Zara), H&M, and GAP. The company's global mission is to grow from a Japanese company to a Japan-born global firm. They strive to be the best apparel manufacturer retailer from Japan, to Asia, and to the world by 2020. To achieve this goal UNIQLO needs to employ and nurture managers to develop business throughout the world. However, UNIQLO is known as a company that has a traditionally Japanese working culture. It has a company standards manual book, which is translated into various languages and is distributed globally to ensure that everyone follows the same global standards. The main principles include Global One ("global approach") and Zen-in Keiei ("all employees with the mindset of a manager"). UNIQLO trains employees to embody these standards in their work. While it makes sense for a global company to share same standards and regulations, due to cultural differences and management styles, it leads to a high turnover ratio especially overseas. In order to tackle this diversity issue, UNIQLO supports women's progress, and gives importance to advancing a regional regular employee program, allowing temporary employees to become permanent employees.

SOURCES: Based on information from Fast Retailing Website, http://www.fastretailing.com/, accessed February 8, 2017; and Tadashi Yanai, "The Fast Retailing in 2020: My Views on Management," Fast Retailing, https://www.fastretailing.com/eng/ir/library/pdf/presen080903_Yanai.pdf, accessed February, 2017.

One of the most competitive and difficult aspects of Strategy Implementation is a move to extend business operations outside of the home country of the company.

Global Strategy is the sum total of the activities that an organization takes in order to compete in markets outside its home country. Given that one of the three pillars of this text is globalization you will note that we have crafted a global issues section into every chapter, have utilized global organizations as examples and have addressed unique concerns that arise with the operation of a global organization. Many companies start with sales outside the country in which the business begins and virtually every company eventually has sales in many other countries. However, running a truly global organization is far more than simply selling goods & services around the world, it is an operational mindset that has its own unique issues and concerns.

In this chapter, we will address some of the unique issues that arise in the move to and the running of a truly global business. This will include means of entry, international coordination, stages of international development, international employment and measurement of performance.

International Entry

9-1. Describe the means of entry by which an organization can do business in another country

Research indicates that shareholders reward companies who grow faster outside of the United States and that growing internationally is positively associated with firm profitability.[1] Tumi (the high-end luggage company) aggressively pushed a global expansion strategy and reported record sales and earnings in 2016, despite foreign exchange issues.[2] A corporation can select from several strategic options regarding the most appropriate method for entering a foreign market or establishing facilities in another country. The options vary from simple exporting to acquisitions to management contracts.

Some of the most popular options for international entry are as follows:

- **Exporting:** A good way to minimize risk and experiment with a specific product is **exporting**, shipping goods produced in the company's home country to other countries for marketing. The company could choose to handle all critical functions itself, or it could contract these functions to an export management company. Exporting is popular for small businesses because of the Internet and rapid advance of overnight express services, which has reduced the once-formidable costs of exporting. About 10% of the sales of High West Distillery in Park City, UT comes from exports to the United Kingdom, Canada, Australia, Hong Kong and others.[3]

- **Licensing:** Under a **licensing** agreement, the licensing firm grants rights to another firm in the host country to produce and/or sell a product. The licensee pays compensation to the licensing firm in return for technical and sometimes marketing expertise. This is an especially useful strategy if the trademark or brand name is well known but the company does not have sufficient funds to finance its entering the country directly, the technology is unique and not easily replicable or if the country makes entry via investment difficult or impossible. Rovi Corporation (guides and recommendation engines for online searches) signed a license agreement with Funai Electric Co. Ltd., covering Japan and Europe that enabled Funai to use Rovi's patent portfolio for digital consumer electronics.[4] This strategy is also important if the country makes entry via investment either difficult or impossible.

- **Franchising:** Under a **franchising** agreement, the franchiser grants rights to another company to open a retail store using the franchiser's name and operating system. In exchange, the franchisee pays the franchiser a percentage of its sales as a royalty. Franchising provides an opportunity for a firm to establish a presence in countries where the population or per capita spending is not sufficient for a major expansion effort.[5] However, the more important element of franchising is the ability of the franchisor to expand rapidly with minimal capital investment. Franchising has enabled McDonald's to grow to a worldwide powerhouse. More than 80% of their worldwide locations and nearly 90% of the locations in the United States are franchised.[6]

- **Joint ventures:** Forming a **joint venture** between a foreign corporation and a domestic company has been one of the most popular strategies used to enter a new country.[7] Companies often form joint ventures to combine the resources and expertise needed to develop new products or technologies. A joint venture may be an association between a company and a firm in the host country or a government agency in that country. A quick method of obtaining local management, it also reduces the risks of expropriation and harassment by host country officials. A joint venture may also enable a firm to enter a country that restricts foreign ownership. The corporation can enter another country with fewer assets at stake and thus lower risk. Under Indian law, for example, foreign retailers are permitted to own no more than 51% of shops selling single-brand products, or to sell to others on a wholesale basis. These and other restrictions deterred supermarket giants Tesco and Carrefour from entering India. As a result, 97% of Indian retailing is composed of small, family-run stores. Eager to enter India, Wal-Mart's management formed an equal partnership joint venture in 2007 with Bharti Enterprises to start wholesale operations. Under the name Best Price, they opened their first store in 2009 and had opened 21 retail stores by 2016.[8]

- **Acquisitions:** A relatively quick way to move into an international area is through acquisitions—purchasing another company already operating in that area. Synergistic benefits can result if the company acquires a firm with strong complementary product lines and a good distribution network. For example, Belgium's InBev purchased Anheuser-Busch in 2008 for US$52 billion to obtain a solid position in the profitable North American beer market. Before the acquisition, InBev had only a small presence in the United States, but a strong one in Europe and Latin American, where Anheuser-Busch was weak.[9] Research suggests that wholly owned subsidiaries are more successful in international undertakings than are strategic alliances, such as joint ventures.[10] This is one reason why firms more experienced in international markets take a higher ownership position when making a foreign investment.[11] Cross-border Merger and Acquisitions amounted to more than US$441 billion in the first half of 2015, up 136% from the same time period in 2014.[12] In some countries, however, acquisitions can be difficult to arrange because of a lack of available information about potential candidates. Government restrictions on ownership, such as the U.S. requirement that limits foreign ownership of U.S. airlines to 49% of nonvoting and 25% of voting stock, can also discourage acquisitions.

- **Green-field development:** If a company doesn't want to purchase another company's problems along with its assets, it may choose **green-field development** and build its own manufacturing plant and distribution system. Research indicates that firms possessing high levels of technology, multinational experience, and diverse product lines prefer green-field development to acquisitions.[13] This is usually a far more complicated and expensive operation than acquisition, but it allows a company more freedom in designing the plant, choosing suppliers, and hiring a workforce. For example, Nissan, Honda, and Toyota built auto factories in rural areas of Great Britain and then hired a young workforce with no experience in the industry. BMW did the same thing when it built its auto plant in Spartanburg, South Carolina, to make its Z3 and Z4 sports cars. In early 2016, BMW announced it had exported its 2,000,000 vehicles built in South Carolina. Seventy percent of the vehicles made in Spartanburg are shipped around the world through the Port of Charleston.[14]

■ **Production sharing:** Coined by Peter Drucker, the term **production sharing** generally refers to the process of combining the higher labor skills and technology available in developed countries with the lower-cost labor available in developing countries. Often called *outsourcing*, many companies have moved data processing, programming, and customer service activities "offshore" to Ireland, India, Barbados, Jamaica, the Philippines, and Singapore, where wages are lower, English is spoken, and strong telecommunications networks are in place. Payroll outsourcing is the fastest growing segment of global human resource outsourcing. It is expected to grow at a compound annual growth rate of 4.4% between 2016 and 2020.[15]

■ **Turnkey operations: Turnkey operations** are typically contracts for the construction of operating facilities in exchange for a fee. The facilities are transferred to the host country or firm when they are complete. The customer is usually a government agency of a country that has decreed that a particular product must be produced locally and under its control. For example, Fiat built an auto plant in Togliatti, Russia, for the Soviet Union in the late 1960s to produce an older model of Fiat under the brand name of Lada. MNCs that perform turnkey operations are frequently industrial equipment manufacturers that supply some of their own equipment for the project and that commonly sell replacement parts and maintenance services to the host country. They thereby create customers as well as future competitors. Interestingly, Renault purchased a 25% stake in the same Togliatti factory and in 2013 was allowed to purchase a majority stake in the business along with their partner Nissan. By 2016 it employed more than 44,000 people.[16]

■ **BOT concept:** The **BOT (Build, Operate, Transfer) concept** is a variation of the turnkey operation. Instead of turning the facility (usually a power plant or toll road) over to the host country when completed, the company operates the facility for a fixed period of time during which it earns back its investment, plus a profit. It then turns the facility over to the government at little or no cost to the host country. In 2013 the State of North Carolina contracted with the Spanish firm Cintra Infraestructuras to build toll lanes on I77. They had previously built the Chicago Skyway and the Indiana East-West Toll Road. North Carolina will contribute $88 million toward the $655 million project with Cintra paying the remaining amount. For that, Cintra will receive toll revenues for 50 years before turning it back over the State. Construction work began in late 2015 and is expected to be completed within three-and-a-half years.[17]

■ **Management contracts:** A large corporation operating throughout the world is likely to have a large amount of management talent at its disposal. **Management contracts** offer a means through which a corporation can use some of its personnel to assist a firm in a host country for a specified fee and period of time. Management contracts are common when a host government expropriates part or all of a foreign-owned company's holdings in its country. The contracts allow the firm to continue to earn some income from its investment and keep the operations going until local management is trained.[18]

International Coordination

9-2. Explain the elements of International Strategic Alliances that lead to success

An international company is one that engages in any combination of activities, from exporting/importing to full-scale manufacturing, in foreign countries. A **multinational corporation (MNC)**, in contrast, is a highly developed international company with a deep involvement throughout the world, plus a worldwide perspective in its management and decision making. For an MNC to be considered global, it must manage its worldwide operations as if they were totally interconnected. This approach works best when the industry has moved from being *multidomestic* (each country's industry is essentially separate from the same industry in other countries) to *global* (each country is a part of one worldwide industry).

The global MNC faces the dual challenge of achieving scale economies through standardization while at the same time responding to local customer differences.

The design of the organization is strongly affected by the sophistication of its international activities and the types of industries in which the company is involved. Strategic alliances may complement or even substitute for an internal functional activity.

INTERNATIONAL STRATEGIC ALLIANCES

Strategic alliances, such as joint ventures and licensing agreements, between an MNC and a local partner in a host country are becoming increasingly popular as a means by which a corporation can gain entry into other countries, especially countries that limit foreign ownership. The key to the successful implementation of these strategies is the selection of the local partner. Each party needs to assess not only the strategic fit of each company's project strategy but also the fit of each company's respective resources. A successful joint venture may require years of prior contacts between the parties. A prior relationship helps to develop a level of trust, which facilitates openness in sharing knowledge and a reduced fear of opportunistic behavior by the alliance partners. This is especially important when the environmental uncertainty is high.[19]

Research reveals that firms favor past partners when forming new alliances.[20]

Key drivers for strategic fit between alliance partners are the following:

- Partners must agree on fundamental values and have a shared vision about the potential for joint value creation.
- Alliance strategy must be derived from business, corporate, and functional strategy.
- The alliance must be important to both partners, especially to top management.
- Partners must be mutually dependent for achieving clear and realistic objectives.
- Joint activities must have added value for customers and the partners.
- The alliance must be accepted by key stakeholders.
- Partners contribute key strengths but protect core competencies.[21]

Stages of International Development

9-3. Discuss the stages of International Development

Corporations operating internationally tend to evolve through five common stages, both in their relationships with widely dispersed geographic markets and in the manner in which they structure their operations and programs. These **stages of international development** are:

- **Stage 1 (Domestic company):** The primarily domestic company exports some of its products through local dealers and distributors in the foreign countries. The impact on the organization's structure is minimal because an export department at corporate headquarters handles everything. Eden Brewery is a UK microbrewery that joined a trade mission organized by UK Trade and Investment, after Eden identified Japan as a potential market for its craft beer. While there the company met with distributors and outlets interested in importing the beer to Japan.[22] The whole process can take some time to set up, but is run fairly simply from an organizational perspective.

- **Stage 2 (Domestic company with export division):** Success in Stage 1 leads the company to establish its own sales company with offices in other countries to eliminate the middlemen and to better control marketing. Because exports have now become more important, the company establishes an export division to oversee foreign sales offices.

- **Stage 3 (Primarily domestic company with international division):** Success in earlier stages leads the company to establish manufacturing facilities in addition to sales and service offices in key countries. The company now adds an international division with responsibilities for most of the business functions conducted in other countries.

- **Stage 4 (Multinational corporation with multidomestic emphasis):** Now a full-fledged MNC, the company increases its investments in other countries. The company establishes a local operating division or company in the host country, such as Ford of Britain, to better serve the market. The product line is expanded, and local manufacturing capacity is established. Managerial functions (product development, finance, marketing, and so on) are organized locally. Over time, the parent company acquires other related businesses, broadening the base of the local operating division. As the subsidiary in the host country successfully develops a strong regional presence, it achieves greater autonomy and self-sufficiency. The operations in each country are, nevertheless, managed separately as if each is a domestic company.

- **Stage 5 (MNC with global emphasis):** The most successful MNCs move into a fifth stage in which they have worldwide human resources, R&D, and financing strategies. Typically operating in a global industry, the MNC denationalizes its operations and plans product design, manufacturing, and marketing around worldwide considerations. Global considerations now dominate organizational design. The global MNC structures itself in a matrix form around some combination of geographic areas, product lines, and functions. All managers are responsible for dealing with international as well as domestic issues.

Research provides some support for stages of international development, but it does not necessarily support the preceding sequence of stages. For example, a company may initiate production and sales in multiple countries without having gone through the steps of exporting or having local sales subsidiaries. In addition, any one corporation can be at different stages simultaneously, with different products in different markets at different levels. Firms may also leapfrog across stages to a global emphasis.

International Employment

9-4. Explain how companies can improve their staffing efforts as they expand beyond their home country

Implementing a strategy of international expansion takes a lot of planning and can be very expensive. Nearly 80% of midsize and larger companies send some of their employees abroad – known as expatriation and the employees are known as expats. The Economist reported that over three-quarters of companies report spending two to three times an expat's annual salary on a typical assignment.[23] Research tells us that between 20% and 45% of expatriate assignments are failures with managers sent abroad returning early because of job dissatisfaction or difficulties in adjusting to a foreign country. Of those who stayed for the duration of their assignment, nearly one-third did not perform as well as expected. One-fourth of those completing an assignment left their company within one year of returning home—often leaving to join a competitor.[24] One common mistake is failing to educate the person about the customs and values in other countries.

Primarily due to cultural differences, managerial style and human resource practices must be tailored to fit the particular situations in other countries. Only 11% of human resource managers have ever worked abroad, most have little understanding of a global assignment's unique personal and professional challenges and thus fail to develop the training necessary for such an assignment.[25] This is complicated by the fact that 90% of companies select employees for an international assignment based on their technical expertise while ignoring other areas.[26] A lack of knowledge of national and ethnic differences can make managing an international operation extremely difficult. One such example that shows the issues that have to be dealt with exists in Malaysia. Three ethnic groups live in Malaysia (Malay, Chinese, and Indian), each with their own language and religion, attending different schools, and a preference to not work in the same factories with each other. Because of the importance of cultural distinctions such as these, multinational corporations (MNCs) are now putting more emphasis on intercultural training for managers being sent on an assignment to a foreign country..[27]

To improve organizational learning, many MNCs are providing their managers with international assignments lasting as long as five years. Upon their return to headquarters, these expatriates have an in-depth understanding of the company's operations in another part of the world. This has value to the extent that these employees communicate this understanding to others in decision-making positions. Research indicates that an MNC performs at a higher level when its CEO has international experience.[28] Global MNCs, in particular, emphasize international experience, have a greater number of senior managers who have been expatriates, and have a strong focus on leadership development through the expatriate experience.[29] Unfortunately, not all corporations appropriately manage international assignments. While out of the country, a person may be overlooked for an important promotion (out of sight, out of mind). Upon his or her return to the home country, co-workers may discount the out-of-country experience as a waste of time. The perceived lack of organizational support for international assignments increases the likelihood that an expatriate will return home early.[30]

Recent work on the subject has led to a set of recommendations to improve the entire expatriation process:

- Have a compelling reason for sending a current employee to a new country. Vague ideas about broadening a person will quickly lead to frustration and loss of productivity. A business case should be made for every assignment.

- Choose individuals who are open to the assignment and committed to adapt to the new environment.

- Assign sponsors/mentors in both the home country and the new country.

- Develop a means of maintaining very open, frequent communication throughout the assignment.

- Design a plan for repatriation. Communication should begin six months before the end of the assignment to discuss the process. The employee should outline the top skills, qualifications, and insights achieved during the assignment and express how he or she would like to incorporate them at the home office (or in some cases on the next assignment).

- Craft an approach for sharing the experiences and lessons learned within the company. One organization asks assignees to blog about their experiences — both during and after the assignment. These posts are shared via internal social media and commented on by others throughout the company.[31]

Once a corporation has established itself in another country, it generally hires and promotes people from the host country into higher-level positions. For example, most large MNCs attempt to fill managerial positions in their subsidiaries with well-qualified citizens of the host countries. One of the fastest growing MNCs in the past few years has been Uber. Uber had grown to almost 400 cities worldwide by 2016 and tries to hire general managers with local experience.[32] This policy serves to placate nationalistic governments and to better attune management practices to the host country's culture. The danger in using primarily foreign nationals to staff managerial positions in subsidiaries is the increased likelihood of suboptimization (the local subsidiary ignores the needs of the larger parent corporation). This makes it difficult for an MNC to meet its long-term, worldwide objectives. To a local national in an MNC subsidiary, the corporation as a whole can be an abstraction. Communication and coordination across subsidiaries become more difficult. As it becomes harder to coordinate the activities of several international subsidiaries, an MNC will have serious problems operating in a global industry.

Another approach to staffing the managerial positions of MNCs is to use people with an "international" orientation, regardless of their country of origin or host country assignment. This is a widespread practice among European firms. For example, Electrolux, a Swedish firm, had a French director in its Singapore factory. Using third-country "nationals" can allow for more opportunities for promotion than does Uber's policy of hiring local people, but it can also result in more misunderstandings and conflicts with the local employees and with the host country's government.

MNCs with a high level of international interdependence among activities need to provide their managers with significant international assignments and experiences as part of their training and development. Such assignments provide future corporate leaders with a series of valuable international contacts in addition to a better personal understanding of international issues and global linkages among corporate activities.[33] Research reveals that corporations using cross-national teams, whose members have international experience and communicate frequently with overseas managers, have greater product development capabilities than others.[34] Executive recruiters have reported that more major corporations are now requiring candidates to have international experience.[35]

Since an increasing number of multinational corporations are primarily organized around business units and product lines instead of geographic areas, product and SBU managers who are based at corporate headquarters are often traveling around the world to work personally with country managers. These managers and other mobile workers are being called *stealth expatriates* because they are either cross-border commuters (especially in the EU) or the accidental expatriate who goes on many business trips or temporary assignments due to offshoring and/or international joint ventures.[36]

Measurement of Performance

9-5. Discuss the unique issues related to Measuring Organizational performance that are presented with the administration of a truly international company

The three most widely used techniques for international performance evaluation are ROI, budget analysis, and historical comparisons. In one study, 95% of the corporate officers interviewed stated that they use the same evaluation techniques for foreign and domestic operations. Rate of return was mentioned as the single most important measure.[37] However, ROI can cause problems when it is applied to international operations: Because of foreign currencies, different accounting systems, different rates of inflation, different tax laws, and the use of transfer pricing, both the net income figure and the investment base may be seriously distorted.[38] To deal with different accounting systems throughout the world, the London-based International Accounting Standards Board developed International Financial Reporting Standards (IFRS) to harmonize accounting practices. The Financial Accounting Standards Board (FASB) oversees the Generally Accepted Accounting Principles (GAAP) that is used in the United States. For over a decade, these two groups worked to merge their systems and there was hope that there would be a single set of standards by 2015, however much like bringing the metric system to the United States, implementation has not gone as planned. More than 116 countries worldwide adopted IFRS while the United States and seven other countries have maintained their own standards.[39]

Nevertheless, enforcement and cultural interpretations of the international rules can still vary by country and may undercut what is hoped to be a uniform accounting system.[40]

A study of 79 MNCs revealed that *international transfer pricing* from one country unit to another is primarily used not to evaluate performance but to minimize taxes.[41] Taxes are an important issue for MNCs, given that corporate tax rates vary from 40% in the United States to 33% in Japan, 35% in India, 30% in Mexico, 20% in the United Kingdom, 24% in South Korea, 26% in Canada, 25% in China, 17% in Singapore, 15% in Albania, and 0% in Bahrain and the Cayman Islands.[42] Recently there has been an uproar about the issue with companies moving operations / headquarters to Ireland with its 12.5% corporate tax rate. In 2016, Apple was being investigated by regulators who had accused the iPhone maker of using subsidiaries in Ireland to avoid paying taxes on revenue generated outside the United States.[43]

Parts made in a subsidiary of a Japanese MNC in a low-tax country such as Singapore could be shipped to its subsidiary in a high-tax country like the United States at such a high price that the U.S. subsidiary reports very little profit (and thus pays few taxes), while the Singapore subsidiary reports a very high profit (but also pays few taxes because of the lower tax rate). A Japanese MNC could, therefore, earn more profit worldwide by reporting less profit in high-tax countries and more profit in low-tax countries. Transfer pricing can thus be one way the parent company can reduce taxes and "capture profits" from a subsidiary. Other common ways of transferring profits to the parent company (often referred to as the *repatriation of profits*) are through dividends, royalties, and management fees.[44]

Among the most important barriers to international trade are the different standards for products and services. There are at least three categories of standards: safety/ environmental, energy efficiency, and testing procedures. Existing standards have been drafted by such bodies as the British Standards Institute (BSI-UK) in the United Kingdom, the Japanese Industrial Standards Committee (JISC), AFNOR in France, DIN in Germany, CSA in Canada, and the American Standards Institute in the United States. These standards traditionally created entry barriers that served to fragment various industries, such as major home appliances, by country. The International Electrotechnical Commission (IEC) standards were created to harmonize standards in the European Union and eventually to serve as worldwide standards, with some national deviations to satisfy specific needs. Because the European Union (EU) was the first to harmonize the many different standards of its member countries, the EU shaped standards for the rest of the world. In addition, the International Organization for Standardization (ISO) published detailed international standards. These standards provided a foundation for regional associations to build upon. CANENA, the Council for Harmonization of Electrotechnical Standards of the Nations of the Americas, was created in 1992 to further coordinate the harmonization of standards in North and South America.[45]

Authorities in international business recommend that the control and reward systems used by a global MNC be different from those used by a multidomestic MNC.[46]

A *MNC* should use loose controls on its foreign units. The management of each geographic unit should be given considerable operational latitude, but it should be expected to meet some performance targets. Because profit and ROI measures are often unreliable in international operations, it is recommended that the MNC's top management, in this instance, emphasize budgets and non-financial measures of performance such as market share, productivity, public image, employee morale, and relations with the host country government.[47] Multiple measures should be used to differentiate between the worth of the subsidiary and the performance of its management.

A *global MNC*, however, needs tight controls over its many units. To reduce costs and gain competitive advantage, it is trying to spread the manufacturing and marketing operations of a few fairly uniform products around the world. Therefore, its key operational decisions must be centralized. Its environmental scanning must include research not only into each of the national markets in which the MNC competes but also into the "global arena" of the interaction between markets. Foreign units are thus evaluated more as cost centers, revenue centers, or expense centers than as investment or profit centers because MNCs operating in a global industry do not often make the entire product in the country in which it is sold.

End of Chapter SUMMARY

Addressing global issues is simply an expectation of the modern organization. The question becomes how and when to expand operations beyond the borders of the company's home country. Six Flags theme parks were looking for a means of expanding their opportunities outside of their core parks in North America (United States, Canada & Mexico). In 2016 they announced a licensing arrangement with NaVi Entertainment in Vietnam to build a theme park and a water park in Vietnam using the Six Flags and Six Flags Hurricane Harbor brand names, respectively. The move allows the largest regional theme park company to expand outside the borders while minimizing the downside risk.[48]

This approach is often a prelude the full-blown multi-national company. Zara Stores are the flagship operation of Inditex and headquartered in the Spanish coastal town of A Coruña. Zara had expanded to over 7,000 stores worldwide by early 2016. Sales grew by more than 15% from the previous year driven by sales outside of Spain. The company runs an MNC on the retail side of the business growing not only their store footprint (they added over 300 new stores worldwide in 2015), but also growing an extensive set of innovative Internet Shopping sites that were in 29 market locations, many of which were in Asia. The company controls the fundamental elements of the business from Spain. All textile design, manufacturing and distribution facilities are located in Spain.[49] MNC's that operate in many countries with full resources within those countries include companies such as Coca-Cola, Wal-Mart, and BMW.

Pearson MyLab Management®

Go to **mymanagementlab.com** to complete the problems marked with this icon ⭐.

KEY TERMS

Acquisition (p. 283)
BOT (Build, Operate, Transfer) concept (p. 284)
Exporting (p. 282)
Franchising (p. 282)
Green-field development (p. 283)

Joint venture (p. 283)
Licensing (p. 282)
Management contracts (p. 284)
Multinational Corporation (MNC) (p. 284)
Production sharing (p. 284)

Stages of international development (p. 285)
Global strategy (p. 285)
Turnkey operations (p. 284)

Pearson MyLab Management®

Go to **mymanagementlab.com** for the following Assisted-graded writing questions:

9-1. What are the nine means by which a company can enter a new international market?
9-2. What are the advantages of using a Strategic alliance when operating in a new country?

DISCUSSION QUESTIONS

9-3. What are the stages of International Development?
9-4. How can an expat program be improved to the benefit of the organization?

9-5. Why is strategic flexibility important for strategy formulation when an organisation is at the growth stage?

NOTES

1. J. Cryan, "4 Real Benefits from International Expansion," *Chief Executive*, April 16, 2012 (http://chiefexecutive.net/4-real-benefits-from-international-expansion/); A. Delios and P. W. Beamish, "Geographic Scope, Product Diversification, and the Corporate Performance of Japanese Firms," *Strategic Management Journal* (August 1999), pp. 711–727.
2. "Tumi Holdings Inc. Earnings: Global Expansion Fuels Profit Growth," *The Motley Fool*, February 26, 2016 (http://www.fool.com/investing/general/2016/02/26/tumi-holdings-inc-earnings-global-expansion-fuels.aspx).
3 K. Kulp, "Your local booze gets the world drunk," *The Daily Beast*, March 19, 2016 (http://www.thedailybeast.com/articles/2016/03/19/how-craft-distillers-are-selling-their-drinks-to-the-world.html).
4. "Rovi Extends Product and Entertainment Discovery Patent License Agreement to Funai," Multichannel News, July 29, 2015 (http://www.multichannel.com/prfeed/rovi-extends-product-and-entertainment-discovery-patent-license-agreement-funai/392591).
5. E. Elango and V. H. Fried, "Franchising Research: A Literature Review and Synthesis," *Journal of Small Business Management* (July 1997), pp. 68–81.
6. http://www.aboutmcdonalds.com/mcd/our_company/business-model.html.
7. J. E. McCann III, "The Growth of Acquisitions in Services," *Long Range Planning* (December 1996), pp. 835–841.
8. http://www.wal-martindia.in/about-us/.
9. A Bid for Bud," *The Economist* (June 21, 2008), p. 77.
10. B. Voss, "Strategic Federations Frequently Falter in Far East," *Journal of Business Strategy* (July/August 1993), p. 6 S. Douma, "Success and Failure in New Ventures," *Long Range Planning* (April 1991), pp. 54–60.
11. A. Delios and P. W. Beamish, "Ownership Strategy of Japanese Firms: Transactional, Institutional, and Experience Approaches," *Strategic Management Journal* (October 1999), pp. 915–933.
12. "Recovery in Cross-Border Mergers and Acquisitions," *Global Investment Trends Monitor*, United Nations (UNCTAD), November 17, 2015 (unctad.org/en/publicationslibrary/webdiaeia2015d5_en.pdf).
13. K. D. Brouthers and L. E. Brouthers, "Acquisition or Greenfield Start-up? Institutional, Cultural, and Transaction Cost Influences," *Strategic Management Journal* (January 2000), pp. 89–97.
14. K. Bolster, "SCPA and BMW celebrate two-millionth vehicle export," Wistv.com, March 18, 2016 (http://www.wistv.com/story/31497619/scpa-and-bmw-celebrate-two-millionth-vehicle-export).
15. "Global Payroll Outsourcing Market 2016-2020," *PRNewswire*, February 15, 2016 (www.prnewswire.com/news-releases/global-payroll-outsourcing-market-2016-2020-300220297.html)..
16. G. Jackson, "Renault profit up but headlights on struggling Russian unit," *Yahoo!News*, February 12, 2016 (news.yahoo.com/Renault-net-profit-russian-unit-drag-091727015.html).

17. S. Lyttle, "NC has a bidder for I-77 toll lanes," *The Charlotte Observer*, April 11, 2014 (www.charlotteobserver.com /news/local/article9111983.html); J. Naisbitt, *Megatrends Asia* (New York: Simon & Schuster, 1996), p. 143 http:// www.ncdot.gov/projects/I-77ExpressLanes/.

18. For additional information on international entry modes, see D. F. Spulber, *Global Competitive Strategy* (Cambridge, UK: Cambridge University Press, 2007) and K. D. Brouthers and J-F Hennart, "Boundaries of the Firm: Insights from International Entry Mode Research," *Journal of Management* (June 2007), pp. 395–425.

19. R. Krishnan, X. Martin, and N. G. Noorderhaven, "When Does Trust Matter to Alliance Performance," *Academy of Management Journal* (October 2006), pp. 894–917.

20. S. X. Li and T. J. Rowley, "Inertia and Evaluation Mechanisms in Interorganizational Partner Selection: Syndicate Formation Among U.S. Investment Banks," *Academy of Management Journal* (December 2002), pp. 1104–1119.

21. M. U. Douma, J. Bilderbeek, P. J. Idenburg, and J. K. Loise, "Strategic Alliances: Managing the Dynamics of Fit," *Long Range Planning* (August 2000), pp. 579–598; W. Hoffmann and R. Schlosser, "Success Factors of Strategic Alliances in Small and Medium-Sized Enterprises—An Empirical Survey," *Long Range Planning* (June 2001), pp. 357–381; Y. Luo, "How Important Are Shared Perceptions of Procedural Justice in -Cooperative Alliances?" *Academy of Management Journal* (August 2005), pp. 695–709.

22. "Cumbrian micro-brewery aims to start exporting to Japan," *The News and Star*, March 23, 2016 (http://www .newsandstar.co.uk/news/business/Cumbrian-micro -brewery-aims-to-start-exporting-to-Japan-c886f335-dc68 -4c8c-b36e-2b773fc15c29-ds).

23. "Expatriate costs and assignments," *The Economist,* July 24, 2012 (http://www.economist.com/blogs /graphicdetail/2012/07/focus-3).

24. S. Mahoney, "Can you afford to throw away £2 million of your organisation's money on a failed Expat Assignment?" *Business Reporter*, May 21, 2015 (http://business- reporter.co.uk/2015/05/21/can-you-afford-to-throw-away-2 -million-of-your-organisations-money-on-a-failed-expat -assignment/); J. S. Black and H. B. Gregersen, "The Right Way to Manage Expats," *Harvard Business Review*.

25. Ibid, p. 54.

26. J. I. Sanchez, P. E. Spector, and C. L. Cooper, "Adapting to a Boundaryless World: A Developmental Expatriate Model," *Academy of Management Executive* (May 2000), pp. 96–106.

27. R. L. Tung, *The New Expatriates* (Cambridge, MA: Ballinger, 1988); J. S. Black, M. Mendenhall, and G. Oddou, "Toward a Comprehensive Model of International Adjustment: An Integration of Multiple Theoretical Perspectives," *Academy of Management Review* (April 1991), pp. 291–317.

28. M. A. Carpenter, W. G. Sanders, and H. B. Gregersen, "Bundling Human Capital with Organizational Context: The Impact of International Assignment Experience on Multinational Firm Performance and CEO Pay," *Academy of Management Journal* (June 2001), pp. 493–511.

29. P. M. Caligiuri and S. Colakoglu, "A Strategic Contingency Approach to Expatriate Assignment Management," *Human Resource Management Journal* (Vol. 17, No. 4, 2007), pp. 393–410.

30. M. A. Shaffer, D. A. Harrison, K. M. Gilley, and D. M. Luk, "Struggling for Balance Amid Turbulence on International -Assignments: Work-Family Conflict, Support, and Commitment," *Journal of Management* (Vol. 27, No. 1, 2001), pp. 99–121.

31. A. Molinsky & M. Hahn, "5 Tips for Managing Successful Overseas Assignments," *Harvard Business Review*, March 16, 2016 (https://hbr.org/2016/03/5-tips-for-managing -successful-overseas-assignments).

32. E. Huet, "Uber's Global Expansion In Five Seconds," *Forbes*, December 11, 2014 (http://www.forbes.com /sites/ellenhuet/2014/12/11/ubers-global-expansion /#1f91997f7a7a); https://www.uber.com/our-story/.

33. K. Roth, "Managing International Interdependence: CEO Characteristics in a Resource-Based Framework," *Academy of Management Journal* (February 1995), pp. 200–231.

34. M. Subramaniam and N. Venkatraman, "Determinants of Transnational New Product Development Capability: Testing the Influence of Transferring and Deploying Tacit Overseas Knowledge," *Strategic Management Journal* (April 2001), pp. 359–378.

35. J. S. Lublin, "An Overseas Stint Can Be a Ticket to the Top," *The Wall Street Journal* (January 29, 1996), pp. B1, B2.

36. "Expatriate Employees: In Search of Stealth," *The Economist* (April 23, 2005), pp. 62–64.

37. S. M. Robbins and R. B. Stobaugh, "The Bent Measuring Stick for Foreign Subsidiaries," *Harvard Business Review* (September–October 1973), p. 82.

38. J. D. Daniels and L. H. Radebaugh, *International Business*, 5th ed. (Reading, MA: Addison-Wesley, 1989), pp. 673–674.

39. R. Ball, "IFRS – Ten Years Later: The Perspectives In 2005 & 2015," *University of Chicago via ValueWalk*, March 10, 2016 (http://www.valuewalk.com/2016/03 /ifrs-global-accounting/).

40. D. Henry, "A Better Way to Keep the Books," *BusinessWeek* (September 15, 2008), p. 35 "International Accounting: Speaking in Tongues," *The Economist* (May 19, 2007), pp. 77–78; C. Hackett, "Convergence of U.S. GAAP and IFRS: Where Do Things Stand?" (http://www.cshco. com/News/-Articles/Convergence_of_U.S._GAAP_and _IFRS%3A_Where_do_things_stand%3F/).

41. W. A. Johnson and R. J. Kirsch, "International Transfer Pricing and Decision Making in United States Multinationals," *International Journal of Management* (June 1991), pp. 554–561.

42. *KPMG's Corporate Tax Rate Table 2016*, (https://home. kpmg.com/xx/en/home/services/tax/tax-tools-and- resources/tax-rates-online/corporate-tax-rates-table .html).

43. R. McHugh, "Apple Irish tax controversy continues," *BusinessWorld*, January 15, 2016 (https://www.business- world.ie/technology-news/Apple-Irish-tax-controversy- continues—562567.html).

44. J. M. L. Poon, R. Ainuddin, and H. Affrim, "Management Policies and Practices of American, British, European, and Japanese Subsidiaries in Malaysia: A Comparative Study," *International Journal of Management* (December 1990), pp. 467–474.

45. http://www.canena.org/about-canena/international-and-regional-partners/ (accessed March 16, 2016); M. Egan, "Setting Standards: Strategic Advantages in International Trade," *Business Strategy Review* (Vol. 13, No. 1, 2002), pp. 51–64; L. Swatkowski, "Building Towards International Standards," *Appliance* (December 1999), p. 30.

46. C. W. L. Hill, P. Hwang, and W. C. Kim, "An Eclectic Theory of the Choice of International Entry Mode," *Strategic Management Journal* (February 1990), pp. 117–128; D. Lei, J. W. Slocum, Jr., and R. W. Slater, "Global Strategy and Reward Systems: The Key Roles of Management Development and Corporate Culture," *Organizational Dynamics* (Autumn 1990), pp. 27–41; W. R. Fannin and A. F. Rodrigues, "National or Global?—Control vs. Flexibility," *Long Range Planning* -(October 1986), pp. 84–188.

47. A. V. Phatak, *International Dimensions of Management*, 2nd ed. (Boston: Kent, 1989), pp. 155–157.

48. "International Expansion Accelerates as Two Six Flags-Branded Parks to Open in Vietnam," *Financial Content*, March 21, 2016 (http://markets.financialcontent.com /stocks/news/read?GUID=31759161).

49. "Zara owner's profits soar on higher sales, expansion," The Peninsula: Qatar's Daily Newspaper, March 9, 2016 (http://thepeninsulaqatar.com/business/international-business/373515/zara-owner-s-profits-soar-on-higher-sales-expansion_); http://www.inditex.com/en/our_group /facilities.

50. http://www.inc.com/inc5000/

CHAPTER **10**

Strategy Implementation:
Organizing and Structure

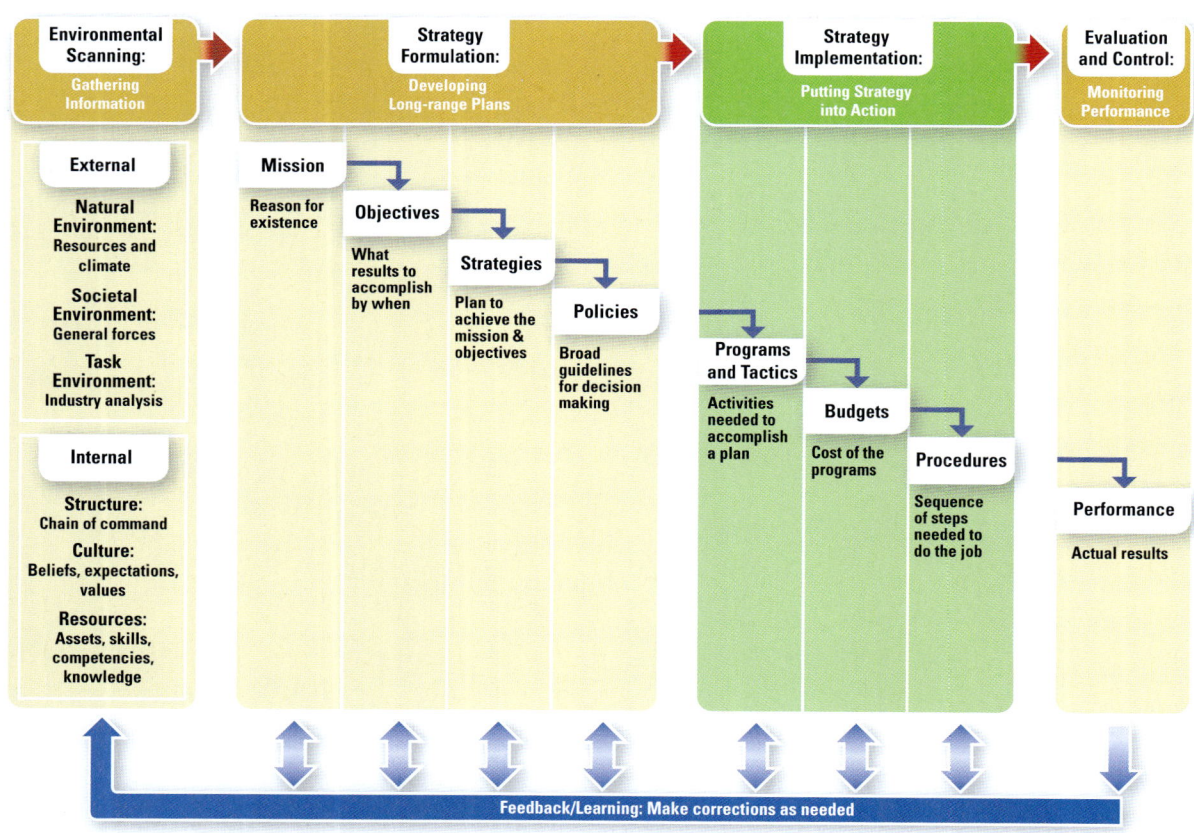

Pearson MyLab Management®

⭐ **Improve Your Grade!**

Over 10 million students improved their results using the Pearson MyLabs. Visit **mymanagementlab.com**
for simulations, tutorials, and end-of-chapter problems.

Learning Objectives

After reading this chapter, you should be able to:

10-1. Describe the major issues that impact successful strategy implementation

10-2. Explain how you would develop programs, budgets, and procedures to implement strategic change

10-3. List the stages of corporate development and the structure that characterizes each stage

10-4. Explain how matrix, network and modular structures are used to implement strategy

10-5. Discuss the issues related to centralization versus decentralization in structuring organizations

Tesla Drives to Change the Structure of an Industry

Every car manufacturer who sells in the United States does so through a network of locally-owned dealerships. The car manufacturers have structured their business to deal with the only sales channel allowed by law in most states. Into this arena comes Tesla. Much to the surprise of many, Tesla was not founded by Elon Musk, but by Martin Eberhard and Marc Tarpenning in 2003 with the goal of utilizing an AC induction motor patented in 1888 by Nikola Tesla to prove that battery-powered cars could be better than gas-powered cars. Their primary investor was PayPal co-founder Elon Musk who then served as Chairman until 2008 when he also became the CEO.

While certainly not a mass-market car (the Tesla Roadster started out at US$109,000), the company had no problem selling every car they made. Tesla opened car information locations at malls in the United States where customers would learn about the car, its features, and how to order one. Customers can use a Web site to select the features they want, pay a deposit, and wait for Tesla to build their car. Tesla offers financing and accepts third-party loans, but delivers the cars directly to the customer that ordered it. The organization has been structured around a retail concept that is more oriented toward providing information rather than selling. The price of the vehicle is not negotiated and every feature is clearly labelled on the Web site. There are no teams of employees working with franchisees, no logistics teams negotiating car allotments, no sales groups crafting the next "big" sale/marketing campaign.

General Motors has almost 4,900 franchise dealers in North America and the company is prohibited from selling directly to consumers because of contracts with those dealers and state laws that protect the dealerships from factory competition. General Motors has invested significant resources in attempting to prevent Tesla from entering markets. They successfully prevented a move into Michigan, but failed in the courts of Massachusetts.

If Tesla is forced to deal through a franchise dealer system it will radically affect the structure and design of the organization. Sometimes the reality of the markets dictates how a company is organized.

SOURCES: "Tesla Takes on the Dealerships—and GM," *Bloomberg BusinessWeek*, March 7–13, 2016, pp. 28–32; N. Chambers, "Tesla is Turning the Car Sales Model on Its Head," *AutoTrader,* November 2011 (http://www.autotrader.com/car-news/tesla-is-turning-the-car-sales-model-on-its-head-132587); B. Schreiber, "Tesla Motors," *Encyclopedia Britannica* (http://www.britannica.com/topic/Tesla-Motors); https://www.teslamotors.com/about.

Strategy Implementation

10-1. Describe the major issues that impact successful strategy implementation

Strategy implementation is the sum total of the activities and choices required for the execution of a strategic plan. It is the process by which objectives, strategies, and policies are put into action through the development of programs and tactics, budgets, and procedures. Implementation should be evaluated as strategy is being formulated although many companies separate the two. Implementation is the key part of strategic management for without implementation we have nothing. Strategy formulation and strategy implementation should be considered as two sides of the same coin.

Poor implementation has been blamed for a number of strategic failures. Merger and acquisitions activities are clear types of very visible implementations. Some studies have shown that half of all acquisitions fail to achieve what was expected of them while recent studies have reported that 83% of companies fail to achieve the goals of a merger.[1] The most mentioned problems reported in post-merger integration were poor communication, unrealistic synergy expectations, structural problems, missing master plans, lost momentum, lack of top management commitment, and unclear strategic fit. A study by A. T. Kearney found that a company has just two years in which to make an acquisition perform. After the second year, the window of opportunity for forging synergies has mostly closed. Kearney's study was supported by further independent research by Bert, MacDonald, and Herd. Among the most successful acquirers studied, 70% to 85% of all merger synergies were realized within the first 12 months, with the remainder being realized in year two.[2]

The implementation process requires strategy makers to consider these questions:

- *Who* are the people who will carry out the strategic plan?
- *What* must be done to align the company's operations in the new intended direction?
- *How* is everyone going to work together to do what is needed?

These questions and similar ones should have been addressed initially when the pros and cons of strategic alternatives were analyzed. They must also be addressed again before successful implementation plans can be made. Unless top management can answer these basic questions satisfactorily, even the best planned strategy is unlikely to provide the desired outcome.

A survey of 93 Fortune 500 firms revealed that more than half of the corporations experienced the following 10 big issues when they attempted to implement a strategic change. These problems are listed in order of frequency.

1. Implementation took more time than originally planned.
2. Unanticipated major problems arose.
3. Activities were ineffectively coordinated.

4. Competing activities and crises took attention away from implementation.
5. The involved employees had insufficient capabilities to perform their jobs.
6. Lower-level employees were inadequately trained.
7. Uncontrollable external environmental factors created problems.
8. Departmental managers provided inadequate leadership and direction.
9. Key implementation tasks and activities were poorly defined.
10. The information system inadequately monitored activities.[3]

WHO IMPLEMENTS STRATEGY?

Depending on how a corporation is organized, those who implement strategy will probably be a much more diverse set of people than those who formulate it. From large, multi-industry corporations to small entrepreneurial ventures, the reality is that the implementers of strategy are everyone in the organization. Vice presidents of functional areas and directors of divisions or strategic business units (SBUs) work with their subordinates to put together large-scale implementation plans. Plant managers, project managers, and unit heads put together plans for their specific plants, departments, and units. SaaS-based company presidents work with their project managers and developers to meet the latest needs of their customers. Therefore, every operational manager down to the first-line supervisor and every employee is involved in some way in the implementation of corporate, business, and functional strategies.

Many of the people in the organization who are most crucial to successful strategy implementation probably had little to do with the development of the corporate and even business strategy. Therefore, they might be entirely ignorant of the vast amount of data and work that went into the formulation process. Unless changes in mission, objectives, strategies, and policies and their importance to the company are communicated clearly to every person in the organization, there can be a lot of resistance and foot-dragging. Some line managers might hope to influence top management into abandoning its new plans and returning to its old ways. This is one reason why involving people from all organizational levels in the formulation and implementation of strategy tends to result in better organizational performance.[4]

What Must Be Done?

10-2. Explain how you would develop programs, budgets, and procedures to implement strategic change

The managers of divisions and functional areas work with their fellow managers to develop programs, budgets, and procedures for the implementation of strategy. They also work to achieve synergy among the divisions and functional areas in order to establish and maintain a company's distinctive competence.

DEVELOPING PROGRAMS, BUDGETS, AND PROCEDURES

Strategy implementation involves establishing programs and tactics to create a series of new organizational activities, budgets to allocate funds to the new activities, and procedures to handle the day-to-day details.

Programs and Tactics

The purpose of a **program** or a tactic is to make a strategy action-oriented. As we discussed in **Chapter 1**, the terms are somewhat interchangeable. In practice, a program is a collection of tactics and a tactic is the individual action taken by the organization as an element of the effort to accomplish a plan. For example, when Xerox Corporation undertook a turnaround strategy, it needed to significantly reduce its costs and expenses. Management introduced *Lean Six Sigma*. This program was developed to identify and improve a poorly performing process. Xerox first trained its top executives in the program and then launched around 250 individual Six Sigma projects throughout the corporation. The result was US$6 million in savings in one year, with even more expected the next.[5] (Six Sigma is explained later in this chapter.)

Most corporate headquarters have around 10 to 30 programs in effect at any one time.[6] The U.S. Army instituted the Lean Six Sigma Excellence Awards Program, known as LEAP to celebrate the successes within the Army. One project applied distance learning practices, eliminated all travel temporary duty assignment from the training delivery and achieved the removal of 97% of recurring labor hours and reduced process cycle time from 124 days to five days.[7] Apple used a program to find a recycled and yet elegant pulp tray to hold the original iPhone that became the inspiration for a business out to change the way bottles are produced. For more information on this innovative approach to bottle design, see the **Sustainability Issue** feature.

Competitive Tactics

Studies of decision making report that half the decisions made in organizations fail because of poor tactics.[8] A tactic is a specific operating plan that details how a strategy

SUSTAINABILITY issue

A BETTER BOTTLE—ECOLOGIC BRANDS

Some of the ideas that transform business practice are born in the simplest of places. Julie Corbett's started when she bought her first iPhone in 2007. She was fascinated by the paper pulp tray that it arrived in. The tray was elegant, sturdy, and biodegradable. She immediately thought of how it could be used to reduce the vast amounts of plastic needed for plastic bottles holding liquids. Combining the sturdiness of the paper pulp with an interior bladder to hold the liquid, she created Ecologic Brands.

Winner of the 2012 Gold Award from the Industrial Designers Society of America, the "bottle" is instantly recognizable as eco-friendly and yet extremely comfortable to touch and use. The bottles use 70% less plastic than regular ones and are the first of their type to hit store shelves. In addition, the bottle shells are made from 100% recycled cardboard and newspaper. The company didn't need to use any exotic materials or techniques to create the bottles.

However, they have patents on the processes for connecting the components and have new products on the way. Ecologic is creating a demand for pulp paper in an industry that has been battered for many years.

Seventh Generation Laundry Detergent was one of the first brands to use the bottles and saw a 19% increase in sales after switching. The company has designed packaging for such widely varying companies as Bodylogix protein powder and Truett Hurst wine.

The company has received several significant rounds of funding and in 2013 opened a 60,000 square foot facility in an economically depressed area of California. They are on a path to make the Ecologic bottle comparable in cost to the plastic competition.

....

SOURCES: J. Griffin, "Good things come in reusable packages," *Entrepreneur*, January 13, 2015 (entrepreneur.com/article/241059); "Bottles Inspired by the iPhone," *Bloomberg Businessweek*, October 29, 2012, p. 45 http://www.ecologicbrands.com/about_eco.html; http://www.fastcodesign.com/1664838/tk-years-in-the-making-a-cardboard-jug-for-laundry-detergent.

is to be implemented in terms of when and where it is to be put into action. By their nature, tactics are narrower in scope and shorter in time horizon than are strategies. Tactics, therefore, may be viewed (like policies) as a link between the formulation and implementation of strategy. Some of the tactics available to implement competitive strategies are timing tactics and market location tactics.

Timing Tactics: When to Compete

A **timing tactic** deals with *when* a company implements a strategy. The first company to manufacture and sell a new product or service is called the **first mover** (or pioneer). Some of the advantages of being a first mover are that the company is able to establish a reputation as an industry leader, move down the learning curve to assume the cost-leader position, and earn temporarily high profits from buyers who value the product or service very highly. A successful first mover can also set the standard for all subsequent products in the industry. A company that sets the standard "locks in" customers and is then able to offer further products based on that standard.[9] Microsoft was able to do this in software with its Windows operating system by being the first to commercialize the product successfully. Research does indicate that moving first or second into a new industry or foreign country results in greater market share and shareholder wealth than does moving later.[10] Some studies have found that being first provides a company profit advantages for about 10 years in consumer goods and about 12 years in industrial goods.[11] This is true, however, only if the first mover has sufficient resources to both exploit the new market and to defend its position against later arrivals with greater resources.[12] Gillette, for example, has been able to keep its leadership of the razor category (70% market share) by continuously introducing new products.[13]

Being a first mover does, however, have its disadvantages. These disadvantages can be, conversely, advantages enjoyed by late-mover firms. **Late movers** may be able to imitate the technological advances of others (and thus keep R&D costs low), keep risks down by waiting until a new technological standard or market is established, and take advantage of the first mover's natural inclination to ignore market segments.[14] Research indicates that successful late movers tend to be large firms with considerable resources and related experience.[15] Microsoft is one example. Once Netscape had established itself as the standard for Internet browsers in the 1990s, Microsoft used its huge resources to directly attack Netscape's position with its Internet Explorer. It did not want Netscape to also set the standard in the developing and highly lucrative intranet market inside corporations. By 2004, Microsoft's Internet Explorer dominated Web browsers, and Netscape was only a minor presence. Nevertheless, research suggests that the advantages and disadvantages of first and late movers may not always generalize across industries because of differences in entry barriers and the resources of the specific competitors.[16]

Market Location Tactics: Where to Compete

A **market location tactic** deals with *where* a company implements a strategy. A company or business unit can implement a competitive strategy either offensively or defensively. An *offensive tactic* usually takes place in an established competitor's market location. A *defensive tactic* usually takes place in the firm's own current market position as a defense against possible attack by a rival.[17]

Offensive Tactics.　Some of the methods used to attack a competitor's position are:

■ **Frontal assault:** The attacking firm goes head to head with its competitor. It matches the competitor in every category from price to promotion to distribution channel. To be successful, the attacker must have not only superior resources, but also the willingness to persevere. This is generally a very expensive tactic and may serve to awaken a sleeping giant, depressing profits for the whole industry. This is what Kimberly-Clark did when it introduced Huggies disposable diapers against P&G's market-leading Pampers. The resulting competitive battle between the two firms depressed Kimberly-Clark's profits.[18]

- **Flanking maneuver:** Rather than going straight for a competitor's position of strength with a frontal assault, a firm may attack a part of the market where the competitor is weak. Texas Instruments, for example, avoided competing directly with Intel by developing microprocessors for consumer electronics, cell phones, and medical devices instead of computers. Taken together, these other applications are worth more in terms of dollars and influence than are computers, where Intel dominates.[19]

- **Bypass attack:** Rather than directly attacking the established competitor frontally or on its flanks, a company or business unit may choose to change the rules of the game. This tactic attempts to cut the market out from under the established defender by offering a new type of product that makes the competitor's product unnecessary. For example, instead of competing directly against Microsoft's Pocket PC and Palm Pilot for the handheld computer market, Apple introduced the iPod as a personal digital music player. It was the most radical change to the way people listen to music since the Sony Walkman. By redefining the market, Apple successfully sidestepped both Intel and Microsoft, leaving them to play "catch-up."[20]

- **Encirclement:** Usually evolving out of a frontal assault or flanking maneuver, encirclement occurs as an attacking company or unit encircles the competitor's position in terms of products or markets or both. The encircler has greater product variety (e.g., a complete product line, ranging from low to high price) and/or serves more markets (e.g., it dominates every secondary market). For example, Steinway was a major manufacturer of pianos in the United States until Yamaha entered the market with a broader range of pianos, keyboards, and other musical instruments. The company was taken private in 2013 and focuses almost exclusively on the very high end of the market producing their 600,000th piano in 2015.[21] Oracle is using this strategy in its battle against market leader SAP for enterprise resource planning (ERP) software by "surrounding" SAP with acquisitions.[22]

- **Guerrilla warfare:** Instead of a continual and extensive resource-expensive attack on a competitor, a firm or business unit may choose to "hit and run." Guerrilla warfare is characterized by the use of small, intermittent assaults on different market segments held by the competitor. In this way, a new entrant or small firm can make some gains without seriously threatening a large, established competitor and evoking some form of retaliation. To be successful, the firm or unit conducting guerrilla warfare must be patient enough to accept small gains and avoid pushing the established competitor to the point that it must respond or else lose face. Microbreweries, which make beer for sale to local customers, use this tactic against major brewers such as AB InBev.

Defensive tactics. According to Porter, defensive tactics aim to lower the probability of attack, divert attacks to less threatening avenues, or lessen the intensity of an attack. Instead of increasing competitive advantage per se, they make a company's or business unit's competitive advantage more sustainable by causing a challenger to conclude that an attack is unattractive. These tactics deliberately reduce short-term profitability to ensure long-term profitability.[23]

- **Raise structural barriers.** Entry barriers act to block a challenger's logical avenues of attack. Some of the most important, according to Porter, are to:

  1. Offer a full line of products in every market segment to close off any entry points (for example, Coca-Cola offers unprofitable non-carbonated beverages to keep competitors off store shelves).

  2. Block channel access by signing exclusive agreements with distributors.

  3. Raise buyer switching costs by offering low-cost training to users.

  4. Raise the cost of gaining trial users by keeping prices low on items new users are most likely to purchase.

  5. Increase scale economies to reduce unit costs.

  6. Foreclose alternative technologies through patenting or licensing.

  7. Limit outside access to facilities and personnel.

  8. Tie up suppliers by obtaining exclusive contracts or purchasing key locations.

  9. Avoid suppliers that also serve competitors.

  10. Encourage the government to raise barriers, such as safety and pollution standards or favorable trade policies.

- **Increase expected retaliation:** This tactic is any action that increases the perceived threat of retaliation for an attack. For example, management may strongly defend any erosion of market share by drastically cutting prices or matching a challenger's promotion through a policy of accepting any price-reduction coupons for a competitor's product. This counterattack is especially important in markets that are very important to the defending company or business unit. For example, when Clorox Company challenged P&G in the detergent market with Clorox Super Detergent, P&G retaliated by test marketing its liquid bleach of the time, Lemon Fresh Comet, in an attempt to scare Clorox into retreating from the detergent market. Research suggests that retaliating quickly is not as successful in slowing market share loss as a slower, but more concentrated and aggressive response.[24]

- **Lower the inducement for attack:** A third type of defensive tactic is to reduce a challenger's expectations of future profits in the industry. Like Southwest Airlines, a company can deliberately keep prices low and constantly invest in cost-reducing measures. With prices kept very low, there is little profit incentive for a new entrant.[25]

Budgets

After programs and tactical plans have been developed, the **budget** process begins. Planning a budget is the last real check a corporation has on the feasibility of its selected strategy. An ideal strategy might be found to be completely impractical only after specific implementation programs and tactics are costed in detail. Mondelez is the world's largest buyer of cocoa and in 2012 made a commitment to dramatically increase the supply of sustainably grown cocoa in the six big cocoa producing countries. The company budgeted US$400 million to reach over 200,000 cocoa farmers by 2022.[26]

Procedures

After the divisional and corporate budgets are approved, **procedures** must be developed. Often called *Standard Operating Procedures (SOPs)*, they typically detail the various activities that must be carried out to complete a corporation's programs and tactical plans. Also known as *organizational routines*, procedures are the primary means by which organizations accomplish much of what they do.[27] Once in place, procedures must be updated to reflect any changes in technology as well as in strategy. For example, a company following a differentiation competitive strategy manages its sales force more closely than does a firm following a low-cost strategy. Differentiation requires long-term customer relationships created out of close interaction with the sales force. An in-depth understanding of the customer's needs provides the foundation for product development and improvement.[28]

In a retail store, procedures ensure that the day-to-day store operations will be consistent over time (that is, next week's work activities will be the same as this week's) and consistent among stores (that is, each store will operate in the same manner as the others). Properly planned procedures can help eliminate poor service by making sure that employees do not use excuses to justify poor behavior toward customers.

Before a new strategy can be successfully implemented, current procedures may need to be changed. For example, in order to implement The Home Depot's strategic move into services, such as kitchen and bathroom installation, the company had to first improve its productivity. Store managers were drowning in paperwork designed for a smaller and simpler company. "We'd get a fax, an e-mail, a call, and a memo, all on the same project," reported store manager Michael Jones. One executive used just three weeks of memos to wallpaper an entire conference room, floor to ceiling, windows included. Then CEO Robert Nardelli told his top managers to eliminate duplicate communications and streamline work projects. Directives not related to work orders had to be sent separately and only once a month. The company also spent US$2 million on workload-management software.[29]

ACHIEVING SYNERGY

One of the goals to be achieved in strategy implementation is synergy between and among functions and business units. This is the reason corporations commonly reorganize after an acquisition. **Synergy** is said to exist for a divisional corporation if the return on investment of each division is greater than what the return would be if each division were an independent business. According to Goold and Campbell, synergy can take place in one of six forms:

- **Shared know-how:** Combined units often benefit from sharing knowledge or skills. This is a leveraging of core competencies. One reason that Procter & Gamble purchased Gillette was to combine P&G's knowledge of the female consumer with Gillette's knowledge of the male consumer.

- **Coordinated strategies:** Aligning the business strategies of two or more business units may give a corporation significant advantage by reducing interunit competition and developing a coordinated response to common competitors (horizontal strategy). The merger between Comcast and NBC Universal in 2011 gave the combined company significant bargaining strength and flexibility with advertisers in the increasingly competitive television media industry.

- **Shared tangible resources:** Combined units can sometimes save money by sharing resources, such as a common manufacturing facility or R&D lab. The big pharmaceutical companies were all looking for savings with the big mergers in the industry, such as Pfizer-Wyeth, Novartis-Alcon, and Roche-Genentech.

- **Economies of scale or scope:** Coordinating the flow of products or services of one unit with that of another unit can reduce inventory, increase capacity utilization, and improve market access. This was a reason United Airlines bought Continental Airlines.

- **Pooled negotiating power:** Units can combine their volume of purchasing to gain bargaining power over common suppliers to reduce costs and improve quality. The same can be done with common distributors. The acquisitions of Macy's and the May Company enabled Federated Department Stores (which changed its name to Macy's) to gain purchasing economies for all of its stores.

- **New business creation:** Exchanging knowledge and skills can facilitate new products or services by extracting discrete activities from various units and combining them in a new unit or by establishing joint ventures among internal business units. Google has acquired more than 100 companies over the past five years.[30]

How Is Strategy to Be Implemented?
Organizing for Action

10-3. List the stages of corporate development and the structure that characterizes each stage

Before plans can lead to actual performance, a corporation should be organized to take advantage of its competitive advantages, programs should be adequately staffed, and activities should be directed toward achieving desired objectives. (Organizing activities are reviewed briefly in this chapter; staffing, directing, and control activities are discussed in **Chapters 10** and **11**.)

Any change in corporate strategy is very likely to require some sort of change in the way an organization is structured and in the kind of skills needed in particular positions. Managers must, therefore, closely examine the way their company is structured in order to decide what, if any, changes should be made in the way work is accomplished. Should activities be grouped differently? Should the authority to make key decisions be centralized at headquarters or decentralized to managers in distant locations? Should the company be managed like a "tight ship" with many rules and controls, or "loosely" with few rules and controls? Should the corporation be organized into a "tall" structure with many layers of managers, each having a narrow span of control (that is, few employees per supervisor) to better control his or her subordinates; or should it be organized into a "flat" structure with fewer layers of managers, each having a wide span of control (that is, more employees per supervisor) to give more freedom to his or her subordinates?

STRUCTURE FOLLOWS STRATEGY

In a classic study of large U.S. corporations such as DuPont, General Motors, Sears, and Standard Oil, Alfred Chandler concluded that **structure follows strategy**—that is, changes in corporate strategy lead to changes in organizational structure.[31] He also concluded that organizations follow a pattern of development from one kind of structural arrangement to another as they expand. According to Chandler, these structural changes occur because the old structure, having been pushed too far, has caused inefficiencies that have become too obviously detrimental to bear. Chandler, therefore, proposed the following as the sequence of what occurs:

1. New strategy is created.
2. New administrative problems emerge.
3. Economic performance declines.
4. New appropriate structure is created.
5. Economic performance rises.

Chandler found that in their early years, corporations such as DuPont tend to have a centralized, functional, organizational structure that is well suited to producing and selling a limited range of products. As they add new product lines, purchase their own sources of supply, and create their own distribution networks, they become too complex for highly centralized structures. To remain successful, this type of organization needs to shift to a decentralized structure with several semiautonomous divisions (referred to in **Chapter 5** as *divisional structure*).

Alfred P. Sloan, past CEO of General Motors, detailed how GM conducted such structural changes in the 1920s.[32] He saw decentralization of structure as "centralized policy determination coupled with decentralized operating management." After top management had developed a strategy for the total corporation, the individual divisions (Chevrolet, Buick, and so on) were free to choose how to implement that strategy. Patterned after DuPont, GM found the decentralized multidivisional structure to be extremely effective in allowing the maximum amount of freedom for product development. Return on investment was used as a financial control. (ROI is discussed in more detail in **Chapter 11**.)

Research generally supports Chandler's proposition that structure follows strategy (as well as the reverse proposition that structure influences strategy).[33] As mentioned earlier, changes in the environment tend to be reflected in changes in a corporation's strategy, thus leading to changes in a corporation's structure. In 2016, TiVo (the company that brought the world more control over their viewing options) announced a change in their strategy in response to strong moves by their competitors. They reorganized the company around just three areas—partnerships, international expansion, and innovation. The goal was to take the already growing firm and accelerate that growth around its core strengths.[34]

Strategy, structure, and the environment need to be closely aligned; otherwise, organizational performance will likely suffer.[35] For example, a business unit following a differentiation strategy needs more freedom from headquarters to be successful than does another unit following a low-cost strategy.[36]

Although it is agreed that organizational structure must vary with different environmental conditions, which, in turn, affects an organization's strategy, there is no agreement about an optimal organizational design. What was appropriate for DuPont and General Motors in the 1920s might not be appropriate today. Firms in the same industry do, however, tend to organize themselves similarly to one another. For example, automobile manufacturers tend to emulate General Motors' divisional concept, whereas consumer-goods producers tend to emulate the brand-management concept (a type of matrix structure) pioneered by Procter & Gamble Company. See the **Innovation Issues** feature to see how P&G's structural decisions ended up derailing their innovation efforts. The general conclusion seems to be that firms following similar strategies in similar industries tend to adopt similar structures.

STAGES OF CORPORATE DEVELOPMENT

Successful, large conglomerate organizations have tended to follow a pattern of structural development as they grow and expand. Beginning with the simple structure of the entrepreneurial firm (in which everybody does everything), these organizations tend to get larger and organize along functional lines, with marketing, production, and finance departments. With continuing success, the company adds new product lines in different industries and organizes itself into interconnected divisions. The differences among these three structural **stages of corporate development** in terms of typical problems,

INNOVATION issue

THE P&G INNOVATION MACHINE STUMBLES

As we have discussed throughout this text, innovation is a key element needed to organically grow a company. Developing an ever-widening portfolio of businesses has been a strategic approach used by many companies. None has been more successful with this approach than Procter & Gamble (P&G). Their 175-year history is filled with consumer-oriented product innovations including Ivory Soap (1879), Crisco (1911), Dreft which became Tide (1933), Crest (1955), Pampers (1961), Pringles (1968), Fabreze (1993), Swiffer (1998), and Crest Whitestrips (2002).

Known for their heavy investment in research and development, the company invested more than US$2 billion in R&D in 2012. For most of its history, the company used a highly centralized R&D group to generate new ideas. This all came to an end in 2000 when then-CEO A. G. Lafley decentralized the operations to the operating units and opened product innovation to outside partners. Taking his cue for the dramatic growth in social media and crowd-sourcing, Lafley sought to have 50% of innovative new products generated from people not employed by the company. The operating units were expected to be more closely tied to the consumers and thus be in a better position to know the potential for each new product idea.

Between 2003 and 2008, the sales of new launches shrank by half. The company's pipeline became focused on reformulating old products, adding scents to successful product lines, and adjusting the sizes that were sold.

In 2009, new CEO Bob McDonald started recentralizing R&D operations in an attempt to reverse the deterioration of innovation at the company. By 2012, between 20 and 30% of R&D had been centralized. The loss of focus cost the company a decade of innovations while competitors rolled out new products in virtually every product category in which P&G competes. There is no single means for generating innovative ideas or for turning those ideas into a blockbuster new product. Companies seek to organize their businesses so they can own the next big thing.

Big changes were in store for the company. In 2014 they announced a dramatic restructuring of the organization into four large industry groups and plans to sell off half the brands in the company portfolio. The company wanted to focus on specific areas of strength and then grow those areas with innovation. Whereas centralization failed to generate organic growth under the old structure, tightly focused areas could benefit from specifically-focused R&D facilities. In 2015, P&G announced plans to build a 500,000 square foot research and development center specifically for its new Beauty Division. It will be interesting to see if this carefully restructured organization grows its innovation engine again.

....

SOURCES: B. Brunsman, "P&G to build massive R&D center in Mason," *Cincinnati Business Courier*, March 17, 2015 (*bizjournals.com/Cincinnati/news/2015/03/17/p-g-to-build-massive-r-d-center-in-mason.html*); "Procter & Gamble to sell off half its brands," *Associated Press via CBC News*, August 1, 2014 (http://www.cbc.ca/news/business/procter-gamble-to-sell-off-half-its-brands-1.2725214); *pg.com/en_US/downloads/investors/annual_reports/2013/2013_auunualreport.pdf*; L. Coleman-Lochner and C. Hymowitz, "At P&G, the Innovation Well Runs Dry," *Bloomberg Businessweek* (September 10, 2012), pp. 24–26; http://www.pg.com/en_US/brands/index.shtml

objectives, strategies, reward systems, and other characteristics are specified in detail in **Table 10–1**.

Stage I: Simple Structure

Stage I is typified by the entrepreneur or a small team, who founds a company to promote an idea (a product or a service). The entrepreneur or team tends to make all the important decisions and is involved in every detail and phase of the organization. The Stage I company has little formal structure, which allows the entrepreneur or team to directly supervise the activities of every employee (see **Figure 5–3** for an illustration of the simple, functional, and divisional structures). Planning is usually short range or reactive. The typical managerial functions of planning, organizing, directing, staffing, and controlling are usually performed to a very limited degree, if at all. The greatest strengths of a Stage I corporation are its flexibility and dynamism. The drive of the

TABLE 10–1 Factors Differentiating Stage I, II, and III Companies

Function	Stage I	Stage II	Stage III
1. Sizing up: Major problems	Survival and growth dealing with short-term operating problems	Growth, rationalization, and expansion of resources, providing for adequate attention to product problems	Trusteeship in management and investment and control of large, increasing, and diversified resources. Also, important to diagnose and take action on problems at division level
2. Objectives	Personal and subjective	Profits and meeting functionally-oriented budgets and performance targets	ROI, profits, earnings per share
3. Strategy	Implicit and personal; exploitation of immediate opportunities seen by owner-manager	Functionally oriented moves restricted to "one product" scope; exploitation of one basic product or service field	Growth and product diversification; exploitation of general business opportunities
4. Organization: Major characteristic of structure	One unit, "one-man show"	One unit, functionally specialized group	Multiunit general staff office and decentralized operating divisions
5. (a) Measurement and control	Personal, subjective control based on simple accounting system and daily communication and observation	Control grows beyond one person; assessment of functional operations necessary; structured control systems evolve	Complex formal system geared to comparative assessment of performance measures, indicating problems and opportunities and assessing management ability of division managers
5. (b) Key performance indicators	Personal criteria, relationships with owner, operating efficiency, ability to solve operating problems	Functional and internal criteria such as sales, performance compared to budget, size of empire, status in group, personal relationships, etc.	More impersonal application of comparisons such as profits, ROI, P/E ratio, sales, market share, productivity, product leadership, personnel development, employee attitudes, public responsibility
6. Reward–punishment system	Informal, personal, subjective; used to maintain control and divide small pool of resources for key performers to provide personal incentives	More structured; usually based to a greater extent on agreed policies as opposed to personal opinion and relationships	Allotment by "due process" of a wide variety of different rewards and punishments on a formal and systematic basis. Companywide policies usually apply to many different classes of managers and workers with few major exceptions for individual cases.

SOURCE: Donald H. Thain, "Stages of Corporate Development," *Ivey Business Journal* (formerly *Ivey Business Quarterly*), Winter 1969, p. 37. Copyright © 1969, Ivey Management Services. One-time permission to reproduce granted by Ivey Management Services.

entrepreneur energizes the organization in its struggle for growth. Its greatest weakness is its extreme reliance on the entrepreneur to decide general strategies as well as detailed procedures. If the entrepreneur falters, the company usually flounders. This is labeled by Greiner as a *crisis of leadership*.[37]

Stage I describes the early life of Oracle Corporation, the computer software firm, under the management of its co-founder and then CEO Lawrence Ellison. The company adopted a pioneering approach to retrieving data, called Structured Query Language (SQL). When IBM made SQL its standard, Oracle's success was assured. Unfortunately, Ellison's technical wizardry was not sufficient to manage the company. Often working at home, he lost sight of details outside his technical interests. Although the company's sales were rapidly increasing, its financial controls were so weak that management had to restate an entire year's results to rectify irregularities. After the company recorded its first loss, Ellison hired a set of functional managers to run the company while he retreated to focus on new product development.

Stage II: Functional Structure

Stage II is the point at which the entrepreneur is replaced by a team of managers who have functional specializations. The transition to this stage requires a substantial managerial style change for the chief officer of the company, especially if he or she was the Stage I entrepreneur. He or she must learn to delegate; otherwise, having additional staff members yields no benefits to the organization. The previous example of Ellison's retreat from top management at Oracle Corporation to new product development manager is one way that technically brilliant founders are able to get out of the way of the newly empowered functional managers. In Stage II, the corporate strategy favors protectionism through dominance of the industry, often through vertical and horizontal growth. The great strength of a Stage II corporation lies in its concentration and specialization in one industry. Its great weakness is that all its eggs are in one basket.

By concentrating on one industry while that industry remains attractive, a Stage II company, such as Oracle Corporation in computer software, can be very successful. Once a functionally structured firm diversifies into other products in different industries, however, the advantages of the functional structure break down. A *crisis of autonomy* can now develop, in which people managing diversified product lines need more decision-making freedom than top management is willing to delegate to them. The company needs to move to a different structure.

Stage III: Divisional Structure

Stage III is typified by the corporation's managing diverse product lines in numerous industries; it decentralizes the decision-making authority. Stage III organizations grow by diversifying their product lines and expanding to cover wider geographical areas. They move to a divisional structure with a central headquarters and decentralized operating divisions—with each division or business unit a functionally organized Stage II company. They may also use a conglomerate structure if top management chooses to keep its collection of Stage II subsidiaries operating autonomously. A *crisis of control* can now develop, in which the various units act to optimize their own sales and profits without regard to the overall corporation, whose headquarters seems far away and almost irrelevant.

Over time, divisions have been evolving into SBUs to better reflect product–market considerations. Headquarters attempts to coordinate the activities of its operating divisions or SBUs through performance, results-oriented control, and reporting systems, and by stressing corporate planning techniques. The units are not tightly controlled but are held responsible for their own performance results. Therefore, to be effective, the company has to have a decentralized decision process. The greatest strength of a Stage III corporation is its almost unlimited resources. Its most significant weakness is that it is usually so large and complex that it tends to become relatively inflexible. General Electric, DuPont, and General Motors are examples of Stage III corporations.

Stage IV: Beyond SBUs

Even with the evolution into SBUs during the 1970s and 1980s, the divisional structure is not the last word in organization structure. The use of SBUs may result in a *red tape crisis* in which the corporation has grown too large and complex to be managed through formal programs and rigid systems, and procedures take precedence over problem solving.[38] For example, Pfizer's acquisitions of Warner-Lambert and Pharmacia resulted in 14 layers of management between scientists and top executives and thus forced researchers to spend most of their time in meetings.[39] Under conditions of (1) increasing environmental uncertainty, (2) greater use of sophisticated technological production methods and information systems, (3) the increasing size and scope of worldwide business corporations, (4) a greater emphasis on multi-industry competitive strategy, and (5) a more educated cadre of managers and employees, new advanced forms of organizational structure are emerging. These structures emphasize collaboration over competition in the managing of an organization's multiple overlapping projects and developing businesses.

The matrix and the network are two possible candidates for a fourth stage in corporate development—a stage that not only emphasizes horizontal over vertical connections between people and groups but also organizes work around temporary projects in which sophisticated information systems support collaborative activities. According to Greiner, it is likely that this stage of development will have its own crisis as well—a sort of *pressure-cooker crisis*. He predicts that employees in these collaborative organizations will eventually grow emotionally and physically exhausted from the intensity of teamwork and the heavy pressure for innovative solutions.[40]

Blocks to Changing Stages

Corporations often find themselves in difficulty because they are blocked from moving into the next logical stage of development. Blocks to development may be internal (such as lack of resources, lack of ability, or refusal of top management to delegate decision making to others) or external (such as economic conditions, labor shortages, or lack of market growth). For example, Chandler noted in his study that the successful founder/CEO in one stage was rarely the person who created the new structure to fit the new strategy, and as a result, the transition from one stage to another was often painful. This was true of General Motors Corporation under the management of William Durant, Ford Motor Company under Henry Ford I, Polaroid Corporation under Edwin Land, eBay under Pierre Omidyar, and Yahoo under Jerry Yang and David Filo.

Entrepreneurs who start businesses generally have four tendencies that work very well for small new ventures but become Achilles' heels for these same individuals when they try to manage a larger firm with diverse needs, departments, priorities, and constituencies:

- **Loyalty to comrades:** This is good at the beginning but soon becomes a liability; seen as "favoritism."
- **Task oriented:** Focusing on the job is critical at first but then becomes excessive attention to detail.
- **Single-mindedness:** A grand vision is needed to introduce a new product but can become tunnel vision as the company grows into more markets and products.
- **Working in isolation:** This is good for a brilliant scientist but disastrous for a CEO with multiple constituencies.[41]

This difficulty in moving to a new stage is compounded by the founder's tendency to maneuver around the need to delegate by carefully hiring, training, and grooming his or her own team of managers. The team tends to maintain the founder's influence throughout the organization long after the founder is gone. This is what happened at Walt Disney Productions when the family continued to emphasize Walt's policies and plans long after he was dead. The refrain that was often heard was "What would Walt have done?" Although in some cases this may be an organization's strength, it can also be a weakness—to the extent that the culture supports the status quo and blocks needed change.

ORGANIZATIONAL LIFE CYCLE

Instead of considering stages of development in terms of structure, the organizational life cycle approach places the primary emphasis on the dominant issue facing the corporation. Organizational structure becomes a secondary concern. The **organizational life cycle** describes how organizations grow, develop, and eventually decline. It is the organizational equivalent of the product life cycle in marketing. These stages are Birth (Stage I), Growth (Stage II), Maturity (Stage III), Decline (Stage IV), and Death (Stage V). The impact of these stages on corporate strategy and structure is summarized in **TABLE 10–2**. Note that the first three stages of the organizational life cycle are similar to the three commonly accepted stages of corporate development mentioned previously. The only significant difference is the addition of the Decline and Death stages to complete the cycle. Even though a company's strategy may still be sound, its aging structure, culture, and processes may be such that they prevent the strategy from being executed properly. Its core competencies become *core rigidities* that are no longer able to adapt to changing conditions—thus the company moves into Decline.[42]

Movement from Growth to Maturity to Decline and finally to Death is not, however, inevitable. A Revival phase may occur sometime during the Maturity or Decline stages. The corporation's life cycle can be extended by managerial and product innovations.[43] Developing new combinations of existing resources to introduce new products or acquiring new resources through acquisitions can enable firms with declining performance to regain growth—so long as the action is valuable and difficult to imitate.[44] We have seen this play out with Apple. It was clearly in decline in the mid-1980s and many believed well on its way to dying. The company was rejuvenated with the return of Steve Jobs and a seemingly continuous stream of new products that took the company into numerous new markets. This can occur during the implementation of a turnaround

TABLE 10–2	Organizational Life Cycle				
	Stage I	**Stage II**	**Stage III**[*]	**Stage IV**	**Stage V**
Dominant Issue	Birth	Growth	Maturity	Decline	Death
Popular Strategies	Concentration in a niche	Horizontal and vertical growth	Concentric and conglomerate diversification	Profit strategy followed by retrenchment	Liquidation or bankruptcy
Likely Structure	Entrepreneur dominated	Functional management emphasized	Decentralization into profit or investment centers	Structural surgery	Dismemberment of structure

NOTE: *An organization may enter a Revival phase either during the Maturity or Decline stages and thus extend the organization's life, especially if it has significant financial reserves.

strategy.[45] Nevertheless, the fact that firms in decline are less likely to search for new technologies suggests that it is difficult to revive a company in decline.[46]

Unless a company is able to resolve the critical issues facing it in the Decline stage, it is likely to move into Stage V, Death—also known as bankruptcy. This is what happened to Montgomery Ward, Pan American Airlines, Mervyn's, Borders, Eastern Airlines, Circuit City, Orion Pictures, and Levitz Furniture, as well as many other firms. As in the cases of Johns-Manville, Bennigan's, Macy's, and Kmart—all of which went bankrupt—a corporation can rise like a phoenix from its own ashes and live again under the same or a different name. The company may be reorganized or liquidated, depending on individual circumstances. For example, Kmart emerged from **Chapter 11** bankruptcy in 2003 with a new CEO and a plan to sell a number of its stores to The Home Depot and Sears. These sales earned the company close to US$1 billion. Although store sales continued to erode, Kmart had sufficient cash reserves to continue with its turnaround. It used that money to acquire Sears in 2005. Unfortunately, however, fewer than 20% of firms entering **Chapter 11** bankruptcy in the United States emerge as going concerns; the rest are forced into liquidation (also known as **Chapter 7**).

Few corporations will move through these five stages in order. Some corporations, for example, might never move past Stage II. Others, such as General Motors, might go directly from Stage I to Stage III. A large number of entrepreneurial ventures jump from Stage I or II directly into Stage IV or V. Hayes Microcomputer Products, for example, went from the Growth to Decline stage under its founder Dennis Hayes. The key is to be able to identify indications that a firm is in the process of changing stages and to make the appropriate strategic and structural adjustments to ensure that corporate performance is maintained or even improved.

Flexible Types of Organizational Structure

10-4. Explain how matrix, network and modular structures are used to implement strategy

The basic structures (simple, functional, divisional, and conglomerate) are discussed in **Chapter 5** and summarized under the first three stages of corporate development in this chapter. A new strategy may require more flexible characteristics than the traditional functional or divisional structure can offer. Today's business organizations are becoming less centralized with a greater use of cross-functional work teams. Although many variations and hybrid structures exist, two forms stand out: the matrix structure and the network structure.

THE MATRIX STRUCTURE

Most organizations find that organizing around either functions (in the functional structure) or products and geography (in the divisional structure) provides an appropriate organizational structure. The matrix structure, in contrast, may be very appropriate when organizations conclude that neither functional nor divisional forms, even when combined with horizontal linking mechanisms such as SBUs, are right for their situations. In **matrix structures**, functional and product forms are combined simultaneously at the same level of the organization. (See **Figure 10–1**.) Employees have two superiors, a product or project manager, and a functional manager. The "home" department—that is, engineering, manufacturing, or sales—is usually functional and is reasonably permanent. People from these functional units are often assigned temporarily to one or more product units or projects. The product units or projects are usually temporary and act like divisions in that they are differentiated on a product-market basis.

FIGURE 10–1
Matrix and
Network Structures

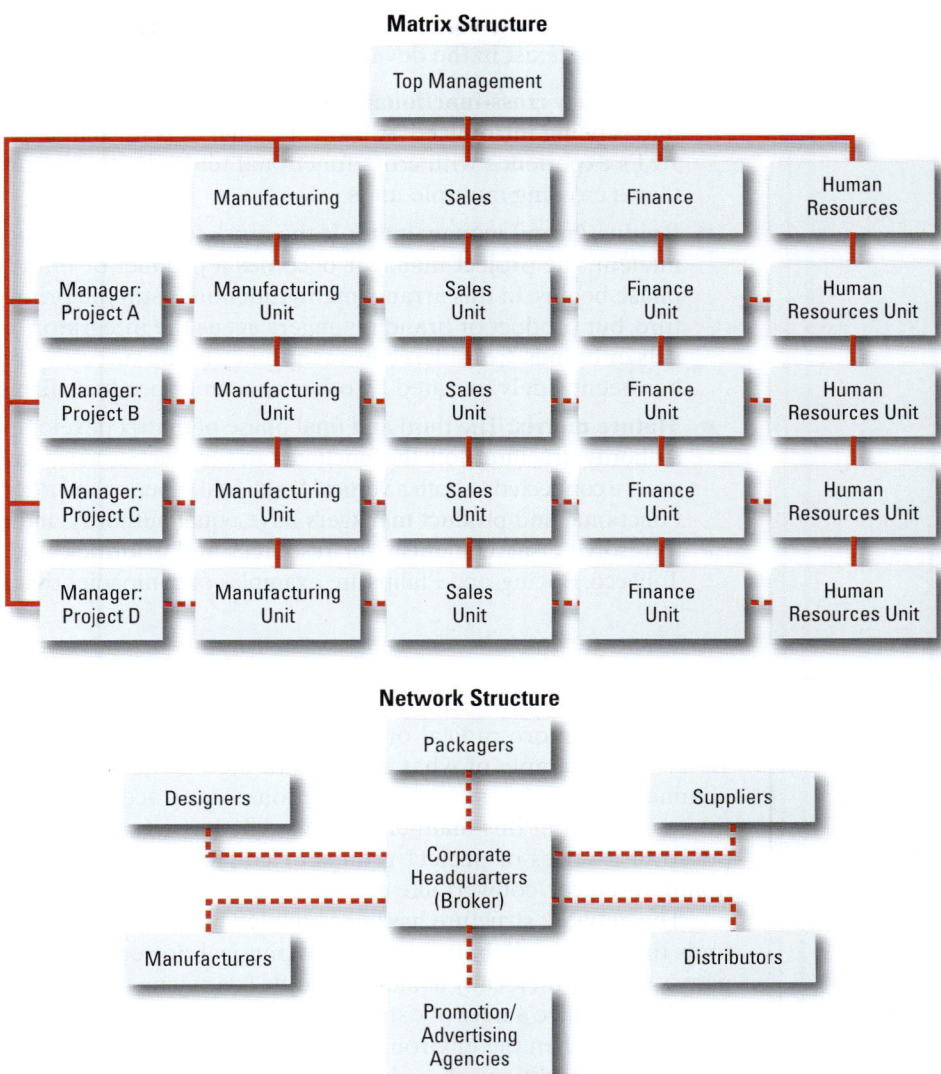

Pioneered in the aerospace industry, the matrix structure was developed to combine the stability of the functional structure with the flexibility of the product form. The matrix structure is very useful when the external environment (especially its technological and market aspects) is very complex and changeable. It does, however, produce conflicts revolving around duties, authority, and resource allocation. To the extent that the goals to be achieved are vague and the technology used is poorly understood, a continuous battle for power between product and functional managers is likely. The matrix structure is often found in an organization or SBU when the following three conditions exist:

- Ideas need to be cross-fertilized across projects or products.
- Resources are scarce.
- Abilities to process information and to make decisions need to be improved.[47]

Davis and Lawrence, authorities on the matrix form of organization, propose that *three distinct phases* exist in the development of the matrix structure:[48]

- **Temporary cross-functional task forces:** These are initially used when a new product line is being introduced. A project manager is in charge as the key horizontal link. J&J's experience with cross-functional teams in its drug group led it to emphasize teams crossing multiple units.

- **Product/brand management:** If the cross-functional task forces become more permanent, the project manager becomes a product or brand manager and a second phase begins. In this arrangement, function is still the primary organizational structure, but product or brand managers act as the integrators of semipermanent products or brands. Considered by many a key to the success of P&G, brand management has been widely imitated by other consumer products firms around the world.

- **Mature matrix:** The third and final phase of matrix development involves a true dual-authority structure. Both the functional and product structures are permanent. All employees are connected to both a vertical functional superior and a horizontal product manager. Functional and product managers have equal authority and must work well together to resolve disagreements over resources and priorities. Vodafone, British American Tobacco, Boeing, and Philips are examples of companies that use a mature matrix.

NETWORK STRUCTURE—THE VIRTUAL ORGANIZATION

A somewhat more radical organizational design, the **network structure** (see **Figure 10–1**) is an example of what could be termed a "non-structure" because of its virtual elimination of in-house business functions. Many activities are outsourced. A corporation organized in this manner is often called a **virtual organization** because it is composed of a series of project groups or collaborations linked by constantly changing nonhierarchical, cobweb-like electronic networks.[49]

The network structure has been enabled by the rapid development of Internet-based tools that allow collaboration without physical presence. Rather than satisfying a company's needs with locally available people (or paying to relocate people) more and more companies utilize a network structure to get the best and brightest. This structure is also quite useful when the environment of a firm is unstable and is expected to remain so.[50] Under such conditions, there is usually a strong need for innovation and quick response. Instead of having salaried employees, the company may contract with people for a specific project or length of time. Long-term contracts with suppliers and distributors replace services that the company could provide for itself through vertical integration. Electronic markets and sophisticated information systems reduce the transaction costs of the marketplace, thus justifying a "buy" over a "make" decision. Rather than being located in a single building or area, the organization's business functions are scattered worldwide. The organization is, in effect, only a shell, with a small headquarters acting as a "broker," electronically connected to some completely owned divisions, partially owned subsidiaries, and other independent companies. In its purist form, a network organization is a series of independent firms or business units linked together by computers in an information system that designs, produces, and markets a product or service.[51]

Developments in information technology are changing the way business is being done internationally. See the **Global Issue** feature to learn about the latest issue related to international outsourcing of IT.

Entrepreneurial ventures often start out as network organizations. For example, Randy and Nicole Wilburn of Dorchester, Massachusetts, ran real estate, consulting, design, and baby food companies out of their home. Nicole, a stay-at-home mom and

GLOBAL issue

OUTSOURCING COMES FULL CIRCLE

What happens when international companies who have developed their business model on cheaper labor in remote countries have to hire employees back in the originating country because the work demands local labor? That is exactly what is happening to many Indian firms who established their businesses as U.S. companies were seeking highly skilled, well-educated employees who worked for one-tenth the wage of U.S. workers. This was the classic cost-cutting model of the past two decades and no area on earth benefited as much as India. By 2011, U.S. companies were spending just shy of US$28 billion on outsourcing.

The mood of the United States swung during the recession of 2009–2011 and the country instituted tough new regulations limiting the number of foreign nationals who could work in the United States. This effort coincided with a wave of companies trying to pitch speed, local knowledge, and U.S. employment growth as competitive factors in their business.

Bangalore-based Infosys acquired Marsh Consumer BPO and its 87 employees based in Des Moines, Iowa,

and the gigantic Cognizant Technology Solutions, which, while based in New Jersey, has most of its 145,000 employees in India, and acquired centers in Iowa and North Dakota employing almost 1000 employees. The complexity of managing the workforces and catering to clients that simultaneously want cost controls, efficient work, and local expertise can be daunting. By 2015 the outsourced workforce in India was approaching 1.5 million.

Indian outsourcing companies moved to an adaptive model where they kept offices and operations in the home countries of their clients all around the world. This provided not only for better communication, but allowed for rapid response operations in addition to low-cost development.

....

SOURCES: E. Haaramo, "Indian outsourcing is booming in the Nordic countries," Computer Weekly, April 9, 2015 (*computer-weekly.com/news/4500244037/indian-outsourcing-is-booming-in-the-nordic-countries*); "Indian Companies Seek a Passage to America," *Bloomberg Businessweek* (October 29, 2012), pp. 26–27; D. Thoppil, "Indian Outsourcing Firms Hire in the U.S.," *The Wall Street Journal* (August 7, 2012); http://online.wsj.com/article/SB10000872396390443517104577572930208453186.html

graphic designer, farmed out design work to freelancers and cooked her own line of organic baby food. For US$300, an Indian artist designed the logo for Nicole's "Baby Fresh Organic Baby Foods." A London freelancer wrote promotional materials. Instead of hiring a secretary, Randy hired "virtual assistants" in Jerusalem to transcribe voice-mail, update his Web site, and design PowerPoint graphics. Retired brokers in Virginia and Michigan deal with his real estate paperwork.[52]

Large companies such as Nike, Reebok, and Benetton use the network structure in their operations function by subcontracting (outsourcing) manufacturing to other companies in low-cost locations around the world. For control purposes, the Italian-based Benetton maintains what it calls an "umbilical cord" by assuring production planning for all its subcontractors, planning materials requirements for them, and providing them with bills of labor and standard prices and costs, as well as technical assistance to make sure their quality is up to Benetton's standards.

The network organizational structure provides an organization with increased flexibility and adaptability to cope with rapid technological change and shifting patterns of international trade and competition. It allows a company to concentrate on its distinctive competencies, while gathering efficiencies from other firms that are concentrating their efforts in their areas of expertise. The network does, however, have disadvantages. Some believe that the network is really only a transitional structure because it is inherently unstable and subject to tensions.[53] The availability of numerous potential partners can be a source of trouble. Contracting out individual activities to separate suppliers/

distributors may keep the firm from discovering any internal synergies by combining these activities. If a particular firm overspecializes on only a few functions, it runs the risk of choosing the wrong functions and thus becoming noncompetitive.

CELLULAR/MODULAR ORGANIZATION: A NEW TYPE OF STRUCTURE?

Some authorities in the field propose that the evolution of organizational forms is leading from the matrix and the network to the cellular (also called modular) organizational form. According to Miles and Snow et al., "a **cellular/modular organization** is composed of cells (self-managing teams, autonomous business units, etc.) which can operate alone but which can interact with other cells to produce a more potent and competent business mechanism." This combination of independence and interdependence allows the cellular/modular organizational form to generate and share the knowledge and expertise needed to produce continuous innovation. The cellular/modular form includes the dispersed entrepreneurship of the divisional structure, customer responsiveness of the matrix, and self-organizing knowledge and asset sharing of the network.[54] Bombardier, for example, broke up the design of its Continental business jet into 12 parts provided by internal divisions and external contractors. The cockpit, center, and forward fuselage were produced in-house, but other major parts were supplied by manufacturers spread around the globe. The cellular/modular structure is used when it is possible to break up a company's products into self-contained modules or cells and when interfaces can be specified such that the cells/modules work when they are joined together.[55] The cellular/modular structure is similar to a current trend in industry of using internal joint ventures to temporarily combine specialized expertise and skills within a corporation to accomplish a task which individual units alone could not accomplish.[56]

The impetus for such a new structure is the pressure for a continuous process of innovation in all industries. Each cell/module has an entrepreneurial responsibility to the larger organization. Beyond knowledge creation and sharing, the cellular/modular form adds value by keeping the firm's total knowledge assets more fully in use than any other type of structure.[57] It is beginning to appear in firms that are focused on rapid product and service innovation—providing unique or state-of-the-art offerings in industries such as automobile manufacture, bicycle production, consumer electronics, household appliances, power tools, computing products, and software.[58]

Reengineering and Strategy Implementation

10-5. Discuss the issues related to centralization versus decentralization in structuring organizations

Reengineering is the radical redesign of business processes to achieve major gains in cost, service, or time. It is not in itself a type of structure, but it is an effective program to implement a turnaround strategy.

Business process reengineering strives to break away from the old rules and procedures that develop and become ingrained in every organization over the years. They may be a combination of policies, rules, and procedures that have never been seriously questioned because they were established years earlier. These may range from "Credit decisions are made by the credit department" to "Local inventory is needed for good customer service." These rules of organization and work design may have been based on assumptions about technology, people, and organizational goals that may no longer be relevant. Rather than attempting to fix existing problems through minor adjustments and the fine-tuning of existing processes, the key to reengineering is asking "If this were a new company, how would we run this place?"

Michael Hammer, who popularized the concept of reengineering, suggests the following principles for reengineering:

- **Organize around outcomes, not tasks:** Design a person's or a department's job around an objective or outcome instead of a single task or series of tasks.

- **Have those who use the output of the process perform the process:** With computer-based information systems, processes can now be reengineered so that the people who need the result of the process can do it themselves.

- **Subsume information-processing work into the real work that produces the information:** People or departments that produce information can also process it for use instead of just sending raw data to others in the organization to interpret.

- **Treat geographically dispersed resources as though they were centralized:** With modern information systems, companies can provide flexible service locally while keeping the actual resources in a centralized location for coordination purposes.

- **Link parallel activities instead of integrating their results:** Instead of having separate units perform different activities that must eventually come together, have them communicate while they work so they can do the integrating.

- **Put the decision point where the work is performed and build control into the process:** The people who do the work should make the decisions and be self-controlling.

- **Capture information once and at the source:** Instead of having each unit develop its own database and information processing activities, the information can be put on a network so all can access it.[59]

Studies of the performance of reengineering programs show mixed results. Several companies have had success with business process reengineering. For example, the Mossville Engine Center, a business unit of Caterpillar Inc., used reengineering to decrease process cycle times by 50%, reduce the number of process steps by 45%, reduce human effort by 8%, and improve cross-divisional interactions and overall employee decision making.[60]

One study of North American financial firms found that "the average reengineering project took 15 months, consumed 66 person-months of effort, and delivered cost savings of 24%."[61] In a survey of 782 corporations using reengineering, 75% of the executives said their companies had succeeded in reducing operating expenses and increasing productivity.[62] A study of 134 large and small Canadian companies found that reengineering programs resulted in (1) an increase in productivity and product quality, (2) cost reductions, and (3) an increase in overall organization quality, for both large and small firms.[63] Other studies report, however, that anywhere from 50% to 70% of reengineering programs fail to achieve their objectives.[64] Reengineering thus appears to be more useful for redesigning specific processes like order entry, than for changing an entire organization.[65]

SIX SIGMA

Originally conceived by Motorola as a quality improvement program in the mid-1980s, Six Sigma has become a cost-saving program for all types of manufacturers. Briefly, **Six Sigma** is an analytical method for achieving near-perfect results on a production line. Although the emphasis is on reducing product variance in order to boost quality and efficiency, it is increasingly being applied to accounts receivable, sales, and R&D. In statistics, the Greek letter *sigma* denotes variation in the standard bell-shaped curve. One sigma equals 690,000 defects per 1 million. Most companies are able to achieve only three sigma, or 66,000 defects per million. Six Sigma reduces the defects to only 3.4 defects per million—thus saving money by preventing waste. The process of Six Sigma encompasses five steps.

1. *Define* a process where results are poorer than average.
2. *Measure* the process to determine exact current performance.
3. *Analyze* the information to pinpoint where things are going wrong.
4. *Improve* the process and eliminate the error.
5. *Establish* controls to prevent future defects from occurring.[66]

Savings attributed to Six Sigma programs have ranged from 1.2% to 4.5% of annual revenue for a number of Fortune 500 firms. Firms that have successfully employed Six Sigma include General Electric, Allied Signal, ABB, and Ford Motor Company.[67] Fifty-three percent of the Fortune 500 companies now have a Six Sigma program in place and more than 83% of the Fortune 100 have it in place despite its manufacturing origins.[68] At Dow Chemical, each Six Sigma project has resulted in cost savings of US$500,000 in the first year. According to Jack Welch, GE's past CEO, Six Sigma is an appropriate change program for the entire organization.[69] Six Sigma experts at 3M have been able to speed up R&D and analyze why its top salespeople sold more than others. A disadvantage of the program is that training costs in the beginning may outweigh any savings. The expense of compiling and analyzing data, especially in areas where a process cannot be easily standardized, may exceed what is saved.[70] Another disadvantage is that Six Sigma can lead to less-risky incremental innovation based on previous work than on riskier "blue-sky" projects.[71]

The newer version of this is called *Lean Six Sigma* and as we pointed out earlier, it is becoming increasingly popular in companies. This program incorporates the statistical approach of Six Sigma with the lean manufacturing program originally developed by Toyota. Like reengineering, it includes the removal of unnecessary steps in any process and fixing those that remain. This is the 'lean' addition to Six Sigma. The U.S. Navy has employed Lean Six Sigma with a wide variety of efforts with spectacular success. One group eliminated more than 580,000 documents in the recruiting process while another group reduced 118 man hours from the candidate tracking system used by the Navy.[72]

DESIGNING JOBS TO IMPLEMENT STRATEGY

Organizing a company's activities and people to implement strategy involves more than simply redesigning a corporation's overall structure; it also involves redesigning the way jobs are done. With the increasing emphasis on reengineering, many companies are beginning to rethink their work processes with an eye toward phasing unnecessary people and activities out of the process. Process steps that have traditionally been performed sequentially can be improved by performing them concurrently using cross-functional work teams. Harley-Davidson managed to reduce total plant employment by 25% while reducing by 50% the time needed to build a motorcycle. Restructuring through needing fewer people requires broadening the scope of jobs and encouraging teamwork. The design of jobs and subsequent job performance are, therefore, increasingly being considered as sources of competitive advantage.

Job design refers to the study of individual tasks in an attempt to make them more relevant to the company and to the employee(s). To minimize some of the adverse consequences of task specialization, corporations have turned to new job design techniques: *job enlargement* (combining tasks to give a worker more of the same type of duties to perform), *job rotation* (moving workers through several jobs to increase variety), *job characteristics* (using task characteristics to improve employee motivation), and *job enrichment* (altering the jobs by giving the worker more autonomy and control over activities). Although each of these methods has its adherents, no one method seems to work in all situations.

A good example of modern job design is the introduction of team-based production by the glass manufacturer Corning Inc., in its Blacksburg, Virginia, plant. With union approval, Corning reduced job classifications from 47 to 4 to enable production workers to rotate jobs after learning new skills. The workers were divided into 14-member teams that, in effect, managed themselves. The plant had only two levels of management: The Plant Manager and two line leaders who only advised the teams. Employees worked very demanding 12 ½-hour shifts, alternating three-day and four-day weeks. The teams made managerial decisions, imposed discipline on fellow workers, and were required to learn three "skill modules" within two years or else lose their jobs. As a result of this new job design, a Blacksburg team, made up of workers with interchangeable skills, can retool a line to produce a different type of filter in only 10 minutes—six times faster than workers in a traditionally designed filter plant. The Blacksburg plant earned a US$2 million profit in its first eight months of production instead of losing the US$2.3 million projected for the startup period. The plant performed so well that Corning's top management acted to convert the company's 27 other factories to team-based production.[73]

CENTRALIZATION VERSUS DECENTRALIZATION

A basic dilemma an MNC faces is how to organize authority centrally so it operates as a vast interlocking system that achieves synergy and at the same time decentralize authority so that local managers can make the decisions necessary to meet the demands of the local market or host government. To deal with this problem, MNCs tend to structure themselves either along product groups or geographic areas. They may even combine both in a matrix structure—the design chosen by 3M Corporation, Philips, and Asea Brown Boveri (ABB), among others.[74] One side of 3M's matrix represents the company's product divisions; the other side includes the company's international country and regional subsidiaries.

Two examples of the usual international structure are Nestlé and American Cyanamid. Nestlé's structure is one in which significant power and authority have been decentralized to geographic entities. This structure is similar to that depicted in **Figure 10–2**, in which each geographic set of operating companies has a different group of products. In contrast, American Cyanamid has a series of centralized product groups with worldwide responsibilities. To depict Cyanamid's structure, the geographical entities in **Figure 10–2** would have to be replaced by product groups or SBUs.

The **product-group structure** of American Cyanamid enables the company to introduce and manage a similar line of products around the world. This enables the corporation to centralize decision making along product lines and to reduce costs. The **geographic-area structure** of Nestlé, in contrast, allows the company to tailor products to regional differences and to achieve regional coordination. For instance, Nestlé markets 200 different varieties of its instant coffee, Nescafé. The geographic-area structure decentralizes decision making to the local subsidiaries.

As industries move from being multidomestic to being more globally integrated, MNCs are increasingly switching from the geographic-area to the product-group structure. Nestlé, for example, found that its decentralized area structure had become increasingly inefficient. As a result, operating margins at Nestlé have trailed those at rivals Unilever, Group Danone, and Kraft Foods by as much as 50%. Then CEO Peter Brabeck-Letmathe acted to eliminate country-by-country responsibilities for many functions. In one instance, he established five centers worldwide to handle most coffee and cocoa purchasing.[75]

FIGURE 10–2
Geographic Area
Structure for an MNC

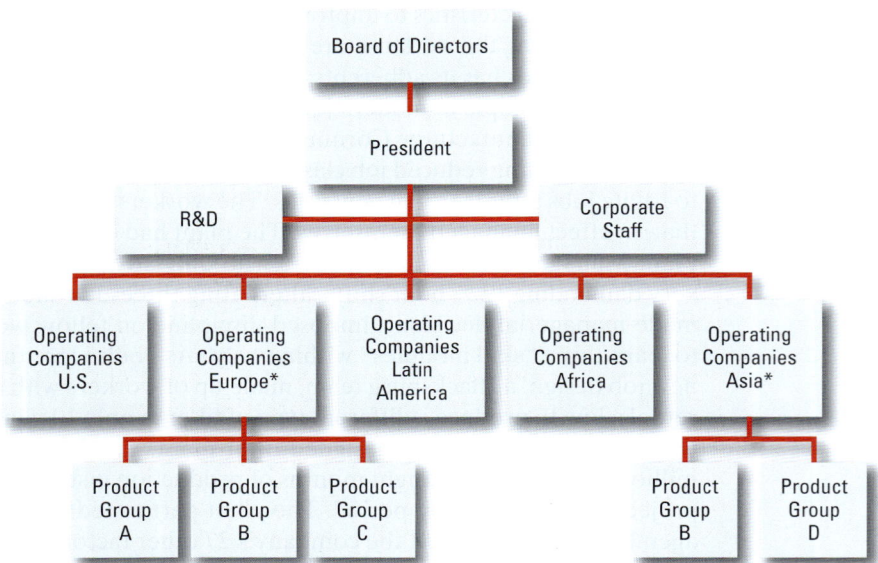

*NOTE: Because of space limitations, product groups for only Europe and Asia are shown here.

Simultaneous pressures for decentralization to be locally responsive and centralization to be maximally efficient are causing interesting structural adjustments in most large corporations. This is what is meant by the phrase "think globally, act locally." Companies are attempting to decentralize those operations that are culturally oriented and closest to the customers—manufacturing, marketing, and human resources. At the same time, the companies are consolidating less visible internal functions, such as research and development, finance, and information systems, where there can be significant economies of scale.

End of Chapter SUMMARY

Strategy implementation is where "the rubber hits the road." Environmental scanning and strategy formulation are crucial to strategic management but are only the beginning of the process. The failure to carry a strategic plan into the day-to-day operations of the workplace is a major reason why strategic planning often fails to achieve its objectives. It is discouraging to note that in one study nearly 70% of the strategic plans were never successfully implemented.[76]

For a strategy to be successfully implemented, it must be made action-oriented. This is done through a series of programs that are funded through specific budgets and contain new detailed procedures. This is what Sergio Marchionne did when he implemented a turnaround strategy as the new Fiat Group CEO in 2004. He attacked the lethargic, bureaucratic system by flattening Fiat's structure and giving younger managers a larger amount of authority and responsibility. He and other managers worked to reduce the number of auto platforms from 19 to 6 by 2012. The time from the completion of the design process to new car production was cut from 26 to 18 months. By 2008, the Fiat auto unit was again profitable. Marchionne reintroduced Fiat to the U.S. market in 2012 after a 27-year absence.[77] Unfortunately, Fiat struggled to gain any traction in the U.S. market. Despite a strong marketing campaign and a number of cars designed specifically for the market, by 2016 sales had stalled at 44,000 cars a year. The company has remained strongly profitable and even acquired 100% of Chrysler in 2014.[78]

This chapter explains how jobs and organizational units can be designed to support a change in strategy. We will continue with staffing and directing issues in strategy implementation in the next chapter.

Pearson MyLab Management®

Go to **mymanagementlab.com** to complete the problems marked with this icon .

KEY TERMS

budget (p. 301)
cellular/modular organization
   (p. 314)
first mover (p. 299)
geographic-area structure (p. 317)
job design (p. 316)
late movers (p. 299)
market location tactic (p. 299)

matrix structures (p. 310)
network structure (p. 312)
organizational life cycle (p. 309)
procedures (p. 301)
product-group structure (p. 317)
program (p. 298)
reengineering (p. 314)

Six Sigma (p. 315)
stages of corporate development
   (p. 304)
strategy implementation (p. 296)
structure follows strategy (p. 303)
synergy (p. 302)
timing tactic (p. 299)
virtual organization (p. 312)

Pearson MyLab Management®

Go to **mymanagementlab.com** for the following assisted-graded writing questions:

10-1. How do timing tactics impact the strategy implementation efforts of a company?

10-2. What issues would you consider to be the most important for a company that is considering the use of a functional structure?

DISCUSSION QUESTIONS

10-3. Staffing decisions are considered an important component of strategic planning and the management process. Why? How is strategy implementation process connected to the decisions resulting from a staffing strategy?

⭐ **10-4.** Why is it necessary for an organization to align its managers with the corporate strategy to ensure better organizational performance?

10-5. Is downsizing a good strategy for revamping an organization's competitiveness when it is facing major competitive threats in the market?

⭐ **10-6.** Can organizations be controlled by culture? Explain.

⭐ **10-7.** How is an international staffing strategy different from a domestic one?

STRATEGIC PRACTICE EXERCISE

The Synergy Game
Yolanda Sarason and Catherine Banbury

Setup

Put three to five chairs on either side of a room, facing each other, in the front of the class. Put a table in the middle, with a bell in the middle of the table.

Procedure

The instructor/moderator divides the class into teams of three to five people. Each team selects a name for itself. The instructor/moderator lists the team names on the board. The first two teams come to the front and sit in the chairs facing each other. The instructor/moderator reads a list of products or services being provided by an actual company. The winning team must identify (1) possible sources of synergy and (2) the actual company being described. For example, if the products/services listed are family restaurants, airline catering, hotels, and retirement centers, the synergy is *standardized food service and hospitality settings* and the company is **The Marriott Corporation**. The first team to successfully name the company *and* the synergy wins the round.

After one practice session, the game begins. Each of the teams is free to discuss the question with other team members. When one of the two teams thinks it has the answer to both parts of the question, it must be the first to ring the bell in order to announce its answer. If it gives the correct answer, it is deemed the winner of round one. Both parts of the answer must be given for a team to have the correct answer. If a team correctly provides only one part, that answer is still wrong—there is no partial credit. The instructor/moderator does not say which part of the answer, if either, was correct. The second team then has the opportunity to state the answer. If the second team is wrong, both teams may try once more. If neither chooses to try again, the instructor/moderator may (1) declare no round winner and both teams sit down, (2) allow the next two teams to provide the answer to round one, or (3) go on to the next round with the same two teams. Two new teams then come to the front for the next round. Once all groups have played once, the winning teams play each other. Rounds continue until there is a grand champion. The instructor should provide a suitable prize, such as candy bars, for the winning team.

SOURCE: This exercise was developed by Professors Yolanda Sarason of Colorado State University and Catherine Banbury of St. Mary's College and Purdue University and presented at the Organizational Behavior Teaching Conference, June 1999. Copyright © 1999 by Yolanda Sarason and Catherine Banbury. Adapted with permission.

Note from Wheelen, Hunger, Hoffman, and Bamford

The *Instructors' Manual* for this book contains a list of products and services with their synergy and the name of the company. In case your instructor does not use this exercise, try the following examples:

Example 1: Motorcycles, autos, lawn mowers, generators

Example 2: Athletic footwear, Rockport shoes, Greg Norman clothing, sportswear

For each example, did you guess the company providing these products/services and the synergy obtained?

Example 1: Engine technology by Honda

Example 2: Marketing and distribution for the athletically oriented by Reebok

NOTES

1. Y. Weber, C. Oberg, S. Tarba, "The M&A Paradox: Factors of Success and Failure in Mergers and Acquisitions," *Financial Times Press*, January 16, 2014 (ftpress.com/articles/article.aspx?p=2164982); J. W. Gadella, "Avoiding Expensive Mistakes in Capital Investment," *Long Range Planning* (April 1994), pp. 103–110; B. Voss, "World Market Is Not for Everyone," *Journal of Business Strategy* (July/August 1993), p. 4.

2. A. Bert, T. MacDonald, and T. Herd, "Two Merger Integration Imperatives: Urgency and Execution," *Strategy & Leadership*, Vol. 31, No. 3 (2003), pp. 42–49.

3. L. D. Alexander, "Strategy Implementation: Nature of the Problem," *International Review of Strategic Management*, Vol. 2, No. 1, edited by D. E. Hussey (New York: John Wiley & Sons, 1991), pp. 73–113. See also L. G. Hrebiniak, "Obstacles to Effective Strategy Implementation," *Organizational Dynamics* (Vol. 35, Issue 1, 2006), pp. 12–31 for six obstacles to implementation.

4. L. G. Hrebiniak (2006).

5. F. Arner and A. Aston, "How Xerox Got Up to Speed," *BusinessWeek* (May 3, 2004), pp. 103–104.

6. J. Darragh and A. Campbell, "Why Corporate Initiatives Get Stuck?" *Long Range Planning* (February 2001), pp. 33–52.

7. "Army Organizations earn 10 Lean Six Sigma Excellence Awards," *Military Spot*, September 25, 2015 (http://www.militaryspot.com/news/army-organizations-earn-10-lean-six-sigma-excellence-awards).

8. P. C. Nutt, "Surprising But True: Half the Decisions in Organizations Fail," *Academy of Management Executive* (November 1999), pp. 75–90.

9. Some refer to this as the economic concept of "increasing returns." Instead of the curve leveling off when the company reaches a point of diminishing returns when a product saturates a market, the curve continues to go up as the company takes advantage of setting the standard to spin off new products that use the new standard to achieve higher performance than competitors. See J. Alley, "The Theory That Made Microsoft," *Fortune* (April 29, 1996), pp. 65–66.

10. H. Lee, K. G. Smith, C. M. Grimm, and A. Schomburg, "Timing, Order and Durability of New Product Advantages with Imitation," *Strategic Management Journal* (January 2000), pp. 23–30; Y. Pan and P. C. K. Chi, "Financial Performance and Survival of Multinational Corporations in China," *Strategic Management Journal* (April 1999), pp. 359–374; R. Makadok, "Can First-Mover and Early-Mover

Advantages Be Sustained in an Industry with Low Barriers to Entry/Imitation?" *Strategic Management Journal* (July 1998), pp. 683–696; B. Mascarenhas, "The Order and Size of Entry into International Markets," *Journal of Business Venturing* (July 1997), pp. 287–299.

11. At these respective points, cost disadvantages vis-à-vis later entrants fully eroded the earlier returns to first movers. See W. Boulding and M. Christen, "Idea—First Mover Disadvantage," *Harvard Business Review* (Vol. 79, No. 9, 2001), pp. 20–21 as reported by D. J. Ketchen Jr., C. C. Snow, and V. L. Hoover, "Research on Competitive Dynamics: Recent Accomplishments and Future Challenges," *Journal of Management* (Vol. 30, No. 6, 2004), pp. 779–804.

12. M. B. Lieberman and D. B. Montgomery, "First-Mover (Dis) Advantages: Retrospective and Link with the Resource-Based View," *Strategic Management Journal* (December, 1998), pp. 1111–1125; G. J. Tellis and P. N. Golder, "First to Market, First to Fail? Real Causes of Enduring Market Leadership," *Sloan Management Review* (Winter 1996), pp. 65–75.

13. S. Bertoni, "Razor Wars: Harry's Raises $75 Million to fight Gillette and Dollar Shave Club," *Forbes*, July 7, 2015 (*forbes.com/sites/stevenbertoni/2015/07/07/razor-wars-harrys-raises-75-million-to-fight-gillette-and-dollar-shave-club/#374e5cc8846a*).

14. S. K. Ethiraj and D. H. Zhu, "Performance Effects of Imitative Entry," *Strategic Management Journal* (August 2008), pp. 797–817; G. Dowell and A. Swaminathan, "Entry Timing, Exploration, and Firm Survival in the Early U.S. Bicycle Industry," *Strategic Management Journal* (December 2006), pp. 1159–1182. For an in-depth discussion of first- and late-mover advantages and disadvantages, see D. S. Cho, D. J. Kim, and D. K. Rhee, "Latecomer Strategies: Evidence from the Semiconductor Industry in Japan and Korea," *Organization Science* (July–August 1998), pp. 489–505.

15. J. Shamsie, C. Phelps, and J. Kuperman, "Better Late than Never: A Study of Late Entrants in Household Electrical Equipment," *Strategic Management Journal* (January 2004), pp. 69–84.

16. T. S. Schoenecker and A. C. Cooper, "The Role of Firm Resources and Organizational Attributes in Determining Entry Timing: A Cross-Industry Study," *Strategic Management Journal* (December 1998), pp. 1127–1143.

17. Summarized from various articles by L. Fahey in *The Strategic Management Reader*, edited by L. Fahey (Englewood Cliffs, NJ: Prentice Hall, 1989), pp. 178–205.

18. M. Boyle, "Dueling Diapers," *Fortune* (February 17, 2003), pp. 115–116.

19. C. Edwards, "To See Where Tech Is Headed, Watch TI," *BusinessWeek* (November 6, 2006), p. 74.

20. P. Burrows, "Show Time," *BusinessWeek* (February 2, 2004), pp. 56–64.

21. L. Murphy and J. Xu, "Steinway agrees to be bought by Paulson for $512 million," *BloombergBusiness*, August 14, 2013 (*Bloomberg.com/news/articles/2013-08-14/Paulson-co-to-buy-piano-maker-steinway-for-512-million*; "Steinway & Sons unveils its 600,000th piano," Luxuo, June 15, 2015 (*luxuo.com/luxury-trends/Steinway-piano-the-fibonacco.html*; A. Serwer, "Happy Birthday, Steinway," *Fortune* (March 17, 2003), pp. 94–97.

22. "Programmed for a Fight," *The Economist* (October 20, 2007), p. 85.

23. This information on defensive tactics is summarized from M. E. Porter, *Competitive Advantage* (New York: The Free Press, 1985), pp. 482–512.

24. H. D. Hopkins, "The Response Strategies of Dominant U.S. Firms to Japanese Challengers," *Journal of Management* (Vol. 29, No. 1, 2003), pp. 5–25.

25. For additional information on defensive competitive tactics, see G. Stalk, "Curveball Strategies to Fool the Competition," *Harvard Business Review* (September 2006), pp. 115–122.

26. "Mondelez International reports strong progress in cocoa life sustainability program," Vending Market Watch, February 23, 2016 (vendingmarketwatch.com/news/12173329/mondelez-international-reports-strong-progress-in-cocoa-life-sustainability-program).

27. M. S. Feldman and B. T. Pentland, "Reconceptualizing Organizational Routines as a Source of Flexibility and Change," *Administrative Science Quarterly* (March 2003), pp. 94–118.

28. S. F. Slater and E. M. Olson, "Strategy Type and Performance: The Influence of Sales Force Management," *Strategic Management Journal* (August 2000), pp. 813–829.

29. B. Grow, "Thinking Outside the Box," *BusinessWeek* (October 25, 2004), pp. 70–72.

30. http://www.google.com/about/company/

31. A. D. Chandler, *Strategy and Structure* (Cambridge, MA: MIT Press, 1962).

32. A. P. Sloan Jr., *My Years with General Motors* (Garden City, NY: Doubleday, 1964).

33. T. L. Amburgey and T. Dacin, "As the Left Foot Follows the Right? The Dynamics of Strategic and Structural Change," *Academy of Management Journal* (December 1994), pp. 1427–1452; M. Ollinger, "The Limits of Growth of the Multidivisional Firm: A Case Study of the U.S. Oil Industry from 1930–90," *Strategic Management Journal* (September 1994), pp. 503–520.

34. J. Langley, "TiVo Inc. (TIVO) to Post Q2 2016 Earnings of $0.05 Per Share, Jefferies Group Forecasts," *Financial Market News*, March 5, 2016 (*http://www.financial-market-news.com/tivo-inc-tivo-to-post-q2-2016-earnings-of-0-05-per-share-jefferies-group-forecasts/924013/*); J. Baumgartner, "TiVo cuts 50 jobs amid restructuring," *Multichannel News*, February 29, 2016 (multichannel.com/news/content/tivo-cuts-50-jobs-amid-restructuring/402924).

35. D. F. Jennings and S. L. Seaman, "High and Low Levels of Organizational Adaptation: An Empirical Analysis of Strategy, Structure, and Performance," *Strategic Management Journal* (July 1994), pp. 459–475; L. Donaldson, "The Normal Science of Structured Contingency Theory," in *Handbook of Organization Studies*, edited by S. R. Clegg, C. Hardy, and W. R. Nord (London: Sage Publications, 1996), pp. 57–76.

36. A. K. Gupta, "SBU Strategies, Corporate-SBU Relations, and SBU Effectiveness in Strategy Implementation," *Academy of Management Journal* (September 1987), pp. 477–500.

37. L. E. Greiner, "Evolution and Revolution as Organizations Grow," *Harvard Business Review* (May–June 1998), pp. 55–67. This is an updated version of Greiner's classic 1972 article.

38. K. Shimizu and M. A. Hitt, "What Constrains or Facilitates Divestitures of Formerly Acquired Firms? The Effects of Organizational Inertia," *Journal of Management* (February 2005), pp. 50–72.

39. A. Weintraub, "Can Pfizer Prime the Pipeline?" *Business-Week* (December 31, 2007), pp. 90–91.

40. Ibid, p. 64. Although Greiner simply labeled this as the *"?" crisis*, the term *pressure-cooker* seems apt.

41. J. Hamm, "Why Entrepreneurs Don't Scale," *Harvard Business Review* (December 2002), pp. 110–115. See also C. B. Gibson and R. M. Rottner, "The Social Foundations for Building a Company Around an Inventor," *Organizational Dynamics* (Vol. 37, Issue 1, January–March 2008), pp. 21–34.

42. W. P. Barnett, "The Dynamics of Competitive Intensity," *Administrative Science Quarterly* (March 1997), pp. 128–160; D. Miller, *The Icarus Paradox: How Exceptional Companies Bring About Their Own Downfall* (New York: Harper Business, 1990).

43. D. Miller and P. H. Friesen, "A Longitudinal Study of the Corporate Life Cycle," *Management Science* (October 1984), pp. 1161–1183.

44. J. L. Morrow Jr., D. G. Sirmon, M. A. Hitt, and T. R. Holcomb, "Creating Value in the Face of Declining Performance: Firm Strategies and Organizational Recovery," *Strategic Management Journal* (March 2007), pp. 271–283; C. Zook, "Finding Your Next Core Business," *Harvard Business Review* (April 2007), pp. 66–75.

45. J. P. Sheppard and S. D. Chowdhury, "Riding the Wrong Wave: Organizational Failure as a Failed Turnaround," *Long Range Planning* (June 2005), pp. 239–260.

46. W-R. Chen and K. D. Miller, "Situational and Institutional Determinants of Firms' R&D Search Intensity," *Strategic Management Journal* (April 2007), pp. 369–381.

47. L. G. Hrebiniak and W. F. Joyce, *Implementing Strategy* (New York: Macmillan, 1984), pp. 85–86.

48. S. M. Davis and P. R. Lawrence, *Matrix* (Reading, MA: Addison-Wesley, 1977), pp. 11–24.

49. J. G. March, "The Future Disposable Organizations and the Rigidities of Imagination," *Organization* (August/November 1995), p. 434.

50. M. A. Schilling and H. K. Steensma, "The Use of Modular Organizational Forms: An Industry-Level Analysis," *Academy of Management Journal* (December 2001), pp. 1149–1168.

51. M. P. Koza and A. Y. Lewin, "The Coevolution of Network Alliances: A Longitudinal Analysis of an International Professional Service Network," *Organization Science* (September/October 1999), pp. 638–653.

52. P. Engardio, "Mom-and-Pop Multinationals," *Business-Week* (July 14 and 21, 2008), pp. 77–78.

53. For more information on managing a network organization, see G. Lorenzoni and C Baden-Fuller, "Creating a Strategic Center to Manage a Web of Partners," *California Management Review* (Spring 1995), pp. 146–163.

54. R. E. Miles, C. C. Snow, J. A. Mathews, G. Miles, and H. J. Coleman Jr., "Organizing in the Knowledge Age: Anticipating the Cellular Form," *Academy of Management Executive* (November 1997), pp. 7–24.

55. N. Anand and R. L. Daft, "What Is the Right Organization Design?" *Organizational Dynamics* (Vol. 36, No. 4, 2007), pp. 329–344.

56. J. Naylor and M. Lewis, "Internal Alliances: Using Joint Ventures in a Diversified Company," *Long Range Planning* (October 1997), pp. 678–688.

57. G. Hoetker, "Do Modular Products Lead to Modular Organizations?" *Strategic Management Journal* (June 2006), pp. 501–518.

58. Anand and Daft, pp. 336–338.

59. Summarized from M. Hammer, "Reengineering Work: Don't Automate, Obliterate," *Harvard Business Review* (July–August 1990), pp. 104–112.

60. D. Paper, "BPR: Creating the Conditions for Success," *Long Range Planning* (June 1998), pp. 426–435.

61. S. Drew, "BPR in Financial Services: Factors for Success," *Long Range Planning* (October 1994), pp. 25–41.

62. "Do As I Say, Not As I Do," *Journal of Business Strategy* (May/June 1997), pp. 3–4.

63. L. Raymond and S. Rivard, "Determinants of Business Process Reengineering Success in Small and Large Enterprises: An Empirical Study in the Canadian Context," *Journal of Small Business Management* (January 1998), pp. 72–85.

64. K. Grint, "Reengineering History: Social Resonances and Business Process Reengineering," *Organization* (July 1994), pp. 179–201; A. Kleiner, "Revisiting Reengineering," *Strategy+Business* (3rd Quarter 2000), pp. 27–31.

65. E. A. Hall, J. Rosenthal, and J. Wade, "How to Make Reengineering *Really* Work," *McKinsey Quarterly* (1994, No. 2), pp. 107–128.

66. M. Arndt, "Quality Isn't Just for Widgets," *Business-Week* (July 22, 2002), pp. 72–73.

67. T. M. Box, "Six Sigma Quality: Experiential Learning," *SAM Advanced Management Journal* (Winter 2006), pp. 20–23.

68. L. Bodell, "5 Ways Process Is Killing Your Productivity," *Fast Company* (May 15, 2012), http://www.fastcompany.com/1837301/5-ways-process-killing-your-productivity

69. J. Welch and S. Welch, "The Six Sigma Shotgun," *BusinessWeek* (May 21, 2007), p. 110.

70. Arndt, p. 73.

71. B. Hindo, "At 3M, a Struggle Between Efficiency and Creativity," *BusinessWeek IN* (June 11, 2007), pp. 8–16.

72. S. Thornbloom, "NSTC Implements Lean Six Sigma to Improve its Core Processes," *America's Navy*, November 3, 2014 (*navy.mil/submit/display.asp?story_id=84231*).

73. J. Hoerr, "Sharpening Minds for a Competitive Edge," *BusinessWeek* (December 17, 1990), pp. 72–78.

74. C. A. Bartlett and S. Ghoshal, "Beyond the M-Form: Toward a Managerial Theory of the Firm," *Strategic Management Journal* (Winter 1993), pp. 23–46.

75. C. Matlack, "Nestle Is Starting to Slim Down at Last," *BusinessWeek* (October 27, 2003), pp. 56–57; "Daring, Defying to Grow," *The Economist* (August 7, 2004), pp. 55–58.

76. J. Sterling, "Translating Strategy into Effective Implementation: Dispelling the Myths and Highlighting What Works," *Strategy & Leadership* (Vol. 31, No. 3, 2003), pp. 27–34.

77. "Rebirth of a Carmaker," *The Economist* (April 26, 2008), pp. 87–89; D. Kiley, "Fiat Headed Back to U.S. after 27 Years," *AOL Autos* (February 14, 2011), http://autos.aol .com/article/fiat-500-coming-to-america/

78. R. Abrams, "Fiat completes acquisition of Chrysler," *New York Times*, January 21, 2014 (http://dealbook.nytimes .com/2014/01/21/fiat-completes-acquisition-of-chrysler/?_ r=0); B. Snavely, "Fiat hopes new 500X pulls brand out of sales slump," *Detroit Free Press*, August 31, 2015 (http:// www.freep.com/story/money/cars/chrysler/2015/08/31 /fiat-brand-sales-slump-chrysler-fca-marchionne/32000385/).

CHAPTER **11**

Strategy Implementation:
Staffing and Directing

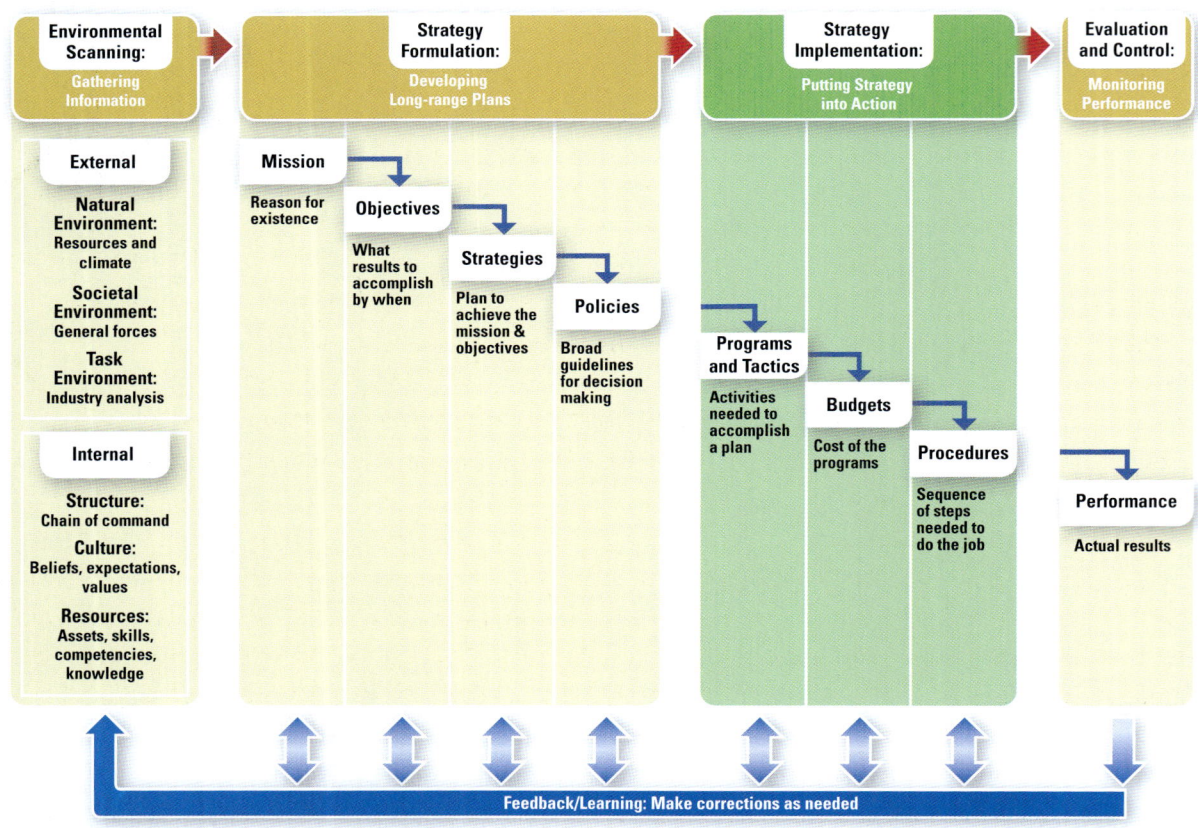

Pearson MyLab Management®

⭐ Improve Your Grade!

Over 10 million students improved their results using the Pearson MyLabs. Visit **mymanagementlab.com** for simulations, tutorials, and end-of-chapter problems.

Learning Objectives

After reading this chapter, you should be able to:

11-1. Explain the link between strategy and staffing decisions

11-2. Discuss how leaders manage corporate culture

11-3. Utilize an action planning framework to implement an organization's MBO and TQM initiatives

Workplace Discrimination and Public Image

While the legal context of what constitutes workplace discrimination is constantly evolving, public perception can impact companies in virtually any industry. In 2015, the U.S. Equal Employment Opportunity Commission (EEOC) received almost 90,000 charges of workplace discrimination. These included discrimination complaints related to race, color, sex, age, religion, pregnancy, disability, genetic information, and national origin.

One of the more contentious issues has developed around the Affordable Care Act (ACA), a movement nationwide to recognize same-sex marriages, and the LGBT community. Companies including Wal*Mart, BNSF Railroad, Saks Fifth Avenue, SkyWest Airlines, and Pepperdine University have cases pending against them in the federal court system. These plaintiffs argue that they are being discriminated against because of their sex.

Wal*Mart extended spousal health coverage to same-sex marriages (where legal) in January 2014, however those denied prior to that point have formed a class action suit against the company for discriminating based upon the sex of the partner. As the country moved toward increasing recognition of same-sex marriage (37 states had statutes on the books before the June 2015 Supreme Court ruling that allowed same-sex couples to marry) more and more companies decided to include same-sex married couples in their employees benefit offerings. Today, it presents not only a business issue, but a public perception issue. Should Wal*Mart fight the retroactive assignment of benefits or should the company settle with plaintiffs?

SOURCES: "If You Are Anti Are You Anti?" *Bloomberg BusinessWeek*, February 22–28, 2016, pp. 23–24; "State Same-Sex Marriage State Laws Map," Governing, (http://www.governing.com/gov-data/same-sex-marriage-civil-unions-doma-laws-by-state.html) (Accessed 3/17/16); S. Heasley, "Workplace Disability Discrimination Claims At Record High," Disability Scoop, February 17, 2016 (https://www.disabilityscoop.com/2016/02/17/workplace-claims-record-high/21926/).

This chapter discusses strategy implementation in terms of staffing and leading. **Staffing** focuses on the selection and use of employees. **Leading** emphasizes the use of programs to better align employee interests and attitudes with a new strategy.

Staffing

11-1. Explain the link between strategy and staffing decisions

The implementation of new strategies and policies often calls for new human resource management priorities and a different use of personnel. Such staffing issues can involve hiring new people with new skills, firing people with inappropriate or substandard skills, and/or training existing employees to learn new skills. Research demonstrates that companies with enlightened talent-management policies and programs have higher returns on sales, investments, assets, and equity.[1] This is especially important given that the total U.S. market for talent acquisition has been estimated at US$124 billion with the average cost per hire at US$5,700.[2]

If growth strategies are to be implemented, new people may need to be hired and trained. Experienced people with the necessary skills need to be found for promotion to newly created managerial positions. When a corporation follows a growth through acquisition strategy, it may find that it needs to replace several managers in the acquired company. The percentage of an acquired company's top management team that either quit or is asked to leave is around 25% after the first year, 35% after the second year, 48% after the third year, 55% after the fourth year, and 61% after five years.[3] In addition, executives who join an acquired company after the acquisition quit at significantly higher-than-normal rates beginning in their second year. Executives continue to depart at higher-than-normal rates for nine years after the acquisition.[4] Turnover rates of executives in firms acquired by foreign firms are significantly higher than for firms acquired by domestic firms, primarily in the fourth and fifth years after the acquisition.[5]

It is one thing to lose excess employees after a merger, but it is something else to lose highly skilled people who are difficult to replace. In a study of 40 mergers, 90% of the acquiring companies in the 15 successful mergers identified key employees and targeted them for retention within 30 days after the announcement. In contrast, this task was carried out only in one-third of the unsuccessful acquisitions.[6] To deal with integration issues such as these, some companies are appointing special **integration managers** to shepherd companies through the implementation process. The job of the integrator is to prepare a competitive profile of the combined company in terms of its strengths and weaknesses, draft an ideal profile of what the combined company should look like, develop action plans to close the gap between the actuality and the ideal, and establish training programs to unite the combined company and make it more competitive.[7] To be a successful integration manager, a person should have (1) a deep knowledge of the acquiring company, (2) a flexible management style, (3) an ability to work in cross-functional project teams, (4) a willingness to work independently, and (5) sufficient emotional and cultural intelligence to work well with people from all backgrounds.[8]

If a corporation adopts a retrenchment strategy, however, a large number of people may need to be laid off or fired (in many instances, being laid off is the same as being fired)—and top management, as well as the divisional managers, needs to specify the criteria to be used in making these personnel decisions. Should employees be fired on the basis of low seniority or on the basis of poor performance? Sometimes corporations find it easier to close or sell off an entire division than to choose which individuals to fire.

STAFFING FOLLOWS STRATEGY

As in the case of structure, staffing requirements should follow a change in strategy. For example, promotions should be based not only on current job performance but also on whether a person has the skills and abilities to do what is needed to implement the new strategy.

Changing Hiring and Training Requirements

Having formulated a new strategy, a corporation may find that it needs to either hire different people or retrain current employees to implement the new strategy. Consider the introduction of team-based production at Corning's filter plant mentioned in **Chapter 9**. Employee selection and training were crucial to the success of the new manufacturing strategy. The plant manager sorted through 8,000 job applications before hiring 150 people with the best problem-solving abilities and a willingness to work in a team setting. Those selected received extensive training in technical and interpersonal skills. During the first year of production, 25% of all hours worked were devoted to training, at a cost of US$750,000.[9]

One way to implement a company's business strategy, such as overall low cost, is through training and development. According to the Association for Talent Development (formerly ASTD), the average annual expenditure per employee on corporate training and development is US$1,229 per employee.[10] Training is especially important for a differentiation strategy emphasizing quality or customer service. At innovative online retailer Zappos, the whole company strategy is built around extraordinary customer service. Employees are screened and then screened again. At the end of each new employee training session, Zappos offers new employees US$2,000 to quit. The company has found that less than 2% accept that offer each year. They are not interested in employees that are simply there to get a paycheck. Training lasts seven weeks and there are tests along the way. A trainee has to graduate to be an employee.[11] Training is also important when implementing a retrenchment strategy. As suggested earlier, successful downsizing means that a company has to invest in its remaining employees. General Electric's Aircraft Engine Group used training to maintain its share of the market even though it had cut its workforce from 42,000 to 33,000 in the 1990s.[12]

Matching the Manager to the Strategy

Executive characteristics influence strategic outcomes for a corporation.[13] It is possible that a current CEO may not be appropriate to implement a new strategy. Research indicates that there may be a career life cycle for top executives. During the early years of executives' tenure, for example, they tend to experiment intensively with product lines to learn about their business. This is their learning stage. Later, their accumulated knowledge allows them to reduce experimentation and increase performance. This is their harvest stage. They enter a decline stage in their later years, when they reduce experimentation still further, and performance declines. Thus, there is an inverted U-shaped relationship between top executive tenure and the firm's financial performance. Some executives retire before any decline occurs. Others stave off decline longer than their counterparts. Because the length of time spent in each stage varies among CEOs, it is up to the board to decide when a top executive should be replaced.[14]

The most appropriate type of general manager needed to effectively implement a new corporate or business strategy depends on the desired strategic direction of that firm or business unit. Executives with a particular mix of skills and experiences may be classified as an **executive type** and paired with a specific corporate strategy. For example, a corporation following a concentration strategy emphasizing vertical or horizontal growth would probably want an aggressive new chief executive with a great deal of experience in that particular industry—a *dynamic industry expert*. A diversification strategy, in contrast, might call for someone with an analytical mind who is highly knowledgeable in other industries and can manage diverse product lines—an *analytical portfolio manager*. A corporation choosing to follow a stability strategy would probably want as its CEO a *cautious profit planner*, a person with a conservative style, a production or engineering background, and experience with controlling budgets, capital expenditures, inventories, and standardization procedures.

Weak companies in a relatively attractive industry tend to turn to a type of challenge-oriented executive known as a *turnaround specialist* to save the company. Julia Stewart started her career as an IHOP (International House of Pancakes) waitress. Years later she left the Applebee's restaurant chain to become CEO of IHOP, she worked to rebuild the company with better food, better ads, and a better atmosphere. Six years later, a much improved IHOP acquired the struggling Applebee's restaurant chain. CEO Stewart vowed to turnaround Applebee's within a year by improving service and food quality and by focusing the menu on what the restaurant does best: riblets, burgers, and salads. She wanted Applebee's to again be the friendly, neighborhood bar and grill that it once was. As of 2016 that was still a work in progress. With sales dropping year after year, she announced a new plan to break through the clutter in the market. Despite all the effort, Applebee's was still not a distinctive destination restaurant.[15]

If a company cannot be saved, a *professional liquidator* might be called on by a bankruptcy court to close the firm and liquidate its assets. This is what happened to Montgomery Ward Inc., the nation's first catalog retailer, which closed its stores for good in 2001, after declaring bankruptcy for the second time.[16] Research supports the conclusion that as a firm's environment changes, it tends to change the type of top executive needed to implement a new strategy.[17]

For example, during the 1990s when the emphasis was on growth in a company's core products/services, the most desired background for a U.S. CEO was either in marketing or international experience. With the current decade's emphasis on mergers, acquisitions, and divestitures, the most desired background is finance. One study found that one out of five American and UK CEOs are former Chief Financial Officers, twice the percentage during the previous decade.[18]

This approach is in agreement with Chandler, who proposes (see **Chapter 9**) that the most appropriate CEO of a company changes as a firm moves from one stage of development to another. Because priorities certainly change over an organization's life, successful corporations need to select managers who have skills and characteristics appropriate to the organization's particular stage of development and position in its life cycle. For example, founders of firms tend to have functional backgrounds in technological specialties, whereas successors tend to have backgrounds in marketing and administration.[19] A change in the environment leading to a change in a company's strategy also leads to a change in the top management team. For example, a change in the U.S. utility industry's environment in 1992 supporting internally focused, efficiency-oriented strategies, led to top management teams being dominated by older managers with longer company and industry tenure, and with efficiency-oriented backgrounds in operations, engineering, and accounting.[20] Research reveals that executives having a specific personality characteristic (external locus of control) are more effective in regulated industries than are executives with a different characteristic (internal locus of control).[21]

Other studies have found a link between the type of CEO and a firm's overall strategic type. (Strategic types were presented in **Chapter 4**.) For example, successful prospector firms tended to be headed by CEOs from research/engineering and general management backgrounds. High-performance defenders tended to have CEOs with accounting/finance, manufacturing/production, and general management experience. Analyzers tended to have CEOs with a marketing/sales background.[22]

A study of 173 firms over a 25-year period revealed that CEOs in these companies tended to have the same functional specialization as the former CEO, especially when the past CEO's strategy continued to be successful. This may be a pattern for successful corporations.[23] In particular, it explains why so many prosperous companies tend to recruit their top executives from one particular area. At Procter & Gamble (P&G)—a good example of an analyzer firm—the route to the CEO's position has traditionally been through brand management, with a strong emphasis on marketing—and more recently international experience. In other firms, the route may be through manufacturing, marketing, accounting, or finance—depending on what the corporation has always considered its core capability (and its overall strategic orientation).

SELECTION AND MANAGEMENT DEVELOPMENT

Selection and development are important not only to ensure that people with the right mix of skills and experiences are initially hired but also to help them grow on the job so they might be prepared for future promotions. For an interesting view of executive selection, take a look at the **Innovation Issue** on keeping Apple "cool."

INNOVATION issue

HOW TO KEEP APPLE "COOL"

Arguably, one of the most iconic "cool" companies in the past few decades has to be Apple. The designs, the feel of the products, and the ease with which the products work has made the company a standout with consumers. The innovative demands of a company that has the "cool" cache requires a balance of creative new products while maintaining a feel for what it means to be an Apple product. Much of this innovative ability was attributed to cofounder Steve Jobs. With his death in 2011, the company turned to Phil Schiller (then–Vice President of Product Marketing) to maintain the cache of the brand. Inside Apple, Phil Schiller was known as "mini-me"—a reference from the Austin Powers films that equated Phil Schiller with Steve Jobs.

Apple determined long ago that it took a consistent and persistent voice to develop and maintain the look and feel of something that would be called an Apple. Eschewing the approach of much of corporate America, Apple placed that authority in one person. This exposes the innovation engine of an organization to both a staffing issue as well as a leading issue.

Schiller has been referred to as overly controlling and virtually dictatorial. Insiders called him "Dr. NO" for the way he dealt with most new ideas. While potentially a positive when controlling content, this approach may be seen as a reticence within the corporation to be creative. If anything happens to Schiller, the company would face a big issue if it tried to either pass the baton to another executive or revert to standard corporate practice and create guidelines for designers to follow. This is a very similar path to that taken by Sony as it transitioned in the 1990s. Unfortunately, Sony became mired in its own procedures and lost its cache as the "cool" product company.

In late 2015, having been a part of the Apple Watch effort along with new editions of the iPhone, iPad and Apple TV, Shiller was placed in charge of the most important area of growth and innovation in the company—The App Store and all of its components. The company sees this as the area of greatest opportunity to maintain and grow its influence.

Does Apple still have that "cool" feel to it? Are the products /offerings innovative?

....

SOURCES: C. Welsh, "Apple's Phil Schiller is now in charge of the App Store," The Verge, December 17, 2015 (http://www.theverge.com/2015/12/17/10412204/apple-phil-schiller-now-leads-app-store); P. Burrows and A. Satariano, "Can This Guy Keep Apple Cool?" *Bloomberg Businessweek* (June 11, 2012), pp. 47–48; http://www.apple.com/pr/bios/philip-w-schiller.html; E. Kolawole, "Apple Reveals iPhone 5: But Is It Innovative?" *The Washington Post* (September 12, 2012), http://www.washingtonpost.com/blogs/innovations/post/apple-reveals-iphone-5-but-is-it-innovative/2012/09/12/ffb257a4-fcda-11e1-8adc-499661afe377_blog.html

Executive Succession: Insiders vs. Outsiders

Executive succession is the process of replacing a key top manager. The average tenure of a chief executive of a large U.S. company declined from nearly 10 years in 2000 to six years in 2015.[24] Given that two-thirds of all major corporations worldwide replace their CEO at least once in a five-year period, it is important that the firm plan for this eventuality.[25] It is especially important for a company that usually promotes from within to prepare its current managers for promotion. For example, companies using so-called "relay" executive succession, in which a particular candidate is groomed to take over the CEO position, have significantly higher performance than those that hire someone from the outside or hold a competition between internal candidates.[26] These "heirs apparent" are provided special assignments including membership on other firms' boards of directors.[27] Nevertheless, only half of large U.S. companies have CEO succession plans in place.[28]

Companies known for being excellent training grounds for executive talent are AlliedSignal, Bain & Company, Bankers Trust, Boeing, Bristol Myers Squibb, Cititcorp, General Electric, Hewlett-Packard, McDonald's, McKinsey & Company, Microsoft, Nike, Pfizer, and P&G. For example, one study showed that hiring 19 GE executives into CEO positions added US$24.5 billion to the share prices of the companies that hired them. One year after people from GE started their new jobs, 11 of the 19 companies they joined were outperforming their competitors and the overall market.[29]

Some of the best practices for top management succession are encouraging boards to help the CEO create a succession plan, identifying succession candidates below the top layer, measuring internal candidates against outside candidates to ensure the development of a comprehensive set of skills, and providing appropriate financial incentives.[30] Succession planning has become the most important topic discussed by boards of directors.[31]

Prosperous firms tend to look outside for CEO candidates only if they have no obvious internal candidates.[32] Eighty percent of the CEOs selected to run S&P 500 companies in 2014 were insiders, according to executive search firm Spencer Stuart.[33] Hiring an outsider to be a CEO is a risky gamble. CEOs from the outside tend to introduce significant change and high turnover among the current top management.[34] For example, in one study, the percentage of senior executives that left a firm after a new CEO took office was 20% when the new CEO was an insider, but increased to 34% when the new CEO was an outsider.[35] CEOs hired from outside the firm tend to have a low survival rate. According to RHR International, 40% to 60% of high-level executives brought in from outside a company failed within two years.[36] A study of 392 large U.S. firms revealed that only 16.6% of them had hired outsiders to be their CEOs. The outsiders tended to perform slightly worse than insiders but had a very high variance in performance. Compared to that of insiders, the performance of outsiders tended to be either very good or very poor. Although outsiders performed much better (in terms of shareholder returns) than insiders in the first half of their tenures, they did much worse in their second half. As a result, the average tenure of an outsider was significantly less than for insiders.[37]

Firms in trouble, however, overwhelmingly choose outsiders to lead them.[38] For example, one study of 22 firms undertaking turnaround strategies over a 13-year period found that the CEO was replaced in all but two companies. Of 27 changes of CEO (several firms had more than one CEO during this period), only seven were insiders—20 were outsiders.[39] The probability of an outsider being chosen to lead a firm in difficulty increases if there is no internal heir apparent, if the last CEO was fired, and if the board of directors is composed of a large percentage of outsiders.[40] Boards realize that the best way to force a change in strategy is to hire a new CEO who has no connections to the current strategy.[41] For example, outsiders have been found to be very effective in leading strategic change for firms in **Chapter 11** bankruptcy.[42]

Identifying Abilities and Potential

A company can identify and prepare its people for important positions in several ways. One approach is to establish a sound *performance appraisal system* to identify good performers with promotion potential. A survey of 34 corporate planners and human resource executives from 24 large U.S. corporations revealed that approximately 80% made some attempt to identify managers' talents and behavioral tendencies so they could place a manager with a likely fit to a given competitive strategy.[43] Companies select those people with promotion potential to be in their executive development training program. GE spends more than US$1 billion per year for employee training at the company's famous Leadership Development Center in Crotonville, New York.[44] Doug Pelino, chief talent officer at Xerox, keeps a list of about 100 managers in middle management and at the vice presidential levels who have been selected to receive special training, leadership experience, and mentorship to become the next generation of top management.[45]

A company should examine its human resource system to ensure not only that people are being hired without regard to their racial, ethnic, or religious background, but also that they are being identified for training and promotion in the same manner. Management diversity can be a competitive advantage in a multiethnic world. With more women in the workplace, an increasing number are moving into top management, but are demanding more flexible career ladders to allow for family responsibilities.

Many large organizations are using *assessment centers* to evaluate a person's suitability for an advanced position. Corporations such as AT&T, Rolls Royce, KPMG, and GE have successfully used assessment centers. Because each is specifically tailored to its corporation, these assessment centers are unique. They use special interviews, management games, in-basket exercises, leaderless group discussions, case analyses, decision-making exercises, and oral presentations to assess the potential of employees for specific positions. Promotions into these positions are based on performance levels in the assessment center. Assessment centers have generally been able to accurately predict subsequent job performance and career success.[46]

Job rotation—moving people from one job to another—is also used in many large corporations to ensure that employees are gaining the appropriate mix of experiences to prepare them for future responsibilities. Rotating people among divisions is one way that a corporation can improve the level of organizational learning. General Electric, for example, routinely rotates its executives from one sector to a completely different one to learn the skills of managing in different industries. Jeffrey Immelt, who took over as CEO from Jack Welch, had managed businesses in plastics, appliances, and medical systems.[47] Companies that pursue related diversification strategies through internal development make greater use of interdivisional transfers of people than do companies that grow through unrelated acquisitions. Apparently, the companies that grow internally attempt to transfer important knowledge and skills throughout the corporation in order to achieve some sort of synergy.[48]

PROBLEMS IN RETRENCHMENT

In 2016, Office Depot/Office Max announced that it would close 400 stores in an effort to return the company to health. Meanwhile, major U.S. retail chains like Wal*Mart, Barnes & Noble, Walgreens, and American Eagle Outfitters announced triple-digit store closing plans.[49] **Downsizing** (sometimes called "rightsizing" or "resizing") refers to the planned elimination of positions or jobs. This program is often used to implement retrenchment strategies. Because the financial community is likely to react favorably to announcements of downsizing from a company in difficulty, such a program may provide some short-term benefits such as raising the company's stock price. If not done properly, however, downsizing may result in less, rather than more, productivity. One study found that a 10% reduction in people resulted in only a 1.5% reduction in costs, profits increased in only half the firms downsizing, and the stock prices of downsized firms increased over three years, but not as much as did those of firms that did not downsize.[50] Why were the results so marginal?

A study of downsizing at automobile-related U.S. industrial companies revealed that at 20 out of 30 companies, either the wrong jobs were eliminated or blanket offers of early retirement prompted managers, even those considered invaluable, to leave. After the layoffs, the remaining employees had to do not only their work but also the work of the people who had gone. Because the survivors often didn't know how to do the work of those who had left the company, morale and productivity plummeted.[51] Downsizing can seriously damage the learning capacity of organizations.[52] Creativity drops significantly (affecting new product development), and it becomes very difficult to keep high performers from leaving the company.[53] In addition, cost-conscious executives tend to defer maintenance, skimp on training, delay new product introductions, and avoid risky new businesses—all of which leads to lower sales and eventually to lower profits.[54] These are some of the reasons why layoffs worry customers and have a negative effect on a firm's reputation.[55]

A good retrenchment strategy can thus be implemented well in terms of organizing but poorly in terms of staffing. A situation can develop in which retrenchment feeds on itself and acts to further weaken instead of strengthen the company. Research indicates that companies undertaking cost-cutting programs are four times more likely than others to cut costs again, typically by reducing staff.[56] This has been the story at such well-known operations like Sears, Gannet, RIM, HSBC, and Borders, which eventually went into bankruptcy.[57] In contrast, successful downsizing firms undertake a strategic reorientation, not just a bloodletting of employees. Research shows that when companies use downsizing as part of a larger restructuring program to narrow company focus, they enjoy better performance.[58] This was the situation at Starbucks in 2008 as it closed stores and laid off more than 7,000 people in its effort to refocus the business on the coffee experience. In the ensuing years, the company roared back to life without having to revert to layoffs again.

Consider the following guidelines that have been proposed for successful downsizing:

- **Eliminate unnecessary work instead of making across-the-board cuts:** Spend the time to research where money is going and eliminate the task, not the workers, if it doesn't add value to what the firm is producing. Reduce the number of administrative levels rather than the number of individual positions. Look for interdependent relationships before eliminating activities. Identify and protect core competencies.

- **Contract out work that others can do cheaper:** We have discussed this topic extensively throughout the text. Outsourcing may be cheaper than vertical integration.

- **Plan for long-run efficiencies:** Don't simply eliminate all expenses that could be potentially postponed, such as maintenance, R&D, and advertising, in the unjustifiable hope that the environment will become more supportive. Continue to hire, grow, and develop—particularly in critical areas.

- **Communicate the reasons for actions:** Tell employees not only why the company is downsizing but also what the company is trying to achieve. Promote educational programs.

- **Invest in the remaining employees:** Because most "survivors" in a corporate downsizing will probably be doing different tasks from what they were doing before the change, firms need to draft new job specifications, performance standards, appraisal techniques, and compensation packages. Additional training is needed to ensure that everyone has the proper skills to deal with expanded jobs and responsibilities. Empower key individuals/groups and emphasize team building. Identify, protect, and mentor people who have leadership talent.

- **Develop value-added jobs to balance out job elimination:** When no other jobs are currently available within the organization to transfer employees to, management must consider other staffing alternatives. Harley-Davidson worked with the company's unions to find other work for surplus employees by moving into Harley plants work that had previously been done by suppliers.[59]

Leading

11-2. Discuss how leaders manage corporate culture

Implementation also involves leading through coaching people to use their abilities and skills most effectively and efficiently to achieve organizational objectives. Without direction, people tend to do their work according to their personal view of what tasks should be done, how, and in what order. They may approach their work as they have in the past or emphasize those tasks that they most enjoy—regardless of the corporation's priorities. This can create real problems, particularly if the company is operating internationally and must adjust to customs and traditions in other countries. This direction may take the form of management leadership, communicated norms of behavior from the corporate culture, or agreements among workers in autonomous work groups. For an example of how a company can lead by radically changing the business model and the way it is staffed, see the **Sustainability Issue** feature. It may be accomplished more formally through action planning or through programs, such as Management by Objectives and Total Quality Management. Procedures can be changed to provide incentives to motivate employees to align their behavior with corporate objectives.

MANAGING CORPORATE CULTURE

Because an organization's culture can exert a powerful influence on the behavior of all employees, it can strongly affect a company's ability to shift its strategic direction. A problem for a strong culture is that a change in mission, objectives, strategies, or policies and tactics is not likely to be successful if it is in opposition to the accepted culture of the company. Corporate culture has a strong tendency to resist change because its very reason for existence often rests on preserving stable relationships and patterns of behavior. For example, when Robert Nardelli became CEO at The Home Depot in 2000, he changed the corporate strategy to growing the company's small professional supply business (sales to building contractors) through acquisitions and making the mature retail business cost-effective. He attempted to replace the old informal entrepreneurial collaborative culture with one of military efficiency. Before Nardelli's arrival, most store managers had based their decisions upon their personal knowledge

SUSTAINABILITY issue

PANERA AND THE "PANERA CARES COMMUNITY CAFÉ"

Sometimes the staffing model for a business can be adapted to provide long-term value to the community and help that company lead an industry. As of early 2016, Panera Bread Company had just shy of 2,000 restaurants in 46 states, had sales of more than US$2.6 billion and net income of US$149 million. The company had grown into an institution in the United States, catering to those who could afford to eat there (in other words, those who are employed). They steadfastly refused to lower prices during the latest recession and posted sales gains through that time period.

In an effort to lead in the business community as well as provide work for individuals in training programs supported by the company, Panera came up with a creative business approach when it opened its pilot "Panera Cares Community Café" in Clayton, Missouri, in 2010. Known by most as the "pay what you want" restaurant, the restaurant offered suggested donation levels instead of prices.

To make the business model work, the company created the Panera Bread Foundation in order to separate it from the for-profit business. Consumers who are most able to pay are asked to donate extra, while those who are short on cash can pay less, and those who can't pay anything can volunteer for an hour to pay for their meal.

As of 2016, the Foundation had four stores open in Clayton, MO, Dearborn, MI, Portland, OR, and Boston, MA. An additional store in Chicago, IL was closed when the lease ran out and the business model was failing to work as planned.

The company limits 'free' meals (that is meals to people who cannot pay) to one per week, but provides an opportunity to work in the store for one hour and earn a meal voucher. To date the stores are bringing in approximately 75% of retail value with approximately 60% of people leaving the suggested donation, 15–20% leaving more and the rest leaving less or nothing.

....

SOURCES: http://paneracares.org/faqs/; D. Goodison, "Pay-What-You-Can Panera Donation Café Will Grace Hub," (November 5, 2012), E. York, "Panera to Open First Local Pay-What-You-Can Café in Lakeview," *Chicago Tribune* (June 20, 2012), http://articles.chicagotribune.com/2012-06-20/business/chi-panera-adds-paywhatyoucan-cafe-in-chicago-20120620_1_ron-shaich-lakeview-open-first; *ATPs://www.panerabread.com/en-us/company/about-panera/our-history.html; http://www.nasdaq.com/symbol/pnra/financials*

of their customers' preferences. Under Nardelli, they were given weekly sales and profit targets. Underperforming managers were asked to leave the company. The once-heavy ranks of full-time employees were replaced with cheaper part-timers who had far less experience to help the DIY customer. In this "culture of fear," morale fell and The Home Depot's customer satisfaction score dropped to last place among major U.S. retailers. Nardelli was asked to leave the company in 2007 and the company's resurgence over the next few years as it moved back to its roots is a testament to the strength of corporate culture.

There is no one best corporate culture. An optimal culture is one that best supports the mission and strategy of the company of which it is a part. This means that *corporate culture should support the strategy*. Unless strategy is in complete agreement with the culture, any significant change in strategy should be followed by a modification of the organization's culture. Although corporate culture can be changed, it often takes a long time, and it requires a lot of effort. At The Home Depot, for example, CEO Nardelli attempted to change the corporate culture by hiring GE veterans like himself into top management positions, hiring ex-military officers as store managers, and instituting a top-down command structure.

A key job of management involves managing corporate culture. In doing so, management must evaluate what a particular change in strategy means to the corporate culture, assess whether a change in culture is needed, and decide whether an attempt to change the culture is worth the likely costs.

Assessing Strategy-Culture Compatibility

When implementing a new strategy, a company should take the time to assess *strategy-culture compatibility.*(See **Figure 11–1**.) Consider the following questions regarding a corporation's culture:

1. **Is the proposed strategy compatible with the company's current culture?** *If yes*, full steam ahead. Tie organizational changes into the company's culture by identifying how the new strategy will achieve the mission better than the current strategy does. *If not . . .*

2. **Can the culture be easily modified to make it more compatible with the new strategy?** *If yes*, move forward carefully by introducing a set of culture-changing activities such as minor structural modifications, training and development activities, and/or hiring new managers who are more compatible with the new strategy. When Proctor & Gamble's top management decided to implement a strategy aimed at reducing costs, for example, it made some changes in how things were done, but it did not eliminate its brand-management system. The culture adapted to these modifications over a couple of years and productivity increased. *If not . . .*

FIGURE 11–1 Assessing Strategy–Culture Compatibility

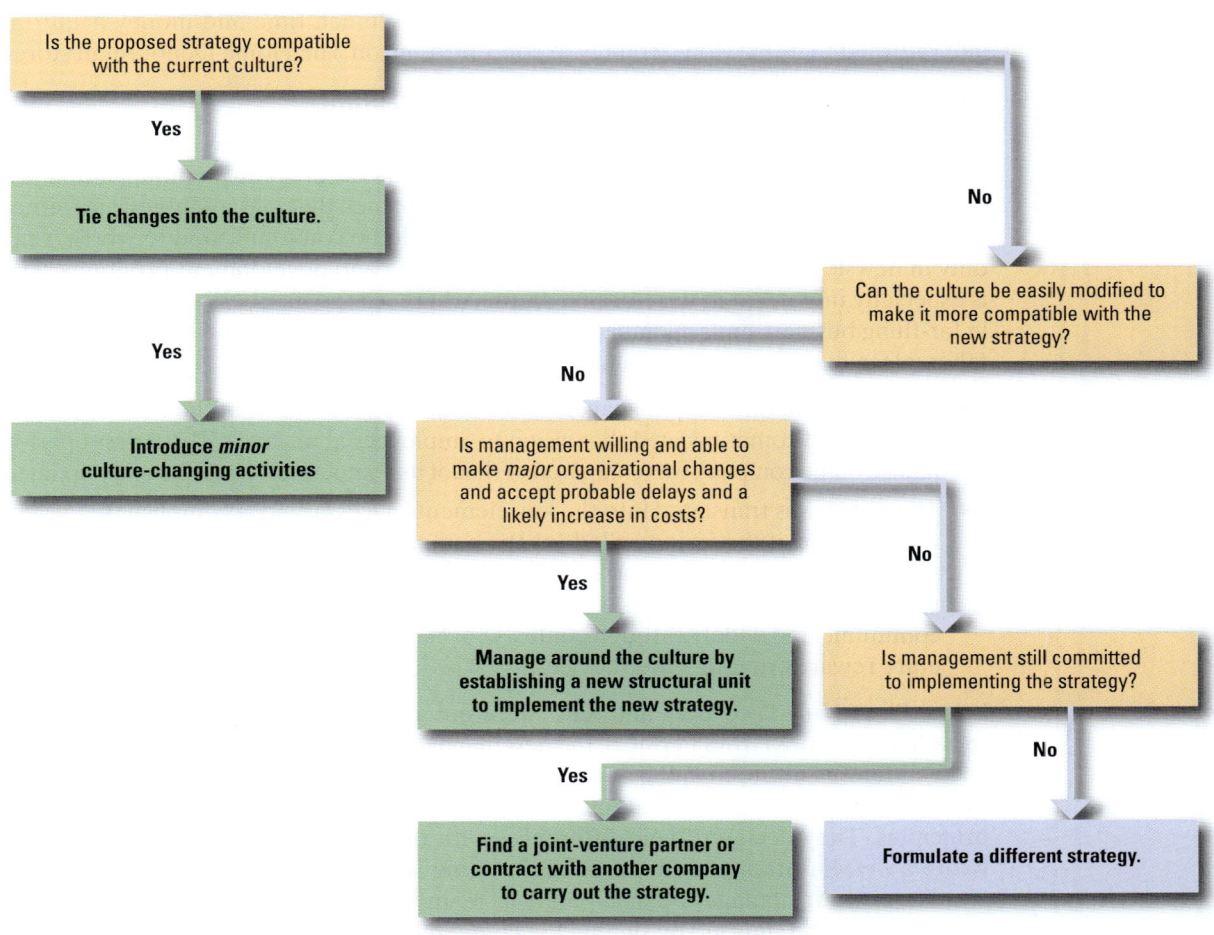

3. **Is management willing and able to make major organizational changes and accept probable delays and a likely increase in costs?** *If yes,* manage around the culture by establishing a new structural unit to implement the new strategy. In 2012, Saab Automobile Parts AB established a subsidiary to provide original parts in the United States after running into a decade of issues resulting from a lack of focus on U.S. Saab owners. By creating a separate subsidiary whose sole responsibility was providing U.S. customers with spare parts for their cars, the company was able to bypass the established focus of the company, which was clearly not on U.S. Saab owners. *If not . . .*

4. **Is management still committed to implementing the strategy?** *If yes,* find a joint-venture partner or contract with another company to carry out the strategy. *If not,* formulate a different strategy.

Based on Robert Nardelli's decisions when he initially started as The Home Depot's CEO, he probably answered "no" to the first question and "yes" to the second question—thus justifying his many changes in staffing and leading. Unfortunately, these changes didn't work very well. Instead, he should have replied "no" to the first and second questions and stopped at the third question. As suggested by this question, he should have considered a different corporate strategy, such as growing the professional side of the business without changing the collegial culture of the retail stores. Not surprisingly, once Nardelli was replaced by a new CEO, the company divested the professional supply companies that Nardelli had spent so much time and money acquiring and returned to its previous strategy of concentrating on The Home Depot retail stores.

Managing Cultural Change through Communication

Communication is key to the effective management of change. A survey of 3,199 worldwide executives by McKinsey & Company revealed that ongoing communication and involvement was the approach most used by companies that successfully transformed themselves.[60] Rationale for strategic changes should be communicated to workers not only in newsletters and speeches, but also in training and development programs. This is especially important in decentralized firms where a large number of employees work in far-flung business units. Companies in which major cultural changes have successfully taken place had the following characteristics in common:

- The CEO and other top managers had a strategic vision of what the company could become and communicated that vision to employees at all levels. The current performance of the company was compared to that of its competition and constantly updated.

- The vision was translated into the key elements necessary to accomplish that vision. For example, if the vision called for the company to become a leader in quality or service, aspects of quality and service were pinpointed for improvement, and appropriate measurement systems were developed to monitor them. These measures were communicated widely through contests, formal and informal recognition, and monetary rewards, among other devices.

When Pizza Hut, Taco Bell, and KFC were purchased by Tricon Global Restaurants (now Yum! Brands) from PepsiCo, the new management knew that it had to create a radically different culture than the one at PepsiCo if the company was to succeed. To begin, management formulated a statement of shared values—"How We Work Together" principles. They declared their differences with the "mother country" (PepsiCo) and wrote a "Declaration of Independence" stating what the new company would stand for. Restaurant managers participated in team-building activities at the corporate headquarters and finished by signing the company's "Declaration of Independence" as "founders" of the company. Since then, "Founders Day" has become an annual event celebrating the culture of the company. Headquarters was renamed the "Restaurant Support Center," signifying the cultural value the restaurants held as the central focus of the company. People measures were added to financial measures and customer measures, reinforcing the "putting people first" value. In an unprecedented move in the industry, restaurant managers were given stock options and stock was added to the list of performance incentives. The company created values-focused 360-degree performance reviews, which were eventually pushed to the restaurant manager level.

Managing Diverse Cultures Following an Acquisition

When merging with or acquiring another company, top management must give some consideration to a potential clash of corporate cultures. According to a Hewitt Associates survey of 218 major U.S. corporations, integrating culture was a top challenge for 69% of the reporting companies. Cultural differences are even more problematic when a company acquires a firm in another country. Daimler-Benz has dealt with this on a number of occasions, including its merger with Chrysler in 1998 and its purchase of a controlling interest in Mitsubishi Motors in 2001. Resistance to change led Daimler-Benz to eject both organizations from the parent company. It's dangerous to assume that the firms can simply be integrated into the same reporting structure. The greater the gap between the cultures of the acquired firm and the acquiring firm, the faster executives in the acquired firm quit their jobs and valuable talent is lost. Conversely, when corporate cultures are similar, performance problems are minimized.

There are four general methods of managing two different cultures. (See **Figure 11–2.**) The choice of which method to use should be based on (1) how much members of the acquired firm value preserving their own culture and (2) how attractive they perceive the culture of the acquirer to be.

1. *Integration* involves a relatively balanced give-and-take of cultural and managerial practices between the merger partners, and no strong imposition of cultural change on either company. It merges the two cultures in such a way that the separate cultures of both firms are preserved in the resulting culture. This is what occurred

FIGURE 11–2
Methods of Managing the Culture of an Acquired Firm

Integration

Equal merger of both cultures into a new corporate culture

Assimilation

Acquiring firm's culture kept intact, but subservient to that of acquiring firm's corporate culture

Separation

Conflicting cultures kept intact, but kept separate in different units

Deculturation

Forced replacement of conflicting acquired firm's culture with that of the acquiring firm's culture

SOURCES: Suggested by A. R. Malezadeh and A. Nahavandi in "Making Mergers Work in Managing Cultures," *Journal of Business Strategy* (May/June 1990), pp. 53–57 and "Acculturation in Mergers and Acquisitions," *Academy of Management Review* (January 1988), pp. 79–90.

when France's Renault purchased a controlling interest in Japan's Nissan Motor Company and installed Carlos Ghosn as Nissan's new CEO to turn the company around. Ghosn was very sensitive to Nissan's culture and allowed the company room to develop a new corporate culture based on the best elements of Japan's national culture. His goal was to form one successful auto group from two very distinct companies.

2. *Assimilation* involves the domination of one organization over the other. The domination is not forced, but it is welcomed by members of the acquired firm, who may feel for many reasons that their culture and managerial practices have not produced success. The acquired firm surrenders its culture and adopts the culture of the acquiring company. This was the case when Maytag Company (now part of Whirlpool) acquired Admiral. Because Admiral's previous owners had not kept the manufacturing facilities up to date, quality had drastically fallen over the years. Admiral's employees were willing to accept the dominance of Maytag's strong quality-oriented culture because they respected it and knew that without significant changes at Admiral, they would soon be out of work. In turn, they expected to be treated with some respect for their skills in refrigeration technology.

3. *Separation* is characterized by a separation of the two companies' cultures. They are structurally separated, without cultural exchange. When Boeing acquired McDonnell-Douglas, known for its expertise in military aircraft and missiles, Boeing created a separate unit to house both McDonnell's operations and Boeing's own military business. McDonnell executives were given top posts in the new unit and other measures were taken to protect the strong McDonnell culture. On the commercial side, where Boeing had the most expertise, McDonnell's commercial operations were combined with Boeing's in a separate unit managed by Boeing executives.

4. *Deculturation* involves the disintegration of one company's culture resulting from unwanted and extreme pressure from the other to impose its culture and practices. This is the most common and most destructive method of dealing with two different cultures. It is often accompanied by much confusion, conflict, resentment, and stress. This is a primary reason why so many executives tend to leave after their firm is acquired. Such a merger typically results in poor performance by the acquired company and its eventual divestment. This is what happened when AT&T acquired NCR Corporation in 1990 for its computer business. It replaced NCR managers with an AT&T management team, reorganized sales, forced employees to adhere to the AT&T code of values (called the "Common Bond"), and even dropped the proud NCR name (successor to National Cash Register) in favor of a sterile GIS (Global Information Solutions) nonidentity. By 1995, AT&T was forced to take a US$1.2 billion loss and lay off 10,000 people. The NCR unit was consequently sold.

Action Planning

11-3. Utilize an action planning framework to implement an organization's MBO and TQM initiatives

Activities can be directed toward accomplishing strategic goals through action planning. At a minimum, an **action plan** states what actions are going to be taken, by whom, during what time frame, and with what expected results. After a program has been selected to implement a particular strategy, an action plan should be developed to put the program in place. **Table 11–1** shows an example of an action plan for a new advertising and promotion program.

Take the example of a company choosing forward vertical integration through the acquisition of a retailing chain as its growth strategy. Once it owns its own retail outlets,

TABLE 11–1 Example of an Action Plan

Action Plan for Jan Lewis, Advertising Manager, and Rick Carter, Advertising Assistant, Ajax Continental

Program Objective: To run a new advertising and promotion campaign for the combined Jones Surplus/Ajax Continental retail stores for the coming Christmas Season within a budget of $XX.

Program Activities:

1. Identify three best ad agencies for new campaign.
2. Ask three ad agencies to submit a proposal for a new advertising and promotion campaign for combined stores.
3. Agencies present proposals to marketing manager.
4. Select best proposal and inform agencies of decision.
5. Agency presents winning proposal to top management.
6. Ads air on TV and promotions appear in stores.
7. Measure results of campaign in terms of viewer recall and increase in store sales.

Action Steps	Responsibility	Start–End
1. A. Review previous programs	Lewis & Carter	1/1–2/1
B. Discuss with boss	Lewis & Smith	2/1–2/3
C. Decide on three agencies	Lewis	2/4
2. A. Write specifications for ad	Lewis	1/15–1/20
B. Assistant writes ad request	Carter	1/20–1/30
C. Contact ad agencies	Lewis	2/5–2/8
D. Send request to three agencies	Carter	2/10
E. Meet with agency acct. execs	Lewis & Carter	2/16–2/20
3. A. Agencies work on proposals	Acct. Execs	2/23–5/1
B. Agencies present proposals	Carter	5/1–5/15
4. A. Select best proposal	Lewis	5/15–5/20
B. Meet with winning agency	Lewis	5/22–5/30
C. Inform losers	Carter	6/1
5. A. Fine-tune proposal	Acct. Exec	6/1–7/1
B. Presentation to management	Lewis	7/1–7/3
6. A. Ads air on TV	Lewis	9/1–12/24
B. Floor displays in stores	Carter	8/20–8/30
7. A. Gather recall measures of ads	Carter	9/1–12/24
B. Evaluate sales data	Carter	1/1–1/10
C. Prepare analysis of campaign	Carter	1/10–2/15

it must integrate the stores into the company. One of the many programs it would have to develop is a new advertising program for the stores. The resulting action plan to develop a new advertising program should include much of the following information:

1. **Specific actions to be taken to make the program operational:** One action might be to contact three reputable advertising agencies and ask them to prepare a proposal for a new radio and newspaper ad campaign based on the theme "Jones Surplus is now a part of Ajax Continental. Prices are lower. Selection is better."

2. **Dates to begin and end each action:** Time would have to be allotted not only to select and contact three agencies, but to allow them sufficient time to prepare a

detailed proposal. For example, allow one week to select and contact the agencies, plus three months for them to prepare detailed proposals to present to the company's marketing director. Also allow some time to decide which proposal to accept.

3. **Person (identified by name and title) responsible for carrying out each action:** List someone—such as Jan Lewis, advertising manager—who can be put in charge of the program.

4. **Person responsible for monitoring the timeliness and effectiveness of each action:** Indicate that Jan Lewis is responsible for ensuring that the proposals are of good quality and are priced within the planned program budget. She will be the primary company contact for the ad agencies and will report on the progress of the program once a week to the company's marketing director.

5. **Expected financial and physical consequences of each action:** Estimate when a completed ad campaign will be ready to show top management and how long it will take after approval to begin to air the ads. Estimate the expected increase in store sales over the six-month period after the ads are first aired. Indicate whether "recall" measures will be used to help assess the ad campaign's effectiveness, plus how, when, and by whom the recall data will be collected and analyzed.

6. **Contingency plans:** Indicate how long it will take to get an acceptable ad campaign to show top management if none of the initial proposals is acceptable.

Action plans are important for several reasons. First, action plans serve as a link between strategy formulation and evaluation and control. Second, the action plan specifies what needs to be done differently from the way operations are currently carried out. Third, during the evaluation and control process that comes later, an action plan helps in both the appraisal of performance and in the identification of any remedial actions, as needed. In addition, the explicit assignment of responsibilities for implementing and monitoring the programs may contribute to better motivation.

MANAGEMENT BY OBJECTIVES

Management by Objectives (MBO) is a technique that encourages participative decision making through shared goal setting at all organizational levels and performance assessment based on the achievement of stated objectives. MBO links organizational objectives and the behavior of individuals. Because it is a system that links plans with performance, it is a powerful implementation technique.

The MBO process involves:

1. Establishing and communicating organizational objectives.

2. Setting individual objectives (through superior-subordinate interaction) that help implement organizational ones.

3. Developing an action plan of activities needed to achieve the objectives.

4. Periodically (at least quarterly) reviewing performance as it relates to the objectives and including the results in the annual performance appraisal.

MBO provides an opportunity for the corporation to connect the objectives of people at each level to those at the next higher level. MBO, therefore, acts to tie together corporate, business, and functional objectives, as well as the strategies developed to achieve them. Although MBO originated in the 1950s, 90% of surveyed practicing managers feel that MBO is applicable today. The principles of MBO are a part of self-managing work teams and quality circles.

One of the real benefits of MBO is that it can reduce the amount of internal politics operating within a large corporation. Political actions within a firm can cause conflict and create divisions between the very people and groups who should be working together to implement strategy. People are less likely to jockey for position if the company's mission and objectives are clear and they know that the reward system is based not on game playing, but on achieving clearly communicated, measurable objectives.

TOTAL QUALITY MANAGEMENT

Total Quality Management (TQM) is an operational philosophy committed to *customer satisfaction* and *continuous improvement*. TQM is committed to quality/excellence and to being the best in all functions. Because TQM aims to reduce costs and improve quality, it can be used as a program to implement an overall low-cost or a differentiation business strategy. Many TQM principles have been incorporated into the ISO 9000 series of standards and certifications. While TQM is focused upon employee participation, refinement, and improvement, the ISO standards are tied to the reporting and data analysis of the process. The two can go hand in hand with ISO 9000 series approaches used to document and measure the efforts.

According to TQM, faulty processes, not poorly motivated employees, are the cause of defects in quality. The program involves a significant change in corporate culture, requiring strong leadership from top management, employee training, empowerment of lower-level employees (giving people more control over their work), and teamwork in order to succeed in a company. TQM emphasizes prevention, not correction. Inspection for quality still takes place, but the emphasis is on improving the process to prevent errors and deficiencies. Thus, quality circles or quality improvement teams are formed to identify problems and to suggest how to improve the processes that may be causing the problems.

TQM's essential ingredients are:

- **An intense focus on customer satisfaction:** Everyone (not just people in the sales and marketing departments) understands that their jobs exist only because of customer needs. Thus all jobs must be approached in terms of how they will affect customer satisfaction.

- **Internal as well as external customers:** An employee in the shipping department may be the internal customer of another employee who completes the assembly of a product, just as a person who buys the product is a customer of the entire company. An employee must be just as concerned with pleasing the internal customer as in satisfying the external customer.

- **Accurate measurement of every critical variable in a company's operations:** This means that employees have to be trained in what to measure, how to measure, and how to interpret the data. A rule of TQM is that *you only improve what you measure.*

- **Continuous improvement of products and services:** Everyone realizes that operations need to be continuously monitored to find ways to improve products and services.

- **New work relationships based on trust and teamwork:** Important is the idea of empowerment—giving employees wide latitude in how they go about achieving the company's goals. Research indicates that the keys to TQM success lie in executive commitment, an open organizational culture, and employee empowerment.[61]

See the **Global Issue** feature to learn how differences in national and corporate cultures created conflict when Upjohn Company of the United States and Pharmacia AB of Sweden merged.

GLOBAL issue

CULTURAL DIFFERENCES CREATE IMPLEMENTATION PROBLEMS IN MERGER

When Upjohn Pharmaceuticals of Kalamazoo, Michigan, and Pharmacia AB of Stockholm, Sweden, merged in 1995, employees of both sides were optimistic for the newly formed Pharmacia & Upjohn, Inc. Both companies were second-tier competitors fighting for survival in a global industry. Together, the firms would create a global company that could compete scientifically with its bigger rivals.

Because Pharmacia had acquired an Italian firm in 1993, it also had a large operation in Milan. U.S. executives scheduled meetings throughout the summer of 1996—only to cancel them when their European counterparts could not attend. Although it was common knowledge in Europe that most Swedes take the entire month of July for vacation and that Italians take off all of August, this was not common knowledge in Michigan. Differences in management styles became a special irritant. Swedes were used to an open system, with autonomous work teams. Executives sought the whole group's approval before making an important decision. Upjohn executives followed the more traditional American top-down approach. Upon taking command of the newly merged firm, Dr. Zabriskie (who had been Upjohn's CEO), divided the company into departments reporting to the new London headquarters. He required frequent reports, budgets, and staffing updates. The Swedes reacted negatively to this top-down management hierarchical style. "It was degrading," said Stener

Kvinnsland, head of Pharmacia's cancer research in Italy before he quit the new company.

The Italian operations baffled the Americans, even though the Italians felt comfortable with a hierarchical management style. Italy's laws and unions made layoffs difficult. Italian data and accounting were often inaccurate. Because the Americans didn't trust the data, they were constantly asking for verification. In turn, the Italians were concerned that the Americans were trying to take over Italian operations. At Upjohn, all workers were subject to testing for drug and alcohol abuse. Upjohn also banned smoking. At Pharmacia's Italian business center, however, waiters poured wine freely every afternoon in the company dining room. Pharmacia's boardrooms were stocked with humidors for executives who smoked cigars during long meetings. After a brief attempt to enforce Upjohn's policies, the company dropped both the no-drinking and no-smoking policies for European workers.

In order to assert more control over the whole operation, the company moved its HQ back to the United States in 1998. In 2000, the company acquired Monsanto and Searle, both large pharmaceutical companies. The new company, called Pharmacia, didn't last long. The company was bought out by Pfizer in 2003.

....

SOURCES: Summarized from R. Frank and T. M. Burton, "Cross-Border Merger Results in Headaches for a Drug Company," *The Wall Street Journal* (February 4, 1997), pp. A1, A12; http://www.pfizer.com/about/history/pfizer_pharmacia.jsp

End of Chapter SUMMARY

Strategy is implemented by modifying structure (organizing), selecting the appropriate people to carry out the strategy (staffing), and communicating clearly how the strategy can be put into action (leading). A number of programs, such as organizational and job design, reengineering, Six Sigma, MBO, TQM, and action planning, can be used to implement a new strategy. Executives must manage the corporate culture and find the right mix of qualified people to put a strategy in place.

Research on executive succession reveals that it is very risky to hire new top managers from outside the corporation. Although this is often done when a company is in trouble, it can be dangerous for a successful firm. This is also true when hiring people for non-executive positions. An in-depth study of 1,052 stock analysts at 78 investment banks revealed that hiring a star (an outstanding performer) from another company did not improve the hiring company's performance. When a company hires a star, the star's performance plunges, there is a sharp decline in the functioning of the team the person works with, and the company's market value declines. Their performance dropped about 20% and did not return to the level before the job change—even after five years. Interestingly, around 36% of the stars left the investment banks that hired them within 36 months. Another 29% quit in the next 24 months.

This phenomenon occurs not because a star doesn't suddenly become less intelligent when switching firms, but because the star cannot take to the new firm the firm-specific resources that contributed to her or his achievements at the previous company. As a result, the star is unable to repeat the high performance in another company until he or she learns the new system. This may take years, but only if the new company has an aligned support system in place. Otherwise, the performance may never improve. For these reasons, companies rarely obtain competitive advantage by hiring stars from the outside. Instead, they should emphasize growing their own talent and developing the infrastructure necessary for high performance.[62]

It is important to not ignore the majority of the workforce who, while not being stars, are the solid performers that keep a company going over the years. An undue emphasis on attracting stars often wastes money and destroys morale. The CEO of McKesson, a pharmaceutical wholesaler, calls these B players "performers in place. . . . They are happy living in Dubuque. I have more time and admiration for them than the A player who is at my desk every six months asking for the next promotion." With few exceptions, coaches who try to forge a sports team composed of stars courts disaster.

Pearson MyLab Management®

Go to **mymanagementlab.com** to complete the problems marked with this icon .

KEY TERMS

action plan (p. 338)
downsizing (p. 332)
executive succession (p. 330)
executive type (p. 327)

integration managers (p. 326)
leading (p. 326)
Management by Objectives
    (MBO) (p. 340)

staffing (p. 326)
Total Quality Management
    (TQM) (p. 341)

Pearson MyLab Management®

Go to **mymanagementlab.com** for the following assisted-graded writing questions:

11-1. What are the critical issues that a company must consider when trying to match its staffing to its strategy?
11-2. What are the unique impacts on a company that must staff in international settings?

DISCUSSION QUESTIONS

11-3. What skills should a person have for managing a business unit following a differentiation strategy? Why? What should a company do if no one is available internally and the company has a policy of promotion from within?

11-4. Does staffing really follow strategy? Are the job applicants' knowledge, skills, and abilities the key, or is it the corporate strategy?

11-5. What are some ways to implement a retrenchment strategy without creating a lot of resentment and conflict with labor unions?

11-6. How can corporate culture be changed?

11-7. Provide local examples to show the relevance of Hofstede's dimensions in effective staffing and directing.

STRATEGIC PRACTICE EXERCISE

The role of human resources has grown increasingly more complex and challenging in today's fast-paced, ever-evolving business world. The truth is, in recent years, there has been a slew of unparalleled transformations in companies in the Emirates that have punctuated the region's workforce. Tenured staff has to handle technological breakthroughs, fluctuating market environments, and the global crises. The additional challenge, of course, is the Millennial Generation! These fresh-driven, young graduates born between 1982 and 2002 come from shifting demographics and changing organizational structures. They are diversified: the new, powered globalization's workforce! The youth has changed the very fabric of the Middle East's ultracompetitive employment landscape, reaffirming the need for world-class human resource practices that place employment engagement at the core of every corporation's business ethos. The third millennium needs a corporate environment that is conducive to productivity, creativity, and innovation, one which is the key to optimizing peak performance, maintaining low employee turnover, and achieving long-term business goals. An example of such a company, at present operating in the Arab Gulf, is Proctor & Gamble (P&G). At P&G, the human resource managers, who have generated an approach that has helped guide the company, are its building blocks of success. The business world is riddled with instability, cynicism, and doubt. Fresh graduates are not readily employed nor do they easily build a career within that organization up until retirement. The rules of the game have radically changed. Every industry suffers from increased job mobility, mounting recruitment costs, and low retention rates. P&G understood the importance of cultivating a high-performing, collaborative, and loyal workforce. The company's vision led to a nomination in Aon Hewitt's Top 5 Best Employers list for 2013. Corporations today need to foster a corporate culture where workers identify with and are motivated by their employer. What this means is nurturing a heightened connection between an employee and his/her job, organization, manager, and co-workers. In fact, recent studies show that employees who are committed and dedicated to their work on an emotional level tend to outperform those who are not. This, of course, begs the question: how can organizations effectively deliver human resource services that can meet the needs of today's layered, multigenerational workforce as it simultaneously guarantees organizational success?

Layer and Divide the Work

Companies need to include everyone in the HRM plan. The ecosystem structures organizational outcomes, and safeguards employee engagement. Leadership skills drive excellence, and create meaningful challenging work that employees "own" and are held accountable for. Pivotal engagement drivers not only motivate employees but also help build strong teams. The new ecosystem shapes a flexible learning and development path: providing employees with deserving rewards, recognition, and enhanced compensation; offering a career trajectory forecast and related guidance; embedding the company's core values; celebrating the organization's overall success and individual accomplishments; creating a transparent, direct line of communication with employees; developing a culture of interdependent teamwork; and lastly, involving employees in corporate social responsibilities initiatives. The new ecosystem is a corporate climate that centers on value, accomplishment, and commitment in the UAE, and across the global market.

11-8. Based on what you read, what are P&G's concepts on handling its staff?

11-9. List P&G's guidelines.

11-10. Do you believe that P&G's guidelines are universal, or should they be tailored to fit different cultures?

NOTES

1. S. Caudron, "How HR Drives Profits," *Workforce Management* (December 2001), pp. 26–31 as reported by L. L. Bryan, C. I. Joyce, and L. M. Weiss in "Making a Market in Talent," *McKinsey Quarterly* (2006, No. 2), pp. 1–7.
2. "Talent Acquisition Up 6% in 2011 and Average Cost Per Hire About $3,500 per New Bersin & Assoc. Factbook," *Shaker* (November 28, 2011), *http://shakerrecruitment.ning.com/profiles/blogs/talent-acquisition-up-6-in-2011-and-average-cost-per-hire-about-3*.
3. The numbers are approximate averages from three separate studies of top management turnover after mergers. See M. Lubatkin, D. Schweiger, and Y. Weber, "Top Management Turnover in Related M&Ss: An Additional Test of the Theory of Relative Standing," *Journal of Management* (Vol. 25, No. 1, 1999), pp. 55–73.
4. J. A. Krug, "Executive Turnover in Acquired Firms: A Longitudinal Analysis of Long-Term Interaction Effects," paper presented to the annual meeting of *Academy of Management*, Seattle, WA (2003).
5. J. A. Krug and W. H. Hegarty, "Post-Acquisition Turnover Among U.S. Top Management Teams: An Analysis of the Effects of Foreign vs. Domestic Acquisitions of U.S. Targets," *Strategic Management Journal* (September 1997), pp. 667–675; J. A. Frug and W. H. Hegarty, "Predicting Who Stays and Leaves After an Acquisition: A Study of Top Managers in Multinational Firms," *Strategic Management Journal* (February 2001), pp. 185–196.
6. D. Harding and T. Rouse, "Human Due Diligence," *Harvard Business Review* (April 2007), pp. 124–131.

7. A. Hinterhuber, "Making M&A Work," *Business Strategy Review* (September 2002), pp. 7–9.

8. R. N. Ashkenas and S. C. Francis, "Integration Managers: Special Leaders for Special Times," *Harvard Business Review* (November–December 2000), pp. 108–116.

9. J. Hoerr, "Sharpening Minds for a Competitive Edge," *BusinessWeek* (December 17, 1990), pp. 72–78.

10. "ASTD 2015 State of the Industry Report: Organizations Continue to Invest in Workplace Learning," *ASTD*, November 2015, (https://www.td.org/Publications /Research-Reports/2015/2015-State-of-the-Industry).

11. "The Happy Wackiness of Zappos.com," *ABC News* (October 26, 2011), http://abcnews.go.com/blogs/business /2011/10/the-happy-wackiness-of-zappos-com/; J. Edwards, "Check Out the Insane Lengths Zappos Customer Service Reps Will Go To," *Business Insider* (January 29, 2012), *http://articles.businessinsider.com/2012-01-09/ news/30606433_1_customer-service-zappos-center-services*

12. R. Henkoff, "Companies that Train Best," *Fortune* (March 22, 1993), pp. 62–75.

13. D. C. Hambrick, "Upper Echelons Theory: An Update," *Academy of Management Review* (April 2007), pp. 334–343.

14. D. Miller and J. Shamsie, "Learning Across the Life Cycle: Experimentation and Performance Among the Hollywood Studio Heads," *Strategic Management Journal* (August 2001), pp. 725–745. An exception to these findings may be the computer software industry in which CEOs are at their best when they start their jobs and steadily decline during their tenures. See A. D. Henderson, D. Miller, and D. C. Hambrick, "How Quickly Do CEOs Become Obsolete? Industry Dynamism, CEO Tenure, and Company Performance," *Strategic Management Journal* (May 2006), pp. 447–460.

15. L. Jennings, "DineEquity aims to 'boldly change the story' at Applebee's," *Nation's Restaurant News*, February 24, 2016 (http://nrn.com/applebees/dineequity-aims-boldly -change-story-applebee-s); B. Hrowvitz, "New CEO Puts Comeback on the Menu at Applebee's," *USA Today* (April 28, 2008), pp. 1B, 2B.

16. A study of former General Electric executives who became CEOs categorized them as cost controllers, growers, or cycle managers on the basis of their line experience at GE. See B. Groysberg, A. N. McLean, and N. Nohria, "Are Leaders Portable?" *Harvard Business Review* (May 2006), pp. 92–100.

17. D. K. Datta and N. Rajagopalan, "Industry Structure and CEO Characteristics: An Empirical Study of Succession Events," *Strategic Management Journal* (September 1998), pp. 833–852; A. S. Thomas and K. Ramaswamy, "Environmental Change and Management Staffing: A Comment," *Journal of Management* (Winter 1993), pp. 877–887; J. P. Guthrie, C. M. Grimm, and K. G. Smith, "Environmental Change and Management Staffing: An Empirical Study," *Journal of Management* (December 1991), pp. 735–748.

18. J. Greco, "The Search Goes On," *Journal of Business Strategy* (September/October 1997), pp. 22–25; W. Ocasio and H. Kim, "The Circulation of Corporate Control: Selection of Functional Backgrounds on New CEOs in Large U.S. Manufacturing Firms, 1981–1992," *Administrative Science Quarterly* (September 1999), pp. 532–562; R. Dobbs, D. Harris, and A. Rasmussen, "When Should CFOs Take the Helm?" *McKinsey Quarterly Online* (November 2006); "How to Get to the Top," *The Economist* (May 31, 2008), p. 70.

19. R. Drazin and R. K. Kazanjian, "Applying the Del Technique to the Analysis of Cross-Classification Data: A Test of CEO Succession and Top Management Team Development," *Academy of Management Journal* (December 1993), pp. 1374–1399; W. E. Rothschild, "A Portfolio of Strategic Leaders," *Planning Review* (January/February 1996), pp. 16–19.

20. R. Subramanian and C. M. Sanchez, "Environmental Change and Management Staffing: An Empirical Examination of the Electric Utilities Industry," *Journal of Business Strategies* (Spring 1998), pp. 17–34.

21. M. A. Carpenter and B. R. Golden, "Perceived Managerial Discretion: A Study of Cause and Effect," *Strategic Management Journal* (March 1997), pp. 187–206.

22. J. A. Parnell, "Functional Background and Business Strategy: The Impact of Executive-Strategy Fit on Performance," *Journal of Business Strategies* (Spring 1994), pp. 49–62.

23. M. Smith and M. C. White, "Strategy, CEO Specialization, and Succession," *Administrative Science Quarterly* (June 1987), pp. 263–280.

24. H. Long, "More CEOs are becoming like Warren Buffett," *CNN Money*, December 29, 2015 (http://money.cnn .com/2015/12/29/investing/ceo-tenure-longer/index.html); "Making Companies Work," *The Economist* (October 25, 2003), p. 14 C. H. Mooney, C. M. Dalton, D. R. Dalton, and S. T. Cero, "CEO Succession as a Funnel: The Critical, and Changing Role of Inside Directors," *Organizational Dynamics* (Vol. 36, No. 4, 2007), pp. 418–428. Note, however, that the tenures of CEOs of family firms typically exceed 15 years. See I. Le Breton-Miller and D. Miller, "Why Do Some Family Businesses Out-Compete? Governance, Long-Term Orientations, and Sustainable Capability," *Entrepreneurship Theory and Practice* (November 2006), pp. 731–746.

25. A. Bianco, L. Lavelle, J. Merrit, and A. Barrett, "The CEO Trap," *BusinessWeek* (December 11, 2000), pp. 86–92.

26. Y. Zhang and N. Rajagopalan, "When the Known Devil Is Better than an Unknown God: An Empirical Study of the Antecedents and Consequences of Relay CEO Succession," *Academy of Management Journal* (August 2004), pp. 483–500; W. Sheen and A. A. Cannella Jr., "Will Succession Planning Increase Shareholder Wealth? Evidence from Investor Reactions to Relay CEO Successions," *Strategic Management Journal* (February 2003), pp. 191–198.

27. G. A. Bigley and M. F. Wiersema, "New CEOs and Corporate Strategic Refocusing: How Experience as Heir Apparent Influences the Use of Power," *Administrative Science Quarterly* (December 2002), pp. 707–727.

28. J. L. Bower, "Solve the Succession Crisis by Growing Inside-Outside Leaders," *Harvard Business Review* (November 2007), pp. 91–96; Y. Zhang and N. Rajagopalan, "Grooming for the Top Post and Ending the CEO Succession Crisis," *Organizational Dynamics* (Vol. 35, Issue 1, 2006), pp. 96–105.

29. "Coming and Going," Survey of Corporate Leadership," *The Economist* (October 25, 2003), pp. 12–14.

30. D. C. Carey and D. Ogden, *CEO Succession: A Window on How Boards Do It Right When Choosing a New Chief Executive* (New York: Oxford University Press, 2000).

31. "The King Lear Syndrome," *The Economist* (December 13, 2003), p. 65.

32. Y. Zang and N. Rajagopalan, "Grooming for the Top Post and Ending the CEO Succession Crisis," *Organizational Dynamics* (Vol. 35, Issue 1, 2006), pp. 96–105.

33. "2014 CEO Transitions," *Spencer Stuart,* (February, 2015, (*https://www.spencerstuart.com/research-and-insight/2014-ceo-transitions*).

34. M. S. Kraatz and J. H. Moore, "Executive Migration and Institutional Change," *Academy of Management Journal* (February 2002), pp. 120–143; Y. Zhang and N. Rajagopalan, "When the Known Devil Is Better than an Unknown God: An Empirical Study of the Antecedents and Consequences of Relay CEO Succession" *Academy of Management Journal* (August 2004), pp. 483–500; W. Shen and A. A. Cannella Jr., "Revisiting the Performance Consequences of CEO Succession: The Impacts of Successor Type, Post-Succession Senior Executive Turnover, and Departing CEO Tenure," *Academy of Management Journal* (August 2002), pp. 717–733.

35. K. P. Coyne and E. J. Coyne Sr., "Surviving Your New CEO," *Harvard Business Review* (May 2007), pp. 62–69.

36. N. Byrnes and D. Kiley, "Hello, You Must Be Going," *BusinessWeek* (February 12, 2007), pp. 30–32.

37. C. Lucier and J. Dyer, "Hiring an Outside CEO: A Board's Best Moves," *Directors & Boards* (Winter 2004), pp. 36–38. These findings are supported by a later study by Booz Allen Hamilton in which 1595 worldwide companies during the years from 1995 to 2005 showed the same results. See J. Webber, "The Accidental CEO," *BusinessWeek* (April 23, 2007), pp. 64–72.

38. Q. Yue, "Antecedents of Top Management Successor Origin in China," paper presented to the annual meeting of the *Academy of Management*, Seattle, WA (2003); A. A. Buchko and D. DiVerde, "Antecedents, Moderators, and Consequences of CEO Turnover: A Review and Reconceptualization," paper presented to *Midwest Academy of Management* (Lincoln, NE: 1997), p. 10 W. Ocasio, "Institutionalized Action and Corporate Governance: The Reliance on Rules of CEO Succession," *Administrative Science Quarterly* (June 1999), pp. 384–416.

39. C. Gopinath, "Turnaround: Recognizing Decline and Initiating Intervention," *Long Range Planning* (December 1991), pp. 96–101.

40. K. B. Schwartz and K. Menon, "Executive Succession in Failing Firms," *Academy of Management Journal* (September 1985), pp. 680–686; A. A. Cannella Jr., and M. Lubatkin, "Succession as a Sociopolitical Process: Internal Impediments to Outsider Selection," *Academy of Management Journal* (August 1993), pp. 763–793; W. Boeker and J. Goodstein, "Performance and Succession Choice: The Moderating Effects of Governance and Ownership," *Academy of Management Journal* (February 1993), pp. 172–186.

41. W. Boeker, "Executive Migration and Strategic Change: The Effect of Top Manager Movement on Product-Market Entry," *Administrative Science Quarterly* (June 1997), pp. 213–236.

42. E. Brockmann, J. J. Hoffman, and D. Dawley, "A Contingency Theory of CEO Successor Choice and Post-Bankruptcy Strategic Change," paper presented to annual meeting of *Academy of Management*, Seattle, WA (2003).

43. P. Lorange and D. Murphy, "Bringing Human Resources into Strategic Planning: System Design Characteristics," in C. J. Fombrun, N. M. Tichy, and M. A. Devanna (Eds.), *Strategic Human Resource Management* (New York: John Wiley & Sons, 1984), pp. 281–283.

44. *http://www.ge.com/company/culture/leadership_learning.html*

45. S. Armour, "Playing the Succession Game," *USA Today* (November 24, 2003), p. 3B.

46. *https://www.assessmentday.co.uk/assessmentcentre/real-examples.html;* D. A. Waldman and T. Korbar, "Student Assessment Center Performance in the Prediction of Early Career Success," *Academy of Management Learning and Education* (June 2004), pp. 151–167.

47. "Coming and Going, Survey of Corporate Leadership," *The Economist* (October 25, 2003), pp. 12–14.

48. R. A. Pitts, "Strategies and Structures for Diversification," *Academy of Management Journal* (June 1997), pp. 197–208.

49. http://retailindustry.about.com/od/USRetailStoreClosingInfoFAQs/fl/US-2016-Store-Closings-All-Retail-Chain-Store-Locations-To-Be-Closed_2.htm

50. K. E. Mishra, G. M. Spreitzer, and A. K. Mishra, "Preserving Employee Morale During Downsizing," *Sloan Management Review* (Winter 1998), pp. 83–95.

51. B. O'Reilly, "Is Your Company Asking Too Much?" *Fortune* (March 12, 1990), p. 41. For more information on the emotional reactions of survivors of downsizing, see C. R. Stoner and R. I. Hartman, "Organizational Therapy: Building Survivor Health & Competitiveness," *SAM Advanced Management Journal* (Summer 1997), pp. 15–31, 41.

52. S. R. Fisher and M. A. White, "Downsizing in a Learning Organization: Are There Hidden Costs?" *Academy of Management Review* (January 2000), pp. 244–251.

53. T. M. Amabile and R. Conti, "Changes in the Work Environment for Creativity During Downsizing," *Academy of Management Journal* (December 1999), pp. 630–640; A. G. Bedeian and A. A. Armenakis, "The Cesspool Syndrome: How Dreck Floats to the Top of Declining Organizations," *Academy of Management Executive* (February 1998), pp. 58–67.

54. For a more complete listing of the psychological and behavioral reactions to downsizing, see M. L. Marks and K. P. De Meuse, "Resizing the Organization: Maximizing the Gain While Minimizing the Pain of Layoffs, Divestitures, and Closings," *Organizational Dynamics* (Vol. 34, No. 1, 2005), pp. 19–35.

55. D. J. Flanagan and K. C. O'Shaughnessy, "The Effect of Layoffs on Firm Reputation," *Journal of Management* (June 2005), pp. 445–463.

56. *The Wall Street Journal* (December 22, 1992), p. B1.

57. V. Giang, "14 of the Biggest Mass Layoffs of 2011," *Business Insider* (August 28, 2011), http://www.businessinsider.com/companies-with-the-biggest-layoffs-in-2011-2011-8?op=1

58. R. D. Nixon, M. A. Hitt, H. Lee, and E. Jeong, "Market Reactions to Announcements of Corporate Downsizing Actions and Implementation Strategies," *Strategic Management Journal* (November 2004), pp. 1121–1129; G. D. Bruton, J. K. Keels, and C. L. Shook, "Downsizing the Firm: Answering the Strategic Questions," *Academy of Management Executive* (May 1996), pp. 38–45; E. G. Love and N. Nohria, "Reducing Slack: The Performance Consequences

of Downsizing by Large Industrial Firms, 1977–93," *Strategic Management Journal* (December 2005), pp. 1087–1108; C. D. Zatzick and R. D. Iverson, "High-Involvement Management and Workforce Reduction: Competitive Advantage or Disadvantage?" *Academy of Management Journal* (October 2006), pp. 999–1015.

59. M. A. Hitt, B. W. Keats, H. F. Harback, and R. D. Nixon, "Rightsizing: Building and Maintaining Strategic Leadership and Long-Term Competitiveness," *Organizational Dynamics* (Autumn 1994), pp. 18–32. For additional suggestions, see W. F. Cascio, "Strategies for Responsible Restructuring," *Academy of Management Executive* (August 2002), pp. 80–91, and T. Mroczkowski and M. Hanaoka, "Effective Rightsizing Strategies in Japan and America: Is There a Convergence of Employment Practices?" *Academy of Management Executive* (May 1997),

pp. 57–67. For an excellent list of cost-reduction programs for use in short, medium, and long-term time horizons, see F. Gandolfi, "Cost Reductions, Downsizing-Related Layoffs, and HR Practices," *SAM Advanced Management Journal* (Spring 2008), pp. 52–58.

60. M. Meaney, C. Pung, and S. Kamath, "Creating Organizational Transformations," *McKinsey Quarterly Online* (September 10, 2008).

61. T. C. Powell, "Total Quality Management as Competitive Advantage: A Review and Empirical Study," *Strategic Management Journal* (January 1995), pp. 15–37.

62. B. Groysberg, A. Nanda, and N. Nohria, "The Risky Business of Hiring Stars," *Harvard Business Review* (May 2004), pp. 92–100.

63. D. Keirsey, *Please Understand Me II* (Del Mar, CA: Prometheus Nemesis Book Co., 1998).

CHAPTER 12

Evaluation and Control

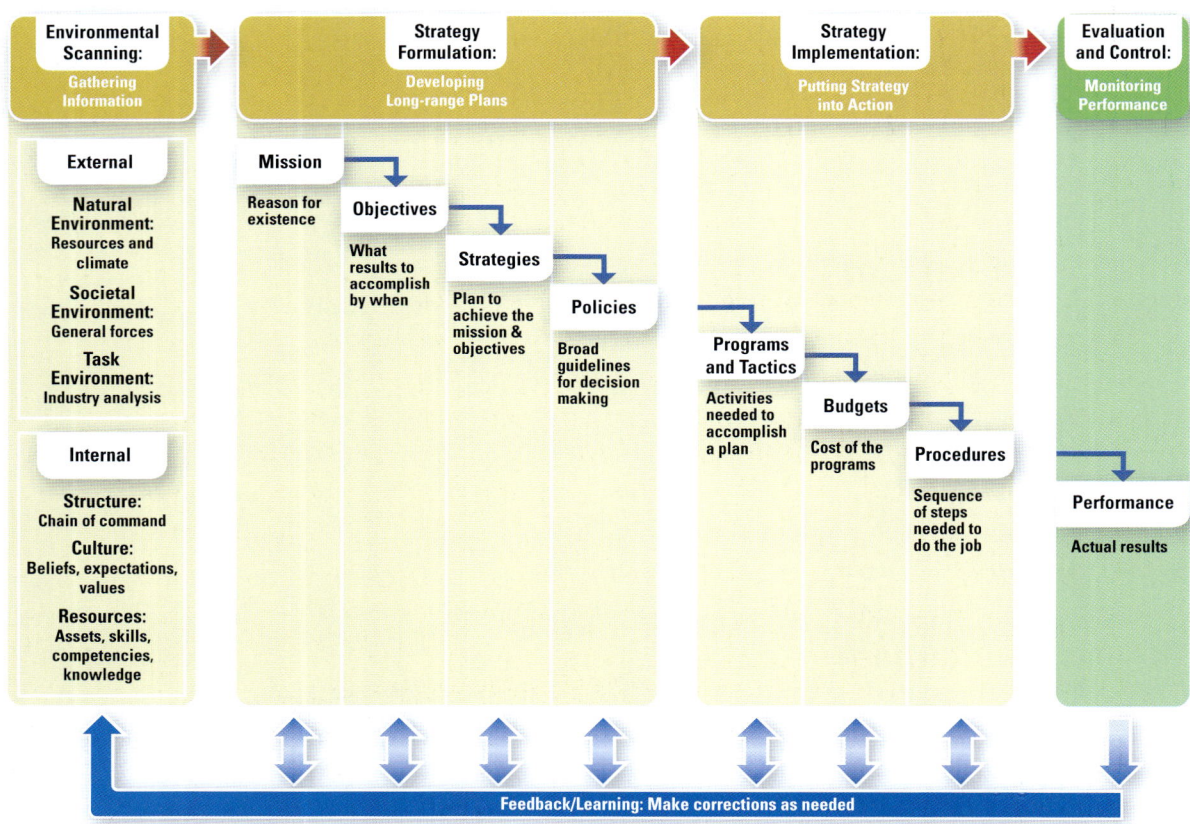

Pearson MyLab Management®

⭐ Improve Your Grade!

Over 10 million students improved their results using the Pearson MyLabs. Visit **mymanagementlab.com** for simulations, tutorials, and end-of-chapter problems.

Learning Objectives

After reading this chapter, you should be able to:

12-1. Explain how various types of measures and controls are utilized to properly assess performance including activity-based costing, ERM, ROI, and EVA

12-2. Develop a balanced scorecard to examine key performance measures of a company

12-3. Apply the benchmarking process to a function or an activity

12-4. Explain how strategic information systems are being utilized to support specific strategies

12-5. Discuss the issues with measuring organizational performance and how organizations can establish proper controls to achieve objectives

Stuck in the Middle – Pizza Hut

If you want to be in a business with thousands of competitors, then you must execute exceptionally well and keep up with the competitive environment. While Pizza Hut was growing their business, they failed to keep up with the changes in the industry. Pizza Hut was founded in 1958 and in 2016 had more than 14,100 locations in over 90 countries and was still the number one pizza chain in the world with sales in excess of US$5.5 billion. Unfortunately, that number was down 3.5% from the previous year as competitors who are more attuned to the customer have taken market share.

Making pizza is a staple of restaurants around the world and there is little rocket science in the effort. What has changed over time is the means by which customers want to order, what they want as ingredients and how they want to consume their pizza. Online and mobile ordering now accounts for more than 50% of rival Domino's business. Customers are demanding fresh ingredients, gluten-free options, and high-speed preparation. The advent of fast-casual restaurants where customers watch the preparation of their food has only exasperated this situation.

Into this new era comes a Pizza Hut empire that was built around a hidden kitchen, pizzas that take 15–20 minutes to prepare and a 1950s style eating area that is anything but comfortable. After evaluating the best way to address the new reality, Pizza Hut began experimenting with new ovens that could cook a pizza in three-and-a-half minutes, redesigned interiors that included a bar and new, simpler procedures for running a store-front. After testing the new ideas at two restaurants in Texas, Pizza Hut announced plans to remodel 700 of its U.S. stores a year through 2022.

Tracking the effect of these changes and crafting those changes systemwide will be a true evaluation and control challenge for the organization.

SOURCES: B. Sozzi, "Pizza Hut Continues Its U.S. Revival," *The Street*, March 16, 2016 (http://www.thestreet.com /story/13496112/1/pizza-hut-continues-its-u-s-revival.html); "Pizza Hut's Shrinking Piece of the Pie," *Bloomberg BusinessWeek*, January 25-31, 2016, pp. 20-21 http://www.yum.com/brands/ph.asp

Measuring Performance

12-1. Explain how various types of measures and controls are utilized to properly assess performance including activity-based costing, ERM, ROI, and EVA

Evaluation and control information consists of performance data and activity reports (gathered in Step 3 in **Figure 12–1**). If undesired performance results because the strategic management processes were inappropriately used, operational managers must know about it so they can correct the employee activity. Top management need not be involved. If, however, undesired performance results from the processes themselves, top managers, as well as operational managers, must know about it so they can develop new implementation programs or procedures. Evaluation and control information must be relevant to what is being monitored. One of the obstacles to effective control is the difficulty in developing appropriate measures of important activities and outputs. **Performance** is the end result of activity. Select measures to assess performance based on the organizational unit to be appraised and the objectives to be achieved. The objectives that were established earlier in the strategy formulation part of the strategic management process (dealing with profitability, market share, and cost reduction, among others) should certainly be used to measure corporate performance once the strategies have been implemented.

APPROPRIATE MEASURES

Some measures, such as return on investment (ROI) and earnings per share (EPS), are appropriate for evaluating a corporation's or a division's ability to achieve a profitability objective. This type of measure, however, is inadequate for evaluating additional corporate objectives such as social responsibility or employee development. Even though profitability is a corporation's major objective, ROI and EPS can be computed only after profits are totaled for a period. It tells what happened after the fact—not what is happening or what will happen. A firm, therefore, needs to develop measures that predict likely profitability. These are referred to as **steering controls** because they measure variables that influence future profitability. Every industry has its own set of key metrics that tend to predict profits. Airlines, for example, closely monitor cost per available seat mile (CASM). In 2002, Southwest's cost per passenger mile was 7.4¢, the lowest among the major airlines in the industry, contrasted with U.S. Airways 11.6¢, the highest

FIGURE 12–1
Evaluation and
Control Process

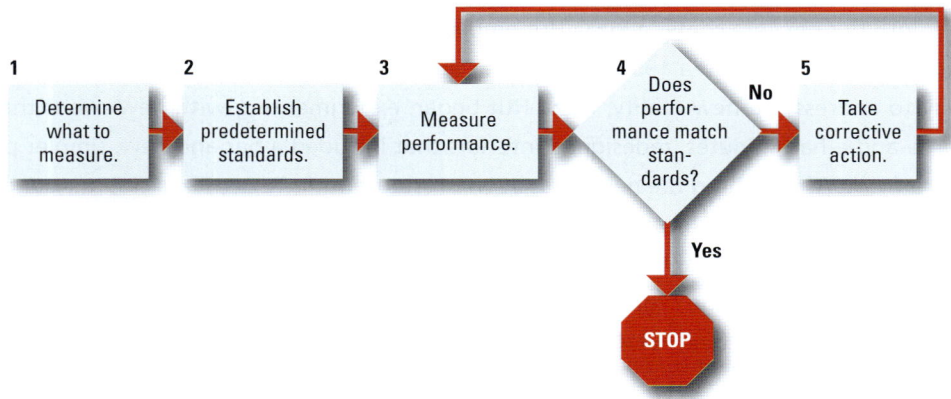

in the industry. Its low costs gave Southwest a significant competitive advantage. By 2015, Southwest's costs had risen substantially to 12.4¢, while U.S. Airways had moved to 12.7¢ just ahead of its merger with American Airlines. In the meantime, Southwest had been replaced as the most low-cost airline by Spirit Airlines, whose cost per ASM in 2015 was 10.1¢.[1]

An example of a steering control used by retail stores is the *inventory turnover ratio*, in which a retailer's cost of goods sold is divided by the average value of its inventories. This measure shows how hard an investment in inventory is working; the higher the ratio, the better. Not only does quicker moving inventory tie up less cash in inventories, it also reduces the risk that the goods will grow obsolete before they're sold—a crucial measure for computers and other technology items. For example, Office Depot increased its inventory turnover ratio from 6.9 in one year to 7.5 the next year, leading to improved annual profits.[2]

Another steering control is customer satisfaction. Research reveals that companies that score high on the *American Customer Satisfaction Index (ACSI),* a measure developed by the University of Michigan's National Research Center, have higher stock returns and better cash flows than those companies that score low on the ACSI. A change in a firm's customer satisfaction typically works its way through a firm's value chain and is eventually reflected in quarterly profits.[3] Other approaches to measuring customer satisfaction include Oracle's use of the ratio of quarterly sales divided by customer service requests and the total number of hours that technicians spend on the phone solving customer problems. To help executives keep track of important steering controls, Netsuite developed *dashboard* software that displays critical information in easy-to-read computer graphics assembled from data pulled from other corporate software programs.[4]

TYPES OF CONTROLS

Controls can be established to focus on actual performance results (output), the activities that generate the performance (behavior), or on resources that are used in performance (input). **Output controls** specify what is to be accomplished by focusing on the end result of the behaviors through the use of objectives and performance targets or milestones. **Behavior controls** specify how something is to be done through policies, rules, standard operating procedures, and orders from a superior. **Input controls** emphasize resources, such as knowledge, skills, abilities, values, and motives of employees.[5]

Output, behavior, and input controls are not interchangeable. Output controls (such as sales quotas, specific cost-reduction or profit objectives, and surveys of customer satisfaction) are most appropriate when specific output measures have been agreed on but the cause–effect connection between activities and results is not clear. Behavior controls (such as following company procedures, making sales calls to potential customers, and getting to work on time) are most appropriate when performance results are hard to measure, but the cause–effect connection between activities and results is relatively clear. Input controls (such as number of years of education and experience) are most appropriate when output is difficult to measure and there is no clear cause–effect relationship between behavior and performance (such as in college teaching). Corporations following the strategy of conglomerate diversification tend to emphasize output controls with their divisions and subsidiaries (presumably because they are managed independently of each other), whereas, corporations following concentric diversification use all three types of controls (presumably because synergy is desired).[6] Even if all three types of control are used, one or two of them may be emphasized more than another depending on the circumstances. For example, Muralidharan and Hamilton propose that as a multinational corporation moves through its stages of development, its emphasis on control should shift from being primarily output at first, to behavioral, and finally to input control.[7]

Examples of increasingly popular behavior controls are the ISO 9000 and 14000 Standards Series on quality and environmental assurance, developed by the International Standards Association of Geneva, Switzerland. Using the **ISO 9000 Standards Series** (now a family of standards with eight management principles which we discussed in **Chapter 11**) is a way of objectively documenting a company's high level of quality operations. The **ISO 14000 Standards Series** establishes how to document the company's impact on the environment. A company wanting ISO 9000 certification would document its process for product introductions, among other things. ISO 9001 would require this firm to separately document design input, design process, design output, and design verification—a large amount of work. ISO 14001 would specify how companies should establish, maintain and continually improve an environmental management system. The benefits from ISO certification are partially in cost savings, but primarily they are a signal to suppliers and buyers about the focus of the company.[8] For an example of how one company that is steeped in controls is using an innovative idea to improve their systems, see the **Innovation Issue** feature.

Many corporations view ISO 9000 certification as assurance that a supplier sells quality products. Companies in more than 119 countries require ISO 9000 and/or ISO 14000 certification of their suppliers.[9]

INNOVATION issue

SOLAR POWER AND THE GRID

No industry is more concerned about established procedures and minimizing fluctuations in their business model than the electric utility industry. Beyond storms that bring down the power grid, the biggest issue is dealing with fluctuations in power demand. Backup generators, purchasing power from other utilities, and keeping excess power available has been used for decades. However, the wide-scale introduction of solar arrays has added a whole new wrinkle to the issue in the industry. While solar arrays work quite well when the sun is shining, even modest cloud cover can cause large fluctuations in output.

Duke Energy in partnership with startup Aquion Energy's environmentally developed batteries in combination with ultracapacitors made by Maxwell, is looking to smooth out fluctuations in the power grid. Not only would the system be good for the environment, but it would provide an innovative solution to a known problem in the industry. Duke Energy had over 600 megawatts of solar capacity by early 2016.

Ultracapacitors are like a battery, but store energy in an electric field instead of a chemical reaction. Ultracapacitors can provide short bursts of high power, while the grid batteries can deliver lower sustained power over several hours. Some utilities are using lithium-ion batteries similar to those used in laptops and automobiles. Elon Musk publically stated that the demand for Tesla Grid Batteries had been enormous. One study found that the market for energy storage in the United States grew 243% last year and is expected to reach a value of $2.5 billion by 2020. The batteries developed by Aquion are low cost, non-toxic batteries made from salt water, carbon, and manganese oxide.

Duke sees battery systems as a means for smoothing out sudden swings in output from solar arrays, thus helping the whole grid work more smoothly. The solar arrays could be used to provide power (when the sun is shining) to the grid, as well as to the recharging of battery systems.

....

SOURCES: K. Fehrenbacher, "Unusual Battery Plugs Into North Carolina Power Grid," *Fortune*, March 10, 2016 (*http://fortune.com/2016/03/10/duke-energy-unusual-battery-north-carolina-grid/*); http://www.duke-energy.com/news/releases/2015042201.asp; B. Henderson, "Duke to Test Uses for EV Batteries," *The Charlotte Observer* (November 16, 2012), pg. 2B.

Airmax is a fleet management company that earned its ISO 14000 certification in 2013 by rigorously working to improve its environmental efforts. This included creating a monitor that tracked the actual CO_2 output of their vehicle fleet based on actual fuel burn and not the estimates generally used in the industry.

Another example of a behavior control is a company's monitoring of employee phone calls and PCs to ensure that employees are behaving according to company guidelines. In a survey done in 2015, 67.3% of U.S. employers reported using some form of electronic monitoring in the workplace. The average time spent online on non-work issues by employees has been estimated at one to three hours per day. In one company, a disgruntled supervisor was spending six to seven hours a day doing everything from job searching to looking up recipes and downloading coupons.[10]

ACTIVITY-BASED COSTING

Activity-based costing (ABC) is an accounting method for allocating indirect and fixed costs to individual products or product lines based on the value-added activities going into that product.[11] This accounting method is very useful in constructing a value-chain analysis of a firm's activities for making outsourcing decisions. Traditional cost accounting, in contrast, focuses on valuing a company's inventory for financial reporting purposes. To obtain a unit's cost, cost accountants typically add direct labor to the cost of materials. Then they compute overhead from rent to R&D expenses, based on the number of direct labor hours it takes to make a product. To obtain unit cost, they divide the total by the number of items made during the period under consideration.

Traditional cost accounting is useful when direct labor accounts for most of total costs and a company produces just a few products requiring the same processes. This may have been true of companies during the early part of the twentieth century, but it is no longer relevant today, when overhead may account for as much as 70% of manufacturing costs. The appropriate allocation of indirect costs and overhead is crucial for decision making. The traditional volume-based cost-driven system systematically understates the cost per unit of products with low sales volumes and products with a high degree of complexity. Similarly, it overstates the cost per unit of products with high sales volumes and a low degree of complexity.[12] When Chrysler used ABC, it discovered that the true cost of some of the parts used in making cars was 30 times what the company had previously estimated.[13]

ABC accounting allows accountants to charge costs more accurately than the traditional method because it allocates overhead far more precisely. For example, imagine a production line in a pen factory where black pens are made in high volume and blue pens in low volume. Assume that it takes eight hours to retool (reprogram the machinery) to shift production from one kind of pen to the other. The total costs include supplies (the same for both pens), the direct labor of the line workers, and factory overhead. In this instance, a very significant part of the overhead cost is the cost of reprogramming the machinery to switch from one pen to another. If the company produces 10 times as many black pens as blue pens, 10 times the cost of the reprogramming expenses will be allocated to the black pens as to the blue pens under traditional cost accounting methods. This approach underestimates, however, the true cost of making the blue pens.

ABC accounting, in contrast, first breaks down pen manufacturing into its activities. It is then very easy to see that it is the activity of changing pens that triggers the cost of retooling. The ABC accountant calculates an average cost of setting up the machinery and charges it against each batch of pens that requires retooling, regardless of the size of the run. Thus, a product carries only those costs for the overhead it actually consumes. Management is now able to discover that its blue pens cost almost twice as much as do the black pens. Unless the company is able to charge a higher price for its blue pens, it cannot make a profit on these pens. Unless there is a strategic reason why it must offer blue pens (such as a key customer who must have a small number of blue pens with every large order of black pens or a marketing trend away from black to blue pens), the company will earn significantly greater profits if it completely stops making blue pens.[14]

ENTERPRISE RISK MANAGEMENT

Enterprise Risk Management (ERM) is a corporatewide, integrated process for managing the uncertainties that could negatively or positively influence the achievement of the corporation's objectives. In the past, managing risk was done in a fragmented manner within functions or business units. Individuals would manage process risk; safety risk; and insurance, financial, and other assorted risks. As a result of this fragmented approach, companies would take huge risks in some areas of the business while over-managing substantially smaller risks in other areas. ERM is being adopted because of the increasing amount of environmental uncertainty that can affect an entire corporation. As a result, the position Chief Risk Officer is one of the fastest growing executive positions in U.S. corporations.[15] Microsoft uses scenario analysis to identify key business risks. According to Microsoft's treasurer, Brent Callinicos, "The scenarios are really what we're trying to protect against."[16] The scenarios were the possibility of an earthquake in the Seattle region and a major downturn in the stock market.

The process of rating risks involves three steps:

1. Identify the risks using scenario analysis, brainstorming, or by performing risk self-assessments.

2. Rank the risks, using some scale of impact and likelihood.

3. Measure the risks, using some agreed-upon standard.

Some companies are using value at risk, or VAR (effect of unlikely events in normal markets), and stress testing (effect of plausible events in abnormal markets) methodologies to measure the potential impact of the financial risks they face. DuPont uses earnings at risk (EAR) measuring tools to measure the effect of risk on reported earnings. It can then manage risk to a specified earnings level based on the company's "risk appetite." With this integrated view, DuPont can view how risks affect the likelihood of achieving certain earnings targets.[17] Research has shown that companies with integrative risk management capabilities achieve superior economic performance.[18]

PRIMARY MEASURES OF CORPORATE PERFORMANCE

The days when simple financial measures such as ROI or EPS were used alone to assess overall corporate performance have generally come to an end. Analysts recommend a broad range of methods to evaluate the success or failure of a strategy. Some of these methods are stakeholder measures, shareholder value, and the balanced scorecard approach. Even though each of these methods has supporters as well as detractors, the current trend is clearly toward more complicated financial measures and an increasing use of non-financial measures of corporate performance. For example, research indicates that companies pursuing strategies founded on innovation and new product development now tend to favor non-financial over financial measures.[19]

Traditional Financial Measures

The most commonly used measure of corporate performance (in terms of profits) is **return on investment (ROI)**. It is simply the result of dividing net income before taxes by the total amount invested in the company (typically measured by total assets). Although using ROI has several advantages, it also has several distinct limitations. While ROI gives the impression of objectivity and precision, it can be easily manipulated.

Earnings per share (EPS), which involves dividing net earnings by the amount of common stock, also has several deficiencies as an evaluation of past and future performance. First, because alternative accounting principles are available, EPS can have several different but equally acceptable values, depending on the principle selected for its computation. Second, because EPS is based on accrual income, the conversion of income to cash can be near term or delayed. Therefore, EPS does not consider the time value of money. **Return on equity (ROE)**, which involves dividing net income by total equity, also has limitations because it is also derived from accounting-based data. In addition, EPS and ROE are often unrelated to a company's stock price.

Operating cash flow, the amount of money generated by a company before the cost of financing and taxes, is a broad measure of a company's funds. This is the company's net income plus depreciation, depletion, amortization, interest expense, and income tax expense.[20] Some takeover specialists look at a much narrower **free cash flow**: the amount of money a new owner can take out of the firm without harming the business. This is net income plus depreciation, depletion, and amortization less capital expenditures and dividends. The free cash flow ratio is very useful in evaluating the stability of an entrepreneurial venture.[21] Although cash flow may be harder to manipulate than earnings, the number can be increased by selling accounts receivable, classifying outstanding checks as accounts payable, trading securities, and capitalizing certain expenses, such as direct-response advertising.[22]

Because of these and other limitations, ROI, EPS, ROE, and operating cash flow are not by themselves adequate measures of corporate performance. At the same time, these traditional financial measures are very appropriate when used with complementary financial and non-financial measures. For example, some non-financial performance measures used by Internet business ventures are *stickiness* (length of Web site visit), *eyeballs* (number of people who visit a Web site), and *mindshare* (brand awareness). Mergers and acquisitions may be priced on multiples of *MUUs* (monthly unique users) or even on registered users.

Shareholder Value

Because of the belief that accounting-based numbers such as ROI, ROE, and EPS are not reliable indicators of a corporation's economic value, many corporations are using shareholder value as a better measure of corporate performance and strategic management effectiveness.

Shareholder value can be defined as the present value of the anticipated future stream of cash flows from the business plus the value of the company if liquidated. Arguing that the purpose of a company is to increase shareholder wealth, shareholder value analysis concentrates on cash flow as the key measure of performance. The value of a corporation is thus the value of its cash flows discounted back to their present value, using the business's cost of capital as the discount rate. As long as the returns from a business exceed its cost of capital, the business will create value and be worth more than the capital invested in it. For example, Deere and Company charges each business unit a cost of capital of 1% of assets a month. Each business unit is required to earn a shareholder value-added profit margin of 20%, on average, over the business cycle. Financial rewards are linked to this measure.[23]

The New York consulting firm Stern Stewart & Company devised and popularized two shareholder value measures: economic value added (EVA) and market value added (MVA). A basic tenet of EVA and MVA is that businesses should not invest in projects unless they can generate a profit above the cost of capital. Stern Stewart argues that a deficiency of traditional accounting-based measures is that they assume the cost of capital to be zero.[24] Well-known companies, such as Coca-Cola, General Electric, AT&T, Whirlpool, Quaker Oats, Eli Lilly, Georgia-Pacific, Polaroid, Sprint, Toyota, and Tenneco have adopted MVA and/or EVA as the best yardstick for corporate performance.

Economic value added (EVA) has become an extremely popular shareholder value method of measuring corporate and divisional performance and may be on its way to replacing ROI as the standard performance measure. EVA measures the difference between the pre-strategy and post-strategy values for the business. Simply put, EVA is after-tax operating income minus the total annual cost of capital. The formula to measure EVA is:

$$\text{EVA} = \text{after-tax operating income} - (\text{investment in assets} \times \text{weighted average cost of capital})^{26}$$

The cost of capital combines the cost of debt and equity. The annual cost of borrowed capital is the interest charged by the firm's banks and bondholders. To calculate the cost of equity, assume that shareholders generally earn about 6% more on stocks than on government bonds. If long-term treasury bills are selling at 2.5%, the firm's cost of equity should be 8.5%—more if the firm is in a risky industry. A corporation's overall cost of capital is the weighted-average cost of the firm's debt and equity capital. The investment in assets is the total amount of capital invested in the business, including buildings, machines, computers, and investments in R&D and training (allocating costs annually over their useful life). Because the typical balance sheet understates the investment made in a company, Stern Stewart has identified more than 160 possible adjustments, before EVA is calculated.[26] Multiply the firm's total investment in assets by the weighted-average cost of capital. Subtract that figure from after-tax operating income. If the difference is positive, the strategy (and the management employing it) is generating value for the shareholders. If it is negative, the strategy is destroying shareholder value.[27]

Roberto Goizueta, past-CEO of Coca-Cola, explained, "We raise capital to make concentrate, and sell it at an operating profit. Then we pay the cost of that capital. Shareholders pocket the difference."[28] Managers can improve their company's or business unit's EVA by: (1) earning more profit without using more capital, (2) using less capital, and (3) investing capital in high-return projects. Studies have found that companies using EVA outperform their median competitor by an average of 8.43% of total return annually.[29] EVA does, however, have some limitations. For one thing, it does not control for size differences across plants or divisions. As with ROI, managers can manipulate the numbers. As with ROI, EVA is an after-the-fact measure and cannot be used like a steering control.[30] Although proponents of EVA argue that EVA (unlike return on investment, equity, or sales) has a strong relationship to stock price, other studies do not support this contention.[31]

Market value added (MVA) is the difference between the market value of a corporation and the capital contributed by shareholders and lenders. Like net present value, it measures the stock market's estimate of the net present value of a firm's past and expected capital investment projects. As such, MVA is the present value of future EVA.[32] To calculate MVA:

1. Add all the capital that has been put into a company—from shareholders, bondholders, and retained earnings.

2. Reclassify certain accounting expenses, such as R&D, to reflect that they are actually investments in future earnings. This provides the firm's total capital. So far, this is the same approach taken in calculating EVA.

3. Using the current stock price, total the value of all outstanding stock, adding it to the company's debt. This is the company's market value. If the company's market value is greater than all the capital invested in it, the firm has a positive MVA—meaning that management (and the strategy it is following) has created wealth. In some cases, however, the market value of the company is actually less than the capital put into it, which means shareholder wealth is being destroyed.

Studies have shown that EVA is a predictor of MVA. Consecutive years of positive EVA generally lead to a soaring MVA.[33] Research also reveals that CEO turnover is significantly correlated with MVA and EVA, whereas ROA and ROE are not. This suggests that EVA and MVA may be more appropriate measures of the market's evaluation of a firm's strategy and its management than are the traditional measures of corporate performance.[34] Nevertheless, these measures consider only the financial interests of the shareholder and ignore other stakeholders, such as environmentalists and employees.

Climate change is likely to lead to new regulations, technological remedies, and shifts in consumer behavior. It will thus have a significant impact on the financial performance of many corporations. To see how companies are using new techniques that are simultaneously good for the environment as well as being good for the company, see the **Sustainability Issue** feature.

SUSTAINABILITY issue

THE END OF THE CASH REGISTER RECEIPT

More than 9 million trees are cut down each year to make cash register receipts in the United States and most of those receipts are simply thrown away. A number of companies were moving toward e-receipts in the late 1990s, but the dot-com bust brought all that to a temporary end. In 2005, Apple introduced e-receipts at its stylish Apple stores and the wave began.

E-receipts not only save on unnecessary printing and landfill waste; they also provide the customer with an electronic record of purchases (for taxes, expense reports, or gift returns). While thousands of companies have gone to an e-receipts option, some are taking it all a step further. Wal*Mart has developed an e-receipts locker app that keeps all purchase receipts easily available for the customer. The advantage beyond cost savings for the retailer is having the customer's e-mail address for use with promotions.

Some companies are using this new opportunity to provide real value to the consumer with the creation of the "smart receipt." The smart receipt shows up in your e-mail and might include links to videos on how to install the product or links to social media. It might have links to coupons or surveys. Meanwhile, all sorts of information is being gathered by the retailer so you can be targeted more precisely.

....

SOURCES: J. Kelly, "We may be hearing the last of, 'Do you just want the receipt in the bag?"' *The Washington Post*, June 8, 2015 (https://www.washingtonpost.com/local/we-may-be-hearing-the-last-of-do-you-just-want-the-receipt-in-the-bag/2015/06/08/bb81e340-0ba7-11e5-a7ad-b430fc1d3f5c_story.html); C. Tode, "Walmart builds ereceipts platform for better mobile in-store experiences," *Mobile Commerce Daily*, May 20, 2014 (http://www.mobilecommercedaily.com/walmart-builds-ereceipts-platform-for-better-mobile-in-store-experiences); W. Koch, "Retailers Find Profits with Paperless Receipts," *USA Today* (November 3, 2012), http://www.usatoday.com/story/news/nation/2012/11/03/retailers-e-mail-digital--paperless-receipts/1675069/#; S. Clifford, "Shopper Receipts Join Paperless Age," *The New York Times* (August 7, 2011), http://www.nytimes.com/2011/08/08/technology/digital-receipts-at-stores-gain-in-popularity.html?_r=0

Balanced Scorecard Approach: Using Key Performance Measures

12-2. Develop a balanced scorecard to examine key performance measures of a company

Rather than evaluate a corporation using a few financial measures, Kaplan and Norton suggested a "balanced scorecard" that includes non-financial as well as financial measures.[35] This approach is especially useful given that research indicates that non-financial assets explain 50% to 80% of a firm's value.[36] The **balanced scorecard** combines financial measures that tell the results of actions already taken with operational measures on customer satisfaction, internal processes, and the corporation's innovation and improvement activities—the drivers of future financial performance. Thus, steering controls are combined with output controls. In the balanced scorecard, management develops goals or objectives in each of four areas:

- **Financial:** How do we appear to shareholders?
- **Customer:** How do customers view us?
- **Internal business perspective:** What must we excel at?
- **Innovation and learning:** Can we continue to improve and create value?[37]

Each goal in each area (for example, avoiding bankruptcy in the financial area) is then assigned one or more measures, as well as a target and an initiative. These measures can be thought of as **key performance measures**—measures that are essential for achieving a desired strategic option.[38] For example, a company could include cash flow, quarterly sales growth, and ROE as measures for success in the financial area. It could include market share (competitive position goal), customer satisfaction, and percentage of new sales coming from new products (customer acceptance goal) as measures under the customer perspective. It could include cycle time and unit cost (manufacturing excellence goal) as measures under the internal business perspective. It could include time to develop next-generation products (technology leadership objective) under the innovation and learning perspective.

A 2013 global survey by Bain & Company reported that 73% of Fortune 1,000 companies in North America were projected to use a version of the balanced scorecard.[39] A study of the Fortune 500 firms in the United States and the Post 300 firms in Canada revealed the most popular non-financial measures to be customer satisfaction, customer service, product quality, market share, productivity, service quality, and core competencies. New product development, corporate culture, and market growth were not far behind.[40] DuPont's Engineering Polymers Division uses the balanced scorecard to align employees, business units, and shared services around a common strategy involving productivity improvements and revenue growth.[41] Corporate experience with the balanced scorecard reveals that a firm should tailor the system to suit its situation, not just adopt it as a cookbook approach. When the balanced scorecard complements corporate strategy, it improves performance. Using the method in a mechanistic fashion without any link to strategy hinders performance and may even decrease it.[42]

Evaluating Top Management and the Board of Directors

Through its strategy, audit, and compensation committees, a board of directors is charged with closely evaluating the job performance of the CEO and the top management team. A recent study found that 98% of Boards used financial measures as the key criteria for CEO and top management team performance evaluation while less than half of organizations look at more qualitative measures, such as customer satisfaction (37%) or innovation (24%).[43] The board, however, is also concerned with other factors.

Members of the compensation committees of today's boards of directors generally agree that a CEO's ability to establish strategic direction, build a management team, and provide leadership are more critical in the long run than are a few quantitative measures. The board should evaluate top management not only on the typical output-oriented quantitative measures, but also on behavioral measures—factors relating to its strategic management practices. According to the same survey by Hay Group, some softer skills such as leadership (77%) and succession planning (65%) were reported as showing up in evaluations. The specific items that a board uses to evaluate its top management should be derived from the objectives that both the board and top management agreed on earlier. If better relations with the local community and improved safety practices in work areas were selected as objectives for the year (or for five years), these items should be included in the evaluation. In addition, other factors that tend to lead to profitability might be included, such as market share, product quality, or investment intensity.

Performance evaluations of the overall board's performance were generally standard practice, but not mandated prior to 2013. After that date, boards were required to make a statement in the Board's report indicating how formal evaluations were made by the Board of its own performance and that of its committees and most importantly the individual directors.[44]

Chairman-CEO Feedback Instrument. Many companies evaluate their CEO by using a 17-item questionnaire developed by Ram Charon, an authority on corporate governance. The questionnaire focuses on four key areas: (1) company performance, (2) leadership of the organization, (3) team-building and management succession, and (4) leadership of external constituencies.[45] The difficulty that some board members have is understanding what a CEO should be evaluated on beyond financial performance. One recommendation is to have Board members "grade" the CEO on six characteristics: (1) vision, (2) HR, (3) proper capital allocation, (4) culture of the organization, (5) decision making, and (6) performance.[46] These approaches are aimed at improving the conversation, mentoring, and effectiveness of the CEO.[47]

Management Audit. **Management audits** are very useful to boards of directors in evaluating management's handling of various corporate activities. Management audits have been developed to evaluate activities such as corporate social responsibility, functional areas like the marketing department, and divisions such as the international division. These can be helpful if the board has selected particular functional areas or activities for improvement.

Strategic Audit. The strategic audit, presented in the **Chapter 1 Appendix 1.A**, is a type of management audit. The strategic audit provides a checklist of questions, by area or issue, that enables a systematic analysis of various corporate functions and activities to be made. It is a type of management audit and is extremely useful as a diagnostic tool to pinpoint corporatewide problem areas and to highlight organizational strengths and weaknesses.[48] A strategic audit can help determine why a certain area is creating problems for a corporation and help generate solutions to the problem. As such, it can be very useful in evaluating the performance of top management.

PRIMARY MEASURES OF DIVISIONAL AND FUNCTIONAL PERFORMANCE

Companies use a variety of techniques to evaluate and control performance in divisions, strategic business units (SBUs), and functional areas. If a corporation is composed of SBUs or divisions, it will use many of the same performance measures (ROI or EVA, for instance) that it uses to assess overall corporate performance. To the extent that it can isolate specific functional units such as R&D, the corporation may develop responsibility centers. It will also use typical functional measures, such as market share and sales per employee (marketing), unit costs and percentage of defects (operations), percentage of sales from new products and number of patents (R&D), and turnover and job satisfaction (HRM). FedEx used Enhanced Tracker software with its COSMOS database to track the progress of its 2.5 to 3.5 million shipments daily. As a courier was completing her or his day's activities, the Enhanced Tracker asked whether the person's package count equals the Enhanced Tracker's count. If the count was off, the software helped reconcile the differences.[49]

During strategy formulation and implementation, top management approves a series of programs and supporting *operating budgets* from its business units. During evaluation and control, actual expenses are contrasted with planned expenditures, and the degree of variance is assessed. This is typically done on a monthly basis. In addition, top management will probably require *periodic statistical reports* summarizing data on such key factors as the number of new customer contracts, the volume of received orders, and productivity figures.

RESPONSIBILITY CENTERS

Control systems can be established to monitor specific functions, projects, or divisions. Budgets are one type of control system that is typically used to control the financial indicators of performance. **Responsibility centers** are used to isolate a unit so it can be evaluated separately from the rest of the corporation. Each responsibility center, therefore, has its own budget and is evaluated on its use of budgeted resources. It is headed by the manager responsible for the center's performance. The center uses resources (measured in terms of costs or expenses) to produce a service or a product (measured in terms of volume or revenues). There are five major types of responsibility centers. The type is determined by the way the corporation's control system measures these resources and services or products.

- **Standard cost centers: Standard cost centers** are primarily used in manufacturing facilities. Standard (or expected) costs are computed for each operation on the basis of historical data. In evaluating the center's performance, its total standard costs are multiplied by the units produced. The result is the *expected* cost of production, which is then compared to the *actual* cost of production.

- **Revenue centers:** With **revenue centers**, production, usually in terms of unit or dollar sales, is measured without consideration of resource costs (for example, salaries). The center is thus judged in terms of effectiveness rather than efficiency. The effectiveness of a sales region, for example, is determined by comparing its actual sales to its projected or previous year's sales. Profits are not considered because sales departments have very limited influence over the cost of the products they sell.

- **Expense centers:** Resources are measured in dollars, without consideration for service or product costs. Thus, budgets will have been prepared for engineered expenses (costs that can be calculated) and for discretionary expenses (costs that can be only estimated). Typical **expense centers** are administrative, service, and research departments. They cost a company money, but they only indirectly contribute to revenues.

■ **Profit centers:** Performance is measured in terms of the difference between revenues (which measure production) and expenditures (which measure resources). A **profit center** is typically established whenever an organizational unit has control over both its resources and its products or services. By having such centers, a company can be organized into divisions of separate product lines. The manager of each division is given autonomy to the extent that he or she is able to keep profits at a satisfactory (or better) level.

Some organizational units that are not usually considered potentially autonomous can, for the purpose of profit center evaluations, be made so. A manufacturing department, for example, can be converted from a standard cost center (or expense center) into a profit center; it is allowed to charge a transfer price for each product it "sells" to the sales department. The difference between the manufacturing cost per unit and the agreed-upon transfer price is the unit's "profit."

Transfer pricing is commonly used in vertically integrated corporations and can work well when a price can be easily determined for a designated amount of product. Transfer pricing is being increasingly scrutinized by tax authorities around the world. The latest survey suggests that companies are utilizing either a Mutual Agreement Procedure (28%) or the Advance Pricing Agreement Process (26%). At the same time 28% of companies reported having unresolved transfer pricing examinations.[50] When a price cannot be set easily, however, the relative bargaining power of the centers, rather than strategic considerations, tends to influence the agreed-upon price. Top management has an obligation to make sure that these political considerations do not overwhelm the strategic ones. Otherwise, profit figures for each center will be biased and provide poor information for strategic decisions at both the corporate and divisional levels.

■ **Investment centers:** Because many divisions in large manufacturing corporations use significant assets to make their products, their asset base should be factored into their performance evaluation. Thus, it is insufficient to focus only on profits, as in the case of profit centers. An **investment center's** performance is measured in terms of the difference between its resources and its services or products. For example, two divisions in a corporation make identical profits, but one division owns a $3 million plant, whereas the other owns a $1 million plant. Both make the same profits, but one is obviously more efficient; the smaller plant provides the shareholders with a better return on their investment. The most widely used measure of investment center performance is ROI.

Most single-business corporations, such as Buffalo Wild Wings, tend to use a combination of cost, expense, and revenue centers. In these corporations, most managers are functional specialists and manage against a budget. Total profitability is integrated at the corporate level. Multidivisional corporations with one dominating product line (such as ABInBev) that have diversified into a few businesses but that still depend on a single product line (such as beer) for most of their revenue and income, generally use a combination of cost, expense, revenue, and profit centers. Multidivisional corporations, such as General Electric, tend to emphasize investment centers—although in various units throughout the corporation other types of responsibility centers are also used. One problem with using responsibility centers, however, is that the separation needed to measure and evaluate a division's performance can diminish the level of cooperation among divisions that is needed to attain synergy for the corporation as a whole. (This problem is discussed later in this chapter, under "Suboptimization.")

Using Benchmarking To Evaluate Performance

12-3. Apply the benchmarking process to a function or an activity

According to Xerox Corporation, the company that pioneered this concept in the United States, **benchmarking** is "the continual process of measuring products, services, and practices against the toughest competitors or those companies recognized as industry leaders."[51] Benchmarking, an increasingly popular program, is based on the concept that it makes no sense to reinvent something that someone else is already using. It involves openly learning how others do something better than one's own company so that the company not only can imitate, but perhaps even improve upon its techniques. The benchmarking process usually involves the following steps:

1. Identify the area or process to be examined. It should be an activity that has the potential to determine a business unit's competitive advantage.

2. Find behavioral and output measures of the area or process and obtain measurements.

3. Select an accessible set of competitors and best-in-class companies against which to benchmark. These may very often be companies that are in completely different industries, but perform similar activities. For example, when Xerox wanted to improve its order fulfillment, it went to L.L.Bean, the successful mail order firm, to learn how it achieved excellence in this area.

4. Calculate the differences among the company's performance measurements and those of the best-in-class and determine why the differences exist.

5. Develop tactical programs for closing performance gaps.

6. Implement the programs and then compare the resulting new measurements with those of the best-in-class companies.

Benchmarking has been found to produce best results in companies that are already well managed. Apparently poorer performing firms tend to be overwhelmed by the discrepancy between their performance and the benchmark—and tend to view the benchmark as too difficult to reach.[52] Nevertheless, a 2015 survey by Bain & Company of companies of various sizes across the globe found that benchmarking was the second most used tool (tied with strategic planning).[53] Benchmarking can also increase sales, improve goal setting, and boost employee motivation.[54] Manco Inc., a small Cleveland-area producer of duct tape, regularly benchmarks itself against Wal-Mart, Rubbermaid, and PepsiCo to enable it to better compete with giant 3M. APQC (American Productivity & Quality Center), a Houston research group, established the Open Standards Benchmarking Collaborative database, composed of more than 1,200 commonly used measures and individual benchmarks, to track the performance of core operational functions. Firms can submit their performance data to this online database to learn how they compare to top performers and industry peers (see www .apqc.org).

In an odd twist to benchmarking, an issue in international trade is counterfeiting/piracy. Firms in developing nations around the world make money by making counterfeit/pirated copies of well-known name-brand products and selling them globally as well as locally. See the **Global Issue** feature to learn about this important problem.

GLOBAL issue

COUNTERFEIT GOODS AND PIRATED SOFTWARE: A GLOBAL PROBLEM

"We know that 15% to 20% of all goods in China are counterfeit," states Dan Chow, a law professor at Ohio State University. This includes products from Tide detergent and Budweiser beer to Marlboro cigarettes. There is a saying in Shanghai, China: "We can copy everything except your mother." Yamaha estimates that five out of every six bikes bearing its brand name are fake. Fake Cisco network routers (known as "Chiscos") and counterfeit Nokia mobile phones can be easily found throughout China. Procter & Gamble estimates that 15% of the soaps and detergents under its Head & Shoulders, Vidal Sassoon, Safeguard, and Tide brands in China are counterfeit, costing the company $150 million in lost sales.

In Yiwu, a few hours from Shanghai, one person admitted to a *60 Minutes* reporter that she could make 1,000 pairs of counterfeit Nike shoes in 10 days for $4.00 a pair. According to the market research firm Automotive Resources, the profit margins on counterfeit shock absorbers can reach 80% versus only 15% for the real ones. The World Custom Organization estimates that 7% of the world's merchandise is bogus.

Tens of thousands of counterfeiters are active in China. They range from factories mixing shampoo and soap in back rooms to large state-owned enterprises making copies of soft drinks and beer. Other factories make everything from car batteries to automobiles. Mobile CD factories with optical disc-mastering machines counterfeit music and software. *60 Minutes* found a small factory in Donguan making fake Callaway golf clubs and bags at a rate of 500 bags per week. Factories in the southern Guangdong and Fujian provinces truck their products to a central distribution center, such as the one in Yiwu. They may also be shipped across the border into Russia, Pakistan, Vietnam, or Burma. Chinese counterfeiters have developed a global reach through their connections with organized crime.

As much as 35% of software on personal computers worldwide is pirated, according to the Business Software Alliance and ISDC, a market research firm. The worldwide cost of software piracy was estimated to be around $63 billion in 2016. For example, 21% of the software sold in the United States is pirated. That figure increases to 26%–30% in the European Union, 83% in Russia, Algeria, and Bolivia, to 86% in China, 87% in Indonesia, and 90% in Vietnam.

....

SOURCES: T. Miracco, "The Hidden Cost Of Software Piracy In The Manufacturing Industry," *MBT Magazine*, Februrary 2016 (http://www.mbtmag.com/article/2016/02/hidden-cost-software-piracy-manufacturing-industry); "The Sincerest Form of Flattery," *The Economist* (April 7, 2007), pp. 64–65; F. Balfour, "Fakes!" *BusinessWeek* (February 7, 2005), pp. 54–64; "PC Software Piracy," *The Economist* (June 10, 2006), p. 102 "The World's Greatest Fakes," *60 Minutes*, CBS News (August 8, 2004); "Business Software Piracy," *Pocket World in Figures 2004* (London: Economist & Profile Book, 2003), p. 60 D. Roberts, F. Balfour, P. Magnusson, P. Engardio, and J. Lee, "China's Piracy Plague," *BusinessWeek* (June 5, 2000), pp. 44–48.

Strategic Information Systems

12-4. Explain how strategic information systems are being utilized to support specific strategies

Before performance measures can have any impact on strategic management, they must first be communicated to the people responsible for formulating and implementing strategic plans. Strategic information systems can perform this function. They can be computer-based or manual, formal or informal. One of the key reasons given for the bankruptcy of International Harvester was the inability of the corporation's top management to precisely determine income by major class of similar products. Because of this inability, management kept trying to fix ailing businesses and was unable to respond flexibly to major changes and unexpected events. In contrast, one of the key reasons for the success of Wal-Mart has been management's use of the company's sophisticated information system to control purchasing decisions. Checkout registers in Wal-Mart retail stores transmit information hourly to computers at the company headquarters.

Consequently, managers know every morning exactly how many of each item were sold the day before, how many have been sold so far in the year, and how this year's sales compare to last year's. The information system allows all reordering to be done automatically by computers, without any managerial input. It also allows the company to experiment with new products without committing to big orders in advance. In effect, the system allows the customers to decide through their purchases what gets reordered.

ENTERPRISE RESOURCE PLANNING

Many corporations around the world have adopted **enterprise resource planning (ERP)** software. ERP unites all of a company's major business activities, from order processing to production, within a single family of software modules. The system provides instant access to critical information to everyone in the organization, from the CEO to the factory floor worker. Because of the ability of ERP software to use a common information system throughout a company's many operations around the world, it is becoming the business information systems' global standard. The major providers of this software are SAP, Oracle, and Infor.

The German company SAP AG originated the concept with its R/3 software system. Microsoft, for example, used R/3 to replace a tangle of 33 financial tracking systems in 26 subsidiaries. Even though it cost the company $25 million and took 10 months to install, R/3 annually saves Microsoft $18 million. Coca-Cola uses the R/3 system to enable a manager in Atlanta to use her personal computer to check the latest sales of 20-ounce bottles of Coke Classic in India. Owens-Corning envisioned that its R/3 system allowed salespeople to learn what was available at any plant or warehouse and to quickly assemble orders for customers.

ERP may not fit every company, however. The system is extremely complicated and demands a high level of standardization throughout a corporation. Its demanding nature often forces companies to change the way they do business. There are three reasons ERP could fail: (1) insufficient tailoring of the software to fit the company, (2) inadequate training, and (3) insufficient implementation support.[55] Over the two-year period of installing R/3, Owens-Corning had to completely overhaul its operations. Because R/3 was incompatible with Apple's very organic corporate culture, the company was able to apply it only to its order management and financial operations, but not to manufacturing. Other companies that had difficulty installing and using ERP are Whirlpool, Hershey Foods, Volkswagen, and Stanley Works. At Whirlpool, SAP's software led to missed and delayed shipments, causing The Home Depot to cancel its agreement for selling Whirlpool products.[56] One survey found that 65% of executives believed that ERP had a moderate chance of hurting their business because of implementation problems. Nevertheless, the payoff from ERP software can be worth the effort. In an industry where one company implements ERP ahead of its competitors, it can be used to gain some competitive advantage, streamline operations, and help manage a lean manufacturing system.[57]

RADIO FREQUENCY IDENTIFICATION AND NEAR FIELD COMMUNICATION

Radio frequency identification (RFID) is an electronic tagging technology used in a number of companies to improve supply-chain efficiency while near field communication (NFC) stands for contactless communication between devices like smartphones or tablets. By tagging containers and items with tiny chips, companies use the tags as wireless barcodes to track inventory more efficiently. Both Wal-Mart and the U.S. Department of Defense began requiring their largest suppliers to incorporate RFID tags in their goods in 2003. After trying to implement RFID for the past decade, the UK-based supermarket chain Tesco postponed their full implementation of RFID technology in late 2012. Tesco had planned to deploy RFID tags and readers in 1,400 stores and in its distribution centers by the middle of 2012. However, it had installed RFID tags in only 40 stores and one depot before it brought the program to a halt.[58]

Nevertheless, some suppliers and retailers of expensive consumer products view the cost of the tag as worthwhile because it reduces losses from counterfeiting and theft. Decathlon uses RFID technology at its 43 distribution centers and 1,030 stores to improve on-shelf availability and reduce shrinkage while Qinshan Nuclear Power Plant (Zhejiang, the People's Republic of China) uses RFID to track its 7,000 workers. RFID technology is currently in wide use as wireless commuter passes for toll roads, tunnels, and bridges. A take on this type of communication is NFC which has been used by Targetto transform the in-store shopping experience and is the means being used by Apple and Samsung to take over how mobile payments are transacted.[59]

DIVISIONAL AND FUNCTIONAL IS SUPPORT

At the divisional or SBU level of a corporation, the information system should be used to support, reinforce, or enlarge the business-level strategy through its decision support system. An SBU pursuing a strategy of overall cost leadership could use its information system to reduce costs either by improving labor productivity or improving the use of other resources such as inventory or machinery. Kaiser Health had 37 hospitals, 15,857 physicians, and 9 million plus members all tied together in a single system that allowed the organization to improve health services and increase its ability to reduce problems in the system. An internal study of heart attacks among 46,000 patients in Northern California who were 30 years and older showed a decline of 24%. Kaiser has also reduced mortality rates by 40% since 2008 for its hospital patients who contract sepsis, a dangerous infectious disease.[60] Another SBU, in contrast, might want to pursue a differentiation strategy. It could use its information system to add uniqueness to the product or service and contribute to quality, service, or image through the functional areas. FedEx wanted to use superior service to gain a competitive advantage. It invested significantly in several types of information systems to measure and track the performance of its delivery service. Together, these information systems gave FedEx the fastest error-response time in the overnight delivery business.

Problems in Measuring Performance

12-5. Discuss the issues with measuring organizational performance and how organizations can establish proper controls to achieve objectives

The measurement of performance is a crucial part of evaluation and control. The lack of quantifiable objectives or performance standards and the inability of the information system to provide timely and valid information are two obvious control problems. Without objective and timely measurements, it would be extremely difficult to make operational, let alone strategic, decisions. Nevertheless, the use of timely, quantifiable standards does not guarantee good performance. The very act of monitoring and measuring performance can cause side effects that interfere with overall corporate performance. Among the most frequent negative side effects are a short-term orientation and goal displacement.

SHORT-TERM ORIENTATION

Top executives report that in many situations, they analyze neither the long-term impli-cations of present operations on the strategy they have adopted nor the operational impact of a strategy on the corporate mission. Long-term evaluations may not be con-ducted because executives (1) don't realize their importance, (2) believe that short-term considerations are more important than long-term considerations, (3) aren't personally evaluated on a long-term basis, or (4) don't have the time to make a long-term analy-sis.[61] There is no real justification for the first and last reasons. If executives realize the importance of long-term evaluations, they make the time needed to conduct them. Even though many chief executives point to immediate pressures from the investment community and to short-term incentive and promotion plans to support the second and third reasons, evidence does not always support their claims.[62]

At one international heavy-equipment manufacturer, managers were so strongly motivated to achieve their quarterly revenue target that they shipped unfinished prod-ucts from their plant in England to a warehouse in the Netherlands for final assembly. By shipping the incomplete products, they were able to realize the sales before the end of the quarter—thus fulfilling their budgeted objective and making their bonuses. Unfortunately, the high cost of assembling the goods at a distant location (requiring not only renting the warehouse but also paying additional labor) ended up reducing the company's overall profit.[63]

Many accounting-based measures, such as EPS and ROI, encourage a **short-term orientation** in which managers consider only current tactical or operational issues and ignore long-term strategic ones. Because growth in EPS (earnings per share) is an important driver of near-term stock price, top managers are biased against investments that might reduce short-term EPS.[64] This is compounded by pressure from financial analysts and investors for quarterly *earnings guidance*—that is, esti-mates of future corporate earnings.[65] Hewlett-Packard (HP) acquired British firm Autonomy for $11.1 billion in 2011 and had to write down (eliminate from the finan-cial reports) $8.8 billion of that amount in 2012 as the company found significant accounting errors. Multiple lawsuits were filed against HP, its officers, directors, and the accounting firms involved with Autonomy before the acquisition.[66] HP later broke up into two companies and HP Enterprise was able to use some unique capa-bilities that Autonomy owned in order to dramatically push into cloud computing with developers.[67]

One of the limitations of ROI as a performance measure is its short-term nature. In theory, ROI is not limited to the short run, but in practice it is often difficult to use this measure to realize long-term benefits for a company. Because managers can often manipulate both the numerator (earnings) and the denominator (investment), the resulting ROI figure can be meaningless. Advertising, maintenance, and research efforts can be reduced. Estimates of pension-fund profits, unpaid receivables, and old inventory, are easy to adjust. Optimistic estimates of returned products, bad debts, and obsolete inventory inflate the present year's sales and earnings.[68]

Expensive retooling and plant modernization can be delayed as long as a man-ager can manipulate figures on production defects and absenteeism. In one survey of financial executives, 80% of the managers stated that they would decrease spending on research and development, advertising, maintenance, and hiring in order to meet earnings targets. More than half said they would delay a new project even if it meant sacrificing value.[69]

Mergers can be undertaken that will do more for the present year's earnings (and the next year's paycheck) than for the division's or corporation's future profits. For example, research on 55 firms that engaged in major acquisitions revealed that even though the firms performed poorly after the acquisition, the acquiring firms' top management still received significant increases in compensation.[70] Determining CEO compensation on the basis of firm size rather than performance is typical and is particularly likely for firms that are not monitored closely by independent analysts.[71]

Research supports the conclusion that many CEOs and their friends on the board of directors' compensation committee manipulate information to provide themselves a pay raise.[72] For example, CEOs tend to announce bad news—thus reducing the company's stock price—just before the issuance of stock options. Once the options are issued, the CEOs tend to announce good news—thus raising the stock price and making their options more valuable.[73] Board compensation committees tend to expand the peer group comparison outside their industry to include lower-performing firms to justify a high raise to the CEO. They tend to do this when the company performs poorly, the industry performs well, the CEO is already highly paid, and shareholders are powerful and active.[74]

GOAL DISPLACEMENT

If not carefully done, monitoring and measuring of performance can actually result in a decline in overall corporate performance. **Goal displacement** is the confusion of means with ends and occurs when activities originally intended to help managers attain corporate objectives become ends in themselves—or are adapted to meet ends other than those for which they were intended. Two types of goal displacement are behavior substitution and suboptimization.

Behavior Substitution

Behavior substitution refers to the phenomenon of pursuing substitute activities that do not lead to goal accomplishment instead of activities that do lead to goal accomplishment because the wrong activities are being rewarded. Managers, like most other people, tend to focus more of their attention on behaviors that are clearly measurable than on those that are not. Employees often receive little or no reward for engaging in hard-to-measure activities such as cooperation and initiative. However, easy-to-measure activities might have little or no relationship to the desired good performance. Rational people, nevertheless, tend to work for the rewards that the system has to offer. Therefore, people tend to substitute behaviors that are recognized and rewarded for behaviors that are ignored, without regard to their contribution to goal accomplishment. A research study of 157 corporations revealed that most of the companies made little attempt to identify areas of non-financial performance that might advance their chosen strategy. Only 23% consistently built and verified cause-and-effect relationships between intermediate controls (such as number of patents filed or product flaws) and company performance.[75]

A U.S. Navy quip sums up this situation: "What you inspect (or reward) is what you get." If the reward system emphasizes quantity while merely asking for quality and cooperation, the system is likely to produce a large number of low-quality products and unsatisfied customers.[76] A proposed law governing the effect of measurement on behavior is that *quantifiable measures drive out non-quantifiable measures*.

A classic example of behavior substitution happened at Sears. Sears' management thought it could improve employee productivity by tying performance to rewards. It, therefore, paid commissions to its auto shop employees as a percentage of each repair bill. Behavior substitution resulted as employees altered their behavior to fit the reward system. The results were over-billed customers, charges for work never done, and a scandal that tarnished Sears' reputation for many years.[77]

Suboptimization

Suboptimization refers to the phenomenon of a unit optimizing its goal accomplishment to the detriment of the organization as a whole. The emphasis in large corporations on developing separate responsibility centers can create some problems for the corporation as a whole. To the extent that a division or functional unit views itself as a separate entity, it might refuse to cooperate with other units or divisions in the same corporation if cooperation could in some way negatively affect its performance evaluation. The competition between divisions to achieve a high ROI can result in one division's refusal to share its new technology or work process improvements. One division's attempt to optimize the accomplishment of its goals can cause other divisions to fall behind and, thus, negatively affect overall corporate performance. Interestingly, Sears in 2016 is a classic example of this type of dysfunction. For over a decade, the company has spiraled downward at the hand of investor and CEO Eddie Lampert. An Ayn Rand fan, he split the company into more than 30 autonomous units, each with its own executives and board of directors, to boost "visibility and accountability." Instead, the divisions engaged in cutthroat competition and sabotage. Incentives were tied to the success of the individual divisions, which often came at the expense of other parts of the company.[78]

GUIDELINES FOR PROPER CONTROL

In designing a control system, top management should remember that controls should follow strategy. Unless controls ensure the use of the proper strategy to achieve objectives, there is a strong likelihood that dysfunctional side effects will completely undermine the implementation of the objectives. The following guidelines are recommended:

1. **Control should involve only the minimum amount of information needed to give a reliable picture of events:** Too many controls create confusion. Focus on the strategic factors by following the **80/20 rule**: *Monitor those 20% of the factors that determine 80% of the results.*

2. **Controls should monitor only meaningful activities and results, regardless of measurement difficulty:** If cooperation between divisions is important to corporate performance, some form of qualitative or quantitative measure should be established to monitor cooperation.

3. **Controls should be timely so that corrective action can be taken before it is too late:** Steering controls, controls that monitor or measure the factors influencing performance, should be stressed so that advance notice of problems is given.

4. **Long-term *and* short-term controls should be used:** If only short-term measures are emphasized, a short-term managerial orientation is likely.

5. **Controls should aim at pinpointing exceptions:** Only activities or results that fall outside a predetermined tolerance range should call for action.

6. **Emphasize the reward of meeting or exceeding standards rather than punishment for failing to meet standards:** Heavy punishment of failure typically results in goal displacement. Managers will "fudge" reports and lobby for lower standards.

If corporate culture complements and reinforces the strategic orientation of a firm, there is less need for an extensive formal control system. In their book *In Search of Excellence,* Peters and Waterman state that "the stronger the culture and the more it was directed toward the marketplace, the less need was there for policy manuals, organization charts, or detailed procedures and rules. In these companies, people way down the line know what they are supposed to do in most situations because the handful of guiding values is crystal clear."[79] For example, at Eaton Corporation, the employees are expected to enforce the rules themselves. If someone misses too much work or picks fights with co-workers, other members of the production team point out the problem. According to Randy Savage, a long-time Eaton employee, "They say there are no bosses here, but if you screw up, you find one pretty fast."[80]

ALIGNING INCENTIVES

To ensure congruence between the needs of a corporation as a whole and the needs of the employees as individuals, management and the board of directors should develop an incentive program that rewards desired performance. This reduces the likelihood of the agency problems (when employees act to feather their own nests instead of building shareholder value) mentioned earlier in **Chapter 2**. Incentive plans should be linked in some way to corporate and divisional strategy. Research reveals that firm performance is affected by its compensation policies.[81] Companies using different strategies tend to adopt different pay policies. For example, a survey of 600 business units indicated that the pay mix associated with a growth strategy emphasizes bonuses and other incentives over salary and benefits, whereas the pay mix associated with a stability strategy has the reverse emphasis.[82] Research indicates that SBU managers having long-term performance elements in their compensation program favor a long-term perspective and thus greater investments in R&D, capital equipment, and employee training.[83] The average CEO pay package in 2015 was US$22.6 million about a third of which was in cash.[84] There is some evidence that stock options are being replaced by greater emphasis on performance-related pay.[85]

The following three approaches are tailored to help match measurements and rewards with explicit strategic objectives and time frames:[86]

- **Weighted-factor method:** The **weighted-factor method** is particularly appropriate for measuring and rewarding the performance of top SBU managers and group-level executives when performance factors and their importance vary from one SBU to another. Using portfolio analysis, one corporation's measurements might contain the following variations: the performance of high-performing (star) SBUs is measured equally in terms of ROI, cash flow, market share, and progress on several future-oriented strategic projects; the performance of low-growth, but strong (cash cow) SBUs, in contrast, is measured in terms of ROI, market share, and cash generation; and the performance of developing question mark SBUs is measured in terms of development and market share growth with no weight on ROI or cash flow. (Refer to **Figure 12–2**.)

- **Long-term evaluation method:** The **long-term evaluation method** compensates managers for achieving objectives set over a multiyear period. An executive is promised some compensation based on long-term performance. A board of directors, for example, might set a particular objective in terms of growth in earnings per share during a five-year period. The giving of awards would be contingent on the corporation's meeting that objective within the designated time. Any executive who leaves the corporation before the objective is met receives nothing. The typical emphasis on stock prices makes this approach more applicable to top management than to business unit managers.

FIGURE 12–2
Business Strength/ Competitive Position

Business Strength/Competitive Position

Industry Attractiveness	High	Low
High	**Star** ROI (25%) Cash Flow (25%) Strategic Funds (25%) Market Share (25%)	**Question Mark** ROI (0%) Cash Flow (0%) Strategic Funds (50%) Market Share Growth (50%)
Low	**Cash Cow** ROI (20%) Cash Flow (60%) Strategic Funds (0%) Market Share (20%)	**DOG** ROI (50%) Cash Flow (50%) Strategic Funds (0%) Market Share (0%)

SOURCE: Suggested by Paul J. Stomach in "The Performance Measurement and Reward System: Critical to Strategic Management," *Organizational Dynamics,* (Winter 1984), pp. 45–57.

- **Strategic-funds method:** The **strategic-funds method** encourages executives to look at developmental expenses as being different from expenses required for current operations. The accounting statement for a corporate unit enters strategic funds as a separate entry below the current ROI. It is, therefore, possible to distinguish between expense dollars consumed in the generation of current revenues and those invested in the future of a business. Therefore, a manager can be evaluated on both a short- and a long-term basis and has an incentive to invest strategic funds in the future. For example, begin with the total sales of a unit ($12,300,000). Subtract cost of goods sold ($6,900,000) leaving a gross margin of $5,400,000. Subtract general and administrative expenses ($3,700,000) leaving an operating profit/ROI of $1,700,000. So far, this is standard accounting procedure. The strategic-funds approach goes one step further by subtracting an additional $1,000,000 for "strategic funds/development expenses." This results in a pretax profit of $700,000. This strategic-funds approach is a good way to ensure that the manager of a high-performing unit (e.g., star) not only generates $700,000 in ROI, but also invests $1 million in the unit for its continued growth. It also ensures that a manager of a developing unit is appropriately evaluated on the basis of market share growth and product development and not on ROI or cash flow.

An effective way to achieve the desired strategic results through a reward system is to combine the three approaches:

1. Segregate strategic funds from short-term funds, as is done in the strategic-funds method.
2. Develop a weighted-factor chart for each SBU.
3. Measure performance on three bases: The pretax profit indicated by the strategic-funds approach, the weighted factors, and the long-term evaluation of the SBUs' and the corporation's performance.

Walt Disney Company, Dow Chemical, IBM, and General Motors are just some firms in which top management compensation is contingent upon the company's achieving strategic objectives.

The board of directors and top management must be careful to develop a compensation plan that achieves the appropriate objectives. One reason why top executives are often criticized for being overpaid (the ratio of CEO to average worker pay is currently 373to 1)[87] is that in a large number of corporations the incentives for sales growth exceed those for shareholder wealth, resulting in too many executives pursuing growth to the detriment of shareholder value.[88]

End of Chapter SUMMARY

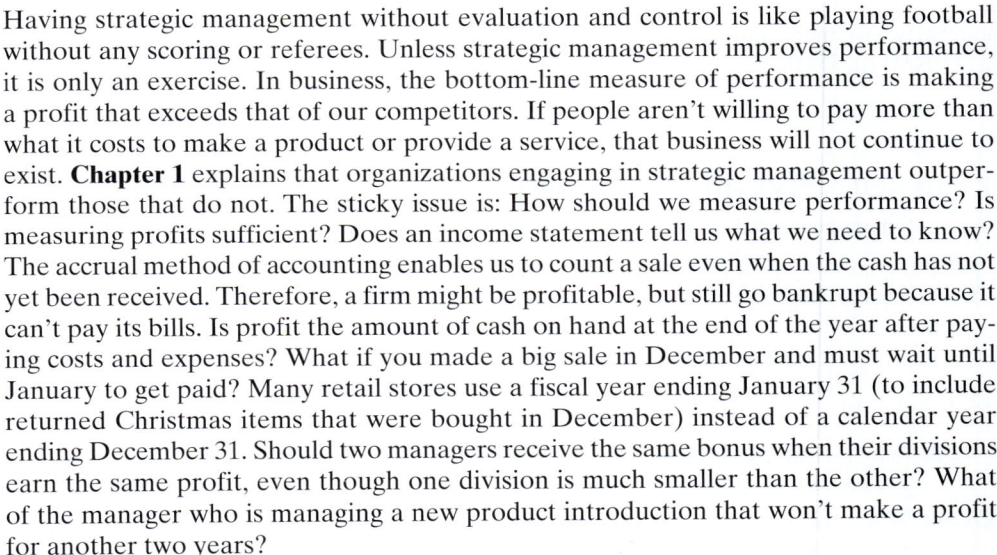

Having strategic management without evaluation and control is like playing football without any scoring or referees. Unless strategic management improves performance, it is only an exercise. In business, the bottom-line measure of performance is making a profit that exceeds that of our competitors. If people aren't willing to pay more than what it costs to make a product or provide a service, that business will not continue to exist. **Chapter 1** explains that organizations engaging in strategic management outperform those that do not. The sticky issue is: How should we measure performance? Is measuring profits sufficient? Does an income statement tell us what we need to know? The accrual method of accounting enables us to count a sale even when the cash has not yet been received. Therefore, a firm might be profitable, but still go bankrupt because it can't pay its bills. Is profit the amount of cash on hand at the end of the year after paying costs and expenses? What if you made a big sale in December and must wait until January to get paid? Many retail stores use a fiscal year ending January 31 (to include returned Christmas items that were bought in December) instead of a calendar year ending December 31. Should two managers receive the same bonus when their divisions earn the same profit, even though one division is much smaller than the other? What of the manager who is managing a new product introduction that won't make a profit for another two years?

Evaluation and control is one of the most difficult parts of strategic management. No one measure can tell us what we need to know. That's why we need to use not only the traditional measures of financial performance, such as net earnings, ROI, and EPS, but we need to consider using EVA or MVA and a balanced scorecard, among other possibilities. On top of that, science informs us that just attempting to measure something changes what is being measured. The measurement of performance can and does result in short-term–oriented actions and goal displacement. That's why experts suggest we use multiple measures of only those things that provide a meaningful and reliable picture of events: Measure those 20% of the factors that determine 80% of the results. Once the appropriate performance measurements are taken, it is possible to get closer to determining whether the strategy was successful. As shown in the model of strategic management depicted at the beginning this chapter, the measured results of corporate performance allow us to decide whether we need to reformulate the strategy, improve its implementation, or gather more information about our competition.

Pearson MyLab Management®

Go to **mymanagementlab.com** to complete the problems marked with this icon .

KEY TERMS

80/20 rule (p. 368)

activity-based costing (ABC) (p. 353)

balanced scorecard (p. 358)

behavior controls (p. 351)

behavior substitution (p. 367)

benchmarking (p. 362)

earnings per share (EPS) (p. 355)

economic value added (EVA) (p. 356)

enterprise resource planning (ERP) (p. 364)

enterprise risk management (ERM) (p. 354)

expense centers (p. 361)

free cash flow (p. 355)

goal displacement (p. 367)

input controls (p. 351)

investment center (p. 361)

ISO 9000 Standards Series (p. 352)

ISO 14000 Standards Series (p. 352)

key performance measures (p. 358)

long-term evaluation method (p. 369)

management audits (p. 359)

market value added (p. 356)

operating cash flow (p. 355)

output controls (p. 351)

performance (p. 350)

profit center (p. 361)

responsibility centers (p. 360)

return on equity (ROE) (p. 355)

return on investment (ROI) (p. 355)

revenue centers (p. 360)

shareholder value (p. 355)

short-term orientation (p. 366)

standard cost centers (p. 360)

steering controls (p. 350)

strategic-funds method (p. 370)

suboptimization (p. 368)

transfer pricing (p. 361)

weighted-factor method (p. 369)

Pearson MyLab Management®

Go to **mymanagementlab.com** for the following assisted-graded writing questions:

12-1. Explain why ROI might not be the best measure of firm performance.

12-2. What are the best methods for evaluating the performance of the top management team?

DISCUSSION QUESTIONS

12-3. Why is strategic control important in monitoring the process of strategy implementation?

12-4. What are some examples of behavior controls? Output controls? Input controls?

12-5. Why is EVA an important component of the strategic management process?

12-6. Is the balanced scorecard a useful tool for developing, controlling and enhancing the strategy implementation process of an organisation? Why or why not?

12-7. Is the evaluation and control process appropriate for a corporation that emphasizes creativity? Are control and creativity compatible?

STRATEGIC PRACTICE EXERCISE

A noteworthy investment company, Dubai Group, based in the United Arab Emirates, is the subsidiary of Dubai Holdings. Founded in 2000 as The Investment Office, the company was renamed Dubai Group in 2005. Through its companies, the group focuses on banking, investments, and insurance both in the United Arab Emirates and globally. Dubai Group has been able to maintain its success through appropriate control despite difficult times. Based on a clear objective, Dubai Group restructured its debt of U.S. $10 billion. Borrowing from banks between 2006 and 2008 to fund its acquisitions across the boom years led to a credit-market that was dried-up to its core. As a result of the global financial and the real-estate crises, local government was forced to reassess itself. It found itself unable to manage its obligations, and was forced to renegotiate tens of billions of dollars of debt. Consequently, Dubai Holdings, that includes France's Natixis and Dubai's Emirates NBD, agreed to loan the money. "It's not perfect, but it's a major milestone for both the Emirate and the banks that were exposed to the Dubai government-related entities," noted a creditor bank. The final deal involves creditors extending maturities up to 12 years, with the length of time dependent on the level of security against specific debts. This means that Dubai Group's assets can recover in value before being sold to meet obligations. While the company has signed the document, formal completion means that lenders have to sign an amended inter-creditor agreement that removes references to the loan secured against Dubai Group's holding in Malaysia's Bank Islam. The stake was sold at the end of last year to BIMB Holdings, when the money from the divestment had been delivered to those banks that held security against the asset. Some of these lenders had held off signing the restructuring deal until the cash was placed with them. This, in effect, meant that the formal deal closing time was missed—the end of 2013. Creditors have two parts to the restructuring document: Part One—specific claim against the company, which has been formally completed, and Part Two—inter-creditor agreement that manages the overall restructuring. Out of its $10 billion total debt, $6 billion is owed to banks, and the remaining $4 billion is classed as intercompany loans.

Try One of These Exercises

12-8. How well has Dubai Group monitored its performance?

12-9. Which steps should be taken to properly monitor its ongoing performance as a leading investment bank?

SOURCE: D. French, "Dubai Signs $10 B Debt Restructuring," *The Daily Star (January 17, 2014)*, p. 6.

NOTES

1. http://ir.spirit.com/releasedetail.cfm?ReleaseID=878527; http://web.mit.edu/airlinedata/www/2014%2012%20Month%20Documents/Expense%20Related/Total/System%20Total%20Expense%20per%20Available%20Seat%20Mile%20(CASM%20ex%20Transport%20Related).htm

2. R. Barker, "A Surprise in Office Depot's In-Box," *BusinessWeek* (October 25, 2004), p. 122.

3. C. W. Hart, "Customer Service: Beating the Market with Customer Satisfaction," *Harvard Business Review* (March 2007), pp. 30–32.

4. S. E. Ante, "Giving the Boss the Big Picture," *BusinessWeek* (February 13, 2006), pp. 48–51.

5. R. Muralidharan and R. D. Hamilton III, "Aligning Multinational Control Systems," *Long Range Planning* (June 1999), pp. 352–361. These types are based on W. G. Ouchi, "The Relationship Between Organizational Structure and Organizational Control," *Administrative Science Quarterly* (Vol. 20, 1977), pp. 95–113 and W. G. Ouchi, "A Conceptual Framework for the Design of Organizational Control Mechanisms," *Management Science* (Vol. 25, 1979), pp. 833–848. Muralidharan and Hamilton refer to Ouchi's clan control as input control.

6. W. G. Rowe and P. M. Wright, "Related and Unrelated Diversification and Their Effect on Human Resource Management Controls," *Strategic Management Journal* (April 1997), pp. 329–338.

7. R. Muralidharan and R. D. Hamilton III, "Aligning Multinational Control Systems," *Long Range Planning* (June 1999) pp. 356–359.

8. B. Manders and H. de Vries, "Does ISO 9001 Pay? Analysis of 42 Studies," *ISO* (October 2012), http://www.iso.org/iso/home/news_index/news_archive/news.htm?refid=Ref1665

9. http://www.iso.org/iso/home/about/iso_members.htm

10. P. Rains, Improper employee monitoring could result in lawsuits," *The Tennessean*, September 30, 2015 (http://www.tennessean.com/story/money/2015/09/30/improper-employee-monitoring-could-result-lawsuits/73108864/); S. Heathfield, "What Are an Employer's Alternatives to Monitoring Employees Online?" *About Money*, December 15, 2015 (http://humanresources.about.com/od/technology/a/alternatives-to-employee-internet-monitoring.htm).

11. J. K. Shank and V. Govindarajan, *Strategic Cost Management* (New York: The Free Press, 1993).

12. R. Gruber, "Why You Should Consider Activity-Based Costing," *Small Business Forum* (Spring 1994), pp. 20–36.

13. "Easier Than ABC," *The Economist* (October 25, 2003), p. 56.

14. T. P. Pare, "A New Tool for Managing Costs," *Fortune* (June 14, 1993), pp. 124–129. For further information on the use of ABC with EVA, see T. L. Pohlen and B. J. Coleman, "Evaluating Internal Operations and Supply Chain Performance Using EVA and ABC," *SAM Advanced Management Journal* (Spring 2005), pp. 45–58.

15. K. Hopkins, "The Risk Agenda," *BusinessWeek*, Special Advertising Section (November 22, 2004), pp. 166–170.

16. T. L. Barton, W. G. Shenkir, and P. L. Walker, "Managing Risk: An Enterprise-wide Approach," *Financial Executive* (March/April 2001), p. 51.

17. T. L. Barton, W. G. Shenkir, and P. L. Walker, "Managing Risk: An Enterprise-Wide Approach," pp. 48–51; P. L. Walker, W. G. Shenkir, and T. L. Barton, "Enterprise Risk Management: Putting It All Together," *Internal Auditor* (August 2003), pp. 50–55.

18. T. J. Andersen, "The Performance Relationship of Effective Risk Management: Exploring the Firm-Specific Investment Rationale," *Long Range Planning* (April 2008), pp. 155–176.

19. C. K. Brancato, *New Corporate PerformanceMeasures* (New York: Conference Board, 1995); C. D. Ittner, D. F. Larcker, and M. V. Rajan, "The Choice of Performance Measures in Annual Bonus Contracts," working paper reported by K. Z. Andrews in "Executive Bonuses," *Harvard Business Review* (January–February 1996), pp. 8–9; J. Low and T. Siesfeld, "Measures That Matter: Wall Street Considers Non-Financial Performance More Than You Think," *Strategy & Leadership* (March/April 1998), pp. 24–30.

20. A similar measure, EBITDA (Earnings Before Interest, Taxes, Depreciation, and Amortization), is also used.

21. J. M. Laderman, "Earnings, Schmernings: Look at the Cash," *BusinessWeek* (July 24, 1989), pp. 56–57.

22. H. Greenberg, "Don't Count on Cash Flow," *Fortune* (May 13, 2002), p. 176 A. Tergesen, "Cash-Flow Hocus-Pocus," *BusinessWeek* (July 15, 2002), pp. 130–132.

23. "Green Revolutionary," *The Economist* (April 7, 2007), p. 66.

24. E. H. Hall Jr., and J. Lee, "Diversification Strategies: Creating Value of Generating Profits?" paper presented to the annual meeting of the *Decision Sciences Institute*, Orlando, FL (November 18–21, 2000).

25. P. C. Brewer, G. Chandra, and C. A. Hock, "Economic Value Added (EVA): Its Uses and Limitations," *SAM Advanced Management Journal* (Spring 1999), pp. 4–11.

26. D. J. Skyrme and D. M. Amidon, "New Measures of Success," *Journal of Business Strategy* (January/February 1998), p. 23 http://www.investopedia.com/articles/fundamental/03/031203.asp#axzz2Cgj4StE0

27. G. B. Stewart III, "EVA Works—But Not if You Make These Common Mistakes," *Fortune* (May 1, 1995), pp. 117–118.

28. S. Tully, "The Real Key to Creating Wealth," *Fortune* (September 20, 1993), p. 38.

29. A. Ehrbar, "Using EVA to Measure Performance and Assess Strategy," *Strategy & Leadership* (May/June 1999), pp. 20–24.

30. P. C. Brewer, G. Chandra, and C. A. Hock, "Economic Value Added (EVA): Its Uses and Limitations," *SAM Advanced Management Journal* (Spring 1999), pp. 7–9.

31. R. Sarbapriya, "Efficacy of Economic Value Added Concept in Business Performance Measurement," *Advances in Information Technology and Management* (Vol. 2, No. 2), pp. 260–267; Pro: K. Lehn and A. K. Makhija, "EVA and MVA as Performance Measures and Signals for Strategic Change," *Strategy & Leadership* (May/June 1996), pp. 34–38; Con: D. I. Goldenberg, "Shareholder Value Debunked," *Strategy & Leadership* (January/ February 2000), pp. 30–36.

32. A. Ehrbar, "Using EVA to Measure Performance and Assess Strategy," *Strategy & Leadership* (May/June 1999), p. 21.

33. A. B. Fisher, "Creating Stockholder Wealth: Market Value Added," *Fortune* (December 11, 1995), pp. 105–116.

34. K. Lehn and A. K. Makhija, "EVA and MVA as Performance Measures and Signals for Strategic Change," p. 37.

35. R. S. Kaplan and D. P. Norton, "Using the Balanced Scorecard as a Strategic Management System," *Harvard Business Review* (January–February 1996), pp. 75–85; R. S. Kaplan and D. P. Norton, "The Balanced Scorecard—Measures That Drive Performance," *Harvard Business Review* (January–February, 1992), pp. 71–79.

36. D. I. Goldenberg, "Shareholder Value Debunked," p. 34.

37. In later work, Kaplan and Norton used the term "perspectives" and replaced "internal business perspective" with "process perspective" and "innovation and learning" with "learning and growth perspective." See R. S. Norton and D. P. Norton, "How to Implement a New Strategy Without Disrupting Your Organization," *Harvard Business Review* (March 2006), pp. 100–109.

38. C. K. Brancato, *New Performance Measures* (New York: Conference Board, 1995).

39. D. Rigby and B. Bilodeau, "Management Tools and Trends 2011," *Bain and Company*, http://www.bain.com/Images/BAIN_BRIEF_Management_Tools.pdf

40. B. P. Stivers and T. Joyce, "Building a Balanced Performance Management System," *SAM Advanced Management Journal* (Spring 2000), pp. 22–29.

41. Kaplan and Norton (March, 2006), p. 107.

42. G. J. M. Braam and E. Nijssen, "Performance Effects of Using the Balanced Scorecard: A Note on the Dutch Experience," *Long Range Planning* (August 2004), pp. 335–349; H. Ahn, "Applying the Balanced Scorecard Concept: An Experience Report," *Long Range Planning* (August 2001), pp. 441–461.

43. "CEO Performance Evaluations Rely Heavily on Financials Over Qualitative Metrics, Hay Group/Agenda Study Finds," *Reuters*, November 2, 2015 (*http://www.reuters.com/article/pa-hay-group-idUSnBw025258a+100+BSW20151102*).

44. "Performance Evaluation of Boards and Directors," Deloitte, March 2014 (*http://www2.deloitte.com/content/dam/Deloitte/in/Documents/risk/Corporate%20Governance/in-cg-performance-evaluation-of-boards-and-directors-noexp.pdf*).

45. R. Charan, *Boards at Work* (San Francisco: Jossey-Bass, 1998), pp. 176–177.

46. J. Trammell, "How Do You Evaluate CEO Performance? 6 Ways To Grade The Chief," *Forbes*, August 18, 2013 (http://www.forbes.com/sites/joeltrammell/2013/08/18/how-do-you-evaluate-ceo-performance-6-ways-to-grade-the-chief/#62c9145741da).

47. T. D. Schellhardt, "Directors Get Tough: Inside a CEO Performance Review," *The Wall Street Journal Interactive Edition* (April 27, 1998).

48. T. L. Wheelen and J. D. Hunger, "Using the Strategic Audit," *SAM Advanced Management Journal* (Winter 1987), pp. 4–12; G. Donaldson, "A New Tool for Boards: The Strategic Audit," *Harvard Business Review* (July–August 1995), pp. 99–107.

49. H. Threat, "Measurement Is Free," *Strategy & Leadership* (May/June 1999), pp. 16–19; http://www.fedex.com/ma/about/overview/innovation.html

50. 2013 Global Transfer Pricing Survey, EY; http://www.ey.com/GL/en/Services/Tax/2013-Global-Transfer-Pricing-Survey

51. H. Rothman, "You Need Not Be Big to Benchmark," *Nation's Business* (December 1992), p. 64.

52. C. W. Von Bergen and B. Soper, "A Problem with Benchmarking: Using Shaping as a Solution," *SAM Advanced Management Journal* (Autumn 1995), pp. 16–19.

53. http://www.bain.com/publications/articles/management-tools-and-trends-2015.aspx

54. "Just the Facts: Numbers Runners," *Journal of Business Strategy* (July/August 2002), p. 3 L. Mann, D. Samson, and D. Dow, "A Field Experiment on the Effects of Benchmarking and Goal Setting on Company Sales Performance," *Journal of Management* (Vol. 24, No. 1, 1998), pp. 73–96.

55. S. McAlary, "Three Pitfalls in ERP Implementation," *Strategy & Leadership* (October/November/December 1999), pp. 49–50.

56. J. B. White, D. Clark, and S. Ascarelli, "This German Software Is Complex, Expensive—And Wildly Popular," *The Wall Street Journal* (March 14, 1997), pp. A1, A8; D. Ward, "Whirlpool Takes a Dive with Software Snarl," *Des Moines Register* (April 29, 2000), p. 8D.

57. J. Verville, R. Palanisamy, C. Bernadas, and A. Halingten, "ERP Acquisition Planning: A Critical Dimension for Making the Right Choice," *Long Range Planning* (February 2007), pp. 45–63.

58. http://www.rfidblog.org/entry/tesco-postpones-rfid-implementation-at-its-stores/.

59. M. Roberti, "Awards Finalists Highlight the Maturation of RFID," *RFID Journal*, March 14, 2016 (http://www.rfidjournal.com/articles/view?14187); C. Krivda, "RFID After Compliance: Integration and Payback," Special Advertising Section, *BusinessWeek* (December 20, 2004), pp. 91–98.

60. D. Leonard and J. Tozzi, "Why Don't More Hospitals Use Electronic Health Records?" *Bloomberg Businessweek* (June 21, 2012), *http://www.businessweek.com/articles/2012-06-21/why-dont-more-hospitals-use-electronic-health-records*

61. R. M. Hodgetts and M. S. Wortman, *Administrative Policy*, 2nd ed. (New York: John Wiley & Sons, 1980), p. 128.

62. J. R. Wooldridge and C. C. Snow, "Stock Market Reaction to Strategic Investment Decisions," *Strategic Management Journal* (September 1990), pp. 353–363.

63. M. C. Jensen, "Corporate Budgeting Is Broken—Let's Fix It," *Harvard Business Review* (November 2001), pp. 94–101.

64. C. M. Christensen, S. P. Kaufman, and W. C. Smith, "Innovation Killers: How Financial Tools Destroy Your Capacity to Do New Things," *Harvard Business Review* (January 2008), pp. 98–105.

65. P. Hsieh, T. Keller, and S. R. Rajan, "The Misguided Practice of Earnings Guidance," *McKinsey Quarterly* (Spring 2006), pp. 1–5.

66. "Audit Firms Sued in HP's Autonomy Acquisition," *Reuters* (November 28, 2012), (http://www.reuters.com/article/2012/11/29/hp-autonomy-auditors-idUSL1E8MS8ZX20121129).

67. D. Clark, "HP Enterprise Bets on 'Machine Learning' Cloud Service," *Wall Street Journal*, March 13, 2016 (http://www.wsj.com/articles/hp-enterprise-bets-on-machine-learning-cloud-service-1457901556).

68. D. Henry "Fuzzy Numbers," *BusinessWeek* (October 4, 2004), pp. 79–88.

69. A. Rappaport, "10 Ways to Create Shareholder Value," *Harvard Business Review* (September 2006), pp. 66–77.

70. D. R. Schmidt and K. L. Fowler, "Post-Acquisition Financial Performance and Executive Compensation," *Strategic Management Journal* (November–December 1990), pp. 559–569.

71. H. L. Tosi, S. Werner, J. P. Katz, and L. R. Gomez-Mejia, "How Much Does Performance Matter? A Meta-Analysis of CEO Pay Studies," *Journal of Management* (Vol. 26, No. 2, 2000), pp. 301–339; P. Wright, M. Kroll, and D. Elenkov, "Acquisition Returns, Increase in Firm Size, and Chief Executive Officer Compensation: The Moderating Role of Monitoring," *Academy of Management Journal* (June 2002), pp. 599–608; S. Werner, H. L. Tosi, and L. Gomez-Mejia, "Organizational Governance and Employee Pay: How Ownership Structure Affects the Firm's Compensation Strategy," *Strategic Management Journal* (April 2005), pp. 377–384.

72. X. Zhang, K. M. Bartol, K. G. Smith, M. D. Pfarrer, and D. M. Khanin, "CEOs on the Edge: Earnings Manipulation and Stock-based Incentive Misalignment," *Academy of Management Journal* (April 2008), pp. 241–258; L. Bebchuk and J. Fried, *Pay Without Performance: The Unfulfilled Promise of Executive Compensation* (Boston: Harvard University Press, 2004); L. A. Bebchuk and J. M. Fried, "Pay Without Performance: Overview of the Issues," *Academy of Management Perspectives* (February 2006), pp. 5–24.

73. D. Jones, "Bad News Can Enrich Executives," *Des Moines Register* (November 26, 1999), p. 8S.

74. J. F. Porac, J. B. Wade, and T. G. Pollock, "Industry Categories and the Politics of the Comparable Firm in CEO Compensation," *Administrative Science Quarterly* (March 1999), pp. 112–144. For summaries of current research on executive compensation and performance, see C. E. Devers, A. A. Cannella Jr., G. P. Reilly, and M. E. Yoder, "Executive Compensation: A Multidisciplinary Review of Recent Developments," *Journal of Management* (December 2007), pp. 1016–1072; M. Chan, "Executive Compensation," *Business and Society Review* (March 2008), pp. 129–161; and S. N. Kaplan, "Are CEOs Overpaid?" *Academy of Management Perspective* (May 2008), pp. 5–20.

75. C. D. Ittner and D. F. Larcker, "Coming Up Short," *Harvard Business Review* (November 2003), pp. 88–95.

76. See the classic article by S. Kerr, "On the Folly of Rewarding A, While Hoping for B," *Academy of Management Journal* (Vol. 18, December 1975), pp. 769–783.

77. W. Zellner, E. Schine, and G. Smith, "Trickle-Down Is Trickling Down at Work," *BusinessWeek* (March 18, 1996), p. 34.

78. "The Problem With Sears Holdings Isn't Tesla, Uber, or Amazon," *The Motley Fool*, March 15, 2016 (http://www.fool.com/investing/general/2016/03/06/the-problem-with-sears-holdings-isnt-tesla-uber-or.aspx); For more information on how goals can have dysfunctional side effects, see D. C. Kayes, "The Destructive Pursuit of Idealized Goals," *Organizational Dynamics* (Vol. 34, Issue 4, 2005), pp. 391–401.

79. T. J. Peters and R. H. Waterman, *In Search of Excellence* (New York: Harper Collins, 1982), pp. 75–76.

80. T. Aeppel, "Not All Workers Find Idea of Empowerment as Neat as It Sounds," *The Wall Street Journal* (September 8, 1997), pp. A1, A13.

81. R. S. Allen and M. M. Helms, "Employee Perceptions of the Relationship Between Strategy, Rewards, and Organizational Performance," *Journal of Business Strategies* (Fall 2002), pp. 115–140; M. A. Carpenter, "The Price of Change: The Role of CEO Compensation in Strategic Variation and Deviation from Industry Strategy Norms," *Journal of Management* (Vol. 26, No. 6, 2000), pp. 1179–1198; M. A. Carpenter and W. G. Sanders, "The Effects of Top Management Team Pay and Firm Internationalization on MNC Performance," *Journal of Management* (Vol. 30, No. 4, 2004), pp. 509–528; J. D. Shaw, N. Gupta, and J. E. Delery, "Congruence Between Technology and Compensation Systems: Implications for Strategy Implementation," *Strategic Management Journal* (April 2001), pp. 379–386; E. F. Montemazon, "Congruence Between Pay Policy and Competitive Strategy in High-Performing Organizations," *Journal of Management* (Vol. 22, No. 6, 1996), pp. 889–908.

82. D. B. Balkin and L. R. Gomez-Mejia, "Matching Compensation and Organizational Strategies," *Strategic Management Journal* (February 1990), pp. 153–169.

83. C. S. Galbraith, "The Effect of Compensation Programs and Structure on SBU Competitive Strategy: A Study of

Technology-Intensive Firms," *Strategic Management Journal* (July 1991), pp. 353–370.

84. T. Mullaney, "Why corporate CEO pay is so high, and going higher," *CNBC*, May 18, 2015 (http://www.cnbc.com/2015/05/18/why-corporate-ceo-pay-is-so-high-and-going-higher.html).

85. "The Politics of Pay," *The Economist* (March 24, 2007), pp. 71–72.

86. P. J. Stonich, "The Performance Measurement and Reward System: Critical to Strategic Management," *Organizational Dynamics* (Winter 1984), pp. 45–57.

87. T. Mullaney, "Why corporate CEO pay is so high, and going higher," *CNBC*, May 18, 2015 (http://www.cnbc.com/2015/05/18/why-corporate-ceo-pay-is-so-high-and-going-higher.html); M. Chan, "Executive Compensation," *Business and Society Review* (March 2008), pp. 129–161.

88. S. E. O'Byrne and S. D. Young, "Why Executive Pay Is Failing," *Harvard Business Review* (June 2006), p. 28.

89. http://fortune.com/worlds-most-admired-companies/ (accessed March 15, 2016)

90. A. Harrington, "America's Most Admired Companies," *Fortune* (March 8, 2004), pp. 80–81.

PART 5

Introduction to
Case Analysis

CHAPTER 13
Suggestions for Case Analysis

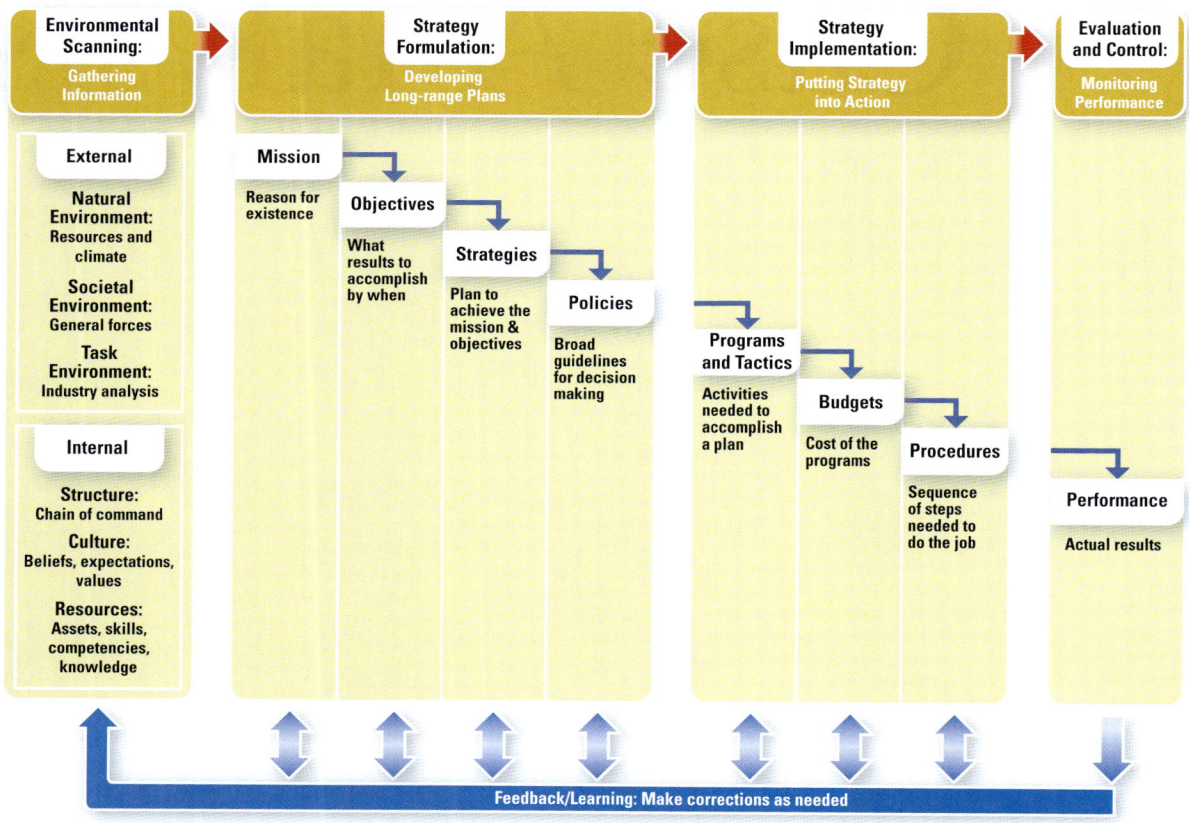

Pearson MyLab Management®

⭐ **Improve Your Grade!**

Over 10 million students improved their results using the Pearson MyLabs. Visit **mymanagementlab.com** for simulations, tutorials, and end-of-chapter problems.

Learning Objectives

After reading this chapter, you should be able to:

13-1. Explain the issues involved in researching a case situation

13-2. Analyze financial statements using ratio analysis, common-size statements, Z-values and economic measures

13-3. Employ the strategic audit as a method of organizing and analyzing case information

Finding the Problems in the Friendly Skies

United Airlines agreed to merge with Continental Airlines in 2010 and the passenger nightmare began. Rather than merge each of the big systems (Reservations, Websites & Frequent Flyer Programs) over time, they merged all three on the same day. The entire operation came to a standstill as the system lost track of pilots and assigned flights to pilots who were retired or deceased. A litany of problems plagued the airline for the next five years as a series of senior leadership teams tried to figure out how to fix the business. From 2012 to 2015 United was at or close to the bottom of most airline performance metrics including delays, cancellations, bumped passengers, complaints filed, and lost bags. In 2015 it was ranked last among the non-discount airlines by J.D. Power & Associates in their customer satisfaction survey.

The stunning number of poor business decisions just exasperated the situation:

1. The new CEO of the airline spent thousands of hours and over a year to pick the coffee for the organization

2. The company moved to a chute system of boarding that encouraged passengers to get in their chutes long before the plane even landed

3. The new uniforms were cheap and did not hold up to repeated cleanings.

A new CEO took over in late 2014 and the company got to work systematically examining what it would take to bring the organization back. The company began surveying customers collecting 8,000 surveys a day and they sent "customer experience" teams to fully evaluate the current situation.

Looking both internally and externally the company found a large number of both small and large items that needed to be corrected and got to work. Easier issues included matching the other major carriers method for boarding planes, quickly selecting a far better type of coffee, and establishing a group to re-vamp the uniforms. Bigger issues were addressed including settling all the union-related issues (the company agreed to a moratorium on outsourcing some jobs until 2017), revamping the travel patterns of planes to minimize weather disruptions, and changing the baggage handling procedures.

Analyzing and systematically repairing the company appeared to be working by early 2016. Rates for mishandled bags, missed connections, and on-time performance were improving dramatically.

This type of in-depth, investigative analysis is a key part of analyzing strategy cases. This chapter provides various analytical techniques and suggestions for conducting this kind of case analysis.

SOURCES: D. Bennett, "The United Way," *Bloomberg BusinessWeek*, January 18–24, 2016, pp. 50–55; http://www.jdpower.com/sites/default/files/2015057%20NA%20Airline_%20(FINAL).pdf; B. Mutzabaugh, "Era of airline merger mania comes to a close with last US Airways flight," *USA Today*, October 16, 2015 (http://www.usatoday.com/story/travel/flights/todayinthesky/2015/10/15/airline-mergers-american-delta-united-southwest/73972928/).

The Case Method

13-1. Explain the issues involved in researching a case situation

The analysis and discussion of case problems has been the most popular method of teaching strategy and policy for many years. Furthermore, most of the big consulting companies use case analysis as their primary means of selecting candidates for on-site interviews. The case method offers the opportunity to move from a narrow, specialized view that emphasizes functional techniques to a broader, less precise analysis of the overall corporation. Cases present actual business situations and enable you to examine both successful and unsuccessful corporations. In case analysis, you might be asked to critically analyze a situation in which a manager had to make a decision of long-term corporate importance. This approach gives you a feel for what it is like to face making and implementing strategic decisions.

Researching the Case Situation

13-2. Analyze financial statements using ratio analysis, common-size statements, Z-values and economic measures

You should not restrict yourself only to the information and timing of when the case was written unless your instructor states otherwise. You should, if possible, undertake outside research about the environmental setting. Check the decision date of each case (typically the latest date mentioned in the case) to find out when the situation occurred and then screen the business periodicals for that time period. An understanding of the economy during that period will help you avoid making a serious error in your analysis—for example, suggesting a sale of stock when the stock market is at an all-time low or taking on more debt when the prime interest rate is over 15%. Information about the industry will provide insights into its competitive activities. *Important Note: Don't go beyond the decision date of the case in your research unless directed to do so by your instructor.*

Use industry information services such as Compustat, Compact Disclosure (for older cases), and a wide variety of information sources available on the Internet. Hoover's online corporate directory (www.hoovers.com) and the U.S. Securities and Exchange Commission's EDGAR database (www.sec.gov) provide access to corporate annual reports and 10-K forms. Most companies post their annual reports along with all filings on the investor page of their company website. This background will give you an appreciation for the situation as it was experienced by the participants in the case. Use a search engine such as Google or Bing to find additional information about the industry and the company.

A company's **annual report** and **SEC 10-K form** from the year of the case can be very helpful. According to the Yankelovich Partners survey firm, 8 out of 10 portfolio managers and 75% of security analysts use annual reports when making decisions.[1] They contain not only the usual income statements and balance sheets, but also cash flow statements and notes to the financial statements indicating why certain actions were taken. On 10-K forms you will find detailed information not usually available in an annual report. **SEC 10-Q forms** include quarterly financial reports. **SEC 14-A forms** include detailed information on members of a company's board of directors and proxy statements for annual meetings. Some resources available for research into the economy and a corporation's industry are suggested in **Appendix 13.A**.

A caveat: Before obtaining additional information about the company profiled in a particular case, ask your instructor if doing so is appropriate for your class assignment. Your strategy instructor may want you to stay within the confines of the case information provided in the book. In this case, it is usually acceptable to at least learn more about the societal environment at the time of the case.

Financial Analysis: A Place to Begin

13-3. Employ the strategic audit as a method of organizing and analyzing case information

Once you have read a case, a good place to begin your analysis is with the financial statements. **Ratio analysis** is the calculation of ratios from data in these statements. It is done to identify possible financial issues. A review of key financial ratios can help you assess a company's overall situation and pinpoint some problem areas. Ratios are useful regardless of firm size and enable you to compare a company's ratios with industry averages. **Table 13–1** lists some of the most important financial ratios, which are (1) **liquidity ratios**, (2) **profitability ratios**, (3) **activity ratios**, and (4) **leverage ratios**.

ANALYZING FINANCIAL STATEMENTS

In your analysis, do not simply make an exhibit that includes all the ratios (unless your instructor requires you to do so), but select and discuss only those ratios that have an impact on the issues you are addressing about that company. For instance, accounts receivable and inventory provide a source of funds. If receivables and inventories are double the industry average, reducing them will provide needed cash. In this situation, the case report should include not only sources of funds but also the number of dollars freed for use. Compare these ratios with industry averages to discover whether the company is out of line with others in the industry. Annual and quarterly industry ratios can be found in the library or on the Internet. (See the resources for case research in **Appendix 13.A**.) In the years to come, expect to see financial entries for the trading of CERs (Certified Emissions Reductions). This is the amount of money a company earns from reducing carbon emissions and selling them on the open market.

A typical financial analysis of a firm would include a study of the operating statements for five or so years, including a trend analysis of sales, profits, earnings per share, debt-to-equity ratio, return on investment, and so on, plus a ratio study comparing the

TABLE 13–1 Financial Ratio Analysis

	Formula	How Expressed	Meaning
1. Liquidity Ratios			
Current ratio	$$\frac{\text{Current assets}}{\text{Current liabilities}}$$	Decimal	A short-term indicator of the company's ability to pay its short-term liabilities from short-term assets; how much of current assets are available to cover each dollar of current liabilities.
Quick (acid test) ratio	$$\frac{\text{Current assets} - \text{Inventory}}{\text{Current liabilities}}$$	Decimal	Measures the company's ability to pay off its short-term obligations from current assets, excluding inventories.
Inventory to net working capital	$$\frac{\text{Inventory}}{\text{Current assets} - \text{Current liabilities}}$$	Decimal	A measure of inventory balance; measures the extent to which the cushion of excess current assets over current liabilities may be threatened by unfavorable changes in inventory.
Cash ratio	$$\frac{\text{Cash} + \text{Cash equivalents}}{\text{Current liabilities}}$$	Decimal	Measures the extent to which the company's capital is in cash or cash equivalents; shows how much of the current obligations can be paid from cash or near-cash assets.
2. Profitability Ratios			
Net profit margin	$$\frac{\text{Net profit after taxes}}{\text{Net sales}}$$	Percentage	Shows how much after-tax profits are generated by each dollar of sales.
Gross profit margin	$$\frac{\text{Sales} - \text{Cost of goods sold}}{\text{Net sales}}$$	Percentage	Indicates the total margin available to cover other expenses beyond cost of goods sold and still yield a profit.
Return on investment (ROI)	$$\frac{\text{Net profit after taxes}}{\text{Total assets}}$$	Percentage	Measures the rate of return on the total assets utilized in the company; a measure of management's efficiency, it shows the return on all the assets under its control, regardless of source of financing.
Return on equity (ROE)	$$\frac{\text{Net profit after taxes}}{\text{Shareholders' equity}}$$	Percentage	Measures the rate of return on the book value of shareholders' total investment in the company.
Earnings per share (EPS)	$$\frac{\text{Net profit after taxes} - \text{Preferred stock dividends}}{\text{Average number of common shares}}$$	Dollars per share	Shows the after-tax earnings generated for each share of common stock.
3. Activity Ratios			
Inventory turnover	$$\frac{\text{Net sales}}{\text{Inventory}}$$	Decimal	Measures the number of times that average inventory of finished goods was turned over or sold during a period of time, usually a year.
Days of inventory	$$\frac{\text{Inventory}}{\text{Cost of goods sold} + 365}$$	Days	Measures the number of one day's worth of inventory that a company has on hand at any given time.

TABLE 13–1   Financial Ratio Analysis, (continued)

	Formula	How Expressed	Meaning
Net working capital turnover	$$\frac{\text{Net sales}}{\text{Net working capital}}$$	Decimal	Measures how effectively the net working capital is used to generate sales.
Asset turnover	$$\frac{\text{Sales}}{\text{Total assets}}$$	Decimal	Measures the utilization of all the company's assets; measures how many sales are generated by each dollar of assets.
Fixed asset turnover	$$\frac{\text{Sales}}{\text{Fixed assets}}$$	Decimal	Measures the utilization of the company's fixed assets (i.e., plant and equipment); measures how many sales are generated by each dollar of fixed assets.
Average collection period	$$\frac{\text{Accounts receivable}}{\text{Sales for year} + 365}$$	Days	Indicates the average length of time in days that a company must wait to collect a sale after making it; may be compared to the credit terms offered by the company to its customers.
Accounts receivable turnover	$$\frac{\text{Annual credit sales}}{\text{Accounts receivable}}$$	Decimal	Indicates the number of times that accounts receivable are cycled during the period (usually a year).
Accounts payable period	$$\frac{\text{Accounts payable}}{\text{Purchase for year} \div 365}$$	Days	Indicates the average length of time in days that the company takes to pay its credit purchases.
Days of cash	$$\frac{\text{Cash}}{\text{Net sales for year} \div 365}$$	Days	Indicates the number of days of cash on hand, at present sales levels.

4. Leverage Ratios

	Formula	How Expressed	Meaning
Debt-to-asset ratio	$$\frac{\text{Total debt}}{\text{Total assets}}$$	Percentage	Measures the extent to which borrowed funds have been used to finance the company's assets.
Debt-to-equity ratio	$$\frac{\text{Total debt}}{\text{Shareholders' equity}}$$	Percentage	Measures the funds provided by creditors versus the funds provided by owners.
Long-term debt to capital structure	$$\frac{\text{Long-term debt}}{\text{Shareholders' equity}}$$	Percentage	Measures the long-term component of capital structure.
Times interest earned	$$\frac{\text{Profit before taxes} + \text{Interest charges}}{\text{Interest charges}}$$	Decimal	Indicates the ability of the company to meet its annual interest costs.
Coverage of fixed charges	$$\frac{\text{Profit before taxes} + \text{Interest charges} + \text{Lease charges}}{\text{Interest charges} + \text{Lease obligations}}$$	Decimal	A measure of the company's ability to meet all of its fixed-charge obligations.
Current liabilities to equity	$$\frac{\text{Current liabilities}}{\text{Shareholders' equity}}$$	Percentage	Measures the short-term financing portion versus that provided by owners.

continued

TABLE 13–1   Financial Ratio Analysis, (continued)

	Formula	How Expressed	Meaning
5. Other Ratios			
Price/earnings ratio	$\dfrac{\text{Market price per share}}{\text{Earnings per share}}$	Decimal	Shows the current market's evaluation of a stock, based on its earnings; shows how much the investor is willing to pay for each dollar of earnings.
Divided payout ratio	$\dfrac{\text{Annual dividends per share}}{\text{Annual earnings per share}}$	Percentage	Indicates the percentage of profit that is paid out as dividends.
Dividend yield on common stock	$\dfrac{\text{Annual dividends per share}}{\text{Current market price per share}}$	Percentage	Indicates the dividend rate of return to common shareholders at the current market price.

NOTE: In using ratios for analysis, calculate ratios for the corporation and compare them to the average and quartile ratios for the particular industry. Refer to Standard & Poor's and Robert Morris Associates for average industry data. Special thanks to Dr. Moustafa H. Abdelsamad, former dean, Business School, Texas A&M University—Corpus Christi, Corpus Christi, Texas, for his definitions of these ratios.

firm under study with industry standards. As a minimum, undertake the following five steps in basic financial analysis.

1. **Examine historical income statements and balance sheets:** These two basic statements provide most of the data needed for analysis. Statements of cash flow may also be useful.
2. **Compare historical statements over time** if a series of statements is available.
3. **Calculate changes that occur in individual categories from year to year,** as well as the cumulative total change.
4. **Determine the change as a percentage** as well as an absolute amount.
5. **Adjust for inflation** if that was a significant factor.

Examination of this information may reveal developing trends. Compare trends in one category with trends in related categories. For example, an increase in sales of 15% over three years may appear to be satisfactory until you note an increase of 20% in the cost of goods sold during the same period. The outcome of this comparison might suggest that further investigation into the manufacturing process is necessary. If a company is reporting strong net income growth but negative cash flow, this would suggest that the company is relying on something other than operations for earnings growth. Is it selling off assets or cutting R&D? If accounts receivable are growing faster than sales revenues, the company is not getting paid for the products or services it is counting as sold. Is the company dumping product on its distributors at the end of the year to boost its reported annual sales? If so, expect the distributors to return the unordered product the next month, thus drastically cutting the next year's reported sales.

Other "tricks of the trade" need to be examined. Until June 2000, firms growing through acquisition were allowed to account for the cost of the purchased company through the pooling of both companies' stock. This approach was used in 40% of the value of mergers between 1997 and 1999. The pooling method enabled the acquiring company to disregard the premium it paid for the other firm (the amount above the fair market value of the purchased company often called "good will"). Thus, when PepsiCo agreed to purchase Quaker Oats for $13.4 billion in PepsiCo stock, the $13.4 billion was not found on PepsiCo's balance sheet. As of June 2000, merging firms must use the "purchase" accounting rules in which the true purchase price is reflected in the financial statements.[2]

The analysis of a multinational corporation's financial statements can get very complicated, especially if its headquarters is in another country that uses different accounting standards.

COMMON-SIZE STATEMENTS

Common-size statements are income statements and balance sheets in which the dollar figures have been converted into percentages. These statements are used to identify trends in each of the categories, such as cost of goods sold as a percentage of sales (sales is the denominator). For the income statement, net sales represent 100%: calculate the percentage for each category so that the categories sum to the net sales percentage (100%). For the balance sheet, give the total assets a value of 100% and calculate other asset and liability categories as percentages of the total assets with total assets as the denominator. (Individual asset and liability items, such as accounts receivable and accounts payable, can also be calculated as a percentage of net sales.)

When you convert statements to this form, it is relatively easy to note the percentage that each category represents of the total. Look for trends in specific items, such as cost of goods sold, when compared to the company's historical figures. To get a proper picture, however, you need to make comparisons with industry data, if available, to see whether fluctuations are merely reflecting industry wide trends. If a firm's trends are generally in line with those of the rest of the industry, problems are less likely than if the firm's trends are worse than industry averages. If ratios are not available for the industry, calculate the ratios for the industry's best and worst firms and compare them to the firm you are analyzing. Common-size statements are especially helpful in developing scenarios and pro forma statements because they provide a series of historical relationships (for example, cost of goods sold to sales, interest to sales, and inventories as a percentage of assets) from which you can estimate the future with your scenario assumptions for each year.

Z-VALUE AND THE INDEX OF SUSTAINABLE GROWTH

If the corporation being studied appears to be in poor financial condition, use **Altman's Z-Value Bankruptcy Formula** to calculate its likelihood of going bankrupt. The *Z-value* formula combines five ratios by weighting them according to their importance to a corporation's financial strength. The formula is:

$$Z = 1.2x_1 + 1.4x_2 + 3.3x_3 + 0.6x_4 + 1.0x_5$$

where:

x_1 = Working capital/Total assets (%)
x_2 = Retained earnings/Total assets (%)
x_3 = Earnings before interest and taxes/Total assets (%)
x_4 = Market value of equity/Total liabilities (%)
x_5 = Sales/Total assets (number of times)

A score below 1.81 indicates significant credit problems, whereas a score above 3.0 indicates a healthy firm. Scores between 1.81 and 3.0 indicate question marks.[3] The Altman Z model has achieved a remarkable 94% accuracy in predicting corporate bankruptcies. Its accuracy is excellent in the two years before financial distress, but diminishes as the lead time increases. It has also been found to be the strongest predictor of bankruptcy and it and the current ratio are great tools to assess the financial health of organizations.[4]

The **index of sustainable growth** is useful to learn whether a company embarking on a growth strategy will need to take on debt to fund this growth. The index indicates how much of the growth rate of sales can be sustained by internally generated funds. The formula is:

$$g^* = \frac{[P(1 - D)(1 + L)]}{[T - P(1 - D)(1 + L)]}$$

where:

$$P = (\text{Net profit before tax/Net sales}) \times 100$$
$$D = \text{Target dividends/Profit after tax}$$
$$L = \text{Total liabilities/Net worth}$$
$$T = (\text{Total assets/Net sales}) \times 100$$

If the planned growth rate calls for a growth rate higher than its g*, external capital will be needed to fund the growth unless management is able to find efficiencies, decrease dividends, increase the debt-equity ratio, or reduce assets through renting or leasing arrangements.[5]

USEFUL ECONOMIC MEASURES

If you are analyzing a company over many years, you may want to adjust sales and net income for inflation to arrive at a "true" financial performance in constant dollars. **Constant dollars** are dollars adjusted for inflation to make them comparable over various years. One way to adjust for inflation in the United States is to use the consumer price index (CPI), as given in **Table 13–2**. Dividing sales and net income by the CPI factor for that year will change the figures to 1982–1984 U.S. constant dollars (when the CPI was 1.0). Adjusting for inflation is especially important for companies operating in emerging economies like China and Russia. China's inflation rate was just 1.8% in 2016; while the Russian inflation rate in 2016 was 9.8%.[6]

Another helpful analytical aid provided in **Table 13–2** is the **prime interest rate**, the rate of interest banks charge on their lowest-risk loans. For better assessments of strategic decisions, it can be useful to note the level of the prime interest rate at the time of the case. A decision to borrow money to build a new plant would have been a difficult one in 2007 when the rate was at 8.05%, but far more practical just two years later when the average rate fell to 3.25%.

In preparing a scenario for your pro forma financial statements, you may want to use the **gross domestic product (GDP)** from **Table 13–2**. GDP is used worldwide and measures the total output of goods and services within a country's borders. The amount of change from one year to the next indicates how much that country's economy is growing. Remember that scenarios have to be adjusted for a country's specific conditions. For other economic information, see the resources for case research in **Appendix 13.A**.

Format for Case Analysis: The Strategic Audit

There is no one best way to analyze or present a case. Each instructor has personal preferences for format and approach. Nevertheless, in **Appendix 13.B** we suggest an approach for both written and oral reports that provides a systematic method for

TABLE 13–2	Year	GDP (in $ billions) Gross Domestic Product	CPI (for all items) Consumer Price Index	PIR (in %) Prime Interest Rate
U.S. Economic Indicators	1980	2,862	.824	15.26
	1985	4,346	1.076	9.93
	1990	5,979	1.307	10.01
	1995	7,664	1.524	8.83
	2000	10,284	1.722	9.23
	2005	13,093	1.953	6.19
	2006	13,855	2.016	7.96
	2007	14,477	2.073	8.05
	2008	14,718	2.153	5.09
	2009	14,418	2.143	3.25
	2010	14,964	2.180	3.25
	2011	15,517	2.249	3.25
	2012	16,155	2.295	3.25
	2013	16,663	2.329	3.25
	2014	17,348	2.367	3.25
	2015	17,942	2.370	3.26

NOTES: Gross domestic product (GDP) in billions of dollars; Consumer price index for all items (CPI) (1982–84 = 1.0); Prime interest rate (PIR) in percentages.

SOURCES: Gross domestic product (GDP) from U.S. Bureau of Economic Analysis, National Economic Accounts (www.bea.gov). Consumer price index (CPI) from U.S. Bureau of Labor Statistics (www.bls.gov). Prime interest rate (PIR) (www.federalreserve.gov).

successfully attacking a case. This approach is based on the strategic audit, which is presented at the end of Chapter 1 in **Appendix 1.A**. We find that this approach provides structure and is very helpful for the typical student who may be a relative novice in case analysis. Regardless of the format chosen, be careful to include a complete analysis of key environmental variables—especially of trends in the industry and of the competition. Look at international developments as well.

If you choose to use the strategic audit as a guide to the analysis of complex strategy cases, you may want to use the **strategic audit worksheet** in **Figure 13–1**. Print a copy of the worksheet to use to take notes as you analyze a case. See **Appendix 13.C** for an example of a completed student-written analysis of a 1993 Maytag Corporation case done in an outline form using the strategic audit format. This is one example of what a case analysis in outline form may look like.

Case discussion focuses on critical analysis and logical development of thought. A solution is satisfactory if it resolves important problems and is likely to be implemented successfully. How the corporation actually dealt with the case problems has no real bearing on the analysis because management might have analyzed its problems incorrectly or implemented a series of flawed solutions.

FIGURE 13–1
Strategic Audit
Worksheet

Strategic Audit Heading	Analysis		Comments
	(+) Factors	(−) Factors	
I. Current Situation			
A. Past Corporate Performance Indexes			
B. Strategic Posture: Current Mission Current Objectives Current Strategies Current Policies			
SWOT Analysis Begins:			
II. Corporate Governance			
A. Board of Directors			
B. Top Management			
III. External Environment (EFAS): **Opportunities and Threats (SWOT)**			
A. Natural Environment			
B. Societal Environment			
C. Task Environment (Industry Analysis)			
IV. Internal Environment (IFAS): **Strengths and Weaknesses (SWOT)**			
A. Corporate Structure			
B. Corporate Culture			
C. Corporate Resources			
1. Marketing			
2. Finance			
3. Research and Development			
4. Operations and Logistics			
5. Human Resources			
6. Information Technology			
V. Analysis of Strategic Factors (SFAS)			
A. Key Internal and External Strategic Factors (SWOT)			
B. Review of Mission and Objectives			
SWOT Analysis Ends. Recommendation Begins:			
VI. Alternatives and Recommendations			
A. Strategic Alternatives—pros and cons			
B. Recommended Strategy			
VII. Implementation			
VIII. Evaluation and Control			

NOTE: See the complete Strategic Audit on pages 64–71. It lists the pages in the book that discuss each of the eight headings.

SOURCE: T. L. Wheelen and J. D. Hunger, "Strategic Audit Worksheet." Copyright © 1985, 1986, 1987, 1988, 1989, 2005, and 2009 by T. L. Wheelen. Copyright © 1989, 2005, and 2009 by Wheelen and Hunger Associates. Revised 1991, 1994, and 1997. Reprinted by permission. Additional copies available for classroom use in Part D of the Case Instructor's Manual and on the Prentice Hall Web site (www.prenhall.com/wheelen).

End of Chapter SUMMARY

Using a structured case analysis approach is one of the best ways to understand and remember the strategic management process. By applying the concepts and techniques you have learned to cases, you will be able to remember them long past the time when you have forgotten other memorized bits of information. The use of cases to examine actual situations brings alive the field of strategic management and helps build your analytic and decision-making skills.

Pearson MyLab Management®

Go to **mymanagementlab.com** to complete the problems marked with this icon .

KEY TERMS

activity ratio (p. 381)
Altman's Z-Value Bankruptcy
    Formula (p. 385)
annual report (p. 381)
common-size statement (p. 385)
constant dollars (p. 386)

gross domestic product
    (GDP) (p. 386)
index of sustainable growth (p. 386)
leverage ratio (p. 381)
liquidity ratio (p. 381)
prime interest rate (p. 386)

profitability ratio (p. 381)
ratio analysis (p. 381)
SEC 10-K form (p. 381)
SEC 10-Q form (p. 381)
SEC 14-A form (p. 381)
strategic audit worksheet (p. 387)

Pearson MyLab Management ®

Go to **mymanagementlab.com** for the following assisted-graded writing questions:

13-1. What ratios would you use to begin your analysis of a case?
13-2. What are the five crucial steps to follow in basic financial analysis?

DISCUSSION QUESTIONS

13-3. Why should you begin a case analysis with a financial analysis? When are other approaches appropriate?

13-4. Discuss the importance of the common-size financial statements in strategic evaluation and control process.

13-5. Financial statement analysis is considered useful for students in handling and analyzing case studies. Is this true? Why?

13-6. When is inflation an important issue in conducting case analysis? Why bother?

13-7. Why is strategic audit recommended in case study analysis for students?

STRATEGIC PRACTICE EXERCISE

Convert the following two years of income statements from the Maytag Corporation into common-size statements. The dollar figures are in thousands. What does converting to a common size reveal?

Consolidated Statements of Income: Maytag Corporation

	1992	%	1991	%
Net sales	$3,041,223	100	$2,970,626	100
Cost of sales	2,339,406	—	2,254,221	—
Gross profits	701,817	—	716,405	—
Selling, general, & admin expenses	528,250	—	524,898	—
Reorganization expenses	95,000	—	0	—
Operating income	78,567	—	191,507	—
Interest expense	(75,004)	—	(75,159)	—
Other—net	3983	—	7069	—
Income before taxes and accounting changes	7546	—	123,417	—
Income taxes	(15,900)	—	(44,400)	—
Income before accounting changes	(8354)	—	79,017	—
Effects of accounting changes for postretirement benefits	(307,000)	—	0	—
Net income (loss)	$ (315,354)	—	$79,017	—

NOTES

1. M. Vanac, "What's a Novice Investor to Do?" *Des Moines Register* (November 30, 1997), p. 3G.
2. A. R. Sorking, "New Path on Mergers Could Contain Loopholes," *The* (Ames, IA) *Daily Tribune* (January 9, 2001), p. B7; "Firms Resist Effort to Unveil True Costs of Doing Business," *USA Today* (July 3, 2000), p. 10A.
3. M. S. Fridson, *Financial Statement Analysis* (New York: John Wiley & Sons, 1991), pp. 192–194.
4. M. Awais, F. Hayat, N. Mehar, & W. Ul-Hassan, 2015 "Do Z-Score and Current Ratio have Ability to Predict Bankruptcy?" *Developing Country Studies*, Vol. 5 (13): 30–36. E. I. Altman, "Predicting Financial Distress of Companies: Revisiting the Z-Score and Zeta Models," working paper at pages.stern.nyu.edu/~ealtman/Zscores. pdf (July 2000).
5. D. H. Bangs, *Managing by the Numbers* (Dover, NH: Upstart Publications, 1992), pp. 106–107.
6. Tradingeconomics.com/Russia/inflation-cpi; Tradingeconomics .com/China/inflation-cpi

APPENDIX **13.A**

Resources for Case Research

Company Information

1. Annual reports
2. Moody's *Manuals on Investment* (a listing of companies within certain industries that contains a brief history and a five-year financial statement of each company)
3. Securities and Exchange Commission Annual Report Form 10-K (annually) and 10-Q (quarterly)
4. Standard & Poor's *Register of Corporations, Directors, and Executives*
5. Value Line's *Investment Survey*
6. Findex's *Directory of Market Research Reports, Studies, and Surveys* (a listing by Find/SVP of more than 11,000 studies conducted by leading research firms)
7. Compustat, Compact Disclosure, CD/International, and Hoover's online corporate directory (computerized operating and financial information on thousands of publicly held corporations)
8. Shareholders meeting notices in SEC Form 14-A (proxy notices)

Economic Information

1. Regional statistics and local forecasts from large banks
2. *Business Cycle Development* (Department of Commerce)
3. Chase Econometric Associates' publications
4. U.S. Census Bureau publications on population, transportation, and housing
5. *Current Business Reports* (U.S. Department of Commerce)
6. *Economic Indicators* (U.S. Joint Economic Committee)
7. *Economic Report of the President to Congress*
8. *Long-Term Economic Growth* (U.S. Department of Commerce)
9. *Monthly Labor Review* (U.S. Department of Labor)
10. *Monthly Bulletin of Statistics* (United Nations)
11. *Statistical Abstract of the United States* (U.S. Department of Commerce)
12. *Statistical Yearbook* (United Nations)
13. *Survey of Current Business* (U.S. Department of Commerce)
14. *U.S. Industrial Outlook* (U.S. Department of Defense)
15. *World Trade Annual* (United Nations)
16. *Overseas Business Reports* (by country, published by the U.S. Department of Commerce)

Industry Information

1. Analyses of companies and industries by investment brokerage firms
2. *Bloomberg Businessweek* (provides weekly economic and business information, as well as quarterly profit and sales rankings of corporations)
3. *Fortune* (each April publishes listings of financial information on corporations within certain industries)

4. *Industry Survey* (published quarterly by Standard & Poor's)

5. *Industry Week* (late March/early April issue provides information on 14 industry groups)

6. *Forbes* (mid-January issue provides performance data on firms in various industries)

7. *Inc.* (May and December issues give information on fast-growing entrepreneurial companies)

Directory and Index Information on Companies and Industries

1. *Business Periodical Index* (on computers in many libraries)

2. *Directory of National Trade Associations*

3. *Encyclopedia of Associations*

4. Funk and Scott's *Index of Corporations and Industries*

5. Thomas's *Register of American Manufacturers*

6. *The Wall Street Journal Index*

Ratio Analysis Information

1. *Almanac of Business and Industrial Financial Ratios* (Prentice Hall)

2. *Annual Statement Studies* (Risk Management Associates; also Robert Morris Associates)

3. *Dun's Review* (Dun & Bradstreet; published annually in September–December issues)

4. *Industry Norms and Key Business Ratios* (Dun & Bradstreet)

Online Information

1. *Hoover's Online*—financial statements and profiles of public companies (www.hoovers.com)

2. U.S. Securities and Exchange Commission—official filings of public companies in the EDGAR database (www.sec.gov)

3. Fortune 500—statistics for largest U.S. corporations (www.fortune.com)

4. Dun & Bradstreet's Online—short reports on 10 million public and private U.S. companies (smallbusiness.dnb.com)

5. Competitive Intelligence Guide—information on company resources (www.fuld.com)

6. Society of Competitive Intelligence Professionals (www.scip.org)

7. *The Economist*—provides international information and surveys (www.economist.com)

8. *CIA World Fact Book*—international information by country (http://www.cia.gov)

9. Bloomberg—information on interest rates, stock prices, currency conversion rates, and other general financial information (www.bloomberg.com)

10. CEOExpress—links to many valuable sources of business information (www.ceoexpress.com)

11. *The Wall Street Journal*—business news (www.wsj.com)

12. Forbes—America's largest private companies (http://www.forbes.com/lists/)

13. CorporateInformation.com—subscription service for company profiles (www.corporateinformation.com)

14. Kompass International—industry information (www.kompass.com)

15. CorpTech—database of technology companies (www.corptech.com)

16. ADNet—information technology industry (www.companyfinders.com)

17. CNN company research—provides company information (http://money.cnn.com/news/)

18. Paywatch—database of executive compensation (http://www.aflcio.org/corporatewatch/paywatch/)

19. Global Edge Global Resources—international resources (http://globaledge.msu.edu/resourceDesk/)

20. Google Finance—data on North American stocks (http://www.google.com/finance)

21. World Federation of Exchanges—international stock exchanges (www.world-exchanges.org/)

22. SEC International Registry—data on international corporations (http://www.sec.gov/divisions/corpfin/internatl/companies.shtml)

23. Yahoo Finance—data on North American companies (http://finance.yahoo.com)

Suggested Case Analysis Methodology Using the Strategic Audit

First Reading of the Case

- Develop a general overview of the company and its external environment.
- Begin a list of the possible strategic factors facing the company at this time.
- List the research information you may need on the economy, industry, and competitors.

Over the past six years, increases in yearly revenues have consistently reached 12%. Byte Products Inc., headquartered in the U.S. Midwest, is regarded as one of the largest-volume suppliers of specialized components and is easily the industry leader.

Second Reading of the Case

- Read the case a second time, using the strategic audit as a framework for in-depth analysis. (See **Appendix 1.A** on pages 64–71.) You may want to make a copy of the strategic audit worksheet (**Figure 13–1**) to use to keep track of your comments as you read the case.
- The questions in the strategic audit parallel the strategic decision-making process shown in **Figure 1–5** (pages 58–59).
- The audit provides you with a conceptual framework to examine the company's mission, objectives, strategies, and policies, as well as problems, symptoms, facts, opinions, and issues.
- Perform a financial analysis of the company, using ratio analysis (see **Table 13–1**), and do the calculations necessary to convert key parts of the financial statements to a common-size basis.

Research

- Each case has a decision date indicating when the case actually took place. Your research should be based on the time period for the case.
- See **Appendix 13.A** for resources for case research. Your research should include information about the environment at the time of the case. Find average industry ratios. You may also want to obtain further information regarding competitors and the company itself (10-K forms and annual reports). This information should help you conduct an industry analysis. *Check with your instructor to see what kind of outside research is appropriate for your assignment.*
- Don't try to learn what actually happened to the company discussed in the case. What management actually decided may not be the best solution. It will certainly bias your analysis and will probably cause your recommendation to lack proper justification.

- Analyze the natural and societal environments to see what general trends are likely to affect the industry(s) in which the company is operating.
- Conduct an industry analysis using Porter's competitive forces from **Chapter 4**. Develop an Industry Matrix (**Table 4–4** on page 149).
- Generate 8 to 10 external factors. These should be the *most important* opportunities and threats facing the company at the time of the case.
- Develop an EFAS Table, as shown in **Table 4–5** (page 157), for your list of external strategic factors.
- **Suggestion:** Rank the 8 to 10 factors from most to least important. Start by grouping the three top factors and then the three bottom factors.

Internal Organizational Analysis: IFAS

- Generate 8 to 10 internal factors. These should be the *most important* strengths and weaknesses of the company at the time of the case.
- Develop an IFAS Table, as shown in **Table 5–2** (page 193), for your list of internal strategic factors.
- **Suggestion:** Rank the 8 to 10 factors from most to least important. Start by grouping the three top factors and then the three bottom factors.
- Review the student-written audit of the Maytag case in **Appendix 13.C** for an example.
- Write Parts I to IV of the strategic audit. Remember to include the factors from your EFAS and IFAS Tables in your audit.

Strategic Factor Analysis Summary: SFAS

- Condense the list of factors from the 16 to 20 identified in your EFAS and IFAS Tables to only the 8 to 10 most important factors.
- Select the most important EFAS and IFAS factors. Recalculate the weights of each. The weights still need to add to 1.0.
- This is a good time to reexamine what you wrote earlier in Parts I to IV. You may want to add to or delete some of what you wrote. Ensure that each one of the strategic factors you have included in your SFAS Matrix is discussed in the appropriate place in Parts I to IV. Part V of the audit is *not* the place to mention a strategic factor for the first time.
- Write Part V of your strategic audit.
- This is the place to suggest a revised mission statement and a better set of objectives for the company. The SWOT categorization coupled with revised mission and objectives for the company set the stage for the generation of strategic alternatives.

A. Alternatives

- Develop two to three mutually exclusive strategic alternatives. If appropriate to the case you are analyzing, you might propose one alternative for growth, one for stability, and one for retrenchment.
- Construct a corporate scenario for each alternative. Use the data from your outside research to project general societal trends (GDP, inflation, etc.) and industry trends. Use these as the basis of your assumptions to write pro forma financial statements (particularly income statements) for each strategic alternative for the next five years.
- List pros and cons for each alternative based on your scenarios.

B. Recommendation

- Specify which one of your alternative strategies you recommend. Justify your choice in terms of dealing with the strategic factors you listed in Part V of the strategic audit.
- Develop policies to help implement your strategies.

Implementation

- Develop programs to implement your recommended strategy.

- Specify who is to be responsible for implementing each program and how long each program will take to complete.

- Refer to the pro forma financial statements you developed earlier for your recommended strategy. Use common-size historical income statements as the basis for the pro forma statement. Do the numbers still make sense? If not, this may be a good time to rethink the budget numbers to reflect your recommended programs.

Evaluation and Control

- Specify the type of evaluation and controls you need to ensure that your recommendation is carried out successfully. Specify who is responsible for monitoring these controls.

- Indicate whether sufficient information is available to monitor how the strategy is being implemented. If not, suggest a change to the information system.

Final Draft of Your Strategic Audit

- Check to ensure that your audit is within the page limits set out by your professor. You may need to cut some parts and expand others.

- Make sure your recommendation clearly deals with the strategic factors.

- **Attach your EFAS and IFAS Tables, and SFAS Matrix,** plus your ratio analysis and pro forma statements. Label them as numbered exhibits and refer to each of them within the body of the audit.

- Proof your work for errors. If on a computer, use a spell checker.

SPECIAL NOTE: Depending on your assignment, it is relatively easy to use the strategic audit you have just developed to write a written case analysis in essay form or to make an oral presentation. The strategic audit is just a detailed case analysis in an outline form and can be used as the basic framework for any sort of case analysis and presentation.

Example of Student-Written Strategic Audit

(For the 1993 Maytag Corporation Case)

I. Current Situation

A. Current Performance

Poor financials, high debt load, first losses since 1920s, price/earnings ratio negative.

- First loss since 1920s.
- Laid off 4500 employees at Magic Chef.
- Hoover Europe still showing losses.

B. Strategic Posture

1. **Mission**
   - Developed in 1989 for the Maytag Company: "To provide our customers with products of unsurpassed performance that last longer, need fewer repairs, and are produced at the lowest possible cost."
   - Updated in 1991: "Our collective mission is world class quality." Expands Maytag's belief in product quality to all aspects of operations.

2. **Objectives**
   - "To be the profitability leader in the industry for every product line Maytag manufactures." Selected profitability rather than market share.
   - "To be number one in total customer satisfaction." Doesn't say how to measure satisfaction.
   - "To grow the North American appliance business and become the third largest-appliance manufacturer (in unit sales) in North America."
   - To increase profitable market share growth in the North American appliance and floor care business, 6.5% return on sales, 10% return on assets, 20% return on equity, beat competition in satisfying customers, dealer, builder, and endorser, and move into third place in total units shipped per year. Nicely quantified objectives.

3. **Strategies**
   - Global growth through acquisition, and alliance with Bosch-Siemens.
   - Differentiate brand names for competitive advantage.
   - Create synergy between companies, product improvement, investment in plant and equipment.

4. **Policies**
   - Cost reduction is secondary to high quality.
   - Promotion from within.
   - Slow but sure R&D: Maytag slow to respond to changes in market.

II. Strategic Managers

A. Board of Directors

1. Fourteen members—eleven are outsiders.
2. Well-respected Americans, most on board since 1986 or earlier.
3. No international or marketing backgrounds.
4. Time for a change?

B. Top Management

1. Top management promoted from within Maytag Company. Too inbred?
2. Very experienced in the industry.
3. Responsible for current situation.
4. May be too parochial for global industry. May need new blood.

III. External Environment (EFAS Table; see Exhibit 1)

A. Natural Environment

1. Growing water scarcity
2. Energy availability a growing problem

B. Societal Environment

1. **Economic**
   a. Unstable economy but recession ending, consumer confidence growing—could increase spending for big ticket items like houses, cars, and appliances. **(O)**
   b. Individual economies becoming interconnected into a world economy. **(O)**
2. **Technological**
   a. Fuzzy logic technology being applied to sense and measure activities. **(O)**
   b. Computers and information technology increasingly important. **(O)**
3. **Political–Legal**
   a. NAFTA, European Union, other regional trade pacts opening doors to markets in Europe, Asia, and Latin America that offer enormous potential. **(O)**
   b. Breakdown of communism means less chance of world war. **(O)**
   c. Environmentalism being reflected in laws on pollution and energy usage. **(T)**
4. **Sociocultural**
   a. Developing nations desire goods seen on TV. **(O)**
   b. Middle-aged baby boomers want attractive, high-quality products, like BMWs and Maytag. **(O)**
   c. Dual-career couples increases need for labor-saving appliances, second cars, and day care. **(O)**
   d. Divorce and career mobility means need for more houses and goods to fill them. **(O)**

C. Task Environment

1. North American market mature and extremely competitive—vigilant consumers demand high quality with low price in safe, environmentally sound products. **(T)**

2. Industry going global as North American and European firms expand internationally. **(T)**

3. European design popular and consumer desire for technologically advanced appliances. **(O)**

4. **Rivalry High**. Whirlpool, Electrolux, GE have enormous resources and developing global presence. **(T)**

5. **Buyers' Power Low**. Technology and materials can be sourced worldwide. **(O)**

6. **Power of Other Stakeholders Medium**. Quality, safety, environmental regulations increasing. **(T)**

7. **Distributors' Power High**. Super retailers more important: mom and pop dealers less. **(T)**

8. **Threat of Substitutes Low**. **(O)**

9. **Entry Barriers High**. New entrants unlikely except for large international firms. **(T)**

IV. Internal Environment (IFAS Table; see Exhibit 2)

A. Corporate Structure

1. Divisional structure: appliance manufacturing and vending machines. Floor care managed separately. **(S)**

2. Centralized major decisions by Newton corporate staff, with a time line of about three years. **(S)**

B. Corporate Culture

1. Quality key ingredient—commitment to quality shared by executives and workers. **(S)**

2. Much of corporate culture is based on founder F. L. Maytag's personal philosophy, including concern for quality, employees, local community, innovation, and performance. **(S)**

3. Acquired companies, except for European, seem to accept dominance of Maytag culture. **(S)**

C. Corporate Resources

1. **Marketing**
   a. Maytag brand lonely repairman advertising successful but dated. **(W)**
   b. Efforts focus on distribution—combining three sales forces into two, concentrating on major retailers. (Cost $95 million for this restructuring.) **(S)**
   c. Hoover's well-publicized marketing fiasco involving airline tickets. **(W)**

2. **Finance** (see **Exhibits 4 and 5**)
   a. Revenues are up slightly, operating income is down significantly. **(W)**
   b. Some key ratios are troubling, such as a 57% debt/asset ratio, 132% long-term debt/equity ratio. No room for more debt to grow company. **(W)**
   c. Net income is 400% less than 1988, based on common-size income statements. **(W)**

3. **R&D**
   a. Process-oriented with focus on manufacturing process and durability. **(S)**
   b. Maytag becoming a technology follower, taking too long to get product innovations to market (competitors put out more in last six months than prior two years combined), lagging in fuzzy logic and other technological areas. **(W)**

4. **Operations**
   a. Maytag's core competence. Continual improvement process kept it dominant in the U.S. market for many years. **(S)**
   b. Plants aging and may be losing competitiveness as rivals upgrade facilities. Quality no longer distinctive competence? **(W)**

5. **Human Resources**
   a. Traditionally very good relations with unions and employees. **(S)**
   b. Labor relations increasingly strained, with two salary raise delays, and layoffs of 4500 employees at Magic Chef. **(W)**
   c. Unions express concern at new, more distant tone from Maytag Corporation. **(W)**

6. **Information Systems**
   a. Not mentioned in case. Hoover fiasco in Europe suggests information systems need significant upgrading. **(W)**
   b. Critical area where Maytag may be unwilling or unable to commit resources needed to stay competitive. **(W)**

V. Analysis of Strategic Factors

A. Situational Analysis (SWOT) (SFAS Matrix; see Exhibit 3)

1. **Strengths**
   a. Quality Maytag culture.
   b. Maytag well-known and respected brand.
   c. Hoover's international orientation.
   d. Core competencies in process R&D and manufacturing.

2. **Weaknesses**
   a. Lacks financial resources of competitors.
   b. Poor global positioning. Hoover weak on European continent.
   c. Product R&D and customer service innovation are areas of serious weakness.
   d. Dependent on small dealers.
   e. Marketing needs improvement.

3. **Opportunities**
   a. Economic integration of European community.
   b. Demographics favor quality.
   c. Trend to superstores.

4. **Threats**
   a. Trend to superstores.
   b. Aggressive rivals—Whirlpool and Electrolux.
   c. Japanese appliance companies—new entrants?

B. Review of Current Mission and Objectives

1. Current mission appears appropriate.
2. Some of the objectives are really goals and need to be quantified and given time horizons.

VI. Strategic Alternatives and Recommended Strategy

A. Strategic Alternatives

1. *Growth through Concentric Diversification*: Acquire a company in a related industry such as commercial appliances.
   a. *[Pros]:* Product/market synergy created by acquisition of related company.
   b. *[Cons]:* Maytag does not have the financial resources to play this game.
2. *Pause Strategy*: Consolidate various acquisitions to find economies and to encourage innovation among the business units.
   a. *[Pros]:* Maytag needs to get its financial house in order and get administrative control over its recent acquisitions.
   b. *[Cons]:* Unless it can grow through a stronger alliance with Bosch-Siemens or some other backer, Maytag is a prime candidate for takeover because of its poor financial performance in recent years, and it is suffering from the initial reduction in efficiency inherent in acquisition strategy.
3. *Retrenchment*: Sell Hoover's foreign major home appliance businesses (Australia and UK) to emphasize increasing market share in North America.
   a. *[Pros]:* Divesting Hoover improves bottom line and enables Maytag Corp. to focus on North America while Whirlpool, Electrolux, and GE are battling elsewhere.
   b. *[Cons]:* Maytag may be giving up its only opportunity to become a player in the coming global appliance industry.

B. Recommended Strategy

1. Recommend pause strategy, at least for a year, so Maytag can get a grip on its European operation and consolidate its companies in a more synergistic way.
2. Maytag quality must be maintained, and continued shortage of operating capital will take its toll, so investment must be made in R&D.
3. Maytag may be able to make the Hoover UK investment work better since the recession is ending and the EU countries are closer to integrating than ever before.
4. Because it is only an average competitor, Maytag needs the Hoover link to Europe to provide a jumping off place for negotiations with Bosch-Siemens that could strengthen their alliance.

VII. Implementation

A. The only way to increase profitability in North America is to further involve Maytag with the superstore retailers; sure to anger the independent dealers, but necessary for Maytag to compete.

B. Board members with more global business experience should be recruited, with an eye toward the future, especially with expertise in Asia and Latin America.

C. R&D needs to be improved, as does marketing, to get new products online quickly.

VIII. Evaluation and Control

A. MIS needs to be developed for speedier evaluation and control. While the question of control vs. autonomy is "under review," another Hoover fiasco may be brewing.

B. The acquired companies do not all share the Midwestern work ethic or the Maytag Corporation culture, and Maytag's managers must inculcate these values into the employees of all acquired companies.

C. Systems should be developed to decide if the size and location of Maytag manufacturing plants is still correct and to plan for the future. Industry analysis indicates that smaller automated plants may be more efficient now than in the past.

EXHIBIT 1   EFAS Table for Maytag Corporation 1993

External Factors	Weight	Rating	Weighted Score	Comments
1	2	3	4	5
Opportunities				
▪ Economic integration of European Community	.20	4.1	.82	Acquisition of Hoover
▪ Demographics favor quality appliances	.10	5.0	.50	Maytag quality
▪ Economic development of Asia	.05	1.0	.05	Low Maytag presence
▪ Opening of Eastern Europe	.05	2.0	.10	Will take time
▪ Trend to "Super Stores"	.10	1.8	.18	Maytag weak in this channel
Threats				
▪ Increasing government regulations	.10	4.3	.43	Well positioned
▪ Strong U.S. competition	.10	4.0	.40	Well positioned
▪ Whirlpool and Electrolux strong globally	.15	3.0	.45	Hoover weak globally
▪ New product advances	.05	1.2	.06	Questionable
▪ Japanese appliance companies	.10	1.6	.16	Only Asian presence in Australia
Total Scores	1.00		3.15	

EXHIBIT 2 IFAS Table for Maytag Corporation 1993

Internal Factors	Weight	Rating	Weighted Score	Comments
	1	2	3	4	5
Strengths				
▪ Quality Maytag culture	.15	5.0	.75	Quality key to success
▪ Experienced top management	.05	4.2	.21	Know appliances
▪ Vertical integration	.10	3.9	.39	Dedicated factories
▪ Employer relations	.05	3.0	.15	Good, but deteriorating
▪ Hoover's international orientation	.15	2.8	.42	Hoover name in cleaners
Weaknesses				
▪ Process-oriented R&D	.05	2.2	.11	Slow on new products
▪ Distribution channels	.05	2.0	.10	Superstores replacing small dealers
▪ Financial position	.15	2.0	.30	High debt load
▪ Global positioning	.20	2.1	.42	Hoover weak outside the United Kingdom and Australia
▪ Manufacturing facilities	.05	4.0	.20	Investing now
Total scores	1.00		3.05	

EXHIBIT 3 SFAS Matrix for Maytag Corporation 1993

Strategic Factors (Select the most important opportunities/threats from EFAS, Table 4–5 and the most important strengths and weaknesses from IFAS, Table 5–2)	Weight	Rating	Weighted Score	Duration SHORT	INTERMEDIATE	LONG	Comments
	2	3	4			5	6
▪ S1 Quality Maytag culture (S)	.10	5.0	.50			X	Quality key to success
▪ S5 Hoover's international orientation (S)	.10	2.8	.28	X	X		Name recognition
▪ W3 Financial position (W)	.10	2.0	.20	X	X		High debt
▪ W4 Global positioning (W)	.15	2.2	.33		X	X	Only in N.A., U.K., and Australia
▪ O1 Economic integration of European Community (O)	.10	4.1	.41			X	Acquisition of Hoover
▪ O2 Demographics favor quality (O)	.10	5.0	.50		X		Maytag quality
▪ O5 Trend to super stores (O + T)	.10	1.8	.18	X			Weak in this channel
▪ T3 Whirlpool and Electrolux (T)	.15	3.0	.45	X			Dominate industry
▪ T5 Japanese appliance companies (T)	.10	1.6	.16			X	Asian presence
Total Scores	1.00		3.01				

EXHIBIT 4		1990	1991	1992	1993
Ratio Analysis for Maytag Corporation 1993	**1. LIQUIDITY RATIOS**				
	Current	2.1	1.9	1.8	1.6
	Quick	1.1	1.0	1.1	1.0
	2. LEVERAGE RATIOS				
	Debt to Total Assets	61%	60%	76%	57%
	Debt to Equity	155%	151%	317%	254%
	3. ACTIVITY RATIOS				
	Inventory turnover—sales	5.7	6.1	7.6	6.9
	Inventory Turnover—cost of sales	4.3	4.6	5.8	6.5
	Avg. Collection Period—days	57	55	56	0
	Fixed Asset Turnover	3.9	3.6	3.6	3.6
	Total Assets Turnover	1.2	1.2	1.2	1.1
	4. PROFITABILITY RATIOS				
	Gross Profit Margin	24%	24%	23%	5%
	Net Operating Margin	8%	6%	3%	5%
	Profit Margin on Sales	3%	3%	–0%	2%
	Return on Total Assets	4%	3%	–0%	2%
	Return on Equity	10%	8%	–1%	8%

EXHIBIT 5		1992	1991	1990
Common Size Income Statements for Maytag Corporation 1993	Net sales	100.0%	100.0%	100.0%
	Cost of sales	76.92	75.88	75.50
	Gross profit	23.08	24.12	24.46
	Selling, general/admin. Expenses	17.37	17.67	16.90
	Reorganization expenses	.031	—	—
	Operating income	.026	.064	.075
	Interest expense	(.025)	(.025)	(0.26)
	Other—net	.001	.002	.009
	Income before accounting changes	.002	.042	.052
	Income taxes	.005	.015	.020
	Income before accounting changes	(.002)	.026	.032
	Effect of accounting changes for postretirement benefits other than pensions and income taxes	(.101)	—	—
	Total operating costs and expenses	74.9	76.0	76.3
	Net income	**(.104)**	**.026**	**.032**

EXHIBIT 6	Implementation, Evaluation, and Control Plan for Maytag Corporation 1993					
Strategic Factor	**Action Plan**	**Priority System (1–5)**	**Who Will Implement**	**Who Will Review**	**How Often Review**	**Criteria Used**
Quality Maytag culture	Build quality in acquired units	1	Heads of acquired units	Manufacturing VP	Quarterly	Number defects & customer satisfaction
Hoover's international orientation	Identify ways to expand sales	2	Head of Hoover	Marketing VP	Quarterly	Feasible alternatives generated
Financial position	Pay down debt	1	CFO	CEO	Monthly	Leverage ratios
Global positioning	Find strategic alliance partners	2	VP of Business Development	COO	Quarterly	Feasible alternatives generated
EU economic integration	Grow sales throughout EU	3	Hoover UK Head	Marketing VP	Annually	Sales growth
Demographics favor quality	Simplify controls	3	Manufacturing VP	COO	Annually	Market research user satisfaction
Trend to super stores	Market through Sears	1	Marketing VP	CEO	Monthly	Sales growth
Whirlpool & Electrolux	Monitor competitor performance	1	Competition committee	COO	Quarterly	Competitor sales & new products
Japanese appliance companies	Monitor expansion	4	Head of Hoover Australia	Competition committee	Semi-annually	Sales growth outside Japan

Cases in

Strategic
Management

cases in
strategic management

CONTENTS

alphabetical listing of cases

CASE **1**

The Recalcitrant Director at Byte Products, Inc.

CORPORATE LEGALITY VERSUS CORPORATE RESPONSIBILITY

Dan R. Dalton, Richard A. Cosier, and Cathy A. Enz

BYTE PRODUCTS, INC., IS PRIMARILY INVOLVED IN THE PRODUCTION OF ELECTRONIC components that are used in personal computers. Although such components might be found in a few computers in home use, Byte products are found most frequently in computers used for sophisticated business and engineering applications. Annual sales of these products have been steadily increasing over the past several years; Byte Products, Inc., currently has total sales of approximately $265 million.

Over the past six years, increases in yearly revenues have consistently reached 12%. Byte Products, Inc., headquartered in the midwestern United States, is regarded as one of the largest-volume suppliers of specialized components and is easily the industry leader, with some 32% market share. Unfortunately for Byte, many new firms—domestic and foreign—have entered the industry. A dramatic surge in demand, high profitability, and the relative ease of a new firm's entry into the industry explain in part the increased number of competing firms.

Although Byte management—and presumably shareholders as well—is very pleased about the growth of its markets, it faces a major problem: Byte simply cannot meet the demand for these components. The company currently operates three manufacturing facilities in various locations throughout the United States. Each of these plants operates three production shifts (24 hours per day), seven days a week. This activity constitutes virtually all of the company's production capacity. Without an additional manufacturing plant, Byte simply cannot increase its output of components.

....

This case was prepared by Professors Dan R. Dalton and Richard A. Cosier of the Graduate School of Business at Indiana University and Cathy A. Enz of Cornell University. The names of the organization, individual, location, and/or financial information have been disguised to preserve the organization's desire for anonymity. This case was edited for the *SMBP*– 9th, 10th, 11th, 12th, 13th, 14th and 15th Editions. Reprint permission is solely granted to the publisher, Prentice Hall, for the book, *Strategic Management and Business Policy – 15th Edition* by copyright holders Dan R. Dalton, Richard A. Cosier, and Cathy A. Enz. Any other publication of this case (translation, any form of electronic or other media), or sale (any form of partnership) to another publisher will be in violation of copyright laws, unless the copyright holders have granted an additional written reprint permission.

James M. Elliott, Chief Executive Officer and Chairman of the Board, recognizes the gravity of the problem. If Byte Products cannot continue to manufacture components in sufficient numbers to meet the demand, buyers will go elsewhere. Worse yet is the possibility that any continued lack of supply will encourage others to enter the market. As a long-term solution to this problem, the board of directors unanimously authorized the construction of a new, state-of-the-art manufacturing facility in the southwestern United States. When the planned capacity of this plant is added to that of the three current plants, Byte should be able to meet demand for many years to come. Unfortunately, an estimated three years will be required to complete the plant and bring it online.

Jim Elliott believes very strongly that this three-year period is far too long and has insisted that there also be a shorter-range, stopgap solution while the plant is under construction. The instability of the market and the pressure to maintain leader status are two factors contributing to Elliott's insistence on a more immediate solution. Without such a move, Byte management believes it will lose market share and, again, attract competitors into the market.

Several Solutions

A number of suggestions for such a temporary measure were offered by various staff specialists but rejected by Elliott. For example, licensing Byte's product and process technology to other manufacturers in the short run to meet immediate demand was possible. This licensing authorization would be short term, or just until the new plant could come online. Top management, as well as the board, was uncomfortable with this solution for several reasons. They thought it unlikely that any manufacturer would shoulder the fixed costs of producing appropriate components for such a short term. Any manufacturer that would do so would charge a premium to recover its costs. This suggestion, obviously, would make Byte's own products available to its customers at an unacceptable price. Nor did passing any price increase to its customers seem sensible, for this too would almost certainly reduce Byte's market share as well as encourage further competition.

Overseas facilities and licensing also were considered but rejected. Before it became a publicly traded company, Byte's founders had decided that its manufacturing facilities would be domestic. Top management strongly felt that this strategy had served Byte well; moreover, Byte's majority stockholders (initial owners of the then privately held Byte) were not likely to endorse such a move. Beyond that, however, top management was reluctant to foreign license their goods—or make available by any means the technologies for others to produce Byte products—as they could not then properly control patents. Top management feared that foreign licensing would essentially give away costly proprietary information regarding the company's highly efficient means of product development. There also was the potential for initial low product quality—whether produced domestically or otherwise—especially for such a short-run operation. Any reduction in quality, however brief, would threaten Byte's share of this sensitive market.

The Solution!

One recommendation that has come to the attention of the Chief Executive Officer could help solve Byte's problem in the short run. Certain members of his staff have notified him that an abandoned plant currently is available in Plainville, a small town in the northeastern United States. Before its closing eight years earlier, this plant was used primarily for the manufacture of electronic components. As is, it could not possibly be used to produce Byte products, but it could be inexpensively refitted to do so in as few as three months. Moreover, this plant is available at a very attractive price. In fact, discreet inquiries by Elliott's staff indicate that this plant could probably be leased immediately from its present owners because the building has been vacant for some eight years.

All the news about this temporary plant proposal, however, is not nearly so positive. Elliott's staff concedes that this plant will never be efficient and its profitability will be low. In addition, the Plainville location is a poor one in terms of high labor costs (the area is highly unionized), warehousing expenses, and inadequate transportation links to Byte's major markets and suppliers. Plainville is simply not a candidate for a long-term solution. Still, in the short run, a temporary plant could help meet the demand and might forestall additional competition.

The staff is persuasive and notes that this option has several advantages: (1) there is no need for any licensing, foreign or domestic, (2) quality control remains firmly in the company's hands, and (3) an increase in the product price will be unnecessary. The temporary plant, then, would be used for three years or so until the new plant could be built. Then the temporary plant would be immediately closed.

CEO Elliott is convinced.

Taking the Plan to the Board

The quarterly meeting of the board of directors is set to commence at 2:00 p.m. Jim Elliott has been reviewing his notes and agenda for the meeting most of the morning. The issue of the temporary plant is clearly the most important agenda item. Reviewing his detailed presentation of this matter, including the associated financial analyses, has occupied much of his time for several days. All the available information underscores his contention that the temporary plant in Plainville is the only responsible solution to the demand problems. No other option offers the same low level of risk and ensures Byte's status as industry leader.

At the meeting, after the board has dispensed with a number of routine matters, Jim Elliott turns his attention to the temporary plant. In short order, he advises the 11-member board (himself, 3 additional inside members, and 7 outside members) of his proposal to obtain and refit the existing plant to ameliorate demand problems in the short run, authorizes the construction of the new plant (the completion of which is estimated to take some three years), and plans to switch capacity from the temporary plant to the new one when it is operational. He also briefly reviews additional details concerning the costs involved, advantages of this proposal versus domestic or foreign licensing, and so on.

All the board members except one are in favor of the proposal. In fact, they are most enthusiastic; the overwhelming majority agree that the temporary plant is an excellent—even inspired—stopgap measure. Ten of the eleven board members seem relieved because the board was most reluctant to endorse any of the other alternatives that had been mentioned.

The single dissenter—T. Kevin Williams, an outside director—is, however, steadfast in his objections. He will not, under any circumstances, endorse the notion of the temporary plant and states rather strongly that "I will not be party to this nonsense, not now, not ever."

T. Kevin Williams, the senior executive of a major nonprofit organization, is normally a reserved and really quite agreeable person. This sudden, uncharacteristic burst of emotion clearly startles the remaining board members into silence. The following excerpt captures the ensuing, essentially one-on-one conversation between Williams and Elliott:

Williams: How many workers do your people estimate will be employed in the temporary plant?

Elliott: Roughly 1200, possibly a few more.

Williams: I presume it would be fair, then, to say that, including spouses and children, something on the order of 4000 people will be attracted to the community.

Elliott: I certainly would not be surprised.

Williams: If I understand the situation correctly, this plant closed just over eight years ago, and that closing had a catastrophic effect on Plainville. Isn't it true that a large portion of the community was employed by this plant?

Elliott: Yes, it was far and away the majority employer.

Williams: And most of these people have left the community, presumably to find employment elsewhere?

Elliott: Definitely. There was a drastic decrease in the area's population.

Williams: Are you concerned, then, that our company must attract the 1200 employees to Plainville from other parts of New England?

Elliott: Not in the least. We are absolutely confident that we will attract 1200—even more, for that matter, virtually any number we need. That, in fact, is one of the chief advantages of this proposal. I would think that the community would be very pleased to have us there.

Williams: On the contrary, I would suspect that the community will rue the day we arrived. Beyond that, though, this plan is totally unworkable if we are candid. On the other hand, if we are less than candid, the proposal will work for us, but only at great cost to Plainville. In fact, quite frankly, the implications are appalling. Once again, I must enter my serious objections.

Elliott: I don't follow you.

Williams: The temporary plant would employ some 1200 people. Again, this means the infusion of over 4000 to the community and surrounding areas. Byte Products, however, intends to close this plant in three years or less. If Byte informs the community or the employees that the jobs are temporary, the proposal simply won't work. When the new people arrive in the community, there will be a need for more schools, instructors, utilities, housing, restaurants, and so forth. Obviously, if the banks and local government know that the plant is temporary, no funding will be made available for these projects and certainly no credit for the new employees to buy homes, appliances, automobiles, and so forth.

If, on the other hand, Byte Products does not tell the community of its "temporary" plans, the project can go on. But, in several years when the plant closes (and we here have agreed today that it will close), we will have created a ghost town. The tax base of the community will have been destroyed; property values will decrease precipitously; practically the whole town will be unemployed. This proposal will place Byte Products in an untenable position and in extreme jeopardy.

Elliott: Are you suggesting that this proposal jeopardizes us legally? If so, it should be noted that the legal department has reviewed this proposal in its entirety and has indicated no problem.

Williams: No! I don't think we are dealing with an issue of legality here. In fact, I don't doubt for a minute that this proposal is altogether legal. I do, however, resolutely believe that this proposal constitutes gross irresponsibility. I think this decision has captured most of my major concerns. These, along with a host of collateral problems associated with this project, lead me to strongly suggest that you and the balance of the board reconsider and not endorse this proposal. Byte Products must find another way.

The Dilemma

After a short recess, the board meeting reconvened. Presumably because of some discussion during the recess, several other board members indicated that they were no longer inclined to support the proposal. After a short period of rather heated discussion, the following exchange took place:

Elliott: It appears to me that any vote on this matter is likely to be very close. Given the gravity of our demand capacity problem, I must insist that the stockholders' equity be protected. We cannot wait three years; that is clearly out of the question. I still feel that licensing—domestic or foreign—is not in our long-term interests for any number of reasons, some of which have been discussed here. On the other hand, I do not want to take this project forward on the strength of a mixed vote. A vote of 6–5 or 7–4, for example, does not indicate that the board is remotely close to being of one mind. Mr. Williams, is there a compromise to be reached?

Williams: Respectfully, I have to say no. If we tell the truth—namely, the temporary nature of our operations—the proposal is simply not viable. If we are less than candid in this respect, we do grave damage to the community as well as to our image. It seems to me that we can only go one way or the other. I don't see a middle ground.

The Wallace Group

Laurence J. Stybel

FRANCES RAMPAR, PRESIDENT OF RAMPAR ASSOCIATES, DRUMMED HER FINGERS ON THE desk. Scattered before her were her notes. She had to put the pieces together in order to make an effective sales presentation to Harold Wallace.

Hal Wallace was the President of The Wallace Group. He had asked Rampar to conduct a series of interviews with some key Wallace Group employees, in preparation for a possible consulting assignment for Rampar Associates.

During the past three days, Rampar had been talking with some of these key people and had received background material about the company. The problem was not in finding the problem. The problem was that there were too many problems!

Background on The Wallace Group

The Wallace Group, Inc., is a diversified company dealing in the manufacture and development of technical products and systems (see **Exhibit 1**). The company currently consists of three operational groups and a corporate staff. The three groups include Electronics, Plastics, and Chemicals, each operating under the direction of a Group Vice President (see **Exhibits 2**, **3**, and **4**). The company generates $70 million in sales as a manufacturer of plastics, chemical products, and electronic components and systems. Principal sales are to large contractors in governmental and automotive markets. With respect to sales volume, Plastics and Chemicals are approximately equal in size, and both of them together equal the size of the Electronics Group.

Electronics offers competence in the areas of microelectronics, electromagnetic sensors, antennas, microwaves, and minicomputers. Presently, these skills are devoted primarily to the engineering and manufacture of countermeasure equipment for aircraft.

This includes radar detection systems that allow an aircraft crew to know that they are being tracked by radar units on the ground, on ships, or on other aircraft. Further, the company manufactures displays that provide the crew with a visual "fix" on where they are relative to the radar units that are tracking them.

EXHIBIT 1
An Excerpt from the
Annual Report

To the Shareholders:

This past year was one of definite accomplishment for The Wallace Group, although with some admitted soft spots. This is a period of consolidation, of strengthening our internal capacity for future growth and development. Presently, we are in the process of creating a strong management team to meet the challenges we will set for the future.

Despite our failure to achieve some objectives, we turned a profit of $3,521,000 before taxes, which was a growth over the previous year's earnings. And we have declared a dividend for the fifth consecutive year, albeit one that is less than the year before. However, the retention of earnings is imperative if we are to lay a firm foundation for future accomplishment.

Currently, The Wallace Group has achieved a level of stability. We have a firm foothold in our current markets, and we could elect to simply enact strong internal controls and maximize our profits. However, this would not be a growth strategy. Instead, we have chosen to adopt a more aggressive posture for the future, to reach out into new markets wherever possible and to institute the controls necessary to move forward in a planned and orderly fashion.

The Electronics Group performed well this past year and is engaged in two major programs under Defense Department contracts. These are developmental programs that provide us with the opportunity for ongoing sales upon testing of the final product. Both involve the creation of tactical display systems for aircraft being built by Lombard Aircraft for the Navy and the Air Force. Future potential sales from these efforts could amount to approximately $56 million over the next five years. Additionally, we are developing technical refinements to older, already installed systems under Army Department contracts.

In the future, we will continue to offer our technological competence in such tactical display systems and anticipate additional breakthroughs and success in meeting the demands of this market. However, we also believe that we have unique contributions to make to other markets, and to that end we are making the investments necessary to expand our opportunities.

Plastics also turned in a solid performance this past year and has continued to be a major supplier to Chrysler, Martin Tool, Foster Electric, and, of course, to our Electronics Group. The market for this group continues to expand, and we believe that additional investments in this group will allow us to seize a larger share of the future.

Chemicals' performance, admittedly, has not been as satisfactory as anticipated during the past year. However, we have been able to realize a small amount of profit from this operation and to halt what was a potentially dangerous decline in profits. We believe that this situation is only temporary and that infusions of capital for developing new technology, plus the streamlining of operations, has stabilized the situation. The next step will be to begin more aggressive marketing to capitalize on the group's basic strengths.

Overall, the outlook seems to be one of modest but profitable growth. The near term will be one of creating the technology and controls necessary for developing our market offerings and growing in a planned and purposeful manner. Our improvement efforts in the various company groups can be expected to take hold over the years with a positive effect on results.

We wish to express our appreciation to all those who participated in our efforts this past year.

Harold Wallace
Chairman and President

EXHIBIT 2
Organizational Chart: The Wallace Group (Electronics)

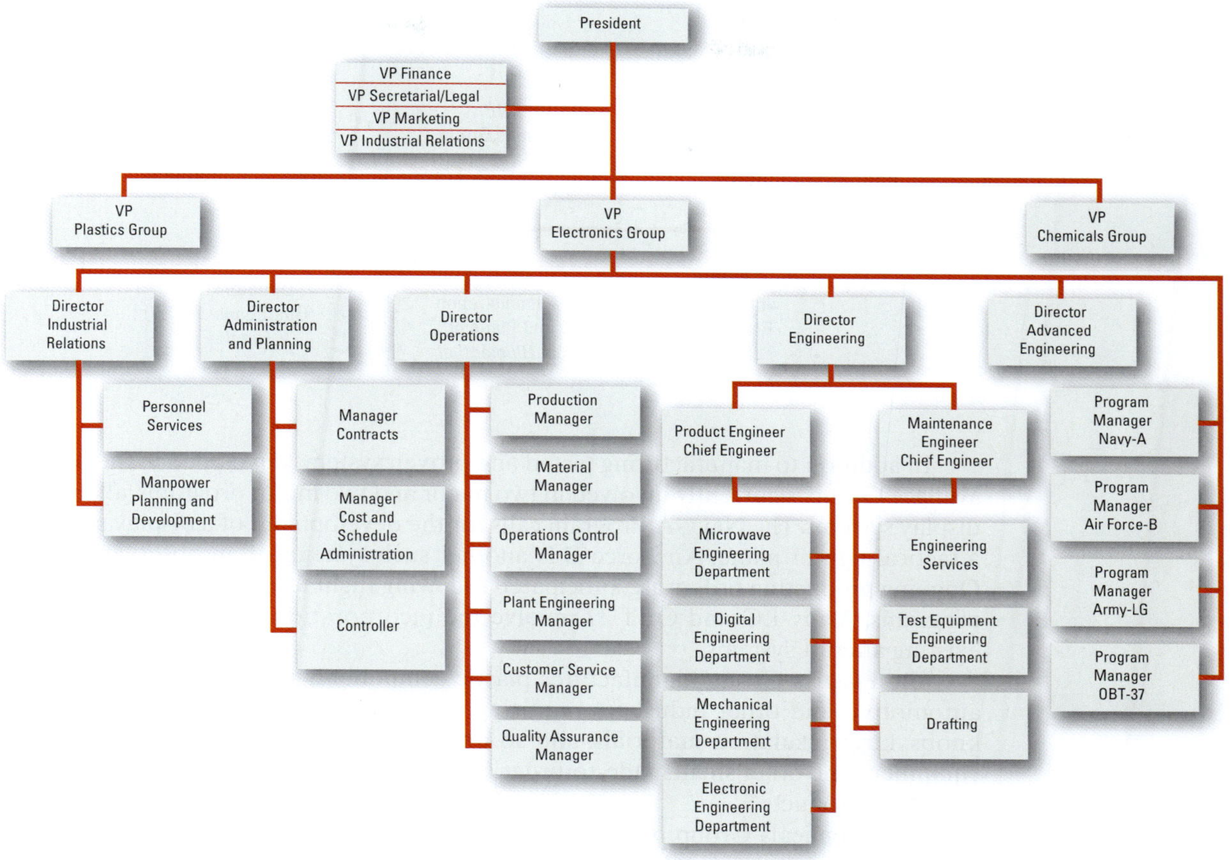

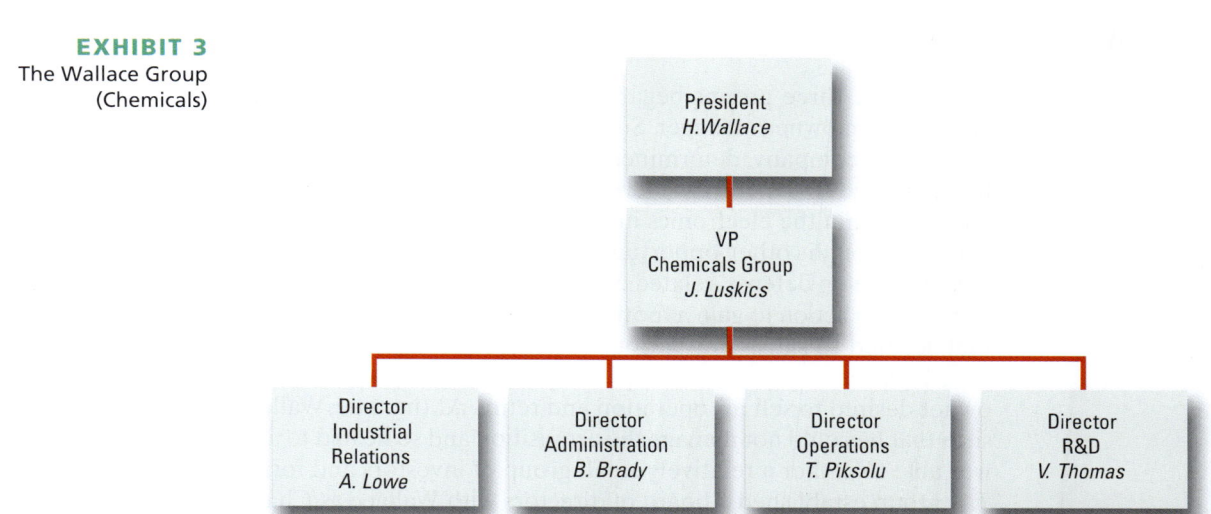

EXHIBIT 3
The Wallace Group
(Chemicals)

EXHIBIT 4
The Wallace Group
(Plastics)

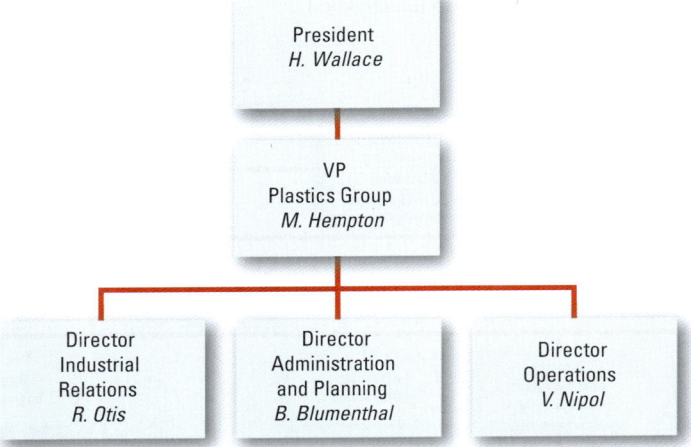

In addition to manufacturing tested and proven systems developed in the past, The Wallace Group is currently involved in two major and two minor programs, all involving display systems. The Navy-A Program calls for the development of a display system for a tactical fighter plane; Air Force-B is another such system for an observation plane. Ongoing production orders are anticipated following flight testing. The other two minor programs, Army-LG and OBT-37, involve the incorporation of new technology into existing aircraft systems.

The Plastics Group manufactures plastic components utilized by the electronics, automotive, and other industries requiring plastic products. These include switches, knobs, keys, insulation materials, and so on, used in the manufacture of electronic equipment and other small made-to-order components installed in automobiles, planes, and other products.

The Chemicals Group produces chemicals used in the development of plastics. It supplies bulk chemicals to the Plastics Group and other companies. These chemicals are then injected into molds or extruded to form a variety of finished products.

History of the Wallace Group

Each of the three groups began as a sole proprietorship under the direct operating control of an owner/manager. Several years ago, Harold Wallace, owner of the original electronics company, determined to undertake a program of diversification. Initially, he attempted to expand his market through product development and line extensions entirely within the electronics industry. However, because of initial problems, he drew back and sought other opportunities. Wallace's primary concern was his almost total dependence on defense-related contracts. He had felt for some time that he should take some strong action to gain a foothold in the private markets. The first major opportunity that seemed to satisfy his various requirements was the acquisition of a former supplier, a plastics company whose primary market was not defense-related. The company's owner desired to sell his operation and retire. At the time, Wallace's debt structure was such that he could not manage the acquisition and so he had to attract equity capital. He was able to gather a relatively small group of investors and form a closed corporation. The group established a board of directors with Wallace as Chairman and President of the new corporate entity.

With respect to operations, little changed. Wallace continued direct operational control over the Electronics Group. As holder of 60% of the stock, he maintained effective control over policy and operations. However, because of his personal interests, the Plastics Group, now under the direction of a newly hired Vice President, Martin Hempton, was left mainly to its own devices except for yearly progress reviews by the President. All Wallace asked at the time was that the Plastics Group continue its profitable operation, which it did.

Several years ago, Wallace and the board decided to diversify further because two-thirds of their business was still defense-dependent. They learned that one of the major suppliers of the Plastics Group, a chemical company, was on the verge of bankruptcy. The company's owner, Jerome Luskics, agreed to sell. However, this acquisition required a public stock offering, with most of the funds going to pay off debts incurred by the three groups, especially the Chemicals Group. The net result was that Wallace now holds 45% of The Wallace Group and Jerome Luskics 5%, with the remainder distributed among the public.

Organization and Personnel

Presently, Harold Wallace serves as Chairman and President of The Wallace Group. The Electronics Group had been run by LeRoy Tuscher, who just resigned as Vice President. Hempton continued as Vice President of Plastics, and Luskics served as Vice President of the Chemicals Group.

Reflecting the requirements of a corporate perspective and approach, a corporate staff has grown up, consisting of Vice Presidents for Finance, Secretarial/Legal, Marketing, and Industrial Relations. This staff has assumed many functions formerly associated with the group offices.

Because these positions are recent additions, many of the job accountabilities are still being defined. Problems have arisen over the responsibilities and relationships between corporate and group positions. President Wallace has settled most of the disputes himself because of the inability of the various parties to resolve differences amongst themselves.

Current Trends

Presently, there is a mood of lethargy and drift within The Wallace Group. Most managers feel that each of the three groups functions as an independent company. And, with respect to group performance, not much change or progress has been made in recent years. Electronics and Plastics are still stable and profitable, but both lack growth in markets and profits. The infusion of capital breathed new life and hope into the Chemicals operation but did not solve most of the old problems and failings that had caused its initial decline. For all these reasons, Wallace decided that strong action was necessary. His greatest disappointment was with the Electronics Group, in which he had placed high hopes for future development. Thus he acted by requesting and getting the Electronics Group Vice President's resignation. Hired from a computer company to replace LeRoy Tuscher, Jason Matthews joined The Wallace Group a week ago.

As of last week, Wallace's annual net sales were $70 million. By group, they were:

Electronics	$35,000,000
Plastics	$20,000,000
Chemicals	$15,000,000

On a consolidated basis, the financial highlights of the past two years are as follows:

	Last Year	Two Years Ago
Net sales	$70,434,000	$69,950,000
Income (pre-tax)	3,521,000	3,497,500
Income (after-tax)	2,760,500	1,748,750
Working capital	16,200,000	16,088,500
Shareholders' equity	39,000,000	38,647,000
Total assets	59,869,000	59,457,000
Long-term debt	4,350,000	3,500,000
Per Share of Common Stock		
Net income	$.37	$.36
Cash dividends paid	.15	.25

Of the net income, approximately 70% came from Electronics, 25% from Plastics, and 5% from Chemicals.

The Problem Confronting Frances Rampar

As Rampar finished reviewing her notes (see **Exhibits 5–11**), she kept reflecting on what Hal Wallace had told her:

> Don't give me a laundry list of problems, Fran. Anyone can do that. I want a set of priorities I should focus on during the next year. I want a clear action plan from you. And I want to know how much this plan is going to cost me!

Fran Rampar again drummed her fingers on the desk.

EXHIBIT 5
Selected Portions of a Transcribed Interview with H. Wallace

Rampar: What is your greatest problem right now?

Wallace: That's why I called you in! Engineers are a high-strung, temperamental lot. Always complaining. It's hard to take them seriously.

Last month we had an annual stockholders' meeting. We have an Employee Stock Option Plan, and many of our long-term employees attended the meeting. One of my managers—and I won't mention any names—introduced a resolution calling for the resignation of the President—me!

The vote was defeated. But, of course, I own 45% of the stock!

Now I realize that there could be no serious attempt to get rid of me. Those who voted for the resolution were making a dramatic effort to show me how upset they are with the way things are going.

I could fire those employees who voted against me. I was surprised by how many did. Some of my key people were in that group. Perhaps I ought to stop and listen to what they are saying.

Businesswise, I think we're okay. Not great, but okay. Last year we turned in a profit of $3.5 million before taxes, which was a growth over previous years' earnings. We declared a dividend for the fifth consecutive year.

We're currently working on the creation of a tactical display system for aircraft being built by Lombard Aircraft for the Navy and the Air Force. If Lombard gets the contract to produce the prototype, future sales could amount to $56 million over the next five years.

Why are they complaining?

Rampar: You must have thoughts on the matter.

Wallace: I think the issue revolves around how we manage people. It's a personnel problem. You were highly recommended as someone with expertise in high-technology human resource management.

I have some ideas on what is the problem. But I'd like you to do an independent investigation and give me your findings. Give me a plan of action.

Don't give me a laundry list of problems, Fran. Anyone can do that. I want a set of priorities I should focus on during the next year. I want a clear action plan from you. And I want to know how much this plan is going to cost me!

Other than that, I'll leave you alone and let you talk to anyone in the company you want.

EXHIBIT 6
Selected Portions
of a Transcribed
Interview with
Frank Campbell,
Vice President of
Industrial Relations

Rampar: What is your greatest problem right now?

Campbell: Trying to contain my enthusiasm over the fact that Wallace brought you in!

Morale is really poor here. Hal runs this place like a one-man operation, when it's grown too big for that. It took a palace revolt to finally get him to see the depths of the resentment. Whether he'll do anything about it, that's another matter.

Rampar: What would you like to see changed?

Campbell: Other than a new President? Rampar: Uh-huh.

Campbell: We badly need a management development program for our group. Because of our growth, we have been forced to promote technical people to management positions who have had no prior managerial experience. Mr. Tuscher agreed on the need for a program, but Hal Wallace vetoed the idea because developing such a program would be too expensive. I think it is too expensive *not* to move ahead on this.

Rampar: Anything else?

Campbell: The IEWU negotiations have been extremely tough this time around, due to the excessive demands they have been making. Union pay scales are already pushing up against our foreman salary levels, and foremen are being paid high in their salary ranges. This problem, coupled with union insistence on a no-layoff clause, is causing us fits. How can we keep all our workers when we have production equipment on order that will eliminate 20% of our assembly positions?

Rampar: Wow.

Campbell: We have been sued by a rejected candidate for a position on the basis of discrimination. She claimed our entrance qualifications are excessive because we require shorthand. There is some basis for this statement since most reports are given to secretaries in handwritten form or on audio cassettes. In fact, we have always required it and our executives want their secretaries to have skill in taking dictation. Not only is this case taking time, but I need to reconsider if any of our position entrance requirements, in fact, are excessive. I am sure we do not want another case like this one.

Rampar: That puts The Wallace Group in a vulnerable position, considering the amount of government work you do.

Campbell: We have a tremendous recruiting backlog, especially for engineering positions. Either our pay scales are too low, our job specs are too high, or we are using the wrong recruiting channels. Kane and Smith [Director of Engineering and Director of Advanced Systems] keep rejecting everyone we send down there as being unqualified.

Rampar: Gee.

Campbell: Being head of human resources around here is a tough job. We don't act. We react.

EXHIBIT 7
Selected Portions of a Transcribed Interview with Matthew Smith, Director of Advanced Systems

Rampar: What is your greatest problem right now?

Smith: Corporate brass keeps making demands on me and others that don't relate to the job we are trying to get done. They say that the information they need is to satisfy corporate planning and operations review requirements, but they don't seem to recognize how much time and effort is required to provide this information. Sometimes it seems like they are generating analyses, reports, and requests for data just to keep themselves busy. Someone should be evaluating how critical these corporate staff activities really are. To me and the Electronics Group, these activities are unnecessary.

An example is the Vice President, Marketing (L. Holt), who keeps asking us for supporting data so he can prepare a corporate marketing strategy. As you know, we prepare our own group marketing strategic plans annually, but using data and formats that are oriented to our needs, rather than Corporate's. This planning activity, which occurs at the same time as Corporate's, coupled with heavy workloads on current projects, makes us appear to Holt as though we are being unresponsive.

Somehow we need to integrate our marketing planning efforts between our group and Corporate. This is especially true if our group is to successfully grow in nondefense-oriented markets and products. We do need corporate help, but not arbitrary demands for information that divert us from putting together effective marketing strategies for our group.

I am getting too old to keep fighting these battles.

Rampar: This is a long-standing problem?

Smith: You bet! Our problems are fairly classic in the high-tech field. I've been at other companies and they're not much better. We spend so much time firefighting, we never really get organized. Everything is done on an ad hoc basis.

I'm still waiting for tomorrow.

EXHIBIT 8
Selected Portions of a Transcribed Interview with Ralph Kane, Director of Engineering

Rampar: What is your greatest problem right now?

Kane: Knowing you were coming, I wrote them down. They fall into four areas:

1. Our salary schedules are too low to attract good, experienced EEs. We have been told by our Vice President (Frank Campbell) that corporate policy is to hire new people below the salary grade midpoint. All qualified candidates are making more than that now and in some cases are making more than our grade maximums. I think our Project Engineer job is rated too low.

2. Chemicals Group asked for—and the former Electronics Vice President (Tuscher) agreed to—"lend" six of our best EEs to help solve problems it is having developing a new battery. That is great for the Chemicals Group, but meanwhile how do we solve the engineering problems that have cropped up in our Navy-A and OBT-37 programs?

3. As you know, Matt Smith (Director of Advanced Systems) is retiring in six months. I depend heavily on his group for technical expertise, and in some areas he depends heavily on some of my key engineers. I have lost some people to the Chemicals Group, and Matt has been trying to lend me some of his people to fill in. But he and his staff have been heavily involved in marketing planning and trying to identify or recruit a qualified successor long enough before his retirement to be able to train him or her. The result is that his people are up to their eyeballs in doing their own stuff and cannot continue to help me meet my needs.

4. IR has been preoccupied with union negotiations in the plant and has not had time to help me deal with this issue of management planning. Campbell is working on some kind of system that will help deal with this kind of problem and prevent them in the future. That's great, but I need help now—not when his "system" is ready.

EXHIBIT 9
Selected Portions
of a Transcribed
Interview with Brad
Lowell, Program
Manager, Navy-A

Rampar: What is your . . . ?

Lowell: . . . great problem? I'll tell you what it is. I still cannot get the support I need from Kane in Engineering. He commits and then doesn't deliver, and it has me quite concerned. The excuse now is that in "his judgment," Sid Wright needs the help for the Air Force program more than I do. Wright's program is one week ahead of schedule, so I disagree with "his judgment." Kane keeps complaining about not having enough people.

Rampar: Why do you think Kane says he doesn't have enough people?

Lowell: Because Hal Wallace is a tight-fisted S.O.B. who won't let us hire the people we need!

Exhibit 10
Selected Portions
of a Transcribed
Interview with Phil
Jones, Director of
Administration and
Planning

Rampar: What is your greatest problem right now?

Jones: Wheel spinning—that's our problem! We talk about expansion, but we don't do anything about it. Are we serious or not?

For example, a bid request came in from a prime contractor seeking help in developing a countermeasure system for a medium-range aircraft. They needed an immediate response and concept proposal in one week. Tuscher just sat on my urgent memo to him asking for a go/no go decision on bidding. I could not give the contractor an answer (because no decision came from Tuscher), so they gave up on us.

I am frustrated because (1) we lost an opportunity we were "naturals" to win, and (2) my personal reputation was damaged because I was unable to answer the bid request. Okay, Tuscher's gone now, but we need to develop some mechanism so an answer to such a request can be made quickly.

Another thing, our MIS is being developed by the Corporate Finance Group. More wheel spinning! They are telling us what information we need rather than asking us what we want! E. Kay (our Group Controller) is going crazy trying to sort out the input requirements they need for the system and understanding the complicated reports that came out. Maybe this new system is great as a technical achievement, but what good is it to us if we can't use it?

Exhibit 11
Selected Portions
of a Transcribed
Interview with Burt
Williams, Director of
Operations

Rampar: What is your biggest problem right now?

Williams: One of the biggest problems we face right now stems from corporate policy regarding transfer pricing. I realize we are "encouraged" to purchase our plastics and chemicals from our sister Wallace groups, but we are also committed to making a profit! Because manufacturing problems in those groups have forced them to raise their prices, should we suffer the consequences? We can get some materials cheaper from other suppliers. How can we meet our volume and profit targets when we are saddled with noncompetitive material costs?

Rampar: And if that issue was settled to your satisfaction, then would things be okay?

Williams: Although out of my direct function, it occurs to me that we are not planning effectively our efforts to expand into nondefense areas. With minimal alteration to existing production methods, we can develop both end-use products (e.g., small motors, traffic control devices, and microwave transceivers for highway emergency communications) and components (e.g., LED and LCD displays, police radar tracking devices, and word processing system memory and control devices) with large potential markets.

   The problems in this regard are:

1. Matt Smith (Director, Advanced Systems) is retiring and has had only defense-related experience. Therefore, he is not leading any product development efforts along these lines.
2. We have no marketing function at the group level to develop a strategy, define markets, and research and develop product opportunities.
3. Even if we had a marketing plan and products for industrial/commercial application, we would still have no sales force or rep network to sell the stuff.
   Maybe I am way off base, but it seems to me we need a Groups/Marketing/Sales function to lead us in this business expansion effort. It should be headed by an experienced technical marketing manager with a proven track record in developing such products and markets.

Rampar: Have you discussed your concerns with others?

Williams: I have brought these ideas up with Mr. Matthews and others at the Group Management Committee. No one else seems interested in pursuing this concept, but they won't say this outright and don't say why it should not be addressed. I guess that in raising the idea with you I am trying to relieve some of my frustrations.

CASE **3**

Everyone Does It

Steven M. Cox and Shawana P. Johnson

JIM WILLIS WAS THE VICE PRESIDENT OF MARKETING AND SALES FOR INTERNATIONAL Satellite Images (ISI). ISI had been building a satellite to image the world at a resolution of one meter. At that resolution, a trained photo interpreter could identify virtually any military and civilian vehicle, as well as numerous other military and non-military objects. The ISI team had been preparing a proposal for a Japanese government contractor. The contract called for a commitment of a minimum imagery purchase of $10 million per year for five years. In a recent executive staff meeting, it became clear that the ISI satellite camera subcontractor was having trouble with the development of a thermal stabilizer for the instrument. It appeared that the development delay would be at least one year and possibly 18 months.

When Jim approached Fred Ballard, the President of ISI, for advice on what launch date to put into the proposal, Fred told Jim to use the published date because that was still the official launch date. When Jim protested that the use of an incorrect date was clearly unethical, Fred said, "Look Jim, no satellite has ever been launched on time. Everyone, including our competitors, publishes very aggressive launch dates. Customers understand the tentative nature of launch schedules. In fact, it is so common that customers factor into their plans the likelihood that spacecraft will not be launched on time. If we provided realistic dates, our launch dates would be so much later than those published by our competitors that we would never be able to sell any advanced contracts. So do not worry about it, just use the published date and we will revise it in a few months." Fred's words were not very comforting to Jim. It was true that satellite launch dates were seldom met, but putting a launch date into a proposal that ISI knew was no longer possible seemed underhanded. He wondered about the ethics of such a practice and the effect on his own reputation.

....

The Industry

Companies from four nations—the United States, France, Russia, and Israel—controlled the satellite imaging industry. The U.S. companies had a clear advantage in technology and imagery clarity. In the United States, three companies dominated: Lockart, Global Sciences, and ISI. Each of these companies had received a license from the U.S. government to build and launch a satellite able to identify objects as small as one square meter. However, none had yet been able to successfully launch a commercial satellite with such a fine resolution. Currently, all of the companies had announced a launch date within six months of the ISI published launch date. Further, each company had to revise its launch date at least once, and in the case of Global Sciences, twice. Each time a company had revised its launch date, ongoing international contract negotiations with that company had been either stalled or terminated.

Financing a Satellite Program

The construction and ongoing operations of each of the programs was financed by venture capitalists. The venture capitalists relied heavily on advance contract acquisition to ensure the success of their investment. As a result, if any company was unable to acquire sufficient advance contracts, or if one company appeared to be gaining a lead on the others, there was a real possibility that the financiers would pull the plug on the other projects and the losing companies would be forced to stop production and possibly declare bankruptcy. The typical advance contract target was 150% of the cost of building and launching a satellite. Since the cost to build and launch was $200 million, each company was striving to acquire $300 million in advance contracts.

Advance contracts were typically written like franchise licensing agreements. Each franchisee guaranteed to purchase a minimum amount of imagery per year for five years, the engineered life of the satellite. In addition, each franchisee agreed to acquire the capability to receive, process, and archive the images sent to them from the satellite. Typically, the hardware and software cost was between $10 million and $15 million per installation. Because the data from each satellite was different, much of the software could not be used for multiple programs. In exchange, the franchisee was granted an exclusive reception and selling territory. The amount of each contract was dependent on the anticipated size of the market, the number of possible competitors in the market, and the readiness of the local military and civilian agencies to use the imagery. Thus, a contract in Africa would sell for as little as $1 million per year, whereas in several European countries $5–$10 million was not unreasonable. The problem was complicated by the fact that in each market there were usually only one or two companies with the financial strength and market penetration to become a successful franchisee. Therefore, each of the U.S. companies had targeted these companies as their prime prospects.

The Current Problem

Japan was expected to be the third largest market for satellite imagery after the United States and Europe. Imagery sales in Japan were estimated to be from $20 million to $30 million per year. Although the principal user would be the Japanese government, for political reasons the government had made it clear that they would be purchasing data through a local Japanese company. One Japanese company, Higashi Trading Company (HTC), had provided most of the imagery for civilian and military use to the Japanese government.

ISI had been negotiating with HTC for the past six months. It was no secret that HTC had also been meeting with representatives from Lockart and Global Sciences. HTC had sent several engineers to ISI to evaluate the satellite and its construction progress. Jim Willis believed that ISI was currently the front-runner in the quest to sign HTC to a $10 million annual contract. Over five years, that one contract would represent one sixth of the contracts necessary to ensure sufficient venture capital to complete the satellite.

Jim was concerned that if a new launch date was announced, HTC would delay signing a contract. Jim was equally concerned that if HTC learned that Jim and his team knew of the camera design problems and knowingly withheld announcement of a new launch date until after completing negotiations, not only his personal reputation but that of ISI would be damaged. Furthermore, as with any franchise arrangement, mutual trust was critical to the success of each party. Jim was worried that even if only a 12-month delay in launch occurred, trust would be broken between ISI and the Japanese.

Jim's boss, Fred Ballard, had specifically told Jim that launch date information was company proprietary and that Jim was to use the existing published date when talking with clients. Fred feared that if HTC became aware of the delay, they would begin negotiating with one of ISI's competitors, who in Fred's opinion were not likely to meet their launch dates either. This change in negotiation focus by the Japanese would then have ramifications with the venture capitalists whom Fred had assured that a contract with the Japanese would soon be signed.

Jim knew that with the presentation date rapidly approaching, it was time to make a decision.

CASE 4

The Audit

Gamewell D. Gantt, George A. Johnson, and John A. Kilpatrick

SUE WAS PUZZLED AS TO WHAT COURSE OF ACTION TO TAKE. SHE HAD RECENTLY STARTED her job with a national CPA firm, and she was already confronted with a problem that could affect her future with the firm. On an audit, she encountered a client who had been treating payments to a large number, but by no means a majority, of its workers as payments to independent contractors. This practice saves the client the payroll taxes that would otherwise be due on the payments if the workers were classified as employees. In Sue's judgment, this was improper as well as illegal and should have been noted in the audit. She raised the issue with John, the senior accountant to whom she reported. He thought it was a possible problem but did not seem willing to do anything about it. He encouraged her to talk to the partner in charge if she didn't feel satisfied.

She thought about the problem for a considerable time before approaching the partner in charge. The ongoing professional education classes she had received from her employer emphasized the ethical responsibilities that she had as a CPA and the fact that her firm endorsed adherence to high ethical standards. This finally swayed her to pursue the issue with the partner in charge of the audit. The visit was most unsatisfactory. Paul, the partner, virtually confirmed her initial reaction that the practice was wrong, but he said that many other companies in the industry follow such a practice. He went on to say that if an issue was made of it, Sue would lose the account, and he was not about to take such action. She came away from the meeting with the distinct feeling that had she chosen to pursue the issue, she would have created an enemy.

Sue still felt disturbed and decided to discuss the problem with some of her co-workers. She approached Bill and Mike, both of whom had been working for the firm for a couple of years. They were familiar with the problem because they had encountered the same issue when doing the audit the previous year. They expressed considerable concern that if she went over the head of the partner in charge of the audit, they could be in big trouble since they had failed to question the practice during the previous audit. They said that they realized it was probably wrong, but they went ahead because it had been ignored in previous years, and they knew their supervisor wanted them to ignore it again this year. They didn't want to cause problems. They encouraged Sue to be a "team player" and drop the issue.

....

This case was prepared by Professors John A. Kilpatrick, Gamewell D. Gantt, and George A. Johnson of the College of Business, Idaho State University. The names of the organization, individual, location, and/or financial information have been disguised to preserve the organization's desire for anonymity. This case was edited for the *SMBP*–9th, 10th, 11th, 12th, 13th, 14th and 15th Editions. Presented to and accepted by the Society for Case Research. All rights reserved to the authors and the SCR. Copyright © 1995 by John A. Kilpatrick, Gamewell D. Gantt, and George A. Johnson. This case may not be reproduced without written permission of the copyright holders. Reprinted by permission.

CASE **5**

Early Warning or False Sense of Security? Concussion Risk and the Case of the Impact-Sensing Football Chinstrap

Clifton D. Petty, Michael R. Shirley
Drury University

> "Anybody who sits down with you and says I have a device that if your child wears it, will either diagnose a concussion or prevent a concussion is lying. Please quote me on that."
> —*DAVE HALSTEAD,*
> *Technical Director of the Southern Impact Research Center*

It wasn't exactly the sort of quote that would help Battle Sports Science, LLC promote its new impact-sensing football chinstrap. National Public Radio (NPR) interviewed Dave Halstead as part of a story titled "*Can that Mouth Guard Really Prevent a Concussion?*" Armed with a promotional e-mail from Battle Sports Science's founder, Chris Circo, the NPR reporter had asked Halstead's opinion on the new device. And, characteristically, Halstead had offered his blunt assessment. Although Halstead hadn't tested the device himself, he elaborated when asked about the potential for the chinstrap to give an early warning to a coach or player: "*The fear here is that you have an individual who has received not much of an impact . . . but has a significant rotational event (whiplash). They in fact have a significant mild traumatic brain injury. But they have a green light on the chin cup.*"(NPR 2011).

....

Battle Sports Science, LLC

Chris Circo and his partners founded Battle Sports Science in 2009. Headquartered in Omaha, Nebraska, the company was built with a focus on "enhancing safety for athletes" (company website). Specifically, the company wanted to protect young athletes who might have suffered a concussion. An elusive and potentially fatal condition, concussions come with the territory of contact sports. In American football, traditional locker room humor lampooned the antics of the disoriented player, who, following a big hit, wandered toward the wrong huddle. But Circo, who suffered five concussions as a young athlete and today takes anti-seizure medication, considered even the so-called "mild" concussion no laughing matter. Many cases of concussion were tragic, like the case of Nathan Stiles. Stiles, a 17-year-old football player from Spring Hill, Kansas, suffered a concussive blow in a game on October 1, 2010. He collapsed during a game on October 28, and later died. An autopsy revealed a re-bleed of an undetected brain injury (subdural hematoma) (NCCSIR 2012).

Battle Sports Science attempted to gain market attention for its $149.99 Impact Indicator (chin strap) through endorsements, and had enlisted a number of NFL players including Ndamukong Suh, Dexter McCluster, Pierre Thomas, and Eddie Royal. (McKewon 2011). The company hoped to sell the device to sports programs (schools) as well as to individual players. In addition to its Impact Sensing chinstrap, Battle Sports Science made a helmet (Battle Helmet) and mouth-guard (Battle Shield) to protect baseball players at bat (company website).

Chris Circo wondered if he should aggressively challenge Dave Halstead's assessment. Battle Sports Science's design team *had* considered whiplash injuries, and believed that the chinstrap would reliably register "rotational events." He might also challenge Halstead directly. Dave Halstead was a research whiz, but possessed neither M.D. nor college engineering degree credentials. Dave Halstead might not be a completely objective reviewer, given that he was a helmet designer and technical advisor to the NFL.

But within a week of the NPR story, a Congressional panel had expressed skepticism over "anticoncussion" equipment, and Senator Tom Udall (D-N.M.) had asked the Federal Trade Commission (FTC) to investigate the claims of companies in this market—including Battle Sports Science. Now the stakes were growing, and CEO Circo realized that he had reached an important milestone for his young company. Pressing ahead meant defying Dave Halstead and other technical skeptics, and facing scrutiny from Congress and the FTC. From this point on, a product failure was likely to doom his young company.

Football and the Concussion Problem

Football is a contact sport, and has long been associated with serious collision-related injuries. President Theodore Roosevelt called on early football enthusiasts to develop rules that reduced these injuries or face government restrictions. But in recent years, many sports medicine experts have commented on the growing number and severity of concussion injuries. Some also noted that the speed and strength of football players had increased significantly in recent decades. And finally, some aspects of the game—including punt returns and spread offenses—increased the likelihood of high-speed contact, as well as the so-called "defenseless player," or blind spot collision. While both professional (NFL) and college (NCAA) rulemaking bodies had recently focused attention on reducing the growing number and severity of traumatic brain injuries, by far the most extensive risk existed at the high school level.

According to the National Federation of State High School Associations, some 1.14 million students annually participated in high school football. Approximately 9%, or at least 140,000 of these young athletes, suffered a concussion each year (Koester 2010). Training programs for high-school football coaches were increasingly focused on concussion recognition. But identification of a player at risk was not an easy matter. According to the Centers for Disease Control (CDC), the symptoms of a concussion were sometimes subtle and athletes often experienced or reported symptoms hours or even days after the concussive event (HHS). Coaches felt pressure to keep talented players on the field, and players often hid their symptoms in order to keep playing. Some high school players took their cues in this regard from professional players:

Both the NFL and NCAA have been sued by players over concussion injuries. A suit was filed against the NCAA on behalf of former Eastern Illinois defensive back Adrian Arrington, 25, who had several concussions between 2006 and 2009. Arrington's suit alleged that the NCAA didn't "set up sufficient guidelines for players with concussions" (Hailey). In addition, 75 former NFL players filed suit in 2010 and alleged that the NFL hid the dangers of concussions from players intentionally (Fendrich 2010).

Product Responsibility and the Impact Indicator

Some recent trends, including the litigation against football leagues and universities, suggest a role for Battle Sports Science's Impact Indicator in both reducing concussive injuries and litigation risk for football organizations and schools. The National Federation of High School (NFHS) has alerted its members that concussion-related litigation is gathering momentum, and is increasingly targeting coaches and school officials at the high school level (Koester). The Impact Indicator identified potential injuries, and helped coaches and players avoid a subsequent collision to an already injured brain. A light on the chin strap shines green until a player is struck in such a way that a head injury is either possible (yellow light) or likely (red light). A coach who spotted the yellow or red light might then sideline the injured player. From this perspective, it might be argued that aggressive promotion of the Impact Indicator should improve safety among players.

Then again, what if Halstead's skepticism was well placed? How will the product have performed in the thousands of complex and high-speed encounters that occur on football fields across the United States? More testing and slower rollout might lower some risk, but it would also provide rivals time to copy the chin strap and beat Battle Science to the market. One thing was certain—the company couldn't stand still now. All the recent publicity—even from critics like Halstead—had pushed the company onto the field with respect to the concussion controversy in football. If Circo had any doubts about his product, it was time to face them before it was too late. Otherwise, it was time to set his strategy for moving forward while managing intense risks and likely controversy.

REFERENCES AND SUGGESTED READINGS

Battle Sports Science, LLC, company website.

Fendrich, Howard (October 20, 2010). NFL concussion saga moves to new phase: Litigation. *Associated Press*.

Hailey, Jim (September 16, 2010). NCAA named in class-action concussion lawsuit. *USA Today*.

Koester, Michael, M.D., (July 2010). NFHS Concussion Rule—What State Associations need to know. *Workshop presentation to the NFHS Sports Medicine Advisory Committee.*

McKewon, Sam (October 14, 2011). Ex-Husker Suh backing safety device. *Omaha World-Herald*.

NPR Interview Transcript (October 5, 2011). Can that mouth guard really prevent a concussion?

(NCCSIR) National Center for Catastrophic Sport Injury Research website.

(HHS) U.S. Department of Health and Human Services, Centers for Disease Control and Prevention (June, 2010). Heads up: Concussion in high school sports.

CASE **6**

The Storm of Governance Reform at the American Red Cross

Jill A. Brown
Bentley University

Anne Anderson
Lehigh University

The Drivers of the Storm

In early 2006, a U.S. Senate Finance Committee began investigating the American Red Cross (ARC) following substantial concerns over the governance effectiveness of the organization and its Board of Governors. This investigation was prompted by concerns over Hurricane Katrina relief efforts, as well as governance concerns regarding the structure and processes of the ARC Board. Consequently, the Finance Committee appointed an Independent Governance Advisory Panel (hereafter referred to as the Panel) to provide recommendations regarding how to overhaul the Board. Later that year, in November 2006, ARC Chairman Bonnie McElveen-Hunter wrote a letter to ARC constituents summarizing the Panel's recommendations, stating, "When an organization is given such an important and sacred trust by the American people, it must do everything in its power not only to ensure that it is worthy of this trust, but to deliver in all areas of its responsibility – and there is no more critical responsibility than in the area of governance, oversight and transparency."

As part of the review, the Panel noted that, "while no such detailed set of practices has emerged for the nonprofit sector due to the variety of organizations in this sector, many leading nonprofit organizations have benchmarked their governance practices against the evolving corporate model, with appropriate modifications for their particular circumstances."[1] The recommended governance practices challenged the way that Chairman McElveen-Hunter and the ARC Board had historically managed the not-for-profit organization, and encouraged them to adopt a more for-profit-like model of governance. McElveen-Hunter had to decide whether to endorse the recommended practices and put them to a Board vote. Ultimately, the Board needed to determine which of the recommendations would lead to more effective governance practices and allow the Red Cross to fulfill its mission.

Brief History of the American Red Cross

The ARC was founded in 1881 by Clara Barton as an affiliate of the International Red Cross, and was chartered by the U.S. Congress in 1905 under the mission of providing services to members of the U.S. armed forces and disaster victims. These services gradually expanded, and by 2008, it had five primary services: providing community services for the needy, supporting military members and their families, collecting and distributing blood, teaching health and related classes and providing disaster services through local and regional chapters. Its annual budget was approximately $4 billion, with most of its revenues coming from donations. As a not-for-profit, charitable organization, the ARC had local and/or regional branches governed by a volunteer board of directors. Membership in the ARC was primarily at the individual level, in contrast to organizations like the United Way of America or Boys and Girls Clubs of America, with memberships that included both organizational and individual members.[2]

The original ARC governance model was mandated under a congressional charter that established a 50-member Board of Governors. The President of the United States appointed eight of the seats, including the chair, while local chapters were responsible for electing 30 of the 50 governors, with the remaining 12 seats filled by governors elected on an at-large basis. The Board of Governors had sole responsibility for decisions ranging from selecting the CEO to approving the budget. Experts considered the ARC to be a "top down organization" with a hierarchy of chapters and affiliates with directors who reported to the Board of Governors.[3] This contrasted with other not-for-profit organizations like the United Way of America, in which the membership elected the board and its officers, and its bylaws were approved or amended by majority vote. Additionally, the ARC operated under an unusually large board that included political appointees and a majority of board members from for-profit organizations (see Appendix A). Each ARC chapter had a local board as well, but these boards did not have fiduciary responsibility for the organization. Instead, each local chapter operated independently, focusing on fund raising within the community, being the local representative for the ARC, and ensuring that the mission of the ARC was delivered effectively to the local community. The Board of Governors made all policy decisions and provided support to the local chapters.

The ARC Board had operated successfully under this model for over 100 years without many governance issues. However, this changed in 2006, when the ARC came under media scrutiny following Hurricane Katrina. In September 2005, Hurricane Katrina devastated the city of New Orleans and brought a level of national attention to the ARC it had never experienced before. CEO Marsha Evans was put under the spotlight to defend the actions of the ARC when it was criticized for not moving quickly enough to assist evacuees in New Orleans. Evans' decision-making power and her relationship with the ARC board were also aired in the media. Like the roll of thunder before the storm, media attention turned toward the ARC and its Board of Governors.

Media Attention

On September 2, 2005 CNN Talk Show host Larry King grilled Secretary of Health and Human Services Michael Leavitt, ARC CEO Evans, and New Orleans Mayor Ray Nagin on the aftermath of one of the worst natural disasters in American history. At that time, four days after the Category 3 hurricane had hit, the ARC had not yet entered New Orleans to rescue hundreds of thousands of victims of the storm. According to Evans, the delay was attributable to various local and state agencies:

> Well, Larry, when the storm came (sic) our goal was prior to landfall to support the evacuation. It was unsafe to be in the city. We were asked by the city not to be there and the Superdome was made a shelter of last resorts and, quite frankly in retrospect, it was a good idea because otherwise those people would have had no shelter at all. We have our shelters north of the city. We're prepared as soon as they can be evacuated . . . but it was not safe to be in the city and it's not been safe to go back into the city. They were also concerned that if we relocated back into the city, people wouldn't leave and they've got to leave.[4]

This answer was highly unsatisfactory to social activist Reverend Jesse Jackson who retorted, "Well, that's ridiculous. I mean the Red Cross' absence in New Orleans; the high point of the crisis is a disaster. It is a sin. We had no real plan for rescue and relief and relocation."[5] He then began to describe his independent rescue of 450 students from Xavier University who were stranded on a bridge for three days. When pressed by Larry King to respond, Evans retorted:

> Well, Larry, we were asked, directed by the National Guard and the city and the state emergency management not to go into New Orleans because it was not safe. We are not a search and rescue organization. We provide shelter and basic support and so we were depending, we are depending on the state and the agencies to get people to our shelters in safe places.[6]

This dialogue began the public fingerpointing that ultimately led to the firing of Federal Emergency Management Association (FEMA) Director Michael Brown and a White House report on Katrina titled, "Lessons Learned."[7] In December 2005, ARC CEO and President Evans resigned after serving for three years in that position. She was the fourth CEO to leave the Red Cross in a decade, and her resignation followed accusations that the ARC had governance problems that had culminated in the mismanagement of the Katrina disaster.[8] On *NewsHour with Jim Lehrer*, governance expert and New York University Professor Paul Light commented, "I think Katrina played a role here. I think that Marsha Evans has become, to some extent, a scapegoat for all that ails the organization, and was having tremendous conflict with the Board and eventually came under fire herself for being too much of an over promiser and an apologist for what had been going wrong down in the Gulf states."[9]

Time for a Review

The media attention on the performance of the ARC in the Katrina disaster, as well as media attention to Evans' resignation spawned the initial decision of the U.S. Senate Finance Committee to review the ARC Board of Governors. In December 2005 and February 2006, Senator Chuck Grassley wrote letters to Chairman McElveen-Hunter expressing his concerns over the board's governance and noting that he had received requests from ARC insiders for more board oversight. At that time, he used the ouster of Evans as his leading example of "board dysfunction."[10] He cited poor attendance at board meetings and reports from volunteers, employees, and former employees who alleged poor governance. Two governance issues were notably highlighted: executive turnover and board composition/structure.

Executive Turnover

In Senator Grassley's letter to the ARC board following Evans' resignation, he reprimanded the board for its inability to retain and get along with its CEOs, and in particular, CEO Evans: "The critical function of a board is whether to hire or fire the CEO," he noted. "The fact, as my staff understands from the briefing provided by the Red Cross' outside counsel, that Ms. Evans' departure took place without any formal action or decision by the entire board is extraordinarily troubling. . . . I am concerned that the CEO is unable to make reforms or changes because an individual or subgroup is 'protected' by a board member."[11]

Senator Grassley suggested that the ARC Board's CEO issues were systemic to the organization. From 1998 to 2005 the position of ARC CEO had been filled by three individuals, including a former U.S. Secretary of Transportation and U.S. Secretary of Labor (Elizabeth Dole), an acclaimed physician and former head of the National Institute of Health (Bernadine Healy), and a Navy Rear Admiral (Marsha Evans) with interim directors serving in-between the executive searches. Each of these appointees and subsequent resignations were controversial. In 1999, ARC CEO Elizabeth Dole resigned after serving eight years as CEO to run for the U.S. Senate. Although Dole's leadership was considered exemplary, her political ties raised concerns that she allowed conservative politics, and specifically her husband's political agenda, to affect Red Cross policies. In 2001, the resignation of CEO Healy came less than two years after Dole's departure. Dr. Healy resigned after she was criticized for the use of 9/11 funds. At the time, the ARC had successfully raised a record $1 billion for its Liberty Fund; however, some donors were upset when they learned that a substantial portion was earmarked for future crises, rather than to help the 9/11 victims. When Healy resigned, she said that she had conflicts with several board members over her decision to cut off dues to the International Red Cross for excluding the Israeli branch from membership. "I had no choice," she said at a news conference.[12] The Board reportedly voted 27–5 in favor of accepting her resignation while also noting that it had lost confidence in her leadership.[13]

When Evans resigned in December 2005 following Katrina, there were rumors that she had clashed with the Board over her removal of several executives. Earlier that year, Chairman McElveen-Hunter told Evans that the Board's executive committee was unhappy with her "command and control" management style.[14] When the ARC announced that Evans was resigning to spend time with her family, many did not believe the explanation. One analyst noted that, "It's unusual to have a board that doesn't get along with four different presidents in such short order. I mean, it is the hiring and firing agency, and it doesn't seem to like anybody that it selects."[15]

Board Composition and Structure

Senator Grassley was particularly concerned about board composition and structure, which he felt contributed to the power struggles and lack of leadership on the board. His first concern was about the size of the board, which he felt was too large for effective decision making as he noted, "when everyone is in charge, no one is in charge." He wrote, "Generally, the non-profit sector, like the commercial sector, has come to recognize that smaller boards—which meet more frequently and have standing committees focused on particular issues relevant to the organization—are more effective than overly large boards which meet infrequently, often by telephone, and whose members sometimes regard board service as an honorary function."[16] He asked Chairman McElveen-Hunter to provide more information on the board composition and urged her to find a way to reduce the size of the board.

Second, Senator Grassley urged the ARC board to revisit board processes within its structure. He noted the lack of participation by board members, "I am troubled by the number of the board of governors, particularly government-appointed board members who rarely attend board meetings and often send representatives who do little more than sit in a chair.... In addition, some of these government officials have a direct conflict with the two hats they wear. For example, the Secretary of Health and Human Services who sits on the Red Cross board also oversees the Food and Drug Administration, which has been engaged in significant oversight of the Red Cross on blood issues."[17] He suggested that McElveen-Hunter investigate these issues and collect additional information for his office.

Time for the Storm

Senator Grassley was not happy with Chairman McElveen-Hunter's response to his two letters requesting information. For one, McElveen-Hunter responded to his first letter with a defense of the ARC structure and its large board. In response, Senator Grassley reprimanded, "The response from the Red Cross to my letter, which points to other organizations with large boards, does not provide a convincing defense of the current 50 person board. Note that The Nature Conservancy's governance review, prompted by the Finance Committee's investigation, came to a very different conclusion about big boards."[18] Second, McElveen-Hunter sent requested documents marked "Confidential," which annoyed the Senator. In response, he declared, "To better inform the public as well as decision-makers, I am releasing today some of the material the Red Cross has provided in response to my letter. A significant portion of material has been marked confidential by the Red Cross. My staff will be discussing this matter further with your counsel. I strongly encourage the Red Cross to be as open and transparent as possible. This is particularly important in light of its designation by Congress to be the lead disaster relief organization for the country in light of the fact that it has board members who are appointed by the President but also depends on the public for the majority of its support."[19]

As media reports of the ARC governance problems grew, Senator Grassley made the decision to investigate the ARC as part of a formal U.S. Senate Finance Committee roundtable session. He scheduled a discussion of the ARC board for a March 2006 meeting.

One of the roles of the Finance Committee was to investigate charities, which included approving tax incentives for donors, investigating executives of not-for-profit institutions, as well as questionable practices. In 2003, for example, the Senate Finance Committee followed up on allegations from whistleblowers regarding conflicts of interest of board members in land transactions under the not-for-profit Nature Conservancy. Two years later, the Committee investigated American University's Board of Trustees regarding the severance pay and compensation paid to the university's former president, Benjamin Ladner. In 2006, when its attention turned to the ARC Board, Senator Grassley cited Ms. McElveen-Hunter's failure to supply adequate justification for the current structure and processes of the ARC Board. After several days of discussion, the Committee decided that it would commission an independent audit of ARC governance procedures.

In response to Senator Grassley's recommendation, the ARC Board of Governors brought in a group of for-profit and not-for-profit experts to evaluate the Board's governance practices.[20] First, the ARC organized a Corporate Governance Summit with the National Association of Corporate Directors to become more informed on "best practices." Then, it formed a separate group of experts to be part of the "Panel." The group included:

- Retired partner of the law firm Crowell & Moring, LLP, Karen Hastie Williams
- Harvard Business School professor and governance expert, Jay Lorsch
- CEO of Governance for Owners USA and former SVP/Chief Counsel for the teachers' retirement fund, TIAA-CREF, Peter Clapman
- Board governance expert and professor at the University of Delaware, Charles Elson
- SVP-Corporate Governance and Associate Counsel of Pfizer, Inc., Margaret Foran
- President of Trinity University, Patricia McGuire
- Professor Emeritus of University of Iowa College of Law, Paul Neuhauser

The Panel was assigned the task of working with the ARC Board's Governance Committee and independent counsel to identify possible governance changes. The Board identified five focus areas for the team to work on as part of a governance audit. Specifically, it identified:

1. The size and composition of the Board, and the independence of governors in the process for selecting candidates for the Board
2. The organization and functioning of the Board, including composition, structure, and roles of the Board's committees
3. The roles and relationships of the Board and management
4. The Board's oversight of the governance practices of the Red Cross chapters
5. The relationships and lines of reporting between the Audit Committee, the outside auditor, and the internal audit function, including the whistleblower process for Red Cross employees and volunteers as well as constituencies serviced by the Red Cross

In April 2006, the Panel formulated a set of recommendations to present to the Board in October of that year. Perhaps in recognition of the importance of the CEO, a large portion of the recommendations focused on the relationship between the Chairman and the CEO. While in previous correspondence with Senator Grassley, Chairman McElveen-Hunter had defended the structure of the ARC, she was now faced with formally assessing her relationship with the Board, and reviewing the Panel's many recommendations regarding better oversight.

Recommendations

The Board

The Panel wrote that the purpose of the Board was to "oversee the operations of the organization in such a manner as will assure effective and ethical management"[21] based on guidelines from the Summit panelists. The Panel compared the ARC to the Corporation for Public Broadcasting, The Nature Conservancy, and Volunteers of America, all of which had recently reviewed the mechanisms by which their boards carried out their oversight functions and created "position descriptions." The Panel recommended the

ARC Bylaws be amended to include more detail about the oversight function of the ARC Board, noting, "Structural, cultural and historical factors (have) blurred the distinction between governance and management functions at the Red Cross."[22] The Panel went on to provide recommendations to the ARC Board that would ensure that it operated as a "true over sight board working in partnership with senior management," while also acknowledging that the board members would also be involved in fundraising.[23] A summary of the Panel's recommendations are provided in Table 1.

TABLE 1		Summary of Governance Issues and Proposed Changes				
Governance Mechanisms	Traditional ARC Board	Proposed Changes	Summary of Reforms	Traditional ARC Board	Proposed Changes
Composition and Size	3-Tier Classification:	Downsize Board to max of 25 members by 2009 and 20 by 2012.	Roles and Functioning	Oversight board that involves "management" of ARC— blurred distinction between governance and management function[27]	Oversight board "in partnership with senior management"[28] and "greater specificity of the oversight role"
	-30 Elected Bd Members by Chapters	Establishment of advisory councils to advise Board and management— National Leadership Council to facilitate communication and Presidentially-appointed Cabinet Council. Cabinet Council to have no fewer than eight and no more than 10 members, with at least one, but no more than three selected from Armed Forces			
	-12 Members at Large				
	-8 Members appointed by President of the United States, including Chairman and 7 "officials of departments and agencies of the U.S. Gov't" including at least one and not more than three from Armed Services			Roles of the Chairman and CEO	Bylaws to be amended to delete references to the Chairman as the "principal officer" of the ARC
					Board to adopt a "more specific, written delegation of authority from the Board to the CEO"
	Staggered Board— 3 yr terms with 1/3 elected each year	Staggered terms, but with single "category" of elected Board members—all nominated and elected through the same process			
Board Oversight of ARC Chapters	Non-Governor Board members like National Chair of Volunteers serves as a non-voting member of Board	No more non-Governor or ex officio members involved in Board meetings	Chairman Selection	Executive Committee of the Board, chaired by incumbent Chair makes a recommendation to Exec Committee which recommends to President	Governance and Board Development Committees recommend candidate to the full Board, which would then recommend to the President

(continued)

TABLE 1	Summary of Governance Issues and Proposed Changes (continued)				
Governance Mechanisms	**Traditional ARC Board**	**Proposed Changes**	**Summary of Reforms**	**Traditional ARC Board**	**Proposed Changes**
Board Selection	Board nominating procedure varied by category of directors 19 members of Committee on Nominations	Board nominating procedure same for all directors. All Board members subject to approval by full Board, except for Chairman, with approval at organization's annual meeting Committee on Nominations reduced to 14 members	CEO Selection	Nominated by Chairman and elected by full Board	Board appoints CEO; President and CEO can be separate
Board Membership of CEO	CEO is not a member of the Board	Board has flexibility to allow CEO as a member of the Board—voting or non-voting	Management Development and Succession	Heavy recruitment of outside CEOs	Compensation and Management Development Committee formed to develop "gifted" management and staff[29]

Size and Composition of the Board

While commenting that "a relatively large Board is justified by the complexity of the Red Cross . . . that can facilitate fundraising," the Panel mentioned that the ARC Board had been criticized for being too large and "unwieldy."[24] It also noted that the Red Cross was the only non-governmental organization (NGO) that had responsibilities closely affiliated with the federal government, and yet Presidential appointees on the ARC Board rarely attended meetings and instead sent non-voting representatives to the meetings. After reviewing comparative information on not-for-profit board size, the Panel recommended dividing the Board into three bodies, based on function:

1. A governing body for oversight and strategic decision making,
2. A chartered "advisory" National Leadership Council for chapters and blood service regions, and
3. An advisory Cabinet Council that would include federal government representatives for "applicable government input and advice."

The ARC Charter provided for Presidential appointees on the Board; however, the Panel noted that some of them had potential conflicts of interest, as was also noted by Senator Grassley in his letter to CEO McElveen-Hunter. The panel recommended reducing the Board's size to 25 under a single category of "directors," with fewer Board seats elected from the chapters, and restructuring so that the Presidential appointees would not have voting rights. The Panel also recommended more Board independence and continuation of six-year director term limits. Additionally, it offered specific recommendations on how to select board members, the CEO, and the Chairman.

Board Selection

Based on comparisons with not-for-profits like the Boy Scouts of America, Goodwill Industries International, and Catholic Charities USA, the Panel recommended changing the current nomination procedure for board members. Instead of having separate nominating procedures for "at large" and chapter board members, the Panel recommended using the same nomination procedure for all board members, with the exception of the Chairman of the Board, who would still be nominated by the President of the United States. It recommended that a new Governance and Board Development Committee, made up exclusively of board members, submit nominations for approval by the full Board with confirmation by delegates at their annual convention. This selection process mirrored practices of for-profit organizations, whereby directors submit nominations for new board members, subject to the approval of shareholders by vote.

Selection of the Chairman of the Board and the CEO

Perhaps in the wake of media attention to CEO turnover, over 13 pages of the Panel's report was dedicated to the topic of selection and responsibilities of the Chairman of the Board and the CEO. Historically, the President of the United States appointed the Chairman of the Red Cross, based on candidates recommended by a subcommittee of the ARC's Executive Committee, chaired by the incumbent Chairman, with the approval of the full Executive Committee. The ARC Chairman nominated a President and CEO for ARC Board approval (these could be two individuals or one individual with dual titles). The Panel noted several concerns with this process. First, it focused on the ARC designation of the Chairman as the "principal officer," with concerns over how this might create confusion and uncertainty about whether management would be accountable to the CEO or to the Chairman. Second, it was concerned about the appointment of the Chairman by the U.S. President without full Board approval. Third, it was concerned about CEO turnover due to the deficiencies it found in the management development and CEO succession planning of the Board. Finally, the panel was critical of the fact that the President and CEO of the ARC had never been a member of the Board before assuming a role at the helm of the organization, a practice that was standard in most not-for-profit organizations where the CEO was an *ex officio*, non-voting member.

As a result, the Panel recommended that the Bylaws be amended to delete reference to the Chairman as the "principal officer" of the ARC. It also recommended clearer written descriptions outlining and delineating the responsibilities of the Chairman and the CEO with clear delegation of authority from the Board to the CEO. Rather than relying exclusively on the President of the United States to recommend the Chairman, the Panel suggested that the Board consider candidates for recommendation to the President. It suggested that the bylaws state that the Chairman could not simultaneously serve as CEO (i.e., no CEO duality) and asked for removal of a bylaw stating that the Chairman nominates the CEO, instead favoring Board appointment of a CEO. After assessing the arguments for and against the CEO as a voting member of the Board, the Panel recommended that the Board have discretion over the voting or nonvoting rights of the CEO. The Panel justified this by noting that, "Concerns about empowering the CEO can be addressed by removing the "principal officer" language from the Charter, developing a position description for the CEO . . . and focusing on enhancing the effectiveness of the partnership between the CEO and the Board."[25]

Board Committees

With regard to the workings of the board committees, the Panel assessed the ARC's eight active committees, which ranged in size from seven to nineteen members, and recommended that these be reduced to six. The recommended committees included:

1. Executive Committee
2. Operational Committees
   a. Biomedical Services
   b. Disaster and Chapter Services
   c. Public Support and International Services
3. Audit Committee
4. Public Support Committee
5. International Services Committee
6. Governance Committee

The Panel was highly critical of the Board being in a position to overstep its role with some of the operational committees, like the Biomedical Services Committee, which was responsible for interacting with the Federal Drug Administration and other regulatory agencies. The Panel also criticized the Governance Committee for lack of succession planning and suggested forming a Compensation and Management Development Committee to take on this task. Therefore, they recommended the formation of five operating committees and an Executive Committee of committee chairs to assist the Board.

Other Issues

The Panel identified other governance issues for improvement, including compliance and governance tools, whistleblower processes, disciplinary practices, and internal audit procedures. However, most of these improvements were in process already at the time of the report. Recommendations included communicating more effectively the new policies and procedures as well as establishing an ombudsman position for independent review of ethics and compliance issues.

The Board's Decision

ARC Chairman McElveen-Hunter reviewed the Panel's recommendations in the fall of 2006. The ARC's close connections with U.S. government agencies and the sheer size of the ARC budget, at $3.45 billion in 2007, seemed to justify many of the for-profit comparisons and the adoption of more for-profit-like governance mechanisms recommended by the Panel.[26] However, the proposed changes reduced the power that McElveen-Hunter had as a "principal officer" in the organization, and she would no longer be able to choose her CEO. With the U.S. Senate Finance Committee awaiting an answer, McElveen-Hunter would have to decide which recommendations from the Panel she would ask the Board to adopt.

Epilogue

The American National Red Cross Governance Modernization Act of 2007 was signed into law on May 11, 2007 and the ARC Board accepted all of the proposed changes. However, even after CEO Evans resigned and governance reforms were put in place, controversies over CEO succession continued. When the ARC announced the appointment of Internal Revenue Service chief Mark Everson to replace Evans as its newest President and CEO, one media blog wrote, "the revolving door to the CEO's office at the ARC has spun yet again"[29] (Rafferty, 2007). After less than two years as president and CEO, the Board fired Everson after learning that he had engaged in a personal relationship with a female subordinate.

Following another interim director, Gail J. McGovern joined the ARC as President and CEO on April 8, 2008, and she serves in that capacity today. A former professor of Marketing at Harvard Business School and former President of Fidelity Personal Investments, she faced a daunting task. In addition to overseeing responses to several high-profile disasters, McGovern had to deal with a $209 million deficit. In her keynote address she stated, "The fact is, this economy is presenting many challenges for not-for-profits. But it's also providing the impetus for the ARC and other not-for-profits to make needed and sometimes overdue changes. Simply put, there's a greater acceptance to change in a crisis."[30] By 2010, McGovern had made significant changes in the organization, including massive layoffs and restructuring and the ARC was once again financially positive. The new ARC Board seemed to be working, and five years after Hurricane Katrina, the ARC released a report called, "Bringing Help, Bringing Hope." The theme of the report was that the ARC was better prepared for future disasters. CEO McGovern reiterated the theme of "rebuilding community" with "strong families, strong communities."[31] This theme seemed to apply as well to the ARC Board of Directors as it revisited its commitment to effective governance.

APPENDIX A ARC Board of Governors*

Board Member	Occupation	Firm	2006–07	2007–08	2008–09	2009–10	2010–11	2011–12
Allan Goldberg	Exec Director	U.S. Medical Affiirs	x	x	x	x	x	x
Allen W. Mathies, Jr	Physician and President	Huntington Mem. Hospital	x					
Ann Kaplan	Partner	Circle Wealth Mgmt	x	x	x	x	x	x
Anna Larsen	Partner	Larsen Consulting Intl	x	x	x	x		
Bonnie MlcEKeen-Hunter	CEO	Pace Communications	x	x	x	x	x	x
Brian Derksen	Deputy CEO	Deloitte & Touche	x	x				
Brian G. Skotko, MD	Physician/ Geneticist	Boston Medical Center	x					
Carlos Gutierrez	Secretary	U.S. Dept of Commerce	x					
Cesar Aristeiguieta	Physician and Director EMS	California EMSA	x	x	x	x		x
Christine K. Wilkinson, PhD	VP & Secretary of ASU	Arizona State University	x					
Condolezza Rice	Secretary	U.S. Dept of State	x					
Douglas Dittrick	President/CEO	Douglas Communications	x					
E. Francine Stokes	Assistant to President	Morgan State University	x	x				
E. Francine Stokes	Chief of Staff	Coppin State			x			
Elaine Lyerly	CEO/President	Lyerly Agency Inc	x	x				
Gail McGovem	CEO/President	American Red Cross				x	x	x
Gen Josue J. Robles	CEO/President	USAA					x	x
Gen. Peter Pace	Chairman	Joint Chief of Staff	x					
Gina Adams	Coporate VP-Gov't affairs	FedEx Corp.	x	x	x	x	x	x
Glenn Sieber	Retired	Accenture	x	x	x			
H. Marshall Schwarz	Retired Chairman/CEO	U.S. Trust	x	x	x	x	x	x
James F. Holmes	Integration Specialist	Harris Corp	x	x				
James Goodwin	Senior Partner	Goodwin & Grant	x	x	x	x	x	
James Keyes	CEO/Chairman	Blockbuster	x	x	x	x	x	x
Joseph Braxton	Attorney and Judge	Treasurer National Bar Assan	x			x	x	
Joseph Pereles	VP Development/ Attorney	Drury Hotels Corp.	x	x	x	x	x	x
Joyce N. Hoffman	Sr. VP & Corporate Secretary	The Principal Financial Group	x					
Hjudith Richards Hope	CEO/Former Chair	MTV Networks						x
Judith Richards Hope	Partner	Hope & Co	x					
Julie Burger	Military SAF Volunteer	U.S. Military	x					
Laurence Paul	Managing Principal	Laurel Crown Partners	x	x	x	x	x	x
M. Victoria Cummock	Owner-Designer	Cummock Designs, Inc	x	x				
Maj. Gen Robert Smolen	U.S. Air Force	U.S. Military	x					

Name	Title	Organization						
Margaret Spellings	Secretary	U.S. Dept of Education	x				x	x
Melanie Sabelhaus	Senior Principal	Jerold Panas, Linzy & Partners	x	x	x	x	x	x
Michael Chertoff	Secretary	U.S. Dept of Homeland Security	x	x				
Michael Hawkins	Partner	Dinsmore & Shohl, LLP	x	x	x	x	x	x
Michael O. Leavitt	Secretary	U.S. Dept of Health	x					
Paula Boggs	Exec VP, General Counsel	Starbucks	x	x	x	x	x	x
R. Bruce LaBoon	Attorney	Lock Lord Bissell & Liddell	x	x	x			
R. James Nicholson	Secretary	U.S. Dept of Veteran Affairs	x					
Richard Davis	CEO/Chairman/President	U.S. Bancorp	x	x	x	x	x	x
Richard Fountain	Attorney	Law Offices of Richard Fountain	x	x	x	x	x	x
Richard M. Niemeic	Senior VP - Corporate Affairs	Blue Cross Blue Shield of Mimes	x					
Richard Patton	Founder/Chief Manager	Courage Capital	x	x	x	x	x	x
Ross H. Ogden	President	Tamarix, Inc	x					
Sanford Belden	Retired President & CEO	Community Bank Systems	x	x	x	x	x	
Sherry Lansing	CEO	The Sherry Lansing Foundation	x	x				
Steven E. Carr	Partner	Fuller & Carr Law Offices	x	x				
Steven Wunning	Group President	Caterpillar	x	x				
Sue B. Hassmiller	Senior Program Officer	Robert Wood Johnson Foundation	x	x	x	x	x	x
Suzanne Johnson	Former Vice Chairman	Goldman Sachs	x	x	x	x	x	x
Theodore R. Parrish	Professor, Health Education	N.C. Central University	x	x				
Walter E. Thornton	Retired		x	x	x			
Wei-Tih Cheng, Ph D.	Retired		x	x				
William F. McConnell, Jr.	Senior VP	Cardiac Rhythm Mgmt	x	x				
William Lucy	SecretaryTreasurer	AFL-CIO	x	x				
William Simon	CEO/President	WalMart				x	x	x
Youngme Moon	Professor	Harvard			x	x	x	x
Number of Board Members			**48**	**28**	**21**	**19**	**18**	**20**

*Data handcollected from SEC filings – DEF14a and 10-K

NOTES

1. "American Red Cross Governance for the 21st Century", Opening Letter dated November 1, 2006. Accessible at http://www.redcross.org/www-files/Documents/Governance/BOG GOvernanceReport.pdf. Herein referred to as "BOG Report".
2. Widmer, C and Houchin, S. K. 1999. "Governance of National Federated Organizations." Board Source E-Book Series, p.7.
3. Ibid., p.18.
4. "Help on the Way for New Orleans." *CNN Larry King Live*. Aired September 2, 2005. Access online transcripts May 2011 at http://transcripts.cnn.com/TRANSCRIPTS/0509/02/lkl.01.html
5. Ibid.
6. Ibid.
7. "The Federal Response to Hurricane Katrina: Lessons Learned," report to President George W. Bush, February 23, 2006, foreword, p.1. Hereafter referred to as White House report. Accessed May 2011 at http://georgewbush-whitehouse.archives.gov/reports/katrina-lessons-learned/foreword.html
8. "Despite Katrina Efforts, Red Cross Draws Criticism," Associated Press, September 28, 2005. Accessed May 2011 at http://www.usatoday.com/news/nation/2005-09-28-katrina-red-cross_x.htm. This is also acknowledged in various parts of the White House report.
9. "American Red Cross Troubles," *NewsHour with Jim Lehrer*. Aired December 14, 2005. Accessed online transcripts May 2011 at http://www.pbs.org/newshour/bb/health-july-dec05-redcross_12-14/
10. Strom, S. "Senator Urges Red Cross to Overhaul its Board. *The New York Times* (February 28, 2006). Accessed February 2012 at (http://www.nytimes.com/2006/02/28/politics/28cross.html).
11. "Grassley Urges Red Cross to Improve Governance, Respond to Volunteers' Concerns." The United States Senate Committee on Finance Report, February 27, 2006. Accessed July 23, 2012 at http://www.finance.senate.gov/newsroom/chairman/release/?id=1e2fce30-51b7-4859-a93f-6a070eea366c herein referred to as "Senate Committee Report."

12. Meckler, L. "Healy to Resign as President of Red Cross," Associated Press, October 26, 2001. Accessed April 2011 at http://www.seattlepi.com/news/article/Healy-to-resign-as-president-of-Red-Cross-1069990.php
13. Nobles, M. E. "The ARC Interim CEO Club: Tempting at the Top Becoming a Regular Occurrence," *The Non-profit Times* February 1, 2006.
14. Salmon, J. March 4, 2006, "Red Cross Gave Ousted Executive $780,000 Deal" Washington Post.com
15. "ARC Troubles." 2005. op.cit., p.3
16. Senate Committee Report, p.3.
17. Ibid.
18. Ibid.
19. Ibid.
20. BOG Report, op. cit., p.20.
21. BOG Report, op. cit., p.33
22. BOG Report, op. cit., p.38
23. BOG Report, op.cit., p.35.
24. Ibid.
25. Ibid., p.78.
26. ARC 2007 fiscal year end report. Accessed September 2011 at http://www.redcross.org/www-files/Documents/pdf/corppubs/14606D.pdf
27. BOG Report, op. cit., p.31.
28. BOG Report, op. cit., p.36.
29. Rafferty, R. J. 2007. "Will New Red Cross CEO Help or Harm Confidence in Disaster Agency?" May 31, 2007 AmericaJR website. Accessed May 2011 at http://americajr.com/news/red-cross-ceo.html
30. "Red Cross Leader Describes First-Year Triumphs, Challenges" ARC announcement dated July 21, 2009. Accessed May 2011 at http://www.prnewswire.com/news-releases/red-cross-leader-describes-first-year-triumphs-challenges-62248512.html
31. "Bringing Help, Bringing Hope" A five-year report following Hurricane Katrina. Accessed May 2011 at http://www.scribd.com/doc/36458115/Katrina-5-Year

Chipotle Mexican Grill, Inc.: Conscious Capitalism by Serving "Food With Integrity"

Alan N. Hoffman
Bentley University

Background

Founded by Steve Ells in 1993, Chipotle Mexican Grill, Inc. (CMG or "Chipotle") quickly became one of the fastest growing restaurant chains in history. A pioneer in the fast-casual segment of the restaurant market, Chipotle focused on changing the way food was processed and delivered to consumers by the restaurant industry.[1] Over the course of 21 years, Chipotle grew to over 1600 restaurants in the United States and 11 internationally. The first restaurant opened its doors in Denver in a renovated Dolly Madison ice cream shop. In 1995, the company added a second and third shop in Denver and eventually expanded to sixteen restaurants in 1998.

Through luck and hard work, Chipotle attracted the attention of MacDonald's Corporation whose investment of $350 million plus expertise in processes, systems, and real estate allowed Chipotle to grow to over 500 restaurants by 2006. Chipotle filed its initial public offering (IPO) that same year. In 2007, McDonald's divested itself of Chipotle,

The author thanks Barbara Gottfried and Bentley University BMBA students Suman Akkinepally, Thomas Daly, Qing He, Donald Khoury, Mena Mahaniah, Craig Richey and Elisaveta Tsvetkova for their research and contributions to this case. Please address all correspondence to: *Dr. Alan N. Hoffman,* Dept. of Management, Bentley University, 175 Forest Street, Waltham, MA 02452-4705, ahoffman@bentley.edu, (781) 891-2287. Printed by permission of Dr. Alan N. Hoffman.

resulting in an impressive return of $1.5 billion on its original investment. However, McDonald's then missed out on CMG's huge growth in share price after the divestiture.[2]

Beginning in 2000, Steve Ells made a concerted effort to serve consumers "food with integrity" utilizing a sustainable and responsible approach to ingredient sourcing, production, and service. For example, CMG began serving naturally raised pork in some of its stores, highlighting the company's commitment to transparency. By 2010, all of the pork served in Chipotle restaurants was naturally raised. In 2002, CMG began serving naturally raised chicken. By 2014 the company sourced 100% of its chicken product from farms that met that standard. And as of 2007, 100% of its beef was naturally raised and 40% of its black beans were organically grown. In 2009, Steve Ells testified before Congress about ways to try to eliminate antibiotics completely from farming.[3]

Chipotle's brand power, customer engagement, and loyalty was evident in 2000 when CMG began to serve naturally raised pork in its burritos. The company was forced to raise the price of its carnitas filling by one dollar, but was rewarded for its efforts rather than punished: sales rose rather than fell, fueling Chipotle's faith that customers would buy responsibly raised food and even pay a premium price for it.[4]

Strategic Direction

According to the company's website, "Chipotle's mission is to change the way people think about and eat fast food."[5] Its vision was to serve delicious food made with fresh ingredients from sustainable resources, and sell it for a reasonable price. All elements of Chipotle's strategic direction were closely aligned and revolved around its flagship program, "Food with Integrity," defined as finding the very best raw ingredients raised in a sustainable way with respect for the animals, the environment, and the farmers who produced the food.[6] Chipotle made a particular effort to use animals raised in a humane way, such that the animals had not been treated with antibiotics or hormones that cause rapid or unnatural growth. It was CMG's firm belief that natural and high-quality ingredients, freshly prepared, resulted in better tasting food as well as better "politics."[7]

Conscious Capitalism: A Higher Purpose

The company's "Food with Integrity" program meant that its supply chain and corporate culture were closely integrated from the time that raw materials (ingredients) were farmed, raised, harvested, and shipped to stores to the time a burrito (the final product) was placed on a customer's serving tray. Chipotle believed that its appeal to its socially responsible customers only deepened as those customers became more aware of the sustainable way Chipotle sourced its ingredients.[8] Unlike its competitors, all of CMG's restaurants were company-owned and supplied by Chipotle's independently owned and operated distribution centers whose suppliers were evaluated on the quality of what they provided and their understanding and empathy with the company's mission.

The Chipotle Business Model: Redefining "Fast Food"

As with any number of other fast-food restaurants, Chipotle's business model was "a few things a thousand ways." Its menu was designed to offer a relatively limited number of menu items (burritos, burrito bowls, tacos, and salads), but with a large variety of extras such as beans, salads, and guacamole such that through extensive recombination of ingredients, customers could create unique and exciting food selections each time they visited, enhancing their overall Chipotle experience.

Even though Chipotle used classic cooking methods with stovetops for heating, knives for chopping, and vessels for mixing, its food was served to customers extremely fast. Its assembly line was seen as one of the most efficient in the business, and unlike competitors such as Starbucks, it didn't take very long for customers to order food and be served. Chipotle saw this customer-oriented culture as key to its success.

Finally, the company made quality assurance and food safety integral to its supply chain.[9] To maintain quality, Chipotle invested heavily in its staff. In many cases, the company mentored future leaders internally, fostering continuity amongst its management team to sustain its explosive growth.[10] Assuring quality and food safety promoted customer loyalty and ongoing engagement.

Ultimately, Chipotle's main objective was profitability achieved through staff and operational efficiencies designed to offset the higher than average cost of its organic ingredients.

Sustainability

CMG's goal was to deliver delicious fast food in a way that was transparent, safe for the environment, and responsible to the animals slaughtered for meat[11] so as to build a reputation as an organization which did not simply pay lip service to the tenets of sustainability, but lived up to those tenets. As the demand for sustainable products grew and became more competitive, Chipotle worked to foster strong relationships with its supply chain to secure and expand its supply of high-quality, natural, organic, and local ingredients. Beginning in 2008, the company embarked on a program to increase local sourcing to 35%. "This seasonable produce program was meant to cut down on fossil fuels used to transport produce, give local family farms a boost and improve the taste of the food served to customers by using ingredients during their peak season."[12] In addition, the company refined its cooking techniques to continually offer customers the very best food possible.

Chipotle followed a similarly innovative path in the way it designed and built its restaurants, looking for more environmentally friendly building materials and systems that made its restaurants more efficient[13] In 2009, the company announced that it had partnered with a renewable energy company to install solar energy systems in Chipotle restaurants across the country, making Chipotle the largest producer and user of solar energy in the restaurant industry.[14]

Competitors

The National Restaurant Association projected total U.S. restaurant sales would hit a record high of $683.4 billion in 2014. Chipotle captured $3.3 billion of total sales revenue in 2013.[15] The industry was divided into three large segments:

- Full Service
- Quick Service
- Fast-Casual

Fast-casual restaurants were seen by consumers as offering a slightly higher quality food, service, and atmosphere than quick-service restaurants, and quickly became the fastest growing segment of the restaurant industry: expanding from 4% growth in sales in 2009 to 9% growth in sales in 2012 and 8% in 2013.[16] According to The NPD Group, fast-casual restaurants had the highest traffic growth in 2013 among all restaurant segments (**Exhibit 1**),[17] evidence of the strength of this segment of the business. "The fast-casual segment always does better than the rest of the industry because it's a

EXHIBIT 1
Change in Customer
Traffic

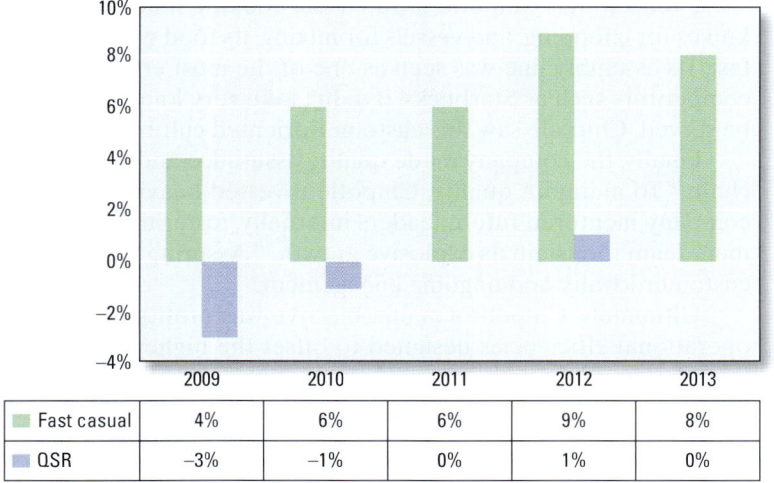

	2009	2010	2011	2012	2013
Fast casual	4%	6%	6%	9%	8%
QSR	−3%	−1%	0%	1%	0%

http://seekingalpha.com/article/2031641-chipotle-mexican-grill-explosive-growth-is
-expected-to-continue

hybrid—it combines the convenience of quick service with the food offerings of higher-check establishments."[18]

Chipotle's business model and strategy were designed to fulfill the expectations of the fast-casual market segment, and its success "has been a market driver for the entire segment, spurring many new players into the fast-casual marketplace."[19] CMG's revenue grew 17.7% in 2013 and 20.3% in 2012. Its strategic philosophy challenged consumers' preconceptions of the fast-food industry, providing high-quality natural products and encouraging multisegment positioning. Redefining fast food meant that Chipotle saw itself as an alternative to traditional fast food and its use of high-quality natural ingredients positioned it at the highest price points in its segment, which overlapped with the low-end price points of the full service segment. According to NPD, guest checks at fast-casual restaurants were, on average, $7.40 in 2013 while average checks for quick service were $5.30 and $13.66 for casual-dining. The higher quality natural products also attracted more health conscious upscale customers who did not traditionally frequent fast-casual or quick-service restaurants.[20]

In addition to being the market leader in the fast-casual market segment, Chipotle also became the market leader in the Mexican fast-casual segment, and successfully competed with Mexican restaurants in all three segments. In the quick-service market segment (formerly known as the fast-food segment) Chipotle competed with YUM! Brands' Taco Bell chain. In the fast-casual market Panera Bread Co, Qdoba Restaurant Corporation, and Panda Restaurant Group were its biggest competitors (**Exhibit 2**). Fresh Enterprises' more than 250 Baja Fresh Mexican Grill fast-casual restaurants were also players in the Mexican fast-casual segment, as were a plethora of single standing and regional chains such as El Pollo Loco Holdings, Inc., Panchero's Franchise Corporation, and Moe's Southwest Grill. By 2014, Mexican food was the third most popular cuisine after American and Italian according to an NPD survey (**Exhibits 3** & **4**). In the full service segment, Chipotle competed with Darden Restaurant Inc.'s Olive Garden and Red Lobster, among others. Food trucks also became important competitors, the latest entrants into the fast-casual and quick-service market segments.

YUM! BRANDS: Taco Bell

As of 2014, Yum! Brands, Inc. operated the Taco Bell, Pizza Hut, KFC, Long John Silver's, and A&W chains. The Yum! Brands corporation was seen by the industry as

EXHIBIT 2
Fast-Casual Industry Segment Perception Map

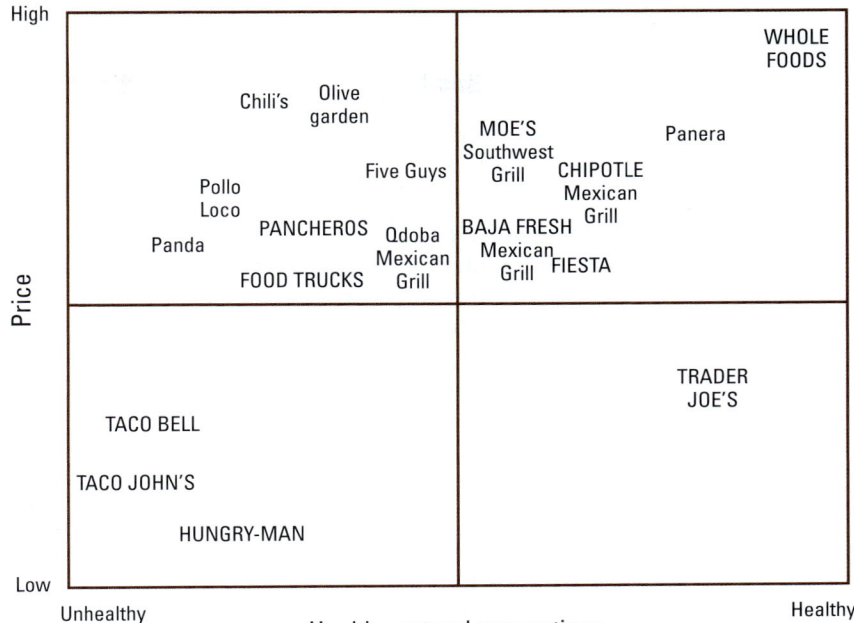

EXHIBIT 3
Survey U.S. Participants Identified Their Favorite Cuisine As Follows:

Survey U.S. Participants Identified Their Favorite Cuisine As Follows:	
American	31%
Italian	23%
Mexican	16%
Chinese	14%
Japanese	5%
Middle-Eastern	3%
Indian	2%

http://www.rkma.com/bentley/rfb14/

EXHIBIT 4
Fast-Food Restaurant Market Leaders

Market Leaders (July 2013)		
Annual Sales Market Leader (USD)		
Bakery Cafe	3.7 billion	Panera Bread
Mexican	2.7 billion	Chipotle Mexican Grill
Asian/noodle	1.8 billion	Panda Express
Sandwich	1.3 billion	Jimmy John's Gourmet Sandwich
Better burger	1.1 billion	Five Guys Burgers and Fries
Chicken	979 million	Zaxby's
Pizza	157 million	Donatos Pizza

http://www.rkma.com/bentley/rfb14/

a major, aggressively expanding international player, operating the largest portfolio of quick-service restaurants in the world with approximately 37,000 locations in more than 100 countries.[21] By 2015, China and India were projected to contribute around $1 billion in annual sales to Yum! Brands. To further its expansion, Taco Bell began testing break-fast meals offerings in 2014, which were expected to contribute $7 billion to its domestic sales over the next decade.[22] Though the trend toward healthier food was seen to have made significant inroads in the restaurant industry, there was also a cultural backlash. Taco Bell understood its mission as serving this health-resistant rebel consumer. Taco Bell's introduction of MTN Dew Kickstart soda, a blend of Mountain Dew and orange juice could be construed as an example of its refusal to "go healthy."

Jack in the Box, Inc.'s Qdoba Mexican Grill

Qdoba Mexican Grill, a wholly owned subsidiary of Jack in the Box, opened in Denver in 1995 under the name Zuma. Qdoba used Zuma, then Z-TECA Mexican Grill to avoid confusion with other Zuma Mexican restaurants. Qdoba was best known for its San Francisco Mission-style burritos customized with options such as roasted chile corn, shredded beef, fajita vegetables, rancho-chile barbecue sauce, and a three-cheese queso.[23] In 2013, the company reported $1.5 billion in sales at more than 600 locations.[24]

Panera Bread Co.

Originally named the St. Louis Bread Company, Panera was purchased in 1993 by the Au Bon Pain Company, a franchiser of fast-casual bakery-cafes. Panera's key menu items were daily baked goods, made-to-order sandwiches, and unique soups. The company reported $2.13 billion in revenue for 2013. Panera's strategy was to straddle the line between affordability and high quality, serving antibiotic-free chicken and turkey, whole grain bread, and some organic and all-natural ingredients, while keeping the cost of an average meal to less than $10.00. Panera also fostered growth by acquiring retail locations from its franchise operators.[25]

Food Trucks

Recently the convenience and variety offered by food trucks began to threaten the stability of the fast-casual segment.[26] In 2013, estimated annual food truck sales were $5 billion, an increase from virtually zero only five years earlier. Several restaurant chains including Qdoba Mexican Grill and Taco Bell decided to compete by outfitting their own food trucks as catering operations and test kitchens on wheels, and taking them to local events to build brand awareness.

In 2013, the food dollar market share of the restaurant industry was 40%; the balance of 60% went to supermarkets.[27] Thus, the biggest substitution threat to restaurants was not so much other restaurants as it was supermarkets that offered a wide breadth of food such as prepared meals and frozen food at lower than restaurant prices.

Financial Operations

Chipotle's financial objectives were simple:

- No long-term debt
- Grow organically, growth funded by retained earnings
- Maintain an operating margin of at least 10%
- Exceed organic growth of occupant safety market

CMG showed a steady growth in terms of both revenue and operating margins from 2004 to 2013. According to the most recent data (**Exhibits 5** & **6**), CMG significantly outperformed the industry average as well as the S&P 500. For instance, CMG's revenue growth rate was approximately 24.41%, nearly 6 times higher than the industry rate (4.3%) and 12 times higher than the S&P 500 index (**Exhibit 7**). While the industry and

EXHIBIT 5
Revenue and
Operating Market

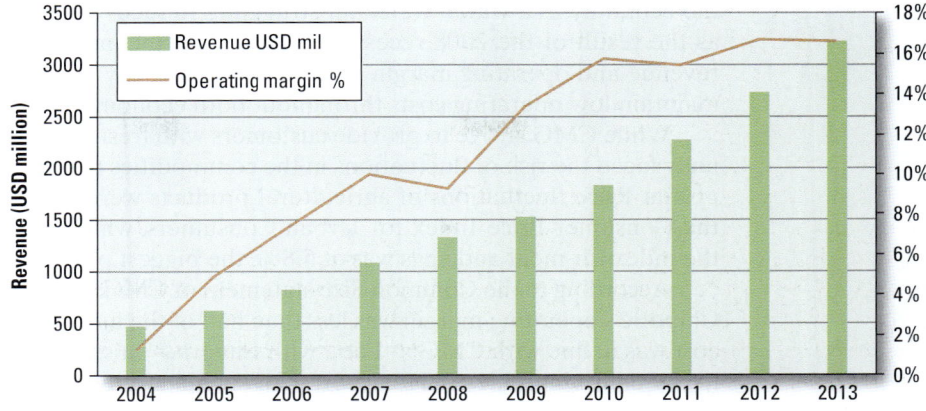

Source: Analysis from Chipotle Annual Report

EXHIBIT 6
Historical Stock Per-
formance for CMG

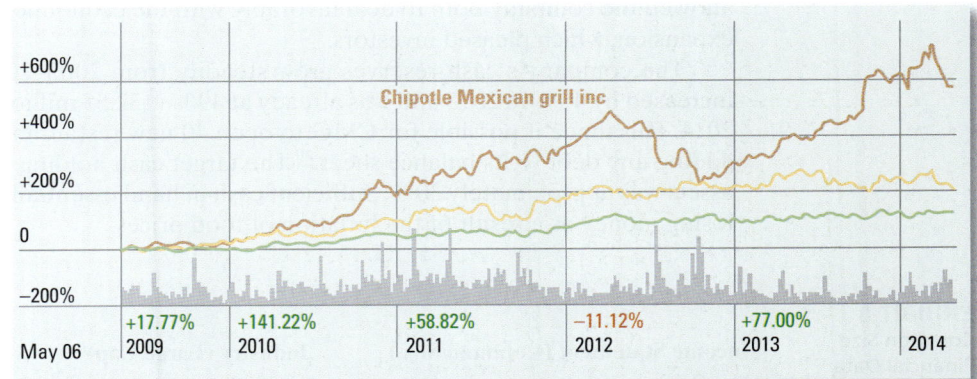

Source: Yahoo Finance

EXHIBIT 7
CMG Growth
Comparison

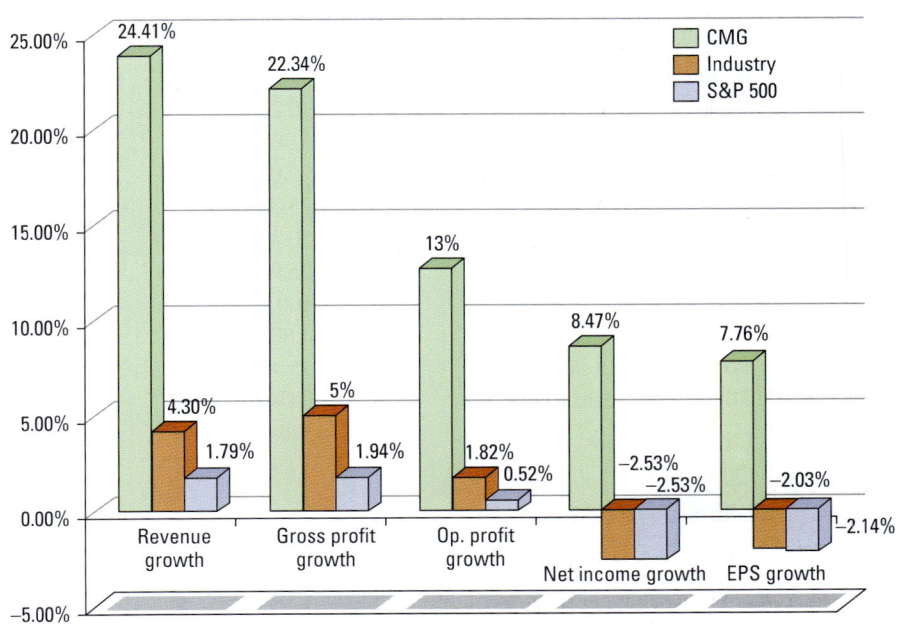

Source: CSI Market

the economy as a whole were still struggling to recover from the negative net income as the result of the 2008 recession, CMG's net income reached 8.47%. The fact that revenue and operating margin grew in line was partly attributable to CMG's ability to maintain low operating costs throughout both economic recession and boom.

While CMG strove to provide customers with fresh and high-quality food, it continually faced the risk of fluctuations in the commodities market that could potentially cut profits. Price fluctuations of agricultural products were often significantly higher than the Consumer Price Index for Urban Consumers, which was at 1.6% in 2013,[28] while the index for meat and eggs was at 5.8%, the biggest price change in the food industry.

According to the Common Size statement of CMG and industry average (**Exhibit 8**), Chipotle's operating margin was less than half of the industry average. The high variable cost was in line with CMG's "Food with Integrity" mission, which focused on high-cost, high-quality ingredients. However, with such a strategy, CMG needed to cut costs in other areas such as operating and labor costs.

As of 2014, CMG had no long-term debt (**Exhibit 9**). Its strong balance sheet allowed the company both to deal favorably with the economic cycle and focus fully on expansion, which pleased investors.

The company's cash reserves grew steadily from 2003–2013. The free cash flow increased by 48% in 2013 and was already at 49% (132.55 million) in the first quarter of 2014. This made it possible for CMG to open 40 new restaurants each quarter without adding any debt to its balance sheet.[29] The target cash holding as a percentage of total assets was approximately 30%. Sufficient cash in hand essentially prevented CMG from losing money as a result of the inflation of food prices.

EXHIBIT 8
Common Size
Financial Data

Income Statement (Common Size)	Industry (Large Cap)	Chipotle
Net Sales	100.00%	100.00%
Gross Margin	63.70%	26.59%
Operating Income	3.40%	16.63%
Net Income	1.50%	10.19%
Balance Sheet (Common Size)		
Cash	10.20%	28.78%
Accounts Receivable	5.40%	1.38%
Inventory	2.50%	0.65%
Total Current Assets	23.70%	33.16%
Property, Plant & Equipment	50.40%	47.94%
Other Non-Current Assets	25.90%	17.81%
Total Assets	100.00%	100.00%
Accounts Payable	4.80%	2.94%
Total Current Liabilities	15.40%	9.92%
Total Long Term Liabilities	34.40%	13.53%
Financial Ratios		
Quick Ratio	1.05	3.04
Current Ratio	1.54	3.34
Inventory Turnover	x26.65	x195.51

http://financials.morningstar.com/ratios/r.html?t=CMG&region=usa&culture=en-US

EXHIBIT 9
Financial Data

	For the years ended December 31				
	2013	2012	2011	2010	2009
Statement of Income:					
Revenue	$ 3,214,591	$ 2,731,224	$ 2,269,548	$ 1,835,922	$ 1,518,417
Food, beverage and packaging costs........	1,073,514	891,003	738,720	561,107	466,027
Labor costs	739,800	641,836	543,119	453,573	385,072
Occupancy costs	199,107	171,435	147,274	128,933	114,218
Other operating costs......	347,401	286,610	251,208	202,904	174,581
General and administrative expenses	203,733	183,409	149,426	118,590	99,149
Depreciation and amortization...........	96,054	84,130	74,938	68,921	61,308
Pre-opening costs	15,511	11,909	8,495	7,767	8,401
Loss on disposal of assets	6,751	5,027	5,806	6,296	5,956
Total operating expenses	2,681,871	2,275,359	1,918,986	1,548,091	1,314,712
Income from operations ...	532,720	455,865	350,562	287,831	203,705
Interest and other income (expense), net	1,751	1,820	(857)	1,230	520
Income before income taxes.................	534,471	457,685	349,705	289,061	204,225
Provision for income taxes	(207,033)	(179,685)	(134,760)	(110,080)	(77,380)
Net income	$ 327,438	$ 278,000)	$ 214,945	$ 178,981	$ 126,845
Earnings per share					
Basic	$ 10,58	$ 8.82	$ 6.89	$ 5.73	$ 3.99
Diluted.............	$ 10.47	$ 8.75	$ 6.76	$ 5.64	$ 3.95
Weighted average common shares outstanding					
Basic	30,957	31,513	31,217	31,234	31,766
Diluted.............	31,281	31,783	31,775	31,735	32,102

	As of December 31				
	2013	2012	2011	2010	2009
Balance Sheet Data:					
Total current assets.......	$ 666,307	$ 546,607	$ 501,192	$ 406,221	$ 297,454
Total assets	$ 2,009,280	$ 1,668,667	$ 1.425,308	$ 1,121,605	$ 961,505
Total current liabilities	$ 199,228	$ 186,852	$ 157,453	$ 123,054	102,153
Total liabilities	$ 470,992	$ 422,741	$ 381,082	$ 310,732	$ 258.044
Total shareholders' equity................	$ 1,538,288	$ 1,245,926	$ 1,044,226	$ 810,873	$ 703,461

CMG Stock

CMG's stock price accelerated consistently, climbing to $500 per share from $22 per share at its initial public offering in 2006.[30] The strong growth underscored CMG's short-term price performance and became a strong indicator of long-performance. From June 2013 to June 2014, CMG's earnings per share (EPS) showed moderate growth from $9.6 to $11.02. Although the growth rate was slightly lower than what outside analysts had expected, it was still higher than the industry average.

Marketing

From the first CMG saw marketing as essential to building its brand recognition.

Though the price point of Chipotle's products was higher than most fast-food competitors and comparable or slightly higher than other fast-casual competitors, the food was of much higher quality than fast food, and more sustainable and slightly higher quality than that of most fast-casual alternatives. This pricing strategy was both a strength and a weakness for CMG. The company was banking on the notion that customers would consider the increase in food quality and sustainability a good value that more than justified the small price premium, which in turn allowed CMG to enjoy a kind of premium brand image and supported above average profit margins. Additionally, as the price was still close to other fast-casual alternatives, younger, value-oriented customers could still be targeted. The weakness of this pricing strategy was the potential exposure to competition entering the fast-casual segment and competing on price. Chipotle feared it would not be able to respond competitively, thereby losing market share.

Location and size were other facets of Chipotle's successful marketing strategy. Typically Chipotle restaurants were smaller than those of its competitors, especially in high traffic areas. This allowed Chipotle to open restaurants in good locations, at somewhat lower rents than its competitors. Building on this strength, Chipotle retained whole ownership of all locations, giving the chain complete control over the look, feel, and design of its restaurants. However, a weakness of Chipotle's typical in-line retail outlet locations and smaller freestanding buildings was that the company generally didn't have exclusive rights over the locations so competitors could, and often did, set up next door.

Analysts (and customers) agreed that Chipotle's major strength was its product. The company's use of high-quality ingredients that tasted better, and custom made-to-order burritos set it a notch above typical fast-food eateries. The simple but customizable menu meant less inventory was required and orders could be processed very quickly. In addition, the healthiness and sustainability of Chipotle's products was consistent with trends in regulation and consumer preferences. The company's main weakness, however, was that nothing was proprietary and its product was very easy to imitate.

Much of Chipotle's success was attributable to its excellent promotional efforts. First, advertising was done in-house which allowed greater flexibility and nimbleness, and insured consistency with company values. Second, in keeping with its reputation for sustainability, Chipotle did not use traditional media, which differentiated CMG from other major players in the market such as McDonalds and Wendy's. However, a weakness of this strategy was that it was hard to scale; thus, recently Chipotle did move into more traditional media promotion with a Super Bowl ad and some radio ads. Chipotle also expanded its use of a highly successful direct mail campaign, but as with traditional media, these promotional practices were not quite consistent with its reputation for sustainability. Finally, a major strength for Chipotle was its focus on brand experience and its drive to create a loyal customer base that didn't just eat at Chipotle but loved the brand and spread Chipotle's mission. A potential weakness with this strategy was that if anyone had a negative experience with the brand, Chipotle would be held responsible for breaking the bond of customer trust. Similarly, critical publicity with regard to CMG business practices could deeply tarnish Chipotle's relationship with its customers.

Human Resources

Chipotle's higher food costs meant smaller margins for operational costs. Chipotle successfully offset those higher food costs by controlling labor costs. The company made the strategic decision to pay above minimum wage, and leverage its positive brand image to attract, motivate, and retain quality employees, who, in turn, produced greater value for the company despite the small price premium. Importantly, Chipotle also promoted 80% of store managers from within, encouraging front line staff, cultivating company loyalty, and insuring that managers had an insider's strong understanding of restaurant operations.

Operational Efficiency

Throughout the industry, Chipotle was renowned for its operational efficiencies of scale. From the beginning, the business was organized from the ground up for efficiency, yielding record-high restaurant throughput rates with data analytics that correlated throughput and repeat purchases, indicating that faster throughput increased customers' willingness to wait in line and to return. In addition, the company fostered operational capabilities to scale up experimental menu items. Chipotle's operational efficiencies were expected to yield mid-single digit growth in 2014.

Chipotle's unique "people culture" also strikingly differentiated it from its competitors, as evidenced by the success stories included on the company's highly dynamic website. Chipotle prides itself on having a strong people culture built on hiring top performing employees, developing and empowering them to deliver an exceptional dining experience for its customers.

The success of many companies, as Chipotle understood quite well, depended not just on innovative products but on the people involved at every level. Analysts concurred, noting that Chipotle's people and its human resource policies were key to its success; and the company's employee retention figures and impressive revenues and efficiencies further validated the key role that employees throughout the company played.

Mobile Payments Coming

In 2014, Chipotle spent $10 million on network upgrades for its restaurants to enable future improvements, especially mobile payments via a barcode. Such payment devices would cost each restaurant hundreds of dollars, however the company expected that the initial outlay would increase its customer base and foster greater efficiency, as the company's own research made clear that in the fast service and fast-casual markets speed of delivery was vital to customer retention.

However, critics pointed out that if cashiers were not the bottleneck for the restaurant's service, mobile payments wouldn't necessarily increase throughput. Regardless, it was felt that the initiative could help Chipotle with marketing efforts as it would also help the company understand its customers better, as mobile payments would allow Chipotle to maintain records of orders, analyze the data, and customize promotions to encourage repeat purchases.

Socially Responsible Strategy

Chipotle always believed that addressing societal concerns could foster innovation and increase productivity. Over the years, the company implemented the following socially responsible initiatives.

- A 10-year project with Good Shepherd Poultry Range to resurrect heritage breeds of chicken that could survive on pastures[31]

- The use of organically grown beans (40%), with another 5% grown using conservation tillage methods, thereby reducing soil erosion

- Refusing to use genetically modified corn even though 65% of American corn came from GM crops as of 2014

- Sourcing lettuce from local farms during the growing season

- Using only organically grown cilantro and working toward the goal of using 10% organic avocados

- Only using dairy products from cows that were never treated with the synthetic hormone rBGH. However, only 30% were pasture-raised, as supply was limited supply. To get to 100%, the chain planned to build its own dairy cooperative.

- Every time two Chipotle restaurants opened, another farmer whose pigs were naturally raised was allowed to join the Niman Ranch network and become a supplier to the chain. When Chipotle began this initiative, there were 50 to 60 such farmers. By 2014 there were between 600 and 700.

- Involvement in community events and charities, and with local farmers and business owners through marketing outreach

- Signing an agreement with the Coalition of Immokalee Workers (CIW) to improve wages and working conditions for tomato pickers in Florida. The company agreed to pay an extra penny per pound of tomatoes purchased for its 1,300 restaurants nationwide, with the money appearing as a bonus in workers' paychecks.

A "Cool" Brand

As noted above, Chipotle's greatest strength and competitive advantage was its brand: edgy, trendy, and cool. People loved Chipotle not just because of the tasty and healthy food but because of the values the brand conveyed. Creative viral marketing techniques such as the scarecrow video[32] that was viewed over 12 million times showcased Chipotle's sustainable sourcing, quality, and integrity as well as distancing the company from the heartless profit-focused giants in the food industry. Chipotle's successful branding showcased its competitive advantage in corporate culture by highlighting its focus on social responsibility. The sense that they were helping make the world a better place together with a preferential internal promotion system enhanced employee satisfaction and attracted high quality employees with low turnover.

Efficient supply chain management, which allowed CMG to use sustainable sourcing and maintain low inventory and accurate forecasting, also contributed to Chipotle's competitive advantage, in turn allowing Chipotle to use more local suppliers than its competitors and offer a higher-quality product at a comparable price. Chipotle's branding, efficient supply chain with sustainable sourcing, and socially responsible corporate culture were consistent and, taken together, supported the company's mission as well as sustained a competitive advantage.

Another important core competence was its restaurant operations expertise in the fast-casual segment. Chipotle could potentially use this expertise as a platform to expand into other fast-casual alternatives. Recently Chipotle tested a pizza as well as an Asian cuisine fast-casual restaurant. Finally, Chipotle declined to franchise its restaurants, thus wholly owns all locations, giving it complete control over the look, feel, design, and management of every location, and allowing it to leverage its restaurant operations expertise.

Key Challenges Facing Chipotle

By 2014, the fast-casual domestic U.S. market was growing, but also becoming increasingly competitive and crowded with many new entrants, especially traditional fast-food players who were attracted by the double-digit revenue growth. Jack in the Box entered the fast-casual market with Qdoba, directly challenging Chipotle. Many new regional fast-casual chains were growing and starting to go national such as Slim Chicken and Q Barbeque. In addition, Chipotle faced increased competition from imitators such as Boloco and Moe's Southwest Grill.

At the same time, Wall Street had extremely high growth and earnings expectations for the company. Speculation on Chipotle's future growth and earnings pushed the share price to 47 times earnings.[33] Chipotle's P/E ratio was the highest of the major companies in its segment, compared to a P/E ratio of thirty for YUM! Brands and twenty-three for Panera. As the fast-casual segment began to reach saturation in the U.S. market and the industry life cycle moved from a high growth phase toward maturity, living up to analysts' expectations was predicted to become increasingly difficult.

Future Growth Opportunities

Despite the challenges within the fast-food industry, analysts saw room for further growth if Chipotle focused on customers and markets previously untapped or underserved. For instance, in 2014, 54% of fast-casual customers were female, yet Chipotle's advertising and large portions were skewed towards males. Females and weight conscious fast-casual customers might be enticed by offering calorie conscious portions and more health and lifestyle advertising that highlighted how wholesome and healthy the food at Chipotle could be.

Chipotle also offered the potential to develop a breakfast menu. In 2014, Taco Bell launched its new breakfast menu that included items such as the "a.m. crunch wrap" and the "waffle taco." At Dulles International Airport, Chipotle was required to be open during breakfast hours. It tested breakfast items but found that early morning customers tended to order regular lunch and dinner menu items so it dropped its experimental breakfast options.[34]

Finally, Chipotle already had a very healthy kids menu that was not very effectively promoted. Additional marketing to health conscious parents could support the expansion into this potential new customer segment.

Chipotle established itself as a successful company practicing "conscious capitalism" by serving "food with integrity." However, by 2014 it had become clear that Chipotle needed to find new markets in order to continue to grow its revenues and keep Wall Street happy.

NOTES

1. Chipotle Mexican Grill, Inc. 2013 Annual Report and Proxy Statement.
2. http://www.businessweek.com/articles/2013-10-03/chipotle-the-one-that-got-away-from-mcdonalds
3. Ibid #1
4. The Chipotle Story. Web: http://www.chipotle.com/en-us/chipotle_story/where_did_we_come_from/where_did_we_come_from.aspx
5. Ibid #1.
6. Chipotle: Food with Integrity. http://www.chipotle.com/en-us/fwi/fwi.aspx
7. Chipotle Mexican Grill, Inc. Announces First Quarter 2014 Results. http://ir.chipotle.com/phoenix.zhtml?c=194775&p=irol-newsArticle_print&ID=1919590&highlight=
8. Ibid #1.
9. Ibid #1.
10. Ibid #5.
11. Subramanian, Ram (2013) Chipotle: Mexican Grill, Inc.: Food with Integrity. Ivey Publishing, https://www.iveycases.com/ProductView.aspx?id=58576
12. Ibid.
13. Ibid.
14. Chips, Salsa, and a Side of Solar Power: http://www.getsolar.com/blog/chips-salsa-and-a-side-of-solar-power/5176/
15. Restaurant, Food and Beverage Research Handbook 2014–2015. Atlanta: Richard K. Miller, 2014. http://www.rkma.com/bentley/rfb14/. Web. May 8, 2014.
16. Ibid.
17. Blackstone Equity Research. Chipotle Mexican Grill: Explosive Growth Is Expected To Continue. http://seekingalpha.com/article/2031641-chipotle-mexican-grill-explosive-growth-is-expected-to-continue. Web. February 19, 2014. Retrieved May 8, 2014
18. Restaurant, Food and Beverage Research Handbook 2014–2015. Atlanta: Richard K. Miller, 2014. http://www.rkma.com/bentley/rfb14/. Web. May 8, 2014.
19. Ibid.
20. Blackstone Equity Research. Chipotle Mexican Grill: Explosive Growth Is Expected To Continue. http://seekingalpha.com/article/2031641-chipotle-mexican-grill-explosive-growth-is-expected-to-continue. Web. 19 Feb. 2014. Retrieved 8 May 2014
21. Business Insights: Essentials http://bi.galegroup.com/essentials/company/888510?u=mlin_m_bent. Web. Retrieved May 8, 2014.
22. S & P CAPITAL IQ. Industry Surveys: Restaurants. New York: McGraw Hill Financial January 2014. Web. http://www.netadvantage.standardandpoors.com/NASApp/NetAdvantage/showIndustrySurvey.do?task=showIndustrySurvey&type=pdf&code=rst
23. Neurdorf, Samantha. America's 15 best Tex-Mex chain restaurants. *USA Today*. Web. http://www.usatoday.com/story/travel/destinations/2014/01/04/best-tex-mex-mexican-restaurants-food/4308625/. January 4, 2014. Retrieved May 8, 2014.
24. Business Insights: Essentials http://bi.galegroup.com/essentials/company/888510?u=mlin_m_bent. Web. Retrieved May 8, 2014.
25. Ibis World. http://clients1.ibisworld.com/reports/us/industry/majorcompanies.aspx?entid=4319#MP9334. Web. Retrieved May 8, 2014.
26. Restaurant, Food and Beverage Research Handbook 2014-2015. Atlanta: Richard K. Miller, 2014. http://www.rkma.com/bentley/rfb14/. Web. May 8, 2014.
27. S & P CAPITAL IQ. Industry Surveys: Restaurants. New York: McGraw Hill Financial , January 2014.
28. http://www.bls.gov/news.release/archives/cpi_02202014.pdf
29. http://www.fool.com/investing/general/2014/04/23/chipotle-mexican-grills-long-term-prospects-remain.aspx
30. http://finance.yahoo.com/q/hp?s=CMG
31. Porter, Michael, Creating Shared Value, *Harvard Business Review*, January 2011.
32. "The Scarecrow by Chipotle." Web: http://youtu.be/lUtnas5ScSE
33. https://finance.yahoo.com/q?s=CMG
34. http://consumerist.com/2014/03/14/no-chipotle-will-not-be-adding-a-breakfast-burrito-to-the-menu/

CASE **8**

Google and the Right to Be Forgotten[1]

Cynthia E. Clark
Bentley University

In 2009, Mario Costeja Gonzalez, a self-employed attorney living in a small town out-side Madrid, Spain, casually "googled" himself and was startled by what came up on his computer screen. Prominently displayed in the search results was a brief legal notice that had appeared more than a decade earlier in a local newspaper, *La Vanguardia*, which listed property seized and being auctioned by a government agency for nonpayments of debts. Among the properties was a home jointly owned by Costeja and his wife.

Costeja immediately realized that this information could damage his reputation as an attorney. Equally troubling, the information was no longer factual. He had paid his debt nearly a decade earlier. Abanlex, Costeja's small law firm, depended on the Internet to gain much of its new business, which was often generated by a Google search. Potential clients might choose not to hire him based on the old auction notice, he reflected. His mind then turned to the possible effects of this kind of information on other people's livelihoods. "There are people who cannot get a job because of content that is irrelevant," he thought.[2] "I support freedom of expression and I do not defend censorship. [However, I decided] to fight for the right to request the deletion of data that violates the honor, dignity and reputation of individuals."[3]

The next week, Costeja wrote to *La Vanguardia* and requested that it remove the article about his debt notice, because it had had been fully resolved a number of years earlier and reference to it now was, therefore, entirely irrelevant.[4] In doing so, he was making use of his rights under Spain's strong data protection policies, which recognized the protection and integrity of personal data as a constitutional right under Section 18 of the nation's Data Protection Act.[5] In response, the newspaper informed him that it had recently uploaded to the Internet all its past archives, dating back to 1881, to allow them to be searched by the public. It also noted that the auction notice had originally been publicly posted in order to secure as many bidders as possible. The newspaper refused

Costeja's request, stating that the information was obtained from public records and had thus been published lawfully.[6]

To be sure, the real problem for Costeja was not that the notice had appeared in *La Vanguardia*'s digital library, but that it had shown up in the results of the most widely used search engine in the world, Google, where potential clients might use it to judge his character.[7] Following this reasoning, Costeja then wrote to Google Spain, the firm's Spanish affiliate, only to be told that the parent company, Google Inc., was the entity responsible for the development of search results.[8] Costeja was taken aback by this development. "The resources Google has at their disposal aren't like those of any other citizens," he reflected.[9] Costeja felt he would be at a disadvantage in a lawsuit against an industry giant like Google.

In March 2010, after his unsuccessful attempts with the newspaper and Google Spain, Costeja turned to Spain's Data Protection Agency (SDPA), the government agency responsible for enforcing the Data Protection Act. "Google in Spain asked me to address myself to its headquarters in the U.S., but I found it too far and difficult to launch a complaint in the U.S., so I went to the agency in Spain to ask for their assistance. They said I was right, and the case went to court," he explained.[10] In a legal filing, Costeja requested, first, that the agency issue an administrative order requiring *La Vanguardia* either to remove or alter the pages in question (so that his personal data no longer appeared) or to use certain tools made available by search engines in order to shield the data from view. Second, he requested that the agency require that Google Spain or Google Inc. remove or conceal his personal data so that it no longer appeared in the search results and in the links to *La Vanguardia*. Costeja stated that his debt had been fully resolved.[11]

With these steps, a small-town Spanish lawyer had drawn one of the world's richest and best-known companies, Google, into a debate over the right to be forgotten.

Google, Inc.

Google Inc. is a technology company that builds products and provides services to organize information. Founded in 1998 and headquartered in Mountain View, CA, Google's mission was to organize the world's information and make it universally accessible and useful. It employed more than 55,000 people and had revenues of $45 billion. The company also had 70 offices in more than 40 countries.

The company's main product, *Google Search*, provided information online in response to a user's search. Google's other well-known products provided additional services. For example, *Google Now* provided information to users when they needed it, and its *Product Listing Ads* offered product image, price, and merchant information. The company also provided *AdWords*, an auction-based advertising program and *AdSense*, which enabled websites that were part of the Google network to deliver ads. *Google Display* was a display advertising network; *DoubleClick Ad Exchange* was a marketplace for the trading of display ad space; and *YouTube* offered video, interactive, and other ad formats.

Search Technology

In its core business, Google conducted searches in three stages: crawling and indexing, applying algorithms, and fighting spam.

Crawlers, programs that browsed the web to create an index of data, looked at web pages and followed links on those pages. They then moved from link to link and brought data about those web pages back to Google's servers. Google would then use this information to create an index of how exactly to retrieve information for its users. Algorithms were the computer processes and formulas that took users' questions and turned them into answers. At the most basic level, Google's algorithms looked up the user's search terms in the index to find the most appropriate pages. For a typical query, thousands, if not millions, of web pages might have helpful information. Google's algorithms relied on more than 200 unique signals or "clues" that made it possible to guess what an individual was really looking for. These signals included the terms on websites, the freshness of content, the region, and the page rank of the web page.[12] Lastly, the company fought spam through a combination of computer algorithms and manual review. Spam sites attempted to game their way to the top of search results by repeating keywords, buying links that passed Google's PageRank process, or putting invisible text on the screen. Google scouted out and removed spam because it could make legitimate websites harder to find. While much of this process was automated, Google did maintain teams whose job was to review sites manually.[13]

Policy on Information Removal

Google's policy on the general removal of information was the following:

> Upon request, we'll remove personal information from search results if we believe it could make you susceptible to specific harm, such as identity theft or financial fraud. This includes sensitive government ID numbers like U.S. Social Security numbers, bank account numbers, credit card numbers and images of signatures. We generally don't process removals of national ID numbers from official government websites because in those cases we consider the information to be public. We sometimes refuse requests if we believe someone is attempting to abuse these policies to remove other information from our results.[14]

Apart from this general policy, Google Inc. also removed content or features from its search results for legal reasons. For example, in the United States, the company would remove content with valid notification from the copyright holder under the Digital Millennium Copyright Act (DMCA), which was administered by the U.S. Copyright Office. The DCMA provided recourse for owners of copyrighted materials who believed that their rights under copyright law had been infringed upon on the Internet.[15] Under the notice and takedown procedure of the law, a copyright owner could notify the service provider, such as Google, requesting that a website or portion of a website be removed or blocked. If, upon receiving proper notification, the service provider promptly did so, it would be exempt from monetary liability.

Google regularly received such requests from copyright holders and those that represented them, such as the Walt Disney Company and the Recording Industry Association of America. Google produced and made public a list of the domain portions of URLs that had been the subject of a request for removal, and noted which ones had been removed. As of July 2015, it had removed more than 600,000 URLs out of more than 2.4 million requests.[16]

Likewise, content on local versions of Google was also removed when required by national laws. For example, content that glorified the Nazi party was illegal in Germany, and content that insulted religion was illegal in India.[17] The respective governments, via a court order or a routine request as described above, typically made these requests. Google reviewed these requests to determine if any content should be removed because it violated a specific country's law.

When Google removed content from search results for legal reasons, it first displayed a notification that the content had been removed and then reported the removal to *www.chillingeffects.org*, a website established by the Electronic Frontier Foundation and several law schools. The Chilling Effects database collected and analyzed legal complaints and requests for removal of a broad set of online materials. It was designed to help Internet users know their rights and understand the law. Researchers could use the data to study the prevalence of legal threats and the source of content removals. This database also allowed the public to search for specific takedown notifications.[18]

Google removed content quickly. Its average processing time across all copyright infringement removal requests submitted via its website was approximately six hours. Different factors influenced the processing time, including the method of delivery, language, and completeness of the information submitted.

The Right to Be Forgotten

The right to be forgotten can be understood as peoples' right to request that information be removed from the Internet or other repositories because it violated their privacy or was no longer relevant. This right assumed greater prominence in the digital era, when people began finding it increasingly difficult to escape information that had accumulated over many years, resulting in expressions such as *"the net never forgets," "everything is in the cloud," "reputation bankruptcy,"* and *"online reputation."*[19] According to Jeffrey Rosen, professor of law at George Washington University, the intellectual roots of the right to be forgotten could be found in French law, which recognized *le droit à l'oubli* — or the "right of oblivion" — a right that allowed a convicted criminal who had served his time and been rehabilitated to object to the publication of the facts of his conviction and incarceration.[20]

Although the right to be forgotten was rooted in expunging criminal records, the rise of the Internet had given the concept a new, more complex meaning. Search engines enabled users to access information on just about any topic with considerable ease. The ease with which information could be shared, stored, and retrieved through online search raised issues of both privacy and freedom of expression. On the one hand, when opening a bank account, joining a social networking website or booking a flight online, a consumer would voluntarily disclose vital personal information such as name, address, and credit card numbers. Consumers were often unsure of what happened to their data and were concerned that it might fall into the wrong hands — that is, that their privacy would be violated.

On the other hand, by facilitating the retrieval of information, search engines enhanced individuals' freedom to receive and impart information. Any interference with search engine activities could, therefore, pose a threat to the effective enjoyment of these rights.[21] As Van Alsenoy, a researcher at the Interdisciplinary Center for Law and Information Communication Technology, argued, "In a world where search engines are used as the main tool to find relevant content online, any governmental interference in the provisioning of these services presents a substantial risk that requires close scrutiny."[22]

Europe

Since the 1990s, both the European Union and its member states (such as Spain) had enacted laws that addressed the right to privacy and, by extension, the right to be forgotten.

A fundamental right of individuals to protect their data was introduced in the EU's original data protection law, passed in 1995. Specifically, the European Data Protection

Directive 95/46 defined the appropriate scope of national laws relating to personal data and the processing of those data. According to Article 3(1), Directive 95/46 applied "to the processing of personal data wholly or partly by automatic means, and to the processing otherwise than by automatic means of personal data which form part of a filing system or are intended to form part of a filing system."[23] Article 2(b) of the EU Data Protection Directive 95/46 defined the processing of personal data as:

> any operation or set of operations which is performed upon personal data, whether or not by automatic means, such as collection, recording, organization, storage, adaptation or alteration, retrieval, consultation, use, disclosure by transmission, dissemination or otherwise making available, alignment or combination, blocking, erasure or destruction.

Individual countries within the European Union also enacted their own laws, which were sometimes stronger than those of the EU. For example, in Spain, the protection of data was a constitutional right. The Spanish Constitution recognized the right to personal privacy, secrecy of communications, and the protection of personal data. These rights were protected through the Data Protection Act (the "Act"), passed in 1999, which incorporated the 1995 European Directive on data protection, and was enforced by the Spanish Data Protection Agency (SDPA). Created in 1993, this agency was relatively inactive until the passing of the Act, which gave it more powers and a mandate to enforce privacy rules in a wide range of situations.[24]

The Spanish agency exercised its powers broadly. For example, in 2013, it fined telecom firm Telefonica SA £0,000 for twice listing an individual's phone number in local phone books without the individual's prior consent. In 2008, the agency fined a marketing company £00 for using "recommend this to a friend" icons on websites, saying that senders of recommendation e-mails had to first request the recipient's permission. The agency had also successfully required anyone using security cameras to clearly mark their presence with a recognizable icon. Supporters of this move have highlighted the importance of transparency in protecting one's privacy.[25]

Over time, however, differences in the way that each EU country interpreted privacy rights led to an uneven level of protection for personal data, depending on where an individual lived or bought goods and services. This led the European high court to take a second look, in 2013, at the original law.[26] A European Commission memo at that time noted that the right "is about empowering individuals, not about erasing past events or restricting freedom of the press."[27] The changes were intended to give citizens more control over their personal data, making it easier to access and improve the quality of information they received about what happened to their data once they decided to share it. An unanswered question, however, was the latitude given to national courts and regulators across Europe to set the parameters by which these requests could be made.[28]

The United States

U.S. courts had taken a very different approach to privacy and to the right to be forgotten. A few U.S. laws recognized the right to be forgotten; the Fair Credit Reporting Act of 1970, for example, gave individuals the right to delete certain negative information about their credit—such as late payments, tax liens, or judgments—seven years from the date of the delinquency. But, for the most part, fundamental differences in legal philosophy made this right less likely to become widely supported in the United States. In an article published in the *Atlantic* in May 2014, Matt Ford suggested that in the U.S. context, one person's right to be forgotten logically imposed a responsibility to forget upon someone else, a notion that was alien to American law. The First Amendment to the Constitution barred the government from interfering with free speech. Law professor

Rosen argued that the First Amendment would make a right to be forgotten virtually impossible, not only to create but to enforce. For example, the U.S. Supreme Court ruled in 1989 that penalizing a newspaper for publishing truthful, lawfully obtained information from the public record was unconstitutional.[29]

The Lawsuit and Court Decision

The main focus of Costeja's complaint before the Spanish Data Protection Agency (SDPA) was his request that *La Vanguardia* remove the debt notice from its archives. In doing so, he was claiming his constitutional right to protect the integrity of his personal data. Costeja's request had two parts: that (1) *La Vanguardia* be required either to remove or alter the pages in question or to use certain tools made available by search engines in order to protect the data and (2) that Google Spain or Google Inc. be required to remove or conceal the personal data relating to him so that the data no longer appeared in search results.

In July 2010, two months after Costeja's original request, the SDPA ordered Google Spain and Google Inc. to take "all reasonable steps to remove the disputed personal data from its index and preclude further access," upholding that part of the complaint.[30] However, the SDPA rejected Costeja's complaint as it related to *La Vanguardia*, because it considered that the publication by it of the information in question was legally justified.[31]

A year later, Google filed an appeal against the decision by the SDPA before the Audiencia Nacional in Madrid, Spain's highest national court. In March 2012, this court referred the case to the European Court of Justice, the EU's high court, for a preliminary ruling.[32]

In their briefs, Google Spain and Google Inc.'s argument hinged on the meaning of "personal data" and "crawling." Crawling, as noted above, was the use of software programs to find multiple websites that responded to requests for information online.[33] These programs were configured to look for information on the Internet, according to a set of criteria that told them where to go and when.[34] Once the relevant web pages had been copied and collected, their content was analyzed and indexed.[35] Google compared its search engine index to an index at the back of a textbook, in that it included information about words and their locations.[36]

Specifically, Google argued before the European Court of Justice that because it crawled and indexed websites "indiscriminately" (that is, without a deliberate intent to process personal data as such), no processing of personal data within the meaning of Article 2 (b) of the EU Data Protection Directive 95/46 actually took place. This absence of intent, the company argued, clearly distinguished Google's activities as a search engine provider from the processing of personal data as interpreted by the Court.

Google's other main argument was that the publisher of the information should be the sole controller of data, not the search engine. After all, its attorneys argued, Google's intervention was purely accessory in nature; it was merely making information published by others more readily accessible. If a publisher, for whatever reason, decided to remove certain information from its website, this information would (eventually) be removed from Google's index and would no longer appear in its search results. As a result, Google's counsel argued, the role of a search engine should be thought of as an "intermediary."

In May 2014, the European Court of Justice ruled against Google. The court found the Internet search provider was responsible for the processing of personal data that appeared on web pages published by third parties. It further required Google to remove links returned in search results based on an individual's name when those results were deemed to be "inadequate, irrelevant or no longer relevant, or excessive." At the heart of the court's logic was the process that Google used to produce its search results. The official ruling explained the court's rationale:

> The Court points out in this context that processing of personal data carried out by such an operator enables any Internet user, when he makes a search on the basis of an individual's name, to obtain, through the list of results, a structured overview of the information relating to that individual on the internet. The Court observes, furthermore, that this information potentially concerns a vast number of aspects of his private life and that, without the search engine, the information could not have been interconnected or could have been only with great difficulty.[37]

In essence, the Court ruled that an activity, "whether or not by automatic means" could be considered to be the "processing of personal data" within the meaning of Article 2(b), even if no intention to process such data existed.[38] The court's ruling applied to any search engine operators that had a branch or a subsidiary in any of the 28 member states of the EU.[39]

Costeja's lawyer, Joaquín Muñoz, was pleased with the ruling. "When you search for something in Google, they don't scour the entire Internet for you and then give you a result. They've stored links, organized them, and they show them based on a criteria they've decided upon."[40] As for Costeja, he expressed satisfaction with the result of his four-year legal crusade. Speaking of the court's decision, he said, "I think this is the correct move. You have to provide a path for communication between the user and the search engine. Now that communication can take place."[41]

Google's Application of the Ruling

For its part, Google—although disappointed with the ruling—set about complying with it. Soon after the court decision, it removed Costeja's disputed information from its search results. But, the company also took more general action.

The Court's decision recognized Google as a data controller, or the operator of the search engine and the party responsible for its data. As such, the court said, Google was required to police its links and put into place a mechanism to address individual concerns. Accordingly, shortly after the ruling was announced, Google set up an online form for users (from the European Union only) to request the right to be forgotten. The company website stated that each request would be evaluated individually and that Google would attempt to "balance the privacy rights of the individual with the public's interest to know and the right to distribute information."[42] Once an individual had filled out the form, he or she received a confirmation. Each request was assessed on a case-by-case basis. Occasionally, Google would ask for more information from the individual. Once Google had made its decision, it notified the individual by e-mail, providing a brief explanation if the decision was against removal. If so, the individual could request that a local data protection authority review Google's decision.

In evaluating a request, Google looked at whether the results included outdated or inaccurate information about the individual. It also weighed whether or not the information was of public interest. For example, Google generally retained the information if it related to financial scams, professional malpractice, criminal convictions, or a government official's public conduct.[43]

At the same time, Google invited eight independent experts to form an advisory council expressly to "advise it on performing the balancing act between an individual's right to privacy and the public's interest in access to information."[44] The committee included three professors (two of law and one of ethics), a newspaper editorial director, a former government official, and three privacy and freedom of speech experts (including one from the United Nations). Google's CEO and chief legal officer served as conveners. The committee's job was to provide recommendations to Google on how to best implement the EU court's ruling.

The majority recommendation of the advisory council, published on February 6, 2015, was that the right to be forgotten ruling should apply only within the 28 countries in the European Union.[45] As a practical matter, this meant that Google was only required to apply removals to European domains, such as Google.fr or Google.co.uk, but not Google.com, even when accessed in Europe. Although over 95% of all queries originating in Europe used European domains, users could still access information that had been removed via the Google.com site.

The report also explained that once the information was removed, it was still available at the source site (e.g., the newspaper article about Costeja in *La Vanguardia*). Removal meant merely that its accessibility to the general public was reduced because searches for that information would not return a link to the source site. A person could still find the information, because only the link to the information had been removed, not the information itself.

The advisory council also recommended a set of criteria Google should use in assessing requests by individuals to "delist" their information (that is, to remove certain links in search results based on queries for that individual's name). How should the operator of the search engine best balance the privacy and data protection rights of the subject with the interest of the general public in having access to the information? The authors of the report felt that whether the data subject experienced harm from such accessibility to the information was relevant to this balancing test. Following this reasoning, they identified four primary criteria for evaluating delisting requests:

- First, what was the data subject's role in public life? Did the individuals have a clear role in public life (CEOs, politicians, sports stars)? If so, this would weigh against delisting.

- Second, what type of information was involved? Information that would normally be considered private (such as financial information, details of a person's sex life, or identification numbers) would weigh toward delisting. Information that would normally be considered to be in the public interest (such as data relevant to political discourse, citizen engagement, or governance) would normally weigh against delisting.

- Third, what was the source of the information? Here, the report suggested that journalistic writing or government publications would normally not be delisted.

- Finally, the report considered the effect of time, given that as circumstances change, the relevance of information might fade. Thus, the passage of time might favor delisting.

The advisory council also considered procedures and recommended that Google adopt an easily accessible and easy-to-understand form for data subjects to use in submitting their requests.

The recommendations of the advisory council were not unanimous. Jimmy Wales, the cofounder of Wikipedia and one of the eight group members, appended a dissenting comment to the report. "I completely oppose the legal situation in which a commercial company is forced to become the judge of our most fundamental rights of expression and privacy, without allowing any appropriate procedure for appeal by publishers whose work in being suppressed," Mr. Wales wrote. "The recommendations to Google contained in this report are deeply flawed due to the law itself being deeply flawed."[46]

DISCUSSION QUESTIONS

1. In what ways has technology made it more difficult for individuals to protect their privacy?

2. Do you believe an individual should have the right to be forgotten, that is, to remove information about themselves from the Internet? If so, should this right be limited, and if so, how?

3. How does public policy with respect to individual privacy differ in the United States and Europe, and what explains these differences?

4. Do you think Google should be responsible for modifying its search results in response to individual requests? If so, what criteria should it use in doing so? Are there limits to the resources the company should be expected to expend to comply with such requests?

5. If you were a Google executive, how would you balance the privacy rights of the individual with the public's interest to know and the right to distribute information?

NOTES

1. Cynthia E. Clark, Bentley University. Copyright © 2015 by the author. Used by permission.

2. "Google Privacy Campaigner Praises Search Engine for Bowing to EU," *Financial Times,* May 30, 2014.

3. "The Man Who Sued Google to be Forgotten," *Newsweek,* May 30, 2014.

4. European Parliament. Judgment of the Court, May 13, 2014, at http://curia.europa.eu/juris/document/document .jsf?docid=152065&doclang=EN

5. "The Unforgettable Story of the Seizure to the Defaulter Mario Costeja González that Happened in 1998," *Derechoaleer,* May 30, 2014, at http://derechoaleer.org/en /blog/2014/05/the-unforgettable-story-of-the-seizure-to-the -defaulter-mario-costeja-gonzalez-that-happened-in-1998.html

6. "Will Europe Censor this Article?" *The Atlantic,* May 13, 2014, www.theatlantic.com

7. "The Unforgettable Story of the Seizure to the Defaulter Mario Costeja González that Happened in 1998," *Derechoaleer,* May 30, 2014, http://derechoaleer.org/en /blog/2014/05/the-unforgettable-story-of-the-seizure-to-the -defaulter-mario-costeja-gonzalez-that-happened-in-1998 .html

8. V. Alsenoy, A. Kuczerawy, and J. Ausloos, "Search Engines after Google Spain: internet@liberty or privacy@ peril?" ICRI Working Paper Series, September 6, 2013, at http://ssrn.com/abstract=2321494

9. "Spain's Everyday Internet Warrior Who Cut Free from Google's Tentacles," *The Guardian,* May 13, 2014, http://www.theguardian.com/technology/2014/may/13 /spain-everyman-google-mario-costeja-gonzalez

10. "The Man Who Sued Google to Be Forgotten," op. cit.

11. Court of Justice, Judgment in Case C-131/12 Google Spain SL, *Google Inc. v. Agencia Española de Protección de Datos, Mario Costeja González.*

12. Information on PageRank is available online at http:// infolab.stanford.edu/~backrub/google.html

13. Information about Google search is available online at www.google.com/insidesearch/howsearchworks/index.html

14. http://www.google.com/insidesearch/howsearchworks /policies.html

15. Information about Digital Millennium Copyright Act ("DMCA") notice procedure is available at www.fosterinstitute .com/legal-forms/dmca-notice

16. Information about the removal process is available online at http://www.google.com/transparencyreport/removals /copyright/domains/?r=all-time

17. http://www.google.com/insidesearch/howsearchworks /policies.html

18. The Berkman Center for Internet & Society at www .chillingeffects.org/pages/about

19. "The Unforgettable Story of the Seizure to the Defaulter Mario Costeja González that Happened in 1998," op. cit.

20. "Will Europe Censor this Article?" op. cit.

21. Alsenoy et al., 2013.

22. Alsenoy et al., 2013.

23. Alsenoy et al., 2013.

24. "Data Protection in Spain" June 24, 2010, at www.i-policy .org/2010/06/data-protection-in-spain.html

25. "Spanish Agency Behind the Google Ruling Lauded by Some, Hated by Others," *The Wall Street Journal,* June 26, 2014.

26. "What is the 'Right to Be Forgotten'?" *The Wall Street Journal,* May 13, 2014.

27. European Commission, "LIBE Committee Vote Backs New EU Data Protection Rules," October 22, 2013, at http:// europa.eu/rapid/press-release_MEMO-13-923_en.htm

28. "What is the 'Right to Be Forgotten'?" op. cit.

29. "Will Europe Censor This Article?" op. cit.

30. Audiencia Nacional. Sala de lo Contencioso, Google Spain SL y Google Inc., S.L. c. Agencia de Protección de Datos, paragraph 1.2, at http://www.poderjudicial.es/search/doAc tion?action=contentpdf&databasematch=AN&reference= 6292979&links=%22725/2010%22&optimize=20120305&p ublicinterface=true

31. "Spanish Agency behind the Google Ruling Lauded by Some, Hated by Others," *The Wall Street Journal,* June 26, 2014 at http://www.wsj.com/articles/spanish-agency -behind-the-google-ruling-lauded-by-some-hated-by -others-1403795717

32. Alsenoy et al., 2013.

33. See http://answers.google.com/answers/threadview /id/33696.html

34. Matt Cutts (Google Quality Group Engineer), *How Search Works,* s30-s44, available at http://www.youtube.com /watch?v=BNHR6IQJGZs

35. Alsenoy et al., 2013.

36. More information about crawling is available online at http://www.google.com/intl/en/insidesearch/howsearch works/crawling-indexing.html

37. Court of Justice. Judgment in Case C-131/12 Google Spain SL, *Google Inc. v Agencia Española de Protección de Datos, Mario Costeja González.*

38. European Parliament. Judgment of the Court. May 13, 2014, at http://curia.europa.eu/juris/document/document .jsf?docid=152065&doclang=EN

39. European Commission, "Fact sheet on the Right to be Forgotten," at http://ec.europa.eu/justice/data-protection/files /factsheets/factsheet_data_protection_en.pdf

40. "Spain's Everyday Internet Warrior Who Cut Free from Google's Tentacles," op. cit.

41. "Google Privacy Campaigner Praises Search Engine for Following to EU," *Financial Times,* May 30, 2014.

42. "Search Removal Request under Data Protection Law in Europe," at https://support.google.com/legal/contact /lr_eudpa?product=websearch

43. Frequently Asked Questions, at http://www.google .com/transparencyreport/removals/europeprivacy/faq /?hl=en#how_does_googles_removals

44. The Advisory Council to Google on the Right to be Forgotten, February 6, 2015, at https://drive.google.com /file/d/0B1UgZshetMd4cEI3SjlvV0hNbDA/view?pli=1

45. "Limit 'Right to Be Forgotten' to Europe, Panel Tells Google," *The New York Times,* February 6, 2015.

46. Ibid.

CASE **9**

Harley Davidson: An Overreliance on Aging Baby Boomers

Alan N. Hoffman
Bentley University

Natalia Gold
Northeastern University

Company Background

In 1903, William S. Harley and Arthur Davidson produced the first Harley-Davidson motorcycle in a 15' x 10' wooden shed with the words 'Harley-Davidson Motor Company' etched into the door. The warehouse was located in Milwaukee, Wisconsin, the company's headquarters to this day. They were soon joined by Arthur's brother Walter, and by 1910, the company had begun to establish itself, using its current "bar and shield" logo for the first time; the logo that it trademarked with the U.S. Patent Office In 1911. In 1981, Harley-Davidson, Inc. purchased the Harley-Davidson Motorcycle Company from AMF Incorporated via a management buyout, incorporated, then went public in 1986. Over the years, Harley-Davidson had made a name for itself as the most well known producer of heavyweight motorcycles in the North American market; and, although its international sales were not significant until the late 1990s, the company then quickly became the most renowned brand in the world.

The authors thank Barbara Gottfried, and Bentley University MBA students Cristina Montalvo, Robert Bondy, Michael Ferriero, and John O'Rourke for their research and contributions to this case. Printed by permission of Dr. Alan N. Hoffman. Please address all correspondence to: Dr. Alan N. Hoffman, Dept. of Management, Bentley University, 175 Forest St Waltham, MA 02452, ahoffman@bentley.edu.

EXHIBIT 1
Harley-Davidson's U.S. and International Dealerships
FULL SERVICE DEALERSHIPS AND SRL'S

	2012	2011	2010	2009	2008	2007	2006
USA	695	706	729	758	787	788	679
Canada	73	74	74	74	74	76	75
Europe region	371	370	364	369	381	370	354
Asia Pacific region	281	274	272	254	200	194	178
Latin America region	47	44	40	40	45	49	31
Totals	1,467	1,468	1,479	1,495	1,487	1,477	1,317

Harley-Davidson, Inc., a publicly traded company listed on the New York Stock Exchange as "HOG," divided its operations into two segments: Motorcycles & Related Products, and Financial Services. The Motorcycles & Related Products segment designed, manufactured, and sold wholesale heavyweight motorcycles, motorcycle parts, accessories, and general Harley-Davidson merchandise to retail customers through a network of independent dealers in North America, Europe, Middle East, Africa, Asia Pacific, and Latin America (**Exhibit 1**). The Financial Services segment, known as Harley-Davidson Financial Services ("HDFS"), provided wholesale and retail financing as well as insurance-related services. HDFS customers were primarily end-users from the Harley-Davidson retail stores, drawn from its networks primarily in the United States and Canada.

Strategic Direction

Harley-Davidson's mission was to design and manufacture premium motorcycles for the heavyweight market. As of 2013, the company offered seven different models: Sportster, Dyna, Softail, V-Rod, Touring, CVO, and Trike. Each model was highly customizable, made to order to customer specifications, creating a Harley-Davidson mystique. As the company's motto so aptly put it:

The company's vision promoted a comprehensive motorcycling experience across a wide demographic through events, rides, and rallies. Its rallies, a crucial part of Harley-Davidson culture, were a way for motorcycle enthusiasts to come together at different locations and tour with each other. Ideally, Harley-Davidson wanted every motorcycle owner to wear a Harley vest, a Harley helmet, and Harley boots, then meet up with other Harley motorcycle owners wearing the same attire—the events, rides, and rallies made this vision come true.

Harley-Davidson's main objectives were: (1) to provide a quality and reliable product; and (2) to allow for highly customized, stylish products. The company was so sure of the quality of its products that it offered a two-year warranty on new motorcycles, and let customers know they came first:

At Harley-Davidson, customers not only purchased a motorcycle, they bought the "rebel" lifestyle Harley signified. This rebel image took a long time to develop and constituted a major competitive advantage for Harley. Nothing promised the same excitement as being on the open road on a Harley, its engine roaring, the wind whipping, the great open spaces of America just down the road. The company also considered the availability of a line of motorcycle parts, accessories, and general merchandise and of financing through HDFS part of its competitive advantage. No other motorcycle company offered its own financing under the same company umbrella.

Harley-Davidson specifically targeted a narrowly defined market of middle-aged males with disposable income. However, as U.S. baby boomers got older, the company recognized that it must look to new markets and demographics to expand sales.

Competition

Harley-Davidson's main competitors were Honda, Suzuki, Yamaha, Ducati, Kawasaki, BMW, and Polaris. Most of Harley's competition was international in focus unlike Harley's more U.S. domestic presence. Other than Honda, most of the other competitors focused on lightweight, sporty, speed bikes. Harley historically targeted the larger, luxury motorcycle market.

According to *Popular Mechanics* magazine, the top 10 best buys for bikes in 2103 were:

1. **2013 Kawasaki Ninja 300**
2. **2013 BMW S1000RR HP4**
3. **2013 Victory Judge**
4. **2013 Harley-Davidson Seventy-Two**
5. **2012 Honda NC700X**
6. **2013 Ducati Monster 696 Anniversary**
7. **2012 Yamaha Super Tenere**
8. **2013 Moto Guzzi V7 Racer**
9. **2013 Suzuki SVF 650**
10. **2013 Zero S**

The Japanese company Honda was always Harley's biggest competitor: Harley-Davidson had the greater domestic market share but Honda had the largest international market share in the entire motorcycle industry, with a history of providing quality products at cheaper prices than comparable American made products. Honda's best selling motorcycle in the United States was the GoldWing. The Harley management was very much aware of Honda as its biggest competitor and consciously strove to stay ahead of Honda in the industry.

The Motorcycle Industry

As with all motorcycle companies, Harley-Davidson operated in a highly regulated industry and had to ensure that it complied with U.S. EPA standards and the National Highway Traffic Safety Administration's National Traffic and Motor Vehicle Safety Act. In most states, motorcyclists had to have a separate license. Some promoters of motorcycles worried that consumers might not want to go through the process of getting a special license to use a motorcycle, which they considered a threat given that any laws implemented against the use of motorcycles could directly affect the acquisition of a motorcycle.

Motorcycle safety regulations were also historically created and implemented at the state level. Each state had a set of individual requirements for motorcycles including: helmet requirements, state funded rider education, eye protection, passenger regulations, and lighting. Even though states had safety regulations in place, trends evidenced an increasing number of motorcycle accidents. A study conducted by the University of Southern California (USC) attributed this increase to two major factors—lack of detection of motorcycles by passenger vehicle drivers and uneducated motorcycle riders. According to the USC study, 92% of motorcyclists who were involved in accidents had no certified training and had not participated in a rider education program. Although some states offered state funded rider education, many did not. Beginning in the 1990s, the rate of motorcycle-related accidents steadily increased, from 61,451 in 1997 to 79,000 in 2003; and fatalities increased from 2,116 to 3,661. This increased risk, it was feared, could deter consumers from purchasing a motorcycle and push them to a safer option such as a small car.

In addition, as baby boomers, Harley-Davidson's main target audience, aged, their concerns about the safety risks of riding a motorcycle grew, which was seen as potentially detrimental to the motorcycle industry as the federal government could then decide to mandate increased safety requirements. Most bikers, it was believed, chose to ride a motorcycle for the cool image; thus, being forced to wear protective gear, helmets, and use extra safety features could hurt the industry's image and sales. If this trend continued, many felt, there could be a potential threat to Harley's ability to retain current customers and attract new ones. The industry could lose profitability, and sales of motorcycles could decrease.

On the other hand, industry leaders argued, rising fuel prices might prompt consumers to switch to motorcycling and bicycling to save money on transportation costs, a trend underpinned by a consumer shift toward eco-friendly practices requiring less (or no) fuel consumption. Thus, demand for these products was expected to rise. By capitalizing on these trends and opening up to a broader consumer market, the industry was expected to grow at an annualized rate of 1.3% to $7.1 billion in the five years leading up to 2018 (IBIS World, 2013).

By the same token, however, the loud vroom Harley-Davidson motorcycles made, once seen as an advantage, became a threat for the brand. While once that noise was seen as a sign of power, customers began to find it both annoying and a sign of conspicuous consumption. Harley needed to see customer dissatisfaction as an opportunity to design new motorcycles that minimized sound to decrease the perception of loud noise and promote a more eco-friendly image.

Finally, while technological enhancements enabled Harley-Davidson to produce a constant stream of appealing technological innovations such as video cameras, GPS, airbag systems, and increased fuel efficiency for its bikes, adding new tech often resulted in higher manufacturing costs, thus higher prices for consumers.

Marketing

One of the primary reasons for Harley-Davidson's success over the past few decades was the positioning of its brand as an American icon. That iconic status was crucial to creating tremendous brand recognition and a strong reputation throughout the world for producing the highest quality bikes in the marketplace. Owners of Harley-Davidson motorcycles swore by them and were extremely unlikely to seek a competitor brand. The brand was so strong the company was even able to generate significant sales of non-motorcycle branded merchandise, including hats, t-shirts, and other household items. Harley was seen as a true "American" brand, something baby boomers supported and were willing to stand behind. Additionally, a sense of community and culture contributed to Harley's brand strength. The company promoted motorcycle rallies, where Harley owners could meet and ride with other Harley owners; and encouraged riders to share their positive experiences through word-of-mouth or online forums set-up for that purpose.

Through all this, the main challenge Harley-Davidson faced from a marketing standpoint was its inability to generate interest and sales from demographics other than its traditional target market: middle-aged men. In 2012, over 65% of sales were made to Caucasian men over 35 (Research and Markets, 2013). The baby-boomer generation had been the main driver of Harley-Davidson sales for more than 20 years, but as boomers aged and lost their desire to purchase and ride, Harley needed to find ways to attract new customers. The younger generation was more attracted to colorful, lightweight bikes, similar to those sold by Kawasaki and Suzuki, two of Harley-Davidson's main competitors, and on top of that, they saw Harleys as appealing to an older demographic, something their fathers would ride but they wouldn't. Thus, the best way for Harley to attract the younger generation was to continue to improve its customization and technological options to appeal to a generation committed to customizing or altering a product to best suit its own needs and desires. Harley-Davidson had been offering customization options for some time, and this allowed potential buyers on its website to build their own Harleys to whatever specifications they desired. Adding yet more customization options in the form of colors and styles, it was hoped, could benefit Harley and increase its chances of attracting new riders. However, some of Harley's competitors such as Kawasaki and Honda were already "on it," offering technological features such as high-quality sound systems, rear-viewing cameras, and GPS system add-on availability for their bikes, a sure-fire way to appeal to younger consumers.

A further challenge for Harley-Davidson was promoting the safety of its bikes versus those of its competitors. Motorcycle riders had become much more safety-conscious than those of previous generations, and as motorcycles were traditionally considered one of the most dangerous forms of transportation, Harley had to meet the challenge of potential buyers' resistance on the grounds of safety in its bid to increase sales.

Operations

By the end of 2012, Harley had over 695 full service dealerships in the United States and 73 in Canada, and another 700 full service dealerships in Europe, the Middle East, Asia, and Latin America (**Exhibit 1**). The availability of full service dealerships was considered the best way to promote sales as it allowed customers to come into a local shop, test drive a bike, look at options, and understand their financing options before actually making a purchase, all of which were crucial for an investment as expensive as a Harley.

Harley-Davidson also believed that flexible manufacturing processes and supply chains combined with cost-competitive and flexible labor agreements were critical to allowing the company to respond to customers in a cost effective manner, restructuring its U.S. manufacturing plants accordingly to maximize efficiency, cost saving, and customer satisfaction. The company also fostered long-term, mutually beneficial relationships with its suppliers. Through these collaborative relationships, the company gained direct access to technical and commercial resources for product design, development, and manufacturing initiatives greatly improving product quality, technology integration, and faster new-vehicle introductions (Research and Markets, 2013).

One of Harley's weaknesses from an operational standpoint was its inability to generate revenue streams from product lines other than motorcycles. Harley had attempted to market various supplemental products in the past, including motorcycle-related parts, Harley-branded trucks, Harley branded snowmobiles and all-terrain vehicles, but all of these ventures proved only marginally successful. Harley also had to face the difficulty that in some regions of the country, especially the Northeast, its products could only be used for a limited number of months per year. As the Northeast was a very large market, critics noted that it would be helpful for Harley to have supplemental products available for sale during the winter months, when riding a motorcycle was not particularly feasible.

Restructuring Plan

Between 2009 and 2014, Harley undertook a number of different restructuring initiatives with the goal of streamlining operations and reducing production costs while maximizing efficiencies. A major restructuring project within its U.S. holdings was the consolidation of its motorcycle production into a single line at the company's motorcycle manufacturing facility in York, Pennsylvania. Additionally, the company ratified a new, more flexible labor agreement at all of its U.S. manufacturing locations. In the first half of fiscal year 2013 the company began implementing "flexible" production capabilities at its York facility by adding flexible workers. By doing this it increased manufacturing production in the first half of 2013 to more closely mirror retail demand for its products.

The company also restructured operations internationally to reduce costs and maximize output, closing one of its major international manufacturing facilities in New Castalloy, Australia, a plant that manufactured the majority of the wheels for the company's products. Instead, the company decided to source these components through existing suppliers, as that would be more efficient and cost effective (Research and Markets, 2013).

Finance

For 2014, Harley-Davidson's main financial objective was to find ways to increase sales and profits and expand sales to new market segments. The company continued to see strong year-over-year growth in sales and net income (**Exhibits 2** and **3**). It also maintained a strong commitment to research and development expenditures, indicative of its drive to continue to search for ways to improve and expand through R & D. While some companies used net profits to pay dividends to investors, Harley-Davidson, like many successful companies, determined that the key to continued success and longevity was reinvestment of profits in the company to fund new product development and improve established products. Another financial strength for Harley was its return of sales and revenue to strong positions after temporary downturns in 2011, following the reorganization and restructuring plans. Finally, the company generally maintained strong cash positions, enabling it to stay liquid and pay down debt balances, should high debt ever become an issue.

Harley-Davidson's main weakness from a financial, and company-wide, perspective was its dependence on a single customer demographic: middle-aged men, its' primary customer base. As boomers aged out of the motorcycle market Harley had to meet an enormous challenge: how to maintain its high sales and revenue volume and grow and diversify its base to replace those boomers. Another challenge was the company's debt to equity ratio, which continued to rise over the five years from 2009 to 2014 as the

EXHIBIT 2
Income Statement

Harley-Davidson, Inc.
Condensed Consolidated Statements of Income
Unaudited
Year Ended December 31, 2013 (In Thousands. Except Per Share Amounts)

	Q1	Q2	Q3	Q4	TOTAL
Motorcycles and related products revenue	$ 1,414,248	$ 1,631,466	$ 1,180,284		$ 4,225,998
Gross profit	519,442	601,870	416,315		1,537,627
Selling, administrative and engineering expense	239,743	249,502	240,198		729,443
Restructuring expense	2,938	(5,297)	646		(1,713)
Operating income from motorcycles and related products	276,761	357,665	175,471	-	809,897
Financial services revenue	156,965	162,841	163,434		483,240
Financial services expense	85,420	88,685	87,366		261,471
Operating income from financial services	71,545	74,156	76,068	-	221,769
Operating income	348,306	431,821	251,539		1,031,666
Investment income	1,615	1,770	1,161		4,546
Interest expense	11,391	11,238	11,369		33,998
Income (loss) before income taxes	338,530	422,353	241,331	-	1,002,214
Provision (benefit) for income taxes	114,401	150,314	78,615	-	343,630
Income (loss) from continuing operations	224,129	271,739	162,716	-	658,584
Income (loss) from discontinued operations, net of tax	-	-	-		-
Net income (loss)	$ 224,129	$ 271,739	$ 162,716	$ -	$ 658,584
Earnings (loss) per common share from continuing operations:					
Basic	$ 1.00	$ 1.22	$ 0.73		
Diluted	$ 0.99	$ 1.21	$ 0.73		
Weighted-average common shares:					
Basic	224,429	223,052	221,936		
Diluted	226,148	224,470	223,486		
Cash dividends per common share	$ 0.21	$ 0.21	$ 0.21		

company took on more and more debt from its restructuring. The high debt balance undercut company flexibility and, it was feared, could present serious problems in the future. Inventory levels also increased at a rate slightly higher than sales, which suggested that sales were not meeting projected levels, resulting in excess inventory. Finally, in recent years, more and more customers chose to pay for their motorcycles through the company's financing program rather than purchase them outright, suggesting that buyers were struggling to afford Harley-Davidson's steep price tag, and perhaps indicating a weakness in the buyer market for Harleys.

EXHIBIT 3
Balance Sheet

Harley-Davidson, Inc.
2013 Quarterly Condensed Consolidated Balance Sheets
Unaudited (In thousands)

ASSETS	March 31,2013	June 30, 2013	Sept 29, 2013
Current assets:			
Cash and cash equivalents	$1,018,759	$1,300,690	$1,029,955
Marketable securities	135,246	133,631	122,234
Accounts receivable, net	259,673	253,819	290,158
Finance receivables held for investment net	2,074,036	2,010,974	1,829,612
Inventories	416,050	307,717	401,199
Restricted cash held by variable interest entities	197,025	212,004	194,329
Other current assets	232,190	235,636	225,188
Total current assets	4,332,979	4,454,471	4,062,675
Finance receivables held for investment net	3,959,903	4,214,612	4,355,278
Other long-term assets	1,042,239	1,038,115	1,036,055
	$ 9,335,121	$ 9,707,198	$ 9,484,008
LIABILITIES AND SHAREHOLDERS' EQUITY			
Current liabilities:			
Accounts payable & accrued liabilities	824,335	794,670	885,940
Short-term debt	687,705	525,745	394.460
Current portion of long-term debt	715,143	776,274	721,316
Total current liabilities	2,227,183	2,096,689	1,981,716
Long-term debt	3,892,469	4,234,352	4,067,733
Pension liability and postretirement! healthcare benefits	426,729	420,096	412,482
Other long-term liabilities	131,692	134,822	140,230
Total shareholders' equity	2,657,048	2,821,239	2,881,847
	$9,335,121	$9,707,198	$9,484,008

Nevertheless, Harley-Davidson sales increased from $5.3 billion in 2011 to $5.6 billion in 2012 while net income increased from $599 million to $624 million during the same time period. Thus, both sales and net income appeared to be trending positively, a good financial sign. Harley also saw some strong percentage sales increases in its international markets during 2012. The units sold in the United States increased 6.6% from 2011 to 2012, compared to a 39% increase in the Latin America region, and a 19.9% increase across the Middle East and Africa. International sales turned out to be a significant growth and expansion opportunity for Harley-Davidson as long as it found ways to participate in international markets without driving costs and related expenses of doing business up too much.

Harley-Davidson's leading position in the U.S. motorcycle market was further attributable to its commitment to research and development. Harley always had a reputation in the industry for its continued investment in research and development. The company even maintained a secret Product Development Center in Milwaukee where it spent hundreds of millions of dollars focusing on the Harley sound, the Harley engine, and various avenues for future motorcycles:

Total research and development expenses were $143.1 million, $136.2 million, $145.4 million and $137.3 million for 2009 through 2012, respectively (sec.gov). Significantly, these research and development figures stayed relatively consistent on a year-over-year basis, even during the recession of 2009 when plagued by sluggish sales and increasing debt,, underscoring the company's unwavering dedication to intracompany investment in research and design, and in the improvement and expansion of its business and product offerings. The hope was that R & D would lead to new models of bikes, new styles, new ways to control emissions, new metals or materials to use on bikes to make them lighter, new ways to improve the safety of the bikes, and any number of other possible improvements that would only strengthen the brand, the product, and the company. The company understood that the lack of the necessary R & D expenditures would quickly be exposed by the competition, as its products would rapidly become outdated.

Ethics: A Priority at Harley Davidson

As a longstanding, well-known American corporation, Harley-Davidson felt it had a responsibility to its shareholders and to the public to maintain a strongly ethical corporate culture. Its human resources and ethics policies were based on five main practices: diversity and inclusion, safety in the work environment, accurate advertising, employee attainment and retention, and environmental awareness.

Diversity and Inclusion

As Harley-Davidson continued to expand its business internationally, the company understood that it was critical to maintain a reputation of diversity and inclusion in its work force. From an external perspective as well, it was important to maintain a public image as a company that promoted diversity, and was not biased in any way with regard to any particular minority group or cause.

Safety in the Work Environment

Maintaining a safe work environment was particularly important for Harley-Davidson as it expanded internationally. Although in the United States there were strict laws governing workplace safety, foreign expansion countries did not necessarily have similarly stringent guidelines, making it even more important that Harley held itself to the same strict regulations internationally as it did nationally.

Accurate Advertising

Harley's success was heavily dependent on its marketing strategies and word-of-mouth buzz. To uphold and build upon this success, Harley recognized that it was imperative to continue to maintain high standards of accurate advertising, as inaccurate advertising was widely regarded as creating negative brand connotations that could deter customers, thus affecting sales and operations.

Employee Attainment and Retention

Employee attainment and retention was a particular concern for the company following the restructuring plans of 2010–2011. The restructuring plans involved letting go thousands of employees both domestically and internationally, which, it was feared, would be detrimental to employee morale, motivation, and production. After the implementation of restructuring, Harley made it a priority to emphasize the importance of employee retention and attainment, increasing efforts to boost employee morale and encourage long-term employment.

Environmental Awareness

As with automobile manufacturers, it was especially important for Harley-Davidson to be aware of and abide by environmental emission regulations. Harley prided itself on the fact that its products constantly met or exceeded all emission laws and regulations. Consistent funding for research and development, even in the face of losses, demonstrated Harley's unwavering commitment to product improvement, especially the never-ending pursuit of ways to cut the environmental impact of emissions.

Core Competencies: A Strong Brand Image

Over more than 100 years, Harley-Davidson established its reputation by building on the core competencies that constituted its competitive advantage: the Harley brand image, its dominant position in the U.S. marketplace, the company's emphasis on research and development, and its extensive international network.

Harley-Davidson created one of the most powerful and recognizable brands in America. Its brand name became an American icon that screamed toughness, masculinity, and quality. Harley developed this brand over many decades through a unique marketing approach. The company spent only 15% of its marketing budget on traditional media outlets, focusing instead on fostering the Harley culture through rallies and events[1] sponsored by the company with the intent of encouraging bonding between riders. Harley believed that these events would bring riders from all different paths of life together to share riding stories and create connections, further strengthening loyalty to the brand. Harley riders span a wide cross section of the population that includes owners with leather jackets and tattoos to doctors and lawyers. A major contributor to this culture was the Harley Owners Group program created in the early eighties with the intent of organizing groups of Harley enthusiasts for rallies and rides. The group grew to over one million members with local chapters around the world through which Harley owners connected and made plans to meet up with other owners. This successful branding work focused specifically on baby boomers, those born in the post World War II era from 1946 to 1964. The company targeted that generation, reputedly the wealthiest ever, when they reached their 40s and 50s, marketing Harleys to them as a way to recapture their youth. Harley Davidson successfully tapped into the baby-boomer market at the right time, which led to tremendous growth and two-year waiting periods for its motorcycles in the late 1990s, a success made possible through effective branding.

Capitalizing on its strong brand name, Harley-Davidson dominated the U.S. heavyweight motorcycle market.

Another core competency for Harley-Davidson was its vast international network. As shown in **Exhibit 1**, Harley established an increasing number of dealerships outside the United States from 2006 to 2012. The company particularly planned to focus on the Asian-Pacific and Latin America countries as growth markets for motorcycle sales. Growth of disposable income from continued development and prosperity, and emphasis on fuel efficiency made these regions particularly desirable markets. As reported in the *Chicago Tribune* in 2013, "From late 2009 through March 2013, [Harley] added 99 new international dealers in emerging markets such as India, China and Brazil as well as in established markets, in line with [its] objective to add 100–150 international dealers through 2014."[2] Harley's expanding footprint across the globe garnered increasing sales as its quality products wooed and wowed new markets.

These core competencies and competitive advantages were the driving factors of Harley-Davidson's success in the 1990s and early 2000s. As the company recovered from the Great Recession, it became imperative for it not merely to return to those core competencies and competitive advantages, but to make them the backbone of its future endeavors.

Opportunities in India, China, and Asia-Pacific

While Harley confronted a saturated heavyweight motorcycle market in the United States and the weakened economy of the EU, sales of lightweight motorcycles in India, China, and the entire Asia-Pacific region experienced double-digit growth after 2010, with India the second largest motorcycle market behind China, where annual sales exceeded 10 million bikes.

In January 2014, Harley-Davidson launched its first lightweight motorcycle since it discontinued the Sprint (350cc) in 1974. The new Street 750 and 500 series were specifically designed for stop and go city traffic with higher street clearance and a better suspension system to accommodate less than perfect Indian roads.

Harley faced stiff price competition from Suzuki, Ducati, Yamaha, and Honda in India. However, the company decided to assemble the new Street 750 in Bawal, India to avoid high import tariffs, thus allowing Harley to be more competitive. The Street 750 price was set at $8,000.

Challenges Ahead

As Harley-Davidson looked forward, its key challenges included its highly leveraged financial position, attributable in part to recent failed mergers and acquisitions; its high inventory levels; its struggle to connect with a younger generation of riders; and its reliance on a strong economy.

Harley-Davidson's debt levels increased significantly over the 10 years since 2002, and in recent years were seen as a deterrent to future growth. The increased debt derived from restructuring charges; discontinuation of certain operations; and defaults associated with the company's lending practices. In the early 2000s, as the demand for Harleys soared, executives determined to increase production, and sustained that increase through 2008, even when demand began tapering off due to the economic downturn. By the end of 2008, at the onset of the Great Recession, the company noticed the inventory building and overhead costs increasing, and implemented a restructuring plan particularly focused on manufacturing. As reported in the *Chicago Tribune*,

"Harley has been revamping its manufacturing operations to cut costs, become more efficient and introduce flexibility in its workforce."[3] The restructuring called for a reduction in employees and plants, and an overall shift to align supply with demand. The restructuring cost Harley-Davidson several hundred million dollars over a three-year period. In 2009, Harley also decided to discontinue the Buell line of sport bikes and focus instead on promoting the Harley-Davidson brand, which led to $125 million in shutdown costs, mostly incurred in 2009.[4] In addition, Harley sold MV Augusta in early 2010, an expensive Italian sport bike company, to the owners they had purchased it from two years earlier with an eye to expanding its network in Europe and attracting younger riders. The plan failed, primarily due to the recession and Harley's lack of knowledge of the European motorcycle marketplace.[5] Ceasing to produce the Buell line and selling MV Augusta back to its original owners between 2009 and 2010, led to $325 million in shutdown and write-down charges and gave the public a glimpse of the financial trouble Harley-Davidson was facing during the Great Recession.

Compounding these difficulties were losses incurred by Harley-Davidson's financial arm. Similar to the problems leading up to the housing crisis of 2008, Harley Davidson's loose lending policies, particularly no-money-down loans, led to significant losses for the company. This resulted in Harley-Davidson writing off $80 million of long-term debt. The mounting losses and increasing expenses eventually led the company to reach out to iconic investor Warren Buffet as a last resort. As part of a one billion dollar debt financing deal, Warren Buffet purchased $300 million of Harley-Davidson's unsecured debt and "In exchange for his good name and millions, Mr. Buffet demanded 15 percent interest from Harley on his investment,"[6] an investment very much needed, both financially and from an investor confidence perspective.

In addition to the high levels of debt associated with the failed mergers and acquisitions and excess inventory, the company also struggled with attracting a younger generation of riders. The company's core customer base was middle-aged men with the means and desire to purchase heavyweight motorcycles for a premium price. However, as its core consumer base aged the company struggled to tap into the younger generation who preferred lighter sport bikes at inexpensive prices from foreign vendors such as Kawasaki and Honda. Harley-Davidson had tried in the past to market a sports bike to tap into this niche market but failed, primarily because the bikes were expensive compared to those of competitors.

It became clear that Harley-Davidson's future success depended on its addressing the weaknesses identified. In 2013, as Harley continued to recover from the Great Recession, the company needed to understand the mistakes and circumstances that led to its high level of debt, failed mergers and acquisitions, excess inventory, inability to attract a younger customer base, and overreliance on the overall state of the economy. Comprehending the import of those weaknesses, it was hoped, would allow Harley to make more prudent business decisions that would lead to a future of strong growth and earnings.

Aging Baby Boomers

Well-documented throughout the financial media world, and specifically recognized by the company, Harley-Davidson's main concern was certainly its aging customer base and struggle to recruit a new pool of younger, more diverse riders. Many of Harley-Davidson's current customers are "baby boomers" over the age of 50.

Over the past two decades leading up to 2014, Harley-Davidson focused its entire strategy on the baby-boomer generation, and was very successful in doing so. However, as boomers hit retirement age, they no longer wanted expensive, heavyweight motorcycles—that phase of their lives was over. The company knew it needed to establish a new strategy that would continue to foster the quality and exclusivity of owning a Harley, but also embrace the tastes and desires of the younger generation, the motorcycle market dominated by the kids of the baby-boomer generation. By connecting with that generation, Harley could hope for another wave of loyal riders that would purchase Harleys throughout their riding lives. In short, to retain its market position and continue to grow, Harley needed to find new demand for its bikes and market toward that demand as it did so successfully with the boomers.

WORKS CITED

Barrett, Rick. "Harley-Davidson takes a Beating on MV Augusta." August 16, 2010. December 1, 2013 http://www.jsonline.com/blogs/business/100759404.html.

Baskin, Jonathan Salem. "Harley-Davidson Will Be A Case History In Social Branding." *Forbes*, July 12, 2013. December 1, 2013. http://www.forbes.com/sites/jonathansalembaskin/2013/07/12/harley-davidson-will-be-a-case-history-in-social-branding/

http://www.forbes.com/sites/greatspeculations/2014/01/16/harley-davidsons-street-750-debuts-in-india/

"Findings from the Hurt Study: Motorcycle Accident Cause Factors and Identification of Countermeasures," http://pages.cs.wisc.edu/~john/vfr/hurt.html

Garrett, Jerry. "Harley-Davidson to Discontinue Buell Sport Bikes." *The New York Times*, October 15, 2009. Accessed on December 1, 2013. http://wheels.blogs.nytimes.com/2009/10/15/harley-davidson-to-discontinue-buell-sport-bikes/?_r=0

Hamner, Susan. "Harley, You're Not Getting Any Younger." *The New York Times*, March 21, 2009. December 1, 2013. http://www.nytimes.com/2009/03/2/business/economy/22harley.html?pagewanted=all

"Harley Davidson 2012 10-K Annual Report." *Sec.gov*. N.p., n.d. Web. December 19, 2013.

"Harley-Davidson – Demographics." 2013. December 1, 2013. http://investor.harley-davidson.com/phoenix.zhtml?c=87981&p=irol-demographics&locale=en_USbmLocale=en_US

"Harley-Davidson in China Encounters Barriers of Entry for Two Wheels: Cars." Bloomberg. http://www.bloomberg.com/news/articles/2011-09-18/harley-davidson-finds-milwaukee-beats-china-as-leisure-motorcycle-market

Harley-Davidson Official U.S. Online Site. Web. December 19, 2013. www.harleydavidson.com

"Harley Davidson SWOT Analysis." *Research and Markets*. N.p., n.d. Web. December 19, 2013.

"Harley Davidson Timeline," http://www.harley-davidson.com/en_US/Content/Pages/HD_Museum/explore/hd-timeline.html

"Harley Earnings on Target as Restructuring Pays Off." *Chicago Tribune*. 25 April 25, 2013. December 1, 2013. http://articles.chicagotribune.com/2013-04-25/business/chi-harley-earnings-20130425_1_harley-davidson-inc-winnebago-industries-sales-volumes

"IBIS World Industry Outlook." December 16, 2013. http://clients1.ibisworld.com/reports/us/industry/industryoutlook.aspx?entid=856

"Motorcycle Accident Statistics," http://www.accidentattorneys.com/motorcycle-accident-lawyer.cfm

"10 Best Buys In 2013 Motorcycles," http://www.popularmechanics.com/cars/motorcycles/g105/10-best-buys-in-2013-motorcycles/

"Product Development Center: Harley-Davidson Motor Company, Milwaukee, WI." Emprise Corporation. 2010. December 1, 2013. http://www.emprise-usa.com/test-facilities/product-development-center/index.php

Richer, Mark-Hans. "Harley-Davidson CMO: We Aren't an Auto Brand." July 10, 2013. Ad Age: CMO Strategy. December 1, 2013. http://adage.com/article/cmo-strategy/cmo-harley-davidson-lifestyle-transportation/242952/

"State Motorcycle Laws," http://americanmotorcyclist.com/Rights/State-Laws-Database

"The U.S. Market for Motorcycles," http://www.marketresearch.com/product/display.asp?productid=1097893&g=1

NOTES

1. Mark-Hans Richer, "Harley-Davidson CMO: We Aren't an Auto Brand," July 10, 2013. Ad Age: CMO Strategy. December 1, 2013 http://adage.com/article/cmo-strategy/cmo-harley-davidson-lifestyle-transportation/242952/

2. 'Harley-Davidson–Demographics," 2013. December 1, 2013, http://investor.harley-davidson.com/phoenix.zhtml?c=87981&p=irol-demographics&locale=en_US&bmLocale=en_US

3. "Harley Earnings on Target as Restructuring Pays Off," *Chicago Tribune*, April 25, 2013. December 1, 2013. http://articles.chicagotribune.com/2013-04-25/business/chi-harley-earnings-20130425_1_harley-davidson-inc-winnebago-industries-sales-volumes

4. Jerry Garrett, "Harley-Davidson to Discontinue Buell Sport Bikes," *The New York Times*, October 15, 2009. December 1, 2013. http://wheels.blogs.nytimes.com/2009/10/15/harley-davidson-to-discontinue-buell-sport-bikes/?_r=0

5. Rick Barrett, "Harley-Davidson takes a Beating on MV Augusta," August 16, 2010. December 1, 2013. http://www.jsonline.com/blogs/business/100759404.html

6. Ibid.

Uber: Feeling the Heat from Competitors and Regulators Worldwide

Alan N. Hoffman
Bentley University

Natalia Gold
Northeastern University

Company Background

Uber, originally known as "UberCab," was started by Travis Kalanick and Garrett Camp in San Francisco, California, in 2009. Its target audience was young, educated, tech-savvy urbanites more likely to rent than own their own homes who generally got around via public transportation, biking, or walking. The company grew rapidly and by 2015 it was providing carpooling services in 300 major cities in 58 countries around the world.[1]

The authors thank Barbara Gottfried and Bentley University MBA students David Miller, Elise Oakes, Scott Marshall, Allison Park, Noelia Taveras, Jessica Tokarz, Mathew Wessells, and Stamoulis Zourmpadelos for their research and contributions to this case. Please address all correspondence to: *Dr. Alan N. Hoffman,* Dept. of Management, Bentley University, 175 Forest Street, Waltham, MA 02452-4705, ahoffman@bentley.edu, (781) 891-2287. Printed by permission of Dr. Alan N. Hoffman.

Garrett Camp, the founder of the successful StumbleUpon, had sold his company to eBay in 2008, and met Travis Kalanick, the founder of the peer-to-peer file sharing network Red Swoosh, in Paris that same year. Both were living in San Francisco and had problems with the taxicab services there. They discussed a plan to share the costs of a driver, a Mercedes S Class, and a garage parking spot using an iPhone app. When that worked for them, they figured others might have had similar problems with taxi services, and expanded their original idea. Uber began as a mix of taxicab and carpooling services that, as a smart phone application ("app"), used GPS to bring together people looking for rides and drivers, who were private contractors driving their own cars.[2] Customers chose a pick up location, the app then notified available drivers in the area, who accepted the pickup location, took the passenger to the requested drop off location, and charged the customer's credit card automatically.[3] In early 2010, the service was launched in New York City with three cars. After a successful beta test in New York it went live for the first time on July 5, 2010, in San Francisco, CA.[4]

After its initial success, Uber expanded across the United States. It was a huge sensation in New York, Chicago, and Washington D.C., and made its international debut in Paris at the end of 2011. From there the company quickly moved to Toronto, London, Sydney, and Johannesburg. In the next couple of years Uber expanded all over the world.[5]

Uber's basic service was UberX, a low cost car service designed to get the customer from point A to point B. Once its original concept was well established in a given location Uber began offering new services such as UberXL, UberBlack, and UberPool. UberXL was similar to UberX except that it was slightly more expensive and offered vehicles with a larger passenger capacity. For a high-end experience UberBlack provided luxury cars for a premium price. Similar to the original concept of UberX, Uberpool was a low cost option which allowed passengers coming from the same area and going in the same direction to share a car at a discounted rate.[6,7]

With Uber's rapid expansion came the need for additional funding. Soon after its official launch in July 2010 Uber closed a $1.25 million financing deal with First Round Capital. By 2011, investors were eager to get a piece of the popular app and Uber raised another $11 million with Benchmark Capital, followed by an additional $37 million from Goldman Sachs later in the year. More funds were raised as Uber continued to spread into new markets. Its largest funding deal came at the end of 2014 when Uber received $1.2 billion from the Chinese search engine Baidu.[8]

As of 2015, Uber was operating worldwide, a hugely successful service unlike any of its predecessors, continually growing and improving. Only the future could tell what was in store for Uber.

Strategic Direction

Uber conceived of its mission as making transportation "as reliable as running water:" a car would show up at the push of a button within 5 minutes, as reliably as getting water by turning on the tap.[4] Uber wanted transportation to be available to everyone so it created both luxury and affordable options. Beyond its core mission, Uber wanted to move things, not just people. The company started doing some experiments to see what might work in different cities. In Los Angeles, Uber tried Uber Fresh for customers to push a button to get lunch delivered in five minutes. In Washington D.C., it was the Uber Corner Store for convenience store deliveries. In New York Uber started Uber Rush, a messenger service. As those at Uber began to realize: if a car could be delivered in five minutes, so could a lot of other things.[4]

At the same time Uber's goal was to remain cheap, fast, and efficient. Being cheap gave Uber a competitive edge. Being fast was part of its differentiation strategy. In short,

Uber sought to be so efficient that for most people using Uber was cheaper than owning a car. Being fast, cheap, and efficient would ultimately help Uber achieve its original corporate objectives of growing revenue and earnings for shareholders.[5] The company conceived of itself as sitting on the border between bits and atoms: bits were the application's code and internet presence; atoms were the physical world cars drove around in. Together bits and atoms represented Uber's ongoing goal of merging intangible code and technology with the tangible world its customers lived in.[5]

Uber's biggest downside was the many legal hurdles it faced from regulators, as it came up against taxi laws written before the concept of Uber even existed.[5]

Uber's Product Offerings

Uber's product offerings grew very quickly, amended by name and objective over the past several years. Each service was designed to meet a different need of consumers to foster complete customer satisfaction. Services as of 2015 included: UberX, UberXL, UberBlack, UberSUV, UberPOOL, UberTaxi, UberSelect, Uber for Business, and UberRUSH (UberEATS).

UberX: the most commonly used, least expensive service, used ordinary, not luxury, cars. Drivers only needed a standard driver's license and to pass a background check. Cars had to be manufactured in 2006 or later, seat four with seatbelts, and pass an independent vehicle inspection.

UberXL: similar to the UberX service, but for six passengers, rather than four.

UberBlack: a professional service that initiated Uber's high-end reputation in the business world (though the name came later). The car had to be a luxury car that seated at least four passengers and newer than the cars used for UberX service. UberBlack catered to wealthy individuals including celebrities, executives, and those using it for a special occasion.

UberSUV: a Black Car service requiring the same standards as UberBlack but for six or more passengers.

UberPOOL: a newer service, created in reaction to one of Uber's most prominent competitors, Lyft, and similar to a carpool service, where riders traveling in the same direction could ride together and split the cost of the service.

UberTaxi: customers would use the Uber app to "hail" a licensed taxi cab driver priced at standard taxi fare and following standard taxi cab regulations.

UberSelect: less widely used in recent years. Similar to UberBlack, except the car was not required to be black, but still had to be high end. The cost sat between UberX and UberBlack This service was only offered in select cities, not worldwide.

Uber for Business: used by companies around the world to offer Uber services to employees, customers, and anyone else interacting with the company for a discounted rate paid by the company. Companies set the policy as to who could use the service, when and where employees could be picked up, then let the application set the guidelines. The service mostly provided UberX cars (Uber for Business, 2015).

UberRUSH: Uber's most recent expansion into the delivery business, available in only three U.S. cities, offering same-day delivery by Uber couriers via bike or car for businesses to consumers at a price range of $5–$6. Also on the docket: further expansion of UberEATS, a food delivery service (Graham, 2015).

Uber also jumped into several short term services to suit the market including Uber ice-cream, which provided delivery services to different neighborhoods, Uberboat, which offered mimic harbor cruises, and UberHealth, providing wellness packs with the option of free flu shots by a registered nurse for up to ten people for a small fee (Verena, 2015). The driving force behind these services was the notion of developing one off programs to meet immediate needs of customers. Additionally, extensive research and development was devoted to anticipating customers' demands and creating complete customer satisfaction.

Existing Competitors

While Uber offered a new take on an old industry using state of the art technology, it faced serious competition from other ride sharing apps with a similar business model, and from city taxi services with a wide range of experience that had been around for decades.

Despite competition, Uber dominated the market, leading in all 132 U.S. cities it entered out of the approximately 147 cities that provided ride sharing app alternatives to taxis. In 54 of the cities Uber dominated it faced no competition from other ride sharing apps.[6]

Uber's most similar market competitor was Lyft, a ride sharing app that copied Uber's business model, linking driver and passenger through the GPS on the user's phone. Other companies offering similar apps such as Curb and Side distinguished themselves by their pricing strategies or advertising but came nowhere close to Uber's market share.[7]

Though Uber was primarily a ride sharing app it was most often compared to the taxi industry, as it provided essentially the same service more cheaply and efficiently. As of the end of 2015, Uber did not have to adhere to the governmental regulations imposed on taxi services, which allowed it to operate with fewer costs. Uber's millennial users preferred its main innovation, its app interface for requesting or locating a ride, to ordering traditional taxi services by phone call or waiting till a cab happened to drive by.

Low Barriers to Entry

Barriers to entering the car services industry typically varied by location but for the most part were pretty low. Imitating the ride sharing app platform was also easy, as evidenced by the proliferation of Uber competitors. Easy entry into the market made it difficult for existing companies to maintain or grow market share, making it crucial for them to differentiate their services. Entering the taxi or luxury car service market had traditionally been fairly easy: a competitor would only need the capital to buy a car and perhaps a taxi medallion—a special permit to operate a taxi in a particular geographic area. Annual fees and rules for acquiring a medallion differed based on local laws.

While Uber had the advantage of being the first mover in the market, imitating its ride sharing app proved to be easy for its competitors. Only a few years after Uber's start, numerous competitors flooded the market at home and abroad such as Lyft, Ola (India), Didi Kuaidi Joint Co. (China), and GrabTaxi (Southeast Asia). As Uber only held limited patents, imitating its platform only cost the amount of designing the app and marketing it which, based on the size of the market and the potential for earnings, seemed worth it to many companies.

Legal & Political Landscape

As of 2015, Uber only owned one patent on its services. Faced with increased competition and seeing an opportunity, the company began filing patents on more than a dozen aspects of its services including "surge pricing" which multiplied rates during peak times, its star rating system for drivers, and its system for calculating tolls. The company felt the patents would give it a competitive edge; and, should the need arise, allow it to bring suit against any competitor infringing on those patents, potentially eliminating some of the competition.

Uber saw further opportunity in the nationwide drunk driving laws prohibiting operation of a moving vehicle with a blood alcohol concentration at or above 0.08%, and positioned itself as the "safe" alternative for those who might have overindulged.

Most importantly, Uber cultivated relationships with local governments, as those local municipalities had the power to regulate how and when Uber operated within their domains, rendering them crucial to Uber's success or failure. The necessity of cultivating these relationships became apparent when Uber came up against governments that did not allow them to operate. In Germany, for example, Uber was not permitted to operate because it was considered unfair competition for taxi drivers, who were required to pay for licenses and operational fees. Uber appealed the court case that banned it and awaited the decision—for it to have any future in Germany it had to win the appeal.[7]

Uber's continued expansion in and beyond the 58 countries it operated in as of 2015 multiplied the complex political and legal scenarios it faced. The legal ramifications of Uber's practices varied from country to country, raising the specter of backlash and criminal litigation. In California, the Labor Commission threatened Uber by ruling that an Uber driver was an employee, not a contractor, and thereby entitled to employee benefits. Further national and state laws could find Uber's operations were breaking the law as the company eschewed any taxi-like licensing and did not follow employee labor practices for its drivers. Political unrest was also a threat in some of the countries Uber operated in. In countries such as France, labor union resistance to Uber's competition with legacy taxi drivers risked injury to people during potential protests, resultant high insurance costs, and potential bad press, all of which made it eminently clear the company needed to carefully consider where it might expand its operations.

Uber's drivers, meanwhile, as "independent contractors" had to consider whether, given their out-of-pocket expenses, driving for Uber really was an attractive proposition yielding sufficient income. Many expenses were tax deductible, yet there was some sense among drivers that true earnings were less than what they had expected, which put a dent in Uber's ability to attract new drivers.

Social and Demographic and Other Income Opportunities

As a company that offered ride and delivery services, in demand by virtually every social and demographic group in the world, Uber was positioned to reach many demographics, broadening services offered by tailoring them to particular constituencies and types of vehicle and technology platform. It was clear that what millennial customers wanted was instant gratification, options, and value for their money. Thus, Uber targeted specific demographics. For money savers, there was the low cost UberX. For quick delivery, there was UberRUSH bicycle delivery. In four cities, Uber introduced UberEATS, an on-demand food delivery service. Uber also tried out a one-day on-demand flu shot clinic in 35 cities by teaming an Uber car with a nurse who delivered 10 doses of flu vaccine per charge and location to allow co-workers and other groups to split the cost of the vaccine service. Uber's app-based, global platform gave it the latitude to test different pilot programs in different markets, then refine those pilots to offer, perhaps, hour rather than over-night flower or gift delivery, and so on rather than as was more common, food or cargo delivery, at more competitive prices.

Uber also saw that it could reach out to various demographics by leveraging holidays or events effectively (e.g., by providing free rides to veterans on Veteran's Day and so on), garnering positive word of mouth that could be parlayed into effective advertising through holiday tie-ins and celebrations in the many different cultures and countries in which it operated.

Beyond its ridesharing services, Uber's ownership of deCarta mapping, which saved it money by decreasing its reliance on Google Maps, potentially provided another business opportunity as Uber could sell the mapping service to its competitors, yielding an additional revenue stream, and protecting those companies from being over-reliant on one source alone. Lastly, Uber could enhance its app by providing more information to both riders and drivers, to ensure a more accurate pick-up process so that the right person was in with the right driver and expectations were met, increasing peace of mind and reducing issues for both.

Driverless Cars

Uber had at least two incentives for an interest in driverless cars. First, much of the cost of an Uber fare went to the driver—driverless cars could cut much of that cost. More importantly, as driverless cars could offer a viable alternative to Uber's ride-sharing services, they could potentially pose a real threat to Uber. Uber, therefore, decided to invest in driverless car R & D, launching a strategic partnership with Carnegie Mellon University to work proactively with experts in the autonomous vehicle industry to understand how Uber might leverage the new technology to its advantage. Otherwise, as industry analysts understood, Uber might potentially be disrupted if it did not take the threat of self-driving cars seriously.[8]

Rapid Global Expansion

In a few short years, Uber's worldwide operations created many opportunities for expansion. What Uber learned from some of the more difficult countries to navigate such as India, Africa, and China positioned Uber to leverage future gains. Its global infrastructure, no small task to create, was potentially a massive advantage Uber had over new or local competition, as it would be better placed to adapt to new markets. Even though those in some countries might not have easy or affordable access to vehicles, or the mobile phones needed to use Uber, or scarce or expensive gasoline, it seemed ever more likely that the demand for ridesharing services would expand with the growth of developing economies worldwide.

Finance

Uber's financial objectives, similar to those of any venture capital backed company were to:

a. maintain/continue to grow the company's revenues throughout the over 300 markets it operated in.

b. expand the number of markets in which it was profitable from 80 to all markets to offset the subsidies provided to drivers and passengers.[9]

c. foster further growth to lead up to a successful Initial Public Offering ("IPO") of stock to allow participants in successive funding rounds to realize a return on their investment.

d. provide sufficient funding for expansion into additional markets and additional product offerings such as services to deliver flu shots.[10]

In January, 2016, General Motors (GM) announced that it was investing $500 million in Uber's main competitor Lyft. Together, GM and Lyft will develop a network of on-demand autonomous vehicles.

Capital Funding

As of 2015, Uber had completed 13 rounds of funding for a total of $8.21 billion from 53 investors including Google, Fidelity, and Baidu (China).[11] These rounds included traditional venture capital funding as well as both private equity and debt financing. While this capital funding provided Uber with a valuation of over $50 billion, it was reported that Uber had initiated yet another funding round in late 2015 seeking more than $2 billion, bringing the potential total valuation of the company to $64.6 billion.[9]

These rounds of funding provided Uber with the financial strength to expand product offerings, especially UberXL and UberPool, and enter new markets, including China in 2015.[12] Without the funding, Uber could not continue to expand at the rate it had in 2015, nor could it continue to sustain the level of loss rumored to have occurred.

Revenue

At the beginning of 2016, Uber remained a privately held company whose revenues were tied to how well it leveraged its product offerings in the various markets it operated in. As the company successfully focused on its services and products, customer loyalty grew, yielding individual market revenues greater than taxi revenues within the same market.[13] In San Francisco, for example, the very first market Uber began operations in, as of early 2015, revenues generated were more than 3 times greater than the revenues generated by the taxi industry and continued to grow as the number of rides used within San Francisco tripled each year, a revenue model which was replicated in other markets as well. For example, in New York City Uber rides quadrupled and in London they quintupled.

The push for greater revenues thus constituted a crucial and successful aspect of Uber's strategy. Reviewing the unaudited statements reported by Gawker indicated that the fiscal period from early 2012 through mid-2013, yielded an average of 69.6% growth in revenues from $1.442 million in the first quarter of 2012 to $19.331 million in the second quarter of 2013. However, while these statements were unaudited and not necessarily reliable, the successful rounds of funding and growing valuation of the company would seem to suggest the reported growth rate was valid.

Net Income

While Uber posted revenue growth that allowed it to return again and again to the venture capital markets, it was not a profitable company, because its entry into new markets incurred many expenses. The company understood it would have to spend heavily to attract both drivers and customers as well as subsidize the rates charged to customers and the fees paid to drivers to allow for the market to properly mature and sustain itself.

By early 2016, reports indicated that Uber was only profitable in about 27% of the markets it operated in (80 out of 300). Nevertheless, it was public knowledge that overall, Uber was operating at a loss as it tried to achieve the appropriate size for operations to support its financial needs.

Surge Pricing

Uber created three different pricing strategies for the marketplace: standard fee, airport rates, and "surge pricing." Its standard fee, comparable to a standard taxi ride, was the most widely used. The Standard Fee included price variations depending on the particular service explained in the product section, as well as geographic location; however, the rates were consistent for each service. The Uber Airport Rate was also comparable to an airport taxi fare, and added a slight increase to the price of the ride to compensate for extended delays while driving to the terminals, increased toll rates or a variety of other inconvenient airport transportation factors (Uber.com, 2015).

It was Uber's third pricing strategy that set the company apart from its competitors. Uber adopted "Surge Pricing," a dynamic pricing model that hinged on the concept of supply and demand. The surge-pricing model, a term coined by Uber, operated on the principle that rides should cost more when demand was greater (Griswold, 2014) or supply lower based on an algorithm developed through significant research and development funding. The system was set up to calculate, based on the current demand (and supply), how much of a "multiple" the service would need to charge to ensure it had reliable vehicles ready for those who might actually need them. Customers would be notified prior to accepting the service that there was an increase in the cost per mile. Although it varied by location, Uber's surge pricing only affected less than 10% of rides (Dickey, 2014) usually around holidays, during bad weather, or on weekend nights.

Uber's prices and fees varied significantly from city to city and especially from country to country. The company charged cancellation fees ranging from $5–$10 depending on the specific service selected for services canceled five minutes or more after the service was ordered. Uber also developed the UberTaxi service with a standard taxi meter rate plus a $1 booking fee and a 20% gratuity automatically added for the driver (Uber.com, 2015). All payments to Uber required a valid credit or debit card selected once the service was chosen. The card information was then saved on the app for future convenience. No additional tip was charged , nor was there a tip option in the app itself.

Uber's Promotional Efforts

Uber's promotional efforts focused on its target market using standard promotional strategies at all locations, as well as a variety of city specific programs to more directly provide services to a particular geographic location.

Uber's most basic promotion was its "First Rider Bonus Coupon," which deposited a credit in the user's account which the customer could use for rides prior to paying any funds to Uber, regardless of the number of rides used. The value of the First Rider Bonus was as high as $30 for new customers, but settled at $22 in the United States. This promotional strategy focused solely on market share and increasing the customer base (Lucky, 2015).

Referrals were the second broadly used promotional strategy, which was focused on networking and provided $30 (at the most) to an Uber user who referred another individual. That other individual entered a promotional code for the recommender to reap the benefit. In 2016, the referral bonus dropped to $20, though Uber occasionally reverted to larger bonuses during select timeframes (Lucky, 2015).

Word of mouth, often the most effective strategy and partly encompassing the two promotional strategies mentioned above, conveniently required the least effort and expense from Uber as it relied on networking without any promotional fees.

In addition to these three preferred and widely used promotional strategies, Uber attempted to quickly generate market share in new cities by providing special promotions as well as posting promotions in already established markets to emphasize Uber's presence and increase brand awareness. For instance, the UberKITTENs helped "deliver smiles and kitten playtime in order to help foster adoptions and awareness for our local shelters. Uber helped connect over 315 kittens and cats to their new families and raised over $40,000 for participating shelters" (Sarah, 2015). Uber's New York City office hosted "The Next Generation of Woman Engineers," a group of aspiring young women entrepreneurs who pitched apps relating to food, safety, news, transportation, and education (Ariella, 2015). The UberMILITARY program pledged to onboard 50,000 service members, veterans, and military spouses as partner drivers (Uber, 2015). And, the Uber back-to-school program focused on bringing together parent drivers, their kids, community organizations, and local officials to hear about parents' experience and foster discussions on how the service could provide benefits to parents, including how to balance all that was involved in caring for children (Ariella, 2015).

Local Marketing

Given the variety of its locales, Uber developed a very decentralized marketing strategy which gave local community operations managers the autonomy to launch campaigns relevant to their particular city. The community managers, essentially the face of the brand in each city, were visible on social media accounts, and their names were attached to Uber's responses related to customer inquiries. In addition, Uber focused on its relationships with riders and drivers in the local community to built up its network, and partnered with local organizations to promote its services. For instance, Uber's Jacksonville team recognized the cultural significance of the NFL's Jacksonville Jaguars to the local community and partnered with the Jaguars to create an integrated service which allowed customers to use the Uber app to purchase same day tickets then coordinate their transportation needs, thereby promoting Uber services by serving the public.[14]

Negative Publicity

Unfortunately for Uber, its aggressive behavior in bending legislative regulations and attitude towards competitors such as Lyft and Sidecar garnered bad press and negative publicity. When entering a new market, Uber's approach was to dive in and deal with the legal consequences later. In Portland, Uber began operations without the formal approval of the city, then went ahead with an "unsanctioned launch party" where partygoers took photos of protest signs with the hashtag#WeWantUberPDX which led to a lawsuit and fines totaling $67K. On top of that, Portland residents felt Uber's aggressive tactics were "icky."[15]

Uber's attitude towards its competitors was even more aggressive and questionable. It was recently discovered that Uber employees ordered rides from Lyft then canceled them to decrease Lyft drivers' availability and increase demand for Uber services instead. Lyft claimed 177 Uber employees canceled more than 5,000 rides in a year, making Uber look like a company that fought dirty and sanctioned disreputable practices to gain advantage over competitors.

Customer Loyalty

As of late 2015, Uber had done little to differentiate itself from competitors such as Lyft and Sidecar (Sidecar went out of business on December 31, 2015), and Uber recognized that to gain more market share and increase customer loyalty, it needed to focus more on branding. To enhance its brand, Uber created UberVIP whereby frequent riders with more than 100 rides could qualify for elite status granting them better access to drivers with high ratings. However, it was not very effective, as most drivers were rated highly so VIP status didn't really garner anything tangible for riders, leaving Uber to face the challenge of creating a better, more effective customer loyalty program to encourage riders to stick with Uber rather than switching back and forth between Uber and its competitors.

Operations

Uber started its ride-sharing operations in San Francisco in 2010. By the end of 2014, the company's U.S. driver base had grown to 160,000 active drivers and 1 million drivers worldwide.[16] Uber also operated in 59 countries and 300 cities around the globe. By early 2016, it seemed as though Uber was expanding to a new city every other day.

Political Lobbying

To combat the legal issues and challenges it faced, Uber built one of the largest and most successful lobbying groups in the United States with 250 lobbyists and 29 lobbying firms representing Uber's interests in major states throughout the United States.[17] Rather than accepting the status quo or waiting for governments to change legislation incrementally, Uber aggressively challenged outdated regulations, oftentimes launching in a new city without approval from the local government as a way of pushing for its agenda to be addressed more quickly.

Mobile App

The intuitive simplicity of Uber's mobile app was one of Uber's greatest strengths, allowing riders to order a car with just two simple clicks and use GPS to see the physical location of the car and the expected wait time with ease, adding utility and value for the customers. Further simplicities included knowing exactly how much the ride would cost ahead of time as pricing was transparent, and saving credit cards to accounts so riders did not have to worry about having cash or tipping. In addition, the app allowed riders to communicate directly with drivers, cutting out the need for dispatchers, which ultimately saved Uber tremendous operating costs.

Dual Rating System

One of Uber's most unusual innovations was its dual rating system whereby after every ride, drivers and passengers rated each other on a scale of one to five, creating accountability on both sides. Drivers who dipped below a certain average rating risked being fired while passengers who received negative scores decreased their likelihood of being picked up by drivers. The dual rating system was designed to encourage a culture of customer service and respect on the part of both parties to foster a more positive rider and driver experience.

Data Privacy

One of the biggest criticisms leveled against Uber pertained to its data privacy policies, which were criticized for violating customers' privacy rights. Allegations surfaced that Uber employees had unfettered access to customer information such as travel records and sensitive geolocation data.[18] As the U.S. Privacy Act and other similar international laws mandated that Personally Identifiable Information on consumers needed to be protected it became necessary for Uber to adjust its data privacy policies. Uber also recently revised its privacy policy for tracking passengers even when they disabled the GPS features on the Uber app.[19] Privacy advocacy groups protested against Uber's aggressive data collection methods and wanted the Federal Trade Commission to restrict the amount of information recorded. Many felt Uber needed to demonstrate greater concern for the misuse of its customers' data as Uber employees as well as external hackers were potential abusers of that data.

Driver App

While Uber's mobile app for riders was widely considered an app of great beauty and simplicity, the app for drivers always lacked the same level of simplicity and utility. Uber recently developed a redesigned app for drivers to use as a management platform to help tend and grow their business and improve their own experience with Uber.[20] The new application allowed drivers to see areas where they were most likely to pick up passengers and whether or not prices were surging. Ultimately, the app was re-designed to help drivers maximize their income, which in the end was meant to attract more drivers to Uber rather than other ride-sharing companies.

Core Competency and Competitive Advantages

Uber's core competency was its ability to create a technology platform that connected people who needed a ride with drivers who could help them. The seamlessness of Uber's service derived from its relentless pursuit of the user experience. The mobile app worked on the principle of providing a service elegant in its simplicity of delivery. In just three simple clicks, users could see how many cars were available within their pickup vicinity, estimate the waiting time and fare, order the car, and pay for the ride with a credit card that already linked to their account. This customer-centric approach added tremendous value to the consumer experience.

However, Uber's core competency of ease of use for customers did not translate to a competitive advantage for the company, especially as Lyft's user interface was an almost exact replica of Uber's and also touted simplicity and beauty. Rather, Uber's competitive advantages derived from four areas of strength: low cost, being first-to-market, product diversity, and fundraising.

Uber's first competitive advantage was that, compared to traditional taxis, Uber offered rides at a much lower cost, largely because its cars were owned by its drivers and not by the company, significantly lowering Uber's costs. In addition, Uber considered drivers contractors, not employees, so drivers were not eligible for costly benefits. Finally, Uber's mobile app allowed drivers and riders to communicate freely, thus eliminating the need for dispatchers. Taken together these three factors enabled Uber's low cost structure.

Uber's second competitive advantage was that it was the first-to-market in the ride-sharing industry which allowed it to develop an extensive global network before other ride-sharing companies really gained traction. As of late 2015, Uber was the only U.S. ride-sharing company to operate outside the United States. Its presence in international markets helped Uber develop a strong brand image worldwide. And, Uber's universal mobile application enabled U.S. citizens traveling abroad as well as international tourists visiting the United States to order Uber cars with the same level of ease as in their home cities.

Third, Uber's differentiation strategy enhanced its competitive edge by offering a wide variety of cars and car services. By the end of its first five years, Uber had seven different tiers of services ranging from simple everyday cars such as UberX to fancy luxury cars in its UberLux line. Its breadth of offerings allowed Uber to cater to many types of passengers while its competitors lacked the same variety of services.

Lastly, Uber's ability to raise capital was a competitive advantage that allowed it to invest in the company's growth, research, and development. In its first five years, Uber raised over $8.21 billion from outside investors enabling the company to innovate by experimenting with ideas such as UberPool and spending heavily to secure a strong foothold in largely populated countries such as India and China.

Key Challenges Facing Uber

On the cusp of 2016, the primary weakness facing Uber was the class-action lawsuit challenging a crucial element of Uber's business strategy: classifying its drivers as independent contractors.[21] If the Federal District Court of San Francisco were to rule against the company and all resulting appeals fail, Uber would be required to classify its drivers as employees who would then qualify for reimbursement for business expenses such as gas and auto insurance, as well as for employee benefits such as health insurance. These additional expenses would increase pressure on Uber's income flow as well as reduce the number of markets in which the company would be profitable. These additional expenses would also undercut Uber's chances of returning to the capital markets to access additional funding.

Uber was also facing challenges in the political realm. Before 2016 ride-sharing services were an unregulated market competing with taxis, limos, and other livery services which, unlike Uber, were subject to a variety of national, state, and local rules and regulations. Being unregulated allowed Uber a lower cost of entry into the market whereas livery services had to deal with the cost of licensing and other regulatory requirements. Markets such as Germany were not open to Uber as regulations prevented access. If other markets were to enact regulatory barriers to entry, it would significantly impact Uber's expansion possibilities as well as potentially force Uber out of some of its current markets.

In addition Uber's whole business-model was seen as relying on customers to download its app thereby limiting its potential customer base to smartphone users and creating an artificial barrier to growing its customer pool. A Pew Internet & American Life Project report from 2013, estimated that 91% of all U.S. adults owned a cell phone but of that 91%, only 61% had a smartphone, a customer pool, in effect, of only of 56% of U.S. adults with access the proper technology for downloading and using the Uber app, a situation likely to be duplicated in Uber's foreign markets as well. [22]

It was clear that in considering further expansion, Uber had to figure out how to sustain its lead in a heavily regulated, controversial, competitive, and ever-changing market while moving forward into various vexed territories. While the market seemed amenable to new and various ride and car sharing innovations, Uber's regulatory/legal status was uncertain at best and very costly at worst, with regard to licensing and employee costs, especially if drivers were reclassified as employees. Finally, Uber also had to continue to effectively differentiate itself from expanding competition and become profitable—all steep challenges indeed.

SOURCES

About. *Uber*. Web. November 8, 2015. https://www.uber.com/about

Ariella. (2015, August 24) *Back-to-School Driver Appreciation Events*. Retrieved November 20, 2015, from Uber Newsroom: http://newsroom.uber.com/2015/08/back-to-school-driver-appreciation-events/

Badger, Emily. "Now We Know How Many Drivers Uber Has - and Have a Better Idea of What They're Making" *Washington Post*. January 20, 2015. Web. November 27, 2015. https://www.washingtonpost.com/news/wonk/wp/2015/01/22/now-we-know-many-drivers-uber-has-and-how-much-money-theyre-making/

Blodget, Henry. "Uber CEO Reveals Mind-Boggling New Statistic That Skeptics Will Hate." *Business Insider*. January 19, 2015. Web. November 21, 2015. http://www.businessinsider.com/uber-revenue-san-francisco-2015-1

Chokkattu, Julian, and Jordan Crook. "A Brief History of Uber." *TechCrunch*. August 14, 2014. Web. December 7, 2015. http://techcrunch.com/gallery/a-brief-history-of-uber/slide/8/

Dickey, M. R. (2014, March 11) *Uber Investor Has The Best Defense Yet Of Surge Pricing*. Retrieved November 20, 2015 , from Business Insider: http://www.businessinsider.com/uber-investor-defends-surge-pricing-2014-3

D'Onfro, Jillian. "Travis Kalanick Says Uber Needs Self-driving Cars to Avoid Ending up like the Taxi Industry." *Business Insider*. October 21, 2015. Web. November 27, 2015. http://www.businessinsider.com/uber-ceo-travis-kalanick-on-self-driving-cars-2015-10

Epitropoulos, Alexa. "Uber to Start Offering Jacksonville Jaguars Tickets at Discounted Rate for In-app Purchase." *Jacksonville Business Journal*. November 17, 2015. Web. November 27, 2015. http://www.bizjour-nals.com/jacksonville/blog/morning-edition/2015/11/jaguars-to-partner-with-uber-in-new-game-day.html

Graham, J. (2015, October 14) *Uber launches delivery service, takes on FedEx*. Retrieved November 20, 2015, from USA Today: http://www.usatoday.com/story/tech/2015/10/14/uber-launches-delivery-service-takes-fedex/73929190/

Griswold, A. (2014, October 27) *In Search of Uber's Unicorn*. Retrieved November 20, 2015, from Slate: http://www.slate.com/articles/business/moneybox/2014/10/uber_driver_salary_the_ride_sharing_company_says_its_drivers_make_great.html

Hempel, Jesse. "Inside Uber's Mission to Give Its Drivers the Ultimate App." *Wired.com*. Conde Nast Digital, October 13, 2015. Web. November 27, 2015. http://www.wired.com/2015/10/uberredesign/

Johnson, David. "Saying Goodbye to Uber? See Where Your Options Are." *Time*. November 21, 2014. Web. Novermber 18, 2015. http://time.com/3598873/uber-alternatives/.

Lemola, Hasse. "Uber CEO Reveals Ambitious Goal of Ending Car Ownership in the World." *Hypebeast*. February 8, 2015. Web. November 9, 2015. http://hypebeast.com/2015/2/uber-ceo-reveals-ambitious-goal-of-ending-car-ownership-in-the-world

Lucky. (2015, January 31) *Uber $30 First Ride Bonus Is Back*. Retrieved November 20, 2015, from One Mile at a Time: http://onemileatatime.boardingarea.com/2015/01/31/uber-30-first-ride-bonus-back

Lyons, Kim. "Uber's Move Toward Transparency Raises Concern Over Customer Data Use." *Government Technology*. July 13, 2015. Web. November 27, 2015. http://www.govtech.com/data/Ubers-Move-Toward-Transparency-Raises-Concern-Over-Customer-Data-Use.html

MacMillan, Douglas. "Uber in Fresh Funding Round That Could Value Company at Up to $64.6 Billion." *Wall Street Journal*. December 3, 2015. Web. December 3, 2015. http://www.wsj.com/articles/uber-in-fresh-funding-round-that-could-value-company-at-up-to-64-6-billion-1449180409

Miks, Jason. "Uber's Mission? 'Transportation as Reliable as Running Water'" *Global Public Square RSS*. CNN, September 17, 2014. Web. November 9, 2015. http://globalpublicsquare.blogs.cnn.com/2014/09/17/ubers-mission-transportation-as-reliable-as-running-water/

Mozur, Paul, and Mike Isaac. "Uber Spends Heavily to Establish Itself in China." *The New York Times*. June 8, 2015. Web. November 21, 2015. http://www.nytimes.com/2015/06/09/technology/uber-spends-heavily-to-establish-itself-in-china.html?smid=tw-share&_r=0

Rawlinson, Kevin. "Uber Service 'banned' in Germany by Frankfurt Court." *BBC News*. September 2, 2015. Web. November 22, 2015. http://www.bbc.com/news/technology-29027803

Sarah. (2015, November 12) *Making A Pawsitive Impact With #UberKITTENS*. Retrieved November 2015, from Uber Newsroom: http://newsroom.uber.com/2015/11/kittensimpact/

Singer, Natasha, and Mike Isaac. "Uber Data Collection Changes Should Be Barred, Privacy Group Urges." *The New York Times*. June 22, 2015. Web. November 27, 2015. http://www.nytimes.com/2015/06/23/technology/uber-data-collection-changes-should-be-barred-privacy-group-urges.html?_r=0

Sterling, Greg. "Pew: 61 Percent In US Now Have Smartphones." *Marketing Land*. June 5, 2013. Web. December 6, 2015. http://marketingland.com/pew-61-percent-in-us-now-have-smartphones-46966

Sun, Lena. "Haven't Got Your Flu Shot? Uber Is Offering One-day, On-demand Vaccinations to Your Doorstep." *Washington Post*. November 17, 2015. Web. November 21, 2015. https://www.washingtonpost.com/news/to-your-health/wp/2015/11/17/no-time-to-get-your-flu-shot-uber-is-offering-on-demand-vaccinations-to-your-doorstep/

"UBER DRIVERS." *Uber Lawsuit Information*. Lichen & Liss-Rioddan, P.C. Web. November 21, 2015. http://uberlawsuit.com/

Uber.com. (2015) *Boston*. Retrieved November 20, 2015, from Uber: https://www.uber.com/cities/boston

"Uber." *Uber*. CrunchBase. Web. November 21, 2015. https://www.crunchbase.com/organization/uber#/entity

Weise, Karen. "How Uber Rolls." *BusinessWeek*. June 29, 2014: 54–59. Print.

"What Is UberX?" *Uber Expansion*. Web. November 8, 2015. http://uberexpansion.com/what-is-uberx/

Uber for Business. (2015) Retrieved November 20, 2015, from Uber: https://www.uber.com/business

Verena, M. (2015, November 17) *Outsmart the Flu with UberHEALTH*. Retrieved November 20, 2015, from Uber Newsroom: https://newsroom.uber.com/2015/11/uberhealth/

Wikipedia. Wikimedia Foundation. Web. November 8, 2015. https://en.wikipedia.org/wiki/Uber_(company).

NOTES

1. "Uber (company)." Wikipedia. Wikimedia Foundation, n.d. Web. November 8, 2015. https://en.wikipedia.org/wiki/Uber_(company).

2. Chokkattu, Julian, and Jordan Crook. "A Brief History of Uber." *TechCrunch*. N.p., August 14, 2014. Web. November 8, 2015. http://techcrunch.com/gallery/a-brief-history-of-uber/slide/8/

3. "What Is UberX?" *Uber Expansion*. N.p., n.d. Web. November 8, 2015. http://uberexpansion.com/what-is-uberx/

4. Miks, Jason. "Uber's Mission? 'Transportation as Reliable as Running Water'" *Global Public Square RSS*. CNN, September 14, 2014. Web. November 9, 2015. http://globalpublicsquare.blogs.cnn.com/2014/09/17/ubers-mission-transportation-as-reliable-as-running-water/

5. Lemola, Hasse. "Uber CEO Reveals Ambitious Goal of Ending Car Ownership in the World." *Hypebeast*. N.p., February 8, 2015. Web. November 9, 2015. http://hypebeast.com/2015/2/uber-ceo-reveals-ambitious-goal-of-ending-car-ownership-in-the-world

6. Johnson, David. "See Where Uber Faces the Biggest Competition." *Time*. November 21, 2014. Web. November 18, 2015. http://time.com/3598873/uber-alternatives/

7. Rawlinson, Kevin. "Uber Service 'banned' in Germany by Frankfurt Court." *BBC News*. September 2, 2014. Web. November 22, 2015. http://www.bbc.com/news/technology-29027803

8. D'onfro, Jillian. "Travis Kalanik says Uber Needs Self-Driving Cars to Avoid Ending up like Taxi Industry." *Business Insider*. October 21, 2015. Web. November 27, 2015. http://www.businessinsider.com/uber-ceo-travis-kalanick-on-self-driving-cars-2015-10

9. MacMillan, Douglas. "Uber in Fresh Funding Round That Could Value Company at Up to $64.6 Billion." *WSJ*. Wall Street Journal. December 3, 2015. Web. December 3, 2015. http://www.wsj.com/articles/uber-in-fresh-funding-round-that-could-value-company-at-up-to-64-6-billion-1449180409

10. Sun, Lena. "Haven't Got Your Flu Shot? Uber Is Offering One-day, On-demand Vaccinations to Your Doorstep." *Washington Post*. November 17, 2015. Web. November 21, 2015. https://www.washingtonpost.com/news/to-your-health/wp/2015/11/17/no-time-to-get-your-flu-shot-uber-is-offering-on-demand-vaccinations-to-your-doorstep/

11. "Uber." *Uber*. CrunchBase. Web. November 21, 2015. https://www.crunchbase.com/organization/uber#/entity

12. Mozur, Paul, and Mike Isaac. "Uber Spends Heavily to Establish Itself in China." *The New York Times*. June 8, 2015. Web. November 21, 2015. http://www.nytimes.com/2015/06/09/technology/uber-spends-heavily-to-establish-itself-in-china.html?smid=tw-share&_r=0

13. Blodget, Henry. "Uber CEO Reveals Mind-Boggling New Statistic That Skeptics Will Hate." *Business Insider*. January 19, 2015. Web. November 21, 2015. http://www.businessinsider.com/uber-revenue-san-francisco-2015-1

14. Epitropoulos, Alexa. "Jaguars to Partner with Uber in New Game-Day Marketing Push". November 17, 2015. Web. November 27, 2015 http://www.bizjournals.com/jacksonville/blog/morning-edition/2015/11/jaguars-to-partner-with-uber-in-new-game-day.html.

15. Weise, Karen. "How Uber Rolls." *BusinessWeek*. Pp. 54-59. June 29, 2014.

16 Badger, Emily. "Now We Know How Many Drivers Uber Has – and Have a Better idea of What They're Making." *Washington Post*. January 22, 2015. Web. November 27, 2015. https://www.washingtonpost.com/news/wonk/wp/2015/01/22/now-we-know-many-drivers-uber-has-and-how-much-money-theyre-making%E2%80%8B/

17. Weise, Karen. "How Uber Rolls." *BusinessWeek*. Pp. 54-59. June 29, 2014.

18. Singer, Natasha and Isaac, Mike. "Uber Data Collection Changes Should Be Barred, Privacy Group Urges." *The New York Times*. June 22, 2015. Web. November 27, 2015. http://www.nytimes.com/2015/06/23/technology/

uber-data-collection-changes-should-be-barred-privacy
-group-urges.html?_r=0

19. Lyons, Kim. "Uber's Move Toward Transparency Raises
Concern Over Customer Data Use." *Government Technology*. July 13, 2015. Web. November 27, 2015. http://www
.govtech.com/data/Ubers-Move-Toward-Transparency
-Raises-Concern-Over-Customer-Data-Use.html

20. Hempel, Jesse. "Inside Uber's Mission to Give Its Drivers the Ultimate App." *Wired Magazine*. October 13, 2015.
Web. November 27, 2015. http://www.wired.com/2015/10
/uberredesign/

21. "UBER DRIVERS." *Uber Lawsuit Information*. Lichten
& Liss-Riordan, P.C. Web. November 21, 2015. http://
uberlawsuit.com/

22. Sterling, Greg. "Pew: 61 Percent In US Now Have
Smartphones." *Marketing Land*. June 5, 2013.
Web. December 6, 2015. http://marketingland.com
/pew-61-percent-in-us-now-have-smartphones-46966

CASE **11**

Pandora Internet Radio (2014): Just Press Play

Gary Stenftennagel and Joyce Vincelette

Introduction

Brian McAndrews was quietly sitting at home listening to a mix of his favorite Pandora stations featuring Elton John, Billy Joel, the Rolling Stones, and Bruce Springsteen.[1] He was putting together a company address to discuss Pandora's recently released 2014 10-K filing and was contemplating the progress the company had made since his arrival. He thought back on the difficulties that the company presented when he joined as the new Chief Executive Officer (CEO) a few months prior. He had come into the role at a crucial time for the company. While Pandora was still experiencing rapid growth in users and listener hours, content acquisition costs were spiraling out of control because the music industry wanted their share of the profits, and listeners were willing to go elsewhere if the company did not offer the music they wanted. In addition, within a few days of being announced the new CEO, the competitive environment heated up considerably when Apple launched iTune Radio, supported by Apple's international reputation and deep pockets. Mr. McAndrews knew that he and Pandora were in a tough spot. If Pandora could not control its costs, acquire the rights to music its listeners wanted, or attain profitability soon, how long could the company possibly survive?

Pandora was built around the idea of providing listeners with only the music that they love. To do so, Pandora fundamentally changed how people listened to music by allowing station customization and the ability to listen to music over the Internet. As technology changed, Pandora evolved from a website-based radio provider and developed a mobile application with which the company could offer its services to customers whenever and wherever they wanted to listen to music. While monetizing the mobile product proved to be difficult and Pandora had not yet attained profitability, it looked like things had started to turn around for Mr. McAndrews and Pandora. By year-end 2013, Pandora's advertising revenue per listener hour showed signs of increasing.[2] Whether this was an anomaly or a positive sign for Pandora's future was yet to be determined. As the company continued to evolve, the industry continued to develop, and competition continued to grow, Pandora had to adapt and change or risk being left behind.

History

Pandora Internet Radio was founded in 2000 when founder Tim Westergren developed an initiative called the Music Genome Project.[3] This project, which mirrored the major breakthroughs of the human genome project, sought to analyze and categorize music based on 450 musical characteristics.[4] As the project grew, he realized that the extensive music database could be used to effectively target, categorize, and recommend music to listeners. He developed one of the smartest music recommendation programs available at the time. Within four years of the start of the project, Pandora Internet Radio was ready for its debut.[5] With the leadership of Chief Executive Officer Joe Kennedy, who joined the company in July 2004, Pandora experienced rapid growth in users, streaming hours, and advertising clients during its early years.[6] However, the road to success was rarely easy for Pandora as the small startup attempted to uproot the traditional radio industry. Pandora had to fight rising royalty costs, combat profitability issues, and attempt to change the status quo in the music industry.

In February 2011, Pandora filed for an initial public offering (IPO).[7] The company was able to leverage its ability to tailor music selections to its listeners' music preferences. Pandora was soon at the forefront of music-oriented technology as the market for Internet radio started to develop. The growth in the company's user base had been strong after the initial public offering in 2011. In January 2011, the company had 80 million registered users who listened to approximately 3.9 billion hours of radio by the year's end.[8] As of December 31, 2013, the company had more than 200 million registered users who listened to 15.31 billion hours of radio by year's end.[9] Within three years, the company had more than doubled its user base and almost quadrupled its listener hours. However, the company also experienced important changes in leadership with the departure of the company's first CEO Joe Kennedy and the arrival of Brian McAndrews as the new CEO in September 2013. In addition, founder Tim Westergren, who served as Pandora's Chief Strategy Officer, left the company in 2014.[10] He continued to serve on Pandora's Board of Directors. Pandora would miss the creative talents and vision of both departing executives who built the company. Mr. McAndrews certainly had large shoes to fill.

By spring 2014, Pandora was the largest Internet radio provider in the United States. The company controlled approximately 70% of the Internet radio market and approximately 8.6% of the overall radio market.[11] As the company grew, it expanded its product offerings through the development of a mobile application and integration with cars and other electronic devices. The company also increased its music offering from 800,000 tracks in 2011 to 1,000,000 tracks in 2013.[12] The company had historically struggled with finances and as of December 31, 2013 had never achieved profitability as a public company.[13] Despite the company's lack of profitability, Pandora remained true to its mission and sought to provide users with only the music they love, whenever they want it, and wherever they want it.

Corporate Governance

Founder[14]

Tim Westergren founded the online radio service in 2000 with the creation of the Music Genome Project and was the company's Chief Strategy Officer until 2014.[15] Prior to founding the company, Mr. Westergren worked in the music industry for over 20 years doing production, audio engineering, film scoring, and live performances. Mr. Westergren continued to help develop Pandora's strategy and vision and traveled the country to connect with Pandora's vast number of listeners.

Executive Officers[16]

Brian McAndrews joined the company in September 2013 as Chief Executive Officer, President, and Chairman of the Board.[17] Prior to joining the company, Mr. McAndrews was a venture partner at Madrona Venture Group. Mr. McAndrews was a Senior Vice President at Microsoft from August 2007 to December 2008 after the firm acquired aQuantive. Mr. McAndrews served as President and CEO of aQuantive from 1999 to 2007. He also worked for ABC, holding senior executive positions at ABC Sports, ABC Entertainment, and ABC Television Network, and as a product manager at General Mills.

Mike Herring served as the Chief Financial Officer of Pandora since February 2013.[18] Prior to joining the company, Mr. Herring was the Vice President of Operations at Adobe Systems Incorporated for three years. Mr. Herring was the Executive Vice President and Chief Financial Officer of Omniture Inc. between 2004 and 2009. He also served as Chief Financial Officer at Ancestry.com, Vice President of Finance at Third Age Media, and Controller at Anergen Inc.

Delida Costin served as the General Counsel of Pandora. Prior to joining the company, Ms. Costin had a private legal practice and was a member of the Attorney Bench at Axiom Legal. Ms. Costin also served as the Vice President and Assistant General Counsel at CNET Networks. She also practiced with two law firms named Goodwin, Proctor LLP and Pillsbury Winthrop Shaw Pittman LLP.

Simon Fleming-Wood served as the Chief Marketing Officer of Pandora since 2011. Prior to joining the company, Mr. Fleming-Wood was the Vice President of Marketing at Pure Digital Technology in charge of developing the Flip Video brand. When the brand was purchased by Cisco, Mr. Fleming-Wood assumed the role of Vice President of Marketing for the Cisco Consumer Products group. He also held senior marketing positions at Sega.com, Mattel, and The Clorox Company.

Tom Conrad served as the interim Head of Product at Pandora. He was also the Chief Technology Officer of Pandora between 2004 and 2014. Prior to joining the company, Mr. Conrad was the Vice President of Engineering at Kenamea, Inc. He also served in various engineering positions at Berkeley Systems, Relevance Technologies, Documentum, Pets.com, and Kenamea. Mr. Conrad began his career at Apple Computer where he helped develop the Mac OS.

John Trimble served as the Chief Revenue Officer of Pandora since March 2009.[19] Prior to joining the company, Mr. Trimble was the Executive Vice President at Glam Media, Inc. Mr. Trimble also served on the executive team tasked with creating Fox Interactive Media and other brands. He has also held the roles of Director of Sales for SportsIllustrated.com and Vice President of Sales for Phase2 Media.

Sara Clemens served as the Chief Strategy Officer of Pandora since February 2014. Prior to joining Pandora, she was an executive at Greylock Partners. Ms. Clemens was also a Vice President of Corporate Development at LinkedIn and an employee at Microsoft Corporation.

Chris Martin served as the Chief Technology Officer of Pandora since March 2014.[20] Prior to joining the company, Mr. Martin worked as an engineer at various companies such as Quintus, Kenamea, and QRS/Inovis.

Kristen Robinson served as the Chief Human Resource Officer since March 2014. Prior to joining Pandora, Ms. Robinson held various roles at Yahoo, Hewlett-Packard, Agilent Technologies, and Verigy.

Board of Directors[21]

Tim Westergren co-founded Pandora in 2000, remained on the Board of Directors and had other limited roles at the company.[22]

Brian McAndrews joined the company in September 2013 as Chief Executive Officer, President, and Chairman of the Board.

Peter Chernin joined the Board of Directors in January 2011. He was the owner of Chernin Entertainment and The Chernin Group, which both focus on media and entertainment initiatives. Prior to joining the company, Mr. Chernin held various positions at News Corporation from 1996 to 2009 such as Chief Executive Officer of Fox Entertainment Group and the head of Twentieth Century Fox Filmed Entertainment and Fox Broadcasting Company. He also served on the Board of Directors at American Express.

Peter Gotcher joined the Board of Directors in September 2005. He was a private investor and venture partner with Redpoint Ventures from 1999 to 2002. Mr. Gotcher was also a partner at Institutional Venture Partners, founder of Digidesign, and Executive Vice President at Avid Technology. He also served on the Board of Directors of Dolby Laboratories.

Robert Kavner joined the Board of Directors in March 2004. He was an independent investor and served as President and Chief Executive Officer of On Command Corporation. Mr. Kavner also held senior management roles at AT&T and AT&T Venture Capital Group. He was also a partner at PricewaterhouseCoopers before joining AT&T.

Elizabeth Nelson joined the Board of Directors in 2013. She was the Executive Vice President and Chief Financial Officer at Macromedia, Inc. Ms. Nelson also held finance and corporate development roles at Hewlett-Packard Company. She also served on the Board of Directors of Nokia, Ancestry.com, CNET Networks, Inc., and other companies.

David Sze joined the Board of Directors in May 2009. Mr. Sze was a partner at Greylock Partners, where he focused on Internet and technology investments. Before joining Greylock Partners, he worked at Excite, Electronic Arts, HBO, and Crystal Dynamics. He started his career at The Boston Consulting Group and Marakon Associates. Mr. Sze also served on the Board of Directors of LinkedIn Corporation.

James Feuille joined the Board of Directors in October 2005. He was a partner at Crosslink Capital where he focused on technology-based investments. Prior to joining Crosslink Capital, Mr. Feuille held roles at UBS, Volpe Brown Whelan & Company, and Robertson Stephens & Company.

Mission, Objectives, And Strategies

Pandora was originally developed to bring the joy and power of music to everyone, everywhere, anytime. This idea, which started with Tim Westergren's development of the Music Genome Project, continued to shape the company's mission and business through the years. Pandora's strategies and business model supported the company's mission, which was outlined in the company's initial SEC filing in 2011. *"Our mission is to enrich people's lives by enabling them to enjoy music they know and discover music they'll love, anytime, anywhere. People connect with music on a fundamentally personal and deeply emotional level. Whether it's a song someone first heard ten years ago or one they've just discovered, if they connect with that music on our service, a strong bond is forged at that moment with Pandora. Just as we value music, we also hold a deep respect for those who create it. We celebrate and hold dear the individuals who have chosen to make music, from megastars to talented new and emerging artists."*[23] This original mission statement had been embodied within Pandora's subsequent mission statements as they evolved over the years, *"To play only music you'll love."*[24] The company recognized how powerful music could be in a person's life. Accordingly, the company continued to strive to increase the size of its music library, improve music recommendations, widen the availability of its service, and make the service seamless and easy to use. Pandora also wanted to grow as a company, increase its user base, and generate revenue, all while minimizing costs. Only by accomplishing its objectives would the company be able to achieve its mission.

Pandora developed key strategies to support the company's objectives. These strategies outlined how the company would expand, improve, and continue to deliver music to millions of people. The first strategy was to widen the availability of its service and "make Pandora available everywhere that there is Internet connectivity."[25] This demonstrated the company's desire to expand geographically and increase the number of devices on which the product was offered. The second strategy was to transform listener hours into revenue through advertisement sales. "Our advertising strategy focuses on developing our core suite of audio, display and video advertising products and marketing these products to advertisers for delivery across traditional computer and mobile and other connected device platforms."[26] The company was trying to provide the most comprehensive advertising suite at competitive rates to both gain new partners and retain old ones. The third strategy focused on growth and financial stability. Pandora sought to "increase the number of listeners and listener hours to increase our market penetration, including the number of listener hours on mobile and other connected devices."[27] In addition to increasing revenue, the company sought to curb content acquisition costs and increase financial stability. The fourth strategy was a long-term plan to expand internationally in order to increase the company's user base and diversify revenue.[28] According to Pandora, international expansion was cost prohibitive.[29] The fifth and last strategy was to better compete with traditional radio for advertising revenue.[30] Pandora was trying to better position itself to court advertising partners and to actively pursue revenue growth.

Marketing

Product

Pandora offered two main products. The first product was the free advertising-supported radio service which launched in 2005.[31] The free alternative was funded through web-based advertisements that appeared intermittently during listening. Pandora sales representatives sold advertisement slots to various companies. The revenue collected from advertisers enabled the company to provide the free streaming service. To use the free alternative, customers only needed to create an account, input personal data, and get started. Based on the personal data and other metrics, advertisements were targeted and user-specific.[32]

The second product Pandora offered was called Pandora One. Pandora One was a subscription-based alternative that offered advertisement-free radio for a fee. When individuals purchased this plan, they experienced seamless and uninterrupted music streaming.

Both products were offered on a variety of platforms that were broken up into two main categories: computer focused or mobile oriented.[33] Users could access Pandora's website through any Internet-enabled computer. The mobile application relied on wireless data or Wi-Fi to function. People could use the product around the house, on the road, or anywhere else they had an Internet connection. This functionality fit in nicely with Pandora's strategy to provide its service to users any place or anytime. The company's product offerings had gone through many changes over the years including the removal of listening limits on free mobile radio. Early on, a listening limit of 40 hours per month was implemented and if listeners exceeded the 40 hour per month listening limit, they had the opportunity to pay $0.99 to get unlimited streaming for the rest of the month.[34] As of September 2013, the company removed the listening cap due to bad publicity.[35]

Pandora's business model was focused on the sale of advertisements delivered to users of the company's free service and from subscription revenue from Pandora One. Pandora made the majority of its revenue from the sale of advertisements delivered in audio, display, and video format.[36] The company offered advertisements to local and national advertisers and provided targeted advertisements based on attributes such as age, gender, zip code, and other preferences.[37] In order to sell advertisement slots to advertisers, the company employed a large sales force to help maintain established clients and recruit new ones. The company's sales force was divided into multiple geographic teams located in California, Illinois, and New York.[38] Advertisements were intermittently shown to users of the free Pandora website and mobile application. Pandora then received revenue for each user listening hour that it registered. In order to quantify the revenue, Pandora developed a metric called Advertising Revenue per Thousand Listener Hours. According to the company's financial filings, one thousand listener hours was worth $29.60 in 2012 and $36.70 in 2013 in advertising revenue.[39] The business model was essentially based on the number of listener hours and the revenue per listening hour generated. If Pandora wanted to generate additional revenue, the company had to increase the number of listener hours or increase its revenue rate per hour.

Pandora also generated revenue through the monthly subscription fee it charged Pandora One subscribers. The Pandora One subscription allowed users to listen to unlimited advertisement-free content.[40] However, with only 3.3 million subscribers, the subscription-based service only made up a fraction of the company's overall revenue, 12% in 2012 and 18% in 2013.[41] Pandora One revenue was dependent on the fee charged for the paid service and the number of customers paying for the service.

Price

Pandora had different pricing schemes for its products. The free Internet radio was subsidized by revenue from advertisement sales. By charging companies for advertising slots, the company was able to offer its free service. This was an attractive product from a consumer's perspective, which was evident in the fact that the majority of Pandora's users were free listeners. In the 11 months ended December 31, 2012 and 2013, 88% and 82% of the company's revenues, respectively, came from advertisement sales.[42] Pandora One was a paid service that, for a small monthly fee, granted customers access to advertisement-free listening.[43] However, due to the popularity of the free alternative, Pandora One only made up a fraction of the company's overall revenue. The percentage of the company's revenue attributable to Pandora One in the 11 months ended December 31, 2012 and 2013 was 12% and 18%, respectively.[44]

Place

Pandora was founded in the United States and grew quickly domestically. The company had become a prominent brand in the United States and was seen as a leader in Internet radio. However, Pandora had no international presence and international expansion was cost prohibitive. Pandora had licensing agreements in place with music rights organizations in the United States. United States copyright laws allowed Pandora to distribute the media domestically but not internationally. Ultimately, this limited Pandora's expansion possibilities. The difficulty of comprehending and the costs associated with international copyright laws had stalled Pandora's international expansion efforts.

Promotion

In order to promote its product, Pandora relied heavily on two forms of free promotion, word of mouth and product integration. As of December 31, 2013, Pandora had 76.2 million monthly active members that used its product.[45] Accordingly, Pandora counted on its current members to inform friends and family about its product. With so many active members, everyone knew someone who used Pandora. With this degree of market penetration, Pandora had decided not to spend on promotion. Pandora was also integrated with cars, televisions, and many other consumer electronics.[46] Car and electronic manufacturers were using Pandora integration as a selling point to draw in potential buyers. As a result, Pandora integration was being promoted at the expense of its partnering companies. Due to the costs involved, Pandora did not produce or air commercials to promote its brand, new features, or new pricing schemes.

Finance

In 2013, Pandora changed its fiscal year to align with the calendar 12 months beginning January 1st and ending December 31st, effective beginning with the year ended December 31, 2013.[47] As a result, Pandora's financial statements are presented on both an 11-month basis from January 31, 2013 to December 31, 2013 and on a 12-month basis from January 31, 2013 to January 31, 2014. Pandora's income statement and consolidated balance sheet are provided in **Exhibit 1** and **Exhibit 2**, respectively.

As shown in **Exhibit 1**, Pandora reported an increase in total revenue from $389.484 million for the 11 months ended December 31, 2012 to $600.233 million for the 11 months ended December 31, 2013, which was a 54% increase. Revenue at Pandora was derived from two significant sources: advertising and subscriptions. Advertising revenue made up the majority of Pandora's revenue. Between the 11 months ended December 31, 2012 and 2013, advertising revenue increased 43% from $343.318 million to $489.340 million while subscription revenue increased 140% from $46.166 million to $110.893 million, as shown in **Exhibit 1**. Despite the rapid growth in revenue, the company had yet to experience profitability due to rising content acquisition costs and sales and marketing expenses.

In order to provide its service, Pandora had to develop licensing agreements with music companies. As the music industry continued to evolve, music rights owners were looking to make more money from licensing agreements. Pandora felt this extra burden as its content acquisition costs continued to rise. As shown in **Exhibit 1**, Pandora reported content acquisition costs of $314.866 million in the 11 months ended December 31, 2013, a 36% increase over the 11 months ended December 31, 2012. These rising costs were constantly an issue for Pandora as the company continued to struggle with profitability.

Sales and marketing expenses were also very high. In order to increase advertising revenue, the company had to sell advertisements to advertisers. To do so, Pandora employed a very large sales team across the country. The team was in charge of bringing in all of the company's advertising revenue. As shown in **Exhibit 1**, Pandora

EXHIBIT 1 Pandora Internet Radio
Consolidated Statement of Operations (All figures in thousands except per share data)

	Twelve Months Ended January 31				Eleven Months Ended December 31	
	2013 (b)	2012 (b)	2011 (a)	2010 (a)	2013 (b)	2012 (b)
Revenue						
Advertising	375,218	239,957	119,333	50,147	489,340	343,318
Subscription and other	51,927	34,383	18,431	5,042	110,893	46,166
Total revenue	427,145	274,340	137,764	55,189	600,233	389,484
Cost of revenue						
Cost of revenue - Content acquisition costs	258,748	148,708	69,357	32,946	314,866	230,731
Cost fo revenue - Other	32,019	22,759	11,559	7,892	41,844	28,740
Total cost of revenue	290,767	171,467	80,916	40,838	356,710	259,471
Gross profit	136,378	102,873	56,848	14,351	243,523	130,013
Operating expenses						
Product development	18,118	13,425	6,736	6,026	29,986	16,191
Sales and marketing	107,715	65,010	36,250	17,426	169,774	94,566
General and administrative	48,247	35,428	14,183	6,358	70,212	43,320
Total operating expenses	174,080	113,863	57,169	29,810	269,972	154,077
Loss from operations	(37,702)	(10,990)	(321)	(15,459)	(26,449)	(24,064)
Other expense	(441)	(5,042)	(1,309)	(1,294)	(474)	(401)
Loss before income taxes	(38,143)	(16,032)	(1,630)	(16,753)	(26,923)	(24,465)
Income tax benefit (expense)	(5)	(75)	(134)	-	(94)	3
Net loss	(38,148)	(16,107)	(1,764)	(16,753)	(27,017)	(24,462)
Deemed dividend on Series D and Series E	-	-	-	(1,443)	-	-
Accretion of redeemable convertible preferred stock	-	(110)	(300)	(218)	-	-
Increase in cumulative dividends payable on conversion of liquidation of redeemable convertible preferred stock	-	(3,648)	(8,978)	(6,461)	-	-
Net loss attributable to common stockholders	(38,148)	(19,865)	(11,042)	(24,875)	(27,017)	(24,462)
Net loss per share, basic and diluted	(0.23)	(0.19)	(1.03)	(3.84)	(0.15)	(0.15)

Notes:

(a) Pandora Internet Radio 2012 10-K, p. 60.

(b) Pandora Internet Radio 2014 10-K, p. 74.

reported sales and marketing expenses of $169.774 million in the 11 months ended December 31, 2013, an 80% increase over the 11 months ended December 31, 2012. Between the 11 months ended December 31, 2012 and 2013, sales and marketing increased by 80% while advertising revenue increased only 43%.

EXHIBIT 2 Pandora Internet Radio
Consolidated Balance Sheets (All figures in thousands except share data)

	As of January 31, 2013 (b)	As of January 31, 2012 (a)	As of January 31, 2011 (a)	As of December 31, 2013 (b)
Assets				
Current Assets				
Cash and cash equivalents	65,725	44,126	43,048	2,45,755
Short-term investments	23,247	46,455	-	98,662
Accounts receivable, net of allowance	103,410	66,738	42,212	1,64,023
Prepaid expenses and other current assets	6,232	2,806	3,516	10,343
Total current assets	198,614	160,125	88,776	5,18,783
Long-term investments	-	-	-	105,686
Property and equipment, net	17,758	15,576	8,683	35,151
Other long-term assets	2,460	2,314	1,750	13,715
Total assets	218,832	178,015	99,209	673,335
Liabilities and stockholders' equity				
Current liabilities:				
Accounts payable	4,471	2,053	1,965	14,413
Accrued liabilities	7,590	3,838	5,532	14,885
Accrued royalties	53,083	33,822	18,080	66,110
Deferred revenue	29,266	19,232	15,910	42,650
Accrued compensation	21,560	11,962	3,815	17,948
Current portion of long-term debt			6,759	
Total current liabilities	115,970	70,907	52,061	156,006
Long-term debt			837	
Preferred stock warrant liability			1,027	
Other long-term liabilities	3,873	2,568	1,632	9,098
Total liabilities	119,843	73,475	55,557	165,104
Redeemable convertible preferred stock			126,662	
Stockholders' equity:				
Preferred Stock, $0.0001 par value				
Common stock, $0.0001 par value	17	16	1	20
Additional paid-in capital	238,552	205,955	2,308	675,103
Accumulated deficit	(139,574)	(101,426)	(85,319)	(166,591)
Accumulated other comprehensive loss	(6)	(5)	-	(301)
Total stockholders' equity	98,989	104,540	(83,010)	508,231
Total liabilities and stockholders' equity	218,832	178,015	99,209	673,335

Notes:

(a) Pandora Internet Radio 2012 10-K, p. 59.

(b) Pandora Internet Radio 2014 10-K, p. 73.

Content acquisition costs and sales and marketing expenses were the most significant costs for Pandora. In 2013, they combined to total $484.640 million, as shown in **Exhibit 1**. These costs were approximately 81% of the total revenue of the company. As a result, the company had not achieved profitability since its IPO in 2011. The company's struggle for profitability was evident in the fact that it had a net loss in both the 11 months ended December 31, 2012 and 2013. In the 11 months ended December 31, 2013, the company reported a net loss attributable to common stockholders of $27.017 million, compared to a loss of $24.462 million in the 11 months ended December 31, 2012, which can be seen in **Exhibit 1**.

Growth

As one of the first companies in the Internet radio market, Pandora initially experienced rapid growth. As with other disruptive technologies, the company took market share from established market leaders. In this case, Pandora grew at the expense of traditional radio as the new technology, which allowed people to listen to radio on the Internet, started to catch on and grow. However, growth opportunities had slowed as the Internet radio market had become saturated with competitors. In order to continue growing, the company had to increase its user base. A few different opportunities such as international expansion and partnerships had been discussed to help spur new growth.

Pandora was almost solely based in the United States. Besides small operations in Australia, Pandora had no international operations. This was mainly the result of complex copyright and licensing laws that did not transfer between countries. As a result, if Pandora wanted to expand internationally, the company would have to negotiate new contracts to stream music to each country individually. Because of this, the cost to expand internationally was extremely high and Pandora had to weigh the costs and benefits of such expansion.

One of Pandora's newest growth initiatives was collaborating with automobile makers and other electronic device makers to integrate the company's service with their products. This initiative, called Pandora Everywhere, focused on providing Internet radio to listeners at home, in the car, and everywhere in between.[48]

In order to capitalize on the fact that Americans spend a lot of time traveling by car, one of the main initiatives of Pandora Everywhere was automobile integration. Pandora had integrated its product with car manufacturers such as BMW, Buick, General Motors, Ford, GMC, and many others.[49] This initiative also helped take away listeners from one of the company's largest competitors, traditional radio. To further increase listening in the car, Pandora collaborated with aftermarket stereo companies such as Pioneer and Sony.[50] Aftermarket stereos are replacement stereos that usually are placed in older or outdated cars.

To further become part of the everyday lives of consumers, Pandora was also integrating its service with household appliances, home theater systems, televisions, and a variety of other home electronic devices. Partnerships with Samsung, LG, Sharp, Philips, and other companies increased the company's exposure to new potential listeners.[51] These strategic partnerships were being formed to both increase the number of individuals who used Pandora and to increase the total number of listening hours. The partnerships helped the company create an easy-to-use product that was available anywhere, on any device, and anytime listeners wanted.

The ability to access and use Pandora anytime and anywhere was the purpose of Pandora's strategic partnerships. Pandora understood that simplicity of use and constant availability of its service was the key to the company becoming the go-to entertainment solution of the future.

Legal Landscape

The music and technology industries had extremely complex legal landscapes. Music licensing was a costly and complicated process but was essential for Pandora to provide its service. The domestic and international music rights laws varied dramatically and presented their own set of issues. Privacy issues and patent disputes could also arise and present legal and financial troubles for companies like Pandora.

Music Licensing

High content streaming acquisition costs were a serious issue for Pandora. Once upon a time the music industry generated revenue by selling CDs and MP3s to fans. As consumers moved toward cheaper and more accessible alternatives, such as Internet radio, record labels attempted to offset declining CD and MP3 sales by increasing the cost to stream music. Music rights owners had significant bargaining power when negotiating rates because without content, companies like Pandora would be unable to survive. This disproportionate bargaining power was evident in the constantly rising content acquisition costs that crippled Pandora.

In order to track licensing costs, Pandora published a statistic called licensing costs per thousand listener hours (LPMs). In the 11 months ended December 31, 2012, the LPMs was $18.30.[52] In 2013 the costs rose over 12% to $20.57.[53] These rising costs had become increasingly problematic for Pandora and the company sought to do a better job of managing costs and monetizing its service.

Domestic versus International Law

Pandora offered its services almost exclusively in the United States and, as a result, was only required to comply with domestic copyright laws. The United States had one of the most developed and complete set of licensing laws in the world. While acquiring streaming rights was extremely expensive domestically, it would be much more difficult internationally. According to Pandora, there were no equivalent laws outside of the United States and other licensing alternatives were not commercially viable.[54] The international landscape was far more complex and decentralized. Pandora would have had to expend substantial time and capital to expand internationally and negotiate the necessary streaming contracts in each country.

Lawsuits

Pandora's lawyers also had to address legal issues concerning privacy and patent infringement because these laws were continuously changing in the United States. While Pandora did everything it could to comply with privacy laws, the company had faced legal action twice over privacy concerns. The first class action lawsuit alleged the company unlawfully accessed and transmitted personal identifiable information in connection with the use of the company's Android application.[55] The second lawsuit claimed Pandora allowed a listener's history to be visible to the public.[56] These lawsuits could be costly for Pandora. As of December 31, 2013, no ruling had been passed for either lawsuit. Pandora also dealt with lawsuits where other companies claimed Pandora infringed on their patents. Pandora had been sued by B.E. Technology, LLC, 1st Technology LLC, and Macrosolve, Inc.[57] As of December 31, 2013, no ruling had been reached on the the B.E. Technology, LLC lawsuit. The 1st Technology LLC lawsuit was settled, and the Macrosolve, Inc. lawsuit was dismissed.[58]

Intellectual Property

A combination of intellectual property rights including copyrights, trademarks, patents, contractual restrictions, and non-disclosure agreements helped protect Pandora's service and brand.[59] Internet-oriented companies usually put strict measures in place to protect their intellectual property. This was particularly important because copying ideas and services had become much easier since the advent of the Internet. For example, Pandora could suffer significant damage to its intellectual property, such as its music recommendation software and Music Genome Project, if a competitor or hacker gained access to the company's computer code.

Accordingly, Pandora had eight patents and purchased additional patents from other technology companies.[60] In addition, in order to protect its name and image, Pandora obtained registered trademarks and domain name rights in the United States and at least nine other countries.[61] The trademark protects the Pandora name, the Music Genome Project, and additional Pandora logos.[62] Pandora also owned Internet domain names for its website at Pandora.com. In addition, if Pandora decided to expand internationally, the company owned additional domain names for Pandora in the United Kingdom, Germany, New Zealand, and India.[63] Despite the company's greatest efforts to protect itself from copycats, the protection of copyrights, trademarks, and patents was only as strong as the country's laws in which it operated. Contractual restrictions and non-disclosure agreements also helped limit the potential negative impact of other companies poaching Pandora employees.

Industry/Competitors

Internet radio as a way to listen to music was a new concept when Pandora was founded and few competitors existed. As the technology landscape changed and with the increased prevalence of the Internet and Internet-connected devices, the age of Internet radio was poised to take over traditional radio. People sought out free and easy-to-use alternatives when listening to music with more customization features and fewer advertisements. As a result of the increasing market desire for Internet radio, competitors emerged in the United States as well as internationally offering both advertisement-based free Internet radio and advertisement-free subscription services. While competition was strong among Internet radio companies, Pandora also faced competition from traditional radio providers and satellite radio providers.

Pandora's competitors could be broken up into three groups, traditional radio, satellite radio, and Internet radio.[64]

Traditional radio was a large and established market with well-defined competitors. Traditional radio was first utilized to air a musical performance in 1907.[65] Traditional table radios soon became integrated into everyday life, eventually becoming the staple form of entertainment in homes before the advent of television and eventually becoming the most common type of radio available in automobiles. Traditional radio stations offered relatively established content including music and talk stations with no customization options. It was a free service but had become outdated as seemingly better alternatives had come to fruition. On average, traditional radio stations aired between 10 and 22 minutes of audio advertisements per hour, which was significantly higher than Pandora.[66]

The main **satellite radio** provider was SiriusXM. SiriusXM was a subscription-based satellite radio service that provided advertisement-free music, sports, comedy, news, weather, and more for a monthly cost between $9.99 and $18.99 per month.[67] There were no free versions available. SiriusXM was the largest radio broadcaster measured by revenue in 2014.[68] The company had approximately 25.8 million subscribers.[69] SiriusXM was available through a mobile application, dedicated SiriusXM devices, and in-car radios. The company had partnerships with all the major automobile manufacturers and was integrated with many of their vehicle offerings. Many Internet radio companies provided advertisement-free subscriptions at a much lower price point than SiriusXM but lacked the diversity of channel offerings, such as sports radio. Satellite radio was created as an alternative to traditional radio and preceded the creation of Internet radio.

The **Internet radio** market had many new and established competitors. Some of the most well-established and well-known services were Spotify and iTunes Radio. These competitors offered free listening alternatives with different options for online versus mobile listening, in different geographical locations, and had drastically different market shares. Pandora commanded a large market share in the United States, with approximately 70% of the Internet radio market share.[70] The company also had 8.6% of the total U. S. radio market making it the largest radio station in most major markets.[71] However, the market had continuously evolved and market share constantly changed.

Spotify was founded in Sweden in 2006.[72] The company quickly expanded and its European presence, in particular, grew. Due to the popularity of its service, Spotify started to offer services in the United States in 2011.[73] The company offered both an advertisement-based free service and an advertisement-free subscription service. This company was very similar to Pandora but also offered the ability to create playlists, listen to individual songs, and listen to top lists, in addition to its radio feature. It was also much more developed and recognized internationally. The company was still expanding internationally and looking to solidify its position in the U. S. market.

iTunes Radio was released by Apple Inc. on September 18, 2013 and was a small part of one of the largest and well-known companies in the world.[74] Accordingly, iTunes Radio had the capital and manpower necessary to succeed. iTunes Radio was an advertisement-based free radio service with a subscription-based advertisement-free alternative. The service was an expansion of the iTunes platform, which was the largest music retailer in the world.[75] While the service was new, Apple's experience in the music industry made it a significant threat and competitor. In 2013, iTunes was available in over 100 countries worldwide.[76] The company's international presence had allowed Apple to expand its service much quicker than Pandora because of its pre-established name brand and knowledge of international music regulations. See **Exhibit 3** for a comparison of competitors' cost (free or paid) and features in further detail.

Pandora also had numerous competitors in the sale of advertisements such as Facebook, Google, Yahoo!, CBS, FOX, the *Wall Street Journal*, and traditional radio.[81] Pandora had to compete based on the effectiveness of the company's advertisements, pricing structure, return on investment to customers, and other criteria. These companies selling advertisements ranged in size but were generally well-established companies in

EXHIBIT 3
Comparison of Competitors' Cost and Features

Service	Cost	Where Available
Pandora [77]	Free or Paid	Mainly the United States
Traditional	Free	Domestic and International
SiriusXM [78]	Paid	Mainly the United States
Spotify[79]	Free or Paid	Domestic and International
iTunes Radio [80]	Free or Paid	Mainly the United States

their respective industries. In addition, with the increase of Internet-based startups, the advertising market had become increasingly competitive as new companies contended for advertising revenue.

Computer Vs. Mobile

When Pandora was founded, the traditional computer market was booming. The main source of Internet usage was from traditional desktop or laptop computers. To target this audience, Pandora developed its Internet radio for use on the computer. Individuals accessed the service through a website. In recent years, the emergence of mobile technology had a tremendous impact on the company's service. Individuals no longer looked to stream music while sitting down at their computer or laptop. Individuals increasingly looked to go mobile and wanted to have access to their music and technology on the road. To capture this changing market, Pandora created a mobile application available on multiple phone operating systems such as iOS and Android. This transition happened rather rapidly and was spurred on by the introduction of the original iPhone.

The transition to mobile computing had major implications on Pandora's revenue stream. When Pandora was created, its advertisement-funded free Internet radio was developed with traditional computing in mind. The company's visual and audio advertisements were tailored to traditional computers and were very lucrative. In the 11 months ended December 31, 2013, traditional computers had advertising revenue per thousand listener hours of $56.79.[82] This was up from $54.51 in 2012.[83] In comparison, mobile computing had advertising revenue per thousand listener hours of $31.97 and $22.80 for 2013 and 2012, respectively.[84] A comparison of the different rates is presented in **Exhibit 4**. Advertisers were less likely to pay for mobile advertisements because listeners paid less attention to the ads and the types of advertisements on

EXHIBIT 4
Comparison of Advertising Revenue per Thousand Listener Hours

	Eleven months ended December 31, 2012	Eleven months ended December 31, 2013
Total Ad RPMs	$29.60	$36.70
Traditional Computer	$54.51	$56.79
Mobile and Other Connected Devices	$22.80	$31.97

Source: Pandora 2013 10-K, p. 44.

mobile devices were limited. As a result, mobile advertisements had a lower rate of advertising revenue per thousand listener hours. The difference was dramatic. Traditional computer advertisements were between 2.5 and three times as valuable to Pandora as their mobile counterparts. As consumers listened to more and more music on their mobile devices, Pandora's advertising revenue per thousand listener hours was expected to decline further. In order to stabilize future revenue, the company had to look for ways to increase advertising revenue and better monetize mobile advertisements.

Technology

Changing Technology

Pandora was developed based on the Music Genome Project that Tim Westergren founded back in 2000. The Music Genome Project started out as an initiative to categorize songs based on musical characteristics. After trained musical analysts characterized the music, the data could be used to help predict user preferences based on similar song choices and allowed Pandora to respond to their tastes. This technology gave Pandora a competitive advantage over its rivals. However, as with all technology, competitors began catching up and Pandora's competitive advantage began to erode. To combat this, Pandora must continue to explore new technological innovations to remain at the forefront of Internet radio technology.

Although the company was still a leader in Internet radio and music recommendation software, it had not adapted to other new technologies and business models. One of the major changes in music streaming technology was the ability to both create radio stations and pick individual songs to play. Pandora lacked the ability for users to listen to individual songs from the company's extensive music database. On Pandora you could only create radio stations based on genres or artists. There was no feature to listen to specific songs or to add them to a playlist. Spotify offered radio stations and the ability to search and play specific songs from their music library. This difference in technology and service had quickly become a differentiating factor for Spotify and because of customer demand for this service Spotify gained market share quickly.[85] Whether Pandora lacked these features because of a shortage of technological development or because of a restriction on Pandora's content streaming agreements was unknown. Pandora was investing in its product and technology development, which was evident in the $16.191 million spent in the 11 months ended December 31, 2012 and the $29.986 million spent in the 11 months ended December 31, 2013 on product development.[86] Continued research and development might deliver the spark the company needed to eventually achieve profitability.

Service Compatibility

In addition to developing new features desired by music listeners, Pandora also had to continue to make its technology compatible with advances in listening devices, including mobile devices, consumer electronic products, and automobiles. If Pandora's services did not work on all of the new devices, the company risked losing customers to competing services. In order to maintain compatibility, Pandora worked with the company's third-party distribution partners on creating compatible technology.[87] This could become increasingly more expensive with an increase in the number of devices supported by Pandora.

Future Outlook

Although Pandora was less than two decades old, the company's technology and business model had revolutionized the way people listened to music. Gone were the days when people predominantly bought music and listened to CDs and MP3s. With the invention of Internet-enabled devices such as smart phones, technology changed music listening habits and Pandora capitalized on this opportunity. However, the entrenched music industry was not easy to combat. Music rights owners still wanted to be paid. As a result, Pandora endured rising content acquisition costs as music companies searched for new ways to make money. Pandora, although successful in creating a platform and business that delivered Internet radio, had done a poor job of managing these rising costs and lacked financial stability. Years after helping revolutionize the music industry, Pandora risked losing out to established competitors and new market entrants. Companies such as Spotify and iTunes Radio were beginning to develop an American audience and could dethrone Pandora as they offered Internet radio with innovative new features and name brand recognition. If Pandora does not effectively manage its rising costs, find ways to diversify its revenue streams, and outpace its competitors with service offerings demanded by its customers, the company might find itself becoming as obsolete as the cassettes and CDs of old. As Steve Jobs once said about revolutionizing the music industry with the opening of the iTunes Music Store, "It will go down in history as a turning point for the music industry. This is landmark stuff. I can't overestimate it!"[88] The music industry might be on the verge of this transformation once more. Pandora needs to plan for the future in order to stay relevant and profitable in this changing industry.

NOTES

1. Web, August 2, 2015 http://investor.pandora.com/phoenix.zhtml?c=227956&p=irol-govBio&ID=212382
2. Pandora, 2014 10K, p. 46. Web August 2, 2015 http://investor.pandora.com/phoenix.zhtml?c=227956&p=proxy
3. Web, August 2, 2015 http://investor.pandora.com/phoenix.zhtml?c=227956&p=irol-govBio&ID=212488
4. Web, August 3, 2015 https://www.pandora.com/about/mgp
5. Web, August 5, 2015 http://thinkofthat.net/2010/02/17/the-story-of-pandora-radio/
6. Web, August 2, 2015 http://techcrunch.com/2013/03/07/pandoras-long-time-ceo-joe-kennedy-abruptly-steps-down-just-as-pandora-starts-making-money-on-mobile/
7. Web, August 5, 2015 http://www.sec.gov/Archives/edgar/data/1230276/000119312511032963/ds1.htm
8. Web, August 2, 2015 http://quote.morningstar.com/stock-filing/Registration/2011/2/11/t.aspx?t=XNYS:P&ft=S-1&d=843511d53f8f977b8241a44e2b11cce9
9. Pandora, 2014 10K, p. 3. Web August 2, 2015 http://investor.pandora.com/phoenix.zhtml?c=227956&p=proxy
10. Web, August 2, 2015 http://investor.pandora.com/phoenix.zhtml?c=227956&p=irol-newsArticle&ID=1853983, http://www.nytimes.com/2014/03/19/business/media/top-technology-officer-at-pandora-steps-down.html?_r=0
11. Web, August 5, 2015 Pandora, 2014 Annual Report, p. 5, Pandora, 2014 Annual Report, p. 41.
12. Web, August 5, 2015 http://www.sec.gov/Archives/edgar/data/1230276/000119312511032963/ds1.htm, p. 1, Pandora, 2013 10K p. 3.
13. Pandora, 2014 10K, p. 63. Web August 2, 2015 http://investor.pandora.com/phoenix.zhtml?c=227956&p=proxy
14. Web, August 5, 2015 http://investor.pandora.com/phoenix.zhtml?c=227956&p=irol-govBio&ID=212488
15. Web, August 5, 2015 http://www.nytimes.com/2014/03/19/business/media/top-technology-officer-at-pandora-steps-down.html?_r=0
16. Web, August 5, 2015 http://investor.pandora.com/phoenix.zhtml?c=227956&p=irol-govManage
17. Web, August 5, 2015 http://investor.pandora.com/phoenix.zhtml?c=227956&p=irol-newsArticle&ID=1853983
18. Web, August 11, 2015 http://investor.pandora.com/phoenix.zhtml?c=227956&p=irol-newsArticle&id=1780880
19. Web, August 11, 2015 http://investing.businessweek.com/research/stocks/people/person.asp?personId=38323298&ticker=P
20. Web, August 12, 2015 http://investor.pandora.com/phoenix.zhtml?c=227956&p=irol-newsArticle&ID=1909735&highlight=
21. Web, August 12, 2015 http://investor.pandora.com/phoenix.zhtml?c=227956&p=irol-govBoard
22. Web, August 12, 2015 http://investor.pandora.com/phoenix.zhtml?c=227956&p=irol-newsArticle&ID=1853983
23. Web, August 11, 2015 http://www.sec.gov/Archives/edgar/data/1230276/000119312511032963/ds1.htm, p. 1.
24. Web, August 11, 2015 http://www.pandora.com/about
25. Pandora, 2014 10K, p. 42. Web August 21, 2015 http://investor.pandora.com/phoenix.zhtml?c=227956&p=proxy

26. Ibid., p. 5.
27. Ibid., p. 11.
28. Ibid., p. 7.
29. Ibid., p. 27.
30. Ibid., p. 42.
31. Ibid., p. 41.
32. Ibid., p. 5.
33. Ibid., p. 4.
34. Ibid., p. 7.
35. Ibid., p. 7.
36. Ibid., p. 4.
37. Ibid., p. 5.
38. Ibid., p. 7.
39. Ibid., p. 44.
40. Ibid., p. 7.
41. Web, August 17, 2015 http://money.cnn.com/2014/03/19 /technology/innovation/pandora-fees/, Pandora, 2014 10K, p. 5.
42. Ibid., p. 47.
43. Ibid., p. 7.
44. Ibid., p. 5.
45. Ibid., p. 41.
46. Ibid., p. 42.
47. Ibid., p. 2.
48. Web, August 17, 2015 http://www.pandora.com/everywhere /home
49. Web, August 17, 2015 http://www.pandora.com/everywhere /auto
50. Web, August 18, 2015 http://www.pandora.com/everywhere /auto
51. Web, August 18, 2015 http://www.pandora.com/everywhere /home
52. Pandora 2014 10K, p. 46. Web August 21, 2015 http://investor .pandora.com/phoenix.zhtml?c=227956&p=proxy
53. Ibid., p. 46.
54. Ibid., p. 27.
55. Ibid., p. 78.
56. Ibid., p. 78.
57. Ibid., p. 78.
58. Ibid., p. 78.
59. Ibid., p. 9.
60. Ibid., p. 9.
61. Ibid., p. 9.
62. Ibid., p. 9.
63. Ibid., p. 9.
64. Ibid., p. 15.
65. Web, August 17, 2015 http://www.historyorb.com/events /date/1907
66. Web, August 19, 2015 http://fivehype.com/fivehype-offers- pandora-advertising/
67. Web, August 19, 2015 http://www.siriusxm.com /ourmostpopularpackages
68. Web, August 19, 2015 http://www.siriusxm.com /corporate
69. Web, August 19, 2015 http://www.siriusxm.com/corporate
70. Pandora, 2014 Annual Report, p. 41. Web August 24, 2015 http://investor.pandora.com/phoenix.zhtml?c= 227956&p=proxy
71. Web, August 29, 2015 http://investor.pandora.com/phoenix .zhtml?c=227956&p=irol-newsArticle&ID=1793860
72. Web, August 29, 2015 http://www.cnn.com/2011/TECH /web/07/21/spotify.fortune.brainstorm/
73. Web, August 29, 2015 http://gigaom.com/2011/06/24 /spotify-us-launch-july/
74. Web, August 30, 2015 http://pitchfork.com/news/52237 -apple-announces-itunes-radio-launch-date/
75. Web, August 30, 2015 http://www.theguardian.com/media/ media-blog/2013/jun/16/itunes-radio-apple-music- streaming
76. Web, August 29, 2015 http://www.apple.com/itunes/affiliates /resources/documentation/available-countries-regions .html
77. Pandora 2014 10K, p. 3, Pandora 201410K, p. 4, Pandora 2014 10K, p. 27. Web August 24, 2015 http://investor .pandora.com/phoenix.zhtml?c=227956&p=proxy
78. Web, September 4, 2015 http://www.siriusxm.com/our mostpopularpackages, http://www.siriusxm.com/corporate, http://www.reuters.com/article/2013/09/26/entertainment -us-siriusxm-international-idUSBRE98P0NN20130926
79. Web, September 4, 2015 http://www.pocket-lint.com /news/125771-spotify-free-vs-spotify-premium-what-s- the-difference, https://support.spotify.com/us/learn-more /faq/#!/article/Availability-in-overseas-territories
80. Web, September 4, 2015 http://adage.com/article/digital /apple-s-itunes-radio-users-pay-avoid-ads/242022/, http://appleinsider.com/articles/14/02/10/apple-begins -international-rollout-for-itunes-radio-launches-in-australia
81. Pandora 2014 10K, p. 16. Web August 2, 2015 http://investor .pandora.com/phoenix.zhtml?c=227956&p=proxy
82. Ibid., p. 44.
83. Ibid., p. 44.
84. Ibid., p. 44.
85. Web, September 4, 2015 http://www.dailyfinance.com/on /why-cant-apple-google-microsoft-beat-spotify-pandora/
86. Pandora 2014 10K, p. 50. Web August 27, 2015 http:// investor.pandora.com/phoenix.zhtml?c=227956&p=proxy
87. Ibid., p. 17.
88. Web, September 4, 2015 http://blogs.wsj.com /digits/2011/08/24/steve-jobss-best-quotes/

CASE **12**

Amazon.com, Inc.

RETAILING GIANT TO HIGH-TECH PLAYER?

Alan N. Hoffman
Bentley University

Overview

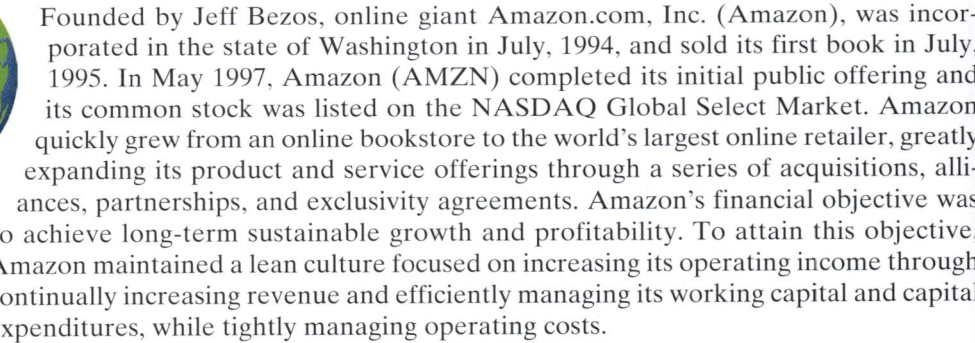

Founded by Jeff Bezos, online giant Amazon.com, Inc. (Amazon), was incorporated in the state of Washington in July, 1994, and sold its first book in July, 1995. In May 1997, Amazon (AMZN) completed its initial public offering and its common stock was listed on the NASDAQ Global Select Market. Amazon quickly grew from an online bookstore to the world's largest online retailer, greatly expanding its product and service offerings through a series of acquisitions, alliances, partnerships, and exclusivity agreements. Amazon's financial objective was to achieve long-term sustainable growth and profitability. To attain this objective, Amazon maintained a lean culture focused on increasing its operating income through continually increasing revenue and efficiently managing its working capital and capital expenditures, while tightly managing operating costs.

The name "Amazon" was evocative for founder Jeff Bezos of his vision of Amazon as a huge natural phenomenon, like the longest river in the world. He envisioned the company to be the largest online marketplace on earth someday.

By 2008, Amazon had become a global brand, with websites in Canada, the United Kingdom, Germany, France, China, and Japan, with order fulfillment in more than 200 countries.[1] Its operations were organized into two principal segments: North America and International Operations, which grew to include Italy in 2010 and Spain in 2011. By 2012, Amazon employed more than 56,200 people around the world working in the corporate office in Seattle, and in software development, order fulfillment, and customer service centers in North America, Latin America, Europe, and Asia.

The authors would like to thank Barbara Gottfried, Jodi Germann, Lauren-Ashley Higson, Faith Naymie, Faina Shakarova, Jamal Ait Hammou, Muntasir Alam, Shaheel Dholakia, Xinxin Zhu, and Will Hoffman for their research and contributions to this case. Please address all correspondence to: Dr. Alan N. Hoffman, Dept. of Management, Bentley University, 175 Forest Street, Waltham, MA 02452-4705, (781) 891-2287, ahoffman@bentley.edu. Printed by permission of Alan N. Hoffman.

Amazon Corporate Governance

Jeff Bezos is the Chairman of the Board and CEO of Amazon and owns 19.4% of the company.

Amazon has three board committees of which two are standard: the audit committee and the governance committee. The third committee, the Leadership Development and Compensation Committee, is uncommon. Most publicly traded companies have a compensation committee; however, it is unusual for the compensation committee to have leadership development as part of its mandate. The Leadership Development and Compensation Committee "monitors and periodically assesses the continuity of capable management, including succession plans for executive officers."

Amazon's board is not populated by CEOs or retired CEOs. It includes several venture capitalists, a number of senior-level executives from varied industries, an eminent scientist, and a representative from the non-profit sector.

Amazon's board has served together for a long time. This implies a deeper understanding of the company and increasing familiarity and even friendship amongst the group. This tends to discourage independent thinking and objectivity.

All of it is further proof that Jeff Bezos is a strong CEO and runs the company.

Retail Operations/Amazon's Superior Website

As people became more comfortable shopping on line, Amazon developed its website to take advantage of increased Internet traffic and to serve its customers most effectively.[2] The hallmarks of Amazon's appeal were ease of use; speedy, accurate search results; selection, price, and convenience; a trustworthy transaction environment; timely customer service; and fast, reliable fulfillment[3]—all of it enabled by the sophisticated technology the company encouraged its employees to develop to better serve its customers. The site, which offered a huge array of products sold both by itself and by third parties, was particularly designed to create a personalized shopping experience that helped customers discover new products and make efficient, informed buying decisions.

Key to Amazon's success was continual website improvement. A huge part of the technological work done for Amazon was dedicated to identifying problems, developing solutions, and enhancing customers' online experience. Jacob Lepley, in his "Amazon Marketing Strategy: Report One," notes that, "when you visit Amazon . . . you can use [it] to find just about any item on the market at an extremely low price. Amazon has made it very simple for customers to purchase items with a simple click of the mouse. . . . When you have everything you need, you make just one payment and your orders are processed."[4] This simple system is the same whether a customer purchases directly from Amazon or from one of its associates.

Pursuing perfection, Amazon was aggressive in analyzing its website's traffic and modifying the website accordingly. Amazon particularly excelled at customer tracking, collecting data from every visit to its website. Utilizing the information, Amazon then directed users to products that it surmised they might be interested in because the item was either related to a product that they had previously searched for or purchased by another Amazon customer looking for a similar product.

Recommendations were also customized based on the information customers provided about themselves and their interests, and their ratings prior purchased. Amazon also collected data on those who had never visited any of its websites, but who had received gifts from those who had used the site.

One of Amazon's most distinctive features was the community created based on the ratings/reviews provided by private individuals to help others make more informed purchasing decisions. Anyone could provide a narrative review and rate a product on a scale of 1–5 stars, and/or comment on others' reviews. Individuals could also create their own "So You'd Like . . . " guides and "Listmania" lists based on Amazon's products offerings and post them or send them to friends and family. To streamline customer research, Amazon also consolidated different versions of a product (e.g., DVD, VHS, Blu-ray disk) into a single product available for commentary that simplified commentary and user accessibility.[5]

To further target potential customers, Amazon engaged in permission marketing, eliciting permission to e-mail customers regarding specific production promotions based on prior purchases on the assumption that a targeted e-mail was more likely to be read than a blanket e-mail. This strategy was hugely appreciated by Amazon customers, further contributing to Amazon's success.

In addition, Amazon purchased pay-per-click advertisements on search engines such as Google to direct browsing customers to its websites. The ads appeared on the left-hand side of the search list results, and Amazon paid a fee for each visitor who clicked on its sponsored link.

At the same time, as "TV and billboard ads were roughly ten times less effective when compared to direct or online marketing when concerning customer acquisition costs"[6], Amazon reduced its offline marketing. The strategy was simple: as customers shopped online, online marketing was key. However, in 2010, Amazon initiated a small television advertising campaign to increase brand awareness.

Finally, to round out its customer care, Amazon expedited shipping by strategically locating its fulfillment centers near airports[7] where rents were also cheaper, giving Amazon the two-pronged advantage of speed and low cost over its competitors. Furthermore, in the United States, the United Kingdom, Germany, and Japan, Amazon offered subscribers to Amazon Prime the added convenience of free express shipping. Amazon Prime's free next-day delivery endeared it to Amazon customers, again contributing to the customer loyalty that was key to Amazon's success. Amazon Prime cost $79 annually to join and included free access to Amazon Instant Video. The overarching objective of the company was to offer low prices, convenience, and a wide selection of merchandise, a pared down, yet wide-reaching strategy that made Amazon such a huge success.

Diversified Product Offerings

Amazon diversified its product portfolio well beyond simply offering books, which in turn allowed it to diversify its customer mix. In 2007, Amazon successfully launched the Kindle, its $79 e-book reader, which offered users more than one million reasonably priced books and newspapers easily accessed on its handheld device. Competitor Apple, Inc., then introduced the iPad, the first tablet computer, in January 2010, sparking further development of mobile e-readers. E-book sales took off immediately, increasing by more than 100%, according to the Association of American Publishers. Eager to compete in a market for which it was uniquely positioned, Amazon quickly developed its own low-cost tablet, the Kindle Fire, an Android-based tablet with a color touchscreen priced at $199, more than $300 lower than the iPad, sacrificing profit margins in search of sales volume and market-share gains. Other tech giants such as RIMM and HP were unable to compete with the iPad. Only the Sony Nook, the Amazon Kindle and Kindle Fire, and the Samsung Galaxy and Series 7 tablets challenged Apple's consistent 60% of market share. Ultimately, however, Amazon's huge growth derived not simply from the sale of Kindle hardware and the growth of e-book sales, but from its diversification and the continual expansion of the easy website access created by mobile devices.

By 2010, 43% of Amazon net sales were from media, including books, music, DVDs/video products, magazine subscriptions, digital downloads, and video games. More than half of all Amazon sales came from computers, mobile devices including the Kindle, Kindle Fire, and Kindle Touch, and other electronics, as well as general merchandise from home and garden supplies to groceries, apparel, jewelry, health and beauty products, sports and outdoor equipment, tools, and auto and industrial supplies.

Amazon also offered its own credit card, a form of co-branding that benefited all parties: Amazon, the credit card company (Chase Bank), and the consumer. Amazon benefited because it received money from the credit card company both directly from Amazon purchases and indirectly from fees generated from non-Amazon purchases. In addition, Amazon benefited from the company loyalty generated by having its own credit card the consumer sees and uses every day. The credit card company gained from Amazon's high visibility, increasing its potential customer base and transactions. And the consumer earned credit toward gift certificates with each use of the card.

Partnerships

Amazon leveraged its expertise in online order taking and order fulfillment and developed partnerships with many retailers whose websites it hosted and managed, including (currently or in the past) Target, Sears Canada, Bebe Stores, Timex Corporation, and Marks & Spencer. Amazon offered services comparable to those it offered customers on its own websites, thus freeing those retailers to focus on the non-website, non-technological aspects of their operations.[8]

In addition, Amazon Marketplace allowed independent retailers and third-party sellers to sell their products on Amazon by placing links on their websites to Amazon.com or to specific Amazon products. Amazon was "not the seller of record in these transactions, but instead earn[ed] fixed fees, revenue share fees, per-unit activity fees, or some combination thereof."[9] Linking to Amazon created visibility for these retailers and individual sellers, adding value to their websites, increasing their sales, and enabling them to take advantage of Amazon's convenience and fast delivery. Sellers shipped their products to an Amazon warehouse or fulfillment center, where the company stored it for a fee, and when an order was placed, shipped out the product on the seller's behalf. This form of affiliate marketing came at nearly no cost to Amazon. Affiliates used straight text links leading directly to a product page and they also offered a range of dynamic banners that featured different content.

Web Services

As a major tech player, Amazon developed a number of web services, including ecommerce, database, payment and billing, web traffic, and computing. These web services provided access to technology infrastructure that developers were able to utilize to enable various types of virtual businesses. The web services (many of which were free) created a reliable, scalable, and inexpensive computing platform that revolutionized the online presence of small businesses. For instance, Amazon's e-commerce Fulfillment By Amazon (FBA) program allowed merchants to direct inventory to Amazon's fulfillment centers; after products were purchased, Amazon packed and shipped. This freed merchants from a complex ordering process while allowing them control over their inventory. Amazon's Fulfillment Web Service (FWS) added to FBA's program. FWS let retailers embed FBA capabilities straight into their own sites, vastly enhancing their business capabilities.

In 2012, Amazon announced a cloud storage solution (Amazon Glacier) from Amazon Web Services (AWS), a low-cost solution for data archiving, backups, and other long-term storage projects where data not accessed frequently could be retained for future reference. Companies often incurred significant costs for data archiving in anticipation of growing backup demand, which led to under-utilized capacity and wasted money. With Amazon Glacier, companies were able to keep costs in line with actual usage, so managers could know the exact cost of their storage systems at all times. With Amazon Glacier, Amazon continued to dominate the space of cold storage, which had first come into prominence in 2009, amidst competitors such as Rackspace (RAX) and Microsoft (MSFT) offering their own solutions.

By 2012, Amazon Web Services were a crucial facet of Amazon's profit base, and Amazon was one of the lead players in the fast-growing retail ecommerce market. Seeing huge growth potential, Amazon made the decision to expand Amazon Web Services (AWS) internationally and invested heavily in technology infrastructure to support the rapid growth in AWS. Though its investments in ecommerce threatened to suppress its near-term margin growth, Amazon expected to benefit in the long term, given the significant growth potential in domestic and, even more so, in international ecommerce.

Amazon's Acquisition of Zappos, Quidsi, Living Social, and Lovefilm

On July 22, 2009, Amazon acquired Zappos, the online shoe and clothing retailer, for $1.2 billion. At that time, Zappos was reporting over $1 billion in annual sales without any marketing or advertising. According to founder Tony Hsieh, the secret to Zappos' success was superior customer service, from its 365-day return guarantee to the company tours with which it regaled visitors, picking them up at the airport, then returning them to the airport afterward. Zappos' employees were also very well treated, earning it a place at the top of the list of the "best companies to work for." Tony Hsieh felt that Amazon was the perfect partner to fuel Zappo's sales growth going forward.

On November 8, 2010, Amazon announced the acquisition of Quidsi, the parent company of Diapers.com, an online baby care specialty site, and Soap.com, an online site for everyday essentials. Amazon paid $500 million in cash, and assumed $45 million in debt and other obligations. As Jeff Bezos explained, "This acquisition brings together two companies who are committed to providing great prices and fast delivery to parents, making one of the chores of being a parent a little easier and less expensive."[12]

On December 2, 2010, Amazon announced that it had invested $175 million in Groupon competitor LivingSocial, a site whose up-to-the-minute research offered users immediate access to the hottest restaurants, shops, activities, and services in a given area, while saving them 50% to 70% through special site deals.

On January 20, 2011, Amazon acquired Lovefilm for £200 million, a 1.6-million-subscriber-strong European Web-based DVD rental service based in London. Lovefilm had followed Netflix's business model, offering unlimited DVD rentals by mail for a monthly subscription fee of £9.99, but planned to challenge Netflix and expand its digital media business by entering the live-streaming subscription business.

Competitors

Competition was fierce for Amazon on all fronts, from catalogue and mail order houses to retail stores from book, music, and video stores to retailers of electronics, home furnishings, auto parts, and sporting goods. Amazon's Kindle contended with

Apple's iPad, among many lesser competitors. And Amazon's competitors in the service sector included other e-commerce and Web service providers. The company faced direct competition from companies such as eBay, Apple, Barnes & Noble, Overstock.com, MediaBay, Priceline.com, PCMall.com, and RedEnvelope.com. Amazon had to compete with companies that provided their own products or services, sites that sold or distributed digital content such as iTunes and Netflix, and media companies such as *The New York Times*. Many of the company's competitors had greater resources (eBay), longer histories (Barnes & Noble), more customers (Apple), or greater brand recognition (iTunes).

The companies offering the most direct threat to Amazon were eBay and Metro AG. Pierre Omidyar founded eBay in 1995, a website that connected individual buyers and sellers, including small businesses to buy and sell virtually anything. In 2010, the total value of goods sold on eBay was $62 billion, making eBay the world's largest online marketplace, serving 39 markets with more than 97 million active users worldwide.[10] eBay and Amazon subscribed to similar growth strategies: each acquired a broad spectrum of companies. Over the 15 years from 1995–2010 eBay acquired PayPal, Shopping.com, StubHub, and Bill Me Later, which have brought new e-commerce efficiencies to eBay.

Metro AG, headquartered in Dusseldorf, Germany, one of the world's leading international retail and wholesale companies, was formed through the merger of retail companies Asko Deutsche Kaufhaus AG, Kaufhof Holding AG and Deutsche SB-Kauf AG. In 2010, the total value of goods sold by Metro AG was €67 billion.[11] Serving 33 countries, Metro AG offered a comprehensive range of products and services designed to meet the specific shopping needs of private and professional customers. Metro AG, like Amazon, focused on customer orientation, efficiency, sustainability, and innovation.

Amazon had to be vigilant, negotiating more favorable terms from suppliers, adopting more aggressive pricing and devoting more resources to technology, infrastructure, fulfillment, and marketing. To maintain competitiveness, Amazon also strengthened its edge by entering into alliances with other businesses (i.e., Amazon Marketplace). Nevertheless, growing competition from global and domestic players continually threatened to erode Amazon's desired share of the market. Across the industries in which it competed, however, Amazon fought to maintain its edge based on its core principles of "selection, price, availability, convenience, information, discovery, brand recognition, personalized services, accessibility, customer service, reliability, speed of fulfillment, ease of use, and ability to adapt to changing conditions, as well as . . . customers' overall experience and trust."[12]

Frustration-Free Packaging

To stay current, Amazon took the initiative to reduce its carbon footprint by implementing a "Frustration Free Packaging" program. Recyclable Frustration Free Packaging came without excess packaging materials such as hard plastic enclosures or wire twists and was designed to be opened by hand without a scissors or a knife. Amazon then went one further and worked with the original manufacturers to package products in Frustration Free Packaging right off the assembly line, further reducing the use of plastic and paper. Units shipped that utilized Frustration Free Packaging has increased very rapidly, from 1.3 million in 2009 to 4.0 million in 2010[13]. Amazon also utilized software to determine the right size box for any product the company shipped, achieving a dramatic reduction in the number of packages shipped in oversized boxes and significantly reducing waste.

Financial Operations

Amazon sales doubled from 2009 to 2011, growing from $24,509 million (2009) to $48,077 million (2011) (see **Exhibits 1a** and **1b**), growth attributable especially to increased sales in electronics and other general merchandise, and the adoption of a new accounting standard update, reduced prices (including free shipping offers), increased in-stock inventory availability, and the impact of the acquisition of Zappos in 2009.[14]

EXHIBIT 1A
Income Statement

Income Statement Currency in (Millions of U.S. Dollars) as of:	Dec 31 2008	Dec 31 2009	Dec 31 2010	Dec 31 2011
Revenues	19,166.0	24,509.0	34,204.0	48,077.0
Total Revenues	**19,166.0**	**24,509.0**	**34,204.0**	**48,077.0**
Cost of Goods Sold	14,896.0	18,978.0	26,561.0	37,288.0
Gross Profit	**4,270.0**	**5,531.0**	**7,643.0**	**10,789.0**
Selling, General, & Admin Expenses, Total	2,419.0	3,060.0	4,397.0	6,864.0
R&D Expenses	1,033.0	1,240.0	1,734.0	2,909.0
Other Operating Expenses	29.0	51.0	106.0	154.0
Other Operating Expenses, Total	**3,481.0**	**4,351.0**	**6,237.0**	**9,927.0**
Operating Income	**789.0**	**1,180.0**	**1,406.0**	**862.0**
Interest Expense	−71.0	−34.0	−39.0	−65.0
Interest and Investment Income	83.0	37.0	51.0	61.0
Net Interest Expense	**12.0**	**3.0**	**12.0**	**−4.0**
Income (Loss) on Equity Investments	−9.0	−6.0	7.0	−12.0
Currency Exchange Gains (Loss)	23.0	26.0	75.0	64.0
Other Non-Operating Income (Expenses)	22.0	−1.0	3.0	8.0
Ebt, Excluding Unusual Items	**837.0**	**1,202.0**	**1,503.0**	**918.0**
Gain (Loss) on Sale of Investments	2.0	4.0	1.0	4.0
Gain (Loss) on Sale of Assets	53.0	—	—	—
Other Unusual Items, Total	—	−51.0	—	—
Legal Settlements	—	−51.0	—	—
Ebt, Including Unusual Items	**892.0**	**1,155.0**	**1,504.0**	**922.0**
Income Tax Expense	247.0	253.0	352.0	291.0
Earnings from Continuing Operations	645.0	902.0	1,152.0	631.0
Net Income	**645.0**	**902.0**	**1,152.0**	**631.0**
Net Income to Common Including Extra Items	**645.0**	**902.0**	**1,152.0**	**631.0**
Net Income to Common Excluding Extra Items	**645.0**	**902.0**	**1,152.0**	**631.0**
Report Data Issue				

EXHIBIT 1B
Balance Sheet

Balance Sheet Currency in Millions of U.S. Dollars as of:	Dec 31 2008	Dec 31 2009	Dec 31 2010	Dec 31 2011
Assets				
Cash and Equivalents	2,769.0	3,444.0	3,777.0	5,269.0
Short-Term Investments	958.0	2,922.0	4,985.0	4,307.0
Total Cash and Short-Term Investments	**3,727.0**	**6,366.0**	**8,762.0**	**9,576.0**
Accounts Receivable	827.0	988.0	1,587.0	2,571.0
Total Receivables	**827.0**	**988.0**	**1,587.0**	**2,571.0**
Inventory	1,399.0	2,171.0	3,202.0	4,992.0
Deferred Tax Assets, Current	204.0	272.0	196.0	351.0
Total Current Assets	**6,157.0**	**9,797.0**	**13,747.0**	**17,490.0**
Gross Property Plant and Equipment	1,078.0	1,517.0	2,769.0	5,143.0
Accumulated Depreciation	−396.0	−418.0	−587.0	−1,075.0
Net Property Plant And Equipment	**682.0**	**1,099.0**	**2,182.0**	**4,068.0**
Goodwill	438.0	1,234.0	1,349.0	1,955.0
Deferred Tax Assets, Long Term	145.0	18.0	22.0	28.0
Other Intangibles	332.0	758.0	795.0	996.0
Other Long-Term Assets	560.0	907.0	702.0	741.0
Total Assets	**8,314.0**	**13,813.0**	**18,797.0**	**25,278.0**
Liabilities and Equity				
Accounts Payable	3,594.0	5,605.0	8,051.0	11,145.0
Accrued Expenses	632.0	901.0	1,357.0	2,106.0
Current Portion of Long-Term Debt/Capital Lease	59.0	—	—	395.0
Current Portion of Capital Lease Obligations	—	—	—	395.0
Unearned Revenue, Current	461.0	858.0	964.0	1,250.0
Total Current Liabilities	**4,746.0**	**7,364.0**	**10,372.0**	**14,896.0**
Long-Term Debt	409.0	109.0	184.0	255.0
Capital Leases	124.0	143.0	457.0	1,160.0
Other Non-Current Liabilities	363.0	940.0	920.0	1,210.0
Total Liabilities	**5,642.0**	**8,556.0**	**11,933.0**	**17,521.0**
Common Stock	4.0	5.0	5.0	5.0
Additional Paid in Capital	4,121.0	5,736.0	6,325.0	6,990.0
Retained Earnings	−730.0	172.0	1,324.0	1,955.0
Treasury Stock	−600.0	−600.0	−600.0	−877.0
Comprehensive Income and Other	−123.0	−56.0	−190.0	−316.0
Total Common Equity	**2,672.0**	**5,257.0**	**6,864.0**	**7,757.0**
Total Equity	**2,672.0**	**5,257.0**	**6,864.0**	**7,757.0**
Total Liabilities and Equity	**8,314.0**	**13,813.0**	**18,797.0**	**25,278.0**
Report Data Issue				

Amazon's annual net income for 2009, 2010, and 2011 were $902 million, $1,152 million, and $645 million, respectively. The significant increase from 2009 to 2010 was due in large part to aggressive net sales growth and a large portion of its expenses and investments being fixed. Management explained that net income decreased from 2010 to 2011 as a result of: (1) selling Kindle hardware at a market price slightly below the cost of manufacture; (2) increased spending on technology infrastructure; and (3) increases in payroll expenses.

Challenges for Amazon

Amazon developed very quickly into a major player in the online retail market, yet challenges remained:

1. From its inception, Amazon was not required to collect state or local sales or use taxes, an exemption upheld by the U.S. Supreme Court. However, in 2012, states began to consider superseding the Supreme Court decision.[15] "If the states were to prevail, Amazon would be forced to collect sales and use tax, creating administrative burdens for it, and putting it at a competitive disadvantage if similar obligations are not imposed on all of its online competitors, potentially decreasing its future sales."[16] Massachusetts and other states were motivated both by the desire (to tap into new sources of revenues for their state budgets and to protect local retailers.

   In 2012, reports had it that Amazon was making deals to collect sales tax in all 50 states, so that they could open warehouses near population centers and provide same-day delivery, a major shift in its business model that would ratchet up competition with big box stores like Best Buy and Target as well as local retailers. However, there were no guarantees of the profitability of same-day delivery, given the added warehouse and delivery costs.

2. With the new social trend of "buying local," Amazon faced the threat of some regular consumers preferring to buy from their local stores rather than from an online retailer.[17]

3. Amazon always had to grapple with the threat of customer preference for instant gratification, the customer's desire to get a product immediately in the store, rather than waiting several days for the product to be shipped to them.

4. Breaches of security from outside parties trying to gain access to its information or data were a continual threat for Amazon.[18] As of 2012, Amazon had systems and processes in place that were designed to counter such attempts; however, failure to maintain these systems or processes could be detrimental to the operations of the company.

5. As more media products were sold in digital formats, Amazon's relatively low-cost physical warehouses and distribution capabilities no longer provided the same competitive advantages. In addition, Amazon had felt that its worldwide free shipping offers and Amazon Prime were effective worldwide marketing tools, and intended to offer them indefinitely, yet it began to suffer from soaring shipping expenses cutting into profits. In quarter three of 2011, Amazon's shipping fees generated $360 million in revenue, which was dwarfed by $918 million in shipping expenses.

6. Amazon had to contend with absorbing losses from its unsuccessful ventures such as its A9 search engine, Amazon Auctions, and Unbox, Amazon's original video-on-demand service.

7. Recent hires from Microsoft, Robert Williams, former senior program manager, and Brandon Watson, head of Windows Phone development prompted speculation that Amazon was developing a smartphone, possibly a Kindle-branded device. Bloomberg reported that Amazon had gone so far as to strike a manufacturing deal with Foxconn, the controversial Taiwanese company responsible for assembling Apple's iPhone and Google Android devices. Amazon has not commented on the reports. A smartphone would have given Amazon another mobile device to

sell, but some analysts felt it wouldn't have made sense for Amazon to enter into the already crowded smartphone arena. "Since tablets skew more heavily toward media consumption than smartphones, they are a natural fit for Amazon's commerce and media platform," said Baird & Co. analyst Colin Sebastian, in a research note. "In contrast, smartphones require specialized native apps (e.g., maps, voice, search, e-mail) that would be costly for Amazon to replicate." Sebastian also noted that hardware is a low-margin business. Amazon's Kindle Fire sold for $199, a price that some analysts believed was below cost, suggesting Amazon hoped the Kindle Fire would more than pay for itself by boosting sales of e-books and other digital content. Thus, by 2012 Amazon had proved itself as a retail giant, yet as with any vibrant company, faced continual challenges, particularly regarding the overarching questions of whether to spend its money developing media products such as the Kindle Smartphone, or to stick with its strengths as an online retailer, perhaps acquiring more holdings such as Zappos, and pushing for same-day delivery despite the added cost to compete with other online retailers, and with the big box stores as well.

In 2012, Amazon was at a crossroads. It needed to decide if it should invest in the infrastructure for same-day delivery, and take on local retailers, or invest in high-technology and compete at a deeper level with Sony, Apple, and Samsung.

REFERENCES

Alexa.com.Amazon.com. 2011. http://www.alexa.com/siteinfo/amazon.com

Amazon.com. 2005 Annual Report. April 2006.

Amazon.com. 2007 Annual Report. April 2008.

Amazon.com. 2008 Annual Report. April 2009.

Amazon.com. 2009 Annual Report. April 2010.

Amazon.com. 2010 Annual Report. April 2011.

Amazon.com. 2011 Corporate Governance: A Message to Shareowners. 2011. http://phx.corporate-ir.net/phoenix.zhtml?c=97664&p=irol-govHighlights

Amazon.com. Amazon Leadership Principles. 2011. http://www.amazon.com/Values-Careers-Homepage/b?ie=UTF8&node=239365011

Amazon.com. Locations. 2011. http://www.amazon.com/Locations-Careers/b?ie=UTF8&node=239366011

Amazon.com. Amazon Certified Frusturation-Free Packaging FAQ. (2011). http://www.amazon.com/gp/help/customer/display.html?nodeId=200285450

Amazon.com. Amazon Annual Meeting of Shareholders Presentation (10Q). June 2011. http://phx.corporate-ir.net/phoenix.zhtml?c=97664&p=irol-presentations

Amazon.com. Q3 2011 Amazon.com Inc Earnings Conference Call. Seattle, WA, USA. 2011.

Amazon.com. Company Facts. 2011. Dec. 2011. http://phx.corporate-ir.net/phoenix.zhtml?c=176060&p=irol-factSheet

Amazon.com FAQs. 2011. Dec. 2011. http://phx.corporate-ir.net/phoenix.zhtml?c=97664&p=irol-faq

Amazon.com. Best Black Friday Ever for Kindle Family: Kindle Sales Increase 4X Over Last Year. Nov. 2011.

Amazon.com. Quarterly Results. http://phx.corporate-ir.net/phoenix.zhtml?c=97664&p=irol-reportsother

Amazon.com. Shipping & Delivery. 2011. http://www.amazon.com/gp/help/customer/display.html/ref=hp_468520_tracking?nodeId=468530

Ante, S. At Amazon, Marketing Is for Dummies. Sept. 2009. http://www.businessweek.com/magazine/content/09_39/b4148053513145.htm

Bange, V. Online Security: Legal Issues. Page 10. New Media Age. Jan. 2007.

Bezos, J. Earth's Most Customer-Centric Company: Differentiating with Technology. MIT, Interviewer. Nov. 2002. http://mitworld.mit.edu/video/1

Bofah, Kofi. What Is the Meaning of Foreign Exchange Risk? eHow Money. http://www.ehow.com/about_6612492_meaning-foreign-exchange-risk_.html

Chaffey, D. Amazon.com Case Study. http://www.davechaffey.com/E-commerce-Internet-marketing-case-studies/Amazon-case-study/

CrunchBase. Amazon. Nov. 2010. http://www.crunchbase.com/company/amazon

Davidson, Paul. Consumers Lifted U.S. Economy Last Quarter. USATODAY.com. Gannett Co. Inc., 27 Oct. 2011. http://www.usatoday.com/money/economy/story/2011-10-27/gdp-q3/50951374/1

eBay Who We Are. 2011. 10 Dec. 2011. http://www.ebayinc.com/who

Elgin, B. Google's Crafty Star Search. UpFront. Sept. 2005.

Federal Trade Commission. About Us. 17 June 2010. http://www.ftc.gov/ftc/about.shtm

Green, Steve. Employee Files lawsuit against Amazon.com. Dec. 2009. http://www.lasvegassun.com/news/2009/dec/01/employee-files-lawsuit-against-amazoncom-seeks-cla/

HR Spectrum. CAHRS Partner Profile: Amazon.com. Nov–Dec 2009. http://www.ilr.cornell.edu/cahrs/hrSpectrum/HR-Profile-Amazon.html

Jeffries Group, Inc. Amazon.com: Undergoing ST Pain for LT Gains. 2011.

Kucera, D. Amazon Profit Plunges After New Products Increase Expenses; Shares Tumble. October 2011. http://www.bloomberg.com/news/2011-10-25/amazon-profit-plunges-after-new-products-increase-expenses-shares-tumble.html

Layton, J. How Amazon Works. Retrieved from How Stuff Works. http://money.howstuffworks.com/amazon3.htm

Legislation.gov.uk. Data Protection Act 1998. http://www.legislation.gov.uk/ukpga/1998/29/contents

Marketing Plan. Marketing Strategies of Amazon.com. http://www.marketingplan.net/amazon-com-marketing-strategies/

Martinez, J. Amazon.com Net Sales, Marketing Expenses Up. July 2011. http://www.dmnews.com/amazoncom-net-sales-marketing-expenses-up/article/208437/

Metro Group. Corporate Strategy. 2011. http://www.metrogroup.de/internet/site/metrogroup/node/10781/Len/index.html

Mind Tools. PEST Analysis—Problem-Solving Training from MindTools.com. Management Training, Leadership Training and Career Training. Mind Tools Ltd. 12 Dec. 2011. http://www.mindtools.com/pages/article/newTMC_09.htm

Morningstar Equity Research. Amazon Is Uniquely Positioned to Remain a Disruptive Force to the traditional retail channel for years to come. Morningstar Equity Research. 2011.

Morningstar Equity Research. Amazon.com Inc Stock Report. 2011.

Morningstar Equity Research. Amazon's Kindle Fire Poised to Be Disruptive Force in Digital. 2011.

The Office of Fair Trading. The Office of Fair Trading. Web. 12 Dec. 2011. http://www.oft.gov.uk/

Rao, Leena. Amazon has Opened 15 Fulfillment Centers in 2011. July 2011. http://techcrunch.com/2011/07/26/amazon-has-opened-15-fulfillment-centers-in-2011-will-build-a-few-more-by-end-of-the-year/

Simmonds, Paul. Amazon Strategic Plan. *Scribd*. Web. 12 Dec. 2011. http://www.scribd.com/doc/24854038/Amazon-Strategic-Plan#

Standard & Poor's Capital IQ. Amazon Inc. Products.

Steinberg, B. For Amazon, a Focus on the New Helps Push Sales of the Old. Advertising Age. Nov. 2011. http://adage.com/article/special-report-marketer-alist/marketing-a-list-amazon/230825/

Supply Chain Digest. Logistics News: Amazon.com in Hot Corner after Reports of Sweltering DC's.2011, "Urgently" Buys $2.4 Million in Air Conditioners. Sept. 2011. http://www.scdigest.com/ontarget/11-09-26-1.php?cid=4995

Tozzi, John. To Beat Recession, Indies Launch Buy-Local Push. Businessweek. Bloomberg L.P., February 2009. http://www.businessweek.com/smallbiz/content/feb2009/sb20090226_752622.htm

Wikipedia, the Free Encyclopedia. Great Firewall of China. 12 Dec. 2011. http://en.wikipedia.org/wiki/Golden_Shield_Project

Yahoo.com. Amazon.com Historical Prices. 2011. http://finance.yahoo.com/q/hp?s=AMZN+Historical+Prices

Yarow, J. Here's How Much a Unique Visitor Is Worth. Jan. 2011. http://articles.businessinsider.com/2011-01-05/tech/30039682_1_facebook-visitor-social-networking

NOTES

1. Chaffey, D. Amazon.com Case Study. http://www.davechaffey.com/E-commerce-Internet-marketing-case-studies/Amazon-case-study/

2. Mind Tools. PEST Analysis – Problem-Solving Training from MindTools.com. Management Training, Leadership Training and Career Training. Mind Tools Ltd. 12 Dec. 2011. http://www.mindtools.com/pages/article/newTMC_09.htm

3. Chaffey, D. Amazon.com Case Study. http://www.davechaffey.com/E-commerce-Internet-marketing-case-studies/Amazon-case-study/

4. Marketing Plan. Marketing Strategies of Amazon.com. http://www.marketingplan.net/amazon-com-marketing-strategies/

5. Layton, J. How Amazon Works. Retrieved from How Stuff Works. http://money.howstuffworks.com/amazon3

6. Marketing Plan. Marketing Strategies of Amazon.com. http://www.marketingplan.net/amazon-com-marketing-strategies/

7. Amazon.com. 2010 Annual Report. April 2011.

8. Marketing Plan. Marketing Strategies of Amazon.com. http://www.marketingplan.net/amazon-com-marketing-strategies/

9. Amazon.com. 2010 Annual Report. April 2011.

10. eBay Who We Are. 2011. 10 December 2011 http://www.ebayinc.com/who

11. Metro Group. Corporate Srategy. 2011. http://www.metrogroup.de/internet/site/metrogroup/node/10781/Len/index.html

12. AMAZON.COM, INC., FORM 10-K, For the Fiscal Year Ended December 31, 2006, page 6. http://www.sec.gov/Archives/edgar/data/1018724/000119312507034081/d10k.htm

13. Amazon.com. Amazon Annual Meeting of Shareholders Presentation (10Q). June 2011. http://phx.corporate-ir.net/phoenix.zhtml?c=97664&p=irol-presentations

14. Amazon.com. 2010 Annual Report. April 2011.

15. Amazon.com. 2010 Annual Report. Page 13–14. April 2011.

16. Amazon.com. 2010 Annual Report. Page 14. April 2011.

17. Tozzi, John. To Beat Recession, Indies Launch Buy-Local Push. *Bloomberg's Businessweek*. Bloomberg L.P., February 2009.http://www.businessweek.com/smallbiz/content/feb2009/sb20090226_752622.htm

18. Amazon.com. 2010 Annual Report. Page 15. April 2011.

Blue Nile, Inc.

"STUCK IN THE MIDDLE" OF THE DIAMOND ENGAGEMENT RING MARKET

Alan N. Hoffman
Bentley University

Built on the premise of making engagement ring selection simpler, Blue Nile, Inc. (formerly known as Internet Diamonds, Inc.) has developed into the largest online retailer of diamond engagement rings. Unlike traditional jewelry retailers, Blue Nile operates completely store-front-free, without in-person consultation services. The business conducts all sales online or by phone and sales include both engagement (70%) and non-engagement (30%) categories.[1] Blue Nile focuses on perfecting its online shopping experience by providing useful guidance and education, extraordinary jewelry, at competitive prices. Blue Nile's vision is to educate its customer base so that customers can make an informed, confident decision no matter what event they are celebrating.[2] It wants to make the entire diamond-buying process easy and hassle-free.[3] In addition, an important part of Blue Nile's vision, as CEO Diane Irvine said in a recent webinar with Kaihan Krippendorf, is for the company to be seen as the "smart" way to buy diamonds, while saving 20%–40% more than one would in the typical jewelry store. Blue Nile is working to become "the Tiffany for the next generation."[4]

Company Background

Blue Nile started in Seattle, Washington, in 1999, when Mark Vadon, the founder of the company, decided to act upon his and his friends' dissatisfaction with their experience in searching for an engagement ring. As a result, to battle their concerns, he created

....

The author would like to thank Abdullah Al-Hadlaq, Rashid Alhamer, Chris Harbert, Sarah Martin, Adnan Rawji, and Will Hoffman for their research. Please address all correspondence to Dr. Alan N. Hoffman, Dept. of Management, Bentley University, 175 Forest Street, Waltham, MA 02452; ahoffman@bentley.edu. Printed by permission of Dr. Alan N. Hoffman.

a company that offered customers education, guidance, quality, and value, allowing customers to shop with confidence.[5]

Blue Nile operates its business through its three websites: www.bluenile.com, www.bluenile.co.uk, and www.bluenile.ca. Customers from the UK and all the member states of the European Union are served by Blue Nile's subsidiary, Blue Nile Worldwide, through the UK website. Canadian customers are served through the Canadian website, and U.S. customers, along with 14 additional countries worldwide, are directed to the primary website. In addition, Blue Nile owns another subsidiary in Dublin, Ireland, named Blue Nile Jewelry, Ltd, which acts as a customer service and fulfillment center.

Furthermore, in order to enhance and facilitate the purchasing process to serve both local and foreign demand, Blue Nile has given customers the choice to purchase their products in 22 foreign currencies, as well as in the U.S. dollar.[6] As of the beginning of 2010, the company has offered sales to customers in over 40 countries worldwide.[7]

Not being built as a traditional brick-and-mortar jewelry company, Blue Nile uses its websites to exhibit its fine jewelry offerings, which include diamond, gold, gemstone, platinum, and sterling silver, as well as rings, earrings, pendants, wedding bands, bracelets, necklaces, and watches. Blue Nile's revolutionary and innovative ways of restructuring industry standards did not just stop with its lack of a physical presence. The company offers a "Diamond Search" tool that lets customers examine their entire directory of diamonds to choose the right one in seconds. It also offers the popular "Build Your Own" tool that helps customers customize their own diamond jewelry and then view it on the computer before executing the order. Moreover, Blue Nile offers customers financing options, insurance for the jewelry, a 30-day return policy and free shipping.[8]

Diamond sales represent the majority of Blue Nile's business and revenues. Diamonds, which are certified for high quality by an "independent diamond grading lab,"[9] are differentiated based on "shape, cut, color, clarity and carat weight."[10] Blue Nile uses a just-in-time ordering system from its suppliers, which is initiated once a diamond purchase is made on the website, eliminating the burden and the costs of keeping high-ticket items in inventory. However, the company does keep in inventory rings, earrings, and pendants that it uses as a base to attach the diamond to, in order to be able to customize diamond jewelry to customer requirements. In order to succeed in this industry, Blue Nile maintains a strong relationship with over 40 suppliers.

After its IPO in 2004, Blue Nile shares traded on the NASDAQ (ticker NILE). The company has been awarded the Circle of Excellence Platinum Award, which customers use to rank the best online company in customer service, by Bizrate.com since 2002. Being the only jeweler to be recognized for this excellence is a true testament to Blue Nile's solid business.[11]

Strategic Direction

Blue Nile is in the business of offering "high-quality diamonds and fine jewelry at outstanding prices."[12] It is a publicly traded company, making its ultimate business objective to achieve the highest return possible for its shareholders. In order to do this, Blue Nile focuses on the following:

1. Cause disruption in the diamond industry by creating a "two-horned dilemma." According to Kaihan Krippendorff, Blue Nile has been able to effectively put its competitors in a position where if they try to compete with Blue Nile directly, they compromise an area of their own business (one edge of the horn), and if they do not choose to compete with Blue Nile, they slowly lose market share

and competitive positioning (the other edge of the horn). Blue Nile's decision to offer the highest-quality diamonds in spite of it operating in an online environment where it could easily position itself purely as a "discounter" has been key to creating this dilemma. Competitors with brick-and-mortar locations are then left to decide whether they should sell their product online at a lower cost than a customer would find in a store in order to compete (knowing that this could negatively impact the brick-and-mortar location) or not go head to head with Blue Nile online.[13] This dilemma helps Blue Nile keep its strong position as the largest online jewelry retailer.

2. Keep the consumer in mind and establish relationships with customers during a very important time in their lives. The idea for Blue Nile was born during an unpleasant shopping experience. The company remains focused on perfecting its user experience by investing in online education tools and resources within its website to help customers make educated decisions.[14] Because Blue Nile's customers cannot view the diamonds in person before a purchase, it provides them with grading reports on their diamonds from two independent diamond graders (GIA or AGSL) and a 30-day return policy.

3. Capture market share and emerge after the recession in a strong competitive position. Some competitors have pulled back during the recession by closing locations, while others have closed their doors all together.[15] Blue Nile has been investing in its website and is working to aggressively grow its market share.[16]

The Jewelry Industry

It is estimated that 2010 U.S. jewelry sales finished at US$49.3 billion for the year, a 2.6% growth over 2009.[17] According to First Research.com, the U.S. retail jewelry industry is considered to be fragmented, as "the top 50 jewelry chains generate less than half of (total) revenue" and there are 28,800 specialty stores that generate around US$30 billion in revenue. Diamond jewelry and loose diamonds account for approximately 45% of total jewelry store sales.[18]

A closer look at this industry reveals that 17.2% of total U.S. jewelry sales took place in non-store retailers. Still though, retail locations continue to be the primary source of jewelry sales, accounting for 50% of total U.S. jewelry sales in 2009 in spite of sales decreasing by 7.8% between 2007 and 2009.[19]

According to Compete.com, Blue Nile controls 4.3%[20] of Internet jewelry sales, and as of 2009 Blue Nile had about 4% of the engagement ring business in the United States,[21] which is 50% of the American online engagement jewelry market.[22]

Blue Nile's Competitors

Blue Nile's many competitors include various different retail outlets like department stores, major jewelry store chains, independently owned jewelry stores, online retailers, catalogue retailers, television shopping retailers, discount superstores, and, lastly, wholesale clubs. Many local jewelers have great relations with their clientele in smaller communities, which poses a challenge for Blue Nile to achieve greater market share. Online retailers include Amazon, Overstock.com, and Bidz.com, which are well-known for their discounting, thus creating tremendous competition for Blue Nile. Most major firms who specialize in jewelry have their own online presence as well, such as Zales, Signet, Tiffany, and Helzberg.

DeBeers

DeBeers, which owns 40% of the world's diamond supply,[23] is establishing its presence online as a trusted advisor, just as Blue Nile has done. Upon visiting DeBeers website, it is clear that Blue Nile's consultative approach online has made an impression on DeBeers, as the website has an "Advice" section under Bridal rings and an "Art of Diamond Jewelry" section that both educates and serves as a source of confidence of quality.

Tiffany & Co.

Tiffany & Co., one of the best-known luxury brand names, had revenues in 2010 of US$2.9 billion, compared to Blue Nile's US$302 million.[24] Tiffany & Co. continues to stand out in the jewelry sector by opening stores in urban America and has shown to be a success because many consumers are willing to pay extra for a well-known brand name. Tiffany also offers great service at its stores through product information. Lastly, owning a piece of jewelry from Tiffany's—and receiving the iconic blue box—has an air of prestige all its own that Blue Nile cannot replicate.[25] In spite of the value associated with the Tiffany name, due to its lean business model, Blue Nile's return on capital is three to four times better than Tiffany's.[26]

Blue Nile's many powerful competitors require the business to compete through differentiation, and so Blue Nile gains an advantage over its competition through its unique operating structure. Its strategy, distribution channel, and supply chain help to keep Blue Nile in the market because it also creates barriers to entry. Some competitive advantages include its partnership with Bill Me Later and its direct contracts with major diamond suppliers. Blue Nile partners with Bill Me Later[27] in order to offer financing for fine jewelry and diamond purchases. Blue Nile also has direct contracts with major diamond suppliers, which in turn allow the company to sell stones online at lower prices than brick-and-mortar locations because it has lower overhead costs and fewer distribution interceptions.

Guild Jewelers

It is difficult to find a competitor that can be compared directly to Blue Nile because of the unique way in which the business operates. While Guild Jewelers are not necessarily a united force that Blue Nile must respond to, Blue Nile CEO Diane Irvine considers Guild Jewelers to be the company's major competitor because Guild has local relationships with potential customers that are difficult for Blue Nile to establish online.[28]

Barriers to Entry/Imitation

Barriers to entry in the jewelry industry are high because the following are needed: capital, strong supplier relationships, and reputation. With regard to capital, traditional jewelry stores must fund their brick-and-mortar locations, onsite inventory, and store labor. Supplier relationships with diamond cutters and distributors are also key, and as seen with Blue Nile, they can greatly impact the profitability of a given retailer. Finally, due to the expense associated with jewelry purchases, Blue Nile's "average ticket" is US$2,000.[29] This helps Blue Nile because customers are looking for a trusted source with a strong reputation.

In regard to imitation, Blue Nile leverages a few unique systems and services that are hard for the competition to imitate. First, Blue Nile's "build your own" functionality online differentiates it from competitors by allowing the customer to personally create their ideal diamond ring, earring, pendant, multiple stone rings, and/or multiple stone pendants. The consumer also has access to an interactive search function, which references an inventory of 50,000 diamonds, including signature diamonds that are hand-selected and cut with extreme precision.[30]

Second, Blue Nile has its own customer service team of diamond and jewelry consultants that offer suggestions and assist customers with their purchases. This online interactive customer service approach creates a barrier to entry as the information technology platform for these functions is complex.

Lastly, Blue Nile also offers exclusive colored diamonds, which include rare diamonds that are red and pink.[31] It has a more diversified product range than its competitors because it does not have to hold inventory in stock.

The threat of new entrants is always a concern, but Blue Nile has been successful thus far at staying ahead of new entrants and has established a reputation as a quality, reputable online service.

One of the most significant resources for jewelers is diamonds, and with DeBeers owning 40% of the world's jewelry supply, diamonds are considered scarce and unique. Large diamond suppliers like DeBeers are not as powerful as they were once were—DeBeers at one time sold 80% of the world's diamonds[32]—but their presence is still felt. In addition, diamonds are generally obtained in politically unstable regions of the world, like Africa, and companies must be aware of the risk of obtaining conflict diamonds. The diamond trade is complex with regard to politics and legal issues, as the majority of diamond mines exist in underdeveloped countries, where corruption is prevalent and the rule of law is not easily enforced. Many of the diamond mines are located in African countries such as Botswana, which currently produces 27% of the global diamond supply.[33] However, recent global initiatives, including the Clean Diamond Trade Act of 2003, and the Kimberly Process Certification Scheme of 2002, have made significant impacts on violence and illegal trade in the last decade.[34]

The lack of legal and political stability in many of the diamond source countries represents a threat to Blue Nile and the industry as a whole. With unstable changes in leadership and power, threats to the global supply chain of a valuable commodity are possible, and perhaps even likely to occur. The takeover of diamond mines by militia groups, government claims of eminent domain, diamond smuggling, and obsolescing contract negotiations with foreign governments all have a potential deleterious impact on the jewelry industry. Finally, given the increased valuation of gold in recent years, this jewelry material has become harder to obtain.

Social and Demographic Trends

There are a number of social and demographic trends that offer opportunities for Blue Nile. First, the average age of first-time newlyweds is increasing in the United States, currently 28[35] for men and 26[36] for women.

A *USA TODAY* analysis of the Census figures shows that just 23.5% of men and 31.5% of women ages 20–29 were married in 2006. (The analysis excludes those who are married but separated.) Both the number and percentage of those in their 20s fell from 2000, when 31.5% of men and 39.5% of women were married.[37]

Higher marrying ages tend to translate into greater spending power for marriage-related items, such as engagement rings.

Next, people nowadays are more receptive to handheld technologies and apps. These on-the-go technologies are an opportunity for Blue Nile to reach busy customers who do not have time to drop by a jewelry store to research their product choices and make a purchase. Mobile sites and apps allow a customer with a Smartphone to make purchases on their own schedule, without adhering to a brick-and-mortar schedule. As this generation ages and people become comfortable with technology, Blue Nile will have more segments to cater to and a broader reach. With online purchases becoming more of a cultural norm, with less associated negative stigma, and as higher percentages of the global population gains reliable access to the Internet, Blue Nile is poised to capitalize on its Web-only strategy.

Finally, with historical events like the marriage of Prince William and Kate Middleton dominating the media, Blue Nile and other jewelry retailers reap the benefits of Kate's sapphire ring being displayed and/or mentioned in countless media venues throughout the world. The jewelers could not have planned such a great publicity stunt, and now have the opportunity to ride the wave for a while.

One social threat Blue Nile faces is tied to issues of Internet fraud and online security in today's environment. The relatively high purchase price for quality jewelry increases the perceived risk for consumers making online purchases.

Another threat is that with each new generation, traditions (such as the purchase and giving of engagement rings) risk becoming outdated or out of fashion. While giving jewelry is highly entrenched in many cultures around the world, it is possible that potential customers in Generation Y and later may perceive lower value in this gifting tradition.

Global Opportunities

Blue Nile wants to expand internationally because it sees great potential in the global marketplace. Currently, non-U.S. sales represent 13% of the total sales at Blue Nile.[38] Blue Nile's international sales have continuously been growing. Recent numbers show that in 2010, sales figures grew by 30.4% compared to the previous year.[39] It is a high priority to grow internationally at Blue Nile. It is important for them to monitor online purchasing rates globally, and expand to those countries accordingly.

One major global threat for Blue Nile is the lack of adoption of online purchasing. Many countries have not yet advanced to American consumer habits. Developed countries are continuing to adopt this as they realize the efficiency, effectiveness, and overall convenience involved. Lack of consumer confidence for high-value online purchases may continue to follow Blue Nile as it expands internationally until it has built a reputation in each foreign country of operations, which may delay return on investment for international expansion programs.

Many consumers in developing nations do not have reliable access to the Internet. Blue Nile currently has no way to tap into the buying power of these would-be customers. Sending huge sums of money and receiving valuable goods when they clear customs is a risk many people are not willing to take, knowing its ramifications. Many countries around the world have a higher incidence of corruption, and thus one cannot be sure that the product will reach the customer safely.

Blue Nile's Finances

Net Sales have been strong each year for Blue Nile since 2006, except in 2008 when the financial crisis impacted the company's performance, as seen in **Exhibit 1.** Sales have grown by US$81.3 million since 2006, a 32% increase. Growth was most substantial in 2007 (26.9%) due to the huge increase in demand for diamond and fine jewelry products ordered through the website. International sales contributed significantly to the surge in demand in 2007, with an increase of 104.8%, due mainly to the new product

EXHIBIT 1
Blue Nile Net Sales
2006-2010
(In Thousands)

Blue Nile Annual Net Sales

Year	2006	2007	2008	2009	2010
Net Sales	$ 251,587.00	$ 319,264.00	$ 295,329.00	$ 302,134.00	$ 332,889.00
Growth		26.90%	−7.50%	2.30%	10.18%

NOTE: All data in Exhibits 1–6 come from the 2010 Blue Nile Annual Report.

offerings and the ability of UK and Canadian customers to purchase in their local currency.[40] Sales decreased by 7.5% in 2008, primarily due to the sluggish economy, which negatively impacted the popularity of luxury goods, and the increase in diamond prices worldwide.[41] In 2009, sales rebounded slightly with an increase of 2.3%, due mostly to an increase of 20% in Q4 year over year. The increase in Q4 is attributed to the boost in international sales, which represented 1.9% of the 2.3% total growth, as a result of the new website enhancements and the ability to purchase in 22 other foreign currencies.[42]

In 2010, sales returned to double-digit growth with an increase of 10.2%. Both U.S. sales and international sales grew considerably with 7.7% and 30.4%, respectively, due mainly to the improving economy, which led to increased consumer spending. Increased marketing focus, better brand recognition, and the favorable exchange rate of foreign currencies against the U.S. dollar contributed to the strong sales in Q4, which reached an all-time record of US$114.8 million.[43] However, although Q1, Q2, and Q4 numbers are growing annually due to events such as Valentine's Day, Mother's Day, Christmas, and New Year's, Q3 continues to present a challenge due to the lack of a special holiday or event.

Net income levels from 2006 to 2010 tracked the performance of net sales, but were more severe as seen in **Exhibits 2** and **3.** Net income increased by 33.64% in 2007, 10.06% in 2009, and 10.48% in 2010, but decreased by −33.39% in 2008. Not including the decrease in earnings during the financial meltdown, the net income numbers are considered healthy for a company that was started 12 years ago.

Gross profit has grown similarly to net sales from 2006–2010, as can be seen in **Exhibit 4.** However, the most telling difference was in year 2009, when it outpaced net sales growth with an increase of 8.91%. The growth was a result of cost savings achieved with regard to sourcing and selling products, which increased the gross profit margin from 20.2% to 21.6%, as can be seen in **Exhibit 4.** Blue Nile's increasing gross profit margin is a good sign for the company since it shows strict financial management and an emphasis on the bottom line.

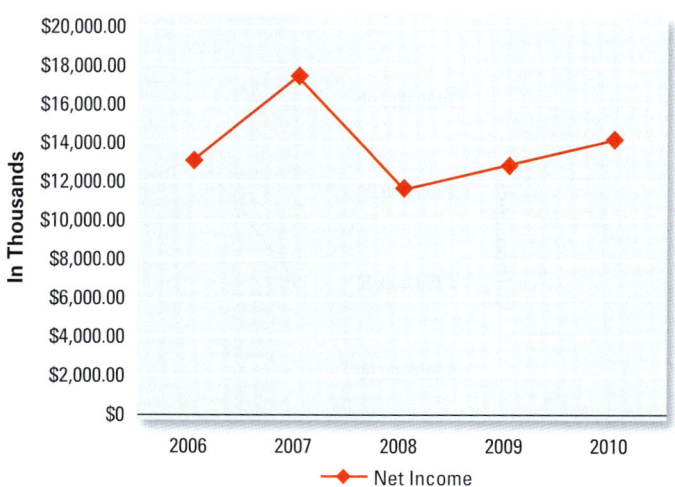

Blue Nile Annual Net Income

Year	2006	2007	2008	2009	2010
Net Income	$ 13,064.00	$ 17,459.00	$ 11,630.00	$ 12,800.00	$ 14,142.00
Growth		33.64%	−33.39%	10.06%	10.48%

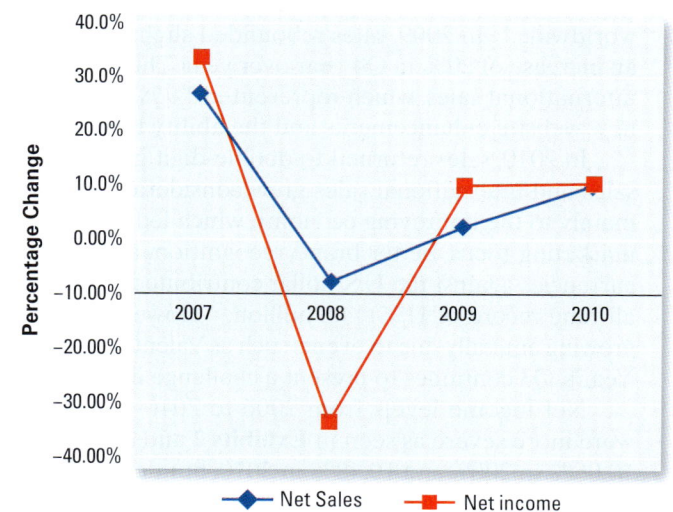

Net Sales vs. Net Income

Growth	2007	2008	2009	2010
Net Sales	26.90%	−7.50%	2.30%	10.18%
Net Income	33.64%	−33.39%	10.06%	10.48%

EXHIBIT 4
Gross Profit Margin
and Operating
Margin

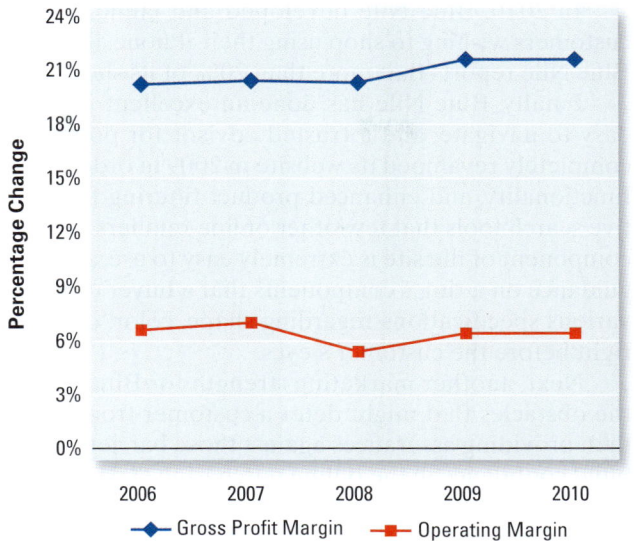

Year	2006	2007	2008	2009	2010
Gross Profit Margin	20.2%	20.4%	20.3%	21.6%	21.6%
Operating Margin	6.600%	7.00%	5.400%	6.400%	6.400%

Blue Nile has no long-term debt. The company only has lease obligations that it needs to pay every year. The lease obligations decreased from US$880,000 in 2007 to US$748,000 in 2010.[44] The long-term debt-to-equity ratio is effectively zero as a result, and even if we include lease obligations, it is minimal, with a value of 0.01, meaning that equity can cover the remaining debt obligations.

Cash at the company is generated mostly through ongoing operations. The increase in cash from 2009 is a result of an increase in accounts payable and the tax benefits received from the execution of stock options. Investing activities also increased the cash amount with the expiration of short-term investment maturity dates. In addition, a slight increase can be attributed to the financing activities coming from the profits of the stock option execution.[45]

In 2011, Blue Nile has only US$79 million in cash. In 2008, the company purchased back 1.6 million shares of stock (US$66.5 million) in order to increase consumer confidence in the stock and because Blue Nile's management team believed the stock was being undervalued.

Blue Nile acquires the majority of its inventory on a just-in-time basis. Moreover, the company is successful in growing cash because its uses for it are minimal, such as improving its website and maintaining facilities and warehouses.[46]

Marketing

Blue Nile's marketing strengths include its use of technology to enhance the customer experience, its dedication to making the diamond-buying process as easy and hassle-free as possible, and its ability to capture market share in spite of the recession.

First, in regard to its use of technology, Blue Nile has been investing in introducing and perfecting online technology that enhances its customer experience. For example, the Blue Nile App, which was launched in September of 2010, gives customers instant access to its inventory of 70,000 diamonds and allows a customer to customize a particular diamond or gem with an ideal setting "while standing at a rival's counter."[47]

In 2010, Blue Nile developed and launched its own mobile site that caters to customers wishing to shop using their iPhone, iPod touch, and Android mobile devices. Blue Nile reports that more than 20% of its shoppers are using the mobile site.

Finally, Blue Nile has done an excellent job of making its website educational, easy to navigate, and a trusted advisor for potential diamond buyers. The company completely revamped its website in 2009 in order to include larger images, better zoom functionality, and enhanced product filtering features.[48] The site also utilizes interactive search tools that few other online retailers can match.[49] The Build Your Own Ring component of the site is extremely easy to use, and fun. Blue Nile provides step-by-step guidance on a ring's components that a buyer can personalize, and based on filling out various specifications regarding shape, color, quality, and size, it builds the ideal ring right before the customer's eyes.

Next, another marketing strength for Blue Nile has been its ability to hone in on the obstacles that might deter a customer from making jewelry purchase online, and then providing assurances against those barriers. Policies like the following all work to build confidence in the online purchasing experience, which works in Blue Nile's favor:

- A 30-day money-back guarantee.[50]
- Orders are shipped fully insured to the customer.
- Grading reports are provided for all certified diamonds, as well as professional appraisals for diamond, gemstone, and pearl jewelry over $1,000.[51]

Finally, in spite of the trying economic environment, Blue Nile has been able to capture market share while many other jewelry sellers have had to close their doors. According to CEO Diane Irvine, the company saw U.S. sales growth of 23% year over year in November and December of 2009, while its competitors ranged from a 12% increase to a 12% decline in the same time-frame.[52] In trying economic times, customers have valued the 20%–40% reduced price found at Blue Nile in comparison to brick-and-mortar retailers.

Although Blue Nile has done a good job of anticipating and catering to the barriers that exist in purchasing an expensive piece of jewelry online, the fact still remains that Blue Nile operates with no storefront locations. This means that customers cannot physically touch and inspect their piece of jewelry before making a purchase. Some traditionally minded members of the jewelry market are not comfortable with this limitation and will not consider Blue Nile a viable alternative. It is also more difficult to develop a lasting, long-term relationship with a customer when the transaction lacks the face-to-face experience found at brick-and-mortar stores. Blue Nile's business is completely dependent in online or phone transactions, making it subject to the adjustment period consumers must go through in order to be comfortable with this purchasing experience.

Building on this weakness is the fact that Blue Nile's online traffic and site visits have been in decline. According to 2010 data from Compete.com, Blue Nile saw its number of unique site visitors decrease year over year in a majority of months, while one of its main competitors, Tiffany's, saw its online traffic increase. Similarly, Compete.com reports that when viewing Blue Nile's unique visitor trend between 2007 and 2009, the company has seen a 36% decrease in unique visitors.[53]

Operations and Logistics

Blue Nile aims to offer a wide range of finished and partially customizable jewelry products to online shoppers, made from ethically sourced materials, via a convenient, hassle-free experience. The company looks to leverage its sourcing power to offer exclusive jewels to exclude competition and retain high selling prices, while maximizing profitability through implementation of just-in-time manufacturing tactics to minimize inventory costs.

Blue Nile employs a flexible manufacturing strategy in its operations. The company heavily advertises the ability for people to customize their desired product—"Build Your Own Ring" is an example of how Blue Nile allows a customer to pick a diamond and an engagement ring setting, and get a unique product.[54] Blue Nile also offers a similar type of customization for earrings, pendants, and other jewelry items.

On the one hand, it seems as though the company would be utilizing an "intermittent job shop" approach. However, while the company does offer full customization through a special order service, the "customization" service is basically allowing online shoppers to pick from a predetermined list of jewels and settings. The jewels are listed in a Blue Nile database (maintained in partnership with its source providers), and the materials are prefabricated in mass production–style to minimize cost.[55]

Using the same methods, Blue Nile makes both finished goods (non-customizable products for direct sale over the Web) and customer-directed finished goods. By using the same supply chain and methods, Blue Nile is able to achieve rapid turnaround of "customized" products, adding value to the service offering.[56]

Blue Nile partners with FedEx for both shipping and returns of all of its products. By maintaining one carrier partnership, the company is able to reach economies of scale in shipping expenditures, and also take advantage of FedEx's international shipping capabilities (other carriers, such as UPS, or USPS, are more limited in their international shipping offers). Also, by partnering with FedEx, Blue Nile is able to take advantage of FedEx's best-in-class shipment tracking functions, which alleviates potential customer concerns about expensive online purchases being "lost in the mail."[57]

Although the majority of revenues for Blue Nile come from the sale of diamonds, it typically does not receive diamonds into inventory until an order is placed, following a just-in-time manufacturing strategy. Instead, Blue Nile partners with its diamond sources, many of them in an exclusive agreement, to provide up-to-date records of available diamond inventory. When a customer places an order for a particular diamond, Blue Nile in turn orders the specified diamond from its supplier, receives the stone, finishes the good, enters the product into inventory, and ships it to the customer.[58]

Financially, this puts the company in a strong position, since it does not have to maintain high inventory carrying costs for the diamonds, which can be valued at several hundred to several thousand dollars each. The company actually produces a positive cash flow of approximately 30–45 days, depending on its contract with a particular supplier.[59]

While partnering with a single distribution partner does provide economic and logistical benefits to the company, it also puts Blue Nile at some degree of risk. Although FedEx has yet to experience a strike by its employees, its rival UPS faced this situation some years ago.[60] If the same situation should occur with FedEx, Blue Nile may be hard-pressed to quickly develop new distribution channels, both domestically and abroad.

In addition, there are also risks associated with Blue Nile's just-in-time inventory approach. First, this approach requires that Blue Nile establish and maintain a direct and accurate path of visibility to its suppliers' diamond inventory. Since many of its diamond suppliers are in less developed regions of the world, this is not an insignificant feat.[61]

Second, since the diamonds are not actually in the possession of Blue Nile at the time the customer places order, it is possible that any type of geo-political disruption (natural disaster, governmental turmoil, etc.) could interrupt the flow of the customer's product, and require subsequent customer service follow up and potential product replacement.

Despite these risks, Blue Nile's success in establishing exclusive sourcing agreements with diamond suppliers and cutters has yielded significant benefits, and is one source of competitive advantage for the organization. By negotiating directly with diamond suppliers and cutters, rather than operating through wholesalers, Blue Nile is able to reduce its diamond procurement costs by more than 20%, compared to other diamond retailers.[62] It is therefore able to offer lower prices than its competition, while simultaneously achieving higher profit margins on its products. Blue Nile's exclusive contracts do offer the company opportunities to be a "sole source" for particular diamond cuts or rare colors, although many diamond retailers have also followed this trend, and each major retailer appears to have its own "exclusive" diamonds.[63]

Human Resources and Ethics

Blue Nile employs 193 full-time workers, with 26 of these full-time positions listed at the executive level (see **Exhibits 5** and **6**).[64] The company maintains employee testimonials on its website as part of its career section, with several comments from employees who have been with the organization for 10 years or more.[65] However, when looking for examples of Blue Nile employee satisfaction outside of the company's own website, the picture is not as rosy. The most common complaints pertain to employee development and retention. Unverified reports of hyper-control by senior management, instead of empowerment and distribution of responsibility to managerial staff, if true, may have a significant impact on Blue Nile's ability to attract and retain high-performance employees, and as a result, grow its business.[66] While the company has made a significant leap forward compared to other jewelry retailers, both brick-and-mortar and Internet-based, if the company focuses exclusively on technology, and not on human talent development, it has little chance to continue its recent growth trends.

While Blue Nile has a significant section of its website devoted to its policies around the ethical sourcing of its diamonds and other materials, the company does not detail any of its policies regarding the handling of its own employees. There are no statements regarding employee diversity, the cultural environment, or employee training/advancement programs. Despite listing nine senior managers listed in the company's investor relations section of its website, not one of the nine is involved in Human Resource Management.[67] This absence, taken with the company's wordage from its corporate reports, paints a picture that suggests attention to human assets is limited at Blue Nile, Inc.

Stuck in the Middle

Operating in a niche segment, Blue Nile is "stuck in the middle" of the diamond engagement ring market. It is not at the top end of the jewelry retail market with the likes of Tiffany & Co. or DeBeers. It is neither at the low end of the market, with the likes of Amazon or Overstock.com. Blue Nile has found a strong growth market by providing high-quality jewelry at discounted prices. Unfortunately, as the company increasingly grows its market share, competitors at the high end and the low end will look to squeeze into the middle niche that Blue Nile currently dominates. Tiffany & Co. and DeBeers have already begun to infuse their online presence with aspects of Blue Nile's approach. Amazon and Overstock.com are likely to look to add higher-priced jewels to their offerings, as broad market acceptance of purchasing jewelry online increases. Michael Porter states that the middle is the worst place to be. The challenge for Blue Nile is how to move up the ladder and become a "high end" diamond retailer—not an easy task for an "online only" retailer.

EXHIBIT 5
Top Management

Harvey Kanter, *Chief Executive Officer, President and Director*

Harvey Kanter, has served as our chief executive officer, president and director since March 30, 2012. He served as the chief executive officer and president of Moosejaw Mountaineering and Backcountry Travel, Inc., a leading multi-channel retailer of premium outdoor apparel and gear, January 2009 to March 2012. From April 2003 to June 2008, Kanter served in various executive positions at Michaels Stores, Inc. ("Michaels"), a specialty retailer of arts and crafts, most recently serving as the Executive Vice President and Managing Director from March 2006 to June 2008. While at Michaels, Kanter also served as the President of Aaron Brothers, Inc., a division of Michaels, from April 2003 to March 2006. From October 1995 to March 2003, Kanter served in various management positions at Eddie Bauer, Inc. ("Eddie Bauer"), a premium outdoor retailer, including serving as the Vice President and Managing Director of Eddie Bauer Home, a division of Eddie Bauer. Prior to Eddie Bauer, Kanter held positions at several other retailers, including Sears Roebuck Company, a multi-line retailer, and Broadway Stores, Inc. (known as, Carter Hawley Hale Department Stores), a department store. Kanter holds an M.B.A from Babson College and a B.S. from Arizona State University.

Vijay Talwar, *General Manager and President of International*

Vijay Talwar has served as our General Manager and President of International since March 30, 2012. He served as our interim chief executive officer from November 2011 to March 2012. He served as our senior vice president and general manager of International from August 2010 to November 2011. From November 2010 to August 2011, he has also served as our interim chief financial officer. From November 2008 to August 2010, Mr. Talwar served as the chief executive officer of the William J. Clinton Foundation India, a global 501©(3) nongovernmental organization established to provide healthcare and sustainability programs across India and South Asia. From February 2008 to September 2008, Mr. Talwar served as the chief operating officer of EL Rothschild LLC, a venture designed to bring international luxury brands to India. From April 2007 to January 2008, Mr. Talwar served as the chief operating officer for the Central Europe, Middle East and Africa region at Nike, Inc., a designer, marketer and distributor of authentic athletic footwear, apparel, equipment and accessories worldwide. From June 2004 to April 2007, Mr. Talwar served as the senior director of strategy and finance at Nike's Global Apparel division. From December 2003 to June 2004, Mr. Talwar served as the director of strategy at Nike's Global Apparel division, and from April 2002 to December 2003, he served as a manager of the global strategic planning group at Nike. Prior to Nike, Mr. Talwar was a consultant at Bain & Company, a management consulting firm; a special projects manager and senior internal auditor at the Kellogg Company, a producer of cereal and convenience foods; and a senior tax consultant and audit assistant at Deloitte & Touche, an accounting firm. Mr. Talwar holds an M.B.A. from University of Chicago, a Master of Accountancy from Miami University and a B.A. in Accountancy from the University of Findlay.

David Binder, *Chief Financial Officer*

David Binder has served as our Chief Financial Officer since August 2011. Mr. Binder joins Blue Nile from Infospace, Inc., an online search and e-commerce company, where he has served as its Chief Financial Officer and Treasurer since January 2008. From October 2004 to December 2007, Mr. Binder was the Vice President of Finance at Infospace. From November 2001 to October 2004, Mr. Binder was the Senior Director of Business Development at Drugstore.com, Inc., an online drugstore. Prior to Drugstore, Mr. Binder served as the Director of Financial Planning and Analysis at Edge2net Inc., a VOIP telecommunications provider; the Director of Finance at Home-Grocer.com, Inc., an e-commerce retailer; and the Director of Planning, Strategy and Competitive Analysis, at AT&T Wireless, a wireless telecommunications business. Mr. Binder holds a master's degree in Economics and Finance and a B.A. degree in Economics from Brandeis University.

Dwight Gaston, *Senior Vice President*

Dwight Gaston has served as Blue Nile's Senior Vice President since September 2005. From July 2003 to March 2005, Mr. Gaston served as Vice President of Operations, and from May 1999 to July 2003, Mr. Gaston served as Blue Nile's Director of Fulfillment Operations. From June 1992 to June 1995 and from August 1997 to May 1999, Mr. Gaston was a consultant with Bain & Company, a management consulting firm. Mr. Gaston holds a B.A. in Economics from Rice University and an M.B.A. from Harvard University.

Terri Maupin, *Chief Accounting Officer*

Terri Maupin has served as Blue Nile's Chief Accounting Officer since August 2011. From July 2004 through August 2011, Ms. Maupin served as Vice President of Finance and Controller, and from October 2004 through January 2010 has served as Corporate Secretary. From September 2003 to July 2004, Ms. Maupin served as Blue Nile's Controller. From February 2001 to September 2003, Ms. Maupin served as the Staff Vice President of Finance and Controller

(continued)

EXHIBIT 5
(Continued)

at Alaska Air Group, Inc. From September 1994 to August 1997, Ms. Maupin served as the Manager of Financial Reporting and from September 1997 to January 2001 as the Director of Financial Reporting for Nordstrom, Inc., a fashion specialty retail company. From October 1993 to September 1994, Ms. Maupin served as Controller at Coastal Transportation Inc., a marine transportation company. From January 1987 to October 1993, Ms. Maupin served in various capacities, most recently as audit manager, with Coopers and Lybrand LLP, an accounting firm. Ms. Maupin holds a B.A. in Accounting from Western Washington University and a CPA-Inactive Certificate from the State of Washington.

Lauren Neiswender, *General Counsel and Corporate Secretary*
Lauren Neiswender has served as the Company's General Counsel since October 2004 and has served as the Company's Corporate Secretary since February 2010. Prior to Blue Nile, Ms. Neiswender was an attorney at Wilson Sonsini Goodrich & Rosati, PC. Ms. Neiswender holds a B.A. in Political Science from Emory University and a J.D. from the University of Virginia.

Jon Sainsbury, *Vice President of Marketing*
Jon Sainsbury has served as Blue Nile's Vice President of Marketing since June 2008. From January 2007 to June 2008, Mr. Sainsbury served as Blue Nile's Director of Marketing and from September 2006 to January 2007, he served as Blue Nile's Senior Marketing Manager. From March 2006 to September 2006, Mr. Sainsbury served as Blue Nile's Search Marketing Manager and from October 2004 to March 2006, he served as Blue Nile's International Program Manager. From September 2002 to October 2004, Mr. Sainsbury served as Blue Nile's Senior Marketing Analyst. Prior to Blue Nile, Mr. Sainsbury was an associate consultant with Bain & Company, a management consulting firm. Mr. Sainsbury holds a B.A. in Physics from Pomona College.

EXHIBIT 6
Board of Directors

Mark Vadon, *Chairman of the Board*
Mark Vadon co-founded Blue Nile and has served as Chairman of the Board since its inception. From February 2008 to August 2011, Mr. Vadon served as Executive Chairman. Prior to February 2008, he served as Chief Executive Officer from its inception and served as President from inception to February 2007. From December 1992 to March 1999, Mr. Vadon was a consultant for Bain & Company, a management consulting firm. Mr. Vadon holds a B.A. in Social Studies from Harvard University and an M.B.A. from Stanford University.

Harvey Kanter, *Director*
Harvey Kanter, has served as our chief executive officer, president and director since March 30, 2012. He served as the chief executive officer and president of Moosejaw Mountaineering and Backcountry Travel, Inc., a leading multi-channel retailer of premium outdoor apparel and gear, January 2009 to March 2012. From April 2003 to June 2008, Kanter served in various executive positions at Michaels Stores, Inc. ("Michaels"), a specialty retailer of arts and crafts, most recently serving as the Executive Vice President and Managing Director from March 2006 to June 2008. While at Michaels, Kanter also served as the President of Aaron Brothers, Inc., a division of Michaels, from April 2003 to March 2006. From October 1995 to March 2003, Kanter served in various management positions at Eddie Bauer, Inc. ("Eddie Bauer"), a premium outdoor retailer, including serving as the Vice President and Managing Director of Eddie Bauer Home, a division of Eddie Bauer. Prior to Eddie Bauer, Kanter held positions at several other retailers, including Sears Roebuck Company, a multi-line retailer, and Broadway Stores, Inc. (known as, Carter Hawley Hale Department Stores), a department store. Kanter holds an M.B.A from Babson College and a B.S. from Arizona State University.

Mary Alice Taylor, *Director*
Mary Alice Taylor has served as a director since March 2000. Ms. Taylor is an independent business executive. She held a temporary assignment as Chairman and Chief Executive Officer of Webvan Group, Inc., an e-commerce company, from July 2001 to December 2001. Prior to that, she served as Chairman and Chief Executive Officer of HomeGrocer.com, an e-commerce company, from September 1999 until she completed a sale of the company to Webvan Group, Inc. in October 2000. From January 1997 to September 1999, Ms. Taylor served as Corporate Executive Vice President of Worldwide Operations and Technology for Citigroup, Inc., a financial services organization. Ms. Taylor also served as a Senior Vice President of Federal Express Corporation, a delivery services company, from September 1991 until December 1996. Ms. Taylor holds a B.S. in Finance from Mississippi State University. Ms. Taylor also serves on the Board of Directors of Allstate Corporation, an insurance company.

EXHIBIT 6
(Continued)

Eric Carlborg, *Director*

Eric Carlborg has served as a director since February 2005. Since June 2010, Mr. Carlborg has served as an investment professional at August Capital, an investment company. From April 2006 to May 2010, Mr. Carlborg was a partner at Continental Investors LLC, an investment company. From September 2005 to March 2006, Mr. Carlborg served as Chief Financial Officer of Provide Commerce, Inc., an e-commerce company. From July 2001 to October 2004, Mr. Carlborg was a Managing Director of Investment Banking with Merrill Lynch & Co., focused on the technology and financial sectors. Prior to his tenure at Merrill Lynch, Mr. Carlborg served in various executive financial positions, including Chief Financial Officer at Authorize.net, Inc. and Chief Strategy Officer at Go2Net, Inc., providers of Internet products and services. Mr. Carlborg also previously served as Chief Financial Officer for Einstein/Noah Bagel Corp. In addition, Mr. Carlborg previously served as a member of the Board of Directors of Big Lots, Inc., a Fortune 500 retailer. Mr. Carlborg holds an M.B.A. from the University of Chicago and a B.A. from the University of Illinois.

Leslie Lane, *Lead Independent Director*

Leslie Lane, age 44, has served as a director since December 2008. Mr. Lane has served as Operating Partner at Altamont Capital Partners, a venture capital company, since May 2011. He served as the Vice President and Managing Director of the Nike Foundation at Nike, Inc., a leading designer, marketer, and distributor of authentic athletic footwear, apparel, equipment, and accessories, from June 2010 to April 2011. From October 2006 to June 2010, he served as Vice President and General Manager of Global Running for Nike, Inc. From March 2004 to October 2006, he served as the Director of Nike Global Footwear Finance and Strategic Planning and, from March 2003 to March 2004, he served as the Director of Nike Subsidiaries. From 1998 to 2002, Lane held various positions at Roll International Corporation, a private holding company, including serving as the Chief Operating Officer of PomWonderful LLC, the Chief Financial Officer of Paramount Citrus, and the Vice President of Strategy of Roll International Corporation. From 1990 to 1998, Lane was a consultant with Bain & Company. He holds an M.A. in Chemistry from Oxford University and an M.B.A. from Harvard University.

Michael Potter, *Director*

Michael Potter has served as a director since October 2007. Mr. Potter served as Chairman and Chief Executive Officer of Big Lots, Inc., a Fortune 500 retailer, from June 2000 to June 2005. Prior to serving as Chief Executive Officer, Mr. Potter served in various capacities at Big Lots, including the role of Chief Financial Officer. Prior to Big Lots, Mr. Potter held various positions at The Limited, Inc., May Department Stores, and Meier & Frank, all retail companies. Mr. Potter currently serves on the Board of Directors of Coldwater Creek, Inc., a triple channel retailer of women's apparel, gifts, and accessories, as well as Newegg, Inc., an online-only retailer specializing in high-tech products. Mr. Potter holds an M.B.A. from Capital University in Ohio and a B.S. in Finance and Management from the University of Oregon.

Steve Scheid, *Director*

Steve Scheid has served as director since October 2007. Mr. Scheid currently serves as the Chairman of the Board of Janus Capital Group, Inc. ("Janus"). From April 2004 until December 2005, Mr. Scheid served as Chief Executive Officer and Chairman of the Board of Janus. Scheid joined the Janus Board in December 2002 and was appointed Chairman in January 2004. Scheid served as Vice Chairman of The Charles Schwab Corporation and President of Schwab's retail group from 2000 to 2002. Prior thereto, Mr. Scheid headed Schwab's financial products and services group and was the firm's Chief Financial Officer from 1996 through 1999. From 2001 to 2002, Mr. Scheid served on the Federal Advisory Council, which provides oversight to the Federal Reserve Board in Washington, D.C. Mr. Scheid holds a B.S. from Michigan State University.

Chris Bruzzo, *Director*

Chris Bruzzo has served as director since July 2011. Mr. Bruzzo has served as the Senior Vice President and Chief Marketing Officer for Seattle's Best Coffee, a subsidiary of Starbucks Corporation, a specialty coffee retailer, since July 2011. From June 2008 to July 2011, he served as Vice President of Global Advertising & Digital Marketing at Starbucks Corporation. From January 2007 to January 2008, Mr. Bruzzo served as the Vice President of Digital Strategy at Starbucks Corporation and from January 2008 to May 2008 he served as the Chief Technology Officer and interim Chief Information Officer at Starbucks Corporation. From July 2006 to October 2006, Mr. Bruzzo served as the Vice President of Marketing and Public Relations at Amazon.com, Inc., an online retailer. From July 2003 to February 2006, Mr. Bruzzo served in various roles at Amazon.com, Inc., including Vice President of Strategic Communications, Content and Initiatives. Prior to Amazon.com, Inc., Mr. Bruzzo was an Assistant Vice President at Regence Blue Shield. Mr. Bruzzo holds a B.A. in Political Studies from Whitworth College.

NOTES

1. Blue Nile, Inc. Datamonitor. www.datamonitor.com. September 10, 2010.
2. http://www.bluenile.com/blue-nile-advantage
3. http://www.bluenile.com/about-blue-nile
4. http://www.kaihan.net/vpw_login.php?img=blue-nile
5. http://www.bluenile.com/blue-nile-history
6. http://www.reuters.com/finance/stocks/companyProfile?symbol=NILE.O
7. Ibid.
8. http://www.bluenile.com/blue-nile-history
9. http://www.bluenile.com/about-blue-nile
10. http://www.reuters.com/finance/stocks/companyProfile?symbol=NILE.O
11. http://www.bluenile.com/about-blue-nile
12. http://www.bluenile.com/blue-nile-advantage
13. Krippendorff, Kaihan. "Creating a Two-Horned Dilemma." *Fast* Company.com. September 8, 2010.
14. http://www.kaihan.net/vpw_login.php?img=blue-nile
15. Blue Nile, Inc. Datamonitor. www.datamonitor.com. September 10, 2010.
16. MacMillan, Douglas. "How Four Rookie CEOs Handled the Great Recession." *Bloomberg Businessweek.* February 18, 2010.
17. Mintel. Accessed May 8, 2011. http://academic.mintel.com/sinatra/oxygen_academic/search_results/show&/display/id=482738/display/id=540585\#hit1.
18. Jewelry Retail Industry Profile. *First* Research.com. February 14, 2011.
19. Mintel. Accessed May 8, 2011. http://academic.mintel.com/sinatra/oxygen_academic/search_results/show&/display/id=482738/display/id=540590\#hit1
20. DeFotis, Dimitra. "No Diamond in the Rough." *Barron's.* February 15, 2010.
21. Plourd, Kate. "I Like Innovative, Disruptive Businesses." *CFO Magazine.* February 1, 2009.
22. Blue Nile, Inc. Datamonitor. www.datamonitor.com. September 10, 2010.
23. Jewelry Retail Industry Profile. *First* Research.com. *February* 14, 2011.
24. DeFotis, Dimitra. "No Diamond in the Rough." *Barron's.* February 15, 2010.
25. https://collab.itc.virginia.edu/access/content/group/dff17973-f012-465d-9e73-a05fa4456644/Research/Memos/MII%20Memos/Archive/Short/S%20-NILE_2.pdf
26. http://www.kaihan.net/vpw_login.php?img=blue-nile
27. http://www.bluenile.com/services_channel.jsp
28. http://www.kaihan.net/vpw_login.php?img=blue-nile
29. "Blue Nile CEO interview." CEO Wire. November 29, 2010. http://ezp.bentley.edu/login?url=http://search.proquest.com/?url=http://search.proquest.com/docview/814841480?accountid=8576
30. http://www.bluenile.com/why-choose-blue-nile
31. http://www.bluenile.com/diamonds/fancy-color-diamonds?keyword_search_value=colored+diamonds
32. Levine, Joshua. "A Beautiful Mine." *The New York Times.* April 17, 2011.
33. (2008), DIAMONDS: Kimberley Process Effective. *Africa Research Bulletin: Economic, Financial and Technical Series,* 44: 17640A-17641A.
34. http://www.kimberleyprocess.com/background/index_en.html
35. http://factfinder.census.gov/servlet/GRTTable?_bm=y&-geo_id=01000US&-_box_head_nbr=R1204&-ds_name=ACS_2009_1YR_G00_&-redoLog=false&-mt_name=ACS_2005_EST_G00_R1204_US30&-format=US-30
36. http://factfinder.census.gov/servlet/GRTTable?_bm=y&-geo_id=D&_box_head_nbr=R1205&ds_name=ACS_2009_1YR_G00_&-_lang=en&-redoLog=false&-format=D&mt_name=ACS_2009_1YR_G00_R1204_US30
37. DeBarros, Anthony and Jayson, Sharon. "Young Adults Delaying Marriage; Data Show 'Dramatic' Surge in Single Twenty-somethings." *USA Today.* September 12, 2007.
38. 2010 Blue Nile Annual Report. Pg 27.
39. 2010 Blue Nile Annual Report. Pg 27.
40. Annual report 2008. Pg 31.
41. Ibid. Pg 30.
42. Annual report 2010. Pg 31.
43. Ibid. Pg 30.
44. Annual report 2010. Pg 33.
45. Ibid. Pg 32.
46. Ibid. Pg 33.
47. Birchall, Jonathan. " Smartphone Apps: Competition Set to Intensify for Online Retailers." FT.com. Nov 13, 2010.
48. Byron Acohido and Edward C. Baig. "Blue Nile Gets a New Look." *USA Today.* September 2, 2009.
49. Blue Nile, Inc. Datamonitor. www.datamonitor.com. September 10, 2010.
50. Ibid.
51. "Blue Nile Unwraps Cyber Monday Promotions." *Information Technology Newsweekly.* December 8, 2009.
52. DeFotis, Dimitra. "No Diamond in the Rough." *Barron's.* February 15, 2010.
53. DeFotis, Dimitra. "No Diamond in the Rough." *Barron's.* February 15, 2010.
54. http://www.bluenile.com/build-your-own-diamond-ring?track=head
55. http://www.glassdoor.com/Reviews/Blue-Nile-Reviews-E11944.htm
56. http://www.glassdoor.com/Reviews/Blue-Nile-Reviews-E11944.htm
57. http://www.fedex.com/us/track/index.html
58. http://www.reuters.com/finance/stocks/companyProfile?symbol=NILE.O
59. http://seekingalpha.com/article/11593-the-bull-and-bear-cases-for-blue-nile-nile
60. http://www.businessweek.com/smallbiz/news/date/9811/e981119.htm
61. http://seekingalpha.com/article/11593-the-bull-and-bear-cases-for-blue-nile-nile
62. http://seekingalpha.com/article/11593-the-bull-and-bear-cases-for-blue-nile-nile
63. http://www.diamondsnews.com/hearts_on_fire.htm
64. http://www.hoovers.com/company/Blue_Nile_Inc/rffxhxi-1.html
65. http://www.bluenile.com/employee_testimonials.jsp
66. http://www.glassdoor.com/Reviews/Blue-Nile-Reviews-E11944.htm
67. http://investor.bluenile.com/management.cfm

CASE **14**

Groupon, Inc.

DAILY DEAL OR LASTING SUCCESS?

Nick Falcone, Eric Halbruner, Ellie A. Fogarty, and Joyce Vincelette

Andrew Mason sat in his office in Chicago, Illinois, thinking about the city. His adult life began there—he graduated from Northwestern in 2003. His business originated there not long after—Groupon began as a local Chicago discount service and became a global phenomenon seemingly overnight. Mason knew that Groupon was a great idea. The company was the first of its kind and changed the way consumers spend, shop, and think about discounts. But how could Groupon, based in such innovation and having experienced such exceptional growth, be in such a precarious position? A wave of competition had swelled, including the likes of technology giants and both general and niche daily deals services, all replicating Groupon's business model. How could Groupon compete against large companies and their expansive resources? Would consumers and merchant partners flock to other services that better suited their needs? Mason worried about the increasingly downward trajectory of Groupon's stock price since the company's initial public offering. The year 2012 had brought additional scrutiny of Groupon from the SEC, as well as the unfortunate title of Worst CEO of 2012 for Mason.[1] He thought about the barrage of competition facing his firm and the related questions regarding the sustainability of its business model. Groupon was a star as it grew from its Illinois roots, but it now had problems on a global scale. Mason looked out his window over the city where it all started, nostalgic for a time when business was easier and wondered what to do.

History

In 2006, three years after graduating from Northwestern University with a degree in Music, Andrew Mason became frustrated when trying to cancel a cell phone contract. He thought about the likely large group of people in similar circumstances and figured "if [he and they] were united in some way, [they] could leverage [their] collective power."[2] He began developing a Web platform based on the "tipping point" principle (the number at which an idea or cause reaches critical mass, popularized by Malcolm Gladwell) that would utilize social media to organize collective action.[3] The company he created was aptly named ThePoint and was designed to be a tool for raising money for various causes. The "tipping point" for a particular cause, which would be set by the fundraiser, was a certain amount of money or signatures needed for the plan to become active.[4] Users could donate with minimal risk because credit cards were not charged unless and until the threshold was met and the cause "tipped."

But ThePoint lacked the focus necessary to survive on its own. "The big problem . . . " Mason said, "is that it's this huge, abstract idea. You can use this platform to do anything from boycotting a multinational company to getting 20% off a subscription to *The Economist* . . . we needed to pick one application of the larger abstract idea and execute it really, really well."[5] The service was too broad to achieve success, but the tipping point element had noticeable potential.

Mason found his "one application" in the most effective campaigns on The Point—those that gave a group of consumers buying power.[6] He began recruiting merchants to offer discounts in online deals that centered on the tipping point principle. In deals that tipped (when enough coupons were purchased), consumers saved money and merchants benefitted from both large-scale sales and market exposure. The concept grew into an entirely new venture: a daily deals service that relied on the power of groups. Groupon—the name is a combination of the words "group" and "coupon"—launched its first deal in October 2008: Buy two pizzas for the price of one from the Motel Bar, located on the first floor of Groupon's Chicago headquarters.[7]

From there, the company grew at an unprecedented rate. In six months, Groupon parlayed its 5000-person Chicago e-mail list into daily deals operations in Boston, New York, and Washington, DC. Groupon's estimated worth was over US$1 billion after just 16 months in business, becoming the second-fastest website to reach that milestone (YouTube reached the mark in 12 months).[8] By 2010, Groupon was serving more than 150 markets in North America, 100 markets in Europe, Asia, and South America, and was boasting 35 million registered users.[9] *Forbes* magazine declared Groupon to be the "fastest growing company ever"[10] in August 2010 and Groupon rejected a US$6 billion acquisition offer from technology giant Google in December of the same year.[11]

In November 2011, the company raised US$700 million in its initial public offering, the largest IPO by a United States Internet company since Google's US$1.7 billion in 2004.[12] But the growth seen in the company's infancy had been largely elusive since its IPO. In the 10 subsequent months, Groupon's stock fell 84% from US$26.11 to close at US$4.15 on August 31, 2012.

Business Model

Groupon described itself as "a local commerce marketplace that connects merchants to consumers by offering goods and services at a discount."[13] The company saw opportunity in bringing the brick-and-mortar world of local commerce onto the Internet, which it said was creating a new way for local merchant partners to attract customers.[14] The "Groupon Promise" was core to the company's customer-service philosophy:

> We're confident in the businesses we feature on Groupon and back them with the Groupon Promise. If the experience using your Groupon ever lets you down, we'll make it right or return your purchase. Simple as that.[15]

Groupon followed specific processes in dealings with consumers and merchants to keep its promise. The company used its technology and scale to target relevant deals based on individual customer preferences.[16] Deals were disseminated primarily via e-mail; consumers subscribed to Groupon's mailing list, chose their locations, and were sent information on deals in their areas. Groupon's mobile application and website were set up to distribute deals to current and potential customers based on proximity to the sponsoring merchant partner.[17] Customers purchased coupons online, which became active only when a deal reached its predetermined critical number of purchases. The coupons had expiration dates.

Merchants wishing to partner with Groupon and feature their products or services in deals were vetted by the company. Only one in eight applicants was accepted. Winning merchants had to be receiving praise on review sites like Yelp, CitySearch, and TripAdvisor, and their Groupon deals had to offer a substantial discount from normal prices and not be similar to other promotions regularly offered by the vendor.[18] A merchant partner signed a contract that specified the percentage of revenue Groupon would collect from a deal (typically 50%) and the number of coupons that would have to be purchased for a deal to "tip" and for the discount to become active. Groupon collected revenue from the deals immediately and made payments to merchants over a 60-day period.[19]

Merchants were not completely at ease with the general model, now utilized by other deal providers, citing the heavy discounts required and low repeat rates from customers as their two biggest concerns.[20] Twenty-three percent of respondents to a merchant survey on daily deals companies said that the discounts were their biggest concern, but 45% said they acquired more customers as a result of offering the promotions.[21] Eighty percent were satisfied with daily-deal companies. Merchant satisfaction and retention were critical to Groupon's strategy for success.

Mission and Strategy

CEO Andrew Mason explained his vision for Groupon in a 2011 Letter to Stockholders. Upon the shoulders of its business model, he wrote, Groupon was setting out to reinvent the multitrillion-dollar local commerce ecosystem. "Today, Groupon is a marketing tool that connects consumers and merchants. Tomorrow, we aim to move upstream and serve as the entry point for local transactions." Groupon's mission, according to Mason, was "to become the operating system for local commerce."[22]

Groupon's objective was to become an essential part of everyday local commerce for consumers and merchants. Key elements of its strategy included the following:[23]

- **Grow subscriber and customer base.** Groupon made significant investments to acquire subscribers through online marketing initiatives, such as search engine marketing, display advertisements, referral programs, and affiliate marketing. In addition, Groupon's subscriber base increased by word of mouth. The company intended to continue to invest in acquiring subscribers; however, it continued to shift its efforts toward converting subscribers into customers who purchase Groupons. Groupon's investment in the growth of its subscriber base and achieving optimal subscriber levels was directly linked to the breadth and location of its merchant partners. As such, while the number of total subscribers was a key metric to measure Groupon's progression over the long term, it was not a key operational metric in the same manner as was the active customer base.

- **Grow the number of merchant partners.** Groupon expanded the number of ways in which consumers could discover deals through its marketplace. The company made significant investments in its sales force, which built merchant partner relationships and local expertise. Merchant partner retention efforts were focused on providing merchant partners with a positive experience by offering targeted placement of their deals to the subscriber base, high-quality customer service, and tools to manage deals more effectively. Groupon routinely solicited feedback from merchant partners to ensure their objectives were met and they were satisfied with its services. Based on this feedback, Groupon believed that merchant partners considered the profitability of the immediate deal, potential revenue generated by repeat customers, and increased brand awareness for the merchant partner and the resulting revenue stream that brand awareness might generate over time. Some merchant partners viewed deals as a marketing expense and might be willing to offer deals with little or no immediate profitability in an effort to gain future customers and increased brand awareness.

- **Position Groupon to benefit from technological changes that may affect consumer behavior.** Groupon believed that as technological advances continued, particularly with the proliferation of affordable Smartphones and tablet computers, the ways in which customers and local merchant partners interacted would change significantly. For example, in December 2011, one quarter of all purchases in its North America segment were made through mobile devices. Groupon believed that it was well positioned to benefit from, and to drive, these changes. The company continued to invest heavily in technology, including through acquisitions.

- **Increase the number and variety of products through innovation.** Groupon launched a variety of new products in 2011 and planned to continue to launch new products to increase the number of customers and merchant partners transacting business through its marketplace. As its local commerce marketplace grew, Groupon believed that consumers would use Groupon not only as a discovery tool for local merchant partners, but also as an ongoing connection point to their favorite merchants.

- **Expand with acquisitions and business development partnerships.** Historically, the core assets Groupon gained from acquisitions were local management teams and small subscriber and merchant partner bases, to which the company then applies its expertise, resources, and brand to scale the business. More recently, Groupon's focus shifted to acquiring businesses with technology and technology talent that could help expand its business. In addition to acquisitions, Groupon entered into agreements with local partners to expand its international presence. Groupon entered into affiliate programs with companies such as eBay, Microsoft, Yahoo, and Zynga, that allowed these partners to display, promote, and distribute Groupon's deals to their users in exchange for a share of the revenue the deals generate.

Corporate Governance

Groupon's Global Code of Conduct and Corporate Governance Guidelines were adopted in the fall of 2011. These documents, and the charters for the Audit, Compensation, and Nominating & Governance Committees, can be found on the company's website at http://investor.groupon.com/governance.cfm.

Board of Directors. [24] The biographies of the eight members of the Board of Directors are as follows:

Eric Lefkofsky, 42, is a co-founder and the Executive Chairman of Groupon. He is also a founder and director of several firms, including InnerWorkings, Inc., a global provider of managed print and promotional solutions; Echo Global Logistics, Inc., a technology-enabled transportation and logistics outsourcing firm; MediaBank, LLC, a leading provider of integrated media procurement technology; and Light-Bank, a venture fund focused on helping disruptive technology businesses. Eric serves on the board of directors of Children's Memorial Hospital and the board of trustees of the Steppenwolf Theatre, the Art Institute of Chicago, and the Museum of Contemporary Art. Eric is also an adjunct professor at the University of Chicago Booth School of Business. He holds a bachelor's degree from the University of Michigan and a Juris Doctor from the University of Michigan Law School.

Peter Barris, 59, joined New Enterprise Associates (NEA) in 1992 and has served as Managing General Partner since 1999. Since joining NEA, Peter has led investments in over 20 information technology companies that have completed public offerings or successful mergers. These include such industry pioneering companies as Amisys, CareerBuilder, InnerWorkings, Neutral Tandem, UUNET, and Vonage. Prior to joining NEA, Peter was President and Chief Operating Officer of Legent Corporation (LGNT) and Senior Vice President of the Systems Software Division of UCCEL Corporation (UCE). Both companies were ultimately acquired at valuations that were record breaking for their time. Earlier, Peter spent almost a decade at General Electric Company in a variety of management positions, including Vice President and General Manager at GE Information Services. Outside interests include serving on the Northwestern University Board of Trustees and the Dartmouth Tuck School Board of Overseers. Peter previously served on the Executive Committee of the Board of the National Venture Capital Association and was also a founding member of Venture Philanthropy Partners, a philanthropic organization in the Washington, DC, area. He has a BS degree in Electrical Engineering from Northwestern and an MBA from Dartmouth. Mr. Barris is the chair of the Compensation Committee and a member of the Nominating and Governance Committee.

Mellody Hobson, 42, is president of Ariel Investments, a Chicago-based money management firm serving institutional clients and individual investors; she also serves as chairman of the board of trustees for Ariel's no-load mutual funds. Beyond her work at Ariel, Mellody has become a nationally recognized voice on financial literacy and investor education. Specifically, she is a regular financial contributor on *Good Morning America,* the featured consumer finance expert on Tom Joyner's *Money Mondays* radio program, and a regular columnist for *Black Enterprise.* Mellody is a director of three public companies: DreamWorks Animation SKG, Inc., The Estée Lauder Companies Inc., and Starbucks Corporation. In addition, she serves on the boards of various civic organizations including The Field Museum, The Chicago Public Education Fund, and the Sundance Institute. Mellody is a graduate of Princeton University where she received her AB degree from the Woodrow Wilson School of Public and International Affairs. She is a member of both the Compensation Committee and the Nominating and Governance Committee.

Brad Keywell, 42, is a founder of MediaBank LLC, Echo Global Logistics, Inc., Groupon Inc., Starbelly, and several other companies. He has served on the Board since Groupon's inception. He is on the Board of the Zell-Lurie Entrepreneurship Institute at the University of Michigan, Big Communications, Warrior Productions, and University of Michigan Hillel Foundation. He was formerly on the Board of Columbia College, as well as the Advisory Committee of the University of Chicago Graduate School of Business Directors' College. Mr. Keywell is a member of the Compensation Committee and the chair of the Nominating and Governance Committee.

Ted Leonsis, 55, is Vice Chairman Emeritus of AOL LLC with more than a decade of experience in global Internet services and media at AOL, where he also served as Vice Chairman and President of several business units. In addition to his work at AOL, Leonsis is the majority owner of the National Hockey League's Washington Capitals and the Women's National Basketball Association's Washington Mystics.

He is also the producer of "Nanking," a documentary film that made its premiere at the 2007 Sundance Film Festival. Mr. Leonsis is the chair of the Audit Committee and a member of the Compensation Committee.

Andrew Mason, 31, is a founder of Groupon and has served as its Chief Executive Officer since its inception in November 2008. Prior to co-founding Groupon and The-Point, Andrew worked as a software developer with Innerworkings, Inc. Andrew received his Bachelor of Arts in Music from Northwestern University.

Daniel Henry, 62, has been the Chief Financial Officer of American Express Company since October 2007. Henry is responsible for leading American Express Company's finance organization and representing American Express to investors, lenders, and rating agencies. He also served as Executive Vice President and Chief Financial Officer of U.S. Consumer, Small Business and Merchant Services and joined American Express as Comptroller in 1990. Prior to joining American Express, Henry was a partner with Ernst & Young. Mr. Henry is a member of the Audit Committee.

Robert Bass, 62, served as a Vice Chairman of Deloitte LLP from 2006 through June 2012, and was a partner in Deloitte from 1982 through June 2012. Mr. Bass specializes in e-commerce, mergers and acquisitions, and SEC filings. At Deloitte, Mr. Bass was responsible for all services provided to Forstmann Little and its portfolio companies and is the advisory partner for Blackstone, DIRECTV, McKesson, IMG, and CSC. He has also previously been the advisory partner for priceline.com, RR Donnelley, Automatic Data Processing, Community Health Systems, and Avis Budget. He is a member of the American Institute of Certified Public Accountants and the New York and Connecticut State Societies of Certified Public Accountants. Mr. Bass is a member of the Audit Committee.

Daniel Henry and Robert Bass joined the Board on April 26 and June 19, 2012, respectively, in a move to bring more accounting and financial expertise to the Board. Mr. Henry replaced Howard Schultz, CEO of Starbucks. Mr. Bass replaced Kevin Efrusy, a partner at the venture-capital firm Accel Partners.[25]

Top Management.[26] The biographical sketches for Groupon's top management team are as follows:

Andrew D. Mason, 31, is a co-founder of Groupon and has served as its Chief Executive Officer and a director since its inception. In 2007, Mr. Mason co-founded ThePoint, a Web platform that enables users to promote collective action to support social, educational, and civic causes, from which Groupon evolved. Prior to co-founding ThePoint, Mr. Mason worked as a computer programmer with InnerWorkings, Inc. Mr. Mason received his Bachelor of Arts from Northwestern University. Mr. Mason brings to the Board the perspective and experience as one of Groupon's founders and as Chief Executive Officer. Mr. Mason was elected to the Board pursuant to voting rights granted to the former holders of Groupon's common stock and preferred stock under Groupon's voting agreement, which terminated as a result of the company's initial public offering.

Jason E. Child, 43, has served as Chief Financial Officer since December 2010. From March 1999 through December 2010, Mr. Child held several positions with Amazon.com, Inc., including Vice President of Finance, International from April 2007 to December 2010, Vice President of Finance, Asia from July 2006 to July 2007, Director of Finance, Amazon Germany from April 2004 to July 2006, Director of Investor Relations from April 2003 to April 2004, Director of Finance, Worldwide

Application Software from November 2001 to April 2003, Director of Finance, Marketing and Business Development from November 2000 to November 2001, and Global Controller from October 1999 to November 2000. Prior to joining Amazon.com, Mr. Child spent more than seven years as a C.P.A. and a consulting manager at Arthur Andersen. Mr. Child received his Bachelor of Arts from the Foster School of Business at the University of Washington.

Joseph M. Del Preto II, 36, has served as Chief Accounting Officer since April 2011. From January 2011 to April 2011, Mr. Del Preto served as Groupon's Global Controller. Prior to joining Groupon, Mr. Del Preto served as Controller and Vice President, Finance of Echo Global Logistics, Inc. from April 2009 to December 2010. From January 2006 to March 2009, Mr. Del Preto served as Controller of InnerWorkings, Inc. Mr. Del Preto began his career at PricewaterhouseCoopers LLP. Mr. Del Preto received his Bachelor of Science degree from Indiana University.

Jason D. Harinstein, 36, has served as Senior Vice President–Corporate Development since March 2011. From June 2005 to February 2011, Mr. Harinstein served in several capacities at Google, Inc., including most recently as Director of Corporate Development. From July 2003 to June 2005, Mr. Harinstein worked as an Equity Research Associate at Deutsche Bank Securities, Inc. where he covered Internet advertising, online search, eCommerce and video game companies. Previously, Mr. Harinstein served as a strategy consultant at iXL, Inc. (now part of Razorfish) from June 1999 to June 2001, and at Andersen Consulting Strategic Services (now Accenture) from September 1997 to June 1999. Mr. Harinstein received his Bachelor of Arts in Economics from Northwestern University and his Master's in Business Administration from the University of Chicago.

Jeffrey Holden, 43, has served as Senior Vice President-Product Management since April 2011. In 2006, Mr. Holden co-founded Pelago, Inc. and served as its Chief Executive Officer until Groupon acquired Pelago in April 2011. Prior to co-founding Pelago, Mr. Holden held several positions at Amazon.com, Inc., including Senior Vice President, Worldwide Discovery, from March 2005 to January 2006, Senior Vice President, Consumer Applications, from April 2004 to March 2005, Vice President, Consumer Applications, from April 2002 to April 2004, and Director, Automated Merchandising and Discovery from February 2000 to April 2002. Mr. Holden joined Amazon.com in May 1997 as Director, Supply Chain Optimization Systems. Mr. Holden received his Bachelor of Science and Master of Science degrees in Computer Science from the University of Illinois at Urbana-Champaign.

David R. Schellhase, 48, has served as General Counsel since June 2011. From March 2010 to May 2011, Mr. Schellhase served as Executive Vice President, Legal of salesforce. com, inc. From December 2004 to March 2010, Mr. Schellhase served as the Senior Vice President and General Counsel of salesforce.com, and he served as Vice President and General Counsel of salesforce.com from July 2002 to December 2004. From December 2000 to June 2002, Mr. Schellhase was an independent legal consultant and authored a treatise entitled Corporate Law Department Handbook. Previously, he served as General Counsel at Linuxcare, Inc., The Vantive Corporation and Premenos Technology Corp. Mr. Schellhase received a Bachelor of Arts from Columbia University and a Juris Doctor from Cornell University.

Brian J. Schipper, 51, has served as Senior Vice President–Human Resources since June 2011. From October 2006 to May 2011, Mr. Schipper served as Senior Vice President and Chief Human Resources Officer of Cisco Systems, Inc. From November 2003 to October 2006, Mr. Schipper served as the Corporate Vice President, Human Resources of Microsoft Corporation. From February 2002 to March 2003,

Mr. Schipper was Partner and Head of Human Resources and Administration for Andor Capital Management LLC. From March 2000 to February 2002, Mr. Schipper served as Senior Vice President of Human Resources and Administration at DoubleClick, Inc. Prior to joining DoubleClick, Mr. Schipper served as Vice President, Human Resources at PepsiCo, Inc. from May 1995 to March 2000. Prior to joining PepsiCo, Mr. Schipper worked at Compaq Computer Corporation, where he was global head of compensation and benefits and head of Human Resources for North America. Mr. Schipper received his Bachelor's from Hope College and his Master's in Business Administration from Michigan State University.

Brian K. Totty, 45, Ph.D., has served as Senior Vice President—Engineering and Operations since November 2010. Dr. Totty was the Chief Executive Officer of Ludic Labs, Inc., a startup venture developing a new class of software applications from January 2006 through November 2007. We acquired Ludic Labs in November 2010. Dr. Totty also was a co-founder and Senior Vice President of Research and Development of Inktomi Corporation from February 1996 to August 2002. Dr. Totty received his Ph.D. in computer science from the University of Illinois at Urbana-Champaign, his Master of Public Administration from Harvard's Kennedy School and his Bachelor of Science from the Massachusetts Institute of Technology.

Operations

Groupon's operations were divided into North America (United States and Canada) and International segments.

One trend that contributed to Groupon's growth was its investment in international markets. In 2009, the company's operations focused entirely on North America. In 2010, however, Groupon began looking abroad for growth, targeting key markets in both Europe and Asia. As a result, the International segment accounted for 36% of total revenues in 2010. As Groupon continued to see growth in 2011, the segment accounted for 60.6%, as shown in **Exhibit 1.** While this rapid expansion of the International segment contributed substantially to the company's growth, it also contributed to its annual net losses. In fact, management blamed the net loss in 2011 primarily on the "rapid expansion of [its] International segment during the year, which involved investing heavily in upfront marketing, sales and infrastructure related to the build out of [its] operations" in early stage countries.[27] Groupon's international segment often felt the impact of unfavorable foreign exchange rates.

To accompany this expansion, Groupon made changes to its distribution of resources, including corporate facilities and employees. The company's principal executive properties are described in **Exhibit 2.** Other facilities were located throughout the world.

EXHIBIT 1

	2009	% of total	2010	% of total	2011	% of total
			Year Ended December 31			
			(dollars in thousands)			
North America	$ 14,540	100.0%	$ 200,412	64.0%	$ 634,980	39.4%
International	—	—	112,529	36.0%	975,450	60.6%
Revenue	$ 14,540	100.0%	$ 312,941	100.0%	$ 1,610,430	100.0%

SOURCE: Groupon, Inc. *10-K* (March 30, 2012), p. 45.

EXHIBIT 2

Description of Use	Square Footage	Operating Segment	Location	Lease Expiration
Corporate office facilities	550,000	North America	Chicago, IL	From 2012 through 2018
Corporate office facilities	30,000	International	Berlin, Germany; Schaffhausen, Switzerland	From 2012 through 2022

SOURCE: Groupon, Inc. *10-K* (March 30, 2012), p. 33.

EXHIBIT 3

Size of sales force	Mar. 31, 2010	June 30, 2010	Sept. 30, 2010	Dec. 31, 2010	Mar. 31, 2011	June 30, 2011	Sept. 30, 2011	Dec. 31, 2011
North America	128	201	348	493	661	990	1,004	1,062
International	—	1,080	1,224	2,080	2,895	3,860	3,849	4,134
Total	128	1,291	1,572	2,573	3,556	4,850	4,853	5,196

SOURCE: Groupon, Inc. *10-K* (March 30, 2012), p. 8.

The size and geographic distribution of Groupon's sales force over time is shown in **Exhibit 3.** Considering Groupon's two-pronged dependence on subscribers and on merchants, many of whom were very small businesses, the company maintained high-touch relationships with its merchants. In addition to its sales team, Groupon employed customer service representatives, editorial staff, marketing planners, merchant research and services teams, and "city planners" who created the schedules for each Groupon city every week.[28]

The growth in Groupon's sales force reflected international operations that began in May 2010 with the acquisition of CityDeal Europe GmbH. CityDeal was founded by Oliver Samwer and Marc Samwer, who have served since the acquisition as consultants and been extensively involved in the development and operations of Groupon's international segment.[29]

Agreements under which Oliver and Marc Samwer provided consulting services were set to expire in October 2012 and October 2013, respectively.[30]

In January 2011, Groupon B.V., a subsidiary, entered into a joint venture along with Rocket Asia GmbH & Co. KG, an entity controlled by the Samwers.[31] Groupon B.V. became part owner of GaoPeng.com, which operates a group buying site offering discounts for products and services to individual consumers and businesses via Internet websites and social and interactive media.[32] GaoPeng.com began offering daily deals in Beijing and Shanghai in March 2011 and subsequently began offering daily deals in other major cities in China.[33]

Such acquisitions and joint ventures were an important part of Groupon's growth strategy. Groupon acquired eight firms in 2010, another nine in 2011, and an additional eight firms as of May 2012.[34]

Finance

Exhibits 4 and **5** show Groupon's consolidated statement of operations and consolidated balance sheet for the fiscal years ended 2008 through 2011.

EXHIBIT 4

Groupon, Inc. Consolidated Statement of Operations (In thousands, except share and per-share amounts)

	Year Ended December 31			
	2008	**2009**	**2010**	**2011**
	(dollars in thousands, except share data)			
Consolidated Statements of Operations Data:				
Revenue (gross billings of $94, $34,082, $745,348 and $3,985,501, respectively)	$ 5	$ 14,540	$ 312,941	$ 1,610,430
Costs and expenses:				
Cost of revenue	88	4,716	42,896	258,879
Marketing	163	5,053	290,569	768,472
Selling, general, and administrative	1,386	5,848	196,637	821,002
Acquisition-related	—	—	203,183	(4,537)
Total operating expenses	1,637	15,617	733,285	1,843,816
Loss from operations	(1,632)	(1,077)	(420,344)	(233,386)
Interest and other income (expense), net	90	(16)	284	5,973
Equity-method investment activity, net of tax	—	—	—	(26,652)
Loss before provision for income taxes	(1,542)	(1,093)	(420,060)	(254,065)
Provision (benefit) for income taxes	—	248	(6,674)	43,697
Net loss	(1,542)	(1,341)	(413,386)	(297,762)
Less: Net loss attributable to non-controlling interests	—	—	23,746	18,335
Net loss attributable to Groupon, Inc.	(1,542)	(1,341)	(389,640)	(279,427)
Dividends on preferred shares	(277)	(5,575)	(1,362)	—
Redemption of preferred stock in excess of carrying value	—	—	(52,893)	(34,327)
Adjustment of redeemable non-controlling interests to redemption value	—	—	(12,425)	(59,740)
Preferred stock distributions	(339)	—	—	—
Net loss attributable to common stockholders	$ (2,158)	$ (6,916)	$ (456,320)	$ (373,494)
Net loss per share of common stock				
Basic	$ (0.01)	$ (0.04)	$ (2.66)	$ (1.03)
Diluted	$ (0.01)	$ (0.04)	$ (2.66)	$ (1.03)
Weighted average number of shares outstanding				
Basic	333,476,258	337,208,284	342,698,772	362,261,324
Diluted	333,476,258	337,208,284	342,698,772	362,261,324

SOURCE: Groupon, Inc. *10-K* (March 30, 2012), p. 38.

For the years ended 2009, 2010, and 2011, Groupon reported revenue of US$14.5 million, US$312.9 million, and US$1.6 billion, respectively.[35] This represented an annual compound growth rate of 380%. From 2010 to 2011 specifically, revenue increased by US$1.3 billion. The company attributed this growth mainly to expanding the scale of its business both domestically and internationally through acquisitions, as well as by entering new markets. Initiatives that contributed to this expansion included an increase in marketing expenditures, as well as an increase in the company's sales force.[36]

Despite such significant revenue growth, operating income remained negative in 2011 (see **Exhibit 4).** Total operating expenses reached over US$1.8 billion in fiscal

EXHIBIT 5

Groupon, Inc. Consolidated Balance Sheets (In thousands, except share and per-share amounts)

	December 31	
	2010	2011
Assets		
Current assets:		
Cash and cash equivalents	$ 118,833	$ 1,122,935
Accounts receivable, net	42,407	108,747
Prepaid expenses and other current assets	12,615	91,645
Total current assets	173,855	1,323,327
Property and equipment, net	16,490	51,800
Goodwill	132,038	166,903
Intangible assets, net	40,775	45,667
Investments in equity interests	—	50,604
Deferred income taxes, non-current	14,544	46,104
Other non-current assets	3,868	90,071
Total assets	$ 381,570	$ 1,774,476
Liabilities and stockholders' equity		
Current liabilities:		
Accounts payable	$ 57,543	$ 40,918
Accrued merchant payable	162,409	520,723
Accrued expenses	98,323	212,007
Due to related parties	13,321	246
Deferred income taxes, current	17,210	76,841
Other current liabilities	21,613	144,427
Total current liabilities	370,419	995,162
Deferred income taxes, non-current	604	7,428
Other non-current liabilities	1,017	70,766
Total liabilities	372,040	1,073,356
Commitments and contingencies (see Note 8)		
Redeemable noncontrolling interests	2,983	1,653
Groupon, Inc. Stockholders' Equity		
Series D, convertible preferred stock, $.0001 par value, 6,560,174 shares authorized and issued, 6,258,297 shares outstanding at December 31, 2010, and no shares outstanding at December 31, 2011	1	—
Series F, convertible preferred stock, $.0001 par value, 4,202,658 shares authorized, issued, and outstanding at December 31, 2010, and no shares outstanding December 31, 2011	1	—
Series G, convertible preferred stock, $.0001 par value, 30,075,690 shares authorized, 14,245,018 shares issued and outstanding at December 31, 2010 and no shares outstanding at December 31, 2011, liquidation preference of $450,000 at December 31, 2010	1	—
Voting common stock, $.0001 par value, 1,000,000,000 shares authorized, 422,991,996 shares issued and 331,232,520 shares outstanding at December 31, 2010 and no shares outstanding at December 31, 2011	4	—
Class A common stock, par value $0.0001 per share, no shares authorized, issued, and outstanding at December 31, 2010; 2,000,000,000 shares authorized, 641,745,225 shares issued and outstanding at December 31, 2011	—	64

(continued)

EXHIBIT 5
(Continued)

	December 31	
	2010	**2011**
Treasury stock, at cost, 93,328,656 shares at December 31, 2010 and no shares outstanding at December 31, 2011	(503,173)	—
Additional paid-in capital	921,122	1,388,253
Stockholder receivable	(286)	—
Accumulated deficit	(419,468)	(698,704)
Accumulated other comprehensive income	9,875	12,928
Total Groupon, Inc. Stockholders' Equity	**8,077**	**702,541**
Noncontrolling interests	(1,530)	(3,074)
Total equity	**6,547**	**699,467**
Total liabilities and equity	**$ 381,570**	**$ 1,774,476**

SOURCE: Groupon, Inc. 10-K (March 30, 2012), p. 65.

year 2011, an increase of 151.4% from that of 2010. Groupon attributed this rise to an increase of US$216 million in the cost of revenue due to increases in credit card processing fees, refunds, and editorial salary costs. Higher volumes of merchant partner transactions and a larger subscriber base contributed to these costs.[37]

The company's greatest increases in operating expenses, however, were in marketing, selling, general, and administrative expenses. For the years ended December 31, 2009, 2010, and 2011, the company reported marketing expenses of US$5.1 million, US$290.6 million, and US$768.5 million, respectively.[38] In its annual report, Groupon made it clear that such increases in marketing expenses have been necessary, stating that "Since our inception, we have prioritized growth, and investments in our marketing initiatives have contributed to our losses."[39] Management viewed investments in marketing as a necessary cost to acquire subscribers. When compared to the profits generated from these subscribers over time, the cost to maintain a subscriber was relatively inexpensive, as interaction was largely limited to e-mails and mobile applications. As its business continued to grow and became established in more markets, Groupon expected that its marketing expense would decrease as a percentage of revenue.

Selling expenses reported in **Exhibit 4** consisted of "payroll and sales commissions for sales representatives, as well as costs associated with supporting the sales function such as technology, telecommunications, and travel."[40] For the years 2009, 2010, and 2011, total selling, general, and administrative expenses were reported at US$5.8 million, US$196.6 million, and US$821.0 million, respectively.[41] Groupon attributed these increases largely to the expansion of its global sales force as well as investments in technology and corporate infrastructure.[42] Like its marketing expense, Groupon expected that selling, general, and administrative expenses would decrease as a percentage of revenue as its operations matured over time.

The underlying concern regarding Groupon's financials was that the company realized a total net loss in income every year since its inception. For the years 2008 through 2011, these losses amounted to US$1.5 million, US$1.3 million, US$413.3 million, and US$297.7 million, respectively.[43] As shown in the statement of retained earnings in **Exhibit 6,** these losses led to an accumulated deficit of US$698.7 million in 2011. In this light, management decided not to pay dividends, intending instead "to retain all of our earnings for the foreseeable future to finance the operation and expansion of our business."[44]

In 2012, Groupon continued to see exceptional growth in revenues. **Exhibit 7** compares the results of operations from the quarter ended March 31, 2012 to the quarter

EXHIBIT 6
Consolidated Statement of Retained Earnings (thousands)

Report Date	12/31/2011	12/31/2010	12/31/2009	12/31/2008
Previous retained earnings (accumulated deficit)	(419,468)	(29,828)	(2,574)	(1,032)
Common stock dividends	—	—	20,338	—
Preferred stock dividends	—	—	5,575	—
Forfeiture of dividends	(191)	—	—	—
Retained earnings (accumulated deficit)	(698,704)	(419,468)	(29,828)	(2,574)

SOURCE: Mergent Online.

Exhibit 7
Groupon, Inc.
Condensed
Consolidated
Statements of
Operations (In
thousands, except
share and per-
share amounts)
(unaudited)

	Three Months Ended March 31	
	2011	2012
(Restated)		
Revenue (gross billings of $668, 174 and $1,354,800, respectively)	$ 295,523	$ 559,283
Costs and expenses:		
Cost of revenue	39,765	119,498
Marketing	230,085	116,615
Selling, general, and administrative	142,821	283,583
Acquisition-related	—	(52)
Total operating expenses	412,671	519,644
(Loss) income from operations	(117,148)	39,639
Interest and other income (expense), net	1,060	(3,539)
Equity-method investment activity, net of tax	(882)	(5,128)
(Loss) income before provision for income taxes	(116,970)	30,972
Provision (benefit) for income taxes	(3,079)	34,565
Net loss:	(113,891)	(3,593)
Less: Net loss (income) attributable to noncontrolling interests	11,223	(880)
Net loss attributable to Groupon, Inc.	(102,668)	(4,473)
Redemption of preferred stock in excess of carrying value	(34,327)	—
Adjustment of redeemable noncontrolling interests to redemption value	(9,485)	(7,222)
Net loss attributable to common stockholders	$ (146,480)	$ (11,695)
Net loss per share:		
Basic	$ (0.48)	$ (0.02)
Diluted	$ (0.48)	$ (0.02)
Weighted average number of shares outstanding:		
Basic	307,849,412	644,097,375
Diluted	307,849,412	644,097,375

SOURCE: Groupon, Inc. *10-Q* (May, 15, 2012), p. 5.

ended March 31, 2011. For the first quarter of 2012, the company reported revenues of US$559.3 million, compared to US$295.5 million for the first quarter of 2011.[45] Total operating expenses continue to rise in 2012, increasing by US$106.9 million from the first quarter of 2011, reflecting significant increases in cost of revenue and selling expenses. Groupon made strides toward cutting marketing spending in 2012, reporting US$116.6 million in marketing expenses compared to US$230.1 million in the first quarter of 2011. The company attributed this expense cut to a strengthening brand name that allowed it to become more established in markets around the globe. As of March 31, 2012, Groupon reported 36.8 million active customers, more than double the 15.3 million reported on March 31, 2011.[46] The amount of revenue that Groupon received per customer had not increased, however; revenue per average active customer was reported at US$72.41 on March 31, 2011, compared to US$71.77 on March 31, 2012.[47] Rather than adding revenue solely by acquiring more customers, Groupon was searching for ways to increase the amount of revenue it received per subscriber from its existing base.

"We Don't Measure Ourselves in Conventional Ways"

Investors and the Securities and Exchange Commission began to question management's reporting of Groupon's financials. Although Groupon disclosed all financial data required by the SEC, management stressed the importance of other, more unconventional metrics. The company, which said that it did not "measure [itself] in conventional ways," placed more importance on metrics such as adjusted consolidated segment operating income, free cash flow, and gross billings, rather than net income.[48] Groupon reported net losses in each of the past three years and believed that unique metrics better reflected its financial progress.

Groupon defined adjusted consolidated segment operating income (CSOI) as "the consolidated segment operating income before new subscriber acquisition costs and certain non-cash charges."[49] It believed that adjusted CSOI was an important measure of the performance of its business since adjusted CSOI excluded expenses that management believed were not indicative of future operating expenses. Free cash flow was defined as cash flow from operations reduced by "purchases of property and equipment"[50] and although the measure could be revealing, Groupon acknowledged that it was a non-GAAP financial measure. Gross billings, another proprietary metric, was the gross amount collected from customers for Groupons sold. Management viewed gross billings as a measurement of growth, but its use in revenue recognition was a source of controversy. Wall Street observers argued that Groupon's use of these non-GAAP measures was simply a strategy to portray its financials favorably in light of its lack of profitability.[51]

In 2011, Groupon had to restate its earnings for the three months ended March 31, 2011 "to correct for an error in its presentation of revenue."[52] Groupon historically reported its revenue as the gross amounts billed to its subscribers. The revision required revenue to be restated as the net of the amounts related to merchant fees. This error prompted the company to report a "material weakness" in its internal control over financial reporting.[53] The Condensed Statement of Operations shown in **Exhibit 8** for the three months ended March 31, 2011, was restated to show the net amount the company retained after paying merchant fees. Several other income statement expenses were changed as well to align with the reporting of revenue on a net basis.

Then, on March 30, 2012, the company announced that it would also have to restate earnings for the fourth quarter of 2011 after a higher-than-expected number of

Exhibit 8
Groupon, Inc.
Notes to Condensed
Consolidated Finan-
cial Statements for
the Three Months
Ended March 31,
2011, In Thousands
(Unaudited)

	As previously reported (unaudited)	Restatement adjustment	As restated
Revenue	$ 644,728	(349,205)	$ 295,523
Cost of revenue	$ 374,728	(334,963)	$ 39,765
Marketing	$ 208,209	21,876	$ 230,085
Selling, general, and administrative	$ 178,939	(36,118)	$ 142,821

SOURCE: Groupon, Inc. *10-Q* (May 15, 2012), p. 11.

customers demanded refunds.[54] Going forward, management planned to improve its internal controls for financial reporting. With significant errors and multiple financial restatements present in Groupon's first year as a publicly traded company, investors continued to question the company's disclosure methods and the reliability of its internal reports. Five federal class action securities complaints, and six federal and two state stockholder derivative lawsuits had been brought against Groupon and its current and former directors and officers since the restatement.[55] The addition of new members of the Board of Directors with accounting and financial expertise was considered necessary to regain investor confidence.[56]

Information Technology

Groupon did not equivocate regarding technology's importance to its operations and business strategy:

> We employ technology to improve the experience we offer subscribers and merchant partners, increase the rate at which our customers purchase Groupons, and enhance the efficiency of our business operations. A component of our strategy is to continue developing and refining our technology.[57]

Almost all of the company's communication with both customers and merchant partners was electronic. It was important for Groupon to adopt an information system that would facilitate efficient communication with both merchants and customers. Groupon used a common information technology platform that enhanced communication while also providing management and merchant partners the ability to track deal performance and analytics for demographic data and capacity. The platform included business operations tools to track internal workflow; applications and infrastructure to serve content at scale; dashboards and reporting tools to display operating and financial metrics for historical and ongoing deals; and a publishing and purchasing system for consumers.[58] Groupon used the platform only in North American operations in 2012, but management planned to merge the system with the company's more segmented international information technology platforms. While there was no timetable in place for this move, Groupon reported that it planned to "enable greater efficiencies and consistency across [its] global organization."[59]

Information system platforms, as well as websites, applications, and back-end business intelligence systems were hosted at data centers in Florida, Texas, California, and overseas in Asia and Europe. For security purposes, Groupon used commercial antivirus, firewall, and patch-management technologies to protect and maintain systems located at the data centers. To ensure the security of its website as well as customer transactions, Groupon also invested in intrusion and pattern detection tools, as well as Secure Socket Layer (SSL) to provide encryption for transferring data. These security measures were easily scalable to accommodate increasing numbers of subscribers.[60]

Marketing

Since the company's founding, marketing had been at the core of Groupon's business strategy. Management's aggressive marketing efforts fueled revenue approaching US$2 billion in three years of existence. A first mover in the daily deal industry, Groupon owned number-one market share in 37 of 48 countries served as of the first quarter of 2012.[61] Specifically in North America, Groupon held 53% market share, as of the second quarter of 2012.[62]

Critical to Groupon's strategy was growing its subscriber and customer base. As stated earlier, the vast majority of its investments to fuel this growth were through online marketing initiatives: search engine marketing, display advertisements, referral programs, and affiliate marketing.[63] Groupon also marketed to merchant partners to grow the number and variety of deals it could offer customers. To further increase merchant partner growth, Groupon utilized a sales force of over 5000 inside and outside representatives. The sales force was responsible for building partner relationships as well as providing local expertise.

The company focused the majority of its marketing efforts on demographics most likely to use a Groupon: relatively young consumers more prone to search for discounts when shopping and most likely to use the Internet or mobile applications to do so. According to Morpace Inc., the majority of Groupon's customers (40.2%) were between the ages of 18 and 34,[64] and although women were historically more likely to purchase online coupons, men and women had been found almost equally likely to use Groupon deals. As with all coupon users, Groupon users had higher income.[65]

Groupon's attempt to participate in national television ads during the 2011 Super Bowl was widely criticized. A series of ads meant to "spoof" typical celebrity-endorsed public service announcements fell flat and many found the ads offensive.[66] Groupon dropped the ads and ultimately stopped working with the advertising agency that created the spots.[67]

Groupon's investments in marketing were substantial. Marketing expenses were largely variable, increasing significantly as revenues grew. For the years ended 2008 through 2011, marketing expenses were reported at US$163 thousand, US$5.05 million, US$290.57 million, and US$768.47 million, respectively (see **Exhibit 4).**

Distribution The distribution of Groupon's deals relied heavily on technology. Deals were distributed to customers directly through daily e-mails, websites, and mobile applications, as well as through social networks. In an effort to reach more potential customers, Groupon also utilized various online affiliates to display and promote deals on their websites. The company's "online affiliates" included eBay, Microsoft, Yahoo, and Zynga.[68] Partnerships allowed for the distribution of daily deals to not only Groupon's customer base, but also to the affiliate's user base. Groupon also partnered with thousands of smaller online affiliates that could embed a Groupon widget on their websites and earn a commission whenever their site's visitors purchased Groupons through the link.[69] Management believed that leveraging affiliate relationships online in this manner would extend the distribution of Groupon deals to a larger customer base.

In an effort to attract more customers and to ease communication with existing customers, Groupon launched a mobile application in March 2010. Deals were offered at no additional cost on the iPhone, Android, BlackBerry, and Windows mobile operating systems. The applications allowed consumers to "browse, purchase, manage and redeem deals on their mobile devices as well as access Groupon Now! Deals that were offered based on the location of the mobile user."[70] In this way, the mobile applications promoted immediate deals based on the customer's desire and location. As of December 31, 2011, the Groupon App had been downloaded over 26 million times.[71]

Groupon began targeting online social networks as another possible distribution channel. Daily deals were published through various social networks, while website and mobile application interfaces also allowed consumers to push notifications of deals to their personal social network. Groupon acknowledged that social networks were not yet a "material portion of customer acquisition."[72]

Products   Founded strictly as a daily deals service, Groupon historically did not offer much variety in terms of deal categories. As its operations grew, however, Groupon made an effort to transition "from offering deals only through email to having a local commerce marketplace where customers can purchase Groupons for a variety of services and products from local, national and online merchants."[73] In 2012, Groupon offered the following types of deals:[74]

- *Featured Daily Deals* were distributed by targeting technology to current and potential customers based on location and personal preferences. Daily deals were sent to subscribers through mass e-mails and posted on the website and mobile application. This product was launched in October 2008 and was offered in all North American and International markets.

- Groupon's primary focus was on local deals, but the company also offered *National Deals* from national merchants to build brand awareness and acquire new customers in the North American market. It featured deals from over 100 national merchant partners, including Domino's Pizza, Sony Electronics, and The Body Shop.

- *Groupon Now!* deals were initiated by a merchant on demand and offered instantly to customers through mobile devices and the Groupon website. These deals targeted current and potential customers within close proximity of the merchant, and the purchased Groupons typically expired within a few hours of the deal launch. This product was launched in the second quarter of 2011.

- *Groupon Goods* enabled customers to purchase vouchers for products directly from the website or mobile application. Deals were offered for a variety of product categories, including electronics, home and garden, and toys. This product was launched in September 2011 in select North American and International markets.

- *Groupon Getaways* are travel deals that feature domestic and international hotels, airfare, and package deals. Groupon Getaways was launched in July 2011.

- *GrouponLive* is a partnership with LiveNation whereby Groupon serves as a local resource for LiveNation events and clients of its global ticketing business, Ticketmaster. GrouponLive is offered as part of the featured daily deals and was launched in May 2011.

- *Groupon Rewards,* a free service to merchant partners that allowed customers to earn reward points through repeat visits that could be used to unlock special deals, were launched in October 2011.

Competition

Groupon rose to prominence in uncertain economic conditions—during the Great Recession and its slow recovery. Consumers began spending less as a result of the financial crisis, and so the demand for coupons increased. At the same time, merchants began looking for new and effective ways of attracting business. This combination could explain why Groupon might owe some of its unprecedented growth to the economic environment into which it was born, but it also explained the more recent blitz of competition Groupon has faced.

Andrew Mason's idea to apply the tipping point principle to online commerce and facilitate the leveraging of consumers' collective power was innovative and established Groupon as a first mover in the daily deals segment. The ease with which the business model could be replicated, however—in concert with the strong demand for discounts—ensured that Groupon would not be the only company competing for market share.

Groupon's competition was fairly broad; the company competed with traditional offline coupon and discount services, as well as newspapers, magazines, and other traditional media companies that provided coupons and discounts on products and services.[75] The most intense competition was with companies utilizing the online daily deals business model—to whatever extent and with whatever focus. Some such competitors offered deals as an add-on to their core business, while others adopted a business model similar to Groupon's.[76] These included GiltCity, DailyDeals.com, Bloomspot, and Eversave. Competition also existed in more narrowly positioned companies that offered services more focused on particular merchant categories or markets. They included Daily Pride, for the Lesbian, Gay, Bisexual, and Transgendered community; Jewpon, for the Jewish community; My Pet Savings, for pet owners; and Group-Price, for online businesses, among others.

Groupon's most directly matched competitor was LivingSocial, a Washington DC, daily-deals website that operated a similar e-mail-based business model. As of December 2011, LivingSocial had about 46 million subscribers spread across 25 countries.[77] The company's deal categories, somewhat more expansive than Groupon's, included nationwide deals and deals for families, escapes, and adventures.[78] LivingSocial, a private company valued in 2010 at US$200 million, was valued in 2011 at US$3 billion after rounds of investing that included funding from the likes of Amazon.com.[79]

Amazon operated its own daily-deals service in addition to its ties to LivingSocial. AmazonLocal launched in mid-2011 and offered customers savings from select businesses in their neighborhoods and nationwide.[80] Around the same time, Google—after its offer to acquire Groupon was rejected in late 2010—began testing its own service, Google Offers.[81] Both Google Offers and AmazonLocal had extensive, available resources from their established and wealthy parent companies, and both Amazon and Google typified the competitors that Groupon expressed concern about in its annual report:

> Many of our current and potential competitors have longer operating histories, significantly greater financial, technical, marketing, and other resources, and larger customer bases than we do. These factors may allow our competitors to benefit from their existing customer base with lower acquisition costs or to respond more quickly than we can to new or emerging technologies and changes in customer requirements. These competitors may engage in more extensive research and development efforts, undertake more far-reaching marketing campaigns and adopt more aggressive pricing policies, which may allow them to build a larger subscriber base or to monetize that subscriber base more effectively than we do. Our competitors may develop products or services that are similar to our products and services or that achieve greater market acceptance than our products and services.[82]

Legal Issues[83]

Regulation   Groupon was subject to a variety of regulations across the jurisdictions where it conducted its business, including, for example, consumer protection, marketing practices, tax and privacy rules, and regulations. Additional areas of concern included the evolving regulation of Internet business, the Credit Card Responsibility and Disclosure (CARD) Act of 2009, gift certificates/cards, disclosure of security breaches of personal data, and liability under the Digital Millennium Copyright Act (DMCA) for linking to third-party websites that include materials that infringe copyrights or other rights.[84] Some of Groupon's merchants raised concerns within their own industries about the appearance of fee-splitting, kickbacks for referrals, and the ethics of using Groupons and other daily deals for health services and the purchase of alcohol.[85,86]

Litigation   As described earlier, Groupon and its current and former directors and officers faced numerous class action lawsuits following its restatement of earnings in 2012. Groupon was also involved in, and at risk of, litigation concerning intellectual property infringement suits and suits by customers (individually or as class actions) alleging, among other things, violation of the Credit Card Accountability, Responsibility and Disclosure Act and state laws governing gift cards, stored value cards, and coupons. The company believed that additional lawsuits alleging that Groupon had violated patent, copyright, or trademark laws would be filed against it.

Looking to the Future

As Groupon continued to grow over the past year, it reported a net loss of only US$3.6 million in the first quarter of 2012, compared to US$113.9 million for that of 2011.[87] Marketing expenses were coming under control. The number of subscribers and merchants continued to grow, and promising new products were being pilot tested in specific markets. The company's prospects looked brighter in 2012 than in years past, but it had yet to record a profit. The question remained whether or not Andrew Mason's Groupon could do so in the future.

NOTES

1. Herb Greenberg, "The Worst CEO for 2012?" *Market Insider, CNBC*. April 12, 2012. http://www.cnbc.com/id/47030593 (last visited August 20, 2012).
2. The Amazing Rise (and Inevitable Fall?) of Groupon. *Online MBA*. http://www.onlinemba.com/the-amazing-rise-of-groupon/ (last visited July 16, 2012).
3. Ibid.
4. Leah Goldman and Alyson Shontell, "Groupon: From The Ashes Of a Dead Startup to a Billion-Dollar Company In 2 Years." *Business Insider*. June 4, 2011.
5. Ibid.
6. Ibid.
7. Bari Weiss, "Groupon's $6 Billion Gambler." *The Wall Street Journal*. December 20, 2010.
8. The Amazing Rise (and Inevitable Fall?) of Groupon.
9. Ibid.
10. Christopher Steiner, "Meet the Fastest Growing Company Ever." *Forbes*. August 30, 2010.
11. Evelyn M. Rusli and Jenna Wortham. "Groupon Said to Reject Google's Offer." *The New York Times, DealBook*. December 3, 2010.
12. Alistair Barr and Clare Baldwin. "Groupon's IPO Biggest by U.S. Web Company since Google." *Reuters*. November 4, 2011.

13. Groupon, Inc. *10-K* (March 30, 2012), p. 3.
14. Ibid.
15. Ibid., p. 6.
16. Ibid.
17. Ibid.
18. Christopher Steiner, "Meet the Fastest Growing Company Ever."
19. Sarah E. Needleman and Shayndi Raice. "Groupon Holds Cash Tight." *The Wall Street Journal.* November 10, 2011.
20. Ari Levy. "Groupon Declines on Concern that Merchants Are Retreating from Daily Deals." *Bloomberg Businessweek.* January 3, 2012.
21. Ibid.
22. Andrew Mason. Groupon, Inc. 2011 Letter to Stockholders. p. 1.
23. Groupon, Inc. *10-K* (March 30, 2012), p. 7–8. This section was quoted directly with minor editing.
24. Groupon, Inc. Investor Relations, http://investor.groupon.com/directors.cfm, (last visited July 15, 2012). This section was quoted directly with minor editing.
25. Brian Womack, "Groupon Bolsters Board with AmEx's Henry, Deloitte's Bass." *Bloomberg Businessweek.* May 1, 2012. http://www.bloomberg.com/news/2012-04-30/groupon-adds-amex-s-henry-deloitte-s-bass-to-bolster-board-1-.html.
26. Groupon, Inc. *10-K* (March 30, 2012), p. 14. This section was quoted directly with minor editing.
27. Groupon, Inc. *10-Q* (May 15, 2012), p. 40.
28. Groupon, Inc. "Meet the Team, Merchant Resources." http://www.grouponworks.com/merchant-resources/meet-the-team (last visited August 25, 2012).
29. Groupon, Inc. *10-K* (March 30, 2012), p. 21.
30. Ibid.
31. Ibid., p. 101.
32. Groupon, Inc. 2012 Proxy Statement (June 19, 2012), p. 13.
33. Ibid.
34. Privco. Groupon Inc. Report on Groupon complied by Privco. March 2012. http://www.privco.com/private-company/groupon-inc.
35. Groupon, Inc. *10-K* (March 30, 2012), p. 38.
36. Ibid., p. 45.
37. Ibid., p. 46.
38. Ibid., p. 44.
39. Ibid., p. 8.
40. Ibid., p. 74.
41. Ibid., p. 44.
42. Ibid., p. 48
43. Mergent Inc., *Mergent Online.* http://www.mergentonline.com.
44. Groupon, Inc. *10-K* (March 30, 2012), p. 31.
45. Groupon, Inc. *10-Q* (May 15, 2012), p. 5.
46. Ibid., p. 25.
47. Ibid.
48. Groupon, Inc. *S-1* (June 2, 2011), p. 1.
49. Ibid., p. 9.
50. Groupon, Inc. *10-K* (March 30, 2012), p. 41.
51. Marielle Segarra. "Groupon CFO Defends Use of Non-GAAP Measures." CFO.com, February 10, 2012. http://www3.cfo.com/article/2012/2/accounting-tax_groupon-cfo-jason-child-defends-non-gaap-metrics.
52. Groupon, Inc. *10-Q* (May, 15, 2012), p. 10.
53. Ibid., p. 15.
54. Shayndi Raice and John Letzing, "Groupon Forced to Revise Results." *The Wall Street Journal.* April 2, 2012.
55. Groupon, Inc. *10-Q* (August 14, 2012), p. 16.
56. Douglas MacMillan, "Groupon Is Said to Seek New Directors After Restatement." Bloomberg Businessweek, April 24, 2012. http://www.bloomberg.com/news/2012-04-24/groupon-is-said-to-seek-new-directors-after-revenue-restatement.html.
57. Groupon, Inc. *10-K* (March 30, 2012), p. 11.
58. Ibid.
59. Ibid.
60. Ibid.
61. Groupon, Inc. Investor Presentation. June 2012.
62. Douglas MacMillan, "Groupon Loses Market Share as Online Daily Deals Decline." *Bloomberg Businessweek,* August 15, 2012. http://www.businessweek.com/news/2012-08-15/groupon-loses-market-share-as-online-daily-deals-decline.
63. Groupon, Inc. *10-K* (March 30, 2012), p. 8.
64. eMarketer, "Groupon and the Online Deal Revolution." *eMarketer,* June 7, 2011.
65. Ibid.
66. Philip Caulfield. "Groupon Super Bowl Ad Falls Flat; Slammed for Making Fun of China-Tibet Conflict." New York Daily News. February 7, 2011. http://articles.nydailynews.com/2011-02-07/entertainment/28536983_1_groupon-ceo-andrew-mason-tibetans-ads-and-one.
67. Rupal Parekh. "Groupon CEO: We Placed Too Much Trust in Agency for Super Bowl Ads." *Advertising Age.* March 21, 2011. http://adage.com/article/news/groupon-ceo-relied-agency-bowl-ads/149498/.
68. Groupon, Inc. *10-K* (March 30, 2012), p. 8.
69. Ibid., p. 10.
70. Ibid.
71. Ibid.
72. Ibid.
73. Ibid., p. 9.
74. Ibid. This section was quoted directly with minor editing.
75. Ibid., p. 11
76. Ibid.
77. Evelyn M. Rusli. "LivingSocial Looks to Raise $400 Million." *The New York Times, DealBook.* December 7, 2011.
78. LivingSocial, home page. www.LivingSocial.com.
79. Thomas Heath and Steven Overly. "LivingSocial, Based in D.C., Raises $400 Million as It Vies with Groupon." *The Washington Post.* April 5, 2011.
80. "Growing Up Fast: AmazonLocal Celebrates First Birthday with Sweepstakes." *The New York Times.* June 1, 2012.
81. Miguel Helft. "Google vs. Groupon." *The New York Times, Bits Blog.* June 1, 2011.
82. Groupon, Inc. 10-K (March 30, 2012), p. 12.
83. Ibid., p. 82.
84. Ibid., p. 12.
85. Kelly Soderlund. "Dental Groupons, Incentives." *ADA News,* November 21, 2011. http://www.ada.org/news/6576.aspx
86. Donna Goodison. "State: Groupon, Online Discounters Can't Offer Alcohol Deals." *Boston Herald.com,* March 14, 2011. http://bostonherald.com/jobfind/news/technology/view/2011_0314massachusetts_groupon_online_discounters_cant_offer_happy_hour_alcohol_deals_state_groupon_online_discounters_cant_offer_alcohol_deals
87. Groupon, Inc. *10-Q* (May, 15, 2012), p. 5.

CASE **15**

Netflix, Inc.

THE 2011 REBRANDING/PRICE INCREASE DEBACLE

Alan N. Hoffman
Bentley University

In 2011, Netflix was the world's largest online movie rental service. Its subscribers paid to have DVDs delivered to their homes through the U.S. mail, or to access and watch unlimited TV shows and movies streamed over the Internet to their TVs, mobile devices, or computers. The company was founded by Marc Randolph and Reed Hastings in August, 1997 in Scotts Valley, California, after they had left Pure Software. Hastings was inspired to start Netflix after being charged US$40 for an overdue video.[1] Initially, Netflix provided movies at US$6 per rental, but moved to a monthly subscription rate in 1999, dropping the single-rental model soon after. From then on, the company built its reputation on the business model of flat fee unlimited rentals per month without any late fees, or shipping and handling fees.

In May 2002, Netflix went public with a successful IPO, selling 5.5 million shares of common stock at the IPO price of US$15 per share to raise US$82.5 million. After incurring substantial losses during its first few years of operations, Netflix turned a profit of US$6.5 million during the fiscal year 2003.[2] The company's subscriber base grew strongly and steadily from 1 million in the fourth quarter of 2002 to over 27 million in July 2012.[3]

By 2012, Netflix had over 100,000 titles distributed via more than 50 shipment centers, insuring customers received their DVDs in one to two business days, which made Netflix one of the most successful dotcom ventures in the past two decades.[4] The company employed almost 4100 people, 2200 of whom were part-time employees.[5] In September 2010, Netflix began international operations by offering an unlimited streaming plan without DVDs in Canada. In September 2011, Netflix expanded its international operations to customers in the Caribbean, Mexico, and Central and South America.

Key to Netflix's success was its no late fee policy. Netflix's profits were directly proportional to the number of days the customer kept a DVD. Most customers wanted to view a new DVD release as soon as possible. If Netflix imposed a late fee, it would

The authors would like to thank Barbara Gottfried, Ashna Dhawan, Emira Ajeti, Neel Bhalaria, Tarun Chugh, and Will Hoffman for their research and contributions to this case. Please address all correspondence to: Dr. Alan N. Hoffman, Dept. of Management, Bentley University, 175 Forest Street, Waltham, MA 02452-4705, voice (781) 891-2287, ahoffman@ bentley.edu. Printed by permission of Alan N. Hoffman.

have to have multiple copies of the new releases and find a way to remain profitable. However, because of the no-late-fee rule, the demand for the newer movies was spread over a period of time, ensuring an efficient circulation of movies.[6]

On September 18, 2011, Netflix CEO and co-founder Reed Hastings announced on the Netflix blog that the company was splitting its DVD delivery service from its online streaming service, rebranding its DVD delivery service Qwikster as a way to differentiate it from its online streaming service, and creating a new website for it. Three weeks later, in response to customer outrage and confusion, Hastings rescinded rebranding the DVD delivery service Qwikster and reintegrating it into Netflix. Nevertheless, by October 24, 2011, only five weeks after the initial split, Netflix acknowledged that it had lost 800,000 U.S. subscribers and expected to lose yet more, thanks both to the Qwikster debacle and the price hike the company had decided was necessary to cover increasing content costs.[7]

Despite this setback, Netflix continued to believe that by providing the cheapest and best subscription-paid, commercial-free streaming of movies and TV shows it could still rapidly and profitably fulfill its envisioned goal to become the world's best entertainment distribution platform.

Online Streaming

By the end of 2011, Netflix had 24.4 million subscribers, making it the largest provider of online streaming content in the world.[8] Subscription numbers had grown exponentially, increasing 250% from 9.3 million in 2008. At the same time, Netflix proactively recognized that the demand for DVDs by mail had peaked, and the future growth would be in online streaming. With 245 million Internet users in the United States, and 2.2 billion[9] worldwide, Netflix saw the opportunity to expand its online streaming base both domestically and internationally to become a dominant world player. In 2011, Netflix expanded into Canada and Central America, and in 2012 into Ireland and the United Kingdom.[10]

The scarce resource for the online video industry was bandwidth, the amount of data that can be carried from one point to another in a given time period.[11] With the introduction of Blu-ray discs, the demand for higher- and better-quality picture and sound streaming increased, which in turn increased the demand for higher bandwidths. At the same time, cheaper Internet connections and faster download speeds made it easier and more affordable for customers to take advantage of the services Netflix and its competitors offered. If the cost of Internet access was to increase, it would directly affect sales in the industry's streaming segment.

Netflix was a leader in developing streaming technologies, increasing its spending on technology and development from US$114 million (2009) to US$258 million in 2011[12] (8% of its revenue),[13] and initiating a US$1 million five-year prize in to improve the existing algorithm of Netflix's recommendation service by at least 10%. Because Netflix had already developed proprietary streaming software and an extensive content library, it had a head start in the online streaming market, and with continued investments in technological enhancements, hoped to maintain its lead.[14] However, increased competition in streaming, ISP fair-use charges, and piracy were some of the major challenges it faced.

In March 2011, Netflix made its services readily available to consumers through Smart-phones, tablets and video game consoles when only 35% of the total U.S. market were using Internet-enabled Smartphones.[15] Thus, the expansion potential for Netflix in this market was substantial. The Great Recession of 2008–2010 was a boon for Netflix as people cut down on high-value discretionary spending, choosing "value for money" Internet offerings instead.[16] However, in its annual letter to shareholders, Netflix acknowledged that many of its customers were among the highest users of data on an ISPs network and in the near future it expected that such users might be forced to pay extra for their data usage, which could be a major deterrent for the growth of Netflix because most of its customers are highly price sensitive.

Demographics

The number of Internet users in the United States had increased from about 205 million in 2005 to 245 million in 2012.[17] According to a research report by Mintel investment research database, the percentage of people using the Internet to stream video has jumped from 5% (2005) to 17% (2011), significantly growing the market for online streaming services such as Netflix. At the same time, the recession of 2008–2010, with its high unemployment and slow economic growth had a significant impact on the spending habits of U.S. consumers. More and more people chose to forego an evening at the movie theatre in favor of home movie rentals to save on costs.[18] By 2011, the crucial 18- to 34-year-old demographic saw the Internet as its prime source of access to entertainment. However, this demographic, was particularly sensitive to price fluctuations. When Netflix changed its pricing structure in the third quarter of 2011, subscriptions immediately dropped off 3%. Mintel Research reported that only 15% of the under 18–25 age bracket of its customers were ready to pay US$16/month for premium content via Netflix. In addition, the proliferation of free content over the Internet—Mega video, for example, with around 81 million unique visitors and a maximum exposure in the 18–33 demographic became a strong competitor for Netflix, further limiting the pricing power Netflix could exercise.[19]

The Mintel report also found that American households with two or more children and a household income of US$50,000 or more had a very favorable attitude toward Netflix;[20] Netflix fostered this trend by cutting a deal with Disney[21] that gave it access to content exclusively targeting young children.

At the same time that Netflix was increasing its customer base among the 18- to 34-year-olds and households with young children, both of whom preferred streaming, it lost ground with affluent Baby Boomers who still preferred to rent the DVDs over the Internet. Thus, Netflix needed to fine-tune its strategy to include this older demographic since people over 60 had US$1 trillion in discretionary income per year, and fewer familial responsibilities, making them a prime target demographic for expanding Netflix's customer base.[22]

The availability of high-speed Internet at home and the shift to online TVs created opportunities for Netflix. The company recognized that to fully leverage the current world of technological convergence, it needed to compete on as many platforms as possible, and created applications for the Xbox, Wii, PS3, iPad, Apple TV, Windows phone, and Android. The company also collaborated with TV manufacturers to integrate Netflix directly into the latest televisions.[23]

Netflix's Competitors

Netflix's great operational advantage in the DVD rental market was its nationwide distribution network, which prevented the entry of many of its potential competitors. While only Netflix provided both mail delivery and online rentals, with the growth of online streaming, Netflix's advantage shrank and it faced increasing competition from Blockbuster, Wal-Mart, Amazon, Hulu, and Redbox.

Netflix's one-time strongest competitor, **Blockbuster** LLC, founded in 1985, and headquartered in McKinney, Texas, provided in-home movie and game entertainment, originally through over 5000 video rental stores throughout the Americas, Europe,

Asia, and Australia, and later by adding DVD-by-mail, streaming video on demand, and kiosks. Its business model emphasized providing convenient access to media entertainment across multiple channels, recognizing that the same customer might choose different ways to access media entertainment on different nights. Competition from Netflix and other video rental companies forced Blockbuster to file for bankruptcy on September 23, 2010, and on April 6, 2011, satellite television provider Dish Network bought it at auction for US$233 million.[24]

Redbox Automated Retail, LLC, a wholly owned subsidiary of Coinstar Inc., specialized in DVD, Blu-ray, and rentals via automated retail kiosks. By June 2011, Redbox had over 33,000 kiosks in over 27,800 locations worldwide,[25] and was considering launching an online streaming service, perhaps for as cheaply as US$3.95 per month.

Vudu, Inc., formerly known as Marquee, Inc., founded in 2004, a content delivery media technology company acquired by **Wal-Mart** in March 2010, worked by allowing users to stream movies and TV shows to Sony PlayStation3, Blu-ray players, HDTVs, computers, or home theaters. VUDU Box and VUDU XL provided access to movies and television shows; users also needed a VUDU Wireless Kit to connect VUDU Box/VUDU XL to the Internet. Based in Santa Clara, California, the company was the third most popular online movie service, with a market share of 5.3%.[26] Vudu had no monthly subscription fee, instead users deposited funds to an online account which was reduced depending on how many movies the user rented. In other words, you paid for only what you watched.

In February 2011, Amazon.com, a multinational electronic commerce company, announced the launch for Amazon Prime members of unlimited, commercial-free instant streaming of all movies and TV shows to members' computers or HDTVs. In addition, Amazon Prime members were given access to the Kindle Owners' Lending Library, allowing them to borrow selected popular titles for free with no due date. For non-Amazon Prime members, 48-hour on-demand rentals were available for US$3.99, or the title could be bought outright.[27]

Hulu Plus was the first ad-supported subscription service for TV shows and films that could be accessed by computers, television sets, mobile phone, or other digital devices. Like Netflix, the streaming service cost US$8 per month, but unlike Netflix, Hulu offered more recent TV episodes and seasons. However, subscribers had to put up with ads, and Hulu's movie selection was much more limited than Netflix's selection.

Marc Schuh, an early financial backer of Netflix, observed that copying software was relatively simple.[28] Anyone could buy the best servers, processors, operating systems, and databases—but timing was crucial.[29] Barnes & Noble waited 17 months to enter the fray against Amazon, so that by 2012, Amazon had eight times the profit and 30 times the market capitalization of Barnes & Noble. Similarly, in the same year that Netflix's profits increased sevenfold, Blockbuster lost over 1 billion dollars.[30] Technology with correct timings can help a company gain competitive advantage over rivals. Other barriers to entry include investments in infrastructure aiding supply chain and delays from major production houses for gaining permission to stream their titles.

Rising Content Costs

In the DVD rental business, the rental company had the first sale doctrine, in which the company was permitted to rent a single disc many times to recover the cost of the content. But this doctrine did not apply to digital content, and the technological shift away from the DVD rental business was in part responsible for the excessive increase in content cost for Netflix.[31]

In addition, Netflix's dependence on outside content suppliers such as the six major movie studios and the top television networks contributed significantly to rising costs for the company. As an example, Liberty Media Corporation's Starz LLC had been an early Netflix supplier. In 2011, Starz demanded US$300 million to renew its deal with Netflix, testament to the power of suppliers in relation to market demand from an increasing number of competitors. On September 1, 2011, Netflix customers learned they would lose access to newer films from the Walt Disney Company and the Sony Corporation after talks to obtain those movies from Starz broke down. The loss created the impression of a major setback, even though the films were making up a smaller share of viewing than previously.

However, Netflix did sign new deals with the CW Network, DreamWorks Animation, and Discovery Communications in 2011.

Global Expansion

Beginning in 2007, Netflix shifted its focus to its streaming business in response to their customers' move to streaming in preference to DVD rentals and the rising cost of mailing DVDs. Conveniently, expanding its streaming business did not require expanding its physical infrastructure. This strategy has proven to be a major differentiator as it expands internationally in the Americas and Europe.

By the end of 2011, the company had started operations in Canada and 43 countries in Latin America, and planned to start European operations in early 2012. At the end of the third quarter of 2011, Netflix had 1.48 million international subscribers with predictions of 2 million by the end of the year.[32] The United Kingdom was considered a huge potential market. Twenty million UK households had broadband Internet, and 60% of those households subscribed to a paid movie service. In Latin America, four times that number had Internet access,[33] making international expansion there especially attractive to subscriber-hungry Netflix.

However, international expansion was potentially risky, as Netflix faced rising content costs from higher studio charges. In addition, international expansion required both broadening its content offerings and tailoring those offerings to meet the specific needs of each of its international markets, which Netflix feared would further increase content costs. It was clear that the correct content mix was crucial, yet a huge challenge for Netflix.

In addition, as Canada and the United Kingdom were already developed markets, Netflix faced local competition from a proliferation of DVD rental/streaming services. In the United Kingdom, for instance, Virgin and Sky already had strong brand recognition and balance sheets, and the Sky network had already contracted exclusive first-pay window rights to movies from all six major American studios, tough competition that could easily delay profitability from international operations.

Lower per capita income and slower Internet speeds, especially in Latin America, were further potential problems for Netflix's international expansion. In Canada, low data usage limits per subscriber were a concern for a data hungry service such as Netflix.

Financial Results

In 2011, Netflix surpassed US$3.2 billion in sales, an annual revenue growth of 50% over 2010 (US$2.1 billion, see **Exhibits 1–3**). Subscriber growth was the most important metric for Netflix because its revenue growth was directly correlated to its subscriber growth. Netflix grew from 12 million subscribers in 2009 to 20 million in 2010, and then to 27 million in 2012. International operations were set to expand to become a major source of sales growth for the company in the coming years.

	Year ended December 31		
	2011	**2010**	**2009**
Revenues	$3,204,577	$2,162,625	$1,670,269
Cost of revenues:			
Subscription	1,789,596	1,154,109	909,461
Fulfillment expenses	250,305	203,246	169,810
Total cost of revenues	2,039,901	1,357,355	1,079,271
Gross profit	1,164,676	805,270	590,998
Operating expenses:			
Marketing	402,638	293,839	237,744
Technology and development	259,033	163,329	114,542
General and administrative	117,937	64,461	46,773
Legal settlement	9,000	—	—
Total operating expenses	788,608	521,629	399,059
Operating income	376,068	283,641	191,939
Other income (expense):			
Interest expense	(20,025)	(19,629)	(6,475)
Interest and other income	3,479	3,684	6,728
Income before income taxes	359,522	267,696	192,192
Provision for income taxes	133,396	106,843	76,332
Net income	$226,126	$160,853	$115,860
Net income per share:			
Basic	$4.28	$3.06	$2.05
Diluted	$4.16	$2.96	$1.98
Weighted-average common shares outstanding:			
Basic	52,847	52,529	56,560
Diluted	54,369	54,304	58,416

	As of December 31	
	2011	**2010**
Assets		
Current assets:		
Cash and cash equivalents	$508,053	$194,499
Short-term investments	289,758	155,888
Current content library, net	919,709	181,006
Prepaid content	56,007	62,217
Other current assets	57,330	43,621
Total current assets	1,830,857	637,231
Non-current content library, net	1,046,934	180,973
Property and equipment, net	136,353	128,570
Other non-current assets	55,052	35,293
Total assets	$3,069,196	$982,067

EXHIBIT 2
(Continued)

	As of December 31	
	2011	**2010**
Liabilities and stockholders' equity		
Current liabilities:		
Content accounts payable	$924,706	$168,695
Other accounts payable	87,860	54,129
Accrued expenses	63,693	38,572
Deferred revenue	148,796	127,183
Total current liabilities	1,225,055	388,579
Long-term debt	200,000	200,000
Long-term debt due to related party	200,000	—
Non-current content liabilities	739,628	48,179
Other non-current liabilities	61,703	55,145
Total liabilities	2,426,386	691,903
Commitments and contingencies (Note 5)		
Stockholders' equity:		
Preferred stock, $0.001 par value; 10,000,000 shares authorized at December 31, 2011 and 2010; no shares issued and outstanding at December 31, 2011 and 2010	—	—
Common stock, $0.001 par value; 160,000,000 shares authorized at December 31, 2011 and 2010; 55,398,615 and 52,781,949 issued and outstanding at December 31, 2011 and 2010, respectively	55	53
Additional paid-in capital	219,119	51,622
Accumulated other comprehensive income	706	750
Retained earnings	422,930	237,739
Total stockholders' equity	642,810	290,164
Total liabilities and stockholders' equity	$3,069,196	$982,067

EXHIBIT 3
Netflix, Inc. Consolidated Statements of Cash Flows[55] (in thousands)

	Year Ended December 31		
	2011	**2010**	**2009**
Cash flows from operating activities:			
Net income	$226,126	$160,853	$115,860
Adjustments to reconcile net income to net cash provided by operating activities:			
Additions to streaming content library	(2,320,732)	(406,210)	(64,217)
Change in streaming content liabilities	1,460,400	167,836	(4,014)
Amortization of streaming content library	699,128	158,100	48,192
Amortization of DVD content library	96,744	142,496	171,298
Depreciation and amortization of property, equipment, and intangibles	43,747	38,099	38,044

SOURCE: http://files.shareholder.com/downloads/NFLX/2097321301x0x561754/3715da18-1753-4c34-8ba7-18dd28e50673/NFLX_10K.pdf

(continued)

EXHIBIT 3
(Continued)

Year Ended December 31			
	2011	**2010**	**2009**
Stock-based compensation expense	61,582	27,996	12,618
Excess tax benefits from stock-based compensation	(45,784)	(62,214)	(12,683)
Other non-cash items	(4,050)	(9,128)	(7,161)
Deferred taxes	(18,597)	(962)	6,328
Gain on sale of business	—	—	(1,783)
Changes in operating assets and liabilities:			
Prepaid content	6,211	(35,476)	(5,643)
Other current assets	(4,775)	(18,027)	(5,358)
Other accounts payable	24,314	18,098	1,537
Accrued expenses	68,902	67,209	13,169
Deferred revenue	21,613	27,086	16,970
Other non-current assets and liabilities	2,883	645	1,906
Net cash provided by operating activities	317,712	276,401	325,063
Cash flows from investing activities:			
Acquisition of DVD content library	(85,154)	(123,901)	(193,044)
Purchases of short-term investments	(223,750)	(107,362)	(228,000)
Proceeds from sale of short-term investments	50,993	120,857	166,706
Proceeds from maturities of short-term investments	38,105	15,818	35,673
Purchases of property and equipment	(49,682)	(33,837)	(45,932)
Proceeds from sale of business	—	—	7,483
Other assets	3,674	12,344	11,035
Net cash used in investing activities	(265,814)	(116,081)	(246,079)
Cash flows from financing activities:			
Principal payments of lease financing obligations	(2,083)	(1,776)	(1,158)
Proceeds from issuance of common stock upon exercise of options	19,614	49,776	35,274
Proceeds from public offering of common stock, net of issuance costs	199,947	—	—
Excess tax benefits from stock-based compensation	45,784	62,214	12,683
Borrowings on line of credit, net of issuance costs	—	—	18,978
Payments on line of credit	—	—	(20,000)
Proceeds from issuance of debt, net of issuance costs	198,060	—	193,917
Repurchases of common stock	(199,666)	(210,259)	(324,335)
Net cash provided by (used in) financing activities	261,656	(100,045)	(84,641)
Net increase (decrease) in cash and cash equivalents	313,554	60,275	(5,657)
Cash and cash equivalents, beginning of year	194,499	134,224	139,881
Cash and cash equivalents, end of year	$508,053	$194,499	$134,224
Supplemental disclosure:			
Income taxes paid	$79,069	$56,218	$58,770
Interest paid	19,395	20,101	3,878

However, by 2012, Netflix faced challenges from its pricing changes in the United States and its expansion into international markets, even stating that it expected revenue per subscriber to drop from its 2011 level of US$11.56[34] as subscribers choose the streaming only option of US$7.99 over the more expensive streaming and DVD delivery option. For future revenue growth, Netflix needed to increase its subscribers numbers both domestically and internationally.

In terms of net income, Netflix had steadily improved its bottom line in conjunction with strong top line growth. The company had a net income of US$226 million in 2011 for a growth rate of 40% over the previous year's US$160 million net income. Over the five years from 2006–2011, the company saw an average net income growth of 31% per year that, coupled with high revenue growth, was instrumental to Netflix's high stock valuation. However, recently, its operating margin slid from 15% in 2010 to 2.9% in 2012, a drop directly attributable to the higher cost of content acquisition.

Until the end of 2007, Netflix had no long-term debt on its books, but it began to acquire long-term debt in 2008 as a result of its decision to invest in building a strong content library and expand overseas. At the end of 2011, Netflix had US$508 million in cash and US$200 million in long-term debt.

Netflix's Success

Netflix went from being a company that exclusively mailed DVDs to the largest media delivery company in the world by making some smart strategic decisions. For instance, Netflix jumped on the streaming bandwagon even though it was not really ready. At the time, the online content available for streaming was extremely limited—less than 10% of the content that was available from Netflix's DVDs holdings.

At that time, Netflix's mail-order DVD business was very popular, and customers did not seem to mind waiting a day or two for their DVDs. Netflix then went ahead and offered streaming content, a bold decision that anticipated an as yet unexpressed need for the immediate gratification of streaming, and made Netflix the first entrant into the market for streamed video. It was clear to Netflix that the use of DVDs would gradually decline, and Netflix's aggressive adoption of streaming videos was a sharp marketing move, that gave it an edge in the global economy.

After its initial launch of online streaming, Netflix kept up to date with new trends and customer preferences, especially the quickly changing preferences of Generation Y, which were influenced by branding, social media, and media saturation. Netflix utilized all the platforms that Generation Y would find appealing, from computers and TVs, to Smartphones and tablets.

Continually bearing in mind that the two most important things for Netflix's customers were price per content, and quality of content, Netflix kept its priorities straight and never stopped improving the quality of its content, or the platforms for delivering that content.

Netflix also focused on increasing customer engagement. It allowed customers to rate movies they viewed, thereby enhancing the customer experience and creating a community of viewers. And, by tracking the movies a customer viewed, Netflix was able to track customer preferences, and offer targeted recommendations for viewing. Netflix also exploited customer loyalty to attract new customers, for instance, through its "refer-a-friend" offer of one free month of service for both the new customer and the referrer to attract new users who wanted to try the service risk-free.

The 2011 Price Increase/Rebranding Debacle

Netflix continued to grow robustly by offering a combined DVD mail and unlimited streaming service at a flat rate of US$9.99 a month, a rate that was key to Netflix's ability to offer a great value for money service. But with increased competition and expensive new content deals, the company found it increasingly difficult to maintain its operating margin levels. In the third quarter of 2011, Netflix implemented a 60% price increase, from US$10 to US$16 a month for unlimited streaming and DVDs by mail, which immediately resulted in the loss of 800,000 subscribers, pointing to the company's very limited latitude with regard to pricing.[35]

In response, Netflix took action that very shortly proved disastrous. In addition to raising its prices and shifting its business model to focus on online streaming, Netflix also attempted to restructure its operations by spinning off its DVD delivery service and rebranding it Qwikster. Rebranding a well-known product or service such as Netflix usually only works if a company was trying to simplify its brand, almost never the other way around, which was, unfortunately what Netflix tried to do. Netflix attempted to introduce a new entity, Qwikster, by splitting the old entity into two: with two separate websites, two separate queues, two separate sets of recommendations, two separate customer bases, two separate billing avenues, and two new sets of rules customer had to learn about. While Netflix had banked on the competitive advantage of offering "affordability, instant access and usability," the introduction of a separate website undercut instant access and usability. Customers, critics, and Wall Street responded harshly.

Apart from losing over 800,000 subscribers after its price increase, and losing half of its market capitalization, Netflix's rebranding strategy did not seem justifiable to its customers.

Netflix botched the rebranding because it neglected due diligence prior to launching it and its price increases. Market research would surely have indicated customer resistance to both. Heavily focused on increasing profits, Netflix did not effectively strategize the rebranding/ repricing plan, nor did it anticipate resistance or prepare strategy implementation scenarios. A new strategy should not only increase revenues and profits, it should consider relationship and brand image gains and losses. In springing the rebranding on customers, Netflix undercut the quality of the experience it had previously offered, and the negative reaction was not mitigated by the company's public apology or its rescinding of its decision to split its services. The botched rebranding led to a dilution of Netflix's brand, and loss of customer trust. Re-establishing its brand image became a priority for Netflix, though it was not very easy to do. The company needed to offer something genuinely useful to its customers at just the right cost, while increasing the quality of the content offered and enhancing customer experience.

Finally, in order for Netflix to expand internationally, it needed to invest in the technological infrastructure in the international markets that it lacked but which it desperately needs due to heavy competitions and other legal concerns that appear there.

Strategic Challenges Ahead for Netflix

Netflix's top management needed to address many issues to maintain the company's leading position in the home video market. A strategic plan was needed to:

1. Repair the PR damage from the rebranding and price increases of 2011.
2. Focus on growing its subscriber base both at home and abroad.

3. Maintain a healthy cash position to meet the growing content cost obligations.
4. Invest in innovative user interface and streaming technologies to create a solid platform for the shift from DVD delivery to streaming.

REFERENCES

Blockbuster Wins 3-Month Restructuring Extension. *Reuters*. 20 Jan 2011. URL: http://t.co/iZPsUi5

Video On Demand, Wikipedia, Accessed: 31-Jan-2011, URL: http://en.wikipedia.org/wiki/Video_on_demand

Netflix Annual SEC Report (2010) URL: http://files.shareholder.com/downloads/NFLX/1159919179x0xS1193125-10-36181/1065280/filing.pdf

http://www.fundinguniverse.com/company-histories/Netflix-Inc-company-History.html

2 10-K Netflix Annual Report – 2010

Hoovers company profile—Netflix Inc.

Datamonitor. Netflix Inc. Company Profile. 23 Jun. 2010

http://money.cnn.com/2011/10/24/technology/netflix_earnings/index.htm

Datamonitor. Blockbuster Inc. Company Profile. 30 Dec. 2010

http://www.redbox.com/release_20110811

http://www.theatlanticwire.com/business/2011/08/walmarts-facebook-powered-future/41843/

http://www.csmonitor.com/Innovation/2011/0713/Five-alternatives-to-Netflix/Amazon-Prime-instant-video

http://facstaff.uww.edu/mohanp/netflix.html

Information System: A Manager's Guide to Harnessing – John Gallaugher

FY 2008, and June 2009 market cap figures for both firms

http://www.barnesandnobleinc.com/newsroom/financial_only.html

http://phx.corporate-ir.net/phoenix.zhtml?c=97664&p=irol-reportsOther

Movies to Go. *The Economist*. July 9, 2005

http://insight.kellogg.northwestern.edu/index.php/Kellogg/article/a_surprising_secret_to_netflixs_runaway_success

http://searchenterprisewan.techtarget.com/definition/bandwidth

http://slatest.slate.com/posts/2011/06/02/nnessee_netflix_law_new_measure_makes_it_illegal_to_share_login_.html

http://www.wired.com/threatlevel/2011/09/netflix-video-privacy/

http://www.reelseo.com/time-warner-netflix-sued-providing-captions-video-streams/

http://news.cnet.com/8301-13578_3-20072619-38/netflix-sued-by-deaf-group-over-lack-of-subtitles/

http://arxiv.org/PS_cache/cs/pdf/0610/0610105v2.pdf

http://www.nytimes.com/2010/03/13/technology/13netflix.html

http://news.cnet.com/8301-10784_3-9926311-7.html

S&P Net Advantage

IDC Technology Research Firm Source: S&P Industry Survey

10-Q Netflix Quarterly Fillings-Q3-2011

10-K Netflix Annual Report – 2010 http://www.cnn.com/2011/08/31/tech/mobile/smartphone-market-share-gahran/index.html

S&P Industry Survey

10-Q Netflix Quarterly Fillings-Q3-2011

Morningstar Analyst Report

Euromonitor Bentley Library Database

http://www.emarketer.com/blog/index.php/time-spent-watching-tv-tops-internet/

Media Usage & Online Behavior—Mintel Report Oct 2011

http://www.reuters.com/article/2011/10/31/us-netflixdisney-idUSTRE79U0O420111031

http://www.businessweek.com/magazine/content/05_43/b3956201.htm

Mintel Investment Research

Annual Shareholder letter Netflix 2011

Consolidated Financial Statement 10k

Netflix 10k 2011

Netflix Factsheet

https://www.google.com/adplanner/planning/site_profile#siteDetails?identifier=megaupload.com Quarterly Letter to the shareholders 3Q 2011

http://www.ibtimes.com/articles/256810/20111128/netflix-estimates-revised-jefferies-guidance-capital-raise.htm

Company Fillings 8k 3Q

Blockbuster Creditors Should Call It Quits, Poll Says, TheStreet, 30 Jan 2011. URL: http://t.co/TcSPlun

Blockbuster Wins 3-month Restructuring Extension, *Reuters*, 20 Jan 2011. URL: http://t.co/iZPsUi5

Grossman, Robert J. Tough Love at Netflix. *HR Magazine* (Apr 2010): 36–41

Fuoco-Karasinski. Netflix Bucks Traditional Total Rewards, WorldatWork workspan (8/07)

Goldfarb, Jeffrey, & Holding, Reynolds. Incentives Play Role in Success of Netflix. *The New York Times*. (May 8, 2011).

http://files.shareholder.com/downloads/NFLX/2097321301x0x561754/3715da18-1753-4c34-8ba7-18dd28e50673/NFLX_10K.pdf

http://ir.netflix.com/management.cfm

NOTES

1. http://www.fundinguniverse.com/company-histories/Netflix-Inc-company-History.html.
2. 10-K Netflix Annual Report – 2010.
3. Hoovers company profile – Netflix Inc.
4. Datamonitor, Netflix Inc. Company Profile. 23 Jun. 2010.
5. Datamonitor, Netflix Inc. Company Profile. 23 Jun. 2010.
6. http://insight.kellogg.northwestern.edu/index.php/Kellogg/article/a_surprising_secret_to_netflixs_runaway_success
7. http://money.cnn.com/2011/10/24/technology/netflix_earnings/index.htm
8. S&P Advantage

9. IDC Technology Research Firm Source: S&P Industry Survey

10. 10-Q Netflix Quarterly Filings – Q3-2011

11. http://searchenterprisewan.techtarget.com/definition/bandwidth

12. Consolidated Financial Statement 10-K

13. 10-K Netflix Annual Report – 2010

14. 10-K Netflix Annual Report – 2010

15. http://www.cnn.com/2011/08/31/tech/mobile/smartphone-market- share-gahran/index.html

16. S&P Industry Survey

17. Euromonitor, Bentley University Library Database

18. S&P Industry Survey

19. https://www.google.com/adplanner/planning/site_profile#siteDetails?identifier=megaupload.com

20. Media Usage & Online Behavior – Mintel Report Oct . 2011

21. http://www.reuters.com/article/2011/10/31/us-netflixdisney-idUSTRE79U0O420111031

22. http://www.businessweek.com/magazine/content/05_43/b3956201.htm

23. Annual Shareholder Letter – Netflix 2011

24. Datamonitor, Blockbuster Inc. Company Profile. 30 Dec . 2010

25. http://www.redbox.com/release_20110811

26. http://www.theatlanticwire.com/business/2011/08/walmarts-facebook-powered-future/41843/

27. http://www.csmonitor.com/Innovation/2011/0713/Five-alternatives-to-Netflix/Amazon-Prime-instant-video

28. http://facstaff.uww.edu/mohanp/netflix.html

29. Information System: A manager's guide to harnessing – John Gallaugher

30. Movies to Go. *The Economist*. July 9, 2005

31. Morningstar Investment Report

32. Quarterly letter to the shareholders 3Q 2011

33. Quarterly letter to the shareholders 3Q 2011

34. Company Filings – 8K 3Q

35. 10-Q Netflix Quarterly Filings – Q3-2011

CASE **16**

Town Sports International Holdings, Inc: Unsquashable

Sarah Stefanelli, Christina Marie Kopka, Jakub Libucha, and Joyce Vincelette

Introduction

Slowing down from a sprint into a slow jog, Richard Giardina reduced the speed on his treadmill and absently gazed out the window of his apartment. He always found escape in exercise, but not even a strenuous workout could keep his mind away from the upcoming Town Sports International Holdings, Inc. (TSI) Q4 earnings call. He had been a part of the company for over 20 years, starting off as a sales manager and working his way up to its helm as the CEO. As Giardina turned off his iPod and wiped his face with a towel, he reminisced back to the days on the gym floor where his biggest concern was a frustrated client. He knew that big challenges lay ahead for the company; the competition for members in the crowded fitness industry would only grow, and the need to provide value that justified higher membership fees would become increasingly important. The year 2013 had brought with it a high rate of membership attrition, expensive damage repairs from Hurricane Sandy, and an exceptionally icy winter that hindered the usual influx of New Year's resolution memberships. Despite these setbacks, Giardina had some new ideas to bring to the table in order to give TSI the kickstart it would need to make 2014 successful. Heading to the shower, he collected his thoughts and prepared himself to begin writing the statement he would deliver to shareholders at the end of the week.

History[1]

Town Sports International Holdings, Inc. (TSI) was founded for love of a sport much older than the modern fitness industry: squash. In the year 1830, at a private institution known as the Harrow School in England, students discovered that punching holes in a rubber "racquets" ball provided an unpredictable bouncing pattern and a more exciting game. By 1864, the game of squash was officially adopted, and four new courts were built at its birthplace. The sport made its North American debut in Canadian prep schools in the 1880s and slowly moved south into the United States, where the newly founded United States Squash Racquets Association began to regulate the game in 1907.

Fast-forward to the early 1970s and Henry Saint's return to his native Pennsylvania from graduate school in Germany. Already a published author of short stories for *Esquire* magazine, Saint was set to pursue a career as a writer until the death of his father forced him to direct his attention to managing family affairs. An avid, yet average, squash player, Saint decided to channel his passion into creating a stronger presence for the sport in the New York metropolitan area. In 1973, Saint founded St. John Squash Racquet Inc. with $300,000 in capital raised from private investors and his wife, Gerarda, who was from a prominent European family with royal connections (and funds).

With his newly formed company, Saint opened the 5th Avenue Squash Club in 1974 that became an almost immediate success. Within its first month of operation, it was cash positive and brought in $150,000 in profits by the end of its second year. As the company grew, Saint sought to bring additional talent onboard and found it in a young graduate named Michael Tascher. Like Saint, Tascher aspired to be a writer but had no concrete plans or direction to make this happen. While most newly minted CEOs would find such a lack of purpose off-putting, Saint saw a potential leader, untainted by industry prejudices and brimming with unconventional ideas.

As the company grew and opened new clubs, Saint changed the name to Town Squash Incorporated. Unfortunately, coupled with increasing competitive pressures, as well as the declining popularity of squash in the late 1970s, Saint and Tascher were forced to adapt their business model to ensure the company's longevity by adding exercise machines and shifting from a pay-per-session model to fully paid memberships. Using this new model, Saint and Tascher expanded beyond New York City opening a club in Washington DC, called Capitol Hill Squash Club. Despite the company's continued success, Saint soon left the business in the hands of Tascher and a newly hired sales manager named Richard Giardina. He had recently divorced his wife, struggled to run a company owned mostly by her family, and yearned to return to a focus on writing. By 1981, he was no longer a part of the business he had created, and Tascher grabbed the reins to steer the organization towards a fitness center model at the urgings of Giardina.

By the mid-1980s, squash was no longer a profitable sport-business. Both Tascher and Giardina realized that in order to survive the company needed to adapt to the newly emerging fitness industry. The company was renamed Town Sports International, allowing it to aggressively grow into a fitness brand while moving away from its core offering of squash courts and equipment. To maintain marketing continuity, the name New York Sports Club was adopted and shortened to NYSC in order to craft a brand and identity out of its past as a New York squash club. The company remained consistent in its naming practices across regions, eventually resulting in the Boston, Philadelphia, and Washington Sports Clubs. Although the "international" aspect of the company seemed incongruous with its New York roots, Saint's ex-wife had opened two clubs in Switzerland in an attempt to recreate the American fitness model in Europe. Tascher and Giardina requested management rights over the clubs, and Gerarda Saint consented. Making a financial pledge to the company, she agreed to assist in funding its growth primarily in the United States while maintaining the two locations in Basel and Zurich.

Unfortunately, tensions between Gerarda's family and Tascher affected his ability to run the organization in a way he saw fit, resulting in his resignation from the CEO position in 1995. As the second largest shareholder in the company, he retained his seat on the board and orchestrated a leveraged buyout of the organization that was eventually accepted by the majority shareholders. Shortly after, Giardina took over as the company's President and Chief Operating Officer while Mark Smith, a former professional squash player and operational manager of the Swiss clubs since 1985, took over as the Chief Executive Officer. With new leadership in place and clubs in New York, Connecticut, and Washington, DC, the company set its sights on the New Jersey and Massachusetts markets with aggressive plans for the future. When Giardina become CEO in 2002, TSI expanded to 150 clubs; four years later, the company went public.[2]

TSI had decided to move forward with its expansion strategy in order to become the most recognized health club network, through both designing and building clubs and through selective acquisitions within its four major markets, Boston, New York, Washington DC, and Philadelphia.[3] TSI set out to accomplish this efficiently and effectively by living by its customer-centric mission, "Improving Lives Through Exercise."[4]

Corporate Governance

Robert Giardina was the only Executive Officer also serving on the Board. As a group, the Board of Directors and Executive Officers (12 persons) owned 2,204,905 shares of TSI common stock, 8.9 percent of total shares, as of March 2014.[5] Beginning in 2013, each Non-Employee Director was required to hold shares of common stock with a Fair Market Value equal to four times the amount of annual cash retainer payable to directors within five years of joining the Board.[6]

After its initial public offering in 2006, TSI separated the positions of Chief Executive Officer and Chairman of the Board of Directors. TSI's leadership felt that the complex business and regulatory environment would best be navigated by an independent board chairman, directly responsible for board activities and company guidance, and a separate Chief Executive Officer, completely focused on running the day-to-day operations of the Company.[7] The names and biographies of the members of the Board of Directors and top management team can be found in the Town Sports International Holdings, Inc. 2013 Proxy Statement.

The U.s. Health And Fitness Industry

As the American people became more aware of the connections between good health and exercise, the health and fitness industry experienced tremendous growth across a variety of sectors. According to IBISWorld in their 2013 report on the Gym, Health, and Fitness Club Industry, the number of establishments classified in the industry in the United States increased from 33,451 in 2008 to 33,527 in 2013.[8]

According to the International Health, Racquet and Sportclub Association (IHRSA), total U.S. fitness club revenues increased at a compound annual growth rate of 3.1 percent from $18.7 billion in 2007 to $21.8 billion in 2012, while total U.S. fitness club memberships increased at a compound annual growth rate of 3.9 percent from 41.5 million in 2007 to 50.2 million in 2012.[9] The steady growth of these businesses generated nearly $26 billion in revenue and grossed $2.2 billion in profits, a 2.5 percent industry growth over the course of 2013 alone. According to IBISWorld, the fitness market had not yet reached saturation and the industry was expected to continue to grow at an average annual rate of 2.9 percent a year to total over $29 billion by the year 2018.[10]

The health and fitness industry in the United States experienced this growth despite consumer uncertainty brought on by events such as the economic crisis of 2008. As the economy continued to recover, the health and fitness industry followed suit as disposable income increased and the United States experienced higher levels of employment. During this period, health and fitness clubs adapted their offerings to meet a variety of consumer needs across a broader spectrum of income levels, making fitness more accessible to the American market at large.

The Gym, Health and Fitness Club industry in the United States was broken into six categories: 1) Gyms and Fitness Clubs (65%); 2) Dance Centers (7%); 3) Ice and Skating Rinks (6%); 4) Tennis Centers (5%); 5) Swimming Pools (7%) and 6) Other (10%). In 2013, Total Industry Revenue was $25.9 billion.

Despite the vast number of options available to consumers seeking to be active, health clubs and fitness centers were by far the most popular choice. Making up 65 percent of total industry revenue,[11] national gym memberships rose from 46.4 million in 2003 to over 52.6 million by 2013.[12] Membership numbers were expected to grow an average of 2 percent annually over the years to 2018.[13]

The "other category" shown in Exhibit 1, although seemingly insignificant, accounted for the innumerable variations and opportunities within the market for physical activity and enhancement. Countless independent studios offered specific discipline training such as yoga or Pilates, while groups like city-based intramural teams or local running clubs attracted members based on camaraderie and low, if any, membership fees. For those who preferred the privacy of their own homes, a plethora of DVD and online exercise programs were available for low, one-time payments. Personal trainers working out of their homes or local gyms provided people with the necessary support to reach their fitness goals. Trademarked events such as the Color Run, the Tough Mudder, and the Spartan Race collected profits and gained strong followings among those with a competitive spirit, while nationally sanctioned events such as the Boston Marathon or the Ironman competition brought competitive fitness opportunities to those seeking to achieve the status of a champion.

So, what did people do when they went to the gym? According to IHRSA, the fitness industry witnessed a shift in the exercise and preferences of health club members from the traditional full-service fitness centers to smaller studios specializing in boxing, yoga, Pilates, group cycling, barre, boot camps, Crossfit, and personal training.[14] These studios required smaller spaces which significantly lowered start-up costs. In addition, those who attended these specialized exercise venues had the same income demographic as those who attended full-service facilities. The American College of Sports Medicine (ACSM) reported on the top ten fitness trends for 2013 in their annual survey of international industry professionals.[15] Fitness sports such as weight training, body weight or "back to basics" training, and childhood obesity prevention programs were the most popular activities among respondents. According to the Centers for Disease Control and Prevention, there was a dramatic increase in obesity among adults in the United States from 1990 to 2010. Though rates varied across states, no state had an obesity level of less than 20 percent in 2012; 41 states had an obesity rate of 25 percent or more, and 13 of these states had a rate of 30 percent or more. Research showed that exercise played a critical role in reducing obesity and ultimately decreased overall healthcare costs by improving wellness.[16] Additionally, functional fitness programs designed to maintain or return functionality to the body placed in the top ten most popular activities,[17] as industry professionals noted a higher demand for programs from older clients.

This overall growth in both memberships and services spelled out a bright future for TSI but also emphasized the need for TSI to understand its current and potential customer base to remain competitive in an increasingly crowded market.

Consumer Profile

Demographic trends helped drive the growth experienced by the fitness industry from 46.4 million Americans holding gym memberships in 2003 to more than 52.6 million by 2013.[18] By year-end 2013, approximately 17 percent of the total U.S. population belonged to a health club indicating substantial growth potential in the industry and a large consumer pool from which to increase membership numbers.[19] The average age of a health club member in 2012 was 38 years old, and more than one-third of health club members were between the ages of 18 and 34 years old. The greatest membership growth in the past few years had been in the demographic group ages 18 to 34 years old, which had grown 31.4 percent from 2008 to 2012 and in the group 35 to 54, where membership grew 6.1 percent from 2008 to 2012. These two age groups made up approximately 70 percent of total U.S. health club members in 2012. The industry also benefited from the aging "baby boomer" and "Eisenhower" generations as they placed greater emphasis on preserving their health by focusing on fitness.[20] The majority of gym and health club members were female, accounting for 57 percent of all membership sales.[21]

Important shifts in American demographics and fitness habits were a driving force behind these masses flocking to the gym. Aging baby boomers looking to preserve their health and combat ailments such as heart disease and arthritis were estimated to hold 20 percent of gym memberships by year-end 2013, indicating a strong demand for programs tailored to meet the needs of this age group.[22] As this generation continues to retire, strong opportunities will be created for health club facilities that focus on this massive market segment. Although most gym-goers fell between the traditional market ages of 18 to 35, the number of younger members grew as well. It was estimated that the demographic ages 6 to 17 accounted for 12 percent of gym memberships.[23] Youth memberships had become one of the fastest growing areas for the fitness club industry due, in part, to public health campaigns such as First Lady Michelle Obama's "Let's Move" initiative. In addition, as public schools cut back on physical fitness classes, parents realizing the importance of fitness to their children's overall wellness had sought alternative activities.

Competition

The health and fitness industry was fiercely competitive with a wide variety of services and providers. The upward trend of more Americans focusing on their health had driven diverse growth and forced businesses to pay attention to how consumers wanted to exercise. Though there were many recognizable fitness clubs in the United States, only a few were publicly traded companies. According to TSI, the principal points of competition in the industry included pricing and ease of payment, required level of members' contractual commitment, level and quality of services, experience and quality of supervisory staff, size and layout of facility, and convenience of location with respect to access to transportation and pedestrian traffic.[24]

TSI considered its primary competitors to include:[25]

- Commercial, multi-recreational, and fitness-only chains, including among others: Equinox Holdings, Inc., Lifetime Fitness, Inc., Crunch, New York Health and Racquet Club, LA Fitness International LLC., Sports Club/LA, 24 Hour Fitness Worldwide, Inc., Bally Total Fitness Holdings Corporation, Gold's Gym International, Inc., Retro Fitness, Snap Fitness, Anytime Fitness, and Planet Fitness. These clubs targeted different income levels and offered different levels of services and amenities.

- Private studios, including among others, Flywheel, Soul Cycle, Barry's Bootcamp, and Cross-Fit, in addition to other private studios offering cycling, yoga, or Pilates.

- The YMCA and similar non-profit organizations.

- Physical fitness and recreational facilities established by local government, hospitals, and businesses.

- Exercise and small fitness clubs; racquet, tennis and other athletic clubs.

- Amenity gyms in apartments, condominiums, and offices.

- Weight reducing salons and country clubs.

The number of competitor clubs that offered lower pricing and a lower level of service had continued to grow in TSI's markets over the last few years.[26] Additionally, TSI faced increased competition from both larger suburban family fitness centers as well as competition from the rising popularity and demand from private studios offering niche boutique experiences. TSI also competed indirectly with other entertainment and retail businesses for the discretionary income of the company's target customers.

Four regions in the United States accounted for 73.1 percent of total health club establishments—Southeast (23 percent), Mid-Atlantic (18.8 percent), the West (16.1 percent), and the Great Lakes region (15.2 percent)—and were primarily located in California, New York, Texas, and Florida.[27]

The industry had a low level of market share concentration with the top four firms accounting for about 12.7 percent of industry sales.[28] Due to the fragmentation in the industry, no competitor held a market share greater than 5 percent (24 Hour Fitness Worldwide Inc. (4.9 percent), Life Time Fitness (4.1 percent), Bally Total Fitness Holding Corporation (3.2 percent) and TSI (2.1 percent)).[29] The industry also had a low level of globalization although this had been increasing as some of the larger competitors, such as Gold's Gym, 24 Hour Fitness, and Curves International, had subsidiaries operating in foreign countries.[30]

Opening a new gym location was a capital-intensive endeavor that required renting or buying a location, purchasing updated equipment, purchasing liability insurance to protect against lawsuits from potential customer injury, furnishing the location, and hiring staff. Unfortunately for TSI and its counterparts, consumer demands for more personalized, varied services provided by studios, individual trainers, and community centers which required smaller spaces with significantly lower start up costs had begun to cause shifts in the industry.

Facilities And Locations

GROWTH AND ACQUISITIONS

Faced with ever-growing competition within the industry, TSI sought to grow as seamlessly and with as little risk as possible. Thus, acquiring already-established clubs was an essential aspect of TSI's growth strategy that minimized the risk of opening a new establishment while ensuring optimum locations, convenience for its current customers, and the opportunity to capitalize on the acquired club's membership base. TSI's two most recent acquisitions were: Fitcorp Clubs of Boston and West End Sports Club in New York City. Prior to the Fitcorp acquisition, approximately thirty-five percent of TSI's clubs (about 50 clubs) were previously privately-owned single and multi-club businesses.[31]

Departing slightly from its traditional health club model, TSI acquired Boston's Fitcorp Clubs in March 2013 for approximately $3.2 million.[32] In addition to owning traditional health and fitness facilities, Fitcorp had managed private fitness centers for companies such as Fidelity Investments, Biogen Idec, Gillette, Raytheon, and Boston Scientific for over forty years. As a result of the acquisition, TSI gained five health and fitness clubs and four managed clubs, including Boston Racquet Club and the 25,000-square-foot fitness club at the Prudential Center in downtown Boston, giving it a considerable presence in the Boston fitness market. All former Fitcorp members were granted access to every TSI facility regardless of location.[33] In addition to these new members, TSI gained Fitcorp's expertise in managing private fitness centers, which provided TSI the opportunity to build its corporate customer base as well as its managed facility business.

In June 2013, TSI leveraged its new acquisitions and launched a new Fitcorp Corporate Fitness Division, capitalizing on the Fitcorp expertise in managing private fitness clubs for both large and small companies, colleges and universities, and private clubs. Fitcorp's founder and CEO, Gary Klencheski, was appointed as the President of this new division tasked with expanding TSI's corporate member base beyond the Boston area and into New York, Philadelphia, and Washington, DC.[34]

In March 2013, TSI acquired West End Sports Club, a New York health and fitness club at 63 & West End Avenue in Manhattan for the purchase price of $560,000.[35] Along with a full service health and fitness club, the deal landed TSI a 75-foot indoor lap pool, the company's first in Manhattan. As a result, all Manhattan club members gained access to a pool, an uncommon luxury considering the lack of available space in the city.[36]

In addition to moving into the management of private fitness clubs with the Fitcorp acquisition, TSI launched a new luxury studio brand called Boutique Fitness Experience studio (BFX Studio) in early 2014 in order to capitalize on the growing consumer demand for smaller, more personalized studio experiences. Each BFX Studio was expected to be about half the size of the average 26,000-foot TSI fitness club.[37] The first two of these studios were scheduled to make their debut during the first half of 2014. Plans were in place for the BFX Studio to feature three services: Ride Republic, a personalized indoor cycling experience, private sessions for personal training, and master classes for defined group exercise practice.[38]

In December 2013, TSI announced an agreement to sell the company's property at 151 East 86th street in NYC for approximately $82 million.[39] In addition to the TSI facility, this property also housed retail space and generated approximately $2 million in rental income for TSI during the 2013 fiscal year. Once sold, TSI was no longer entitled to this rental income.[40] TSI planned to continue operating its NYSC health and fitness club at this location under a two-year lease. At the end of this period, the purchaser could exercise its right to terminate the lease in order to demolish the building and construct a new luxury high-rise, multi-use building. Upon completion of this development, TSI planned to enter into a new lease for a health and fitness club space at this location.[41] All other fitness club facilities as well as corporate office spaces were leased.

LOCATIONS

On December 31, 2013, TSI was the largest owner and operator of fitness clubs in the Northeast and Mid-Atlantic regions of the United States, based on the number of clubs. The company operated 162 fitness clubs, including subsidiaries, under four regional brand names: "New York Sports Clubs" (NYSC), "Boston Sports Clubs" (BSC), "Philadelphia Sports Clubs" (PSC), and "Washington Sports Clubs" (WSC). TSI utilized local brand names for its clubs to create a consistent image within its local markets while reinforcing its corporate identity as a "local network of quality fitness clubs rather than a national chain."[42] Specifically, TSI finished 2013 as the largest fitness club owner and operator in Manhattan with 37 locations and a total of 108 clubs within a 120-mile radius of New York City. The company also owned and operated 29 clubs in the Boston area; 16 clubs (two of which were partially owned) in the Washington, DC area; six clubs in the Philadelphia region; and three clubs in Switzerland.[43]

TSI clubs collectively served 497,000 members by year-end 2013.[44] In addition, the Fitcorp division managed eight private fitness facilities comprised of three university clubs, four managed sites which were acquired as part of the Fitcorp acquisition, and one new managed site which was opened during the fourth quarter of 2013 from the efforts of the Fitcorp Private Fitness Center Division.[45]

The number of clubs TSI acquired, opened or closed, and the total number of clubs operated between 2008 and 2013 can be seen in **Exhibit 1**. The average revenue per club and comparable club revenues during this period can also be found in **Exhibit 1**.

TSI planned to open four to six more health and fitness clubs in the New York and Boston markets and two to four new BFX Studio units during 2014. Expected construction costs for the traditional clubs was $2.5 million per club and $1.5 to 2.25 million per BFX studio.[46] Expansion was expected to be funded with cash on hand or through internally generated cash flows with borrowings under the company's revolving credit facility if necessary.[47]

CLUSTERING

TSI used a clustering strategy when deciding on club locations and potential future acquisitions. In each of TSI's four markets in the United States, the company began its clustering strategy by opening and/or acquiring clubs located in central urban markets and later branching out into suburbs and neighboring communities.[48] In order to serve densely populated, major metropolitan areas, TSI clustered its clubs near the highest concentrations of its target market populations, their residences and employers, as well as transportation hubs, offices, and retail centers. The idea behind this clustering strategy was to offer convenience to its busy members with memberships that allowed them to use multiple gym locations near their work and home (approximately 45 percent of members had a membership that gave them access to multiple clubs).[49] At year-end December 31, 2013, 40 percent of all club usage was by members visiting clubs other than their home club.[50] Clustering also allowed members to retain their status with TSI clubs if they relocated or changed companies within the same region.[51]

TSI's clustering strategy allowed the company to achieve economy of scale and reduce capital-spending needs in regards to sales, marketing, purchasing, general operations, and corporate administrative expenses.[52] The strategy also allowed access to special facilities to all members within a local area, such as swimming pools, and squash, tennis, and basketball courts without the need to offer them at every location.

EXHIBIT 1

Town Sports International Holdings Inc. Selected Consolidated Financial and Other Data						
Fiscal Years Ended December 31,	**2013 (a)**	**2012 (a)**	**2011 (a)**	**2010 (a)**	**2009 (a)**	**2008 (b)**
Clubs Acquired or Opened	6	0	2	0	4	9
Clubs Closed	-4	0	-2	-1	-9	-4
Total Clubs Operated at End of Period (c)	162	160	160	160	161	166
Total Members at End of Period (d)	497,000	510,000	523,000	493,000	486,000	510,000
Comparable Club Revenue (Decrease) Increase (e)	-1.8%	1.6%	-1.8%	-4.3%	-5.6%	2.2%
Revenue per Weighted Average Club (In Thousands) (f)	$2,971	$3,032	$2,934	$2,881	$2,957	$3,142
Average Revenue per Member (g)	$934	$922	$915	$947	$969	$990
Annual Attrition (h)	41.9%	41.0%	39.9%	41.9%	45.2%	40.2%

Notes:

(a) Town Sports International Holdings 2013 10-K, p. 36.

(b) Town Sports International Holdings 2012 10-K, p. 35.

(c) Includes wholly-owned and partly-owned clubs. Not included in the total club count are locations that are managed by Town Sports International Holdings Inc. in which it does not have an equity interest. These managed sites include three managed university locations and four additional managed locations acquired on May 2013 as part of the Fitcorp acquisition as well as one new managed location added during the fourth quarter of 2013.

(d) Represents members at wholly-owned and partly-owned clubs.

(e) Total revenue for a club is included in comparable club revenue increase (decrease) beginning on the first day of the thirteenth full calendar month of the club's operation.

(f) Revenue per weighted average club is calculated as total revenue divided by the product of the total number of clubs and their weighted average months in operation as a percentage of the period

(g) Average revenue per member is total revenue from wholly-owned clubs for the period divided by the average number of memberships from wholly-owned clubs for the period, including restricted memberships, summer student and summer pool memberships, where average number of memberships for the period is derived by dividing the sum of the total memberships at the end of each month during the period by the total number of months in the period.

(h) Annual attrition is calculated as total member losses for the year divided by the average monthly member count over the year excluding pre-sold, summer student and summer pool memberships, and including restricted memberships that began in April 2010, during each respective year.

Even though TSI's clustering strategy offered many advantages, in 2012 the strategy also offered its fair share of complications. On October 29, 2012, 131 clubs were closed due to flooding and power outages brought on by Hurricane Sandy. One of these clubs closed permanently, one closed for over a year and reopened in December of 2013, and 16 were closed for over a week. The clustering strategy ultimately resulted in 131 clubs of TSI's 162 clubs in the region being affected by one storm on the East Coast.[53]

CLUB FORMATS

TSI club formats had evolved over its 40-year history, but TSI remained focused on a singular objective: to cost-effectively construct and efficiently operate fitness clubs in the competitive real estate markets where they were located. TSI fitness-only clubs averaged approximately 21,000 square feet (15,000–25000 square feet). Multi-recreational facilities (about 66 percent of TSI clubs) averaged approximately 37,000 square feet, with the largest club measuring approximately 200,000 square feet. Overall, the average club size of clubs was 26,000 square feet[54] while the new BFX Studios were expected to be approximately 7,500 to 10,000 square feet per studio.[55]

Clubs typically had an open space for cardiovascular and strength-training equipment along with special-purpose rooms for group classes. When developing an individual club format, TSI examined the local potential customer base in detail to see which supplemental services would draw and retain members such as swimming, tennis, squash, basketball, Sports Clubs for Kids programs, and swim lessons for kids.[56]

Membership

In 2013, individual club membership generally ranged from 2,000 to 4,500 members at a club's maturity for TSI's fitness only clubs and multi-recreational facilities.[57] TSI members included a wide age demographic covering the student market to the active mature market. Members generally had annual income levels of between $50,000 and $150,000.[58]

Like its competitors, TSI's success was dependent on its ability to continually attract and retain members in order to maintain membership and revenue levels. According IBISWorld, the average yearly attrition rate for fitness facilities in the U.S. was 37 percent. In addition, the cost of recruiting a new member was estimated to be more than twice the cost of retaining an existing member.[59] For these reasons, it was critical that TSI design membership programs and fees in a way that reduced membership attrition and encouraged new member acquisition. Membership growth tended to be the highest at the beginning of each year and during the summer months. From an industry perspective, 30 percent of all new members acquired signed up for a gym membership during the beginning of the year, making these months critical to the financial performance of the company. TSI estimated the average customer lifecycle was 23 months for unrestricted members and 28 months for restricted members.[60] In addition, with member retention at the core of TSI's success, the company's employees and the culture of each club location played a key role in membership satisfaction, retention, and growth and had the potential to make a club excel above competition that offered similar products and workout experiences.

Membership and attrition rates for TSI from 2008 to 2013 can be found in **Exhibit 2**.

Membership Options

TSI offered three principal membership options.[61]

Passport Membership—The Passport Membership was the most expensive membership option and granted access to all clubs at all times providing members convenient access to fitness near their work and homes as well as while traveling. In the Washington and Philadelphia Sports Club regions, TSI also offered Regional Passport Memberships, allowing members to go to any club at any time within one region. Passport Memberships ranged from $69.99 per month to $99.99 per month. Corporate and group members were priced approximately at $65.00 per month.

Exclusively at two clubs, TSI offered a Passport Premium Memberships (BSC Waltham and BSC Wellesley), which included a greater number of select services and facilities and cost from $105.99 per month to $115.99 per month. TSI's Boston Racquet Club offered a higher level Premium Membership priced from $135.00 to $170.00 that included an exclusive Squash membership that was only available at this club.

Core Membership—A Core Membership allowed members to use one defined club at any time. At year-end 2013, this membership ranged from $39.99 per month to $89.99 per month, dependent upon specific facilities and services, the location's target market, and the length of the membership contract. Core Members could use other TSI clubs at a one-time fee ranging from $9.50 to $12.00 per visit.

Restricted Membership—A Restricted Membership was a lower priced restricted-use month-to-month only membership. In 2010, this membership offering was extended to students, in April of 2011 to teachers, and in September of 2011 to first responders of the 9/11 tragedy. If a Restricted Member wished to use a club between the peak hours of 4:30 pm and 7:30 pm, Monday through Thursday, they were charged a usage fee ranging from $9.50 to $12.00 per visit. The Restricted Passport Membership and the Restricted Core Membership were offered at $39.99 per month and $29.99 per month, respectively. Approximately 87 percent of these restricted members were comprised of restricted student and teacher memberships.

Prior to November 1, 2010, TSI offered a Gold Membership that enabled members to use one club at any time and any club during off-peak times. As of December 2013, 78,000 members, or about sixteen percent of all members continued to hold a Gold Membership.[62] Gold memberships were no longer offered to new members. Gold members paid a fee ranging from $9.50 to $12.00 per visit to use non-home clubs during peak hours.[63]

In an effort to bring in new customers, TSI offered trial periods for the cost of one dollar per day. These trials provided a 30-day membership for $30 dollars to a single club of a customer's choosing. This option appealed to those in the area for a temporary period of time or for those who wanted to try TSI before they committed to a longer-term and more-expensive membership option.

TSI offered two types of membership options. Members could choose a *month-to-month* membership or a *commit* contract. The *month-to-month* option allowed a member to cancel their membership at any time with 30 days' notice. Under the *commit* option, new members committed to a membership for one year. After one year, *commit* members retained membership as a month-to-month member until they chose to cancel. As of December 2013, 80 percent of new TSI members had chosen the *commit* option. At year-end 2013, 72 percent of TSI's total members (380,880 members) were on a *month-to-month* basis.[64] See **Exhibit 2** for TSI's membership types and numbers, and price ranges for each option as of December 31, 2013.

TSI instituted a rate lock guarantee and maintenance fee in May 2011 for new members. Rather than yearly cost of living increases to membership fees, a fee was collected annually from all members. In 2013, this fee was $39.99 and was collected from each member in January. These maintenance fees were recognized in membership revenue during the 12-month period following collection. In January 2013 and January 2012, TSI collected approximately $7.0 million and $5.0 million, respectively, from these fees. Dues were increased on a cost of living basis for those members who joined prior to 2011.[65]

EXHIBIT 2

Town Sports International Holdings Inc.
Membership Types as of December 31, 2013

Membership Type	Percentage of Total Members	Membership Base	Price Range (per month)
Passport Membership (a)	45.0%	~226,000	$69.99–$99.99
Core Membership (b)	31.0%	~152,000	$39.99–$89.99
Gold Membership (c)	16.0%	~78,000	$39.99–$79.99
Restricted Membership (d)	8.0%	~41,000	$29.99–$39.99
Non-Commit Membership Originations (e)	20.0%	~99,000	N/A
Commit Membership Originations (f)	80.0%	~398,000	N/A

Notes:

(a) Allowed unlimited access to all of TSI clubs within a specific cluster.

(b) Allowed unlimited access to a member's home club.

(c) Allowed unlimited access to a designated club and access to all other clubs during off-peak hours. This membership is no longer offered to new members.

(d) Generally sold to students and teachers, provides access to all clubs except during the peak hours of 4:30pm to 7:30pm, Monday through Thursday.

(e) Month-to-month memberships that allow members to cancel at any time with 30-days notice.

(f) Members commit to a one year membership at initiation.

Source: Town Sports International Holdings 2013 10K, p. 8–9.

Programming And Services

MEMBERSHIP SERVICES

Because of the format of TSI's facilities, all clubs, regardless of size, were designed to adapt to current workout trends and compete against private studios with unique specialty offerings without large capital expenditures and while maintaining the company's dedication to fitness training with traditional equipment. Every gym provided the same array of free weights, cardio machines, and strength training equipment as well as personal training, fitness classes, and group workouts. Most clubs had between one and three studios for exercise classes, including one large studio for group fitness classes, a cycling studio, and a mind and body studio used for yoga and Pilates classes.[66]

Traditional classes such as yoga, Pilates, dance, cycling, strength training, boxing, step, and aerobics were available as part of a club membership without additional fees. Additionally, each club had a space reserved for the TRX Exercise Band system that allowed members to incorporate body-weight and suspension training into their workouts. TSI also offered its own branded workouts and training systems. Local club managers worked with regional club managers to ensure uniformity among class content and class schedules.

At certain multi-recreational locations, additional amenities were also offered, including swimming pools, racquet and basketball courts, babysitting services, and pro-shops. In 2012, TSI began to outfit its clubs with a new Ultimate Fitness Experience (UFX) training zone featuring an array of innovative equipment, with 126 clubs having installed the UFX zones as of December 31, 2013. The UFX training zone was open to members for free self-guided workouts and could also be used by personal trainers for their personal training sessions with members and other UFX fee-based workout programs.

ANCILLARY FEE-BASED SERVICES

Non-membership revenues (revenues from services not included in monthly membership fees) as well as certain services provided to non-members had increased from $85.2 million, or 17.5 percent of revenues for the year ended 2009, to $97.1 million, or 20.6 percent of revenues for the year ended December 31, 2013.[67]

The types of fee-based services offered varied depending on the size of the TSI club facility as well as the needs of members and non-members in a particular geographic location. Some of these additional fee-based amenities included conveniences such as babysitting, children's programming, sports massages, pro-shops, overnight locker rentals, laundry services, and specialty fee-based small group exercise classes. TSI believed that these sources of ancillary and other non-membership revenues generated incremental profits with minimal capital investment and assisted in attracting and retaining members.[68] TSI intended to grow its ancillary and other non-membership revenues by focusing on increasing the additional value-added services provided to members and non-members as well as capitalizing on the opportunities for other non-membership revenues such as in-club advertising and retail sales.

Group exercise programming.

In addition to those exercise classes included in the monthly membership fee, TSI also offered an array of offerings for an additional fee, such as the Ultimate Fitness Experience class introduced in 2012. Other fee-based offerings included Small Group Training classes such as Pilates Reformer Technique, Total Body Resistance Exercise (TRX), Kettle Bells, and TSI's Signature Classes which included VBarre and Pilates Tower.[69] TSI was able to change these offerings as dictated by fitness trends and member interests.

Children's programming.

As of December 2013, TSI offered ancillary programs to support club operations under the Sports Clubs for Kids brand in 36 different locations throughout the New York, Boston, and Philadelphia club regions. Sports Clubs for Kids programming included, but was not limited to, day camps, sports camps, swim lessons, hockey and soccer leagues, gymnastics, dance, and birthday parties, dependent upon individual club facilities.

PERSONAL TRAINING

TSI offered its members personal training packages at all of its locations consisting of 1, 4, 8, 12, or 16 personal training sessions per month for an additional fee. Members who purchased this product had to commit to a six-month membership and use their designated number of personal-training sessions per month within the month they were issued. Members could also purchase prepaid single sessions or multi-session packages which were sold at a premium to the personal training membership product.[70] TSI believed that members who participated in a personal training program typically had an extended longevity as a club member.[71] Personal training revenue increased 16.5 percent since 2009 and increased as a percentage of total revenue from 11.7 percent in 2009 to 14.1 percent in 2013.[72] TSI's long-term objective was to generate approximately 20 percent of revenue from personal training.[73]

TSI's revenue streams from 2008 to 2013 from membership dues, joining fees, personal training and other ancillary revenue and fees can be seen in **Exhibit 3**.

EXHIBIT 3

Town Sports International Holdings Inc.

Revenues
($ in Thousands)

Fiscal Years Ended December 31,	2013 (a)		2012 (a)		2011 (b)		2010 (b)		2009 (c)		2008 (c)	
Membership dues	$358,761	76.3%	$366,044	76.4%	$364,536	78.1%	$365,100	79.0%	$387,123	79.8%	$400,874	79.1%
Joining fees	$14,392	3.1%	$11,595	2.4%	$6,824	1.5%	$6,967	1.5%	$12,048	2.5%	$13,723	2.7%
Membership revenue	$373,153	79.4%	$377,639	78.8%	$371,360	79.5%	$372,067	80.5%	$399,171	82.2%	$414,597	81.8%
Personal training revenue	$66,367	14.1%	$65,641	13.7%	$62,394	13.4%	$60,875	13.2%	$56,971	11.7%	$61,752	12.2%
Other ancillary club revenue	$24,720	5.3%	$29,897	6.2%	$28,297	6.1%	$24,684	5.3%	$24,589	5.1%	$24,329	4.8%
Ancillary club revenue	$91,087	19.4%	$95,538	19.9%	$90,691	19.4%	$85,559	18.5%	$81,560	16.8%	$86,081	17.0%
Fees and other revenue	$5,985	1.3%	$5,804	1.2%	$4,890	1.0%	$4,761	1.0%	$4,661	1.0%	$6,031	1.2%
Total Revenue	**$470,225**	100.0%	**$478,981**	100.0%	**$466,941**	100.0%	**$462,387**	100.0%	**$485,392**	100.0%	**$506,709**	100.0%

Notes:

(a) Town Sports International Holdings 2013 10-K, p. 43.

(b) Town Sports International Holdings 2011 10-K, p. 40.

(c) Town Sports International Holdings 2009 10-K, p. 38.

Sales

The constant battle to attract and retain new members meant that much of TSI's success depended on its sales team. The company employed four different channels to reach out to prospective club members: direct sales at club locations, a corporate and group sales division, the company's corporate website, and a dedicated call center introduced in 2010 principally to reach out to former members and to handle specific campaigns.[74]

At year-end 2013, TSI employed over 400 in-club membership sales consultants who were responsible for new membership sales in and around their designated club locations. At the individual club level, each location had two or three membership sales consultants whose compensation was almost entirely incentive-based commission.[75]

Under the Private Fitness Center Division, established in June 2013, 21 full-time employees, located throughout TSI's markets, concentrated on building long-term relationships with local and regional companies and large groups such as Standard & Poors, New York University, Ralph Lauren, Con Edison, Viacom, and Citibank Corporate. Large group and corporate members accounted for approximately 18 percent of the company's sales by year-end 2013.[76] Corporate and group membership sales were typically sold under the higher priced Passport membership at a discount to standard rates with corporations sometimes subsidizing the costs of memberships provided to their employees.

Members of pre-established corporate or group programs were able to make purchases online at www.mysportsclubs.com. The website also allowed for TSI members to provide feedback about service levels and enabled prospective members to sign up for the 30 days for 30 dollars web trial membership. Members who joined on-line accounted for approximately 1.9 percent of memberships sold in 2013.[77] The website also provided information about club locations, program offerings, exercise class schedules, and sales promotions as well as employment and financial information. In 2013, the Company's first member self-service web and mobile site called "My Club," was introduced allowing members to manage their own schedules and book into classes on-line. Enhancements to "My Club" were planned for 2014.[78]

Marketing

TSI recognized that growing the company and remaining profitable depended heavily on the success of the company's marketing efforts. Total advertising costs incurred by TSI for the years ended December 31, 2013, 2012, and 2011 totaled $5,943, $6,158 and $5,999, respectively, and are included in club operating expenses.[79]

As an East Coast fitness franchise, TSI focused heavily on regional culture and current events, leveraging these elements to create unique marketing campaigns. Specifically, the multifaceted strategy was called "clustering" where budgets and strategies were tailored to focus primarily on the regions where its clubs and members were concentrated. This approach was intended to achieve three advertising objectives: grow the membership base, achieve broad regional brand awareness, and become "top of mind" to consumers.[80]

This clustering approach allowed TSI brands the flexibility to adapt messages to their specific regions while the metropolitan locations of its clubs enabled broader reach and higher frequency for advertising dollars spent. Recognizing its audience as upper-middle class, well-educated, and up-to-date on current events, the company's strategy was to play to the wit of their audience rather than bombard them with the traditional images of fit, toned bodies. Advertisements focused on catchy, one-line tags that focused on events in the news, pop culture, or city rivalries that caught a viewer's eye or sense of humor. Boston Sports Clubs took advantage of a years-old rivalry between Boston and New York City and created relevant, if not controversial, taglines such as "Hey Carlos Danger, we give extra attention to our members too" and "Alex, losing $34 million? Don't miss our summer sale. Join today and keep that A-bod."[81]

To deliver the Company's messages, TSI used a mix of just about everything from traditional outlets such as radio, newspapers, and television to targeted digital media, such as paid search, email, and online banners. TSI's use of social media platforms for marketing or consumer relation purposes was minimal as the company had no Twitter profile and only 2,234 "likes" on its corporate Facebook page.[82] Leveraging the metropolitan locations of many of its clubs, TSI also utilized transportation-based advertising slots in subway stations, trains, and buses, achieving high frequency, broad reach to a diverse populace at a maximized cost efficiency.

In keeping with its "top of mind" objective, TSI offered a variety of promotions and incentives for both members and non-members to participate. For example, TSI ran a "Write Our Ad" contest where the public was invited to send in taglines and ad copy for a chance to win a variety of prizes, including yearly memberships to Sports Club gyms and vacations to Jamaica.[83] In addition to general consumer engagement, TSI delivered targeted promotions to draw in new members such as trial memberships, fitness class specials, reduced joining fees, and corporate partnerships that offered employees of participating companies 20 percent off TSI memberships. Additionally, the company offered referral incentives to its current members to encourage "homegrown" growth.

Finally, TSI worked to incorporate public relations opportunities into its marketing strategy that would be beneficial to its image, with appearances in magazines such as *Self, Shape, and Fitness* as well as on television shows such as *Good Morning America* and *CNN*.[84] After the tragedy of 9/11, the New York Sports Clubs offered discounted rates to first responders of the disaster, gaining goodwill in the eyes of consumers and giving back to the community. Most recently, TSI opened its clubs to the public in the wake of Hurricane Sandy, offering free showers, charging stations, and complimentary workouts to the storm's victims. Additionally, the company partnered with New York Cares, a nonprofit that organizes volunteers, to run its "Workout to Help Out" fundraiser for those affected by Hurricane Sandy in New York City.[85]

Despite these well-coordinated efforts, the company lost 13,000 members over the course of 2013, a 2.5 percent drop in membership total year over year. Low enrollment rates from new members in 2013 dropped club revenue by 1.3 percent.[86] Harsh weather in December and January of 2014 further exacerbated the problem by reducing the typical influx of new members brought in by New Year's resolutions and the upcoming spring and summer seasons.

Financial Results

Town Sports International Holdings, Inc. traded on the NASDAQ Global Market under the ticker "CLUB." The company went public in 2006 through an I.P.O. (initial public offering) that raised less money than the company had originally anticipated. Ultimately, the company began trading around $13 per share and the stock's performance provided optimism for shareholders as the price rose to above $23 per share by April of 2007.[87] Economic turmoil across global equity markets along with deteriorating trends in the fitness club industry led to a sharp decline in TSI's stock price. The company traded below $5 per share for all of 2009 and 2010.[88] Since then, the stock price had been gradually climbing back towards pre-recession levels and TSI had been focusing on driving shareholder wealth through positive operating results and distributions, such as the one-time cash dividend of $3.00 per share issued to shareholders in 2012.[89]

Presented in **Exhibits 4** and **5** are TSI's historical balance sheets and income statements for the years ended December 31, 2008 through 2013. In 2013, TSI's total revenues decreased to $470.2 million from $479.0 million in 2012. The company generated most of its revenue from its club operations, but generated approximately $6 million in other revenue in 2012 and 2013 in the form of rental income, marketing revenue, and

EXHIBIT 4

Town Sports International Holdings Inc.						
Consolidated Balance Sheets						
(All figures in thousands except share data)						
Fiscal Years Ended December 31,	2013 (a)	2012 (a)	2011 (b)	2010 (b)	2009 (c)	2008 (c)
Balance Sheets						
Assets						
Current Assets						
Cash and equivalents	73,598	37,758	47,880	38,803	10,758	10,399
Accounts receivable, net	3,704	6,508	5,857	5,258	4,295	4,508
Inventory	473	438	290	217	224	143
Deferred tax assets, net	17,010	19,325	20,218	-	-	-
Prepaid corporate income taxes	6	550	73	7,342	1,274	8,116
Prepaid expenses and other current assets	10,850	11,435	10,599	13,213	10,264	14,154
Total Current Assets	105,641	76,014	84,917	64,833	26,815	37,320
Fixed assets, net	243,992	256,871	286,041	309,371	340,277	373,120
Goodwill	32,870	32,824	32,799	32,794	32,636	32,610
Intangible assets, net	908	-	-	44	149	281
Deferred tax assets, net	11,340	15,728	19,782	41,883	50,581	42,266
Deferred membership costs	8,725	10,811	10,117	5,934	6,079	14,462
Other assets	10,316	12,522	15,886	9,307	10,929	11,579
Total Assets	413,792	404,770	449,542	464,166	467,466	511,638
Liabilities and Stockholders' Equity (Deficit)						
Current Liabilities						
Current portion of long-term debt	3,250	15,787	25,507	14,550	1,850	20,850
Accounts payable	8,116	7,467	9,180	4,008	6,011	7,267
Accrued expenses	31,536	27,053	26,575	27,477	23,656	35,565
Accrued interest	737	89	950	6,579	6,573	523
Dividends payable	259	305	-	-	-	-
Deferred revenue	33,913	37,138	40,822	35,106	35,346	40,326
Total Current Liabilities	77,811	87,839	103,034	87,720	73,436	104,531
Long-term debt	311,659	294,552	263,487	301,963	316,513	317,160
Dividends payable	407	799	-	-	-	-

(Continued)

EXHIBIT 4
(Continued)

Town Sports International Holdings Inc.						
Consolidated Balance Sheets						
(All figures in thousands except share data)						
Fiscal Years Ended December 31,	**2013 (a)**	**2012 (a)**	**2011 (b)**	**2010 (b)**	**2009 (c)**	**2008 (c)**
Deferred lease liabilities	56,882	61,732	65,119	67,180	71,438	69,719
Deferred revenue	2,460	3,889	5,338	3,166	1,488	4,554
Other liabilities	8,089	11,455	12,210	11,082	12,824	14,902
Total Liabilities	457,308	460,266	449,188	471,111	475,699	510,866
Stockholders' Equity (Deficit)						
Common stock	24	24	23	23	23	25
Additional paid-in capital	(13,846)	(16,326)	(19,934)	(21,788)	(22,572)	(18,980)
Accumulated other comprehensive income	2,052	1,226	1,251	2,121	1,327	1,070
Accumulated earnings (deficit)	(31,746)	(40,420)	19,014	12,699	12,989	18,657
Total Stockholders' Equity (Deficit)	(43,516)	(55,496)	354	(6,945)	(8,233)	772
Total Liabilities and Stockholders' Equity (Deficit)	413,792	404,770	449,542	464,166	467,466	511,638

Notes:

(a) Town Sports International Holdings 2013 10-K, p. F-3.

(b) Town sports International Holdings 2011 10-K, p. F-3.

(c) Town Sports International Holdings 2009 10-K, p. F-3.

EXHIBIT 5

Town Sports International Holdings Inc.						
Consolidated Statements of Operations						
(All figures in thousands except share data and per share data)						
Fiscal Years Ended December 31,	**2013 (a)**	**2012 (a)**	**2011 (a)**	**2010 (b)**	**2009 (b)**	**2008 (b)**
Income Statements						
Revenues						
Club Operations	464,240	473,177	462,051	457,626	480,731	500,678
Fees and other	5,985	5,804	4,890	4,761	4,661	6,031
Total Revenue	470,225	478,981	466,941	462,387	485,392	506,709
Operating Expenses						
Payroll and related	174,894	181,632	177,528	185,583	193,891	193,580
Club operating	179,683	178,950	176,463	174,135	178,854	172,409
General and administrative	28,431	24,139	25,799	28,773	31,587	33,952
Depreciation and amortization	49,099	49,391	51,536	52,202	56,533	52,475
Insurance recovery related to damaged property	(3,194)	-	-	-	-	-
Impairment of fixed assets	714	3,436	-	3,254	6,708	3,867

Town Sports International Holdings Inc.

Consolidated Statements of Operations

(All figures in thousands except share data and per share data)

Fiscal Years Ended December 31,	2013 (a)	2012 (a)	2011 (a)	2010 (b)	2009 (b)	2008 (b)
Impairment of internal-use software	-	-	-	-	10,194	-
Impairment of goodwill	-	-	-	-	-	17,609
Total Operating Expenses	429,627	437,548	431,326	443,947	477,767	473,892
Operating Income	40,598	41,433	35,615	18,440	7,625	32,817
Loss on extinguishment of debt	750	1,010	4,865	-	-	-
Interest expense	22,617	24,640	24,274	21,158	20,972	23,902
Interest income	(1)	(43)	(147)	(145)	(3)	(319)
Equity in the earnings of investees and rental income	(2,459)	(2,461)	(2,391)	(2,139)	(1,876)	(2,307)
Income (loss) before benefit for corporate income taxes	19,691	18,287	9,014	(434)	(11,468)	11,541
(Benefit) provision for corporate income taxes	7,367	6,321	2,699	(144)	(5,800)	9,204
Net (loss) income	12,324	11,966	6,315	(290)	(5,668)	2,337
Earnings per Share (Basic)	$ 0.51	0.51	0.28	(0.01)	(0.25)	0.09
Earnings per Share (Diluted)	$ 0.50	0.50	0.27	(0.01)	(0.25)	0.09

Notes:

(a) Town Sports International Holdings 2013 10-K, p. F-4.

(b) Town sports International Holdings 2010 10-K, p. F-4.

management fees. Although revenues had generally been trending in a positive direction since 2010, total revenue still lagged the $506.7 million generated in 2008. Despite variations in the company's revenue trends, TSI was able to manage its bottom line efficiently, improving net income in each year since 2009. As of December 31, 2013, the company was highly leveraged. As seen in **Exhibit 4**, TSI's liabilities exceeded the book value of its assets, leading to a negative book value of equity of $43.5 million.

TSI's struggle to retain members and expand its club base resulted in deteriorating financial results in recent years. Turning to off-balance sheet financing to fund a special cash dividend to pay out to investors, TSI focused its attention on maximizing shareholder wealth. As economic conditions improved following the economic downturn, a predicted turnaround in the fitness club industry should lead to positive growth rates in operating results for TSI.

Future Outlook

Fitness will continue to grow as a priority for the American population, across all demographics. This will mean increased business opportunities as well as competition for established firms and newcomers alike. TSI is operating in an industry that will continue to evolve and challenge the status quo of what constitutes a positive fitness experience. As a powerful regional player in the fitness game, the company's success is directly tied to the health of the economy as well as customer loyalty and satisfaction. Projected increases in consumer discretionary spending signal a bright future for the company over the short term. Going forward, TSI must decide whether or not to maintain its traditional means of retaining customers and generating revenue streams or explore new means of operating. When considering longer-term growth, the company must examine its approach to adapting in a constantly changing environment, its current financial challenges, and its attempts to remain attractive to current and potential members. If the company fails on any of these accounts, what options will it have to recover? Given that many gyms have had to liquidate their facilities and assets in recent years, what steps can TSI take to avoid a similar fate? While some challenges, such as membership retention and attrition, are as old as the industry itself, newer challenges, such as increasing pressure from boutique shops and rapidly changing fitness trends, are pushing the company in ways it has never before experienced. Time will tell if TSI has the flexibility and vision to define its own fate in an environment that is anything but predictable.

NOTES

1. http://www.fundinguniverse.com/company-histories/town-sports-international-inc-history/
2. http://www.nytimes.com/2011/09/04/jobs/04boss.html?_r=0
3. Town Sports International Holdings, Inc. 2013 10K, p. 5.
4. Ibid.
5. Town Sports International Holdings, Inc. March 25, 2014 Proxy Statement, p. 17.
6. Ibid., p.16.
7. Ibid., pp. 4–5.
8. IBISWorld Report on Gyms, Health & Fitness Clubs in the U.S., February 2013, p. 8. www.IBISWorld.com
9. Town Sports International Holdings, Inc. 2013 10K , p. 2.
10. IBISWorld report on Gyms, Health & Fitness Clubs in the U.S., February 2013, p. 4–5 and 10. www.IBISWorld.com
11. Ibid., p.13.
12. Ibid., p. 5.
13. Ibid., p. 12.
14. "IHRSA Top Health Club Trends$ $2012." *IHRSA - Media Center*. International Health, Racquet & Sportclub Association, January 11, 2012. Web. 28 July 2013. http://www.ihrsa.org/media-center/2012/1/11/top-health-club-trends-for-2012.html. Also Town Sports International Holdings, Inc. 2013 10K, p. 3.
15. http://www.acsm.org/about-acsm/media-room/news-releases/2012/10/29/body-weight-training-emerging-trend-in-annual-acsm-fitness-survey
16. Town Sports International Holdings, Inc. 2013 10K, p. 3.
17. http://www.acsm.org/about-acsm/media-room/news-releases/2012/10/29/body-weight-training-emerging-trend-in-annual-acsm-fitness-survey
18. IBISWorld Report on Gyms, Health & Fitness Clubs in the U.S., February 2013, p. 5. www.IBISWorld.com
19. Town Sports International Holdings, Inc. 2013 10K, p. 3.
20. Ibid.
21. IBISWorld Report on Gyms, Health & Fitness Clubs in the U.S., February 2013, p. 15. www.IBISWorld.com
22. Ibid.
23. Ibid., p. 16.
24. Town Sports International Holdings, Inc. 2013 10K , p.14.
25. Ibid.
26. Ibid., p. 15.
27. IBISWorld Report on Gyms, Health & Fitness Clubs in the U.S., February 2013, p. 19. www.IBISWorld.com
28. Ibid., p.20.
29. Ibid., pp.24–26.
30. Ibid., p. 23.
31. Town Sports International Holdings, Inc. 2013 10K , p. 11.
32. Ibid., p. F21.
33. "Town Sports International Signs Deal to Acquire Fitcorp Clubs in Boston." Town Sports International Holdings Press Report, February, 14, 2014. http://investor.mysportsclubs.com/releasedetail.cfm?ReleaseID=740486
34. Ibid.
35. Town Sports International Holdings, Inc. 2013 10K, p. F 21.
36. "Town Sports International Signs Deal to Acquire West End Sports Club." http://investor.mysportsclubs.com/releasedetail.cfm?ReleaseID=740815 Town Sports International Holdings Press Report, February15, 2014.
37. Town Sports International Holdings, Inc. 2013 10K, p. 2.
38. Ibid., p. 5.
39. "Town Sports International Signs Deal to Sell New York City Property for $82 Million." Town sports International Holdings Press Release December, 24, 2013. http://investor.mysportsclubs.com/releasedetail.cfm?ReleaseID=815770
40. Town Sports International Holdings, Inc. 2013 10K , p. 39.
41. "Town Sports International Signs Deal to Sell New York City Property for $82 Million." Town sports International Holdings Press Release December, 24, 2013. http://investor.mysportsclubs.com/releasedetail.cfm?ReleaseID=815770
42. Ibid., p. 1.
43. Ibid.
44. Ibid., p. 38.
45. Ibid., p. 8.
46. Ibid., p. 11.
47. Ibid., p. 5.
48. Ibid., pp. 2 and 38.
49. Ibid., p. 3.
50. Ibid., pp. 3 and 4.
51. Ibid., p. 4.
52. Ibid.
53. Ibid., p. 18.
54. Ibid., p. 10.
55. Ibid., p. 5.
56. Ibid., p. 2.
57. Ibid., p. 10.
58. Ibid., p. 38.

59. IBISWorld Report on Gyms, Health & Fitness Clubs in the U.S., February 2013, p. 20. www.IBISWorld.com
60. Town Sports International Holdings, Inc. 2013 10K , p.58.
61. Ibid., pp. 8-9.
62. Ibid., p. 8.
63. Ibid., p. 9.
64. Ibid.
65. Ibid.
66. Ibid., p. 6.
67. Ibid., p. 5.
68. Ibid.
69. Ibid., p.12.
70. Ibid.
71. Ibid.
72. Ibid., p. 5.
73. Ibid.
74. Ibid., p. 7.
75. Ibid.
76. Ibid.
77. Ibid. p. 8.
78. Ibid., p. 13.
79. Ibid.,p. F-11.
80. Ibid., p. 6
81. http://www.bostonmagazine.com/news/blog/2013/08/12/boston-sports-club-ads-are-the-scourge-of-scandalous-new-yorkers/
82. https://www.facebook.com/MySportsClubs
83. http://www.mysportsclubs.com/contests/write_our_ad.htm
84. Town Sports International Holdings, Inc. 2013 10K , p. 7.
85. Ibid., p. 6.
86. Ibid., p. 40.
87. Town Sports International Holdings, Inc. 2007 10K , p. 26.
88. Ibid., p. 28.
89. Ibid, p. 32.

Zynga, Inc. (2011): Whose Turn Is It?

Zachary Burkhalter, Daniel Zuller, Concetta Bagnato, Joyce Vincelette, and Ellie A. Fogarty

Introduction

As Mark Pincus waited for his friend to play a word, he could not help but think how the Facebook IPO and the growth in mobile gaming would affect his company over the long term. Mr. Pincus, founder and Chief Executive Officer (CEO) of Zynga, had built a company around social gaming. This new type of gaming had transformed the gaming industry on multiple levels and across various platforms. Zynga had originally built its games using the Facebook platform and had capitalized on the company's unique method of social networking that had captured audiences around the world. However, this strong reliance on Facebook and changes in consumer gaming practices caused some concern for outside investors and the future of Zynga. As a result of these concerns, by 2012, Zynga had expanded beyond its almost total reliance on the Facebook platform. The company had developed browser-based games that worked both stand-alone on mobile platforms such as Apple iOS and Google Android and as an application on social networking websites such as Facebook, Zynga.com, Google+, and Tencent.[1]

Zynga was built entirely around the concept of social gaming. It could then be inferred that social gaming took playing video games to a new level. When playing games on platforms such as computers, cell phones, tablets, or other devices, gamers were no longer required to play alone or with a friend physically present. Social gamers were able to play with others, over the Internet, at each other's pace. This was exactly how Zynga's games were played. For example, *Words with Friends* was a game similar to *Scrabble*. One person initiated a game with a friend or random opponent, played a word on a board game, and then waited for the friend to see that it was their move, which could take minutes or days. The friend then played a word and the move was sent back to the other player. This went back and forth until the game was done and, of course, the player with the most points won. All social games followed a somewhat similar format. In some games, like *FarmVille*, a player could plant, plow, and harvest crops without waiting for another player. However, players could help each other farm by sending necessary supplies and fertilizing their friends' crops. Players could even send each other gifts, which could either be bought with coins gathered from harvesting crops or by purchasing coins via real money.

Social games had been known to generate considerable competition between players. In one instance, a *Words with Friends* game became so heated that a celebrity player was kicked-off an airplane for refusing to turn off his cell phone during his turn. However, in the heat of the social gaming battle, Mark Pincus could not help but wonder about a few things concerning Zynga's future. How could Zynga continue to generate new social games to attract the masses? Did Zynga's business model need modifications? Would it be a wise decision to move away from Facebook and toward Zynga's own platform? What was the future of mobile gaming? Where else could Zynga spend its marketing dollars to gain more users and effectively grow its fan base? Were there alternative methods for generating revenues more consistently in the future? How should Zynga spend the approximate US$1 billion generated from its IPO? In addition, Pincus knew that Zynga had to remain aware of the trends in the company's external environment, including its competition, customers, changing technology (cloud computing, apps, increasing and changing platforms, etc.), and the global legal landscape and yet continually create or acquire games that attracted large audiences.

History

After three failed companies, Mark Pincus decided to try yet again and founded Zynga in April 2007 under the name Presidio Media, as a California limited liability company. Presidio converted to a Delaware corporation in October 2007 and its name was changed to Zynga in November 2010.[2] Zynga was named for Mark Pincus's late American Bulldog, Zinga, and the company used an image of a bulldog as their logo.[3] Zynga's first game, *Texas Hold'EM Poker*, now known as *Zynga Poker*, was released on Facebook in July 2007.

The company received two rounds of venture capital financing in 2008 totaling US$39 million. By June of 2008, Zynga had launched *Mafia Wars* on multiple platforms, including Facebook and MySpace and acquired the *YoVille* game in order to expand its game portfolio.[4] Zynga Poker was free to players, and Zynga's revenues were generated through advertisements. Because of its popularity, Zynga decided to sell chips to users in 2008 to generate additional revenues.[5]

In April 2009, Zynga became the #1 Facebook app developer with 40 million monthly active users (MAUs).[6] Soon afterward, Zynga opened a game studio, Zynga East, in Baltimore. In June 2009, Zynga launched *FarmVille*, which quickly became the most popular game on Facebook with 20 million daily active users (DAUs). In the second half of 2009, Zynga launched several other new games, including *Café World*.

In 2010, Zynga saw continued growth from existing games and new game launches, including *FrontierVille* and *CityVille*. In February 2010, Zynga opened a studio in Los Angeles and also the company's first office outside of the United States, Zynga India, in Bangalore.[7] During the second quarter of 2010, Zynga acquired both XPD Media and Challenge Games, which would later become known as Zynga China and Zynga Austin, respectively. In August 2010, Zynga acquired Conduit Labs and renamed it Zynga Boston. At this time, Zynga began its expansion into Europe and acquired Dextrose AG, renamed Zynga Germany. Also during this year, Zynga acquired Bonfire Studios, renamed Zynga Dallas, and Texas-based mobile game developer, Newtoy, Inc., renamed Zynga with Friends. With Newtoy, Zynga acquired the games *Words with*

Friends and *Chess with Friends*. Additional smaller studios were also opened in 2010 in Japan and Seattle. In 2010, Facebook began requiring the use of Facebook Credits for monetization in Zynga games and on May 18, 2010, Zynga and Facebook entered into a five-year relationship to expand the use of Facebook Credits in Zynga games.[8] In December 2010, *CityVille* surpassed *FarmVille* as the company's most popular game with over 61 million MAUs and a base of over 16 million DAUs.[9]

In early 2011, Zynga announced numerous acquisitions, including the New York–based game developer Area/Code, renamed Zynga New York; Boston-based game developer Floodgate Entertainment; and MarketZero, renamed Zynga ATX, an online poker tracker company; Five Mobile, renamed Zynga Toronto, specializing in mobile platforms; as well as a number of smaller acquisitions. Zynga also launched a number of games in 2011, including *Empires and Allies*, the company's first strategy combat game; *Hanging with Friends*, a mobile game that was developed in the company's Zynga with Friends studio; *Indiana Jones Adventure World*; *Words with Friends on Facebook*; and *CastleVille*. In October 2011, Zynga announced plans to create the company's own platform on which users could play games.[10] Although the platform, Project Z, would have ties to Facebook, it would be the first step away from reliance on Facebook. This new platform would be operated as Zynga.com.

Zynga completed its initial public offering in December 2011 and the company's Class A common stock was listed on NASDAQ Global Select Market under the symbol "ZNGA."[11] During its IPO, Zynga issued and sold 100 million shares of Class A common stock at a public offering price of US$10 per share. The company raised a total of US$961.4 million of net proceeds.[12]

In early 2012, Zynga added a puzzle game, *Hidden Chronicles*, to its game portfolio, and also launched *Zynga Slingo*, a casino type game, and *Bubble Safari*, the first game created by Zynga San Diego and the first to be launched simultaneously on two platforms: Zynga.com and Facebook.[13] In March 2012, Zynga announced the purchase of the game company OMGOP, creator of *Draw Something*, a popular mobile game. The largest and most controversial of Zynga's acquisitions, OMGOP cost the company US$180 million.[14] In June 2012, CBS was the winner of a bidding war for the pilot of a TV game show based on *Draw Something*.[15]

In order to develop new titles, in early 2012 Zynga acquired four small mobile game companies, including German company, GameDoctors, maker of the *Zombie-Smash* game; U.S.-based company Page44 Studios, creator of the *World of Goo* game for the Apple iOS platform; San Francisco–based HipLogic; and New York–based Astro Ape Studios.[16] In June 2012, Zynga announced the purchase of video game maker Buzz Monkey, renamed Zynga Eugene. Buzz Monkey was known for working on successful video games such as *Tomb Raider* and *Tony Hawk*, as well as *Zynga's FrontiersVille*.[17]

In March 2012, Zynga launched the new Zynga Platform, Zynga.com, designed to bring players a new way to play social games. On Zynga.com, players were able to play not only Zynga-created games, but also games created by third-party game developers, called Platform Partners. Zynga planned to open up the new Platform and make it more widely available to all third-party game developers through an API by the end of 2012.[18] When launched, Zynga.com was available in 16 languages, including English, French, Italian, German, Spanish, Portuguese, Turkish, Indonesian, Norwegian, Danish, Dutch, Swedish, Chinese, Korean, Japanese, and Thai, and was totally integrated with Facebook.[19] An additional goal was to connect players of various Zynga game titles across multiple platforms. Players could create profiles to show their activity, message friends, discover which games friends were playing, and meet new people based on shared gaming interests.[20]

On June 26, 2012, Zynga launched the cross-platform *Zynga with Friends* network. Zynga described the network as a social lobby where all players could meet and play across all social networks and platforms. This meant that a player on Facebook would be able to play a game with a player on an iOS device.[21] Key features included activity feeds, a new chat interface, multiplayer leaderboards, and a variety of other additions designed to unify the company's titles. The *Zynga with Friends* network put Zynga in direct competition with Facebook as a social networking site.

Mission, Strategy, and Business Model

Mark Pincus, always thought that he would love to work with games and had been quoted as saying, "I've always said that social games are like a great cocktail party. . . . What I thought was the ultimate thing you can do—once you bring all of your friends and their friends together—is play games."[22] The concept behind all of Zynga's games was for them to be available for friends to play with or against each other over the Internet across platforms such as Facebook, mobile phones, Internet connected devices, social networking sites, and any platform that could help enhance a user's experience.[23]

This was consistent with Zynga's mission to: Connect the world through games.[24] To support this mission, Zynga encouraged entrepreneurship and innovation to produce breakthrough innovations, called bold beats.[25]

With the mission in mind, Zynga had achieved significant growth in a short period of time using a unique business model that had been questioned by analysts for its long-term sustainability. Essentially, Zynga's social games were free to play and the company generated revenue through the in-game sale of virtual goods and advertising. Initially, the primary method Zynga used to deliver its games to consumers had been the Facebook platform. Consumers would log on to Facebook to access Zynga games. By 2011, the number of people who played games on Facebook was shrinking. This decline had come as people shifted to playing games on their mobile devices instead of on personal computers. According to Zynga, the number of people who played its games on mobile devices was growing three times faster than the number of those who played on the Internet.

Recognizing these trends, by the fourth quarter of 2011 Zynga had begun investing in its own network infrastructure, with the goal of reducing its reliance on third-party, web-hosting services. By 2012, the company was hosting a significant portion of its game traffic on its own network infrastructure. Zynga also began investing in new distribution channels such as mobile and other platforms, including other social networks and in international markets, to expand its reach and grow its business. The company continued to hire additional employees and acquired companies with experience in developing mobile applications. Zynga also invested resources in integrating and operating some of the company's games on additional platforms, including Google+, mixi, and Tencent.[26]

As a result of the changes in consumer playing habits, Zynga's core business with its Facebook games had suffered. For Zynga, these trends made moving into mobile games and figuring out how to make money from them more important than ever. Zynga's CEO said his vision for mobile games was to connect a large network of game players across a variety of platforms. "I think that there's an opportunity on mobile devices for there to be a connector of these experiences," he said.[27]

Corporate Governance

Zynga's Code of Business Conduct was adopted on October 12, 2011, and Zynga's Corporate Governance Guidelines were adopted in March of 2012. These documents can be found on the company's website at http://investor.zynga.com/governance.cfm.

In September 2011, Zynga adopted a three-class common stock structure which had the effect of concentrating voting control with those stockholders who held the stock prior to the company's initial public offering, including Mark Pincus, founder and CEO, and other executive officers, employees, directors, and their affiliates. Zynga's Class C common stock had 70 votes per share. Mark Pincus was the only holder of Class C common stock. Class B common stock had seven votes per share. Class A common stock has one vote per share. As of December 31, 2011, there were approximately 1461 stockholders of Class B common stock and approximately 109 holders of Class A common stock. The holders of Class C and B common stock collectively held approximately 97.8% of the voting power of the company's outstanding capital stock, with Mark Pincus owning approximately 36.0% of the voting power. Future sales or transfers of Class B or Class C common stock would result in those shares converting to Class A common stock.[28]

Board of Directors.   Zynga's board of directors was comprised of two internal and six external members including: Mark Pincus founder, Chairman, and CEO; John Schappert, Chief Operating Officer (COO); William "Bing" Gordon, Reid Hoffman, Jeffrey Katzenberg, Stanley J. Meresman, Sunil Paul, and Owen Van Natta. Cash compensation had not been granted to non-employee directors for their services. Instead, non-employee directors had been granted options or restricted stock units (ZSUs) to purchase shares of Zynga's common stock under the company's equity incentive plans.[29]

The Zynga Way

Zynga attributed its success to its ability to identify, hire, integrate, develop, motivate, and retain talented employees, particularly game designers, product managers, and engineers under the leadership of Chief People Officer, Colleen McCreary. Zynga had historically hired a number of key personnel through acquisitions. As of March 31, 2012, Zynga was comprised of 2267 full-time employees domestically and internationally.[30] As of December 31, 2011, approximately 54% of Zynga employees had been with the company for less than one year, and approximately 84% for less than two years.[31]

Zynga's corporate headquarters, located in San Francisco, California, was nicknamed The Dog House.[32] Zynga employees enjoyed unique benefits including a gym and personal training, free gourmet meals, access to a nutritionist, pet insurance, massages, haircuts, acupuncture, a coffee shop, gaming arcade, basketball court, lounges with big-screen TVs, poker nights, and a beer bar in the basement with happy hours. Zynga also offered generous benefits packages to its employees. The company paid 100% of the premiums for medical, dental, and vision coverage, life and accident insurance, and short- and long-term disability protection for all U.S. full-time employees, as well as 75% of the premiums for dependents. The company had a unique vacation policy in that there was no formal policy. Instead, Zynga employees were encouraged to take days off when they felt the need.[33]

Zynga was known for its entrepreneurial, execution-focused, fiercely competitive, and stressful culture that worked well for the company pre-IPO but appeared to be more difficult to maintain as a public company obtaining most of its employees through acquisitions. Zynga's culture could be described as one where employees were encouraged to work hard and play hard. Many Zynga employees chose to work and thrived in the hard-driving, performance-driven, results-oriented culture that was often described as meritocratic, but others may not have been willing participants, particularly those who came on board through acquisitions. This had led to varying reports from employees about what it was like to work at Zynga, some very positive and some extremely negative.

Since its beginnings, Zynga utilized an organization structure where the company's studios operated independently from each other in game creation. When Zynga acquired small gaming companies, often their name was changed but the management and creative teams remained intact. The reason for this organizational structure was to encourage and reward creativity. Studio heads set goals and were given the freedom to achieve them any way that was possible.[34] Those who succeeded were rewarded with cash, stock bonuses, and extra resources, such as the ability to hire extra staff. Mark Pincus called this structure "true meritocracy." The approach was designed to motivate everyone to succeed in an environment where all winners were rewarded.[35]

Turning Games to Revenue

In 2012, Zynga generated revenue in primarily two ways: (1) through the in-game sale of virtual goods, and (2) through advertisements.[36]

Sale of Virtual Goods. All Zynga games were offered as live services that allowed players to play for free. Within these games, Zynga provided the opportunity for players to purchase virtual currency to obtain virtual goods that could enhance their game-playing experience. Examples of virtual goods were items used to decorate farms in Farmville, VIP access and chips in Zynga Poker, and gifts that players could buy for their online friends. Gamers could also advance through a game based on their time invested and level of skill, or purchase goods that would allow them to advance more quickly through a game and "skip the line," giving people the option of paying with time, or money.[37] Some forms of virtual currency could be earned through game play, while other forms could only be acquired for cash or, in some cases, by accepting promotional offers from the company's advertising partners.[38]

Virtual goods were the primary source of Zynga's revenues and the company generated US$969 million from the sales of these goods in 2011. Surprisingly, only a small percentage of gamers actually spent money on virtual goods in Zynga games. It was estimated that less than 1% of gamers were responsible for up to half of Zynga's sales, the majority of Zynga gamers did not spend any money.[39]

Zynga believed its players chose to pay for virtual goods for the same reasons they were willing to pay for other forms of entertainment. They enjoyed the additional playing time or added convenience, the ability to personalize their game boards, the satisfaction of leveling up, and the opportunity for sharing creative expressions. Zynga believed players were more likely to purchase virtual goods when they were connected to and playing with friends, whether those friends played for free or also purchased virtual goods.

According to Zynga's May 2010 agreement with Facebook, virtual goods purchased by gamers playing Zynga games on the Facebook Platform must purchase their virtual goods using Facebook Credits as the primary method of payment. Players could purchase Facebook Credits from Facebook, directly through Zynga games, or through game cards purchased from retailers and distributors. When playing Zynga games on platforms other than Facebook, players were able to purchase virtual goods through various payment methods offered in the games, including credit cards, PayPal, Apple iTunes accounts, and direct wires. Players could also purchase game cards from retailers and distributors for use on these platforms.[40]

Advertisements.   The second way Zynga generated revenue was through the company's online advertisements. Although advertising had not been the company's primary emphasis, Zynga was beginning to focus more on online ads as a source of revenue. The types of advertisements that Zynga used included: branded virtual goods and sponsorships that integrated advertising within game play; engagement ads and offers where players could answer certain questions or sign up for third-party services to receive virtual currency; mobile ads through ad-supported free versions of Zynga mobile games; and display ads in Zynga's online Web games that included banner advertisements.[41] Zynga generated US$55 million in revenues in 2011 from advertisements, which accounted for only 5% of the company's total revenues.

Zynga realized the importance of sustaining growth in the sale of virtual goods and increasing advertising revenues. Zynga's revenue growth depended on its ability to attract and retain players and more effectively monetize its player base through the sale of virtual goods and advertising.[42]

Partnerships

Facebook.   Facebook was the primary distribution, marketing, promotion, and payment platform for all Zynga games. In 2012, Zynga generated most of its bookings, revenue, and players through the Facebook platform.[43] In addition, the largest amount of marketing dollars Zynga spent was spent on Facebook ads.[44] In 2011, an estimated 93.25% of Zynga's yearly bookings and revenues were generated through the Facebook platform.[45]

Although Zynga had stated it would like to lessen its reliance on Facebook, it was also aware that if its relationship with Facebook were to deteriorate or if Facebook itself became less popular with consumers, the company's business would suffer and alternatives would have to be created. This would be costly and more than likely not as efficient in generating such large amounts of attention from gamers.[46] Zynga's relationship with Facebook was mutually beneficial. Not only did Zynga generate revenue and a large portion of its players from Facebook, Zynga contributed 12% of Facebook's US$3.711 billion in revenue or US$445 million during 2011.[47]

In May 2010, Zynga entered into a five-year deal with Facebook in order to promote the launch of their new games. This deal required that Zynga be subject to Facebook's standard terms and conditions for application developers that governed the promotion, distribution, and operation of Zynga games through the Facebook platform. These included: that Zynga must notify Facebook a week before a new game launch, that Facebook had control over the release date, and that Zynga game players must be actively logged into Facebook in order to play.[48] In addition to the standard terms, Zynga had an addendum with Facebook that modified the terms and required the use of Facebook Credits as the primary payment method for Zynga games on the Facebook platform. The addendum also required Facebook to remit to Zynga an amount equal to 70% of the face value of Facebook Credits purchased by Zynga game players for use in Zynga games. This addendum with Facebook expires in May 2015.[49]

Hasbro.   In mid-2012, Zynga announced a comprehensive partnership that granted Hasbro Inc. the rights to develop a wide range of toy and gaming experiences based on Zynga's popular social games and brands, such as *Farmville*, *Mafia Wars*, *Words With Friends*, and others. This deal also created opportunities for co-branded merchandise featuring a combination of both Hasbro and Zynga brands. The two companies expected that the first products would be available beginning fall 2012.[50]

New Platform Partners.   In early 2012, Zynga announced new Zynga Platform Partners including: Mob Science, Row Sham Bow, Sava Transmedia, Konami Digital Entertainment, Playdemic, Rebellion, 50 Cubes, Majesco Entertainment, and Portalarium. These partners were able to publish and promote their games on Zynga's new platform, Zynga.com, and not only have access to Zynga players but also the ability to tap into other Zynga features and metrics.[51] Zynga also announced partners for the company's new Zynga Partners for Mobile Program including Atari, Crash Lab, Fat Pebble, Phosphor Games Studio, and Sava Transmedia to help increase Zynga's presence on mobile devices.[52]

American Express.   In May 2012, Zynga and American Express announced a partnership that would link everyday spending to online rewards for Zynga game players through a cobranded prepaid card called Zynga Serve Rewards. Players would be able to add money to their Serve account through any funding source, including a bank account, debit card, credit card, or cash. The Serve Rewards card would be accepted everywhere in the United States that American Express cards were accepted for purchases and would receive online, in-game rewards.[53]

Acquisitions

Acquisitions had become an integral source of new games, international expansion, and employees for Zynga, and the foundation of Zynga's growth strategy. Zynga spent US$147.2 million for 22 companies during 2010 and 2011.[54] In order to develop new game titles for a variety of platforms, this strategy was continued into 2012 with the purchase of six domestic and international companies by mid-year, including OMGOP, creator of *Draw Something*, a popular mobile game.[55] *Draw Something* was the #1 word game in 80 countries when acquired by Zynga, and then experienced a noticeable drop in popularity following the acquisition, as DAUs dropped from 15 million to 10 million in the first month after the acquisition.[56] Mark Pincus was quoted as saying, "We love finding great, accomplished teams that share our mission and vision."[57]

To be successful with the company's acquisition strategy, Zynga must be able to successfully integrate acquired companies into its business and manage the growth associated with these multiple acquisitions. Zynga must also be able to integrate highly talented and creative employees from these acquired companies into Zynga's highly competitive culture. Zynga's headquarters, acquisitions, and studios are listed in **Exhibit 1**.

Operations

In 2007, Zynga was able to meet the demand for its games like Zynga Poker with a simple IT infrastructure using servers stacked in a rented retail data center. Then Zynga released *FarmVille* in 2009 and the company's IT needs changed overnight. Within five months of the game's release, 25 million users were hitting *FarmVille* servers. Zynga was not able to scale its internal infrastructure quickly enough to keep up with demand, so the company shifted most of its IT needs to Amazon Web Services (AWS). AWS allowed Zynga to buy virtual server and storage space, scaling capacity up and down as needed. Zynga relied on Amazon for most of its IT needs throughout 2009 and 2010, and then

EXHIBIT 1
Zynga Headquarters,
Acquisitions, Studios
and Facilities in
June 2012

- Zynga Corporate Headquarters, San Francisco, CA
- Zynga East-Baltimore, Maryland, 2009
- Zynga India-Bangalore, 2010
- Zynga Los Angeles, 2010
- Zynga China, Beijing (formerly XPD media), 2010
- Zynga Austin (formerly Challenge Games), 2010
- Zynga Boston (formerly Conduit Labs), 2010
- Zynga Japan, Tokyo (formerly UNOH games), 2010
- Zynga Germany, Frankfurt (formerly Dextro AG), 2010
- Zynga Dallas (formerly Bonfire Studios), 2010
- Zynga with Friends, McKinney, Texas (formerly Newtoy, Inc.), 2010
- Zynga ATX (formerly MarketZero, Inc.), 2011
- Zynga New York (formerly Area/Code), 2011
- Zynga Seattle, opened 2010
- Floodgate Entertainment, 2011
- Zynga Toronto (formerly Five Mobile), 2011
- OMGOP, 2012
- Wild Needle (casual gaming company specializing in games appealing to females), 2012
- Zynga Eugene (formerly Buzz Monkey Software), 2012
- GameDoctors, Germany, 2012
- Page44 Studios, 2012
- HipLogic, 2012
- Astro Ape Studios, 2012
- Zynga San Diego, 2012
- Additional smaller studios and facilities

realized that they could develop a proprietary system that would be more aligned with the company's business needs and yet be entirely within their own control. For example, with its own system, Zynga could customize its hardware and software to meet the specific needs of *FarmVille*, *Words with Friends*, and all of its other games.[58]

In 2010, Zynga started building data centers on both the east and west coasts. By the end of 2011, about 80% of Zynga game users at any given time were logged onto servers in the company's own data centers, while the other 20% were playing in the Amazon cloud. By 2012, Zynga's internal infrastructure, called zCloud, was able to not only serve the company's social gaming needs but also provide a platform to help third-party developers build social games.[59] Zynga planned to continue to use Amazon to meet some of its server needs and provide increased capacity when needed.

In March 2011, Zynga announced the launch of a new platform, Zynga.com, where players were able to play not only Zynga-created games, but also games created by third-party game developers, called Platform Partners. Zynga planned to open up the new Platform and make it more widely available to all third-party game developers through an API by the end of 2012.[60] The Zynga API would allow third-party game developers to take advantage of Zynga's technology and servers and build their own games on top of Zynga's technology, enhancing online gaming opportunities for smaller startups.

In 2012, Zynga had one operating segment with one business activity, developing, and monetizing social games.[61] In the past, the company's studios specialized in certain types of social games for specific devices. By 2012, all studios created games for mobile devices, indicating the increased importance placed on the development of mobile games for the future success of Zynga.

Marketing

In 2012, Zynga developed, marketed, and operated online social games as live services played over the Internet, on social gaming sites, and on mobile platforms.[62] In 2011, Zynga was the world's leading provider of social games with 240 million MAUs in over 175 countries. Zynga launched the most successful social games in the industry in 2009, 2010, and 2011 and generated over US$1.85 billion in cumulative revenue and over US$2.35 billion in cumulative bookings since the company's inception in 2007.[63]

Products. Zynga had historically depended on a small number of games for the majority of its revenue. Company growth depended on the ability to launch and enhance games that attracted and retained a significant number of players. The games that constituted Zynga's top three games varied over time, but historically, the top three revenue-generating games in any period contributed the majority of Zynga's revenue. Zynga's top three games accounted for 57%, 78%, and 83% of Zynga's online game revenue in 2011, 2010, and 2009, respectively.[64]

From 2007 to 2012, Zynga had regularly created and launched new social games and had improved upon well establish games. All Zynga's games were accessible to players worldwide on mobile platforms such as Apple iOS and Google Android and as an application on social networking websites such as Facebook, Zynga.com, Google+, and Tencent.[65] In 2012, Zynga was actively attempting to increase the number of games offered on multiple platforms, especially mobile platforms, through both internal game development and acquisitions. A list of Zynga Games in mid-2012 can be found in **Exhibit 2**.

In 2012, Zynga created and launched new games in what Zynga called popular "genres." In the *Ville* genre, Zynga was about to launch *FarmVille 2*, and had created *The Ville*, *ChefVille*, and other popular games. In the *Casino* genre, Zynga built on the legacy of *Zynga Poker* and *Zynga Bingo* and created *Zynga Slots* and *Zynga Elite Slots*. Casino games using real money rather than virtual currency were also in the works. In the *Arcade* genre, a new game called *Ruby Blast* became the first game from both Zynga China and Zynga Seattle and the first international cross-collaboration for a game launch. In the *Words with Friends* genre, Zynga was building on the popularity *of Words with Friends* with the creation of *Scramble with Friends,* a find a word game, and *Matching with Friends*, a puzzle game involving matching colors. Additional "genres" were planned.

Zynga's "products" were classified as social games for a variety of platforms, but it needed to be understood that Zynga gave these products to game players for free. Customers were not charged for these products. Zynga generated real revenue and posted real profits from the sale of virtual goods and to a lesser extent advertising.[66] Social game developers found it more difficult to make money from mobile games than from computer console–based games because the smaller screen size resulted in less room for advertisements. In addition, players on mobile devices tended to be more casual players who spent less money for ways to advance quickly in a game, than did the more

EXHIBIT 2
Zynga Games
July 2012

Blackjack	Matching with Friends
Bubble Safari	Pathwords
CastleVille	PetVille
CaféWorld	The Pioneer Trail (formerly FrontierVille)
ChefVille	Ruby Blast
Chess with Friends	Scramble with Friends
CityVille	Sudoku
CityVille Holidaytown	The Ville CityVille
Hometown	Treasure Isle
Draw Something	Vampires: Bloodlust
Dream Heights	Vampire Wars
Dream Pethouse	Word Twist
Dream Zoo	Words with Friends
Drop7	Yakuza Lords
Empires & Allies	YoVille
FarmVille	Zynga Bingo
FarmVille Mobile	Zynga Elite Slots
FishVille	Zynga Poker+
ForestVille	Zynga Slingo
Hanging with Friends	Zynga Slots
Hidden Chronicles (F	Zombie Swipeout
Indiana Jones Adventure World	ZombieSmash
Live Poker	

Upcoming Games
FarmVille2

dedicated players on PCs. These concerns had led to debates about whether mobile games should be free or if players should pay to play up front.[67]

Customers.   To sustain revenue levels, it was necessary to attract, retain, and increase the number of players or more effectively monetize the company's existing players.[68] Mark Pincus said, "The most important predictor of next month's usage is how many people you play with this month."[69]

It was important for Zynga to understand the characteristics of its players for the effective expense of marketing dollars. With over 247 million MAUs in 2011, Zynga had found it difficult to pinpoint the exact characteristics of the company's average gamer.[70] However, studies suggested, somewhat surprisingly, that the average person that engaged in social games was a 43-year-old woman.[71] This demographic made more sense when the characteristics of social games were considered. Social games were simple to play, could be played in a short period of time, and were for the most part offered for free. Women outpaced men with 38% and 29%, respectively, playing social games several times a day. The study also cited that women were more likely to play with real-world friends than men, and men were more likely than women to play with strangers met online. Roughly 95% of social gamers played multiple times per week and almost two-thirds played at least daily.[72] Another survey discovered that gamer age correlated to whether or not the player purchased in-game virtual goods.

It was found that the older the gamer, the more inclined they were to spend money on goods. Forty-two percent of all virtual goods purchases were made by gamers 35 and older, while 18% of virtual good purchases were made by players 18 to 25 years of age.[73]

The number of individuals who accessed the Internet through devices other than a personal computer, such as Smartphones, tablets, televisions, and set-top box devices had increased dramatically and the trend was likely to continue. These devices typically had lower processing speed, power, functionality, and memory and made playing Zynga games through these devices more difficult and the versions developed less compelling to players.

It was estimated that in mid-2012 nearly half of U.S. cell phone subscribers had a Smartphone, up from 36% in 2011. This almost 14% increase was not surprising considering two out of three people who purchased a new device chose a Smartphone.[74] The tablet industry had also been on the rise and in 2012 boasted just under 60 million users.[75] The consumer transition from playing social games on desktop computers to playing these games on mobile platforms happened in a very short period of time requiring social game developers to scramble to make the transition in order to remain profitable.

Advertising.   Zynga generated advertising revenue through paid advertisements and also spent considerable advertising dollars to attract new players to Zynga games and to advertise new games and game upgrades. During 2011, Zynga spent about US$234 million dollars on marketing. This equated to the company spending roughly 36 cents to earn one dollar in sales, up from 14 cents in the third quarter of 2011.[76] Most of the traditional advertising dollars were spent on Facebook advertisements. Zynga, however, acquired most players through unpaid channels and had gained users by the viral and sharing features available on social networking sites.[77] In addition, Zynga tried to stay connected with players through fan pages, generally on Facebook, Twitter, and occasionally hosted live and online player events.[78]

Zynga operated in a highly competitive and fast-paced environment. Zynga competed for the leisure time, attention, and discretionary spending of its players with other social game developers, on a number of factors, including quality-of-player experience, brand awareness and reputation, and access to distribution channels. For Zynga to be successful, the company must fully understand the competition and the changing nature of the company's external environment.

The Legal Landscape

Government Regulations.   Zynga is subject to a number of foreign and domestic laws and regulations that affect companies conducting business on the Internet, many of which are still evolving and subject to interpretation. Because some of Zynga's games, such as *Zynga Poker*, are based on traditional casino games, the company had structured and operated these games with the gambling laws in mind. Zynga also sometimes offered its players various types of sweepstakes, giveaways, and promotional opportunities.[79] Because the U.S. Justice Department has signaled that states could begin developing regulations for online gambling, Zynga had begun investing in state and federal lobbying efforts around gambling with real money. Zynga reported spending some US$75,000 during the second quarter of 2012 on these lobbying efforts. Zynga planned on releasing its first real money gambling program in early 2013.

Privacy issues.   Zynga was subject to federal, state, and foreign laws regarding privacy and protection of player data. This regulatory framework for privacy issues worldwide was currently in flux. During the course of its business, Zynga received, stored, processed, and used personal information and other player data, and enabled its players to share their personal information with each other and third parties, on both the Internet and mobile platforms. These practices had come under increased public scrutiny, and civil claims alleging the liability for the breach of data privacy had been asserted against Zynga.[80]

Cheating Programs and Scams.   Unauthorized third parties operated cheating programs that enabled players to exploit Zynga games, play them in an automated way or obtain unfair advantages over players who played fairly. In addition, unauthorized parties had attempted to scam players with fake offers for virtual goods, disrupting the virtual economy of Zynga games.[81]

Intellectual Property.   Intellectual property in the gaming industry was a very valuable asset; however, it was sometimes hard to protect because the laws were so loosely defined. The laws protected expressions, or codes used to create games, but not ideas. For example, the idea of a farm game could not be protected because of its generality, but the code used to create the games could be protected.[82] Based on the law, if Zynga or any other developer could create a game with the company's own code but used the same concept as another, it was legal. This interpretation of the law had provided a challenge for all game companies in the industry. Copying of successful game ideas had been rampant in the industry with numerous lawsuits filed.

Zynga and its competitors had extensively used this "copying" strategy. If another game developer created a game that saw positive results, Zynga launched a similar version of its own. When Psycho Monkey launched the popular game *Mob Wars*, Zynga came out with *Mafia Wars*.[83] Zynga responded to Playfish's *Restaurant City* with their *Café World*.[84] After Slashkey's *Farm Town* appeared successful, Zynga's quickly created *Farmville*.[85] Many examples could also be found of competitors engaged in similar practices. Mark Pincus believed that the copying of competitor's products was a sound business level strategy.

Industry players had engaged in this strategy because it had worked. It had proven to be a cost-effective formula. Competitors had been able to quickly launch games while making slight improvements based on player experiences. The downside of the strategy was the cost of lawsuits and potential damage to a company's image. Just one lawsuit with Psycho Monkey over the copying of *Mob Wars* cost Zynga US$7 to US$9 million in an out-of-court settlement.[86]

In June 2012, Zynga appeared to have stepped on bigger toes with potentially deeper pockets. Electronic Arts (EA) hit Zynga with a copyright infringement suit stating similarities that were more than coincidental and superficial between *The Sims Social* (launched in August 2011) and Zynga's *The Ville* (released in June 2012) and deemed it a "clear violation" of copyright laws. The lawsuit alleged that Zynga copied everything from design choices and animations to visual style and character motions. Reginald Davis, Zynga's General Counsel, had responded that Zynga planned to defend itself against the EA lawsuit and has stated that *The Ville* was much more innovative than *The Sims Social*.[87]

Lawsuits.   Typing in the keywords "Zynga" and "lawsuit" together in Google's search bar resulted in a whopping 1,210,000 hits as of this writing, which gives the reader an idea of the scope of Zynga's legal concerns. Most of these lawsuits dealt with alleged intellectual property law violations. In July 2012, Zynga was hit with an insider-trading lawsuit alleging that some top executives and investors, including CEO Mark Pincus and Google, engaged in insider trading. Following Zynga's IPO in December 2011, employees and investors were "locked up," unable to sell their shares until May 28th. A group of top executives and shareholders hired underwriters to manage the sale of some of their shares, creating a loophole that allowed them to sell some of their stock at US$12 on April 3. Zynga actually beat Q1 2012 earnings estimates and the "insiders" were not aware of Q2 results prior to selling their stock, but the stock price declined to approximately US$3 per share shortly after the sale, raising investor concerns.[88]

Corporate Philanthropy

Through Zynga's philanthropic arm, Zynga.org, the company raised over US$13 million for its nonprofit partners, including UCSF Benioff Children's Hospital, Save the Children, the World Food Programme, Habitat for Humanity, St. Jude's Children's Research Hospital, Wildlife Conservation Society, Half the Sky Foundation, Direct Relief International, Every Mother Counts, and many others, by selling virtual goods in Zynga games and donating some of the proceeds to charity.[89] In addition, the Knight Foundation and Zynga collaborated to look into the creation of digital games that were not just for entertainment, but also had a philanthropic or social edge. Zynga.org was also focused on working with nonprofits to help them develop suitable online games to raise money for their organizations.

Finance

In addition to traditional financial measures of the company's performance, Zynga used a number of proprietary metrics to evaluate the company's financial and operating results. A description of these metrics can be found in **Exhibit 3**. Zynga's balance sheets, statement of operations, and cash flow statements can be found in **Exhibits 4** through **6**.

From 2008 to 2011, Zynga reported revenue of US$19.4 million, US$121.5 million, US$597.5 million, and US$1.14 billion, respectively, and bookings of US$35.9 million, US$328.1 million, US$838.9 million, and, US$1.16 billion, respectively.[90] The resulting net income from 2008 to 2011 was a loss of US$22.1 million, US$52.8 million, and US$404.3 million in 2008, 2009, and 2011, respectively, and a gain of US$90.6 million in 2010. International revenue as a percentage of the total accounted for 36%, 33%, and 27% in 2011, 2010, and 2009, respectively.[91]

Exhibit 6 shows Zynga's statement of operations for the six months ended June 30, 2012 compared to the six months ended June 30, 2011. As can be seen, Zynga's total revenue was up 25% to US$653.5 million from US$522 million in the prior year. During this same period, the company's cost of revenue had also increased significantly to US$184 million from US$145 million in June 2011. More importantly, Zynga's total costs and expenses as of June 2012 increased nearly 65% to US$777 million from US$472 million during the same in 2011. As a result, Zynga's stock price dropped to US$5.44 as of the close on June 29, 2012. After Zynga announced second-quarter results on July 25, 2012, and slashed the company's 2012 earnings outlook, Zynga's stock plunged to US$3.05, down nearly 70% from the company's IPO price of US$10 in December 2011.

EXHIBIT 3

Zynga Proprietary
Key Financial and
Operating Metrics

Bookings were equal to the revenue recognized in the period in addition to the change in deferred revenue during the period. Bookings were used to evaluate the results of operations, generate future operating plans, and assess company performance. Bookings were the fundamental metric used by Zynga to manage its business. Zynga believed it was a better indicator of the sales activity in a given period.

Adjusted EBITDA was calculated as net income (loss), adjusted for benefit from income taxes; other income (expense), net; interest income; gain (loss) from legal settlements; depreciation; amortization; stock-based compensation; and change in deferred revenue.

DAUs (daily active users of Zynga games) were the number of individuals who played a game during a particular day. Under this metric, an individual who played two different games on the same day was counted as two DAUs. Similarly, an individual who played the same game on two different platforms or on two different social networks on the same day was counted as two DAUs. Average DAUs was the average of the DAUs for each day during the period recorded. Zynga used DAU as a measure of audience engagement.

MAUs (mean monthly active users of Zynga games) were the number of individuals who played a particular game during a 30-day period. Under this metric, an individual who played two different games in the same period was counted as two MAUs. Similarly, an individual who played the same game on two different platforms or on two different social networks during the period was counted as two MAUs. Average MAUs were the average of the MAUs at each month-end during the period. Zynga used MAUs as a measure of total game audience size.

MUUs (mean monthly unique users of Zynga games) were the number of unique individuals who played any Zynga game on a particular platform in a 30-day period. Any individual who played more than one Zynga game during the period was counted as a single MUU. Because many Zynga players played more than one game during a given 30-day period, MUUs were always lower than MAUs in any given period. Average MUUs for a particular period were the average of the MUUs at each month-end. Zynga used MUU as a measure of total audience reach across the company's network of games.

MUPs (monthly unique payers) were the number of unique players who made a payment at least once during the applicable month. If a player made a payment in Zynga games on two different platforms in a period, the player was counted as two unique players in that period. MUPs were presented as a quarterly average of the three months in the applicable quarter.

ABPU (average bookings per user) were defined as Zynga total bookings in a given period, divided by the number of days in that period, divided by the average DAUs during the period. Zynga used ABPU as a measure of overall monetization across all of the company's players through the sale of virtual goods and advertising.

SOURCE: Zynga, Inc., *2011 Form 10-K*, pp. 35–36.

Correspondingly, Zynga's ending cash balance had reduced to US$435 million as of June 2012, compared with US$535 million as of June 2011. This decrease in cash, on top of a falling stock price and costs and expenses increasing more than revenue, suggested concerns about Zynga's future. The Zynga management team listed several reasons for the results, including changes to Facebook's gaming platform making Zynga's most profitable games harder to find, the shift to mobile platforms, a delayed game release, and several games that were poorly rated by users. Zynga had also struggled to get users of its mostly free games to pay real money for virtual items in games.[92]

EXHIBIT 4
Consolidated Balance Sheets: Zynga Inc. (Dollar amounts in thousand, except share and per share information)

	For the Fiscal Year Ended		
	December 31, 2011	December 31, 2010	December 31, 2009
Assets			
Current assets:			
Cash and cash equivalents	$ 1,582,343	$ 187,831	$ 127,336
Marketable securities	225,165	550,259	72,622
Accounts receivable, net of allowance of $163 and $325 at December 31, 2011 and 2010, respectively	135,633	79,974	7,157
Income tax receivable	18,583	36,577	11,298
Deferred tax assets	23,515	24,399	—
Restricted cash	3,846	2,821	653
Other current assets	34,824	24,353	3,082
Total current assets	2,023,909	906,214	222,140
Long-term marketable securities	110,098	—	—
Goodwill	91,765	60,217	—
Other intangible assets, net	32,112	44,001	1,045
Property and equipment, net	246,740	74,959	34,827
Restricted cash	4,082	14,301	—
Other long-term assets	7,940	12,880	836
Total assets	$ 2,516,646	$ 1,112,572	$ 258,848
Liabilities and stockholders' equity (deficit)			
Current liabilities:			
Accounts payable	44,020	33,431	21,503
Other current liabilities	167,271	78,749	35,024
Deferred revenue	457,394	408,470	178,109
Total current liabilities	668,685	520,650	234,636
Deferred revenue	23,251	56,766	45,690
Deferred tax liabilities	13,950	14,123	—
Other non-current liabilities	61,221	38,818	—
Total liabilities	767,107	630,357	28,326
Stockholders' equity			
Convertible preferred stock, $.00000625 par value:			
Authorized, 0 and 351,199 at December 31,2011 and 2010, respectively. Issued and outstanding, 0 and 276,702 shares at December 21, 2011 and 2010, respectively (aggregate liquidation preference of $849,380 at December 31, 2010.	—	394,026	47,672
Common stock, $.00000625 par value:			
Authorized, 2,020,517 (Class A 1,100,000, Class B 900,000, Class C 20,517) and 965,632 (Class A 0, Class B 945,115, Class C 20,517) shares at December 31, 2011 and 2010, respectively. Issued and Outstanding, 721,592 (Class A 121,381, Class B 579, 694, Class C 20,517) and 291,524 (Class A 0, Class B 271,007, Class C 20,517) shares at December 31, 2011 and 2010, respectively;	4	2	2

	For the Fiscal Year Ended		
	December 31, 2011	December 31, 2010	December 31, 2009
Additional paid-in capital	2,426,164	79,335	6,610
Treasury stock	(282,897)	(1,484)	—
Other comprehensive income	362	114	21
Retained earnings (accumulated deficit)	(394,094)	10,222	(75,783)
Total stockholders' equity	1,749,539	482,215	(21,478)
Total equity and liabilities	$ 2,516,646	$ 1,112,572	$ 258,848

SOURCE: Zynga, Inc. 2011 Form 10-K, p.57.

EXHIBIT 5
Consolidated Statement of Operations Data: Zynga Inc. (In thousands, except per share, users, and ABPU data)

	For the Fiscal Year Ended (1)				
		Year Ended December 31,			Period from Inception (April 19, 2007) to December 31,
	2011	2010	2009	2008	2007
Consolidated statements of operations data:					
Revenue	$ 1,140,100	$ 597,459	$ 121,467	$ 19,410	$ 693
Costs and expenses:					
Cost of revenue	330,043	176,052	56,707	10,017	189
Research and development	727,018	149,519	51,029	12,160	869
Sales and marketing	234,199	114,165	42,266	10,982	231
General and administrative	254,456	32,251	24,243	8,834	277
Total costs and expenses	1,545,716	471,987	174,245	41,993	1,566
Income (loss) from operations	(405,616)	125,472	(52,778)	(22,583)	(873)
Interest income	1,680	1,222	177	319	22
Other income (expense), net	(2,206)	365	(209)	187	8
Income (loss) before income taxes	(406,142)	127,059	(52,810)	(22,077)	(843)
(Provision for)/ benefit from income taxes	1,826	(36,464)	(12)	(38)	(3)
Net income (loss)	$ (404,316)	$ 90,595	$ (52,822)	$ (22,115)	$ (846)
Deemed dividend to a Series B-2 convertible preferred stockholder	—	4,590	—	—	—
Net income attributable to participating securities	—	58,110	—	—	—
Net income (loss) attributable to common stockholders	$(404,316)	$27,895	$52,822	$22,115	$(846)
Net income (loss) per share attributable to common stockholders					
Basic	$(1.40)	$0.12	$(0.31)	$(0.18)	$(0.06)
Diluted	$(1.40)	$0.11	$(0.31)	$(0.18)	$(0.06)

(Continued)

EXHIBIT 5
(Continued)

	For the Fiscal Year Ended (1)				
					Period from Inception (April 19, 2007) to December 31,
	Year Ended December 31,				
	2011	**2010**	**2009**	**2008**	**2007**
Weighted average common shares used to compute net income (loss) per share attributable to common stockholders:					
Basic	288,599	223,881	171,751	119,990	14,255
Diluted	288,599	329,256	171,751	119,990	14,255
Other financial and operational data:					
Bookings	1,155,509	$838,896	$328,070	$35,948	$1,351
Adjusted EBITDA	303,274	$392,738	$168,187	$4,549	–$185
Average DAUs (in millions)	57	56	41	NA	NA
Average MAUs (in millions)	233	217	153	NA	NA
Average MUUs (in millions)	151	116	86	NA	NA
ABPU	$ 0.055	$0.041	$0.035	NA	NA

NOTE: Definitions and calculations for "Other Financial and Operational Data" can be found in Exhibit 3.
SOURCE: Zynga, Inc. *2011 Form 10-K*, pp. 29–30.

EXHIBIT 6
Consolidated Statements of Operations for Six Months Ended June 30, 2011 and 2010: Zynga Inc. (In thousands, except per share data) (Unaudited)

	Six Months Ended June 30,	
	2012	**2011**
Revenue		
Online game	$584,328	$493,872
Advertising	69,137	28,162
Total revenue	653,465	522,034
Cost and expenses:		
Cost of revenue	184,963	145,738
Research and development	358,192	167,507
Sales and marketing	112,892	78,254
General and administrative	121,445	81,328
Total costs and expenses	777,492	472,827
Income (loss) from operations	(124,027)	49,207
Interest income	2,375	961
Other income (expense), net	20,108	(536)
Income (loss) before income taxes	(101,544)	49,632
Provision for income taxes	(6,618)	(31,483)
Net income (loss)	$(108,162)	$18,149

SOURCE: Zynga, Inc. Form 10-Q filed on July 30, 2012.

Future Outlook

In the company's short history, Zynga had been able to capitalize on the growth of social gaming and the popularity of the Facebook platform. By mid-2012, Facebook had been showing signs of weakness, and Zynga's growth in bookings had been slowing down. In addition, there was a rapid shift in demand from console-based social games to mobile gaming. Zynga had been preparing for the shift by acquiring companies with mobile gaming experience and developing games for mobile platforms. In addition, Zynga had lessened its reliance on Facebook and had invested considerable resources in infrastructure, including new platforms and networks. The social gaming industry had changed rapidly in just two years and more changes appeared to be on the horizon. Zynga will need to rethink the sustainability of the company's current business model as it plans for future success.

NOTES

1. "About Zynga" (http://company.zynga.com/about).
2. Zynga, Inc., *2011 Form 10-K*, p. 2.
3. http://www.crunchbase.com/company/zynga
4. Zynga, Inc., *2011 Form 10-K*, p. 33.
5. http://venturebeat.com/2011/12/12/zynga-history/view-all/
6. Mack, Christopher, "Zynga Making $100 Million/Year," April 30, 2009, (http://www.insidesocialgames.com/2009/04/30/zyngamaking-100-millionyear/)
7. "Zynga Opens First International Office in India," http://www.businesswire.com/news/home/20100217005531/en/Zynga-Opens-International-Office-India
8. "Facebook and Zynga Enter into a Long-Term Relationship" (http://www.facebook.com/press/releases.php?p=162172)
9. "CityVille Dethrones FarmVille as Biggest Game on Facebook: What's Next for Zynga?" (http://www.Socialtimes.com/2010/12/cityville-dethrones-farmville-as-biggest-game-on-facebookwhats-next-for-zynga/)
10. Anderson, Ash, "Zynga Unveils New Games and a New Platform, Project Z," http://www.hollywoodreporter.com/news/zynga-unveils-new-games-own-246702
11. Zynga, Inc., *2011 Form 10-K*, p. 2.
12. Ibid., p. 63.
13. Zynga company website, http://company.zynga.com/games/featured-games
14. http://www.bloomberg.com/news/2012-04-17/zynga-flashes-1-8-billion-searching-for-the-new-farmville-tech.html
15. Wallenstein, Andrew, "CBS to Adapt Zynga game 'Draw Something' for TV," June 15, 2012, (http://www.variety.com/article/VR1118055570)
16. "Zynga Acquires Four Mobile Gaming Companies," January 19, 2012, (http://www.telecompaper.com/news/zynga-acquires-fourmobile-gaming-companies)
17. Cutler, Kim-Mai, "Zynga Adds 50 People Through Talent Acquisition of Video Game Maker Buzz Monkey," June 4, 2012, (http://techcrunch.com/2012/06/04/zynga-acquires-buzz-monkey/)
18. www.Zynga.com, Press Release, "Zynga Unveils New Platform for Play," March 2012.
19. Ibid.
20. Chang, Alexandra, "Zynga Unleashes New Games and Its Own 'With Friends' Social Network," *Wired*, June 26, 2012, (http://www.wired.com/gadgetlab/2012/06/zynga-unleashed-its-own-social-network-new-games)
21. Eldon, Eric, "Zynga Launches Cross-Platform *Zynga with Friends*, Multiplayer, New Chat Features, and More Games," June 26, 2012, (http://www.techcrunch.com/2012/06/26/zynga-network-adds-social-lobby-for-users-across-all-devices)
22. http://venturebeat.com/2011/12/12/zynga-history/view-all/
23. Zynga, Inc., *2011 Form 10-K*, p. 2.
24. Ibid., p. 2.
25. Ibid., p. 2.
26. Ibid., p. 38.
27. Rice, Shayndi, *The Wall Street Journal*, August 6, 2012, pp. B1–2. http://online.wsj.com/article/SB10000872396390443545504577567762954064098.html?mod=djemjiewrMGdomainid
28. Zynga. Inc., Proxy Statement, June 8, 2012, p. 21.
29. Ibid., pp. 9–12.
30. http://investor.zynga.com/faq.cfm
31. Zynga, Inc., *2011 Form 10-K*, p. 4.
32. "Zynga Slashes Outlook, Denting Iits Stock and Facebook's," http://mobile.reuters.com/article/idUSL2E8IPJFS20120725?irpc=932
33. Hintz-Zambrano, Katie, "Zynga's Stylish Power Players Give Us a Tour of Their Extra-Fun Office" April 12, 2012, (http://www.refinary29.com/zynga-offoce-tour).
34. http://www.cenedella.com/job-search/zynga-org-structure-follows-business-needs/
35. http://blogs.atlassian.com/2010/03/zynga_on_game_development_tools/
36. http://files.shareholder.com/downloads/AMDA-KX1KB/1956019531x0x562957/69c06a79-9713-43a3-8f3a-cead638f00d0/2011AnnualReport.pdf. Also Zynga, Inc., *2011 Form 10-K*, p. 49.
37. http://mashable.com/2012/03/23/zynga-economics/
38. Zynga, Inc., *2011 Form 10-K*, p. 3.

39. http://images.businessweek.com/cms/2011-07-13/tech_zynga29_01_popup.jpg

40. Zynga, Inc., *2011 Form 10-K*, pp. 49 and 34.

41. Ibid, pp. 4 and 34.

42. http://files.shareholder.com/downloads/AMDA-KX1KB/1956019531x0x562957/69c06a79-9713-43a3-8f3a-cead638f00d0/2011_Annual_Report.pdf

43. Zynga, Inc., *2011 Form 10-K*, p. 7.

44. Ibid., p. 4.

45. Ibid., p. 38.

46. Ibid., pp. 7–8.

47. http://seekingalpha.com/article/365781-estimates-on-zynga-s-4q-revenues-from-facebook-s-latest-filing

48. http://articles.businessinsider.com/2011-07-19/tech/29993613_1_zynga-games-facebook-integration-playfish

49. Zynga, Inc., *2011 Form 10-K*, pp. 4, 7, 50 and 65.

50. http://online.wsj.com/article/SB10001424052970204642604577213590333947130.html

51. www.Zynga.com, Zynga Press Releases, "Zynga Welcomes New Platform Partners: Konami, Playdemic, and Rebellion," and "Zynga Unveils New Platform for Play," March 12, 2012.

52. Marlowe, Chris, "Zynga Powers Up Social Gaming Network, Mobile and More," June 26, 2012, (http://www.dmwmedia.com/news/news/2012/06/26/zynga-powers-up-social-gaming-network-mobile-and-more)

53. www.Zynga.com. Zynga Press Release, "Zynga and American Express Launch Zynga Serve Rewards Program," May 22, 2012.

54. Zynga, *2011 Form 10-K*, pp. 71–72.

55. http://www.bloomberg.com/news/2012-04-17/zynga-flashes-1-8-billion-searching-for-the-new-farmville-tech.html

56. http://www.forbes.com/sites/insertcoin/2012/05/04/draw-something-loses-5m-users-a-month-after-zynga-purchase/

57. http://www.bloomberg.com/news/2012-04-17/zynga-flashes-1-8-billion-searching-for-the-new-farmville-tech.html

58. Brodkin, John, "How Amazon Saved Zynga's Butt—and Why Zynga Built a Cloud of Its Own," May 8, 2012, (http://arstechnica.com/business/2012/05/how-amazon-saved-zyngas-buttand-why-zynga-built-a-cloud-of-its-own)

59. http://seekingalpha.com/article/430761-zynga-moves-highlight-amazon-web-services-and-adverse-selection

60 www.Zynga.com. Press Release, "Zynga Unveils New Platform for Play," March 2012.

61. Ibid., p. 63

62. Zynga, Inc., *2011 Form 10-K*, p. 63.

63. Ibid., p. 33.

64. Ibid., p. 34.

65. "About Zynga" (http://company.zynga.com/about)

66. http://online.wsj.com/article/SB10001424053111904823804576502442835413446.html

67. Letzing, John, "Zynga Puts Real Money in Gambling Lobby," pp. B1–B2.

68. Zynga, Inc., *2011 Form 10-K*, p. 9.

69. http://news.cnet.com/8301-1023_3-57461989-93/zyngas-quest-for-player-liquidity/

70. appdata.com/leaderboard/developers?metric_select=mau

71. http://gigaom.com/2010/02/17/average-social-gameris-a-43-year-old-woman/

72. Ibid.

73. http://www.forbes.com/sites/johngaudiosi/2011/12/20/new-report-details-demographics-of-mobile-gamers-buying-virtual-goods/

74. http://www.nielsen.com/us/en/newswire/2012/smartphones-account-for-half-of-all-mobile-phones-dominate-new-phone-purchases-in-the-us.html

75. http://mashable.com/2012/06/07/mobile-commerce-infographic/

76. http://www.businessinsider.com/zynga-sees-limits-to-growthsales-flatten-as-marketing-costs-double-2012-2?op=1

77. Zynga, Inc., *Form 10-K*, p. 4. http://www.astproxyportal.com/ast/17382/index.html?where=eengine.goToPage(1,1)

78. Ibid., p. 4.

79. Ibid., pp. 7 and 18.

80. Zynga, Inc., *2011 Form 10-K*, p. 17.

81. Ibid, p. 15.

82. http://lawofthegame.blogspot.com/2012/03/zynga-vs-every-body-battle-over-online07.html

83. http://techcrunch.com/2009/02/14/mob-wars-creatorsues-zynga-for-copyright-infringement/

84. http://arstechnica.com/gaming/news/2009/12/cloning-or-theftars-explores-game-design-with-jenova-chen.ars

85. http://www.sfweekly.com/2010-09-08/news/farmvillains/

86. http://techcrunch.com/2009/02/14/mob-wars-creatorsues-zynga-for-copyright-infringement/

87. Silwinski, Alexander, "Highlights from EA's lawsuit against Zynga," August 3, 2012, (http://www.joystiQ.com/2012/08/03/highlights-from-eas-lawsuit-against-zynga/) and Eric Kain, "CloneWars: Zynga vs. EA and The Baffling Laziness of Copycat Games," August 10, 2012, (http://www.forbes.com/sites/erikkain/2012/08/10/clone-wars-zynga-vs-ea-and-the-baffling-laziness-of-copycat-games)

88. Primack, Dan, "Fraudville? Zynga Sued for Insider Trading," July 31, 2012, http://finance.fortune.cnn.com/2012/07/31/fraudville-zynga-sued-for-insider-trading/

89. http://www.sfgate.com/technology/article/Zynga-teams-up-with-nonprofits-for-games-3782858.php

90. Zynga, Inc., *2011 Form 10-K*, pp. 2, 31, and 32.

91. Ibid., pp. 40 and 42.

92. Steitfield, David and Wortham, Jenna, "The New Isn't Good in FarmVille," July 25, 2012, (http://www.nytimes.com/2012/07/26/technology/for-zynga-a-reversal-of-fortune.html

CASE **18**

The Boston Beer Company

BREWERS OF SAMUEL ADAMS BOSTON LAGER (MINI CASE)

Alan N. Hoffman

Company History

THE BOSTON BEER COMPANY WAS FOUNDED BY JIM KOCH IN 1984 after the discovery of his great-great-grandfather's family microbrew recipe in the attic of his home in Cincinnati, Ohio. In his kitchen, Jim Koch brewed the first batch of what is today known as Samuel Adams Boston Lager. Through use of the family recipe, Jim handcrafted a higher-quality, more flavorful beer than what was currently available in the United States.

Samuel Adams beers were known for their distinct taste and freshness. Although different brewers had access to the rare, expensive Noble hops that Samuel Adams used, its special ingredients remained a secret and were what gave its brews their distinct flavor. Jim Koch refused to compromise on the components that made up the full, rich, flavorful taste of Samuel Adams beer.

As his business began to grow, Jim moved his brewing operations into an old, abandoned brewery in Pennsylvania. This was subsequently followed by the opening of the extremely popular Boston Brewery in 1988. In the mid-1990s, Jim further expanded his business operations by purchasing the Hudepohl-Schoenling Brewery in his hometown of Cincinnati, Ohio. In 1995, The Boston Beer Company Inc. went public.

Jim Koch was viewed as the pioneer of the American craft beer revolution. He founded the largest craft brewery, brewing over 1 million barrels of 25 different styles of Boston Beer products and employing 520 people. Nevertheless, Boston Beer was

....

This case was prepared by Professor Alan N. Hoffman, Bentley University and Erasmus University. Copyright © 2010 by Alan N. Hoffman. The copyright holder is solely responsible for case content. Reprint permission is solely granted to the publisher, Prentice Hall, for *Strategic Management and Business Policy*, 15th Edition (and the international and electronic versions of this book) by the copyright holder, Alan N. Hoffman. Any other publication of the case (translation, any form of electronics or other media) or sale (any form of partnership) to another publisher will be in violation of copyright law, unless Alan N. Hoffman has granted an additional written permission. Reprinted by permission. The author would like to thank MBA students Peter Egan, Marie Fortuna, Jason McAuliffe, Lauren McCarthy, and Michael Pasquarello at Bentley University for their research.

No part of this publication may be copied, stored, transmitted, reproduced, or distributed in any form or medium whatsoever without the permission of the copyright owner, Alan N. Hoffman.

only the sixth-largest brewer in the United States, producing less than 1% of the total U.S. beer market in 2010.

Since its inception, Jim Koch has had numerous offers from the large brewing companies to buy him out, but he has consistently declined them. He wanted to remain independent and never compromise on the full, rich, flavorful, and fresh taste of Samuel Adams beer. Jim never altered his great-great-grandfather's original recipe created over a century ago.

Corporate Mission and Vision

The mission of the Boston Beer Company was "to seek long-term profitable growth by offering the highest quality products to the U.S. beer drinker."[1] As the largest craft brewer, the Boston Beer Company had been successful for several reasons: (1) premium products produced from the highest-quality ingredients; (2) an unwavering commitment to the freshness of its beer; (3) constant creativity and innovation that resulted in the introduction of a new flavor of beer every year; and (4) the passion and dedication of its employees.

The Boston Beer Company's vision was "to become the leading brewer in the Better Beer category by creating and offering high quality full-flavored beers."[2] The Better Beer category was comprised of craft brewers, specialty beers, and a large majority of the imports. As of 2010, Samuel Adams was the largest craft brewer and "the third largest brand in the Better Beer category of the United States brewing industry, trailing only the imports Corona and Heineken."[3]

In 2007, the Boston Beer Company had revenues of $341 million with COGS of $152 million and $22.5 million of net income. From 2007 to 2009, revenues grew by 22% to $415 million with COGS of $201 million and $31.1 million in net income. Management expected sales to be $430 million in 2010. The Boston Beer Company had no long-term debt and only 14 million shares outstanding. In August 2010, the stock price was $67.

The Beer Industry

The domestic beer market in 2010 was facing many challenges. In 2010, domestic beer overall sales declined 1.2%. Industry analysts predicted inflation-adjusted growth to be only 0.8% through 2012.[4] Decreases in domestic beer sales as a whole were mainly due to decreased alcohol consumption per person. U.S. consumers were drinking less beer because of health concerns, increased awareness of the legal consequences of alcohol abuse, and an increase in options for more flavorful wines and spirits.

To gain more market share in a highly competitive market, the industry was shifting to the mass production of beers, leading to industry consolidation. There were two major players in the brewing industry in the United States: AB InBev (Anheuser-Busch) and SABMiller PLC (SABMiller). SABMiller PLC was a 2007 joint venture of SABMiller and Molson Coors. Anheuser-Busch had been purchased in 2008 by Belgium producer InBev, the second-largest beer producer in the world.

The domestic beer industry also contained some opportunities. Although sales of domestic beer were flat, the past decade showed increases in the domestic consumption of light beer and the craft beer categories. The Better Beer category (comprised of craft, specialty, and import beers) was growing at an annual rate of 2.5% and comprised roughly 19% of all U.S. sales. Beers were classified as "better beers" mainly because of higher quality, taste, price, and image, compared to mass-produced domestic beers. The craft beer segment grew an estimated 9% in 2010. In an industry dominated by male customers, females were viewed as an opportunity. Research showed that women were most concerned about the calories in beer. However, 28% of these same women answered that they were presently drinking more wine.[5]

The growth in craft beer sales was good news for the Boston Beer Company, which positioned itself in this category and was the largest and most successful craft brewer in the United States. It ranked third overall in the U.S. Better Beer category, trailing only two imports: Corona from Mexico and Heineken from The Netherlands.

Domestic Beers

Two major players in the U.S. domestic beer market—AB InBev and MillerCoors—accounted for roughly 95% of all U.S. beer production and sales, minus imports.

MillerCoors LLC controlled roughly 30% of the U.S. beer market. MillerCoors recently entered the Better Beer category by acquiring, in whole or in part, existing craft brewers and by importing and distributing foreign brewers' brands. In 2010, the company experienced double-digit growth with its Blue Moon, Leinenkugel's, and Peroni Nastro Azzurro brands.

AB Inbev was the number-one brewer in the U.S. market in terms of both volume and revenues. Its dominant position allowed it to exert significant influence over distributors, making it difficult for smaller brewers to maintain their market presence or access new markets. Inbev was created in the 2004 merger of the Belgian company Interbrew and the Brazilian brewer AmBev, and subsequently purchased Anheuser-Busch in 2008.

Craft Beer Segment

Sierra Nevada Brewing Company was the second-largest craft beer maker in the United States. Founded in Chico, California, in 1980, the company's mission was to produce the finest-quality beers and ales, and believed that its mission could be accomplished "without compromising its role as a good corporate citizen and environmental steward." Its most successful brands included the hop-flavored Pale Ale, as well as Porter, Stout, and wheat varieties. Sierra Nevada, like Samuel Adams, produced seasonal brews including Summer Fest, Celebration, and Big Foot. Although Sierra Nevada beer had been distributed nationally for some time, sales were still strongest on the West Coast.

New Belgium Brewing Company was founded in 1991 in Fort Collins, Colorado. Its Fat Tire brand made up two-thirds of the company's total sales.[6] New Belgium currently had nine total craft beer brands, in addition to seasonal and limited brands. Its products were offered in 25 western and midwestern states. New Belgium, like Sierra Nevada, focused on being eco-friendly and stressed employee ownership in its mission.

Imports

Grupo Modelo was founded in 1925 and was the market leader in Mexico. Its most successful product, Corona Extra, was the United States' number-one beer import out of 450 imported beers. AB Inbev held a 50% noncontrolling interest in Grupo Modelo.

Heineken, the third-largest brewer by revenue, positioned itself as the world's most valuable international premium beer. Heineken had over 170 international, regional, and local specialty beers and 115 breweries in 65 countries. It had the widest presence of all international brewers due to the sales of Heineken and Amstel products.

Flavored Malt Beverage Category

Samuel Adams also competed in the "flavored malt beverage" (FMB) category with Twisted Tea. The FMB category accounted for roughly 2% of U.S. alcohol consumption. Twisted Tea competed mainly with beverages such as Smirnoff Ice, Bacardi Silver, and Mike's Hard Lemonade. FMB products all targeted relatively the same consumers. Since pricing was similar, these products relied heavily upon advertising and promotions.

Current Challenges

The Boston Beer Company had been growing revenues by 22% over the past two years, and the craft beer industry as a whole continued to experience double-digit growth as well. However, there were some challenges ahead if the company was to successfully achieve its mission and continue this level of growth.

1. Probably the most critical challenge was the increased level of competition in the craft beer industry. "Volume sales within the craft beer industry increased 20% during 2002–2010 to 220 million cases,"[7] and this astonishing growth attracted many players into this market, especially imported beers such as Corona and Heineken, and the top two brewers AB Inbev and MillerCoors.

2. Through mergers and acquisitions, the major competitors achieved cost savings and greater leverage with suppliers and distributors and preferential shelf space and placement with retailers.

3. A continuous increase in production costs of all basic beer ingredients, such as barley malt and hops, as well as packaging materials like glass, cardboard, and aluminum continued into 2010 with further increases in fuel and transportation costs. The global inventory of the company's "Noble" hops declined, and the harvest in recent years of its two key hops suppliers in Germany did not meet the high standards of the Boston Beer Company. As a result, Boston Beer received a lower quantity at a higher price than expected.

4. The company purchased a brewery in Breinigsville, Pennsylvania, in 2008 for $55 million. Although this brewery was expected to increase capacity by 1.6 million barrels of beer annually, it required significant renovations before it could produce quality beer.

United Airlines Dilemma

United Airlines recently approached the Boston Beer Company with an interesting opportunity. United wanted to offer Samuel Adams Boston Lager to fliers on all of its flights. This would provide the Boston Beer Company increased national exposure and could result in a significant increase in beer sales. However, United Airlines would only sell Samuel Adams Boston Lager in cans, not bottles.

The Boston Beer Company had never sold any of its beers in cans because management believed that metal detracts from the flavor of the beer. Management felt that the "full-flavor" of Samuel Adams could only be realized using glass bottles. Should Boston Beer's management rethink its decision not to distribute its beer in cans to take advantage of this opportunity? Many years ago, Jim Koch said that there would never be a "Sam Adams Light Beer," but he eventually reversed that decision and Sam Light became a huge success.

NOTES

1. 2007 Annual Report, http://thomson.mobular.net/thomson/7/2705/3248/.
2. Ibid.
3. Ibid.
4. Mintel—US–Domestic Beer December 2007.
5. Ibid.

6. http://www.rockymountainnews.com/news/2007/nov/24/reuteman-colorado-rides-on-fat-tire-to-beer/.
7. Mintel Report, "Domestic Beer–US–December 2007–Executive Summary," http://academic.mintel.com.ezp.bentley.edu/sinatra/mintel/print/id=311747 (July 15, 2008).

CASE **19**

Panera Bread Company (2010): Still Rising Fortunes?

Joyce P. Vincelette and Ellie A. Fogarty

BREAD—ESSENTIAL AND BASIC, but nonetheless special—has transcended millennia. A master baker combined simple ingredients to create what has been an integral part of society and culture for over 6000 years. Sourdough bread, a uniquely American creation, was made from a "culture" or "starter." Sourdough starter contained natural yeasts, flour, and water and was the medium that made bread rise. In order to survive, a starter had to be cultured, fed, and tended to by attentive hands in the right environment. Without proper care and maintenance, the yeast, or the growth factor, would slow down and die. Without a strong starter, bread would no longer rise.

Ronald Shaich, CEO and Chairman of Panera Bread Company, created the company's "starter." Shaich, the master baker, combined the ingredients and cultivated the leavening agent that catalyzed the company's phenomenal growth. Under Shaich's guidance, Panera's total systemwide (both company and franchisee) revenues rose from US$350.8 million in 2000 to US$1,353.5 million in 2009, consisting of US$1,153.3 million from company-owned bakery-café sales, US$78.4 million from franchise royalties and fees, and US$121.9 million from fresh dough sales to franchisees. Franchise-operated bakery-café sales, as reported by franchisees, were US$1,640.3 million in fiscal 2009.[1] Panera shares have outperformed every major restaurant stock over the last 10 years.[2] Panera's share price has risen over 1600% from US$3.88 a share on December 31, 1999, to US$67.95 a share on December 28, 2009.[3] Along the way, Panera largely led the evolution of what became known as the "fast casual" restaurant category.

Ronald Shaich had clearly nurtured the company's "starter" and had been the vision and driving force behind Panera's success from the company's beginnings until his resignation as CEO and Chairman effective May 13, 2010. For Panera to continue to rise, the company's new CEO, William Moreton, would need to continue to feed and maintain Panera's "starter." In addition to new unit growth, new strategies and initiatives must be folded into the mix.

History

Panera Bread grew out of the company that could be considered the grandfather of the fast casual concept: Au Bon Pain. In 1976, French oven manufacturer Pavailler opened the first Au Bon Pain (a French colloquialism for "where good bread is") in Boston's Faneuil Hall as a demonstration bakery. Struck by its growth potential, Louis Kane, a veteran venture capitalist, purchased the business in 1978.[4] Between 1978 and 1981, Au Bon Pain opened 13, and subsequently closed 10, stores in the Boston area and piled up US$3 million in debt.[5] Kane was ready to declare bankruptcy when he gained a new business partner in Ronald Shaich.[6]

Shortly after opening the Cookie Jar bakery in Cambridge, Massachusetts, in 1980, Shaich, a recent Harvard Business graduate, befriended Louis Kane. Shaich was interested in adding bread and croissants to his menu to stimulate morning sales. He recalled that "50,000 people a day were going past my store, and I had nothing to sell them in the morning."[7] In February 1981, the two merged the Au Bon Pain bakeries and the cookie store to form one business, Au Bon Pain Co. Inc. The two served as co-CEOs until Kane's retirement in 1994. They had a synergistic relationship that made Au Bon Pain successful: Shaich was the hard-driving, analytical strategist focused on operations, and Kane was the seasoned businessperson with a wealth of real estate and finance connections.[8] Between 1981 and 1984, the team expanded the business, worked to decrease the company's debt, and centralized facilities for dough production.[9]

In 1985, the partners added sandwiches to bolster daytime sales as they noticed a pattern in customer behavior—that is, customers were buying sliced baguettes and making their own sandwiches. It was a "eureka" moment, and the birth of the fast casual restaurant category.[10] According to Shaich, Au Bon Pain was the "first place that gave white collar folks a choice between fast food and fine dining."[11] Au Bon Pain became a lunchtime alternative for urban dwellers who were tired of burgers and fast food. Differentiated from other fast-food competitors by its commitment to fresh, quality sandwiches, bread, and coffee, Au Bon Pain attracted customers who were happy to pay more money (US$5 per sandwich) than they would have paid for fast food.[12]

In 1991, Kane and Shaich took the company public. By that time, the company had US$68 million in sales and was a leader in the quick service bakery segment. By 1994, the company had 200 stores and US$183 million in sales, but that growth masked a problem. The company was built on a limited growth concept, what Shaich called, "high density urban feeding."[13] The main customers of the company were office workers in locations like New York, Boston, and Washington, DC. The real estate in such areas was expensive and hard to come by. This strategic factor limited expansion possibilities.[14]

Au Bon Pain acquired the Saint Louis Bread Company in 1993 for US$24 million. Shaich saw this as the company's "gateway into the suburban marketplace."[15] The acquired company, founded in 1987 by Ken Rosenthal, consisted of a 19-store bakery-café chain located in the Saint Louis, Missouri, area. The concept of the café was based on San Francisco sourdough bread bakeries. The acquired company would eventually become the platform for what is now Panera.

Au Bon Pain management spent two years studying Saint Louis Bread Co., looking for the ideal concept that would unite Au Bon Pain's operational abilities and quality food with the broader suburban growth appeal of Saint Louis Bread. The management team understood that a growing number of consumers wanted a unique expression of tastes and styles, and were tired of the commoditization of fast-food service. Shaich and his team wrote a manifesto that spelled out what Saint Louis Bread would be, from the type of food it would serve, to the kind of people behind the counters, and to the look and feel of the physical space.[16]

Au Bon Pain began pouring capital into the chain when Shaich had another "eureka" moment in 1995. He entered a Saint Louis Bread store and noticed a group of business people meeting in a corner. The customers explained that they had no other place to talk.[17] This experience helped Shaich realize that the potential of the neighborhood bakery-café concept was greater than that of Au Bon Pain's urban store concept. The bakery-café concept capitalized on a confluence of current trends: the welcoming atmosphere of coffee shops, the food of sandwich shops, and the quick service of fast food.[18]

While Au Bon Pain was focusing on making Saint Louis Bread a viable national brand, the company's namesake unit was faltering. Rapid expansion of its urban outlets had resulted in operational problems, bad real estate deals,[19] debt over US$65 million,[20] and declining operating margins.[21] Stiff competition from bagel shops and coffee chains such as Starbucks compounded operational difficulties. Au Bon Pain's fast-food ambiance was not appealing to customers who wanted to sit and enjoy a meal or a cup of coffee. At the same time, the café style atmosphere of Saint Louis Bread, known as Panera (Latin for "time for bread") outside the Saint Louis area, was proving to be successful. In 1996, comparable sales at Au Bon Pain locations declined 3% while same-store sales of the Panera unit were up 10%.[22]

Lacking the capital to overhaul the ambiance of the Au Bon Pain segment, the company decided to sell the unit. This allowed the company to strategically focus its time and resources on the more successful Panera chain. Unlike Au Bon Pain, Panera was not confined to a small urban niche and had greater growth potential. On May 16, 1999, Shaich sold the Au Bon Pain unit to investment firm Bruckman, Sherrill, and Co. for US$73 million. At the time of the divestiture, the company changed its corporate name to Panera Bread Company. The sale left Panera Bread Company debt-free, and the cash allowed for the immediate expansion of its bakery-café stores.[23]

Throughout the 2000s, Panera grew through franchise agreements, acquisitions (including the purchase of Paradise Bakery & Café, Inc.), and new company-owned bakery-cafés. By 2009, Panera had become a national bakery-café concept with 1380 company-owned and franchise-operated bakery-café locations in 40 states and in Ontario, Canada. Panera had grown from serving approximately 60 customers a day at its first bakery-café to serving nearly six million customers a week systemwide, becoming one of the largest food-service companies in the United States. The company believed its success was rooted in its ability to create long-term dining concept differentiation.[24] The company operated under the Panera, Panera Bread, Saint Louis Bread Co., Via Panera, You Pick Two, Mother Bread, and Paradise Bakery & Café design trademark names registered in the United States. Others were pending. Panera also had some of its marks registered in foreign countries.[25]

May 13, 2010, marked a significant change in the history of Panera Bread Company. After 28 years, Ronald Shaich stepped down as CEO and Chairman effective immediately following the Annual Stockholders Meeting, and William Moreton, previously the Executive Vice President and co-Chief Operating Officer, assumed the role of CEO. Shaich planned to remain as the company's Executive Chairman. He announced that he expected to focus his time and energy within Panera on a range of strategic and innovation projects and mentoring the senior team. In typical Panera fashion, the transition had been planned for one-and-a-half years to ensure its success.

Concept and Strategy[26]

Concept

At the time when Panera was created, the fast-food industry was described as featuring low-grade burgers, greasy fries, and sugared colas. Shaich decided to create a casual but comfortable place where customers could eat fresh-baked artisan breads and fresh sandwiches, soups, and salads without worrying about whether it was nutritious.[27]

Panera's restaurant concept focused on the specialty bread/bakery-café category. Bread was Panera's platform and entry point to the Panera experience at its bakery-cafés. It was the symbol of Panera quality and a reminder of "Panera Warmth," the totality of the experience the customer received and could take home to share with friends and family. The company endeavored to offer a memorable experience with superior customer service. The company's associates were passionate about sharing their expertise and commitment with Panera customers. The company strove to achieve what Shaich termed "Concept Essence," Panera's blueprint for attracting targeted customers that the company believed differentiated it from competitors. Concept Essence included a focus on artisan bread, quality products, and a warm, friendly, and comfortable environment. It called for each of the company's bakery-cafés to be a place customers could trust to serve high-quality food. Bread was Panera's passion, soul, expertise, and the platform that made all of the company's other food items special.

The company's bakery-cafés were principally located in suburban, strip mall, and regional mall locations and featured relaxing décor and free Internet access. Panera's bakery-cafés were designed to visually reinforce the distinctive difference between its bakery-cafés and those of its competititors.

Panera extended its strong values and concept of fresh food in an unpretentious, welcoming atmosphere to the nonprofit community. The company's bakery-cafés routinely donated bread and baked goods to community organizations in need. Panera's boldest step was the May 2010 opening of the Panera Cares bakery-café in Missouri, which had no set prices; instead, customers were asked to pay what they wanted.[28]

Panera's success in achieving its concept was often acknowledged through customer surveys and awards from the press. From *Advertising Age*[29] to *Zagat*,[30] Panera was touted as one of America's hottest brands and most popular chains. Customers rated Panera fifth overall in the restaurant industry in 2008 and highest among fast casual eateries in an annual customer satisfaction and quality survey conducted by Dandelman & Associates, a restaurant market research firm.[31] In 2009, Panera also was named number one on the "Healthiest for Eating on the Go" list by *Health* magazine for its variety of health menu options, whole grain breads, and half-sized items. Numerous other national and local awards had been received each year for the company's sandwiches, breads, lunches, soups, vegetarian offerings, cleanliness, Wi-Fi, community responsibility, workplace quality, and kids' menu.[32] Panera's own consumer panel testing of 1000 customers showed consistently high value perceptions of the company's products.[33]

Strategy

Panera operated in three business segments: company-owned bakery-café operations, franchise operations, and fresh dough operations. As of December 29, 2009, the company-owned bakery-café segment consisted of 585 bakery-cafés, all located in the United States, and the franchised operations segment consisted of 795 franchise-operated bakery-cafés, located throughout the United States and in Ontario, Canada. The company anticipated 80 to 90 systemwide bakery-cafés opening in 2010 with average weekly sales for company-owned new units of US$36,000 to US$38,000.[34]

EXHIBIT 1   Company-Owned and Franchise-Operated Bakery-Cafés: Panera Bread Company

	For the Fiscal Year Ended				
	December 29, 2009	December 30, 2008	December 25, 2007	December 26, 2006	December 27, 2005
Number of bakery-cafés					
company-owned					
Beginning of period	562	532	391	311	226
Bakery-cafés opened	30	35	89	70	66
Bakery-cafés closed	(7)	(5)	(5)	(3)	(2)
Bakery-cafés acquired from franchisees (1)	—	—	36	13	21
Bakery-cafés acquired (2)	—	—	22	—	—
Bakery-cafés sold to a franchisees (3)	—	—	(1)	—	—
End of period	585	562	532	391	311
Franchise-operated					
Beginning of period	763	698	636	566	515
Bakery-cafés opened	39	67	80	85	73
Bakery-cafés closed	(7)	(2)	(5)	(2)	(1)
Bakery-cafés sold to company (1)	—	—	(36)	(13)	(21)
Bakery-cafés acquired (2)	—	—	22	—	—
Bakery-cafés purchased from company (3)	—	—	1	—	—
End of period	795	763	698	636	566
Systemwide					
Beginning of period	1,325	1,230	1,027	877	741
Bakery-cafés opened	69	102	169	155	139
Bakery-cafés closed	(14)	(7)	(10)	(5)	(3)
Bakery-cafés acquired (2)	—	—	44	—	—
End of period	1,380	1,325	1,230	1,027	877

Notes:

(1) In June 2007, Panera acquired 32 bakery-cafés and the area development rights from franchisees in certain markets in Illinois and Minnesota. In February 2007, the company acquired four bakery-cafés, as well as two bakery-cafés still under construction, and the area development rights from a franchisee in certain markets in California.

In October 2006, Panera acquired 13 bakery-cafés (one of which was under construction) and the area development rights from a franchisee in certain markets in Iowa, Nebraska, and South Dakota. In September 2006, the company acquired one bakery-café in Pennsylvania from a franchisee. In November 2005, Panera acquired 23 bakery-cafés (two of which were under construction) and the area development rights from a franchisee in certain markets in Indiana.

(2) In February 2007, Panera acquired 51% of the outstanding capital stock of Paradise Bakery & Café Inc., which then owned and operated 22 bakery-cafés and franchised 22 bakery-cafés, principally in certain markets in Arizona and Colorado.

(3) In June 2007, Panera sold one bakery-café and the area development rights for certain markets in Southern California to a new area developer.

SOURCES: Panera Bread Company Inc., *2009 Form 10-K*, p. 25 and *2006 Form 10-K*, p. 20.

Exhibit 1 shows the total number of systemwide bakery-cafés for the last five years. As of December 29, 2009, the company's fresh dough operations segment, which supplied fresh dough items daily to most company-owned and franchise-operated bakery-cafés, consisted of 23 fresh dough facilities. Company-owned bakery-café operations accounted for 85.2% of revenues in 2009, up from 78% in 2005. Royalties and fees from franchise operations made up 5.8% of revenues in 2009, down from 8.5% in 2005, and fresh dough operations accounted for 9% of total revenues in 2009, down from 13.5% in 2005.[35]

In addition to the dine-in and take-out business, the company offered Via Panera, a nationwide catering service that provided breakfast assortments, sandwiches, salads, and soups using the same high-quality ingredients offered in the company's bakery-cafés. Via Panera was supported by a national sales infrastructure. The company believed that Via Panera would be a key component of long-term growth.

The key initiatives of Panera's growth strategy focused on growing store profit, increasing transactions and gross profit per transaction, using its capital smartly, and putting in place drivers for concept differentiation and competitive advantage.[36] The company paid careful attention to the development of new markets and further penetration of existing markets by both company-owned and franchised bakery-cafés, including the selection of sites that would achieve targeted returns on invested capital.[37] Panera's strategy in 2009 was different from many of its competitors. When many restaurant companies were focused on surviving the economic meltdown by downsizing employees, discounting prices, and lowering quality, Panera chose to stay the course and continued to execute its long-term strategy of investing in the business to benefit the customer. The result, according to Shaich: "Panera zigged while others zagged."[38]

During the economic downturn, Panera stuck to a simple recipe: Get more cash out of each customer, rather than just more customers. While other recession-wracked restaurant chains discounted and offered meals for as little as US$5 to attract customers, Panera bucked conventional industry wisdom by eschewing discounts and instead targeted customers who could afford to shell out an average of about US$8.50 for lunch. While many of its competitors offered less expensive meals, Panera added a lobster sandwich for US$16.99 at some of its locations. Panera was able to persuade customers to pay premiums because it had been improving the quality of its food.[39] "Most of the world seems to be focused on the Americans who are unemployed," said CEO Ronald Shaich. "We're focused on the 90 percent that are still employed."[40]

Panera's positive financial results contrasted with those of many other casual dining chains, which had posted negative same-store sales due partly to declining traffic and lower-priced food. Some chains found that discounting not only hurt margins but also failed to lure as many customers as hoped. Shaich seemed to thrive on doing the opposite of his competition. During 2009, instead of slashing prices, he raised them twice, one on bagels and once on soup. "We're contrarians to the core," said Shaich. "We don't offer a lower-end strategy. In a world where everyone is cutting back, we want to give more not less."[41] "This is the time to increase the food experience," insisted Shaich, "that is, when consumers least expect it."[42]

Also crucial to Panera's success in 2009 was the company's approach to operations during the recession. Over the years, many restaurant companies told investors they were able to improve labor productivity while running negative comparable store sales. Panera believed that reducing labor in a restaurant taxed the customer by creating longer waits, slower service, and more frazzled team members. Panera took the approach of keeping labor consistent with sales and continuing to invest in its employees as a way to better serve its customers.[43]

The results for 2009 showed that Panera's strategy of zigging while others were zagging paid off. Panera met or exceeded its earnings targets in each quarter of 2009. Panera delivered 25% earnings per share (EPS) growth in 2009 on top of 24% EPS growth in 2008. Panera's stock price increased 115% from December 31, 2007, to March 30, 2010.

Panera's objectives for 2010 included a target of 17%–20% EPS growth through the execution of its key initiatives. To further build transactions, Panera planned to focus on differentiation through innovative salads utilizing new procedures to further improve quality. Panera also planned to test a new way to make paninis using newly designed grills. The company expected to roll out improved versions of several Panera classics while continuing to focus on improving operations, speed of service, and accuracy.[44]

In early 2010, to increase gross profit per transaction and further improve margins while still providing overall value to customers, Panera introduced an initiative called the Meal Upgrade Program. With this program, a customer who ordered an entrée and a beverage was offered the opportunity to purchase a baked good to complete their meal at a "special" price point. Panera intended to test other impulse add-on initiatives, bulk baked goods, and bread as a gift.[45]

"I worry about keeping the concept special," said Shaich. "Is it worth walking across the street to? It doesn't matter how cheap it is. If it isn't special, there's no reason the business needs to exist."[46]

The Fast Casual Segment

Panera's predecessor, Au Bon Pain, was a pioneer of the fast casual restaurant category. Dining trends caused fast casual to emerge as a legitimate trend in the restaurant industry as it bridged the gap between the burgers-and-fries fast-food industry and full service, sitdown, casual dining restaurants.

Technomic Information Services, a food-service industry consultant, coined the term to describe restaurants that offered the speed, efficiency, and inexpensiveness of fast food with the hospitality, quality, and ambiance of a full-service restaurant. Technomic defined a fast casual restaurant by whether or not the restaurant met the following four criteria: (1) The restaurant had to offer a limited service or self-service format. (2) The average check had to be between US$6 and US$9, whereas fast-food checks averaged less than US$5. This pricing scheme placed fast casual between fast food and casual dining. (3) The food had to be made-to-order, as consumers perceived newly prepared, made-to-order foods as fresh. Fast casual menus usually also had more robust and complex flavor profiles than the standard fare at fast-food restaurants. (4) The décor had to be upscale or highly developed. Décor inspired a more enjoyable experience for the customer as the environment of fast casual restaurants was more akin to a neighborhood bistro or casual restaurant. The décor also created a generally higher perception of quality.[47]

The fast casual market was divided into three categories: bread-based chains, traditional chains, and ethnic chains. According to a Mintel 2008 report, bread-based chains, such as Panera, and ethnic chains, such as Chipotle Mexican Grill, had sales momentum and were predicted to grow at the expense of traditional chains such as Steak 'n Shake, Boston Market, Fuddruckers, and Fazoli's, which were weighted down by older concepts. The report also suggested that bread-based and ethnic chains had an edge with respect to consumer perceptions about food healthfulness.[48] Most fast casual brands did not compete in all dayparts (breakfast, lunch, dinner, late-night), but instead focused on one or two. While almost all competitors in this segment had a presence at lunch, many grappled with the question of whether and how to participate in other dayparts.[49] In addition, unlike fast-food restaurants that constructed standalone stores, fast casual chains were typically located in strip malls, small-town main streets, and preexisting properties.

According to Technomic, by offering high-quality food with fast service, fast casual chains had experienced increased traffic in 2009 as diners "traded-down" from casual dining chains and "traded-up" from fast-food restaurants to lower-priced but still higher-quality fresh food.[50] In other words, the desire to eat out did not diminish; only the destination changed. Sales in 2009 for the top 100 fast casual chains reached US$17.5 billion, a 4.5% increase over 2008; and units grew by 4.3% to 14,777 locations,[51] compared to a 3.2% sales decline in the overall restaurant industry.[52] The growth in the fast casual segment was also due to the maturation of two large segments of the U.S. population: baby boomers and their children. Both age groups had little time for cooking and were tired of fast food.

Bakery-café/bagel remained the largest of the fast casual restaurant clusters and the largest menu category, generating US$4.8 billion in U.S. sales in 2009 and jumping from 17% to 21% of the top 100 fast casual restaurants. In 2009, Mexican, with total sales of US$3.8 billion, was the second-largest fast casual cluster of restaurants.[53] Technomic's 2009 Top 100 Fast-Casual Restaurant Report noted that besides burgers (up 16.7%), the fastest growing menu categories reflected the growing interest of consumers in international flavors: Asian/noodle (up 6.4%) and Mexican (up 6.3%).[54]

Exhibit 2 provides a list of the 20 largest fast casual franchises in 2010. Even though Chipotle Mexican Grill was one of Panera's key competitors, it was not included on this list because it did not franchise.

EXHIBIT 2
2010's Twenty Largest Fast Casual Franchises

	2009 United States Sales
1. Panera Bread	$2,796,500
2. Zaxby's	718,250
3. El Polio Loco	582,000
4. Boston Market	545,000
5. Jason's Deli	475,870
6. Five Guys Burgers and Fries	453,500
7. Qdoba Mexican Grill	436,500
8. Einstein Bros. Bagels	378,444
9. Moe's Southwestern Grill	358,000
10. McAlister's Deli	351,960
11. Fuddruckers	320,500
12. Wingstop	306,606
13. Baja Fresh Mexican Grill	300,000
14. Schlotzky's	248,000
15. Corner Bakery Café	235,029
16. Fazoli's	235,000
17. Noodles & Company	230,000
18. Bruegger's Bagel Bakery	196,000
19. Donatos Pizza	185,000
20. Cosi	168,500

Note:
(a) Not all key fast casual competitors are franchised restaurants.

SOURCES: Technomic's 2010 Top 100 Fast-Casual Chain Restaurant Report, www.bluemaumau .cor/9057/2010's-top- twenty-largest-fastcausual-franchises.

Competition

Panera experienced competition from numerous sources in its trade areas. The company's bakery-cafés competed with specialty food, casual dining and quick service cafés, bakeries, and restaurant retailers, including national, regional, and locally owned cafés, bakeries, and restaurants. The bakery-cafés competed in several segments of the restaurant business based on customers' needs for breakfast, AM "chill," lunch, PM "chill," dinner, and take-home through both on-premise sales and Via Panera catering. The competitive factors included location, environment, customer service, price, and quality of products. The company competed for leased space in desirable locations and also for hourly employees. Certain competitors or potential competitors had capital resources that exceeded those available to Panera.[55]

Panera's 2009 sales of nearly US$2.8 billion ranked as the largest of the fast casual chains. The company saw an increase in sales of 7.1% and an increase in units of 4.3% to 1380 stores over 2008. Chipotle Mexican Grill held on to the number two spot, growing U.S. sales 13.9% to US$1.5 billion, and units by 14.2% to 955 locations in 2009.[56]

Panera and Chipotle Mexican Grill, which together made up more than 25% of the fast casual segment, posted double-digit percentage increases in first-quarter 2010 sales over the same period in 2009, driven by opening new outlets and robust increases in same-store sales. By contrast, United States revenues at McDonald's suffered in 2009, and for the first five months of 2010, same-store sales were up 3% over the same period in 2009. Burger King struggled during the same period with revenues in the United States and Canada down 4% for the first three months of 2010.[57] Established restaurant chains were beginning to take notice of the opportunities in the fast casual segment and were considering options. For example, Subway started testing an upscale design in the Washington, DC, market in 2008. New competitors, such as Otarian, were also entering the fast casual segment and testing new concepts, many having a health and wellness or sustainability component to them.

Although Panera continued to learn from its competitors, none of its competitors had yet figured out the formula to Panera's success. While McDonald's had rival Burger King, and Applebee's had T.G.I. Friday's, there was no direct national competitor that replicated Panera's business model. Like Panera, Chipotle sold high-quality food made with fine ingredients—but it was Mexican. Cosi sold quality sandwiches and salads, but lacked pastries and gourmet coffees. Starbucks had fine coffee and pastries but not Panera's extensive food menu. According to Shaich, the reason is that "this is hard to do, . . . what seems simple can be tough. It is not so easy to knock us off."[58]

Corporate Governance

Panera was a Delaware corporation and its corporate headquarters were located in Saint Louis, Missouri.

Board of Directors

Panera's Board was divided into three classes of membership. The terms of service of the three classes of directors were staggered so that only one class expired at each annual meeting. At the time of the May 2010 annual meeting, the Board consisted of six members. Class I consisted of Ronald M. Shaich and Fred K. Foulkes, with terms expiring in 2011; Class II consisted of Domenic Colasacco and Thomas E. Lynch, with terms expiring in 2012; and Class III consisted of Larry J. Franklin and Charles J. Chapmann III, with terms ending in 2010. Mr. Franklin and Mr. Chapman were both nominated for reelection with terms ending in 2013, if elected.[59]

The biographical sketches for the board members are shown next.[60]

Ronald M. Shaich (age 56) was a Director since 1981, co-founder, Chairman of the Board since May 1999, Co-Chairman of the Board from January 1988 to May 1999, Chief Executive Officer since May 1994, and Co-Chief Executive Officer from January 1988 to May 1994. Shaich served as a Director of Lown Cardiovascular Research Foundation, as a trustee of the nonprofit Rashi School, as Chairman of the Board of Trustees of Clark University, and as Treasurer of the Massachusetts Democratic Party. He had a Bachelor of Arts degree from Clark University and an MBA from Harvard Business School. Immediately following the 2010 Annual Meeting, Mr. Shaich planned to resign as Chief Executive Officer and the Board intended to elect him as Executive Chairman of the Board.

Larry J. Franklin (age 61) was a Director since June 2001. Franklin had been the President and Chief Executive Officer of Franklin Sports Inc., a leading branded sporting goods manufacturer and marketer, since 1986. Franklin joined Franklin Sports Inc. in 1970 and served as its Executive Vice President from 1981 to 1986. Franklin served on the Board of Directors of Bradford Soap International Inc. and the Sporting Goods Manufacturers Association (Chairman of the Board and member of the Executive Committee).

Fred K. Foulkes (age 68) was a Director since June 2003. Dr. Foulkes had been a Professor of Organizational Behavior and had been the Director (and founder) of the Human Resources Policy Institute at Boston University School of Management since 1981. He had taught courses in human resource management and strategic management at Boston University since 1980. From 1968 to 1980, Foulkes had been a member of the Harvard Business School faculty. Foulkes wrote numerous books, articles, and case studies. He served on the Board of Directors of Bright Horizons Family Solutions and the Society for Human Resource Management Foundation.

Domenic Colasacco (age 61) was a Director since March 2000, and Lead Independent Director since 2008. Colasacco had been President and Chief Executive Officer of Boston Trust & Investment Management, a banking and trust company, since 1992. He also served as Chairman of its Board of Directors. He joined Boston Trust in 1974 after beginning his career in the research division of Merrill Lynch & Co. in New York City.

Charles J. Chapman III (age 47) was a Director since 2008. Chapman had been the Chief Operating Officer and a Director of the American Dairy Queen Corporation since October 2005. From 2001 to October 2005, Chapman held a number of senior positions at American Dairy Queen. Prior to joining American Dairy Queen, Chapman served as Chief Operating Officer at Bruegger's Bagel's Inc., where he was also President and co-owner of a franchise. He also held marketing and operations positions with Darden Restaurants and served as a consultant with Bain & Company.

Thomas E. Lynch (age 50) was a Director since March 2010 and previous Director from 2003-2006. Lynch served as Senior Managing Director of Mill Road Capital, a private equity firm, since 2005. From 2000 to 2004, Lynch served as Senior Managing Director of Mill Road Associates, a financial advisory firm that he founded in 2000. From 1997 through 2000, Lynch was the founder and Managing Director of Lazard Capital Partners. From 1990 to 1997, Lynch was a Managing Director of the Blackstone Group, where he was a senior investment professional for Blackstone Capital Partners. Prior to Black-stone, Lynch was a senior consultant at the

Monitor Company. He also had previously served on the Board of Directors of Galaxy Nutritional Foods Inc.

The Board had established three standing committees, each of which operated under a charter approved by the Board. The *Compensation and Management Development Committee* included Foulkes (Chair), Franklin, and Colasacco. The *Committee on Nominations and Corporate Governance* included Franklin (Chair), Chapman, and Foulkes. The *Audit Committee* included Colasacco (Chair), Foulkes, and Franklin.[61]

The compensation package of non-employee directors consisted of cash payments and stock and option awards. Total non-employee director compensation ranged from US$29,724 to US$124,851 in fiscal 2009 depending on services rendered.[62]

Top Management

The biographical sketches for some of the key executive officers follow.[63]

Ronald Shaich (age 56) planned to resign as Chief Executive Officer immediately following the May 2010 Annual Meeting. The Board of Directors announced its intentions to elect him as Executive Chairman of the Board at that time. The Board intended to appoint William W. Moreton to succeed Mr. Shaich as Chief Executive Officer and President and to elect him to the Board of Directors.[64]

William M. Moreton (age 50) re-joined Panera in November 2008 as Executive Vice President and Co-Chief Operating Officer. He previously served as Executive Vice President and Chief Financial Officer from 1998 to 2003. From 2005 to 2007, Moreton served as President and Chief Financial Officer of Potbelly Sandwich Works, and from 2004–2005 as Executive Vice President-Subsidiary Brands, and Chief Executive Officer of Baja Fresh, a subsidiary of Wendy's International Inc. Immediately following the conclusion of the 2010 Annual Meeting, upon the resignation of Mr. Shaich, the Board planned for Mr. Moreton to succeed Mr. Shaich as Chief Executive Officer, and the Board intended to appoint him as President and elect him to the Board.

John M. Maguire (age 44) had been Chief Operating Officer and subsequently Co-Chief Operating Officer since March 2008 and Executive Vice President since April 2006. He previously served as Senior Vice President, Chief Company, and Joint Venture Operations Officer from August 2001 to April 2006. From April 2000 to July 2001, Maguire served as Vice President, Bakery Operations, and from November 1998 to March 2000, as Vice President, Commissary Operations. Maguire joined the company in April 1993; from 1993 to October 1998, he was a Manager and Director of Au Bon Pain/Panera Bread/St. Louis Bread.

Cedric J. Vanzura (age 46) had been Executive Vice President and Co-Chief Operating Officer since November 2008 and Executive Vice President and Chief Administrative Officer from March to November 2008. Prior to joining the company, Vanzura held a variety of roles at Borders International from 2003 to 2007.

Mark A. Borland (age 57) had been Senior Vice President and Chief Supply Chain Officer since August 2002. Borland joined the company in 1986 and held management positions within Au Bon Pain and Panera Bread divisions until 2000, including Executive Vice President, Vice President of Retail Operations, Chief Operating Officer, and President of Manufacturing Services. From 2000 to 2001, Borland served as Senior Vice President of Operations at RetailDNA, and then rejoined Panera as a consultant in the summer of 2001.

Jeffrey W. Kip (age 42) had been Senior Vice President and Chief Financial Officer since May 2006. He previously served as Vice President, Finance and Planning, and Vice President, Corporate Development, from 2003 to 2006. Prior to joining Panera, Mr. Kip was an Associate Director and then Director at UBS from 2002 to 2003 and an Associate at Goldman Sachs from 1999 to 2002.

Michael J. Nolan (age 50) had been Senior Vice President and Chief Development Officer since he joined the company in August 2001. From December 1997 to March 2001, Nolan served as Executive Vice President and Director for John Harvard's Brew House, L.L.C., and Senior Vice President, Development, for American Hospitality Concepts Inc. From March 1996 to December 1997, Nolan was Vice President of Real Estate and Development for Apple South Incorporated, a chain restaurant operator, and from July 1989 to March 1996, Nolan was Vice President of Real Estate and Development for Morrison Restaurants Inc. Prior to 1989, Nolan served in various real estate and development capacities for Cardinal Industries Inc. and Nolan Development and Investment.

Other key Senior Vice Presidents included Scott Davis, Chief Concept Officer; Scott Blair, Chief Legal Officer; Rebecca Fine, Chief People Officer; Thomas Kish, Chief Information Officer; Michael Kupstas, Chief Franchise Officer; Michael Simon, Chief Marketing Officer; and William Simpson, Chief Company and Joint Venture Operations Officer. In 2009, the total compensation for the top five highest-paid executive officers ranged from US$939,919 to US$3,354,708.[65]

At year-end 2009, there were two classes of stock: (1) Class A common stock with 30,491,278 shares outstanding and one vote per share, and (2) Class B common stock with 1,392,107 shares outstanding and three votes per share.[66] Class A common stock was traded on NASDAQ under the symbol PNRA. As of March 15, 2010, all directors, director nominees, and executive officers as a group (20 persons) held 1,994,642 shares or 6.22% of Class A common stock and 1,311,690 shares or 94.22% of Class B common stock with a combined voting percentage of 13.23%. Ronald Shaich owned 5.5% of Class A common stock and 94.22% of Class B common stock for a combined voting percentage of 12.42%.[67] In November 2009, Panera's Board of Directors approved a three-year share repurchase program of up to US$600 million of Class A common stock.[68]

Menu[69]

Panera's value-oriented menu was designed to provide the company's target customers with affordably priced products built on the strength of the company's bakery expertise. The Panera menu featured proprietary items prepared with high-quality fresh ingredients as well as unique recipes and toppings. The key menu groups were fresh-baked goods, including a variety of freshly baked bagels, breads, muffins, scones, rolls, and sweet goods; made-to-order sandwiches; hearty and unique soups; hand-tossed salads; and café beverages including custom-roasted coffees, hot or cold espresso, cappuccino drinks, and smoothies.

The company regularly reviewed and updated its menu offerings to satisfy changing customer preferences, to improve its products, and to maintain customer interest. To give its customers a reason to return, Panera had been rolling out new products with fresher ingredients such as antibiotic-free chicken (Panera is the nation's largest buyer[70]). The roots of most new Panera dishes could be traced to its R&D team's twice-yearly retreats to the Adirondacks, where staffers took turns trying to out-do each other in the kitchen. "We start with: What do we think tastes good," said Scott Davis. "We're food people, and if we're not working on something that gets us really excited, it's kind of not worth working on."[71] Panera did not have test kitchens and instead tested all new menu items directly in its cafés.

Panera integrated new product rollouts into the company's periodic or seasonal menu rotations, referred to as "Celebrations." Examples of products introduced in fiscal 2009 included the Chopped Cobb Salad and Barbeque Chicken Chopped Salad, introduced during the 2009 summer salad celebration. Other menu changes in 2009 included a reformulated French baguette, a new line of smoothies, new coffee, a new Napa Almond Chicken Salad sandwich, a new Strawberry Granola Parfait, the Breakfast Power Sandwich, and a new line of brownies and blondies. Three new salmon options, five years in the making, were introduced in early 2010 along with a new Low-Fat Garden Vegetable Soup and a new Asiago Bagel Breakfast Sandwich. New chili offerings were in the planning stages. During this time Shaich had also been busy tweaking things he wanted Panera to do better, such as improving the freshness of Panera's lettuce by cutting the time from field to plate in half. He also improved the freshness of the company's breads by opting to bake all day long, not just in the early morning hours. Panera's changes and improvements were all designed to build competitive advantage by strengthening value. Value, according to the company, meant offering guests an even better "total experience."

In 2008, Panera introduced the antithesis to the microwaved, processed breakfast sandwich, by introducing a made-to-order grilled breakfast sandwich. The new line of breakfast sandwiches were made fresh daily with quality ingredients—a combination of all-natural eggs, Vermont white cheddar cheese, Applewood-smoked bacon or all natural sausage, grilled between two slices of fresh baked ciabatta. Many of the company's competitors had also moved to more protein-based breakfast sandwich offerings because of the growth opportunities in this segment of the market. In order to be competitive, Panera needed to be different.

Not all of Panera's menu innovations had been successful with customers or had added much to the bottom line. Panera redesigned its menu boards in 2009 to draw the customers' eyes toward meals with higher margins, like the soup and salad combo, rather than pricier items, like a strawberry poppy-seed salad, that did not bring as much to the bottom line. The Crispani pizza was discontinued in 2008 after it failed to drive business during evening hours.

To improve margins, Panera was able to anticipate and react to changes in food and supply costs including, among other things, fuel, proteins, dairy, wheat, tuna, and cream cheese costs through increased menu prices and to use its strength at purchasing to limit cost inflation in efforts to drive gross profit per transaction.

Panera believe in being transparent with regard to the ingredients it used. They were one of the first restaurants to serve antibiotic-free chicken even though it was more expensive. Panera chose to be ahead of the curve again when it announced in early 2010 that it would post calorie information on all systemwide bakery-café menu boards by the end of 2010. Panera had for a number of years provided a nutritional calculator on its website so customers could find nutritional information for individual products or build a meal according to their dietetic specifications. Recognizing the health risks associated with transfats, Panera had completely removed all transfat from its menu by 2006.[72] Panera also offered a wide range of organic food products including cookies, milk, and yogurt, which were incorporated into the company's children's menu, Panera Kids, in 2006. Because of its healthy choices, Panera was named "One of the 10 Best Fast-Casual Family Restaurants" by *Parents* magazine in its July 2009 issue.[73]

Site Selection and Company-Owned Bakery-Cafés[74]

As of December 29, 2009, the company-owned bakery-café segment consisted of 585 company-owned bakery-cafés, all located in the United States. During 2009, Panera focused on using its cash to build new high-ROI bakery-cafés and executed a disciplined development process that took advantage of the recession to drive down costs while selecting locations that delivered strong sales volume. In 2009, Panera believed the best use of its capital was to invest in its core business, either through the development of new bakery-cafés or through the acquisition of existing bakery-cafés from franchisees or other similar restaurant or bakery-café concepts, such as the acquisition of Paradise Bakery & Café Inc.

All company-owned bakery-cafés were in leased premises. Lease terms were typically 10 years with one, two, or three 5-year renewal option periods thereafter. Leases typically had charges for a proportionate share of building and common area operating expenses and real estate taxes, and a contingent percentage rent based on sales above a stipulated sales level. Because Panera was considered desirable as a tenant due to its profitable balance sheet and national reputation, the company enjoyed a favorable leasing environment in lease terms and the availability of desirable locations.

The average size of a company-owned bakery-café was approximately 4600 square feet as of December 29, 2009. The average construction, equipment, furniture and fixtures, and signage costs for the 30 company-owned bakery-cafés opened in fiscal 2009 was approximately US$750,000 per bakery-café after landlord allowances and excluding capitalized development overhead. The company expected that future bakery-cafés would require, on average, an investment per bakery-café of approximately US$850,000.

In evaluating potential new locations for both company-owned and franchised bakery-cafés, Panera studied the surrounding trade area, demographic information within the most recent year, and publicly available information on competitors. Based on this analysis and utilizing predictive modeling techniques, Panera estimated projected sales and a targeted return on investment. Panera also employed a disciplined capital expenditure process focused on occupancy and development costs in relation to the market, designed to ensure the right-sized bakery-café and costs in the right market. Panera's methods had proven successful in choosing a number of different types of locations, such as in-line or end-cap locations in strip or power centers, regional malls, drive-through, and freestanding units.

Franchises[75]

Franchising was a key component of Panera's growth strategy. Expansion through franchise partners enabled the company to grow more rapidly as the franchisees contributed the resources and capabilities necessary to implement the concepts and strategies developed by Panera.

The company began a broad-based franchising program in 1996, when the company actively began seeking to extend its franchise relationships. As of December 29, 2009, there were 795 franchise-operated bakery-cafés open throughout the United States and in Ontario, Canada, and commitments to open 240 additional franchise-operated bakery-cafés. At this time, 57.6% of the company's bakery-cafés were owned by franchises comprised of 48 franchise groups. The company was selective in granting franchises, and applicants had to meet specific criteria in order to gain consideration for a franchise. Generally, the franchisees had to be well capitalized to open bakery-cafés, with a minimum net worth of US$7.5 million and meet liquidity requirements (liquid assets of US$3 million),[76] have the infrastructure and resources to meet a negotiated development schedule, have a proven track record as multi-unit restaurant operators, and have a commitment to the development of the Panera brand. A number of markets were still available for franchise development.

Panera did not sell single-unit franchises. Instead, they chose to develop by selling market areas using Area Development Agreements, referred to as ADAs, which required the franchise developer to open a number of units, typically 15 bakery-cafés, in a period of four to six years. If franchisees failed to develop bakery-cafés on schedule or defaulted in complying with the company's operating or brand standards, the company had the right to terminate the ADA and to develop company-owned locations or develop locations through new area developers in that market.

The franchise agreement typically required the payment of an up-front franchise fee of US$35,000 (broken down into US$5000 at the signing of the area development agreement and US$30,000 at or before the bakery-café opens) and continued royalties of 4%–5% on sales from each bakery-café. The company's franchise-operated bakery-cafés followed the same protocol for in-store operating standards, product quality, menu, site selection, and bakery-café construction as did company-owned bakery-cafés. Generally, the franchisees were required to purchase all of their dough products from sources approved by the company.

The company did not generally finance franchise construction or area development agreement purchases. In addition, the company did not hold an equity interest in any of the franchise-operated bakery-cafés. However, in fiscal 2008, to facilitate expansion into Ontario, Canada, the company entered into a credit facility with the Canadian franchisee. By March 2010, Panera had repurchased the three franchises in Toronto in order to be more directly involved in the Canadian market. While the company thought the geographic market represented a good growth opportunity, Panera decided to study and learn from other U.S. firms that had expanded successfully in Canada.[77]

Bakery Supply Chain[78]

According to Ronald Shaich, "Panera has a commitment to doing the best bread in America."[79] Freshly baked bread made with fresh dough was integral to honoring this commitment. System-wide bakery-cafés used fresh dough for sourdough and artisan breads and bagels.

Panera believed its fresh dough facility system and supply chain function provided competitive advantage and helped to ensure consistent quality at its bakery-cafés. The company had a unique supply-chain operation in which dough was supplied daily from one of the company's regional fresh dough facilities to substantially all company-owned and franchise-operated bakery-cafés. Panera bakers then worked through the night shaping, scoring, and glazing the dough by hand to bring customers fresh-baked loaves every morning and throughout the day. In 2009, the company began baking loaves later in the morning to ensure freshness throughout the day and altered the fermentation cycle of its baguettes to make them sweeter.

As of December 29, 2009, Panera had 23 fresh dough facilities, 21 of which were company-owned, including a limited production facility that was co-located with one of the company's franchised bakery-cafés in Ontario, Canada, to support the franchise-operated bakery-cafés located in that market (2 of the fresh dough facilities were franchise operated). All fresh dough facilities were leased. In fiscal 2009, there was an average of 62.5 bakery-cafés per fresh dough facility compared to an average of 62.0 in fiscal 2008.[80]

Distribution of the fresh dough to bakery-cafés took place daily through a leased fleet of 184 temperature-controlled trucks driven by Panera employees. The optimal maximum distribution range for each truck was approximately 300 miles; however, when necessary, the distribution ranges might be up to 500 miles. An average distribution route delivered dough to seven bakery-cafés.

The company focused its expansion in areas served by the fresh dough facilities in order to continue to gain efficiencies through leveraging the fixed cost of its fresh dough facility structure. Panera expected to enter selectively new markets that required the construction of additional facilities until a sufficient number of bakery-cafés could be opened that permitted efficient distribution of the fresh dough.

In addition to its need for fresh dough, the company contracted externally for the manufacture of the remaining baked goods in the bakery-cafés, referred to as sweet goods. Sweet goods products were completed at each bakery-café by professionally trained bakers. Completion included finishing with fresh toppings and other ingredients and baking to established artisan standards utilizing unique recipes.

With the exception of products supplied directly by the fresh dough facilities, virtually all other food products and supplies for the bakery-cafés, including paper goods, coffee, and smallwares, were contracted externally by the company and delivered by vendors to an independent distributor for delivery to the bakery-cafés. In order to assure high-quality food and supplies from reliable sources, Panera and its franchisees were required to select from a list of approved suppliers and distributors. The company leveraged its size and scale to improve the quality of its ingredients, effect better purchasing efficiency, and negotiate purchase agreements with most approved suppliers to achieve cost reduction for both the company and its customers. One company delivered the majority of Panera's ingredients and other products to the bakery-cafés two or three times weekly. In addition, company-owned bakery-cafés and franchisees relied on a network of local and national suppliers for the delivery of fresh produce (three to six times per week).

Marketing[81]

Panera focused on customer research to plan its marketing and brand-building initiatives. According to Panera executives, "everything we do at Panera goes through the customer filter first."[82] Panera's target customers were between 25 and 50 years old, earned US$40,000 to US$100,000 a year, and were seeking fresh ingredients and high-quality choices.[83] The company's customers spent an average of US$8.50 per visit.[84]

Panera was committed to improving the customer experience in ways the company believed rare in the industry. The company leveraged its nationwide presence as part of a broader marketing strategy of building name recognition and awareness. As much as possible, the company used its store locations to market its brand image. When choosing a location to open a new store, Panera carefully selected the geographic area. Better locations needed less marketing, and the bakery-café concept relied on a substantial volume of repeat business.

In 2009, Panera executed a more aggressive marketing strategy than most of its competitors. While many competitors discounted to lure customers back through 2009, Panera focused on offering guests an even better "total experience." Improvements to the "total experience" included new coffee and breakfast items, new salads, new china, smoothies, and mac and cheese. The company focused on improving store profit by increasing transactions as well as increasing gross profit per transaction through the innovation and sales of higher gross profit items. Panera also had a successful initiative to drive add-on sales through the Meal Upgrade program.[85]

In 2010, Panera began modest increases in advertising and additional investments in its marketing infrastructure because the company recognized the importance of marketing as a driver of earnings and sales increases.[86] In spite of these increases, Panera remained very cautious about its marketing investments and focused on the appropriate mix for each market. Panera primarily used radio and billboard advertising, with some television, social networking, and in-store sampling days. Panera found that it benefited when other companies advertised products that Panera also carried, such as McDonald's early 2010 promotion of smoothies. Panera was testing additional television advertising in 20 markets but considered any significant growth in this medium to be a few years away.[87]

Panera's franchise agreements required franchisees to pay the company advertising fees based on a percentage of sales. In fiscal 2009, franchise-operated bakery-cafés contributed 0.7% of their sales to a company-run national advertising fund, paid a marketing administration fee of 0.4% of sales, and were required to spend 2.0% of their sales on advertising in their respective local markets. The company contributed the same sales percentages from company-owned bakery-cafés toward the national advertising fund and marketing administration fee. For fiscal 2010, the company increased the contribution rate to the national advertising fund to 1.1% of sales.[88]

Panera invested in cause-related marketing efforts and community activities through its Operation Dough-Nation program. These programs included sponsoring runs and walks, helping nonprofits raise funds, and the Day-End Dough-Nation program through which unsold bakery products were packaged at the end of each day and donated to local food banks and charities.[89]

Management information Systems[90]

Each company-operated bakery-café had programmed point-of-sale registers to collect transaction data used to generate pertinent information, including transaction counts, product mix, and average check. All company-owned bakery-café product prices were programmed into the system from the company's corporate headquarters. The company allowed franchisees to have access to certain proprietary bakery-café systems and systems support. The fresh dough facilities had information systems that accepted electronic orders from the bakery-cafés and monitored delivery of the ordered product. The company also used proprietary online tools such as eLearning to provide online training for retail associates and online baking instructions for its bakers.

Panera's intranet site, The Harvest, allowed the company to monitor important analytics and provide support to its bakery-cafés. For example, Panera used a weather application on its intranet that tied a bakery-café's historic local weather to the store's historic sales, allowing managers to forecast sales based on weather for any given day. "That helps in staffing and how you're going to allocate labor and what you need in terms of materials," said Greg Rhoades, Panera's senior manager in information services. He called The Harvest "our single source of information." Panera shared news with its employees about food safety and customer satisfaction websites and provided information on daily sales, hourly sales, staffing, product sales, labor costs, and ingredient costs.[91]

The company began offering Wi-Fi in its bakery-cafés in 2003. By 2010, most bakery-cafés provided customers with free Internet access through a managed Wi-Fi network. As a result, Panera hosted one of the largest free public Wi-Fi networks in the country.[92]

In 2010, Panera began to pilot test a loyalty program, "My Panera," in 23 stores. Rather than just a food-discounting program, "My Panera" was intended to provide a deeper relationship with the customer by including participants in events such as the food tasting of new products. The company expected to complete the pilot by year-end 2010 and hoped to begin leveraging the data to better understand its high-frequency customers and to "surprise and delight" them in a way that was tailored to the customers' buying habits.[93]

Human Resources[94]

From the beginning, Panera realized that the key ingredients to the successful development of the Panera brand ranged from the type of food it served to the kind of people behind the counters. The company placed a priority on staffing its bakery-cafés, fresh dough facilities, and support center operations with skilled associates and invested in training programs to ensure the quality of its operations. As of December 29, 2009, the company employed approximately 12,000 full-time associates (defined as associates who average 25 hours or more per week), of whom approximately 600 were employed in general or administrative functions, principally in the company's support centers; approximately 1200 were employed in the company's fresh dough facility operations; and approximately 10,300 were employed in the company's bakery-café operations as bakers, managers, and associates. The company also had approximately 13,200 part-time hourly associates at the bakery-cafés. There were no collective bargaining agreements. The company considered its employee relations to be good.

Panera believed that providing bakery-café operators the opportunity to participate in the success of the bakery-cafés enabled the company to attract and retain experienced and highly motivated personnel, which resulted in a better customer experience. Through a Joint Venture Program, the company provided selected general managers and multi-unit managers with a multi-year bonus program based upon a percentage of the cash flows of the bakery-café they operated. The intent of the program's five-year period was to create team stability, generally resulting in a higher level of stability for that bakery-café and thus lead to stronger associate engagement and customer loyalty. In December 2009, approximately 50% of company-owned bakery-café operators participated in the Joint Venture program.[95]

Finance

Panera reported a 48% increase in net income of US$25,845 million, or US$0.82 per diluted share, during the first quarter of 2010, compared to US$17,432 million, or US$0.57 per diluted share, during the first quarter of 2009. For this same period, Panera reported revenues of US$364,210 million, a 14% gain over revenues of US$320,709 for the same period in 2009.[96] Company-owned comparable bakery-café sales in the first quarter of fiscal 2010 increased 10.0%, due to transaction growth of 3.5% and average check growth of 6.5% over the comparable period in 2009. Franchise-operated comparable bakery-café sales increased 9.2% in the first quarter of 2010 compared to the same period in 2009. As a result, total comparable bakery-café sales increased 9.5% in the first quarter of fiscal 2010 compared to the comparable period in 2009.[97] In addition, average weekly sales (AWS) for newly opened company-owned bakery-cafés during the first quarter of 2010 were US$56,111 compared to US$41,922 in the first quarter of 2009. During the first quarter of 2010, Panera and its franchises opened eight new bakery-cafés systemwide. No bakery-cafés were closed during this period.[98]

Exhibits 3 to **5** provide Panera's consolidated statement of operations, common size income statements, and consolidated balance sheets, respectively, for the company for the fiscal years ended 2005 through 2009.

EXHIBIT 3 Consolidated Statement of Operations: Panera Bread Company

	(Dollar amounts in thousands, except per share information)				
	For the Fiscal Year Ended (1)				
	December 29, 2009	December 30, 2008	December 25, 2007	December 26, 2006	December 27, 2005
Revenues					
Bakery-café sales	$ 1,153,255	$ 1,106,295	$ 894,902	$ 666,141	$ 499,422
Franchise royalties and fees	78,367	74,800	67,188	61,531	54,309
Fresh dough sales to franchisee	121,872	117,758	104,601	101,299	86,544
Total revenue	1,353,494	1,298,853	1,066,691	828,971	640,275
Costs and expenses					
Bakery-café expenses					
Cost of food and paper products	$ 337,599	$ 332,697	$271,442	$ 196,849	$ 143,057
Labor	370,595	352,462	286,238	204,956	151,524
Occupancy	95,996	90,390	70,398	48,602	35,558
Other operating expenses	155,396	147,033	121,325	92,176	70,003
Total bakery-café expenses	959,586	922,582	749,403	542,583	400,142
Fresh dough cost of sales to franchisees	100,229	108,573	92,852	85,951	74,654
Depreciation and amortization	67,162	67,225	57,903	44,166	33,011
General and administrative expenses	83,169	84,393	68,966	59,306	46,301
Pre-opening expenses	2,451	3,374	8,289	6,173	5,072
Total costs and expenses	1,212,597	1,186,147	977,413	738,179	559,180
Operating profit	140,897	112,706	89,278	90,792	81,095
Interest expense	700	1,606	483	92	50
Other (income) expense, net	273	883	333	(1,976)	(1,133)
Income before income taxes	139,924	110,217	88,462	92,676	82,178
Income taxes	53,073	41,272	31,434	33,827	29,995
Net income	86,851	68,945	57,028	58,849	52,183
Less: income (loss) attributable to noncontrolling interest	801	1,509	(428)		
Net income attributable to Panera Bread	$ 86,050	$ 67,436	$ 57,456	$ 58,849	$ 52,183
Per share data					
Earnings per common share attributable to Panera Bread Company					
Basic	$ 2.81	$ 2.24	$ 1.81	$ 1.88	$ 1.69
Diluted	$ 2.78	$ 2.22	$ 1.79	$ 1.84	$ 1.65
Weighted average shares of common and common equivalent shares outstanding					
Basic	30,667	30,059	31,708	31,313	30,871
Diluted	30,979	30,422	32,178	32,044	31,651

Notes:
(1) Fiscal 2008 was a 53-week year consisting of 371 days. All other fiscal years presented contained 52 weeks consisting of 364 days with the exception of fiscal 2005. In fiscal 2005, the company's fiscal week was changed to end on Tuesday rather than Saturday. As a result, the 2005 fiscal year ended on December 27, 2005, instead of December 31, 2005, and, therefore, consisted of 52 and a half weeks rather than the 53 week year that would have resulted without the calender change.

SOURCES: Panera Bread Company Inc., *2009 Form 10-K*, pp. 20–21.

EXHIBIT 4 Common Size Statement: Panera Bread Company

	(Percentages are in relation to total revenues except where otherwise indicated) For the Fiscal Year Ended				
	December 29, 2009	December 30, 2008	December 25, 2007	December 26, 2006	December 27, 2005
Revenues					
Bakery-café sales	85.2%	85.2%	83.9%	80.4%	78.0%
Franchise royalties and fees	5.8	5.8	6.3	7.4	8.5
Fresh dough sales to franchisee	9.0	9.1	9.8	12.2	13.5
Total revenue	100.0%	100.0%	100.0%	100.0%	100.0%
Costs and expenses					
Bakery-café expense (1)					
Cost of food and paper products	29.3%	30.1%	30.3%	29.6%	28.6%
Labor	32.1	31.9	32.0	30.8	30.3
Occupancy	8.3	8.2	7.9	7.3	7.1
Other operating expenses	13.5	13.3	13.6	13.8	14.0
Total bakery-café expenses	83.2	83.4	83.7	81.5	80.0
Fresh dough cost of sales to franchisees (2)	82.2	92.2	88.8	84.5	86.7
Depreciation and amortization	5.0	5.2	5.4	5.3	5.2
General and administrative expenses	6.1	6.5	6.5	7.2	7.2
Pre-opening expenses	0.2	0.3	0.8	0.7	0.8
Total costs and expenses	**89.6**	**91.3**	**91.6**	**89.0**	**87.3**
Operating profit	10.4	8.7	8.4	11.0	12.7
Interest expense	0.1	0.1	0.1	—	—
Other (income) expense, net	—	0.1	—	-0.2	-0.2
Income before income taxes	10.3	8.5	8.3	11.2	12.8
Income taxes	3.9	3.2	2.9	4.1	4.7
Net income	**6.4**	**5.3**	**5.4**	**7.1**	**8.2**
Less: net income attributable to noncontrolling interest	0.1	0.1	—	—	—
Net income attributable to Panera Bread Company	**6.4%**	**5.2%**	**5.4%**	**7.1%**	**8.2%**

Notes:
(1) As a percentage of bakery-café sales.
(2) As a percentage of fresh dough facility sales to franchisees.

SOURCES: Panera Bread Company, Inc. *2009 Form 10-K*, p. 24 and 2006 Form 10-K, p. 19

EXHIBIT 5 Consolidated Balance Sheets: Panera Bread Company

| | **(Dollar amounts in thousands, except share and per share information)** | | | | |
| | **For the Fiscal Year Ended** | | | | |
	December 29, 2009	**December 30, 2008**	**December 25, 2007**	**December 26, 2006**	**December 27, 2005**
Assets					
Current assets					
Cash and cash equivalents	$ 246,400	$ 74,710	$ 68,242	$ 52,097	$ 24,451
Short-term investments	—	2,400	23,198	20,025	36,200
Trade accounts receivable, net	17,317	15,198	25,122	19,041	18,229
Other accounts receivable	11,176	9,944	11,640	11,878	6,929
Inventories	12,295	11,959	11,394	8,714	7,358
Prepaid expenses	16,211	14,265	5,299	12,036	5,736
Deferred income taxes	18,685	9,937	7,199	3,827	3,871
Total current assets	322,084	138,413	152,124	127,618	102,774
Property and equipment, net	403,784	417,006	429,992	345,977	268,809
Other assets					
Goodwill	87,481	87,334	87,092	57,192	48,540
Other intangible assets, net	19,195	20,475	21,827	6,604	3,219
Long-term investments	—	1,726	—	—	10,108
Deposits and other	4,621	8,963	7,717	5,218	4,217
Total other assets	111,297	118,498	116,636	69,014	66,084
Total assets	$ 837,165	$ 673,917	$ 698.752	$ 542,609	$ 437,667
Liabilities and stockholders' equity					
Current liabilities					
Accounts payable	6,417	4,036	6,326	5,800	4,422
Accrued expenses	135,842	109,978	121,440	102,718	81,559
Deferred revenue	—	—	—	1,092	884
Total current liabilities	142,259	114,014	127,766	109,610	86,865
Long-term debt	—	—	75,000	—	—
Deferred rent	43,371	39,780	33,569	27,684	23,935
Deferred income taxes	28,813	—	—	—	5,022
Other long-term liabilities	25,686	21,437	14,238	7,649	4,867
Total liabilities	240,129	175,231	250,573	144,943	120,689
Stockholders' equity					
Common stock, $.0001 par value:					
Class A, 75,000,000 shares authorized: 30,364,915 issued and 30,196,808 outstanding in 2009; 29,557,849 issued and 29,421,877 outstanding in 2008; 30,213,869 issued and 30,098,275 outstanding in 2007.	3	3	3	3	3
Class B, 10,000,000 shares authorized; 1,392,107 issued and outstanding in 2009; 1,398,242 in 2008; 1,398,588 in 2007; 1,400,031 in 2006 and 1,400,621 in 2005.	—	—	—	—	—

(continued)

EXHIBIT 5 (Continued)

Treasury stock, carried at cost;	(3,928)	(2,204)	(1,188)	(900)	(900)
Additional paid-in capital	168,288	151,358	168,386	176,241	154,402
Accumulated other comprehensive income (loss)	224	(394)	—	—	—
Retained earnings	432,449	346,399	278,963	222,322	163,473
Total stockholders' equity	597,036	495,162	446,164	397,666	316,978
Noncontrolling interest	—	3,524	2,015	—	—
Total equity	$ 597,036	$ 498,686	$ 446,164	$ 397,666	$ 316,978
Total equity and liabilities	$ 837,165	$ 673,917	$ 698,752	$ 542,609	$ 437,667

SOURCES: Panera Bread Company, Inc., *2009 Form 10-K*, p. 45; *2008 Form 10-K*, p. 43; and *2006 Form 10-K*, p. 36.

In fiscal 2009, during an uncertain economic environment, Panera bucked industry-wide trends and increased performance on the following key metrics: (1) systemwide comparable bakery-café sales growth of 0.5% (0.7% for company-owned bakery-cafés and 0.5% for franchise-operated bakery-cafés); (2) systemwide average weekly sales increased 1.8% to US$39,926 (US$39,050 for company-owned bakery-cafés and US$40,566 for franchise-operated bakery-cafés); and (3) 69 new bakery-cafés opened systemwide (7 company-owned bakery-cafés and 39 franchise-operated bakery-cafés). In fiscal 2009, Panera earned US$2.78 per diluted share.[99] In addition, average weekly sales (AWS) for newly opened company-owned bakery-cafés in 2009 reached a six-year high for new units.[100] **Exhibit 6** provides 2005–2009 selected financial information about Panera.

Total company revenue in fiscal 2009 increased 4.2% to US$1,353.5 million from US$1,298.9 million in fiscal 2008. This growth was primarily due to the opening of 69 new bakery-cafés systemwide in fiscal 2009 (and the closure of 14 bakery-cafés) and, to a lesser extent, the 0.5% increase in systemwide comparable bakery sales.

Company-owned bakery-café sales increased 4.2% in fiscal 2009 to US$1,153.3 million compared to US$1,106.3 million in fiscal 2008. This increase was due to the opening of 30 new company-owned bakery-cafés and to the 0.7% increase in comparable company-owned bakery-café sales in 2009. Company-owned bakery-café sales as a percentage of revenue remained consistent at 85.2% in both fiscal 2009 and fiscal 2008. In addition, the increase in average weekly sales for company-owned bakery-cafés in fiscal 2009 compared to the prior fiscal year was primarily due to the average check growth that resulted from the company's initiative to drive add-on sales. Franchise royalties and fees in fiscal 2009 were up 4.8% to US$78.4 million, or 5.8% of total revenues, up from US$74.8 million in 2008. Fresh dough sales to franchises increased 3.5% in fiscal 2009 to US$121.9 million compared to US$117.8 million in fiscal 2008.[101]

Panera believed that its primary capital resource was cash generated by operations. The company's principal requirements for cash have resulted from the company's capital expenditures for the development of new company-owned bakery-cafés; for maintaining or remodeling existing company-owned bakery-cafés; for purchasing existing franchise-operated bakery-cafés or ownership interests in other restaurant or bakery-café concepts; for developing, maintaining, or remodeling fresh dough facilities; and for

EXHIBIT 6   Selected Financial Information: Panera Bread Company

(Dollar amounts in thousands)

A. Year to Year Comparable Sales Growth (not adjusted for differing number of weeks)

	For the Fiscal Year Ended				
	December 29, 2009 (52 weeks)	December 30, 2008 (53 weeks)	December 25, 2007 (52 weeks)	December 26, 2006 (52 weeks)	December 27, 2005 (52-1/2 weeks)
Company-owned	0.7%	5.8%	1.9%	3.9%	7.4%
Franchise-operated	0.5%	5.3%	1.5%	4.1%	8.0%
Systemwide	0.5%	5.5%	1.6%	4.1%	7.8%

B. System Wide Average Weekly Sales

	For the Fiscal Year Ended				
	December 29, 2009	December 30, 2008	December 25, 2007	December 26, 2006	December 27, 2005
Systemwide average weekly sales	$ 39,926	$ 39,239	$ 38,668	$ 39,150	$ 38,318

C. Company-owned Bakery-Café Average Weekly Sales

	For the Fiscal Year Ended				
	December 29, 2009	December 30, 2008	December 25, 2007	December 26, 2006	December 27, 2005
Company-owned average weekly sales	39,050	38,066	37,548	37,833	37,348
Company-owned number of operating weeks	29,533	29,062	23,834	176,077	13,280

D. Franchise-owned Bakery-Café Average Weekly Sales

	For the Fiscal Year Ended				
	December 29, 2009	December 30, 2008	December 25, 2007	December 26, 2006	December 27, 2005
Franchise average weekly sales	40,566	40,126	39,433	39,894	38,777
Franchise number of operating weeks	40,436	38,449	34,905	31,220	28,090

SOURCES: Panera Bread Company, Inc., *2009 Form 10-K*, pp. 26–30; *2008 Form 10-K*, pp. 25–27; and *2006 Form 10-K*, pp. 20–23.

other capital needs such as enhancements to information systems and infrastructure. The company had access to a US$250 million credit facility which, as of December 29, 2009, had no borrowings outstanding. Panera believed its cash flow from operations and available borrowings under its existing credit facility to be sufficient to fund its capital requirements for the foreseeable future.[102]

According to Nicole Miller Regan, an analyst at Piper Jaffray, "the key to Panera's success during the recessionary period lies in what the company hasn't done . . . . It hasn't tried to change."[103] "For us, the recession has been the best of times," said CEO Shaich.[104]

NOTES

1. Panera Bread Company Inc., *2009 Form 10-K,* pp. 1–2.
2. John Jannarone, "Panera Bread's Strong Run," *The Wall Street Journal* (January 23, 2010).
3. Christopher Tritto, "Panera's Rosenthal Cashes In," *St. Louis Business Journal* (January 5, 2010), http://stlouis .bizjournals.com/stlouis/stories/2010/01/04/story2.html.
4. "Overview: Panera Bread Company," *Hoover's Inc.*
5. Linda Tischler, "Vote of Confidence," *Fast Company* 65 (December 2002), pp. 102–112.
6. Peter O. Keegan, "Louis I. Kane & Ronald I. Shaich: Au Bon Pain's Own Dynamic Duo," *Nation's Restaurant News* 28 (September 19, 1994), p. 172.
7. Tischler, pp. 102–112.
8. Keegan, p. 172.
9. Robin Lee Allen, "Au Bon Pain's Kane Dead at 69; Founded Bakery Chain," *Nation's Restaurant News* 34 (June 26, 2000), pp. 6–7.
10. Tischler, pp. 102–112.
11. Ibid.
12. Powers Kemp, "Second Rising," *Forbes* 166 (November 13, 2000), p. 290.
13. Tischler, pp. 102–112.
14. Ibid.
15. "Overview: Panera Bread Company," *Hoover's Inc.*
16. Robin Lee Allen, "Au Bon Pain Co. Pins Hopes on New President, Image," *Nation's Restaurant News* 30 (December 2, 1996), pp. 3–4.
17. Tischler, pp. 102–112.
18. Chern Yeh Kwok, "Bakery-Café Idea Smacked of Success from the Very Beginning; Concept Gives Rise to Rapid Growth in Stores, Stock Price," *St. Louis Dispatch* (May 20, 2001), p. E1.
19. Allen (December 2, 1996), pp. 3–4.
20. Kemp, p. 290.
21. Richard L. Papiernik, "Au Bon Pain Mulls Remedies, Pares Back Expansion Plans," *Nation's Restaurant News* 29 (August 28, 1995), pp. 3–4.
22. "Au Bon Pain Stock Drops 11% on News that Loss Is Expected," *The Wall Street Journal* (October 7, 1996), p. B2.
23. Andrew Caffrey, "Heard in New England: Au Bon Pain's Plan to Reinvent Itself Sits Well with Many Pros," *The Wall Street Journal* (March 10, 1999), p. NE.2.
24. Panera Bread Company Inc., *2009 Form 10-K,* p. 1.
25. Ibid., pp. 6–7.
26. Panera Bread Company Inc., *2009 Form 10-K,* pp. 1–2.
27. Bruce Horovitz, "Panera Bakes a Recipe for Success," *USA Today* (July 23, 2009), p. 1.
28. Christopher Leonard, "New Panera Location Says Pay What You Want," Associated Press (May 18, 2010).
29. Emily Bryson York. "Panera: An America's Hottest Brands Case Study," *Advertising Age* (November 16, 2009), http://adage.com/article?article_id=140482.
30. Zagat Survey, http://www.zagat.com/FASTFOOD.
31. Tritto.
32. Panera Company Overview, www.panerabread.com/about /company/awards.php.
33. Panera Bread Company Inc., Second Quarter Earnings Conference Call, July 28, 2010.
34. Panera Press Release (314-633-4282), *Panera Bread Reports Q1 EPS of $.82, up 44% Over Q1 2009, on a 10% Company-owned Comparable Bakery-Café Sales Increase,* pp. 1–10.
35. Ibid., p. 20.
36. Panera Bread Company Inc., Second Quarter Earnings Conference Call, July 28, 2010.
37. Ibid., p. 10.
38. Panera, April 12, 2010 Letter to Stockholders, p. 1.
39. Julie Jargon, "Slicing the Bread but Not the Prices," *The Wall Street Journal* (August 18, 2009), B1.
40. Ibid.
41. Horovitz, p. 1.
42. Ibid.
43. Panera, April 12, 2010 Letter to Stockholders.
44. Ibid.
45. Ibid.
46. Sean Gregory, "How Panera Bread Defies the Recession," *Time* (December 23, 2009), p. 2, www.time.com/time/print out/0,8816,1949371,00.html.
47. G. LaVecchia, "Fast Casual Enters the Fast Lane," *Restaurant Hospitality* 87 (February 2003), pp. 43–47.
48. *MINTEL 2008.*
49. Ibid.
50. Paul Ziobro, "Panera Looks to Bake Up Profit," *The Wall Street Journal* (August 13, 2008), p. B3C.
51. "Fast-Casual Chains Thriving During Tough Economy" (June 24, 2010), www.foodproductdesign.com /news/2010/06/fast-casual-chains-thriving-during-tough-economy.aspx.
52. Lauren Shephard, "Convenience Key to Driving Fast -Casual Sales," *Nations Restaurant News* (June 16, 2010).
53. "Fast-Casual Chains Thriving . . . ."
54. Bob Vosburgh, "The Future of Fast Casual Restaurants" (June 24, 2010), http://supermarketnews.com/blog /future-fast-casual-restaurants
55. Panera Bread Company Inc., *2009 Form 10-K,* p. 8.
56. "Fast-Casual Chains Thriving . . . ."
57. Greg Farrell, "Appetite Grows for US 'Fast Casual Food,'" *Financial Times* (June 18, 2010), http://www.ft.com/cms /s/0/0f452038-7b06-11df-8935-00144feabdc0.html
58. Horovitz, p. 1.
59. Panera Bread Company Inc. Notice of Annual Stockholders Meeting, April 12, 2010, pp. 4–5.
60. Ibid., pp. 5–8.
61. Ibid., pp. 10–12.
62. Ibid., p. 37.
63. Ibid., pp. 14–16.
64. Ibid., p. 5.
65. Ibid., p. 29.
66. Ibid., p. 3.
67. Ibid., p. 40.
68. Ibid., p. 1.
69. Panera Bread Company Inc., *2009 Form 10-K,* p. 4.
70. Kate Rockwood, "Rising Dough: Why Panera Bread Is on a Roll," *Fastcompany.com* (October 1, 2009), www.fast company.com//magazine/139/rising-dough.html.
71. Ibid.
72. www.Datamonitor.com (December 15, 2008), p. 8.

73. www.panerabread.com/menu/café/kids.php.
74. Panera Bread Company Inc., *2009 Form 10-K*, pp. 5–6.
75. Panera Bread Company Inc., *2009 Form 10-K*, p. 7.
76. Panera Bread Franchise Information, www.panerabread.com/about/franchise/, pp. 1–8.
77. Panera Bread Company Inc., Second Quarter Earnings Conference Call, July 28, 2010.
78. Panera Bread Company Inc., *2009 Form 10-K*, p. 7.
79. Tischler, pp. 102–112.
80. Panera Bread Company Inc., *2009 Form 10-K*, p. 28.
81. Panera Bread Company Inc., *2009 Form 10-K*, pp. 3–4.
82. Panera Bread Company Inc., Second Quarter Earnings Conference Call, July 28, 2010.
83. Jargon, p. B1.
84. Ibid.
85. Panera, April 12, 2010 Letter to Stockholders.
86. Panera Bread Company Inc., Second Quarter Earnings Conference Call, July 28, 2010.
87. Ibid.
88. Panera Bread Company Inc., *2009 Form 10-K*, p. 3.
89. Panera Bread Company Inc. http://www.panerabread.com/about/community/.
90. Panera Bread Company Inc., *2009 Form 10-K*, p. 6.
91. Gregg Cebrzynski, "Panera Bread Managers 'Harvest' Key Sales Data via Intranet to Support Internal Marketing Goals," *Nation's Restaurant News* (November 3, 2008), www.nrn.com/article/panera-bread-managers-%E2%80%98harvest%E2%80%99-key-sales-data-intranet-support-internal-marketing-goals.
92. Panera, *2009 Form 10-K*, p. 6.
93. Panera Bread Company Inc., Second Quarter Earnings Conference Call, July 28, 2010.
94. Panera Bread Company Inc., *2009 Form 10-K*, p. 8.
95. Ibid. p. 5.
96. Panera Press Release (314-633-4282), *Panera Bread Reports Q1 EPS of $.82, up 44% Over Q1 2009, on a 10.0% Company-owned Comparable Bakery-Café Sales Increase*, pp. 1–1(
97. Ibid., pp. 1–2.
98. Ibid., p. 2.
99. Panera Bread Company Inc., *2009 Form 10-K*, p. 23.
100. Panera Bread Company Inc., *2009 Form 10-K, Annual Letter to Stockholders*, p. 2.
101. Panera Bread Company Inc., *2009 Form 10-K*, pp. 26–28.
102. Panera Bread Company Inc., *2009 Form 10-K*, pp. 4 and 32–33.
103. Sean Gregory, "How Panera Bread Defies the Recession," *Time* (December 23, 2009), pp. 1–2, www.time.com/time/printout/0,8816,1949371,00.html.
104. Ibid., p. 1.

Whole Foods Market 2010: How to Grow in an Increasingly Competitive Market? (Mini Case)

Patricia Harasta and Alan N. Hoffman

REFLECTING BACK OVER HIS THREE DECADES OF EXPERIENCE IN THE GROCERY BUSINESS, John Mackey smiled to himself over his previous successes. His entrepreneurial history began with a single store that he has now grown into the nation's leading natural food chain. Whole Foods is not just a food retailer but instead represents a healthy, socially responsible lifestyle that customers can identify with. The company has differentiated itself from competitors by focusing on quality, excellence, and innovation that allow it to charge a premium price for premium products. While proud of the past, John had concerns about the future direction in which Whole Foods should head.

Company Background

Whole Foods carries both natural and organic food, offering customers a wide variety of products. "Natural" refers to food that is free of growth hormones or antibiotics, whereas "certified organic" food conforms to the standards, as defined by the U.S. Department of Agriculture (USDA) in October 2002. Whole Foods Market is the world's leading retailer of natural and organic foods, with 193 stores in 31 states, Canada, and the United Kingdom.

This case was prepared by Patricia Harasta and Professor Alan N. Hoffman, Bentley University and Erasmus University. Copyright © 2010 by Alan N. Hoffman. The copyright holder is solely responsible for case content. Reprint permission is solely granted to the publisher, Prentice Hall, for *Strategic Management and Business Policy*, 15th Edition (and the international and electronic versions of this book) by the copyright holder, Alan N. Hoffman. Any other publication of the case (translation, any form of electronics or other media) or sale (any form of partnership) to another publisher will be in violation of copyright law, unless Alan N. Hoffman has granted an additional written permission. Reprinted by permission. The authors would like to thank Will Hoffman, Christopher Ferrari, Robert Marshall, Julie Giles, Jennifer Powers, and Gretchen Alper for their research and contributions to this case. No part of this publication may be copied, stored, transmitted, reproduced, or distributed in any form or medium whatsoever without the permission of the copyright owner, Alan N. Hoffman.

According to the company, Whole Foods Market is highly selective about what it sells, dedicated to stringent quality standards, and committed to sustainable agriculture. It believes in a virtuous circle entwining the food chain, human beings, and Mother Earth: Each is reliant upon the others through a beautiful and delicate symbiosis. The message of preservation and sustainability are followed while providing high-quality goods to customers and high profits to investors.

Whole Foods has grown over the years through mergers, acquisitions, and new store openings. The US$565 million acquisition of its lead competitor, Wild Oats, in 2007 firmly set Whole Foods as the leader in the natural and organic food market and led to 70 new stores. The U.S. Federal Trade Commission (FTC) focused its attention on the merger on antitrust grounds. The dispute was settled in 2009, with Whole Foods closing 32 Wild Oats stores and agreeing to sell the Wild Oats Markets brand.

Although the majority of Whole Foods' locations are in the United States, European expansion provides enormous potential growth due to the large population there and because it has access to a more sophisticated organic-foods market than the United States in terms of suppliers and acceptance by the public. Whole Foods targets its locations specifically by an area's demographics. The company targets locations where 40% or more of the residents have a college degree because its citizens are more likely to be aware of nutritional issues.

Whole Foods Market's Philosophy

Whole Foods Market's company philosophy is to be a sustainable company. While Whole Foods recognizes it is only a supermarket, management is working toward fulfilling their vision within the context of the industry. In addition to leading by example, they strive to conduct business in a manner consistent with their mission and vision. By offering minimally processed, high-quality food, engaging in ethical business practices, and providing a motivational, respectful work environment, the company believes it is on the path to a sustainable future.

Whole Foods incorporates the best practices of each location back into the chain. This can be seen in the company's store product expansion from dry goods to perishable produce, including meats, fish, and prepared foods. The lessons learned at one location are absorbed by all, enabling the chain to maximize effectiveness and efficiency while offering a product line customers love. Whole Foods carries only natural and organic products. The best tasting and most nutritious food available is found in its purest state—unadulterated by artificial additives, sweeteners, colorings, and preservatives.

Employee and Customer Relations

Whole Foods encourages a team-based environment allowing each store to make independent decisions regarding its operations. Teams consist of up to 11 employees and a team leader. The team leaders typically head up one department or another. Each store employs anywhere from 72 to 391 team members. The manager is referred to as the "store team leader." The "store team leader" is compensated by an Economic Value Added (EVA) bonus and is also eligible to receive stock options.

Whole Foods tries to instill a sense of purpose among its employees and has been named for 13 consecutive years as one of the "100 Best Companies to Work For" in America by *Fortune* magazine. In employee surveys, 90% of its team members stated that they always or frequently enjoy their job.

The company strives to take care of its customers, realizing they are the "lifeblood of our business," and the two are "interdependent on each other." Whole Foods' primary objective goes beyond 100% customer satisfaction with the goal to "delight" customers in every interaction.

Competitive Environment

At the time of Whole Foods' inception, there was almost no competition with less than six other natural food stores in the United States. Today, the organic foods industry is growing and Whole Foods finds itself competing hard to maintain its elite presence.

Whole Foods competes with all supermarkets. With more U.S. consumers focused on healthful eating, environmental sustainability, and the green movement, the demand for organic and natural foods has increased. More traditional supermarkets are now introducing "lifestyle" stores and departments to compete directly with Whole Foods. This can be seen in the Wild Harvest section of Shaw's, or the "Lifestyle" stores opened by conventional grocery chain Safeway.

Whole Foods' competitors now include big box and discount retailers who have made a foray into the grocery business. Currently, the United States' largest grocer is Wal-Mart. Not only does Wal-Mart compete in the standard supermarket industry, but it has even begun offering natural and organic products in its supercenter stores. Other discount retailers now competing in the supermarket industry include Target, Sam's Club, and Costco. All of these retailers offer grocery products, generally at a lower price than what one would find at Whole Foods.

Another of Whole Foods' key competitors is Los Angeles–based Trader Joe's, a premium natural and organic food market. By expanding its presence and product offerings while maintaining high quality at low prices, Trader Joe's has found its competitive niche. It has 215 stores, primarily on the west and east coasts of the United States, offering upscale grocery fare such as health foods, prepared meals, organic produce, and nutritional supplements. A low-cost structure allows Trader Joe's to offer competitive prices while still maintaining its margins. Trader Joe's stores have no service department and average just 10,000 square feet in store size.

A Different Shopping Experience

The setup of the organic grocery store is a key component to Whole Foods' success. The store's setup and its products are carefully researched to ensure that they are meeting the demands of the local community. Locations are primarily in cities and are chosen for their large space and heavy foot traffic. According to Whole Foods' 10-K, "approximately 88% of our existing stores are located in the top 50 statistical metropolitan areas." The company uses a specific formula to choose store sites that is based upon several metrics, which include but are not limited to income levels, education, and population density.

Upon entering a Whole Foods supermarket, it becomes clear that the company attempts to sell the consumer on the entire experience. Team members (employees) are well trained and the stores themselves are immaculate. There are in-store chefs to help with recipes, wine tasting, and food sampling. There are "Take Action food centers" where customers can access information on the issues that affect their food such as legislation and environmental factors. Some stores offer extra services such as home delivery, cooking classes, massages, and valet parking. Whole Foods goes out of its way to appeal to the above-average income earner.

Whole Foods uses price as a marketing tool in a few select areas, as demonstrated by the 365 Whole Foods brand name products priced less than similar organic products that are carried within the store. However, the company does not use price to differentiate itself from competitors. Rather, Whole Foods focuses on quality and service as a means of standing out from the competition.

Whole Foods spends much less than other supermarkets on advertising, approximately 0.4% of total sales in fiscal year 2009. It relies heavily on word-of-mouth advertising from its customers to help market itself in the local community. The company advertises in several health-conscious magazines, and each store budgets for in-store advertising each fiscal year.

Whole Foods also gains recognition via its charitable contributions and the awareness that they bring to the treatment of animals. The company donates 5% of its after-tax profits to not-for-profit charities. It is also very active in establishing systems to make sure that the animals used in their products are treated humanely.

The Green Movement

Whole Foods exists in a time where customers equate going green and being environmentally friendly with enthusiasm and respect. In recent years, people began to learn about food and the processes completed by many to produce it. Most of what they have discovered is disturbing. Whole Foods launched a nationwide effort to trigger awareness and action to remedy the problems facing the U.S. food system. It has decided to host 150 screenings of a 12-film series called "Let's Retake Our Plates," hoping to inspire change by encouraging and educating consumers to take charge of their food choices. Jumping on the bandwagon of the "go green" movement, Whole Foods is trying to show its customers that it is dedicated to not only all natural foods, but to a green world and healthy people. As more and more people become educated, the company hopes to capitalize on them as new customers.[1]

Beyond the green movement, Whole Foods has been able to tap into a demographic that appreciates the "trendy" theme of organic foods and all natural products. Since the store is associated with a type of affluence, many customers shop there to show they fit into this category of upscale, educated, new-age people.

The Economic Recession of 2008

The uncertainty of today's market is a threat to Whole Foods. The expenditure income is low and "all natural foods" are automatically deemed as expensive. Because of people being laid off, having their salaries cut, or simply not being able to find a job, they now have to be more selective when purchasing things. While Whole Foods has been able to maintain profitability, it's questionable how long this will last if the recession continues or worsens. The reputation that organic products have of being costly may be enough to motivate people to never enter Whole Foods. In California, the chain is frequently dubbed "Whole Paycheck."[2]

However, management understood that it must change a few things if the company was to survive the decrease in sales felt because customers were not willing to spend their money so easily. They have been working to correct this "pricey" image by expanding offerings of private-label products through their "365 Everyday Value" and "365 Organic" product lines. Private-label sales accounted for 11% of Whole Foods' total sales in 2009, up from 10% in 2008. They have also instituted a policy that their 365 product lines must match prices of similar products at Trader Joe's.[3]

Organic Foods as a Commodity

When Whole Foods first started in the natural foods industry in 1980, the industry was a relatively new concept. During its first decade, Whole Foods enjoyed the benefits of offering a unique value proposition to consumers wanting to purchase high-quality natural foods from a trusted retailer. Over the last few years, however, the natural and organic foods industry has attracted the attention of general food retailers that have started to offer foods labeled as natural or organic at reasonable prices.

By 2007, the global demand for organic and natural foods far exceeded the supply. This is becoming a huge issue for Whole Foods, as more traditional supermarkets with higher purchasing power enter the premium natural and organic foods market. The supply of organic food has been significantly impacted by the entrance of Wal-Mart into the competitive arena. Due to the limited resources within the United States, Wal-Mart began importing natural and organic foods from China and Brazil, which led to it coming under scrutiny for passing off non-natural or organic products as the "real thing." Additionally, the quality of natural and organic foods throughout the entire market has been decreased due to constant pressure from Wal-Mart.

The distinction between what is truly organic and natural is difficult for the consumer to decipher because general supermarkets have taken to using terms such as "all natural," "freerange," and "hormone-free," thus confusing customers. Truly organic food sold in the United States bears the "USDA Organic" label and needs to have at least 95% of the ingredients organic before it can get this distinction.[4]

In May 2003, Whole Foods became America's first Certified Organic grocer by a federally recognized independent third-party certification organization. In July 2009, California Certified Organic Growers (CCOF), one of the oldest and largest USDA-accredited thirdparty organic certifiers, individually certified each store in the United States, complying with stricter guidance on federal regulations. This voluntary certification tells customers that Whole Foods has gone the extra mile by not only following the USDA's Organic Rule, but opening its stores up to third-party inspectors and following a strict set of operating procedures designed to ensure that the products sold and labeled as organic are indeed organic—procedures that are not specifically required by the Organic Rule. This certification verifies the handling of organic goods according to stringent national guidelines, from receipt through repacking to final sale to customers. To receive certification, retailers must agree to adhere to a strict set of standards set forth by the USDA, submit documentation, and open their facilities to onsite inspections—all designed to assure customers that the chain of organic integrity is preserved.

Struggling to Grow in an Increasingly Competitive Market

Whole Foods has historically grown by opening new stores or acquiring stores in affluent neighborhoods targeting the wealthier and more educated consumers. This strategy has worked in the past; however, the continued focus on growth has been impacting existing store sales. Average weekly sales per store have decreased over the last number of years despite the fact that overall sales have been increasing. It is likely that this trend will continue unless Whole Foods starts to focus on growing sales within the stores it has and not just looking to increase overall sales by opening new stores. It is also increasingly difficult to find appropriate locations for new stores that are first and foremost in an area where there is limited competition and also to have the store in a location that is easily accessible by both consumers and the distribution network. Originally, Whole Foods had forecast to open 29 new stores in 2010 but this has since been revised downward to 17.

Opening up new stores or acquiring existing stores is also costly. The average cost to open a new store ranges from US$2 to US$3 million, and it takes on average 8 to 12 months. A lot of this can be explained by the fact that Whole Foods custom builds the stores, which reduces the efficiencies that can be gained from the experience of having opened up many new stores previously. Opening new stores requires the company to adapt its distribution network, information management, supply, and inventory management, and adequately supply the new stores in a timely manner without impacting the supply to the existing stores. As the company expands, this task increases in complexity and magnitude.

The organic and natural foods industry overall has become a more concentrated market with few larger competitors having emerged from a more fragmented market composed of a large number of smaller companies. Future acquisitions will be more difficult for Whole Foods because the FTC will be monitoring the company closely to ensure it does not violate any federal antitrust laws through the elimination of any substantial competition within this market.

Over the last number of years, there has been an increasing demand by consumers for natural and organic foods. Sales of organic foods increased by 5.1% in 2009 despite the fact that U.S. food sales overall only grew by 1.6%.[5] This increase in demand and high-margin availability on premium organic products led to an increasing number of competitors moving into the organic foods industry. Conventional grocery chains such as Safeway have remodeled stores at a rapid pace and have attempted to narrow the gap with premium grocers like Whole Foods in terms of shopping experience, product quality, and selection of takeout foods. This increase in competition can lead to the introduction of price wars where profits are eroded for both existing competitors and new entrants alike.

Unlike low-price leaders such as Wal-Mart, Whole Foods dominates because of its brand image, which is trickier to manage and less impervious to competitive threats. As competitors start to focus on emphasizing organic and natural foods within their own stores, the power of the Whole Foods brand will gradually decline over time as it becomes more difficult for consumers to differentiate Whole Foods' value proposition from that of its competitors.

NOTES

1. "Whole Foods Market; Whole Foods Market Challenge: Let's Retake Our Plates!" *Food BusinessWeek* (April 15, 2010).
2. "Eating Too Fast at Whole Foods," *BusinessWeek* (2005).
3. Katy McLaughlin, "As Sales Slip, Whole Foods Tries Health Push," *The Wall Street Journal* (August 15, 2009).
4. "Whole Foods Markets Organic China California Blend," http://www.youtube.com/watch?v=JQ31Ljd9T_Y (April 10, 2010).
5. Organic Trade Association, http://www.organicnewsroom.com/2010/04/us_organic_product_sales_reach_1.html.

CASE **21**

Burger King (Mini Case)

J. David Hunger

ORIGINALLY CALLED INSTA-BURGER KING, the company was founded in Florida in 1953 by Keith Kramer and Matthew Burns. Their Insta-Broiler oven was so successful at cooking hamburgers that they required all of their franchised restaurants to use the oven. After the chain ran into financial difficulties, it was purchased by its Miami-based franchisees, James McLamore and David Edgerton, in 1955. The new owners renamed the company Burger King, and the restaurant chain introduced the first *Whopper* sandwich in 1957. Expanding to over 250 locations in the United States, the company was sold in 1967 to Pillsbury Corporation.

The company successfully differentiated itself from McDonald's, its primary rival, when it launched the *Have It Your Way* advertising campaign in 1974. Unlike McDonald's, which had made it difficult and time-consuming for customers to special-order standard items (such as a plain hamburger), Burger King restaurants allowed people to change the way a food item was prepared without a long wait.

Pillsbury (including Burger King) was purchased in 1989 by Grand Metropolitan, which in turn merged with Guinness to form Diageo, a British spirits company. Diageo's management neglected the Burger King business, leading to poor operating performance. Burger King was damaged to the point that major franchises went out of business and the total value of the firm declined. Diageo's management decided to divest the money-losing chain by selling it to a partnership private equity firm led by TPG Capital in 2002.

The investment group hired a new advertising agency to create (1) a series of new ad campaigns, (2) a changed menu to focus on male consumers, (3) a series of programs designed to revamp individual stores, and (4) a new concept called the BK Whopper Bar. These changes led to profitable quarters and reenergized the chain. In May 2006, the investment group took Burger King public by issuing an Initial Public Offering (IPO). The investment group continued to own 31% of the outstanding common stock.

Business Model

Burger King was the second-largest fast-food hamburger restaurant chain in the world as measured by the total number of restaurants and systemwide sales. As of June 30, 2010, the company owned or franchised 12,174 restaurants in 76 countries and U.S. territories, of which 1,387 were company-owned and 10,787 were owned by franchisees. Of Burger King's restaurant total, 7,258 or 60% were located in the United States. The restaurants featured flame-broiled hamburgers, chicken and other specialty sandwiches, French fries, soft drinks, and other low-priced food items.

According to management, the company generated revenues from three sources: (1) retail sales at company-owned restaurants; (2) royalty payments on sales and franchise fees paid by franchisees; and (3) property income from restaurants leased to franchisees. Approximately 90% of Burger King restaurants were franchised, a higher percentage than other competitors in the fast-food hamburger category. Although such a high percentage of franchisees meant lower capital requirements compared to competitors, it also meant that management had limited control over franchisees. Franchisees in the United States and Canada paid an average of 3.9% of sales to the company in 2010. In addition, these franchisees contributed 4% of gross sales per month to the advertising fund. Franchisees were required to purchase food, packaging, and equipment from company-approved suppliers.

Restaurant Services Inc. (RSI) was a purchasing cooperative formed in 1992 to act as purchasing agent for the Burger King system in the United States. As of June 30, 2010, RSI was the distribution manager for 94% of the company's U.S. restaurants, with four distributors servicing approximately 85% of the U.S. system. Burger King had long-term exclusive contracts with Coca-Cola and with Dr Pepper/7UP to purchase soft drinks for its restaurants.

Management touted its business strategy as growing the brand, running great restaurants, investing wisely, and focusing on its people. Specifically, management planned to accelerate growth between 2010 and 2015 so that international restaurants would comprise 50% of the total number. The focus in international expansion was to be in (1) countries with growth potential where Burger King was already established, such as Spain, Brazil, and Turkey; (2) countries with potential where the firm had a small presence, such as Argentina, Colombia, China, Japan, Indonesia, and Italy; and (3) attractive new markets in the Middle East, Eastern Europe, and Asia.

Management was also working to update the restaurants by implementing its new 20/20 design and complementary Whopper Bar design introduced in 2008. By 2010, more than 200 Burger King restaurants had adopted the new 20/20 design that evoked the industrial look of corrugated metal, brick, wood, and concrete. The new design was to be introduced in 95 company-owned restaurants during fiscal 2011.

Management was using a "barbell" menu strategy to introduce new products at both the premium and low-priced ends of the product continuum. As part of this strategy, the company introduced in 2010 the premium Steakhouse XT burger line and BK Fire-Grilled Ribs, the first bone-in pork ribs sold at a national fast-food hamburger restaurant chain. At the other end of the menu, the company introduced in 2010 the quarter-pound Double Cheeseburger, the Buck Double, and the US$1 BK Breakfast Muffin Sandwich.

Management continued to look for ways to reduce costs and boost efficiency. By June 30, 2010, point-of-sale cash register systems had been installed in all company-owned restaurants, and in 57% of its franchise-owned restaurants. It had also installed a flexible batch broiler to maximize cooking flexibility and facilitate a broader menu selection while reducing energy costs. By June 30, 2010, the flexible broiler was in 89% of company-owned restaurants and 68% of franchise restaurants.

Industry

The fast-food hamburger category operated within the quick service restaurant (QSR) segment of the restaurant industry. QSR sales had grown at an annual rate of 3% over the past 10 years and were projected to continue increasing at 3% from 2010 to 2015. The fast-food hamburger restaurant (FFHR) category represented 27% of total QSR sales. FFHR sales were projected to grow 5% annually during this same time period. Burger King accounted for around 14% of total FFHR sales in the United States.

The company competed against market-leading McDonald's, Wendy's, and Hardee's restaurants in this category and against regional competitors, such as Carl's Jr., Jack in the Box, and Sonic. It also competed indirectly against a multitude of competitors in the QSR restaurant segment, including Taco Bell, Arby's, and KFC, among others. As the North American market became saturated, mergers occurred. For example, Taco Bell, KFC, and Pizza Hut became part of Yum! Brands. Wendy's and Arby's merged in 2008. Although the restaurant industry as a whole had few barriers to entry, marketing and operating economies of scale made it difficult for a new entrant to challenge established U.S. chains in the FFHR category.

The quick-service restaurant market segment appeared to be less vulnerable to a recession than other businesses. For example, during the quarter ended May 2010, both QSR and FFHR sales decreased 0.5%, compared to a 3% decline at both casual dining chains and family dining chains. The U.S. restaurant category as a whole declined 1% during the same time period.

America's increasing concern with health and fitness was putting pressure on restaurants to offer healthier menu items. Given its emphasis on fried food and saturated fat, the quick service restaurant market segment was an obvious target for likely legislation. For example, Burger King's recently introduced Pizza Burger was a 2,530-calorie item that included four hamburger patties, pepperoni, mozzarella, and Tuscan sauce on a sesame seed bun. Although the Pizza Burger may be the largest hamburger produced by a fast-food chain, the foot-long cheeseburgers of Hardee's and Carl's Jr. were similar entries. A health reform bill passed by the U.S. Congress in 2010 required restaurant chains with 20 or more outlets to list the calorie content of menu items. A study by the National Bureau of Economic Research found that a similar posting law in New York City caused the average calorie count per transaction to fall 6%, and revenue increased 3% at Starbucks stores where a Dunkin Donuts outlet was nearby. One county in California attempted to ban McDonald's from including toys in its high-calorie "Happy Meal" because legislators believed that toys attracted children to unhealthy food.

Issues

Even though Burger King was the second-largest hamburger chain in the world, it lagged far behind McDonald's, which had a total of 32,466 restaurants worldwide. McDonald's averaged about twice the sales volume per U.S. restaurant and was more profitable than Burger King. McDonald's was respected as a well-managed company. During fiscal year 2009 (ending December 31), McDonald's earned US$4.6 billion on revenues of US$22.7 billion. Although its total revenues had dropped from US$23.5 billion in 2008, net income had actually increased from US$4.3 billion in 2008. In contrast to most corporations, McDonald's common stock price had risen during the 2008–2010 recession, reaching an all-time high in August 2010.

In contrast, Burger King was perceived by industry analysts as having significant problems. As a result, Burger King's share price had fallen by half from 2008 to 2010.

During fiscal year 2010 (ending June 30), Burger King earned US$186.8 million on revenues of US$2.50 billion. Although its total revenues had dropped only slightly from US$2.54 billion in fiscal 2009 and increased from US$2.45 billion in 2008, net income fell from US$200.1 million in 2009 and US$189.6 million in 2008. Even though same-store sales stayed positive for McDonald's during the recession, they dropped 2.3% for Burger King from fiscal 2009 to 2010. In addition, some analysts were concerned that expenses were high at Burger King's company-owned restaurants. Expenses as a percentage of total company-owned restaurant revenues were 87.8% in fiscal 2010 for Burger King compared to only 81.8% for McDonald's in fiscal 2009.

McDonald's had always emphasized marketing to families. The company significantly outperformed Burger King in both "warmth" and "competence" in consumers' minds. When McDonald's recently put more emphasis on women and older people by offering relatively healthy salads and upgraded its already good coffee, Burger King continued to market to young men by (according to one analyst) offering high-calorie burgers and ads featuring dancing chickens and a "creepy-looking" king. These young men were the very group who had been hit especially hard by the recession. According to Steve Lewis, who operated 36 Burger King franchises in the Philadelphia area, "overall menu development has been horrible. . . . We disregarded kids, we disregarded families, we disregarded moms." For example, sales of new, premium-priced menu items like the Steakhouse XT burger declined once they were no longer being advertised. One analyst stated that the company had "put a lot of energy into gimmicky advertising" at the expense of products and service. In addition, analysts commented that franchisees had also disregarded their aging restaurants.

Some analysts felt that Burger King may have cannibalized its existing sales by putting too much emphasis on value meals. For example, Burger King franchisees sued the company in 2009 over the firm's double-cheeseburger promotion, claiming it was unfair for them to be required to sell these cheeseburgers for only US$1 when they cost US$1.10. Even though the price was subsequently raised to US$1.29, the items on Burger King's "value menu" accounted for 20% of all sales in 2010, up from 12% in 2009.

New Owners: Time for a Strategic Change?

On September 2, 2010, 3G Capital, an investment group dominated by three Brazilian millionaires, offered US$4 billion to purchase Burger King Holdings Inc. At US$24 a share, the offer represented a 46% premium over Burger King's August 31 closing price. According to John Chidsey, Burger King's Charman and CEO, "It was a call out of the blue." Both the board of directors and the investment firms owning 31% of the shares supported acceptance of the offer. New ownership should bring a new board of directors and a change in top management. What should new management propose to ensure the survival and long-term success of Burger King?

Sonic Restaurants: Does Its Drive-In Business Model Limit Future Growth Potential?

Alan N. Hoffman
Bentley University

Natalia Gold
Northeastern University

Company Background

In 1953 Troy Smith founded the Top Hat in Oklahoma, a restaurant where customers parked their cars and walked up to the root beer stand to order. On a trip to Louisiana a year later, Smith noticed that similar drive-in restaurants used speakers for ordering. Convinced the speakers would be a game changer, Smith implemented the same system at the Top Hat, marking out parking spots for customers and using carhops on roller skates to deliver the orders. The new business model was a hit. Sales tripled instantly, which caught the attention of entrepreneur Charles Pappe, and together he and Smith began franchising in the region. As the name "Top Hat" had already been trademarked, they changed the company's name to Sonic, a play on its slogan, "Service with the Speed of Sound."[1]

Over the next few decades, the company expanded from small towns in Oklahoma to Kansas, New Mexico, Missouri, and Arkansas. From 1967 to 1978, Sonic grew from 41 drive-ins to 1,000. After a change in leadership in 1984, the company sought to redevelop

The author thanks Barbara Gottfried and Bentley University MBA students Brian Piper, Ivor Lee, Turhan Tezol, Vishal Ved, and Cuiwen Zhu for their research and contributions to this case. Please address all correspondence to: Dr. Alan N. Hoffman, Dept. of Management, Bentley University, 175 Forest Street, Waltham, MA 02452-4705, ahoffman@bentley.edu, (781) 891-2287. Printed by permission of Dr. Alan N. Hoffman.

markets that had not been successful in the past. Using a new advertising campaign that featured the talents of singer/actor Frankie Avalon, Sonic quickly became a household name.

In 1991, Sonic became a publicly traded company on the NASDAQ. After the IPO the company renegotiated its current franchise agreements and opened 100–150 new drive-ins per year. By 1998, the company had more than 1,700 restaurants, and decided to redesign them with a new, chic "retro-future" look that became the standard Sonic image.

For its 50th anniversary in 2003 Sonic re-introduced classic items such as Pickle-o's, inaugurating a decade of remarkable growth. During this period Sonic opened its 3,000th drive-in in Shawnee, Oklahoma, then its 3,500th drive-in outside Chicago. The company regularly posted increases in net income and revenues, and increased the efficiency of its process by introducing card readers in the car stalls in its parking lots. However, the 2008 recession hit the company hard, and plans to expand into new markets like Alaska were put on hold. Nevertheless, the company recorded steady growth every year since then, and recently announced plans to add 1,000 new drive-ins by 2024.

Strategic Direction

Sonic Corporation envisioned becoming "America's most loved restaurant brand" by fulfilling America's nostalgia for drive-in restaurants. Its very successful niche was drive-in fast food: hot dogs, hamburgers, sandwiches, lemonade, handmade milk shakes, and shaved ice ordered over speakers and delivered by roller-skating carhops so that customers did not have to leave their cars. Its unique, low cost, drive-up, eat-in-your-car model was designed to be highly customizable and adaptable to indoor dining for cold weather climates, and to a smaller footprint for more developed urban environments. In recent years, the company shifted its innovative focus to developing exciting menu items, products, and processes that were ahead of its competitors, offering customizable drinks, an evolving menu, and a slice of American nostalgia. Yet that model presented challenges.

Sonic's main objective over its 60-year history was growth. New stores were added through franchising, which, simply put, meant opening new stores with other people's money. One of the largest fast-food brands in America as of 2015, the company envisioned further expansion by opening franchises in small towns across America as well as internationally using a new low cost building format.[2] To this end, the company planned to develop some more non-traditional locations, breaking away from its original drive-in concept and shifting to indoor dining while continuing to leverage its fully customizable menu that allowed customers more control over what they ordered than its competitors. However, over the next 10 years Sonic's goal was to open 1,000 new drive-in restaurants, expanding from its current position of 44 states to all 50 states and establishing an international foothold.

Sonic's Competitors

Sonic's competitors in the quick service restaurant sector were always other large fast-food franchises that served breakfast, lunch, and dinner, plus franchised coffeehouses. Its largest competitors by sales were McDonald's, Subway, Starbucks, Wendy's, and Burger King. As of 2013, Sonic was tied for sales with Domino's, although Domino's had 1,464 more franchise units than Sonic, thus Sonic's profitability per franchise was 41.6% greater than Domino's. In terms of franchise unit growth, another important indicator, Sonic's five largest competitors from 2012–2013 were Subway, Dunkin' Donuts, Starbucks, Jimmy John's, and Little Caesars.

Traditionally, the two main barriers to entry into the quick service food industry were brand recognition and infrastructure. The brand built around fast-food establishments was developed over time, and sometimes concentrated in particular regions. Sonic built its brand for over 60 years. The cornerstone of Sonic's branding was its nostalgic carhop/drive-in model, unique in the industry. More recently, the company implemented branding of menu customization options as a differentiator in the market. Many brands such as McDonald's and Dunkin' Donuts also built elaborate branding models extending into markets outside the United States. The history and reach of these brands helped to establish an identity in consumers' eyes.

The cost of infrastructure, that is, the technology and real estate required, was the other major barrier to entry in the quick service industry. Implementing systems and acquiring and/or building out real estate was time-consuming and cost-intensive. To succeed, Sonic developed its Point of Personalized Service System, an intricate technological advantage not easily replicable.

Common belief was that low-income people ate at fast-food restaurants because they were the most affordable alternative for dining out. However, scientists from the University of California, Davis found that fast-food eatery visits increased proportionately with individuals' income, stabilizing for those with annual incomes of $60,000; thus, white collar workers were the main purchaser of fast food.[3] At the same time, regardless of vows to curtail their more questionable marketing practices, fast-food restaurants stepped up their practice of targeting kids.

Finance

For fiscal year 2015 Sonic's financial objectives were:

- Positive same-store sales in the low to mid-single digits.
- Net profit margin in the range of 10%–12%.
- Incremental royalty revenue growth from same-store sales improvements, new unit development, and 900 drive-ins converting to a higher royalty rate structure.
- Drive-in-level margin improvement of between 100 to 150 basis points, reflecting an improving outlook for commodity cost inflation and leverage from company drive-in same-store sales growth.

Prior to 2015, sales derived from company drive-ins (73%) and franchise drive-ins (27%) (**Exhibit 1**). In 2014, same-store sales increased 3.5%, an increase of 3.3% at franchise drive-ins plus an increase of 3.5% at company drive-ins. The company's continued positive same-store sales were a result of successful implementation of initiatives, including product quality improvements, a greater emphasis on personalized service, and a tiered pricing strategy that created a solid foundation for growth. Along with new technology initiatives implemented at drive-in locations during fiscal year 2014, the company continued to focus on key promotional strategies such as increased media effectiveness and its innovative product pipeline to drive same-store sales.

Sales increased from $542.6M in fiscal year 2013 to $552.3M in fiscal year 2014, an increase of 1.8%, attributable to a 6% increase in franchise royalties and fees and an increase in company drive-in sales of 0.76% compared to the previous year. Company drive-in margins improved by 90 basis points, reflecting the leverage of positive same-store sales. The cost of company drive-ins decreased to 84.4% for 2014 from 85.3% in

EXHIBIT 1 : Select Financial Data

[In thousands. except per share data]	Year Ended August 31, 2014	2013	2012	2011	2010
Income Statement Data:					
Company Drive-In sales	$ 405,363	$ 402,296	$ 404,443	$ 410,820	$ 414,369
Franchise Drive-Ins:					
Franchise royalties and fees	138,416	130,737	128,013	125,871	125,137
Lease revenue	4,291	4,785	6,575	6,023	6,879
Other	4,279	4,767	4,699	3,237	4,541
Total revenues	552,349	542,585	543,730	545,951	550,926
Cost of Company Drive-In sales	342,109	343,209	347,470	356,236	354,459
Selling, general and administrative	69,415	66,022	65,173	64,943	66,847
Depreciation and amortization	42,210	40,387	41,914	41,225	42,615
Provision for impairment of long-lived assets	114	1,776	764	824	15,161
Other operating (income) expense, net	(176)	1,943	(531)	(585)	763
Total expenses	453,672	453,337	454,790	462,643	480,045
Income from operations	98,677	89,248	88,940	83,308	70,881
Interest expense, net[1]	24,913	32,949	30,978	54,929	36,073
Income before income taxes	73,764	56,299	57,962	28,379	34,808
Net income-including noncontrolling interests	47,916	36,701	36,085	19,225	25,839
Net income-noncontrolling interests[2]	-	-	-	-	4,630
Net income-attributable to Sonic Corp	$ 47,916	$ 36,701	$ 36,085	$ 19,225	$ 21,209
Income per share:					
Basic	$ 0.87	$ 0.65	$ 0.60	$ 0.31	$ 0.35
Diluted	$ 0.85	$ 0.64	$ 0.60	$ 0.31	$ 0.34
Weighted average shares used in calculation:					
Basic	55,164	56,384	60,078	61,781	61,319
Diluted	56,619	57,191	60,172	61,943	61,576
Cash dividends declared per common share	$ 0.09	$ -	$ -	$ -	$ -
Balance Sheet Data:					
Working capital	$ 16,201	$ 67,792	$ 26,635	$ 22,178	$ 15,320
Property, equipment and capital leases, net	441,969	399,661	443,008	464,875	489,264
Total assets	650,972	660,794	680,760	679,742	737,320
Obligations under capital leases (including current portion)	26,743	26,864	31,676	34,063	36,256
Long-term debt (including current portion)	437,318	447,294	481,793	497,013	591,621
Stockholders' equity	62,675	77,464	59,247	51,833	22,566

[1] Includes net loss from early extinguishment of debt of $4.4 million, $23.0 million and $0.3 million for fiscal years 2013, 2011 and 2010. respectively.

[2] Effective April 1, 2010, we revised our compensation program at the Company Drive-In level. As a result of these changes, noncontrolling interests are immaterial for fiscal years 2014, 2013, 2012 and 2011 and have been included in payroll and other employee benefits.

2013, primarily from a reduction in food and packaging expenses and reduced payroll and other employee benefits.

Sonic's net income for fiscal year 2014 was $47.9M or $0.85 per diluted share compared with $36.7M or $0.64 per diluted share for fiscal year 2013, an increase in net income of 31% as compared to the previous year. Net income as a percentage of total sales increased to 9% in 2014 from 7% in 2013.[4]

As of August 31, 2014, Sonic's long-term debt was $428M. Sonic's cash and cash equivalents amounted to just $27.23M as of February 28, 2015, decreasing from $35.69M as of August 31, 2014. Sonic's cash on hand consisted of highly liquid investments, primarily money market accounts that matured in three months or less from date of purchase, and depository accounts.

As indicated above, Sonic's long-term debt was 15 times its cash on hand as of August 31, 2014. The increase in the company's long-term debt derived mostly from the company's strategic expansion across the country and the implementation of its goal of opening 1,000 more Sonic drive-ins over 10 years. The company invested heavily in buildings and improvements, new drive-in equipment, and brand technology development to achieve its long-term expansion goals. The estimated useful life of these investments was calculated as 8–25 years, 5–7 years, and 2–5 years, respectively.[13] However, if the company were to face tough times in the future, it could have difficulty repaying its debt.

Marketing

As of 2014, Sonic was America's largest drive-in restaurant chain with over 60 years of experience in the quick service sector. Company presence was strong in the southern and Midwestern United States, with plans to expand operations on the East and West coasts primarily through franchise development. As a franchise-centric company offering substantial franchisee support services, a national advertising budget in excess of $100 million annually, and brand differentiation impossible to duplicate, Sonic Drive-In was primed for expansion with a goal of 1,000 new drive-ins in the next 10 years. In 2014, the company forecast growth of over 300 drive-ins in California by 2020, with plans to add new talent to its business development team to achieve this goal.[4]

Over the years Sonic's iconic drive-in style proved hard to duplicate, and its distinct brand differentiation went far beyond that. Its one-of-a-kind menu offered a variety of options not available from other brands, including breakfast all day, real ice-cream desserts, sandwiches, molten cake sundaes, tasty tots, premium hot dogs, and hundreds of unique drink combinations. In addition, Sonic provided convenience to consumers with its strong presence in 44 states nationwide.

Sonic's unique look and feel meant that virtually any space could be customized as a Sonic drive-in; recently, some Sonic franchises in colder locations even began offering indoor seating. As a franchise-centric brand, Sonic made it a major aspect of its growth plan to provide a full range of franchisee support services from help with real estate site selection and negotiation; site design; and construction guidance to comprehensive training programs; continuing education through in-person, online, and mobile learning; human resources and staff selection support; and actionable consumer insights and marketing support. Despite the more than 3,500 Sonic Drive-Ins serving guests every day, the company's 10-year plan envisioned continued franchising opportunities in markets big and small across the country, with no minimum requirement for number of drive-ins.[5]

To enhance its marketing efforts, drive traffic, and reach more consumers while increasing awareness in markets yet to be developed, Sonic substantially increased its national media spending becoming one of the top five burger or sandwich advertisers in most major markets with memorable and recognizable advertising. Although Sonic continued to push expansion, as of 2014 it still had a way to go in establishing its presence in international markets, and even further to go in emerging markets such as India and China. Unlike bigger players such as McDonalds and Burger King, which were established global players, Sonic remained primarily reliant on expansion across America. It became imperative for Sonic to customize menus if it planned to enter emerging markets while maintaining its standard of quality and consistency.

Operations

Over all the years of Sonic's long history its well-known slogan "America's Drive-In" promised a highly recognizable customer experience replicated down to the finest details at each location. All 3,500 locations were branded with the same Sonic Drive-In logo, the same store look and feel, the same food, and the same service. The feeling of familiarity created by such consistent styling quickly became one of the company's greatest strengths.

During the 1990s when competition was particularly stiff, the company used its strong brand image to competitive advantage,[6] distinguishing itself from the competition by iconizing its nostalgic brand, offering menu items reminiscent of the past, and combining these with the strengths of modern management and customer relations methods to create the Sonic Drive-In experience customers grew to know and love. Customer service was a crucial aspect of the Sonic Drive-In experience—just mentioning the company's name conjured up its carhops on roller skates, and those skates became a new source of revenue through sales of identical skates to customers who couldn't get enough of them at the drive-in.[7] In addition, the company reworked its internal mechanisms to make its operations more efficient, resulting in cost savings.

A big part of Sonic's business was based on the franchise model, which was highly dependent on each store accurately reproducing Sonic's nostalgic image in all possible ways. However, one of Sonic's greatest challenges derived from a weakness intrinsic to that model: while the franchise model allowed for financial flexibility in relation to the parent company, it permitted only lesser control over any given franchise, thus increasing risk of improper representation of the brand.

While the company successfully competed with many other quick service restaurants,[8] its niche operational model of reliance on drive-in services allowed the company to provide service only in areas that could accommodate large parking lots, like the outskirts of a city or near highways, while its competitors could position themselves both inside cities and in the same locations as Sonic Drive-Ins. This meant that Sonic was forced to compete for a limited number of locations and could only locate at relatively remote sites.

Human Resources

As of 2014, Sonic Drive-In's headquarters in Oklahoma City employed 25 key personnel, including Chief Executive Officer Clifford Hudson.[9] In the company's 2013 annual report, Hudson mentioned a number of improvements Sonic Drive-In had made to its core processes, menus, services, communication platforms, and advertising campaigns, displaying Sonic's "tone at the top." The company's directors, chiefs of various departments, and senior managers worked to establish and uphold its core values, emphasizing top notch relations with customers and refining processes to best serve them. The company's employee handbook stressed those core values:

- Respect for everyone touched by the Sonic Brand
- Entrepreneurial spirit and the power of the individual
- Importance of relationships as a way of life
- Surprising and delighting everyone touched by the brand by doing things differently.[10]

Themes of working together and caring for both customers other employees were central. Employees were encouraged to create a more fulfilling working space both for themselves and any potential employees, and a positive choice for customers.

While sales volume increased between 2012 and 2014, the number of employees decreased from 12 million to 11 million, a reflection not of downsizing but of an effort to increase employee efficiency. Employees' biggest complaints were not about the company, but about angry customers who were impossible to satisfy.[11] Employees consistently reported that Sonic Drive-In was a good place to work and enjoyed the teamwork Sonic encouraged. The company developed a reputation for providing lots of movement and promotion opportunities, giving employees an incentive to work their best to prove themselves. The company's extensive network of over 3500 stores nationwide combined with fluidity and turnover of positions within stores created frequent opportunities for new recruits to enter the company and current employees to move to new positions.

Technology

Technological improvements were big in 2014 for Sonic Drive-In and this addressed, in a two stage process, the company's need for better data collection and analysis while serving customers in the best, fastest way possible. The first stage was a Point of Sale (POS) system that allowed customers to interact with a monitor to make rapid purchases. In its default state the system served as both an improved ordering system and a conduit for promotional products. The second stage involved improving the POS system by combining its advertising capacities with personalized sales opportunities to create a Point of Personalized Sale (POPS) platform that would build on the POS. Together these platforms would fully personalize customer service, becoming the cornerstone of Sonic's individualized marketing.

In addition, new technologically sophisticated supply chain management helped reduce inventory costs through streamlining inventory purchasing and allowing for better tracking of current inventory. Tracking the food and package inventory through automation also reduced errors of miscalculation and risk of lost inventory due to theft.

Innovation: Culinary Innovation Center

Over the years, a large part of Sonic Drive-In's competitive advantage beyond its iconic drive-in model came from its unique and extensive variety of food and drink choices. The company recognized that investing in a state of the art facility to develop and test new products for customers was crucial, and opened its new R&D facility, the Culinary Innovation Center, in late 2014. Chefs employed there were free to brainstorm, pitch, create, and test new products in a controlled environment before they hit the market. As Sonic's success relied on customers' satisfaction with the food and drinks served, creating a wide and ever changing variety of menu items, and tailoring menus to specific restaurant locations was key. The Culinary Innovation Center gave Sonic an edge, helping it satisfy its goals and ensure the quality and novelty of the menu items customers were accustomed to seeing at Sonic Drive-In.

Location

A key strategy of Sonic's business plan included targeted expansion into small towns in the central United States, as small towns were seen as receptive to new businesses and opportunities and ripe for growth. The benefits of opening a franchise in a small town rather than a large metropolitan area included reduced building costs, lowered land requirements, and higher purchasing power, yielding quicker and greater return on investment for both franchise and franchisee. In addition, franchises in rural areas could leverage local rural tax advantages, from a full refund on all sales taxes and tax credits to reduced state corporate income tax, and tax credits for eligible employees.[12]

According to *Entrepreneur 2014 Franchise 500*, Sonic's brand was estimated to be in the top 6% of franchise brands and the third highest among burger brands. Sonic had invested heavily in its branding and advertising, exceeding 100 million dollars in 2014. *Entrepreneur 2014* also ranked Sonic the 21st fastest-growing franchise, in line with its long term growth plans of even greater expansion. Sonic's 2014 10-year plan included an addition of 1,000 new restaurants and 30% growth, including expansion to all 50 U.S. states. Announcements of franchises in Rochester NY, San Diego CA, and the greater Los Angeles area in 2014 pointed to Sonic's strategy and success in expanding to both small and large markets. While the emphasis was primarily on domestic growth, Sonic also sought strategies for entry into new and emerging international markets within the next decade.[13]

Recent Supply Chain Overhaul

As of 2014 there were 3,500 Sonic locations serving 3 million visitors a day. One of Sonic's core competencies was supply chain operations, yet Sonic felt there was room for improvement and began investing heavily in revamping its supply chain operations to make them more efficient, consistent, and profitable. One of its earliest and biggest areas of improvement was its database cataloguing. The old program that catalogued its inventory included redundant codes that were often used incorrectly, resulting in a fragmented picture of existing inventory which affected how different regions ordered and negotiated with suppliers based on perceived need. A centralized data management system with universal codes was incorporated across all Sonic locations to address this issue, and from then on Sonic noticed a marked increase in its ability to forecast and anticipate demand.

A natural extension of the changes in inventory cataloging was a change in how Sonic negotiated with its suppliers. Prior to these changes, Sonic's orders from suppliers had been inconsistent, which often led to errors and delays. From region to region, negotiations differed with regard to tactics as well as suppliers. With an improved ability to forecast demand once the new system was in place, Sonic was able to standardize which suppliers to use as well as how to negotiate with them. As a result, Sonic was able to leverage suppliers more effectively and lower its overhead.

Franchise Requirements

Sonic's franchisee requirements were considered rigorous, with fees ranging from $1 million to $1.6 million, steep enough to dissuade less committed franchisees. About $100,000–$200,000 of the initial investment was allocated for employee training, evidence of the importance with which Sonic regarded the training of its employees and managers to maintain its brand and reputation. A unique feature of Sonic's training regimen was the creation of an "A-team," the franchisor's store-certified training team. The "A-team" was trained to staff the pre-opening and opening of the franchisee's first three stores to ensure a smooth transition." Sonic also required each franchisee and one full time employee and manager to participate in its career development program; and store managers were also required to complete a Sonic management seminar within six months of hiring at a location. These training seminars served as a way to reinforce both Sonic's core values and its operations to standardize each new franchise.

The typical franchisee term of agreement was 20 years. Franchisees for Sonic were given territorial protection: once a location was selected and approved, Sonic prohibited the establishment of another Sonic franchise within that region.[14]

Key Challenges Facing Sonic

As Sonic considered its 10-year plan in 2014, it faced major challenges:

Cash flows were a major area of concern in Sonic's financials as their debt-to-cash ratio was extremely high as a result of the company's expansion plan. There was concern that not generating enough cash flow in the future could get Sonic into trouble.

The Implementation of the new Obama healthcare law requiring health insurance coverage for all employees could result in higher future labor costs for Sonic, as most of its employees were minimum wage workers.

Sonic's lack of an international presence in the face of direct competitors McDonald's and Burger King's already established international markets, presented a unique challenge. The concern was that Sonic's nostalgia effect was limited to North America as global markets were not likely to have the same emotional connection to carhops and speakers.

Sonic's total franchise model was flawed both because it limited the organizational flexibility of the company, and because franchise owners could face numerous lawsuits from franchisees.

As the fast-food industry scrambled to redefine itself and offer "healthier" options, the growing trend of eating healthy complicated Sonic's mission: how to make a burger and fries appear "healthy"? The lack of healthy foods on its menu and state laws requiring the serving of healthy foods could hurt the company in the future. However, this was not Sonic's biggest hurdle to meeting its 10-year plan goals. Rather, the most daunting challenge to Sonic's expansion was the difficulty of entering urban markets.

By definition, the drive-in model limited where restaurants were located and the number of people Sonic could serve at any given time. The space requirement of a drive-in business model made it difficult for Sonic to enter highly urban environments, yet that space defined the Sonic Drive-in. Where parking lots were tiny, and roads tight, a drive-in restaurant was hardly ideal, especially in the urban markets of the northeast. In cities like Boston, Sonic drive-ins were typically found only in the far suburbs of the city. Only cities in the south had enough space for Sonic to expand into more urban areas.

Sonic's planning team understood that space restrictions placed a limit not only on growth in the United States, but on expansion into international markets as well. While the drive-in model continued to work well in most of North America thanks to nostalgia and the drive-in's iconic history, without that sense of history, the franchise model could fall flat in international markets. Internationally, Sonic would need to rely on the novelty of a drive-in restaurant rather than nostalgia to entice customers, especially as so many of its larger competitors such as McDonald's already had a substantial international presence. Additionally, the space requirement also made it difficult to locate in major cities, the norm for international expansion, highlighting yet again the drive-in model's problems of scale.

The crux of Sonic's problem seemed to be a conundrum: to grow and succeed required moving away from Sonic's iconic drive-in model, yet changing that model removed one of Sonic's main competitive advantages and areas of differentiation: without the drive-in, Sonic was on a slippery slope to becoming just another fast-food burger joint with a customizable menu.

NOTES

1. Sonic Corporate Profile Background. https://corporate.sonicdrivein.com/Profile/Background

2. "SONIC Drive-In, One of America's Largest Restaurant Brands, Aims to Open One Thousand Locations Over the Next 10 Years" http://ir.sonicdrivein.com/releasedetail.cfm?ReleaseID=840772

3. Todd Smith - CMO, Sonic Drive-in, Sonic Corp. San Francisco: Boardroom Insiders, Inc, 2014. ProQuest. Web. April 21, 2015.

4. Investor Relations. Sonicdrivein.com http://ir.sonicdrivein.com/releasedetail.cfm?ReleaseID=840772

5. Investor Relations. Sonicdrivein.com http://ir.sonicdrivein.com/releasedetail.cfm?ReleaseID=840772

6. Lienert, A. (1996). Setting off a Sonic Boom. *Management Review*.

7. (2015, April). Retrieved from Sonic Skates: https://www.sonicskates.com/

8. (2013). *The QSR 50*. QSR Magazine. http://www.qsrmagazine.com/reports/qsr50-2013-top-50-chart

9. (2015). *Sonic Corp. Company Summary*. ReferenceUSA.

10. *Employee Handbook Acknowledgement*. (2015). Retrieved from Esch Group: www.eschgroup.com/.../Employee%20Handbook.pdf

11. *Sonic Reviews*. (April 2015). Retrieved from Glassdoor: http://www.glassdoor.com/Reviews/Sonic-Reviews-E1303.htm

12. "SONIC Drive-In Expands Franchise Development in Small Town, USA." http://ir.sonicdrivein.com/releasedetail.cfm?ReleaseID=773413

13. "SONIC Drive-In, One of America's Largest Restaurant Brands, Aims to Open One Thousand Locations Over the Next 10 Years." http://ir.sonicdrivein.com/releasedetail.cfm?releaseid=840772

14. "Sonic Franchise Cost & Fee, Sonic FDD & Franchise Information | FranchiseDirect.com." http://www.franchisedirect.com/foodfranchises/sonic-franchise-07087/ufoc/

"Breaking Up is Hard to Do": PepsiCo in 2014

Ram Subramanian
Montclair State University

On April 17, 2014, Indra Nooyi, Chief Executive Officer of PepsiCo, a diversified beverage and snack foods company, met with Ian Cook, the Presiding Director of the company's Board, to discuss a response to Nelson Peltz's (the head of Trian Fund Management, an activist fund) latest call for breaking up the company into two independent entities. Peltz had threatened to approach the company's stockholders directly if the Board did not accede to his demands[1]. Having just announced PepsiCo's first quarter results for 2014, Nooyi realized that Peltz was likely to step up his criticism because the results had once again indicated that snack foods were driving PepsiCo's sales and profits while beverages were losing ground to rival Coca-Cola. Both Nooyi and Cook decided that they had to make a decision immediately to respond to Peltz's activism.

Industry Context[2]

Beverages

The term "liquid refreshment beverages" (LRB) referred to the non-alcoholic segment of the beverage industry. Following falls in demand in 2008 and 2009, the LRB segment had turned around to register volume increases of 1.2% in 2010, 0.7% in 2011, and 1.0% in 2012. The segment's increases in recent years had come from significant demand spikes for energy drinks, ready-to-drink coffees, sports drinks, and bottled water, while the segment's biggest contributor, carbonated soft drinks (CSDs) that accounted for 45% of segment revenues, had shown declining demand (in 2013 this segment reported its ninth straight yearly contraction). The CSD segment was highly concentrated with the Coca-Cola Company (42.4% market share), PepsiCo (27.7%), and Dr. Pepper Snapple Group (16.8%) accounting for nearly 87% of the market share in 2012. Coca-Cola's flagship brand, Coke, held the leading market share (17%), while PepsiCo's Pepsi-Cola brand was third with a 2012 share of 8.9% (versus 9.2% in 2011). The Coca-Cola Company and PepsiCo were also numbers 1 and 2 in the overall LRB market with Coca-Cola holding a share of 34.2% and PepsiCo 25.8%. *Beverage Digest*, an industry trade publication assigned the status of "Megabrand" if a product sold more than 100 million 192 oz. cases in a year. Per this classification, PepsiCo's Gatorade was a top ten Megabrand while the company's bottled water brand, Aquafina, lost its top ten Megabrand status (Coca-Cola's bottled water brand, Dasani was a top ten Megabrand) when it was replaced by Nestle's Poland Spring brand.

LRB companies such as Coca-Cola and PepsiCo typically operated as franchisors, holding on to the low-capital, high margin stage of the industry value chain, while passing on the high capital, low margin activity of bottling and distribution to independent franchisees (the bottlers) each of whom had exclusive access to a designated market area. One study estimated that franchisors had a gross margin of 78% and operating margin of 32%, while franchisees had a gross margin of 42% and operating margin (before financing costs) of just 8%.[3] LRBs were sold through a variety of channels with supermarkets accounting for the largest volume, followed by the fountain and vending channels.

Snack Foods

The U.S. snack foods industry (consisting of products such as nuts, chips, and popcorn) was concentrated with the top 50 producers accounting for over 90% of the market share. Potato chips accounted for a 25% share of this industry, followed by corn (and tortilla) chips with 20%, and roasted nuts and seeds with 20%. Frito-Lay (owned by PepsiCo) held a 41% market share in 2013 with its Lays, Doritos, Tostitos, and Rold Gold brands. Industry estimates indicated a 1% volume and a 3% value (due to price increases) growth per year for the next five years. Standard & Poor's summed up the challenges facing snack food companies:

> *Consumers have become increasingly demanding of food and beverage products in recent years, often expecting meals and snacks that go far beyond the basic need of satisfying hunger and thirst. Today, consumers often expect that food and drink, in addition to tasting good, should offer some or all of the following characteristics: be low in calories; provide supplemental vitamins and minerals; create energy; and offer other health benefits. In response, we see major food companies refocusing their best product lines and acquiring brands in encouraging new areas. They are selling off or discontinuing products that don't resonate with consumers.[4]*

Popchips was an example of a response to changing consumer tastes. This product combined low fat content and low calories with innovative new flavors. Apart from Frito-Lay, the leading players in the industry were Mondelez (the snack food spin-off of the erstwhile Kraft Foods International) and Diamond Foods (the leader in salted nuts). Players in the industry followed the traditional business model of owning manufacturing and distribution facilities and selling their product through the retail channel.

PepsiCo—Profile[5]

1n 1893, Caleb Bradham, a pharmacist in North Carolina developed a carbonated cola drink for sale in his store (this was seven years after John Pemberton founded Coca-Cola in Atlanta). He called it, "Pepsi-Cola," and popularized it when he convinced other store owners to sell the product as franchisees. The company's growth was stuttered by two bankruptcies—in 1923 and 1932—but grew by underpricing Coca-Cola and by attacking its rival in its marketing. In 1950, Pepsi-Cola had a 10% market share, second to Coca-Cola's 47%. In 1961, the company merged with Frito-Lay, Inc. (itself formed as a result of a merger between Frito Company and the H.W. Lay Company), a major snack food player. The combined company, now called PepsiCo, grew its beverage and snack food brands both organically (e.g., Diet Pepsi, Ruffles) and via acquisitions (Mountain Dew, Rold Gold). A major turning point in the company's fight with Coca-Cola came in 1974 when PepsiCo launched the "Pepsi Challenge" in Dallas, Texas. This campaign played on the company's findings that more customers preferred Pepsi over Coke in blind taste tests. This campaign, when expanded nationwide, helped Pepsi narrow the market share gap with Coca-Cola. Coca-Cola's launch of the "New Coke" in 1985 was seen as an admission of Pepsi's ascendancy in the market. In fiscal 2014, Pepsi had 22 billion-dollar brands, including Diet Mountain Dew, Brisk (tea), and Starbucks ready-to-drink beverages. It reported net revenues of $66.415 billion (versus $65.492 billion in 2012) and net income of $6.740 billion ($6.178 in 2012). The company employed 274,000 worldwide, with 106,000 in the United States Indra Nooyi was both CEO and Chairman of the Board (**Exhibit 1** has the company's financials in summary form).

EXHIBIT 1
PepsiCo, Inc. Summarized Financial Statements Income Statement (in $ millions, for year ended)

	2013	2012	2011
Net Revenue	66,415	65,492	66,504
Cost of Sales	31,243	31,291	31,593
Selling, General and Administrative Expenses	25,357	24,970	25,145
Amortization of Intangible Assets	110	119	133
Operating Profit*	9,705	9,112	9,633
Net Income	6,740	6,178	6,443

* After a deduction for corporate overhead of $1.246 billion in 2013, $1.162 billion in 2012, and $961 million in 2011.

SOURCE: PepsiCo, 2013 10-K.

Statement of Cash Flows (in $ millions, for year ended)

	2013	2012	2011
Net Cash Provided by Operating Activities	9,688	8,479	8,944
Net Cash Used for Investing Activities	(2,625)	(3,005)	(5,618)
Net Cash Used for Financing Activities	(3,789)	(3,306)	(5,135)

SOURCE: PepsiCo, 2013 10-K.

Balance Sheet (in $ millions, as of December 28, 2013 and December 29, 2012)

	2013	2012
Current Assets	22,203	18,720
Other Assets	55,275	55,918
Total Assets	**77,478**	**74,638**
Current Liabilities	17,839	17,089
Long-Term Debt	24,333	23,544
Other Liabilities	10,917	11,606
Total Liabilities	53,089	52,239
Total Equity	24,389	22,399

SOURCE: PepsiCo, 2013 10-K.

PepsiCo's Business Organization[6]

PepsiCo divided itself into four business units for operational purposes while it reported results for 6 segments (**Exhibit 2** summarizes segment revenues and profits). The business units were: PepsiCo Foods Americas, PepsiCo Americas Beverages, PepsiCo Europe, and PepsiCo Asia, Middle East and Africa (**Exhibit 3** lists a sample of the company's brands).

PepsiCo Foods Americas was responsible for all of the company's activities in both North and Latin America. For reporting purposes, this operating division reported results for three segments. Frito-Lay North America (FLNA) manufactured (in 40 facilities) and distributed (through 1,710 warehouses) branded snack foods through major retail chains as well as independent distributors. Quaker Foods North America (QFNA) manufactured (in 4 owned and 1 leased facility) and distributed cereals, rice, pasta, dairy, and other branded products also through major retail chains (in fiscal 2013, Wal-Mart accounted for 11% of PepsiCo's global sales and 17% of North America sales for all products) and independent distributors. Latin America Foods (LAF) distributed both snack food brands and branded cereals that were manufactured in both company owned (54) and third party plants. In 2013, this division accounted for 14% of total assets and 30% of capital spending.

PepsiCo Americas Beverages (PAB) was the franchisor of brands such as Pepsi, Gatorade, and Mountain Dew that were sold through a variety of channels. Like its competitor, Coca-Cola, periodically PAB bought financially troubled bottlers to bolster its distribution system. In fiscal 2013, the company owned 80 bottling plants and this division accounted for 39% of total assets and 26% of capital spending.

PepsiCo Europe (Europe) made and sold all of the company products in Europe and South Africa. It owned snack and cereal production plants as well as beverage bottling plants. This division was responsible for 24% of total assets and 20% of 2013's capital spending.

EXHIBIT 2

PepsiCo – Segment Revenue and Profit Breakdown (in $ billions)

SEGMENT	2011		2012		2013	
	Revenues	Op. Profits	Revenues	Op. Profits	Revenues	Op. Profits
FLNA	13.3	3.621	13.6	3.646	14.1	3.877
QFNA	2.7	0.797	2.6	0.695	2.6	0.617
LAF	7.2	1.078	7.8	1.059	8.3	1.242
PAB	22.4	3.273	21.4	2.937	21.1	2.955
Europe	13.6	1.210	13.4	1.330	13.8	1.293
AMEA	7.4	0.887	6.7	0.747	6.5	1.174

FLNA = Frito-Lay North America

QFNA = Quaker Foods North America

LAF = Latin America Foods and Snacks

PAB = PepsiCo Americas Beverages

Europe = Beverages, Foods, and Snacks in Europe and South Africa

AMEA = Beverages, Foods, and Snacks in Asia, Middle East, and Africa (except South Africa)

Source: PepsiCo, 2013 10-K.

EXHIBIT 3

PepsiCo's Brands
(Selected)

SEGMENT	BRANDS
FLNA	Lay's
	Doritos
	Cheetos
	Tostitos
	Ruffles
	Fritos
	Santitas
	Sabra
QFNA	Quaker
	Aunt Jemima
	Cap'n Crunch
	Life
	Rice-A-Roni
LAF	Marias Gamesa
	Emperador
PAB	Pepsi, Diet Pepsi
	Gatorade
	Mountain Dew, Diet Mountain Dew
	Aquafina
	7Up (outside the United States)
	Tropicana
	Sierra Mist
	Mirinda
EUROPE	Walkers
	Pepsi Max
AMEA	Kurkure
	Chipsy
	Smith's

Source: PepsiCo, 2013 10-K.

PepsiCo Asia, Middle East, and Africa (AMEA) made and sold the company's products in all of Asia, Middle East, and Africa (except for South Africa). In 2013, this division accounted for 8% of total assets and 19% of capital expenditures.

Nelson Peltz's Case for Breaking Up PepsiCo

Trian Fund Management, L.P, an investment vehicle controlled by activist investor, Nelson Peltz, owned approximately $1.3 billion worth (or 0.81%) of PepsiCo's shares. Starting in mid-2013, Trian had demanded that PepsiCo split up its beverages and snack foods businesses to unlock what they believed was shareholder value that was hidden in the underperforming company. Picking up on what he had started in mid-2013, on March 13, 2014, Peltz sent a letter to the members of PepsiCo's Board demanding rationale as to why the company opposed splitting up the beverage and snack foods units. In the letter, Peltz expressed disappointment at the Board's dismissal of Trian's arguments laid out in a lengthy white paper issued a month earlier.

Peltz's criticism was captured in the opening paragraph of his March 13 letter, where he stated,

> Given the company's prolonged underperformance, we believe the Board and management are obligated to provide shareholders substance and analytics —not just platitudes and rhetoric—to defend the alleged benefits of the "Power of One.[7]

The Economist summarized the thrust of Peltz's argument as:

To buttress his argument, Peltz had pointed out that since 2006, when Indra Nooyi took over as PepsiCo's CEO, the company had delivered a total shareholder return (price appreciation plus dividends) of 47% compared with 103% for the S&P consumer staples index.[8]

Trian's rationale for the breakup centered on the differences between beverages and snack foods and the consequent challenges of operating both under one roof. To Trian, beverages were a capital intensive business where the demand was declining due to health concerns. In contrast, snack foods were a growing business (particularly in the international arena) that needed significant outlays in marketing to parlay the growth into increased revenues. According to Trian, there were not significant synergies in running these businesses together and PepsiCo's insistence on operating them as one unit held back the potential of the snack foods business. To Trian, PepsiCo's decision to invest $21 billion since 2010 to buy back many of its bottlers was poor allocation of capital that took resources away from the snack foods unit. Trian refuted PepsiCo's assertion of the benefits of the "Power of One"—the purported synergies that came from operating beverages and snack foods as one unit. Trian pointed out that if the powerful position of snack foods in a specific market enabled the company to sell more beverages in that market, then why was the company's beverage market share extremely low in Mexico, United Kingdom, Brazil, Spain, and Australia—markets where Frito-Lay was dominant. Likewise, Trian questioned how PepsiCo could lose the lucrative Subway fountain contract to Coke when it supplied Subway with Frito-Lay products. In a strong indictment of how poorly Frito-Lay was run, Trian accused PepsiCo management of using Frito-Lay as management's "piggy bank" by reducing its advertising and hampering its growth[9] (**Exhibit 4** contains a summary of Trian's charges).

PepsiCo's Response to Peltz

Ian Cook, PepsiCo's Presiding Director, summarily dismissed Trian's criticisms (made in a February 2014 letter to PepsiCo's Board) in a letter sent to the Fund on February 27, 2014.0[10] In the letter, Cook accused Trian (and Peltz) of suggesting short-term financial engineering and stated that the company had a well-developed long-term plan as an integrated food and beverage company.

Following a strategic review of the company in 2011, Nooyi announced the creation of a platform termed "The Power of One," to maximize the synergies that came from owning both beverages and snack foods. According to Nooyi, the platform's rationale was based on three significant benefits:

> First, it provides compelling cross leverage across the value chain. It provides compelling scale and cost leverage (with an estimated annual cost savings coming in at $800 million—$1 billion). Second, it enables us to accelerate in-market growth because in market we benefit from the coincidence of snack and beverage consumption occasions. We benefit from the

EXHIBIT 4
Summary of Charges Made Public by Trian Fund Management

- Separation of snacks and beverages into two independent public companies to maximize shareholder value. "Separating snacks and beverages would eliminate PepsiCo's current holding company structure, remove layers of unproductive overhead, drive cost savings to reinvest in the brands, and foster operating and cultural benefits."

- Any synergies (that management argues come from procurement, customer insights, advertising, coordinated national account activity and international expansion) that come from operating snacks and beverages together are more than offset by the significant corporate overhead that is required for these businesses.

- It is wrong to argue (as management does) that a standalone PepsiCo beverage business cannot compete effectively against Coca-Cola. Even with snack foods, PepsiCo has lost beverage market share to Coca-Cola. In addition, Dr. Pepper Snapple has outperformed both Coca-Cola and PepsiCo in earnings per share even with just a beverage business.

- As per CEO Indra Nooyi's own admission, the $21 billion spent on acquiring bottlers was a "mistake." Coca-Cola has a plan to get out of bottling completely by 2020 but PepsiCo does not have a similar plan. Investment in bottling has adversely affected the company's return on invested capital (from 25% when Nooyi became CEO to 14% in fiscal 2013).

- The "Power of One" synergy is a myth both in the domestic and in international markets. Snacks have not helped the beverage business.

- By reducing Frito-Lay's advertising budget to 3% of sales, its sales growth has been adversely affected. In contrast, Hershey spends 8.1% of sales on advertising. "The implication is obvious—Frito-Lay could accomplish great things if it were no longer forced to subsidize an underperforming beverage business and pay for bloated allocated corporate costs.

- PepsiCo's snack foods business account for two-thirds of the company's earnings per share. Even Indra Nooyi has gone on record stating that "if it were a standalone company, Frito-Lay North America might well be the best consumer products company."

Source: Summarized from Trian Partners Press Release of February 20, 2014, http://www.trianpartners.com/content/uploads/2014/02/Trian-%E2%80%93-PEP-Press-Release-2-20-14.pdf, and March 13, 2014 http://www.trianpartners.com/content/uploads/2014/03/Trian-PEP-Press-Release-3-13-14.pdf, both accessed August 26, 2014. All quotes are from the above referenced documents.

commonality of consumer and opportunity to cross-merchandise and promote our products. The third reason is that our operation as one company enables us to share capabilities across geographies and sectors and allows us to attract better talent.[11]

While both Nooyi and Cook realized that Peltz was refuting every one of the company's rationales behind "The Power of One," they believed that their review supported their viewpoint. They wondered how they could convince Peltz that a single diversified beverage and snack foods company was a better option than breaking up PepsiCo into two independent companies.

NOTES

1. Trian Partners March 13, 2014 Press Release, http://www.trianpartners.com/content/uploads/2014/03/Trian-PEP-Press-Release-3-13-14.pdf, accessed August 18, 2014.

2. This section was based on the following sources: Standard & Poor's Industry Surveys: Foods & Nonalcoholic Beverages, June 2013; Statista: Facts on Snack Foods, http://www.statista.com/topics/1496/snack-foods/, accessed August 19, 2014; Euromonitor International, Packaged Foods, http://www.euromonitor.com/sweet-and-savoury-snacks-in-the-us/report, accessed August 19, 2014; *Beverage Digest*, U.S. Beverage Results for 2013, http://www.beverage-digest.com/pdf/top-10_2014.pdf, accessed August 19, 2014.

3. Cited in David B. Yoffie and Renee Kim, "Cola Wars Continue: Coke and Pepsi in 2010," Harvard Business School Case # 9-711-462.

4. Standard & Poor's, op. cit.

5. Based on PepsiCo: Who We Are, http://www.pepsico.com /Company, accessed August 19, 2014.

6. PepsiCo, 2013 10-K.

7. Trian, op. cit.

8. Trian, op. cit.

9. Trian, op. cit.

10. PepsiCo, 8-K, February 27, 2014.

11. "PepsiCo: Management Stands Behind 'Power of One,'" http:// www.gurufocus.com/news/161266/pepsico-management -stands-behind-power-of-one, accessed August 21, 2014.

CASE **24**

Under Armour

Ram Subramanian
Montclair State University

Pradeep Gopalakrishna
Lubin School of Business Pace University

Kevin A. Plank, the founder and Chief Executive Officer of Under Armour (UA), reviewed the press briefing that was to accompany the company's release of the financial performance for the second quarter of fiscal 2010. Plank noted that the second quarter saw the second consecutive decline in footwear sales. UA's footwear sales had declined by 4.5% over second quarter 2009 and was showing a 16.6% decline for the first six months of 2010 over 2009. This was in contrast to apparel, the company's core category, which saw a 32.2% uptick over 2009, and accessories that had gone up by 28% (**Table 1** shows summary performance for the first two quarters of fiscal 2010).[1]

TABLE 20–1	Under Armour's Summary Financials for First Two Quarters of 2010 (in US$ millions)			
	First Quarter 2010	**First Quarter 2009**	**Second Quarter 2010**	**Second Quarter 2009**
Apparel	172,636	132,239	150,205	112,040
Footwear	42,958	56,931	35,820	37,496
Accessories	7,518	5,776	8,857	7,012
Licensing	6,295	5,054	9,904	8,100
Total	229,407	200,000	204,786	164,648

SOURCE: Under Armour 10Q, 2010.

Industry Background

The Sporting Goods Manufacturers Association (SGMA) projected the industry's revenues in the United States to hit US$75.03 billion (wholesale) in 2010, an increase of 4.5% over 2009.[2] Sports apparel and athletic footwear were two important industry categories. Sports apparel accounted for approximately US$30 billion in revenues and was projected to grow at 2.4%, while footwear was US$12.9 billion with a projected growth rate of 5.1%. The women's segment of the sports apparel category was the fastest growing industry segment with an anticipated 42% growth rate. The sporting goods industry was cyclical in nature and was impacted by the macroeconomic business cycle. There was a high correlation between disposable income and industry sales. The 4.3% drop in 2009 industry revenues over 2008 was due to the 2008–2009 recession, and as the economy recovers so will consumer spending on fitness and athletic apparel.

Ten brands accounted for 30% of the sports apparel market share. The rest were spread out among numerous small companies that focused on specific segments. Apparel made from synthetic products was the fastest growing segment of the sports apparel market. This category was referred to as "performance apparel" (the category created by UA), and products in this category were purchased for use in active sports or exercise. Performance apparel consisted of apparel that provided compression, moisture management, and temperature control.

The sports apparel market was fragmented, with Nike (16.4% market share in 2008) and Adidas (13.8%) accounting for less than one-third of the market. Champion, a brand owned by Hanesbrands Inc., was regarded as an up-and-coming player in this segment. The performance apparel segment was concentrated with UA holding a 78% market share in 2009.[3]

The athletic footwear market was dominated by Nike and Adidas (that also owned the Reebok brand). In 2009, Nike had an estimated 35% market share, Adidas 22%, followed by New Balance and Puma.[4]

Sporting goods companies typically designed the product and outsourced manufacturing to contract manufacturers in various Asian countries. In the footwear segment, Vietnam, China, and Indonesia were the leading countries for contract manufacture, while China, Thailand, and Indonesia were the most used by sports apparel companies. Many leading sporting goods companies (Nike, Adidas, and UA, among them) sourced inputs (such as synthetic rubber and fiber, leather, and canvas) to take advantage of purchasing power and pass on the inputs to the contract manufacturers. Nike, for example, also used a Japanese company for global procurement of key inputs. The contract manufacturers were responsible for shipping the finished products either to the client (for sale through company stores or online) or to the warehouses of retail chains. All the leading sporting goods companies had local offices to monitor their contract manufacturers.

Sporting goods were sold in the United States through department stores (such as Sears), mass merchandisers (such as Target and Wal-Mart), sports specialty chains (such as Dick's Sporting Goods, Modell's, and The Sports Authority), and thousands of independent stores, both freestanding and mall-based.[5] According to Standard & Poor's, in 2009,[6] sports specialty stores accounted for 30% of sporting goods sales, followed by 22% for mass merchandisers, and 14% for department stores. Internet retailers, factory stores, and independent outlets accounted for the rest of the retail sales. Leading companies in the industry sold their products through a wide variety of channels, including company owned "flagship" and factory-outlet stores, as well as via the Internet. Consumers faced a number of choices in each category of sporting goods, with some categories like athletic footwear offering 30 plus well-known brands. Sporting goods companies competed on a variety of price points, with most product categories offering some variation of the "good," "better," "best" possibilities.

Competitors

UA regarded its key competitors as Nike and Adidas. In addition, Champion competed with UA in the apparel category.

Nike[7]

Founded in 1964 by Bill Bowerman and Phil Knight, Nike was the world's leading supplier of athletic footwear and apparel. It reported revenues of US$19.014 billion, gross margins of 46.3%, and net income of US$1.907 billion in 2010. It sold US$10.332 billion worth of footwear, US$5.037 of apparel, and U $1.035 million of equipment (the rest of the revenues came from licensing and its other brands such as Cole Haan). Fifty-eight percent of its revenues came from international markets. It sold its products in over 170 countries., and it employed around 30,000 people. The company identified its target market as any individual playing a sport anywhere in the world. It's slogan in this regard was, "If you have a body, you are an athlete." Nike was positioned as a premium brand and the company sought to maximize its brand equity. It sold through 23,000 U.S. and 24,000 international outlets. Its 2010 marketing budget was US$2.356 billion. The company's athletic endorsers included Tiger Woods, Kobe Bryant, LeBron James, and Cristiano Ronaldo. In its 2010 annual report, Nike's CEO, Mark Parker, spoke about China being the next great opportunity for the company. In addition, he identified "action sports" as a key growth category and emphasized the need to leverage the company's Nike, Converse, and Hurley brands in this category. He spoke about the strength of the Nike brand:

> *"The NIKE brand will always be our greatest competitive advantage. It's the source of our most advanced R&D. It delivers insight and scale and leverage to every NIKE, Inc. brand and business. It's the source of our culture and personality that connects so strongly with consumers around the world. The NIKE brand is a source of instant credibility and opportunity that we never take for granted."[8]*

Adidas[9]

The Adidas Group was a Germany-based global industry leader. It was the largest athletic products company in Europe and second in the world, after Nike. It reported 2009 revenues of 10.381 billion euros, a gross profit of 4.712 billion euros, and net income of 245 million euros. It employed 39,596 people and sold products under the Adidas, Reebok, Rockport, and Taylor Made brand names. It used leading athletes such as Lionel Messi and David Beckham to endorse its products. Each of the company's subsidiaries created brands that catered to specific target markets, such as Taylor Made for golf, Rockport for the metropolitan professional, and Reebok Classic for the lifestyle consumer.

Champion[10]

Champion, a leading sports apparel company, was part of Hanesbrands, Inc. Hanesbrands, Inc. was spun off from Sara Lee Corporation and owned brands such as Hanes, Champion, Playtex, and L'eggs. Champion competed in the sports apparel and performance sports apparel segments with T-shirts, shorts, fleece, sports bras, and thermals. The company obtained 89% of its revenues from the United States. It reported revenues of US$3.691 billion in fiscal 2010, gross profits of US$1.265 billion, and net income of US$51.83 million. It employed 47,400 employees.

Under Armour's History[11]

In 1995, Kevin Plank was a walk-on special teams player for the University of Maryland football team. He played on the field goal, punting, and kicking teams. At 5'11" and 228 pounds, Plank tended to sweat a lot during the long, arduous practice sessions. Frustrated by being weighed down by the accumulated sweat in his cotton T-shirt, Plank began to search for alternatives. He began looking for synthetic material that would wick the sweat from his body and make him lighter and faster. He took various promising fabrics to a local fabric store to be sewn as a T-shirt. After spending US$450 on seven prototypes, Plank found a fabric usually used in women's lingerie to work very well as a tight-fitting compression T-shirt. The T-shirt (inner wear) wicked away sweat, thus keeping the outerwear light. Plank used his savings of US$17,000 from a campus flower business to order 500 shirts. Plank gave these shirts to his high school and college teammates and also mailed them to college and professional football player friends from around the country. Plank talked about the importance of player recommendation to the success of the startup company.

These early influencers included Jim Druckenmiller, then a backup quarterback for the San Francisco 49ers, and his teammate, Frank Wycheck (a teammate of Plank's at the University of Maryland). The first big exposure for Plank came serendipitously. A front-page photograph in *USA Today* of then–Oakland Raiders quarterback, Jeff George, showed George wearing the UA mock turtleneck T-shirt visibly under his uniform. This surprised Plank because he hadn't sent a sample to George. While the George photograph gave the fledgling company publicity, it did not turn into sales. Plank sent samples to every equipment manager in the Atlantic Coast Conference. His first big break came when the equipment manager for Georgia Tech University placed an order for 350 T-shirts. North Carolina State University followed with an order and the network of equipment managers soon resulted in sales to other colleges and National Football League teams.

Further exposure came with the release of Oliver Stone's football movie *Any Given Sunday*. Plank had heard about the movie from a former high school classmate and sent samples of his product to the costume designer. It resulted in the movie's star, Jamie Foxx wearing a UA jockstrap prominently in a locker room scene. Anticipating publicity from the movie, Plank paid US$25,000 for an advertisement in *ESPN The Magazine*. The advertisement generated orders worth US$750,000 and the three-year old company was on its way. In effect, Plank had created, using US$17,000 of his own cash and a US$40,000 credit card debt, a new category of sports apparel, one that focused on the athlete's performance, and hence dubbed "performance apparel."

Plank talked about how the company was able to create an entirely new category:

> *"Analysts often ask me: "How was the door left so wide open for UA's entry into the industry?" I tell them that my many detractors did not think consumers would pay $25 to $35 for a T-shirt. But, when you give consumers some tangible benefit, you're able to reinvent entire product categories."*[12]

Plank took the company public in a 2005 IPO. Under Armour was granted the rights to outfit the fictitious Dillon Panthers high school football team when the television show *Friday Night Lights* premiered in 2006 on NBC. The company, headquartered in Baltimore, Maryland, had a market cap of US$2.28 billion in September 2010. Plank owned 25% of UA shares and also controlled 77% of the company's voting shares.[13]

Under Armour's Activities

Products[14]

UA sold products in three categories: apparel, footwear, and accessories (**Table 2** contains a sample list of UA's products). UA sold a wide variety of innerwear and outerwear in the apparel segment, a broad line of footwear, and a line of accessories for both men and women. UA's price points were comparable to those of competitors like Nike, Adidas, and Champion (**Table 3** provides a price comparison of selected products for UA and its competitors).

Under Armour created the performance apparel segment, a sub-segment of the sports apparel category, and had a 78% market in 2009. UA's core apparel product was the tight-fitting compression T-shirt. It was a three-layered synthetic fabric that used moisture wicking technology to speed up the evaporation of sweat.

TABLE 20–2 Sample List of Under Armour Products

Apparel

Men	Women
▪ ColdGear Longsleeve Mock	▪ UA Victory Burnout T
▪ Men's Armour Fleece	▪ UA HeartGear Fitted Shortsleeve
▪ UA Tech Short Sleeve	▪ UA Form Cardio Tank
▪ ColdGear Action Legging	▪ UA Duplicity (A/B Cup)
▪ UA Barrage Jacket (Rainwear)	▪ UA surge Jacket (Rainwear)
▪ HeatGear Zone Socks	▪ Quickstep Lo Cut Liner socks
Footwear	**Accessories**
▪ Men's UA Fleet (Running)	▪ Men's Cage III Batting Glove (Baseball)
▪ Women's UA Proto Interval (Training)	▪ Thief (Eyewear)
▪ Men's UA Blur (Football)	▪ UA Surge Backpack
▪ Men's UA Twin Bill II Mid (Baseball)	▪ Performance Bottle (Water Bottle)

SOURCE: www.underarmour.com

TABLE 20–3 Sample Price Comparison Apparel

Apparel Type	Nike	Under Armour	Champion
Men's Graphic Tee	$25.00	$24.99	$11.99
Men's Jersey	$30.00	$34.99	$40.00
Men's Shorts	$22.00	$24.99	$22.00
Women's Short Sleeve Tee	$20.00	$19.99	$22.00
Women's Track Pant	$60.00	$54.99	$40.00

Shoe Type	Footwear		
	Nike	Under Armour	Adidas
Men's Football Cleats	$129.99	$119.99	$99.99
Men's Baseball Cleats	$104.99	$ 99.99	$89.99
Men's Performance Training shoes	$ 89.99	$ 89.99	$99.99
Women's Running Shoes	$ 89.99	$ 84.99	$84.99
Women's Performance Training Shoes	$ 84.99	$ 89.99	$75.00

SOURCE: Company websites and www.dickssportinggoods.com

In tests, UA demonstrated that its T-shirt was 52% lighter than a cotton T-shirt after 60 minutes of exercise. In addition, tests indicated that a UA T-shirt released 80% of its moisture after 30 minutes, in comparison to a cotton T-shirt that released 39% of its moisture after the same period. UA's T-shirt was also able to keep the body 3.5 degrees cooler than cotton.[15]

The initial product was marketed as HeatGear. The same microfiber technology was used to develop a line of cold weather T-shirts called ColdGear. In 2010, UA had additional products embodying the same technology and was sold under the LooseGear and AllseasonsGear trade names. In addition to the microfiber technology for temperature control, UA also developed "Lockertag" technology to prevent skin irritation from tags and labels. UA's technology heat-sealed the label onto the shirt, thereby preventing the irritation caused by the tag rubbing against the skin. The company's other product technologies included UA Metal and UA Tech for men, and Duplicity sports Bras for women.

UA sold a line of sports accessories that featured items such as sweatbands, headbands, running goggles, backpacks, and water bottles.

The footwear line was launched in 2006 in the form of football cleats, followed by baseball cleats. The company soon established itself as the number-two player (in terms of market share) behind Nike in the niche segment of athletic cleats. A four-product running shoe line (running shoes were a US$5 billion market and the largest segment in athletic footwear) was launched on January 31, 2009. The running shoes featured a proprietary technology, Cartilage, that has, according to a company press release, an "independent suspension system [that] serves as the connective tissue between a runner and his environment to enhance performance and provide an exceptionally stable and smooth ride." Plank believes that Under Armour will surpass Nike as the preferred brand of today's teenagers.

In spite of the high-profile launch, Under Armour couldn't meet their sales expectations for running shoes. UA replaced its head of footwear operations and decided to revamp the line. The company had to mark down its prices to clear inventory, and Wall Street responded by pummeling its stock price. UA announced that it was forgoing any new footwear launch until late 2010 or early 2011. Plank cautioned analysts to be patient while the company navigated its way through the 18-month cycle necessary to bring new models to market.

Operations[16]

UA outsourced almost all of its manufacturing to contract manufacturers in Asia and Latin America. In 2009, 22 manufacturers operating in 17 countries manufactured the company's products. A team from UA evaluated potential contract manufacturers on quality, social compliance, and financial strength prior to certifying them. UA's Hong Kong and Guangzhou, China offices supported and monitored the company's outsourced manufacturing activities for apparel and footwear. Manufacturers procured raw materials (specialty fabrics, canvas, etc.) and provided finished products to the company's distribution facilities. Manufacturing contracts were typically for the short-term and UA ensured that it had multiple manufacturers for a single product.

UA operated a small manufacturing facility in Glen Burnie, Maryland, called Special Make-Up Shop. This 17,000-square-foot shop manufactured apparel products for the company's high-profile athletes, leagues, and teams. The purpose of this operation was to provide superior (and quick) service to special customers. The company treated the cost of operating this facility as a marketing expense.

Distribution[17]

UA operated two leased distribution facilities in Glen Burnie, Maryland, a short distance away from the company's headquarters in Baltimore, Maryland. The first was a 359,000-squarefoot facility, while the second occupied 308,000 square feet. Products were shipped to retailers and company stores via a third-party logistics provider, both in the United States and in Europe. Inventory management was critical because of two factors. Industry practice was for retailers to return defective or improperly shipped merchandise. In addition, because of overseas sourcing, the lead times for design and production was long, which meant that production orders were to be made much before customer orders for new products.

Marketing

UA's 2009 annual report summed up the company's vision as: "The athletic brand of this generation. And next." To guide its marketing, UA also developed a brand mission: "To make all athletes better through passion, science and the relentless pursuit of innovation." UA spent between 12% and 13% of revenues on marketing.[18]

The market for sporting apparel and gear spanned the entire population, although primary users were the sports-oriented and/or active and health conscious segments. Young males constituted a large segment of this market, although recent trends indicated an upsurge in the female and older age group segments. UA targeted individuals in the 15–25 age group.

From the inception of UA, Plank relied on what he called "influencers" to market his products. After high school, determined to get a scholarship to play Division I football, Plank enrolled in Fork Union Military Academy to bulk up, play with top high school athletes, and attract the attention of major programs. Fork Union Military Academy was well-known as a "football mill," that sent a lot of athletes to the top college football programs. The contacts that Plank made at Fork helped him select his first influencers.

An early series of influencers included former and current NFL players such as Jim Druckenmiller, Frank Wycheck, and Eddie George. Later influencers included Brandon Jacobs (of the NFL New York Giants), Heather Mitts (U.S. women's soccer player), Brandon Jennings (of the NBA Milwaukee Bucks), and Lindsay Vonn (a gold medal–winning U.S. skier from the Vancouver Olympics). Plank's former teammate, Eric Ogbogu (who played seven years in the NFL and was dubbed "The Big E") was the company's brand spokesman.

UA's marketing budget was spent on athlete influencers, print, digital and television advertising, and payments to college teams to wear the company's products. Steve Battista, UA's senior vice president of brand, wanted UA's ads featuring professional athletes wearing Under Armour apparel to come across as similar to comic book superheroes.

UA's signature commercial "Protect This House" was featured in numerous college football and NFL stadiums in both print and video forms. Other commercials included "Click-Clack, I Think You Hear Us Coming" (for the footwear line launch), "Athlete's Run" (for running shoes), and "Protect This House, I Will" (for the women's line of products). UA was the official outfitter for around 50 universities (including Auburn University, University of Maryland, and Texas Tech University), while Nike had over a 100 universities under contract. UA paid its universities for the privilege of being named the "Official Outfitter."[19]

UA priced its products competitively on a par with Nike and Adidas. The company supported its product positioning with a policy of full retail pricing, rarely allowing its brand to be discounted. The idea was to add to the company's up-market appeal and position its brand as distinct from competing brands. UA, however, was forced to discount its prices in the running shoe line because of overstock.

In 2009, UA generated approximately 78% of its revenues from its U.S. wholesale distribution channel. UA was highly dependent on its two primary retailers—Dick's Sporting Goods and The Sports Authority—which accounted for 30% of its wholesale distribution. In addition to the two retailers, UA also sold through stores such as Modell's Sporting Goods, Academy Sports and Outdoors in the United States, and Sportcheck International and Sportsman International in Canada. UA's distribution channels also included independent and specialty retailers, institutional athletic departments, leagues and teams, and company-owned stores, as well as its website. When UA got into footwear, it extended its distribution to include footwear chains such as Finish Line and Foot Locker. Worldwide, UA sold its product in over 20,000 stores.

Personnel[20]

In September 2010, UA employed approximately 3,000 people. About half of the employees worked at the company's manufacturing facility, the Special Make-Up Shop, and various company-owned stores. The rest worked at UA's distribution facilities and the corporate headquarters. The company's employees were non-unionized. The company reported that in 2008 it received about 26,000 resumes, of which it hired 215 employees.

Eight executives made up UA's top management team. Kevin A. Plank was the President, Chief Executive Officer, and Chairman of the Board, Wayne A. Marino was the Chief Operating Officer, and Brad Dickerson was the Chief Financial Officer. The operations of the company were divided into apparel (led by Senior Vice President, Henry B. Stafford) and footwear (headed by Senior Vice President, Gene McCarthy). Distribution was the responsibility of Dan J. Sawall (Vice President of Retail), and John S. Rogers (Vice President/General manager of e-Commerce). Finally, Kevin Plank's older brother, J. Scott Plank headed the company's domestic and global business development efforts as an Executive Vice President.

Culture

Football, the sport that gave UA its start, not only dominated the company's product categories, but also permeated its culture. For example, employees were referred to as "teammates." Further, posted on the walls of company offices were "Under Armour Huddles," short, pithy statements that provided guidance to all. Examples were "manage the clock," "execute the play," and "run the huddle."

Plank himself set the aggressive tone for the company by never considering UA to be too small to take on giants such as Nike.

Plank and Marino, the COO, had developed a tradition of meeting at Plank's house every Saturday morning at 6:00 a.m. Accompanied by personal trainers, the two would engage in a strenuous physical workout while talking about Under Armour.

Tori Hanna, UA's director of women's sports marketing, talked about how Plank's belief in playing offense even in a tough economy percolated throughout the company.

Finances

Table 4 contains UA's financials for the last three years. The company broke down its revenues into apparel, footwear, accessories, and licensing.[21] It did not, however, provide category-wise operating margins. The company explained that the 2009 decline in gross profit margins was due to a less favorable footwear and apparel product mix and the liquidation of unsold footwear inventory. The company's finances were affected by seasonality with the last two quarters showing better numbers because of the Fall football season. The company did not break down revenues geographically, although one report indicated that in 2009, UA obtained nearly 94% of its revenues from the United States and Canada.

TABLE 4	Under Armour's Financial Statements Consolidated Balance Sheets (In thousands, except share data)		
	December 31, 2009	**December 31, 2008**	**December 31, 2007**
Assets			
Current assets			
Cash and cash equivalents	$ 187,297	102,042	40,588
Accounts receivable, net	79,356	81,302	93,515
Inventories	148,888	182,232	166,082
Prepaid expenses and other current assets	19,989	18,023	11,642
Deferred income taxes	12,870	12,824	10,418
Total current assets	448,000	396,423	322,245
Property and equipment, net	72,926	73,548	52,332
Intangible assets, net	5,681	5,470	6,470
Deferred income taxes	13,908	8,687	8,173
Other long-term assets	5,073	3,427	1,393
Total assets	$ 545,588	487,555	390,613
Liabilities and Stockholders' Equity			
Current liabilities			
Revolving credit facility	$ —	25,000	—
Accounts payable	68,710	72,435	55,012
Accrued expenses	40,885	25,905	36,111
Current maturities of long-term debt	9,178	7,072	4,111
Current maturities of capital lease obligations	97	361	465
Other current liabilities	1,292	2,337	—
Total current liabilities	120,162	133,110	95,699
Long-term debt, net of current maturities	10,948	13,061	9,298
Capital lease obligations, net of current maturities	—	97	458
Other long-term liabilities	14,481	10,190	4,673
Total liabilities	$ 145,591	156,458	110,128
Stockholders' equity			
Class A Common Stock, $.0003 1/3 par value; 100,000,000 shares authorized as of December 31, 2009 and 2008; 37,747,647 shares issued and outstanding as of December 31, 2009 and 36,808,750 shares issued and outstanding as of December 31, 2008	13	12	12
Class B Convertible Common Stock, $.0003 1/3 par value; 12,500,000 shares authorized, issued and outstanding as of December 31, 2009 and 2008	4	4	4
Additional paid-in capital	197,342	174,725	162,362
Retained earnings	202,188	156,011	117,782
Unearned compensation	(14)	(60)	(182)
Accumulated other comprehensive income	464	405	507
Total stockholders' equity	399,997	331,097	280,485
Total liabilities and stockholders' equity	$ 545,588	487,555	390,613

SOURCE: Under Armour Annual report, 2009.

Consolidated Statements of Income (In thousands, except per-share amounts)

	December 31, 2009	December 31, 2008	December 31, 2007
Net revenues	$856,411	725,244	606,561
Cost of goods sold	443,386	370,296	301,517
Gross profit	413,025	354,948	305,044
Operating expenses			
Selling, general, and administrative expenses	327,752	278,023	218,779
Income from operations	85,273	76,925	86,265
Interest income (expense), net	(2,344)	(850)	749
Other income (expense), net	(511)	(6,175)	2,029
Income before income taxes	82,418	69,900	89,043
Provision for income taxes	35,633	31,671	36,485
Net income	$ 46,785	38,229	52,558
Net income available per common share			
Basic	$0.94	0.78	1.09
Diluted	$0.92	0.76	1.05
Weighted average common shares outstanding			
Basic	49,848	49,086	48,345
Diluted	50,650	50,342	50,141

SOURCE: Under Armour Annual report, 2009.

Consolidated Statements of Cash Flows (In thousands)

	December 31, 2009	December 31, 2008	December 31, 2007
Cash flows from operating activities			
Net income	$46,785	38,229	52,558
Adjustments to reconcile net income to net cash provided by (used in) operating activities: Depreciation and amortization	28,249	21,347	14,622
Unrealized foreign currency exchange rate (gains) losses	(5,222)	5,459	(2,567)
Loss on disposal of property and equipment	37	15	—
Stock-based compensation	12,910	8,466	4,182
Deferred income taxes	(5,212)	(2,818)	(4,909)
Changes in reserves for doubtful accounts, returns, discounts and inventories	1,623	8,711	4,551
Changes in operating assets and liabilities:			
Accounts receivable	3,792	2,634	(24,222)
Inventories	32,998	(19,497)	(83,966)
Prepaid expenses and other assets	1,870	(7,187)	(2,067)
Accounts payable	(4,386)	16,957	11,873
Accrued expenses and other liabilities	11,656	(5,316)	11,825
Income taxes payable and receivable	(6,059)	2,516	3,492
Net cash provided by (used in) operating activities	119,041	69,516	(14,628)

(Continued)

	December 31, 2009	December 31, 2008	December 31, 2007
Cash flows from investing activities			
Purchase of property and equipment	(19,845)	(38,594)	(33,959)
Purchase of intangible assets	—	(600)	(125)
Purchase of trust owned life insurance policies	(35)	(2,893)	—
Proceeds from sales of property and equipment	—	21	—
Purchases of short-term investments	—	—	(62,860)
Proceeds from sales of short-term investments	—	—	62,860
Net cash used in investing activities	(19,880)	(42,066)	(34,084)
Cash flows from financing activities			
Proceeds from revolving credit facility	—	40,000	14,000
Payments on revolving credit facility	(25,000)	(15,000)	(14,000)
Proceeds from long-term debt	7,649	13,214	11,841
Payments on long-term debt	(7,656)	(6,490)	(2,973)
Payments on capital lease obligations	(361)	(464)	(794)
Excess tax benefits from stock-based compensation arrangements	5,127	2,131	6,892
Proceeds from exercise of stock options and other stock issuances	5,128	1,990	3,182
Payments of debt financing costs	(1,354)	—	—
Net cash provided by (used in) financing activities	(16,467)	35,381	18,148
Effect of exchange rate changes on cash and cash equivalents	2,561	(1,377)	497
Net increase (decrease) in cash and cash equivalents	85,255	61,454	(30,067)
Cash and cash equivalents			
Beginning of year	102,042	40,588	70,655
End of year	$187,297	102,042	40,588
Non-cash financing and investing activities			
Fair market value of shares withheld in consideration of employee tax obligations relative to stock-based compensation	$ 608	—	—
Purchase of property and equipment through certain obligations	4,784	2,486	1,110
Purchase of intangible asset through certain obligations	2,105	—	—
Other supplemental information			
Cash paid for income taxes	40,834	29,561	30,502
Cash paid for interest	1,273	1,444	525

SOURCE: Under Armour Annual report, 2009.

The Pursuit of Three Percent

Several experts criticized the company's foray into footwear. Laura Ries, a marketing expert, was quite critical of UA's entry into footwear:

> *"The key to remember is that Under Armour isn't just a great brand; Under Armour pioneered and dominates a great category. Its power comes from the category it owns in the mind, not the brand name it puts on the package. "Under Armour" are the words that represent that category in mind. So putting the Under Armour brand name on another category is not going to guarantee success, especially if that category has little to do with performance clothing. Under Armour is an apparel brand. Nike is a footwear brand. Each might sell other stuff too, but the brands are rooted in these categories and can't grow too far from them. Here is a company (UA) with no credibility in athletic shoes attacking one of the world's most iconic and dominant brands for athletic footwear. Furthermore, Under Armour was doing so with no clear-cut product advantage and with a name that defined a totally different strategy."* [22]

John Horan, publisher of *Sporting Goods Intelligence*, an industry newsletter, talked about the U.S. sports apparel/footwear market becoming a duopoly with Nike and Under Armour. He believes that Under Armour is one of a very small number of companies that has successfully challenged Nike in the marketplace.

But Plank and his team were attracted by the US$31 billion international branded footwear market. Their contention was that even a 3% share of the market would nearly double UA's total revenues. They based their support of the footwear foray on the strength of UA's brand.

In addition, UA's team believed that the strong relationships they had with the distribution channel was a viable foundation to succeed in the new category.

In a number of interviews, Plank and his top management team members had reiterated the importance of the international markets for its apparel products. In fact, Plank's favorite line was "We haven't sold a single T-shirt in China." UA was a company that was largely dependent on the U.S. market for its revenues.

As Plank reflected on UA's second quarter 2010 financial results, he thought about what he wanted UA to be. Should the company attempt to be a leading athletic brand with products beyond apparel, or should UA cement its reputation as the leading U.S. performance apparel maker and extend its dominance globally?

ENDNOTES

1. Under Armour Press Release, July 27, 2010, http://investor.underarmour.com/releases.cfm.
2. http://sgma.com, extracted September 20, 2010.
3. Michels, W, How Stealth Stocks Make it Big, *The Motley Fool*, http://www.fool.com/investing/high-growth/2008/07/09/how-stealth-stocks-make-it-big.aspx, 2008, retrieved on September 20, 2010.
4. Heath, Thomas, Taking on the Giants: How Under Armour Founder Kevin Plank Is Going Head-to-Head with the Industry's Biggest Players, *The Washington Post*, January 24, 2010, www.washingtonpost.com.
5. Websites of Nike and Under Armour.
6. Standard & Poor's Industry Surveys, Apparel and Footwear: retailers and Brands, September 3, 2009.
7. www.nike.com.
8. Ibid., 2010 Annual Report.
9. www.adidas.com.
10. www.hanesbrands.com.
11. This section is drawn from the following sources: Palmisano, Trey, From Rags to Microfiber: Inside the

Rapid Rise of Under Armour, http://si.com, April 9, 2009; Dessauer, Carin, For Under Armour CEO and Kensington Native Kevin Plank, It's Always Been About the Huddle, *Bethesda Magazine*, www.bethesdamagazine.com, March 2009; De Lollis, Barbara, No Sweat: Idea for Athletic Gear Takes Him to Top, *USA Today*, December 12, 2004, http://usatoday.com; and, Heath, Thomas, op. cit.
12. Under Armour, 2006 Annual Report.
13. Yahoo Finance and Heath, Thomas, op. cit.
14. Under Armour, 2009 10K.
15. Under Armour, various 10Ks.
16. Under Armour, 2009 10K.
17. Ibid.
18. Under Armour, 2009 Annual Report.
19. Under Armour, 2009 10K.
20. Under Armour, Investor Relations Website.
21. Under Armour, 2009 10K.
22. http://ries.typepad.com/ries_blog/2009/11/under-armour-too-big-for-its-shirt.html, extracted September 28, 2010.

CASE 25
TOMS Shoes (Mini Case)

J. David Hunger

FOUNDED IN 2006 BY BLAKE MYCOSKIE, TOMS Shoes was an American footwear company based in Santa Monica, California. Although TOMS Shoes was a for-profit business, its mission was more like that of a not-for-profit organization. The firm's reason for existence was to donate to children in need one new pair of shoes for every pair of shoes sold. Blake Mycoskie referred to it as the company's "One for One" business model. While vacationing in Argentina during 2006, Mycoskie befriended children who had no shoes to protect them during long walks to obtain food and water, as well as attend school. Going barefoot was a common practice in rural farming regions of developing countries, where many subsistence farmers could not afford even a single pair of shoes. Mycoskie learned that going barefoot could lead to some serious health problems. Podoconiosis was one such disease in which feet and legs swelled, formed ulcers, emitted a foul smell, and caused intense pain. It affected millions of people across 10 countries in tropical Africa, Central America, and northern India. For millions, not wearing shoes could deepen the cycle of poverty and ruin lives. Upset that such a simple need was being unmet, Mycoskie founded TOMS Shoes in order to provide them the shoes they needed. "I was so overwhelmed by the spirit of the South American people, especially those who had so little,"[1] Mycoskie said. "I was instantly struck with the desire—the responsibility—to do more."[2] The name of his new venture was TOMS Shoes.

History

Blake Mycoskie started his entrepreneurial career by creating a college laundry service in 1997 when he was a student at Southern Methodist University. In his words, "After we expanded EZ Laundry to four colleges, I sold my share. I moved to Nashville to start an outdoor media company that Clear Channel scooped up three years later."[3] In 2002, Blake and his sister Paige formed a team to compete on the CBS reality show

This case was prepared by Professor J. David Hunger, Iowa State University and St. John's University. Copyright © 2015 by J. David Hunger. The copyright holder is solely responsible for case content. Reprint permission is solely granted to the publisher, Prentice Hall, for *Strategic Management and Business Policy*, 15th Edition (and the international and electronic versions of this book) by the copyright holder, J. David Hunger. Any other publication of the case (translation, any form of electronics or other media) or sale (any form of partnership) to another publisher will be in violation of copyright law, unless J. David Hunger has granted an additional written permission. Reprinted by permission.

The Amazing Race, coming in second. One of the places that they visited during the filming was Argentina. Fascinated by South America, Blake returned to Argentina in 2006 for a vacation. "On my visit I saw lots of kids with no shoes who were suffering from injuries to their feet. I decided a business would be the most sustainable way to help, so I founded TOMS, which is short for a 'better tomorrow,'"[4] explained Mycoskie.

While in Argentina, Mycoskie had taken to wearing *alpargatas*—resilient, light-weight, slip-on shoes with a breathable canvas top and soft leather insole traditionally worn by Argentine workers, but worn casually by most people in that country. Mycoskie spent two months meeting with shoe and fabric makers in Argentina. Although he modeled his shoe after the espadrille-like alpargata, he used brighter colors and different materials. "No one looked twice at alpargatas, but I thought they had a really cool style,"[5] said Mycoskie. "I'm a fan of Vans, but they can be clunky and sweaty. These aren't. They fit your foot like a glove but are sturdy enough for a hike, the beach, or the city."[6]

Founding his new company that year in Santa Monica, California, the 30-year-old Blake Mycoskie began his third entrepreneurial venture. With a staff of seven full-time employees (including former Trovata clothing line designer John Whitledge), six sales representatives, and eight interns, TOMS Shoes introduced 15 styles of men's and women's shoes plus limited edition artist versions in June 2006. The shoes were quickly selected for distribution by stores like American Bag and Fred Segal in Los Angeles and Scoop in New York City. By Fall 2006, the company had sold 10,000 pairs of shoes, averaging US$38 each, online and through 40 retail stores.

As promised, Mycoskie returned to Argentina in October 2006 with two dozen volunteers to give away 10,000 pairs of shoes along 2,200 miles of countryside. Mycoskie wryly explained what he learned from this experience. "I always thought that I'd spend the first half of my life making money and the second half giving it away. I never thought I could do both at the same time."[7] The next year, TOMS Shoes gave away 50,000 pairs of shoes in "shoe drops" to children in Argentina plus shoe drops to South Africa. More countries were added to the list over the next three years.

Business Model

Realizing that a not-for-profit organization would be heavily dependent upon sponsors and constant fundraising, Mycoskie chose to create an innovative for-profit business model to achieve a charitable purpose. For every pair of shoes the company sold, it would donate one pair to a child in need. Mycoskie felt that this model would be more economically sustainable than a charity because sales would be used to achieve the company's mission. He saw this to be a form of social entrepreneurship in which a new business venture acted to improve society through product donations at the same time it lived off society through its sales.

Mycoskie believed that the firm's One-for-One model would be self-sustaining because the company could make and sell shoes at a price similar to other shoe companies, but with lower costs. "Selling online (www.toms.com) has allowed us to grow pretty rapidly, but we're not going to make as much as another shoe company, and the margins are definitely lower,"[8] he admits. "But what we do helps us to get publicity. Lots of companies give a percentage of their revenue to charity, but we can't find anyone who matches one for one."[9]

Marketing and Distribution

TOMS Shoes kept expenses low by spending only minimally on marketing and promotion. The company's marketing was primarily composed of presentations by Blake Mycoskie, fan word-of-mouth, and promotional events sponsored by the firm. The company won the 2007 People's Design Award at Cooper-Hewitt's National Design Awards. Two years later, Mycoskie and TOMS received the annual ACE award given by U.S. Secretary of State Hillary Clinton. This award recognized companies' commitment to corporate social responsibility, innovation, exemplary practices, and democratic values worldwide. Mycoskie spoke along with President Bill Clinton at the Opening Plenary session of the Second Annual Clinton Global Initiative Conference in 2007. With other business leaders, he also met with President Obama's senior administration in March 2009 to present solutions and ideas to support small businesses. In addition, he was featured in a CNBC segment titled "The Entrepreneurs," in which he and TOMS Shoes was profiled.

Mycoskie explained why he spent so much time speaking to others about TOMS Shoes. "My goal is to inspire the next generation of entrepreneurs and company leaders to think differently about how they incorporate giving into their business models. Plus, many of the people who hear me speak eventually purchase a pair of Toms, share the story with others, or support our campaigns like *One Day Without Shoes*, which has people go barefoot for one day a year to raise awareness about the children we serve."

Celebrities like Olivia Wilde, Karl Lagerfeld, and Scarlett Johansson loved the brand and what it stood for. Actress Demi Moore promoted the 2010 *One Day Without Shoes* campaign on *The Tonight Show with Jay Leno*. It didn't hurt that Mycoskie's fame was supported by his Bill Clinton–like charisma, Hollywood good looks, and his living on a boat in Marina del Rey with "TOMS" sails. Famed designer Ralph Lauren asked Mycoskie to work with him on a few styles for his Rugby collection, the first time Lauren had collaborated with another brand.

TOMS Shoes and Blake Mycoskie were profiled in the *Los Angeles Times*, as well as *Inc.*, *People*, *Forbes*, *Fortune*, *Fast Company*, and *Time* magazines. Mycoskie pointed out that the 2009 *Los Angeles Times* article, "TOMS Shoes the Model: Sell 1, Give 1," resulted in 2,200 orders for shoes in just 12 hours after the article appeared. In February 2010, *FastCompany* listed TOMS Shoes as #6 on its list of "Top Ten Most Innovative Retail Companies."[10]

By early 2007, TOMS Shoes had orders from 300 retail stores, including Nordstrom's, Urban Outfitters, and Bloomingdale's, for 41,000 pairs of shoes from its spring and summer collections. The company introduced a line of children's shoes called Tiny TOMS in May 2007 and unveiled a pair of leather shoes in Fall of that year. By September 2010, the company added Whole Foods to its distribution network and had given over 1,000,000 pairs of new shoes to children in need living in more than 20 countries in the Americas (Argentina, El Salvador, Guatemala, Haiti, Honduras, Nicaragua, and Peru), Africa (Burundi, Ethiopia, Lesotho, Malawi, Mali, Niger, Rwanda, South Africa, Swaziland, Uganda, and Zambia), Asia (Cambodia and Mongolia), and Eurasia (Armenia). The shoes were now selling for US$45 to US$85 a pair.

Operations and Management

TOMS shoes were manufactured in Argentina, China, and Ethiopia. The company required the factories to operate under sound labor conditions, pay fair wages, and follow local labor standards. A code of conduct was signed by all factories. In addition to its production staff routinely visiting the factories to ensure that they were maintaining good working standards, third parties annually audited the factories. The company's original line of alpargata shoes was expanded to include children's shoes, leather shoes, cordones youth shoes, botas, and wedges. In January 2009, the company collaborated with Element Skateboards to create a line of shoes, skateboard decks, and longboards. For each pair of TOMS Element shoes and/ or skateboard bought, one of the same was given to children at the Indigo Skate Camp in the village of Isithumba in Durban, South Africa.

Blake Mycoskie was the company's Chief Executive Officer and joked that he was also its "Chief Shoe Giver." He spent much of his time traveling the country to speak at universities and companies about the TOMS Shoes' business model. According to CEO Mycoskie in a June 2010 article in *Inc.*, "The reason I can travel so much is that I've put together a strong team of about ten people who pretty much lead the company while I am gone. Candice Wolfswinkel is my chief of staff and the keeper of the culture. . . . I have an amazing CFO, Jeff Tyler, and I'll check in with him twice a week. I talk to my sales managers on a weekly basis. I also call my younger brother, Tyler, a lot—he's head of corporate sales."[11] The company had 85 employees plus interns and volunteers. In 2009, more than 1000 people applied for 15 summer internship positions.

The company depended upon many volunteers to promote the company and to distribute its shoes to needy children. For example, Friends of TOMS was a registered nonprofit affiliate of TOMS Shoes that had been formed to coordinate volunteer activities and all shoe drops. The company sponsored an annual "Vagabond Tour" to reach college campuses. Volunteers were divided into five regional teams to reach campuses throughout the United States to spread information about the One-for-One movement. To capture volunteer enthusiasm, the company formed a network of college representatives at 200 schools to host events, screen a documentary about the brand, or throw shoe decorating parties.

Mycoskie believed that a key to success for his company was his generation's desire to become involved in the world. "This generation is one that thrives off of action. We don't dream about change, we make it happen. We don't imagine a way to incorporate giving into our daily lives—we do it. TOMS has so many young supporters who are passionate about the One-for-One movement, and who share the story and inspire others every day they wear their TOMS. Seeing them support this business model is proof that this generation is ready and able to create a better tomorrow."

Mission Accomplished: Next Steps?

When Blake Mycoskie originally proposed his One-for-One business model in 2006, few had much confidence in his ability to succeed. He never generated a business plan or asked for outside support. Mycoskie used the money he had earned from his earlier entrepreneurial ventures to fund the new business. Looking back on those days, Mycoskie stated, "A lot of people thought we were crazy. They never thought we could make a profit."[12] Much to everyone's surprise, TOMS Shoes had its first profitable year in 2008, only two years after being founded. The company's sales kept increasing throughout the "great recession" of 2008–2009 and continued being marginally profitable. Mycoskie admitted that the company would have to sell about a million pairs of shoes annually to be really profitable. Nevertheless, TOMS Shoes did not take on any outside investors and did not plan to do so.

In September 2010, Blake Mycoskie celebrated TOMS Shoes' total sales of one million pairs of shoes by returning to Argentina to give away the millionth pair. Looking forward to returning to where it all began, Mycoskie mused: "To reach a milestone like this is really amazing. We have been so busy giving shoes that we don't even think about the scope of what we've created and what we've done."[13]

What should be next for TOMS Shoes? Blake Mycoskie invested a huge amount of his own time, energy, and enthusiasm in the growth and success of TOMS Shoes. Was the company too dependent upon its founder? How should it plan its future growth?

NOTE

1. Source: http://www.toms.com/corporate-info

J.C. Penney Company, Inc.: Surviving the Ron Johnson (CEO) Era

Alan N. Hoffman
Bentley University

Company Background

James Cash Penney was born on September 16, 1875 in Hamilton, Missouri. In 1898, Penney began working for the Golden Rule Stores, a small chain known for selling quality goods at low prices. In 1902, Penney became a partner and opened his first Golden Rule Store in Kemmerer, Wyoming. In 1907, Penney purchased the Golden Rule Stores by buying out his other two partners. In 1913, the company incorporated and changed its name to the J.C. Penney Company. The first company headquarters was located in Salt Lake City, Utah. In 1914, the company moved its headquarters from Salt Lake to New York City. By 1922, the company had grown to 371 stores in 27 states (JCPenney). The stores were typically located in downtown areas that made shopping convenient for people working in the city. The company then began to introduce the first of its own private label brands that included Gaymode hosiery, Silver Moon lingerie, Big Mac work clothes, and Towncraft menswear.

On October 23, 1929 J.C. Penney Company became a publicly traded company. One week later the stock market crashed—an event that became known as Black

The author thanks Barbara Gottfried and Bentley MBA students Jennifer Cherry, Olger Bostanxhi, Elizabeth Papp, Lawrence Perreira at Bentley University for their research and contributions to this case. Please address all correspondence to: *Dr. Alan N. Hoffman*, Dept. of Management, Bentley University, 175 Forest Street, Waltham, MA 02452-4705, ahoffman@bentley.edu, (781) 891-2287. Printed by permission of Dr. Alan N. Hoffman.

Tuesday, the beginning of the Great Depression. During the Depression, J.C. Penney actually grew—growth driven by the company's reputation for high quality and low prices, and the company gave back considerably to the community as well (Encylopedia.com).

During the mid-1970s, when shopping trends changed from consumers walking downtown to shoppers driving to malls, J.C. Penney became an anchor, or foundational, store in malls around the country. In 1983, J.C. Penney shifted its business model, refocusing its product offerings on soft goods, and no longer selling automotive services, appliances, paint, hardware, or fabrics, then stopped carrying sporting goods, consumer electronics, and photographic equipment in 1987. The company introduced additional private label apparel brands during this time, choosing to become a department store rather than a mass merchandiser (Encylopedia.com). In 1988, the company headquarters relocated to Plano, Texas and J.C. Penney Telemarketing was established to take catalogue phone orders and provide telemarketing services for other companies. In the late 1980s, although it had historically been a middle of the road store, J.C. Penney attempted to move up-market by enlisting fashion designer Halston to provide the latest fashions. This fashion line ultimately failed, and the company decided rather to continue to develop its own brands. In the 1990s, the company successfully shifted its focus to women's fashion, allocating 41% of store space to it, which had a positive impact on financials (Encylopedia.com).

At the same time, catalogue sales grew with the introduction of the private label brand Arizona Jeans and a marketing campaign about "doing it right" (Encylopedia.com). In 1994, the company launched www.jcp.com, becoming one of the first national retailers to embrace the Internet. New sales growth came from private label brands like Arizona Jeans, Worthington, and St. John's Bay. The company focused on both dual income modern families (ages 25 to 54) and families that were just starting out (35 and under) to serve its middle of the road, primarily female demographic, while catalogue sales transitioned to online commerce (Encylopedia.com).

In 2009, J.C. Penney opened its first store in Manhattan just down the block from Macy's flagship store on W. 34th Street. The company exited the catalogue sales business In 2010 and stopped printing its large seasonal catalogues, exploiting press coverage about its being the last of the print catalogues to cease operations, and heralding the end of an era. In that same year, J.C. Penney became the exclusive retailer of the iconic Liz Claiborne brand and international fast fashion brand MNG by Mango, which was set up using the store-within-a-store concept. In 2011, J.C. Penney became the exclusive department store retailer for ALDO's Call It Spring brand, again embracing a store-within-a-store concept, and launched its Modern Bride experience in its fine jewelry department (JCPenney). In late 2011, J.C. Penney acquired the worldwide rights for the Liz Claiborne family of brands, including the fashion jewelry brand Monet, for about $288 million. The deal positioned Penney's department stores as the exclusive destination for Monet as well as Liz Claiborne.

The Ron Johnson (CEO) Era: 17 months

Ron Johnson, the architect behind Apple's wildly successful retail stores and 15-year Target veteran, became J.C. Penney's new CEO on November 1, 2011. J.C. Penney had high hopes for Johnson, who proceeded to make drastic changes to the company including a new logo and a new spokesperson (Ellen DeGeneres). His vision included transforming 700 of the largest J.C. Penney stores into collections of some 100 branded shops with a central "town square" gathering area for services including free haircuts for kids, and small shops around the perimeter. Johnson further planned to implement a simplification of the company's pricing strategy including a reduction in the number of times prices were marked down. Johnson knew that transforming J.C. Penney's 1100 department stores nationwide would take considerable time and effort, and that changes at J.C. Penney would also involve job cuts, including nearly 1,000 employees at its head-quarters, and the closing of one of its three call centers.

J.C. Penney fired Ron Johnson after just 17 months, following a disastrous decline in business directly attributable to the failure of the new business plan. Ex-CEO Mike Ullman then rejoined the company and was charged with stabilizing the retail chain, which was in a free fall after racking up almost a billion dollars in losses in 2012 as revenue plunged nearly 25%. At that point, it was not clear if Ullman would con-tinue with Johnson's plans to remake the legacy department store chain; however, it appeared that Ullman planned to return J.C. Penney to its roots while developing a point of differentiation and competitive advantage in the present day market, rather than simply implementing Johnson's vision. J.C. Penney very quickly learned that it needed to listen to its customers and drive desired changes, rather than implement a drastic overhaul.

Mr. Ullman, 66, brought almost eight years of senior executive leadership to the organization, along with specific company and industry knowledge, as well as a sensitiv-ity to the "voice of the customer" and an altruistic intent to "fix" the company:

> Given that Ullman decided on the spot to take the job, and to do so with no employment agreement for only $1 million in salary a year, we believe his interest is purely in fixing J.C. Penney and leaving a legacy that ends on a high note. His experience and the respect he has in the department store industry is already apparent, as the company has secured a loan from Goldman Sachs and vendors have continued to support the team despite dif-ficult financial results (Swinand, 2013).

At the same time, J.C. Penney learned a hard lesson about the risks associated with workforce reductions—that seasoned store veterans with tribal knowledge of the company and its operations, and the industry as a whole, offered a unique competitive advantage, thus letting them go was a huge risk. This realization was duly noted in its 2012 10-k explanation of its reductions to shareholders:

> These reductions, combined with our voluntary early retirement plan initiated in 2011 and voluntary departures of employees have resulted in a substantial amount of turnover of officers and line managers with specific knowledge relating to us, our operations and our industry that could be difficult to replace. We now operate with significantly fewer individuals who have assumed additional duties and responsibilities and we could have additional workforce reductions in the future . . . These workforce changes may negatively impact communication, morale, management cohesiveness and effective decision-making, which could have an adverse impact on our operating efficiency cursor (J.C. Penney Company, 2013).

Strategic Direction

J.C. Penney wanted to be "America's favorite store" and the company that treated its customers "fair and square" according to the traditional values of the Golden Rule Stores (MarketLine, 2012, p. 24). The company was in the business of physical and online department store sales in the fashion and home goods market segments. Subsets of the department store included women's apparel, men's apparel, home goods, men's and women's accessories, children's apparel, footwear, make up, and fine jewelry. Some stores ventured into services, offering design consulting, wedding registries, hair styling, optical offerings, and portrait photography (MarketLine, 2012). In its bid to recoup its losses after the Johnson debacle, J.C. Penney invoked its trusted history, positioning itself as the department store that listened to its customers and was a "better place to shop." It strove to meet the needs of families through its private label brands and selections for all segments of the population. It also sought ethical suppliers and chose to "give back" to improve relations with local communities.

J.C. Penney's strategic goals included profitability, growth, increased market share, efficiency, accuracy of inventory, appropriate levels of quality, and customer-oriented service. Aligning its 2,500 domestic and foreign suppliers with its objectives was imperative for ordering the right goods at the right time in the right quantities through its purchasing subsidiary. Maintaining quality and having all of its suppliers operate ethically was of utmost importance, thus the company operated inspection offices in 15 countries to implement these objectives (MarketLine, 2012).

To achieve a competitive advantage, J.C. Penney focused on differentiation and location. It used customer service and strong private label brands as well as national brand name offerings to create points of distinction. Offering these brands within the store and opening its doors to partner boutiques, J.C. Penney became a retailer with "shops within the shop." The company competed on "price, quality, style, service, product mix, convenience, and credit availability" (MarketLine, 2012, p. 21). It used a basic defender strategy to maintain market position, yet the company was not a technological leader—it did not make innovative changes to push its stores to new levels. It did, however, try to adapt to the current environment and make its traditional philosophy fit new trends.

Competitors

J.C. Penney operated within the Department Store industry, a sector that included large, multi-department retail and discount stores retailing a wide range of general merchandise such as apparel, jewelry, cosmetics, and home furnishings/household products, but excluded supercenters and warehouse clubs. According to Mintel, this industry had 64.9 billion in sales in 2011 (Mintel, 2013).

By definition, the retail industry was always highly competitive with few barriers to entry. J.C. Penney's strongest rivals in the apparel and home furnishing retailers industry included Macy's Inc., Kohl's Corporation, Sears, and other department stores. Macy's had the highest percentage of the market share, approximately $16.3 billion (or 21.73%), followed by Kohl's with $11.3B (or 15.06%), and lastly J.C. Penney with $2.6B (or 3.47%). Kohl's and Sears were traditionally considered low-end department stores and Macy's was seen as high end, while J.C. Penney was traditionally viewed as middle of the market in terms of pricing. The remainder of the market was held by smaller companies' department stores (Yahoo, 2013).

Macy's Inc.

Headquartered in Cincinnati, OH, with 175,700 employees working in 850 stores in 45 states, Macy's was, in 2013, the top competitor in the apparel and home furnishing retail industry with $27.7 billion in sales for the year ending February 2013. A retail company operating stores and websites under two brands, Macy's and Bloomingdale's, its operations purveyed a wide range of merchandise from apparel and accessories for men, women, and children to home furnishing and other consumer goods. The company expanded globally under Bloomingdale's stores and through license agreements with Al Tayer Insignia in Dubai. Macy's had always attracted customers by offering superior selections and convenient locations. The company also had high-end makeup boutiques within its stores, the store within a store configuration that J.C. Penney wished to emulate (Yahoo, 2013).

Kohl's Corporation

With over 1,150 family-oriented department stores and a website, and 30,000 employees, Kohl's Corporation, headquartered in Menomonee Falls, WI, was another major competitor in the apparel and home furnishings retail industry, selling apparel, footwear, and accessories for women, men, and children; soft home products; and housewares. Kohl's apparel and home fashions were designed to appeal to classic, modern classic, and contemporary customers. The company had $19.279 billion in sales for the year ending February 2, 2013, and it was thus well positioned as the second largest player in the apparel and home furnishing retail industry. Kohl's began reaching out to technologically savvy customers by equipping all the stores with Wi-Fi, continuing to improve digital mobile sales platforms, and building the infrastructure to allow shipping on-line from its stores (Yahoo, 2013).

Sears Holding Corporation

Sears Holding Corporation, a retailer with 2,019 full-line and 54 specialty retail stores in the United States and 475 full-line and specialty stores in Canada had, as of February, 2013, approximately 246,000 employees in the United States and approximately 28,000 employees in Canada. At that time, Sears was the leading home appliance retailer in the United States and offered a broad range of apparel labels as well, including Land's End, Jaclyn Smith, Sandra Lee Levi's, etc. The company operated in three segments: Kmart, Sears Domestic, and Sears Canada with $39.85 billion in revenues for the period ending February 2, 2013 (Yahoo, 2013).

Sustainability and Technology

In October of 2013, J.C. Penney reported that over 500 of its stores qualified for Energy Star certifications. According to Katheryn Burchett, SVP of Property Development, "stores that proudly display the ENERGY STAR label generate fewer greenhouse emissions than non-certified structures, and each certified building saves the Company thousands of dollars in energy costs every year" (JCPenney, 2013). The improvements were important for both cost reductions and company perception, particularly from an environmentally sustainable perspective.

Social media (Facebook, Twitter, Pinterest, Google+, and YouTube) also presented marketing opportunities that capitalized on the latest digital technologies, which J.C. Penney worked hard to leverage as an effective means to market and connect with consumers.

J.C. Penney was looking to implement RFID technology in its inventory management systems under CEO Ron Johnson, but in early 2013 the company elected to move away from the initiative as part of a cost-saving effort. Implementing RFID tags would have enabled J.C. Penney to reduce costs, but the initial investment was too large for the company to take on as it tried to bounce back from major losses.

Marketing

J.C. Penney's marketing efforts were designed to increase both foot traffic to J.C. Penney retail locations and visits to jcpenney.com [also known as jcp.com] to increase sales. Marketing collateral also positioned the J.C. Penney brand according to the vision and mission of the organization, further communicating the company's points of differentiation (private and national brands, ease of walking around store, price) that drove consumers to choose J.C. Penney over a competitor.

Analysts pointed out that J.C. Penney could improve its segmentation efforts through marketing messages that catered to segments other than its traditional target market of American middle class families (all age ranges and genders). In response, J.C. Penney revitalized its focus on families just starting out, primarily speaking to women, or dual income families in the 1990s. However, when, under Ron Johnson, J.C. Penney changed the way it communicated its pricing, and positioned pricing as three tiers of deals, it lost 10% of its female customers, its primary demographic. (MarketLine, 2012, p. 21).

Market research revealed crucial information that J.C. Penney's needed to consider to maximize its marketing efforts. First of all, a Mintel survey indicated that shoppers actually visited a J.C. Penney's or other comparable department stores only relatively infrequently: 38% visited less than once a month, and 21% once a month. The research also indicated that social media efforts were geared to 18–24 year olds, yet online conversations indicated shoppers saw J.C. Penney's as primarily for Baby Boomers, pointing to a brand positioning and segmentation issue as well as suggesting that the company's efforts to "speak" to a younger demographic were missing their mark. Nonetheless, the 18–24-year-old demographic recorded the highest percentage of visits to the store per month, and women of all ages were more likely than men to shop there. It was important for the company to keep in mind that women and young adults, its two primary demographics, were the most likely to be price sensitive. In addition, young adults shied away from department stores that were not conveniently located. Finally, further market research made clear that when segmenting marketing messages, the company needed to pay attention to the 35–44-year-old demographic, as well as to Hispanics, the two demographics most likely to shop for the whole family across the departments of the store rather than just visit one section (Mintel, 2013).

A wide range of income levels reported shopping at J.C. Penney; however, the highest number of people who visited a J.C. Penney's had household incomes of $75,000 to $99,999. In terms of race, the Mintel survey of shoppers indicated that J.C. Penney's customers crossed all races. 50% of white survey respondents, 48% of blacks, 44% of Asians, and 56% of Hispanics had shopped at a J.C. Penney. In terms of marital status, the Mintel survey indicated that 48% of single respondents, 49% of partnered individuals, 52% of married respondents, and 45% of separated or divorced respondents had shopped at a J.C. Penney's; therefore, marital status did not significantly affect shopping at J.C. Penney. In terms of family size, the highest percentage, 61%, of those shopping at J.C. Penney's, were families of four, while the lowest percentage, 40%, were singles. Thus, families were the main segment of J.C. Penney shoppers. Employment was not a significant factor in the decision to shop at J.C. Penney's as 50% of each category (employed, unemployed, self-employed) had shopped at a J.C. Penney's. Nor was age: 50% of the millennials, Generation X, and baby boomers surveyed had shopped at the store, though only 39% of the World War II generation had. Millennials were the main demographic to have shopped at J.C. Penney on line (Mintel, 2013). To increase its market share, J.S. Penney could cultivate older shoppers as a potential growth market looking for particular styles and conveniences.

Shopkick

In October 2013, J.C. Penney announced that it was teaming up with shopkick, a mobile shopping app set up to recommend products in participating stores near users, who in turn earned points by entering participating stores and by making purchases. The points earned were called kicks and were redeemable for gift cards (shopkick). By the end of 2013 shopkick had over 6 million users and had already partnered with several other retailers, including Macy's, Old Navy, Best Buy, J.C. Penney, Crate & Barrel, Sports Authority, and Target.

As part of its initial promotion, J.C. Penney offered users additional kicks. According to Cyriac Roeding, CEO and co-founder of shopkick:

> J.C. Penney's nationwide rollout of shopkick makes shopping more inspiring and rewarding. For shoppers, we delight them by rewarding them for behaviors they are already doing while shopping. For retailers, like J.C. Penney, we are driving incremental traffic and sales and ensuring that marketing dollars are invested in driving actual foot traffic — it's a win-win (JCPenney, 2013).

In addition, J.C. Penney needed to pursue further mobile marketing opportunities, including native applications for the iPad, iPhone, and android devices; a mobile friendly website; and mobile coupon functionality.

Brand positioning

J.C. Penney had always been a middle of the road department store, competing heavily with the higher end Macy's and the lower end Sears. Under its new CEO, J.C. Penney attempted to position itself as more affordable yet more "with it" (or to position itself a bit lower in the ranking of department stores, as businesses in the middle often have to move up or down for growth). As part of its reinvention, J.C. Penney updated its logo to "jcpenney" in 2011. A college student at the University of Cincinnati won the logo competition, bolstering the company's desire to engage its stakeholders and reach the younger generation who would be more apt to be drawn in by its new lower prices. The all lowercase text highlighted the brand's recognition of more casual trends, and the fact that some of the text was outside of the box was meant as a graphic representation of J.C. Penney's move away from the traditional storefront of the past. The problem was that, in actuality, the new logo upset customers, as it did not match either J.C. Penney's image or customers' nostalgia for the J.C. Penney of their childhoods. It became clear that the association in customers' minds was more "Old Navy" than a classy department store (Brand New, 2013). In addition, J.C. Penney stopped using Saatchi & Saatchi, the marketing agency it had been using for the past five years, when it discovered that 99% of the 590 promotions it ran in 2011 had been ignored by consumers (Green, 2013).

Further changes in 2012 reduced the logo simply to JCP in light of the trend toward shorter names in the age of social media, and to coincide with its price-oriented marketing goals. However, like the original re-design, this also caused alarm with consumers as no one called J.C. Penney "JCP," reducing brand recognition to 56% (Brand New, 2011). The company then attempted to promote its lower prices positioning with a campaign highlighting that J.C. Penney treated its customers "fair and square," capitalizing on the square around the JCP in its logo. It also added blue to its traditional red and white color scheme, playing on patriotism to push J.C. Penney as "America's favorite store" (Brand New, 2012). As part of its lower price positioning, the number of promotions was reduced to 12, as the idea was that rather than having sales, the company maintained everyday low prices with monthly communications created by a different marketing agency, Peterson Milla Hooks (Green, 2013). In market research conducted for J.C. Penney, 26% of customers reported lower price positioning would lead to an increase in shopping at J.C. Penney; only 8% said it would reduce their shopping. However, in actuality, sales dropped (Lubin, 2012). Rather than showing savings, the pricing was a three-tier structure: the everyday low price, the monthly special price, and the best price (J.C. Penney Corporation, Inc., 2012). After the implementation of the lower price positioning, customer surveys revealed that consumers perceived the prices as higher, and only 16% of respondents associated low prices with J.C. Penney, making it clear that most customers did not see the value of "fair and square" (Edwards, 2012). This was partly because the store did not play into psychological techniques such as $19.99 pricing—the pricing was rounded to the nearest dollar. Customers also reported missing coupons as they could no longer brag that they saved X percent (Lubin, 2012). Thus, customers' perception was that prices were increasing rather than decreasing, while the quality remained the same, causing much customer confusion: was the brand moving up in the market or lower in the market?

Ultimately, J.C. Penney's re-branding fractured customers' sense of the company: there were several versions of the J.C. Penney logo circulating; Google searches turned up only bits and pieces of the company's website; and the site's functionality needed to be optimized for new tablets and other mobile devices. Thus, the site was fragmented and required reassessment for usability such that all its pieces could be accessed from jcpenney.com or jcp.com with easy access to investor relations, media relations, and history, sections currently hidden under a "full site" button.

Despite all these marketing issues, J.C. Penney did succeed with Ellen DeGeneres as a spokesperson even though a few Christian groups complained about rainbow pride (J.C. Penney Corporation, Inc., 2012).

2012: Firing Ron Johnson amidst Apologies

When J.C. Penney realized the three-tiered pricing was a mistake, it reinstated coupons offering a $10 gift card at the end of 2012 and a 30% off-sale (MarketLine, 2012, p. 21). Throughout 2013, discounting the suggested retail price became the corporate pricing strategy, with emails about savings events and price tags showing the difference between the suggested price and the actual price (Mintel, 2013).

In 2013, "It's No Secret," an apology ad acknowledging that J.C. Penney's changes in marketing and brand image had ventured away from its roots, ran on TV and YouTube. The YouTube video stated that the good news was the company was listening to its customers and learning. It encouraged customers to talk with the company on Facebook and "come back to J.C. Penney" (Brand New, 2013). Three-tiered, no coupon pricing had been disastrous for J.C. Penney, so towards the end of 2012, the decision was made to return to the Macy's way. Analysts pointed out that the company must continue to find pricing at levels customers would accept for the perceived value. The company also reverted to offering deep deals and discounts to drive sales and these promotions were smoothly integrated into the home page of the company's website and other marketing channels.

Also in 2013, J.C. Penney reverted to its pre-2011 logo and began to re-upscale its image from the low-end image it had experimented with by capitalizing on brand nostalgia to regain consumer trust. Its other logos were still in use in various marketing capacities, however, pending streamlining to one logo. At that point, skeptics continued to insist that the old logo was bland and questioned how the company would use its historic position to gain competitive advantage in the current marketplace (Brand New, 2013).

In its return to simpler times, J.C. Penney also reinvested in its core brand value with a focus on its private labels St. John's Bay, Stafford, and jcp Home, as well as on sales of other classic brands such as Levi's, Nike, Carter's, Dockers, Alfred Dunner, Vanity Fair, and Izod. Focus again shifted to connecting with customers and positioning J.C. Penney as a "better place to shop," increasing customer service levels which, it was hoped, would translate to better customer satisfaction, despite the human resources challenges involved. The company sought to find the right mix of private, exclusive, and national brand offerings and the right inventory levels. Progress as of October 2013 indicated a small increase in sales (J.C. Penney, 2013). Its strength lay in developing its private label brands and the images associated with those brands, which were exclusive to J.C. Penney. The company also decided to pursue partnerships with trendy brands and well recognized actors. For its children's line, J.C. Penney began offering Disney toys, role-play options, and Disney apparel. As Macy's had traditionally featured high-end makeup lines in its stores, J.C. Penney decided to open additional Sephora locations inside its stores to offer high-end makeup to its shoppers. Thus, the company began to focus on providing "shops" within the shop such that by entering J.C. Penney's, the customer felt she or he was entering a mini mall with partner brands.

Women's clothing was the biggest draw to the store (Mintel, 2013). In all departments, J.C. Penney combined private label brands—brands only available at J.C. Penney—with national brand offerings, most recently incorporating Martha Stewart's products, including a joint website of J.C. Penney and Martha Stewart products. There was a problem with this move, however, as Martha Stewart had a contract with Macy's which resulted in a lawsuit and poor press coverage. Eventually, J.C. Penney was permitted to sell Martha Stewart items without using her name (Lutz, 2013).

The company dedicated sections of its stores to Liz Claiborne, Olsenboye (founded by Mary-Kate and Ashley Olsen), IZOD, Supergirl by Nastia (a lifestyle line for girls founded with Olympic gymnast Nastia Liuin), Royal Velvet, ALDO, One Koss by Cindy Crawford and a new exclusive brand for basic fashion—jcp. In fact, J.C. Penney acquired the exclusive rights to the Liz Claiborne brand name and its subset, Monet. This exclusivity and the exclusivity of partnerships with other famous brands either through the sale of existing brands or the creation of new brands like Supergirl, it was hoped, would prove a strength, as J.C. Penney tried to differentiate its products. The company's staple sections within its store included Levi's, Arizona Jean Co., I jeans by Buffalo, MNG by Mango, and Sephora. Other brands offered included: The jcpenney, Okie Dokie, Worthington, east 5th, a.n.a, St. John's Bay, Ambrielle, Decree, Linden Street, Article 365, Uproar, Stafford, J. Ferrar, jcpenney Home Collection, Studio by jcpenney (MarketLine, 2012) [**Exhibit 1**].

In addition, the company re-focused on jcp.com or jcpenney.com where sales of home goods were strongest, followed by women's, men's, and children's clothing. Creating jcp.com as a home fashion hub, offering seasonal "catalogue" type campaigns/sales, and really capitalizing on what sells well— the home goods—were seen as the best strategies to reposition J.C. Penney for future competitive advantage (J.C. Penney, 2013), especially as a Mintel Survey of 2,000 U.S. retail shoppers over 18 conducted online revealed that 52% of respondents had shopped at J.C. Penney, second only to Kohl's, and, 50% of respondents had shopped online. Thus, J.C. Penney was beginning to transition to an online retailer from a brick-and-mortar catalogue solution (Mintel, 2013)

EXHIBIT 1
Private Labels

2012 Sales

	% of total
Women's apparel	25
Men's apparel & accessories	20
Home	15
Women's accessories, including Sephora	12
Children's apparel	12
Family footwear	7
Fine jewelry	4
Services & other	5
Total	100

J.C. Penney Company, Inc. Austin: Dun and Bradstreet, Inc., 2013. *ProQuest.* Web. November 11, 2013.

Selected Private and Exclusive Labels

- Ambrielle (intimate apparel)
- American Living (apparel and home furnishings)
- a.n.a. (casual women's apparel)
- Arizona
- Bisou Bisou
- Cindy Crawford
- Crazy Horse by Liz Claiborne (exclusive third-party brand)
- Decree
- east5th
- Every Day Matters
- Hunt Club
- J. Ferrar
- Jacqueline Ferrar
- JCPenney Home Collection (bedding, furniture, window coverings)
- Linden Street
- Liz & Co.
- nicole by Nicole Miller
- Okie Dokie
- Olsenboye
- St. John's Bay
- Sephora
- Stafford
- The Chris Madden for JCPenney Home
- Worthington

[**Exhibit 2**]. In particular, J.C. Penney capitalized on holiday promotions offering QR code gift messages attached to gift purchases during the holiday season (Mintel, 2013). In 2012, for the holidays, J.C. Penney demonstrated digital innovation with email footers to click to gift ideas, gift cards, and store hours. The footer was used as a best practice in documentation from ExactTarget, an email service provider (2013 Holiday Inspirations). In addition, a holiday TV promotion using music focusing on the holiday spirit was recognized for being upbeat and focusing on the fun meanings of Christmas rather than sales and gimmicks (Mintel, 2013).

EXHIBIT 2
Mintel, Department Store Retailing US, Feb. 2013

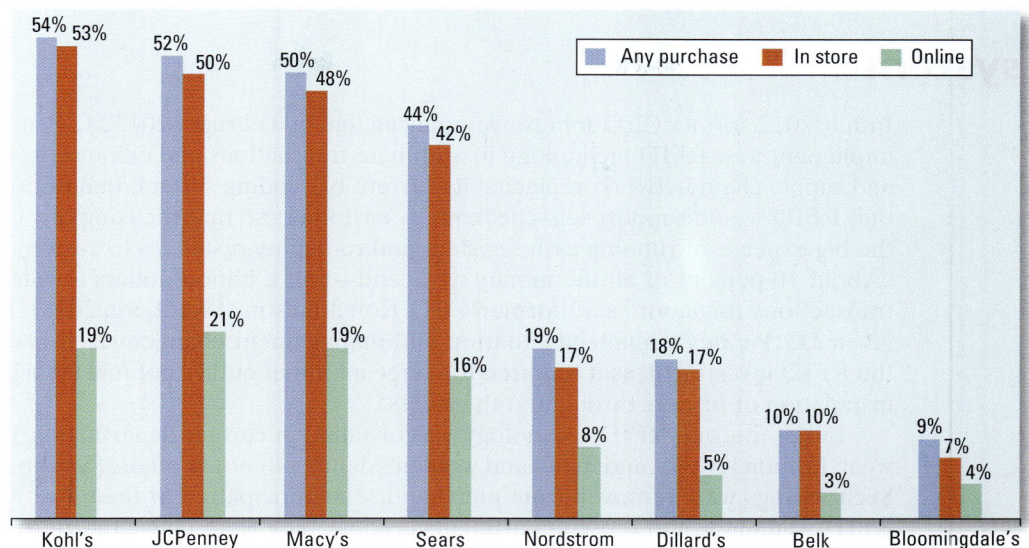

With regard to social media engagement, J.C. Penney ranked in the middle in relation to other department stores, gaining a market share of 12% of online discussion. Customers interacting with J.C. Penney on Facebook, specifically 18–24 year olds, liked salon services and complained about product cuts. (Mintel, 2013).

Store Layout "Shops," "Street," "Square"

The new store layout, designed to improve customer flow around "shops" within the larger store and implemented with renovations earlier in 2013, yielded some positive results, especially merchandising opportunities and pleased consumers. The Home department added furniture and "small shops featuring an entire line from one brand, like the Liz Claiborne shop or the Levi jean shop elsewhere in the store. If a customer liked the colors featured in the Royal Velvet collection or those in the Studio line, all the matching towels and bedding products could be found together (Lindeman, 2013). This made it more convenient for the customer, rather than having items spread throughout the store, and had the added benefit of helping to move inventory. J.C. Penney store customers, Ms. Sullivan and Ms. Pinti, said they "like the wider aisles and the brighter, cleaner look of the store" (Lindeman, 2013). Even Mr. Ullman commented, "From my perspective, J.C. Penney has made very good progress over the last 18 months, improving how our stores look, and how our brand assortments, like Joe Fresh and Happy Chic by Jonathan Adler, look in our stores" (Lindeman, 2013).

This new layout of "Shops," "Street," and "Square" was designed to present "a streamlined visual display for our customers" (J.C. Penney Company, 2013). However, although it was inviting to customers, and made the merchandising of products from the same brand easier for customers to find, it reduced the amount of space for merchandise display. Diminished space for display meant that the Operations team needed to tighten processes and execute with more precision; the store staff needed to keep the shops organized and stocked with merchandise in the correct locations; and the sourcing and inventory management teams needed to ensure merchandise was restocked quickly, as empty displays earned no revenue. Management also recognized that the new layout might only work in its larger stores, not in its smaller stores.

RFID system

In July 2012, former CEO Johnson announced that by February 2013 J.C. Penney would implement new RFID technology to automate transactions and enhance its inventory and supply chain network, replacing its current bar coding system. In addition, he said that RFID would support self–checkout by customers so that the company could save the big expense of running cash registers, and re-deploy resources to customer service. "About 10 percent of all the money we spend—half a billion dollars a year—goes to transactions for labor" said former CEO Ron Johnson (Swedberg, 2013). However, given J.C. Penney's financial situation and management changeover, it had to defer the RFID investment, as it required too large an initial outlay, not just for tags, but the installation of readers throughout the stores.

In the interim, RFID technology was installed in certain departments: bras, foot-wear, fashion jewelry, and men's and women's denim but not in others (Swedberg, 2013). Security tags were removed from merchandise in anticipation of the move to the new RFID system even in those departments because they would have interfered with the radio frequency devices. However, that turned out to be a big mistake as that, in com-bination with a change to a "friendlier" returns policy which did not require receipts to return items, resulted in a spike in theft in the third quarter, as "shoplifting took a full percentage point off the department store chain's profit margins" according to CEO Ullman (Kapner, 2013).

The Ron Johnson Legacy: Disastrous Financials

J.C. Penney always operated in a highly competitive industry, serving a wide range of customers. Its sales were dependent on the ability to predict and respond to changes in fashion trends and customer preferences. In order to capture a broad range of custom-ers the company offered several types of products. Percentage of sales from 2008–2012 segregated by different lines of businesses were as follows:

	2012	2011	2010	2009	2008
Women's apparel	23%	25%	24%	24%	24%
Men's apparel and accessories	21%	20%	20%	19%	20%
Home	12%	15%	18%	19%	19%
Women's accessories, including Sephora	13%	12%	12%	11%	11%
Children's apparel	12%	12%	11%	11%	10%
Family footwear	7%	7%	7%	7%	6%
Fine jewelry	7%	4%	4%	4%	5%
Services and other	5%	5%	4%	5%	5%
	100%	100%	100%	100%	100%

All divisions experienced a decline in sales from 2011 to 2012. The Home division posted the largest decline, while women's and men's apparel posted the lowest. Impor-tantly, the changes in marketing that occurred during this time period were focused on trendy clothing and barely touched home goods.

After its failed attempt in 2012, J.C. Penney continued to try to turn-around its busi-ness. From 2008–2012 the company did not perform well. In 2010 sales decreased by approximately $930 million or 5%, compared to 2009. The company recovered in 2011;

however, it declined again in 2012. As noted in the following table the total net sales decreased between 20% and 30% each quarter during 2011 and 2012:

($ in millions)	First Quarter	Second Quarter	Third Quarter	Fourth Quarter
2012	$ 3,152	$ 3,022	$ 2,927	$ 3,884
2011	$ 3,943	$ 3,906	$ 3,986	$ 5,425
Decrease	$ (791)	$ (884)	$ (1,059)	$ (1,541)
	−20%	−23%	−27%	−28%

(J.C. Penney Company, 2013)

For the 26 weeks ending August 3, 2013 revenues from retail sales decreased by 14% to $4.87 billion and online sales decreased by approximately 12% to $432 million. In fact, sales had fallen short of expectations for the four consecutive quarters (Morning Star, 2013), as indicated below in a comparison of actual to estimated sales ($ in millions):

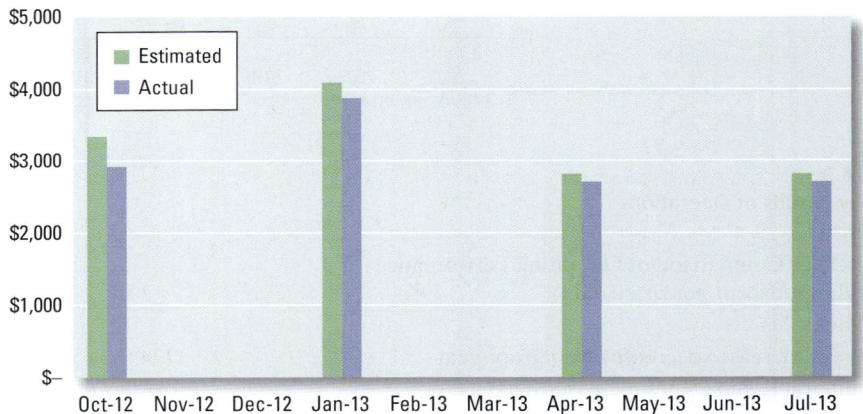

Gross Margins

The company's gross margins depended highly on the ability to manage appropriate inventory levels and quickly respond to both customers' demands and fashion trends. J.C. Penney's profit margin declined in 2011 and 2012 due to the change in its business model and lower consumer confidence. From the period 2009 through 2013 gross margins declined from 39% to 29%, as shown here:

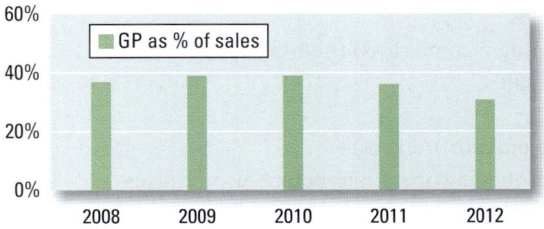

The same pattern of decrease in gross margins persisted in quarterly gross margins for the first three quarters of 2013 compared to 2012. In the first quarter in 2013 gross margins decreased by 6%; in the second quarter they decreased by 7%; and third quarter by 4% when compared to the corresponding quarters in 2012. Decreases in gross margins during 2012 were directly related to the high markdown of inventory and lower margins achieved on clearance items (Morning Star, 2013).

Net Income

J.C Penny did not respond quickly to the continuous drop in sales even though it was in the process of implementing cost savings initiatives, resulting in net income decreasing at a higher rate than sales. Operating expenses as percent of sales were 41%, 36%, 35%, 36%, and 31% for the period 2012 to 2009. The higher percentages toward 2012 were attributable to the inability of the company to leverage expense reduction against lower sales (**Exhibit 3**). Also interest expenses increased by approximately 19% during 2012 compared to 2011.

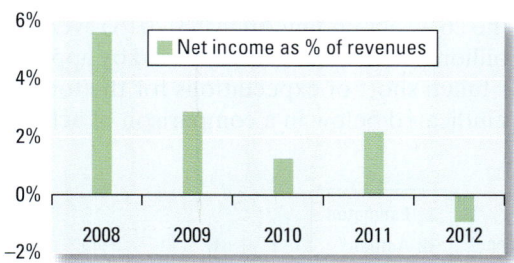

EXHIBIT 3
JC Penney Results of Operations

Three-Year Comparison of Operating Performance (in millions, except per share data)	2012	2011	2010
Total net sales	$ 12,985	$ 17,260	$ 17,759
Percent increase/(decrease) from prior year	(24.8)% [1]	(2.8)%	1.2%
Comparable store sales increase/(decrease) [2]	(25.2)%	0.2%	2.5%
Gross margin	4,066	6,218	6,960
Operating expenses/(income):			
Selling, general and administrative	4,506	5,109	5,358
Pension	353	121	255
Depreciation and amortization	543	518	511
Real estate and other, net	(324)	21	(28)
Restructuring and management transition	298	451	32
Total operating expenses	5,376	6,220	6,128
Operating income/(loss)	(1,310)	(2)	832
As a percent of sales	(10.1)%	(0.0)%	4.7%
Adjusted operating income/(loss) (non-GAAP) [3]	(939)	536	1,085
As a percent of sales	(7.2)%	3.1%	6.1%
Net interest expense	226	227	231
Bond premiums and unamortized costs	-	-	20
Income/(loss) from continuing operations before income taxes	(1,536)	(229)	581
Income tax (benefit)/expense	(551)	(77)	203
Income/(loss) from continuing operations	$ (985)	$ (152)	$ 378
Adjusted income/(loss) from continuing operations (non-GAAP) [3]	$ (766)	$ 207	$ 533
Diluted EPS from continuing operations	$ (4.49)	$ (0.70)	$ 1.59
Adjusted diluted EPS from continuing operations (non-GAAP) [3]	$ (3.49)	$ 0.94 [4]	$ 2.24
Weighted average shares used for diluted EPS	219.2	217.4	238.0

Net income in 2012 was also affected by onetime costs like markdowns related to alignment of inventory with the new business model introduced in 2011 and 2012; restructuring; management transition charges; and non-cash primary pension plan expenses. These costs were offset by a net gain on the sale of non-operating assets (Morning Star, 2013).

Long-term Debt & Cash

As illustrated in the table below, J.C. Penney's long-term debt over **five years ranged in 2009 to 2010** from $3.5B to $2.9B. During 2013, the company increased proceeds from financing activities and by mid-2013 it held $4.9 billion in long-term debt.

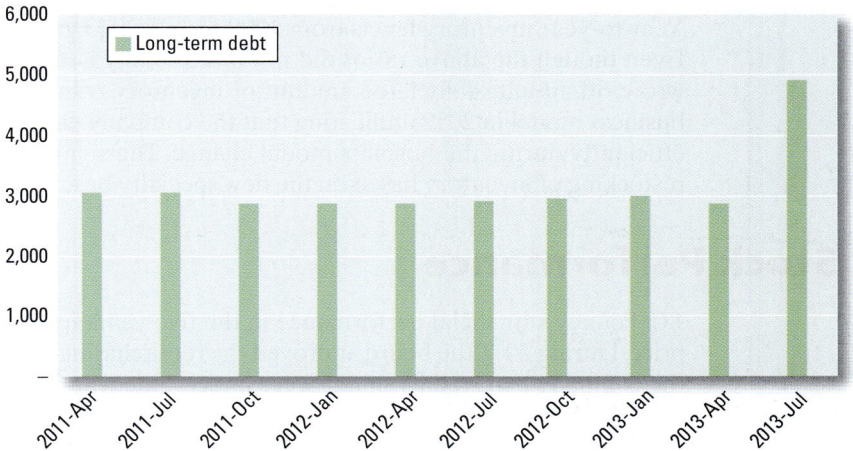

The long-term debt to equity ratio steadily increased from .65 in April 2011 to 2.09 in July 2013. The increase in long-term debt was intended to fund working capital requirements, invest in capital improvement plans, and service the outstanding indebtedness. In 2012, the company spent considerable resources developing a new everyday low pricing strategy that was then abandoned, requiring stores to be re-merchandised (Morning Star, 2013).

In 2009 and 2010, J.C. Penney had $2.4B and $3B in cash and $3.5B and $3B in long-term debt, which approximated 67% and 100% cash to long-term debt, respectively, indicating that the company was well positioned to pay off its long-term obligations from operating cash flow with sufficient funds remaining to fund its working capital and invest in properties, acquisitions, or other expansion plans. The cash to long-term debt changed in 2010 and 2011 as the company implemented a repurchase of its own stock and also planned to change its business model. In 2010, the company bought back 900 million shares under the belief that the company's stock was undervalued. From 2010 to 2012, the cash to long-term debt decreased from 100% to 30%, and remained in the 30% level each quarter in 2013.

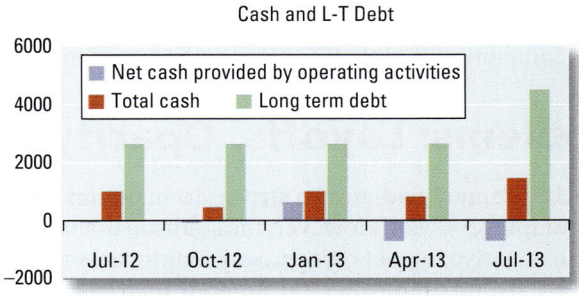

As shown above, the company had a difficult time generating cash from its opera-tions in the five quarters from mid-2012 to mid-2013; the cash on hand at year's end came from financing and investing activities. The last two quarters ending in April 2013 and July 2013, were the worst, as the company had to borrow money to meet its cash requirements. J.C. Penney's inability to generate cash, it was felt, could adversely impact its business, requiring the company to satisfy more restrictive covenants, which could lead to higher financing costs or be dilutive for current shareholders (Morning Star, 2013).

Inventory

Year-to-year inventory levels from 2009 to July 2013 grew in proportion to sales levels. Even though the above ratios did not indicate any issues with inventory, the company wrote off an unusually large amount of inventory resulting from the failure of its new business model in 2012, indicating that the company was not able to manage inventory efficiently during the business model change. The significant write down was offset by restocking of inventory based on the new specialty business model (Morning Star, 2013).

JCP Stock Performance

J.C. Penney's financial performance in the five years from 2008–2012 dictated its stock price. During 2011 the board approved the repurchasing of 900 million shares, suggesting the company believed its shares were undervalued, and the turnaround would succeed. As shown below, J.C. Penney's stock value fell significantly, reaching a five year low of $6.42 per share on October 21, 2013.

J.C. Penny, Inc. Stock Price

The stock price in 2013 was even lower than during the recession, when many stocks hit bottom. Toward the end of 2013, J.C. Penny's stock began to show signs of life as the company stated that its sales outlook had improved (Morning Star, 2013).

Morale Problems: Layoffs, Opacity, Instability

J.C. Penney had always striven to maintain a positive work environment and treat its employees well. However, the Johnson management team made some changes that had a negative impact on company employees, mainly in the form of layoffs. J.C. Penney let go 19,000 employees throughout its transformation, according to CNBC's Courtney

Reagan, including in-store associates, middle managers, salon receptionists, call center workers, corporate employees, and others (Bhasin, 2013). Under Johnson, supervisors in stores were reportedly instructed to color-code their employees in preparation for future firings. "Red" meant the worker should be eliminated; "yellow" was the designation for employees who needed more coaching; "green" signified strong employee performance (Bhasin, 2013).

When the new management team was installed at J.C. Penney and Johnson was made CEO in 2011, the internal culture of the company became opaque, rather than transparent. As an executive who had worked in the previous era claimed, "Corporate culture is very different than it was one year ago. There is no protocol or process in the company anymore. The direction given on product changes very frequently." "There are no memos or written directives anymore," another J.C. Penney home office executive stated. "Last one I saw was almost eight months ago. Everything gets communicated verbally and without too much detail. They do not leave any opportunity for anyone to ask questions," the executive continued. "While working at the home office, we do not get any insight to store operations and changes" (Bhasin, 2013). This opacity created a human resources opportunity to improve employee morale and communication and to standardize processes to decrease fears. As it was felt that explaining decisions and involving employees more in the decision-making process could help revitalize the company, more open communication with employees was implemented after Johnson's departure.

Under Johnson, the J.C. Penney's dress code changed to reflect a more casual environment, but upon his return, Ullman found that customers had trouble locating store workers and reinstated a business-casual requirement in May 2013. Name tags for store workers were changed from paper lanyards to small magnetic pieces in 2012, and by late 2013 to newly designed larger name tags to identify team members. Analysts considered the lack of a consistent appearance for store workers a weakness that would not be overcome until J.C. Penney codified what store associates wore.

Under Johnson, morale at J.C. Penney headquarters was undermined by having to deal with a distant management staff: Johnson and former executive vice presidents Ben Fay and Laurie Miller all commuted by private plane from California to Plano, Texas; the former CCO Michael Fisher and senior design and trends executive Nick Wooster flew from New York; and the construction executive Bob Laughrea commuted from Boston. The company paid for all of these commutes, which company employees resented, as the company was paying for these expensive commutes while struggling financially (Maheshwari, 2013).

To obtain a competitive advantage J.C. Penney adopted a location-oriented strategy early on, selecting and accumulating store locations over a long period and adapting its locations to changing consumer behaviors, especially keeping in mind shoppers' preference for short travel and easy access. By 1922 the company had 371 stores in 27 states and by the late 1920s the company had expanded to approximately 1,400 stores. As of 2013 the company operated over 1,100 department stores across the United States and Puerto Rico, mostly in malls. Replicating its location advantage would be very difficult and costly for new entrants.

The company also focused on differentiation, adding value through distinctive private label brands. For example, Arizona Jeans saw a spike in popularity when they were first introduced. In moving forward after the Johnson debacle J.C. Penney needed to assess these private brands and capitalize on their potential markets. Moreover, as home goods were a sales leader online, adding private label brands to its Home department, it was felt, would fuel future online sales, while focusing on private label Women's apparel would boost in-store sales as women's apparel drove sales in stores.

Operationally, J.C. Penney was always a store that gave back to the community. While this was not always marketed as a source of competitive advantage, positioning the company behind the Golden Rule and highlighting its corporate giving and sustainability initiatives, it was considered, could resonate with the consumer and become a point of differentiation particularly if the company invested in being even more progressive in this arena. At the same time, the company's supplier communications and oversight proved to be core competencies in maintaining effective relationships and practices.

While J.C. Penney continued to develop its overall market segments and marketing messaging, it also successfully targeted Hispanics, gaining operational knowledge of Hispanic consumers through opening its first Mexican department store in Monterrey in 1995, and continuing to expand in Mexico until it sold its six Mexican department stores to Grupo Sanborns S.A. de C.V. of Mexico City in 2003. The growth of the Hispanic population in the United States, their high frequency of departments store visits, and the company's knowledge of Hispanic shopping habits helped J.C. Penney, as market research confirmed that Hispanics were more likely to shop at J.C. Penney than Kohl's or Sears. Continuing to court this demographic by putting up signs in both Spanish and English and using bilingual sales representatives and cashiers was considered crucial to future growth.

J.C. Penney's over 100 years of successful business strategy was attributable to the establishment and understanding of its primary demographic; customer profiling, and outperforming its competition by developing appealing products and services that appealed to its core customers. The company changed and adapted as preferences and the competitive environment changed. In recent years, the company lost its focus on aligning its business with its customer profile, in particular, the female demographic. Under Johnson, the company lost 10% of its female customers, because they were looking for discounts, not every day pricing. In 2012, the company also shifted its efforts to focus on reaching 18–24 year olds, alienating its bread and butter demographic of female heads of households. It became clear that if the company did not re-invent itself by catering to both its core customer and other market segmentations, it would be selected out. It was imperative, therefore, for J.C. Penney to determine its key customer segments, and then provide merchandise and messaging that reached all of them effectively without alienating any of them.

Moreover, effective management of inventory was also key to sustaining profitability; merchandise had to be distributed among the stores in an efficient and timely manner. If the company overestimated customer demand, it had to markdown its inventory, thus taking a loss; yet if the company underestimated customer demand it experienced inventory shortage, thereby missing sales opportunities and eventually losing customers. In 2012, the company marked down its inventory by $155 million, indicating that the company had not managed its inventory effectively.

Uncertainty Going Forward

In trying to change too quickly at too great a cost at a time when the economy was weak in the aftermath of the recession, J.C. Penney suffered an identity crisis, no longer able to answer to the question, "Who are we?" In 2009, the economy was down but J.C. Penney was still doing relatively well compared to other stores. Growth and profits were flattening during this time period, however, and for any public company, that was disheartening. Trying to determine how to increase growth, J.C. Penney's radical board member, Mr. Ackman, advocated re-branding the company through the leadership of a new CEO, Ron Johnson.

Ron Johnson spent a lot of money at an inopportune time. In 2005, J.C. Penney's debt was equal to its cash. By 2013, the company had only 30% cash on hand compared to its long-term debt. This horrendous financial situation was brought on by large debts incurred to rebrand the company at a time when operations were shrinking. Rather than revitalizing the company, the rebranding confused customers who couldn't tell anymore if J.C. Penney was a higher end store or a lower priced store. The company reconceived its inventory to incorporate higher end boutique items, yet it was still effectively discounting its clothing. The "fair and square" three-tiered pricing system worked against psychological research about pricing, as customers confirmed when they saw these "low prices" as high and the lack of sales/discounts as off-putting. At the same time that J.C. Penney incurred high interest expenses to pay for its overhauls, it also bought back shares—this poor timing resulted in lingering weak financials.

Had J.C. Penney changed slowly over time, responding to market trends and testing the waters for new set ups, the outcome could have been different, but the company failed to test its changes—for instance, its initial logo change was designed by a competition and then immediately implemented, without market research. Even before the major changes of 2011 to 2012, J.C. Penney still needed to develop a strategy for growth in an increasingly competitive environment and in the middle of a market position highly dependent on economic conditions for sales. Analysts saw that, to survive, J.C. Penney would need to develop and closely monitor an effective turnaround strategy to regain the trust of both customers and Wall Street. Only time would tell if they would be successful.

On January 15, 2014, J.C. Penney announced its plan to close 33 stores and eliminate 2,000 jobs, potentially saving the retail giant $65 million a year. The move came as chief executive Mike Ullman worked desperately to bolster a company that had gone nine straight quarters without a profit.

REFERENCES

Associated Press. (2013, August 1). JC Penney: CIT supporting supplier deliveries. Retrieved December 1, 2013 from Yahoo: http://news.yahoo.com/jc-penney-cit-supporting-supplier-deliveries-110307489.html

Associated Press. (2009, July 19). Once-drab J.C. Penney taking on Manhattan. Retrieved December 1, 2013 from NBC NEWS: http://www.nbcnews.com/id/31994583/#.UpbUfIIo5yQ

Austin, Dun and Bradstreet, Inc. (2013). J.C. Penney Company, Inc. Retrieved November 11, 2013 from Proquest.

Bhasin, K. (2013, March 1). Business Insider. Retrieved November 17, 2013 from http://www.businessinsider.com/jcpenney-total-layoffs-2013-3

Bhasin, K. (2013, August 20). J.C. Penney's New CEO Is Gradually Eliminating Any Trace Of His Predecessor. Retrieved November 17, 2013 from Huffington Post: http://www.huffingtonpost.com/2013/08/20/jc-penney-new-ceo_n_3787106.html

Bhasin, K. (2013, March 1). Ron Johnson Has Fired 19,000 People Since Taking Over JC Penney. Retrieved November 17, 2013 from Business Insider: http://www.businessinsider.com/jcpenney-total-layoffs-2013-3

Brand New. (2011, February 23). A Penney for your Thoughts. Retrieved November 21, 2013 from Brand New: http://www.underconsideration.com/brandnew/archives/a_penney_for_your_thoughts.php#.Uq_WZfRDuYh

Brand New. (2012, January 26). jcpenney Nails the American Look. Retrieved November 21, 2013 from Brand New: http://www.underconsideration.com/brandnew/archives/jcpenney_nails_the_american_look.php#.Uq_WffRDuYi

Brand New. (2013, October 23). Old Logo for JCPenney. Retrieved November 11, 2013 from Brand New: http://www.underconsideration.com/brandnew/archives/old_logo_for_jcpenney.php#.Uq_MA_RDuYg

Carvajal, D. (2013, November 4). European Borders Tested as Money is Moved to Shield Wealth. Retrieved December 8, 2013 from The New York Times: http://www.nytimes.com/2013/11/04/world/europe/european-borders-tested-as-money-is-moved-to-shield-wealth.html?gwh=CCE90077B0FD3BAE961A2EE5224750EB&gwt=pay

Cherney, A. (2012, August 13). Bloomberg Businessweek. Retrieved November 17, 2013 from http://www.businessweek.com/articles/2012-08-13/two-questions-haunting-j-dot-c-dot-penney

Coinnews Media Group. (2013). Retrieved November 28, 2013 from US Inflation Calculator: http://www.usinflationcalculator.com/inflation/historical-inflation-rates/

CSR Hub. (2013). Retrieved December 1, 2013 from CSR Hub: http://www.csrhub.com/CSR_and_sustainability_information/J-C-Penney-Company-Inc/

Devnath, A., & Shannon, S. (2013, May 2). Wal-Mart to J.C. Penney Join Bangladesh Safety Talks. Retrieved December 1, 2013 from *Bloomberg Law*: http://about.bloomberglaw.com/legal-news/wal-mart-to-j-c-penney-join-bangladesh-safety-talks/

Dickey, T. (2013, November 3). Retrieved November 10, 2013 from *Retail Technology Trends*: http://retailtechnologytrends.com/

Dodes, R. (2010, May 4). *The Wall Street Journal*. Retrieved November 17, 2013 from http://online.wsj.com/news/articles/SB10001424052748704093204575216530311509768

Edwards, J. (2012, June 15). BRUTAL: JC Penney Rebranding Is Driving Its Core Customers AWAY From The Store. Retrieved November 10, 2013 from *Business Insider*: http://www.businessinsider.com/brutal-jc-penney-rebranding-is-driving-its-core-customers-away-from-the-store-2012-6

Edwards, J., & Minato, C. (2013, April 8). *Business Insider*. Retrieved November 10, 2013 from http://www.businessinsider.com/ron-johnson-disaster-timeline-apple-guru-failed-at-jcpenney-2013-4

eliteAds. (2013, May 7). It's No Secret JC Penney TV Commercial. Retrieved November 10, 2013 from You-Tube: http://www.youtube.com/watch?feature=player_embedded&v=ACAkN6w86XM

Encyclopaedia Britannica. (2010, January 7). *Encyclopaedia Britannica*. Retrieved November 17, 2013 from http://www.britannica.com/EBchecked/topic/450063/JC-Penney-Corporation-Inc

Encylopedia.com. (n.d.). JC Penney Company, Inc. Retrieved November 3, 2013 from Encylopedia.com: http://www.encyclopedia.com/topic/J.C._Penney_Company_Inc.aspx

Everett, N. (2013, August). Department Stores in the U.S. Retrieved December 1, 2013 from *IBISWorld*: http://clients1.ibisworld.com/reports/us/industry/default.aspx?entid=1090

Farfan, B. (n.d.). After 107 Years, J.C. Penney Will Get a Brand Makeover in 2010. Retrieved December 8, 2013 from *About*: http://retailindustry.about.com/od/retailtrendsetters/ig/2010-US-Retail-Store-Openings/JC-Penney-2010-Store-Openings.htm

Farfan, B. (2013, November 12). JC Penney Mission Statement - Winning Together Principles For Superior Service. Retrieved December 2, 2013 from *About*: http://retailindustry.about.com/od/retailbestpractices/ig/Company-Mission-Statements/JC-Penney-Mission-Statement.htm

Green, D. (2013, May 8). JCPenney Redesigned Its Logo So Many Times Nearly Half Of America No Longer Recognizes It. Retrieved November 10, 2013 from *Business Insider*: http://www.businessinsider.com/jcpenneys-new-logo-2013-5

Guinto, J. (2013, November). Who Wrecked J.C. Penney? Retrieved December 2013, 2013 from *D Magazine:* http://www.dmagazine.com/Home/D_CEO/2013/November/Who_Wrecked_JC_Penney.aspx

Halkias, M. (2013, November 2). *Dallas News*. Retrieved November 17, 2013 from http://www.dallasnews.com/business/retail/20131102-morale-at-j.c.-penney-is-mending.ece

IBISWorld. (2013, November). Consumer Confidence Index. Retrieved December 2, 2013 from *IBISWorld Business Environment Profiles*: http://clients1.ibisworld.com/reports/us/bed/default.aspx?entid=93

IBISWorld. (2013, September). Per capita disposable income. Retrieved November 27, 2013 from *IBISWorld Business Environment Profiles*: http://clients1.ibisworld.com/reports/us/bed/default.aspx?entid=33

IBISWorld. (2013, May). Population. Retrieved November 28, 2013 from *IBISWorld Business Environment Profiles:* http://clients1.ibisworld.com/reports/us/bed/default.aspx?bedid=1

Internet Wire. (2005, November 28). VCF and RCC Recognize JCPenney With "Retail Industry Innovator of the Year" Award. Retrieved December 15, 2013 from *Highbeam Business:* http://business.highbeam.com/436102/article-1G1-139209623/vcf-and-rcc-recognize-jcpenney-retail-industry-innovator

J.C. Penney Company, I. (2013, March 30). Retrieved November 28, 2013 from 2012 Form 10-K: http://ir.jcpenney.com/phoenix.zhtml?c=70528&p=irol-reportsannual

J.C. Penney. (2013, March 1). Conflict Minerals Policy. Retrieved November 28, 2013 from JCPenney: http://ir.jcpenney.com/phoenix.zhtml?c=70528&p=irol-govCSR

J.C. Penney Corporation, Inc. (2012, March 27). 2011 Form 10-K. Retrieved December 15, 2013 from JCPenney: http://media.corporate-ir.net/media_files/IROL/70/70528/reports/JCP_2011I10K/HTML2/default.htm

J.C. Penney. (2013). Evironmental Principles. Retrieved December 15, 2013 from JCPenney: http://ir.jcpenney.com/phoenix.zhtml?c=70528&p=irol-govCSR

J.C. Penney. (2013, November 7). J. C. Penney Company, Inc. Provides Update on Continued Progress of Turnaround. Retrieved November 21, 2013 from *Company News*: http://ir.jcpenney.com/phoenix.zhtml?c=70528&p=irol-newsCompanyArticle&ID=1873694&highlight=

J.C. Penney. (2013). JCP Cares. Retrieved December 15, 2013 from J.C. Penney: http://www.jcpmediaroom.com/jcpcares

J.C. Penney. (2013). *Product Recalls*. Retrieved December 15, 2013 from JCPenney: http://www.jcpenney.net/Customers/Product-Recalls.aspx?page=1

JCPenney. (2013, October 31). *Company News*. Retrieved November 10, 2013 from JCPenney: http://ir.jcpenney.com/phoenix.zhtml?c=70528&p=irol-newsCompanyArticle&ID=1871032&highlight

JCPenney. (2013, October 25). *Company News*. Retrieved November 10, 2013 from JCPenney: http://ir.jcpenney.com/phoenix.zhtml?c=70528&p=irol-newsCompanyArticle&ID=1868695&highlight=

JCPenney. (2013, November 7). *Financial News*. Retrieved November 10, 2013 from JCPenney: http://ir.jcpenney.com/phoenix.zhtml?c=70528&p=irol-newsFinancial_SalesArticle&ID=1873694&highlight

JCPenney. (n.d.). *JCP*. Retrieved November 17, 2013 from http://jcp.tcgdevbox.com/jcpenney-Media-Room/jcp-Facts/History-Timeline

Jolly, D. (2013, October 25). Small, Steady Growth for Europe's Economy. Retrieved December 8, 2013 from *The New York Times*: http://www.nytimes.com/2013/10/25/business/international/europes-economy-shows-modest-signs-of-life.html?_r=0&gwh=D2E2682129909D5FB483E01C5089F3B0&gwt=pay

Kahn, G. (2003, September 11). Made to Measure: Invisible Supplier Has Penney's Shirts All Buttoned Up. Retrieved December 15, 2013 from *WSJ*: http://online.wsj.com/news/articles/SB106323446110491600

Kanter, J. (2013, November 13). E.U. Identifies Problems in Its Members' Economies. Retrieved December 8, 2013 from *The New York Times*: http://www.nytimes.com/2013/11/14/business/international/eu-presses-countries-to-improve-economies.html

Kapner, S. (2013, November 21). Jump in Shoplifting Hurt Penney. Retrieved December 15, 2013 from *WSJ*: http://online.wsj.com/news/articles/SB10001424052702303653004579209642603738408

Krugman, P. (2013, November 14). The Money Trap. Retrieved December 10, 2013 from *The New York Times*: http://www.nytimes.com/2013/11/15/opinion/krugman-the-money-trap.html?_r=0

Lauricella, T. (2013, September 26). Goldman's Various Relationships With J.C. Penney Spark Questions. Retrieved December 1, 2013 from *WSJ*: http://blogs.wsj.com/moneybeat/2013/09/26/goldmans-various-relationships-with-j-c-penney-spark-questions/

Lindeman, T. F. (2013, June 27). J.C. Penney Betting on Improvements in Display, Inventory to Draw Customers. Retrieved December 15, 2013 from *Pittsburgh Post-Gazette*: http://www.post-gazette.com/businessnews/2013/06/27/J-C-Penney-betting-on-improvements-in-display-inventory-to-draw-customers/stories/201306270389

Lubin, G. (2012, March 30). A Big Survey of JC Penney Customers Says the New Model Is a Hit. Retrieved November 10, 2013 from *Business Insider*: http://www.businessinsider.com/survey-customers-like-the-new-jc-penney-2012-3

Lubin, G. (2012, March 28). JC Penney May Have Overestimated the Intelligence of the American Consumer. Retrieved November 10, 2013 from *Business Insider*: http://www.businessinsider.com/jc-penney-overestimating-customer-intelligence-2012-3

Lublin, J. S., & Mattioli, D. (2013, April 8). Penney CEO Out, Old Boss Back In. Retrieved November 28, 2013 from *WSJ*: http://online.wsj.com/news/articles/SB10001424127887324504704578411031708241800

Lutz, A. (2013, April 12). Victory for Jcpenney: Judge Rules Martha Stewart Can Sell Her Home Line in Stores. Retrieved November 10, 2013 from *Business Insider*: http://www.businessinsider.com/martha-stewart-and-macys-court-ruling-2013-4

Maheshwari, S. (2013, March 21). *Bloomberg*. Retrieved November 17, 2013 from http://www.bloomberg.com/news/2013-03-20/j-c-penney-plane-commute-executives-seen-hurting-revamp.html

MarketLine. (2012). *Company Profile J. C. Penney Company, Inc.* London: MarketLine.

Miller, G. (2013, September 19). *Upstream Commerce*. Retrieved November 17, 2013 from http://upstreamcommerce.com/blog/2013/09/19/retailers-worry-trillion-effects-retail-technology-human-behavior-vice-versa

Mintel. (2013, February). *Department Store Retailing US*. Retrieved November 21, 2013

Morning Star. (2013). Investment Research Center. Retrieved December 3, 2013 from *Morning Star*: http://library.morningstar.com.ezp.bentley.edu/stock/quote?t=JCP&region=USA

Payne, D. (2013, December 6). *Kiplinger's Economic Outlooks*. Retrieved December 7, 2013 from Kiplinger: http://www.kiplinger.com/tool/business/T019-S000-kiplinger-s-economic-outlooks/

shopkick. (n.d.). Retrieved December 3, 2013 from shopkick: http://www.shopkick.com/about

Stout, H. (2013, October 21). Ruling Near, J.C. Penney Capitulates to Macy's. Retrieved November 29, 2013 from *The New York Times*: http://www.nytimes.com/2013/10/22/business/ruling-near-jc-penney-capitulates-to-macys.html?_r=0

Swedberg, C. (2013, January 30). Retrieved November 10, 2013 from *RFID Journal:* http://www.rfidjournal.com/articles/view?10368

Swedberg, C. (2013, January 30). J.C. Penney Defers Its RFID Dreams. Retrieved December 15, 2013 from *RFID Journal*: http://www.rfidjournal.com/articles/view?10368/

Swinand, P. (August 23, 2013). We've Said Penney's Transformation Will Take Time; Near-term Cash Burn Will Be the Critical Factor. Retrieved December 1, 2013 from *Morning Star*.

Trading Economics. (2013). *Inflation Rate Forecast*. Retrieved November 28, 2013 from *Trading Economics*: http://www.tradingeconomics.com/forecast/inflation-rate

Weisenthal, J. (2011, March 8). Guess What Surging Cotton Prices Do to the Cost of Blue Jeans. Retrieved November 10, 2013 from *Business Insider*: http://www.businessinsider.com/guess-what-surging-cotton-prices-do-to-the-cost-of-blue-jeans-2011-3

Yahoo. (2013, December 1). Retrieved December 1, 2013 from *Yahoo Finance*: http://finance.yahoo.com/q;_ylt=AoL.cj2f-SncLeQ4CwJbWOxOiuYdG;_ylu=X3oDMTBxdGVyNzJxBHNlYwNVSCAzIERlc2t0b3AgU2VhcmNoIDEx;_ylg=X3oDMTBsdWsyY2FpBGxhbmcDZW4tVVMEcHQDMgR0ZXN0Aw--;_ylv=3;_ylc=X1MDMjE0MjQ3ODk0OARfcgMyBGZyA3VoM19maW5hbmNlX3dlb9ncwRmcjIDc2EtZ3AEZ3 *(truncated in source)*

Young, V. M., & Lockwood, L. (2013, August 13). *Women's Wear Daily*. Retrieved November 17, 2013 from http://www.wwd.com/business-news/human-resources/ackman-quits-penneys-board-7086346

CASE **27**

Best Buy Co. Inc. (2009): Sustainable Customer-Centricity Model?

Alan N. Hoffman
Bentley University

BEST BUY CO. INC., HEADQUARTERED IN RICHFIELD, MINNESOTA, was a specialty retailer of consumer electronics. It operated over 1100 stores in the United States, accounting for 19% of the market. With approximately 155,000 employees, it also ran more than 2800 stores in Canada, Mexico, China, and Turkey. The company's subsidiaries included Geek Squad, Magnolia Audio Video, and Pacific Sales. In Canada, Best Buy operated under both the Best Buy and Future Shop labels.

Best Buy's mission was to make technology deliver on its promises to customers. To accomplish this, Best Buy helped customers realize the benefits of technology and technological changes so they could enrich their lives in a variety of ways through connectivity: "To make life fun and easy,"[1] as Best Buy put it. This was what drove the company to continually increase the tools to support customers in the hope of providing end-to-end technology solutions.

As a public company, Best Buy's top objectives were sustained growth and earnings. This was accomplished in part by constantly reviewing its business model to ensure it was satisfying customer needs and desires as effectively and completely as possible.

....

This case was prepared by Professor Alan N. Hoffman, Bentley University and Erasmus University. Copyright © 2015 by Alan N. Hoffman. The copyright holder is solely responsible for case content. Reprint permission is solely granted to the publisher, Prentice Hall, for *Strategic Management and Business Policy,* 15th Edition (and the international and electronic versions of this book) by the copyright holder, Alan N. Hoffman. Any other publication of the case (translation, any form of electronics or other media) or sale (any form of partnership) to another publisher will be in violation of copyright law, unless Alan N. Hoffman has granted an additional written permission. Reprinted by permission. The author would like to thank MBA students Kevin Clark, Leonard D'Andrea, Amanda Genesky, Geoff Merritt, Chris Mudarri, and Dan Fowler for their research. No part of this publication may be copied, stored, transmitted, reproduced, or distributed in any form or medium whatsoever without the permission of the copyright owner, Alan N. Hoffman.

The company strived to have not only extensive product offerings but also highly trained employees with extensive product knowledge. The company encouraged its employees to go out of their way to help customers understand what these products could do and how customers could get the most out of the products they purchased. Employees recognized that each customer was unique and thus determined the best method to help that customer achieve maximum enjoyment from the product(s) purchased.

From a strategic standpoint, Best Buy moved from being a discount retailer (a low-price strategy) to a service-oriented firm that relied on a differentiation strategy. In 1989, Best Buy changed the compensation structure for sales associates from commission-based to noncommissioned-based, which resulted in consumers having more control over the purchasing process and in cost savings for the company (the number of sales associates was reduced). In 2005, Best Buy took customer service a step further by moving from peddling gadgets to a customer-centric operating model. It was now gearing up for another change to focus on store design and providing products and services in line with customers' desire for constant connectivity.

Company History[2]

From Sound of Music to Best Buy

Best Buy was originally known as Sound of Music. Incorporated in 1966, the company started as a retailer of audio components and expanded to retailing video products in the early 1980s with the introduction of the videocassette recorder to its product line. In 1983, the company changed its name to Best Buy Co. Inc. (Best Buy). Shortly thereafter, Best Buy began operating its existing stores under a "superstore" concept by expanding product offerings and using mass marketing techniques to promote those products.

Best Buy dramatically altered the function of its sales staff in 1989. Previously, the sales staff worked on a commission basis and was more proactive in assisting customers coming into the stores as a result. Since 1989, however, the commission structure has been terminated and sales associates have developed into educators that assist customers in learning about the products offered in the stores. The customer, to a large extent, took charge of the purchasing process. The sales staff's mission was to answer customer questions so that the customers could decide which product(s) fit their needs. This differed greatly from their former mission of simply generating sales.

In 2000, the company launched its online retail store: BestBuy.com. This allowed customers a choice between visiting a physical store and purchasing products online, thus expanding Best Buy's reach among consumers.

Expansion Through Acquisitions

In 2000, Best Buy began a series of acquisitions to expand its offerings and enter international markets:

2000: Best Buy acquired Magnolia Hi-Fi Inc., a high-end retailer of audio and video products and services, which became Magnolia Audio Video in 2004. This acquisition allowed Best Buy access to a set of upscale customers.

2001: Best Buy entered the international market with the acquisition of Future Shop Ltd, a leading consumer electronics retailer in Canada. This helped Best Buy increase revenues, gain market share, and leverage operational expertise. The same year, Best Buy also opened its first Canadian store. In the same year, the company purchased Musicland, a mall-centered music retailer throughout the United States (divested in 2003).

2002: Best Buy acquired Geek Squad, a computer repair service provider, to help develop a technological support system for customers. The retailer began by incorporating in-store Geek Squad centers in its 28 Minnesota stores, then expanding nationally, and eventually internationally in subsequent years.

2005: Best Buy opened the first Magnolia Home Theater "store-within-a-store" (located within the Best Buy complex).

2006: Best Buy acquired Pacific Sales Kitchen and Bath Centers Inc. to develop a new customer base: builders and remodelers. The same year, Best Buy also acquired a 75% stake in Jiangsu Five Star Appliance Co., Ltd, a China-based appliance and consumer electronics retailer. This enabled the company to access the Chinese retail market and led to the opening of the first Best Buy China store on January 26, 2007.

2007: Best Buy acquired Speakeasy Inc., a provider of broadband, voice, data, and information technology services, to further its offering of technological solutions for customers.

2008: Through a strategic alliance with the Carphone Warehouse Group, a UK-based provider of mobile phones, accessories, and related services, Best Buy Mobile was developed. After acquiring a 50% share in Best Buy Europe (with 2414 stores) from the Carphone Warehouse, Best Buy intended to open small-store formats across Europe in 2011.[3] Best Buy also acquired Napster, a digital download provider, through a merger to counter the falling sales of compact discs. The first Best Buy Mexico store was opened.

2009: Best Buy acquired the remaining 25% of Jiangsu Five Star. Best Buy Mobile moved into Canada.

Industry Environment

Industry Overview

Despite the negative impact the financial crisis had on economies worldwide, in 2008 the consumer electronics industry managed to grow to a record high of US$694 billion in sales—a nearly 14% increase over 2007. In years immediately prior, the growth rate was similar: 14% in 2007 and 17% in 2006. This momentum, however, did not last. Sales dropped 2% in 2009, the first decline in 20 years for the electronics giant.

A few product segments, including televisions, gaming, mobile phones, and Blu-ray players, drove sales for the company. Television sales, specifically LCD units, which accounted for 77% of total television sales, were the main driver for Best Buy, as this segment alone accounted for 15% of total industry revenues. The gaming segment continued to be a bright spot for the industry as well, as sales were expected to have tremendous room for growth. Smartphones were another electronics industry segment predicted to have a high growth impact on the entire industry.

The consumer electronics industry had significant potential for expansion into the global marketplace. There were many untapped markets, especially newly developing countries. These markets were experiencing the fastest economic growth while having the lowest ownership rate for gadgets.[4] Despite the recent economic downturn, the future for this industry was optimistic. A consumer electronics analyst for the European Market Research Institute predicted that the largest growth will be seen in China (22%), the Middle East (20%), Russia (20%), and South America (17%).[5]

Barriers to Entry

As globalization spread and use of the Internet grew, barriers to entering the consumer electronics industry were diminished. When the industry was dominated by brick-and-mortar companies, obtaining the large capital resources needed for entry into the market was a barrier for those looking to gain any significant market share. Expanding a business meant purchasing or leasing large stores that incurred high initial and overhead costs. However, the Internet significantly reduced the capital requirements needed to enter the industry. Companies like Amazon.com and Dell utilized the Internet to their advantage and gained valuable market share.

The shift toward Internet purchasing also negated another once strong barrier to entry: customer loyalty. The trend was that consumers would research products online to determine which one they intended to purchase and then shop around on the Internet for the lowest possible price.

Even though overall barriers were diminished, there were still a few left, which a company like Best Buy used to its advantage. The first, and most significant, was economies of scale. With over 1000 locations, Best Buy used its scale to obtain cost advantages from suppliers due to high quantity orders. Another advantage was in advertising. Large firms had the ability to increase advertising budgets to deter new entrants into the market. Smaller companies generally did not have the marketing budgets for massive television campaigns, which were still one of the most effective marketing strategies available to retailers. Although Internet sales were growing, the industry was still dominated by brick-and-mortar stores. Most consumers looking for electronics—especially major electronics—felt a need to actually see their prospective purchases in person. Having the ability to spend heavily on advertising helped increase foot traffic to these stores.

Internal Environment

Finance

While Best Buy's increase in revenue was encouraging (see **Exhibit 1),** recent growth had been fueled largely by acquisition, especially Best Buy's fiscal year 2009 revenue growth. At the same time, net income and operating margins had been declining (see **Exhibits 2** and **3**). Although this could be a function of increased costs, it was more likely due to pricing pressure. Given the current adverse economic conditions, prices of many consumer electronic products had been forced down by economic and competitive pressures. These lower prices caused margins to decline, negatively affecting net income and operating margins.

EXHIBIT 1
Quarterly Sales, Best Buy Co., Inc.

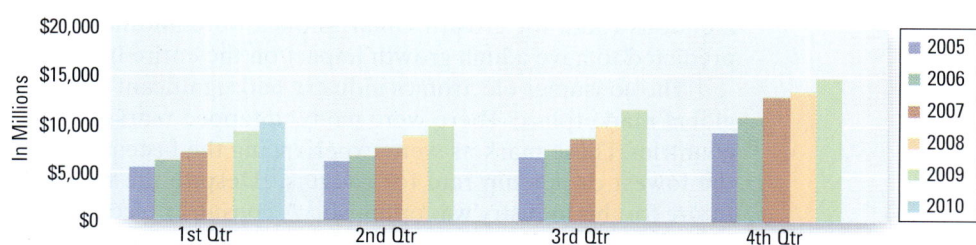

SOURCE: Best Buy Co., Inc.

Exhibit 2
Quarterly Net
Income, Best Buy
Co., Inc.

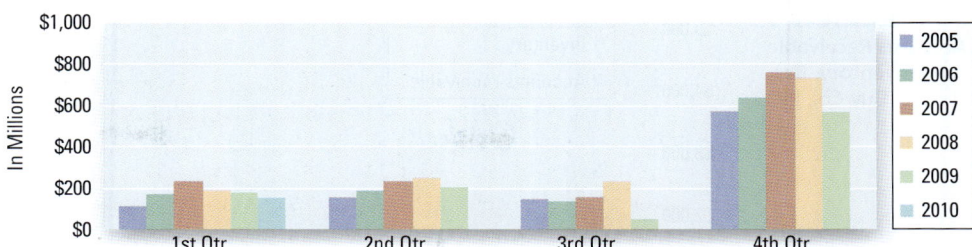

SOURCE: Best Buy Co., Inc.

Exhibit 3
Operating Margin,
Best Buy Co., Inc.

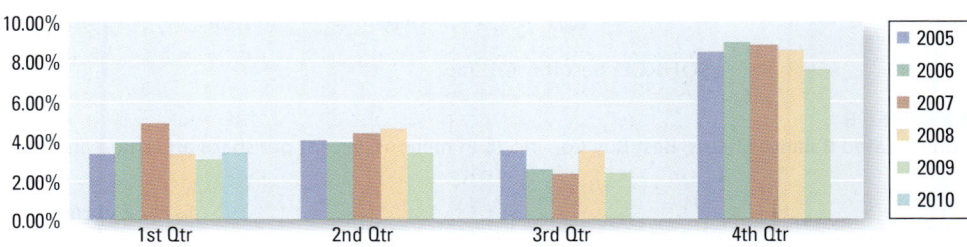

SOURCE: Best Buy Co., Inc.

Exhibit 4
Long-Term Debt and
Cash, Best Buy Co.,
Inc.

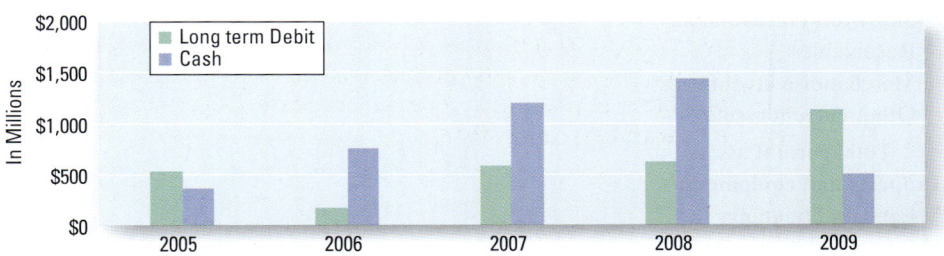

SOURCE: Best Buy Co., Inc.

Best Buy's long-term debt increased substantially from fiscal 2008 to 2009 (see **Exhibit 4),** which was primarily due to the acquisition of Napster and Best Buy Europe. The trend in available cash has been a mirror image of long-term debt. Available cash increased from fiscal 2005 to 2008 and then was substantially lower in 2009 for the same reason.

While the change in available cash and long-term debt were not desirable, the bright side was that this situation was due to the acquisition of assets, which led to a significant increase in revenue for the company. Ultimately, the decreased availability of cash would seem to be temporary due to the circumstances. The more troubling concern was the decline in net income and operating margins, which Best Buy needed to find a way to turn around. If the problems with net income and operating margins were fixed, the trends in cash and long-term debt would also begin to turn around.

At first blush, the increase in accounts receivable and inventory was not necessarily alarming since revenues were increasing during this same time period (see **Exhibit 5.** However, closer inspection revealed a 1% increase in inventory from fiscal 2008 to 2009 and a 12.5% increase in revenue accompanied by a 240% increase in accounts receivable. This created a potential risk for losses due to bad debts. (For complete financial statements, see **Exhibits 6** and **7).**

EXHIBIT 5
Accounts Receivable and Inventory, Best Buy Co., Inc.

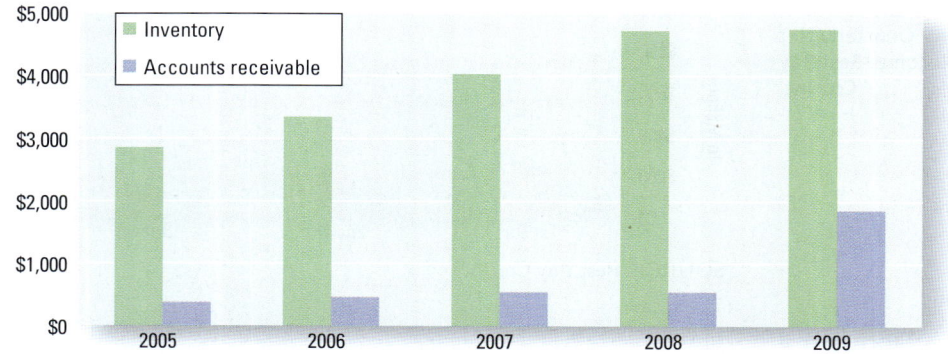

SOURCE: Best Buy Co., Inc.

EXHIBIT 6

Consolidated Balance Sheets, Best Buy Co., Inc. ($ in millions, except per share and share amounts)

	February 28, 2009	March 1, 2008
Assets		
Current assets:		
Cash and cash equivalents	$498	$1,438
Short-term investments	11	64
Receivables	1,868	549
Merchandise inventories	4,753	4,708
Other current assets	1,062	583
Total current assets	8,192	7,342
Property and equipment:		
Land and buildings	755	732
Leasehold improvements	2,013	1,752
Fixtures and equipment	4,060	3,057
Property under capital lease	112	67
	6,940	5,608
Less accumulated depreciation	2,766	2,302
Net property and equipment	4,174	3,306
Goodwill	2,203	1,088
Tradenames	173	97
Customer relationships	322	5
Equity and other investments	395	605
Other assets	367	315
Total assets	$15,826	$12,758
Liabilities and shareholders' equity		
Current liabilities:		
Accounts payable	$4,997	$4,297
Unredeemed gift card liabilities	479	531
Accrued compensation and related expenses	459	373
Accrued liabilities	1,382	975
Accrued income taxes	281	404
Short-term debt	783	156
Current portion of long-term debt	54	33
Total current liabilities	8,435	6,769

EXHIBIT 6
(Continued)

	February 28, 2009	March 1, 2008
Long-term liabilities	1,109	838
Long-term debt	1,126	627
Minority interests	513	40
Shareholders' equity:		
Preferred stock, $1.00 par value: Authorized—400,000 shares; Issued and outstanding—none	—	—
Common stock, $0.10 par value: Authorized—1.0 billion shares; Issued and outstanding—413,684,000 and 410,578,000 shares, respectively	41	41
Additional paid-in capital	205	8
Retained earnings	4,714	3,933
Accumulated other comprehensive (loss) income	(317)	502
Total shareholders' equity	4,643	4,484
Total liabilities and shareholders' equity	$15,826	$12,758

SOURCE: *Best Buy Co., Inc. 2009 Form 10-K*, p. 56.

EXHIBIT 7
Consolidated Statements of Earnings, Best Buy Co., Inc. ($ in millions, except per share amounts)

Fiscal Years Ended	February 28, 2009	March 1, 2008	March 3, 2007
Revenue	$45,015	$40,023	$35,934
Cost of goods sold	34,017	30,477	27,165
Gross profit	10,998	9,546	8,769
Selling, general and administrative expenses	8,984	7,385	6,770
Restructuring charges	78	—	—
Goodwill and tradename impairment	66	—	—
Operating income	1,870	2,161	1,999
Other income (expense)			
Investment income and other	35	129	162
Investment impairment	(111)	—	—
Interest expense	(94)	(62)	(31)
Earnings before income tax expense, minority interests and equity in income (loss) of affiliates	1,700	2,228	2,130
Income tax expense	674	815	752
Minority interests in earnings	(30)	(3)	(1)
Equity in income (loss) of affiliates	7	(3)	—
Net earnings	$1,003	$1,407	$1,377
Earnings per share			
Basic	$2.43	$3.20	$2.86
Diluted	$2.39	$3.12	$2.79
Weighted-average common shares outstanding (in millions)			
Basic	412.5	439.9	482.1
Diluted	422.9	452.9	496.2

SOURCE: *Best Buy Co., Inc. 2009 Form 10-K*, p. 57.

Marketing

Best Buy's marketing goals were four-fold: (1) to market various products based on the customer-centricity operating model, (2) to address the needs of customer lifestyle groups, (3) to be at the forefront of technological advances, and (4) to meet customer needs with end-to-end solutions.

Best Buy prided itself on customer centricity that catered to specific customer needs and behaviors. Over the years, the retailer created a portfolio of products and services that complemented one another and added to the success of the business. These products included seven distinct brands domestically, as well as other brands and stores internationally:

Best Buy: This brand offered a wide variety of consumer electronics, home office products, entertainment software, appliances, and related services.

Best Buy Mobile: These stand-alone stores offered a wide selection of mobile phones, accessories, and related e-services in small-format stores.

Geek Squad: This brand provided residential and commercial product repair, support, and installation services both in-store and onsite.

Magnolia Audio Video: This brand offered high-end audio and video products and related services.

Napster: This brand was an online provider of digital music.

Pacific Sales: This brand offered high-end home improvement products, primarily including appliances, consumer electronics, and related services.

Speakeasy: This brand provided broadband, voice, data, and information technology services to small businesses.

Starting in 2005, Best Buy initiated a strategic transition to a customer-centric operating model, which was completed in 2007. Prior to 2005, the company focused on customer groups such as affluent professional males, young entertainment enthusiasts, upscale suburban mothers, and technologically advanced families.[6] After the transition, Best Buy focused more on customer lifestyle groups such as affluent suburban families, trendsetting urban dwellers, and the closely knit families of Middle America.[7] To target these various segments, Best Buy acquired firms with aligned strategies, which were used as a competitive advantage against its strongest competition, such as Circuit City and Wal-Mart. The acquisitions of Pacific Sales, Speakeasy, and Napster, along with the development of Best Buy Mobile, created more product offerings, which led to more profits.

Marketing these different types of products and services was a difficult task. That was why Best Buy's employees had more training than competitors. This knowledge service was a value-added competitive advantage. Since the sales employees no longer operated on a commission-based pay structure, consumers could obtain knowledge from salespeople without being subjected to high-pressure sales techniques. This was generally seen to enhance customer shopping satisfaction.

Operations

Best Buy's operating goals included increasing revenues by growing its customer base, gaining more market share internationally, successfully implementing marketing and sales strategies in Europe, and having multiple brands for different customer lifestyles through M&A (Merger and Acquisition).

Domestic Best Buy store operations were organized into eight territories, with each territory divided into districts. A retail field officer oversaw store performance through district managers, who met with store employees on a regular basis to discuss operations strategies such as loyalty programs, sales promotion, and new product introductions.[8] Along with domestic operations, Best Buy had an international operation segment, originally established in connection with the acquisition of Canada-based Future Shop.[9]

In fiscal 2009, Best Buy opened up 285 new stores in addition to the European acquisition of 2414 Best Buy Europe stores. It relocated 34 stores and closed 67 stores.

Human Resources

The objectives of Best Buy's human resources department were to provide consumers with the right knowledge of products and services, to portray the company's vision and strategy on an everyday basis, and to educate employees on the ins and outs of new products and services. Best Buy employees were required to be ethical and knowledgeable. This principle started within the top management structure and filtered down from the retail field officer through district managers, and through store managers to the employees on the floor. Every employee had to have the company's vision embedded in their service and attitude.

Despite Best Buy's efforts to train an ethical and knowledgeable employee force, there were some allegations and controversy over Best Buy employees, which gave the company a black eye in the public mind. One lawsuit claimed that Best Buy employees had misrepresented the manufacturer's warranty in order to sell its own product service and replacement plan. The lawsuit accused Best Buy of "entering into a corporate-wide scheme to institute high-pressure sales techniques involving the extended warranties" and "using artificial barriers to discourage consumers who purchased the 'complete extended warranties' from making legitimate claims."[10]

In a more recent case (March 2009), the U.S. District Court granted Class Action certification to allow plaintiffs to sue Best Buy for violating its "Price Match" policy. According to the ruling, the plaintiffs alleged that Best Buy employees would aggressively deny consumers the ability to apply the company's "price match guarantee."[11] The suit also alleged that Best Buy had an undisclosed "Anti-Price Matching Policy," where the company told its employees not to allow price matches and gave financial bonuses to employees who complied.

Competition

Brick-and-Mortar Competitors

Wal-Mart Stores Inc., the world's largest retailer, with revenues over US$405 billion, operated worldwide and offered a diverse product mix with a focus on being a low-cost provider. In recent years, Wal-Mart increased its focus on grabbing market share in the consumer electronics industry. In the wake of Circuit City's liquidation,[12] Wal-Mart was stepping up efforts by striking deals with Nintendo and Apple that would allow each company to have their own in-store displays. Wal-Mart also considered using Smartphones and laptop computers to drive growth.[13] It was refreshing 3500 of its electronics departments and was beginning to offer a wider and higher range of electronic products.

These efforts should help Wal-Mart appeal to the customer segment looking for high quality at the lowest possible price.[14]

GameStop Corp. was the leading video game retailer with sales of almost US$9 billion as of January 2009, in a forecasted US$22 billion industry. GameStop operated over 6000 stores throughout the United States, Canada, Australia, and Europe, as a retailer of both new and used video game products including hardware, software, and gaming accessories.[15]

The advantage GameStop had over Best Buy was the number of locations: 6207 GameStop locations compared to 1023 Best Buy locations. However, Best Buy seemed to have what it took to overcome this advantage—deep pockets. With significantly higher net income, Best Buy could afford to take a hit to its margins and undercut GameStop prices.[16]

RadioShack Corp. was a retailer of consumer electronics goods and services, including flat panel televisions, telephones, computers, and consumer electronics accessories. Although the company grossed revenues of over US$4 billion from 4453 locations, RadioShack consistently lost market share to Best Buy. Consumers had a preference for RadioShack for audio and video components, yet preferred Best Buy for their big box purchases.[17]

Second tier competitors were rapidly increasing. Wholesale shopping units were becoming more popular, and companies such as Costco and BJ's had increased their piece of the consumer electronics pie over the past few years. After Circuit City's bankruptcy, mid-level electronics retailers like HH Gregg and Ultimate Electronics were scrambling to grab Circuit City's lost market share. Ultimate Electronics, owned by Mark Wattles, who was a major investor in Circuit City, had a leg up on his competitors. Wattles was on Circuit City's board of executives and had firsthand access to profitable Circuit City stores. Ultimate Electronics planned to expand its operations by at least 20 stores in the near future.

Online Competitors

Amazon.com Inc., since 1994, had grown into the United States' largest online retailer with revenues of over US$19 billion in 2008 by providing just about any product imaginable through its popular website. Created as an online bookstore, Amazon soon ventured into various consumer electronics product categories including computers, televisions, software, video games, and much more.[18]

Amazon.com gained an advantage over its supercenter competitors because it was able to maintain a lower cost structure compared to brick-and-mortar companies like Best Buy. Amazon was able to push those savings through to its product pricing and selection/diversification. With an increasing trend in the consumer electronics industry to shop online, Amazon.com was positioned perfectly to maintain strong market growth and potentially steal some market share away from Best Buy.

Netflix Inc. was an online video rental service, offering selections of DVDs and Blu-ray discs. Since its establishment in 1997, Netflix had grown into a US$1.4 billion company. With over 100,000 titles in its collection, the company shipped for free to approximately 10 million subscribers. Netflix began offering streaming downloads through its website, which eliminated the need to wait for a DVD to arrive.

Netflix was quickly changing the DVD market, which had dramatically impacted brick-and-mortar stores such as Blockbuster and Hollywood Video and retailers who offered DVDs for sale. In a responsive move, Best Buy partnered with CinemaNow to enter the digital movie distribution market and counter Netflix and other video rental providers.[19]

Core Competencies

Customer-Centricity Model

Most players in the consumer electronics industry focused on delivering products at the lowest cost (Wal-Mart—brick-and-mortar; Amazon—web-based). Best Buy, however, took a different approach by providing customers with highly trained sales associates who were available to educate customers regarding product features. This allowed customers to make informed buying decisions on big-ticket items. In addition, with the Geek Squad, Best Buy was able to offer and provide installation services, product repair, and ongoing support. In short, Best Buy provided an end-to-end solution for its customers.

Best Buy used its customer-centricity model, which was built around a significant database of customer information, to construct a diversified portfolio of product offerings. This let the company offer different products in different stores in a manner that matched customer needs. This in turn helped keep costs lower by shipping the correct inventory to the correct locations. Since Best Buy's costs were increased by the high level of training needed for sales associates and service professionals, it had been important that the company remain vigilant in keeping costs down wherever it could without sacrificing customer experience.

The tremendous breadth of products and services Best Buy was able to provide allowed customers to purchase all components for a particular need within the Best Buy family. For example, if a customer wanted to set up a first-rate audio-visual room at home, he or she could go to the Magnolia Home Theater store-within-a-store at any Best Buy location and use the knowledge of the Magnolia or Best Buy associate in the television and audio areas to determine which television and surround sound theater system best fit their needs. The customer could then employ a Geek Squad employee to install and set up the television and home theater system. None of Best Buy's competitors offered this extensive level of service.

Successful Acquisitions

Through its series of acquisitions, Best Buy had gained valuable experience in the process of integrating companies under the Best Buy family. The ability to effectively determine where to expand was important to the company's ability to differentiate itself in the marketplace. Additionally, Best Buy was also successfully integrating employees from acquired companies. Best Buy had a significant global presence, which was important because of the maturing domestic market. This global presence provided the company with insights into worldwide trends in the consumer electronics industry and afforded access to newly developing markets. Best Buy used this insight to test products in different markets in its constant effort to meet and anticipate customer needs.

Retaining Talent

Analyzing Circuit City's demise, many experts concluded one of the major reasons for the company's downfall was that Circuit City let go of their most senior and well-trained sales staff in order to cut costs. Best Buy, on the other hand, had a reputation for retaining talent and was widely recognized for its superior service. Highly trained sales professionals had become a unique resource in the consumer electronics industry, where technology was changing at an unprecedented rate, and was a significant source of competitive advantage.

Challenges Ahead

Economic Downturn

Electronics retailers like Best Buy sold products that could be described as "discretionary items, rather than necessities."[20] During economic recessions, however, consumers had less disposable income to spend. While there was optimism about a possible economic turnaround in 2010 or 2011, if the economy continued to stumble, this could present a real threat to sellers of discretionary products.

In order to increase sales revenues, many retailers, including Best Buy, offered customers low-interest financing through their private-label credit cards. These promotions were tremendously successful for Best Buy. From 2007 to 2009, these private-label credit card purchases accounted for 16%–18% of Best Buy's domestic revenue. Due to the credit crisis, however, the Federal Reserve issued new regulations that could restrict companies from offering deferred interest financing to customers. If Best Buy and other retailers were unable to extend these credit lines, it could have a tremendous negative impact on future revenues.[21]

Pricing and Debt Management

The current depressed economic conditions, technological advances, and increased competition put a tremendous amount of pricing pressure on many consumer electronics products. This was a concern for all companies in this industry. The fact that Best Buy did not compete strictly on price structure alone made this an even bigger concern. Given the higher costs that Best Buy incurred training employees, any pricing pressure that decreased margins put stress on Best Buy's financial strength. In addition, the recent acquisition of Napster and the 50% stake in Best Buy Europe significantly increased Best Buy's debt and reduced available cash. Even in prosperous times, debt management was a key factor in any company's success, and it became even more important during the economic downturn. (See **Exhibits 6** and **7** for Best Buy's financial statements.)

Products and Service

As technology improved, product life cycles, as well as prices, decreased. As a result, margins decreased. Under Best Buy's service model, shorter product life cycles increased training costs. Employees were forced to learn new products with higher frequency. This was not only costly but also increased the likelihood that employees would make mistakes, thereby tarnishing Best Buy's service record and potentially damaging one of its most important, if not its most important, differentiators. In addition, more resources would be directed at research of new products to make sure Best Buy continued to offer the products consumers desire.

One social threat to the retail industry was the growing popularity of the online marketplace. Internet shoppers could browse sites searching for the best deals on specific products. This technology allowed consumers to become more educated about their purchases, while creating increased downward price pressure. Ambitious consumers could play the role of a Best Buy associate themselves by doing product comparisons and information gathering without a trip to the store. This emerging trend created a direct threat to companies like Best Buy, which had 1023 stores in its domestic market alone. One way Best Buy tried to continue the demand for brick-and-mortar locations and counter the threat of Internet-based competition was by providing value-added services in stores. Customer service, repairs, and interactive product displays were just a few examples of these services.[22]

Leadership

The two former CEOs of Best Buy, Richard Shultze and Brad Anderson, were extremely successful at making the correct strategic moves at the appropriate times. With Brad Anderson stepping aside in June 2009, Brian Dunn replaced him as the new CEO. Although Dunn worked for the company for 24 years and held the key positions of COO and President during his tenure, the position of CEO brought him to a whole new level and presented new challenges, especially during the economic downturn. He was charged with leading Best Buy into the world of increased connectivity. This required a revamping of products and store setups to serve customers in realizing their connectivity needs. This was a daunting task for an experienced CEO, let alone a new CEO who had never held the position.

Wal-Mart

Best Buy saw its largest rival, Circuit City, go bankrupt. However, a new archrival, Wal-Mart, was expanding into consumer electronics and stepping up competition in a price war Wal-Mart hoped to win. Best Buy needed to face the competition not by lowering prices, but by coming up with something really different. Best Buy had to determine the correct path to improve its ability to differentiate itself from competitors, which was increasingly difficult given an adverse economic climate and the company's financial stress. How Best Buy could maintain innovative products, top-notch employees, and superior customer service while facing increased competition and operational costs was an open question.

NOTES

1. Best Buy Co. Inc., *Form 10-K*. Securities and Exchange Commission, February 28, 2009.
2. Ibid.
3. Ibid.
4. Greg Keller, "Threat Grows by iPod and Laptop," *The Columbus Dispatch*, May 18, 2009, http://www.dispatch.com/live/content/business/stories/2009/05/18/greener_gadgets.ART_ART_05-18-09_A9_TMDSJR8.html (July 10, 2009).
5. Larry Magid, "Consumer Electronics: Future Looks Bright," *CBSNews.com*, May 2, 2008, http://www.cbsnews.com/stories/2008/05/02/scitech/pcanswer/main4067008.shtml (July 10, 2009).
6. Best Buy Co. Inc., *Form 10-K*, 2009.
7. Ibid.
8. Ibid.
9. Ibid.
10. Manhattan Institute for Policy Research, "They're Making a Federal Case Out of It . . . in State Court," *Civil Justice Report* 3, 2001, http://www.manhattan-institute.org/html/cjr_3_part2.htm.
11. "Best Buy Bombshell!" *HD Guru*, March 21, 2009, http://hdguru.com/best-buy-bombshell/.
12. Circuit City Stores Inc. was an American retailer in brand-name consumer electronics, personal computers, entertainment software, and (until 2000) large appliances. The company opened its first store in 1949 and liquidated its final American retail stores in 2009 following a bankruptcy filing and subsequent failure to find a buyer. At the time of liquidation, Circuit City was the second-largest U.S. electronics retailer, after Best Buy.
13. Z. Bissonnette, "Wal-Mart Looks to Expand Electronics Business," Bloggingstocks.com, May 18, 2009, http://www.bloggingstocks.com/2009/05/18/wal-mart-looks-to-expand-electronics-business/.
14. N. Maestrie, "Wal-Mart Steps Up Consumer Electronics Push," *Reuters*, May 19, 2009, http://www.reuters.com/article/technologyNews/idUSTRE54I4TR20090519.

15. Capital IQ, "GameStop Corp. Corporate Tearsheet," *Capital IQ,* 2009.

16. E. Sherman, "GameStop Faces Pain from Best Buy, Downloading," *BNET Technology,* June 24, 2009, http://industry .bnet.com/technology/10002329/gamestop-faces-pain-from-best-buy-downloading/.

17. T. Van Riper, "RadioShack Gets Slammed," *Forbes.com,* February 17, 2006, http://www.forbes.com/2006/02/17/radioshack-edmondson-retail_cx_tr_0217radioshack.html.

18. Capital IQ, "Amazon.com Corporate Tearsheet," *Capital IQ,* 2009.

19. T. Kee, "Netflix Beware: Best Buy Adds Digital Downloads with CinemaNow Deal," *paidContent.org,* June 5, 2009, http://paidcontent.org/article/419-best-buy-adds-digital-movie-downloads-with-cinemanow-deal/.

20. Best Buy Co., Inc., *Form 10-K,* 2009.

21. Ibid.

22. Ibid.

Target Corp's Tarnished Reputation: Failure in Canada and a Massive Data Breach

Alan N. Hoffman
Bentley University

and

Natalia Gold
Northeastern University

Company Background

Target Corporation's vision was to offer customers everyday essentials and fashionable, differentiated merchandise at discount prices, including apparel and accessories, home décor and furniture, electronics, office supplies, toys, health and beauty products, food, pet supplies, and pharmacy products and services.[1] Traditionally, Target sold its own brands, as well as specialized merchandise through periodic exclusive design and creative partnerships. The company also generated revenue from in-store amenities such as Target Photo, and leased or licensed departments such as Target Optical and Starbucks. For the fiscal year ending January 31, 2015, the company generated over $72.6 billion in annual revenue from continuing operations at its 1,790 stores spread across all 50 states in the United States, a figure that represented an increase of $1.34 billion or 1.9% over the previous fiscal year's revenue.

The author thanks Barbara Gottfried and Bentley University MBA students Mohammad Almodaifer, Shailja Dedakia, Tejaswini Rao, Soumya Shetty and Lindsey Theriault for their research and contributions to this case. Please address all correspondence to: Dr. Alan N. Hoffman, Dept. of Management, Bentley University, 175 Forest Street, Waltham, MA 02452-4705, ahoffman@bentley.edu, (781) 891-2287. Printed by permission of Dr. Alan N. Hoffman.

Founded by George Dayton, a bank and real estate investor, Target began as the Dayton Dry Goods Company in Minneapolis, Minnesota in 1902. Dayton and his department store chain became known for dependable merchandise, fair business practices, and a generous spirit of giving, the core of the business from its inception through its more than 100-year history. When Dayton passed away in 1938, his son and grandsons took over and began to grow the Dayton Company into a nationwide retailer. In 1961, Douglas Dayton and his leadership team saw an opportunity to develop a new kind of mass-market discount store that catered to value-oriented shoppers seeking high quality that would become "Target." After significant growth on a regional scale, the company was ready for national expansion with an Initial Public Offering (IPO) on October 18, 1967.[2] The common stock was listed on the New York Stock Exchange under the symbol "TGT." Doug Dayton's vision for the company was to create "a shopping experience that would be fun, delightful, and welcoming to the entire family, [in] stores that would include wide aisles, easy-to-shop displays, fast checkout, and well-lighted parking [lots]."[3] Doug Dayton and his brothers also prioritized programs that fostered strong leadership in its store managers, founding the company's "Target Business College" which worked toward developing and retaining superior managerial talent. The Dayton brothers shared a passion for volunteerism as well, and established a renowned corporate-giving program. From 1946 on, the corporation gave 5% of its pretax profit back to the community in support of education, the arts, social services, and volunteerism.

By 1979, Target Stores had reached an organizational milestone of $1 billion in annual sales from 74 stores in 11 states. Over the next decade, Target invested in innovative technology and became the first mass merchandiser to introduce UPC scanning at its stores and distribution centers. UPC scanning made for a more efficient shopping experience for customers and team members, as it improved Target's inventory management system, increased automation, and reduced the wait time in checkout lines. Throughout the 1990s and 2000s, Target continued to innovate in ways that improved customer experience. The company introduced a grocery section in many stores and became a USDA certified organic produce retailer; created the ClearRx pharmacy program with easy-to-read medicine bottles and color-coded rings; and unveiled GO International to provide affordable fashion created by emerging designers around the world. In the years after 2008, Target made a conscious effort to build its mobile and online presence so that customers could use those platforms to navigate Target stores, refill prescriptions, browse the weekly Ad, and pick up online orders in stores. Target also began expanding into urban areas by creating CityTarget stores which offered an assortment of everyday essential products appropriately sized for city dwellers.

2013: The Data Breach

As discount retailing became ever more competitive, Target faced significant challenges. Competitors such as Wal-mart put downward pressure on prices at Target, which in turn had to match those prices to satisfy customers. Amazon also emerged as a fierce competitor, and Target had to struggle to leverage technological innovation and interact with consumers to the same degree as its competitors.

During the fourth quarter holiday season in 2013, Target learned of a massive data breach in its system, and had to acknowledge that criminal hackers had stolen the credit and debit card information of 40 million customers. In 2014, the company revealed that additional personal information, such as email and mailing addresses, had been stolen from 70 million to 110 million people with some overlap between the two groups. After these revelations, Target sales weakened significantly, and cashiers temporarily stopped asking shoppers if they were interested in participating in Target's REDcard program. In a bid to rescue its image and its business, Target announced plans to invest $5 million in new security measures and offered customers a free year of credit monitoring and identity theft protection. While Target's management did not expect the incident to have a long-term impact on the company's relationship with its customers, the breach nevertheless had a negative impact on Target's reputation and sales. In March 2015, Target agreed to a $10 million dollar settlement with the victims of the data breach, who stood to collect up to $10,000 each in damages.

The Disastrous Canadian Expansion (2011–2014)

Target also met with disastrous results in its expansion into the Canadian market. In 2011, Target acquired 133 Zellers sites across Canada that it reopened as Target stores in 2013. However, the stores failed to meet demand due to inventory software constraints and other expansion issues. A major reason for the operational failure was the company's entering into the Canadian market by purchasing all the stores of a failed retailer, a move that seemed prudent but actually saddled the Canadian unit with inconveniently located stores that weren't built for Target's well-known layout.

Opening so many stores at once in a brand new market strained the company's logistics infrastructure and left Canadians staring at empty shelves. At the same time, this increase in operational scale made it difficult for the company to scale down during times of slowing sales. Target's major operational failure in Canada turned out to be a huge loss for the company. After careful review of all options, the company was unable to find a realistic scenario that could get Target Canada to profitability before 2021 and decided instead to close all 189 of its Canadian stores in January 2015.[4]

Strategic Direction

Target's brand promise, "Expect More. Pay Less" succinctly expressed its mission to become customers' preferred shopping destination by offering high quality affordable products and services, continuous innovation, and exceptional customer experiences to satisfy customer needs, simplify their lives, and deliver outstanding value. To do so in the face of stiff competition, Target differentiated itself by combining the better quality fashion aspect of a higher-end retailer with the low prices of a discount store. It also offered price matching and an additional 5% savings when customers used its REDcard loyalty program as part of its commitment to making sure customers got "more for their money" every time they shopped.

To further distinguish itself, Target prioritized innovative design, positive employer/employee relations for positive employee attitudes, diversity, and strong community relations through community giving. Its store layouts were designed to create a fun, energetic, and inviting atmosphere to engage shoppers, and its employees were encouraged to see themselves as "team members" to enhance customer experience by providing friendly and efficient service. In addition, the company strove to foster an inclusive culture, hiring a diverse workforce and making sure everyone felt welcome, valued, and respected. Team members were supported with training and development opportunities, and encouraged to innovate, contribute ideas, and discover solutions to improve customer experience. Diversity was viewed as intrinsic to every aspect of Target's business, from team membership, to those in its supply chain, to the communities in which the company operated, important for developing lasting relationships and leveraging partners' talents to drive innovation and success. Finally, community giving was fundamental to the company ethos: Target regularly pledged 5% of its income to local groups and encouraged employees to donate their time, talent, and business strengths to various community initiatives.[5]

At a recent investors meeting, Target Chairman and CEO Brian Cornell and his leadership team presented the vision and strategies they hoped would transform Target's competitive edge in the near future with renewed emphasis on innovation and putting customers first. They planned to increase focus on the company's omni-channel evolution; further develop merchandise categories that would differentiate Target from its competitors; tailor a more personal approach for individual customers; and implement more flexible store formats such as TargetExpress and City Target. A thorough strategic analysis of the business revealed that customers who shopped both in Target stores and on Target's website generated three times as many sales as those who shopped only in the stores.[6] In response, the company decided to take a channel neutral approach to growing its business, driving a total Target experience across stores, online, and on mobile platforms. However, Target's perhaps appropriately aggressive sales objectives—to grow in-store sales by 2 to 3% annually and online sales by 40%—would require significant enhancements to the company's technology, supply chain, and inventory management systems.

In 2014, four merchandise categories (style, baby, kids, and wellness) accounted for more than 25% of Target's sales. Moving forward, Target planned to invest more resources in those key areas, focusing on newness and differentiation for greater consumer value. Another corporate objective was to create a more customer-centric experience by using demographics, climate, location, and other customer-led factors to drive store and online purchasing, and build up its data analytics to deliver a more personalized digital experience by tailoring promotional offerings to specific customers. The company also planned store expansions that would focus on new, more flexible formats to cater to rapidly growing dense urban populations, testing new layouts to ensure that each store opened was the right fit for each community. Target hoped to realize cost savings of $2 billion over the two years 2015–2016 by establishing leaner operations to make the company more agile, even while planning to invest $1 billion in technology and supply chain improvements in 2015.

Target's Competitors

Target's prime competitors in the discount retail chain market were Wal-Mart Stores Inc., Costco Wholesale Corporation, Sears Holdings, and Amazon.com. The company's competitors in related industries such as electronics, grocery, drug, department, and home furnishings stores were Macy's, Burlington Stores, Dillard's Inc., Dollar General Corporation, Dollar Tree Inc., Family Dollar Stores, J.C Penney, and Kohl's. As of 2015, Target was the second largest discount store chain in the United States, with a market share of about 2.5% in the retail category.

Wal-Mart Inc.

In the fiscal year 2014 Wal-Mart, a top competitor in the discount stores segment, generated revenue of $485.65B. Prior to 2014, Wal-Mart had seen its revenues rise by 16% while Target's revenues only increased by 12.9%.

Like Target, Wal-Mart maintained a reputation for convenience, value for money, and offering a wide range of products all in one store. Its core competencies in information systems and cost leadership strategy were used very effectively to identify better ways to perform tasks, manage stores, and stock the shelves. Its size allowed Wal-Mart to exercise power in relation to suppliers by demanding lower prices; and its best practices allowed it the flexibility to improvise its inventory and supply chain management whenever necessary. Wal-Mart's international success and Target's failure in Canada posed a huge threat to Target's future operations.

Amazon Inc.

Target was slow to provide customers with a satisfying online retail shopping experience. Amazon, its biggest competitor in that realm, reported revenues of $88.99B, constantly edging out Wal-Mart and Target in online sales for a variety of products (though it was necessary for shoppers to keep close tabs on Amazon's fluctuating prices). Amazon had had the foresight to build its fulfillment centers near airports, which proved a highly successful strategy for providing expedited shipping. While Amazon's major weakness, its lack of profit on its financial statements, raised concerns for its investors, its stellar record of innovation and reshaping the consumer experience on line assured its number one place in online retailing.

Barriers to Entry/Imitation

Historically, three major barriers to entry into the discounted retail segment industry—customer captivity, proprietary technology, and economies of scale—tamped down competition as the companies already occupying this segment had daunting competitive advantages in these categories. For example, Amazon and Wal-Mart were ahead in deploying technology for inventory management and supply chain; Target had the advantage of providing customers with relatively high-quality products at low prices. The companies in this segment were huge, yet their operating margins were low. A company could enter this market only if it could compete with the prices that were offered by these retail giants, which would require massive capital investment and access to prime locations.

Target had stronger product quality than its main competitors, and exclusive partnerships with designers. Its differentiation strategy of offering designer brands, owned brands, and signature national brands had proved very successful. Twenty percent of the brands sold in Target Stores were private; and 22 of those brands were sold exclusively at Target. For example, Target partnered with Peter Pilotto for apparel, Chris March for Halloween wigs, and Justin Timberlake for his special edition CD. Target's image, compared to that of Amazon and Wal-mart, was that of an upscale discount retailer. Target's strong customer service component also distinguished it. For example, 43% of Target's customers were parents with children, thus Target designed its new shopping carts with built in baby seats for customer convenience. Target also gained substantial PR from its huge number of followers on Instagram and YouTube.

Sustainability

In recent years, critics, investors, and customers have become increasingly concerned with all companies' ongoing environmental sustainability efforts. Wal-Mart took the lead in this important area. Rising demand for organic and eco-friendly products required companies to abide by laws regulating sustainability, follow sustainable practices, and ensure their suppliers followed environmentally friendly practices. Target made commitments to ensure its packaging included recycled and renewable content; to build an energy efficient IT network and implement technology that reduced greenhouse gas emissions; and to create buildings that used space more efficiently and that were located in areas convenient to customers and team members, and enhanced local communities.

Finance

Analysts considered Target a seasonal business because its Q4 (Oct–Dec) and Q1 (Jan–Mar) were its highest revenue periods. While the company had been growing for decades, it had a hectic year in 2014 after its data breach and failed expansion into Canada. Its 2013 strategy in Canada had been to cut prices below its COGS just to increase its market share in Canada, but that led to shrinking its overall margins.

By the end of Q1 FY2015 Target sales had topped $ 21.75 billion—its peak seasonal sales as compared to $20.893 billion for Q4 of FY2014, a 4.1% increase (see **Exhibits 1 & 2**)

EXHIBIT 1
Target Income Statement

Consolidated Statements of Operations

(millions, except per share data)	2014	2013	2012
Sales	$ 72.618	$ 71,279	$ 71,960
Credit card revenues	—	—	1,341
Total revenues	72,618	71,279	73,301
Cost of sales	51,278	50,039	50,568
Selling, general and administrative expenses	14,676	14,465	14,643
Credit card expenses	—	—	467
Depreciation and amortization	2,129	1,996	2,044
Gain an receivables transaction	—	(391)	(161)
Earnings from continuing operations before interest expense and income taxes	4,535	5,170	5,740
Net interest expense	882	1.049	684
Earnings from continuing operations before income taxes	3,653	4,121	5,056
Provision for income taxes	1,204	1,427	1,741
Net earnings from continuing operations	2,449	2,694	3,315
Discontinued operations, net of tax	(4,085)	(723)	(316)
Net (loss)/earnings	$ (1,636)	$ 1,971	$ 2,999
Basic (loss)/earnings per share			
Continuing operations	$ 3.86	$ 4.24	$ 5.05
Discontinued operations	(6.44)	(1.14)	(0.48)
Net (loss)/earnings per share	$ (2.58)	$ 3.10	$ 4 57
Diluted (loss)/earnings per share			
Continuing operations	$ 3.83	$ 4 20	$ 5 00
Discontinued operations	(6.38)	(1.13)	(0.48)
Net (loss)/earnings per share	$ (2.56)	$ 3.07	$ 4 52
Weighted average common shares outstanding			
Basic	634.7	635.1	656.7
Dilutive effect of share-based awards	5.4	6.7	6.6
Diluted	640.1	641.3	663.3
Antidilutive shares	3.3	2.3	5.0

See accompanying Notes to consolidated Financial Statements

Consolidated Statements of Comprehensive Income

(millions)	2014	2013	2012
Net (loss)/income	$ (1,636)	$ 1,971	$ 2,999
Other comprehensive income/(loss), net of tax			
Pension and other benefit liabilities, net of (benefit)/provision for taxes of $(90), $71 and $58	(139)	110	02
Currency translation adjustment and cash flow hedges, net of provision for taxes of $2, $11 and $8	431	(425)	13
Other comprehensive income/(loss)	292	(315)	105
Comprehensive (loss)/income	$ (1,344)	$ 1,656	$ 3,104

See accompanying Notes to consolidated Financial Statements.

EXHIBIT 2
Target Balance Sheet

Consolidated Statements of Financial Position

(millions, except footnotes)	January 31, 2015	February 1, 2014
Assets		
Cash and cash equivalents, including short-term investments of $1.520 and $3	$ 2.210	$ 670
Inventory	8,790	8,278
Assets of discontinued operations	1,333	793
Other current assets	1,754	1,832
Total current assets	14,087	11,573
Properly and equipment		
Land	6.127	6.143
Buildings and improvements	26,614	25.984
Fixtures and equipment	5,346	5,199
Computer hardware and software	2,553	2,395
Construction-in-progress	424	757
Accumulated depreciation	(15.106)	(14.066)
Property and equipment, net	25,958	26,412
Noncurrent assets of discontinued operations	442	5,461
Other noncurrent assets	917	1,107
Total assets	$ 41,404	$ 44,553
Liabilities and shareholders' investment		
Accounts payable	$ 7.759	$ 7.335
Accrued and other current liabilities	3,783	3,610
Current portion of long-term debt and other borrowings	91	1,143
Liabilities of discontinued operations	103	689
Total current liabilities	11,736	12,777
Long-term debt and other borrowings	12,705	11.429
Deferred income taxes	1,321	1,349
Noncurrent liabilities of discontinued operations	193	1,296
Other noncurrent liabilities	1,452	1,471
Total noncurrent liabilities	15,671	15,545

(continued)

EXHIBIT 2
(continued)

Shareholders' investment		
Common stock	53	53
Additional paid-in capital	4,899	4,470
Retained earnings	9,644	12,599
Accumulated other comprehensive loss		
Pension and other benefit liabilities	(561)	(422)
Currency translation adjustment and cash flow hedges	(38)	(469)
Total shareholders' investment	13,997	16,231
Total liabilities and shareholders' investment	$ 41,404	$ 44,553

Common Stock Authorized 6,000,000,000 shares, $0.0833 par value; 640,213,987 shares Issued outstanding at January 31, 2015;632,930,740 shares issued and outstanding at February 1, 2014.

Preferred Stock Authorized 5,000,000 shares, $0.01 par value; no shares were Issued or outstanding at January 31, 2015 or February 1, 2014.

See accompanying Notes to Consolidated Financial Statements.

even as pressure from the market for low prices during peak seasons had forced Target to cut its prices. Annual growth from FY2014 to FY2015 was 1.9%. Its net operating margin shrank during FY2014 and FY2015 as a result of price cutting in its Canadian stores where income margins fell to 1.34% in Q2 FY2015, compared to 4.2% in Q2 FY2013. However, the company predicted margins would recover after it shut down its Canadian stores, and the day Target announced the termination of its Canadian operations, its stock price rose 37% from $60 to $82.

Marketing

In fiscal 2014, Target Corporation spent $1.7 billion on advertising, $.3 billion more than the $1.4 billion spent in fiscal 2013. Newspaper circulars, Internet ads, and broadcast media made up the majority of the company's advertising costs. Target was facing increased downward pressure on prices from online retailers, particularly Amazon, and also had to adapt to the "showrooming" that occurred when customers browsed items in Target stores then used their smartphones to check prices and buy from cheaper online sites. To stay competitive, Target decided to match Amazon's prices and offered free Wi-Fi in its stores, in-store pickup of online orders, and in-store concierges offering tips, recommendations, and other enhanced customer services.

Target further committed to improving its own online customer experience, launching a pilot program, Target Subscriptions, and establishing an innovation center in San Francisco to foster online and mobile business growth. In its advertising the company increasingly emphasized the value pricing promised in its slogan, "Expect More, Pay Less," over its earlier emphasis on differentiation. This shift of focus to pricing and value succeeded in improving the company's competitiveness, enabling the company to tap the constantly growing market of customers opting for lower priced merchandise. Target's website was redesigned to include product recommendations, enhanced registries and lists, integrated community features, and social networking integration. Target also focused on increasing its online presence through acquisitions.

The key to Target's success was its strategy of positioning itself as a high-style brand despite its low prices to attract shoppers who would ordinarily avoid discount retailers. It did this with clever, eye-catching marketing and a series of partnerships with high-profile design-oriented suppliers. Target Corp. provided an excellent example of a content-based strategy with "A Bullseye View." Revamped and re-launched, its website told "a deeper story" about Target to media members and other influencers, significant in terms of online marketing as many brands were only just beginning to focus on content, whereas Target was ahead of the curve in presenting its audience with innovative content. With celebrity assets such as Jay Leno, Solange Knowles, and Maria Sharapova, Target's Internet marketing strategy generated about 40 million-plus unique monthly visitors and its website became the fourth most-visited retail website in the United States.

Target also applied an integrated design philosophy to everything from visually appealing building exteriors and an award-winning mobile app, to innovative tools and systems such that all aspects of the Target interface cohered to create a satisfying customer experience. The Target mobile app was very successful in offering personal, easy, and convenient options for customers to shop whenever and however they wanted. Target's marketing 2015 campaign featured three of its solutions-focused initiatives—subscriptions, store pickup, and Cartwheel, which was designed to help customers save time and money and stay organized—which were highlighted in TV spots and online educational videos explaining how they worked.

Also key for Target was its "REDcard," its proprietary credit and debit card, that encouraged customer loyalty and drove sales by offering customers a 5% discount every time they used their REDcards.

Operations and Logistics

Target had always combined great leadership and operational savvy with cutting-edge technologies to optimize its supply chain network. After its operational failure in Canada, Target's primary objective was to operate as a single segment throughout the United States. The company decided that the leadership team for each store would include at least seven executive level managers counting the Store Team Leader or General Manager, and each would be assigned a strategic department of expertise: Soft Lines, Hard Lines, Asset Protection, Guest Services/Front End, Logistics, Human Resources, and Store Team Leader. High volume and SuperTarget stores would have at least one additional Logistics/Replenishment Executive Team Leader, an Executive Operations Team Leader, and an Executive Food Team Leader. The company also turned its attention to its business-to-business subsidiary, Target Commercial Interiors (TCI), which operated about a half-dozen showrooms in Illinois, Minnesota, and Wisconsin providing office products and services. The interior design company, whose clients included some of America's largest companies, wanted to expand by marketing its products and services to small and midsize companies.

Through store level data analysis techniques, Target identified opportunities that were lost when data was aggregated at the chain level rather than store by store—opportunities that, the company predicted, could substantially improve its week-in/week-out ability to forecast sales, plan promotions, and optimize its supply chain. Logistic operational experts, who went on to work for the Capital Ladder Advisory Group, were hired to streamline the early morning logistic process at Target to help the company increase profitability and deliver a clean, clutter-free experience to customers every day. The success of this partnership effectively saved Target $475 million in expenses over the three years from 2012 through 2014. Target continued to foster its greatest strength—its ability to do outbound logistics—which helped it to differentiate from other low cost leaders by emphasizing its brand as more upscale and trendier, and to capitalize on the weaknesses of other low cost leaders by creating a higher scale in-store atmosphere, and more space.

Target also realized it needed to build on relationships already established with suppliers rather than abusing them from a price/profit standpoint simply because they could, a strategy that wouldn't foster long-term relationships or even fit its partnership philosophy. However, it became increasingly clear that Target needed to better understand its own systems such as TLO and POL; even its supply chain experts had a hard time understanding how to fix opportunities. Target suffered a huge decline in overall net profit growth during the financial crisis that began in 2008, partly because its operational size could not be scaled down fast enough. While the thousands of Wal-Mart stores operated 24 hours a day, Target stores did not, a disadvantage in times of crisis. Logistic processes were the heart of Target Store operations, and accounted for much of the operational effectiveness of any given store. If the logistic process was broken, the chain's entire operation was also broken. The leadership teams knew operations could be fixed, but that it would take increased proficiency levels to achieve operational success and respond to customer demand more effectively.

One weak spot for Target was its inventory system software whose main function was to fuel the logistics processes. The company itself seemed to recognize the system's deficiencies, as it added an In-Stocks process. The flawed inventory system software also added to employment and labor costs, especially as the logistics work center became the source of the highest rate of attrition at Target. The inventory and logistics processes simply did not operate the way they should have, hurting the company's overall net profit. In short Target's scalability left it more vulnerable to downturns in the economy than Wal-Mart.

Human Resources

Target had made it a goal to offer a wide variety of job opportunities throughout its operations, from its retail stores to its distribution centers and corporate offices. Over the 20 years prior to 2015, Target scaled stores to achieve levels of productivity outlined by executive level managers. Based on the operational demands of the average Target store,

Target determined that the appropriate mix of full-time and part-time employees was a 63–37 split in favor of full-time employees. This ratio of full to part time was among the retail industry's highest. In addition, Target implemented many important human resource policies, from its hiring practices and diversity efforts, to the benefits offered employees. Target defined diversity as individuality incorporating differences of race, gender, sexual orientation, education and life experiences, and physical ability, and instituted specific recruiting efforts to hire teams characterized by diversity on all of these fronts.

Target was always known as a reputable company and fun place to work with good benefits, yielding very high employee satisfaction. As one of its most effective benefits, Target provided educational opportunities for employees to build on their skills, thereby attracting a significant number of young college graduates as an appealing stepping stone for those just starting their careers. At the same time, Target's hiring philosophy consisted of not only hiring recent grads but seasoned retail management team leaders from outside the company as well. Whereas Wal-Mart hired both graduates and non-graduates with equivalent management experience as leadership personnel for their stores, only 10% of Target's Executive Team leadership were promoted from within without four-year college degrees, landing it among the bottom 15% of *Fortune* 500 companies when it came to promoting from within. Nevertheless, Target's hiring practices resulted in benefit to the consumer, as the average Target Executive Team Leader was much more customer focused than the average Wal-Mart Executive/ Assistant manager.

One downside of Target's large organizational structure was that it required a lot of meetings and red tape. Decisions often needed to go through many layers, and unless an employee was specifically on a strategy team or at the director level, strategic vision was typically not a primary focus. Rising labor costs also became a major concern for those responsible for Target's bottom line: the federal minimum wage, which had remained at $5.15 per hour since 1998, increased to $5.85 per hour in 2008, $6.55 per hour in 2009, and $7.25 per hour in 2010, with further hikes projected, and many states and municipalities had minimum wage rates even higher than $7.25 per hour in response to higher costs of living. Rising wage and healthcare costs had the potential to hold down profit margins. In addition, Target's failed expansion into Canada had significant one-time costs. Target Canada had 133 stores across the country and employed approximately 17,600 people. To ensure fair treatment of Target Canada employees, the Target Corporation sought the Court's approval to make voluntary cash contributions of C$70 million (approximately US$59 million) to an Employee Trust that would provide Target Canada-based employees not required for the full wind-down period a minimum of 16 weeks' compensation, including wage and benefits coverage while Target Canada stores remained open during the liquidation process. This operational failure resulted in a huge financial loss for the company.

Core Competencies

First and foremost, Target made sure its brand was widely recognized in the U.S. market, by utilizing strategic placement of its logo on all merchandise, media communications, and events. According to a recent survey conducted by Target, 96 % of Americans recognized the Target bullseye logo. At the same time, Target traditionally differentiated itself by providing exclusive private brands and designer products along with everyday essentials at attractive prices, capitalizing on quality products and affordable prices. The company introduced its first design partnership in 1999, in collaboration with the architect Michael Graves. By 2015, Target had over $1 billion of owned and exclusive brands. The company also formed partnerships with high-profile, design-oriented suppliers including Neiman Marcus, Lilly Pulitzer, Burt's Bees, Massimo, Isaac Mizrahi, Liz Lange, Kashi, and many more, launching these brands and partnerships through limited edition lines or by stocking the brands for a limited time. These designer brands generally yielded higher margins than equivalent national brands and represented a significant portion of Target's overall sales. The company further enhanced the value of these brands by using celebrities such as Jay Leno, Solange Knowles, and Maria Sharapova to promote them.

Ultimately, Target struck an effective balance between fashion and price, and its strong product/service assortment became one of its key competitive advantages. Target had always positioned itself as an upscale discount chain with a bright and attractive environment, known for carrying discount designer clothes and home decor under the same roof as detergent and dishwashing liquid. Target thus positioned itself to attract customers from a wide spectrum of demographics, and as the U.S. economy exited one of its worst slowdowns, consumers evidenced more willingness to spend on Target's quality and exclusive products.

Another aspect of Target's success was its goal of providing a more pleasing shopping experience than that of its competitors. Target recognized that many customers preferred wider aisles, less crowding, easier checkouts, with pricing that remained competitive. In addition, the company provided effective on-floor assistance (such as price checkers, on-floor customer service representatives, etc.), as well as savings programs through options such as the REDcard. According to industry analysts, new REDcard holders spent 50% to 150% more than typical customers, and made 8–10 more visits per year, evidence customers were satisfied with the program and benefiting from it.

Target's Challenges Going Forward

Especially after the Canada debacle, it became clear that Target had challenges that had to be met. Its inventory management system was inefficient and costly, leading to empty shelves, which had a direct negative impact on customers and thus on brand perception. The flawed inventory system software also added to employment and labor costs for Target. The company saw the greatest attrition from the logistics work center. The in-stocks team process was designed to cover every shelf space and SKU in the store. The team aimed to scan every SKU during the course of a week to monitor shelved product levels so that in-stock products could to be brought to the sales floor from the backroom should the shelved product be low or out, and out of stock products could be re-ordered. However, the in-stock process essentially duplicated the efforts of the logistics processes. Unfortunately, the inventory system employed by Target was prone to errors and created artificial holes in the logistic process that the in-stock team aimed to fill. The logistic process was supposed to fill the shelves according to the inventory system software that dictated what was needed on the sales floor and what should be sent directly to the backroom when it arrived on the daily 53' trailer, but it did not.

Further, the company's inability to scale the inventory up or down depending on economic conditions and demand was a primary reason why Target failed in its expansion efforts in Canada. The improvements needed required not only investment in technology but also investment in centralized teams assigned to assess and monitor current systems and recommend changes as needed.

Target's online presence was another area of weakness. While the company had made some improvements in its website and mobile applications, it struggled to attract and retain a base of online shoppers. As online shopping was so prevalent, it became increasingly important that Target innovate in this area to keep its market share on a par with competitors such as Wal-Mart and Amazon.

Finally, Target had difficulty accurately forecasting consumer demand. From the company's earliest days as an apparel company, it kept its inventory lean to preserve profits in an industry known for low margins. However, the downside of lean inventory was missing out on sales and disappointing customers who got to the store only to find empty shelves. An example of keeping the inventory too lean undercut Target's recent partnership with Lilly Pulitzer, an American fashion brand featuring bright, colorful, floral prints. It was wildly successful: Lilly for Target items sold out within hours of the brand's debut on Target's website. Loyal Target customers were frustrated and voiced their opinion that faulty insight into consumer demand was indicative of larger problems at Target. Even with a robust inventory management system in place, Target ran out of products and could not meet consumer demand. The situation was particularly problematic for Target because it prevented the company from fulfilling its core mission; if items were out-of-stock, Target was not able to meet customers' expectations, and customers would then leave the store empty-handed and frustrated. The situation was complicated by an inefficient inventory management system that required manual fixes by in-store teams to combat system errors, which resulted in higher labor, storage, and transportation costs than those incurred by Target's competitors.

REFERENCES

1. http://www.bidnessetc.com/25361-target-corporation-will-new-strategies-turn-it-around/2/
2. https://corporate.target.com/about/history/Target-through-the-years
3. https://corporate.target.com/article/2013/07/a-vision-on-target-remembering-doug-dayton
4. http://fortune.com/target-new-ceo/
5. http://www.sec.gov/Archives/edgar/data/27419/000002741915000012/tgt-20150131x10k.htm
6. http://finance.yahoo.com/news/target-shares-roadmap-transform-business-213100357.html

Staples: The Fierce Battle Between Brick and Mortar vs. Online Sales

Alan N. Hoffman
Bentley University

Natalia Gold
Northeastern University

Company Background

In 1985, when Tom Stemberg couldn't find a replacement printer cartridge over a holiday weekend, he came up with the idea of making office supplies more accessible and affordable, founding Staples, Inc. in November 1985 with Leo Kahn. The first Staples Office Superstore opened in May,1986 in Brighton, Massachusetts, offering one-stop shopping for office supplies, computers, and furniture.[1] In 1989, Staples went public and raised $36 million through its IPO.[1] In 1990, Staples began purchasing products overseas and formed a subsidiary, Total Global Sourcing, Inc., to handle international buying. By the end of that same year, Staples had expanded into Brighton, Massachusetts, California, with sales nearly reaching the $300 million mark, then invested in its first foreign venture, The Business

The author would like to thank Barbara Gottfried and Pamela Miller and Bentley University students Alana Aharonov, Mike Burton, James Duong, Gregory Dwyer, Nick Morganis, and Zach Cantor for their research and contributions to this case. Please address all correspondence to: *Dr. Alan N. Hoffman*, Dept. of Management, Bentley University, 175 Forest Street, Waltham, MA 02452-4705, ahoffman@bentley.edu. (781) 891-2287. Printed by permission of Dr. Alan N. Hoffman.

Depot, Ltd., a new Canadian office superstore it bought out in 1994. In 1992, Staples further expanded in the United States through the purchase of Office Mart Holding Corporation, thereby acquiring ten Workplace stores in Florida, and competing directly with the Florida-based Office Depot. Later that year, Staples expanded into Germany by acquiring a 48% interest in MAXI-Papier which operated in five German cities. Staples also signed a partnership agreement with Kingfisher plc, in the United Kingdom to further its European expansion. By1995, Staples had bought out both Maxi-Papier and Kingfisher plc.[1] Ten years later, Staples had expanded further into Europe and launched its expansion into Latin American countries and China, then Taiwan through a joint venture. By the time of the 2014 announcement that it would close 225 stores, Staples had grown to be the largest office supplies superstore chain in the world, with more than 2,200 stores in Europe, Asia, North and South America, and Australia.[2]

In addition to acquisitions and expansion, Staples offered new innovative services. Following its west coast expansion in 1990, Staples introduced a new retail concept known as Staples Express, designed to appeal to small business operators in urban areas and geared towards quick trips and impulse buying during lunch breaks or after work. These stores were typically only a third as large as the suburban stores, with half the stock.[1] The Express stores were part of Staples's strategy to dominate the office supplies market through three distribution channels: suburban superstores, urban mini-stores, and phone-in direct delivery service.[1] In 2003, Staples introduced its "Easy" brand which focused on converting stores from a warehouse design to a boutique look to make it easier and faster for customers to find what they were looking for.[1] In 2010, Staples launched Staples Advantage, its business-to-business website for customers to order everything they needed for their business from one website and have it shipped directly to their office, reducing supplier invoices and red tape through one accountable and convenient ordering site.[3] In 2011, Staples went on to make ordering even more convenient by creating a mobile app that allowed customers to purchase all of their supplies directly from their mobile devices.

In 2012, Staples introduced "smart-size" boxes, custom-made to fit each customer's order. This innovative idea was more convenient for customers as they did not need to break down oversized boxes; it reduced Staples' carbon footprint by 30,200 tons (or 120,000 trees); and it increased operational efficiency by allowing more shipments to fit on each line haul and more orders in each delivery truck.[3]

Strategic Direction

Staples' vision was to provide every product that your business needs to succeed. Its main objectives were to provide superior value via a broad selection of products and services, and to accelerate growth in its online businesses. The company's focus on convenience and a wide range of product offerings made it the world's largest and the Internet's second largest office supplies retailer,[4] with a dominant 36.5% of the office supplies industry. In 2012, Staples generated $24.38 billion in sales with an expected low single digit increase in 2013. Staples carried $1.9 billion in debt with a debt to assets ratio of 16.38% [**Exhibit 1**]. At that time, the company employed 50,020 full-time and 35,067 part-time associates worldwide. The company worked to achieve its goals by continuing to improve growth platforms, reshape its business, and create funds for its future, all the time taking appropriate measures to remain the industry leader and fulfill its vision for the future.

EXHIBIT 1
Balance Sheet and Income Statement (Staples Annual Report: 2013)

STAPLES, INC. AND SUBSIDIARIES
Consolidated Balance Sheets
(Dollar Amounts in Thousands, Except Share Data)

	February 1, 2014	February 2, 2013
ASSETS		
Current assets:		
Cash and cash equivalents	$ 492,532	$ 1,334,302
Receivables, net	1,838,714	1,815,586
Merchandise inventories, net	2,328,299	2,314,058
Deferred income tax assets	179,566	218,899
Prepaid expenses and other current assets	400,447	346,773
Current assets of discontinued operations	—	170,819
Total current assets	5,239,558	6,200,437
Property and equipment:		
Land and buildings	990,324	1,015,225
Leasehold improvements	1,306,987	1,300,258
Equipment	2,778,294	2,625,949
Furniture and fixtures	1,078,876	1,088,669
Total property and equipment	6,154,481	6,030,101
Less: Accumulated depreciation	4,283,762	4,066,926
Net property and equipment	1,870,719	1,963,175
Intangible assets, net of accumulated amortization	382,700	384,609
Goodwill	3,233,597	3,221,162
Other assets	448,302	510,622
Total assets	$ 11,174,876	$ 12,280,005
LIABILITIES AND STOCKHOLDERS' EQUITY		
Current liabilities:		
Accounts payable	$ 1,997,494	$ 1,896,040
Accrued expenses and other current liabilities	1,266,974	1,405,752
Debt maturing within one year	103,982	987,161
Current liabilities of discontinued operations	—	129,672
Total current liabilities	3,368,450	4,418,625
Long-term debt, net of current maturities	1,000,205	1,001,943
Other long-term obligations	665,386	723,343

See notes to consolidated financial statements

(continued)

EXHIBIT 1
(Continued)

STAPLES, INC. AND SUBSIDIARIES
Consolidated Balance Sheets
(Dollar Amounts in Thousands, Except Share Data)

Stockholders' equity:

Preferred stock, $.01 par value, 5,000,000 shares authorized: no shares issued	—	—
Common stock, $.0006 par value. 2,100,000,000 shares authorized; issued and outstanding 938,722,858 and 652,860,207 shares at February 1, 2014 and 932,246,614 shares and 669,182,785 shares at February 2, 2013, respectively	563	559
Additional paid-in capital	4,866,467	4,711,113
Accumulated other comprehensive loss	(507,154)	(388,773)
Retained earnings	7,001,755	6,694,207
Less: Treasury stock at cost, 285,862,651 shares at February 1, 2014 and 263,063,829 shares at February 2, 2013	(5,229,368)	(4,888,953)
Total Staples, Inc. stockholders' equity	6,132,263	6,128,153
Noncontrolling interests	8,572	7,941
Total stockholders' equity	6,140,835	6,136,094
Total liabilities and stockholders' equity	$ 11,174,876	$ 12,280,005

STAPLES, INC. AND SUBSIDIARIES
Consolidated Statements of Income
(Dollar Amounts in Thousands, Except Share Data)

	Fiscal Year		
	February 1, 2014	**February 2, 2013**	**January 28, 2012**
Sales	$ 23,114,263	$ 24,380,510	$ 24,664,752
Cost of goods sold and occupancy costs	17,081,978	17,889,249	17,974,884
Gross profit	6,032,285	6,491,261	6,689,868
Operating expenses:			
Selling, general and administrative	4,735,294	4,884,284	4,991,195
Impairment of goodwill and long-lived assets	—	810,996	—
Restructuring charges	64,085	207,016	—
Amortization of intangibles	55,405	78,900	64,902
Total operating expenses	4,854,784	5,981,196	5,056,097
Operating income	1,177,501	510,065	1,633,771
Other (expense) income:			
Interest income	4,733	5,340	7,370
Interest expense	(119,329)	(162,477)	(173,394)
Loss on early extinguishment of debt	—	(56,958)	—
Other income (expense), net	(100)	(30,547)	(3,103)

See notes to consolidated financial statements.

Income from continuing operations before income taxes	1,062,805	265,423	1,464,644
Income tax expense	355,801	426,270	477,247
Income (loss) from continuing operations, including the portion attributable to the noncontrolling interests	707,004	(160,847)	987,397
Discontinued Operations:			
Loss from discontinued operations, net of income taxes	(86,935)	(49,978)	(3,564)
Consolidated net income (loss)	620,069	(210,825)	983,833
Loss attributed to the noncontrolling interests	—	(119)	(823)
Income (loss) attributed to Staples, Inc.	$ 620,069	$ (210,706)	$ 984,656
Amounts attributable to Staples, Inc.:			
Income (loss) from continuing operations	$ 707,004	$ (160,728)	$ 988,220
Loss from discontinued operations	(86,935)	(49,978)	(3,564)
Income (loss) attributed to Staples, Inc.	$ 620,069	$ (210,706)	$ 984,656
Basic Earnings Per Common Share:			
Continuing operations attributed to Staples, Inc.	$ 1.08	$ (0.24)	$ 1.42
Discontinued operations attributed to Staples, Inc.	$ (0.13)	(0.07)	—
Net income (loss) attributed to Staples, Inc.	$ 0.95	$ (0.31)	$ 1.42
Diluted Earnings per Common Share:			
Continuing operations attributed to Staples, Inc.	$ 1.07	$ (0.24)	$ 1.40
Discontinued operations attributed to Staples, Inc.	(0.13)	(0.07)	—
Net income (loss) attributed to Staples, Inc.	$ 0.94	$ (0.31)	$ 1.40
Dividends declared per common share	$ 0.48	$ 0.44	$ 0.40

STAPLES, INC. AND SUBSIDIARIES
Consolidated Statements of Comprehensive Income
(Dollar Amounts in Thousands)

	Fiscal Year Ended		
	February 1, 2014	**February 2, 2013**	**January 28, 2012**
Consolidated net income (loss)	$ 620,069	$ (210,825)	$ 983,833
Other comprehensive (loss) income, net of tax:			
Foreign currency translation adjustments	(126,735)	36,602	(191,972)
Disposal of foreign business, net	8,308	—	—

(continued)

EXHIBIT 1
(Continued)

STAPLES, INC. AND SUBSIDIARIES
Consolidated Statements of Comprehensive Income
(Dollar Amounts in Thousands)

	Fiscal Year Ended		
	February 1, 2014	February 2, 2013	January 28, 2012
Changes in the fair value of derivatives, net	—	2,022	(1,505)
Deferred pension and other post-retirement benefit costs, net	737	(106,656)	(27,520)
Other comprehensive loss, net of tax	(117,750)	(68,032)	(220,997)
Consolidated comprehensive income (loss)	502,319	(278,857)	762,836
Comprehensive income attributed to noncontrolling interests	631	879	990
Comprehensive income (loss) attributed to Staples, Inc.	$ 501,688	$ (279,736)	$ 761,846

Competitors

Staples, Inc. was positioned in the specialty retail industry in the services sector. Its major competitors were other high-volume office suppliers such as Office Depot and Lyreco; mass merchants such as Wal-mart, Target, and Tesco; warehouse clubs such as Costco; electronics retail stores such as Best Buy; specialty technology stores such as Apple; copy and print businesses such as FedEx Office; online retailers such as Amazon. com; and additional discount retailers.[5]

Office Depot Inc.

Office Depot, headquartered in Boca Raton, Florida, was founded in 1986, and, like Staples, operated in the Specialty Retail industry. As of 2014, the company, with North American Retail, North American Business Solutions, and International divisions,[6] had a market cap of 1.60 billion, 38,000 full time employees, and 1,629 office supply stores worldwide. In the 1990s, a merger of Staples and Office Depot was halted by the Federal Trade Commission due to the potential for near-monopoly pricing power.[7] However, in November 2013, Office Depot and OfficeMax merged, combining the second and third-largest U.S. office-supply chains in an attempt to better compete with Staples.[8] In May 2014, Office Depot announced that it planned to close 400 stores as fallout from the merger.

W.B. Mason

W.B. Mason, the largest privately owned office products dealer in the United States, was founded in 1898 as a rubber stamp maker headquartered in Brockton, Massachusetts, and employed 1700 workers as of 2013. Over the years, the company carved out a niche for itself largely by contracting with small-to-midsized businesses in the Northeast and Mid-Atlantic states with the objective of providing the best overall solution.[9] W.B. Mason became competition for Staples through its office supply centers as well as its Whatta Bargain stores that sold office furniture and business equipment.[10]

Amazon Hints at Future Drone Delivery

Amazon.com, founded in 1994 and headquartered in Seattle, Washington, began operations in the Catalog & Mail Order Houses industry in the Services sector as an online retailer in North America and internationally. As of 2014, the company operated retail websites, Amazon Web Services, and Kindle Direct Publishing, employing 88,400, and with a market cap of 168.98B. From Staples' perspective, Amazon retail websites were significant competition, offering merchandise and content purchased for resale from vendors or offered by third-party sellers.[11]

Amazon's innovative new drone technology with the potential to deliver packages in as little as 30 minutes in a radius surrounding its fulfillment centers could be an industry game changer, further intensifying Staples' competition with Amazon.

Wal-mart Stores Inc.

Wal-mart, founded in 1945 and based in Bentonville, Arkansas, segmented its company worldwide into Wal-mart U.S., Wal-mart International, and Sam's Club in the Discount, Variety Stores industry in the Services sector, operating 11,000 stores in 27 countries and employing 2,200,000 people worldwide. Wal-mart became a threat to Staples when it began to offer office supplies, office furniture, software, paper goods, and electronics in its extensive product mix.[12]

Low Barriers to Entry

Industry-wide, the office supply sector really had no barriers to entry as capital costs were low compared to other retail industries. No licensing requirements were necessary, easing the burden on new entrants; however, competition and market awareness were likely to threaten new entrants. The low level of differentiation of goods between one office supply store and the next, forced new entrants to provide either niche or specialty products to compete. On top of that challenge, industry competition came not only from traditional office supply stores, but from discount retailers, warehouse clubs, supercenters, and e-commerce websites that could undercut smaller businesses, making conditions difficult for new entrants. Ultimately, new entrants found that it was relatively easy to enter the office supply industry, but competing against large companies made it difficult to become profitable.[13]

Staples' established relationships, convenience of access via its website Staples.com, and its many retail store locations increased its brand awareness and gave the chain a competitive edge over newer and smaller companies. Its experienced management team, helpful customer service, wide variety of available products and services, and competitive pricing also constituted advantages for Staples, as did its efforts to differentiate its offerings from those of its competitors. In addition, Staples continued to invest in information technology to enhance Staples.com to improve usability, efficiency, and overall customer experience, an important companywide goal.

Through its sheer size Staples optimized economies of scale for further competitive advantages including enhanced efficiencies in purchasing, distribution, advertising, and general and administrative expenses. The company believed that its network of stores and online businesses enhanced its profitability by allowing it to leverage marketing, distribution, and supervisory costs. Staples particularly focused on leveraging synergies between Staples.com and its retail stores with the introduction of new concepts including ship to store, online retail store inventory lookup, reserve online pickup in store, as well as mobile and tablet optimized websites.[14]

Focus on Sustainability

Sustainability was crucial to Staples' vision. The company ranked in the top 25 of the EPA's Green Power Partner List. To achieve this standard Staples developed many programs over the years to position itself as a green company including:

- An environmentally friendly paper policy to increase the amount of post-consumer recycled paper available for sale.
- Phasing out products originating from endangered forests to preserve the environment in threatened parts of the world.
- Modifying its fulfillment center in Hanover, Maryland, to be fully powered by a 1.01 megawatt solar initiative.

By abiding by governmental standards and attempting to influence political ideals, Staples both acquired a reputation as a green company and chalked up millions of dollars a year in savings as a result of new power reduction strategies.

Staples also implemented sustainability strategies in its copy and print centers. The premise of the program was that copiers would enter sleep mode in as little as 15 minutes after use. This not only saved money but cut over 11 million pounds of carbon monoxide from release into the atmosphere, resonating with another hot topic in the legal and political world. These programs garnered Staples an FSSI 2, an exclusive contract with the U.S. government for office supplies. Other programs with legal and political implications Staples participated in included AbilityOne, Eco-Conscious, and the Trade Agreement Act. The AbilityOne program was the largest source of employment for blind or disabled people in the United States. The Eco-Conscious program, designed to be "easy on the planet," and the Trade Agreement Act advocated that items not produced by countries permitted by the TAA be referred to as "Open Market Buy" items.

Core Competencies

Staples' core competencies were its extensive product offerings, competitive pricing, large and diversified market segmentation, and a strong brand perception. From its beginnings, Staples offered a wide variety of office supplies and services as well as office machines and related products, computers and related products, and office furniture. All products and services were marketed and delivered via various distribution channels. Through such a wide range of product offerings, Staples offered the distinct advantage of "one-stop-shopping" that provided "everything your business needs," the motive behind all its product expansion decisions. To expand further, Staples began offering items in adjacent product categories such as break-room and facilities; medical; safety; office décor; and packaging and shipping supplies.

In addition, Staples strongly reinforced its wide assortment of product offerings to customers through its in-stock guarantee and strong pricing message supported by its loyalty programs. By offering products that were competitively priced, in-stock, and easy to find (in store and online), Staples positioned itself as the "easy" and convenient choice in comparison to its competitors. In recent years, Staples also launched a "price-match guarantee" initiative to compete with Amazon, its top Internet competitor,[15,16]

Staples customer base could be classified into three segments [**Exhibit 2**]:home offices/small businesses; mid-size businesses classified as organizations with 20 to 500 office workers; and large businesses classified as greater than 500 office workers, including fortune 1000 companies.[17] According to Staples, each of these market segments was able to benefit from separate sales channels. For example, the retail stores and Staples .com website were most convenient for the small business and home office segment while the Staples catalog and Staples Advantage program were best suited for the mid- to large-size companies. Each of these sales avenues attracted different customers and each customer group exhibited distinct purchasing behaviors.[18] By understanding the needs and buying behaviors of these three separate segments, Staples was better able to meet the demands of its large and diversified market, and to better provide its customers with new products and services.

The Staples brand, best described as "easy," was designed to provide a "hassle-free" experience for any and all of the company's customers. In 2005, Staples partnered with Prophet, a strategic brand and marketing consulting agency, to cultivate its "That Was Easy" marketing campaign. The implementation of the "That Was Easy" tagline and the Easy button campaign led to many operational improvements and increased brand awareness worldwide.[19] Staples overtook Office Depot as the number one office supply superstore in the United States in 2005, and remained in the number one spot through 2013. Alongside the notion of the ease of shopping at Staples, the company also offered customers quality products competitively priced.

Operations

The main strength of Staples' retail store operations was the sheer number of stores in each operating sector, so customers could easily find a Staples retail store near them. The North American Stores & Online segment included over 1,880 stores, 1,547 in the United States and 339 in Canada,[20] selling a wide variety of office products such as ink and toner, paper, and virtually every other office necessity. Staples' newest strategic plan incorporated venturing further into all aspects of the office environment to provide facilities and break-room supplies, in addition to expanding its copy and print and technology services. Staples' sheer number of stores created incredible distribution channels, allowing it to leverage marketing, distribution, and supervision costs. The transition to

EXHIBIT 2
Sales Breakdown by Products (Staples Annual Report: 2013)

	Fiscal Year Ended		
	February 2, 2013	**January 28, 2012**	**January 29, 2011**
Office supplies	43.9%	44.6%	44.0%
Services	6.7%	5.7%	5.3%
Office machines and related products	29.7%	29.4%	29.9%
Computers and related products	14.1%	15.2%	15.6%
Office furniture	5.6%	5.1%	5.2%
	100.0%	100.0%	100.0%

online helped cut costs and increase company value by developing full mobile and tablet optimized website to help customers look up inventory for an item at any retail store and reserve online pickup at a store or ship items to a specific store.

The North American Commercial segment's operations were designed to sell and deliver office products and services directly to businesses in the United States and Canada as well as the Staples Advantage and Quill.com services. Commercial's main operating function was expanding the retail stores' general sales of office supplies to customers that needed more, or a wider variety, of specific items. Staples Advantage served mid-sized businesses up to Fortune 1000 companies which required more than a traditional retail store could provide for their operations, products that would otherwise be difficult to get ahold of as easily as a giant company could. Quill.com's operations were quite different as an Internet and catalog business focused on serving small to mid-sized businesses with very specific needs or services. For instance, one business under Quill.com's umbrella was Medical Arts Press, Inc., which provided specialized office supplies and products for healthcare companies, a totally different market from the rest of Staples' business.

Staples' International Operations segment built up operations in 23 countries in Europe, Australia, South America, and Asia. This segment was less unified and more troubled than the North American segments. The products and services offered to the different countries across this segment varied widely with no set standard to follow. There were 283 retail stores in the European section, largely in the United Kingdom, the Netherlands, Germany, and Portugal. There was also a direct mail service and online center with sales primarily in the United Kingdom, Italy, and France. Staples' main goal was to standardize and optimize the European segment to streamline the systems used and create a standard of products to follow; further e-commerce sales; and expand the array of business services offered, thus following the same plan as Staples' North American successes. However, economic conditions in the European Union necessitated the closing of underperforming stores and those that were creating financial strain to improve the profitability of the European segment and secure profits. The Staples Australia segment of International Operations fared better than Europe as it had government contracts and customers in Australia and New Zealand to provide stable income. Staples in Asia and South America were fragmented, but retail and delivery businesses were established in China and delivery businesses also operated in Taiwan, Argentina, and Brazil, with an arrangement for a franchise in India underway.

Supply Chain

The massive size of Staples' segments and the sheer number of Staples stores necessitated the development of two North American supply chain networks for stocking and deliveries. However, the North American stores and online had only four distribution centers across the United States for retail operations, significantly cutting labor costs while saving on merchandise costs, as the centralizing of all functions relating to replenishment created an economy of scale that allowed for huge amounts of inventory to be dispersed quickly and efficiently. North American Commercial, on the other hand, maintained sixty-six fulfillment centers across North America operating as a separate distribution channel to prevent complexity in the distribution network.

The de-centralized European supply and distribution chains lacked the efficiency and depth of the North American sector, pushing Staples to initiate measures to reduce redundancy and complexity to cut costs and increase efficiency. The company realized that implementing centralized distribution would streamline resupplying and distributing inventory, rendering the system significantly more efficient and less costly.

Human Resources

Staples' main business was its retail stores staffed by Staples associates who interacted directly with customers, providing assistance as well as pushing sales for various products and services. As of the end of FY2012, Staples had 50,020 full-time and 35,067 part-time associates, most of whom were paid at or near minimum wage, saving the company money at the cost of employee apathy and high turnover rates. The Staples workforce garnered quite a lot of publicity during the 2012 Presidential election, as Republican presidential candidate Mitt Romney served on Staples' board of directors, which seemed to many an example of the rich getting richer on the backs of a minimum wage work-force.[21] However, attempts to unionize in an effort to raise wages to the level of wages at competitor Costco wholesale were firmly rebuffed by management, despite its large number of minimum-wage employees.[22] One Staples store successfully unionized in September 2013 and negotiated a 2% wage increase.[23]

In 2012, Staples updated its corporate values policy that provided guidelines for associates' interactions with customers and each other, part of its efforts to prevent human resource issues and avoid the kind of problems that could occur at such a low wage level. A major aspect of its corporate values was "Staples Soul," or responsible corporate citizenship, coordinated by its chief cultural officer and designed to articulate how Staples' financial success translated into benefits for its various constituencies: associates, communities, and the planet through four aspirational goals.

First, Staples aimed to show that ethics was part of the Staples' culture by maintaining ethical business practices, and assuring employees that they could voice their opinions without fear of reprisal. As part of the hiring process, the company's training program included an ethics lesson to demonstrate the impact of unethical decisions and the negative effect they could have on stakeholders and the company, as well as on the reputation of the brand.

Next, Staples aimed to generate business while protecting the environment and benefiting the community through sustainable business practices such as selling recyclable products and green services and improving energy efficiency. The green movement provided Staples both with social opportunities in terms of reputation and community goodwill, and with financial opportunities by aligning the company with the green market, thus benefiting all parties involved.

The third aspect of Staples Soul, diversity, involved acknowledging that the company's success came from diverse people of all races, ages, sexes, sexual orientations, backgrounds, and nationalities; and encouraging the recruitment of diverse associates to spur new opportunities for innovation and growth.

The last component of Staples Soul, community, focused on providing job skills and educational opportunities such as career development to associates and literacy training and tutoring to disadvantaged youth through financial contributions to various charitable organizations and grants from the non-profit Staples Foundation funded by the corporation. Over the years, the Foundation assisted 6,500 organizations in local communities in 26 different countries, and worked tirelessly to encourage customer and associate volunteer efforts in the community.

Financial Operations

For the three years from 2011 to 2014, Staples' sales revenues were flat at around $24 billion, though fluctuating as much as $400 million on a year-to-year basis. The company's sales revenue derived primarily from the sale of office supplies, which accounted for 43.9% of revenues in FY2012 [**Exhibit 3**]. This figure represented a fall of 0.7% from FY2011, as the company pushed further growth of its services sector of the business, which represented only 6.7% of sales revenue in FY2012.[24]

A major obstacle to Staples' financial strength was the goodwill impairment of $771.5 million the company recorded in the third quarter of 2012, which resulted in a net loss of $210.7 million for FY2012.[24] The impairment was attributable to losses in the European retail and Europe catalog reporting units, incurred as a result of ongoing economic weakness in Europe. Further impairment of goodwill, it was feared, might arise from a variety of factors including the lessening of consumer spending; worsening industry and macroeconomic conditions; changes in the price of Staples stock; and the future profitability of the businesses.[25] Though the goodwill impairment was a non-cash loss on the business, it altered the balance sheet and the overall financial strength of the company. Analysts predicted further impairment for 2013, which did not bode well for investors and pointed to the weakness of Staples' European business in relation to overall revenue for the company.

Another important financial risk factor for Staples was its long-term debt, ringing up at over $1 billion, with other long-term obligations at over $700 million. This amount of debt, it was feared, could create a substantial roadblock to financing further working capital for business operations; could disadvantage Staples in relation to its less debt-burdened competitors; could require the company to borrow at a higher rate to secure financing; and could place it at risk should the economy face trouble or its business was no longer sustainable, as the company would still be required to repay its obligations. This last risk was mitigated, however, thanks to Staples' maintaining a large cash balance. Cash from operations was $1.22 billion in 2012, providing a balance of cash on hand of $1.33 billion, more than enough to cover long-term financing debt if it became a liability,[24] suggesting that Staples' long-term debt was fully under control thanks to its cash reserve policy initiated in 2012, and thus presented no real long-term concern for the business in the future.

As of 2013, Staples' North American segment was its largest at almost $20 billion total deriving from two sources: its retail stores—North American Stores & Online at $11.8 billion, and North American Commercial, previously known as North American Delivery, at $8.1 billion.[24] The segment's primary purpose was selling and delivering office products and services directly to businesses; as such this segment included the Staples Advantage and Quill.com service.

The North American Stores & Online segment's sales only gradually increased year-to-year, with a 0.7% increase in sales revenue from FY2011 and a 1.7% increase from FY2010 to FY2011. However, FY2012 included an extra week from 2012, resulting in a 53-week fiscal year that added $221.4 million to FY2012; not counting this extra week,

EXHIBIT 3
Sales Revenue over
Five Years (Staples
Annual Report: 2013)

Sales revenue (net) for Staples Inc. (SPLS)

sales in 2012 actually decreased by 1.2% from 2011. However, the next year FY2013's third quarter filings showed a 5.3% decrease from FY2012 in the North American Stores and Online: $3 billion as opposed to $3.18 billion.[24]

For the North American Commercial segment, sales increased by 1.7% in FY2012, this again included the extra week from 2012; excluding the extra week, sales from North American Commercial actually decreased by 0.3% from 2011.[24] As of Q3 FY2013, sales for this segment increased by 0.7% from $2.075 billion to $2.089 billion.[24]

Same-Store Sales and Profit Margins: Two Major Problems for Staples

From 2010 through 2013, same-store sales consistently fell for Staples [**Exhibit 5**], in line with other financial information such as sales revenue and net income. The low margin of office supplies store sales coupled with the loss of sales from the closing of underperforming stores correlated with the figures of consistent decreases in same-store sales in the exhibit. Thus, the majority of Staples' positive sales revenue numbers for the past few years came either from online sales or new store sales to make up for the decrease in same-store sales.

Staples' profit and operating margins were exceptionally low during this time period as well At 1.1% for FY2012 and 4.5% for the year before, such profit margins were unlikely to attract new entrants to the industry. Operating margins were similar at 6.4% for FY2012 and 6.5% for FY2011,[24] which explained why net income [**Exhibit 4**]. was so small compared to sales revenue and why any type of abnormal fluctuations such as goodwill impairment had a real and material effect on the bottom line. Essentially, the only reason Staples made any type of income from the office supply business derived from economies of scale and efficiency. Any other kind of startup simply would not have made any real money. Thus, it became necessary for Staples to optimize and cut costs through efficiency, or there would not be much growth in terms of net income other than from an increase in sales volume.

Staples' stock price [**Exhibit 5**]. hovered in the $11–$15 range in 2013 [**Exhibit 4**], in keeping with its poor performance in the five years prior to that during which it lost about half its value. In response, Staples heralded new business strategies for growth to gain investor confidence such as its online restructuring. Yet its low margins, only $500–$700 million net income from $24–$25 billion in sales, continued to dismay investors. Growth and earnings, the end-goal of all public companies, was simply not there for Staples or for the industry as a whole. Until there was a complete overhaul of Staples'

EXHIBIT 4
Net Income over Five Years (Staples Annual Report: 2013)

Net-Income (Loss) for Staples Inc. (SPLS)

EXHIBIT 5
Stock Price (2009–2013)
(Staples Annual
Report: 2013)

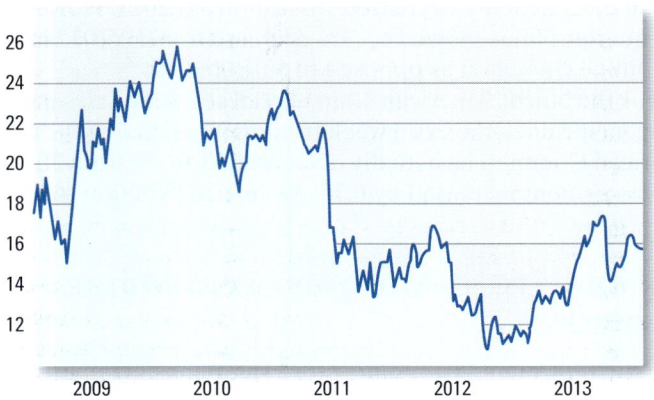

business plan to better manage these costs and improve margins, Staples' stock, it was feared, would continue to underperform.

Global Operations

Staples' overseas operations in 26 countries—18% of its revenues (31% consolidated revenues)—often exposed the company to global conditions. In 2012, Staples recorded $36.6 million in currency translation loses. Staples' international operations represented a loss of $21 million in 2012 net income.

In 2013, Staples began working on creating a more efficient distribution system in Europe by consolidating its facilities, an opportunity to increase margins and make operations more profitable. However, building its overseas distribution network required significant capital, raising the concern that the company might overspend in expanding its global presence.

The International Operations segment sales decreased by 10.2% from 2011, including $80.8 million in sales from the extra week in FY2012; excluding this week, International Operations sales in 2012 dropped by 11.8%. The continued decline of European and Australian business sales as well as a $180.6 million negative impact due to unfavorable exchange rates accounted for much of this sharp drop in sales figures. Importantly, $303.3 million and $468.1 million, respectively, in goodwill impairment attributed to the European Retail and Europe Catalog reporting units was not included in these figures. Additional losses included over $177 million in restructuring costs from the closing of retail stores across Europe.[24] Given these losses, it became clear that the European side of Staples' International Operations was not faring well and might face continued restructuring costs from the closing of stores as well as continued goodwill impairment as the value of these European sectors continued to fall.

Many Challenges Facing Staples

Staples' greatest weaknesses were its difficulty in competing in the online realm and the company's lack of e-commerce and mobile intelligence, weaknesses stemming from its reactive nature and behind the curve thinking. As the retail industry had been trending towards online sales for quite a while, and Staples' traditional brick and mortar stores were costing Staples a pretty penny, Staples' new reinvention strategy was aimed at reducing square footage and transitioning in-store customers to online customers.

These steps were necessary to ensure a fighting chance against online superstores such as Amazon, which had begun offering the same products as Staples at rock-bottom prices. By investing in online and mobile technologies, Staples demonstrated its promise to meet customers' needs. Yet, Staples lacked consumer-facing marketing that would direct customers to its website rather than its retail outlets. Its game plan to convert its in-store customers to online customers was to promote purchasing online while customers were in still in the store. For example, Staples planned to equip sales associates with tablets to constantly check inventory and help customers order online. When customers first entered the "omnichannel" store, they would be greeted by a "business lounge" decked out with computer workstations, charging stations, and kiosks so they could browse the online store.[26] The decision to use the retail stores as the place to encourage online purchases was Staples' solution for transitioning its existing customers to online sales. Overall, Staples planned to combat its marketing weaknesses by reducing square footage and tripling the size of its e-commerce and IT staff, fundamental shifts necessary for Staples to remain the number one office supply superstore.

By 2014, an important challenge for Staples was decreasing product margins across all three of its market segments. Staples' low product margins meant that in order to really be profitable it needed to sell huge quantities of products and services. In 2012, Staples had sales revenue of $25.02 billion and a net-income of $984.66 million for an effective profit margin of approximately 3.9% of sales revenue.

Staples' main challenge was its complacency as the global office supplies industry leader. Many analysts concurred that Staples spent too much time and effort reacting to a changing industry and merely maintaining leadership, rather than focusing on innovation and driving change in the industry. In recent years, Staples began restructuring through the closing of stores and centralizing of its European distribution system, but these were seen as efficiency measures to adapt to a changing industry, not growth strategies addressing the company's stagnant sales.

In March 2014, Staples announced that it would close 225 stores by the end of 2015 to focus on its online business. In May 2014, Office Depot announced that it would close 400 stores due to its merger with OfficeMax. The entire office supply industry was changing and under pressure from online retailers.

NOTES

1. "About Staples Advantage - Our Structure, Staples Soul, Awards, News." *About Staples Advantage - Our Structure, Staples Soul, Awards, News.* N.p., n.d. Web. November 17, 2013.
2. "Staples, Inc.Company Information." *Staples, Inc.* N.p., n.d. Web. November 17, 2013.
3. "Staples Delivers Custom Box Sizes With Every Order for More Convenience, Reduced Waste." *Staples Online Newsroom.* N.p., n.d. Web. November 17, 2013.
4. Staples, Inc. 2012 Annual report, Dec. 2012. Investor relations corporate website http://investor.staples.com /phoenix.zhtml?c=96244&p=irol-reportsannual
5. "SPLS FY2012 10-K." *Sec.gov.* N.p., n.d. Web. Decemer 8, 2013.
6. "Office Depot, Inc. Company Profile." *Yahoo! Finance.* N.p., n.d. Web. December 8, 2013.
7. Broder, John M. "Office Depot and Staples Merger Halted." *The New York Times.* July 1, 1997. Web. December 8, 2013.
8. Townsend, Matt. "Staples May Be Winner in Office Depot-OfficeMax Merger." Bloomberg.com. Bloomberg, February 20, 2013. Web. December 6, 2013.
9. "About W.B. Mason." *W.B. Mason.* N.p., n.d. Web. December 8, 2013.
10. "W.B. Mason Company Sales Preparation." *W.B. Mason Company.* N.p., n.d. Web. December 8, 2013.
11. "Amazon.com Inc. Company Profile." *Yahoo! Finance.* N.p., n.d. Web. December 8, 2013.
12. "Wal-Mart Stores Inc. Company Profile." *Yahoo! Finance.* N.p., n.d. Web. December 8, 2013.
13. "Competitive Landscape." *IBISWorld.* N.p., n.d. Web. December 8, 2013.
14. "SPLS FY2012 10-K." *Sec.gov.* N.p., n.d. Web. December 8, 2013.
15. Luna, Taryn. "Staples Will Match Amazon Prices." Boston Globe.com. N.p., n.d. Web. December 9, 2013. http://www .bostonglobe.com/business/2013/10/10/staples-matches-amazon -prices-stores-online/sdli8Z32OkduHdLsssLDBN/story.html

16. Douglas, Craig. "Staples Launches New Online Pricing Strategy to Reverse Recent Sales Slip." *Boston Business Journal*. N.p., n.d. Web. December 1, 2013. http://www.bizjournals.com/boston/blog/mass_roundup/2013/10/staples-launches-new-online-pricing.html

17. "Staples, Inc. 2012 Annual Report." *Staples, Inc. 2012 Annual Report*. N.p., n.d. Web. November 2, 2013. http://thomson.mobular.net/thomson/7/3359/4770/

18. Ibid.

19. "Growth through a Refined Target Audience." *Staples*. N.p., n.d. Web. November 22, 2013. http://www.prophet.com/impact/projects/staples

20. Staples, Inc. *Annual Report 2012*. Retrieved from http://investor.staples.com/phoenix.zhtml?c=96244&p=irol-IRHome

21. Primack, Dan. "Staples Founder: Why I'm Supporting Romney." *CNNMoney*. Cable News Network, August 29, 2012. Web. December 8, 2013. http://finance.fortune.cnn.com/2012/08/29/staples-founder-why-im-supporting-romney/

22. NELP. "Big Business, Corporate Profits, and Minimum Wage." *NELP*. National Employment Law Sponsor, July 2012. Web. December 8, 2013. http://nelp.3cdn.net/e555b2e361f8f734f4_sim6btdzo.pdf

23. UCFW. "Staples Workers Make History." *Ecocide Alert*. UCFW, September 20, 2013. Web. December 8, 2013. http://ecocidealert.com/?p=1637

24. Staples, Inc. *Annual Report 2012*. Retrieved from http://investor.staples.com/phoenix.zhtml?c=96244&p=irol-IRHome

25. Staples, Inc. *Quarterly Report Q2* 2013. Retrieved from http://investor.staples.com/phoenix.zhtml?c=96244&p=irol-IRHome

26. Luna, Taryn. "A Big Box King Learns to Think Small." *Boston Globe*. June 22, 2013. ProQuest. Web. December 9, 2013.

CASE **30**

Tesla Motors, Inc.:

THE FIRST U.S. CAR COMPANY IPO SINCE 1956

Alan N. Hoffman
Bentley University

Tesla Motors, Inc. is in the business of developing, manufacturing, and selling technology for high-performance electric automotives and power train components. Hoping to develop a greater worldwide acceptance of electric vehicles as an alternative to the traditional internal combustion, petroleum-based vehicles that dominate the market, Tesla is the first company that commercially produced a federally compliant electric vehicle with the design styling and performance characteristics of a high-end performance automobile. Tesla currently offers one vehicle, the Roadster, for sale, as well as supplying electric power train components to Daimler for use in its Smart EV automobile. Additionally, Tesla has a partnership with Toyota Motors to develop and supply an electric power train for Toyota's Rav4 SUV.

Company Background

Tesla Motors was founded in Silicon Valley in 2003 by Martin Eberhard and Marc Tarpenning to create efficient electric cars for driving aficionados. The founders acquired their first round of financing from PayPal and SpaceX founder Elon Musk who subsequently took over as CEO in 2008. The company unveiled its first car, a two-seat sports car named the Roadster, in 2006 after raising $150 million and going through four years of technological and internal struggles.[1] Powered by a three-phase, four-pole AC induction motor, the Roadster has a top speed of 130 mph and accelerates from 0 to 60 mph in under four seconds, all completely silent.[2] Production of the Roadster began in March of 2008 with a first-year production run of 600 vehicles.[3] In June 2008, Tesla announced that it would be building a four-door, five-passenger sedan called the Model S to be

This teaching case was compiled from published sources. The author would like to thank Lindsay Pacheco, Patrick Toomey, Ned Coffee, William Gormly, and Will Hoffman for their research. Please address all correspondence to Dr. Alan N. Hoffman, Dept. of Management, Bentley University, 175 Forest Street, Waltham, MA 02452; ahoffman@bentley.edu. Printed by permission of Dr. Alan N. Hoffman.

built in California and be available for sale in 2012.[4] The Model S is slated to retail for approximately $57,400 and be offered with battery options for 160-, 230-, or 300-mile ranges per charge. The company went public in June 2010 with an initial public offering at $17 a share, raising about $226.1 million in the first stock debut of a car maker since the Ford Motor Company held its initial public offering in 1956.[5]

Tesla has also used its innovative technology to partner with traditional automobile manufacturers on their electric vehicle offerings. In 2009, Tesla signed a deal to provide Daimler with the battery technology to power 1000 electric Smart city cars.[6] Tesla will supply battery packs and electric power trains to Daimler and in return it will receive auto manufacturing and design expertise in areas including safety requirements and mass production of vehicles.[7] Later in that same year, Daimler announced that it had acquired a "nearly 10 percent" stake in Tesla.[8] On October 6, 2010, Tesla entered into a Phase 1 Contract Services Agreement with Toyota Motor Corporation for the development of a validated power train system, including a battery, power electronics module, motor, gearbox, and associated software, which will be integrated into an electric vehicle version of the RAV4 for which Tesla received US$60 million.[9]

In May 2010, Tesla purchased the former NUMMI factory in Fremont, California, one of the largest, most advanced and cleanest automotive production plants in the world, where it will build the Model S sedan and future Tesla vehicles.[10] Additionally, Toyota invested US$50 million in Tesla and together the two companies will cooperate on the development of electric vehicles, parts, and production system and engineering support.[11]

Strategic Direction

Tesla desires to develop alternative energy electric vehicles for people who love to drive. While most car companies are developing small, compact electric cars, Tesla has focused on a high-priced, high-performance electric vehicle that competes against traditional performance cars such as those offered by BMW and Porsche. The company has also devoted many resources to research and development in an effort to produce an electric power train that has both long mileage between recharges and the high performance that car enthusiast's desire.

Tesla's main objectives are to achieve both growth in sales and profits, provide technological leadership in the field of electric vehicles, and foster sustainability and social responsibility. The company desires for growth are served with its development and sale of the Model S vehicle that is expected to retail for almost half of the Roadster price and thus create higher demand and revenue. The company further strives for growth through its strategic partnerships with Toyota and Daimler to supply electric power trains to those companies for use in their electric vehicle designs.

The company's objectives of sustainability and social responsibility are shown through its desire to develop automobiles that are not powered by petroleum products and produce very little carbon emissions. The company won the Globe Sustainability Innovation Award 2009.

Tesla's Competition

Tesla's products participate in the automotive market based on its power train technology. It currently competes with a number of vehicles in the non-petroleum powered (alternative fuel) automobile segment from companies such as Mitsubishi, Nissan, General Motors (Chevy), Toyota, BMW, and Honda to name a few. Within this market segment, there are four primary means of power train propulsion which differentiate the various competitors in this market:

- *Electric Vehicles (EV)* are vehicles powered completely by a single on-board energy storage system (battery pack or fuel cell) which is refueled directly from an electricity source. Both the Tesla Roadster and the Model S are examples of electric vehicles.

- *Plug-in Hybrid Vehicles (PHEV)* are vehicles powered by both a battery pack with an electric motor and an internal combustion engine that can be refueled both with traditional petroleum fuels for the engine and electricity for the battery pack. The internal combustion engine can either work in parallel with the electric motor to power the wheels, such as in a parallel plug-in hybrid vehicle, or be used only to recharge the battery, such as in a series plug-in hybrid vehicle like the Chevrolet Volt.

- *Hybrid Electric Vehicles (HEV)* are vehicles powered by both a battery pack with an electric motor and an internal combustion engine but which can only be refueled with traditional petroleum fuels as the battery pack is charged via regenerative braking, such as used in a hybrid electric vehicle like the Toyota Prius.[12]

- *Hydrogen Vehicles* are vehicles powered by liquefied hydrogen fuel cells. The power plants of such vehicles convert the chemical energy of hydrogen to mechanical energy either by burning hydrogen in an internal combustion engine, or by reacting hydrogen with oxygen in a fuel cell to run electric motors.[13] These vehicles are required to refuel their hydrogen fuel cells at special refueling stations. Examples of these types of vehicles are the BMW Hydrogen 7 and the Honda Clarity.

Mitsubishi i-MiEV

Established in Japan in 1970, Mitsubishi Motors Corporation is a member of the Mitsubishi conglomerate of 25 distinct companies. Mitsubishi Motors is headquartered in Tokyo, Japan, and employs roughly 31,000 employees. The company sells automobiles in 160 countries worldwide and in 2010 sold 960,000 units.[14] Within the United States, the company had a meager 0.5% of the market share in 2010 with 55,683 units sold.[15] Along with traditional gasoline engine automobiles, the company has long been involved in the R&D of electric vehicles. Mitsubishi has been involved in electric vehicle research and development since the 1960s with a partnership with the Tokyo Electric Power Company (TEPCO).[16] Since 1966 to the present, the company has dabbled in electric vehicle and battery research and development with numerous prototype vehicles produced.

In 2009. Mitsubishi released its newest EV car called the i-MiEV (Mitsubishi Innovative Electric Car). The i-MiEV is a small, four-passenger, all-electric car with a top speed of approximately 80 MPH and a quoted range of 75 miles on a single charge based on U.S. driving habits and terrain.[17] The car is based on lithium-ion battery technology. In October 2010, the company announced that it had reached the 5000 production unit mark for the car.[18] Currently the i-MiEV is being sold in Japan, other Asian countries, Costa Rica, and 14 countries in Europe. The Japanese price of the i-MiEV was originally US$50,500 but was reduced to US$42,690 in mid-2010 due to competition from other car companies. Mitsubishi plans on introducing the i-MiEV to the U.S. market in the fall of 2011.

Nissan Leaf

The Nissan Motor Company, formed in 1933, is headquartered in Yokohama, Japan and employs over 158,000 workers. Currently, it builds automobiles in 20 countries and offers products and services in 160 countries around the world.[19] In 2010, it sold globally over

3 million vehicles in its first three fiscal quarters (April 2010–December 2010) with over 700,000 of those being sold in the United States.[20] The company operates two brands, Nissan and Infinity, which design and sell both passenger vehicles and luxury passenger vehicles.

On December 3, 2010, Nissan introduced the LEAF, which it billed as the world's first 100% electric, zero-emission car designed for the mass market.[21] The LEAF is a five-passenger electric car with a top speed of 90 mph and a quoted range of 100 miles on a single charge using lithium-Ion battery technology. The current 2011 price in the United States for the LEAF is approximately US$33,000, which is also eligible for the US$7500 electric vehicle tax credit. It is reported that Nissan had sold 3657 LEAFs by the end of February 2011 with 173 of the sales within the United States and the rest in Japan.[22]

Chevy Volt

Chevrolet Motor Company was formed in 1911 and joined the General Motors Corporation in 1918.[23] GM has its global headquarters in Detroit, Michigan, and employs 209,000 people in every major region of the world and does business in more than 120 countries.[24] In 2010, Chevrolet sold 4.26 million vehicles worldwide and 1.57 million in the United States.[25]

In mid-December 2010, Chevy began delivery of a four-passenger, plug-in hybrid electric vehicle called the Volt. The Volt operates by using an electric engine until the batteries are discharged and then a gasoline engine kicks in for what Chevy calls "extended-range" driving. The car is quoted as having a range of 35 miles in electric mode and an additional 340 miles of extended driving using the gasoline engine.[26] It is reported that Chevy had sold 928 Volts by the end of February 2011; all within the United States.[27] The current 2011 price in the United States for the Volt is approximately US$42,000, which is also eligible for the US$7500 electric vehicle tax credit.

Toyota Prius

The Toyota Motor Company was established in 1937 and is headquartered in Toyota City, Japan. It employs over 320,000 employees worldwide with 51 overseas manufacturing companies in 26 countries and regions.[28] Toyota's vehicles are sold in more than 170 countries and regions. For fiscal year 2010, Toyota sold over 7.2 million vehicles worldwide, of which 1.76 million were sold in the United States.[29]

In 1997, Toyota introduced a five-passenger, gasoline-electric hybrid automobile called the Prius. The Prius has both a gasoline engine and an electric motor, which is used under lighter load conditions to maximize the car's fuel economy. The electric batteries are recharged via the gasoline engine only. On April 5, 2011, Toyota announced that it had sold its 1 millionth Prius in the United States and had surpassed 2 million global sales 6 months earlier in October 2010.[30] Currently, Toyota offers four versions of the Prius in the United States with prices ranging from US$23,000 to US$28,000. The company has announced a plug-in version of the Prius, which is slated for sale in 2012.

BMW Hydrogen 7

Bayerische Motoren Werke (BMW) was established in 1916 in Bavaria, Germany. Originally, the company started manufacturing airplane engines, but after World War I, Germany was not allowed to manufacture any airplane components as part of the terms of the armistice.[31] The company turned its focus to motorcycle engine development and subsequently, in 1928, developed its first automobile. Presently, the company is head-quartered in Munich, Germany, and employs approximately 95,000 workers. In 2010, BMW sold approximately 1.2 million vehicles.[32]

In 2006, BMW introduced the four-passenger Hydrogen 7 automobile that was the world's first hydrogen-drive luxury performance automobile.[33] The car is a dual-fuel vehicle capable of running on either liquid hydrogen or gasoline with just the press of a button on the steering wheel.[34] The combined range for the car is approximately 425 miles with the hydrogen tank contributing 125 miles and the gasoline providing the rest. To date, BMW has only produced 100 units of the vehicle, which have been leased/loaned to public figures. The car has not been made available for purchase to the general public and no sale price has been quoted.

Honda Clarity

The Honda Motor Company was established in the 1940s in Japan originally as a manu-facturer of engines for motorcycles.[35] Honda produced its first production automobile in 1963 and has been a global supplier since then. In 2010, Honda sold 3.4 million auto-mobiles worldwide with 1.4 million being sold in the United States.[36] In 2008, Honda began production of its four-passenger FCX Clarity, the world's first hydrogen-powered fuel-cell vehicle intended for mass production.[37] The FCX Clarity FCEV is basically an electric car because the fuel cell combines hydrogen with oxygen to make electricity which powers an electric motor, which in turn propels the vehicle.[38] The car can drive 240 miles on a tank, almost as far as a gasoline car, and also gets higher fuel efficiency than a gasoline car or hybrid, the equivalent of 74 miles per gallon of gas.[39] The company planned to ship 200 of the Clarity to customers in Southern California who can lease it for three years at US$600 a month.

Barriers to Entry and Imitation

The barriers to entry into the non-petroleum-powered automobile market segment are high. The hybrid technology for vehicles such as the Prius is well understood by the major automobile companies and many of them have developed and marketed their own version of electric/gasoline hybrid vehicles. The all-electric and hydrogen fuel-cell automobiles are unique technologies that require resources to develop. In this segment, the energy storage and motor technologies are barriers to new competitors. Recharge-able battery systems and fuel cells are newer technologies that require large investments in research and development. A competitor would need to develop its own technologies or partner with another company to acquire these resources.

Proprietary Technology

As electric vehicles are a newer technology, Tesla's innovation has led it to have some unique resources in technology and intellectual property over its competitors. Tesla's proprietary technology includes cooling systems, safety systems, charge balancing sys-tems, battery engineering for vibration and environmental durability, customized motor design and the software and electronics management systems necessary to manage bat-tery and vehicle performance under demanding real-life driving conditions. These tech-nology innovations have resulted in an extensive intellectual property portfolio—as of

February 3, 2011, the company had 35 issued patents and approximately 280 pending patent applications with the United States Patent and Trademark Office and internationally in a broad range of areas.[40] These patents and innovations are not easily duplicated by competitors.

A second unique resource that a company developing electric vehicles would require would be its battery cell design. Tesla's current battery strategy incorporates proprietary packaging using cells from multiple battery suppliers.[41] This allows the company to limit the power of its battery supply chain. The company also has announced a partnership with Panasonic to jointly collaborate on next-generation battery development.

Inherent to the requirements for an electric automobile company is the knowledge and skills of the workforce. Tesla believes that its roots in Silicon Valley have enabled it to recruit engineers with strong skills in electrical engineering, power electronics, and software engineering to aid it in development of its electric vehicles and components.[42] Being one of the first to market with a high-performance EV also gives the company a first-mover advantage in experience and branding.

Tesla has an agreement with the automobile manufacture Lotus for the supply of its Roadster vehicle bodies. The company entered into a supply agreement in 2005 with Lotus that requires Tesla to purchase a certain number of vehicle chassis and any additional chassis will require a new contract of redesign to a new supplier.[43] This places a large dependence on Lotus to both fulfil the existing contract and also gives them significant power in the event that Tesla requires additional Roadster units.

Tesla is dependent on its single battery cell supplier. The company designed the Roadster to be able to use cells produced by various vendors, but to date there has only been one supplier for the cells fully qualified. The same is also true for the battery cells used for battery packs that Tesla supplies to other OEMs.[44] Any disruption in the supply of battery cells from its vendors could disrupt production of the Roadster or future vehicles and the battery packs produced for other automobile manufacturers.[45]

External Opportunities and Threats

Electric vehicle companies may be able to take advantage of many of the opportunities with the continuous shift toward green energy. President Barack Obama has publicly committed to funding "green" or alternative energy initiatives through various vehicles.[46] In his 2011 State of the Union Address, the President set a goal of getting one million electric cars on the road by 2015.[47] Within the United States, various federal and state governmental agencies are currently supporting loan programs through the likes of the Department of Energy and the California Zero-Emission Vehicle (ZEV) program. The tragic Louisiana BP oil spill that took place from April to May 2010 intensified the focus on decreasing U.S. dependence on petroleum products. It also highlighted the fact that while alternative energy is currently more expensive to produce than conventional energy, there are hidden environmental and human costs that must be taken into consideration when making this comparison. This increased focus on alternative energy has been beneficial for the EV industry, benefiting both Tesla and its competitors. Due in part to this increase in funding, Tesla is competing in an industry that is expanding, making its absolute market share less relevant than how fast it is growing its market share.

Despite the new dawn of interest and pledges for funding alternative energy, many plans for funding will never come to fruition. Currently in the United States, there is a massive budget deficit, and members of the Republican Party have focused their demands for budget cuts in the "discretionary spending" arena, which is where alternative energy funding falls. Notably, some of the cuts proposed would seriously affect programs funding energy efficiency, renewable energy, and the DOE Loan Guarantee Authority.[48] The EV industry has very few lobbyists compared to the traditional car and petroleum industry, and so is more vulnerable to being targeted in budget cuts. These cuts represent a serious threat to the continued development of the alternative energy and electric car industry. For EVs to come into widespread use, the United States must develop an EV-charging infrastructure, and this will need the support of both state and federal government in the form of both funding and regulation.

Not only is the federal government facing budget cuts, but the state of California is also dealing with massive shortfalls and reductions in services and funding. This is especially important to Tesla since it operates its manufacturing in California, and one of its largest target markets is California, due to the strict emissions regulation and traditional green focus of Californians.

There are also many regulations to which companies developing electric vehicles are subjected. A topic of current interest is the upcoming change in how the range of electric vehicles is calculated—a regulation determined by the EPA. It is thought that the new calculation will result in a lower advertised range for all the electric vehicles, which may make their superiority over traditional petroleum-based vehicles less prevalent. There are also numerous safety requirements that EVs must adhere to, governed by the National Highway Traffic Safety Administration. Companies that produce less than 5000 cars for sale and have three product lines or less can qualify for a gradual phase-in regulation for advanced airbag systems and other safety requirements. Similarly, in Europe, smaller companies are currently exempt from many of the safety testing regulations, and are currently allowed to operate under the "Small Series Whole Vehicle Type Approval."

Additionally, battery safety and testing is regulated by the Pipeline and Hazardous Materials Safety Administration, which is based on UN guidelines regarding the safe transport of hazardous materials. These guidelines ensure that the batteries will perform or travel safely when undergoing changes in altitude, temperature, vibrations, shocks, external short circuiting, and overcharging.

Other regulatory issues include automobile manufacturer and dealer regulations, which are set on a state-by-state basis. In some United States states, such as Texas, it is not legal for the dealer and manufacturer to be owned by the same company. Therefore, these regulations would impact the market penetration levels that a company wishing to utilize a distribution model based on being able to both manufacture and sell its cars through its own wholly owned dealerships would be able to reach in certain states.

An interesting, though potentially costly, new regulation is the minimum noise requirements, mandated by the Pedestrian Safety Enhancement Act of 2010 signed in January 2011. There have been concerns that since electric cars are so much quieter than their combustion-engine counterparts that their design must be somehow altered to increase the amount of noise they generate in order to make them easier to hear by people with impaired vision. These regulations are likely to take effect by 2013 and could alter electric vehicle designs.

The macroeconomic conditions of 2011 and the outlook for the near future is slow but continued growth,[49] in contrast to the past several years of economic retraction. In recent years, American buyers, and indeed buyers in most parts of the world, have cut back on discretionary purchases in light of high unemployment and general economic uncertainty. The economic recovery has created more demand for higher-priced luxury vehicles.

The largest component of what makes an electric vehicle attractive from a financial standpoint is the savings in traditional fuel costs. There is a huge difference between the cost of electricity to recharge an electric vehicle versus the cost of gas to fuel a conventional vehicle. Hence, as oil prices increase, the financial incentive to purchase an electric vehicle increases as well. Additionally, the variability of oil prices means that owners of conventionally powered vehicles cannot predict what their fuel costs for the year will be with any confidence. Thus, the much more stable costs of electricity make an electric vehicle more desirable. It is not likely that the cost of oil will ever see a sustained and significant drop in price, nor is it likely that the cost of oil will ever be as stable as the cost of electricity, creating a sustained advantage over traditionally powered vehicles.

Electric vehicle manufacturers are currently riding the wave of environmental consciousness that began in the 1960s, and has been slowly gaining momentum since. The "Green movement" encourages people to make choices that lessen their negative impact on the environment, and to use resources that are renewable. Alternative fuel products fit this description, by both reducing consumer demand for oil and eliminating harmful emissions during use. For the time being, electric vehicles still leave a noticeable "footprint," though one not nearly as large as a conventional car.

Challenges to Adoption of Electric Cars: Consumer Perceptions

Consumer perceptions of electric vehicles are a huge challenge to adoption. Many people think of electric vehicles as being underpowered, clunky looking, hard to charge, quirky, and undependable. Public experience with traditional vehicles and their concerns about the newness of alterative fuel vehicles must be overcome.

Additionally, the absence of a public infrastructure for recharging electric vehicle batteries introduces a "Which came first – the chicken or the egg?" paradox: There is no infrastructure because there are not enough electric vehicles, and part of the reason why there are not many electric vehicles is because there is no infrastructure to support them. For the time being, consumers must charge their vehicles either at home, or possibly at their place of work. This limits the electric vehicle driving range, which has a negative impact on the image of electric vehicles with consumers.

Another concern that consumers have when considering an alternative energy vehicle is the cost. Electric vehicles, as well as most alternative fuel vehicles, cost significantly more than traditional vehicles of similar style and performance. This is due both to the cost of the research and development and the high cost of materials, particularly for the battery cells.[50] Additionally, the production of low environmental impact products is in most cases more expensive than their conventionally produced counterparts. So long as there are areas of the world willing to sacrifice the environment (natural resources, air, water, waste production) to create low-cost products, this dynamic will continue.

The EV industry is hampered by the public view of the limited range of vehicles in comparison to traditional gasoline cars. In recent years, there has been much advancement in the ways of sustainable energy. High gas prices along with increased awareness on environmental impacts have become the catalysts for new research into sustainability. There has been an increase in new battery technology that is an opportunity for the electric vehicle industry. Currently, the most viable battery for an electric vehicle, that also provides performance, is the lithium-ion battery (is the same type found in your laptop). Companies like Planar Energy are now coming out with "solid state, ceramic-like" batteries that could potentially provide more energy for a lower cost.[51] With these new advances, there is a distinct opportunity for electric car companies to create a better performing and less expensive vehicle. Electric vehicle companies that can develop battery architectures that cross this limited mileage chasm will have positive implications in the public view. Tesla is credited to have one of the industry's best batteries, and it is on the cutting edge of innovative technology. This type of innovative technology is what distinguishes Tesla from other competitors in its industry, and will continue to set it apart across contexts in the market.

Electric vehicles are also reliant on a network of available power sources. Though infrastructure is currently limited, companies like GE are already planning a rollout of EV charging stations to be sold to households, companies, and local governments.[52] The U.S. government has set out to aid in the building of electric vehicle charging stations, with government grants supporting the installation of the electric-car charging stations in areas such as San Francisco and Oregon, which will soon host 15,000 stations around the state, some of them public.[53] An increase in charging station technology and infrastructure should broaden the demand for electric vehicles that is still encumbered by beliefs of limited service and "refueling" capabilities.

Along with the advantages of technological innovations in electric vehicle designs, there are also respective weaknesses to consider, including the amount of time necessary to charge a battery and the limited driving range per charge. Currently, Tesla has reduced the recharge time of its battery cell to 45 minutes, but this is a long time compared to the few minutes that it takes cars to refuel at the gas pump. Coupled with the recharge time of the battery cells is the limited range of electric vehicles. For owners of conventional cars who are used to having a range of 300 miles or more, with a refilling time of 3 to 4 minutes, the limited range and recharging options of EVs can seem very restrictive. However, the average American driver travels only 35 miles per day, and the average trip length is only 10 miles.[54] More importantly, long distance trips (more than 100 miles, accounting for less than 1% of all trips) made by American drivers have a median distance of 194 miles.[55] This indicates that most drivers will very infrequently be driving non-stop for more than 245 miles, making range a virtual non-issue. However, while the facts may be different from perception, it is the perception of consumers that will drive their purchasing behavior, thus still making the range issue a serious concern for EV manufacturers.

The second issue with batteries is their end-of-life concerns. Rechargeable batteries, over time, will become less efficient, and will no longer hold their charge as well as when the battery was new. The same issue exists with electric vehicle batteries. Tesla estimates that after 100,000 miles or seven years, the Roadster's battery will only operate at 60%–65% efficiency.[56] This decrease in battery performance will decrease the range of the car, and will start taking place well before the 100,000 mile/7-year marker. Proper battery disposal is another issue. At this time, there are not many battery disposal facilities due to the limited electric vehicle market to date.

Finally, maintenance of electric vehicles is a concern, given the paucity of many adequately trained repair facilities and the low market penetration of the cars. There simply are not many EVs on the road, and conventional car repair shops do not have proper training in the repair of electric vehicles. This can have a detrimental effect on adoption of EVs.

In recent years, international emerging markets have increased their infrastructures and stratification of wealth and the current consumer demographic is better equipped to afford more expensive vehicles as a result. Additionally, there is a growing global awareness and commitment to developing sustainable and "green" energy and innovations. These factors may increase opportunities for sales of EVs in these markets.

Oil Price

The rising cost of oil is also a major opportunity for electric vehicle manufacturers to cultivate a great presence in the market, due to the demand of consumers to seek alternative types of vehicles, including electric. The global future of the EV market is promising based on the current trends in oil cost, consumption, and awareness about conservation.

Global economic policies, such as the Kyoto protocol, advance the cause of environmentally sustainable products, such as electric vehicles. However, every country has the choice to either ratify these protocols, or not. This lack of accountability means that the financial and political support of environmentally sustainable products are highly variable, and can affect the favorability and feasibility of selling electric vehicles in every country in which they are sold or manufactured.

Finances

Revenues at Tesla Motors are derived from sales that are recognized from two sources, sales of the Roadster and sales of Tesla's patented electric power train components (see **Exhibit 1**). Coinciding with the sales of the Roadster, Tesla recognizes income from the sale of vehicle options and accessories, vehicle service and maintenance, and the sale of Zero-Emission Vehicle (ZEV) credits.

Zero-Emission Vehicle credits are required by the State of California to ensure auto manufacturers design vehicles to meet strict eco-friendly guidelines. Credits are acquired by producing and selling vehicles that meet a minimum emission level in an attempt to offset the pollutants produced by mainstream vehicles. If a manufacturer chooses not to design ZEV vehicles, it is able to purchase credits from companies such as Tesla, who only produces electric vehicles and does not have to accrue credits. Tesla has realized sales of US$14.5 (see **Exhibit 2),** million in ZEV credits since 2008.

Total quarterly revenues at Tesla have been increasing steadily throughout 2010, but no definitive year-over-year positive trends can be established from Tesla's sales data. Two trends that do appear to be gaining in the most recent fiscal year are foreign sales and sales of power train components and related sales.

Tesla's cash position (see **Exhibit 5)** is currently in a less than optimal position. Through its IPO, Tesla was able to raise US$226 million in June of 2010 and has also

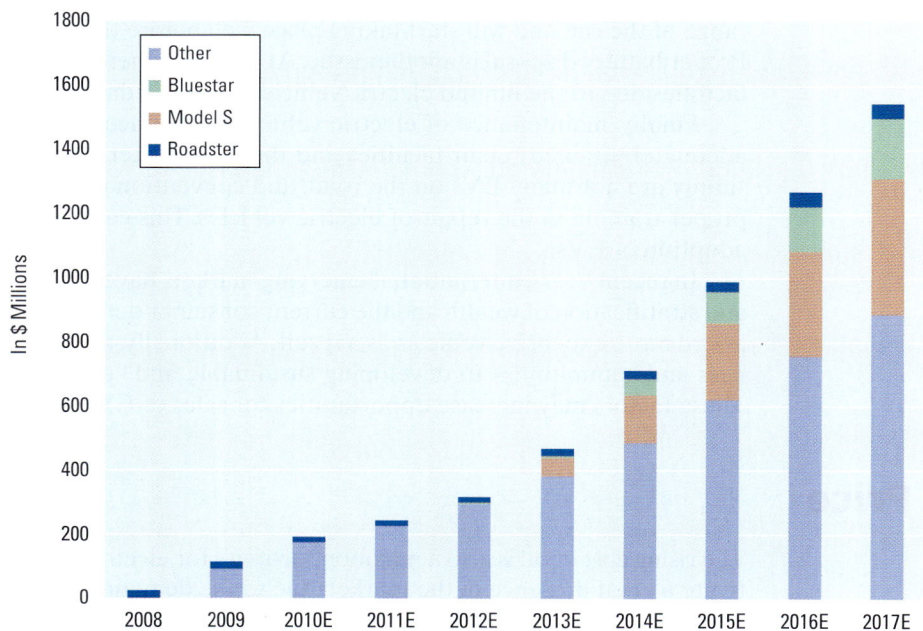

EXHIBIT 1
Tesla Projected
Sales, in US$ millions

EXHIBIT 2
Automotive Sales

Automotive sales consisted of the following for the periods presented (in thousands):

	2010	2009	2008
Vehicle, options and related sales	US$75,459	$111,555	$14,742
Power train component and related sales	21,619	388	—
	$97,078	$111,943	$14,742

been able to take advantage of state and federal programs to raise capital at low prices due to its investment in alternative energy pi grams. These sources of cash offer the company the ability to meet its current obligations, but revenues (see **Exhibits 3** and **4**) have not been able to match expenses, resulting in the company's largest net loss yet of US$51 million in December of 2010. The United States Department of Energy (DOE) loaned Tesla US$465 million at the beginning of the year, so no matter what, Tesla has to manage a "mountain of debt."[57] This specific loan has various restrictions that are structured around the progress of the Model S and several financial ratios. Tesla stands to lose revenue if the Model S delays, since the DOE loan pays in installments as the Model S reaches various development and production benchmarks. Although debt as a

EXHIBIT 3
Income Statement
(2010)

The following table includes selected quarterly results of operations data for the years ended December 31, 2010 and 2009 (in thousands, except per share data):

	Three Months Ended			
	Mar 31	Jun 30	Sept 30	Dec 31
2010				
Total Revenue	US$20,812	$28,405	$31,241	$36,286
Gross profit	3,852	6,261	9,296	11,321
Net loss	(29,519)	(38,517)	(34,935)	(51,158)
Net loss per share, basic and diluted	(4.04)	(5.04)	(0.38)	(0.54)
2009				
Total Revenue	$20,886	$26,945	$45,527	$18,585
Gross profit	(2,046)	2,101	7,699	1,781
Net loss	(16,016)	(10,867)	(4,615)	(24,242)
Net loss per share, basic and diluted	(2.31)	(1.56)	(0.66)	(3.43)

EXHIBIT 4
Revenue by Region

The following table sets forth revenue by geographic area (in thousands):

Revenues			C f
	2010	2009	2008
North America	$ 41,866	$ 90,833	$14,742
Europe	70,542	21,110	—
Asia	4,336	—	—
	$116,744	$111,943	$14,742

EXHIBIT 5
Tesla 2010
Financial
Highlights

All info as of 12/31/2010 (in thousands)

Sales: US$97,078
Net Profit: (US$154,328)
Operating Margin: (125.78%)
Receivables: US$6710
Cash Assets: US$99,558
Inventory: US$45,182
Total Debt: US$71,828

percent of total capital increased at Tesla Motors, Inc. over the last fiscal year to 25.96%, it is still in line with the automobile industry's norm. Additionally, there are enough liquid assets to satisfy current obligations.[58]

Marketing

Tesla's internal marketing situation has to operate with many limitations stemming from the company's infancy and its lack of resources. Looking at the product offerings, the only vehicle Tesla currently has on the market is the Roadster, a sporty two-seater priced at US$108,000 and up. The high price tag puts it firmly in competition with other luxury vehicles as opposed to other electric vehicles. The key demographic market for luxury cars are white males, 45 and older, who are married, have no kids, and make over US$75,000 a year. Primary considerations for this group when purchasing a luxury vehicle are performance, design, and safety, while factors such as financing, the environment, and gas mileage are not important.[59] The Roadster does deliver on aesthetics and performance, but it is questionable whether or not its electric motor will be an effective differentiator. Bearing this in mind, Tesla needs to focus on early adopters and environmentalists, who also have the resources to afford their car. One could argue that this is a narrow market segment.

In 2012, Tesla will roll out the Model S, a premium four-door sedan that will be variably priced at US$57,000 for the lowest range, US$67,000 for the mid range, and US$77,000 at the top of the range. This lower-priced vehicle will target larger families and a greater-sized market. Unless it can lower the price point, this will still be a difficult sell, as households with children have less disposable income and accumulated wealth. Demand for electric cars is also estimated to remain below 10% until at least 2016, because of perceptions of high cost for marginal utility.[60] Two advantages Tesla does have on price, however, are the US$7500 government tax credit for buying fuel-efficient vehicles, and the low cost of maintenance and fuel.

Aside from a minimal product offering, Tesla is also limited by its distribution and fulfilment infrastructure. At the moment, Tesla has a mix of brick-and-mortar dealerships in premium locations, along with regional sales representatives, and online ordering. North America has 10 stores and four reps, Europe has seven stores and four reps, and Asia has one store and two reps. Over the next few years, Tesla plans to open 50 stores in preparation of the Model S rollout. To ease its current lack of fulfilment capabilities, Tesla sales representatives will arrange a test drive in your location and organize vehicle delivery. This is an inexpensive way to increase its distribution capabilities without investing in physical stores. This might also hinder sales though, given that the key demographic for luxury vehicles rely on car dealerships as the second most influential outlet on what car to buy.[61]

Tesla could ramp up distribution by allowing existing dealerships to sell its cars but chooses not to, preferring a customized sales approach where it has complete control over its message. To compliment direct sales, the company has avoided traditional advertising in lieu of product placement, Internet ads, and event marketing. It is adept at turning current customers into vocal brand ambassadors. The company website is littered with quotes from owners and industry reviewers singing its praises. This promotion strategy is a clear strength for Tesla, especially considering that recommendations from friends and relatives, as well as general word of mouth, are the most influential factors for a luxury/sports car's key demographic.

The Tesla brand is also inherently tied to the environmental/green movement. Because of this, it has been able to generate a lot of free media publicity.

Operations

Tesla is headquartered in Palo Alto, California, where it also manufactures its power trains, battery packs, motors, and gearbox. The body and chassis for the Roadster are manufactured by Lotus in Hethel, England, and then are fully assembled in Menlo Park, California, for U.S. buyers, or Wymondham, England, for European and Asian customers. For the upcoming launch of the Model S, Tesla is building a new factory in Fremont, California, that will have a capacity of 20,000 cars per year.

Tesla's main operating strength lies in its intellectual property and its patents. Currently, Tesla has 35 issued patents with another 280 pending. Proprietary components include power train technology, safety systems, charge balancing, battery engineering for vibration and environmental durability, motor design, and the electricity management system. The company also owns the proprietary software systems that are used to manage efficiency, safety, and controls. Tesla's software is designed to be updatable, and many aspects of the vehicle architecture have been designed so it can be used on multiple future models.

To boost operational know-how and supplement the revenue Tesla gets from sales of the Roadster, it also sells Zero-Emission Vehicle credits, and supplies power train and battery pack components to original equipment manufacturers. Currently, Tesla has strategic partnerships with Daimler and Toyota, and is providing their electric vehicle expertise in the development of Daimler's Smart Car and Toyota's new RAV4. These partnerships are an opportunity for Tesla to diversify its revenue streams and network and access greater supply chains.

As previously mentioned, Tesla has decided to distribute through its own network of stores and regional sales staff as opposed to selling through established dealer networks. Despite fulfilment implications, Tesla considers owning its own distribution channel as a competitive advantage. Channel ownership not only allows for greater operating efficiency through inventory control, but also gives Tesla control over its sales message, warranty, price, brand image, and user feedback. The drawbacks to this strategy include the high capital costs of buying real estate and constructing showrooms and the cost of additional sales staff.

Currently, over 2000 parts are sourced from 150 suppliers. One major issue with the current supply structure is that many vendors are the single source. This leaves Tesla vulnerable to delays and increased costs. Due to limited economies of scale, (as of December 31, 2010 only 1500 Roadsters were sold) production costs also run high. The first Roadster was sold in early 2008, but revenues didn't exceed the costs of production until the second quarter of 2009. Tesla is still struggling to bring the costs of the Model S down so it can be profitably sold at US$57,000.

Servicing vehicles presents another challenge for Tesla. Given the complex and proprietary components of their cars, the average mechanic won't be able to diagnose and fix issues. Lacking the appropriate physical infrastructure, Tesla sends maintenance technicians (which it refers to as Rangers) to wherever the car owner lives. The cars themselves also have advanced diagnostic systems that link up to a server at Tesla's headquarters. Issues can be determined prior to sending Rangers out to fix the car, which saves time and resources. Overall though, this system isn't as convenient as having a worldwide infrastructure of third-party repair shops.

This Ranger service system may work for the time being, with only 1500 cars on the road, but with the anticipated sales of the Model S and subsequent vehicles, the services infrastructure will have to be greatly expanded. Two ideas that Tesla hopes will come to fruition are an increase in fast charge stations, and the creation of a battery replacement network. The latter harkens back to the days where cowboys would exchange tired horses for fresh steeds. In anticipation of this, the Model S will incorporate removable battery packs.

Human Resources

Tesla Motors operates more like a software company than a car company, and innovation is top priority. CEO Elon Musk is a serial entrepreneur who has stocked his executive team with half-techie, half-business hybrid employees who are former industry leaders. Taking a cue from Google, the environment is fast paced and culturally unstructured. Employees are encouraged to challenge norms, think outside the box, and commit time to innovation. In order to boost teamwork and eliminate departmental silos, most staff work in an open room with no walls. Tesla prides itself on solutions created through an integration of all departments working side by side. An explanation for this corporate culture can be found in the hiring of Human Resources director, Arnnon Geshuri, who was the former director of staffing and operations at Google. Because of the emphasis on technology and innovation, the majority of manufacturing is done in California, as opposed to areas with lower labor costs, due to the abundance of top-quality engineers.

Due to the extreme importance of Tesla's intellectual capital, it is imperative to have happy employees. Aside from being able to get in on the ground floor of an innovative new company, employees are also given competitive salaries, benefits, an aesthetically pleasing office space, and "meaningful equity."

Currently, Tesla has about 900 employees, including 212 in the power train and R&D department, 170 in vehicle design and engineering, 121 in sales and marketing, 79 in the service department, and 213 in the manufacturing department. Tesla is currently looking to hire more graduating engineering students and sales staff, especially those who have had some hands-on experience. Recruiting and retaining the best talent is a paramount goal, because of difficulties arising from Tesla's capacity to design, test, manufacture, and sell at the same time.

Tesla's Future: Success or Bust?

In a nutshell, Tesla has limited sales in a limited market, and is making low margins due to high product costs and the lack of economies of scale. However, if oil prices continue to climb toward US$200 a barrel and new electric cars, such as the Chevy Volt and Nissan Leaf, catch on with consumers, the upside for Tesla could be enormous. Can Tesla reach the tipping point? Or will it become just a footnote in automotive history? Time will tell.

NOTES

1. NYTimes.com. (2010) Tesla Motors. http://topics.nytimes.com/top/news/business/companies/tesla_motors/index.html

2. Blanco, Sebastian. (2006) Roadster Unveiled in Santa Monica. http://green.autoblog.com/2006/07/20/tesla-roadster-unveiled-in-santa-monica/

3. U.S. Dept. of Energy. (2008) Tesla Motors Starts Production of Its Electric-Only Roadster http://apps1.eere.energy.gov/news/news_detail.cfm/news_id=11645

4. Tesla Motors. (2008) Tesla Motors to Manufacture Sedan in California. http://www.teslamotors.com/about/press/releases/tesla-motors-manufacture-sedan-california

5. http://topics.nytimes.com/top/news/business/companies/tesla_motors/index.html

6. Chuck Squatriglia. "Tesla Motors Joins Daimler on a Smart EV," Wired.com, January 13, 2009. http://www.wired.com/autopia/2009/01/tesla-motors-jo/

7. Eric Loveday. AllCarsElectric.com. "Daimler Announces New Strategic Partner Tesla Motors." http://www.allcarselectric.com/blog/1020804_daimler-announces-new-strategic-partner-teslamotors

8. Jim Motavalli. "Daimler Takes a Stake in Tesla Motors," The New York Times, May 9, 2011. http://wheels.blogs.nytimes.com/2009/05/19/daimler-takes-a-stake-in-tesla-motors/

9. Tesla Motors. (2010) Tesla Notifies SEC of Agreement with Toyota to Develop Electric Version of RAV4. http://www.tesla-motors.com/about/press/releases/tesla-notifies-sec-agreement-toyota-develop-electric-version-rav4

10. Tesla Motors. (2010) Tesla Motors Announces Factory in Northern California. http://www.teslamotors.com/about/press/releases/tesla-motors-announces-factory-northern-california

11. Edmunds InsideOnline.com. (2010, May 21). Toyota and Tesla to Make Electric Vehicles at Mothballed NUMMI Plant. http://www.insideline.com/tesla/toyota-and-tesla-to-make-electric-vehicles-at-mothballed-nummi-plant.html

12. Tesla Motors, Inc. (March 3, 2011) 2010 10-K Annual Report. Pg. 28.

13. Wikipedia. Hydrogen vehicle. http://en.wikipedia.org/wiki/Hydrogen_vehicle

14. Mitsubishi Motors. (2011). Overview of Mitsubishi Motors. Retrieved from http://www.mitsubishi-motors.com/en/corporate/aboutus/profile/index.html

15. Wall Street Journal.com. (2011, May 3). Sales and Share of Total Market by Manufacturer. http://online.wsj.com/mdc/public/page/2_3022-autosales.html\#autosalesE

16. Mitsubishi Motors. (2011). History of Mitsubishi Motors' EV Development. Retrieved from http://global.ev-life.com/

17. Brad Berman. (2010, March 9). Mitsubishi i. Retrieved from http://www.plugincars.com/mitsubishi-i-miev/review

18. PureGreenCars.com. (2010, November 24) http://puregreencars.com/Green-Cars-News/markets-finance/mitsubishi-i-miev-production-hits-5000-units.html

19. Nissan Motors. (2011). Corporate Information. Retrieved from http://www.nissan-global.com/EN/COMPANY/PROFILE/

20. Nissan Motors. (2011, February 9).FY2010 3rd Quarter Financial Results [Press Release]. http://www.nissan-global.com/EN/IR/FINANCIAL/

21. Nissan Motors. 100% Electric Zero-Emission Nissan LEAF Debuts in Japan Start of Sales on December 20th [Press Release]. http://www.nissan-global.com/EN/NEWS/2010/_STORY/101203-01-e.html

22. Eric Loveday. (2011, March 11). AutoBlog.com. "Nissan Leaf sales hit 3,657; that's like four times more than the Chevy Volt." http://green.autoblog.com/2011/03/11/nissan-leaf-sales-3657-four-times-more-chevy-volt/

23. Chevrolet. (2011). History & Heritage. Retrieved from http://www.chevrolet.com/experience/history/

24. GM. (2011). About GM. http://www.gm.com/content/gmcom/home/company/aboutGM.html

25. GM. (2011). http://www.gm.com/investors/sales-production/pressrelease.jsp?id=/content/Pages/news/cn/en/2011/Jan/0118.html

26. Chevrolet. (2011). 2011 Volt. Retrieved from http://www.chevrolet.com/volt/

27. Eric Loveday. "Nissan Leaf sales hit 3,657; that's like four times more than the Chevy Volt."

28. Toyota Motor Corporation. (2011). Worldwide Operations. Retrieved from http://www.toyota-global.com/company/profile/facilities/worldwide_operations.html

29. Toyota Motor Corporation. (2011). Overview. Retrieved from http://www.toyota-global.com/company/profile/overview/

30. Toyota Motor Corporation. (2011, April 6). *Toyota Sells One-Millionth Prius in the U.S.* [Press Release]. http://pressroom.toyota.com/article_display.cfm?article_id=2959

31. BMW. (2011). BMW History. Retrieved from http://www.bmwdrives.com/bmw_history/bmw-1910.php

32. BMW Group. (2011). BMW Group in Figures. Retrieved from http://annual-report.bmwgroup.com/2010/gb/en/facts-and-figures-2010/bmw-group-in-figures.html

33. DistroCars.com. (2006, Sept. 12). 2007 BMW Hydrogen 7 Series Reducing Fuel Consumption. http://www.distrocars.com/2007-bmw-hydrogen-7-series

34. Hydrogen Fuel Cars Now. (2011). BMW Hydrogen 7. http://www.hydrogencarsnow.com/bmw-hydrogen7.htm

35. Honda. (2011) History. http://world.honda.com/history/limit-lessdreams/encounter/text01/index.html

36. Honda Motor Company, LTD. Annual Report 2010. Retrieved May 2, 2011 from http://world.honda.com/investors/library/annual_report/2010/honda2010ar-all-e.pdf

37. Martin Fackler. "Latest Honda Runs on Hydrogen, Not Petroleum," The New York Times, June 17, 2008. http://www.nytimes.com/2008/06/17/business/worldbusiness/17fuelcell.html

38. Honda Motor Company. (2011) How FCX Clarity FCEV Works. Retrieved from http://automobiles.honda.com/fcx-clarity/how-fcx-works.aspx

39. Martin Fackler. "Latest Honda Runs on Hydrogen, Not Petroleum"

40. Tesla Motors, Inc. (March 3, 2011) 2010 10-K Annual Report. Pg 29

41. Tesla Motors, Inc. (2010, Jan. 11). *Tesla and Panasonic Collaborate to Develop Next-Generation Battery Cell Technology* [Press Release]. http://www.teslamotors.com/about/press/releases/tesla-and-panasonic-collaborate-develop-nextgeneration-battery-cell-technology

42. Tesla Motors, Inc. (March 3, 2011) 2010 10-K Annual Report. Pg 4

43. Ibid. Pg 48

44. Ibid. Pg 50

45. Ibid. Pg 50

46. http://apps1.eere.energy.gov/news/progress_alerts.cfm/pa_id=152

47. http://www.washingtonpost.com/wp-dyn/content/article/2011/02/07/AR2011020705616.html

48. http://www.nationaljournal.com/house-gop-proposes-cuts-to-scores-of-sacred-cows-20110209

49. http://dailyreckoning.com/us-data-indicate-slow-economic-growth/

50. http://green.autoblog.com/2010/06/10/ask-abg-why-are-electric-vehicles-so-expensive/

51. Planar Energy, "Department of Energy Awards $4 million to Planar Energy Under Its Advanced Research Project Agency–Energy Initiative," http://www.planarenergy.com/Press%20Releases/DOE%20Awards%20Planar%20Energy%20$4M%20Grant.pdf, April 29, 2010.

52. "Electric Vehicle Equipment from GE." *GE Industrial Systems.* Web. May 11, 2011. http://www.geindustrial.com/products/static/ecomagination-electric-vehicles/?kmed=ppc.

53. http://techland.time.com/2011/05/10/san-francisco-to-offer-free-electric-car-charging-stations/

54. http://www.bts.gov/publications/highlights_of_the_2001_national_household_travel_survey/html/executive_summary.html

55. http://www.bts.gov/publications/highlights_of_the_2001_national_household_travel_survey/html/table_a22.html

56. Tesla Motors, Inc. (March 3, 2011) 2010 10-K Annual Report. Pg 37

57. Tyler Matuella, J. and Ajayi, Mannie (March 28, 2011). Why Electric Carmaker Tesla Motors Will Likely Be Acquired. *Business Insider.* Retrieved on April 21, 2011, from, http://www.businessinsider.com/why-electric-carmaker-tesla-motors-is-unlikely-to-succeed-on-its-own-2011-3.

58. Bloomberg Businessweek (May 3, 2011) from, http://investing.businessweek.com/businessweek/research/stocks/financials/financials.asp?ticker=TSLA:US&dataset=balanceSheet&period=A&currency=native

59. Mintel – Auto Market – Sports and Luxury Cars – U.S. 2003

60. Bloomburg.com, "Hybrid, Battery Car Demand Limited by Cost, Utility, J.D. Power Says," Alan Ohnsman, April 2011

61. Mintel – Auto Market – Sports and Luxury Cars – U.S. 2003

CASE **31**

TomTom

NEW COMPETITION EVERYWHERE!

Alan N. Hoffman
Bentley University

TOMTOM WAS ONE OF THE LARGEST PRODUCERS OF SATELLITE NAVIGATION SYSTEMS IN THE
WORLD. Its products were comprised of both stand-alone devices and applications.
TomTom led the navigation systems market in Europe and was second in the
United States. TomTom attributed its position as a market leader to the following
factors: the size of its customer and technology base, its distribution power, and
its prominent brand image and recognition.[1]

   With the acquisition of Tele Atlas, TomTom became vertically integrated and
also controlled the map creation process. This helped TomTom establish itself as
an integrated content, service, and technology business. The company was Dutch by
origin and had its headquarters based in Amsterdam, The Netherlands. In terms of
geography, the company's operations spanned from Europe to Asia Pacific, covering
North America, the Middle East, and Africa.[2]

   TomTom was supported by a workforce of 3300 employees from 40 countries. The
company's revenues had grown from €8 million in 2002 to €1.674 billion in 2008. (See
Exhibits 1 and **2.**)

....

This case was prepared by Professor Alan N. Hoffman, Bentley University and Erasmus University. Copyright © 2015 by Alan N. Hoffman. The copyright holder is solely responsible for the case content. Reprint
permission is solely granted to the publisher, Prentice Hall, for *Strategic Management and Business Policy,*
14th Edition (and the international and electronic versions of this book) by the copyright holder, Alan N.
Hoffman. Any other publication of the case (translation, any form of electronics or other media) or sale (any
form of partnership) to another publisher will be in violation of copyright law, unless Alan N. Hoffman has
granted an additional written permission. The author would like to thank Will Hoffman, Mansi Asthana,
Aakashi Ganveer, Hing Lin, and Che Yii for their research. Please address all correspondence to: Professor
Alan N. Hoffman, Bentley University, 175 Forest Street, Waltham, MA 02452 or ahoffman@bentley.edu.
Printed by permission of Dr. Alan N. Hoffman.

   RSM Case Development Centre prepared this case to provide material for class discussion rather than
to illustrate either effective or ineffective handling of a management situation. Copyright © 2010, RSM Case
Development Centre, Erasmus University. No part of this publication may be copied, stored, transmitted,
reproduced, or distributed in any form or medium whatsoever without the permission of the copyright owner,
Alan N. Hoffman.

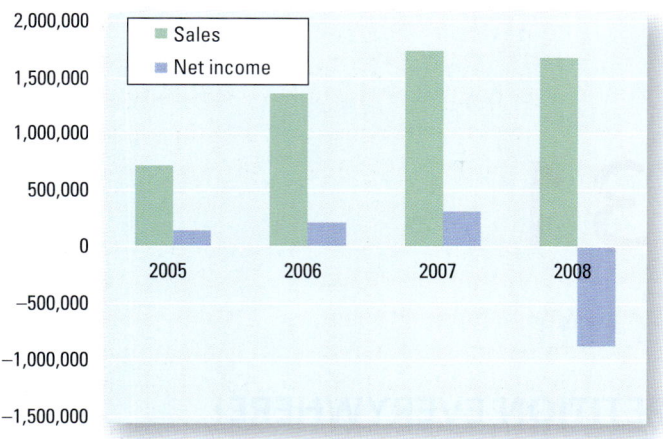

EXHIBIT 2
Quarterly Sales:
TomTom (Amount
in millions of €)

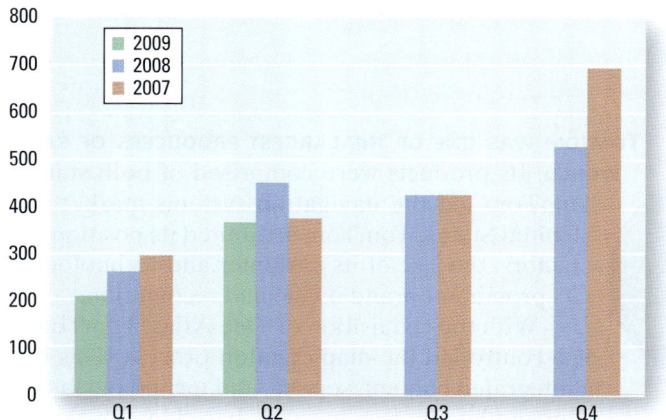

However, because of the Tele Atlas acquisition and the current economic downturn, the company has recently become a cause of concern for investors. On July 22, 2009, TomTom reported a decline in its net income at the end of the second quarter of 2009.

TomTom was in the business of navigation-based information services and devices. The company had been investing structurally and strategically in research and development to bring new and better products and services to its customers. The company's belief in radical innovation helped it remain at the cutting edge of innovation within the navigation industry.

The vision of TomTom's management was to improve people's lives by transforming navigation from a "don't-get-lost solution" into a true travel companion that gets people from one place to another safer, faster, cheaper, and better informed. This vision helped the company become a market leader in every marketplace in the satellite navigation information services market.[3]

The company's goals focused around radical advances in three key areas:

- **Better maps:** This goal was achieved by maintaining TomTom's high-quality map database, which was continuously kept up to date by a large community of active users who provided corrections, verifications, and updates to TomTom. This was supplemented by inputs from TomTom's extensive fleet of surveying vehicles.[4]

- **Better routing:** TomTom had the world's largest historical speed profile database IQ Routes, facilitated by TomTom HOME, the company's user portal.[5]
- **Better traffic information:** TomTom possessed a unique, real-time traffic information service called TomTom HD traffic, which provided users with high-quality, real-time traffic updates.[6] These three goals formed the base of satellite navigation, working in conjunction to help TomTom achieve its mission.

TomTom's Products

TomTom offered a wide variety of products ranging from portable navigation devices to software navigation applications and digital maps. The unique features in each of these products made them truly "the smart choice in personal navigation."[7] Some of these products are described next.

TomTom Go and TomTom One

These devices came with an LCD screen that made it easy to use with fingertips while driving. They provided Points of Interest (POI) that helped in locating petrol stations, restaurants, and places of importance and traffic information.

TomTom Rider

These were portable models especially designed for bikers. The equipment consisted of an integrated GPS receiver that could be mounted on any bike, and a wireless headset inside the helmet. Similar to the car Portable Navigation Devices (PNDs), the TomTom Rider models had a number of POI applications. The interfaces used in TomTom Rider were user-friendly and came in a variety of languages.[8]

TomTom Navigator and TomTom Mobile

These applications provided navigation software along with digital maps. Both of these applications were compatible with most mobiles and PDAs provided by companies like Sony, Nokia, Acer, Dell, and HP. These applications came with TomTom HOME, which could be used to upgrade to the most recent digital maps and application versions.[9]

TomTom for iPhone

On August 17, 2009, TomTom released TomTom for the iPhone.

The TomTom app for iPhone 3G and 3GS users included a map of the United States and Canada from Tele Atlas, and was available for US$99.99.

The TomTom app for iPhone included the exclusive IQ Routes technology. Instead of using travel time assumptions, IQ Routes based its routes on the actual experience of millions of TomTom drivers to calculate the fastest route and generate the most accurate arrival times in the industry. TomTom IQ Routes empowered drivers to reach their destination faster up to 35% of the time.

Company History

TomTom was founded as "Palmtop" in 1991 by Peter-Frans Pauwels and Pieter Geelen, two graduates from Amsterdam University, The Netherlands. Palmtop started out as a software development company and was involved in producing software for handheld computers, one of the most popular devices of the 1990s. In the following few years, the company diversified into producing commercial applications including software for personal finance, games, a dictionary, and maps. In the year 1996, Corinne Vigreux joined Palmtop as the third partner. In the same year, the company announced the launch of Enroute and RouteFinder, the first navigation software titles. As more and more people using PCs adopted Microsoft's operating system, the company developed applications which were compatible with it. This helped the company increase its market share. In 2001, Harold Goddijn, the former Chief Executive of Psion, joined the company as the fourth partner. This proved to be a turning point in the history of TomTom. Not only did Palmtop get renamed to TomTom, but it also entered the satellite navigation market. TomTom launched TomTom Navigator, the first mobile car satnav system.

In 2002, the company generated revenue of €8 million by selling the first GPS-linked car navigator, the TomTom Navigator, for PDAs. The upgraded version, Navigator 2, was released in early 2003. Meanwhile, the company made efforts to gain technical and marketing personnel. TomTom took strategic steps to grow its sales. The former CTO of Psion, Mark Gretton, led the hardware team, while Alexander Ribbink, a former top marketing official, looked after sales of new products introduced by the company.

TomTom Go, an all-in-one car navigation system, was the company's next major launch. With its useful and easy-to-use features, TomTom Go was included in the list of successful products of 2004. In the same year, the company launched TomTom Mobile, a navigation system that sat on top of Smartphones.[10]

TomTom completed its IPO on the Amsterdam Stock Exchange in May 2005, raising €469 million (US$587 million). The net worth of the company was nearly €2 billion after the IPO. A majority of the shares were held by the four partners.[11] From the years 2006 to 2008, TomTom strengthened itself by making three key strategic acquisitions. Datafactory AG was acquired to power TomTom WORK through WEBfleet technology, while Applied Generics gave its technology for Mobility Solutions Services. However, the most prominent of these three was the acquisition of Tele Atlas.[12]

In July of 2007, TomTom bid for Tele Atlas, a company specializing in digital maps. The original bid price of €2 billion was countered by a €2.3 billion offer from Garmin, TomTom's biggest rival. When TomTom raised its bid price to €2.9 billion, the two companies initiated a bidding war for Tele Atlas. Although there was speculation that Garmin would further increase its bid price, in the end management decided not to pursue Tele Atlas any further. Rather, Garmin struck a content agreement with Navteq. TomTom's shareholders approved the takeover in December 2007.[13]

TomTom's Customers

TomTom was a company that had a wide array of customers, each with their own individual needs and desires. TomTom had a variety of products to meet the requirements of a large and varied customer base. As an example, its navigational products ranged from US$100–$500 in the United States, spanning lower-end products with fewer capabilities to high-end products with advanced features.

The *first* group was the individual consumers who bought stand-alone portable navigation devices and services. The *second* group was automobile manufacturers. TomTom teamed with companies like Renault to develop built-in navigational units to install as an option in cars. A *third* group of customers was the aviation industry and pilots with personal planes. TomTom produced navigational devices for air travel at affordable prices. A *fourth* group of customers was business enterprises. Business enterprises referred to companies such as Wal-Mart, Target, or The Home Depot, huge companies with large mobile workforces. To focus on these customers, TomTom formed a strategic partnership with a technology company called Advanced Integrated Solutions to "optimize business fleet organization and itinerary planning on the TomTom pro series of navigation devices." This new advanced feature on PNDs offered ways for fleet managers and route dispatchers to organize, plan, and optimize routes and to provide detailed mapping information about the final destination. TomTom's *fifth* group of customers, the Coast Guard, was able to use TomTom's marine navigational devices for its everyday responsibilities.

Mergers and Acquisitions

TomTom made various mergers and acquisitions as well as partnerships, which positioned the company well. In 2008, TomTom acquired a digital mapping company called Tele Atlas. The acquisition significantly improved TomTom customers' user experience and created other benefits for the customers and partners of both companies, including more accurate navigation information, improved coverage, and new enhanced features such as map updates and IQ Routes.

In 2005, TomTom partnered with Avis, adding its user-friendly navigation system to all Avis rental cars. This partnership began in Europe, and soon the devices had made their way into Avis rental cars in North America as well as many other countries where Avis operated.

TomTom acquired several patents for its many different technologies. By having these patents for each of its ideas, the company protected itself against its competition and other companies trying to enter into the market.

TomTom prided itself on being the industry innovator and always being a step ahead of the competition in terms of its technology.

TomTom had a strong brand name/image. It positioned itself well throughout the world as a leader in portable navigation devices. The company marketed its products through its very user-friendly online website and also through large companies such as Best Buy and Wal-Mart. TomTom also teamed up with Locutio Voice Technologies and Twentieth Century Fox Licensing & Merchandising to bring the original voice of Homer Simpson to all TomTom devices via download. "Let Homer Simpson be your TomTom co-pilot" was one of the many interesting ways TomTom marketed its products and name to consumers.[14]

TomTom's Resources and Capabilities

The company believed that there were three fundamental requirements to a navigation system—digital mapping, routing technology, and dynamic information. Based on these requirements, three key resources could be identified that really distinguished TomTom from its competition.

The first of these resources was the in-house **routing algorithms.** These algorithms enabled TomTom to introduce technologies like IQ Routes that provided a "community based information database." IQ Routes calculated customer routes based on the real average speeds measured on roads at that particular time.

The second unique resource was Tele Atlas and the **digital mapping technology** that the TomTom group specialized in. Having the technology and knowledge in mapping that the company brought to TomTom allowed it to introduce many unique features to its customers. First, TomTom came out with a map update feature. The company recognized that roads around the world were constantly changing and, because of this, it used the technology to come out with four new maps each year, one per business quarter. This allowed its customers to always have the latest routes to incorporate into their everyday travel. A second feature it introduced is its Map Share program. The idea behind this is that customers of TomTom who notice mistakes in a certain map are able to go in and request a change to be made. The change was then verified and checked directly by TomTom and was shared with the rest of the global user community.

The third unique resource was **automotive partnerships** with two companies in particular: Renault and Avis. At the end of 2008, TomTom reached a deal with Renault to install its navigation devices in its cars as an option. The clincher was the new price of the built-in navigation units. The cost of a navigation device installed in Renault's cars before TomTom was €1500. Now, with the TomTom system, it cost only €500. As mentioned earlier, TomTom also partnered with Avis in 2005 to offer its navigation devices, specifically the model GO 700, in all Avis rental cars, first starting in Europe and then expanding into other countries where Avis operated.

Traditional Competition

TomTom faced competition from two main companies. The first of these was Garmin, which held 45% of the market share, by far the largest and double TomTom's market share (24%). Garmin was founded in 1989 by Gary Burrell and Min H. Kao. The company was known for its on-the-go directions since its introduction into GPS navigation in 1989. At the end of 2008, Garmin reported annual sales of US$3.49 billion. Garmin had competed head to head in 2009 with TomTom in trying to acquire Tele Atlas for its mapmaking. Garmin withdrew its bid when it became evident that it was becoming too expensive to own Tele Atlas. Garmin executives made a decision that it was cheaper to work out a long-term deal with its current supplier, Navteq, than to try to buy out a competitor.

The second direct competitor was Magellan, which held 15% of the market share. Magellan was part of a privately held company under the name of MiTac Digital Corporation. Similar to Garmin, Magellan products used Navteq-based maps. Magellan was the creator of Magellan NAV 100, the world's first commercial handheld GPS receiver, which was created in 1989. The company was also well-known for its award-winning RoadMate and Maestro series portable car navigation systems.

Together these three dominant players accounted for about 85% of the total market. Other competitors in the personal navigation device market were Navigon, Nextar, and Nokia. Navigon and Nextar competed in the personal navigation devices with TomTom, Magellan, and Garmin, who were the top three in the industry. But Navigon competed in the high-end segment, which retailed for more than any of the competitors but offered a few extra features in its PNDs. Nextar competed in the low-end market and its strategy was low cost. Finally, Nokia was mentioned as a competitor in this industry because the company acquired Navteq, a major supplier of map services in this industry. Along with that, Nokia had a big market share in the cell phone industry and planned on incorporating GPS technology in every phone, making it a potential key player to look for in the GPS navigation industry.

New Competition Everywhere!

Cell Phones

Cell phones were widely used by people all around the world. With the 2005 FCC mandate that required the location of any cell phone used to call 911 to be tracked, phone manufacturers included a GPS receiver in almost every cell phone. Due to this mandate, cell phone manufacturers and cellular services were able to offer GPS navigation services through the cell phone for a fee.

AT&T Navigator

GPS Navigation with AT&T Navigator and AT&T Navigator Global Edition feature real-time GPS-enabled turn-by-turn navigation onAT&T mobile Smartphones (iPhones and BlackBerrys) or static navigation and Local Search on a non-GPS AT&T mobile Smartphone.

AT&T Navigator featured Global GPS turn-by-turn navigation—Mapping and Point of AT&T Interest content for three continents, including North America (United States, Canada, and Mexico), Western Europe, and China, where wireless coverage was available from AT&T or its roaming providers. The AT&T Navigator was sold as a subscription service and cost US$9.99 per month.

Online Navigation Applications

Online navigation websites that were still popular among many users for driving directions and maps were MapQuest, Google Maps, and Yahoo Maps. Users were able to use these free sites to get detailed directions on how to get to their next destination. In the current economic downturn, many people were looking for cheap (or if possible, free) solutions to solve their problems. These online websites offered the use of free mapping and navigation information that would allow them to get what they needed at no additional cost. However, there were downsides to these programs: They were not portable and could have poor visualization designs (such as vague images or text-based output).[15]

Built-in Car Navigation Devices

In-car navigation devices first came about in luxury, high-end vehicles. Currently, it has become more mainstream and is now being offered in mid- to lower-tier vehicles. These built-in car navigation devices offered similar features to the personal navigation device but didn't have the portability, so users wouldn't have to carry multiple devices. However, they came with a hefty price. Some examples of these are Kenwood, Pioneer, and Eclipse units, which are all installed in cars. These units tended to be expensive and overpriced because they were brand-name products and required physical installation. For example, the top-of-the-line Pioneer unit was US$1,000 for the monitor and another US$500 for the navigation device plus the physical labor. When buying such products, a customer spent a huge amount of money on a product that was almost identical to a product TomTom offered at a significantly lower price.

Physical Maps

Physical maps were the primary option for navigating for decades until technology improved them. Physical maps provided detailed road information to help a person get from point A to point B. Although more cumbersome to use than some of the modern technology alternatives, it was an alternative for people who were not technically savvy or for whom a navigation device was an unnecessary luxury.

Potential Adverse Legislation and Restrictions

In the legal and political realm, TomTom faced two issues that were not critical now, but that might have significant ramifications to not only TomTom in the future, but also the entire portable navigation device industry. The reaction of TomTom's management to each of these issues will determine whether or not there was an opportunity for gain or a threat of a significant loss to the company.

The most important issue TomTom dealt with was the possible legislative banning of all navigational devices from automobiles. In Australia, the government was considering banning PNDs completely from automobiles. There was a similar sentiment in Ontario, Canada, where a law that was currently under review would ban all PNDs that were not mounted either to the dashboard or to the windshield itself.[16]

With the increase in legislation adding to the restrictions placed on PND devices, the threat that the PND market in the future will be severely limited could not be ignored. All of the companies within the PND industry, not just TomTom, must create a coordinated and united effort to stem this wave of restrictions as well as provide reassurance to the public that they were also concerned with the safe use of their products. This effort can be seen in the heavily regulated toy industry. Many companies within the toy industry had combined to form the International Council of Toy Industries[17] to be proactive in regard to safety regulations, as well as lobby governments against laws that may unfairly threaten the toy industry.[18]

The other issue within the legal and political spectrum that TomTom must focus on was the growing use of GPS devices as tracking devices. Currently, law enforcement agents were allowed to use their own GPS devices to track the movements and locations of individuals they deemed suspicious. However, if budget cuts reduced the access to these GPS devices, then the simple solution will be to use the PND devices already installed in many automobiles.

This issue also required the industry as a whole to proactively work with the consumers and the government to come to an amicable resolution. The threat of having every consumer's GPS information at the fingertips of either the government or surveillance company will most certainly stunt or even completely halt any growth within the PND industry.

Another alarming trend was the rise in PND thefts around the country.[19] With the prices for PNDs at a relatively high level, thieves were targeting vehicles that had visible docking stations for PNDs either on the dashboard or the windshield. The onus will be on TomTom to create new designs that will not only hide PNDs from would-be thieves but also deter them from trying to steal one. Consumers who were scared to purchase PNDs because of this rise in crime will become an issue if this problem is not resolved.

There was also a current trend, labeled the GREEN movement,[20] that aimed to reduce any activities that would endanger the environment. This movement was a great opportunity for TomTom to tout its technology as the smarter and more environmentally safe tool if driving is an absolute necessity. Not only can individuals tout this improved efficiency, but more importantly on a larger scale, businesses that require large amounts of materials to be transported across long stretches can show activists that they too are working toward becoming a green company.

It is ironic that the core technology used in TomTom's navigation system, the GPS system, has proliferated into other electronic devices at such a rapid pace that it has caused serious competition to the PND industry. GPS functionality was a basic requirement for all new Smartphones that entered the market and soon will become a basic functionality in regular cellular phones. TomTom will be hard pressed to compete with these multifunctional devices unless it can improve upon its designs and transform itself into a single focused device.

Another concern for not only TomTom, but also every company that relies heavily on GPS technology, was the aging satellites that supported the GPS system. Analysts predicted that these satellites will be either replaced or fixed before there are any issues, but this issue was unsettling due to the fact that TomTom had no control over it.[21] TomTom will have to devise contingency plans in case of catastrophic failure of the GPS system, much like what happened to Research in Motion when malfunctioning satellites caused disruption in its service.

TomTom was one of the leading companies in the PND markets in both Europe and the United States. Although they were the leader in Europe, that market was showing signs of becoming saturated. Even though the U.S. market was currently growing, TomTom could not wait for the inevitable signs of that market's slowdown as well.

The two main opportunities for TomTom to expand—creating digital maps for developing countries and creating navigational services—can either be piggybacked or can be taken in independent paths. The first-mover advantage for these opportunities will erect a high barrier of entry for any companies that do not have large amounts of resources to invest in the developing country. TomTom was already playing catch-up to Garmin and its already established service in India.

Globalization of any company's products did not come without a certain set of issues. For TomTom, the main threat brought on by foreign countries was twofold. The first threat, which may be an isolated instance, but could also be repeated in many other countries, was the restriction of certain capabilities for all of TomTom's products. Due to security and terrorism concerns, GPS devices have not been allowed in Egypt since 2003.[22] In times of global terrorism, TomTom must be vigilant of the growing trend for countries to become overly protective of foreign companies and their technologies.

Internal Environment

Finance

TomTom's financial goals were to diversify and become a broader revenue-based company. The company not only sought to increase the revenue base in terms of geographical expansion but also wanted to diversify its product and service portfolio. Additionally, another important goal the company strived to achieve was reducing its operating expenses.

Sales Revenue and Net Income

Exhibit 2 shows that from 2005 to 2007 there was a consistent growth in sales revenue, as well as a corresponding increase in net income. However, year 2008 was an exception to this trend. In this year, sales revenue decreased by 3.7% and the net income decreased by 136%. In fact, in the first quarter the net income was actually negative, totaling −€37 million. The decrease in sales can be accounted for by the downturn in the economy. According to its 2008 annual report, the sales are in line with market expectations. However, the net income plummeted much more than the decrease in sales. This was actually triggered by its acquisition of the digital mapping company—Tele Atlas—which was funded by both cash assets and debt.

Quarterly sales. In the second quarter of 2009, TomTom received sales revenue of €368 million, compared to €213 million in the first quarter and €453 million in the same quarter in 2008 **(Exhibit 3).** By evaluating quarterly sales for a three-year period from 2007 until the present, it was apparent that the sales followed a seasonal trend in Tom-Tom, with highest sales in the last quarter and lowest in the first quarter. However, focusing on just the first and second quarter for three years, one can infer that the sales revenue as a whole was also going down year after year. To investigate further on the causes of this scenario, the company will have to delve deeper into its revenue base. TomTom's sources of revenue can be broadly grouped into two categories—market segment and geographic location.

Revenue per Segment

TomTom's per segment revenue stream can be divided into PNDs and others, where others consisted of services and content. Evaluating the first quarter of 2008 against that of 2009 and the last quarter of 2008, TomTom experienced steep declines of 40% and 68% (see **Exhibit 4).** This could be a consequence of the compounded effect of the following: (1) The number of devices (PNDs) decreased by a similar amount during both time periods. (2) The average selling price of PNDs had also been decreasing consistently. In a technology company, a decrease in average selling price is a part of doing business in a highly competitive and dynamic marketplace. Nevertheless, the revenue stream from business units other than PNDs had seen a steady increase in both the scenarios.

Revenue per Region

TomTom's per region revenue stream can be further divided into Europe, North America, and the rest of the world. Comparing the first quarter of 2009 against 2008, it can be seen that revenue from both Europe and North America was on the decline, with a decrease of 22% and 52%, respectively (see **Exhibit 5).** At the same time, revenue from

EXHIBIT 3
Revenue per Segment: Tom-Tom (Amount in millions of €)

(in € millions)	Q 1'09	Q 1'08	y.o.y	Q 4'08	q.o.q.
Revenue	172	264	−35%	473	−64%
PNDs	141	234	−40%	444	−68%
Others	31	29	5%	29	5%
# of PNDs sold (in thousands)	1,419	1,997	−29%	4,443	−68%
Average Selling Price (€)	99	117	−15%	100	−1%

EXHIBIT 4
Revenue per Region: Tom-Tom (Amount in millions of €)

	Quarter 1 of 2009	Quarter 1 of 2009	Difference
Europe	178,114	146,549	−22%
North America	84,641	55,558	−52%
Rest of world	1,087	10,976	90%
Total	263,842	213,083	−24%

EXHIBIT 5
Cash versus Long-Term Debt (Amount in thousands of €)

	2005	2006	2007	2008	2009
Long Term Debt	301	338	377	4,749	4,811
Cash Assets	178,377	437,801	463,339	321,039	422,530
Borrowings	0	0	0	1,241,900	1,195,715

EXHIBIT 6
Operating Margin: TomTom

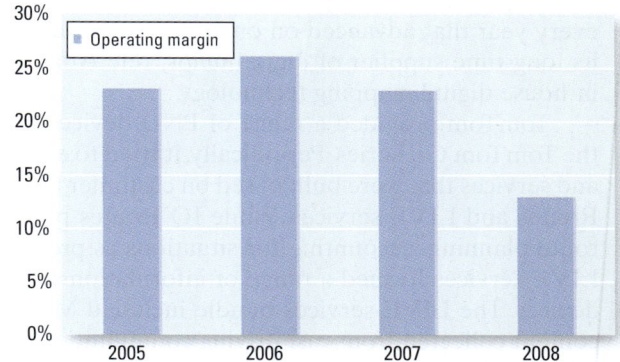

the rest of the world had seen a huge increase of 90%. Both of these analyses supported TomTom's current goal to increase its revenue base and is aligned with its long-term strategy of being a leader in the navigation industry.

Long-term debt.   In 2005, TomTom was a cash-rich company. However, the recent acquisition of Tele Atlas, which amounted to €2.9 billion, was funded by cash, the release of new shares, and long-term debt (see **Exhibit 6),** in this case a €1.2 billion loan. These combined to use up TomTom's cash reserves. Currently, TomTom's debt was €1,006 million.

Operating margin.   TomTom saw a consistent increase in operating margin until 2006. However, since 2007, operating margin has been decreasing for the firm. In fact, by the end of 2008 it came down to 13%, compared to 26% in 2006.

Marketing

Traditionally, high quality and ease of use of solutions have been of utmost importance to TomTom. In a 2006 interview, TomTom's Marketing Head, Anne Louise Hanstad, emphasized the importance of simplicity and ease of use with its devices. This underlined TomTom's belief that people prefer fit-for-purpose devices that are developed and designed to do one specific thing very well. At that time, both of these were core to TomTom's strategy as its targeted customers were *early adopters.* Now, however, as the navigation industry moved from embryonic to a growth industry, TomTom's current customers were *early majority.* Hence, simplicity and ease alone could no longer provide it with a competitive advantage.

Recently, to be in line with its immediate goal of diversifying into different market segments, TomTom was more focused on strengthening its brand name. In December 2008, TomTom's CEO stated " . . . we are constantly striving to increase awareness of our brand and strengthen our reputation for providing smart, easy-to-use, high-quality portable navigation products and services."[23]

Along with Tele Atlas, the TomTom group has gained depth and breadth of expertise over the last 30 years, which made it a trusted brand. Three out of four people were aware of the TomTom brand across the markets. The TomTom group has always been committed to the three fundamentals of navigation: mapping, routing algorithm, and dynamic information. Tele Atlas' core competency was the digital mapping database, while TomTom's was routing algorithms and guidance services using dynamic information. Together, the group created synergies that enabled it to introduce products almost every year that advanced on one or a combination of these three elements. Acquiring its long-time supplier of digital maps, Tele Atlas, in 2008 gave TomTom an edge with in-house digital mapping technology.

TomTom provided a range of PND devices like TomTom One, TomTom XL, and the TomTom Go Series. Periodically, it tried to enhance those devices with new features and services that were built based on customer feedback. Examples of services were IQ Routes and LIVE services. While IQ Routes provided drivers with the most efficient route planning, accounting for situations as precise as speed bumps and traffic lights, LIVE services formed a range of information services delivered directly to the LIVE devices. The LIVE services bundle included Map Share and HD Traffic, bringing the content collected from vast driving communities directly to the end-user.

These products and services accentuated effective designs and unique features, and required TomTom to work with its customers to share precise updates and also get feedback for future improvements. Hence, effective customer interaction became essential to its long-term goal of innovation. In 2008, J. D. Power and Associates recognized TomTom for providing outstanding customer service experience.[24] Although it awarded TomTom for customer service satisfaction, J. D. Power and Associates ranked Garmin highest in overall customer satisfaction. TomTom followed Garmin in the ranking, performing well in the routing, speed of system, and voice direction factors.[25]

As mentioned previously, when the navigation industry was still in its embryonic stages, features, ease of use, and the high quality of its solutions gave TomTom products a competitive edge. Eventually, the competition increased in the navigation industry and even substitutes posed a substantial threat to market share. TomTom offered PNDs in different price ranges, broadly classified into high-range and mid-range PNDs, with an average selling price of €99. There were entry-level options that allowed a savvy shopper to put navigation in his/her car for just over US$100. Higher-end models added advanced features and services that were previously described.

TomTom sold its PNDs to consumers through retailers and distributors. After acquiring Tele Atlas, it was strategically placed to gain the first mover advantage created by its rapid expansion of geographical coverage.[26] This was of key importance when it came to increasing its global market share.

TomTom directed its marketing expenditure toward B2B advertising that was directed to retailers and distributors. TomTom also invested in an official blog website, as well as search optimization, which placed it in premium results in online searches. This enabled TomTom to do effective word-of-mouth promotion while keeping flexible marketing spending, in accordance with changes in the macroeconomic environment or seasonal trends.[27] Although this approach gave TomTom spending flexibility, it lacked a direct B2C approach. In 2009, only 21% of U.S. adults owned PNDs, whereas 65% of U.S. adults neither owned nor used navigation.[28] By not spending on B2C marketing, TomTom discounted on the opportunity both to attract first-tier noncustomers and glean an insight of needs of second-tier noncustomers.[29]

Operations

The focus of operations had always been on innovation. More recently, TomTom's operational objective had been to channel all its resources and core capabilities to create economies of scale so as to be aligned with its long-term strategy. TomTom aimed to focus and centralize R&D resources to create scale economies to continue to lead the industry in terms of innovation.[30]

Implementation of this strategy was well underway and the changes were visible. By the second quarter of 2009, mid-range PNDs were introduced with the capabilities of high-range devices. In addition, 50% of PNDs were sold with IQ Routes technology. The first in-dash product was also launched in alliance with Renault, and the TomTom iPhone application was also announced.[31]

After acquiring Tele Atlas to better support the broader navigation solutions and content and services, the group underwent restructuring. The new organizational structure consisted of four business units that had a clear focus on a specific customer group and were supported by two shared development centers.

The four business units were CONSUMER (B2C), composed of retail sales of PND, on-board, and mobile; AUTOMOTIVE (B2B), composed of auto industry sales of integrated solutions and content & services; LICENSING (B2B), composed of PND, automotive, mobile, Internet, and GIS content and services; and WORK (B2B), composed of commercial fleet sales of Webfleet & Connected Solutions.

TomTom's supply chain and distribution model was outsourced. This increased TomTom's ability to scale up or down the supply chain, while limiting capital expenditure risks. At the same time, however, it depended on a limited number of third parties—and in certain instances sole suppliers—for component supply and manufacturing, which increased its dependency on these suppliers.

TomTom's dynamic content sharing model used high-quality digital maps along with the connected services, like HD Traffic, Local Search with Google, and weather information. This provided customers with relevant real-time information at the moment they needed it, which helped them deliver the benefits of innovative technology directly to the end-user at affordable prices. Although the network externalities previously mentioned were among the advantages of TomTom's LIVE, it had also increased TomTom's dependency on the network of the connected driving community. The bigger the network, the more effective the information gathered from the guidance services.

Furthermore, in order to reduce operating expenses and strengthen the balance sheet, heavy emphasis had been placed on the cost-cutting program. In 2009, the cost reductions were made up of reduction of staff, restructuring and integration of Tele Atlas, reduced discretionary spending, and reduction in the number of contractors and marketing expenditures. However, if not executed wisely, it could hamper TomTom's long-term objective of being a market leader. For example, one of the core capabilities of any technology company was its staff; reducing it could hinder future innovative projects. This may also occur when reducing the marketing expenditures in a market that still held rich prospects of high growth. Among U.S. adults, 65% did not own any kind of navigation system.[32]

Human Resources

Like in any other technology company, the success of individual employees was very important to TomTom. Additionally, TomTom had a vision that company success should also mean success for the individual employee. Therefore, at TomTom, employee competency was taken very seriously and talent development programs were built around it. There was a personal navigation plan that provided employees with a selection of courses based on competencies in their profile. In 2008, TomTom completed its Young Talent Development Program, which was aimed at broadening the participants' knowledge while improving their technical and personal skills.

TomTom's motto was to do business efficiently and profitably, as well as responsibly. This underlined its corporate social responsibility. TomTom's headquarters was one of the most energy-efficient buildings in Amsterdam. As previously mentioned, earlier navigation was oriented toward making the drivers arrive at their destination without getting lost. TomTom was the pioneer in introducing different technology that actually helped drivers make their journeys safer and more economical. This showed TomTom's commitment to its customer base as well as to the community as a whole.

Issues of Concern for TomTom

First, TomTom was facing increasing competition from other platforms using GPS technology, such as cell phones and Smartphones. In the cell phone industry, Nokia was leading the charge in combining cell phone technology with GPS technology. Around the same time TomTom acquired Tele Atlas, Nokia purchased Navteq, a competitor to Tele Atlas. With the acquisition of Navteq, Nokia hoped to shape the cell phone industry by merging cell phone, Internet, and GPS technology.

The Smartphone industry was emerging with the iPhone and the Palm Pre. There was also a shift in how people were able to utilize these technologies as a navigation tool. A big trend in Smartphones was applications. Because of the ease of developing software on platforms for Smartphones, more and more competitors were coming to the forefront and developing GPS navigation applications. On October 28, 2009, Google announced the addition of Tom Tom and Garmin Ltd. as competitors. Google was adding driving directions to its Smartphones.

For TomTom, both of these sectors might signal that major change was on the horizon and that there was no longer a need for hardware for GPS navigation devices. The world seemed to be heading toward a culture where consumers wanted an all-in-one device such as a cell phone or Smartphone that would do everything needed, including offering GPS navigation services. A recent study done by Charles Golvin for Forrester suggested that by 2013 phone-based navigation will dominate the industry. The reason was due to Gen Y and Gen X customers who were increasingly reliant on their mobile phone and who would demand that social networking and other connected services be integrated into their navigation experience.[33]

Secondly, TomTom faced a maturing U.S. and European personal navigation device market. After three years of steady growth in the PND market, TomTom had seen decreasing growth rates for PND sales. Initially entering the European market 12 months before entering the U.S. market, TomTom witnessed a 21% dip in sales for the European market. Although TomTom experienced some growth in the U.S. market for 2008, the growth rate was not as good as in prior years.

NOTES

1. TomTom AR-08, "TomTom Annual Report 2008," *TomTom Annual Report 2008,* December 2008.
2. Ibid.
3. TomTom, "TomTom, Portable GPS Car Navigation Systems," http://investors.tomtom.com/overview.cfm.
4. Ibid.
5. Ibid.
6. Ibid.
7. TomTom AR-08, "TomTom Annual Report 2008," *TomTom Annual Report 2008,* December 2008.
8. Ibid.
9. Ibid.
10. Ibid.
11. "TomTom NV," http://www.answers.com/topic/tomtom-n-v.
12. Ibid.
13. Thomson Reuters, "TomTom Launches 2.9 bln Euro Bid for Tele Atlas," http://www.reuters.com/article/technology-media-telco-SP/idUSL1839698320071119 (November 19, 2007).
14. *Boston Business* Article, http://www.boston.com/business/ticker/2009/06/let_homer_simps.html.
15. Magellan website, http://www.magellangps.com/Company/About-Us.
16. Tanya Talaga and Rob Ferguson, *TheStar.com,* October 28, 2008, http://www.thestar.com/News/Ontario/article/525697 (July 29, 2009).
17. ICTI, 2009, http://www.toy-icti.org/ (July 29, 2009).
18. Ibid.
19. *GPS Magazine,* September 23, 2007, http://gpsmagazine.com/2007/09/gps_thefts_rise.php (July 29, 2009).
20. "Webist Media," *Web Ecoist,* August 17, 2008, http://webecoist.com/2008/08/17/a-brief-history-of-the-modern-green-movement/ (July 29, 2009).
21. Nick Jones, *Garnter,* January 5, 2009, http://www.gartner.com/id=1007612
22. *US News,* October 14, 2008, http://usnews.rankingsandreviews.com/cars-trucks/daily-news/081014-GPS-Devices-Banned-in-Egypt/ (July 29, 2009).
23. TomTom AR-08, "TomTom Annual Report 2008," *TomTom Annual Report 2008,* December 2008.
24. Reuters, "TomTom Inc. Recognized for Call Center Customer Satisfaction Excellence by J.D. Power," January 7, 2008, http://www.reuters.com/article/pressRelease/idUS141391+07-Jan-2008+PRN20080107.
25. J. D. Power and Associates, "Garmin Ranks Highest in Customer Satisfaction with Portable Navigation Devices," October 23, 2008, http://www.jdpower.com/corporate/news/releases/pressrelease.aspx?ID=2008221.
26. TomTom AR-08, "TomTom Annual Report 2008," *TomTom Annual Report 2008,* December 2008.
27. Ibid.
28. Forrestor Research, "Phone-Based Navigation Will Dominate by 2013," March 27, 2009.
29. W. Chan Kim and Mauborgne, *Blue Ocean Strategy* (Boston: Harvard Business School Press, 2005).
30. TomTom AR-08, "TomTom Annual Report 2008," *TomTom Annual Report 2008,* December 2008.
31. Ibid.
32. Forrestor Research, "Phone-Based Navigation Will Dominate by 2013," March 27, 2009.
33. Ibid.

CASE **32**

General Electric, GE Capital, and the Financial Crisis of 2008:

THE BEST OF THE WORST IN THE FINANCIAL SECTOR?

Alan N. Hoffman
Bentley University

Company Background

For more than a century, General Electric (GE), has been a global leader and iconic brand known for innovation and leadership in a wide range of endeavors. Its diversified portfolio of products is organized into four strategic business units: energy, technology infrastructure, GE Capital, and home and business solutions.

GE began in 1878 when Thomas Edison formed the Edison General Electric Company (EGEC). Though Edison was best known for inventing the first incandescent light bulb, he also pioneered systems design for generating and distributing electricity, eventually holding over 1000 patents. Within a few years, the rival Thomas Houston Company, which held key patents in the same area, challenged EGEC's position in the marketplace. In 1892, the two companies merged, forming General Electric. GE then parlayed the demand for electricity into the invention of home heating, stoves and other appliances, and refrigeration, transforming American households, and went on to become an innovator in myriad fields, from medicine, aviation, and transportation to plastics and financial services. GE created the GE Credit Corporation (later GE Capital) in the wake of the Great Depression to facilitate the sale of household appliances and provide the option of extended payments for consumers. Innovation defined the organization, and the commitment to research and development remained key.[1]

The authors would like to thank Barbara Gottfried, Patrick DeCourcy, Keith Dugas, Kaitlin Mackie, Desiree Ouellette, Jason Tate, and Will Hoffman for their research and contributions to this case.

Please address all correspondence to: Dr. Alan N. Hoffman, Dept. of Management, Bentley University, 175 Forest Street, Waltham, MA 02452-4705, voice (781) 891-2287, ahoffman@bentley.edu. Printed by permission of Alan N. Hoffman.

GE was one of the original 12 companies that formed the Dow Jones Industrial Average, and the only one of those companies that was still part of the DJIA in 2012. GE was also recognized for cultivating leaders such as Charles Wilson, Ralph Cordiner, Fred Borch, Reginald Jones, and John Welch.[2] In the early 1970s under Fred Borch, GE was one of the first companies with a diversified infrastructure to formalize strategic planning at both corporate and business unit levels with its creation of strategic business units.[3]

GE always saw itself as striving to create a world that worked better, "making what few in the world can, but everyone needs."[4] The company's strategic philosophy centered on innovation, superior technology, and demonstrating leadership in growth markets. GE sought to maintain a strong competitive advantage through innovation, smart capital allocation, and solidifying customer relationships. The strategy also included transitioning from an industrial conglomerate to an infrastructure leader to maximize the core strengths of its existing businesses. Diversification and expansion of its business portfolio was a central focus, designed to minimize volatility and create stability through varying growth cycles. Another facet of GE's strategy was to invest for the long-term in high-growth market opportunities that were closely related to its core businesses. For instance, in 2010 the company launched the GE Advantage Program that focused on process excellence and innovation to improve margins in industrial projects.[5]

One of GE's biggest operational strengths lay in its ability to cut costs and maximize return for shareholders. In the 1990s, GE CEO Jack Welch implemented the Six Sigma approach to business management. This approach helped decrease variability and errors to help cut down waste and build a consistent product, one of the many ways GE trained employees to succeed and build their expertise. GE was also able to cut costs because its reputation as a market leader with a large network of businesses and strong alliances with other major corporations enabled it to leverage long-standing relationships to employ the best human, equipment, and capital resources to ensure quality and consistency at a low cost. It acquired many businesses that provided useful resources, and sold off business units that did not contribute to its success.

In 2011, GE's strategic accomplishments included 22% growth (defined as a 22% increase in operating EPS excluding impact of the preferred stock redemption) and a 20% rise in operating earnings. Over the two-year period through 2011, GE's dividends increased a total of 70%. GE was positioned for continued success in 2012 with a record industrial backlog of US$200 billion, US$85 billion cash, and equivalents offering significant financial flexibility. Internationally, GE saw 18% growth in industrial revenue, and U.S. exports were up US$1 billion from 2010. At the same time, GE's management demonstrated their continued commitment to innovation by investing 6% of the firm's industrial revenue in R&D.[6] General Electric was divided into six Operating Segments (five Industrial): Aviation, Energy Infrastructure, Healthcare, Home & Business Solutions, Transportation, and GE Capital.

By 2012, under the leadership of Jeffrey Immelt, General Electric was a powerful conglomerate employing approximately 300,000 people globally and operating in more than 100 countries,[7] ranked the sixth-largest American corporation and the 14th most profitable by *Forbes*. Immelt had replaced the highly regarded Jack Welch as CEO and Chairman of the Board in 2001 and had been named as one of the "World's Best CEOs" three times by *Barron's*. GE's board of directors was composed of 17 members, of whom two-thirds were considered to be "independent." The board was in continuous dialogue with GE's top management. Together they emphasized strategy and risk management while monitoring strategic initiatives personally through site visits.

Fast Company ranked GE the 19th most innovative company; *Fortune* listed GE as the 15th most admired company; and Interbrand cited GE as the number 5 best global brand.[8] General Electric's objectives were, and continued to be, earnings growth, increasing margins, and returning cash to investors, as well as organic growth, increased financial flexibility, and larger U.S. exports. While pursuing these ambitious objectives, GE, at the same time, committed itself to social and environmental responsibility

GE's Diversified Industrial Products Competitors

Diversified international industrial conglomerates, such as GE, have by definition many strong, direct competitors spanning many industries, as the total market capitalization for this industry is over US$137 billion.[9] Aside from GE, the three industrial conglomerates with the best relative performance (based on fundamental and technical strength) were Siemens, Phillips Electronics, and 3M.[10]

Siemens AG, the largest European electronic engineering and manufacturing conglomerate, based in Munich, Germany, and operating worldwide,[11] is split into four sectors: Energy, Healthcare, Industry, and Infrastructure and Cities, yielding 19 divisions with over 360,000 employees and €73.5 billion (US$96.2 billion) in sales in 2011. Its focus is on sustainable value creation, innovation-driven growth markets, customer relations, and capitalizing on core competencies.

Royal Phillips Electronics, based in the Netherlands, is split into three overlapping sectors: Healthcare, Lighting, and Consumer Lifestyle, with many subdivisions in 60 countries,[12] over 125,000 employees, and €20.1 billion (US$26.3 billion) in sales in 2011. Phillips' focus is on improving people's lives through meaningful innovation, delivering a quality product, and building value for customers and shareholders.

3M, based in Minnesota, operates in the markets of consumer goods, office supplies, display and graphics, health care, industrial goods, transportation goods, and safety, security, and protection services. With over 80,000 employees and a presence in more than 65 countries, 3M amassed more than US$27 billion of sales revenue in 2011. As a diversified technology company, 3M focuses on ingenious, innovative products and building global market share.[13]

GE Capital

GE Capital, the largest of GE's four strategic business units in 2012, was created in 1932 as GE Contracts, an internal business unit to help finance consumer purchases of GE appliances (see **Exhibits 1** and **2**).[14] Particularly in the midst of the Great Depression,

EXHIBIT 1

GE Capital (in millions)	2011	2010	2009	2008	2007
Revenues	45,730	46,422	48,906	65,900	65,625
Net Income	6,549	3,158	1,325	7,841	12,179

EXHIBIT 2

GE (Parent Company) (in millions)	2011	2010	2009
Revenues	147,300	149,593	154,438
Net Income	13,120	11,344	10,725

consumers were hesitant to invest in what at the time were considered superfluous products. To encourage consumers, GE Contracts offered comparatively low monthly payments to make its parent company's products more affordable.

Renamed GE Capital in 1987, the former appliance financing unit grew to incorporate interests beyond those of its GE corporate parent, such as investment banking, retail stores, television channels, and auto/truck leasing. It also acquired a significant market share in private-label credit cards, including those of JCPenney, Montgomery Ward, and Wal-Mart. Early on in its history, GE Capital benefited particularly from its association with its GE parent's strong asset base and creditworthiness, garnering both lower borrowing rates and easy access to cheap capital to generate investment beyond its profits. Through the early 2000s, GE Capital continued to expand its product lines, delving into property and casualty insurance, life insurance, mortgages, and real estate.[15]

As the unit grew, GE Capital became an increasingly significant contributor to its GE parent's success. While in the past most people had thought of GE as an industrial company, GE Capital, a finance company, grew to represent nearly half of its GE parent's annual profits.[16] As of 2012, there were five major components of GE Capital:[17]

1. **Commercial Lending and Leasing:** This division provides loans to outside businesses for a range of uses, including company acquisition, internal restructuring, and even leasing office space. Additionally, the Commercial Lending unit maintains fleets of cars and heavy industrial equipment available for leasing.

2. **Consumer Financing:** Within the U.S., GE Capital's retail financing arm represents their private-label credit card interests, and retail purchase financing that includes automobiles, furniture, and other costly items consumers often don't pay for with cash.

3. **Energy Financial Services:** GE Energy owned stakes in energy interests worldwide, providing financing for companies to invest and expand, often in conjunction with its GE parent's efforts to educate and supply companies with necessary equipment.

4. **Aviation Services:** GE Capital Aviation is involved in passenger aircraft purchasing and leasing, and aircraft part financing, including various engines that its GE parent produced, and airport expansion financing.

5. **Real Estate:** GE Capital Real Estate specializes in various real estate transactions, including property acquisition, debt refinancing, and joint venture investments. Many of its properties are office buildings, but it also owns stakes in multi-family developments and hotels.

GE Capital's Strategic Direction

GE Capital's main expertise is in mid-market banking, providing financing for a range of industries from aviation and energy to health care, and for the purchase, lease, distribution, and maintenance of large fleets and equipment.[18] It also provides capital for corporate acquisitions and restructuring. It is GE Capital's vision to be more than just a banker—to align itself with GE's corporate objective of supporting growth not simply by providing capital, but by helping customers invent more and build more[19] through leveraging its global experience and industry expertise.[20]

However, the financial services industry was, by definition, volatile, and GE Capital was particularly hard hit by the economic recession of 2008. With the credit markets illiquid and financial markets falling, GE Capital found that it was overexposed to commercial real estate and foreign residential mortgages. At this point, GE's parent corporation stepped in, began reorganizing GE Capital, and significantly downsized the unit.

GE Capital sold most of its insurance lines, completely left the U.S. mortgage market, and substantially tightened its consumer underwriting guidelines. However, the company still was on the lookout for under-priced assets, and purchased several lending lines from even more troubled Citigroup, as well as a large commercial real estate portfolio from Merrill Lynch financing.

By 2012, GE Capital was smaller, leaner, and more focused on specialty financing especially mid-market lending and leasing.[21] However, like its parent company, GE Capital hoped to see continued sustainable earnings growth with growing margins and lower portfolio risk, and to return money to investors and resume paying dividends to its parent company.[22]

GE Capital's Competitors

GE Capital's main competition came primarily from specialty corporate financial lenders, such as CIT Group, and larger companies that offered diverse and comprehensive financial services, such as Bank of America and Citigroup, according to Hoovers.[23]

In 2012, *Bank of America*[24] was one of the largest and most identifiable banks in the United States with over US$2.1 trillion in assets. Its goal was to be accessible to every sort of customer at any stage of their financial lives by offering both a variety of products and easy accessibility with over 5700 locations and 17,000 ATMs. Beyond the arena of specialty lending, Bank of America served consumers and companies ranging from small sole proprietorships to multinational global corporations with banking, investments, and asset management. While the company was successful in building market share, it faced a multitude of difficulties from major lawsuits deriving from its acquisitions of Countrywide and Merrill Lynch, and from its "robo-signing" foreclosure practices.

Bank of America attempted to return to profitability after declaring a US$2.2 billion loss in 2010 and only a US$1.5 billion profit in 2011, focusing on strengthening its capital reserves and integrating lean initiatives to cut costs and improve efficiency. However, legislation that reduced its two major sources of revenue, interest earnings and fee revenue, in conjunction with depressed consumer and investor confidence levels, heralded a difficult road ahead for the company.

Like Bank of America, *Citigroup* is a behemoth in the financial services industry, made up of a number of units including brokerage, investment bank, and wealth management and consumer lending divisions, with over US$1.9 trillion in total assets and maintaining more than 200 million customer accounts in over 160 countries. The 2008 financial crisis and its aftermath hit Citigroup very hard, resulting in US$90 billion in losses, which led to selling off or divesting from underperforming industries. Citigroup then sold several commercial lending lines to GE Capital, fully exited the student loan market, and planned to sell its CitiMortgage and CitiFinancial divisions. Going forward, Citigroup refocused on traditional banking and continued unloading toxic assets and non-core business units.

Perhaps most similar to GE Capital, *CIT Group Inc*[25] specialized in commercial lending and financing for small and mid-sized businesses, managing US$45 billion in total assets. In addition to its general corporate finance arm, CIT group offered transportation equipment financing, vendor finance, and a smaller branch of consumer lending. Hit severely by the financial crisis, CIT Group briefly declared chapter 11 in 2009, stemming from extreme losses in its subprime mortgage and student loan portfolios. It subsequently improved its balance sheet and reduced debt obligations, refocusing on its commercial lending division by building up its loan and lease accounts and hoping to increase deposit accounts by acquiring already established banks.

Financials

With operations in over 100 countries and 53% of its revenues coming from outside the United States, GE's growth depended on its ability to successfully navigate the political risks associated with international business dealings that could affect its growth and profitability.[26]

Change and instability in the financial markets had a significant effect on GE, especially GE Capital. Historically, GE had relied on commercial paper and long-term debt as major sources of its funding, but the increasing difficulty and cost of obtaining those sources of funding potentially threatened GE's ability to grow and maintain its level of profitability.[27] After the financial crisis of 2008, the deterioration of the real estate market, for example, adversely affected GE Capital. GE Capital subsequently tried to secure other sources of funding, including bank deposits, securitization, and other asset-based funding to mitigate its risks. These economic setbacks affected not only GE and GE Capital, but trickled down to the corporations, large and small, they did business with, along with GE's governmental customers around the world.

Nevertheless, GE's credit rating with the major analysts helped stem the tide of negativity and control the costs of funds, margins, and access to capital markets. As of 2012, GE boasted a AA+ Rating (2nd out of 21 ratings) from Standard and Poor's and an Aa2 rating (3rd out of 21 ratings) from Moody's, solidifying its rating with the major analysts. Any reduction in these ratings would negatively impact GE's profitability.[28]

In the three years after the financial crisis, from 2009 to 2011, both GE and GE Capital's sales revenue declined sharply (see also **Exhibits 3** thru **8**).

Consistent quarterly revenue losses slightly rebounded beginning in Q1 2010 (from double-digit to single-digit losses in both GE and GE Capital), yet sales revenue at GE Capital declined again from US$12.814 billion to US$10.745 billion from

EXHIBIT 3
Quarterly Sales Growth[50]

		Quarterly Sales Growth	
Year		**GE**	**GE Capital**
2008	Q1	7.7%	3.2%
	Q2	13.3%	10.4%
	Q3	10.8%	1.7%
	Q4	−3.2%	−18.4%
2009	Q1	−8.7%	−19.9%
	Q2	−15.5%	−29.3%
	Q3	−20.0%	−30.8%
	Q4	−10.8%	−14.5%
2010	Q1	−6.0%	−11.5%
	Q2	−6.2%	−5.0%
	Q3	−5.8%	−5.1%
	Q4	−1.1%	−5.1%
2011	Q1	−4.8%	−4.6%
	Q2	−4.5%	−9.1%
	Q3	−1.1%	−7.9%
	Q4	−7.8%	−16.1%
2012	Q1	3.4%	−6.6%

Quarterly Net Income Growth

Year		GE	GE Capital
2008	Q1	–11.7%	–27.9%
	Q2	–3.5%	14.8%
	Q3	–12.4%	–37.6%
	Q4	–43.4%	–84.2%
2009	Q1	–34.5%	–60.1%
	Q2	–46.6%	–86.8%
	Q3	–45.2%	–94.4%
	Q4	–21.6%	–79.2%
2010	Q1	–19.4%	–48.7%
	Q2	11.3%	100.0%
	Q3	26.6%	590.3%
	Q4	28.7%	807.2%
2011	Q1	47.0%	252.2%
	Q2	10.5%	117.0%
	Q3	3.7%	86.3%
	Q4	0.6%	60.7%
2012	Q1	–11.2%	1.4%

Quarterly Net Profit Margins

Year		GE	GE Capital
2007	Q1	12.7%	19.5%
	Q2	13.7%	14.0%
	Q3	12.1%	17.8%
	Q4	14.3%	17.4%
2008	Q1	10.4%	13.6%
	Q2	11.7%	14.6%
	Q3	9.6%	10.9%
	Q4	8.3%	3.4%
2009	Q1	7.5%	6.8%
	Q2	7.4%	2.7%
	Q3	6.6%	0.9%
	Q4	7.3%	0.8%
2010	Q1	6.4%	3.9%
	Q2	8.8%	5.7%
	Q3	8.8%	6.4%
	Q4	9.5%	7.9%
2011	Q1	9.9%	14.5%
	Q2	10.1%	13.7%
	Q3	9.3%	13.0%
	Q4	10.4%	15.1%

EXHIBIT 6
GE Income
Statement[53]
(All numbers in
thousands)

Period Ending	31-Dec-11	31-Dec-10	31-Dec-09
Total Revenue	147,300,000	149,593,000	154,438,000
Cost of Revenue	71,190,000	74,725,000	78,938,000
Gross Profit	76,110,000	74,868,000	75,500,000
Operating Expenses			
Research and Development	—	—	—
Selling, General, and Administrative	37,384,000	38,054,000	37,354,000
Non-recurring	4,083,000	7,176,000	10,585,000
Others	—	—	—
Total Operating Expenses	—	—	—
Operating Income or Loss	34,643,000	29,638,000	27,561,000
Income from Continuing Operations			
Total Other Income/Expenses Net	—	—	—
Earnings Before Interest and Taxes	34,643,000	29,638,000	27,561,000
Interest Expense	14,545,000	15,553,000	17,697,000
Income Before Tax	20,098,000	14,085,000	9,864,000
Income Tax Expense	5,732,000	1,033,000	−1,142,000
Minority Interest	−292,000	−535,000	−200,000
Net Income From Continuing Ops	14,366,000	13,052,000	11,006,000
Non-recurring Events			
Discontinued Operations	77,000	−873,000	219,000
Extraordinary Items	—	—	—
Effect of Accounting Changes	—	—	—
Other Items	—	—	—
Net Income	14,151,000	11,644,000	11,025,000
Preferred Stock and Other Adjustments	−1,031,000	−300,000	−300,000
Net Income Applicable to Common			
Shares	13,120,000	11,344,000	10,725,000

NOTE: Currency in USD.

Period Ending	30-Dec-11	30-Dec-10	30-Dec-09
Assets			
Current Assets			
Cash and Cash Equivalents	84,501,000	78,943,000	70,488,000
Short-Term Investments	47,374,000	43,938,000	51,343,000
Net Receivables	307,470,000	329,204,000	30,514,000
Inventory	13,792,000	11,526,000	11,987,000
Other Current Assets	—	—	—
Total Current Assets	453,137,000	463,611,000	164,332,000
Long-Term Investments	—	—	319,247,000
Property, Plant, and Equipment	66,450,000	103,099,000	103,081,000
Goodwill	72,625,000	64,388,000	65,076,000
Intangible Assets	12,068,000	9,971,000	11,751,000
Accumulated Amortization	—	—	—
Other Assets	112,962,000	106,724,000	118,414,000
Deferred Long-Term Asset Charges	—	—	—
Total assets	**717,242,000**	**747,793,000**	**781,901,000**
Liabilities			
Current Liabilities			
Accounts Payable	58,373,000	56,943,000	32,860,000
Short/Current Long-Term Debt	166,869,000	147,977,000	129,869,000
Other Current Liabilities	59,891,000	67,328,000	50,788,000
Total Current Liabilities	285,133,000	272,248,000	213,517,000
Long-Term Debt	243,459,000	293,323,000	336,172,000
Other Liabilities	70,647,000	55,271,000	104,995,000
Deferred Long-Term Liability Charges	−131,000	2,753,000	2,081,000
Minority Interest	1,696,000	5,262,000	7,845,000
Negative Goodwill	—	—	—
Total liabilities	**600,804,000**	**628,857,000**	**664,610,000**
Stockholders' equity			
Misc Stocks Options Warrants	—	—	—
Redeemable Preferred Stock	—	—	—
Preferred Stock	—	—	—
Common Stock	702,000	702,000	702,000
Retained Earnings	137,786,000	131,137,000	126,363,000
Treasury Stock	−31,769,000	−31,938,000	−32,238,000
Capital Surplus	—	—	—
Other Stockholder Equity	9,719,000	19,035,000	22,464,000
Total stockholder equity	**116,438,000**	**118,936,000**	**117,291,000**
Net tangible assets	**31,745,000**	**44,577,000**	**40,464,000**

NOTE: Currency in USD.

EXHIBIT 8 Summary of Operating Segments[55] (In millions)

	General Electric Company and consolidated affiliates				
	2011	**2010**	**2009**	**2008**	**2007**
Revenues					
Energy infrastructure	$ 43,694	$ 37,514	$ 40,648	$ 43,046	$ 34,880
Aviation	18,859	17,619	18,728	19,239	16,819
Healthcare	18,083	16,897	16,015	17,392	16,997
Transportation	4,885	3,370	3,827	5,016	4,523
Home & business solutions	8,465	8,648	8,443	10,117	11,026
Total industrial revenues	93,986	84,048	87,661	94,810	84,245
GE Capital	45,730	46,422	48,906	65,900	65,625
Total segment revenues	139,716	130,470	136,567	160,710	149,870
Corporate items and eliminations[a]	7,584	19,123	17,871	19,127	20,094
Consolidated revenues	$147,300	$149,593	$154,438	$179,837	$169,964
Segment profit					
Energy infrastructure	$ 6,650	$ 7,271	$ 7,105	$ 6,497	$ 5,238
Aviation	3,512	3,304	3,923	3,684	3,222
Healthcare	2,803	2,741	2,420	2,851	3,056
Transportation	757	315	473	962	936
Home & business solutions	300	457	370	365	983
Total industrial segment profit	14,022	14,088	14,291	14,359	13,435
GE Capital	6,549	3,158	1,325	7,841	12,179
Total segment profit	20,571	17,246	15,616	22,200	25,614
Corporate items and eliminations[a]	(359)	(1,105)	(593)	1,184	1,441
GE interest and other financial charges	(1,299)	(1,600)	(1,478)	(2,153)	(1,993)
GE provision for income taxes	(4,839)	(2,024)	(2,739)	(3,427)	(2,794)
Earnings from continuing operations	14,074	12,517	10,806	17,804	22,268
Earnings (loss) from discontinued operations, net of taxes	77	(873)	219	(394)	(60)
Consolidated net earnings attributable to the company	$ 14,151	$ 11,644	$ 11,025	$ 17,410	$ 22,208

NOTE:

See accompanying notes to consolidated financial statements in Part II, Item 8. "Financial Statements and Supplementary Data" of this Form 10-K Report.

[a]Includes the result of NBCU, our formerly consolidated subsidiary, and our current equity method investment in NBCUniversal LLC.

Q4 2010 to Q4 2011, marking a return to double-digit quarterly revenue losses. GE Capital's Q1 2012 revenue loss shrank again to single digits at 6.6%, while revenue grew at GE as a whole in Q1 2012 by 3.4% from the industrial division's strong performance (14% quarterly revenue growth).[29] Annually from 2010 to 2011, GE and GE Capital respectively reported 1.9% and 1.5% sales revenue losses. Much of the poor performance was attributable to macroeconomic risk factors, causing unstable demand for the products of the industrial business units, as well as restrictions in the global credit markets, which severely hampered GE Capital's ability to perform as it did prior to the recession (US$65.435 billion revenue in FY 2007, US$45.730 billion in FY 2011). From FY2009 on, GE Capital began strategically transforming its portfolio to be less focused on risky lending and more focused on middle market lending and specialty finance to industrial division customers.[30] This strategy required reducing leverage, improving liquidity, and shedding assets—all of which cut into previous top-line sales revenue performance.[31]

Despite the overall top-line losses, GE was organized as a global corporation that generated revenue in a number of regions worldwide. Although U.S. revenues were down 7.9% in 2011 (from US$75.8 billion in FY2010 to US$69.8 billion in FY2011) and Western European revenues decreased 12 %, global revenues (excluding the U.S.) increased 4% overall, from US$74.5 billion in 2010 to US$77.5 billion in 2011.[32] The strong international performance was tied to revenue growth in emerging markets such as Latin America (29%), China (28%), and Australia (46%).

GE recorded massive net income losses from FY2007 to FY2009, peaking between FY2008 and FY2009 (with net income losses of 38% for GE and 78.3% for GE Capital), driven by the global financial crisis and recession. The performance of GE as a whole was largely tied to that of GE Capital, its largest and formerly most profitable business unit. GE Capital had become deeply ensnared in both the collapse of the credit markets through the excessive use of leverage leading up to FY2009 and the subprime mortgage crisis because it had bought a subprime mortgage company and heavily invested in commercial real estate.[33]

GE Capital had made some ill-advised marketing decisions prior to the financial collapse in 2008. Rather than retaining its focus on middle market and specialty finance for GE industrial product customers, GE Capital began to market itself as a credit card financing entity as well as a mortgage financier.[34] Financing subprime mortgages and commercial real estate soon followed, and eventually GE Capital was engaging in the financing of very risky assets, including derivatives and credit default swaps. This market strategy led to the highly leveraged structure that almost caused the entire corporation to collapse in 2008 during the financial crisis.

GE's long-term debt began growing in FY2007 and hit a high of US$377 billion in 2009, but was reduced slightly in FY2010 and FY2011, resulting in flat growth for the five years from 2007–12. Most of the debt on GE's balance sheet was from GE Capital. During the financial crisis of 2008–09, GE Capital's highly leveraged structure—combined with its risky ventures in interest rate swaps, subprime mortgages, commercial real estate, and massive commercial paper—almost led to the financial collapse of the entire GE Corporation.[35] A record influx of equity capital and the sale of preferred stock stabilized a 10% daily hemorrhage in the stock price that began on October 1, 2008. After that, GE capital aggressively cut its long-term debt from US$304 billion in FY2007 to US$234 billion in FY2011 through strategic de-leveraging and restructuring of the scope of its financing activities.

Both GE and GE capital also took steps to significantly increase their cash balances to better manage risk. From FY2007 to FY2011, GE increased its cash balance from US$18 billion to US$87 billion, and GE Capital's increased from US$11 billion to US$43 billion. However, as of 2012, neither GE nor GE Capital was on completely solid footing, with a LT debt-to-equity ratio of 2.67 and 2.93, respectively.

GE Capital had been forced to scale back in the wake of the recession, and due to pressures to meet stricter regulatory standards. These strictures streamlined GE Capital's operations, helping it better understand its best practices for lending and its other financial endeavors. GE Capital also moved to expand its operational base in the aftermath of the recession by creating new partnerships with companies like Ducati and

Sophos. These new partnerships were important to GE Capital's operations to offset "shrinking its asset base and tightening underwriting standards."[36] Nevertheless, the decrease in year-over-year earnings was evidence that GE Capital had to operate with fewer resources and adjust its internal infrastructure to utilize more limited resource availability.

GE Capital returned some of its profits to its GE parent company through the issuance of a dividend. GE Capital resumed paying a dividend to GE in May 2012.

New Directions for Growth: Green Energy and Health Care

In the new millennium, General Electric was uniquely positioned to take advantage of financial incentives, subsidies, and lucrative partnerships available for innovators in the green energy sector.[37] It was spurred both by an interest in the environment, and the desire for financial security due to volatility in fossil fuel prices and concerns over climate change. Having spent more money than any other single corporation on governmental lobbying, General Electric used its political capital for growth opportunities.[38] For example, GE, especially its electrical energy divisions, was able to leverage its political strength to benefit from tax incentives associated with the green energy movement.

In addition, the GE Energy Group took a leadership role in the manufacture and distribution of wind turbines—a critical component of the renewable energy sector, particularly in Oregon, where the largest wind turbine farm in the United States was powered entirely by GE-built wind turbines.[39] GE also branched out into the management and financing of solar energy projects, including a solar farm in Australia developed by a consortium of companies, including GE.[40] GE was one of the leading manufacturers of LED lighting and had signed a distribution deal with Marriot hotels that saved it 66% in power use for lighting, without compromising on the look or quality of the light.[41] GE perceived the opportunity to become the best-in-class manufacturer and distributor of certain elements of clean energy infrastructure, as well as other innovative forms of clean energy, and is poised to continue to innovate as the sector grows.

Over the past decade GE Healthcare Group established itself as a leading innovator in emerging health care technology. Diagnostic medicine became a key area of health care sector investment—the market is projected to grow 11% annually from US$232 billion,[42] and GE developed some creative tools for diagnostic imaging, including a handheld ultrasound device, with which primary care doctors could be more accurate in their initial diagnoses, prior to ordering expensive follow up diagnostics.[43] GE also launched a US$100 million open innovation competition related to cancer diagnostics[44] and invested in life science offerings, with a US$4 billion portfolio that projects to double over the next few years.[45] As the Baby Boomer generation entered retirement age, the health care demand began to rise, expanding the need for new health care technologies. GE Healthcare was poised to capitalize on this new demand.

Core Competencies

General Electric's key strengths—its operational efficiencies, sheer size, history, and reputation—all worked to create competitive advantages for GE. One of GE's biggest operational strengths lay in its ability to cut costs and maximize return for shareholders, as with GE CEO Jack Welch's implementation of the Six Sigma approach in the 1990s to business management, as mentioned earlier. GE was also able to cut costs because its reputation as a market leader, its large network of businesses, and its strong alliances with other major corporations, enabled it to leverage long-standing relationships to employ the best human, equipment, and capital resources to ensure quality and consistency at a low cost. It acquired many businesses that provided useful resources, and sold off business units that did not contribute to its success. In addition, GE's history of innovation, from Edison inventing the light bulb to its pioneering of green energy medical diagnostic technology contributed to GE's long-term success.

In addition to the operational excellence that came from GE's experience and unparalleled commitment to growth, the sheer size of GE also created a tremendous competitive advantage, from distribution channels in over a hundred companies to dozens of lines of business. Few other companies were big enough to compete with the variety and breadth of resources GE brought to the table.

Globally recognized and ubiquitous in American homes, GE's history and reputation was also a key competitive advantage. Its reputation and political influence garnered favorable treatment from the U.S. and other governments. Smaller firms tried to compete with GE in individual industries, but GE's reputation and brand awareness made it difficult for them to succeed.

Finally, GE's strong company culture empowered and motivated employees, creating a workforce that stayed with the company long-term and moved internally, building a strong, knowledgeable employee base, and its focus on sustainability and the greater community helped inspire employees and improve GE's image overall.

Challenges Facing GE

By the end of 2012, GE faced many challenges. First, the parent company's comfort in mature industries such as industrial appliances and jet engines rendered it reluctant to explore different markets, or identify and move into innovative industries at the beginning of their life cycles when potential growth and earnings are greatest. While this defensive strategy was more pronounced with former CEO Jack Welch, under whose direction GE maintained a near-zero marketing budget and focus on efficiency, many within the company perceived that there was still room for growth in innovative markets, particularly the green energy market, where GE could utilize its strength of scalability to establish a competitive advantage.

Second, for many years, GE relied on its staunch traditional methods to train workers, especially general managers. Throughout the 1990s, CEO Jack Welch focused on the bottom line through lean practices and overall cost cutting, creating an extremely efficient, process-conscious organization that prioritized meeting budgets, but lagged in innovation. While these strategies did increase net earnings, it became clear that they would not yield sustainable growth, as cutting additional costs began to outweigh the savings. GE began to see that the long-term solution was to train employees and management to focus on creating new technology and products that both earn profitable returns and open new growth opportunities.

GE also needed to acknowledge potential weaknesses stemming from being such a large and diverse organization. For instance, it occasionally underperformed in Asian and European markets. Greater understanding of the operational differences and difference in business practices between the U.S. and these countries could explain in part why GE's growth there did not meet projections.

Another challenge for GE was potential changes to the tax code. In 2012, GE filed a 57,000-page tax return, the single largest tax return in the United States.[46] While GE benefited from a number of tax incentives, tax code reform constantly loomed on the horizon, and GE would be one of the companies most affected by changes to the tax code.

Although GE had a strong global brand associated with product excellence and market leadership in several industrial categories, it came under attack for being synonymous with corporate greed. GE was accused of not paying its fair share of taxes, and protestors forcefully interrupted Jeff Immelt's speeches alleging that[47] using legitimate accounting techniques to pay lower effective tax rates, GE only paid an effective tax rate of 2.3% for more than 10 years, and that GE realized US$14 billion in profits yet paid no taxes in 2011.[48] Also, GE was the recipient of a US$140 billion bailout in 2008, to cover massive losses at GE Capital.[49] These allegations did not help their name, tarnishing the reputation of an otherwise well-managed brand. Furthermore, GE was the fourth-largest producer air and water pollution globally. Although top management's focus on sustainability was considered a strength, GE needed to develop ways to become more "green" without hurting its bottom line.

What to Do with GE Capital?

Despite General Electric's market-leading portfolio and strong brand-name recognition, in the recent financial crisis, the dangers of a company's reliance on financial services became apparent. What had begun as a financing arm to catalyze GE appliance sales had grown into a dominating financial services company that surpassed the earnings of the rest of the company to account for over 50% of GE's total net income.

This concentration of resources in GE Capital paid excellent dividends during strong economic times, yet the financial sector's volatility rendered GE Capital vulnerable to large, rapid losses. Unless GE hedged against financial slowdowns by reducing its exposure to GE Capital, it might occasionally suffer losses that could put the company as a whole at risk. Further, like many financial firms, GE Capital was tempted by the large potential returns of what were later seen as risky investments, such as mortgage-backed securities and real estate. Unless GE Capital decreased its portfolio of risky assets, it could be prone to future losses that might have a negative impact on its GE parent.

In the years leading up to the financial crisis, GE, according to some industry analysts, had become complacent, and corporate growth and earnings consequently stagnated. GE focused too heavily on cutting costs and relied too heavily on the fortunes of GE Capital, which suffered from massive losses during the 2008–2009 financial crisis. When the recession forced GE to reduce the scope of GE Capital's activities, GE was not able to invest and innovate elsewhere to bolster its financials and satisfy stockholders. GE also did not have enough significant new ideas to mitigate GE Capital's financial setback, such that GE Capital's losses had a major negative impact on the growth and earnings of the corporation as a whole.

The key question facing GE's top management and board of directors at the end of 2012 was to what degree should they reduce GE Capital as a percentage of the entire company. Or, more to the point, should GE Capital be spun off altogether to allow the GE parent corporation to focus on the industrial products segment it had historically excelled in and where there is less competition and government regulation?

NOTES

1. "Explore GE Innovations by Title." General Electric Company. Web. 21 Apr. 2012. http://www.ge.com/innovation/timeline/index.html.

2. "GE Past Leaders." General Electric Company. Web. 21 Apr. 2012. http://www.ge.com/company/history/past_leaders.html.

3. Joseph, John and Ocasio, William. *Rise and Fall-or Transformation? The evolution of Strategic Planning at the General Electric Company.* http://www.elsevier.com/locate/lrp.

4. *GE 2011 Annual Report.* http://www.ge.com/ar2011/pdf/GE_AR11_EntireReport.pdf.

5. Ibid.

6. *GE 2011 Annual Report.* http://www.ge.com/ar2011/pdf/GE_AR11_EntireReport.pdf.

7. *GE 2011 Annual Report.* http://www.ge.com/ar2011/pdf/GE_AR11_EntireReport.pdf.

8. "General Electric." *Wikipedia.* Wikimedia Foundation, 05 Apr. 2012. Web. 21 Apr. 2012. http://en.wikipedia.org/wiki/General_Electric.

9. "Industrial Conglomerates Industry Snapshot - NYTimes.com." *NYTimes.com.* New York Times, 02 May 2012. Web. 02 May 2012. http://markets.on.nytimes.com/research/markets/usmarkets/industry.asp?industry=52311.

10. Stone, Mallory. "Top 5 Companies in the Industrial Conglomerates Industry with the Best Relative Performance (SI, GE, PHG, MMM, TYC)." *Comtex News Network.* Comcast, 16 Mar. 2012. Web. 02 May 2012. http://finance.comcast.net/stocks/news_body.html?ID_OSI=85473.

11. *Siemens USA.* Web. 05 May 2012. http://www.usa.siemens.com/entry/en/.

12. *Phillips Global.* Web. 05 May 2012. http://www.philips.com/global/index.page.

13. 3M Global. Web. 05 May 2012. http://www.3m.com/.

14. Ramirez, Diane. "General Electric Capital Corporation Profile." *Hoovers* D&B Company. http://www.hoovers.com/company/General_Electric_Capital_Corporation/.

15. Ramirez, Diane. "General Electric Capital Corporation Profile." *Hoovers* D&B Company. http://www.hoovers.com/company/General_Electric_Capital_Corporation/

16. Colvin, Geoffrey. "GE under Siege (pg. 2)." *CNNMoney.* Cable News Network, 10 Oct. 2008. Web. 23 Apr. 2012. http://money.cnn.com/2008/10/09/news/companies/colvin_ge.fortune/index2.htm

17. *GE Capital: Our Businesses.* 2012. General Electric. http://www.gecapital.com/en/our-company/our-businesses.html?gemid2=gtnav0502

18. "Start Building." *GE Capital Business Model & Fact Sheet.* Web. 21 Apr. 2012. http://www.gecapital.com/en/our-company/company-overview.html?gemid2=gtnav0501.

19. "GE Capital: The Capital Difference." *Fact Sheet.* General Electric Company. Web. 21 Apr. 2012. http://www.gecapital.com/en/pdf/GE_Capital_Fact_Sheet.pdf.

20. Ibid.

21. *GE 2011 Annual Report.* http://www.ge.com/ar2011/pdf/GE_AR11_EntireReport.pdf.

22. Ibid.

23. Ramirez, Diane. "General Electric Capital Corporation Profile." *Hoovers* D&B Company. http://www.hoovers.com/company/General_Electric_Capital_Corporation/.

24. Ramirez, Diane. "Bank of America Corporation Profile." *Hoovers* D&B Company. http://www.hoovers.com/company/Bank_of_America_Corporation/.

25. Ramirez, Diane. "CIT Group IncProfile." *Hoovers* D&B Company. http://www.hoovers.com/company/CIT_Group_Inc.

26. *GE 2011 Annual Report.* http://www.ge.com/ar2011/pdf/GE_AR11_EntireReport.pdf.

27. Ibid.

28. *GE 2011 Annual Report.* http://www.ge.com/ar2011/pdf/GE_AR11_EntireReport.pdf.

29. General Electric. *GE Q1'12 Earnings.* Www.ge.com. General Electric Company, 20 Apr. 2012. Web. 25 Apr. 2012. http://www.ge.com/pdf/investors/events/04202012/ge_webcast_pressrelease_04202012.pdf.

30. Protess, Ben. "Revenue Drops at GE Capital." *The New York Times.* The New York Times Company, 20 Apr. 2012. Web. 23 Apr. 2012. http://dealbook.nytimes.com/2012/04/20/revenues-drop-at-ge-capital/.

31. GE *2011 Annual Report.* Page 5 http://www.ge.com/ar2011/pdf/GE_AR11_EntireReport.pdf.

32. Ibid., page 47.

33. Protess, Ben. "Revenue Drops at GE Capital." *The New York Times.* The New York Times Company, 20 Apr. 2012. Web. 23 Apr. 2012. http://dealbook.nytimes.com/2012/04/20/revenues-drop-at-ge-capital/.

34. Colvin, Geoffrey. "GE under Siege (pg. 2)." *CNNMoney.* Cable News Network, 10 Oct. 2008. Web. 23 Apr. 2012. http://money.cnn.com/2008/10/09/news/companies/colvin_ge.fortune/index2.htm.

35. Ibid.

36. Andrejczak, Matt. "Industrial Operations Key to GE Earnings Report." *Market Watch.* The Wall Street Journal, 19 Apr. 2012. Web. 29 Apr. 2012. http://articles.marketwatch.com/2012-04-19/industries/31366115_1_ge-capital-ge-shares-chief-executive-jeff-immelt.

37. "DSIRE: DSIRE Home." *DSIRE USA.* Web. 28 Apr. 2012. http://www.dsireusa.org/.

38. Mosk, Matthew. "General Electric Wages Never-Say-Die Campaign for Jet Engine Contract." ABD News 7 March 2012.

39. *GE 2011 Annual Report.* Page 18 http://www.ge.com/ar2011/pdf/GE_AR11_EntireReport.pdf.

40. "GE Set to Soar on Clean Energy Projects—Seeking Alpha." *Stock Market News & Financial Analysis.* 17 Apr. 2012. Web. 28 Apr. 2012. http://seekingalpha.com/article/503701-ge-set-to-soar-on-clean-energy-projects.

41. Ibid.

42. "$232 Billion Personalized Medicine Market to Grow 11 Percent Annually, Says PricewaterhouseCoopers." *NEW YORK, Dec. 8/ PRNewswire/.* Web. 28 Apr. 2012. http://www.prnewswire.com/news-releases/232-billion-personalized-medicine-market-to-grow-11-percent-annually-says-pricewaterhousecoopers-78751072.html.

43. "DOTmed.com - GE Launches Handheld Ultrasound Tool." *Dotmed.com.* 2010. Web. 28 Apr. 2012. http://www.dotmed.com/news/story/11669.

44. *GE 2011 Annual Report.* Page 27 http://www.ge.com/ar2011/pdf/GE_AR11_EntireReport.pdf.

45. Ibid., page 5.
46. McCormack, John. "GE Filed 57,000-Page Tax Return, Paid No Taxes on $14 Billion in Profits." Weekly Standard. 17 November 2011.
47. Shepardson, David. "GE CEO Defends Tax Rate after Protestors Disrupt Speech." *The Detroit News*. 24 Apr. 2012. Web. 24 Apr. 2012. http://www.detroitnews.com /article/20120424/BIZ/204240397/GE-CEO-defends-tax -rate-after-protesters-disrupt-speech?odyssey=tabltopnew sltextlFRONTPAGE.
48. "GE Filed 57,000-Page Tax Return, Paid No Taxes on $14 Billion in Profits." *The Weekly Standard*. 17 Nov. 2011. Web. 24 Apr. 2012. http://www.weeklystandard.com/blogs /ge-filed-57000-page-tax-return-paid-no-taxes-14-billion- profits_609137.html.
49. Hill, Vernon. "General Electric Gets a $140B Bailout - What's the Point of AAA? - Seeking Alpha." *Stock Market News & Financial Analysis*. 14 Nov. 2008. Web. 24 Apr. 2012. http://seekingalpha.com/article/105984-general -electric-gets-a-140b-bailout-what-s-the-point-of-aaa.
50. Source: http://www.ge.com/ar2011/.
51. Ibid.
52. Ibid.
53. Ibid.
54. Ibid.
55. Ibid.

Snap-on Tools: A Victim of Its Own Success

Alan N. Hoffman
Bentley University

SNAP-ON TOOLS' HISTORY BEGAN IN 1920, WHEN JOSEPH JOHNSON AND WILLIAM Seidemann used their idea of interchangeable sockets and wrench handles to form the Snap-on Wrench Company. The concept of ten sockets that "snapped on" to five interchangeable handles revolutionized the tool industry. Through the years since then, Snap-on continued to innovate and create new tools and products.

To sell their products, the company's founders turned to Stanton Palmer, who demonstrated the benefits of bringing tools directly to customers at their places of business. This became the cornerstone of the company's marketing success. Snap-on's founders expanded on the concept of bringing products to customers through fully stocked walk-in vans, thus pioneering the familiar franchisee van channel. This strong connection and one-on-one relationship with customers allowed the company to thrive. The franchises introduced and demonstrated to customers all new products—top quality, modern design, hand tools; power tools built for demanding situations; attractive and neat tool storage; and intelligent and powerful diagnostics products. In addition to the canny design of basic mechanics' tools such as interchangeable sockets or the Flank Drive® wrenching system, Snap-on's line card grew until it offered nearly 14,000 products featuring innovative designs and precision manufacturing.[1]

The author would like to thank Barbara Gottfried and Pamela Miller and Bentley University MBA students Gintaras Lenkutis, Konstantin Mikhailov, Mary-Helen Nsangou, Jonathan Safran, and Safiya Samms for their research and contributions to this case. Please address all correspondence to: *Dr. Alan N. Hoffman,* Dept. of Management, Bentley University, 175 Forest Street, Waltham, MA 02452-4705, ahoffman@bentley.edu, (781) 891-2287. Printed by permission of Dr. Alan N. Hoffman.

Snap-on's innovation led to manufacturing tools for industries including aviation and aerospace, agriculture, construction, government and military, mining, natural resources, power generation and technical education.[2] Over the past decade, education also became an important focus for Snap-On: it was the company's belief that it was in its best interest to train up-and-coming auto mechanics who would become its future customers, and that developing a skilled labor force was an issue of national concern. Though Snap-on was never a mainstream company, it always felt that its greatest means of promotion was word-of-mouth testimonials. Its visible association with motor sports, and its professional relationship with auto racing for more than 70 years served it very well.

As of 2013, Snap-on was a $2.9 billion, S&P 500 company headquartered in Kenosha, Wisconsin, which offered products and services around the world. The company was divided into four business groups: (1) the Commercial & Industrial Group; (2) the Snap-on Tools Group; (3) the Repair Systems & Information Group; and (4) Financial Services.

Strategic Direction

Snap-on's mission was to manufacture and distribute premium hand and power tools, serving the global vehicle services industry with productivity solutions including tools, equipment, diagnostics, repair information, and systems solutions. Its vision was to be seen as the first choice of employers, franchisees, business partners, and investors and to support serious professionals in the automotive industry, while at the same time innovating and expanding its product lines to engineering industries including aerospace, aviation, and oil and gas.

Snap-on had three major strategic objectives:

1. Enhancing its franchise network—Snap-on worked closely with franchisees to improve their profitability and increase their sales. To strengthen its outreach to this customer segment, the company created the "Snap-on Masters of Metal Tour." Each event showcased a customized truck dubbed the "Rock 'n Roll Cab Express" which highlighted a variety of tool storage units and accessories that offered automotive technicians the opportunity to try Snap-on's tools and meet Snap-on factory associates.

2. Expansion in the garage—Snap-on sought to expand its presence with owners and managers of vehicle service and repair facilities by providing them with better, more efficient performance solutions. To do so, Snap-on came up with the "Integrity Test Drive by John Bean," a system which quickly performed a detailed vehicle inspection. Winner of the 2012 *MOTOR Magazine* Top 20 Tools award, the system integrated several products that together enabled the shop to quickly diagnose problems, fix vehicles on the first visit, and increase revenue.

3. Building in Emerging Markets—As repair industries developed in emerging markets, Snap-on sought to expand to these rapidly growing economies and participate in the building of repair infrastructure. In 2012, it opened its fourth manufacturing facility in Kunshan, China, where it manufactured undercar equipment, an important, high-value product line for the local market. Kunshun joined existing Snap-On facilities for power tools, cutting tools, and tool storage manufacturing plants, as well as a modern engineering and research and development center.

When the Snap-on Wrench Company was formed in 1920, it was built on innovation. The original Snap-on wrench set revolutionized the tool market by creating a new product in an old industry. By 2013, Snap-on had 600 patents either confirmed or pending in the United States, and held 1,500 globally. Even its website encouraged would-be inventors to register their ideas through Snap-on, and it developed a direct method to purchase or share in the value of these ideas. In November of 2013, Snap-on was the recipient of five innovation awards[3] in the areas of lighting, tool storage, lab scopes, tire/wheel service, and shop equipment. Clearly Snap-on's focus on creating the newest and best products had buoyed them to great success: for over 90 years, the cornerstone of Snap-on's strategic philosophy remained innovation.

Snap-on actively pursued and relied on patent protection, trade secret protection, copyrights, and/or trademarks and domain names to protect its intellectual property and position in its markets.

Snap-on also focused its strategic efforts on customer relations. Snap-on's founders began by bringing their products directly to customers to demonstrate their use and receive direct feedback. This evolved into the fully loaded walk-in vans, described earlier, which helped build lasting relationships with customers by providing them with Snap-on's most current and innovative tools while allowing them at the same time to conduct focused and immediate market research. In addition, Snap-on was the first in the industry to offer lines of credit to their customers that guaranteed a long-term relationship as well as a foundation of trust. Ultimately, Snap-on Tools was successful because it adhered staunchly to its core beliefs:

1. Non-negotiable product and workplace safety
2. Uncompromising quality
3. Passionate customer care
4. Fearless innovation
5. Rapid and continuous improvement[4]

These clearly articulated and tangible ideals led directly to product delivery that insured Snap-on's success. The company never had to compromise in any way to turn a profit.

Competitors

More recently, Snap-on faced strong competition in each of its four business groups in the areas of product quality and performance, product line breadth and depth, service, brand awareness and imagery, technological innovation, and availability of financing. Price competition, especially during the economic recession, was intense, as pricing pressures from competitors and customers increased.[5] The concern was that such high levels of competition could limit the company's ability to maintain or increase its market share.[6] Given this increased competition, Snap-on Tools had to maintain high customer satisfaction in all segments to ensure that its premium image and reputation remained stable. By successfully maintaining its image, the company strove to dictate premium pricing in its industries.

While there was no single company in competition with Snap-on across all product lines and distribution channels, various companies competed in one or more of these areas. Major competitors who sold diagnostics, shop equipment, and information to automotive dealerships and independent repair shops included original equipment manufacturers (OEMs) and their proprietary electronic parts catalogs, diagnostics, and information systems, as well as other companies serving this sector.[7] According to Hoover's, Inc., a business research company, Snap-on Tools' top competitors were Stanley Black & Decker, Inc. (SWK), Danaher (DHR), and The Home Depot, Inc. (HD).

Snap-on also competed with companies selling tools and equipment to automotive technicians through retail stores and online, including Sears Holdings, Home Depot, and Lowe's Companies. It further competed with auto parts supply outlets such as AutoZone and The Pep Boys - Manny, Moe & Jack; and tool supply warehouses/distributorships such as Integrated Supply Network.

Snap-on's major competitors in the power tools industry included Ingersoll-Rand, Makita, Atlas Copco, and Techtronic Industries. In the industrial sector, major competitors included Cooper Industries and W.W. Grainger. The major competitors selling diagnostics and shop equipment and information to automotive dealerships, independent repair shop owners, and managers in the vehicle service and repair sector were Corghi, SPX, Dover, Car-O-Liner, and Infomedia.

Stanley Black & Decker, Inc. (SWK)

After the merger of Stanley Works and rival Black & Decker in 2010 the new entity, Stanley Black & Decker, continued to sell its products through home centers and mass-merchant distributors, as well as through third-party distributors.[9] The newly merged company boasted operations in the United States, Canada, Europe, and Asia. The United States accounted for about 48% of its revenue, followed by Europe (31%), Canada (6%), and emerging markets (15%). Stanley Black & Decker's business operations were divided into three segments: Construction & Do-It-Yourself; Security; and Industrial. One of the United States' top toolmakers, Stanley Black & Decker successfully marketed mechanics', power, pneumatic, and hydraulic tools. After the merger of Stanley and Black and Decker, the company's tool shed expanded to include garden tools, plumbing products (Pfister), and cleaning items (Dustbuster), as well as security hardware (Kwikset) and door products. In addition to Stanley and Black & Decker named products, the company sold brands such as Bostitch, Mac Tools, and DEWALT. The company saw positive sales increases from 2008 through 2013: it logged an 8% revenue rise in fiscal 2012 as compared to 2011, while profits increased by 31%.

Danaher (DHR)

Danaher, another of Snap-on's competitors, was viewed in the industry as a well-diversified industrial and medical conglomerate whose products were designed to test, analyze, and diagnose. Its subsidiaries designed, manufactured, and marketed products and offered services geared to worldwide professional, medical, industrial, and commercial markets. As of 2013, Danaher had around 240 manufacturing and distribution facilities worldwide, 125 in the United States in more than 40 states; and roughly 120 outside the United States in over 50 countries throughout Asia, Europe, North America, South America, and Australia. Over half the company's revenue was generated by North America, primarily the United States. Built largely through acquisitions, Danaher's five business segments reflected a well-balanced portfolio. Top segments "Life Sciences" and "Test & Measurement" accounted for 35% and 19%, respectively, of revenues for fiscal 2012. Danaher enjoyed three straight years of unprecedented growth. Its revenues rose by 13% from $16.1 billion in 2011 to roughly $18.3 billion in 2012. Profits were also up by 10% from $2.2 billion to nearly $2.4 billion in 2012.[10]

The Home Depot, Inc. (HD)

As of 2013, The Home Depot was the world's largest home improvement chain and one of the largest US retailers, selling building materials, home improvement, and lawn and garden products; installing carpeting, flooring, cabinets, countertops, and water heaters; and providing home maintenance and professional service programs for do-it-yourself, do-it-for-me, and professional customers, homeowners, professional remodelers, general contractors, repairmen, small business owners, and tradespeople. Challenged by the deep recession and the housing crisis in the United States after 2008, the company began to regain its footing by focusing on its core Home Depot stores, and exiting China.[11] As of September 26, 2013, the company operated 2,258 retail stores in 50 states, the District of Columbia, Puerto Rico, U.S. Virgin Islands, Guam, 10 Canadian provinces, and Mexico.[12]

Barriers to Entry

Because Snap-on's tools, systems, and financial services were standard in design and function, they were easily replicable. However, Snap-on raised significant barriers to entry through strong and established distribution channels, patent and other intellectual property protections, the strength of its brand, allegiance to its products by users, and its relationships with key partners and industry players. Thus, the risk of competition was relatively low because the basic tools that Snap-on manufactured were differentiated from its competitors by the quality of the product and the strength of the brand name. In addition, Snap-on focused increasingly on both its own and its customers' productivity through innovative productivity-enhancing products. As the company developed new tools and systems, and patented them, competition was cut further, as the products and systems were not easily replicable. Finally, though Snap-on's price point was often higher, so was the quality of its products: customers found it was worth paying the higher price as a one-time buy was usually all that was necessary.

Skilled Labor Shortage

By early 2014, factories and service centers built in the United States had far fewer workers than in the past, but the skill-sets required of those workers demanded versatile technical skills and training to work with current technology. Economists forecast a manufacturing renaissance in the United States[13] that would create increased demand for skilled labor, but according to the Boston Consulting Group, appropriately skilled labor was getting increasingly difficult to find. Certain areas in the United States were already predicted to experience a shortage of skilled workers, especially Virginia's tobacco lands manufacturing plants, which, it was estimated, would require 6,840 skilled workers by 2017, while only about 5,800 were likely to be available. In the past, U.S. labor shortfalls had been made up by the influx of highly skilled immigrant labor, but by 2014 that was no longer the case. These combined threats to the U.S. labor market were made worse by the lack of a German model of a vast network of technical schools tied to apprenticeship programs. Snap-on foresaw these labor issues and successfully partnered with technical institutions across the United States, while its CEO Ken Pinchuck publically emphasized the importance of making technical careers attractive for young people.

An Over Dependence on the US Market

Snap-on's greatest challenge was perhaps the lack of diverse markets for its products and services: 65% of its sales were US based; Europe, its second-largest market, accounted for 21% of sales; and 10% of its total sales were Asia-Pacific–based[14] [Exhibit A]. The fear was that its overdependence on the U.S. market could make its business and operations vulnerable to country-specific trends, as 65% of all revenue from one region was a risky figure even with a global presence. And there was also concern that the concentration of operations in the United States could increase the

EXHIBIT A
Sales by Region

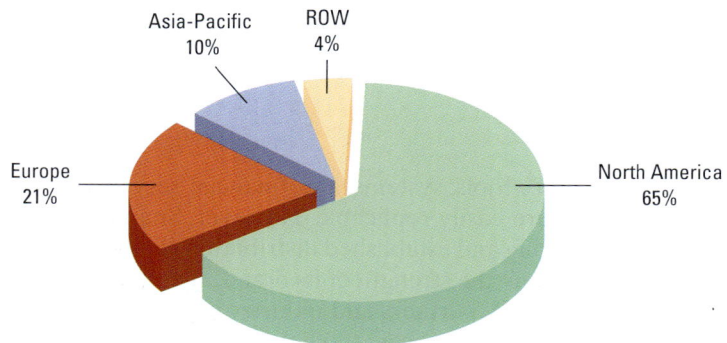

Broad Geographic Reach: Sales by Geography

Asia-Pacific 10%

ROW 4%

Europe 21%

North America 65%

Source: Snap-On, Inc. 2012 Annual Report

company's exposure to local factors such as severe weather conditions, labor strikes, or changes in regulations, thus increasing its business risk.[15]

Uncertain Economic Recovery in Europe

In 2012, the Eurozone entered into a worse recession than in 2009. The debt-wracked Eurozone suffered through a dreaded double-dip recession with the second contraction actually lasting longer than the first downturn. The GDP for the 17 countries using the euro shrank for the sixth straight quarter during the first three months of 2013."[16] It was feared that the ongoing debt crisis in Europe would have a detrimental impact on the global economic recovery, which might, in turn, cut demand for Snap-on's products and services in Europe, creating a major problem for Snap-on, as 21% of its revenues were generated by European sales. In short, the company's future growth, profitability, and financial liquidity were under threat from decreased demand for its products and services[17] from depressed consumer and business confidence in the developed region of Europe.

Improving Global Automotive Retail

As the production and demand for automobiles outside the United States grew, the demand for Snap-on Tools' products increased proportionately. Although the global automotive retail sector fell into decline in 2009, it recovered strongly in 2010 and 2011, with solid growth projected through the end of 2016.[18] According to MarketLine the global automotive retail sector generated total revenues of $4.9 Trillion in 2011, representing a CAGR of 2.2% between 2007 and 2011, with performance forecast to accelerate to an anticipated CAGR of 8% for the five-year period 2011–16, driving the sector to a value of $7.2 trillion by the end of 2016.[19] Such growth in the global automotive retail sector was expected to generate increased demand for Snap-on's products and services.[20]

Marketing

Snap-on's main marketing objectives were always to:

1. Maintain premium brand and high-quality image
2. Utilize franchisees as a key marketing tool

3. Expand to emerging markets

4. Grow and support U.S. Tech Education

As Glenn Rifkin put it, "the way to create a world-class brand was to give customers what they needed when they needed it, and never let them out of your sight."[21] For over 90 years, Snap-on Tools was known as the #1 brand for manufacturing all different types, shapes, and sizes of tools. Its Facebook page read: "From the smallest bit socket to the biggest roll cab, one thing is certain; our customers live by their Snap-on tools."

Snap-on's greatest marketing strengths were its brand recognition and awareness, extensive product selection, franchisee network, annual festivals and events, and support of technical education in the United States. Its marketing campaigns reached its customers through several channels: franchises, company-direct, distributors, and the Internet. The company reported advertising and promotion expenses of $50.1 million in 2012, compared to $46.3 million in 2011,[22] an important positive increase in advertising expenditures. However, as Snap-on was valued at close to $6B, many felt its marketing budget should be further increased to support the objective of maintaining its premium image and brand awareness. While in the United States approximately 300,000 vehicle repair shops were using Snap-on tools and 1 million technicians were visiting the company's 4500 franchised vans, the possibility still existed of increasing even those strong numbers if more of the budget were allocated to advertising.

To expand their marketing, in November 2013, the company even published a Snap-on Holiday Gift Guide called The Toy Catalog for Techs.

Beyond regular and holiday sales, Snap-on's products and services were appealing enough to some to interest them in selling those products and services. Franchises became one of Snap-on's key marketing tools, a great business opportunity for entrepreneurial people to run their own trade with Snap-on's logo, which worked very effectively for Snap-on for more than 90 years. The company provided many compelling reasons for becoming a Snap-On franchisee:

1. More than 4,200 franchises worldwide

2. Most in-demand product in the category

3. Financing available through Snap-on Credit

4. Protected list of calls

5. No real estate investment

6. Exceptional training and support

7. Proven franchise model

Each franchise dealer owned his own truck, visiting 200 to 300 customers in his territory every week on a regular rotation. Out of pocket start-up expenses for a standard franchise ranged from $30,095 to $79,265 and when used, the financing through Snap-on included $9,432 to $19,863 of working capital.[24] To support and celebrate its franchisees, Snap-on held an annual Franchisee Conference in Nashville. In 2013 more than 2850 franchisees attended the three-day business conference, and the gathering of more than 7,000 total represented the largest Snap-on event in the company's 93-year history.

Another venue for appealing to its customers was Snap-on's Masters of Metal Festivals. The company used these events to showcase its newest products and innovations, and to regale automotive service technicians "with customized semi-trailers full of the latest and greatest Snap-on tools and equipment." The interactive tour celebrated automotive service technicians as the "masters of their trade" and provided these "masters" with a hands-on experience of the newest and most exciting products Snap-on had to offer. As Snap-on promoted it, "The Snap-on Masters of Metal Tour [wa]s the perfect chance to see firsthand [its] latest innovations and hottest tool offerings."[25]

The final prong of Snap-on's marketing strategy was its stress on the importance of technical education in the United States. Over a number of years, Snap-on had begun to see the impact of a wide gap in U.S. employees' technical skills between the older baby boomer generation and younger mid–career-level workers. Snap-on's CEO Nick Pinchuk himself noted, "Add in the fact that the experienced baby boomers are leaving America's workforce—with 10,000 turning 65 every day for the next 19 years—and it is easy to see that America's already significant skills gap will only become more challenging, and must be addressed now."[26] The company realized that to bring manufacturing jobs back to the country, companies in the manufacturing sector needed to invest in technical education. In the 10 years prior to 2013, Snap-on began to invest heavily in educational programs, grants, and trainings. In particular, Snap-on supported SkillsUSA, a national non-profit dedicated to fostering a partnership of students, teachers, and industry to ensure a skilled workforce for America. In 2013 Snap-on's CEO, Nick Pinchuk, was honored with SkillsUSA's Champion of the Year award. Additionally, the company funded grants for young talented students in this field to help them with the cost of getting a technical degree. Nonetheless, some worried that these measures were too little too late, and that the manufacturing industry in the United States would have a hard time bouncing back from the loss of baby boomers' technical skills in the workforce.

In the final analysis, Snap-on was always a very traditional manufacturing company. As of 2013, its CEO, Nick Pinchuk, was 66 years old, and many of its other the executive officers were of a similar age, perhaps an explanation for Snap-on's conservative marketing strategies. Snap-on not only resisted the lure of new and innovative marketing tools such as social media and heavy online advertising, it did not even use such traditional marketing channels as television ads. This lack of general exposure became an issue in building Snap-on's brand awareness. While the company's reputable brand was well known to people involved in manufacturing, auto, and other such areas, it was largely unknown to the general public. There was a strong sense that without more investment in advertising, the company's brand would likely start to diminish.

Human Resources

Snap-on always espoused strong values for its employees:

> *"Our behaviors define our success: We demonstrate Integrity. We tell the Truth. We respect the Individual. We promote Teamwork. We Listen."* (2012 annual report)

By the end of January 2013 Snap-on employed approximately 11,200 people, slightly lower than the 11,500 people employed at the end of January 2012. Approximately 2,700 of these employees, or 24% of Snap-on's worldwide workforce, were represented by unions and/or covered under collective bargaining agreements. In the years leading up to 2013 Snap-on had not experienced any significant work slow-downs, stoppages, or other labor disruptions, indicating a relatively stable and contented workforce.

A scan of on-line comment boards, however, reflected a somewhat different reality from that professed in the company's values. Past and present employee reviews on Indeed.com revealed a mix of experiences with the work environment, including good relationships with coworkers but trouble with the politics of management. Negative comments especially pointed to management's expectations of very long work hours without much flexibility for dealing with family or personal matters. Although employees reported a practice of management giving quarterly reviews, reflecting a good feedback culture, reports revealed evidence of better growth trajectories for managers than for lower-level workers. Finally, the employees posting on-line were mostly either early or late in their careers, suggesting problems with attracting and retaining a workforce through the middle years of employment.

Taken together, the gamut of these anonymous on-line employee commentaries exposed a potential crisis in Snap-on's labor force. Faced with retiring baby boomers on one end, and a lack of skilled younger workforce on the other, together with organizational challenges in retaining and advancing employees through their middle years, it became clear that Snap-on faced a potential hollowing out of its U.S. workforce unless it changed its human resource practices and culture.

Financials

Rebounding from the recession that took its toll on end-of-year numbers in 2009, Snap-on gained nearly 10.77% on revenue in 2010, continuing to increase its revenue stream by 11% through 2011. Sales in 2012, however, grew only 4%. According to the company's 2012 annual report, the Commercial & Industrial business segment produced 32% of 2012 revenue, an increase of 2%.[27] Higher sales in emerging Asian markets offset lower sales of hand tools in the economically fragile European market. Through this large business segment, Snap-on moved toward achieving its financial objectives including extension to critical industries and emerging markets.[28]

The Snap-on Tools Group posted an increase in organic net sales of 10.7% growth to $1.27 billion in 2012. Financial Services revenue was up 11.7% in 2012, year over year. Two areas of concern remained, however, as both Snap-on's Commercial & Industrial and its Repair Systems & Information Groups only increased net sales by 2.2% and 1.7%, respectively.[29] At the beginning of fiscal year 2013, the company posted a slight rise in net income in comparison with sales trends, perhaps attributable to a decrease in operating costs from the restructuring of operations in Europe as a result of the European economic downturn.[30]

At the same time, Snap-on's operating margins increased over the four years from 2008 to 2012, with a slight dip in Q2 of FY2012.[31] A comparison of Snap-on's operating margin to that of the Danaher Corporation, one of its major competitors, showed that Snap-on gained on Danaher, a company with much higher revenues, indicating a competitive, high-quality company making $0.18 on every $1 of sales in Q2 of 2013.[32]

Snap-on's long-term debt began to plateau in 2009, which was to be expected from a responsible company in an economic downturn. Cash and cash equivalents decreased into 2012 as the company continued spending without accumulating more debt. At the end of 2012, Snap-on's long-term debt to equity ratio equaled 0.54. The long-term debt was 4.53 times the amount of cash and cash equivalents.[33]

EXHIBIT B
Balance Sheet

(Amounts in millions)	Operations*		Financial Services	
	2013	2012	2013	2012
ASSETS				
Current assets				
Cash and cash equivalents	$ 214.4	$ 211.2	$ 3.2	$ 3.3
Intersegment receivables	15.3	14.1	–	–
Trade and other accounts receivable—net	531.1	497.5	0.5	0.4
Finance receivables—net	–	–	374.6	323.1
Contract receivables—net	7.0	7.4	61.4	55.3
Inventories—net	434.4	404.2	–	–
Deferred income tax assets	71.1	68.8	14.3	13.0
Prepaid expenses and other assets	88.1	88.3	1.3	1.0
Total current assets	1,361.4	1,291.5	455.3	396.1
Property and equipment—net	390,9	373.2	1.6	2.0
Investment in Financial Services	193.7	165.3	–	–
Deferred income tax assets	56.8	110.2	0.3	0.2
Intersegment long-term notes receivable	9.6	–	–	–
Long-term finance receivables—net	–	–	560.6	494.6
Long-term contract receivables—net	12.0	12.1	205.1	182.3
Goodwill	838.8	807.4	–	–
Other intangibles—net	190.5	187.2	–	–
Other assets	58.9	65.3	1.1	1.1
Total assets	$ 3,112.6	$ 3,012.2	$ 1,224.0	$ 1,076.3

(Amounts in millions)	Operations*		Financial Services	
	2013	2012	2013	2012
LIABILITIES AND EQUITY				
Current liabilities				
Notes payable and current maturities of long-term debt	$ 13.1	$ 5.2	$ 100.0	$ –
Accounts payable	150.7	142.1	4.9	0.4
Intersegment payables	–	–	15.3	14.1
Accrued benefits	48.1	50.6	–	–
Accrued compensation	91.9	84.9	3.6	3.4
Franchisee deposits	59,4	54.7	–	–
Other accrued liabilities	229.5	207.8	22.2	46.9
Total current liabilities	592.7	545,3	146.0	64.8

Long-term debt and intersegment long-term debt	–	143.2	868.5	827.2
Deferred income tax liabilities	142.7	125.7	1.1	1.4
Retiree health care benefits	41.7	48.4	–	–
Pension liabilities	135.8	260.7	–	–
Other long-term liabilities	69.3	69.9	14.7	17.6
Total liabilities	982.2	1,193.2	1,030.3	911.0
Total shareholders' equity attributable to Snap-on Inc.	2,113.2	1,802.1	193.7	165.3
Noncontrolling interests	17.2	16.9	–	–
Total equity	2,130.4	1,819.0	193.7	165.3
Total liabilities and equity	$ 3,112.6	$ 3,012.2	$ 1,224.0	$ 1,076.3

*Snap-on with Financial Services on the equity method.

Slow to Enter Emerging Markets

Snap-on Tools faced a real difficulty in promoting their premium products in emerging markets. Snap-on envisioned expansion to emerging markets as key to its future growth. However, given the impact of the recent recession and pessimistic economic results in the rest of the world, some worried that it would be hard for the company to push its premium high-quality and high-priced products to cost-sensitive economies. Many companies, especially small size auto shops, would have to evaluate their options before going with Snap-on, a premium brand. Thus, the Snap-on brand was both a successful competitive differentiator and at the same time, a key barrier to entry.

Nevertheless, increasing numbers of aging vehicles requiring continued maintenance offered an opportunity to sustain Snap-on's growth, as did the emerging market of China, even though cars there were relatively new. Additionally, management saw opportunities to expand the product line to various industries including aerospace, aviation, and energy production.[34] The increase in new car sales as the American and European economies rebounded also constituted a long-term opportunity for Snap-on as these cars would eventually age and require maintenance.[35]

As repair industries rapidly developed in emerging markets, Snap-on Tools had great opportunities to utilize its brand recognition to expand its manufacturing capabilities into these rapidly growing economies. Even though it had already opened its fourth manufacturing facility in Kunshan, China, Snap-on needed to continue expanding to gain a bigger manufacturing market share. Additionally, the Asia-Pacific region constituted about 32% of the global automotive retail sector. Snap-on Tools, therefore, needed to focus its attention on this rapidly developing region to garner the biggest possible market share there.

EXHIBIT C
Income Statement

Results of Operations
2013 vs. 2012
Results of operations for 2013 and 2012 are as follows:

(*Amounts in millions*)	2013		2012		Change	
Net sales	$ 3,056.5	100.0%	$ 2,937.9	100.0%	$ 118.6	4.0%
Cost of goods sold	(1,583.6)	−51.8%	(1,547.9)	−52.7%	(35.7)	−2.3%
Gross profit	1,472.9	48.2%	1,390.0	47.3%	82.9	6.0%
Operating expenses	(1,012.4)	−33.1%	(980.3)	−33.4%	(32.1)	−3.3%
Operating earnings before financial services	460.5	15.1%	409.7	13.9%	50.8	12.4%
Financial services revenue	181.0	100.0%	161.3	100.0%	19.7	12.2%
Financial services expenses	(55.3)	−30.6%	(54.6)	−33.8%	(0.7)	−1.3%
Operating earnings from financial services	125.7	69.4%	106.7	66.2%	19.0	17.8%
Operating earnings	586.2	18.1%	516.4	16.7%	69.8	13.5%
Interest expense	(56.1)	−1.7%	(55.8)	−1.8%	(0.3)	−0.5%
Other income (expense)–net	(3.9)	−0.1%	(0.4)	–	(3.5)	NM
Earnings before income taxes and equity earnings	526.2	16.3%	460.2	14.9%	66.0	14.3%
Income tax expense	(166.7)	−5.2%	(148.2)	−4.8%	(18.5)	−12.5%
Earnings before equity earnings	359.5	11.1%	312.0	10.1%	47.5	15.2%
Equity earnings, net of tax	0.2	–	2.6	0.1%	(2.4)	−92.3%
Net earnings	359.7	11.1%	314.6	10.2%	45.1	14.3%
Net earnings attributable to noncontrolling interests	(9.4)	−0.3%	(8.5)	−0.3%	(0.9)	−10.6%
Net earnings attributable to Snap. on Inc.	$ 350.3	10.8%	$ 306.1	9.9%	$ 44.2	14.4%

NM: Not meaningful

A Victim of its own Success

Snap-on was always a strategic slow mover. The company rarely responded quickly enough to trends and opportunities. Firmly rooted in an old-fashioned industry, the leadership behaved in old-fashioned ways. The strong spirit of its innovation department did not extend to the whole company. Evidence of this strategic slowness included the following:

■ Snap-on did not act quickly enough to respond to demand for tools and basic repair equipment in emerging markets—China in particular. The Tools group didn't grow fast enough to build facilities and generate product that kept pace with opportunities in those markets, opening up the possibility that a fast-moving competitor could move in and supplant them.

■ Snap-on did not anticipate and adapt to obvious demographic trends in the United States. Baby Boomers began hitting retirement age in the ten years leading up to 2013; Snap-on never considered the impact of the loss of these skilled workers, nor worked to avoid the prospect of worker attrition by adapting its corporate culture to enable retention and professional development.

■ Similarly, Snap-on's ambitions to offer technical education to build the skilled labor base in the United States were not enacted quickly enough to provide a pipeline of skilled laborers for the company or the industry.

■ The company was not aggressive enough in its reinvestment and expansion policies in the commercial and industrial sectors in which it sought to expand and diversify its operations, such as aerospace and oil and gas.

Snap-on's innovative, high-quality products were always both its greatest strength and one of its greatest weaknesses: the company became a victim of its own success, as its customers never needed to buy new replacement products. Its greatest weakness, however, reflected a fundamental organizational irony: that this well-regarded company, whose competitive edge was product innovation, was not innovative in its organizational management approach and strategic decision making.

NOTES

1. "Company History." *Company History*. Snap-on Tools, n.d. Web. December 1, 2013. http://www1.snapon.com /corporate/companyhistory.nws

2. Ibid.

3. Snap-on Receives Five Top Innovation Awards From Professional Tool & Equipment News. Snap-on Receives Five Top Innovation Awards From Professional Tool & Equipment News. N.p., 2013. Web. December 18, 2013.

4. Snap-on Inc. "Company Beliefs/Values." *Company Beliefs/ Values*. N.p., n.d. Web. December 18, 2013.

5. *Snap-on 2012 Annual Report*. Snap-on Incorporated. Web. December 1, 2013. http://www1.snapon.com/display/233 /Snap_on_2012_Annual_Report_Final.pdf

6. "Snap-on Incorporated SWOT Analysis." Snap-on, Inc. SWOT Analysis (2013): 1–7. Business Source Premier. Web. December 10, 2013.

7. *Snap-on 2012 Annual Report*. Snap-on Incorporated. Web. December 1, 2013. http://www1.snapon.com/display/233 /Snap_on_2012_Annual_Report_Final.pdf

8. Snap-on Incorporated. Austin: Dun and Bradstreet, Inc, 2013. *ProQuest*. Web. December 1, 2013.

9. *Stanley Black & Decker, Inc. Austin: Dun and Bradstreet, Inc, 2013. ProQuest*. Web. December 1, 2013.

10. Danaher. Austin: Dun and Bradstreet, Inc, 2013. *ProQuest*. Web. December 1, 2013.

11. The Home Depot, Inc. Austin: Dun and Bradstreet, Inc, 2013. *ProQuest*. Web. December 1, 2013.

12. "HD Profile | Home Depot, Inc. (The) Common S Stock - Yahoo! Finance." HD Profile | Home Depot, Inc. (The) Common S Stock - Yahoo! Finance. Yahoo Finance, n.d. Web. Deceber 1, 2013. http://finance.yahoo.com/q /pr?s=HD

13. Foroohar, R "Made In The USA" Nation Manufacturing, Blackboard.

14. Rep. N.p.: n.p., n.d. *Snap-on 2012 Annual Report*. Snap-on Incorporated. Web. December 1, 2013. http://www1.snapon .com/display/233/Snap_on_2012_Annual_Report_Final.pdf

15. "Snap-on Incorporated SWOT Analysis." Snap-on, Inc. SWOT Analysis (2013): 1-7. Business Source Premier. Web. December 10, 2013.

16. "The Bears Were Right: Europe's Double-Dip Recession." *Canadian Business* 86.11/12 (2013): 12. Business Source Premier. Web. December 10, 2013.

17. "Snap-on Incorporated SWOT Analysis." Snap-on, Inc. SWOT Analysis (2013): 1–7. Business Source Premier. Web. December 10, 2013.

18. Ibid.

19. "Automotive Retail Industry Profile: Global." Automotive Retail Industry Profile: Global (2012): 1–39. Business Source Premier. Web. December 10, 2013.

20. "Snap-on Incorporated SWOT Analysis." Snap-on, Inc. SWOT Analysis (2013): 1–7. Business Source Premier. Web. December 10, 2013.

21. Rifkin, Glenn. "How Snap-on Tools Ratchets Its Brand." *Strategy+business*. N.p., Januaru 1, 1998. Web. December 1, 2013. http://www.strategy-business.com/article/9598

22. MLA - Snap-on Incorporated. Austin: Dun and Bradstreet, Inc, 2013. *ProQuest*. Web. November 13, 2013. http://search .proquest.com.ezp.bentley.edu/hooverscompany/docview /230616956/141B9B882431ABB9056/1?accountid=8576#

23. "New Snap-on Holiday Gift Guide: The Toy Catalog for Techs." *PRNewswire*. N.p., November 12, 2013. Web. December 1, 2013. http://www.prnewswire.com/news -releases/new-Snap-on-holiday-gift-guide-the-toy-catalog -for-techs-231630301.html

24. "Snap-on Financing" Snap-on Financing. Snap-on Tools, n.d. Web. December 1, 2013. http://www1.snapon.com /franchise/us/investment-information

25. Rifkin, Glenn. "How Snap-on Tools Ratchets Its Brand." *Strategy+business*. N.p., January 1, 1998. Web. December 1, 2013. http://www.strategy-business.com/article/9598

26. "Snap-on CEO Nick Pinchuk Is SkillsUSA's Champion of the Year." *PRWeb*. N.p., September 6, 2012. Web. December 1, 2013. http://www.prweb.com/releases/2012/9 /prweb9876883.htm

27. Exhibits C & D.

28. Snap-on Inc. (2012) Annual Report 2012. p 4.

29. Snap-on Inc. (2012) Annual Report 2012. p 4–6.

30. Exhibits C & D.

31. Ibid.

32. Ibid.

33. Ibid.

34. Hilgert, R. "Investment Thesis" 10/4/2013–Morningstar.

35. National Independent Automobile Dealers Association. Manheim. 2013 Used Car Market Report.

WORKS CITED

"An Interview With Nick Pinchuk, Recipient Of CTE Foundation Award." Techniques: Connecting Education & Careers 86.5 (2011): 14-15. Academic Search Premier. Web. 10 Dec. 2013.

Bloomberg LP. "Nicholas Pinchuk, Ceo, Snap-On Tools, Is Interviewed." *CEO Wire* (2013): n. page. Print

Compustat North America. (n.d.). *Snap-on Tools, Inc. (SNA)* [Comparative Statistics]. Retrieved November 16, 2013, from FactSet database.

Compustat North America. (n.d.). *Stanley Black & Decker, Inc. (SWK)* [Comparative Statistics]. Retrieved November 16, 2013, from FactSet database.

Compustat North America. (n.d.). *Danaher Corporation (DHR)*. [Comparative Statistics]. Retrieved November 16, 2013, from FactSet database.

Danaher. Austin: Dun and Bradstreet, Inc, 2013. *ProQuest*. Web. 1 Dec. 2013.

Foroohar, R "Made In The USA" Nation Manufacturing, Blackboard.

Harvard Business Review, December 2013, How Diversity Can Drive Innovation, by Sylvia Ann Hewlett, Melinda Marshall, and Laura Sherbin.

Hasson, Sara. NAMAD Diversity Luncheon: Drive Sales by Targeting Hispanic Buyers. 11 Apr. 13. <http://corporate.univision .com/2013/content-types/articles/namad-diversity-luncheon -drive-sales-by-targeting-hispanic-buyers/#.UrEZBlCsiSo.

"HD Profile | Home Depot, Inc. (The) Common S Stock - Yahoo! Finance." HD Profile | Home Depot, Inc. (The) Common S Stock - Yahoo! Finance. Yahoo Finance, n.d. Web. 1 Dec. 2013. http://finance.yahoo.com/q/pr?s=HD.

Hilgert, R. (2013, October 4). *Snap-on, Inc.* [Analyst report]. "Investment Thesis." Retrieved from Morningstar Investment Research Database.

Hilgert, R. (2013, October 4). *Snap-on, Inc.* [Analyst report]. "Economic Moat." Retrieved from Morningstar Investment Research Database.

MLA - Snap-on Incorporated. Austin: Dun and Bradstreet, Inc, 2013. *ProQuest*. Web. 13 Nov. 2013. http://search .proquest.com.ezp.bentley.edu/hooverscompany/docview /230616956/141B9B882431ABB9056/1?accountid=8576#.

"New Snap-on Holiday Gift Guide: The Toy Catalog for Techs." *PRNewswire*. N.p., 12 Nov. 2013. Web. 1 Dec. 2013. http://

www.prnewswire.com/news-releases/new-Snap-on-holi day-gift-guide-the-toy-catalog-for-techs-231630301.html

NIADA National Independent Automobile Dealers Association. Manheim. 2013 Used Car Market Report. http://www.niada.com /uploads/dynamic_areas/wp6QIPSw6C83LYM1dGrU/287 /Manheim%202013%20UCMR.PDF.

Snap-on 2012 Annual Report. Snap-on Incorporated. Web. 1 Dec. 2013. http://www1.snapon.com/display/233/Snap_ on_2012_Annual_Report_Final.pdf.

Rifkin, Glenn. "How Snap-on Tools Ratchets Its Brand." *Strategy+business*. N.p., 1 Jan. 1998. Web. 1 Dec. 2013. http://www.strategy-business.com/article/9598.

SNA v. S&P 500. Yahoo Finance. 13 Dec. 2013. finance.yahoo.com.

"Snap-on CEO Nick Pinchuk Is SkillsUSA's Champion of the Year." *PRWeb*. N.p., 6 Sept. 2012. Web. 1 Dec. 2013. http:// www.prweb.com/releases/2012/9/prweb9876883.htm.

"Snap-on Financing" Snap-on Financing. Snap-on Tools, n.d. Web. 1 Dec. 2013. http://www1.snapon.com/franchise/us /investment-information.

Snap-on Inc. (2012) Annual Report 2012. Retrived from http:// www1.snapon.com/display/233/Snap_on_2012_Annual_ Report_Final.pdf.

Snap-on Incorporated. Austin: Dun and Bradstreet, Inc, 2013. *ProQuest*. Web. 1 Dec. 2013.

Snap-on Incorporated Company Profile, www.marketline.com Aug. 2013.

"Snap-on Incorporated; Snap-on Raises Dividend 15.8%." *Investment Weekly News* (2013): 633. *ProQuest*. Web. 15 Dec. 2013.

Snap-on Receives Five Top Innovation Awards From Professional Tool & Equipment News. Snap-on Receives Five Top Innovation Awards From Professional Tool & Equipment News. N.p., 2013. Web. 18 Dec. 2013.

Stanley Black & Decker, Inc. Austin: Dun and Bradstreet, Inc, 2013. ProQuest. Web. 1 Dec. 2013.

"Supplier Code of Conduct." Snap-on, Inc, n.d. Web

The Home Depot, Inc. Austin: Dun and Bradstreet, Inc, 2013. ProQuest. Web. 1 Dec. 2013.

Vuru. Snap-on Inc. Competitive Industry. Web. 15 Dec. 2013. www.vuru.co/analysis/SNA/economicMoat.

Wikiwealth."Snap-on Stock Research". Web. 15Dec. 2013 www .wikiwealth.com/research:sna

GLOSSARY

360-degree performance appraisal An evaluation technique in which input is gathered from multiple sources.

80/20 rule A rule of thumb stating that one should monitor those 20% of the factors that determine 80% of the results.

Absorptive capacity A firm's ability to value, assimilate, and utilize new external knowledge.

Acquisition The purchase of a company that is completely absorbed by the acquiring corporation.

Action plan A plan that states what actions are going to be taken, by whom, during what time frame, and with what expected results.

Activity-based costing (ABC) An accounting method for allocating indirect and fixed costs to individual products or product lines based on the value-added activities going into that product.

Activity ratios Financial ratios that indicate how well a corporation is managing its operations.

Adaptive mode A decision-making mode characterized by reactive solutions to existing problems, rather than a proactive search for new opportunities.

Advisory board A group of external business people who voluntarily meet periodically with the owners/managers of the firm to discuss strategic and other issues.

Affiliated directors Directors who, though not really employed by the corporation, handle the legal or insurance work for the company or are important suppliers.

Agency theory A theory stating that problems arise in corporations because the agents (top management) are not willing to bear responsibility for their decisions unless they own a substantial amount of stock in the corporation.

Altman's Z-Value Bankruptcy Formula A formula used to estimate how close a company is to declaring bankruptcy.

Analytical portfolio manager A type of general manager needed to execute a diversification strategy.

Andean Community A South American free-trade alliance composed of Columbia, Ecuador, Peru, Bolivia, and Chile.

Annual report A document published each year by a company to show its financial condition and products.

Assessment center An approach to evaluating the suitability of a person for a position by simulating key parts of the job.

Assimilation A strategy that involves the domination of one corporate culture over another.

Association of Southeast Asian Nations (ASEAN) A regional trade association composed of the Asian countries of Brunei Darussalam, Cambodia, Indonesia, Laos, Malaysia, Myanmar, Philippines, Singapore, Thailand, and Vietnam. ASEA+3 includes China, Japan, and South Korea.

Autonomous (self-managing) work teams A group of people who work together without a supervisor to plan, coordinate, and evaluate their own work.

Backward integration Assuming a function previously provided by a supplier.

Balanced scorecard Combines financial measures with operational measures on customer satisfaction, internal processes, and the corporation's innovation and improvement activities.

Bankruptcy A retrenchment strategy that forfeits management of the firm to the courts in return for some settlement of the corporation's obligations.

Basic R&D Research and development that is conducted by scientists in well-equipped laboratories where the focus is on theoretical problem areas.

BCG (Boston Consulting Group) Growth-Share Matrix A simple way to portray a corporation's portfolio of products or divisions in terms of growth and cash flow.

Behavior control A control that specifies how something is to be done through policies, rules, standard operating procedures, and orders from a superior.

Behavior substitution A phenomenon that occurs when people substitute activities that do not lead to goal accomplishment for activities that do lead to goal accomplishment because the wrong activities are being rewarded.

Benchmarking The process of measuring products, services, and practices against those of competitors or companies recognized as industry leaders.

Best practice A procedure that is followed by successful companies.

Blind spot analysis An approach to analyzing a competitor by identifying its perceptual biases.

Board of director responsibilities Commonly agreed obligations of directors, which include: setting corporate strategy, overall direction, mission or vision; hiring and firing the CEO and top management; controlling, monitoring, or supervising top management; reviewing and approving the use of resources; and caring for shareholder interest.

Board of directors' continuum A range of the possible degree of involvement by the board of directors (from low to high) in the strategic management process.

BOT (build-operate-transfer) concept A type of international entry option for a company. After building a facility, the company operates the facility for a fixed period of time during which it earns back its investment, plus a profit.

Brainstorming The process of proposing ideas in a group without first mentally screening them.

Brand A name that identifies a particular company's product in the mind of the consumer.

Budget A statement of a corporation's programs in terms of money required.

Business model The mix of activities a company performs to earn a profit.

Business plan A written strategic plan for a new entrepreneurial venture.

Business policy A previous name for strategic management. It has a general management orientation and tends to look inward with primary concern for integrating the corporation's many functional activities.

Business strategy Competitive and cooperative strategies that emphasize improvement of the competitive position of a corporation's products or services in a specific industry or market segment.

Cannibalize To replace popular products before they reach the end of their life cycle.

Capability A corporation's ability to exploit its resources.

Cap-and-trade A government-imposed ceiling (cap) on the amount of allowed greenhouse gas emissions combined with a system allowing a firm to sell (trade) its emission reductions to another firm whose emissions exceed the allowed cap.

Capital budgeting The process of analyzing and ranking possible investments in terms of the additional outlays and additional receipts that will result from each investment.

Captive company strategy Dedicating a firm's productive capacity as primary supplier to another company in exchange for a long-term contract.

Carbon footprint The amount of greenhouse gases being created by an entity and released into the air.

Cash cow A product that brings in far more money than is needed to maintain its market share.

Categorical imperatives Kant's two principles to guide actions: A person's action is ethical only if that person is willing for that same action to be taken by everyone who is in a similar situation, and a person should never treat another human being simply as a means but always as an end.

Cautious profit planner The type of leader needed for a corporation choosing to follow a stability strategy.

Cellular/modular organization A structure composed of cells (self-managing teams, autonomous business units, etc.) that can operate alone but can interact with other cells to produce a more potent and competent business mechanism.

Center of excellence A designated area in which a company has a core or distinctive competence.

Center of gravity The part of the industry value chain that is most important to the company and the point where the company's greatest expertise and capabilities lay.

Central American Free Trade Agreement (CAFTA) A regional trade association composed of El Salvador, Guatemala, Nicaragua, Honduras, Costa Rica, the United States, and the Dominican Republic.

Clusters Geographic concentrations of interconnected companies and industries.

Code of ethics A code that specifies how an organization expects its employees to behave while on the job.

Codetermination The inclusion of a corporation's workers on its board of directors.

Collusion The active cooperation of firms within an industry to reduce output and raise prices in order to get around the normal economic law of supply and demand. This practice is usually illegal.

Commodity A product whose characteristics are the same regardless of who sells it.

Common-size statements Income statements and balance sheets in which the dollar figures have been converted into percentages.

Common thread A unifying theme for the whole organization to rally around and provide focus for organizational efforts.

Competency A cross-functional integration and coordination of capabilities.

Competitive intelligence A formal program of gathering information about a company's competitors.

Competitive scope The breadth of a company's or a business unit's target market.

Competitive strategy A strategy that states how a company or a business unit will compete in an industry.

Competitors The companies that offer the same products or services as the subject company.

Complementor A company or an industry whose product(s) works well with another industry's or firm's product and without which that product would lose much of its value.

Concentration A corporate growth strategy that concentrates a corporation's resources on competing in one industry.

Concentric diversification A diversification growth strategy in which a firm uses its current strengths to diversify into related products in another industry.

Concurrent engineering A process in which specialists from various functional areas work side by side rather than sequentially in an effort to design new products.

Conglomerate diversification A diversification growth strategy that involves a move into another industry to provide products unrelated to its current products.

Conglomerate structure An assemblage of legally independent firms (subsidiaries) operating under one corporate umbrella but controlled through the subsidiaries' boards of directors.

Connected line batch flow A part of a corporation's manufacturing strategy in which components are standardized and each machine functions like a job shop but is positioned in the same order as the parts are processed.

Consensus A situation in which all parties agree to one alternative.

Consolidated industry An industry in which a few large companies dominate.

Consolidation The second phase of a turnaround strategy that implements a program to stabilize the corporation.

Constant dollars Dollars adjusted for inflation.

Continuous improvement A system developed by Japanese firms in which teams strive constantly to improve manufacturing processes.

Continuous systems Production organized in lines on which products can be continuously assembled or processed.

Contraction The first phase of a turnaround strategy that includes a general across-the-board cutback in size and costs.

Cooperative strategies Strategies that involve working with other firms to gain competitive advantage within an industry.

Co-opetition A term used to describe simultaneous competition and cooperation among firms.

Core competency A collection of corporate capabilities that cross divisional borders and are widespread within a corporation, and that a corporation can do exceedingly well.

Core rigidity/deficiency A core competency of a firm that over time matures and becomes a weakness.

Corporate brand A type of brand in which the company's name serves as the brand name.

Corporate capabilities See *capability*.

Corporate culture A collection of beliefs, expectations, and values learned and shared by a corporation's members and transmitted from one generation of employees to another.

Corporate culture pressure A force from existing corporate culture against the implementation of a new strategy.

Corporate entrepreneurship Also called intrapreneurship; the creation of a new business within an existing organization.

Corporate governance   The relationship among the board of directors, top management, and shareholders in determining the direction and performance of a corporation.

Corporate parenting   A corporate strategy that evaluates the corporation's business units in terms of resources and capabilities that can be used to build business unit value as well as generate synergies across business units.

Corporate reputation   A widely held perception of a company by the general public.

Corporate scenario   Pro forma balance sheets and income statements that forecast the effect that each alternative strategy will likely have on return on investment.

Corporate stakeholders   Groups that affect or are affected by the achievement of a firm's objectives.

Corporate strategy   A strategy that states a company's overall direction in terms of its general attitude toward growth and the management of its various business and product lines.

Corporation   A mechanism legally established to allow different parties to contribute capital, expertise, and labor for their mutual benefit.

Cost focus   A low-cost competitive strategy that concentrates on a particular buyer group or geographic market and attempts to serve only that niche.

Cost leadership   A low-cost competitive strategy that aims at the broad mass market.

Cost proximity   A process that involves keeping the higher price a company charges for higher quality close enough to that of the competition so that customers will see the extra quality as being worth the extra cost.

Crisis of autonomy   A time when people managing diversified product lines need more decision-making freedom than top management is willing to delegate to them.

Crisis of control   A time when business units act to optimize their own sales and profits without regard to the overall corporation. See also *suboptimization*.

Crisis of leadership   A time when an entrepreneur is personally unable to manage a growing company.

Cross-functional work teams   A work team composed of people from multiple functions.

Cultural integration   The extent to which units throughout an organization share a common culture.

Cultural intensity   The degree to which members of an organizational unit accept the norms, values, or other culture content associated with the unit.

Deculturation   The disintegration of one company's culture resulting from unwanted and extreme pressure from another to impose its culture and practices.

Dedicated transfer line   A highly automated assembly line making one mass-produced product and using little human labor.

Defensive centralization   A process in which top management of a not-for-profit retains all decision-making authority so that lower-level managers cannot take any actions to which the sponsors may object.

Defensive tactic   A tactic in which a company defends its current market.

Delphi technique   A forecasting technique in which experts independently assess the probabilities of specified events. These assessments are combined and sent back to each expert for fine-tuning until an agreement is reached.

Devil's advocate   An individual or a group assigned to identify the potential pitfalls and problems of a proposal.

Dialectical inquiry   A decision-making technique that requires that two proposals using different assumptions be generated for consideration.

Differentiation   A competitive strategy that is aimed at the broad mass market and that involves the creation of a product or service that is perceived throughout its industry as unique.

Differentiation focus   A differentiation competitive strategy that concentrates on a particular buyer group, product line segment, or geographic market.

Differentiation strategy   See *differentiation*.

Dimensions of national culture   A set of five dimensions by which each nation's unique culture can be identified.

Directional strategy   A plan that is composed of three general orientations: growth, stability, and retrenchment.

Distinctive competencies   A firm's competencies that are superior to those of their competitors.

Diversification   A corporate growth strategy that expands product lines by moving into another industry.

Divestment   A retrenchment strategy in which a division of a corporation with low growth potential is sold.

Divisional structure   An organizational structure in which employees tend to be functional specialists organized according to product/market distinctions.

Dogs   A business that does not seem to provide any remaining opportunities for growth.

Downsizing   Planned elimination of positions or jobs.

Due care   The obligation of board members to closely monitor and evaluate top management.

Durability   The rate at which a firm's underlying resources and capabilities depreciate or become obsolete.

Dynamic industry expert   A leader with a great deal of experience in a particular industry appropriate for executing a concentration strategy.

Dynamic capabilities   Capabilities that are continually being changed and reconfigured to make them more adaptive to an uncertain environment.

Dynamic pricing   A marketing practice in which different customers pay different prices for the same product or service.

Earnings per share (EPS)   A calculation that is determined by dividing net earnings by the number of shares of common stock issued.

Economic value added (EVA)   A shareholder value method of measuring corporate and divisional performance. Measures after-tax operating income minus the total annual cost of capital.

Economies of scale   A process in which unit costs are reduced by making large numbers of the same product.

Economies of scope   A process in which unit costs are reduced when the value chains of two separate products or services share activities, such as the same marketing channels or manufacturing facilities.

EFAS (External Factor Analysis Summary) table   A table that organizes external factors into opportunities and threats and how well management is responding to these specific factors.

Electronic commerce   The use of the Internet to conduct business transactions.

Engineering (or process) R&D   R&D concentrating on quality control and the development of design specifications and improved production equipment.

Enterprise resource planning (ERP) software   Software that unites all of a company's major business activities, from order processing to production, within a single family of software modules.

Enterprise risk management (ERM)   A corporatewide, integrated process to manage the uncertainties that could negatively or positively influence the achievement of the corporation's objectives.

Enterprise strategy   A strategy that explicitly articulates a firm's ethical relationship with its stakeholders.

Entrepreneur   A person who initiates and manages a business undertaking and who assumes risk for the sake of a profit.

Entrepreneurial characteristics   Traits of an entrepreneur that lead to a new venture's success.

Entrepreneurial mode   A strategy made by one powerful individual in which the focus is on opportunities, and problems are secondary.

Entrepreneurial venture   Any new business whose primary goals are profitability and growth and that can be characterized by innovative strategic practices.

Entry barrier   An obstruction that makes it difficult for a company to enter an industry.

Environmental scanning   The monitoring, evaluation, and dissemination of information from the external and internal environments to key people within the corporation.

Environmental sustainability   The use of business practices to reduce a company's impact upon the natural, physical environment.

Environmental uncertainty   The degree of complexity plus the degree of change existing in an organization's external environment.

Ethics   The consensually accepted standards of behavior for an occupation, trade, or profession.

European Union (EU)   A regional trade association composed of 27 European countries.

Executive leadership   The directing of activities toward the accomplishment of corporate objectives.

Executive succession   The process of grooming and replacing a key top manager.

Executive type   An individual with a particular mix of skills and experiences.

Exit barrier   An obstruction that keeps a company from leaving an industry.

Expense center   A business unit that uses money but contributes to revenues only indirectly.

Experience curve   A conceptual framework that states that unit production costs decline by some fixed percentage each time the total accumulated volume of production in units doubles.

Expert opinion   A nonquantitative forecasting technique in which authorities in a particular area attempt to forecast likely developments.

Explicit knowledge   Knowledge that can be easily articulated and communicated.

Exporting   Shipping goods produced in a company's home country to other countries for marketing.

External environment   Forces outside an organization that are not typically within the short-run control of top management.

Externality   Costs of doing business that are not included in a firm's accounting system, but that are felt by others.

External strategic factor   Environmental trend with both a high probability of occurrence and a high probability of impact on the corporation.

Extranet   An information network within an organization that is available to key suppliers and customers.

Extrapolation   A form of forecasting that extends present trends into the future.

Family business   A company that is either owned or dominated by relatives.

Family directors   Board members who are descendants of the founder and own significant blocks of stock.

Financial leverage   The ratio of total debt to total assets.

Financial strategy   A functional strategy to make the best use of corporate monetary assets.

First mover   The first company to manufacture and sell a new product or service.

Flexible manufacturing   A type of manufacturing that permits the low-volume output of custom-tailored products at relatively low unit costs through economies of scope.

Follow-the-sun-management   A management technique in which modern communication enables project team members living in one country to pass their work to team members in another time zone so that the project is continually being advanced.

Forward integration   Assuming a function previously provided by a distributor.

Four-corner exercise   An approach to analyzing a competitor in terms of its future goals, current strategy, assumptions, and capabilities, in order to develop a competitor's response profile.

Fragmented industry   An industry in which no firm has large market share and each firm serves only a small piece of the total market.

Franchising   An international entry strategy in which a firm grants rights to another company/individual to open a retail store using the franchiser's name and operating system.

Free cash flow   The amount of money a new owner can take out of a firm without harming the business.

Full integration   Complete control of the entire value chain of the business.

Full vertical integration   A growth strategy under which a firm makes 100% of its key supplies internally and completely controls its distributors.

Functional strategy   An approach taken by a functional area to achieve corporate and business unit objectives and strategies by maximizing resource productivity.

Functional structure   An organizational structure in which employees tend to be specialists in the business functions important to that industry, such as manufacturing, sales, or finance.

Geographic-area structure   A structure that allows a multinational corporation to tailor products to regional differences and to achieve regional coordination.

Global industry   An industry in which a company manufactures and sells the same products, with only minor adjustments for individual countries around the world.

Globalization   The internationalization of markets and corporations.

Global warming   A gradual increase in the Earth's temperature leading to changes in the planet's climate.

Goal   An open-ended statement of what one wants to accomplish, with no quantification of what is to be achieved and no time criteria for completion.

Goal displacement Confusion of means with ends, which occurs when activities originally intended to help managers attain corporate objectives become ends in themselves or are adapted to meet ends other than those for which they were intended.

Good will An accounting term describing the premium paid by one company in its purchase of another company that is listed on the acquiring company's balance sheet.

Grand strategy Another name for directional strategy.

Green-field development An international entry option to build a company's manufacturing plant and distribution system in another country.

Greenwash A derogatory term referring to a company's promoting its environmental sustainability efforts with very little action toward improving its measurable environmental performance.

Gross domestic product (GDP) A measure of the total output of goods and services within a country's borders.

Growth strategies A directional strategy that expands a company's current activities.

Hierarchy of strategy A nesting of strategies by level from corporate to business to functional, so that they complement and support one another.

Horizontal growth A corporate growth concentration strategy that involves expanding the firm's products into other geographic locations and/or increasing the range of products and services offered to current markets.

Horizontal integration The degree to which a firm operates in multiple geographic locations at the same point in an industry's value chain.

Horizontal strategy A corporate parenting strategy that cuts across business unit boundaries to build synergy across business units and to improve the competitive position of one or more business units.

House of quality A method of managing new product development to help project teams make important design decisions by getting them to think about what users want and how to get it to them most effectively.

HRM strategy A functional strategy that makes the best use of corporate human assets.

Human diversity A mix of people from different races, cultures, and backgrounds in the workplace.

Hypercompetition An industry situation in which the frequency, boldness, and aggressiveness of dynamic movement by the players accelerates to create a condition of constant disequilibrium and change.

Idea A concept that could be the foundation of an entrepreneurial venture if the concept is feasible.

IFAS (Internal Factor Analysis Summary) table A table that organizes internal factors into strengths and weaknesses and how well management is responding to these specific factors.

Imitability The rate at which a firm's underlying resources and capabilities can be duplicated by others.

Index of R&D effectiveness An index that is calculated by dividing the percentage of total revenue spent on research and development into new product profitability.

Index of sustainable growth A calculation that shows how much of the growth rate of sales can be sustained by internally generated funds.

Individual rights approach An ethics behavior guideline that proposes that human beings have certain fundamental rights that should be respected in all decisions.

Individualism-collectivism (IC) The extent to which a society values individual freedom and independence of action compared with a tight social framework and loyalty to the group.

Industry A group of firms producing a similar product or service.

Industry analysis An in-depth examination of key factors within a corporation's task environment.

Industry matrix A chart that summarizes the key success factors within a particular industry.

Industry scenario A forecasted description of an industry's likely future.

Information technology strategy A functional strategy that uses information systems technology to provide competitive advantage.

Input control A control that specifies resources, such as knowledge, skills, abilities, values, and motives of employees.

Inside director An officer or executive employed by a corporation who serves on that company's board of directors; also called management director.

Institutional advantage A competitive benefit for a not-for-profit organization when it performs its tasks more effectively than other comparable organizations.

Institution theory A concept of organizational adaptation that proposes that organizations can and do adapt to changing conditions by imitating other successful organizations.

Integration A process that involves a relatively balanced give-and-take of cultural and managerial practices between merger partners, with no strong imposition of cultural change on either company.

Integration manager A person in charge of taking an acquired company through the process of integrating its people and processes with those of the acquiring company.

Intellectual property Special knowledge used in a new product or process developed by a company for its own use, and which is usually protected by a patent, copyright, or trademark, and is sometimes treated as a trade secret.

Interlocking directorate A condition that occurs when two firms share a director or when an executive of one firm sits on the board of a second firm.

Intermittent system A method of manufacturing in which an item is normally processed sequentially, but the work and the sequence of the processes vary.

Internal environment Variables within the organization not usually within the short-run control of top management.

Internal strategic factors Strengths (core competencies) and weaknesses that are likely to determine whether a firm will be able to take advantage of opportunities while avoiding threats.

International transfer pricing A method of minimizing taxes by declaring high profits in a subsidiary located in a country with a low tax rate, and small profits in a subsidiary located in a country with a high tax rate.

Intranet An information network within an organization that also has access to the Internet.

Investment center A unit in which performance is measured in terms of the difference between the unit's resources and its services or products.

ISO 9000 Standards Series   An internationally accepted way of objectively documenting a company's high level of quality operations.

ISO 14000 Standards Series   An internationally accepted way to document a company's impact on the environment.

Job characteristics model   An approach to job design that is based on the belief that tasks can be described in terms of certain objective characteristics, and that those characteristics affect employee motivation.

Job design   The design of individual tasks in an attempt to make them more relevant to the company and more motivating to the employee.

Job enlargement   Combining tasks to give a worker more of the same type of duties to perform.

Job enrichment   Altering jobs by giving the worker more autonomy and control over activities.

Job rotation   Moving workers through several jobs to increase variety.

Job shop   One-of-a-kind production using skilled labor.

Joint venture   An independent business entity created by two or more companies in a strategic alliance.

Justice approach   An ethical approach that proposes that decision makers be equitable, fair, and impartial in the distribution of costs and benefits.

Just-in-time   A purchasing concept in which parts arrive at the plant just when they are needed rather than being kept in inventories.

Key performance measures   Essential measures for achieving a desired strategic option—used in the balanced scorecard.

Key success factors   Variables that significantly affect the overall competitive position of a company within a particular industry.

Late movers   Companies that enter a new market only after other companies have done so.

Law   A formal code that permits or forbids certain behaviors.

Lead director   An outside director who calls meetings of the outside board members and coordinates the annual evaluation of the CEO.

Lead user   A customer who is ahead of market trends and has needs that go beyond those of the average user.

Leading   Providing direction to employees to use their abilities and skills most effectively and efficiently to achieve organizational objectives.

Lean Six Sigma   A program incorporating the statistical approach of Six Sigma with the lean manufacturing program developed by Toyota.

Learning organization   An organization that is skilled at creating, acquiring, and transferring knowledge and at modifying its behavior to reflect new knowledge and insights.

Levels of moral development   Kohlberg proposed three levels of moral development: preconventional, conventional, and principled.

Leveraged buyout   An acquisition in which a company is acquired in a transaction financed largely by debt—usually obtained from a third party, such as an insurance company or an investment banker.

Leverage ratio   An evaluation of how effectively a company utilizes its resources to generate revenues.

Licensing   An agreement in which the licensing firm grants rights to another firm in another country or market to produce and/or sell a branded product.

Lifestyle company   A small business in which the firm is purely an extension of the owner's lifestyle.

Line extension   Using a successful brand name on additional products, such as Arm & Hammer brand first on baking soda, and then on laundry detergents, toothpaste, and deodorants.

Linkage   The connection between the way one value activity (for example, marketing) is performed and the cost of performance of another activity (for example, quality control).

Liquidation   The termination of a firm in which all its assets are sold.

Liquidity ratio   The percentage showing to what degree a company can cover its current liabilities with its current assets.

Logical incrementalism   A decision-making mode that is a synthesis of the planning, adaptive, and entrepreneurial modes.

Logistics strategy   A functional strategy that deals with the flow of products into and out of the manufacturing process.

Long-term contract   Agreements between two separate firms to provide agreed-upon goods and services to each other for a specified period of time.

Long-term evaluation method   A method in which managers are compensated for achieving objectives set over a multiyear period.

Long-term orientation (LT)   The extent to which society is oriented toward the long term versus the short term.

Lower-cost strategy   A strategy in which a company or business unit designs, produces, and markets a comparable product more efficiently than its competitors.

Management audit   A technique used to evaluate corporate activities.

Management By Objectives (MBO)   An organization-wide approach ensuring purposeful action toward mutually agreed-upon objectives.

Management contract   Agreements through which a corporation uses some of its personnel to assist a firm in another country for a specified fee and period of time.

Market development   A marketing functional strategy in which a company or business unit captures a larger share of an existing market for current products through market penetration or develops new markets for current products.

Marketing mix   The particular combination of key variables (product, place, promotion, and price) that can be used to affect demand and to gain competitive advantage.

Marketing strategy   A functional strategy that deals with pricing, selling, and distributing a product.

Market location tactics   Tactics that determine where a company or business unit will compete.

Market position   Refers to the selection of specific areas for marketing concentration and can be expressed in terms of market, product, and geographical locations.

Market research   A means of obtaining new product ideas by surveying current or potential users regarding what they would like in a new product.

Market segmentation   The division of a market into segments to identify available niches.

Market value added (MVA)   The difference between the market value of a corporation and the capital contributed by shareholders and lenders.

Masculinity-femininity (MF)   The extent to which society is oriented toward money and things.

Mass customization   The low-cost production of individually customized goods and services.

Mass production A system in which employees work on narrowly defined, repetitive tasks under close supervision in a bureaucratic and hierarchical structure to produce a large amount of low-cost, standard goods and services.

Matrix of change A chart that compares target practices (new programs) with existing practices (current activities).

Matrix structure A structure in which functional and product forms are combined simultaneously at the same level of the organization.

Mercosur/Mercosul South American free-trade area including Argentina, Brazil, Uruguay, and Paraguay.

Merger A transaction in which two or more corporations exchange stock, but from which only one corporation survives.

Mission The purpose or reason for an organization's existence.

Mission statement The definition of the fundamental, unique purpose that sets an organization apart from other firms of its type and identifies the scope or domain of the organization's operations in terms of products (including services) offered and markets served.

Modular manufacturing A system in which preassembled subassemblies are delivered as they are needed to a company's assembly-line workers who quickly piece the modules together into finished products.

Moore's law An observation of Gordon Moore, co-founder of Intel, that microprocessors double in complexity every 18 months.

Morality Precepts of personal behavior that are based on religious or philosophical grounds.

Moral relativism A theory that proposes that morality is relative to some personal, social, or cultural standard, and that there is no method for deciding whether one decision is better than another.

Most-favored nation A policy of the World Trade Organization stating that a member country cannot grant one trading partner lower customs duties without granting them to all WTO member nations.

Multidomestic industry An industry in which companies tailor their products to the specific needs of consumers in a particular country.

Multinational corporation (MNC) A company that has significant assets and activities in multiple countries.

Multiple sourcing A purchasing strategy in which a company orders a particular part from several vendors.

Multipoint competition A rivalry in which a large multibusiness corporation competes against other large multibusiness firms in a number of markets.

Mutual service consortium A partnership of similar companies in similar industries that pool their resources to gain a benefit that is too expensive to develop alone.

Natural environment That part of the external environment that includes physical resources, wildlife, and climate that are an inherent part of existence on Earth.

Net present value (NPV) A calculation of the value of a project that is made by predicting the project's payouts, adjusting them for risk, and subtracting the amount invested.

Network structure An organization (virtual organization) that outsources most of its business functions.

New entrants Businesses entering an industry that typically bring new capacity to an industry, a desire to gain market share, and substantial resources.

New product experimentation A method of test marketing the potential of innovative ideas by developing products, probing potential markets with early versions of the products, learning from the probes, and probing again.

No-change strategy A decision to do nothing new; to continue current operations and policies for the foreseeable future.

North American Free Trade Agreement (NAFTA) Regional free trade agreement between Canada, the United States, and Mexico.

Not-for-profit organization Private nonprofit corporations and public governmental units or agencies.

Objectives The end result of planned activity stating what is to be accomplished by when, and quantified if possible.

Offensive tactic A tactic that calls for competing in an established competitor's current market location.

Offshoring The outsourcing of an activity or function to a provider in another country.

Open innovation A new approach to R&D in which a firm uses alliances and connections with corporate, government, and academic labs to learn about new developments.

Operating budget A budget for a business unit that is approved by top management during strategy formulation and implementation.

Operating cash flow The amount of money generated by a company before the costs of financing and taxes are figured.

Operating leverage The impact of a specific change in sales volume on net operating income.

Operations strategy A functional strategy that determines how and where a product or service is to be manufactured, the level of vertical integration in the production process, and the deployment of physical resources.

Opportunity A strategic factor considered when using the SWOT analysis.

Orchestrator A top manager who articulates the need for innovation, provides funding for innovating activities, creates incentives for middle managers to sponsor new ideas, and protects idea/product champions from suspicious or jealous executives.

Organizational analysis Internal scanning concerned with identifying an organization's strengths and weaknesses.

Organizational learning theory A theory proposing that an organization adjusts to changes in the environment through the learning of its employees.

Organizational life cycle How organizations grow, develop, and eventually decline.

Organizational structure The formal setup of a business corporation's value chain components in terms of work flow, communication channels, and hierarchy.

Organization slack Unused resources within an organization.

Output control A control that specifies what is to be accomplished by focusing on the end result of the behaviors through the use of objectives and performance targets.

Outside directors Members of a board of directors who are not employees of the board's corporation; also called non–management directors.

Outsourcing A process in which resources are purchased from others through long-term contracts instead of being made within the company.

Parallel sourcing A process in which two suppliers are the sole suppliers of two different parts, but they are also backup suppliers for each other's parts.

Parenting strategy The manner in which management coordinates activities and transfers resources and cultivates capabilities among product lines and business units

Pattern of influence A concept stating that influence in strategic management derives from a not-for-profit organization's sources of revenue.

Pause/proceed-with-caution strategy A corporate strategy in which nothing new is attempted; an opportunity to rest before continuing a growth or retrenchment strategy.

Penetration pricing A marketing pricing strategy to obtain dominant market share by using low price.

Performance The end result of activities, actual outcomes of a strategic management process.

Performance appraisal system A system to systematically evaluate employee performance and promotion potential.

Performance gap A performance gap exists when performance does not meet expectations.

Periodic statistical report Reports summarizing data on key factors such as the number of new customer contracts, volume of received orders, and productivity figures.

Phases of strategic management A set of four levels of development through which a firm generally evolves into strategic management.

Piracy The making and selling of counterfeit copies of well-known name-brand products, especially software.

Planning mode A decision-making mode that involves the systematic gathering of appropriate information for situation analysis, the generation of feasible alternative strategies, and the rational selection of the most appropriate strategy.

Policy A broad guideline for decision making that links the formulation of strategy with its implementation.

Political strategy A strategy to influence a corporation's stakeholders.

Population ecology A theory that proposes that once an organization is successfully established in a particular environmental niche, it is unable to adapt to changing conditions.

Portfolio analysis An approach to corporate strategy in which top management views its product lines and business units as a series of investments from which it expects a profitable return.

Power distance (PD) The extent to which a society accepts an unequal distribution of influence in organizations.

Prediction markets A forecasting technique in which people make bets on the likelihood of a particular event taking place.

Pressure-cooker crisis A situation that exists when employees in collaborative organizations eventually grow emotionally and physically exhausted from the intensity of teamwork and the heavy pressure for innovative solutions.

Primary activity A manufacturing firm's corporate value chain, including inbound logistics, operations process, outbound logistics, marketing and sales, and service.

Primary stakeholders A high priority group that affects or is affected by the achievement of a firm's objectives.

Prime interest rate The rate of interest banks charge on their lowest-risk loans.

Private nonprofit corporation A nongovernmental not-for-profit organization.

Privatization The selling of state-owned enterprises to private individuals. Also the hiring of a private business to provide services previously offered by a state agency.

Procedures A list of sequential steps that describe in detail how a particular task or job is to be done.

Process innovation Improvement to the making and selling of current products.

Product champion A person who generates a new idea and supports it through many organizational obstacles.

Product development A marketing strategy in which a company or unit develops new products for existing markets or develops new products for new markets.

Product innovation The development of a new product or the improvement of an existing product's performance.

Product life cycle A graph showing time plotted against sales of a product as it moves from introduction through growth and maturity to decline.

Product/market evolution matrix A chart depicting products in terms of their competitive positions and their stages of product/market evolution.

Product-group structure A structure of a multinational corporation that enables the company to introduce and manage a similar line of products around the world.

Production sharing The process of combining the higher labor skills and technology available in developed countries with the lower-cost labor available in developing countries.

Product R&D Research and development concerned with product or product-packaging improvements.

Professional liquidator An individual called on by a bankruptcy court to close a firm and sell its assets.

Profitability ratios Ratios evaluating a company's ability to make money over a period of time.

Profit center A unit's performance, measured in terms of the difference between revenues and expenditures.

Profit-making firm A firm depending on revenues obtained from the sale of its goods and services to customers, who typically pay for the costs and expenses of providing the product or service plus a profit.

Profit strategy A strategy that artificially supports profits by reducing investment and short-term discretionary expenditures.

Program A statement of the activities or steps needed to accomplish a single-use plan in strategy implementation.

Propitious niche A portion of a market that is so well suited to a firm's internal and external environment that other corporations are not likely to challenge or dislodge it.

Public governmental unit or agency A kind of not-for-profit organization that is established by government or governmental agencies (such as welfare departments, prisons, and state universities).

Public or collective good Goods that are freely available to all in a society.

Pull strategy A marketing strategy in which advertising pulls the products through the distribution channels.

Punctuated equilibrium A point at which a corporation makes a major change in its strategy after evolving slowly through a long period of stability.

Purchasing power parity (PPP) A measure of the cost, in dollars, of the U.S.-produced equivalent volume of goods that another nation's economy produces.

Purchasing strategy A functional strategy that deals with obtaining the raw materials, parts, and supplies needed to perform the operations functions.

Push strategy   A marketing strategy in which a large amount of money is spent on trade promotion in order to gain or hold shelf space in retail outlets.

Quality of work life   A concept that emphasizes improving the human dimension of work to improve employee satisfaction and union relations.

Quasi-integration   A type of vertical growth/integration in which a company does not make any of its key supplies but purchases most of its requirements from outside suppliers that are under its partial control.

Question marks   New products that have the potential for success and need a lot of cash for development.

R&D intensity   A company's spending on research and development as a percentage of sales revenue.

R&D mix   The balance of basic, product, and process research and development.

R&D strategy   A functional strategy that deals with product and process innovation.

Ratio analysis   The calculation of ratios from data in financial statements to identify possible strengths or weaknesses.

Real options   An approach to new project investment when the future is highly uncertain.

Red flag   An indication of a serious underlying problem.

Red tape crisis   A crisis that occurs when a corporation has grown too large and complex to be managed through formal programs.

Reengineering   The radical redesign of business processes to achieve major gains in cost, service, or time.

Regional industry   An industry in which multinational corporations primarily coordinate their activities within specific geographic areas of the world.

Relationship-based governance   A government system perceived to be less transparent and have a higher degree of corruption.

Repatriation of profits   The transfer of profits from a foreign subsidiary to a corporation's headquarters.

Replicability   The ability of competitors to duplicate resources and imitate another firm's success.

Resources   A company's physical, human, and organizational assets that serve as the building blocks of a corporation.

Responsibility center   A unit that is isolated so that it can be evaluated separately from the rest of the corporation.

Retired executive directors   Past leaders of a company kept on the board of directors after leaving the company.

Retrenchment strategy   Corporate strategies to reduce a company's level of activities and to return it to profitability.

Return on equity (ROE)   A measure of performance that is calculated by dividing net income by total equity.

Return on investment (ROI)   A measure of performance that is calculated by dividing net income before taxes by total assets.

Revenue center   A responsibility center in which production, usually in terms of unit or dollar sales, is measured without consideration of resource costs.

Reverse engineering   Taking apart a competitor's product in order to find out how it works.

Reverse stock split   A stock split in which an investor's shares are reduced for the same total amount of money.

RFID   A technology in which radio frequency identification tags containing product information are used to track goods through inventory and distribution channels.

Risk   A measure of the probability that one strategy will be effective, the amount of assets the corporation must allocate to that strategy, and the length of time the assets will be unavailable.

Rule-based governance   A governance system based on clearly stated rules and procedures.

Rules of thumb   Approximations based not on research, but on years of practical experience.

Sarbanes–Oxley Act   Legislation passed by the U.S. Congress in 2002 to promote and formalize greater board independence and oversight.

Scenario box   A tool for developing corporate scenarios in which historical data are used to make projections for generating pro forma financial statements.

Scenario writing   A forecasting technique in which focused descriptions of different likely futures are presented in a narrative fashion.

SEC 10-K form   An SEC form containing income statements, balance sheets, cash flow statements, and information not usually available in an annual report.

SEC 10-Q form   An SEC form containing quarterly financial reports.

SEC 14-A form   An SEC form containing proxy statements and information on a company's board of directors.

Secondary stakeholders   Lower-priority groups that affect or are affected by the achievement of a firm's objectives.

Sell-out strategy   A retrenchment option used when a company has a weak competitive position resulting in poor performance.

Separation   A method of managing the culture of an acquired firm in which the two companies are structurally divided, without cultural exchange.

SFAS (Strategic Factors Analysis Summary) matrix   A chart that summarizes an organization's strategic factors by combining the external factors from an EFAS table with the internal factors from an IFAS table.

Shareholder value   The present value of the anticipated future stream of cash flows from a business plus the value of the company if it were liquidated.

Short-term orientation   The tendency of managers to consider only current tactical or operational issues and ignore strategic ones.

Simple structure   A structure for new entrepreneurial firms in which the employees tend to be generalists and jacks-of-all-trades.

Six Sigma   A statistically based program developed to identify and improve a poorly performing process.

Skim pricing   A marketing strategy in which a company charges a high price while a product is novel and competitors are few.

Small-business firm   An independently owned and operated business that is not dominant in its field and that does not engage in innovative practices.

Social capital   The goodwill of key stakeholders, which can be used for competitive advantage.

Social entrepreneurship   A business in which a not-for-profit organization starts a new venture to achieve social goals.

Social responsibility   The ethical and discretionary responsibilities a corporation owes its stakeholders.

Societal environment   Economic, technological, political-legal, and sociocultural environmental forces that do not directly touch on the short-run activities of an organization but influence its long-run decisions.

Sole sourcing Relying on only one supplier for a particular part.

SO, ST, WO, WT strategies A series of possible business approaches based on combinations of opportunities, threats, strengths, and weaknesses.

Sources of innovation Drucker's proposed seven sources of new ideas that should be monitored by those interested in starting entrepreneurial ventures.

Sponsor A department manager who recognizes the value of a new idea, helps obtain funding to develop the innovation, and facilitates the implementation of the innovation.

Stability strategy Corporate strategies to make no change to the company's current direction or activities.

Staffing Human resource management priorities and use of personnel.

Stages of corporate development A pattern of structural development that corporations follow as they grow and expand.

Stages of international development The stages through which international corporations evolve in their relationships with widely dispersed geographic markets and the manner in which they structure their operations and programs.

Stages of new product development The stages of getting a new innovation into the marketplace.

Stage-gate process A method of managing new product development to increase the likelihood of launching new products quickly and successfully. The process is a series of steps to move products through the six stages of new product development.

Staggered board A board on which directors serve terms of more than one year so that only a portion of the board of directors stands for election each year.

Stakeholder An individual or entity with an interest in the activities of the organization

Stakeholder analysis The identification and evaluation of corporate stakeholders.

Stakeholder measure A method of keeping track of stakeholder concerns.

Stakeholder priority matrix A chart that categorizes stakeholders in terms of their interest in a corporation's activities and their relative power to influence the corporation's activities.

Stall point A point at which a company's growth in sales and profits suddenly stops and becomes negative.

Standard cost center A responsibility center that is primarily used to evaluate the performance of manufacturing facilities.

Standard operating procedures Plans that detail the various activities that must be carried out to complete a corporation's programs.

Star Market leader that is able to generate enough cash to maintain its high market share.

Statistical modeling A quantitative technique that attempts to discover causal or explanatory factors that link two or more time series together.

STEEP analysis An approach to scanning the societal environment that examines socio-cultural, technological, economic, ecological, and political-legal forces. Also called PESTEL analysis.

Steering control Measures of variables that influence future profitability.

Stewardship theory A theory proposing that executives tend to be more motivated to act in the best interests of the corporation than in their own self-interests.

Strategic alliance A partnership of two or more corporations or business units to achieve strategically significant objectives that are mutually beneficial.

Strategic audit A checklist of questions by area or issue that enables a systematic analysis of various corporate functions and activities. It's a type a management audit.

Strategic audit worksheet A tool used to analyze a case.

Strategic business unit (SBU) A division or group of divisions composed of independent product-market segments that are given primary authority for the management of their own functions.

Strategic choice The evaluation of strategies and selection of the best alternative.

Strategic choice perspective A theory that proposes that organizations adapt to a changing environment and have the opportunity and power to reshape their environment.

Strategic decision-making process An eight-step process that improves strategic decision making.

Strategic decisions Decisions that deal with the long-run future of an entire organization and are rare, consequential, and directive.

Strategic factors External and internal factors that determine the future of a corporation.

Strategic flexibility The ability to shift from one dominant strategy to another.

Strategic-funds method An approach that separates developmental expenses from expenses required for current operations.

Strategic group A set of business units or firms that pursue similar strategies and have similar resources.

Strategic inflection point The period in an organization's life in which a major change takes place in its environment and creates a new basis for competitive advantage.

Strategic management A set of managerial decisions and actions that determine the long-run performance of a corporation.

Strategic management model A rational, prescriptive planning model of the strategic management process including environmental scanning, strategy formulation, strategy implementation, and evaluation and control.

Strategic myopia The willingness to reject unfamiliar as well as negative information.

Strategic piggybacking The development of a new activity for a not-for-profit organization that would generate the funds needed to make up the difference between revenues and expenses.

Strategic planning staff A group of people charged with supporting both top management and business units in the strategic planning process.

Strategic R&D alliance A coalition through which a firm coordinates its research and development with another firm(s) to offset the huge costs of developing new technology.

Strategic rollup A means of consolidating a fragmented industry in which an entrepreneur acquires hundreds of owner-operated small businesses resulting in a large firm with economies of scale.

Strategic sweet spot A market niche in which a company is able to satisfy customers' needs in a way that competitors cannot.

Strategic type A category of firms based on a common strategic orientation and a combination of structure, culture, and processes that are consistent with that strategy.

Strategic vision A description of what the company is capable of becoming.

Strategic window A unique market opportunity that is available only for a particular time.

Strategic-funds method An evaluation method that encourages executives to look at development expenses as being different from expenses required for current operations.

Strategies to avoid Strategies sometimes followed by managers who have made a poor analysis or lack creativity.

Strategy A comprehensive plan that states how a corporation will achieve its mission and objectives.

Strategy-culture compatibility The match between existing corporate culture and a new strategy to be implemented.

Strategy formulation Development of long-range plans for the effective management of environmental opportunities and threats in light of corporate strengths and weaknesses.

Strategy implementation A process by which strategies and policies are put into action through the development of programs, budgets, and procedures.

Structure follows strategy The process through which changes in corporate strategy normally lead to changes in organizational structure.

Stuck in the middle A situation in which a company or business unit has not achieved a generic competitive strategy and has no competitive advantage.

Suboptimization A phenomenon in which a unit optimizes its goal accomplishment to the detriment of the organization as a whole.

Substages of small business development A set of five levels through which new ventures often develop.

Substitute products Products that appear to be different but can satisfy the same need as other products.

Supply chain management The formation of networks for sourcing raw materials, manufacturing products or creating services, storing and distributing goods, and delivering goods or services to customers and consumers.

Support activity An activity that ensures that primary value-chain activities operate effectively and efficiently.

SWOT analysis Identification of strengths, weaknesses, opportunities, and threats that may be strategic factors for a specific company.

Synergy A concept that states that the whole is greater than the sum of its parts; that two units will achieve more together than they could separately.

Tacit knowledge Knowledge that is not easily communicated because it is deeply rooted in employee experience or in a corporation's culture.

Tactic A short-term operating plan detailing how a strategy is to be implemented.

Takeover A hostile acquisition in which one firm purchases a majority interest in another firm's stock.

Taper integration A type of vertical integration in which a firm internally produces less than half of its own requirements and buys the rest from outside suppliers.

Task environment The part of the business environment that includes the elements or groups that directly affect the corporation and, in turn, are affected by it.

Technological competence A corporation's proficiency in managing research personnel and integrating their innovations into its day-to-day operations.

Technological discontinuity The displacement of one technology by another.

Technological follower A company that imitates the products of competitors.

Technological leader A company that pioneers an innovation.

Technology sourcing A make-or-buy decision that can be important in a firm's R&D strategy.

Technology transfer The process of taking a new technology from the laboratory to the marketplace.

Time to market The time from inception to profitability of a new product.

Timing tactics Tactics that determine when a business will enter a market with a new product.

Tipping point The point at which a slowly changing situation goes through a massive, rapid change.

Top management responsibilities Leadership tasks that involve getting things accomplished through, and with, others in order to meet the corporate objectives.

Total Quality Management (TQM) An operational philosophy that is committed to customer satisfaction and continuous improvement.

TOWS matrix A matrix that illustrates how external opportunities and threats facing a particular company can be matched with that company's internal strengths and weaknesses to result in four sets of strategic alternatives.

Transaction cost economics A theory that proposes that vertical integration is more efficient than contracting for goods and services in the marketplace when the transaction costs of buying goods on the open market become too great.

Transferability The ability of competitors to gather the resources and capabilities necessary to support a competitive challenge.

Transfer pricing A practice in which one unit can charge a transfer price for each product it sells to a different unit within a company.

Transformational leader A leader who causes change and movement in an organization by providing a strategic vision.

Transparent The speed with which other firms can understand the relationship of resources and capabilities supporting a successful firm's strategy.

Trends in governance Current developments in corporate governance.

Triggering event Something that acts as a stimulus for a change in strategy.

Trigger point The point at which a country has developed economically so that demand for a particular product or service is increasing rapidly.

Turnaround specialist A manager who is brought into a weak company to salvage that company in a relatively attractive industry.

Turnaround strategy A plan that emphasizes the improvement of operational efficiency when a corporation's problems are pervasive but not yet critical.

Turnkey operation Contracts for the construction of operating facilities in exchange for a fee.

Turnover A term used by European firms to refer to sales revenue. It also refers to the amount of time needed to sell inventory.

Uncertainty avoidance (UA) The extent to which a society feels threatened by uncertain and ambiguous situations.

Union of South American Nations An organization formed in 2008 to unite Mercosur and the Andean Community.

Utilitarian approach A theory that proposes that actions and plans should be judged by their consequences.

Value chain A linked set of value-creating activities that begins with basic raw materials coming from suppliers and ends with distributors getting the final goods into the hands of the ultimate consumer.

Value-chain partnership A strategic alliance in which one company or unit forms a long-term arrangement with a key supplier or distributor for mutual advantage.

Value disciplines An approach to evaluating a competitor in terms of product leadership, operational excellence, and customer intimacy.

Vertical growth A corporate growth strategy in which a firm takes over a function previously provided by a supplier or distributor.

Vertical integration The degree to which a firm operates in multiple locations on an industry's value chain from extracting raw materials to retailing.

Virtual organization An organizational structure that is composed of a series of project groups or collaborations linked by changing nonhierarchical, cobweb-like networks.

Virtual team A group of geographically and/or organizationally dispersed co-workers who are assembled using a combination of telecommunications and information technologies to accomplish an organizational task.

Vision A view of what management thinks an organization should become.

VRIO framework Barney's proposed analysis to evaluate a firm's key resources in terms of value, rareness, imitability, and organization.

Web 2.0 A term used to describe the evolution of the Internet into wikis, blogs, RSSs, social networks, podcasts, and mash-ups.

Weighted-factor method A method that is appropriate for measuring and rewarding the performance of top SBU managers and group-level executives when performance factors and their importance vary from one SBU to another.

Whistle-blower An individual who reports to authorities incidents of questionable organizational practices.

World Trade Organization A forum for governments to negotiate trade agreements and settle trade disputes.

Z-value A formula that combines five ratios by weighting them according to their importance to a corporation's financial strength to predict the likelihood of bankruptcy.

NAME INDEX

SUBJECT INDEX